Great Women Writers

Great Women Writers

The Lives and Works of 135 of the World's Most
Important Women Writers, from
Antiquity to the Present

Frank N. Magill, Editor
Introduction by Rosemary Canfield Reisman

ROBERT HALE • LONDON

CONTENTS

CONTRIBUTING REVIEWERS

Timothy Dow Adams
Patrick Adcock
Jacob H. Adler
Terry L. Andrews
Marilyn Arnold
Jane Augustine
Melissa E. Barth
Kate Begnal
Todd K. Bender
Mary Berg
Randi Birn
Jo-Ellen Lipman Boon
Allyson Booth
Harold Branam
Anne Kelsch Breznau
David Bromige
Mitzi M. Brunsdale
Karen Carmean
G. A. Cevasco
Balance Chow
John W. Crawford
Paul J. deGategno
K. Z. Derounian
Ayne C. Durham
Doris Earnshaw
Grace Eckley
Wilton Eckley
Robert P. Ellis
Ann Willardson Engar
Bernard F. Engel
Nettie Farris
Howard Faulkner
William L. Felker
Robert J. Forman
Margot K. Frank
Jean C. Fulton
Kenneth E. Gadomski
Kristine Otteson Garrigan
Donna Gerstenberger
Richard F. Giles
Peter W. Graham
Angela Hague

Natalie Harper
Nelson Hathcock
Terry Heller
Erwin Hester
Ann R. Hill
Jane Hill
Helen Mundy Hudson
Archibald E. Irwin
Helen Jaskoski
Alfred W. Jensen
Betty H. Jones
Jane Anderson Jones
Deborah Kaplan
Catherine Kenney
Karen A. Kildahl
Anne Mills King
James Reynolds Kinzey
Paula D. Kopacz
Lawrence F. Laban
Brooks Landon
Norman Lavers
Katherine Lederer
Mary S. LeDonne
Robert W. Leutner
Robert Emmet Long
Michael Loudon
John D. Lyons
Fred B. McEwen
Richard D. McGhee
Victoria E. McLure
Lois A. Marchino
Paul Marx
Kenneth W. Meadwell
Vasa D. Mihailovich
Sally Mitchell
Carol J. Murphy
Stella A. Nesanovich
Anne Newgarden
Evelyn S. Newlyn
Martha Nochimson
Makarand Paranjape
Carole Deering Paul

Alice Hall Petry
Chapel Louise Petty
Linda Schelbitzki Pickle
Susan L. Piepke
Janet Polansky
Honora Rankine-Galloway
Rosemary M. Canfield Reisman
Helene M. Kastinger Riley
Samuel L. Rogal
Mary Rohrberger
Amelia A. Rutledge
Dale Salwak
Lucy M. Schwartz
Barbara Kitt Seidman
Vasant A. Shahane
D. Dean Shakelford
John C. Shields
Hugh Short
Jan Sjåvik
Katherine Snipes
George Soule
Jenny S. Spencer
Sharon Spencer
P. Jane Splawn
Karen F. Stein
L. Robert Stevens
Louise M. Stone
W. J. Stuckey
Catherine Swanson
Thomas J. Taylor
John Clendenin Townsend
John Michael Walsh
Judith Weise
John P. Welle
Craig Werner
Barbara Wiedemann
Roger E. Wiehe
Cynthia Wong
Jennifer L. Wyatt
Mary F. Yudin

INTRODUCTION

In *A Room of One's Own* (1929), the feminist writer Virginia Woolf considers what would have happened to a sister of William Shakespeare if she had been as gifted as he. Sadly, she concludes that such a woman would have been denied an outlet for her talent. Her plays would never have been performed, and if she did not escape from her own frustrations through madness or suicide, Shakespeare's sister would probably have become one of the those peculiar women who lived in isolation and were suspected of being witches.

Although Woolf's scenario is purely speculative, it is based on an indisputable fact. During some thirty centuries of Western civilization, women writers were the exception rather than the rule. In all of Greek and Roman literature, only one woman is generally remembered, the poet Sappho; during the Middle Ages and the Renaissance, at most there are a dozen, including Christine de Pisan and Marie de France. The seventeenth, eighteenth, and nineteenth centuries were only slightly better. Even though one might point to the established reputations of Jane Austen, Emily Dickinson, Elizabeth Barrett Browning, Charlotte Brontë, and Emily Brontë as proof that at least by the nineteenth century, women writers no longer had to overcome insuperable obstacles, in actuality such achievements were as out of the ordinary as Sappho's. The statistics speak for themselves. More than eighty percent of the women writers included in this volume are products of the twentieth century. If creativity is a gift awarded equally to the sexes, in the past there must have been as many women who were denied a voice as men whose words have been preserved.

Women living in ancient Greece and in Renaissance Europe were prevented from writing by the same conditions and attitudes. One problem was their lack of education. No matter how high their level of society, no matter how literate their fathers, their brothers, and their husbands, women were expected to concern themselves not with reading, thinking, and writing, but with running households and rearing children. Therefore girls did not receive a general education, but instead were trained for a specific job. Once they married, their intellectual development was further hampered by a lack of time and of energy. They were burdened with domestic responsibilities and exhausted by frequent pregnancies, which often left them in poor health or sentenced them to early death. Furthermore, as long as the reading public was limited to members of the upper class, there was no audience for works by women. Believing that women were, at worst, irrational and, at best, inferior to them in intelligence, educated men were not interested in reading what women might write. On the other hand, while women would have welcomed some reflection of their own life experiences or at least some distraction from everyday life, most were unable to read.

During the seventeenth and eighteenth centuries, the rapid extension of literacy into the middle classes remedied one of these problems—the lack of an audience. At last the printed word was not reserved for a small, elite group; instead, there was a large new reading public, made up of women as well as of men, eager to pay their money for books that would inform and instruct them and quite willing to be entertained in the process. They were delighted with the new novels, which enabled them to read pious sentiments while they enjoyed the adventures of Daniel Defoe's Robinson Crusoe or were titillated by the sexual exploits of his Moll Flanders and Roxana. Interestingly, Defoe's heroines were ostensibly real women, telling their stories in the first person. They were soon to be followed by actual women authors.

Although in the seventeenth century Aphra Behn had brought out the popular philosophical tale *Oroonoko: Or, The History of the Royal Slave* (1688), it was not until the late eighteenth century that women authors began to claim a substantial share of the novel-reading public. Perhaps their efforts were accepted more easily because the genre was considered frivolous. As long as the stories women wrote for women were not morally reprehensible, men tended to think of them, and their authors, as harmlessly amusing. Many of the women writers of that period, such as the Gothic novelist Ann Radcliffe, are not read today except by specialists. Others, such as Mary Wollstonecraft Shelley, the creator of *Frankenstein* (1818), and the inimitable Jane Austen, have attained permanent popularity. In any case, these writers established a tradition and set a precedent. It was socially acceptable for a woman to be a professional writer.

Eventually, as they became better educated and were able to demonstrate their capacity for serious thought, women proved to the male publishing establishment and to the world that their works were worthy of a general audience. In viewing life from a woman's perspective, such contemporary women writers as Margaret Atwood, Gail Godwin, Nadine Gordimer, and Alice Walker have revealed new truths about society and about the universal human condition. They also emphasize the difficulties that creative and ambitious women still face: pressures from the past, uncertainties about identity, and, always, the need for time, energy, and space, an emotional and physical "Room of One's Own."

The final decades of the twentieth century saw not only an explosion of literary production among women but also an intense interest in the lives and works of women writers, present and past. This volume was designed to meet the needs of general readers who are interested in such authors. While space limitations dictate the omission of many worthy writers, past and present, the 135 authors whose works are discussed here represent the whole spectrum of writing by women—in poetry, drama, the novel, and short fiction and from antiquity to the end of the twentieth century. Traditional favorites such as Austen and Dickinson are covered along with contemporary figures such as Toni Morrison and Sandra Cisneros. Also notable is the linguistic, ethnic, and cultural diversity of the writers represented.

The articles are arranged in alphabetical order, beginning with the Russian poet Anna Akhmatova and concluding with the French novelist Marguerite Yourcenar. Each article is prepared by an academic specialist and follows the same accessible format, including a list of works, a biographical sketch, critical analysis, and a bibliography. An index lists authors, terms, and the individual works or collections that are discussed in the text. *Great Women Writers* will serve as an invaluable chairside reference, as an aid to study, and, perhaps most important, as a stimulus to further reading and to the development of new insights.

Rosemary M. Canfield Reisman

Great Women Writers

ANNA AKHMATOVA
Anna Andreyevna Gorenko

Born: Bol'shoy Fontan, near Odessa, Russian Empire;
June 23, 1889

Died: Domodedovo, near Moscow, Soviet Union;
March 5, 1966

Principal poetry

Vecher, 1912; *Chetki*, 1914; *Belaia staia*, 1917; *Podorozhnik*, 1921; *Anno Domini MCMXXI*, 1922, 1923; *Iz shesti knig*, 1940; *Izbrannye stikhotvoreniia*, 1943; *Stikhotvoreniia*, 1958, 1961; *Poema bez geroa*, 1960 (*A Poem Without a Hero*, 1973); *Rekviem*, 1963 (*Requiem*, 1964); *Beg vremeni*, 1965; *Sochineniia*, 1965; *Poems of A.*, 1973; *Selected Poems*, 1976; *Requiem, and Poem Without a Hero*, 1976.

Other literary forms

In addition to poetry, Anna Akhmatova wrote an unfinished play and many essays on Russian writers. Her spirited book *O Pushkine: Stat' i i zametki* (1977), published in its complete version posthumously, is one of the most discerning tributes to Alexander Pushkin by a fellow poet. Akhmatova also translated poems from the Old Egyptian, Hindu, Armenian, Chinese, French, Italian, and many other languages, most of these in collaboration with native speakers.

Achievements

Akhmatova enriched Russian literature immeasurably, not only with the quality of her poetry but also with the freshness and originality of her talent. Through Acmeism, a literary movement of which she was one of the founders and leading members, she effected a significant change of direction in Russian poetry in the second decade of the twentieth century. The Acmeists' insistence on clarity and precision of expression—much in the spirit of the Imagists, although the two movements developed independently of each other—represented a reaction against the intricate symbols and otherworldly preoccupations of the Symbolists. Akhmatova's youthful love poems brought her early fame, and her reputation was further enhanced during the long reign of terror in her country, through which she was able to preserve her dignity, both as a human being and as a poet. With Boris Pasternak, Osip Mandelstam, and Marina Tsvetayeva, Akhmatova is universally regarded as one of the four great poets of postrevolutionary Russia. Having been generously translated into English, Akhmatova's works are constantly gaining stature in world literature as well.

Biography

Anna Akhmatova—the pen name of Anna Andreyevna Gorenko—was born in a suburb of Odessa in 1889, into the family of a naval officer. Akhmatova began to write poetry when she was eleven, and her first poem was published in 1907. She achieved great popularity with her first books, *Vecher* and *Chetki*. After joining the literary movement called Acmeism, she played an important part in it together with Osip Mandelstam and with her husband, Nikolay Gumilyov, from whom she was later divorced. During World War I and the Russian Revolution, Akhmatova stood by her people even though she did not agree with the ideas and methods of the revolutionaries. Never politically inclined, she saw in the war and the revolution an evil that might eventually destroy the private world in which she had been able to address herself exclusively to her own problems. When the end of that world came, she refused to accept it, believing that she would be able to continue her sequestered life. She also refused to emigrate, saying that it took greater courage to stay behind and accept what came. The effect of the revolution on her life and creativity was not immediately evident, for she subsequently published two more collections of poetry. When her former husband and fellow Acmeist Gumilyov was shot, however,

Akhmatova realized that the new way of life was inimical to her own. Compelled to silence, she ceased to exist publicly, instead remaining an inner émigré for eighteen years and occupying herself mostly with writing essays and translating. This silence may have saved her life during the purges of the 1930's, although she was not spared agony while trying to ascertain the fate of her only son, a promising scholar of Asian history, who had been sent to a labor camp three times. Only World War II brought a change to Akhmatova's dreary and dangerous life. Like many Soviet writers and intellectuals, she once again sided with her people, suppressing her reservations and complaints. She spent the first several months of the war in besieged Leningrad and then was evacuated to Tashkent, where she stayed almost to the end of the war. In Tashkent, she was brought closer to the other part of her ancestry, for her grandmother, from whom she took her pen name, was a Tartar.

When the war was over and the authorities again resorted to repression, Akhmatova was among the first to be victimized. In a vitriolic speech by Andrei Zhdanov, the cultural dictator at that time, she and the satirist Mikhail Zoshchenko were singled out as exam-ples of anti-Soviet attitudes among intellectuals and charged with harmful influence on the young. They were expelled from the Writers' Union, and their works ceased to be published. Thus, Akhmatova vanished from public view once again in 1946, this time involuntarily, and did not reappear until ten years later. In 1958, a slender collection of her poems was published as a sign of rehabilitation. A few more of her books were subsequently published, both at home and abroad, thus reinstating the poet as an active member of society. During the last decade of her life, she wrote some of the best poetry of her career. Shortly before her death, she received two richly deserved accolades for her work. Ironically, the recognition came from abroad: She was awarded the prestigious Italian Etna Taormina Prize in 1964 and an honorary doctorate from Oxford University in 1965. Ravaged by long illness, she died in 1966, having preserved her dignity and independence by asking for and receiving a church funeral according to the Russian Orthodox rites. After her death, Akhmatova was almost unanimously eulogized as the finest woman poet in all Russian literature.

Analysis

Anna Akhmatova's poetry can conveniently be divided into three distinct periods: 1912 to 1923, 1940 to 1946, and 1956 to 1966 (with a few poems published in 1950). The interim periods were those of enforced silence. The first silence, from 1923 to 1940, came as a result of tacit admission on her part that the changed way of life in Russia was not fully acceptable to her. The second, from 1946 to 1956, was a direct result of the authorities' intervention. Needless to say, Akhmatova kept busy by further refining her poetry, by writing essays, and by translating.

Akhmatova's development as a poet can be traced from book to book. Her first books, *Vecher* and *Chetki*, impressed readers with the freshness of a young woman's concern about her feelings of love. In almost all the poems having love as a focal point, Akhmatova presents love from a woman's point of view, in a form resembling a diary. The beloved is almost always silent, never fully revealed or described, and at times he seems to be almost secondary—only a catalyst for the woman's feelings. She is so entranced by his mere presence that, in her anguish, she draws her "left-hand glove upon [her] right." The poet expresses the whole spectrum of love—from the playfulness of a young woman trying to dismay her partner in order to prove that she, too, can wield some power over him, to moments of flaming passion. To be sure, passion is presented implicitly, in the time-honored tradition of Russian literature, yet it is also vividly indicated in unique ways. As she says, "In human intimacy there is a secret boundary,/ Neither the experience of being in love nor passion can cross it/ Though the lips be joined together in awful silence/ And the heart break asunder with love." Her fervent passion is coupled with fidelity to her partner, but as her loyalty is professed time and again, a note of frustration and a fear of incompatibility and rejection become noticeable. The prospect of unrequited love is confirmed by betrayal and parting. The ensuing feeling of loneliness leads to despair and withdrawal. The woman's reaction shows a mixture of anger, defiance, even resignation: "Be accursed . . ./ But I swear by the garden of angels/ By the holy icon I swear,/ By the passionate frenzy of our nights,/ I will never go back to you!" (These lines prompted Zhdanov, in his merciless attack many years later, to call Akhmatova "a nun and a harlot.") Thus, celebration, parting, and suffering receive equal play in Akhmatova's approach to love, although the ultimate outcome is a markedly un-happy one. Her love poetry is a vivid testimony both to the glories and to the miseries of her sex.

The feminine "I" of the poems seeks refuge, release, and salvation in religion, nature, and poetry. The refuge in religion is especially evident in *Chetki*. The work has a peculiar religious tone, pervaded, like Akhmatova's sentiments of love, with a mood of melancholy and inexplicable sadness. The persona seems to have found consolation for unhappiness in love when she says: "The King of Heaven has healed my/ Soul with the icy calm of love's/ Absence." Her prayers are mostly in the form of confession or intercession. It is easy to see, however, that they are used primarily to compensate for her feeling of loneliness and weariness of life. Thus, privations and misfortunes are closely tied to her religious feelings; sin and atonement are inseparable, and her passions of the flesh are tempered by spiritual fervor. Akhmatova's po-ems with religious overtones have little in common with customary religious experience. They are also much more complex and psychologically laden than any of her other poetry.

In Akhmatova's third collection, *Belaia staia*, a new theme joins those of love and religion: a presentiment of doom. Nourished by the horrors of war and revolution, this presentiment grows into a wake for a world on the verge of annihilation. As the revolution dragged on, Akhmatova's mood turned bleaker and more hopeless. She sought rapport with the events by writing poetry with political motifs, but to no avail. The poems in *Anno Domini MCMXXI* clearly reveal Akhmatova's state of mind and emotions at this difficult time, as well as her awareness that an era had come to an end. "All is sold, all is lost, all is plundered,/ Death's wing has flashed black on our sight,/ All's gnawed bare with sore, want, and sick longing," she laments in one poem. She refused to emigrate, however, knowing instinctively, as did Boris Pasternak many years later when he was threatened with expulsion from the Soviet Union, that for a poet to leave his or her native land is tantamount to a death worse than physical death. She did not hesitate to criticize those who had left their country in its worst hour: "Poor exile, you are like a prisoner/ To me, or one upon the bed/ Of sickness. Dark your road, O wanderer,/ Of wormwood smacks your alien bread." These lines were quoted often by Soviet critics for propaganda purposes, although Akhmatova wrote them sincerely, as a poet who could not tear herself away from her own land.

In the poems in which Akhmatova grappled with the problems of present-day reality, a gradual shift away from intimate love poetry toward more worldly themes can be seen. This shift can be considered as an overture to another kind of Akhmatova's poetry. Tormented by the turbulent years of war and revolution, in which she made many personal sacrifices and witnessed many tragedies, she was forced to face reality and to express her feelings and opinions about it. The silence imposed on her in 1923 only postponed further development in that direction. When she was allowed to reappear shortly before World War II, she wrote little in her old idiom. In many poems written during the war, she extols the beauty of her land and the magnitude of the martyrdom of her people under attack by a ruthless enemy. Leningrad, the city of her life and of her dreams, is especially the object of her affection. Tsarskoe Selo—a settlement near Len-ingrad that was the residence of the czars, the town of young Alexander Pushkin, and the town of Akhmatova's favorite poetry teacher, Innokenty Annensky, as well as of her own youth—remained vividly and forever etched in her memory, even when she saw it almost totally destroyed in the war.

Leningrad and Tsarskoe Selo were not the only places to which Akhmatova paid homage; indeed, all Russia was her home. From her earliest poems to her last, Akhmatova expressed the same feeling for Russia, a strange mixture of abstract love for her country, on the one hand, and down-to-earth concern for its people, on the other. In the poem "Prayer," for example, she prays to the Lord to take even her child and to destroy "the sweet power of song" that she possesses if it would help to change "the storm cloud over Russia . . . into a nimbus ablaze." This willingness to sacrifice what is dearest to her if it would benefit her country is no mere affecta-tion—it is expressed with utmost sincerity and convic-tion. In a poem written almost thirty years later, "From an Airplane," she again expresses her love for her coun-try in no less sincere terms: "It is all mine—and nothing can divide us,/ It is my soul, it is my body, too." Perhaps the most profound and meaningful testimony to her patriotism can be found in the poem "Native Land," written in the last years of her life. For her, her country was "the mud on our gumboots, the grit in our teeth . . . And we mill, and we mix, and we crumble/ This innocent earth at our feet,/ But we rest in this earth at the roots of the flowers,/ Which is why we so readily say: It is ours!"

Akhmatova did not limit her gaze to European Russia,

where she was reared and where she spent most of her life. Through her experiences in Tashkent, the city in which her ancestors had resided, she acquired a great admiration for, and understanding of, the Asian mind and soul. A mystical bond with Asia inspired her to write some of her most beautiful descriptive poems, such as "From the Oriental Notebook."

Nevertheless, Akhmatova could not close her eyes to the Soviet reality, in which she was personally caught in a most tragic way. In a unified cycle of poems, *Requiem*, a masterpiece left unpublished in the Soviet Union, she expresses her deep sorrow not only about her personal loss but also about the suffering to which the Russian people were subjected. *Requiem* was her closest approach to public castigation of the regime in her country. The tone for the entire work is set by the motto, which sadly admits that the circumstances are not those of a foreign country but, more personally, those of the poet's own country and people. In a short foreword in prose, Akhmatova tells how during the horrible years of the purges she spent seventeen months waiting in line in front of a prison in order to discover the fate of her son. Another woman recognized her and whispered, "Can you describe this?" "Yes, I can," Akhmatova replied. She kept her promise by writing *Requiem*. Although much of it reflects the universal sorrow and despair of a mother on the verge of losing her son, it is the injustice of her suffering that most pains the poet. Using her personal sorrow to speak for all human beings who suffer unjustly, the poet created in *Requiem* a work of lasting value. Moreover, there is much encouragement to be gained from *Requiem*. The persona does not lose hope and courage. She perseveres, knowing that the victims are unjustly persecuted and that she is not alone in suffering. In the epilogue, she recalls the trying hours and the faces she has seen in those seventeen months; in her final words, she begs that her monument be erected in front of the prison where she has stood for "three hundred hours," so that the thawing snow from the face of her monument will glide like tears. Even if overt references to the political terror are overlooked, *Requiem* is still one of the twentieth century's most eloquent poetic testimonies to human tragedy.

Akhmatova's poetry from the last decade of her life shows the greater maturity and wisdom of old age. Her approach to poetic themes is more epic and historical, with a deeper perspective. This mature poetry is also more philosophical and psychological. The best example is the autobiographical *A Poem Without a Hero*, a panoramic view of the nineteenth century as it pertains to the twentieth. It is a subtle and at times complex poem, difficult to fathom without a proper key. In her last poems, she speaks as if she has realized that her active role is over and that nothing else can hurt her. Her work at this time shows a mixture of sadness, resignation, relief, and even slight bewilderment as to what life really is after more than seven decades of coping with it: "The grim epoch diverted me/ As if I were a river./ I have been given a different life. In a new bed/ The river now flows, past the old one,/ And I cannot find my shores. . . ." She finds solace in her increasing loneliness, contemplating the past, trying to reevaluate it and to find the correct perspective on it. In one of her last poems, written slightly more than a year before her death, she speaks of the "Supreme Mystery." It has been on her mind from the beginning, changing its face from period to period. In her early poetry, it was the mystery of the romantic relationship. Later, it became the mystery of the human relationship, with the emphasis on cruelty. In her last years, it became the mystery of the relationship of humankind to eternity, indeed the mystery of the meaning of existence. Through such organic development, Akhmatova reached the pinnacle of her poetic power, the power found in Pasternak's late poetry and in the work of other great poets of the twentieth century.

The stylistic aspect of Akhmatova's poetry is just as important as the thematic one, if not more so. She shows several peculiarly Akhmatovian features. Above all, there is the narrative tone that points to a definite affinity with prose. It is this affinity that enables her to switch easily from emotion to description. Connected with this skill is a dramatic quality, expressed through either inner monologue or dialogue. The second striking feature is the brief lyric form, usually consisting of three to four stanzas, rarely five to seven, and never more than seven. (Later in her career, Akhmatova wrote many poems in free verse.) Parallel to the brevity of form is a pronounced laconism: A few carefully selected details suffice to convey an entire picture. Akhmatova's economy of words, spare almost to the point of frugality, led her to the epigrammatic form and to fragmentation, understatement, and improvisation. As a result, her sentences are sometimes verbless and even without a subject (that being quite possible in Russian). Another peculiarity is the concreteness of her images, especially with reference to space and time. She tells the reader exactly where and when, almost to the minute, the events in her poem take place. The colors are vividly and exactly given. She avoids metaphors, instead using pointed, explanatory epithets. Finally, her intonation, never scrupulously measured or regulated, is that of a syncopated rhythm, approaching the rhythm of some forms of folk poetry.

Many of these stylistic features result from her adherence to the tenets of Acmeism, but many others are uniquely her own and are easily recognizable as such. Akhmatova is a poet without whom modern Russian literature is unthinkable and by whom world literature has been significantly enriched.

Other major work

NONFICTION: *O Pushkine: Stat' i i zametki*, 1977.

Bibliography

Amert, Susan. *In a Shattered Mirror: The Later Poetry of Anna Akhmatova*. Stanford, Calif.: Stanford University Press, 1992.

Driver, Sam N. *Anna Akhmatova*. New York: Twayne, 1972.

Eikhenbaum, Boris. *Anna Akhmatova: Opyt analiza*. Paris: Lev, 1923.

Haight, Amanda. *Anna Akhmatova: A Poetic Pilgrimage*. New York: Oxford University Press, 1976.

Verheul, Kees. *The Theme of Time in the Poetry of Anna Akhmatova*. The Hague: Mouton, 1971.

LOUISA MAY ALCOTT

Born: Germantown, Pennsylvania; November 29, 1832

Died: Boston, Massachusetts; March 6, 1888

Principal long fiction

Moods, 1864; *Little Women*, 1868-1869; *An Old-Fashioned Girl*, 1870; *Little Men*, 1871; *Work: A Story of Experience*, 1873; *Eight Cousins*, 1875; *Rose in Bloom*, 1876; *Jo's Boys*, 1886.

Other literary forms

In addition to her novels, Louisa May Alcott wrote many short stories. Her first book, *Flower Fables* (1854), was a collection of fairy tales written for Ralph Waldo Emerson's daughter, Ellen. During the 1850's, Alcott wrote sentimental stories, most of which were published under a pseudonym, and in the 1860's she published sensational thrillers both anonymously and under a pseudonym. She also tried her hand at poetry, signing her first newspaper poems with the name "Flora Fairchild," and she succeeded in publishing many historical and feminist essays later in her career. Having written dramas and home theatricals since childhood, she was pleased to see her farce *Nat Bachelor's Pleasure Trip* presented at the Howard Atheneum on May 4, 1860. Letters written home during her short stint as a Civil War nurse were published with a narrative frame as *Hospital Sketches* (1863). As editor of a girls' magazine, *Merry's Museum*, she wrote poetry, stories, and advice columns, the latter under the pseudonym "Aunty Wee."

Achievements

Alcott was a prolific and versatile writer. Her remarkable versatility was slow to come to public recognition, however, because she often wrote anonymously and under various pseudonyms, many of which were only discovered by historians and scholars a century later. Her career and her life illustrate the difficulties that a woman in mid-nineteenth century America had trying to live independently and to avoid the stultifying conventions of the day—conventions of which Alcott was keenly and personally aware.

Although she had published many stories in journals such as *The Atlantic Monthly* and *Olive Branch*, Alcott did not become known as a serious writer until *Hospital Sketches*. The work that made her name and established her professional identity, however, was the novel *Little Women*. As shown by most of her writings, Alcott knew how to appeal to a given audience, in this case young girls; the themes of growing to maturity, of dealing with adversity, and of recognizing the moral authority of the family circle may account for the novel's continued popularity.

Alcott struggled her entire life to make a difference in the world. Because her famous father, Bronson Alcott, was never a good provider and ceased early on even to try, Louisa assumed the role of caretaker to her family, eventually extending this responsibility to take in her niece Louisa, whom the family called Lulu, after the death of May Alcott Nierecker, Louisa's youngest sister. Time and time again, Louisa put her own interests second to those of her family, and she devoted her last years to caring for Lulu and for her father. As a result of her dedication to her family, she sacrificed her own desires for adventure and travel and wrote the kind of fiction that would sell.

Nevertheless, even under the domestic serenity for which her writing is known, feminist themes and issues emerge. The difficulty of women in finding gratifying and respectable employment is an enduring theme throughout the Alcott corpus. Her heroines are often women who are independent, lively, and spirited. The sensational writings betray Alcott's enthusiasm for willful, strong women who triumph over the restrictions of their time. In her later years, Alcott used her celebrity status to endorse the women's movement, attending congresses, writing public letters supporting the suffrage movement, and campaigning for the vote in Concord, Massachusetts, where she was the first woman to register to vote. Recent and growing awareness of the extent and variety of her writings has brought new interest in the life of Alcott, and she is beginning to receive the serious and respectful study that she genuinely deserves.

Biography

Louisa May Alcott was born on November 29, 1832, the second daughter of four to Amos Bronson and Abba May Alcott. Although born in Germantown, Pennsylvania, Alcott is associated with Concord and Boston, Massachusetts, where she lived and worked most of her life. Her father was the friend of the leading intellectuals in Concord, the famous Transcendentalists Ralph Waldo Emerson and Henry David Thoreau, and Emerson virtually became Louisa's idol.

Bronson Alcott was a man of vision, commitment, and imagination, but few practical skills—certainly without the talent and inclination necessary to support a family of six. Shortly after the birth of Louisa, he moved his family to Boston, where he organized and ran the Temple School. Like many of Bronson Alcott's ventures, the school was impressive in its philosophy but unsuitable in its realization. The school employed many teaching techniques that have since come into vogue, and one of its teachers was Margaret Fuller. The Temple School was more liberal than many Bostonians could tolerate, however, and after six years Alcott was forced to close its doors and shoulder much of the school's debt. This rupture was to have great significance to the young Louisa, for it was the last time her father would have anything resembling a steady income. After this period, the family's financial state was always critical, and when she was old enough, Louisa herself assumed the family's financial burdens.

After a trip to England and the subsequent failure of his experiment in utopian living, Fruitlands, Bronson finally had a nervous breakdown, and his wife, Abba, became the head of the household. It was at this point that the Alcott girls confronted their future of poverty and sought odd jobs to ease their financial instability. While poverty is never welcome, Louisa's experiences nevertheless provided her with both the substance and the vision for much of her later writing. She learned at first hand the lack of economic opportunity available to women and the extent to which they were restricted by the conventions and mores of mid-nineteenth century America. On the positive side, she also experienced the family bonding that adversity sometimes brings and learned respect for women who stand up to life's hard times.

As the family moved around to various Massachusetts towns, Louisa adopted the pattern of living for a few months in Boston, picking up odd jobs and writing, and then returning to the family when she earned a little money. Thus the family became the focus of her life—living with them when possible and working for them when away. Her own wishes for travel and adventure were postponed in favor of earning some money to help the family at home. The themes of self-denial and family loyalty that run through her writings stem from the reality of her own life. So too, the bold and adventurous heroines who create opportunities and triumph against the odds even if they must employ unscrupulous methods reveal the other side of Alcott's frustration with her life.

Thus Alcott wrote under duress, for the sole purpose of earning money. In 1851, the poem "Sunlight" was published in *Peterson's Magazine*, but Alcott quickly realized that poetry did not pay as well as fiction and began to write short stories. In 1852, her first story, "The Rival Painters: A Tale of Rome," was published in *Olive Branch*, followed by other stories in the *Saturday Evening Gazette* and *The Atlantic Monthly*. For a decade, Alcott churned out the sentimental tales for which readers of the period clamored.

In 1862, Alcott became a hospital nurse for Union troops in Washington, D.C. In a very short time, however, she contracted typhoid fever and had to return home to recuperate. While she recovered enough to write, she never regained the vitality of her youth, suffering perhaps as much from the mercury "cure" as from the disease itself. She had seen and experienced much, and she converted her letters into a series of sketches with a narrative frame, published as *Hospital Sketches*. While the volume did not earn much money, it did gain for her a literary reputation and helped to crystallize her style.

In the 1860's, Alcott wrote sensational stories, many

of which were published under the pseudonym "A. M. Barnard." Among these stories are fantasies of female revenge and power that contrast sharply with the domestic idealism of her novels for young girls, the fiction for which she is known. Indeed, when Thomas Niles of Roberts Brothers publishers invited her to write a story for young girls, Alcott agreed only reluctantly. *Little Women* was an enormous success from the beginning of its serialization, and in 1868, she moved to Boston and wrote a chapter a day on the second half until it was completed. *Little Women* established Alcott's reputation as a writer of children's books, and while the sequels

were many, none was as successful as her first.

In the 1870's, having achieved wide recognition, Alcott involved herself publicly with such women's issues as suffrage, wrote children's books that would sell, and composed essays and letters advocating women's rights. After the death of her mother in 1879, the care of Bronson fell on her even more heavily, although both father and daughter suffered from ill health as they aged. Bronson Alcott died during the night on March 4, 1888, and Louisa May Alcott died two days later. They had a joint funeral and were buried in Sleepy Hollow Cemetery in Concord, Massachusetts.

Analysis

Alcott is best known for her enormously successful and enduringly popular *Little Women*. While the novel was written at the instigation of Thomas Niles, who was looking for a best-seller, Alcott managed to throw herself into the work and create a novel that would speak to the Victorian era, become part of the American family mythos, and provide a good read as well. Readers were enchanted with the story of the March family: Marmee and her four daughters Meg, Jo, Amy, and Beth.

Little Women appeared in an era when sentimentality was appreciated by readers, and the novel has its share of sentimental events and speeches. The most obvious occurs with the obligatory death of young Beth. Perhaps Alcott was pandering to the Victorian fascination with death in this episode, or perhaps she was basing the event, as she does others, on her own home life (her sister Elizabeth had died at an early age). Whatever the reason, it certainly did not hurt sales to have the best, the most loved, the most generous, the most serene of all the sisters die an early death. So good Beth succumbs, using even her illness and death to encourage others to lead a better life.

The novel has a strong didactic tone throughout. Beth's virtues are clearly to be emulated, but she is not the only character concerned with developing a stronger moral core. Indeed, early in the novel a parallel with John Bunyan's *The Pilgrim's Progress* (1678, 1684) is established: Just as the girls as children used to play at pilgrim's progress in a game that would take them physically from basement to attic, now they are encouraged to challenge themselves morally to reach higher levels of goodness. Each of the little women has a particular flaw to which to attend—Amy's selfishness, Meg's vanity,

Jo's wild spirit and roughness, and Beth's shyness. Many chapter titles use the allegorical names of Bunyan, such as "Meg Goes to Vanity Fair," the title of chapter 9, and in this way the novel's episodes take on an archetypal and instructional significance without constant outright preaching. While seizing upon a concept crucial in its own period, *Little Women* has eased the way to adulthood for generations of young women by providing several models for self-improvement among different personality types.

Some of the virtues held up for women were generosity, self-sacrifice, docility, and respect for authority. Marmee and the girls are so poor at Christmas that it promises to be a grim holiday. Nevertheless, the young women find ways to give in the spirit of Christmas, and there is always enough to share with people even poorer than they. Marmee consistently cares for the sick, and when she cannot because she must nurse Father, who is ill in Washington, D.C., the girls take over for her. Indeed, the scarlet fever that Beth contracts comes when she assumes Marmee's visits of charity to a family in the neighborhood. Beth never fully recovers, and her act of charity initiates the slow decline into her premature but most saintly death. She has sacrificed her health, her life, for others, and all are aware of her consummate goodness.

There are other kinds of self-sacrifice lauded in the novel as well. Meg gives up her dreams of parties, fashions, and social events to marry a respectable young man and become the mother of twins. Jo gives up her freedom and tomboyish behavior to work as companion to a crotchety aunt so that she can help the family financially. All this self-sacrifice occurs under the watchful eye of Marmee, who is clearly the moral center of the family since Father is away. Yet even she submits to the undisputed authority of Father, supporting the strong family hierarchy for which the Victorian period is known. Being docile and respecting authority were virtues that all the girls practice, although such behavior is clearly more difficult for Jo than for any of the others.

A tight family circle is another crucial theme in *Little Women*. Just as one can recall the Victorian era's stiff family portraits, the image of Marmee and her four girls warming themselves at the fire as they do hand work of various kinds and chat is an image of family unity that lingers long after a reader turns the final pages. Indeed, so strong is the ideal of the family circle that even marriage, an undisputed goal for young women and an economic necessity during this period, was seen as a potential threat to family solidarity. Consequently, when Meg decides to marry, her decision is received not so much with exultation as with regret for the inevitable. The other girls must sacrifice their interest in retaining the family circle that has been so supportive and so warm in the hope of Meg's greater happiness.

A reader at first might find it curious that Father is absent in a novel that so valorizes the family. Marmee's husband is away working as a chaplain during the Civil War. His presence in the family comes only by way of letters he sends home, exhorting the girls to become better. His is a moral presence, not a physical one, and the entire family looks to him for ethical guidance and eagerly anticipates his return. No doubt Alcott was far more comfortable writing about women than about men, her own father being so inconsequential in effecting family stability. Having Mr. March absent himself from the novel in such a respectable way was a triumph in economy for Alcott, who could then focus on the female characters with whom she was comfortable and the female audience that she was assigned to reach.

As readers have taken a second look at *Little Women*, no character has evoked more debate than Jo, the most spirited, disgruntled, and outspoken of the little women.

Because Jo rejects the marriage proposal of Laurie, the boy next door who had been her companion for many years, many readers see Jo's later marriage to stuffy Professor Bhaer as a capitulation to convention. Bhaer sets a clear hierarchy that puts Jo in a subservient position: He is older than Jo; he is better educated and has taught her German; and he first manages to get her to stop writing her sensational stories, then keeps her too busy with his boys' school to do much of anything creative. Many of the traits that had made Jo so endearing and interesting are sacrificed. Because Alcott herself never married and evidenced feminist concerns all of her life, the outcome she devises for Jo seems to some a sell-out that is unworthy of her.

Yet these critics and readers forget that Alcott's real intention with *Little Women* was to write something that would please, and please it did—both the young girls who were the intended audience and their parents, who wanted their daughters to be taught the lessons that they wanted them to learn. This was no time to be radical, to indulge in one's own fancies, but to write what people wanted to read. In this Alcott was highly successful; her success was a personal triumph, for she earned the money she needed and established her literary reputation.

When Alcott was not concerned about writing according to conventions, she freely indulged her desires for women to be powerful, enactors of their revenge and passion, rather than passive recipients of male commands. Her novels for adults, such as *Moods* and *Work*, and especially the sensational stories, characterize women differently from the docile creatures of the domestic fiction for children. In the fiction for adults, women often succeed by subterfuge, carry out their revenge, consummate their passion, and realize their own identities rather than those designed for them by men. Although Alcott is best known for her children's literature, today's mature readers and students of nineteenth century literature find her adult literature fascinating to study, exciting to read, and worthy of the avowed feminist that Alcott came to be.

Other major works

NOVEL: *A Modern Mephistopheles*, 1877.

SHORT FICTION: *Flower Fables*, 1854; *Behind a Mask: The Unknown Thrillers of Louisa May Alcott*, 1975; *Plots and Counterplots: More Unknown Thrillers of Louisa May Alcott*, 1976; *A Double Life: Newly Discovered Thrillers of Louisa May Alcott*, 1988.

PLAY: *Nat Bachelor's Pleasure Trip*, pr. 1860.

NONFICTION: *Hospital Sketches*, 1863; *Transcendental Wild Oats*, 1915.

Bibliography

Bedell, Madelon. *The Alcotts: Biography of a Family.* New York: Clarkson N. Potter, 1980.

Elbert, Sarah. *A Hunger for Home: Louisa May Alcott and Little Women.* Philadelphia: Temple University Press, 1984.

MacDonald, Ruth K. *Louisa May Alcott.* Boston: Twayne, 1983.

Saxton, Martha. *Louisa May: A Modern Biography of Louisa May Alcott.* Boston: Houghton Mifflin, 1977.

Stern, Madeleine, ed. *Critical Essays on Louisa May Alcott.* Boston: G. K. Hall, 1984.

ISABEL ALLENDE

Born: Lima, Peru; August 2, 1942

Principal long fiction

La casa de los espíritus, 1982 (*The House of the Spirits*, 1985); *De amor y de sombra*, 1984 (*Of Love and Shadows*, 1987); *Eva Luna*, 1987 (English translation, 1988); *El plan infinito*, 1991 (*The Infinite Plan*, 1993).

Other literary forms

In addition to her novels, Isabel Allende is well known for her collection of short stories *Cuentos de Eva Luna* (1990; *The Stories of Eva Luna*, 1991) and for her many hundreds of newspaper columns and articles, interviews, plays, and short stories for children. Some of her humorous essays, originally published in the magazine *Paula*, were collected under the title *Civilice a su troglodita: Los Impertinentes de Isabel Allende* (1974). One of her books for children, *La gorda de porcelana* (1984), weaves reality and fantasy together, as in her novels for adults.

Achievements

Allende's novels have been instant and enduring best-sellers, translated into many languages and published in many editions. These novels, her short stories, and her frequent public appearances have established Allende as one of the best-known contemporary Latin American writers and as a spokesperson for her country and for human rights. Her novels are romantic love stories that also speak eloquently of the problems of those who are often voiceless: the poor, the politically oppressed, agricultural workers and servants, recent immigrants, factory workers, soldiers in Vietnam, and, above all, women of all classes and cultures.

Biography

Isabel Allende was born to Chilean parents living in Lima, Peru, on August 2, 1942. After her parents' divorce when she was three, she moved to Chile with her mother and lived in her maternal grandparents' home in Santiago. It is these eccentric and articulate grandparents who later served as models for Clara and Esteban Trueba in *The House of the Spirits*, and Allende has often spoken of the wonderful stories they told her. She learned how to read when she was very young, and she read constantly. She speaks of especially loving the works of Jules Verne, Emilio Sagari, and Charles Dickens and William Shakespeare's plays. She says that she has always loved to invent tales, and that as a child she listened to radio soap operas and to the maids' stories in the kitchen, believing that these were all true tales.

When she was ten years old, her mother married a Chilean diplomat, and they lived in Bolivia, Europe, and the Middle East. When she was fifteen and living in Lebanon, diplomats were asked to send their families home because of political tensions, so Allende went back to Santiago to live with her grandparents. When she finished high school at sixteen, she began to work for the Santiago office of the Food and Agriculture Organization of the United Nations, which soon had her appearing on television in a program on world hunger. This was so successful that a new career of television appearances was launched. By the age of seventeen, she had begun to contribute articles to newspapers and to the magazine *Paula*. She married Miguel Frías, a civil engineer, when she was nineteen, and they had two children, Paula and Nicolás. In Santiago, she continued to write columns and articles, had her own interview program on television, and wrote children's stories for *Mampato* magazine. She says that she enjoyed every aspect of journalism and wrote everything from horoscopes to humorous advice columns, feature articles, interviews, and even recipes. She was also involved with theater, writing four plays between 1970 and 1975.

Allende was much affected, as were all Chileans, by the military coup that overthrew her uncle, the first democratically elected Marxist president of Chile, Salvador Allende, on September 11, 1973. Initially, Isabel

Allende and her husband intended to remain in Chile, believing that the dictatorship would be only temporary, but when they realized that their presence and their efforts to help others were endangering themselves and their families, they decided to leave. She has said that when she left Chile in 1975, she took along a small suitcase, family photographs, a small bag of Chilean soil, and a volume of Pablo Neruda's poetry. Once established in Venezuela in 1975, Allende wrote a weekly column in the newspaper *El Nacional* for eight years, but was otherwise unable to find much other work as a journalist. She worked as a school administrator and started writing fiction. Upon hearing that her beloved grandfather in Santiago was dying, she began to write him a letter, which grew longer and longer and eventually turned into her first novel, *The House of the Spirits*. After its publication in Spain in 1982, it became an immediate best-seller.

Divorced from her first husband, Allende married a U.S. citizen, William Gordon, in 1988. They moved to San Rafael, California, near San Francisco. She often speaks of the importance of her family and comments that, if ever she thinks of herself as an individual entity, "it's an entity that includes my children, my grandchildren, my mother, my relatives," and all those who matter to her. The death of her daughter Paula in 1992 was a tragedy which deeply affected her. She says that her refuge from pain is in writing, in storytelling, in meeting her responsibility as one who takes seriously the recording of the history of her family, her country, and her time.

Analysis

The House of the Spirits, Isabel Allende's first novel, is an ambitious account of Chilean twentieth century history and of four generations of strong women. At the center of the novel are the women of the del Valle/Trueba family: Nivea, an early feminist and suffragette; her daughter Clara, clairvoyant but also charitable and compassionate; Clara's daughter Blanca, trapped between her duty to her family and the great love of her life; and Blanca's daughter Alba, who becomes a bridge between her conservative grandfather and her revolutionary lover. It is through Alba's eyes that one sees the repression of the military takeover. The country in which *The House of the Spirits* is set is never named, but is clearly Chile, just as the poet and the Candidate (later the President) unmistakably represent Pablo Neruda and Salvador Allende. Much of the novel is a fictionalized version of real experiences and family memories.

Magic and metaphor intertwine with realistic description in the novel; memory slips into myth and legend, and the supernatural becomes another dimension of the events recounted. Clara's sister Rosa has the green hair and uncanny beauty of a mermaid, and Clara herself has a remarkable (however sporadic and unreliable) ability to foresee certain events, although this prescience is more entertaining than useful, since no one believes her serious predictions of earthquakes or other disasters.

The novel is narrated retrospectively by Alba, who bases her account on her grandmother Clara's notebooks and on all the family stories she has heard, as well as upon her own experience. Another first-person voice throughout the novel is that of Esteban Trueba, who is Nivea's son-in-law, Clara's husband, Blanca's father, and Alba's grandfather. Esteban Trueba is a traditional, energetic, dominating landlord and patriarch whose conservative views of justice and power cause him to oppose socialism and champion the military coup of 1973 until he is made to see that its abuses of human rights are unacceptable by any moral standard.

Of Love and Shadows, Allende's second novel, also presents a series of contrasts between love and violence, light and shadow, freedom and repression, and order and chaos. It is the story of Irene Beltrán, a woman's magazine journalist reared to be an upper-class lady, who gradually realizes what kind of oppressive reality surrounds her. Her companion in this political awakening is Francisco Leal, son of idealistic Spanish Civil War exiles, a photographer, and an active opponent of the military regime. Irene and Francisco find their love for each other as they lose their political innocence. When they are sent by the magazine to cover what initially seems to be a nonpolitical story (the seizures or mystic trances of a fifteen-year-old village girl), it eventually leads them to the discovery of a mine shaft full of the dismembered bodies of political prisoners who have disappeared, a horror which they manage to publicize with the help of the Catholic church. This aspect of the novel is based upon the actual discovery in 1978 of unmarked graves at Lonquén, an incident which was also reported by church authorities. Like *The House of the Spirits*, *Of Love and Shadows* is set in an unnamed country, but there is no doubt that it portrays specific Chilean experience of the 1970's. The novel is about the importance of bearing witness and of opposing institutional violence even when it is disguised as protective law enforcement.

In *Eva Luna*, an adventurous storyteller recounts the major events of her life in an unnamed country that is clearly Venezuela. Daughter of a displaced servant and a dying Indian gardener, the child is named Eva, which her mother believes means "life," and Luna, for her father's tribe, the Children of the Moon. Like all Allende's heroines, Eva grows up nourished by stories. According to Eva, her mother's tales "sowed in my mind the idea that reality is not only what we see on the surface; it has a magical dimension as well and, if we so desire, it is legitimate to enhance it and color it to make our journey through life less trying."

Eva's account of her own life alternates with chapters about Rolf Carlé, beginning with his childhood in Austria just before World War II; predictably, the two story lines fuse at the end of the book when Eva and Rolf fall in love. Rolf Carlé's career as a news photographer has brought him into contact with Huberto Naranjo, a guerrilla commander Eva has known since they were homeless street children together. Like Alba and her guerrilla lover in *The House of the Spirits* and like Irene and Francisco in *Of Love and Shadows*, Eva and Rolf are joined together in the end of *Eva Luna* by their collaboration in active opposition to the government—in this case, the escape of political prisoners from a penal colony.

Eva's tale is a picaresque account of successive displacements and enduring intermittent friendships. As she moves from place to place living by her wits, she is employed in a series of different jobs which allow her to see the whole spectrum of society from top to bottom. She is sheltered by a succession of strong, protective women: her mother, her godmother, Elvira the cook, a schoolteacher, and Mimí/Melesio, a beautiful transvestite. Gradually, Eva finds her own voice as a storyteller. She writes a fantastically successful script for a television series and, at the end, when the story of the confrontation between the military and the guerrillas in the prison escape is officially suppressed, she writes a factual account of this action into her television script so that the truth may be known. Like *The House of the Spirits*, which was a clandestine best-seller in Chile during the most repressive period of the military dictatorship and was used secretly as a textbook of contemporary history in schools in Chile when no other accounts of events of the 1970's were available, the fiction within the fiction of

Eva Luna serves not only to make sense of real events but also to provide the most basic information about these situations.

Allende's eagerness to dramatize the connections between individual personal lives and social contexts remains apparent in her fourth novel, *The Infinite Plan*, which is set in the United States and recounts the life story of a male protagonist, Gregory Reeves. Like *The House of the Spirits, The Infinite Plan* is both a family saga and a scrutiny of a half century of social change which culminates in physical violence: American participation in the Vietnam War. In both books, as in *Of Love and Shadows* and *Eva Luna*, this eruption of violence and the protagonists' involvement in it constitute the emotional center of the stories.

The reader first meets Gregory Reeves as a child, when he is zigzagging across the United States with his eccentric family: his messianic preacher-father who is obsessed with spreading the word about his all-explanatory "Infinite Plan"; his vague and unworldly mother; his sister, who will later become obese and focus her life exclusively upon mothering; and their bizarre friend Olga, steeped in natural remedies and fortune-telling. Their wanderings come to an end when Gregory's father becomes ill, and the family settles in a Latino immigrant barrio in East Los Angeles. Gregory survives the harsh experiences of public school and neighborhood gangs, and he is sustained by the loving concern of a Mexican family whose children, Juan José and Carmen, will be his lifelong friends. As in all Allende's novels, extremes of good and evil are set in epic opposition. Gregory makes enemies and friends, foolish decisions and wise ones. Berkeley, California, of the 1960's, with its flower children and ubiquitous drugs, is described as Gregory makes his way through chaotic undergraduate and law school years. He stumbles through two disastrous marriages that result in two seriously troubled children, as well as the horrors of the Vietnam War, unsatisfying jobs, and finally psychotherapy, which brings him to the point where he can tell his story: His is the first-person narration, which alternates with and complements a more omniscient third-person account. American values of the 1970's and 1980's are examined and found lacking: Rampant consumerism and inadequate human relationships afflict not only Gregory but also the society around him. The end of the novel, as with *The House of the Spirits, Of Love and Shadows*, and *Eva Luna*, offers the possibility of true love as panacea and resolution, but the social fragmentation portrayed in *The Infinite Plan* is resistant to analysis or transformation. Gregory Reeves tells the unnamed woman to whom he is recounting the story of his life: "Look how far I've come to reach this point and find there is no infinite plan, just the strife of living, I told you that day. Maybe, you answered, maybe everyone carries a plan inside, but it's a faded map that's hard to read and that's why we wander around and sometimes get lost." Gregory eventually takes responsibility for one of his impaired children, simplifies his life by stripping away all of his material possessions, finishes his course of therapy, and feels energetic and restored. Finally, he says, he is "aware of who I truly am, and at last . . . in control of my destiny."

Other major works

SHORT FICTION: *Cuentos de Eva Luna*, 1990 (*The Stories of Eva Luna*, 1991).
NONFICTION: *Civilice a su troglodita: Los Impertinentes de Isabel Allende*, 1974.
CHILDREN'S LITERATURE: *La gorda de porcelana*, 1984.

Bibliography

Earle, Peter G. "Literature as Survival: Allende's *The House of the Spirits*." *Contemporary Literature* 28 (Winter, 1987): 543-554.

Hart, Patricia. *Narrative Magic in the Fiction of Isabel Allende*. Rutherford, N.J.: Fairleigh Dickinson University Press, 1989.

Levine, Linda Gould. "A Passage to Androgyny: Isabel Allende's *La casa de los espíritus*." In *In the Feminine Mode: Essays on Hispanic Women Writers*, edited by Noël Valis and Carol Maier. Lewisburg, Pa.: Bucknell University Press, 1990.

Meyer, Doris. "Exile and the Female Condition in Isabel Allende's *De amor y de sombra*." *The International Fiction Review* 15 (Summer, 1988): 151-157.

Riquelme Rojas, Sonia, and Edna Aguirre Rehbein, eds. *Critical Approaches to Isabel Allende's Novels*. New York: P. Lang, 1991.

Schiminovich, F. H. "Two Modes of Writing the Female Self: Isabel Allende's *The House of the Spirits* and Clarice Lispector's *The Stream of Life*." In *Redefining Autobiography in Twentieth-Century Women's Fiction*, edited by Janice Morgan and Colette Hall. New York: Garland, 1991.

MAYA ANGELOU
Marguerite Johnson

Born: St. Louis, Missouri; April 4, 1928

Principal poetry

Just Give Me a Cool Drink of Water 'fore I Diiie, 1971; *Oh Pray My Wings Are Gonna Fit Me Well*, 1975; *And Still I Rise*, 1978; *Shaker, Why Don't You Sing?*, 1983; *Maya Angelou: Poems*, 1986 (contains her four previously published volumes); *Now Sheba Sings the Song*, 1987; *I Shall Not Be Moved*, 1990; "On the Pulse of Morning," 1993.

Other literary forms

Maya Angelou is renowned for her autobiographies, which include *I Know Why the Caged Bird Sings* (1970), *Gather Together in My Name* (1974); *Singin' and Swingin' and Gettin' Merry Like Christmas* (1976), *The Heart of a Woman* (1981), and *All God's Children Need Traveling Shoes* (1986). Angelou has also written for the stage, the screen, and television. Her television work includes scripts for the 1968 series *Blacks, Blues, Black*, the 1975 series *Assignment America*, and the African American-themed specials "The Legacy" and "The Inheritors," both shown in 1976.

Achievements

Angelou's achievements can be understood in the context of her life as she has documented it in her autobiographies. These works have generated great interest because of their connections with, and differences from, autobiographical narratives by prominent African American men such as Frederick Douglass, Booker T. Washington, W. E. B. Du Bois, and Malcolm X. The dominant pattern of Angelou's life is that of one woman's struggle to relate her personal experience to the general condition of African Americans, so that the individual's chaotic life is given order through the social awareness of its being related to the communal experience. As a chronicle of her quest for a voice and an identity of her own, Angelou's autobiographies are important documents of the black woman's place in twentieth century America.

Although Angelou's poetry has not generated as much enthusiasm as her autobiographies, like them it also merits attention as a testimony, in lyrical rather than narrative terms, to her struggle to create order out of chaos, a struggle which critic Pricilla Ramsey characterizes as the transformation of "the elements of a stultifying and personal, social, political and historical milieu into a sensual and physical refuge," and the "glorification of life and sensuality which produces a transcendence over all which could otherwise destroy and create her despair." Angelou has extended the personal struggle to the construction of a civic culture promoting democracy in the United States. By taking upon her shoulders the burden of a public mission, she has given poetry a new role to play in a multicultural society. The televised reading of her poem "On the Pulse of Morning" at President Bill Clinton's inauguration ceremony in January, 1993, was thus an appropriate crowning moment for Angelou. It also reminds her readers that Angelou is first and foremost a poet.

Biography

Maya Angelou was born Marguerite Johnson on April 4, 1928, in St. Louis, Missouri; her brother, Bailey, called her "Mya Sister," which became "Maya." At the age of three, upon the divorce of her parents, she and her brother were sent to Stamps, Arkansas, to live with their paternal grandmother in her general store. A woman of strength and independent will, she had a formative influence on Angelou.

When Angelou was barely eight, while spending a few months with her mother (then a nurse) in St. Louis, she was often left alone with her mother's suitor, Mr. Freeman, who eventually raped her. After Angelou disclosed the secret, Freeman was kicked to death by her uncles. Horrified by the event, Angelou suffered from a self-imposed silence that lasted five years; she attributed the loss of her voice to her belief that her voice could kill. After returning to Stamps, thanks to the encouragement and patience of her teacher, Bertha Flowers, Angelou overcame her trauma, recovered her voice, and started writing poetry. Angelou's love and command of literature can be traced back to this period.

In 1940, after graduating from the eighth grade at the top of her class, Angelou and her brother went to live with their mother in San Francisco. While attending George Washington High School, she took drama and dance lessons at the California Labor School, where her talents in dance, theater, and music were developed. By this time, her mother had become a professional gambler and the operator of a rooming house.

Such an environment had an unhealthy influence on Angelou. In 1944, at sixteen, she became pregnant and gave birth to a son, Clyde Johnson (who later changed his name to Guy). She tried a number of odd jobs and ended up as a nightclub waitress in San Diego, in the process involving herself in prostitution. A few years of chaotic life ensued, including drug abuse, until she married a former sailor of Greek origins named Tosh Angelos (from which she derived "Angelou"). The marriage failed a few years later, and Angelou found herself dancing in a strip bar for a living.

The dancing job proved to be the turning point in Angelou's life. She was discovered by performers of the Purple Onion company and was invited to work with them. Thus began Angelou's professional involvement with the entertainment business. In 1954-1955, she toured twenty-two countries with the musical *Porgy and Bess* as a featured dancer. Her travels in Africa proved to be among the most significant events in her life because they gave her a sense of self-worth and of being connected to something larger.

Returning to the United States after the performance tours, Angelou stayed in show business. In 1959, she moved to New York, where she became acquainted with James Baldwin and other literary figures. This led to her participation in the Harlem Writers Guild and her vision of becoming a writer.

During this time, on one occasion, she attended a rally in New York featuring a speech given by Martin Luther King, Jr., who had just been released from a Birmingham jail. Moved by the speech, Angelou worked with Godfrey Cambridge to produce the play *Cabaret for Freedom* (1960) to raise money for the Southern Christian Leadership Conference (SCLC). The show was so successful that she was appointed as the northern coordinator of SCLC. Around the same time, she also worked on a committee devoted to Malcolm X.

In late 1961, Angelou left the United States for Cairo with Vusumzi Make, a South African freedom fighter. They lived together for several years, but this romantic liaison was a disastrous one because of Make's amorous adventures and financial mismanagement. To bring in more money, Angelou sought employment and became an editor of the *Arab Observer*. The move exacerbated her souring relationship with Make and prompted her to leave for Ghana, where she stayed for three years. Although Angelou's protracted stay there was occasioned by the serious injury of her son in a car accident, it turned out to be the most positive experience of her life because Ghana, under President Kwame Nkrumah, was then the center of an African cultural renaissance. It was in Ghana that Angelou found the spiritual and cultural ties needed to uplift her life. While in Ghana, she also became friends with Malcolm X, who was visiting there.

After working for several years in Ghana as an editor, writer, and lecturer, Angelou returned to the United States during the mid-1960's. She actively involved herself in cinema and television, winning an impressive number of nominations and awards for her scripts, productions, and acting. Despite Angelou's success in show business, her focus gradually shifted to writing after she recorded "The Poetry of Maya Angelou" in 1969 and published the first of her autobiographical series, *I Know Why the Caged Bird Sings*, in 1970. Since then, her books have earned critical acclaim, and some have won nominations for major prizes. Angelou has been favored by academic institutions with grants, scholarships, fellowships, professorships, and honorary degrees. In 1982, she began teaching at Wake Forest University in Winston-Salem, North Carolina, as Reynolds Professor of American Studies.

Analysis

Angelou's poetry is characterized by simplicity both in form and in technique. This apparent simplicity can be deceptive both for general readers who accept it readily and for critics who resist it out of sophistication. As Angelou has explained in *The Paris Review*, a simple style can contain meanings that go deep beneath the surface of language. Known as "deep talk," Angelou's style is based on Hawthorne's notion that "Easy reading is damn hard writing." Such a "deep talk" approach contributes to the sense of oral performance in Angelou's poetry, which appeals to the ear and the heart rather than to the eye. The spoken voice is reinforced by a singing voice which, as critic Judson Jerome suggests, is derived from the rhythms of spirituals and chants, with influences from jazz and the blues also evident.

The poems of *Just Give Me a Cool Drink of Water 'fore I Diiie* are typical of Angelou's work in that they employ two related voices to address individual as well as communal issues. Eventually, the personal voice merges with, and becomes indistinguishable from, the communal voice; the communal voice transcends the personal at the end of the struggle. The two voices are evident from the two divisions of the book.

Part 1, "Where Love Is a Scream of Anguish," focuses on various kinds of male-female relationships and employs the "I" persona. Some of these relationships are love affairs filled with bittersweet emotions ("Remembering" and "Tears"). Even at the most tender and most intimate moments, the shadow of insecurity and loss looms large ("After"); the shadow is especially prominent in relationships that are somewhat abnormal ("They Went Home" and "No Loser No Weeper"). At times, the woman even indulges in the morose premonition of her own death ("Mourning Grace"). Despite the gloom dominating part 1, one poem signals the persona's desire to transcend the impasse. In "On Diverse Deviations," the persona, out of exasperation, expresses her wish to be carried off "To a shore,/ Where love is the scream of anguish/ And no curtain drapes the door." The poem also serves as a transitional link to the next section, which can be understood as the other "shore."

Part 2, "Just Before the World Ends," deals with communal, social, and political issues. The poems are unified by their social realism and criticism with regard to the predicament of African Americans ("Times-Square-Shoeshine-Composition" and "When I Think About Myself"). Social realism is often inseparable from social satire, which can be directed at white society ("The Calling of Names") or the black community ("Sepia Fashion Show"). At times, satire gives way to sarcastic protest: In "My Guilt," for example, the persona declares in bitterness that her guilt is making music out of slavery's chains, her crime is being alive to tell of heroes, dead and gone, and her sin is hanging from a tree without screaming aloud.

At her best, Angelou is able to combine satire and protest into a powerful indictment. One remarkable example is "Miss Scarlett, Mr. Rhett, and Other Latter-Day Saints," where the lynching of blacks on a plantation combines with a grotesquely surrealistic Christian ritual in which victims turn out to be Jesus and Ku Klux Klan members serve as priests for "King Kotton" as God. The ritual is even complete with a "little Eva" as the "Virgin Mary of Dixie" who, in order to guard the relics of her intact hymen, plays a part in "daily putting to death,/ into eternity,/ The stud, his seed." Angelou's relentless indictments come close to an apocalyptic vision when given the occasion: In "Riot: 60's," the reader gets a glimpse of "Lighting: a hundred Watts/ Detroit, Newark and New York," where Negroes are shot by nervous national guards; in "No No No No" (which contains the line that gives the volume its title), the colonial, racial, and global violence perpetuated by the West compels the persona to deny the possibility of love and forgiveness. The nihilism in this kind of bitterness is accentuated by the threat of a nuclear war, the subject of "On a Bright Day, Next Week," which contains the subtitle of part 2.

The two parts of the book are tied together: The poignant emotions and personal sufferings of part 1 are juxtaposed with the activist militancy and critical reflections of part 2, as if to suggest that the individual's failures and distresses in life and love ought to be understood and measured in the context of the community's historical and social conditions. The framework of the book is closely related to the title of the volume itself, which refers to Angelou's "belief that we as individuals in a species are still so innocent that we could ask our murderer just before he puts the final wrench upon the throat, 'Would you please give me a cool drink of water?'" Symbolically, it is the innocence—and the courage—to ask for such a "cool drink of water" that allows the communal persona in part 2 to voice its understanding and critique of the anguishes and tribulations of the individual persona in part 1. The black woman may have suffered much both as an individual and as a collective persona, but as "The Mothering Blackness" suggests, Angelou's interest is in highlighting her return to the mother's waiting arms "blameless," "black," and "tall as was Sheba's daughter."

In *Oh Pray My Wings Are Gonna Fit Me Well*, which was inspired by a song, Angelou's purpose was "to put all the things bothering me—my heavy load—in that book, and let them pass." The book continues the pattern of ordering chaos by merging individual and communal voices, but there is an increasing amount of humor, wit, tenderness, and meditation. The first two parts, which deal with love in its various guises ranging from consolation ("Conceit") to frustration ("Poor Girl"), are intensely personal. The success of these poems lies mainly in their drama, which is enacted against the backdrop (in parts 3 through 5) of historical and contemporary realities, including the alienation of the poor ("Alone"), the abandonment of the underprivileged ("Request"), the victimization of women ("Chicken-Licken"), and various other social injustices ("Southeast Arkansas"). This sense of heaviness is directly related to the failure of the American Dream for African Americans, but Angelou's goal here is not to condemn but to rediscover the real America ("America") and, as an antidote, to appreciate the new Africa emerging from colonialism and learn about African civilization itself ("Africa"). Linking the two continents together by means of space (the ocean) and time (history), Angelou comes to terms with her identity and ethnicity in a series of carefully crafted poems which includes "Child Dead in Old Seas," "Song for the Old Ones," and "Elegy." These poems are characterized by a combination of poignancy and triumph, thus indicating the poet's belief that her race has never been broken.

And Still I Rise further develops Angelou's pattern of turning chaos into order, and order dominates. Part 1, entitled "Touch Me, Life, Not Softly," consists of poems about love, but here Angelou treats it as a subject of study and critique rather than an experience in which to indulge. In part 2, "Traveling," the analytical mind is also brought into play in case-study portraits of various types of people. In these vignettes, Angelou's clinical observations of society and her mockery of reality are also infused with a strong sense of compassion, as if to prepare the reader for the next section. The subtitle of part 3, "And Still I Rise," is taken from the first poem of the section. "And Still I Rise" is one of the most important aphorisms by which Angelou's poetry can be understood. The poem opens with a mundane but powerful simile: "You may write me down in history/ With your bitter, twisted lies,/ You may trod me in the very dirt/ But still, like dust, I'll rise." The poem then continues in a proud, even haughty tone, which through a series of stanzas rises steadily in pitch, in dauntless challenge to the history and reality of oppression, and in self-congratulatory celebration of dignity, strength, and survival. The kind of bitterness found in earlier volumes is conspicuously absent, indicating that perhaps a process of sublimation and transcendence has taken place upon the triumphant close of the civil rights era.

As a poet, Angelou reached a new maturity with the publication of *And Still I Rise* because she found her voice, her self, her history, her race, and her God; order came into shape out of the chaos of her life and of her world. The volumes that have followed constitute further attempts to reinforce this order, but each volume contains some new elements. For example, there is a feminist sensuality in *Now Sheba Sings the Song*, which promotes a mythical image of Sheba as a black woman of beauty in body and in spirit.

Other major works

PLAYS: *Cabaret for Freedom*, 1960 (with Godfrey Cambridge); *The Least of These*, 1966; *Ajax*, 1974 (adapted from Sophocles); *And Still I Rise*, 1976.
SCREENPLAYS: *Georgia, Georgia*, 1972; *All Day Long*, 1974; *I Know Why the Caged Bird Sings*, 1979.
TELEVISION SCRIPTS: *Blacks, Blues, Black*, 1968; *Assignment America*, 1975; "The Legacy," 1976; "The Inheritors," 1976; "Sister, Sister," 1982.
NONFICTION: *I Know Why the Caged Bird Sings*, 1970; *Gather Together in My Name*, 1974; *Singin' and Swingin' and Gettin' Merry Like Christmas*, 1976; *The Heart of a Woman*, 1981; *All God's Children Need Traveling Shoes*, 1986; *Wouldn't Take Nothing for My Journey Now*, 1993.

Bibliography

Elliot, Jeffrey M., ed. *Conversations with Maya Angelou*. Jackson: University Press of Mississippi, 1989.

Jerome, Judson. "Uncage the Songbird." *Writer's Digest* 65 (March, 1985): 12-14.

McPherson, Dolly A. *Order out of Chaos: The Autobiographical Works of Maya Angelou*. New York: P. Lang, 1990.

Plimpton, George, ed. "Maya Angelou." In *Writers at Work: The Paris Review Interviews*. 8th Series. New York: Penguin Books, 1988.

Ramsey, Pricilla R. "Transcendence: The Poetry of Maya Angelou." *Current Bibliography on African Affairs* 17, no. 2 (1984-1985): 139-153.

Tate, Claudia, ed. *Black Women Writers at Work*. New York: Continuum, 1983.

MARGARET ATWOOD

Born: Ottawa, Ontario, Canada; November 18, 1939

Principal long fiction

The Edible Woman, 1969; *Surfacing*, 1972; *Lady Oracle*, 1976; *Life Before Man*, 1979; *Bodily Harm*, 1981; *The Handmaid's Tale*, 1986; *Cat's Eye*, 1989; *The Robber Bride*, 1993.

Other literary forms

A skillful and prolific writer, Margaret Atwood has published many volumes of poetry. *Double Persephone* (1961), *The Animals in That Country* (1968), *The Journals of Susanna Moodie* (1970), *Procedures for Underground* (1970), *Power Politics* (1971), *You Are Happy* (1974), *Selected Poems* (1976), *Two-Headed Poems* (1978), *True Stories* (1981), *Interlunar* (1984), and *Selected Poems II* (1987) have enjoyed a wide and enthusiastic readership, especially in Canada. During the 1960's, Atwood published in limited editions poems and broadsides illustrated by Charles Pachter: *The Circle Game* (1964), *Kaleidoscopes Baroque: A Poem* (1965), *Speeches for Dr. Frankenstein* (1966), *Expeditions* (1966), and *What Was in the Garden* (1969). Atwood has also written and illustrated books for children, including *Up in the Tree* (1978) and *Anna's Pet* (1980). Her volumes of short stories, a collection of short fiction and prose poems (*Murder in the Dark*, 1983), a volume of criticism (*Survival: A Thematic Guide to Canadian Literature*, 1972), and a collection of literary essays (*Second Words*, 1982) further demonstrate Atwood's wide-ranging talent. In 1982, Atwood coedited the revised version of *The Oxford Book of Canadian Poetry*. She has also written articles and critical reviews too numerous to list. She has contributed prose and poetry to literary journals such as *Acta Victoriana* and *Canadian Forum*, and her teleplays have been aired by the Canadian Broadcasting Corporation.

Achievements

Early in her career, Atwood's work was recognized for its distinction. This is particularly true of her poetry, which has earned her numerous awards, including the E. J. Pratt Medal in 1961; the President's Medal from the University of Western Ontario in 1965; and the Governor-General's Award, Canada's highest literary honor, for *The Circle Game* in 1966. Twenty years later, Atwood again won this prize for *The Handmaid's Tale*. Atwood won first prize from the Canadian Centennial Commission Poetry Competition in 1967, and won a prize for poetry from the Union League Civic and Arts Foundation in 1969. Honorary doctorates have been conferred by Trent University and Queen's University. Additional prizes include the Bess Hokins Prize for poetry (1974); the City of Toronto Award (1977); the Canadian Bookseller's Association Award (1977); the St. Lawrence Award for Fiction (1978); the Canada Council Molson Prize (1980); and the Radcliffe Medal (1980).

Biography

Margaret Atwood was born in Ottawa, Ontario, Canada, on November 18, 1939, the second of Carl Edmund and Margaret Killam Atwood's three children. At the age of six months, she was backpacked into the Quebec wilderness, where her father, an entomologist, pursued his special interests in bees, spruce budworms, and forest tent caterpillars. Throughout her childhood, Atwood's family spent several months of the year in the bush of Quebec and northern Ontario. She did not attend school full-time until she was twelve.

Though often interrupted, Atwood's education seems to have been more than adequate. She was encouraged by her parents to read and write at an early age, and her creative efforts started at five, when she wrote stories, poems, and plays. Her serious composition, however, did not begin until she was sixteen.

In 1961, Atwood earned her B.A. in the English honors program from the University of Toronto, where she studied with poets Jay Macpherson and Margaret Avison. Her M.A. from Radcliffe followed in 1962. Continuing graduate work at Harvard in 1963, Atwood interrupted her studies before reentering the program for two more years in 1965. While she found graduate studies interesting, Atwood's energies were largely directed toward her creative efforts. To her, the Ph.D. program was chiefly a means of support while she wrote. Before writing her doctoral thesis, Atwood left Harvard.

Returning to Canada in 1967, Atwood accepted a position at Sir George Williams University in Montreal. By this time, her poetry was gaining recognition. With the publication of *The Edible Woman* and the sale of its film rights, Atwood was able to concentrate more fully on writing, though she taught at York University and was writer-in-residence at the University of Toronto. In 1973, Atwood divorced her American husband of five years, James Polk. After the publication of *Surfacing*, she was able to support herself through her creative efforts. Atwood moved to a farm near Alliston, Ontario, with Canadian novelist Graeme Gibson. Their daughter, Eleanor Jess Atwood Gibson, was born in 1979. In 1980, Atwood's family returned to Toronto, where Atwood and Gibson became active in the Canadian Writers' Union, Amnesty International, and the International Association of Poets, Playwrights, Editors, Essayists, and Novelists (PEN).

Analysis

For Margaret Atwood, an unabashed Canadian, literature is a means to cultural and personal self-awareness. "To know ourselves," she writes in *Survival*, "we must know our own literature; to know ourselves accurately, we need to know it as part of literature as a whole." Thus, when she defines Canadian literary concerns, she relates her own as well, for Atwood's fiction grows out of this tradition. In her opinion, Canada's central reality is the act of survival: Canadian life and culture are decisively shaped by the demands of a harsh environment. Closely related, in Atwood's view, to this defining act of survival is the Canadian search for territorial identity.

Atwood's heroines invariably discover themselves to be emotional refugees, strangers in a territory they can accurately label but one in which they are unable to feel at home. Not only are they alienated from their environment, but also they are alienated from language itself; for them, communication becomes a decoding process. To a great degree, their feelings of estrangement extend from a culture that, having reduced everything to products, threatens to consume them. Women are particularly singled out as products, items to be decorated and sold as commodities, though men are threatened as well.

Atwood often couches their struggle in terms of a journey, which serves as a controlling metaphor for inner explorations: The unnamed heroine of *Surfacing* returns to the wilderness of Quebec, Lesje Green of *Life Before Man* wanders through imagined Mesozoic jungles, and Rennie Wilford of *Bodily Harm* flies to the insurgent islands of Ste. Agathe and St. Antoine. By setting contemporary culture in relief, these primitive sites define the difference between nature and culture and allow Atwood's heroines to gain new perspectives on their own realities. They can see people and places in relation to one another, not as isolated entities. Ultimately, however, this resolves little, for Atwood's novels end on a tenuous note. Although her heroines come to terms with themselves, they remain estranged.

Supporting her characters' ambivalence is Atwood's versatile narrative technique. Her astringent prose reflects their emotional numbness; its ironic restraint reveals their wariness. Frequent contradictions suggest not only the complexity of her characters but also the antagonistic times they must survive. By skillful juxtaposition of past and present through the use of flashbacks, Atwood evokes compelling fictional landscapes which ironically comment on the untenable state of modern men and women. Still, there remains some hope, for her characters survive with increased understanding of their world.

The first of Atwood's novels to arouse critical praise and commentary, *Surfacing* explores new facets of the *Bildungsroman*. What might have been a conventional novel of self-discovery develops into a resonant search for self-recovery imbued with mythic overtones and made accessible through Atwood's skillful use of symbol and ritual. At the same time, Atwood undercuts the romantic literary conventions on which *Surfacing* is built by exposing the myth of ultimate self-realization as a plausible conclusion. To accept the heroine's final emergence as an end in itself is to misread this suggestively ironic novel.

The unnamed heroine of *Surfacing*, accompanied by her lover Joe and a married couple named David and Anna, returns to the Canadian wilderness where she was reared in the hope of locating her missing father. His sudden disappearance has recalled her from a city life marked by personal and professional failures which have left her emotionally anesthetized. While her external search goes forward, the heroine conducts a more important internal investigation to locate missing "gifts" from both parents. Through these, she hopes to rediscover her lost ability to feel. In order to succeed, however, she will need to expose the fiction of her life.

At the outset of her narrative, the heroine warns her readers that she has led a double life when she recalls Anna's question, "Do you have a twin?" She denies having one, for she apparently believes the elaborate fiction she has created, a story involving a spurious marriage, divorce, and abandonment of her child. As additional protection, the heroine has distanced herself from everyone. She refers to her family as "they," "as if they were somebody else's family." Her relationship with Joe is notable for its coolness, and she has only known Anna, described as her best friend, for two months. She describes herself both as a commercial artist, indicating her sense of having sold out, and as an escape artist. Reluctantly approaching the past she sought to escape, the heroine feels as if she is in foreign territory.

That she feels alienated by the location of her past is not surprising, for she is an outsider in a number of telling ways: of English descent in French territory; a non-Catholic, indeed nonreligious, person among the devout; a woman in a man's world. Her French is so halting that she could be mistaken for an American, representing yet another form of alienation—displacement by foreigners. Most of all, she is a stranger to herself. Rather than focusing on her self-alienation, she is consumed by the American usurpation of Canada, its wanton rape of virgin wilderness, in order to avoid a more personal loss of innocence.

Canada's victimization by Americans reflects the heroine's victimization by men. Having been subjected to the concept that "with a paper bag over their head they're all the same," the protagonist is perceived as either contemptible or threatening. Her artistic skills are denigrated by a culture in which no "important" artists have been women. Even her modest commercial success is treated as a personal assault by Joe, who has an "unvoiced claim to superior artistic skills." By telling herself that the wilderness can never recover from abuse, the protagonist denies her own recovery. Although she feels helpless at the beginning of the novel, she soon rediscovers her own capabilities, and as these are increasingly tested, she proves to be a powerful survivor. Thus, the wilderness, a self-reflection, provides the key to self-discovery.

Perhaps the most important lesson the heroine learns is that the wilderness is not innocent. Her encounter and response to a senselessly slaughtered heron evoke a sense of complicity, leading her to reflect on similar collusion in her brother's animal experiments when they were children. Finding her refuge in childhood innocence blocked, the heroine goes forward with her search. Once again, nature provides information, for in discovering her father's body trapped underwater, she finally recognizes her aborted child, her complicity in its death by yielding to her lover's demands. On a broader scale, she acknowledges death as a part of life and reclaims her participation in the life process by conceiving a child by Joe.

In a ceremony evocative of primitive fertility rites, she seduces her lover. Then, assured of her pregnancy, she undergoes a systematic purgation in order to penetrate to the very core of reality. During this process, the protagonist discovers her parents' gifts—her father's sense of sight and her mother's gift of life. With body and mind reunited, she takes an oath in which she refuses to be a victim. Whole, she feels free to reenter her own time, no longer either victim or stranger.

Atwood's procedure for bringing her heroine to this state of consciousness is remarkable for its intricacy. Though she distrusts language, the protagonist proceeds to tell her story by describing what she sees. Since she has lost her ability to feel, much of this description seems to be objective—until the reader realizes just how unreliable her impressions can be. Contradictions abound, creating enormous uncertainty as intentional and unintentional irony collide, lies converge, and opinion stated as fact proves to be false. Given this burden of complexity, any simple conclusion to *Surfacing* is out of the question. Clearly, Atwood hints at a temporary union with Joe, but this is far from resolving the heroine's dilemma. Outer reality, after all, has not altered. Thus, Atwood's open-ended conclusion is both appropriate and plausible, for to resolve all difficulties would be to give in to the very romantic conventions that her fiction subverts.

In *The Handmaid's Tale*, Atwood's fiction turns from the realistic to the speculative, though she merely takes the political bent of the 1980's to its logical—and chilling—conclusion. Awash in a swill of pollution, promiscuity, pornography, and sexually transmitted disease, late twentieth century America erupts into political and religious battles. Rising from the ashes is the Republic of Gilead, a theocracy so conservative in its reactionary bent that women are channeled into roles as Daughters, Wives, Marthas (maids), Econowives, and Handmaids (mistresses).

The narrator, Offred (referring to her status as a possession of her master), is among the first group of Handmaids, fertile women assigned to high-ranking government officials. Weaving between her past and present in flat, almost emotionless prose, Offred draws a terrifyingly real picture of a culture retreating to fundamentalist values in the name of stability. At first, her prose seems to be accurate, a report from an observer. Deeper in the story, readers come to understand that Offred is numb from all that has changed in her life. She does not trust anyone, least of all herself. Still, as a survivor, she determines to stay alive, even if that means taking risks.

Her loss of freedom and identity create new hungers in Offred: curiosity about the world, a subversive desire for power, a longing for feeling, a need to take risks. In many ways, *The Handmaid's Tale* is a novel about what loss creates. Gilead, in fact, is created partially in response to men's loss of feeling, according to Fred, Offred's Commander. Yet Offred takes little comfort in his assurance that feeling has returned.

As she knows, feeling is ephemeral, often unstable, impossible to gauge. Perhaps this is why her characterization of others in the novel seems remote. While Offred observes gestures, facial movements, and voice tone, she can only guess at intent. Implicit in the simplest statement may be an important message. Thus, Offred decodes all kinds of communication, beginning with the Latin inscription she finds scratched in her wardrobe: "Nolite te bastardes carborundorum." Even this injunction, however, which becomes her motto, is a corruption. Though desperate for communication, Offred cautiously obscures her own message. Her struggle to understand reflects Atwood's familiar theme of the inability to understand truly another person, another situation.

By having Offred acknowledge the impossibility of accurately decoding messages, Atwood calls attention to the narrative itself. Another interesting fictional element is the narrative's remove in time. Offred tells her story in the present, except when she refers to her life before becoming a Handmaid. Ironically, readers learn not only that she is telling her story after events but also that her narrative has been reconstructed and presented to an audience at a still greater temporal remove. All of this increases the equivocal quality of the novel and its rich ambiguity. Perennial issues of a woman's place, the value of her work, and her true role in society are at the center of this novel.

Atwood's vision is as informed and humane as that of any contemporary novelist. Challenging her readers to form their own judgments, she combines the complexity of the best modern fiction into the moral rigor of the great nineteenth century novelists. Atwood's resonant symbols, her ironic reversals, and her example challenge readers and writers alike to confront the most difficult and important issues of the contemporary world.

Other major works

SHORT FICTION: *Dancing Girls*, 1977; *True Stories*, 1982; *Murder in the Dark*, 1983; *Bluebeard's Egg*, 1983; *Wilderness Tips*, 1991.

POETRY: *Double Persephone*, 1961; *The Circle Game*, 1964; *Talismans for Children*, 1965; *Kaleidoscopes Baroque: A Poem*, 1965; *Speeches for Dr. Frankenstein*, 1966; *Expeditions*, 1966; *The Animals in That Country*, 1968; *What Was in the Garden*, 1969; *The Journals of Susanna Moodie*, 1970; *Procedures for Underground*, 1970; *Power Politics*, 1971; *You Are Happy*, 1974; *Selected Poems*, 1976; *Two-Headed Poems*, 1978; *True Stories*, 1981; *Snake Poems*, 1983; *Interlunar*, 1984; *Selected Poems II*, 1987.

NONFICTION: *Survival: A Thematic Guide to Canadian Literature*, 1972; *Second Words: Selected Critical Prose*, 1982; *Margaret Atwood: Conversations*, 1990.

CHILDREN'S LITERATURE: *Up in the Tree*, 1978; *Anna's Pet*, 1980 (with Joyce Barkhouse).

EDITED TEXT: *The Oxford Book of Canadian Poetry*, 1982.

Bibliography

Davey, Frank. *Margaret Atwood: A Feminist Poetics*. Vancouver: Talonbooks, 1984.

Davidson, Arnold E., and Cathy N. Davidson, eds. *The Art of Margaret Atwood: Essays in Criticism*. Toronto, Canada: Anansi, 1981.

Grace, Sherrill E., and Lorraine Weir. *Margaret Atwood: Language, Text, and System*. Vancouver: University of British Columbia Press, 1983.

Hite, Molly. *The Other Side of the Story: Structures and Strategies of Contemporary Feminist Narrative*. Ithaca, N.Y.: Cornell University Press, 1989.

Mendez-Egle, Beatrice, ed. *Margaret Atwood: Reflection and Reality*. Edinburg, Tex.: Pan American University Press, 1987.

Rosenberg, Jerome H. *Margaret Atwood*. Boston: Twayne, 1984.

St. Andrews, Bonnie. *Forbidden Fruit: On the Relationship Between Women and Knowledge in Doris Lessing, Selma Lagerlöf, Kate Chopin, Margaret Atwood*. Troy, N.Y.: Whitson, 1986.

JANE AUSTEN

Born: Steventon, England; December 16, 1775

Died: Winchester, England; July 18, 1817

Principal long fiction

Sense and Sensibility, 1811; *Pride and Prejudice*, 1813; *Mansfield Park*, 1814; *Emma*, 1815; *Northanger Abbey*, 1818; *Persuasion*, 1818; *Sanditon*, 1974.

Other literary forms

In addition to her six novels, Jane Austen was the author of various short juvenile pieces, most of them literary burlesques mocking the conventions of the eighteenth century novel. Her other works are *Lady Susan*, a story told in letters and written c. 1805; *The Watsons*, a fragment of a novel written about the same time (both appended by J. E. Austen-Leigh to his 1871 *Memoir of Jane Austen*); and *Sanditon*, another fragmentary novel begun in 1817 and not published under that title until 1974. All these pieces appear in *Minor Works* (Vol. VI of the *Oxford Illustrated Jane Austen*, 1954, R. W. Chapman, editor). Jane Austen's surviving letters have also been edited and published by Chapman.

Achievements

Austen, who published her novels anonymously, was not a writer famous in her time, nor did she wish to be. From the first, though, her novels written in and largely for her own family circle, gained the notice and esteem of a wider audience. Among her early admirers were the Prince Regent and the foremost novelist of the day, Sir Walter Scott, who deprecated his own aptitude for the "big Bow-Wow" and praised her as possessing a "talent for describing the involvements and feelings and characters of ordinary life which is to me the most wonderful I ever met with." Since the days of Scott's somewhat prescient praise, her reputation has steadily grown. The critical consensus now places Jane Austen in what F. R. Leavis has termed the "Great Tradition" of the English novel. Her talent was the first to forge, from the eighteenth century novel of external incident and internal sensibility, an art form that fully and faithfully presented a vision of real life in a particular segment of the real world. Austen's particular excellences—the elegant economy of her prose, the strength and delicacy of her judgment and moral discrimination, the subtlety of her wit, the imaginative vividness of her character drawing—have been emulated but not surpassed by subsequent writers.

Biography

Jane Austen's life contained little in the way of outward event. Born in 1775, she was the seventh of eight children. Her father, the Reverend George Austen, was a scholarly clergyman, the rector of Steventon in rural Hampshire. Mrs. Austen shared her husband's intelligence and intellectual interests, and the home they provided for their children was a happy and comfortable one, replete with the pleasures of country life, genteel society, perpetual reading, and lively discussion of ideas serious and frivolous. Jane Austen, who never married, was devoted throughout her life to her brothers and their families, but her closest relationship was with her older sister Cassandra, who likewise remained unmarried and whom Austen relied upon as her chief critic, cherished as a confidante, and admired as the ideal of feminine virtue.

On the rector's retirement in 1801, Austen moved with her parents and Cassandra to Bath. After the Reverend George Austen's death in 1804, the women continued to live for some time in that city. In 1806, the Austens moved to Southampton, where they shared a house with Captain Francis Austen, Jane's older brother, and his wife. In 1808, Edward Austen (who subsequently adopted the surname Knight from the relations whose two estates he inherited) provided his mother and sisters with a permanent residence, Chawton Cottage, in the

Hampshire village of the same name. At this house, Austen was to revise her manuscripts that became *Sense and Sensibility, Pride and Prejudice*, and *Northanger Abbey* and to write *Mansfield Park, Emma*, and *Persuasion*. In 1817, it became evident that she was ill with a serious complaint whose symptoms seem to have been those of Addison's disease. To be near medical help, she and Cassandra moved to lodgings in Winchester in May, 1817. Austen died there less than two months later.

Analysis

Jane Austen's novels unite subtlety and common sense, good humor and acute moral judgment, charm and conciseness, deftly marshaled incident and carefully rounded character. Austen's detractors have spoken of her as a "limited" novelist, one who, writing in an age of great men and important events, portrays small towns and petty concerns, who knows (or reveals) nothing of masculine occupations and ideas, and who reduces the range of feminine thought and deed to matrimonial scheming and social pleasantry. Her tales, like her own life, are set in country villages and at rural seats, from which the denizens venture forth to watering places or travel to London. Her characters tend to be members of her own order, that prosperous and courteous segment of the middle class called the gentry. Unlike her novel-writing peers, Austen introduced few aristocrats into the pages of her novels, and the lower ranks, though glimpsed from time to time, are never brought forward. The happenings of her novels would not have been newsworthy in her day. She depicts society at leisure rather than on the march, and in portraying pleasures her literary preference is modest.

Yet these limitations are the self-drawn boundaries of a strong mind rather than the innate restrictions of a weak or parochial one. In focusing on the manners and morals of rural middle-class English life, particularly on the ordering dance of matrimony that gives shape to society and situation to young ladies, Austen emphasizes rather than evades reality. The microcosm she depicts is convincing because she understands, though seldom explicitly assesses, its connections to the larger order. Her characters have clear social positions but are not just social types; the genius of such comic creations as Mrs. Bennet, Mr. Woodhouse, and Miss Bates is that each is a sparkling refinement on a quality or set of qualities existing at all times and on all levels. A proof of Austen's power (no one questions her polish) is that she succeeds in making whole communities live in the reader's imagination with little recourse to the stock device of the mere novelist of manners: descriptive detail.

Sense and Sensibility, Austen's first published novel, is generally considered her weakest, largely because of Austen's struggle with the eighteenth century antithetical pattern suggested in the novel's title. According to this formula, opposing qualities of temperament or mind are presented in characters (generally female, often sisters) who despite their great differences are sincerely attached to each other. In *Sense and Sensibility*, the antithetical characters are Elinor and Marianne Dashwood, the respective embodiments of cool, collected sense and prodigal, exquisite sensibility. The great flaw of *Sense and Sensibility* is that the polarities presented in the persons of Elinor and Marianne are too genuinely antithetical to be plausible or dynamic portraits of human beings. Elinor has strong feelings, securely managed though they may be, and Marianne has some rational powers to supplement her overactive imagination and emotions, but the young ladies do not often show themselves to be more than mere embodiments of sense and sensibility. In her second published novel, *Pride and Prejudice*, Austen makes defter use of two sisters whose values are the same but whose minds and hearts function differently. The book is a paragon of "classic" literature in which the conventions and traditions of the eighteenth century novel come to full flowering yet are freshened and transformed by Austen's distinctive genius.

The title *Pride and Prejudice*, with its balanced alliterative abstractions, might suggest a second experiment in schematic psychology, and indeed the book does show some resemblances to *Sense and Sensibility*. Here again, the reader encounters a pair of sisters, the elder (Jane Bennet) serene, the younger (Elizabeth) volatile. Unlike the Dashwoods, however, these ladies both demonstrate deep feelings and perceptive minds. The qualities alluded to in the title refer not to a contrast between sisters but to double defects shared by Elizabeth and Fitzwilliam Darcy, a wealthy and wellborn young man she meets when his easygoing friend Charles Bingley leases Netherfield, the estate next to the Bennets' Longbourn. If so rich and vital a comic masterpiece could be reduced to a formula, it might be appropriate to say that the main thread of *Pride and Prejudice* involves the twin correction of these faults. As Darcy learns to moderate his tradition-based view of society and to recognize individual excellence (such as Elizabeth's, Jane's, and their Aunt and Uncle Gardiner's) in ranks below his own, Elizabeth becomes less dogmatic in her judgments, and in particular more aware of the real merits of Darcy, whom she initially dismisses as a haughty, unfeeling aristocrat. The growing accord of Elizabeth and Darcy is one of the most perfectly satisfying courtships in English literature. Their persons, minds, tastes, and even phrases persuade the reader that they are two people truly made for each other; their union confers fitness on the world around them.

Elizabeth and Darcy's slow-growing love may be *Pride and Prejudice*'s ideal alliance, but it is far from being the only one, and a host of finely drawn characters surround the heroine and hero. In Jane Bennet and Charles Bingley, whose early mutual attraction is temporarily suspended by Darcy and the Bingley sisters (who deplore, not without some cause, the vulgarity of the amiable Jane's family), Austen presents a less sparkling but eminently pleasing and well-matched pair. William Collins—the half pompous, half obsequious, totally asinine cousin who, because of an entail, will inherit Longbourn and displace the Bennet females after Mr. Bennet's demise—aspires to marry Elizabeth but, when rejected, gains the hand of her plain and practical friend Charlotte Lucas. Aware of her suitor's absurdities, Charlotte is nevertheless alive to the advantages of the situation he can offer. Her calculated decision to marry gives a graver ring to the irony of the novel's famous opening sentence: "It is a truth universally acknowledged, that a single man in possession of a good fortune, must be in want of a wife." The last of the matches made in *Pride and Prejudice* is yet more precariously based. A lively, charming, and amoral young officer, George Wickham, son of the former steward of Pemberley, Darcy's estate, and source of many of Elizabeth's prejudices against that scrupulous gentleman, first fascinates Elizabeth, then elopes with her youngest sister, mindless, frivolous Lydia. Only through Darcy's personal and financial intervention is Wickham persuaded to marry the ill-bred girl, who never properly understands her disgrace—a folly she shares with her mother. Mrs. Bennet, a woman deficient in good humor and good sense, is—along with her cynical, capricious husband, the ponderous Collins, and the tyrannical Lady Catherine de Bourgh—one of the great comic creations of literature.

Most of these characters could have seemed odious if sketched by another pen, but so brilliant is the sunny intelligence playing over the world of *Pride and Prejudice* that even fools are golden.

Mansfield Park, begun in 1811 and finished in 1813, is the first of Austen's novels to be a complete product of her maturity. The longest, most didactic, least ironic of her books, it is the one critics generally have most trouble reconciling with their prevailing ideas of the author. Pleased with and proud of *Pride and Prejudice*, Austen nevertheless recorded her impression of its being "rather too light, and bright, and sparkling"—in need of shade. That darkness she found wanting is supplied in *Mansfield Park*, which offers the antithesis to *Pride and Prejudice*'s generous, humorous, spirited social vision.

Austen's next novel, *Emma*, might be thought of as harmonizing the two voices heard in *Pride and Prejudice* and *Mansfield Park*. For this book, Austen claimed to be creating "a heroine whom no one but myself will much like," an "imaginist" whose circumstances and qualities of mind make her the self-crowned queen of her country neighborhood. Austen was not entirely serious or accurate: Emma certainly has her partisans, and even those readers who do not like her tend to find her fascinating. She is a spirited, imaginative, healthy young woman who, like *Mansfield Park*'s Mary Crawford, has potential to do considerable harm to the fabric of society but on whom, like Elizabeth Bennet, her creator generously bestows life's greatest blessing: union with a man whose virtues, talents, and assets are the best complement for her own.

Emma's eventual marriage to Mr. Knightley of Donwell Abbey is the ultimate expression of one of Austen's key assumptions: that marriage is a young woman's supreme act of self-definition. Unlike any other Austen heroine, Emma has no pressing need to marry. As the opening sentence of the book implies, Emma's situation makes her acceptance or rejection of a suitor an act of unencumbered will: "Emma Woodhouse, handsome, clever, and rich, with a comfortable home and happy disposition, seemed to unite some of the best blessings of existence; and had lived nearly twenty-one years in the world with very little to distress or vex her."

Free though circumstance allows her to be, Emma has not been encouraged by her lot in life to acquire the discipline and self-knowledge that, augmenting her innate intelligence and taste, would help her to choose wisely. Brought up by a doting valetudinarian of a father and a perceptive but permissive governess, Emma has been encouraged to think too highly of herself. Far from vain about her beauty, Emma has—as Mr. Knightley, the only person who ventures to criticize her, observes—complete yet unfounded faith in her ability to judge people's characters and arrange their lives. The course of *Emma* is Miss Woodhouse's education in judgement, a process achieved through repeated mistakes and humiliations.

As the novel opens, the young mistress of Hartfield is at loose ends. Her beloved governess has just married Mr. Weston, of the neighboring property, Randalls. To fill the newly made gap in her life, Emma takes notice of Harriet Smith, a pretty, dim "natural daughter of somebody," and a parlor-boarder at the local school. Determined to settle her protégée into the sort of life she deems suitable, Emma detaches Harriet from Robert Martin, a young farmer who has proposed to her, and embarks upon a campaign to conquer for Harriet the heart of Mr. Elton, Highbury's unmarried clergyman. Elton's attentiveness and excessive flattery convince Emma of her plan's success but at the same time show the reader what Emma is aghast to learn at the end of Book I: that Elton scorns the nobody and has designs upon the heiress herself.

With the arrival of three new personages in Highbury, Book II widens Emma's opportunities for misconception. The first newcomer is Jane Fairfax, an elegant and accomplished connection of the Bates family and a girl whose prospective fate, the "governess trade," shows how unreliable the situations of well-bred young ladies without fortunes or husbands tend to be. Next to arrive is the suave Mr. Frank Churchill, Mr. Weston's grown son, who has been adopted by wealthy relations of his mother and who has been long remiss in paying a visit to Highbury. Finally, Mr. Elton brings home a bride, the former Augusta Hawkins of Bristol, a pretentious and impertinent creature possessed of an independent fortune, a well-married sister, and a boundless fund of self-congratulation. Emma mistakenly flatters herself that the dashing Frank Churchill is in love with her, and then settles on him as a husband for Harriet; she suspects the reserved Miss Fairfax, whose cultivation she rightly perceives as a reproach to her own untrained talents, of a clandestine relationship with a married man. She despises Mrs. Elton, as would any person of sense, but fails to see that the vulgar woman's offensiveness is an exaggerated version of her own officiousness and snobbery.

Thus, the potential consequences of Emma's misplaced faith in her judgment intensify, and the evidence of her fallibility mounts. Thoroughly embarrassed to learn that Frank Churchill, to whom she has retailed all her hypotheses regarding Jane Fairfax, has long been secretly engaged to that woman, Emma suffers the death-blow to her smug self-esteem when Harriet announces that the gentleman whose feelings she hopes to have aroused is not, as Emma supposes, Churchill but the squire of Donwell. Emma's moment of truth is devastating and complete, its importance marked by one of Jane Austen's rare uses of figurative language: "It darted through her, with the speed of an arrow, that Mr. Knightley must marry no one but herself!" Perhaps the greatest evidence of Emma's being a favorite of fortune is that Mr. Knightley feels the same as she does on this matter. Chastened by her series of bad judgments, paired with a gentleman who for years has loved and respected her enough to correct her and whom she can love and respect in turn, Emma participates in the minuet of marriage with which Austen concludes the book, the other couples so united being Miss Fairfax and Mr. Churchill and Harriet Smith (ductile enough to form four attachments in a year) and Robert Martin (stalwart enough to persist in his original feeling).

Emma Woodhouse's gradual education, which parallels the reader's growing awareness of what a menace to the social order her circumstances, abilities, and weaknesses combine to make her, is one of Austen's finest pieces of plotting. The depiction of character is likewise superb. Among a gallery of memorable and distinctive characters are Mr. Woodhouse; Miss Bates, the stream-of-consciousness talker who inadvertently provokes Emma's famous rudeness on Box Hill; and the wonderfully detestable Mrs. Elton, with her self-contradictions and her fractured Italian, her endless allusions to Selina, Mr. Suckling, Maple Grove, and the *barouche landau*. Life at Hartfield, Donwell, and Highbury is portrayed with complexity and economy. Every word, expression, opinion, and activity—whether sketching a portrait, selecting a dancing partner, or planning a strawberry-picking party—becomes a gesture of self-revelation. *Emma* demonstrates how, in Austen's hands, the novel of manners can become a statement of moral philosophy.

Other major works

SHORT FICTION: *Minor Works*, 1954 (Vol. 6 of the *Oxford Illustrated Jane Austen*, R. W. Chapman, editor).
NONFICTION: *Jane Austen's Letters*, 1952 (R. W. Chapman, editor).

Bibliography

Bush, Douglas. *Jane Austen*. New York: Macmillan, 1975.

Grey, J. David, ed. *The Jane Austen Companion*. New York: Macmillan, 1986.

Halperin, John, ed. *Jane Austen: Bicentenary Essays*. New York: Cambridge University Press, 1975.

Hardy, Barbara. *A Reading of Jane Austen*. New York: New York University Press, 1976.

Honan, Park. *Jane Austen: Her Life*. New York: St. Martin's Press, 1987.

Lane, Maggie. *Jane Austen's England*. New York: St. Martin's Press, 1986.

Mooneyham, Laura G. *Romance, Language, and Education in Jane Austen's Novels*. New York: St. Martin's Press, 1986.

Sulloway, Alison. *Jane Austen and the Province of Womanhood*. Philadelphia: University of Pennsylvania Press, 1989.

Thompson, James. *Between Self and World: The Novels of Jane Austen*. University Park: Pennsylvania State University, 1988.

Williams, Michael. *Jane Austen: Six Novels and Their Methods*. New York: St. Martin's Press, 1986.

ANN BEATTIE

Born: Washington, D.C.; September 8, 1947

Principal short fiction

Distortions, 1976; *Secrets and Surprises*, 1978; *Jacklighting*, 1981; *The Burning House*, 1982; *Where You'll Find Me*, 1986; *What Was Mine and Other Stories*, 1991.

Other literary forms

While Ann Beattie's reputation rests primarily on her short stories, particularly those that first appeared in *The New Yorker*, she has also written several novels. The first, *Chilly Scenes of Winter* (1976), appeared simultaneously with *Distortions*, a rare occurrence in the publishing world, especially for a first-time author. Her second novel, *Falling in Place* (1980), is her most ambitious and her best. In *Love Always* (1985), she uses an approach that is closer to that of her short stories than in either of the previous novels. The subject matter is narrower, and the characters are more distanced from the narrative voice. Her novel *Picturing Will* was published in 1989. In 1986 and 1987, she worked on her first nonfiction project, the text to accompany a monograph containing twenty-six color plates of the paintings of Alex Katz.

Achievements

Beattie has been called the most imitated short-story writer in the United States, an amazing claim for a woman whose publishing career began in the early 1970's. Along with such writers as Raymond Carver, she is a premier practitioner of minimalism, the school of fiction-writing that John Barth has characterized as the "less is more" school. In 1977, she was named Briggs-Copeland Lecturer in English at Harvard, where she was apparently uncomfortable. She used a Guggenheim grant to leave Harvard and move back to Connecticut, where she had attended graduate school. She has also received an award of excellence from the American Academy and Institute of Arts and Letters (1980).

Biography

Born on September 8, 1947, Ann Beattie grew up with television, rock music, and all the other accoutrements of the baby-boomers. The child of a retired Health, Education, and Welfare Department administrator, Beattie took a B.A. in English at American University in 1969 and completed her M.A. at the University of Connecticut in 1970. She began, but did not complete, work on her Ph.D. In 1972 she was married to, and was later divorced from, David Gates, a writer for *Newsweek* and a singer. Together they had one son. Before her appointment at Harvard, Beattie taught at the University of Virginia in Charlottesville. After living in the Connecticut suburbs and in New York City, she returned to Charlottesville and the university in 1985. She appeared as a waitress in the film version of *Chilly Scenes of Winter* and, after her divorce, was named one of the most eligible single women in America. In 1985, Beattie met painter Lincoln Percy, whom she later married. The couple settled in Charlottesville.

Analysis

Ann Beattie has been called the spokesperson for a new lost generation, a sort of Ernest Hemingway for those who came of age during the 1960's and 1970's. Many of her themes and much about her style support the assertion that she, like Hemingway, voices a pervasive and universal feeling of despair and alienation, a lament for lost values and lost chances for constructive action. Yet to limit one's understanding of Beattie's work to this narrow interpretation is a mistake.

Beattie's primary themes are loneliness and friendship, family life, love and death, materialism, art, and, for want of a better term, the contemporary scene. Her short fiction tends to be spare and straightforward. Her vocabulary and her sentence structure are quite accessible, or minimalist, to use a more literary label. Even when the stories contain symbols, their use is most often direct and self-reflexive.

Her combination of subject matter and style leads to a rather flat rendering of the world, and Beattie is sometimes criticized for that flatness. Because her narrators usually maintain a significant distance from the stories and their characters, critics and readers sometimes assume that Beattie is advocating such remove and reserve as the most feasible posture in contemporary life. Even her most ironic characters and narrative voices, however, experience a profound longing for a different world. Despite the ennui that dominates the texture of their lives, Beattie's characters hold on to the hope of renewal and redemption, often with great fierceness, even though the fierceness frequently suggests that these people are clutching at hope so hard that they are white-knuckling their way through life. If members of the generation about which she writes are indeed lost, they have not accepted their condition, even though they recognize it. They are still searching for the way out, for a place in which to find themselves or to be found.

"Dwarf House," the first story in *Distortions*, establishes an interest in the grotesque, the bizarre, and the slightly askew that surfaces several times in this first of Beattie's collections. The main characters of the story are James and MacDonald, brothers who struggle to find understanding and respect for each other and to deal with their possessive and intrusive mother. Because James, the older of the two, is a dwarf, Beattie immediately plays upon the collection's title and places the story beyond the plane of realism.

The irony of the story develops as the reader realizes that MacDonald's supposedly normal life is as distorted as the life of his sibling. When MacDonald goes to visit James in the dwarf house, where he lives along with several other dwarfs and one giant, he finds himself repulsed by the foreign environment. Yet, when he gets home, he cannot face his own "normal" world without his martinis. He is as alienated and isolated at home and at work as he would be if he were a dwarf. Beattie uses the ludicrous, the exaggerated scenario of James's life, complete with his wedding to a fellow dwarf, conducted by a hippie minister and culminating in the releasing of

a caged parrot as a symbol of hope and the new freedom of married life, to bring into focus the less obvious distortions of regular American life.

MacDonald wants to make his brother's life more normal—that is, get him out of the dwarf house, the one place where James has ever been happy, and back into their mother's home, where James and MacDonald will both be miserable. MacDonald is motivated not by malice toward James but by an overdeveloped sense of guilt and responsibility toward his mother, a trait he shares with many of Beattie's young male characters. By the story's end, the reader cannot say who is better off: James, whose life is distorted but productive and satisfying to him, or MacDonald, who has everything a man could want but still lacks an understanding of what it is he should do with what he has.

If *Distortions* emphasizes the outward manifestations of the disordered contemporary world, *Secrets and Surprises*, the second collection, turns inward, as its title suggests. "A Vintage Thunderbird" features a woman who comes to New York to have an abortion against the wishes of her husband. The friends to whom she turns, Karen and Nick, have their own problems in love. By mirroring the sense of loss that follows the abortion with the sense of loss felt by Karen and Nick when she sells the vintage car of the title, Beattie addresses the connection between spiritual and emotional needs and material needs.

Very few of the people in Beattie's fiction suffer for want of material goods; almost all suffer from lack of spiritual and emotional fulfillment. The interesting aspect of this dichotomy is that the characters do not, as a rule, actively pursue material well-being. Their money is often inherited, as are their houses and many of their other possessions. The money earned by these characters is almost always earned halfheartedly, without conspicuous ambition or enthusiasm. These are not Yuppies, who have substituted acquisition for all human emotion; they are people who, by accident of birth or circumstance, have not had to acquire material wealth. For whatever reason, wealth comes to them. What does not come is peace, satisfaction, or contentment. When a material object does provide emotional pleasure, as the Thunderbird does for Karen and Nick, Beattie's characters tend to confuse the emotion with the symbol and to conclude, erroneously, that ridding themselves of the object will also rid them of the gnawing doubts that seem to accompany contentment and satisfaction.

In *The Burning House*, Beattie's third collection, she turns to the darker, more richly textured veins of her standard subject matter to produce stories that are less humorous but more humane, less ironic but wiser than those in the earlier collections. Infidelity, divorce, love gone bad—all standard Beattie themes—are connected to parenthood and its attendant responsibilities, to homosexuality, to death, and to birth defects. The affairs and the abortions that were entered into, if not concluded, with a "me-generation" bravado suddenly collide with more traditional values and goals.

Many of Beattie's characters, both married and single, have lovers. In fact, having a lover or having had one at some time during a marriage is almost standard. In "The Cinderella Waltz," Beattie adds a further complication to the *de rigueur* extramarital affair by making the husband's lover a man. Yet, in much the same way that she makes the unusual work in a story such as "Dwarf House," Beattie manages to make this story more about the pain and suffering of the people involved than about the nontraditional quality of the love relationship.

The wife in "The Cinderella Waltz," left to understand what has happened to her marriage and to help her young daughter to reach her own understanding, finds herself drawn into a quiet, resigned acceptance of her husband's relationship with his lover. She laments the loss of innocence in the world, for her child and for them all, but she chooses to go forward with the two men as part of her life and the child's. She rejects—really never even considers—the negative, destructive responses that many women would have. "The Cinderella Waltz" ends with images of enormous fragility—glass elevators and glass slippers. Yet they are images that her characters embrace and cling to, recognizing that fragile hope is better than none. The cautious nature of such optimism is often mistaken for pessimism in Beattie's work, but her intention is clearly as affirmative as it is tentative.

Another story from *The Burning House*, "Winter: 1978," offers a glimpse of most of Beattie's concerns and techniques. An unusually long story for Beattie, "Winter: 1978" features a selfish mother who is hosting a wake for her younger son, who has drowned in a midwinter boating accident. His death is mystifying, for there were life preservers floating easily within his reach, a fact that suggests the ultimate despair and surrender often present in Beattie's characters. An older son blames the mother for placing too much guilt and responsibility on the dead son, but he himself has done nothing to assume some of

that burden. His former wife, their child, his current girlfriend, and his best friend are all present at the wake. The best friend's girlfriend is alone back in California, having her uterus cauterized. His former wife seems inordinately grief stricken until it is revealed that the dead man was her lover. During the course of the wake, which lasts several days, she becomes the lover of her former husband's best friend. This extremely baroque and convoluted situation contains much that is ironically humorous, but it also reflects deep pain on the part of all the characters, not only the pain of having lost a loved one but also the pain of reexamining their own lives and measuring them against the idea of death.

"Winter: 1978" concludes with the absentee father, the surviving son, taking his own child upstairs for a bedtime story. The little boy, like the daughter in "The Cinderella Waltz," is far too wise to take comfort from the imaginary world of the story; he has been exposed to far too much of the confused adult world of his parents. On this occasion, however, he pretends to believe, and he encourages his father's tale about the evolution of deer. According to the story, deer have such sad eyes because they were once dinosaurs and cannot escape the sadness that comes with having once been something else.

This story serves as a metaphor for the melancholy cast of characters in this and Beattie's other collections of short fiction. Almost all of her characters have a Keatsian longing to connect with a better, more sublime existence that seems to be part of their generational collective consciousness. Far too aware and too ironic to follow the feeling and thereby to transcend reality, they linger in their unsatisfactory lesser world and struggle to accommodate their longing to their reality.

More than her other collections, *Where You'll Find Me* displays Beattie's awareness of her own reputation as a writer. In particular, in a story called "Snow," she appears to write a definition of the kind of story her work has come to define. Less than three pages long, the story takes a single image, that of snow, and uses it not only as a symbol of the lost love the narrator is contemplating but also as a metaphor for storytelling as practiced by the author.

The remembered lover has explained to the narrator at one point that "any life will seem dramatic if you omit mention of most of it." The narrator then tells a story, actually one paragraph within this story, about her return to the place where the lovers had lived in order to be with a dying friend. She offers her story-within-the-story as an example of the way in which her lover said stories should be told.

The narrator goes on to say that such efforts are futile, bare bones without a pattern to establish meaning. For her, the single image, snow in this case, does more to evoke the experience of her life with the man than does the dramatized story with the details omitted. In the story's final paragraph, the narrator concludes that even the single image is too complex for complete comprehension. The mind itself, let alone the narratives it creates, is incapable of fully rendering human experience and emotion. The best a writer, a storyteller, can do is to present the essence of the experience in the concrete terms in which his or her consciousness has recorded it.

The characters in this fourth collection are generally older and wiser than their predecessors. They have, as a rule, survived an enormous loss and are still hoping for a richer, more rewarding life, or at least one in which they feel less out of place and alone. Andrea, the real-estate agent who is the main character of "Janus," is typical. Safely married to a husband who is interesting and financially secure, she is also successful in her career. The two of them take great pleasure in the things that they have accumulated. Yet Andrea takes most pleasure in a relatively inexpensive and quite ordinary-looking ceramic bowl, a gift from a former lover who asked her to change her life, to live with him.

Although she has long since turned him down, Andrea finds herself growing increasingly obsessed with the bowl. She begins to believe that all of her career success comes from the bowl's being precisely placed in the homes that she shows to her clients. A mystery to her, the bowl seems to be connected to the most real, the most private parts of herself. She loves the bowl as she loves nothing else and is terrified at the thought that it might disappear. She has lost the chance that the lover represents, choosing instead stasis and comfort, remaining intransigent about honoring her previous commitments.

Sometimes Andrea goes into her living room late at night and sits alone, contemplating the bowl. She thinks, "In its way, it was perfect; the world cut in half, deep and smoothly empty." Such is the world that Beattie observes, but Beattie is, after all, an artist, not a real-estate agent. All that Andrea can do is contemplate. Beattie can fill the bowl, to use a metaphor, with whatever she chooses. She can capture, again and again, the story behind the "one small flash of blue, a vanishing point on the horizon," that Andrea can only watch disappear.

Beattie's fiction is a lesson in the psychological reality of a certain segment of American life: well-educated, upper-middle-class men and women of the baby-boom generation. Although she sometimes writes about other types of people, it is these with whom she is most often identified. While the scope of her short fiction may be somewhat narrow, her finely detailed canvases yield a rich reward.

Other major works

NOVELS: *Chilly Scenes of Winter*, 1976; *Falling in Place*, 1980; *Love Always*, 1985; *Picturing Will*, 1989.
NONFICTION: *Alex Katz*, 1987.
CHILDREN'S LITERATURE: *Goblin Tales*, 1975; *Spectacle*, 1985.

Bibliography

Atwood, Margaret. "Stories from the American Front." *The New York Times Book Review*, September 26, 1982, 1, 34.
Barth, John. "A Few Words About Minimalism." *The New York Times Book Review,* December 28, 1986, 1, 2, 25.
Beattie, Ann. "An Interview with Ann Beattie." Interview by Steven R. Centola. *Contemporary Literature* 31 (Winter, 1990): 405-422.
Gelfant, Blanche H. "Ann Beattie's Magic Slate: Or, The End of the Sixties." *New England Review* 1 (1979): 374-384.
Hansen, Ron. "Just Sitting There Scared to Death." *The New York Times Book Review,* May 26, 1991, 3, 14.

ELIZABETH BISHOP

Born: Worcester, Massachusetts; February 8, 1911   **Died:** Boston, Massachusetts; October 6, 1979

Principal poetry

North & South, 1946; *Poems: North & South—A Cold Spring*, 1955; *Questions of Travel*, 1965; *The Complete Poems*, 1969; *Geography III*, 1976; *The Complete Poems, 1927-1979*, 1983.

Other literary forms

In addition to her poetry, Bishop wrote short stories and other prose pieces. She is also known for her translations of Portuguese and Latin American writers. *The Collected Prose*, edited and introduced by Robert Giroux, was published in 1984. It includes "In the Village," an autobiographical revelation of Bishop's youthful vision of, and later adult perspective on, her mother's brief return home from a mental hospital. Like her poetry, Bishop's prose is marked by precise observation and a somewhat withdrawn narrator, although the prose works reveal much more about Bishop's life than the poetry does. Editor Giroux has suggested that this was one reason many of the pieces were unpublished during her lifetime. *The Collected Prose* also includes Bishop's observations of other cultures and provides clues as to why she chose to live in Brazil for so many years.

Achievements

Bishop was often honored for her poetry. Among many awards and prizes, she received the 1956 Pulitzer Prize for Poetry and the 1969 National Book Award for Poetry. Yet, as John Ashbery said, in seconding her presentation as the winner of the *Books Abroad*/Neustadt International Prize for Literature in 1976, she is a "writer's writer." Despite her continuing presence for more than thirty years as a major American poet, Bishop never achieved great popular success. Perhaps the delicacy of much of her writing, her restrained style, and her ambiguous questioning and testing of experience made her more difficult and less approachable than poets with showier technique or more explicit philosophies.

For critics, however, and certainly for other poets—those as different as Marianne Moore and Robert Lowell, or Randal Jarrell and Ashbery—hers is a voice of influence and authority. Writing with great assurance and sophistication from the beginning of her career, she achieved in her earliest poetry the quiet, though often playful, tone, the probing and examining of reality, the exactness of language, and the lucidity of vision that mark all of her best poetry. Her later poetry is slightly more relaxed than her earlier, the formal patterns often less rigorous; but her concern and her careful eye never waver. Because of the severity of her self-criticism, her collected poems, although relatively few in number, are of a remarkably even quality.

Bishop's place in American poetry, in the company of such other twentieth century poets as Moore, Wallace Stevens, and Richard Wilbur, is among the celebrators and commemorators of the things of this world, in her steady conviction that by bringing the light of poetic intelligence, the mind's eye, on those things, she will enrich her readers' understanding of them and of themselves.

Biography

Elizabeth Bishop is a poet of geography, as the titles of her books testify, and her life itself was mapped out by travels and visits as surely as is her poetry. Eight months after Bishop's birth in Massachusetts, her father died. Four years later, her mother suffered a nervous breakdown and was hospitalized, first outside Boston, and later in her native Canada.

Elizabeth was taken to Nova Scotia, where she spent much of her youth with her grandmother; later, she lived for a time with an aunt in Massachusetts. Although her mother did not die until 1934, Bishop did not see her again after a brief visit home from the hospital in 1916—

the subject of "In the Village."

For the rest of her life, Bishop traveled: in Canada, in Europe, in North and South America. She formed friendships with many writers: Robert Lowell, Octavio Paz, and, most influentially, Marianne Moore, who read drafts of many of her poems and offered suggestions. In 1951, Bishop began a trip around South America, but during a stop in Brazil she suffered an allergic reaction to some food she had eaten and became ill. After recovering, she remained in Brazil for almost twenty years. During the last decade of her life, she continued to travel and to spend time in Latin America, but she settled in the United States, teaching frequently at Harvard, until her death in 1979.

Analysis

In Elizabeth Bishop's poem "Sandpiper," the title bird runs along the shore, ignoring the sea that roars on his left and the beach that "hisses" on his right, disregarding the interrupting sheets of water that wash across his toes, sucking the sand back to sea. His attention is focused. He is watching the sand between his toes; "a student of Blake," he attempts to see the world in each of those grains. The poet is ironic about the bird's obsessions: In looking at these details he ignores the great sweeps of sea and land on either side of him. The poet seems to chide the bird in his darting search for "something, something, something," but then in the last two lines of the poem the irony subsides; as Bishop carefully enumerates the varied and beautiful colors of the grains of sand, she joins the bird in his attentiveness. The reward, the something one can hope to find, lies simply in the rich and multivalent beauty of what one sees.

The irony in the poem is self-mocking, for the bird is a metaphor for Bishop, its vision like her own, its situation that of many of her poetic personae. Like the sandpiper, Bishop is an obsessive observer. As a poet, her greatest strength is her pictorial accuracy. Whether her subject is as familiar as a fish, a rooster, or a filling station, or as strange as a Brazilian interior or a moose in the headlights of a bus, she enables the reader to see. The world for the sandpiper is sometimes "minute and vast and clear," and because Bishop observes the details so lucidly, her vision becomes truly vast.

Although the world for the sandpiper is sometimes clear, it is also sometimes a mist, and Bishop describes a more clouded vision as well. In her translation of "Objects and Apparitions," a poem by Paz, the objects are

In her early poem "The Map," Bishop writes that "More delicate than the historians' are the map-makers' colors." Her best poetry, although only indirectly autobiographical, is built from those mapmakers' colors. Nova Scotian and New England seascapes and Brazilian and Parisian landscapes become the geography of her poetry. At the same time, her own lack of permanent roots and her sense of herself as an observer suggest the lack of social relationships one feels in Bishop's poetry, for it is a poetry of observation, not of interaction, of people as outcasts, exiles, and onlookers, not as social beings. The relationships that count are with the land and sea, with primal elements, with the geography of Bishop's world.

those details, the grains of sand that reveal the world once they are tipped toward the light, and the apparitions occur when one sees the world through the mist and when one turns vision inward, as in the world of dreams. Objects and apparitions, mist and vision, land and sea, history and geography, travel and home, ascent and fall, dawn and night—these oppositions supply the tension in Bishop's poetry. The tensions are never resolved by giving way; in Bishop's world, one is a reflection of the other, and "reflection" becomes a frequent pun: that of a mirror and that of thought.

No verbs are more prevalent or important in Bishop's poetry than those of sight: look, watch, see, stare, she admonishes the reader. The end of all art is to make that which is invisible—too familiar to be noticed, too small to be important, too strange to be comprehended—visible. In "The Man-Moth," the normal human being of the first stanza cannot even see the moon, but after the man-moth comes above ground and climbs a skyscraper—trying to climb out through the moon, which he thinks is a hole in the sky—he falls back and returns to life below ground, riding the subway backward through his memories and dreams. The poet addresses the readers, cautioning them to examine the man-moth's eye, from which a tear falls. If the "you" is not paying attention, the man-moth will swallow his tear and his most valuable possession will be lost, but "if you watch," he will give it up, cool and pure, and the fruit of his vision will be shared.

To see the world afresh, even as briefly as does the man-moth, to gain that bitter tear of knowledge, one must, according to Bishop, change perspectives. This is the theme of Bishop's "Over 2000 Illustrations and a Complete Concordance." The poet is looking at the illustrations in a gazetteer, comparing the engraved and serious pictures in the book with her remembered travels. In the first section of the poem, the poet lists the illustrations, the familiar, even tired Seven Wonders of the World, moving away from the objects pictured to details of the renderings, until finally the "eye drops" away from the real illustrations which spread out and dissolve into a series of reflections on past travels. These too begin with the familiar: with Canada and the sound of goats, through Rome, to Mexico, to Marrakesh. Then, finally, she goes to a holy grave, which, rather than reassuring the viewer, frightens her, as an amused Arab looks on. Abruptly, the poet is back in the world of books, but this time her vision is on the Bible, where everything is "connected by 'and' and 'and.' " She opens the book, feeling the gilt of the edges flake off on her fingertips, and then asks, "Why couldn't we have seen/ this old Nativity while we were at it?" The colloquial last words comprise a casual pun, implying physical presence or accidental benefit. The next four lines describe the nativity scene, but while the details are familiar enough, Bishop's language defamiliarizes them. The poet ends with the statement that had she been there she would have "looked and looked our infant sight away"—another pun rich with possibilities. Is it that she would have looked repeatedly, so that the scene would have yielded meaning and she could have left satisfied? Do the lines mean to look away, as if the fire that breaks in the vision is too strong for human sight? The gazetteer into which the poet first looked, that record of human travels, has given way to Scripture; physical pictures have given way to reflected visions and reflections.

Bishop participates in the traditional New England notion that nature is a gazetteer, a geography, a book to be read. In her poem "The Riverman," the speaker gets up in the night—night and dawn, two times of uncertain light, are favorite times in Bishop's poetic world—called by a river spirit, though at first the dolphin-spirit is only "glimpsed." The speaker follows and wades into the river where a door opens. Smoke rises like mist, and another spirit speaks in a language the narrator does not know but understands "like a dog/ although I can't speak it yet." Every night he goes back to the river, to study its language. He needs a "virgin mirror," a fresh way of seeing, but those that he finds are spoiled. "Look," he says significantly, "it stands to reason" that everything one needs can be obtained from the river, which draws from the land "the remedy." The river sucks the earth "like a child," and the riverman, like the poet, must study the earth and the river to read them and find the remedy of sight.

Not only do the spirits of nature speak, but so too for Bishop does art itself. Her poetry is pictorial not only in the sense of giving vivid descriptions of natural phenomena but also in its use of artificial objects to reflect on the self-referential aspect of art. In "Large Bad Picture," the picture is an uncle's painting, and after five stanzas describing the artist's attempt to be important by drawing everything oversized—miles of cliffs hundreds of feet high, hundreds of birds—the painting, at least in the narrator's mind, becomes audible, and she can hear the birds crying. In the much later "Poem," Bishop looks at another but much smaller painting by the same uncle, and this time the painting speaks to her memory. Examining the brushstrokes in a detached and slightly contemptuous manner, she suddenly exclaims, "Heavens, I recognize the place, I know it!" The voice of her mother enters, and then she concludes, "Our visions coincided"; life and memory have merged in this painting as in this poem: "how touching in detail/—the little that we get for free."

Bishop's poetry is not unequivocally optimistic or affirmative. There are finally more ambiguities than certainties, and questions, rhetorical and conversational, are at the heart of these poems. Bishop's ambiguity is not that of unresolved layers of meaning in the poetry, but in the unresolvable nature of the world she tests. "Which is which?" she asks about memory and life in "Poem." "What has he done?" the poet asks of a chastised dog in the last poem of *Geography III*. "Can countries pick their colors?" she asks in "The Map." *Questions of Travel* begins with a poem questioning whether this new country, Brazil, will yield "complete comprehension"; it is followed by another poem which asks whether the poet should not have stayed at home: "Must we dream our dreams/ and have them, too?" Bishop poses more questions than she answers. Indeed, at the end of "Faustina," Faustina is poised above the dying woman she has cared for, facing the final questions of the meaning that death gives to life: Freedom or nightmare, it begins, but the question becomes "proliferative," and the poet says that "There is no way of telling./ The eyes say only either." Knowledge, like the sea, like tears, is salty and bitter, and even answering the questions, achieving a measure of knowledge, is no guarantee of permanence. Yet, even though knowledge for Bishop is bitter, is fleeting, though the world is often inscrutable or inexplicable, hers is finally a poetry of hope.

Bishop's poetry is often controlled by elaborate formal patterns of sight and sound. She makes masterful use of such forms as the sestina and villanelle, avoiding the appearance of mere exercise by the naturalness and wit of the repetitions and the depth of the scene. Her favorite sound devices are alliteration and consonance. In "The Map," for example, the first four lines include "shadowed," "shadows," "shallows," "showing"; "edges" rhymes with "ledges," "water" alliterates with "weeds." The repetition of sounds suggests the patterning that the poet finds in the map, and the slipperiness of sounds in "shadows"/"shallows" indicates the ease with which one vision of reality gives place to another. The fifth line begins with another question: "Does the land lean down to lift the sea," the repeated sound changing to a glide. "Along the fine tan sandy shelf/ is the land tugging at the sea from under?" repeats the patterning of questions and the *sh* and *l* alliteration, but the internal rhyme of "tan" and "sandy," so close that it momentarily disrupts the rhythm and the plosive alliteration of "tan" and "tugging," implies more strain.

Being at the same time a pictorialist, Bishop depends heavily on images. Again in "The Map," Norway is a hare that "runs south in agitation." The peninsulas "Take the water between thumb and finger / like women feeling for the smoothness of yard-goods." The reader is brought up short by the aptness of these images, the familiar invigorated. In the late poem "In the Waiting Room," a young Elizabeth sits in a dentist's waiting room, reading through a *National Geographic*, looking at pictures of the scenes from around the world. The experience causes the young girl to ask who she is, what is her identity and her similarity, not only with those strange people in the magazine but also with the strangers there in the room with her, and with her Aunt Consuela whose scream she hears from the inner room. Bishop's poetry is like the pictures in that magazine; its images offer another geography, so that readers question again their own identity.

This sense of seeing oneself in others, of doubled vision and reflected identities, leads to another of Bishop's favorite devices, the conceit. In "Wading at Wellfleet," the waves of the sea, glittering and knifelike, are like the wheels of Assyrian chariots with their sharp knives affixed, attacking warriors and waders alike. In "The Imaginary Iceberg," the iceberg is first an actor, then a jewel, and finally the soul, the shifting of elaborated conceits duplicating the ambiguous nature of the iceberg. The roads that lead to the city in "From the Country to the City" are stripes on a harlequin's tights, and the poem a conceit with the city the clown's head and heart, its neon lights beckoning the traveler.

Formal control, a gently ironic but appreciative tone, a keen eye—these are hallmarks of Bishop's poetry. They reveal as well her limitation as a poet: a deficiency of passion. The poetry is so carefully controlled, the patterns so tight, the reality tested so shifting, and the testing so detached, that intensity of feeling is minimized. There is little love in Bishop's poetry. At the end of "Filling Station," the grubby, but "comfy" design of the family-owned station suggests that "Somebody loves us all," but this love is detached and observed, not felt. Even in "Four Poems," the most acutely personal of Bishop's poems and the only ones about romantic love, the subject is lost love, the conversation internal. "Love should be put into action!" screams a hermit at the end of "Chemin de Fer," but his only answer is an echo.

History, writes Bishop in "Objects and Apparitions," is the opposite of art, for history creates ruins, while the artist, out of ruins, out of "minimal, incoherent fragments," simply creates. Bishop's poetry is a collection of objects and apparitions, of scenes viewed and imagined, made for the moment into a coherent whole. The imaginary iceberg in the poem of that name is a part of a scene "a sailor'd give his eyes for," and Bishop asks that surrender of her readers. Her poetry, like the iceberg, behooves the soul to see. Inner and outer realities are in her poetry made visible, made one.

Other major works

NONFICTION: *Brazil*, 1962.
TRANSLATION: *The Diary of "Helena Morley,"* 1957 (by Alice Brant).
MISCELLANEOUS: *The Collected Prose*, 1984.

Bibliography

Bloom, Harold. *Elizabeth Bishop: Modern Critical Views.* New York: Chelsea House, 1985.

Goldensohn, Lorrie. *Elizabeth Bishop: The Biography of a Poetry.* New York: Columbia University Press, 1991.

Harrison, Victoria. *Elizabeth Bishop's Poetics of Intimacy.* New York: Cambridge University Press, 1993.

Kalstone, David. *Becoming a Poet: Elizabeth Bishop with Marianne Moore and Robert Lowell.* New York: Farrar, Straus & Giroux, 1989.

Millier, Brett C. *Elizabeth Bishop: Life and the Meaning of It.* Berkeley: University of California Press, 1993.

Parker, Robert Dale. *The Unbeliever: The Poetry of Elizabeth Bishop.* Urbana: University of Illinois Press, 1988.

Schwartz, Lloyd, and Sybil P. Estess. *Elizabeth Bishop and Her Art.* Ann Arbor: University of Michigan Press, 1983.

Travisano, Thomas. *Elizabeth Bishop: Her Artistic Development.* Charlottesville: University Press of Virginia, 1988.

ELIZABETH BOWEN

Born: Dublin, Ireland; June 7, 1899

Died: London, England; February 22, 1973

Principal long fiction

The Hotel, 1927; *The Last September,* 1929; *Friends and Relations,* 1931; *To the North,* 1932; *The House in Paris,* 1935; *The Death of the Heart,* 1938; *The Heat of the Day,* 1949; *A World of Love,* 1955; *The Little Girls,* 1964; *Eva Trout,* 1968.

Other literary forms

The first seven of Elizabeth Bowen's novels were republished by Jonathan Cape in Cape Collected Editions between the years 1948 and 1954, when Cape also republished four of her short-story collections: *Joining Charles* (1929), *The Cat Jumps and Other Stories* (1934), *Look at All Those Roses* (1941), and *The Demon Lover* (1945). The other books of short stories are *Encounters* (1923), *Ann Lee's and Other Stories* (1926), *Stories by Elizabeth Bowen* (1959), and *A Day in the Dark and Other Stories* (1965). *The Demon Lover* was published in New York under the title *Ivy Gripped the Steps* (1946) and, as the original title indicates, has supernatural content which scarcely appears in the novels. Bowen's nonfiction consists of *Bowen's Court* (1942), a description of her family residence in Ireland; *Seven Winters* (1942), an autobiography; *English Novelists* (1946), a literary history; *Collected Impressions* (1950), essays; *The Shelbourne* (1951), a work about the hotel in Dublin; *A Time in Rome* (1960), travel essays; and *Afterthought* (1962), broadcasts and reviews. A play, coauthored with John Perry and entitled *Castle Anna* was performed in London in March, 1948, but remains unpublished.

Achievements

Considered a great lady by those who knew her, Bowen draws an appreciative audience from readers who understand English gentility—the calculated gesture and the controlled response. Bowen's support has come from intellectuals who recognize the values of the novel of manners and who liken her work to that of Jane Austen and Henry James. Her contemporaries and colleagues included members of the Bloomsbury Group and of Oxford University, where the classical scholar C. M. Bowra was a close friend. Many readers know Bowen best through her novel *The Death of the Heart* and her short stories, especially "The Demon Lover," "Joining Charles," and "Look at All Those Roses," which are frequently anthologized in college texts. Bowen was made a Commander of the British Empire in 1948, and was awarded the honorary Doctor of Letters degree at Trinity College, Dublin, in 1949, and at Oxford University in 1957. She was made a Companion of Literature in 1965.

Biography

Although born in Ireland, Elizabeth Dorothea Cole Bowen came from a pro-British family who received land in County Cork as an award for fighting with Oliver Cromwell in 1649. The family built Bowen's Court in 1776—what the Irish call a "big house"—as a Protestant stronghold against the mainly Catholic Irish and lived there as part of the Anglo-Irish ascendancy. Bowen was educated in England and spent some summers at Bowen's Court. Not until after the Irish Rising in 1916 did she come to realize the causes of the Irish struggle for independence; and in writing *Bowen's Court,* she admitted that her family "got their position and drew their power from a situation that shows an inherent wrong."

Her barrister father, when he was nineteen, had disobeyed forewarnings and carried home smallpox, which killed his mother and rendered his father mad. Preoccupied with the desire for a son, the attempt to have one nearly killed his wife in 1904, and burdened with the debts of Bowen's Court, he suffered severe mental breakdowns in 1905 and 1906 and again in 1928. He was the cause of Elizabeth's removal to England where, as an Irish outcast, her defense was to become excessively British. Living in a series of locations with her mother, she was kept uninformed of family circumstances; and, as an adult, her novels provided for her an outlet for her sense of guilt, the result of feeling responsible for the unexplained events around her. Her lack of roots was intensified with the death of her mother in 1912.

Bowen studied art, traveled in Europe, and worked as an air-raid warden in London during World War II. In 1923, she* married Alan Charles Cameron, who was employed in the school system near Oxford, and they lived there for twelve years. She inherited Bowen's Court in 1928 when her father died; and in 1952, she and her husband returned there to live. Bowen's husband,

however, died that year. She sold the home in 1960 and returned to Oxford.

Bowen's career as novelist spanned years of drastic change, 1927 to 1969, and, except for *The Last September*, she wrote about the present; her war experiences are reflected in the short-story collection *The Demon Lover* and in the novel *The Heat of the Day*. After 1935, she also wrote reviews and articles for *The New Statesman* and other publications, the Ministry of Information during World War II, *The Tatler* (in the 1940's), and helped edit the *London Magazine* in the late 1950's. Afflicted with a slight stammer, Bowen lectured infrequently but effectively; two of her BBC broadcasts, "left as they were spoken," may be read in *Afterthought*. After a visit to Ireland in 1973, she died in London, leaving an unfinished autobiographical work, "Pictures and Conversations," which was intended to be published the next year.

Analysis

Elizabeth Bowen had a special talent for writing the conversations of children around the age of nine, as she does in *The House in Paris*. Somewhat corresponding to her personal experience, her novels often present a homeless child, orphaned and shunted from one residence to another, or a child with one parent who dies and leaves the adolescent in the power of outwardly concerned but mainly selfish adults. Frequently, management by others prolongs the protagonist's state of innocence into the twenties, when the woman must begin to assert herself and learn to manage her own affairs. (At the age of twenty-four, for example, Eva Trout does not know how to boil water for tea.) On the other side of the relationship, the controlling adult is often a perfectly mannered woman of guile, wealthy enough to be idle and to fill the idleness with discreet exercise of power over others. The typical Bowen characters, then, are the child, the unwanted adolescent, the woman in her twenties in a prolonged state of adolescence, and the "terrible woman" of society. Young people, educated haphazardly but expensively, are culturally mature but aimless. Genteel adults, on the other hand, administer their own selfish standards of what constitutes an impertinence in another person; these judgments disguise Bowen's subtle criticism of the correct English.

Typical Bowen themes follow as "loss of innocence," "acceptance of the past," or "expanding consciousness." The pain and helplessness attendant upon these themes

and the disguise of plentiful money make them unusual. Although she writes about the privileged class, three of her four common character types do not feel privileged. To handle her themes, Bowen frequently orders time and space by dividing the novels into three parts, with one part set ten years in the past and with a juxtaposition of at least two locations. The ten-year lapse provides a measure of the maturity gained, and the second location, by contrast, jars the consciousness into revaluation of the earlier experience.

The three-part structure of Bowen's novels is most fully realized in *The Death of the Heart*; the parts are labeled "The World," "The Flesh," and "The Devil," which follow the seasons of winter, spring, and summer. The world of Windsor Terrace, the Quaynes's residence in London, is advanced and sterile. Portia enters into this world at age fifteen, an orphan and stepsister to the present Thomas Quayne. Thomas' wife Anna, who has miscarried twice and is childless, secretly reads Portia's diary and is indignant at the construction Portia puts on the household events. Portia sees much "dissimulation" at Windsor Terrace, where doing the "right" thing does not mean making a moral choice. As one of Bowen's radical innocents who has spent her youth in hotels and temporary locations, Portia says no one in this house knows why she was born. She has only one friend in this, her first home: the head-servant Matchett who gives Portia some religious training. Of the three male friends who wait upon Anna—St. Quentin Martin, Eddie, and Major Brutt—Portia fastens on the affections of Eddie.

Spring, in part 2, brings a much-needed vacation for the Quaynes. Thomas and Anna sail for Capri, and Portia goes to stay with Anna's former governess at Seale-on-Sea. At the governess' home, dubbed Waikiki, Portia is nearly drowned in sensuality—the sights, smells, sounds, feelings—of a vulgar and mannerless household. Portia invites Eddie to spend a weekend with her at Seale-on-Sea, which further educates her in the ways of the flesh.

Portia's more open nature, on her return to London in part 3, is immediately apparent to Matchett, who says she had been "too quiet." The Devil's works are represented both obviously and subtly in this section, and they take many identities. St. Quentin, Anna, Eddie, even the unloving atmosphere of Windsor Terrace make up the Devil's advocacy. St. Quentin, a novelist, tells Portia that Anna has been reading her diary, a disloyalty and an invasion of privacy with which, after some contemplation, Portia decides she cannot live. Herein lies the death of her teenage heart, what Bowen calls a betrayal of her innocence, or a "mysterious landscape" that has perished.

Summer at Windsor Terrace brings maturity to Portia, as well as others: Anna must confront her own culpability, even her jealousy of Portia; St. Quentin, his betrayal of Anna's reading of the diary; Thomas, his neglect of his father and his father's memory; and even Matchett takes a terrified ride in the unfamiliar cab, setting out in the night to an unknown location to pick up Portia. They all share in the summer's maturation that Portia has brought to fruition.

William Shakespeare's Portia preferred mercy to justice, paralleling the Portia in this novel. Bowen's Portia observes everything with a "political seriousness." The scaffolding of this novel supports much allusion, metaphor, and drama—all artfully structured. The world, the flesh, and the Devil as medieval threats to saintliness are reinterpreted in this context; they become the locations of the heart that has been thrust outside Eden and comprise a necessary trinity, not of holiness but of wholeness. This novel earns critics' accord as Bowen's best.

Ranked by many critics as a close second to *The Death of the Heart* is *The Heat of the Day*. In this novel, Bowen uses the war to purge the wasteland conditions that existed before and during the years from 1940 through 1945. Middle-class Robert Kelway has returned from Dunkirk with a limp that comes and goes according to the state of his emotions. At the individual level, it reflects the psychological crippling of his youth; at the national level, it is the culmination of the condition expressed by the person who says "Dunkirk was waiting there in us."

Upper-class Stella Rodney has retreated from the privileges of her past into a rented apartment and a war job. Having grown impassive with the century, divorced with a son (Roderick) in the army, she has taken Robert as her lover. She has become so impassive, in fact, that in 1942, a sinister and mysterious government spy named Harrison tells her that Robert has been passing information to the enemy, and she says and does nothing.

Critics have commented frequently on this novel's analogies to *Hamlet* (1600-1601), an obvious example being Holme Dene (Dane home), Robert Kelway's country home. Psychologically weak, Robert is ruled by his destructive mother, who also had stifled his father and planted the seeds of Robert's defection from English ways. While Stella visits Holme Dene and learns to understand Robert, her son visits a cousin who tells him that Stella did not divorce her husband, as was commonly thought, but rather was divorced by him while he was having an affair, although he died soon after the divorce. Roderick, however, has managed to survive Stella's homelessness with a positive and manly outlook and, when he inherits an estate in Ireland, finds that it will give him the foundation for a future.

In *Eva Trout*, the various autobiographical elements of Bowen's work come to life: Bowen's stammer in Eva's reticence, the tragic deaths of both parents, the transience and sporadic education, the delayed adolescence, the settings of hotels and train stations. Eva Trout lives with a former teacher, Iseult Arbles, and her husband Eric while she waits for an inheritance. She turns twenty-four and receives the inheritance, which enables her to leave their home, where the marriage is unstable, to buy a home filled with used furniture. She also escapes the clutches of Constantine, her guardian who had been her father's male lover.

Eva discovers that a woman with money is suddenly pursued by "admirers," and Eric visits her in her new home. Eva subsequently lets Iseult think that Eric has fathered her child, whom she has adopted in America. After eight years in American cities, where Eva seeks help for the deaf-mute child Jeremy, Eva and Jeremy return to England. From England, they flee to Paris where a doctor and his wife begin the successful training of Jeremy. Back in England, Eva attempts the next phase of reaching security and a normal life. She seeks a husband and persuades the son of Iseult's vicar to stage a wedding departure with her at Victoria Station. All her acquaintances are on hand to see the couple off, but Jeremy—brought from Paris for the occasion—playfully points a gun (he thought a toy) at Eva and shoots her. In the midst of revelry, on the eve of her happiness, Eva drops dead beside the train.

Eva Trout makes a poignant and haunting last heroine for the Bowen sequence and a final bitter statement on the elusiveness of security and happiness.

Other major works

SHORT FICTION: *Encounters*, 1923; *Ann Lee's and Other Stories*, 1926; *Joining Charles*, 1929; *The Cat Jumps and Other Stories*, 1934; *Look at All Those Roses*, 1941; *The Demon Lover*, 1945 (published in the United States as *Ivy Gripped the Steps*, 1946); *The Early Stories*, 1951; *Stories by Elizabeth Bowen*, 1959; *A Day in the Dark and Other Stories*, 1965; *Elizabeth Bowen's Irish Stories*, 1978; *The Collected Stories of Elizabeth Bowen*, 1981.

PLAY: *Castle Anna*, 1948 (with John Perry).

NONFICTION: *Bowen's Court*, 1942; *Seven Winters*, 1942; *English Novelists*, 1946; *Collected Impressions*, 1950; *The Shelbourne: A Center of Dublin Life for More Than a Century*, 1951; *A Time in Rome*, 1960; *Afterthought: Pieces About Writing*, 1962; *Pictures and Conversations*, 1975; *The Mulberry Tree: Writings of Elizabeth Bowen*, 1986.

CHILDREN'S LITERATURE: *The Good Tiger*, 1965.

Bibliography

Austin, Allan. *Elizabeth Bowen*. Rev. ed. Boston: Twayne, 1989.

Craig, Patricia. *Elizabeth Bowen*. London: Penguin Books, 1986.

Davenport, Guy. "Elizabeth Bowen and the Big House." *Southern Humanities Review* 8 (1974): 27-34.

Glendinning, Victoria. *Elizabeth Bowen*. New York: Alfred A. Knopf, 1978.

Lee, Hermione. *Elizabeth Bowen: An Estimation*. New York: Barnes & Noble Books, 1981.

KAY BOYLE

Born: St. Paul, Minnesota; February 19, 1903

Died: Mill Valley, California; December 27, 1992

Principal long fiction

Plagued by the Nightingale, 1931; *Year Before Last*, 1932; *Gentlemen, I Address You Privately*, 1933; *My Next Bride*, 1934; *Death of a Man*, 1936; *Monday Night*, 1938; *Primer for Combat*, 1942; *Avalanche*, 1943; *A Frenchman Must Die*, 1946; *1939*, 1948; *His Human Majesty*, 1949; *The Seagull on the Step*, 1955; *Three Short Novels*, 1958; *Generation Without Farewell*, 1960; *The Underground Woman*, 1975.

Other literary forms

Although she has published some fifteen novels, Kay Boyle's principal recognition has been for her shorter works. First published in the small magazines of the 1920's, her stories were collected in *Wedding Day and Other Stories* (1930) and *First Lover and Other Stories* (1933). The 1930's, declared her vintage period by critics, brought an O. Henry Prize for the title story of *The White Horses of Vienna and Other Stories* (1936), followed in 1941 by another for "Defeat," a story on the French collapse which also appeared in *Primer for Combat*. Two volumes of short stories, *The Smoking Mountain: Stories of Postwar Germany* (1951) and *Nothing Ever Breaks Except the Heart* (1966), reflect wartime and postwar Europe.

Her poetry, also first published in small magazines, was collected in *A Glad Day* (1938) and *Collected Poems* (1962). *American Citizen Naturalized in Leadville, Colorado* (1944), based on the experience of an Austrian refugee in the United States military, is dedicated to Carson McCullers, "whose husband is also overseas," and *Testament for My Students and Other Poems* (1970) concerns "that desperate year, 1968." *This Is Not a Letter and Other Poems* (1985) appeared fifteen years later.

Boyle wrote nonfiction prose of both journalistic and literary distinction, including her reportage of the war crimes trial of Heinrich Babb for *The New Yorker* and her essays on civil rights and the military establishment. Two memoirs, her edition of *The Autobiography of Emanuel Carnevali* (1967) and her chapters in Robert McAlmon's *Being Geniuses Together, 1920-1930* (1968), capture the literary underground of that period, while a subsequent collection, *The Long Walk at San Francisco State and Other Essays* (1970), reflects the antiwar movement of the 1960's. She also published three illustrated children's novels: *The Youngest Camel* (1939) and the Pinky novels.

Achievements

Perhaps more consistently and tenaciously than any other twentieth century American writer, Boyle sought to unite the personal and political, the past and present, the feminine and the masculine. Recognized in both the literary and the popular realms, her rich oeuvre unites the American and the European experience of twentieth century history.

Helpful though it may be as an outline, the conventional division of Boyle's achievement into an aesthetic period before 1939 and a polemical period after may obscure Boyle's constant focus upon the dialectic between subject and object. In the exploration of personal experience, her intense imaginative reconstruction posits the integration of conflicting aspects of the self, the struggle between self-abnegation and self-assertion, and the liberation of the individual from repressive aspects of personal or family relationships. Usually presented as a union of archetypally masculine and feminine characteristics in an individual or in a couple, often a pair of same-sex friends, Boyle's image of the completed self is one of growth beyond confining roles.

In her exploration of the self as a political creature, Boyle asserts the life-affirming potential of the individual and the community against destructive authoritarian or absolutist constructs, whether within the family or in the larger society. In her evocation of personal awakening to political morality, Boyle's synthesis reaches beyond the narrowly ideological to affirm the human search for tenderness in a landscape which, although distorted by repression, gives hope for regeneration.

Biography

The cross between Kay Boyle's Midwestern roots and cosmopolitan experience produced the distinctive flavor of her work. Although born into an upper-class St. Paul family, Boyle spent her early years not in the Midwest but in the eastern United States, France, Austria, and Switzerland, and especially in the mountains, which become a symbol of human transcendence in her work. The aesthetic and creative aspect of her childhood is expressed in the family custom of gathering sketches and stories into marbled covers for gift books. Her mother, Katherine Evans Boyle, introduced her daughter to the most avant-garde of European art and literature, as well as the most progressive of American populist politics.

Never having been "properly through the eighth grade," Boyle pursued writing on her own, a training she later advocated for her students. Less than twenty years old, she moved from Cincinnati to New York, attended a few classes at Columbia, worked as a secretary, and met Greenwich Village literati of a progressive bent. She worked for *Broom*, a journal of European and American experimentalism, and became acquainted with William Carlos Williams, who became her friend and mentor. Described as a shy, timid ingenue, Boyle appears in Williams' memoirs attending Fourteenth Street parties with John Reed, Louise Bryant, Jean Toomer, Kenneth Burke, and Hart Crane.

In 1921, Boyle married Richard Brault, a French student whom she had met in Ohio, and she returned with him to his family's provincial seat. Williams recalls meeting a lonely and isolated Boyle in the vicinity of Le Havre, in which atmosphere her first two novels take place. When the marriage deteriorated and ended a few years later, Boyle remained in Paris and the Riviera, playing a central role in the literary underground of American exiles and the European avant-garde. Centered on the publication of small magazines, these groups brought Boyle together with Ernest Walsh, an effervescent poet, critic, and editor whose death from lung injuries incurred as a pilot is recounted in *Year Before Last*.

The aesthetic of Boyle's group was eclectic, drawing on the work of Ernest Hemingway, James Joyce, Gertrude Stein, Ezra Pound, William Carlos Williams, and Carl Sandburg. This loosely knit group ascribed to an informal creed known as Orphism that advocated a rhythmic, "hallucinatory" style cognizant of current psychological and anthropological lore and inimical to standard realism and the genteel tradition. It was in this milieu that Boyle developed the lyrical subjectivism reflected in her early poems and stories.

Following Walsh's death and the birth of her first child, Boyle briefly joined a communal art colony led by Raymond Duncan, Isadora's brother, whose personal charisma and exploitative idealism are reflected in a number of her novels. Boyle spent her next years in the French and British settings that are reflected in her novels of this period. In 1931, she married the scholar and poet Laurence Vail, and in the following years bore three more daughters.

Emerging aboveground in the late 1930's with a Simon & Schuster contract, Boyle published a major short-story collection, *The White Horses of Vienna*, which introduced the Lippizanner horses that became an important symbol in later works. Three highly praised short novels and two longer ones followed, and she received a Guggenheim Fellowship to pursue the metaphor of aviation for human history. Before the fall of France in 1939, she wrote about the collapse of Europe's democracies before Fascism. The war novels of that period are usually set in small French villages where an expatriated woman becomes involved in the political choices of various men, usually Austrians made nationless by the Anschluss. The conflict between resistance and collaboration addressed in her novels surfaced in Boyle's private life as well when Vail disapproved of her efforts to secure visas for Jewish refugees, citing the "historical necessity" of Fascism. Following their divorce, Boyle married Baron Joseph Von Franckenstein, an Austrian refugee whose experiences are reflected in *American Citizen Naturalized in Leadville, Colorado* and in *His Human Majesty*.

After the fall of France, the popular novels *Avalanche* and *A Frenchman Must Die* brought the resistance experience to American audiences but received negative reviews. Despite this criticism, Boyle continued to address the question of individual political choice in short novels such as *Decision*, set in post-Civil War Spain, and in *The Seagull on the Step*, which points out the growing inappropriateness of American occupation policy. After the war, Boyle's work became even more journalistic in her role as a European correspondent, and she also commented on European moral and political conditions in her short stories of the period.

Returning in 1953 to an America caught up in the events of McCarthyism, Boyle lost her job with *The New Yorker*, while Von Franckenstein was removed from his state department post for his "questionable" loyalty in associating with Boyle. After frequent testimony by both before Internal Security committees, Von Franckenstein was reinstated in 1957. In 1958, the first American edition of *Three Short Novels*, including *The Crazy Hunter, The Bridegroom's Body*, and *Decision*, appeared, followed by *Generation Without Farewell*, Boyle's most ambitious postwar novel.

Following Von Franckenstein's death from cancer in 1963, Boyle continued her political commitment and her writing during the anti-Vietnam War movement. The

Christmas Eve of 1967, which Boyle spent in jail for her part in a sit-in at an Oakland induction center, is drawn upon in her novel *The Underground Woman*. As a teacher of creative writing at San Francisco State, she courted dismissal to join the student protest. Having received the San Francisco Art Commission's Award of Honor in 1978, Boyle retired from teaching in 1980, the year in which *Fifty Stories* appeared. She died on December 27, 1992, a few months short of her ninetieth birthday.

Analysis

From *Plagued by the Nightingale*, published in the early 1930's, to *The Underground Woman* in the 1970's, Kay Boyle's novels explore a complex dialectic between the personal and the political. Within the individual psyche and the social world as well there is a conflict between the human will to liberation and the authoritarian will to dominance. Not autobiographical in the usual sense, most of Boyle's early novels are imaginative reconsiderations of episodes which, although recognizable in outline in her personal life, are universalized into paradigms of human experience. Her first novel, *Plagued by the Nightingale*, which Hart Crane admired, introduced an expatriate American bride to her husband's family in their decaying French provincial seat. A crippling congenital disease afflicting all the family males, an emblem of general social decay, prevents the young husband, Nicole, from asserting independence, and requires the family to be always on the lookout to perpetuate itself. Bridget, the young wife, and Luc, a family friend whose energy and vivacity have earmarked him for marriage to one of Nicole's three sisters, are alternately drawn into and repelled by the patriarchal family's power to protect and engulf. By making the birth of an heir the condition upon which the young couple's inheritance depends, Nicole's father threatens to bring them entirely within the control of the patriarchal family. Freeing both herself and Nicole from the grasp of this decaying culture, Bridget chooses to bear a child not by Nicole, whose tainted genes would continue the cycle, but by Luc, a vigorous outsider whose health and vitality promise liberation and autonomy. Although ostensibly a narrative of personal life, this first novel becomes political in its exploration of the relationship between the self and the family, the will to immerse oneself in the group or to aspire to self-determination. The decaying and yet

compelling power of the patriarchal family becomes a metaphor for Western culture itself in its paralyzing traditionalism and sacrifice of the individual to authority.

In two novels addressing the postwar period of occupation, *The Seagull on the Step* and *Generation Without Farewell*, Boyle's vision of the dialectic between the personal and the political becomes more fully a clash between the human and the totalitarian impulses in the heart and in history. In *Generation Without Farewell*, a study of the human response to authoritarianism, hunters stalk their prey in an occupied German village. Both Germans and Americans, led by the American Colonel Roberts, the universal authoritarian, hunt a wild boar believed hidden in the seemingly primeval forest surrounding the village. An expression of the people's will to survive and affirm the positive aspects of their nationality against the dead hand of their Nazi past, the boar is identified by an American observer, Seth Honerkamp, with an anti-Fascist spirit and the great composers of the past. Jaeger, an anti-Nazi German searching for his roots in a past not distorted by Fascism, sees in the hunt his people's historic tendency to create an "other" whose extermination becomes an obsession, destroying human liberty and ultimately the very source of the culture. The will to liberty breaks free, however, when Robert's wife Catherine and daughter Milly, both expressions of the reproductive and nurturing power contained in the Demeter-Persephone myth so pervasive in Boyle, join Jaeger and Christoph Horn. Horn is Milly's lover, whose identification with the Lippizanner horses in his care connects him with the most fertile and, at the same time, the most transcendent elements of the national spirit they represent. This identification is shared by Milly, whose pregnancy by Horn parallels the mare's pregnancy in a particularly female vision of the survival and continuity of the culture itself. Although the repressive qualities of both German and American authority unite in the hunt for the boar, an attempt to ship the horses to Brooklyn, and an epidemic of polio—the essentially American disease which fatally strikes Horn despite Jaeger's and Honerkamp's efforts to secure an iron lung—Catherine joins Milly to protect the coming child, leaving a revitalized Jaeger and Honerkamp to continue their pursuit for the life-affirming aspects of both German and American culture.

The myth of the sorrowing mother in search of her daughter appears again in *The Underground Woman*. Against the background of the American antiwar movement, Athena Gregory's psychic restoration is connected to a vision of human transcendence expressed in a community of women. Athena, a university classics teacher, her husband lost to cancer and her daughter to a satanic cult, finds herself jailed during a sit-in at an induction center. Through a process of bonding not only with the other war protesters but also with the black, Hispanic, and poor white women there, she finds personal and

political transformation in an intense female friendship with Calliope, another older woman whose intuitive, emotional nature balances Athena's own rational, analytical one. She also forms a friendship with a young woman musician, who replaces Athena's daughter Melanie, irrevocably lost to a cult serving Pete the Redeemer, an exploitative, charismatic leader who demands complete surrender of the will. Released from jail and from her mourning, Athena asserts her new self in a symbolic defense of all daughters when she successfully resists Pete's attempt to commandeer her home. In this affirmative vision of female power, Athena resolves the conflict between her two selves, the respectable, aboveground Athena sprung from Zeus's head and heir to his rationality, and the more emotional, intuitive "underground woman," as she joins Calliope to save the deer from the hunters and the Hispanic prostitute's children from the state. In this late novel, Kay Boyle's vision of personal and political self-affirmation advances the dialectic between subjective experience and objective reality which always marked her work.

Other major works

SHORT FICTION: *Short Stories*, 1929; *Wedding Day and Other Stories*, 1930; *First Lover and Other Stories*, 1933; *The White Horses of Vienna and Other Stories*, 1936; *The Crazy Hunter and Other Stories*, 1940; *Thirty Stories*, 1946; *The Smoking Mountain: Stories of Postwar Germany*, 1951; *Nothing Ever Breaks Except the Heart*, 1966; *Fifty Stories*, 1980; *Life Being the Best and Other Stories*, 1988.

POETRY: *A Glad Day*, 1938; *American Citizen Naturalized in Leadville, Colorado*, 1944; *Collected Poems*, 1962; *Testament for My Students and Other Poems*, 1970; *This Is Not a Letter and Other Poems*, 1985.

NONFICTION: *Breaking the Silence: Why a Mother Tells Her Son About the Nazi Era*, 1962; *The Autobiography of Emanuel Carnevali*, 1967; *Being Geniuses Together, 1920-1930*, 1968 (with Robert McAlmon); *The Long Walk at San Francisco State and Other Essays*, 1970; *Enough of Dying! An Anthology of Peace Writings*, 1972; *Words That Must Somehow Be Said: The Selected Essays of Kay Boyle, 1927-1984*, 1985.

CHILDREN'S LITERATURE: *The Youngest Camel*, 1939, 1959; *Pinky, the Cat Who Liked to Sleep*, 1966; *Pinky in Persia*, 1968.

EDITED TEXT: *365 Days*, 1936 (with others).

Bibliography

Carpenter, Richard C. "Kay Boyle: The Figure in the Carpet." *Critique: Studies in Modern Fiction* 7 (Winter, 1964-1965): 65-78.

Ford, Hugh. *Four Lives in Paris*. San Francisco: North Point Press, 1987.

Howard, Richard. "Poetry Chronicle." Review of *Collected Poems*, by Kay Boyle. *Poetry* 102 (July, 1963): 250-259.

Spanier, Sandra Whipple. *Kay Boyle: Artist and Activist*. Carbondale: Southern Illinois University Press, 1986.

Yalom, Marilyn. *Women Writers of the West Coast: Speaking of Their Lives and Careers*. Santa Barbara, Calif.: Capra Press, 1983.

ANNE BRADSTREET

Born: Northampton, England; 1612(?)

Died: Andover, Massachusetts; September 16, 1672

Principal poetry

The Tenth Muse Lately Sprung Up in America, 1650; *Several Poems Compiled with Great Variety of Wit and Learning*, 1678.

Other literary forms

Anne Bradstreet's published collections in 1650 and 1678 consist entirely of poetry, and her reputation rests on her poems. She left in manuscript the prose "Meditations Divine and Morall" (short, pithy proverbs) and a brief autobiography written especially for her children.

Achievements

One of Bradstreet's distinctive poetic strengths is her generic variety. She wrote epics, dialogues, love lyrics, public elegies, private elegies, a long meditative poem, and religious verse. Few other Puritan poets successfully tackled so many genres.

Although Bradstreet's contemporaries admired her early imitative poetry, her later personal poetry is what endures. Poems included in *The Tenth Muse Lately Sprung Up in America* fall within an essentially Renaissance tradition, while those in *Several Poems Compiled with Great Variety of Wit and Learning* initiate a distinctive tradition of American literature. Bradstreet's love poems to her husband are admired for their wit, intricate construction, emotional force, and frank admission of the physical side of marriage. Bradstreet's personal elegies on her grandchildren skillfully dramatize the Puritans' unremitting battle between worldliness (grieving for the dead) and unworldliness (rejoicing in their salvation). Yet her masterpiece is probably her long meditative poem "Contemplations," praised for its maturity, complexity, and lyricism. Her love poems, personal elegies, and "Contemplations" reveal the human side of Puritanism from a woman's vantage point.

Biography

Through her poetic voices, Anne Bradstreet assumes a clear (but complex) presence, yet factual data about her are surprisingly scant. Joseph McElrath, editor of *The Complete Works of Anne Bradstreet* (1981), shows that even her birth date is uncertain. She was probably born in 1612 in Northampton, England, but may have been born as late as 1613, one of Thomas Dudley and Dorothy Yorke's six children.

In 1619, the family moved to Sempringham, where Dudley became steward to the earl of Lincoln. Both Thomas Dudley and his employer allowed the prospective poet an unusually good education for a woman. Scholars even speculate that she had access to the earl's library. In 1621, Simon Bradstreet joined the earl's household to assist Dudley; but in 1624, the Dudleys moved to Boston, England, and Simon Bradstreet left to work for the countess of Warwick.

When the poet was about sixteen, as she records in her autobiographical prose, "the Lord layd his hand sore upon me & smott mee with the small pox." After her recovery in 1628, she and Simon Bradstreet married, and two years later, the Dudley and Bradstreet families left for America aboard the *Arbella*.

For Anne Bradstreet, the transition was not entirely smooth, and her prose autobiography speaks of "a new World and new manners at which my heart rose, But after I was convinced it was the way of God, I submitted to it & joined to the chh., at Boston." After brief spells in Salem, Boston, Cambridge, and Ipswich, the Bradstreets moved to North Andover, Massachusetts, where Anne Bradstreet reared eight children, wrote, and shared her husband's life as he rose from judge to governor of the colony. Although the poet was susceptible to many illnesses and was childless for several years, her supremely happy marriage compensated for, and helped her to overcome, these "trials."

As the governor's wife, Bradstreet enjoyed a socio-economic status conducive to writing. In the mid-1640's, Bradstreet had completed the poems which appeared in her first collection. Bradstreet herself did not supervise their printing; John Woodbridge, her brother-in-law, probably carried the manuscript to London, where it was published in 1650. Bradstreet expressed mixed feelings about its publication, largely because of the printing errors. The poem "The Author to Her Book" mildly chides "friends, less wise than true" who exposed the work "to publick view." Poems in the collection are mainly public in tone and content, while those in her second collection (published posthumously in 1678) are mainly private and personal.

Bradstreet was a known, respected, and loved poet in both the Old and New Worlds. Her death in 1672 called forth elegies and eulogies. These lines from the preface to *The Tenth Muse Lately Sprung Up in America*, probably written by Woodbridge, best convey Bradstreet's qualities: "It is the Work of a Woman, honoured, and esteemed where she lives, for her gracious demeanour, her eminent parts, her pious conversation, her courteous disposition, [and] her exact diligence in her place."

Analysis

Anne Bradstreet wrote poetry from the 1640's to her death in 1672. Her public voice, which dominates the early poetry, is eulogistic, imitative, self-conscious, and less controlled in metaphor and structure; most of the poems in *The Tenth Muse Lately Sprung Up in America* illustrate these traits. Her private voice—more evident in *Several Poems Compiled with Great Variety of Wit and Learning*—is often elegiac, original, self-confident, and better controlled in metaphor and structure. It is convenient to consider representative elegies from three roughly chronological stages in Bradstreet's work: "poetic" involvement, conventional involvement, and personal involvement.

Almost all the verse in her first collection conveys Bradstreet's public, poetic involvement. Specifically, in secular poems such as the "Quaternions," "The Four Monarchies," and the elegies on famous Elizabethans, Bradstreet as professional poet or bard dominates and controls. "In Honour of Du Bartas" (1641) contains the typical Renaissance characteristics of public content, imitative style, classical allusions, and secular eulogy. The poem's content could hardly be more public, since it dutifully details the accomplishments of Bradstreet's mentor Guillaume de Salluste Du Bartas—his learning, valor, wit, and literary skill. Although Bradstreet contrasts her meager poetic powers with Du Bartas' unlimited powers, her involvement is not personal; rather, it eventually points a favorite moral for Renaissance poets. No matter how bad the writer, the dead person (in this case a poet, too) will "live" in the poem's lines.

An extension of public content and bardic involvement is imitative style. For example, "In Honour of Du Bartas" contains conventional images such as the simile comparing Bradstreet's muse to a child, the hyperbole declaring that Du Bartas' fame will last "while starres do stand," and the oxymoron in "senslesse Sences." Although Bradstreet's early imitative style is skillful, it hinders her from expressing the unique voice of her later work. Furthermore, tradition compels her to scatter her public poems with classical allusions.

Finally, these lengthy early poems may contain secular eulogy, also a characteristic of the pastoral elegy, and hyperbole, common in the debate form. The opening lines of "In Honour of Du Bartas," for example, state that Du Bartas is "matchlesse knowne" among contemporary poets. In such a richly literary age, Bradstreet obviously uses hyperbole and eulogy to emphasize Du Bartas' greatness for her.

The second phase—conventional involvement—includes religious poems within a public or orthodox context. A few such poems are from *The Tenth Muse Lately Sprung Up in America*; more are from her second collection. In this poetry, Bradstreet moves closer to mainstream Puritan verse. The elegies on her parents are conventionally formal and fit the pattern of the New England funeral elegy, whose hallmark was public praise of the dead one's life and virtues to overcome personal grief. "The Flesh and the Spirit," "As weary pilgrim, now at rest," and "Of the vanity of all worldly creatures" treat the theme of worldliness versus unworldliness generally and impersonally to reach orthodox conclusions.

Bradstreet's elegy on her father, "To the memory of my dear and ever honoured Father Thomas Dudley," begins with an apparently personal touch: Bradstreet's claim to write from filial duty, not custom. Even so, as she reminds her readers, this filial duty allows her to praise her father's virtues fully and publicly, not partially and privately. In later elegies, Bradstreet does not explain so defensively why she follows certain conventions; indeed, she frequently modifies or ignores them. In this early elegy, however, these conventions constrain Bradstreet's own voice so that she writes forced lines such as these: "In manners pleasant and severe / The Good him lov'd, the bad did fear, / And when his time with years was spent / If some rejoyc'd, more did lament." Lacking are the emotional force, personal involvement, and dramatic struggle between flesh and spirit found in the later poems.

One characteristic apparent in the second phase is Bradstreet's use of fairly standard poetic structure, such as the dialogue/debate form, the meditation, and the Puritan elegy. Standard, often biblical, imagery is another distinct aspect of the second phase. While this imagery is to some extent present in the earlier and later phases, it is particularly evident in the middle stage. In the first stage, Bradstreet's images are traditionally Renaissance, and in the third stage, they are biblical but infused with emotive and personal force. The elegy on Thomas Dudley illustrates the traditionally biblical images of the second phase: Dudley has a "Mansion" prepared above; and, like a ripe shock of wheat, he is mowed by the sickle Death and is then stored safely. The other orthodox poems also use biblical images almost exclusively.

Universality and individuality form the special strength of Bradstreet's masterpiece, "Contemplations." This thirty-three verse meditative poem fits best into the second stage because of its spiritual content. Given the poem's importance, however, it must be discussed separately. Bradstreet skillfully evokes a dramatic scene— she walks at dusk in the countryside—then uses it to explore the relationships among man, God, and nature.

In stanzas 1 to 7, the poet acknowledges nature's potency and majesty by looking first at an oak tree and then at the sun. If they are glorious, she muses, how much more glorious must their creator be? Stanzas 8 to 20 recall humanity's creation and fall, extending from Adam and Eve to Cain and Abel and finally to Bradstreet's own day. The answer to human misery, however, is not nature worship. Instead, humans must acknowledge that God made them alone for immortality. In stanzas 21 to 28, the poet considers the amoral delight of nature—the elm, the river, the fish, and the nightingale— incapable of the tortures of free will. Stanzas 29 to 33

show that beyond the natural cycle, only humans can be resurrected within the divine cycle.

"Contemplations" contains some of Bradstreet's most original and inspired poetry within the three-part structure of the seventeenth century meditation. These parts correspond to the mental faculties of memory, understanding, and will. The person creates or recalls a scene in the first part, analyzes its spiritual significance in the second part, and responds emotionally *and* intellectually by prayer and devotion in the last. Clearly, these are the three basic structural elements of "Contemplations." Although Bradstreet ultimately returns to orthodoxy, this poem is no mere religious exercise; it is "the most finished and musical of her religious poems."

The third phase of Bradstreet's poetry includes love lyrics, elegies on grandchildren and a daughter-in-law, and other works inspired by private matters (the burning of Bradstreet's house, the publication of her first collection, the poet's eight children). Yet, unlike the poems of the previous stage, which are overwhelmingly spiritual, the poems of the third phase are primarily secular. If they deal with religious matters—as the elegies do, for example—it is within a personal context. One critic calls Bradstreet "the worldly Puritan," and these late poems show the material face of Puritanism. Bradstreet's personal involvement affects structure, tone, rhythm, and metaphor. "In memory of my dear grand-child Elizabeth Bradstreet" illustrates many of these changes.

Because she was more comfortable writing of private matters in a private voice, Bradstreet's poetic structure arises naturally from content and context. The elegy on Elizabeth, for example, divides into two seven-line stanzas (it is a variation of the sonnet form). In stanza 1, the poet says farewell to her grandchild and questions why she should be sad since little Elizabeth is in Heaven. In stanza 2, Bradstreet explains that nature's products perish only when they are ripe; therefore, if a newly blown "bud" perishes, it must be God's doing. The structure aptly complements the poet's grief, disbelief, and final resignation. Both stanzas effortlessly follow the rhyme scheme *ababccc*. Bradstreet's love poems are also constructed in an intricate but uncontrived way. Both poems entitled "Another [Letter to her Husband]" show careful attention to structure. The first poem of this title personifies the sun and follows the sun's daily course; the second ties together three images and puns suggesting marital harmony (*dear/deer, heart/hart,* and *hind/hind*).

A marked difference in the poetry of the third phase is

its tone. Instead of sounding self-conscious, bookish, derivative, overambitious, or staunchly orthodox, Bradstreet's later poetry is poised, personal, original, modest, and unwilling to accept orthodoxy without question. Another tonal change is subtlety, which the elegy on Elizabeth illustrates well. Throughout the poem, Bradstreet hovers between the worldly response of grief and the unworldly one of acceptance. This uneasy balance, finally resolved when Bradstreet accepts God's will, makes the elegy especially poignant. The poet's other late elegies on her grandchildren Anne and Simon and her daughter-in-law Mercy are also poignant. The secular love poetry that Bradstreet wrote to her husband—often while he was away on business—conveys playfulness, longing, and, above all, boundless love. The tone of Bradstreet's late poetry tends to be more varied and complex than the tone of her early poetry, the only notable exception being "Contemplations."

Bradstreet's rhythm reflects her increased poetic self-confidence. Gone are the strained lines and rhythms characteristic of the "Quaternions" and "The Four Monarchies"; instead, the opening lines of Bradstreet's elegy on Elizabeth show how private subject matter lends itself to natural, personal expression: "Farewel dear babe, my hearts too much content, / Farewel sweet babe, the pleasure of mine eye, / Farewel fair flower that for a space was lent. / Then ta'en away unto Eternity." The delicate antithesis in the first to third lines and the repetition of "Farewel" add emotional force to the content and emphasize Bradstreet's difficulty in accepting Elizabeth's death. The other late elegies are rhythmically varied and use antithesis to underscore life's ever-present duality:

flesh/spirit, worldliness/unworldliness. For example, within the elegy on three-year-old Anne, Bradstreet conveys her problem in coming to terms with yet another grandchild's death when she uses this forced, monosyllabic rhythm, "More fool then I to look on that was lent. / As if mine own, when thus impermanent." The love poetry is also written with special attention to rhythmic variety.

The poet's metaphoric language in the later works is free of bookishness and imitativeness. She does not resort to classical allusions or literary images but chooses familiar, often domestic or biblical, metaphors. In the elegy on Elizabeth, the entire second stanza comprises a series of images drawn from nature. Bradstreet heightens her grandchild's death by saying how unnatural it is compared to the natural cycle of trees, fruit, corn, and grass. The love poetry draws on nature images too—the sun, fish, deer, and rivers. In her late personal poetry, Bradstreet also feels comfortable using some extended images.

The elegies on Du Bartas, Thomas Dudley, and Elizabeth Bradstreet are representative of stages in Bradstreet's poetic career. Critics agree on her importance as one of the two foremost Colonial poets, with Edward Taylor. Until recently, scholarship on her work focused on biographical and historical concerns. Modern criticism, on the other hand, concentrates on structure, style, theme, and text. This move toward aesthetic analysis has deepened scholarly appreciation of Bradstreet's talent. In addition, the rise of women's studies ensures her place as a significant female voice in American poetry.

Other major works

MISCELLANEOUS: *The Complete Works of Anne Bradstreet*, 1981 (Joseph R. McElrath and Allan P. Robb, editors).

Bibliography

Cowell, Pattie, and Ann Stanford, eds. *Critical Essays on Anne Bradstreet*. Boston: G. K. Hall, 1983.

Martin, Wendy. *An American Triptych: Anne Bradstreet, Emily Dickinson, Adrienne Rich*. Chapel Hill: University of North Carolina Press, 1984.

Piercy, Josephine K. *Anne Bradstreet*. New York: Twayne, 1965.

Rich, Adrienne. "Anne Bradstreet and Her Poetry." Foreword to *The Works of Anne Bradstreet*. Cambridge, Mass.: The Belknap Press of Harvard University Press, 1967.

Stanford, Ann. *Anne Bradstreet: The Worldly Puritan*. New York: Burt Franklin, 1974.

Tyler, Moses C. *A History of American Literature During the Colonial Period*. New York: G. P. Putnam's Sons, 1897.

White, Elizabeth Wade. *Anne Bradstreet: The Tenth Muse*. New York: Oxford University Press, 1971.

CHARLOTTE BRONTË

Born: Thornton, England; April 21, 1816

Died: Haworth, England; March 31, 1855

Principal long fiction

Jane Eyre, 1847; *Shirley*, 1849; *Villette*, 1853; *The Professor*, 1857.

Other literary forms

The nineteen poems which Charlotte Brontë selected to print with the work of her sisters Anne and Emily in *Poems by Currer, Ellis, and Acton Bell* (1846) were her only other works published during her lifetime. The juvenilia produced by the four Brontë children—Charlotte, Emily, Anne, and Branwell—between 1824 and 1839 are scattered in libraries and private collections. Some of Charlotte's contributions have been published in *The Twelve Adventurers and Other Stories* (1925), *Legends of Angria* (1933), *The Search After Hapiness*, (1969), *Five Novelettes* (1971), and *The Secret and Lily Hart* (1979). A fragment of a novel written during the last year of Brontë's life was published as *Emma* in *Cornhill Magazine* in 1860 and is often reprinted in editions of *The Professor*. *The Complete Poems of Charlotte Brontë* appeared in 1923. Other brief selections, fragments, and ephemera have been printed in *Transactions and Other Publications of the Brontë Society*. *The Shakespeare Head Brontë* (1931-1938), edited by T. J. Wise and J. A. Symington, contains all the novels, four volumes of life and letters, two volumes of miscellaneous writings, and two volumes of poems.

Achievements

Brontë brought to English fiction an intensely personal voice. Her books show the moral and emotional growth of a protagonist almost entirely by self-revelation. Her novels focus on individual self-fulfillment; they express the subjective interior world not only in thoughts, dreams, visions, and symbols but also by projecting inner states through external objects, secondary characters, places, events, and weather. Brontë's own experiences and emotions inform the narrative presence. "Perhaps no other writer of her time," wrote Margaret Oliphant in 1855, "has impressed her mark so clearly on contemporary literature, or drawn so many followers into her own peculiar path."

The personal voice, which blurs the distance between novelist, protagonist, and reader, accounts for much of the critical ambivalence toward Brontë's work. Generations of unsophisticated readers have identified with Jane Eyre; thousands of romances and modern gothics have used Brontë's situations and invited readers to step into the fantasy. Brontë's novels, however, are much more than simply the common reader's daydreams. They are rich enough to allow a variety of critical approaches. They have been studied in relation to traditions (gothic, provincial, realistic, Romantic); read for psychological, linguistic, Christian, social, economic, and personal interpretations; and analyzed in terms of symbolism, imagery, metaphor, viewpoint, narrative distance, and prose style. Because the novels are so clearly wrought from the materials of their author's life, recent psychoanalytic and feminist criticism has proved rewarding. In Brontë's work, a woman author makes significant statements about issues central to women's lives. Most of her heroines are working women; each feels the pull of individual self-development against the wish for emotional fulfillment, the tension between sexual energies and social realities, the almost unresolvable conflict between love and independence.

Biography

Charlotte Brontë was the third of six children born within seven years to the Reverend Patrick Brontë and his wife Maria Branwell. Patrick Brontë was perpetual curate of Haworth, a bleak manufacturing town in Yorkshire. In 1821, when Charlotte Brontë was five years old, her mother died of cancer. Three years later, the four elder girls were sent to the Clergy Daughter's School at Cowan Bridge—the school which appears as Lowood in

Jane Eyre. In the summer of 1825, the eldest two daughters, Maria and Elizabeth, died of tuberculosis. Charlotte and Emily were removed from the school and brought home. There were no educated middle-class families in Haworth to supply friends and companions. The Brontë children lived with a noncommunicative aunt, an elderly servant, and a father much preoccupied by his intellectual interests and his own griefs.

In their home and with only one another for company, the children had material for both educational and imaginative development. In 1826, Branwell was given a set of wooden soldiers which the four children used for characters in creative play. These soldiers gradually took on personal characteristics and acquired countries to rule. The countries needed cities, governments, ruling families, political intrigues, legends, and citizens with private lives, all of which the children happily invented. In 1829, when Charlotte Brontë was thirteen, she and the others began to write down materials from these fantasies, producing a collection of juvenilia that extended ultimately to hundreds of items: magazines, histories, maps, essays, tales, dramas, poems, newspapers, wills, speeches, scrapbooks. This enormous creative production in adolescence gave concrete form to motifs that were later transformed into situations, characters, and concerns of Charlotte Brontë's mature work. It was also a workshop for literary technique; the young author explored prose style, experimented with viewpoint, and discovered how to control narrative voice.

In 1831, when she was almost fifteen, Charlotte Brontë went to Miss Wooler's School at Roe Head. After returning home for a time to tutor her sisters, she went back to Miss Wooler's as a teacher. Over the next several years, all three sisters held positions as governesses in private families, but they all suffered when separated from their shared emotional and creative life. A possible solution would have been to open their own school, but they needed some special qualification to attract pupils. Charlotte conceived a plan for going abroad to study languages. In 1842, she and Emily went to Brussels to the Pensionnat Héger. They returned in November because of their aunt's death, but in the following year Charlotte went back to Brussels alone to work as a pupil-teacher. An additional reason for her return to

Brussels was that she desired to be near Professor Constantine Héger, but at the end of the year she left in misery after Héger's wife had realized (perhaps more clearly than did Charlotte herself) the romantic nature of the attraction.

In 1844, Charlotte Brontë established herself permanently at Haworth and tried to set up a school, but no pupils applied. Charlotte spent nearly two years in deep depression: Her yearning for love was unsatisfied and she had repressed her creative impulse because she was afraid her fantasies were self-indulgent. Then, with the discovery that all three had written poetry, the sisters found a new aim in life. A joint volume of poems was published in May, 1846, though it sold only two copies. Each wrote a short novel; they offered the three together to publishers. Emily Brontë's *Wuthering Heights* (1847) and Anne Brontë's *Agnes Grey* (1847) were accepted. Charlotte Brontë's *The Professor* was refused, but one editor, George Smith, said he would like to see a three-volume novel written by its author. *Jane Eyre* was by that time almost finished; it was sent to Smith on August 24, 1847, and impressed him so much that he had it in print by the middle of October. *Jane Eyre* was immediately successful, but there was barely any time for its author to enjoy her fame and accomplishment. Within a single year, her three companions in creation died: Branwell on September 24, 1848; Emily on December 19; and Anne on May 28, 1849.

Charlotte Brontë's sense that she was plain, "undeveloped," and unlikely to be loved seems to have been partly the product of her own psychological condition. She had refused more than one proposal in her early twenties. In 1852 there was another, from Arthur Bell Nicholls, curate at Haworth. Patrick Brontë objected violently and dismissed his curate. Gradually, however, the objections were worn away. On June 29, 1854, Charlotte Brontë and the Reverend Nicholls were married and, after a brief honeymoon tour, took up residence in Haworth parsonage. After a few months of apparent content—which did not prevent her from beginning work on another novel—Charlotte Brontë died on March 31, 1855, at the age of thirty-eight; a severe cold made her too weak to survive the complications of early pregnancy.

Analysis

Few writers of English prose have so successfully communicated the emotional texture of inner life while still constructing fictions with enough verisimilitude to appear realistic as has Charlotte Brontë. Brontë startled the Victorians because her work was so little influenced by the books of her own era. Its literary forebears were the written corporate daydreams of her childhood and the Romantic poets she read during the period when the fantasies took shape. Certain characters and situations that crystallized the emotional conflicts of early adolescence became necessary components of emotional satisfaction. The source of these fantasies was, to a degree, beyond control, occurring in the region the twentieth century has termed "the unconscious"; by writing them down from childhood on, Brontë learned to preserve and draw on relatively undisguised desires and ego conflicts in a way lost to most adults.

The power and reality of the inner life disturbed Brontë after she had passed through adolescence; she compared her creative urge to the action of opium and was afraid that she might become lost in her "infernal world." When she began to think of publication, she deliberately used material from her own experience and reported scenes and characters in verifiable detail. In this way, she hoped to subdue the exaggerated romanticism—and the overwrought writing—of the fantasy-fictions. Her drawing from life was so accurate that the curates and the Yorkes in *Shirley* were recognized at once by people who knew them, and Brontë lost the protection that her pseudonym had provided.

The years of practice in writing fiction that satisfied her own emotional needs gave Brontë the means to produce powerful psychological effects. She uses a variety of resources to make readers share the protagonist's subjective state. The truth of the outside world is only that truth which reflects the narrator's feelings and perceptions. All characters are aspects of the consciousness that creates them: Brontë uses splitting, doubling, and other fairy-tale devices; she replicates key situations; and she carefully controls the narrative distance and the amount of information readers have at their disposal.

The unquietness which Brontë's readers often feel grows from the tension between direct emotional satisfactions (often apparently immature) on the one hand, and, on the other, mature and realistic conflicts in motive, reason, and sense of self. Read as a sequence, the four completed novels demonstrate both Brontë's development and the story of woman's relationship to the world. Brontë's heroines find identity outside the enclosed family popularly supposed to circumscribe nineteenth century women. Isolation allows the heroines' self-development, but it impedes their romantic yearning

to be thoroughly lost in love.

In *Jane Eyre*, Brontë created a story that has the authority of myth. Everything that had deeply affected her was present in the book's emotional content. The traumatic experiences of maternal deprivation, the Clergy Daughters' School, and Maria's death create the events of Jane's early life. The book also taps universal feelings of rejection, victimization, and loneliness. Rochester's compelling power as a lover derives from neither literal nor literary sources—Rochester is the man Brontë had loved for twenty years, the Duke of Zamorna who dominates the adolescent fantasies, exerting a power on both Jane and the reader. Jane defied literary convention because she was poor, plain, and a heroine; she defied social convention by refusing to accept any external authority. Placed repeatedly in situations that exemplify male power, Jane resists and survives. At the end of the narrative, she is transformed from Cinderella to Prince Charming, becoming the heroine who cuts through the brambles to rescue the imprisoned sleeper. Identification is so immediate and so close that readers often fail to notice Brontë's control of distance, in particular the points of detachment when an older Jane comments on her younger self and the direct addresses from Jane to the reader that break the spell when emotions become too strong.

Place controls the book's structure. Events at Gateshead, Lowood, Thornfield, and Moor House determine Jane's development; a brief coda at Fearndean provides the resolution. Each of the four major sections contains a figure representing the sources of male power over women: John Reed (physical force and the patriarchal family), Reverend Brocklehurst (the social structures of class, education, and religion), Rochester (sexual attraction), and St. John Rivers (moral and spiritual authority). Jane protects herself at first by devious and indirect means—fainting, illness, flight—and then ultimately, in rejecting St. John Rivers, by direct confrontation. Compelled by circumstances to fend for herself, she comes—at first instinctively, later rationally—to rely on herself.

The book's emotional power grows from its total absorption in Jane's view of the world and from the images, symbols, and structures that convey multiple interwoven reverberations. The red room—which suggests violence, irrationality, enclosure, rebellion, rebirth, the bloody chamber of emerging womanhood—echoes throughout the book. The Bridewell charade, Jane's paintings, the buildings and terrain, and a multitude of other details have both meaning and function. Characters double and split: Helen Burns (mind) and Bertha Mason (body) are aspects of Jane as well as actors in the plot. Recurring images of ice and fire suggest fatal coldness without and consuming fire within. Rochester's sexuality is the most threatening and ambiguous aspect of masculine power because of Jane's own complicity and her need for love. Her terrors and dreams accumulate as the marriage approaches; there are drowning images, abyss images, loss of consciousness. She refuses to become Rochester's mistress, finally, not because of the practical and moral dangers (which she does recognize) but because she fears her own willingness to make a god of him. She will not become dependent; she escapes to preserve her self.

As Jane takes her life into her own hands, she becomes less needy. After she has achieved independence by discovering a family and inheriting money, she is free to seek out Rochester. At the same time, he has become less omnipotent, perhaps a code for the destruction of patriarchal power. Thus, the marriage not only ends the romance and resolves the moral, emotional, and sexual conflicts but also supplies a satisfactory woman's fantasy of independence coupled with love.

Villette is Brontë's most disciplined novel. Lucy Snowe is a woman without money, family, friends, or health. She is not, however, a sympathetic friendly narrator like Jane Eyre. Her personality has the unattractiveness that realistically grows from deprivation; she has no social ease, no warmth, no mental quickness. Furthermore, her personality creates her pain, loneliness, and disengagement.

In the book's early sections, Lucy is not even the center of her narrative. She watches and judges instead of taking part; she tells other people's stories instead of her own. She is so self-disciplined that she appears to have neither feelings nor imagination, so restrained that she never reveals the facts about her family or the incidents of her youth that might explain to readers how and why she learned to suppress emotion, hope, and the desire for human contact. Despite—or perhaps because of—her anesthetized feeling and desperate shyness, Lucy Snowe drives herself to actions that might have

been inconceivable for a woman more thoroughly socialized. Thrust into the world by the death of the elderly woman whose companion she had been, she goes alone to London, takes a ship for the Continent, gets a job as nursemaid, rises through her own efforts to teach in Madame Beck's school, and begins laying plans to open a school of her own.

The coincidental and melodramatic elements of the story gain authenticity because they grow from Lucy's inner life. When she is left alone in the school during vacation, her repressed need to be heard by someone drives her to enter the confessional of a Catholic church. Once the internal barrier is breached, she immediately meets the Bretton family. Realistically, she must have known they were in Villette; she knew that "Dr. John" was Graham Bretton, but she withheld that information from the reader both because of her habitual secretiveness and also because she did not really "know" the Brettons were accessible to her until she was able to admit her need to reach out for human sympathy. The characterization of Paul Emanuel gains richness and detail in such a manner that readers realize—before Lucy herself dares admit it—that she is interested in him. The phantom nun, at first a night terror of pure emotion, is revealed as a prankish disguise when Lucy is free to express feelings directly.

The novel's ending, however, is deliberately ambiguous, though not in event. (Only the most naïve readers dare accept Brontë's invitation to imagine that Paul Emanuel escapes drowning and to "picture union and a happy succeeding life.") The ambiguity grows from Lucy's earlier statement: "M. Emanuel was away for three years. Reader, they were the three happiest years of my life." In those years, Lucy Snowe prospered, became respected, expanded her school. Her happiness depends not on the presence of her beloved but rather on the knowledge that she is loved. With that knowledge, she becomes whole and independent. No longer telling others' stories, she speaks directly to the reader about her most private concerns. Only when her lover is absent, perhaps, can a woman treasure love and emotional satisfaction while yet retaining the freedom to be her own person.

Other major works

POETRY: *Poems by Currer, Ellis, and Acton Bell,* 1846 (with Emily Brontë and Anne Brontë); *The Complete Poems of Charlotte Brontë,* 1923.

CHILDREN'S LITERATURE: *The Twelve Adventurers and Other Stories*, 1925 (C. K. Shorter and C. W. Hatfield, editors); *Legends of Angria*, 1933 (Fannie E. Ratchford, compiler); *The Search After Hapiness*, 1969; *Five Novelettes*, 1971 (Winifred Gérin, editor); *The Secret and Lily Hart*, 1979 (William Holtz, editor).
MISCELLANEOUS: *The Shakespeare Head Brontë*, 1931-1938 (T. J. Wise and J. A. Symington, editors, 19 volumes).

Bibliography

Fraser, Rebecca. *The Brontës: Charlotte Brontë and Her Family*. New York: Crown, 1988.
Gaskell, Elizabeth C. *The Life of Charlotte Brontë*. 1857. Reprint. London: Penguin Books, 1975.
Gérin, Winifred. *Charlotte Brontë: The Evolution of Genius*. Oxford, England: Clarendon Press, 1967.
Lloyd Evans, Barbara, and Gareth Lloyd Evans. *The Scribner Companion to the Brontës*. New York: Charles Scribner's Sons, 1983.
McGregor, Ian, ed. *The Brontës: A Collection of Critical Essays*. Englewood Cliffs, N.J.: Prentice-Hall, 1970.
Nestor, Pauline. *Charlotte Brontë*. Savage, Md.: Barnes & Noble Books, 1987.

EMILY BRONTË

Born: Thornton, England; July 30, 1818   **Died:** Haworth, England; December 19, 1848

Principal long fiction

Wuthering Heights, 1847.

Other literary forms

Poems by Currer, Ellis, and Acton Bell (1846) contains poems by Charlotte, Emily, and Anne Brontë. Juvenilia and early prose works on the imaginary world of Gondal have all been lost.

Achievements

Brontë occupies a unique place in the annals of literature. Her reputation as a major novelist stands on the merits of one relatively short novel that was misunderstood and intensely disliked upon publication, yet no study of British fiction is complete without a discussion of *Wuthering Heights*. The names of its settings and characters, particularly Heathcliff, have become part of the heritage of Western culture. Several film versions, the two most popular in 1939 and 1970, have helped perpetuate this familiarity.

The literary achievement of *Wuthering Heights* lies in its realistic portrayal of a specific place and time and in its examination of universal patterns of human behavior. Set in Yorkshire in the closing years of the eighteenth century, the novel delineates the quality of life in the remote moors of northern England and also reminds the reader of the growing pains of industrialization throughout the nation. In addition, more than any other novel of the period, *Wuthering Heights* presents in clear dialectic form the conflict between two opposing psychic forces, embodied in the settings of the Grange and the Heights and the people who inhabit them. The novel may be most fully appreciated as a study of the nature of perception and its ultimate failure in understanding human behavior.

Biography

Emily Jane Brontë was born at Thornton, in Bradford Parish, Yorkshire, on July 30, 1818, the fifth child of the Reverend Patrick and Maria Brontë. Patrick Brontë was a schoolteacher and tutor before obtaining his B.A. from the University of Cambridge in 1806. He was then ordained to curacies, first in Essex and then in Hartshead, Yorkshire. He married Maria Branwell, of Penzance, in Hartshead on December 19, 1812, and in 1817, they moved to Thornton. The other children at the time of Emily's birth were Maria, Elizabeth, Charlotte, and Patrick Branwell; another daughter, Anne, was born two years later. Charlotte and Anne also became writers.

In early 1820 the family moved to Haworth, four miles from the village of Keighley, where the Reverend Brontë was perpetual curate until his death in 1861. Maria Brontë died on September 15, 1821, and about a year later, an elder sister, Elizabeth Branwell, moved in to take care of the children and household. She remained with them until her own death in 1842.

Life at Haworth was spartan but not unpleasant. There was a close and devoted relationship among the children, especially between Charlotte and Emily. Reading was a favorite pastime, and a wide range of books, including the novels of Sir Walter Scott and the poetry of William Wordsworth and Robert Southey, as well as the more predictable classics, were available to the children. Outdoor activities included many hours of wandering through the moors and woods. Their father wanted the children to be hardy and independent, intellectually and physically, indifferent to the passing fashions of the world.

Maria, Elizabeth, and Charlotte had already been sent away to a school for clergymen's daughters, at Cowan's Bridge, when Emily joined them in November, 1824. Emily was not happy in this confined and rigid environment and longed for home. Two of the sisters, Elizabeth and Maria, became ill and were taken home to die during 1825; in June, Charlotte and Emily returned home as well.

From 1825 to 1830, the remaining Brontë children

lived at Haworth with their father and Miss Branwell. In June, 1826, their father gave them a set of wooden soldiers, a seemingly insignificant gift that stimulated their imaginative and literary talents. The children devoted endless energy to creating an imaginary world for these soldiers. During these years, Charlotte and brother Branwell created in their minds and on paper the land of "Angria," while Emily and Anne were at work on "Gondal." Although all these early prose works have been lost, some of Emily's poetry contains references to aspects of the Gondal-Angria creations.

In July, 1835, Emily again joined Charlotte, already a teacher, at the Roe Head School. She remained only three months, returning home in October. Three years later, she accepted a position as governess in a school in Halifax for about six months, but returned to Haworth in December; Charlotte joined her there early in the following year. During 1839 and 1840, the sisters were planning to establish their own school at Haworth, but the plan was never carried through. Charlotte left home again to serve as a governess in 1841, and in February, 1842, she and Emily went to Mme. Héger's school in Brussels to study languages. They returned to Haworth in November because of Miss Branwell's death. Charlotte went back to Brussels to teach in 1843, but Emily never left Yorkshire again.

From August, 1845, the Brontë children were again united at Haworth. They did not have much contact with neighbors, whose educational level and intellectual interests were much inferior to theirs. They kept busy reading and writing, both fiction and poetry. *Wuthering Heights* was probably begun in October, 1845, and completed sometime in 1846, although it was not published until December, 1847, after the success of Charlotte's *Jane Eyre* (1847).

Meanwhile, the sisters published *Poems by Currer, Ellis, and Acton Bell* in May, 1846. Finding a press was very difficult and pseudonyms were chosen to avoid personal publicity and to create the fiction of male authorship, more readily acceptable to the general public. The reaction was predictable, as Charlotte reports: "Neither we nor our poems were at all wanted." The sisters were not discouraged, however, and they continued to seek publishers for their novels.

The first edition of *Wuthering Heights* was published in 1847 by T. C. Newby, with Anne's *Agnes Grey* as the third volume. It was a sloppy edition and contained many errors. The second edition, published in 1850, after the author's death, was "corrected" by Charlotte. The public reaction to *Wuthering Heights* was decidedly negative; readers were disturbed by the "wickedness" of the characters and the "implausibility" of the action. Until Charlotte herself corrected the misconception, readers assumed that *Wuthering Heights* was an inferior production by the author of *Jane Eyre*.

In October, 1848, Emily became seriously ill with a cough and cold. She suffered quietly and patiently, even refusing to see the doctor who had been called. She died of tuberculosis at Haworth on December 19, 1848. She was buried in the church alongside her mother, her sisters Maria and Elizabeth, and her brother Branwell.

These facts about Emily Brontë's life and death are known, but her character will always remain a mystery. Her early prose works have been lost, only three personal letters survive, and her poems give little insight to her own life. Most information about the Brontës' family life and background comes from Mrs. Elizabeth Gaskell's biography of Charlotte and the autobiographical comments on which she based her work. Charlotte comments that Emily was "not a person of demonstrative character" and that she was "stronger than a man, simpler than a child." She had a nature that "stood alone." The person behind this mystery is revealed only in a reading of *Wuthering Heights*.

Analysis

Wuthering Heights is constructed around a series of dialectic motifs which interconnect and unify the elements of setting, character, and plot. The novel grows from a coherent imaginative vision demonstrating that all human perception is limited and failed. The fullest approach to Emily Brontë's novel is through the basic patterns that support this vision.

Wuthering Heights concerns the interactions of two families, the Earnshaws and Lintons, over three genera-tions. The novel is set in the desolate moors of Yorkshire and covers the years from 1771 to 1803. The Earnshaws and Lintons are in harmony with their environment, but their lives are disrupted by an outsider and catalyst of change, the orphan Heathcliff. Heathcliff is, first of all, an emblem of the social problems of a nation entering the age of industrial expansion and urban growth. Although Brontë sets the action of the novel entirely within the locale familiar to her, she reminds the reader continually of the contrast between that world and the larger world outside.

Besides Heathcliff's background as a child of the streets and the description of urban Liverpool from which he is brought, there are other reminders that Yorkshire, long insulated from change and susceptible only to the forces of nature, is no longer as remote as it once was. The servant Joseph's religious cant, the class distinctions obvious in the treatment of Nelly Dean as well as of Heathcliff, and Lockwood's pseudosophisticated urban values, are all reminders that Wuthering Heights cannot remain as it has been, that religious, social, and economic change is rampant. Brontë clearly signifies in the courtship and marriage of young Cathy and Hareton that progress and enlightenment *will* come and the wilderness *will* be tamed. Heathcliff is both an embodiment of the force of this change and its victim. He brings about a change but cannot change himself. What he leaves behind, as Lockwood attests and the relationship of Cathy and Hareton verifies, is a new society, at peace with itself and its environment.

It is not necessary, however, to examine in depth the Victorian context of *Wuthering Heights* to sense the dialectic contrast of environments. Within the limited setting that the novel itself describes, society is divided between two opposing worlds, Wuthering Heights, ancestral home of the Earnshaws, and Thrushcross Grange, the Linton estate. Wuthering Heights is rustic and wild; it is open to the elements of nature and takes its name from "atmospheric tumult." The house is strong, built with narrow windows and jutting cornerstones, fortified to withstand the battering of external forces. It is identified with the outdoors and nature, and with strong, "masculine" values. Its appearance, both inside and out, is wild, untamed, disordered, and hard. The Grange expresses a more civilized, controlled atmosphere. The house is neat and orderly and there is always an abundance of light—to Brontë's mind, "feminine" values. It is not surprising that Lockwood is more comfortable at the Grange, since he takes pleasure in "feminine" behavior (gossip, vanity of appearance, adherence to social decorum, romantic self-delusion), while Heathcliff, entirely "masculine," is always out of place there.

Indeed, all the characters reflect, to greater or lesser degrees, the masculine and feminine values of the places they inhabit. Hindley and Catherine Earnshaw are as wild and uncontrollable as the Heights: Catherine claims even to prefer her home to the pleasures of heaven. Edgar and Isabella Linton are as refined and civilized as the Grange. The marriage of Edgar and Catherine (as well as the marriage of Isabella and Heathcliff) is ill-fated from the start, not only because she does not love him, as her answers to Nelly Dean's catechism reveal, but also because each is so strongly associated with the values of his (or her) home as to lack the opposing and necessary personality components. Catherine is too willful, wild, and strong; she expresses too much of the "masculine" side of her personality, while Edgar is weak and effeminate. They are unable to interact fully with each other because they are not complete individuals themselves. This lack leads to their failures to perceive each other's true needs.

Even Catherine's passionate cry for Heathcliff, "Nelly, I *am* Heathcliff," is less love for him as an individual than the deepest form of self-love. Catherine cannot exist without him, but a meaningful relationship is not possible, because she sees Heathcliff only as a reflection of herself. Heathcliff, too, has denied an important aspect of his personality. Archetypally masculine, Heathcliff acts out only the aggressive, violent parts of himself. Only Hareton and young Cathy, each of whom embodies the psychological characteristics of both Heights and Grange, can successfully sustain a mutual relationship.

This dialectic structure extends into the roles of the narrators as well. The story is reflected through the words of Nelly Dean—an inmate of both houses, a participant in the events of the narrative, and a confidante of the major characters—and Lockwood, an outsider who witnesses only the results of the characters' interactions. Nelly is a companion and servant in the Earnshaw and Linton households, and she shares many of the values and perceptions of the families. Lockwood, an urban sophisticate on retreat, misunderstands his own character as well as others'. His brief romantic "adventure" in Bath and his awkwardness when he arrives at the Heights (he thinks Cathy will fall in love with him; he mistakes the dead rabbits for puppies) exemplify his obtuseness. His perceptions are always to be questioned. Occasionally, however, even a denizen of the conventional world may gain a glimpse of the forces at work beneath the surface of reality. Lockwood's dream of the dead Catherine, which sets off his curiosity and Heathcliff's final plans, is a reminder that even the placid, normal world may be disrupted by the psychic violence of a willful personality.

Taken together, the setting, plot, characters, and structure combine into a whole when they are seen as parts of the nature of existence. In a world where opposing forces are continually arrayed against each other in the environment, in society, in families, and in relationships, as well as within the individual, there can be no easy route to perception of another human soul. *Wuthering Heights* convincingly demonstrates the complexity of this dialectic and portrays the limitations of human perception.

Other major works

POETRY: *Poems by Currer, Ellis, and Acton Bell*, 1846 (with Charlotte Brontë and Anne Brontë); *The Complete Poems of Emily Jane Brontë*, 1941 (C. W. Hatfield, editor).

Bibliography

Benvenuto, Richard. *Emily Brontë*. Boston: G. K. Hall, 1982.
Fraser, Rebecca. *The Brontës: Charlotte Brontë and Her Family*. New York: Crown, 1988.
Gaskell, Elizabeth C. *The Life of Charlotte Brontë*. 1857. Reprint. London: Penguin Books, 1975.
Hewish, John. *Emily Brontë: A Critical and Biographical Study*. New York: St. Martin's Press, 1969.
Smith, Anne, ed. The Art of Emily Brontë. New York: Barnes & Noble Books, 1976.
Spark, Muriel, and Derek Stanford. Emily Brontë: Her Life and Work. New York: Coward, McCann, 1966.

ANITA BROOKNER

Born: London, England; July 16, 1938

Principal long fiction

A Start in Life, 1981 (published in the United States as The Debut, 1981); *Providence*, 1982; *Look at Me*, 1983; *Hotel du Lac*, 1984; *Family and Friends*, 1985; *The Misalliance*, 1986; *A Friend from England*, 1987; *Latecomers*, 1988; *Lewis Percy*, 1989; *Brief Lives*, 1990; *A Closed Eye*, 1991; *Fraud*, 1992; *Dolly*, 1993.

Other literary forms

A distinguished historian of eighteenth and nineteenth century French art and culture, Anita Brookner wrote several books of nonfiction before she began to write novels. *Watteau* (1968) is an assessment of the early eighteenth century French artist Antoine Watteau. *The Genius of the Future, Studies in French Art Criticism: Diderot, Stendhal, Baudelaire, Zola, the Brothers Goncourt, Huysmans* (1971) is a collection of six essays on seven French writers; each writer is considered in the context of his time. The greatest space is given to Charles Baudelaire. *Greuze: The Rise and Fall of an Eighteenth-Century Phenomenon* (1972) is a study of the French painter Jean-Baptiste Greuze in a successful attempt to locate the background of a sentimental genre that is distinct from both Rococo and classicism. *Jacques-Louis David* (1980), a biography of the foremost painter of the French revolutionary period, explores the relationship between David's life and work, places that work in the context of contemporary French painting, and details a career that spanned some of the most turbulent years in French history. Brookner's translations include *Utrillo* (1960) and *The Fauves* (1962).

Achievements

Brookner suddenly began to write fiction during her middle years, while still an active teacher and scholar. Although she continued her academic career, she quickly found equal success as a novelist. With the publication of several novels, she gained an international following and widespread critical acclaim. In 1984, Great Britain's prestigious Booker Prize for fiction was awarded to *Hotel du Lac*. Brookner was praised for her elegant and precise prose, her acute sense of irony, and her subtle insights into character and social behavior. Her witty explorations of manners and morals suggest to many a literary kinship to Jane Austen and Barbara Pym. While Brookner's somber, more complex moral vision disallows any sustained comparison to Pym, Austen and Brookner undeniably share a common concern for intelligent, subtle, clever heroines who seek to satisfy both private sensibility and public expectations.

To regard Brookner's novels as simply traditional novels of manners, however, is to misconstrue her art. Brookner's intentions greatly exceed this conventional genre; her achievements, indeed, take her far beyond it.

Perhaps it is more useful to note the singularity of her contribution to British letters. Her highly developed pictorial sense; her baroque diction, with its balance of reason and passion; and her allusive, richly textured narratives, haunting in their resonances, reflect at every turn her extensive knowledge of the materials and motifs of eighteenth and nineteenth century paintings and literature.

Her works have been generously admired, but some dissenting voices have been raised. She is occasionally brought to task for fictive worlds too narrow in scope and claustrophobic in their intensity; for overzealous, self-conscious, schematic fiction; and for excessive sentimentality that unfortunately evokes the pulp romance. Brookner's worlds, however, are invariably shaped toward significant moral revelations; technique rarely intrudes to the detriment of story; and her ability to maintain an ironic distance from her characters, one that allows her to reveal sentimentality, to make judgments dispassionately, is one of her greatest strengths as a writer.

Biography

Anita Brookner was born in London, England, on July 16, 1938, to Newsom and Maude Brookner. She was educated at James Allen's Girls' School and King's College, University of London, and received a Ph.D. in art history from the Courtauld Institute of Art in London. From 1959 to 1964, she was visiting lecturer at the University of Reading, Berkshire. In 1968, she was Slade Professor at Cambridge University, the first woman to hold this position. From 1977 to 1987 she taught at the Courtauld Institute of Art, where she lectured on neoclassicism and the Romantic movement. She was awarded the Booker Prize in 1984.

Analysis

Anita Brookner established her reputation as a novelist with four books published in rapid succession between 1981 and 1984. Written in austerely elegant prose, each of these four novels follows essentially the same course. Each centers on a scholarly, sensitive, morally earnest young woman who leads an attenuated life. None of these heroines has intended a life so circumscribed. As their stories begin, they seek change, liberation from boredom and loneliness. They seek connection to a wider world. While these women are intelligent, endlessly introspective, and possessed of a saving ironic wit, they do not know how to get the things they most desire: the love of, and marriage to, a man of quality. With compassion, rue, and infinite good humor, Brookner makes it abundantly clear that these worthy women, these good daughters, good writers, and good scholars are unknowing adherents to a romantic ideal. Like the shopgirls and "ultrafeminine" women they gaze upon with such wonder and awe, these intellectually and morally superior women accept without question the cultural assumption that marriage is a woman's greatest good. Consistently undervaluing their own considerable talents and professional achievements, these heroines look to love and marriage as a way of joining the cosmic dance of a rational, well-ordered society. Their intense yearning for a transforming love shapes their individual plots; in each case, the conflict between what the romantic imagination wants and what it indeed does get impels these narratives forward. Brookner's concern is to illuminate the worthiness, the loneliness, the longing of these heroines for love and a more splendid life.

Before their stories can end, these women must abandon sentiment and accept their solitary state. Their triumph lies in their ability to confront their fall from romantic innocence and recognize it for what it is. These novels build inexorably toward an ending that is both startling and profoundly moving. While Brookner's heroines must struggle with sentimentality, Brookner herself does not. Her vision is bleak, unsparing. In telling their stories, she raises several other themes: The most notable of these are filial obligation, the "romantic" versus the "realistic" apprehension of life, truth and its relationship to self-knowledge, the determination of proper behavior in society, and the small pleasures that attend the trivia of daily life. Brookner presents her major and minor themes against the background of fictive worlds so powerfully realized that her novels seem to be absorbed as much as read. These are novels of interior reality. Little that is overt happens; dramatic action rests in the consciousness of the heroine, who is always center stage.

Edith Hope, the heroine of *Hotel du Lac*, Brookner's fourth novel and the winner of the 1984 Booker Prize, is a writer who produces pulp romances for a living. Until she learns better, she believes that romance is only her business, not her frame of mind. Edith is indeed a romantic, although an unknowing one. Edith begins her stay at the Hotel du Lac in ignorance of her true nature; she leaves enlightened as to the deeper, more recessed aspects of her moral being.

It was not Edith's choice to leave England and travel to Switzerland, the setting of *Hotel du Lac*. Edith was sent away because of her severe breach of social decorum: She chose not to appear at her own wedding, thus profoundly humiliating a good man and eminently suitable husband. Her action was shocking to all, including Edith herself. Modest, unassuming, and usually anxious to please, Edith is in many ways a typical Brooknerian heroine. She spends too much time alone, condemned to her own introspection. Her marriage would have broken that isolation. Edith's revolt and subsequent removal to Switzerland provide a context for the discussion of numerous moral and psychological questions. While Edith's story is always foremost, the novel itself alternates between first- and third-person narratives, with philosophical positions being argued, accepted, or dismissed. The central fact that emerges about Edith is her passionate love for a married man whom she only seldom sees. Edith's David is exceedingly handsome, elegant, intelligent, and remote. For love of him, Edith jilted her dull but safe fiancé. At the Hotel du Lac, Edith's interactions with the other residents move her to a greater understanding of truth, self-knowledge, and the differences between romance and reality. Numerous other themes are present here as well, including that of "ultrafeminine" as opposed to "feminist" women. Edith understands these women as models of feminine response to feminine experience. In relative isolation at this Swiss hotel, she studies these models and rejects both. The will to power, the utility of egotism as a serviceable instrument in the world, a recurrent Brooknerian theme, also receives much discussion here.

What Edith eventually learns as she evaluates her exchanges and relationships with her fellow guests is accorded significant status by the mythological underpinnings of this novel. Inside the hotel, characters are both particular and types, acting out self-assigned roles in a grand comedy of manners. All the inhabitants exhibit a theatrical sense of themselves; they "present" themselves to this community consciously, deliberately. Such attention to the pictorial, personal presentation is a constant of Brookner's fiction. The details of clothes, manners, and mannerisms convey aspects of self and morality in Brookner's works as they do in the works of Henry James, to whom Brookner alludes in this novel. If inside the hotel the characters are on parade, making their statements with dress, or gesture, once outside the hotel, they are subsumed to the mythicized landscape. Gray mist, conveying a sense of menace and oppression, surrounds everything. Characters make journeys that are important only for their mythic impact. Much movement against this dreary landscape takes place as characters are directed toward crucial, definitive moral choices. The landscape helps Edith to perceive her dilemmas; she is finally able to reject a diabolical figure, who offers marriage without love. He forces Edith to recognize her romanticism for what it is. At least in the end, however, when she returns to England and her married lover, Edith knows that she has chosen a cold and solitary path. Her self-determination represents a triumph for her and for this book. Edith is finally transformed by her successful journey to knowledge.

Having laid claim with her first four novels to a sharply defined fictional territory, Brookner has shown in subsequent books a willingness to extend her range. The book with which Brookner departed most radically from the pattern established in her first four novels was *Family and Friends*; perhaps because it violated readers' expectations, it was sharply criticized by some reviewers. Written in the historical present with virtually no dialogue, *Family and Friends* is an extended meditation on the French tradition. It stems from the ruminations of a narrator who quickly disappears, makes only glancing reappearances, and is curiously never identified. Here, Brookner's concern is not with a particular heroine, but with the Dorn family, rich, most likely German immigrants who fled to England before the start of World War II. The war, when it comes, receives but scant attention; the novel focuses always on the small, interior world of the Dorn family. Little seems to exist outside the family and their immediate interests, sparking again charges of a work too narrow in range.

The lives of the Dorn family and their associates are followed over a period of time. Sofka, the gentle but strong matriarch of the family, is the moral center of the work. Widowed early in life, she rejects the idea of remarriage, directing her loving attentions to her family, instead. Mimi and Betty are her two daughters. While Betty is selfish, willful, theatrical, tricking her family into giving her an independent life quite early, she is nevertheless the child Sofka secretly loves best. Sofka, beautiful and contained, admires her younger daughter's spirit. Mimi is virtuous, dreamy, passive, frozen into inertia in young womanhood when an early feeble attempt to reach out for love was unsuccessful. Mimi languishes for years afterward, until her mother urges her into marriage, and thereby respectability, with a gentle, good man who would normally be her social inferior. Also playing a significant part in the novel are Sofka's two sons: the sensitive, intelligent, responsible Alfred and his handsome, charming brother Frederick. Interestingly, it is Alfred's plight that mirrors the situation of the usual Brooknerian heroine. It is he who is trapped by filial obligation into a life he had not intended; it is he who suffers forever afterward from an unsatisfying search for love and a desire for a larger, more extended world. It is also he who ultimately becomes inured to long-established habits of insularity.

This, then, is the saga of a family whose interior lives and moral relations are acutely realized. Important themes here include familial relations, especially filial obligation, the search for a transcendent love, and the need to venture, to dare, if one is to "win" in life. Structured around four wedding pictures, the novel impresses with its unity and intensity of tone; the pervasive, elegant irony; the discerning moral judgments; and the engrossing character portraits. Especially effective is the novel's lament for the loss of youthful promise, energy, and innocence. The once-vibrant Betty, trapped in middle-aged stasis, is a case in point. Dominating this entire work is a rich narrative voice, stern, compassionate, and often sad. The Dorn family seems to exist in a twilight, dreamlike world outside time. Yet this world, while admittedly narrow, is nevertheless mesmerizing.

Brookner's novels brought her remarkable success within a very short time. Her taut, spare narratives share distinctive qualities: grace, precision, and elegance of language; ironic commentaries on character and social behavior that both instruct and delight; a tone compounded of the comic and the melancholy; and a moral vision that is both rigorous and compassionate.

Other major works

NONFICTION: *Watteau*, 1968; *The Genius of the Future, Studies in French Art Criticism: Diderot, Stendhal, Baudelaire, Zola, the Brothers Goncourt, Huysmans*, 1971; *Greuze: The Rise and Fall of an Eighteenth-Century Phenomenon*, 1972; *Jacques-Louis David*, 1980.

TRANSLATIONS: *Utrillo*, 1960 (of Waldemar George's biography); *The Fauves*, 1962 (of Jean Paul Crespelle's book).

Bibliography

Haffenden, John. *Novelists in Interview*. London: Methuen, 1985.
Kenyon, Olga. *Women Novelists Today*. New York: St. Martin's Press. 1988.
Lasdun, James. "Pre-Modern, Post Modernist." *Encounter* 64 (February, 1985): 42.
Sadler, Lynn Veach. *Anita Brookner*. Boston: Twayne, 1990.
Samarth, Manimi Mayar. "The Internalized Narrative: A Study of Lyricism and Irony in the Novels of Anita Desai and Anita Brookner." *DAI* 49 (September, 1988): 513A.
Schlueter, Paul, and June Schlueter, eds. *An Encyclopedia of British Women Writers*. New York: Garland, 1988.

GWENDOLYN BROOKS

Born: Topeka, Kansas; June 7, 1917

Principal poetry

A Street in Bronzeville, 1945; *Annie Allen*, 1949; *The Bean Eaters*, 1960; *Selected Poems*, 1963; *In the Mecca*, 1968; *Riot*, 1969; *Family Pictures*, 1970; *Aloneness*, 1971; *Beckonings*, 1975; *Primer for Blacks*, 1980; *To Disembark*, 1981; *The Near-Johannesburg Boy*, 1986; *Blacks*, 1987; *Gottschalk and the Grand Tarantelle*, 1988.

Other literary forms

In addition to the poetry on which her literary reputation rests, Gwendolyn Brooks has published a novel, *Maud Martha* (1953); a book of autobiographical prose, *Report from Part One* (1972); and volumes of children's verse. An episodic novel, *Maud Martha* makes some use of autobiographical materials and shares many of the major concerns of Brooks's poetry, particularly concerning the attempts of the person to maintain integrity in the face of crushing environmental pressures. *Report from*

Part One recounts the personal, political, and aesthetic influences that culminated in Brooks's movement to a black nationalist stance in the late 1960's. Since that time she has written introductions to, and edited anthologies of, the works of younger black writers. These introductions frequently provide insight into her own work. Several recordings of Brooks reading her own work are available.

Achievements

Working comfortably in relation to diverse poetic traditions, Brooks has been widely honored. Early in her career, she received numerous mainstream literary awards, including the Pulitzer Prize for Poetry in 1950 for *Annie Allen*, and was named Poet Laureate of Illinois in 1969. Equally significant, numerous writers associated with the Black Arts movement recognize her as an inspirational figure linking the older and younger generations of black poets. Brooks's ability to appeal both to poetic establishments and to a sizable popular audience, especially among young blacks, stems from her pluralistic voice which echoes a wide range of precursors while remaining unmistakably black. Her exploration of America in general and Chicago in particular links her with Walt Whitman and Carl Sandburg. Her exploration of the interior landscape of humanity in general and women in particular places her in the tradition of Emily Dickinson and Edna St. Vincent Millay. At once the technical heir of Langston Hughes in her use of the rhythms of black street life and of Robert Frost in her exploration of traditional forms such as the sonnet, Brooks nevertheless maintains her integrity of vision and voice.

This integrity assumes special significance in the context of African American writing of the 1950's and 1960's. A period of "universalism" in black literature, the 1950's brought prominence to such poets as Brooks, LeRoi Jones, and Robert Hayden, all of whom provided clear evidence that African American poets matched the technical and intellectual range of their white counterparts. During this period of intellectual and aesthetic integration, Brooks never abandoned her social and racial heritage to strive for the transcendent (and deracinated) universalism associated by some African American critics with T. S. Eliot. Brooks demonstrates unambiguously that an African American writer need not be limited in relevance by concentrating on the black experience.

The 1960's, conversely, encouraged separatism and militancy in African American writing. Even while accepting the Black Arts movement's call for a poetry designed to speak directly to the political condition of the black community, Brooks continued to insist on precision of form and language. While Jones changed his name to Amiri Baraka and radically altered his poetic voice, Brooks accommodated her new insights to her previously established style. An examplar of integrity and flexibility, she both challenges and learns from younger black poets such as Haki R. Madhubuti (Don L. Lee), Sonia Sanchez, Carolyn Rodgers, and Etheridge

Knight. Like Hughes, she addresses the black community without condescension or pretense. Like Frost, she writes technically stunning "universal" poetry combining clear surfaces and elusive depths.

A recipient of more than fifty honorary doctorates, Brooks was appointed to the Presidential Commission on the National Agenda for the Eighties; she was the first black woman elected to the National Institute of Arts and Letters. She was named Consultant in Poetry to the Library of Congress for 1985-1986.

Biography

Gwendolyn Brooks's poetry bears the strong impress of Chicago, particularly of the predominantly black South Side where she has lived most of her life. Although she was born in Topeka, Kansas, Brooks was taken to Chicago before she was a year old. In many ways she has devoted her career to the physical, spiritual, and, more recently, political exploration of her native city.

Brooks's life and writings are frequently separated into two phases, with her experience at the 1967 Black Writers' Conference at Fisk University in Nashville serving as a symbolic transition. Prior to the conference, Brooks was known primarily as the first black Pulitzer Prize winner in poetry. Although not politically unaware, she held to a somewhat cautious attitude. The vitality she encountered at the conference crystallized her sense of the insufficiency of universalist attitudes and generated close personal and artistic friendships with younger black poets such as Madhubuti, Walter Bradford, and Knight. Severing her ties with the mainstream publishing firm of Harper & Row, which had published her first five books, Brooks transferred her work and prestige to the black-owned and operated Broadside Press of Detroit, Third World Press of Chicago, and Black Position Press, also of Chicago. Her commitment to black publishing houses remains unwavering despite distribution problems which render her later work largely invisible to the American reading public.

Educated in the Chicago school system and at Wilson Junior College, Brooks learned her craft under Inez Cunningham Stark (Boulton), a white woman who taught poetry at the South Side Community Art Center in the late 1930's and 1940's. Brooks's mother, who had been a teacher in Topeka, had encouraged her literary interests from an early age. Her father, a janitor, provided her with ineffaceable images of the spiritual strength and dignity of "common" people. Brooks married Henry Blakely in 1939 and her family concerns continued to play a central role in shaping her career. The eleven-year hiatus between the publication of *Annie Allen* and *The Bean Eaters* resulted at least in part from her concentration on rearing her two children, born in 1940 and 1951. Her numerous poems on family relationships reflect both the rewards and the tensions of her own experiences. Her children grown, Brooks concentrated on teaching, supervising poetry workshops, and speaking publicly. These activities brought her into contact with a wide range of younger black poets, preparing her for her experience at Fisk. As Poet Laureate of Illinois, a position she has held since 1969, she continues to encourage the development of younger poets through personal contact and formal competitions.

The division between the two phases of Brooks's life should not be overstated. She evinced a strong interest in the Civil Rights movement during the 1950's and early 1960's; her concern with family continued in the 1980's. Above all, Brooks continues to live with and write of and for the Chicagoans whose failures and triumphs she sees as deeply personal, universally resonant, and specifically black.

Analysis

The image of Gwendolyn Brooks as a readily accessible poet is at once accurate and deceptive. Capable of capturing the experiences and rhythms of black street life, she frequently presents translucent surfaces which give way suddenly to reveal ambiguous depths. Equally capable of manipulating traditional poetic forms such as the sonnet, rhyme royal, and heroic couplet, she employs them to mirror the uncertainties of characters or personae who embrace conventional attitudes to defend themselves against internal and external chaos. Whatever form she chooses, Brooks consistently focuses on the struggle of people to find and express love, usually associated with the family, in the midst of a hostile environment. In constructing their defenses and seeking love, these persons typically experience a disfiguring pain. Brooks devotes much of her energy to defining and responding to the elusive forces, variously psychological and social, that inflict this pain. Increasingly in her later poetry, Brooks traces the pain to political sources and expands her concept of the family to encompass all black people. Even while speaking of the social situation of blacks in a voice crafted primarily for blacks, however, Brooks maintains the complex awareness of the multiple perspectives relevant to any given experience. Her ultimate concern is to encourage every individual, black or white, to "Conduct your blooming in the noise and whip of the whirlwind" ("The Second Sermon on the Warpland").

A deep concern with the everyday circumstances of black people living within the whirlwind characterizes many of Brooks's most popular poems. From the early "Of De Witt Williams on His Way to Lincoln Cemetery" and "A Song in the Front Yard," through the later "The Life of Lincoln West" and "Sammy Chester Leaves 'Godspell' and Visits UPWARD BOUND on a Lake Forest Lawn, Bringing West Afrika," she focuses on characters whose experiences merge the idiosyncratic and the typical. She frequently draws on black musical forms to underscore the communal resonance of a character's outwardly undistinguished life. By tying the refrain of "Swing Low Sweet Chariot" to the repeated phrase "Plain black boy," Brooks transforms De Witt Williams into an Everyman figure. Brooks describes his personal search for love in the poolrooms and dance halls, but stresses the representative quality of his experience by starting and ending the poem with the musical allusion.

"We Real Cool," perhaps Brooks's single best-known poem, subjects a similarly representative experience to an intricate technical and thematic scrutiny, at once loving and critical. The poem is only twenty-four words long, including eight repetitions of the word "we." It is suggestive that the subtitle of "We Real Cool" specifies the presence of only seven pool players at the "Golden Shovel." The eighth "we" suggests that poet and reader share, on some level, the desperation of the group-voice that Brooks transmits. The final sentence, "We/ die soon," restates the *carpe diem* motif in the vernacular of Chicago's South Side.

The poem is crafted to hint at an underlying coherence in the defiance. The intricate internal rhyme scheme echoes the sound of nearly every word. Not only do the first seven lines end with "we," but the penultimate words of each line in each stanza also rhyme (cool/school,

late/straight, sin/gin, June/soon). In addition, the alliterated consonant of the last line of each stanza is repeated in the first line of the next stanza (Left/lurk, Strike/sin, gin/June) and the first words of each line in the middle two stanzas are connected through consonance (Lurk/strike, Sing/thin). The one exception to this suggestive texture of sound is the word "Die" which introduces both a new vowel and a new consonant into the final line, breaking the rhythm and subjecting the performance to ironic revaluation. Ultimately, the power of the poem derives from the tension between the celebratory and the ironic perspectives on the lives of the plain black boys struggling for a sense of connection.

Although her political vision influences every aspect of her work, Brooks maintains a strong sense of enduring individual pain and is aware that black nationalism offers no simple panacea. "The Blackstone Rangers," a poem concerning one of the most powerful Chicago street gangs, rejects as simplistic the argument, occasionally advanced by writers associated with the Black Arts movement, that no important distinction exists between the personal and the political experience. Specifically, Brooks doubts the corollary that politically desirable activity will inevitably increase the person's ability to love. Dividing "The Blackstone Rangers" into three segments—"As Seen by Disciplines," "The Leaders," and "Gang Girls: A Rangerette"—Brooks stresses the tension between perspectives. After rejecting the sociological-penal perspective of part 1, she remains suspended between the uncomprehending affirmation of the Rangers as a kind of government-in-exile in part 2, and the recognition of the individual person's continuing pain in part 3.

Brooks undercuts the description of the Rangers as "sores in the city/ that do not want to heal" ("As Seen by Disciplines") through the use of off-rhyme and a jazz rhythm reminiscent of "We Real Cool." The disciplines, both academic and corrective, fail to perceive any coherence in the Rangers' experience. Correct in their assumption that the Rangers do not want to "heal" themselves, the disciplines fail to perceive the gang's strong desire to "heal" the sick society. Brooks suggests an essential coherence in the Rangers' experience through the sound texture of part 1. Several of the sound patterns echoing through the brief stanza point to a shared response to pain (there/thirty/ready, raw/sore/corner). Similarly, the accent cluster on "Black, raw, ready" draws attention to the pain and potential power of the Rangers. The descriptive voice of the disciplines, however, provides only relatively weak end rhymes (are/corner, ready/city), testifying to the inability of the distanced, presumably white, observers to comprehend the experiences they describe. The shifting, distinctively black, jazz rhythm further emphasizes the distance between the voices of observers and participants. Significantly, the voice of the disciplines finds no rhyme at all for its denial of the Rangers' desire to "heal."

This denial contrasts sharply with the tempered affirmation of the voice in part 2 which emphasizes the leaders' desire to "cancel, cure and curry." Again, internal rhymes and sound echoes suffuse the section. In the first stanza, the voice generates thematically significant rhymes, connecting Ranger leader "*Bop*" (whose name draws attention to the jazz rhythm which is even more intricate, though less obvious, in this section than in part 1) and the militant black leader "*Rap*" Brown, both nationalists whose "country is a Nation on no *map*." "Bop" and "Rap," of course, do not rhyme perfectly, attesting Brooks's awareness of the gang leader's limitations. Her image of the leaders as "Bungled trophies" further reinforces her ambivalence. The only full rhyme in the final two stanzas of the section is the repeated "night." The leaders, canceling the racist association of darkness with evil, "translate" the image of blackness into a "monstrous pearl or grace." The section affirms the Blackstone Rangers' struggle; it does not pretend to comprehend fully the emotional texture of their lives.

Certain that the leaders possess the power to cancel the disfiguring images of the disciplines, Brooks remains unsure of their ability to create an alternate environment where love can blossom. Mary Ann, the "Gang Girl" of part 3, shares much of the individual pain of the characters in Brooks's early poetry despite her involvement with the Rangers. "A rose in a whiskey glass," she continues to live with the knowledge that her "laboring lover" risks the same sudden death as the pool players of "We Real Cool." Forced to suppress a part of her awareness—she knows not to ask where her lover got the diamond he gives her—she remains emotionally removed even while making love. In place of a fully realized love, she accepts "the props and niceties of non-loneliness." The final line of the poem emphasizes the ambiguity of both Mary Ann's situation and Brooks's perspective. Recommending acceptance of "the rhymes of Leaning," the line responds to the previous stanza's question concerning whether love will have a "gleaning." The full rhyme paradoxically suggests acceptance of off-rhyme, of love consummated leaning against an alley wall, without expectation of safety or resolution. Given the political tension created by the juxtaposition of the disciplines and the leaders, the "Gang Girl" can hope to find no sanctuary beyond the reach of the whirlwind. Her desperate love, the more moving for its precariousness, provides the only near-adequate response to the pain that Brooks continues to see as the primary fact of life.

Other major works

NOVEL: *Maud Martha*, 1953.
NONFICTION: *Report from Part One*, 1972; *Young Poet's Primer*, 1980.
CHILDREN'S LITERATURE: *Bronzeville Boys and Girls*, 1956; *The Tiger Who Wore White Gloves*, 1974; *Very Young Poets*, 1983.
ANTHOLOGY: *Jump Bad: A New Chicago Anthology*, 1971.
MISCELLANEOUS: *The World of Gwendolyn Brooks*, 1971.

Bibliography

Kent, George E. *A Life of Gwendolyn Brooks*. Lexington: University Press of Kentucky, 1990.
Melhem, D. L. *Gwendolyn Brooks: Poetry and the Heroic Voice*. Lexington: University Press of Kentucky, 1987.
Mootry, Maria K., and Gary Smith, eds. *A Life Distilled: Gwendolyn Brooks, Her Poetry and Fiction*. Urbana: University of Illinois Press, 1987.
Shaw, Harry B. *Gwendolyn Brooks*. Boston: Twayne, 1980.
_____. "Perceptions of Men in the Early Works of Gwendolyn Brooks." In *Black American Poets Between Worlds, 1940-1960*, edited by R. Baxter Miller. Tennessee Studies in Literature 30. Knoxville: University of Tennessee Press, 1986.

ELIZABETH BARRETT BROWNING

Born: Durham, England; March 6, 1806

Died: Florence, Italy; June 29, 1861

Principal poetry

The Battle of Marathon, 1820; *An Essay on Mind, with Other Poems*, 1826; *The Seraphim and Other Poems*, 1838; *Poems, by Elizabeth Barrett Barrett*, 1844; *Poems*, 1850 (including *Sonnets from the Portuguese*); *Casa Guidi Windows*, 1851; *Aurora Leigh*, 1856; *Poems Before Congress*, 1860; *Last Poems*, 1862.

Other literary forms

Elizabeth Barrett Browning was an accomplished Greek scholar, and from her translations she learned much of her own prosody. In 1833, she published a weak translation of Aeschylus' *Prometheus Bound*. In 1850, she included in her collected poems an entirely new and substantially improved version of the same play. "The Daughters of Pandarus," a selection from the *Odyssey* (c. 800 B.C.), was translated for Anna Jameson's *Memoirs and Essays Illustrative of Art, Literature, and Social Morals* in 1846. She modernized selections from Geoffrey Chaucer's *The Canterbury Tales* (1387-1400) for R. H. Horne's edition of the work in 1841. She submitted occasional translations to periodicals, such as three hymns of Gregory Nazianzen which appeared in the *Athenaeum*, January 8, 1842. Browning also published a modest amount of prose criticism. Four articles on Greek Christian poets appeared anonymously in the *Athenaeum* during 1842. For the same journal, she published five articles reviewing an anthology of English verse entitled *The Book of the Poets* (1842). Later in the same year, she reviewed a new edition of William Wordsworth's poetry. In 1843, she reviewed Horne's *Orion: An Epic Poem in Three Books* (1843) for the *Athenaeum*, and then she gave up literary criticism in order to devote more time to her poetry.

Achievements

Literary critics since Browning's time have insisted upon thinking of her as a great woman poet, or as the Sappho of the age, or as the first woman to write a sustained sequence of sonnets. Her husband, the poet Robert Browning, thought of her simply as having written the finest sonnets since William Shakespeare. The headnote to "The Seraphim" indicates specifically that she invited comparison with Aeschylus. "A Drama of Exile" is a continuation of the Adamic drama just beyond the events described by John Milton and clearly invites comparison with him. Her sonnets can be compared with those of Petrarch, Shakespeare, Milton, and William Wordsworth. Whether she meets the measure of these models is problematic in some cases, doubtful in others. Still, her aim is consistently high and her achievement is historically substantial. She gave a strong voice to the democratic revolution of the nineteenth century; she was a vigorous antagonist of those she thought were the enemies of children, of the world's dispossessed, and of popular government.

Biography

In 1861, Elizabeth Barrett Browning died in her husband's arms in a rented apartment (unfurnished for the sake of economy). She had been born in one of the twenty marbled bedrooms of her father's estate, Coxhoe Hall. When Elizabeth was three years old, her family moved to a still larger home, Hope End, in Herefordshire. This was to be her home until the abolition of slavery brought about sharp retrenchments in the Barrett family's affairs in 1832. After three years at Sidmouth, on the channel coasts, the family moved to London. Her family's congregational Protestantism and its strong support for the Reform Bill of 1832 had already helped to establish the intellectual landmarks of her poetry—Christian idealism and a sharp social conscience. In London, as her weak lungs became a source of chronic anxiety, the dark and reclusive habits which were to lend a fearful realism to

Elizabeth Barrett's ideals became fixed in her mode of life.

Such anxiety found its consolations in a meditative piety which produced an increasingly intense inwardness in the poet. Eventually, she even gave up attending chapel services. In 1838, her lungs racked by a persistent cough, she left London for Torquay, hoping the sea air would afford her some relief. When her brother Edward ("Bro") had concluded his visit there and planned to return to London, Elizabeth pleaded with him to stay. He did so, but in the summer of 1840, as he was boating with friends, a sudden squall capsized the boat; Bro was drowned. Elizabeth, who had been using laudanum fairly steadily since arriving in Torquay, almost lost her mind from guilt and distress. Elizabeth, more nervous and withdrawn than ever, returned to the family home at 50 Wimpole Street in London. She rarely descended the stairs, and in the darkened room came to depend ever more heavily on the morphine that dulled her physical and spiritual pains. She called her room a "hermitage," a "convent," a "prison."

In January of 1845, Robert Browning, then an obscure poet, wrote to thank Elizabeth for praising him in a poem she had recently published. She replied to the letter but was not anxious to meet him. She had already declined twice to receive calls from the venerable Wordsworth, whom she had met earlier. She did receive Browning several months later, however, and their famous courtship began. Both parties claimed that they had never been in love before, yet both did have a history of strong attachments. Still, for these two idealists, love was something quite particular, not a vague sentiment, and their claim seems authentic enough. The principal obstacle to their courtship was Elizabeth's father. Strong-willed, pietistic, politically liberal, Edward Moulton Barrett saw Robert Browning as a footloose adventurer with a barely supportable claim to being a sometime-poet. Browning had no reliable means of support, and Mr. Barrett was certain that if the two were married Browning would merely live off Elizabeth's ample but not boundless fortune.

On September 12, 1846, while her family was away, Elizabeth, nearly fainting with fear, made her way to Saint Marylebone Parish Church. Robert met her there, and they were married. It was the first time he had seen her away from Wimpole Street. She returned home for one week and then slipped out of the house to begin the long journey to Italy with her husband. She never saw her father again. He wrote her a cruelly condemnatory letter, disinherited her, and sent her books out of the house to be stored (the bills to go to Elizabeth). She was forty years old, a poet widely respected in England and America.

The Brownings' most enduring home in Italy was at Florence in the Casa Guidi, a fifteenth century palace located very near the palace of the Grand Duke of Tuscany. Although Elizabeth's health was a constant concern to them, it is nevertheless clear that in Italy she recovered something of the vitality of her youth. Elizabeth's health was in fact sufficiently improved that on March 9, 1849, she was able to deliver a child—her only one—without the expected complications. Indeed, she became exhilarated and active just after the birth of her son, seeming much stronger than when she first married.

During the last ten years of her life, Browning traveled extensively between Venice, Paris, and England. She found England, however, a somewhat alien place, more unyielding in manner than the Continent. When she was in London, she wrote seeking a reconciliation with her father, asking him at least to see her child. In reply, she received two packets containing the letters she had written home in the years since her marriage—all unread.

At the close of 1856, back in Italy, Browning published a "novel in verse," *Aurora Leigh*. Critics gave the book a somewhat ungenerous reception, but the public bought out issue after issue. It was a genuine best-seller. She was by then a true celebrity. In her next (and last) volume of poems, *Poems Before Congress*, she praised Louis Napoleon, who had raised the fears of England. English friends alleged that Browning was politically unsophisticated for supporting the French. Browning replied, however, that this Napoleon would pry Italy loose from Austrian fingers. The freedom of her adopted land would not be abandoned just because it caused fears at home.

As the Italian national movement gained strength, however, Browning's strength waned. She could no longer keep up with her husband's vitality and languished under the long struggle with her weak lungs. On a June night in 1861, protesting the fuss made over her, she lay down to sleep. Later she roused and, struggling to cough, relaxed into death.

Analysis

Elizabeth Barrett Browning did not think it a kindness when critics praised her as a "woman poet." She would think it much closer to essentials if she were praised instead as a Christian poet. An evangelical of an old Victorian strain, she prized learning, cultivated Greek as the language of the Christian revelation, studied the work of the church fathers, and brought a fine intellectual vigor to the manifestly Christian ethos which shapes her work.

Like her husband, Browning suffered somewhat at the close of the nineteenth century from the uncritical applause of readers who praised the religious thought in her work merely as religious thought. A century after her death—and again like her husband—Browning began to enjoy the approbation of more vigorous critics who called attention to an element of intellectual toughness in her work which earlier critics had ignored. Now it is widely agreed that her poetry constitutes a coherent working out of evangelical principles into a set of conclusions which bear on the most pressing issues of modern times: the progress of liberal democracy, the role of militant nationalism, the ambivalences of the "woman question," and the task of the poet in a world without decisive voices.

Evangelicalism has often encouraged a strong antiintellectual bias among its followers. Since redemption is a matter of divine grace extended to childlike faith, there is no great need for secular learning. Browning, however, worked out a reconciliation of the dilemma: Fallen human beings can govern themselves well by a system of checks and balances which allows the many to restrain the venality of the powerful few. As a result, the poet was able to maintain a rather rigorous evangelicalism which was progressive, yet was not so facile and glibly optimistic as her early readers sometimes supposed.

In her second major volume, *Poems, by Elizabeth Barrett Barrett*, Browning makes two important advances over her first. The first is that her leading poem, "A Drama of Exile," is no longer a mere account of events. Rather, there is more invention and conflict than in earlier poems: Outside the garden, surrounded by a sinister-seeming nature, Eve meets Lucifer for the first time since her fall. On this occasion she rejects him. Then, in a mystical vision, Adam and Eve see and hear the omnipotent Christ rebuking the taunting spirits of fallen nature and the pride of the triumphant Lucifer. Eve now forgives Lucifer and Christ forgives Eve. Here, the poet ventures a dramatic representation of her views with a series of invented situations which constitute a small episode in her effort to build a poetically Christian mythology.

The second advance of this volume over her previous one is technical. It is at this point in her career that Browning begins to experiment with the sonnet. The volume contains twenty-eight sonnets on various subjects. All are Italian in form (divided between an octet and a sestet), and in all cases the first eight lines rhyme *abba abba*. In the last six lines, however, Browning uses two different patterns. Some of the poems end with a *cdcdcd* pattern; others end *cdecde*. The profit to the poet is that her attempts with the sonnet force on her a verbal economy that is more rigorous than that in her earlier volumes. Browning occasionally restricts herself to four rhyme values in a single sonnet—*abcd*. This practice imposes upon her vocabulary even stricter limits than those imposed by either the Petrarchan or the Shakespearean form. Furthermore, the sonnets—some about grief, tears, and work, with two about George Sand—force her to be less diffuse. They force her to find the concrete image that will quickly communicate a complex feeling.

It is also in *Poems, by Elizabeth Barrett Barrett* that she includes the romance "Lady Geraldine's Courtship," which was to have significant repercussions for her. It is in this poem that she praises Robert Browning—eliciting his first letter to her—and it is here that she first attempts a theme that will not be fully realized until *Aurora Leigh*: that romance is plausible but handicapped in an unromantic (that is, an industrial, mercantile) age.

The last poem in this volume, though brief, is an important one in the poet's canon. "The Dead Pan" produces just the image necessary to give Browning's religious thought the freshness, clarity, and invention necessary if she is to avoid mere clichés of faith in the search for an authenticating power in her poems. The subject of the poem is the ancient claim made by Plutarch (in *De Oraculorum Defectu*) that at the very hour of Christ's Crucifixion a supernatural cry went out across the sea, "Great Pan is dead," and that from that moment the pagan oracles lost their vision and power. In the poem, Browning utters a long roll call of the pagan deities to witness that the prophetic power of an old world has been subsumed by Christianity.

The poem is also a challenge to the skepticism and

materialism of the poet's own age. For Browning, the oracular voice of the modern world is heard in poetry. Some nineteenth century thinkers believed that, with the death of the mythopoeic consciousness, humans had entered an age of rational secularism from which there could be no historical return. Against this sort of plaintive skepticism Browning raised her protest. The Christian narrative constitutes the mythos of modern times, and the oracular voice of poetry constantly reinvigorates this mythology. The creativity and the virtuoso invention of Christian poets proves the vitality of the myths from which they draw, to which they add their stories and songs. Pan is dead, but the spirit—now illuminated by science—is as quick as ever.

Browning's next collection appeared six years later, after her famous elopement to Italy. *Poems* is marked by the distinction of containing *Sonnets from the Portuguese*, which prior to this time had been available only in a small private edition. These forty-four sonnets had been completed in 1847. They are technically more sure-handed than the earlier ones. The same Italian octet is here *abbaabba*, but Browning has decided unequivocally on a sestet which rhymes *cdcdcd*. The *e* rhyme has disappeared. She limits herself to four rhyme values in each sonnet. The effect is a tight, organically unified sequence of sonnets. This impression of technical unity is enhanced by the single-minded theme of the poems: "this very love which is my boast." The poet has nevertheless avoided sameness in the sonnets by avoiding clichés and by writing from her own varied experience of love. For her, love had been exhilarating and risky during the days of her engagement; it had cruelly forced on her the determination to defy her father; it had sorrowfully juxtaposed her frailty to Robert's vigor; it had pitted her will to live against her expectation of an early death. These experiences provide the images that keep her poems from being merely conventional and confessional. Throughout them all there is a grim sense of herself which tries to avoid melodramatic self-deprecation on the one hand, while expressing an honest sense of her own limits on the other. This ironic view of herself gives the poems an underlying psychological realism that holds their Romanticism in check.

Browning's *Aurora Leigh* is a narrative poem fulfilling her earlier wish to set a romance in an unromantic age. The ironies of such a circumstance are resolved for her when it becomes manifest to the protagonists that love is not only a "romantic" experience, but also a universal ethic. It therefore disarms the meanness of spirit, the poverty of values which the poet associated with the growing skepticism of a scientific and industrial age. The poem consists of nine books of approximately twelve hundred lines each, all in unrhymed iambic pentameter—blank verse. Although this poem has a more detailed narrative framework than most of Browning's poems, it still is characterized by long reflective passages in which she devotes intense thought to the important ideas that arise from the narrative events. While her characters are not persuasive, the incidents seem improbable, and the diction is uniformly stilted, the themes discussed are confronted with a directness and boldness almost unequaled among Victorian poets.

Aurora Leigh is born in Italy of an English father and an Italian mother. Orphaned early, she travels to England to be reared by her father's sister. She becomes a retiring, moderately successful poet. Her cousin Romney, who has inherited the Leigh title and fortune, is a deeply compassionate Christian socialist with a strongly activist disposition. Aurora and Romney are drawn to each other, yet they so little understand each other that there is constant friction between them. After years of circling about each other, proposed marriages to third parties, and the exhaustion of Romney's fortune on an ungrateful community of the poor, Aurora and Romney recognize that their ambivalence toward each other is actually a rigorous—that is, not a very sentimental—form of love.

The issues of the poem are resolved in the most comprehensive working out of these problems that Browning ever undertook. Romney acknowledges that his social activism has been too doctrinaire, too manipulative; it has ignored the practical realities of human experiences. Aurora acknowledges that the ferocity of her independence has masked a deep need for intimacy. Each finds that love—as both an ethic and a sentiment—gives complexity and vitality both to the social question (Romney's problem) and to individual identity (Aurora's problem). The poet believes that this kind of love is grounded in an eternal Divine and is therefore the key to resolving the antinomies in an age of conflict—nationalists against empires, poor against rich, men against women, faith against doubt.

Other major works

NONFICTION: *The Letters of Elizabeth Barrett Browning*, 1897; *The Letters of Robert Browning and Elizabeth Barrett Barrett*, 1899; *Diary by E. B. B.: The Unpublished Diary of Elizabeth Barrett Browning, 1831-1832*, 1969 (Philip Kelly and Ronald Hudson, editors).

MISCELLANEOUS: *Prometheus Bound, Translated from the Greek of Aeschylus: And Miscellaneous Poems*, 1833.

Bibliography

Dally, Peter. *Elizabeth Barrett Browning: A Psychological Portrait*. London: Macmillan, 1989.

Forster, Margaret. *Elizabeth Barrett Browning: A Biography*. London: Chatto & Windus, 1988.

Hewlett, Dorothy. *Elizabeth Barrett Browning: A Life*. New York: Alfred A. Knopf, 1952.

Leighton, Angela. *Elizabeth Barrett Browning*. Brighton, England: Harvester Press, 1986.

Mermin, Dorothy. *Elizabeth Barrett Browning: The Origins of a New Poetry*. Chicago: University of Chicago Press, 1989.

Stephenson, Glennis. *Elizabeth Barrett Browning and the Poetry of Love*. Ann Arbor: University of Michigan Research Institute, 1989.

Taplin, Gardner. *The Life of Elizabeth Barrett Browning*. London: John Murray, 1957.

PEARL S. BUCK

Born: Hillsboro, West Virginia; June 26, 1892

Died: Danby, Vermont; March 6, 1973

Principal long fiction

East Wind: West Wind, 1930; *The Good Earth*, 1931; *Sons*, 1932; *The Mother*, 1934; *A House Divided*, 1935; *House of Earth*, 1935; *This Proud Heart*, 1938; *The Patriot*, 1939; *Other Gods: An American Legend*, 1940; *Dragon Seed*, 1942; *China Sky*, 1942; *The Promise*, 1943; *China Flight*, 1945; *Portrait of a Marriage*, 1945; *The Townsman*, 1945 (as John Sedges); *Pavilion of Women*, 1946; *The Angry Wife*, 1947 (as John Sedges); *Peony*, 1948; *Kinfolk*, 1949; *The Long Love*, 1949 (as John Sedges); *God's Men*, 1951; *The Hidden Flower*, 1952; *Bright Procession*, 1952 (as John Sedges); *Come, My Beloved*, 1953; *Voices in the House*, 1953 (as John Sedges); *Imperial Woman*, 1956; *Letter from Peking*, 1957; *Command the Morning*, 1959; *Satan Never Sleeps*, 1962; *The Living Reed*, 1963; *Death in the Castle*, 1965; *The Time Is Noon*, 1967; *The New Year*, 1968; *The Three Daughters of Madame Liang*, 1969; *Mandala*, 1970; *The Goddess Abides*, 1972; *All Under Heaven*, 1973; *The Rainbow*, 1974.

Other literary forms

An overwhelmingly prolific writer, Pearl S. Buck wrote short stories, juvenile fiction and nonfiction, pamphlets, magazine articles, literary history, biographies, plays (including a musical), educational works, an Oriental cookbook, and a variety of books on the United States, democracy, Adolf Hitler and Germany, Japan, China, Russia, the mentally retarded, the sexes, and the Kennedy women. In addition, she translated *Shui Hu Chuan* (*All Men Are Brothers*, 1933) and edited a book of Oriental fairy tales, several Christmas books, and a book of Chinese woodcuts. Besides *The Good Earth*, her finest works are her biographies of her parents, *The Exile* (1936) and *Fighting Angel: Portrait of a Soul* (1936). Buck also delivered several important addresses that reveal much about her own literary philosophy, including her Nobel Prize lecture on the Chinese novel.

During World War II, Buck delivered many speeches and published articles, letters, and pamphlets on the Asian view of the war, particularly on colonial rule and imperialism. Buck's canon further includes personal works, such as the autobiographical *My Several Worlds: A Personal Record*, (1954) and *A Bridge for Passing* (1962). Several of her plays were produced off-Broadway or in summer stock.

Achievements

Buck has been enormously successful with popular audiences, more so than with the literati. She is the most widely translated author in all American literary history. In Denmark, for example, her popularity exceeded that of Ernest Hemingway and John Steinbeck in the 1930's, and in Sweden, ten of her books were translated between 1932 and 1940, more than those of any other American author. *The Good Earth*, her most famous work, has been translated into more than thirty languages (seven different translations into Chinese alone) and made into a play and a motion picture.

Buck's early novels received much acclaim. *The Good Earth* was awarded the Pulitzer Prize; in 1935, she was awarded the William Dean Howells medal by the American Academy of Arts and Letters for the finest work in American fiction from 1930 to 1935, and in 1936, she was elected to membership in the National Institute of Arts and Letters. In 1938, she was awarded the Nobel Prize, the third American to receive it and the fourth woman, for her "rich and generous epic description of Chinese peasant life and masterpieces of biography." *The Good Earth*, a staple of high school and undergraduate reading, is undoubtedly a masterpiece; and her missionary biographies, *The Exile* and *Fighting Angel*, though currently neglected, have merit in the depth of their analysis. Three other books of the 1930's—*Sons*, *The Mother*, and *The Patriot*—have effective passages. In all of her works, Buck evinces a deep humanity, and she did much to further American understanding of Asian culture.

Buck has not fared so well with the literary establishment. Critics of the 1930's disdained her work because she was a woman, because her subjects were not "American," and because they thought she did not deserve the Nobel Prize. Her success in writing best-seller after best-seller and her optimistic faith in progress and humanity have irked later critics. Her innate storytelling ability does "please," "amuse," and "entertain" (her three criteria for good writing), but even the kindest of her admirers wish that she had written less and spent more time exploring the minds of her characters and polishing her work.

Biography

Pearl S. Buck was born Pearl Comfort Sydenstricker on June 26, 1892, in the family home at Hillsboro, West Virginia, to Absalom and Caroline (Stulting) Sydenstricker. Her parents were missionaries in China, home on a furlough. After five months she was taken to China. Buck grew up in Chinkiang, an inland city on the Yangtze River. In 1900, during the Boxer Rebellion, her family was forced to flee and she experienced the horrors of racism.

Buck's early literary influences included her parents and her old Chinese nurse. Her parents encouraged her to read the Bible and told her tales of their American homeland, while her nurse told her fantastic Buddhist and Taoist legends of warriors, devils, fairies, and dragons. She learned to speak Chinese before English, but she learned to read and write in English sooner than in Chinese. Her education included one year at boarding school in Shanghai and four years at Randolph-Macon Women's College in Virginia.

In 1917, she married John Lossing Buck, an agricultural specialist. They lived in Nanhsuchon in Anhwei province (the setting of *The Good Earth*). After five years, they moved southward to Nanking, where her husband taught agriculture and she taught English at the university. She published her first article in *The Atlantic* (January, 1923); "In China, Too" described the growing Western influence in China.

Tragedy struck Buck's life with the birth of Carol, her only natural child, who was mentally retarded (she later adopted eight children). She took Carol to the United States for medical treatment in 1925. When her husband took a year's leave of absence, Buck studied English at Cornell University and received her master's degree. Her first published novel, *East Wind: West Wind*, combined two short stories, one of which was originally published in 1925 in *Asia* magazine. On March 2, 1931, *The Good Earth* appeared, creating a literary sensation. The Bucks were divorced in 1932, and that same year Pearl married her publisher, Richard J. Walsh, president of John Day and editor of *Asia* magazine. Their marriage lasted until his death in 1960.

Buck's humanitarian efforts began in 1941 with the founding of the East and West Association, which endeavored to increase understanding between diverse cultures. During World War II, Buck actively spoke against racism, against the internment of Japanese Americans, and against the yielding of democratic privileges during wartime. In 1949, she and her husband founded Welcome House, an adoption agency for Amerasian children. In 1954, her letter of protest to *The New York Times* led to the changing of a policy which put immigrants in federal prisons with criminals. In 1964, she founded the Pearl S. Buck Foundation to care for Amerasian children who remain overseas. She also worked for the Training School, a school for the retarded in Vineland, New Jersey. For her many humanitarian efforts, she received the Brotherhood Award of the National Conference of Christians and Jews, the Wesley Award for Distinguished Service to Humanity, and more than a dozen honorary degrees from American colleges and universities.

Along with her extensive humanitarian activities, Buck continued to write. Because her American novels *This Proud Heart* and *Other Gods* were not well received, Buck assumed the pen name "John Sedges" to write with freedom on American subjects. Between 1945 and 1953, five novels were published under this name while she wrote Asian stories under her own name. Unfortunately, as Buck's humanitarian efforts increased, the quality of her fiction declined. Its strident and moralistic tone reflected her growing concern with social issues rather than artistic technique. She continued writing, however, and by the time of her death in 1973 had written more than eighty novels and novellas.

Analysis

Pearl S. Buck's reputation for excellence as a writer of fiction rests solely on *The Good Earth* and segments of a few of her other novels of the 1930's. The appeal of *The Good Earth* is undeniable and easy to explain: Its universal themes are cloaked in the garments of an unfamiliar and fascinating Chinese culture. Echoing many elements of life, the book speaks of animosity between town and country, love of land, decadent rich and honest poor, marital conflicts, interfering relatives, misunderstandings between generations, the joys of birth and sorrows of old age and death, and the strong bonds of friendship. Added to these universal themes are the cyclical movement of the growth and decay of the crops, the decline of the House of Hwand and the ascent of the House of Wang, the changes of the years, and the birth and death of the people.

Buck fittingly chose to tell her story in language reminiscent of the Bible, with its families and peoples who rise and fall. Her style also owes something to that of the Chinese storytellers, to whom she paid tribute in her Nobel Prize lecture, a style which flows along in short words "with no other technique than occasional bits of description, only enough to give vividness to place or person, and never enough to delay the story." Most of Buck's sentences are long and serpentine, relying on balance, parallelism, and repetition for strength. While the sentences are long, the diction is simple and concrete. She chooses her details carefully: Her descriptions grow out of close observation and are always concise. The simplicity of the diction and the steady, determined flow of the prose fit the sagalike plot. In Chinese folk literature, the self-effacing author, like a clear vessel, should transmit life but not color it with his or her personality. So, also, Buck presents her story objectively. Her authorial presence never intrudes, though her warm feeling for the characters and her own ethical beliefs are always evident.

The strength of the novel also lies in its characterization, particularly that of the two main characters, O-lan and her husband Wang Lung. Whereas characters in Buck's later novels too easily divide into good and bad, the characters of *The Good Earth*, like real people, mix elements of both. Ching, Wang Lung's faithful, doglike friend and later overseer, early in the novel joins a starving mob that ransacks Wang Lung's home for food; Ching takes Wang Lung's last handful of beans. The eldest son is a pompous wastrel, but he does make

the House of Hwang beautiful with flowering trees and fish ponds and he does settle into the traditional married life his father has planned for him. Even O-lan, the almost saintly earth mother, seethes with jealousy when Wang Lung takes a second wife, and she feels contempt and bitterness for the House of Hwang in which she was a slave. Her major flaw is her ugliness. Wang Lung delights the reader with his simple wonder at the world and with his perseverance to care for his family and his land, but he, too, has failings. In middle age, he lusts for Lotus, neglecting the much-deserving O-lan, and in old age, he steals Pear Blossom from his youngest son. Rather than confusing the morality of the novel, the intermingling of good and bad increases its reality. Buck acknowledged literary indebtedness to Émile Zola, and the influence of naturalism is evident in *The Good Earth* in its objective, documentary presentation and its emphasis on the influence of environment and heredity. Unlike the naturalists, however, Buck also credits the force of free will

The Good Earth aroused much fury in some Chinese scholars, who insisted that the novel portrays a China that never was. Younghill Kang criticized the character of Wang Lung. Professor Kiang Kang-Hu said that Buck's details and her knowledge of Chinese history were inaccurate. Buck defended herself by granting that customs differed in the many regions of China. In later novels, she retaliated by harshly portraying Chinese scholars such as Kang and Kiang, who, she believed, distorted the picture of the real China either because of their ignorance of peasant life or because of their desire to aid propagandistic efforts of the Chinese government. Other native Chinese, including Phio Lin Yutang, sprang to Buck's defense, insisting on the accuracy of her portrayal.

As Buck became more interested in social and political issues and in the media—magazines, film, and radio—her fiction began to deteriorate. She claimed, "The truth is I never write with a sense of mission or to accomplish any purpose whatever except the revelation of human character through a life situation." Her fiction, however, did not demonstrate this belief: More and more it became a forum for her own social and political ideas rather than an exploration of human character and life. Further, American films and women's magazines began to influence her stories: They became drippingly romantic.

Buck's power as a novelist derived from her intelligence, her humanity, her interesting stories, and her ability to make Chinese culture real to readers from all over the world. Her weaknesses as a novelist included didacticism, sentimentalism, and an inability to control her energy long enough to explore deeply, revise, and improve. In her later novels, she lost control of her point of view, her language, and her characterization. Her legacy is an enduring masterpiece, *The Good Earth*, and an inestimable contribution to cultural exchange between China and the West.

Other major works

SHORT FICTION: *The First Wife and Other Stories*, 1933; *Today and Forever*, 1941; *Twenty-Seven Stories*, 1943; *Far and Near: Stories of Japan, China and America*, 1947; *American Triptych*, 1958; *Hearts Come Home and Other Stories*, 1962; *The Good Deed and Other Stories*, 1969; *Once Upon a Christmas*, 1972; *East and West*, 1975; *Secrets of the Heart*, 1976; *The Lovers and Other Stories*, 1977; *The Woman Who Was Changed and Other Stories*, 1979.

NONFICTION: *East and West and the Novel*, 1932; *The Exile*, 1936; *Fighting Angel: Portrait of a Soul*, 1936; *The Chinese Novel*, 1939; *Of Men and Women*, 1941, 1971; *American Unity and Asia*, 1942; *What America Means to Me*, 1943; *China in Black and White*, 1945; *Talk About Russia: With Masha Scott*, 1945; *Tell the People: Talks with James Yen About the Mass Education Movement*, 1945; *How It Happens: Talk About the German People, 1914-1933, with Erna von Pustau*, 1947; *American Argument: With Eslanda Goods*, 1949; *The Child Who Never Grew*, 1950; *My Several Worlds: A Personal Record*, 1954; *Friend to Friend: A Candid Exchange Between Pearl Buck and Carlos F. Romulo*, 1958; *A Bridge for Passing*, 1962; *The Joy of Children*, 1964; *Children for Adoption*, 1965; *The Gifts They Bring: Our Debt to the Mentally Retarded*, 1965; *The People of Japan*, 1966; *To My Daughters with Love*, 1967; *China As I See It*, 1970; *The Kennedy Women: A Personal Appraisal*, 1970; *The Story Bible*, 1971; *Pearl S. Buck's America*, 1971; *China Past and Present*, 1972.

CHILDREN'S LITERATURE: *The Young Revolutionist*, 1932; *Stories for Little Children*, 1940; *One Bright Day and Other Stories for Children*, 1952; *Johnny Jack and His Beginnings*, 1954; *The Man Who Changed China: The Story of Sun Yat-sen*, 1953; *Fourteen Stories*, 1961; *The Chinese Story Teller*, 1971.

TRANSLATION: *All Men Are Brothers*, 1933.

Bibliography

Cavasco, G. A. "Pearl Buck and the Chinese Novel." *Asian Studies* 5 (1967): 437-450.

Doyle, Paul A. *Pearl S. Buck*. Rev. ed. Boston: Twayne, 1980.

Harris, Theodore F. *Pearl S. Buck: A Biography*. 2 vols. New York: John Day, 1969.

Spencer, Cornelia. *Revealing the Human Heart: Pearl S. Buck*. Chicago: Encyclopædia Britannica, 1964.

FANNY BURNEY

Born: King's Lynn, Norfolk, England; June 13, 1752   **Died:** London, England; January 6, 1840

Principal long fiction

Evelina: Or, The History of a Young Lady's Entrance into the World, 1778; *Cecilia: Or, Memoirs of an Heiress*, 1782; *Camilla: Or, A Picture of Youth*, 1796; *The Wanderer: Or, Female Difficulties*, 1814.

Other literary forms

In addition to editing the memoirs of her father—the eminent organist, composer, and music historian, Dr. Charles Burney (1726-1814)—Fanny Burney wrote an *Early Diary, 1768-1778* (1889) and then a later *Diary and Letters, 1778-1840* (1842-1846). The first work, not published until 1889, contains pleasant sketches of Samuel Johnson, James Boswell, David Garrick, and Richard Brinsley Sheridan. Notable figures from government and the arts march across the pages of the early diary, which scholars have claimed surpasses her fiction in literary quality. The latter diary and correspondence appeared between 1842 and 1846; the seven volumes are notable for the record of the writer's meeting in her garden with the insane George III of England, the account of her glimpse of Napoleon I, and the recollections of her chat with the weary Louis XVIII of France.

Of her eight dramatic productions, three are worthy of mention: *The Witlings* (never published); *Edwy and Elgiva*, written in 1790, performed at Drury Lane on March 21, 1795, and withdrawn after the first night; and *Love and Fashion*, written in 1800, accepted by the manager at Covent Garden, but never performed. Finally, Burney published, in 1793, a political essay entitled *Brief Reflections Relative to the French Emigrant Clergy*, an address to the women of Great Britain in behalf of the French emigrant priests.

Achievements

Burney produced fiction at a time in history when a lady of means and social standing could not easily write fiction and still be considered a lady. Adding to that inhibition was the fact that both her father and his influential friends held literary standards not always easy for a self-educated young woman to attain. She burned her early manuscript efforts, wrote secretly at night, and published anonymously. Nevertheless, Burney succeeded as a novelist and achieved significance as a contributor to the history and development of the English novel. She brought to that genre an ability to observe the natural activities and reactions of those about her and to weave those observations through narrative structures and character delineations similar to those employed by her predecessors: Samuel Johnson, Henry Fielding, Samuel Richardson, Tobias Smollett, Aphra Behn, Mary De La Riviere Manley, Eliza Heywood, and Clara Reeve. For Burney, the novel would be the means by which to portray realistic persons and to represent the times in which they functioned.

Although Burney's four novels were published anonymously, the sophisticated readers of the day recognized the woman's point of view and immediately set the works apart from those of her contemporaries. The female readership, especially, both appreciated and praised the woman's view of the contemporary world; on the other hand, men scoffed at the novels' heroines as comic sentimentalists, products of blatant amateurism, and characteristic examples of a sex that would continue to be dominated by men. Burney's popularity, however, rests with her ability to develop fully the effects of female intelligence upon and within a society dominated by men and to persuade her audience that coexistence between the sexes was far more beneficial than the dominance of one over the other.

As a woman writing about women, Burney could not cling too long to the models that the past century had provided for her. She determined early to purge her fictional environment of masculine influence. In its place, she would establish the importance of her title characters as working parts in the machinery of eighteenth century British society. As a group, Burney's heroines are meant to be carbon copies of one another; individually, each portrays a young lady in pursuit of traditional goals: marriage, money, and the discovery of the self.

Biography

Fanny (Frances) Burney, later Madame D'Arblay, the third of six children of Charles Burney and Esther Sleepe Burney, was born on June 13, 1752, at King's Lynn, Norfolk, where her father served as church organist while recuperating from tuberculosis. In 1760, his health completely restored, Burney moved his family to London, where he resumed his professional involvements in teaching, composition, and music history. Upon the death of Esther Burney on September 28, 1761, two of the children went to school in Paris, while Frances remained at home. Dr. Burney seemed prepared to send Frances to join her sisters when, in 1766, he married Mrs. Stephen Allen. Thus, the fourteen-year-old girl remained at home in London, left to her own educational aims and directions, since her father had no time to supervise her learning. She had, at about age ten, begun to write drama, poetry, and fiction; on her fifteenth birthday, she supposedly burned her manuscripts because she felt guilty about wasting her time with such trifles.

Nevertheless, the story of Evelina and her adventures did not die in the flames of her fireplace. After securing her father's permission, Burney gave *Evelina* to the London publisher Thomas Lowndes, who issued it in January, 1778. Its success and popularity owed some debt to Dr. Burney, who passed the novel on to Mrs. Thrale, a prominent figure in London's literary society. From there, it made its way to Samuel Johnson, Joshua Reynolds, and Edmund Burke. Shortly afterward, Fanny Burney met Mrs. Thrale, who took the new novelist into her home and introduced her to Johnson, Reynolds, Sheridan, and Arthur Murphy—all of whom pressed her to write drama. The result took the form of *The Whitlings*, a dramatic piece that, principally because of her father's displeasure over the quality of the work, she never published.

Returning to the form that produced her initial success, Burney published *Cecilia* in the summer of 1782, further advancing her literary reputation and social standing. Mary Delany, an intimate of the royal family, helped secure for her an appointment in July, 1786, as second keeper of the Queen's robes. Her tenure at court proved to be more of a confinement than a social or political advantage because of the menial tasks, the rigid schedule, and the stiffness of Queen Charlotte Sophia and her attendants.

The activities and events at court, however, did contribute to the value of Burney's diaries, though her health suffered. She continued in service until July, 1791, at which time she gained permission to retire on a pension of one hundred pounds per annum. On July 31, 1793, she married General Alexandre D'Arblay, a comrade of the Marquis de Lafayette. The couple's entire income rested with Madame D'Arblay's pension, and thus she sought to increase the family's fortunes through her writing. A tragic play, *Edwy and Elgiva*, lasted but a single night's performance at Drury Lane, but a third novel, *Camilla*, generated more than three thousands pounds from subscriptions and additional sales, although the piece failed to achieve the literary merit of *Evelina* or *Cecilia*.

In 1801, General D'Arblay returned to France to seek employment but managed only a pension of fifteen hundred francs. His wife and son, Alexander, joined him the next year, and the family spent the succeeding ten years at Passy, in a state of quasi-exile that lasted throughout the Napoleonic wars. Madame D'Arblay and her son returned to England in 1812, and there, the novelist attended her aged father until his death in April, 1814. Her last novel, begun in France in 1802 and entitled *The Wanderer*, appeared early in 1814. Again, the financial returns far exceeded the literary quality of the piece. After Napoleon's exile, the novelist returned to her husband in Paris; she then went to Brussels after the emperor's return from Elba. General D'Arblay, meanwhile, had been seriously injured by the kick of a horse, which brought an end to his military career. The family returned to England to spend the remainder of their years: General D'Arblay died on May 3, 1818, and Alexander died on January 19, 1837. In November, 1839, Madame D'Arblay suffered a severe illness and died on January 6, 1840, in her eighty-seventh year.

Analysis

Despite the relative brevity of her canon, Fanny Burney's fiction cannot be dismissed with the usual generalizations from literary history: specifically that the author shared the interests of her youthful heroines in good manners. She possessed a quick sense for the comic in character and situation, and those talents distinctly advanced the art of the English novel in the direction of Jane Austen. From one viewpoint, she indeed exists as an important transitional figure between the satiric allegories of the earlier eighteenth century and the instruments that portrayed middle-class manners in full flourish during the first quarter of the nineteenth century.

Burney's contemporaries understood both her method and her purpose. Samuel Johnson thought her a "real wonder," one worth being singled out for her honest sense of modesty and her ability to apply it to fiction. Edmund Burke seemed amazed by her knowledge of human nature. Three years after her death, Thomas Babington Macaulay proclaimed that the author of *Evelina* and *Cecilia* had done for the English novel what Jeremy Collier, at the end of the seventeenth century, did for the drama: maintain rigid morality and virgin delicacy. Macaulay proclaimed that Fanny Burney had indeed vindicated the right of woman "to an equal share in a fair and noble promise of letters" and had accomplished her task in clear, natural, and lively "woman's English."

Nevertheless, Burney contributed more to the English novel than simply the advancement of her sex's cause. Her heroines are mentally tormented and yet emerge as wiser and stronger human beings. The fictional contexts into which she placed her principal characters are those that readers of every time and place could recognize: situations in which the proponents of negative values seem to prosper and the defenders of virtue cling tenaciously to their ground. Burney's women must learn the ways of a difficult world, a society composed of countless snares and endless rules; they must quickly don the accoutrements for survival: modesty, reserve, submission, and (above all else) manners. What makes Burney's depiction of women in society particularly poignant is the knowledge that the author herself had to endure trials of survival. An awareness of the author's accounts of actual struggles for social survival, then, becomes a necessity for understanding and appreciating the problems confronted by her fictional characters.

In Burney's first novel, *Evelina*, the title character brings with her to London and Bristol two qualities most difficult for a young provincial girl to defend: her sense of propriety and her pure innocence—the latter quality not to be confused with ignorance. In London, Evelina stumbles into false, insecure situations because she does not comprehend the rules of the social game. During the course of eighty-five epistles, however, she learns. The learning process is of utmost importance to Burney, for it serves as both plot for her fiction and instruction for her largely female readership. Once in London, life unfolds new meanings for Evelina Anville, as she samples the wares of urbanity: assemblies, amusements, parks and gardens, drawing rooms, operas, and theaters. Accompanying the activities is a corps of sophisticates by whose rules Evelina must play: Lord Orville, the well-bred young man and the jealous lover; Sir Clement Willoughby, the obnoxious admirer of Evelina who tries (through forged letters) to breach the relationship between Orville and Evelina; Macartney, the young poet whom Evelina saves from suicide and against whom Orville exercises his jealous streak; Captain Mirvan, the practical joker who smiles only at the expense of others; Mrs. Beaumont, who would have the heroine believe that good qualities originate from pride rather than from principles; Lady Louisa Larpent, the sullen and distraught (but always arrogant) sister of Lord Orville who tries to separate her brother from Evelina; Mr. Lovel, a demeaning fop who constantly refers to Evelina's simple background; and the Watkins sisters, who chide Evelina because they envy her attractiveness to young men.

Despite these obstacles of situation and character, however, Evelina does not lack some protection. The Reverend Arthur Villars, her devoted guardian since the death of her mother, guides and counsels the seventeen-year-old girl from his home in Dorsetshire. Villars receives the major portion of Evelina's letters; in fact, he initially advises her to be wary of Lord Orville, but then relents when he learns of his ward's extreme happiness. Since Evelina cannot count on immediate assistance from Villars, she does rely on several people in London. Mrs. Mirvan, the amiable and well-bred wife of the captain, introduces Evelina to a variety of social affairs, while their daughter, Maria, becomes the heroine's only real confidante, sharing mutual happiness and disappointment. Finally, there is the Reverend Villars' neighbor, Mrs. Selwyn, who accompanies Evelina on a visit to Bristol Hot Wells. Unfortunately, the one person closest to Evelina during her London tenure, her maternal grandmother, Madame Duval, proves of little use and even less assistance. A blunt, indelicate, and severe woman, she is bothered by her granddaughter's display of independence and vows that the young lady will not share in her inheritance.

Villars emerges as the supporting character with the

most depth, principally because he is ever present in the letters. From the novel's beginning, the heroine reaches out to him for guidance and support, scarcely prepared "to form a wish that has not [his] sanction." The local clergyman, Villars serves as parent for a motherless and socially fatherless young lady who, for the first time, is about to see something of the world. Thus, Villars' caution and anxiety appear natural, for he knows the bitter effects of socially unequal marriages, as in the cases of Evelina's own parents and grandparents. He naturally mistrusts Lord Orville and fears the weakness of the young girl's imagination. Everyone knows that, as long as Evelina remains obedient to Villars' will, no union between her and Orville can occur. Once the girl's father, Sir John Belmont, repents for his many years of unkindness to his daughter and then bequeaths her thirty thousand pounds, however, the guardian cleric no longer remains the dominant influence. Lord Orville proceeds to put his own moral house in order and supplants his rivals; the reserve felt by Evelina because of the Reverend Villars' fears and anxieties gradually disintegrates, and the romance proceeds toward its inevitable conclusion.

The process may be inevitable, but it is sufficiently hampered by a series of struggles and conflicts, as is typical of the late eighteenth century novel of manners. Both her grandmother and Mrs. Mirvan provide Evelina with fairly easy access to fashionable society, but the socialites in that society involve the girl in a number of uncomfortable and burdensome situations. For example, Biddy and Polly Branghton and Madam Duval use Evelina's name in requesting the use of Lord Orville's coach. Evelina realizes the impropriety of the request and knows that Orville's benevolence would never permit him to refuse it. Furthermore, Tom Branghton, an admirer of Evelina, solicits business from Orville also by relying on Evelina's name; he does so after damaging the borrowed vehicle. Evelina's innocence forces her to bear the responsibility for her relatives' actions and schemes, although she opposes all that they attempt. Fortunately, the fierce determination with which she advances her innocence and honesty enables her to endure such problems until rescued, in this case, by Lord Orville and Mrs. Selwyn. Vulgarity (Madam Duval), ill breeding (the Branghtons), and impertinence (Sir Clement Willoughby) eventually fall before the steadfastness and the force of Evelina's emerging wisdom and strength. Burney here demonstrates the specific means by which an eighteenth century woman could surmount the perplexities of that era.

Burney's ability to depict the misgivings of those who are driven by external circumstances to earn a livelihood through unaccustomed means is powerful. In coming to grips with an obvious and serious problem of her time, she demonstrated how her major fictional characters and herself, as a character from the real world, could indeed rely successfully on the resources endowed upon all individuals, female as well as male. If nothing else, the novelist showed her society and the generations that followed not only how well women could function in the real world but also how much they could contribute and take advantage of opportunities offered them. In a sense, Burney's compositions belong to social history as much as to literature.

Other major works

PLAYS: *Edwy and Elgiva*, 1790; *Love and Fashion*, 1800.
NONFICTION: *Brief Reflections Relative to the French Emigrant Clergy*, 1793; *The Early Diary of Frances Burney, 1768-1778*, 1889; *Diary and Letters, 1778-1840*, 1842-1846 (7 volumes).
EDITED TEXT: *Memoirs of Dr. Charles Burney*, 1832.

Bibliography

Bloom, Harold, ed. *Fanny Burney's "Evelina": Modern Critical Interpretations*. New York: Chelsea House, 1988.
Doody, Margaret Anne. *Frances Burney*. New Brunswick, N.J.: Rutgers University Press, 1988.
Epstein, Julia L. *The Iron Pen: Frances Burney and the Politics of Women's Writing*. Madison: University of Wisconsin Press, 1989.
Simons, Judy. *Fanny Burney*. Totowa, N.J.: Barnes & Noble Books, 1987.
Straub, Kristina. *Divided Fictions: Fanny Burney and Feminine Strategy*. Lexington: University Press of Kentucky, 1987.

ANGELA CARTER

Born: Eastbourne, Sussex, England; May 7, 1940   **Died:** London, England; February 16, 1992

Principal long fiction

Shadowdance, 1966 (published in the United States as *Honeybuzzard*, 1967); *The Magic Toyshop*, 1967; *Several Perceptions*, 1968; *Heroes and Villains*, 1969; *Love*, 1971, revised 1987; *The Infernal Desire Machines of Doctor Hoffman*, 1972 (published in the United States as *The War of Dreams*, 1974); *The Passion of New Eve*, 1977; *Nights at the Circus*, 1984; *Wise Children*, 1992.

Other literary forms

Angela Carter is nearly as well known for her short fiction as she is for her novels. Her short-story collections include *Fireworks: Nine Profane Pieces* (1974), *Black Venus* (1985; published in the United States as *Saints and Strangers*, 1986), and the highly praised *The Bloody Chamber and Other Stories* (1979), which contains her transformations of well-known fairy tales into adult tales with erotic overtones. She also wrote a number of fantastic stories for children, including *Miss Z, the Dark Young Lady* (1970), *The Donkey Prince* (1970), and a translated adaptation of the works of Charles Perrault, *Sleeping Beauty and Other Favourite Fairy Tales* (1982). In 1978, she published her first book of nonfiction, *The Sadeian Woman: And the Ideology of Pornography*, a feminist study of the Marquis de Sade that remains controversial among both literary and feminist critics. Other nonfiction essays were published by British journals; *Nothing Sacred: Selected Writings* (1982) is a collection of her journalistic pieces. She also cowrote the screenplay for the British film *The Company of Wolves* (1985), based on her short story of the same title. *Come unto These Yellow Sands* (1985) is a collection of various other scripts adapted from her fiction.

Achievements

With the publication of her first novels in the late 1960's, Carter received wide recognition and acclaim in Great Britain for blending gothic and surreal elements with vivid portrayals of urban sufferers and survivors. She was awarded the John Llewellyn Rhys Memorial Prize for *The Magic Toyshop* and the Somerset Maugham Award for *Several Perceptions*. Critics have praised her wit, inventiveness, eccentric characters, descriptive wealth, and strongly sustained narrative while sometimes questioning her depth of purpose and suggesting a degree of pretentiousness. Such adverse criticism is mostly directed at such novels as *Heroes and Villains* and *The Infernal Desire Machines of Doctor Hoffman*, which are set in postapocalyptic or metaphysical landscapes. Her imaginative transformation of folkloric elements and examination of their mythic impact on sexual relationships began to be fully appreciated on the appearance of *The Bloody Chamber and Other Stories*, which received the Cheltenham Festival of Literature Award. *Nights at the Circus*, recipient of the James Tait Black Memorial Prize, helped to establish firmly for Carter a transatlantic reputation as an extravagant stylist of the Magical Realist school. She became noted for her provocative observations and commentary on contemporary social conditions.

Biography

Angela Carter (neé Stalker) was born in Eastbourne, Sussex, England, on May 7, 1940. After working as a journalist from 1958 to 1961 in Croyden, Surrey, she attended Bristol University, from which she received a B.A. in English literature in 1965. She traveled widely and lived for several years in Japan. From 1976 to 1978, she served as Arts Council of Great Britain Fellow in Creative Writing at Sheffield University. She was a visiting professor at Brown University, the University of Texas, Austin, and the University of Iowa, and made her home in London, England, where she died on February 16, 1992, of cancer.

Analysis

The search for self and for autonomy is the underlying theme of most of Angela Carter's fiction. Her protagonists, usually described as bored or in some other way detached from their lives, are thrust into an unknown landscape or enter on a picaresque journey in which they encounter representatives of a vast variety of human experience and suffering. These encountered characters are often grotesques or exaggerated parodies reminiscent of those found in the novels of Charles Dickens or such Southern gothic writers as Flannery O'Connor. They also sometimes exhibit the animalistic or supernatural qualities of fairy-tale characters. The protagonists undergo a voluntary or, more often, forced submission to their own suppressed desires. By internalizing the insights gained through such submission and vicariously from the experiences of their antagonists and comrades or lovers, the protagonists are then able to garner some control over their own destinies. This narrative structure is borrowed from the classic folktales and fairy tales with which Carter was closely associated. Carter does not merely retell such tales in modern dress; rather, she probes and twists the ancient stories to illuminate the underlying hierarchical structures of power and dominance, weakness and submission.

In addition to the folkloric influence, Carter drew from a variety of other writers, most notably Lewis Carroll, Jonathan Swift, the Marquis de Sade, and William Blake. The rather literal-minded innocent abroad in a nightmarish wonderland recalls both Alice and Gulliver, and Carter acknowledged, both directly and obliquely, her borrowings from *Alice's Adventures in Wonderland* (1865) and *Gulliver's Travels* (1726). She also was influenced by the Swiftian tool of grotesque parody used in the service of satire. It is through Swiftian glasses that she read Sade. While deploring the depredations on the human condition committed by both the victims and victimizers in Sade's writings, she interpreted these as hyperbolic visions of the actual social situation, and she employed in her novels derivatively descriptive situations for their satiric shock value. Finally, the thematic concerns of Blake's visionary poetry—the tension between the contrarieties of innocence and experience, rationality and desire—were integral to Carter's outlook. The energy created by such tension creates the plane on which Carter's protagonists can live most fully.

Certain symbolic motifs appear regularly in her novels. Carter is particularly intrigued by the possibilities of roses, wedding dresses, swans, wolves, tigers, bears, vampires, mirrors, tears, and vanilla ice cream. Menacing father figures, prostitute mothers, and a kaleidoscope of circus, fair, and Gypsy folk people most of her landscapes. It is unfair, however, to reduce Carter's novels to a formulaic mode. She juggles traditional and innovative elements with a sometimes dazzling dexterity and is inevitably a strong storyteller.

At the opening of *The Magic Toyshop*, fifteen-year-old Melanie is entranced with her budding sexuality. She dresses up in her absent mother's wedding gown to dance on the lawn in the moonlight. Overwhelmed by her awakening knowledge and the immense possibilities the night offers, she is terrified and climbs back into her room by the childhood route of the apple tree—shredding her mother's gown in the process. Her return to childhood becomes catastrophic when a telegram arrives announcing the death of Melanie's parents in a plane crash. Melanie, with her younger brother and sister, is thrust from a safe and comfortable existence into the constricted and terrifying London household of her Uncle Philip Flower, a toy maker of exquisite skill and sadistically warped sensibility. He is a domestic tyrant whose Irish wife, Margaret, was inexplicably struck dumb on her wedding day. The household is also inhabited by Margaret's two younger brothers, Finn and Francie Jowle; the three siblings form a magic "circle of red people" which is alternately seductive and repulsive to Melanie. Uncle Philip is a creator of the mechanical. He is obsessed by his private puppet theater, his created world to which he enslaves the entire household. In aligning herself with the Jowle siblings, Melanie asserts her affirmation of life but becomes aware of the thwarted and devious avenues of survival open to the oppressed. The growing, but ambivalent, attraction between her and Finn is premature and manipulated by Uncle Philip. Even the love that holds the siblings together is underlined by a current of incest. Finn is driven to inciting his uncle to murder him in order to effect Philip's damnation. The crisis arises when Uncle Philip casts Melanie as Leda in a puppet extravaganza. Her symbolic rape by the immense mechanical swan and Finn's destruction of the puppet release an orgiastic, yet purifying, energy within the "circle of red people." The ensuing wrath of Uncle Philip results in the conflagration and destruction of the house. Finn and Melanie are driven out, Adam-and-Eve-like, to face a new world "in a wild surmise."

In fairy-tale fashion, Melanie is threatened by an evil father figure, protected by the good mother, and rescued by the young hero. Even in this early novel, however, Carter skews and claws at the traditional fabric. The Jowle brothers, grimy, embittered, and twisted by their victimization at the hands of Philip Flower, are as dangerous as they are endangered. They are unable to effect their own freedom. Melanie's submission to Uncle Philip's swan catalyzes not only her own rescue but also, indeed, the release of the Jowle siblings. Melanie's sacrifice breaks the magic spell that held the Jowles imprisoned.

Parody and satire are major elements in Carter's three novels that are often classified as science fiction or science fantasy. In *Heroes and Villains*, *The Infernal Desire Machines of Doctor Hoffman*, and *The Passion of New Eve*, Carter's protagonists dwell in societies that are described in metaphysical iconography. Carter seems to be questioning the nature and values of received reality. Marianne's world in *Heroes and Villains* is divided into high-technology enclaves containing Professors, the Soldiers who protect them, and the Workers who serve them. Outside the enclaves, in the semijungle/semicesspool wildernesses, dwell the tribes of nomadic Barbarians and the Out-people, freaks created by nature gone awry. Marianne, the daughter of a Professor, motivated mainly by boredom, escapes from her enclave with Jewel, a young Barbarian chieftain, during a raid. In *The Infernal Desire Machines of Doctor Hoffman*, the aging Desiderio narrates his heroic exploits as a young man when he saved his City during the Reality War. Doctor Hoffman besieges the City with mirages generated from his Desire Machines. Sent by the Minister of Determination to kill Doctor Hoffman, Desiderio is initiated into the wonders of desires made manifest, Nebulous Time, and the juggled samples of cracked and broken reality. His guide is Hoffman's daughter, Albertina, who appears to Desiderio as an androgynous ambassador, a black swan, the young valet of a vampiric count, and finally as his one true love, the emanation of his whole desire. The United States in *The Passion of New Eve* is torn apart by racial, class, and sexual conflicts. Evelyn, a young British teacher, travels through this landscape and is recreated. The unconsciously exploitive and disinterestedly sadistic narrator suffers a wild revenge when captured by an Amazon-like community of women. He is castrated, resexed, raped, forcibly wed and mated, and ultimately torn from his wife's love by a gang of murder-ous puritanical boys. Each of these protagonists experiences love but only seems to be able to achieve wholeness through the destruction of the loved one. Symbolically, the protagonists seem to consume the otherness of the loved ones, reincorporating these manifest desires back into their whole beings. Each, however, is left alone at the end of the novel.

Symbolic imagery of a harshly violent though rollicking nature threatens to overwhelm these three novels. The parody is at times wildly exaggerated and at times cuts very close to reality (for example, in *The Passion of New Eve*, the new Eve is incorporated into a polygamous family that closely resembles the Charles Manson cult). Although some critics have decried Carter's heavy reliance on fantasies, visions, and zany exuberance, it is probably these qualities that have appealed to a widening audience. It must also be given to Carter that, within her magical realms, she probed and mocked the repressive nature of institutionalized relationships and sexual politics.

With *Nights at the Circus*, Carter wove the diverse threads of her earlier novels into brilliantly realized tapestry. This novel has two protagonists—Fevvers, the Cockney Venus, a winged, six-foot, peroxide-blonde aerialist, who was found "hatched out of a bloody great egg" on the steps of a benevolent whorehouse (her real name is Sophia), and Jack Walser, an American journalist compiling a series of interviews entitled "Great Humbugs of the World," who joins Colonel Kearney's circus, the Ludic Game, in order to follow Fevvers and who is "Not hatched out, yet . . . his own shell don't break, yet." It is 1899, and a New World is about to break forth. The magic in this novel comes in the blurring between fact and fiction, the intense unbelievability of actual reality and the seductive possibilities of imaginative and dreamlike visions. As in most Magical Realist fiction, Carter is probing the lines between art and artifice, creation and generation, in a raucous and lush style.

With shifting narrative focuses, Carter unfolds the rebirths of Walser and Fevvers through their own and each other's eyes. Walser's shells of consciousness are cracked as he becomes a "first-of-May" clown, the waltzing partner to a tigress, the Human Chicken, and, in losing consciousness, an apprentice shaman to a primitive Finno-Urgic tribe. As star of Kearney's circus, Fevvers is the toast of European capitals: an impregnable, seductive freak, secure in and exploitive of her own singularity. On the interminable train trek through Siberia, she becomes less a freak and more a woman, but she remains determined to hatch Walser into her New Man. As he had to forgo his socially conditioned consciousness in order to recognize Sophia, however, so she has to allow him to hatch himself. It is as confident seers that Sophia/Fevvers and Jack Walser love at the close of the novel. With *Nights at the Circus*, Angela Carter, too, entered a confident, strong period in her remarkable literary career.

Other major works

SHORT FICTION: *Fireworks: Nine Profane Pieces*, 1974; *The Bloody Chamber and Other Stories*, 1979; *Black Venus*, 1985 (published in the United States as *Saints and Strangers*, 1986).

SCREENPLAYS: *Come unto These Yellow Sands*, 1985 (based on her short fiction); *The Company of Wolves*, 1985 (based on her short story).

NONFICTION: *The Sadeian Woman: And the Ideology of Pornography*, 1979; *Nothing Sacred: Selected Writings*, 1982.

CHILDREN'S LITERATURE: *Miss Z, the Dark Young Lady*, 1970; *The Donkey Prince*, 1970.

TRANSLATIONS: *The Fairy Tales of Charles Perrault*, 1979; *Sleeping Beauty and Other Favourite Fairy Tales*, 1982 (adaptation of Perrault's tales).

Bibliography

Haffenden, John. "Angela Carter." In *Novelists in Interview*. New York: Methuen, 1985.

Palumbo, Donald, ed. *Erotic Universe: Sexuality and Fantastic in Literature*. London: Greenwood Press, 1986.

Punter, David. "Angela Carter: Supersessions of the Masculine." *Critique: Studies in Modern Fiction* 25 (Summer, 1984): 209-222.

Sheets, Robin. "Angela Carter." In *An Encyclopedia of British Women Writers*, edited by Paul Schlueter and June Schlueter. New York: Garland, 1988.

Vannatta, Dennis P., ed. *The English Short Story, 1945-1980: A Critical History*. Boston: Twayne, 1985.

WILLA CATHER

Born: Back Creek Valley, near Gore, Virginia; December 7, 1873

Died: New York, New York; April 24, 1947

Principal long fiction

Alexander's Bridge, 1912; *O Pioneers!*, 1913; *The Song of the Lark*, 1915; *My Ántonia*, 1918; *One of Ours*, 1922; *A Lost Lady*, 1923; *The Professor's House*, 1925; *My Mortal Enemy*, 1926; *Death Comes for the Archbishop*, 1927; *Shadows on the Rock*, 1931; *Lucy Gayheart*, 1935; *Sapphira and the Slave Girl*, 1940.

Other literary forms

Willa Cather was a prolific writer, especially as a young woman. By the time her first novel was published when she was thirty-eight, she had written more than forty short stories, at least five hundred columns and reviews, numerous magazine articles and essays, and a volume of poetry. She collected three volumes of her short stories: *The Troll Garden* (1905), *Youth and the Bright Medusa* (1920), and *Obscure Destinies* (1932). Since her death, three additional volumes have been published that contain the rest of her known stories: *The Old Beauty and Others* (1948), *Willa Cather's Collected Short Fiction: 1892-1912* (1965), and *Uncle Valentine and Other Stories: Willa Cather's Collected Short Fiction, 1915-1929* (1973). Many of her early newspaper columns and reviews have been collected in *The King-*dom of Art: Willa Cather's First Principles and Critical Statements, 1893-1896* (1966) and in *The World and the Parish: Willa Cather's Articles and Reviews, 1893-1902* (1970, 2 volumes). Three volumes of essays, which include prefaces to the works of writers she admired, have been published. Cather herself prepared the earliest volume, *Not Under Forty* (1936), for publication. The other two, *Willa Cather on Writing* (1949) and *Willa Cather in Europe* (1956), appeared after her death. Only one of Cather's novels, *A Lost Lady*, has been adapted for the screen. A second screen version of that novel was so distasteful to her that in her will she prohibited any such attempts in the future. Cather's will also forbids the publication of her letters.

Achievements

Over the years, Cather published stories in such national magazines as *Century*, *Collier's*, *Harper's*, *Ladies' Home Journal*, *Woman's Home Companion*, *Saturday Evening Post*, and *McClure's*, the popular journal for which she served as an editor for several years. During her affiliation with *McClure's*, Cather traveled widely gathering materials for stories and making contacts with contributors to the magazine. She helped many struggling young writers to find a market, and she worked regularly with already prominent writers. Cather had been a student of the classics since childhood, and she was unusually well-read. She was also a devoted and knowledgeable student of art and music. She was friendly with several celebrated musicians, including Metropolitan Opera soprano Olive Fremstad, after whom she patterned Thea Kronborg in *The Song of the Lark*.

Known primarily as a novelist, in the late twentieth century Cather has enjoyed a growing reputation as a writer of short fiction. She was awarded the Pulitzer Prize for *One of Ours*, and an ardent admirer, Sinclair Lewis, was heard to remark that she was more deserving than he of the Nobel Prize he won. Cather is particularly appealing to readers who like wholesome, value-centered art. She is held in increasingly high regard among critics and scholars of twentieth century literature and is recognized as one of the finest stylists in American letters.

Biography

Willa Cather was born in Back Creek Valley, Virginia, on December 7, 1873, the first of seven children. Her father's side of the family came to Virginia during colonial terms. Her grandfather, William Cather, did not believe in slavery and favored the Union cause during the Civil War, creating a rift in a family of Confederate sympathizers. Her grandfather on her mother's side, William Boak, served three terms in the Virginia House of Delegates. He died before Cather was born, while serving in Washington in the Department of the Interior. Cather's grandmother, Rachel Boak, returned with her children to Back Creek Valley and eventually moved to Nebraska with her son-in-law Charles, Willa Cather's father, and his wife, Mary Virginia. Rachel Boak is an important figure in Cather's life and fiction. A courageous and enduring woman, she appears as Sapphira's daughter Rachel in Cather's last completed novel and as the grandmother in a late story, "Old Mrs. Harris." Rachel's maiden name was Seibert, a name that Cather adopted (spelling it "Sibert" after her uncle William Sibert Boak) as a young woman and then later dropped.

In 1883, when Cather—named Wilella, nicknamed Willie, and later renamed Willa by her own decree—was nine years old, her family sold their holdings at Back Creek and moved to Webster County, Nebraska. That move from a lush Virginia countryside to a virtually untamed prairie proved to be the most significant single event in her young life. The move was a shock, but a shock that was the beginning of love both for the land and the people, and for the rest of her life, Cather was to draw from this experience in creating her fiction.

Cather always had a special affection for her father; he was a gentle, quiet-mannered man who, after eighteen months on his parents' prairie homestead, moved his family into Red Cloud, sixteen miles away. There, he engaged in various business enterprises with no great success and reared his family. Unlike her husband, Mary Cather was energetic and driving, a hard disciplinarian but generous and life-loving. A good many scenes and people from Cather's years on the farm and in Red Cloud appear in her fiction. Her third novel, *The Song of the Lark*, though its central character is a singer, recounts some of Cather's own struggles to develop her talent amid the strictures and jealousies of small-town life.

Cather's years at the university in Lincoln were extremely busy ones. Lincoln was many times larger than Red Cloud, and Cather gratefully discovered the joys of the theater and of meeting people with broad interests and capabilities. At first she planned to study science but switched to the humanities when she saw an essay of hers printed in the newspaper. While at the university, she was active in literary circles. The year after her graduation,

in 1895, she began writing for the weekly Lincoln *Courier* as well as for the *Nebraska State Journal* and published her first story in a magazine of national circulation, the *Overland Monthly*. Then in June, 1896, she left Nebraska to take a position with the *Home Monthly*, a small, rather weak family magazine in Pittsburgh.

Cather knew she had to leave Red Cloud to forward her career, and even the drudgery of the *Home Monthly* was an important opportunity. Later, she secured a position with the Pittsburgh *Daily Leader*, and she then taught high school English and Latin for five years. It was in Pittsburgh that she met Isabelle McClung, who was to become her dearest friend. For a time, Cather lived with Isabelle and her parents, and in their home she enjoyed the quiet seclusion she needed for her writing. Cather's big break in her journalistic career came in 1903 when an interview with S. S. McClure, the dynamic publisher of *McClure's* magazine, eventually led to an important position that allowed Cather to devote her full energies to the writing of fiction. The publication of *The Troll Garden* in 1905 announced that a major new talent had arrived on the literary scene.

Cather's first novel, *Alexander's Bridge*, was written while she was still with *McClure's*, and it was first conceived as a serial for the magazine. It appeared as a novel in 1912, the year she left *McClure's* to try writing on her own. Still, it was not until *O Pioneers!* came to fruition the next year that Cather discovered herself as a novelist. In this book, she turned to her memories of the Nebraska prairie and wrote powerfully of immigrant efforts to come to terms with the land. In 1920, she began a long and satisfying professional relationship with Alfred A. Knopf, who became her publisher and remained so for the rest of her life.

Cather lived most of her professional life in New York City with a friend and literary associate, Edith Lewis. Her many trips to Europe confirmed her great admiration for France and the French people, an appreciation that receives repeated expression in her novels. She also visited the American West a number of times and drew upon her experiences there for some of her work. She developed a special affection for the area around Jaffrey, New Hampshire, where she liked to go for uninterrupted work. She even chose to be buried there. Prior to her death on April 24, 1947, Cather was working on a novel that was set in medieval France. After her death, the unfinished manuscript, as she had requested, was destroyed.

Analysis

Willa Cather once said in an interview that the Nebraska landscape was "the happiness and the curse" of her life. That statement points up the ambivalence in Cather that produced in her a lifelong tug-of-war between the East and the western prairie. That ambivalence is the central tension in her novels. As long as her parents were alive, she made repeated trips back home to see them and each time she crossed the Missouri River, she said, "the very smell of the soil tore [her] to pieces." As a young woman in Red Cloud and Lincoln, however, she was chafed by narrow attitudes and limited opportunities. She knew that she had to leave the prairie in order to fulfill her compelling desire for broader experiences and for art. Like Thea Kronborg in *The Song of the Lark*, Cather knew she would never find fulfillment unless she left her home. At the same time, however, she also discovered that her very being was rooted in the landscape of her childhood. Thus, going back to it, even if only in memory, was essential and inescapable.

Cather's second novel, *O Pioneers!*, her first to use Nebraska materials, presents the conflict between the land and civilization and the threat of destructive materialism as its major concerns. The novel's principal character, Alexandra Bergson, is something of an earth mother, a being so closely linked with the soil and growing things that her very oneness with the earth seems to convert the harsh wild land into rich acreage that willingly yields its treasures. From the first, she believes in the land and loves it, even when her brothers and neighbors grow to despise and curse it. Two of Alexandra's brothers have such a fear of financial failure that they cannot see the land's potential.

Cather, however, does not simply present Alexandra's struggle and eventual triumph. There is another value, opposed to the land but equally important, with which Alexandra must contend. Her youngest brother, Emil, is sensitive in a way that does not lend itself to life on the Continental Divide, and she wants him to have opportunities that are available only in centers of civilization. His finely tuned spirit, though, leads him to disaster in a prairie environment where passions can run high, untempered by civilizing influences. Emil falls in love with Marie Shabata, a free, wild creature, and both of them are killed by her enraged husband. The book's final vision, however, returns to an affirmation of the enduring qualities of the land and the value of human union with it.

The conflict between the landscape of home and art is played out dramatically in the central character of *The Song of the Lark*. Thea Kronborg is in many ways the young Willa Cather, fighting the narrowness of small-town life on the prairie, needing to leave Moonstone to develop her talent, but needing also to integrate the landscape of home with her artistic desire. Thea has to leave home, but she also has to have it with her in order to reach her potential as an opera singer. Much that she has set aside in her quest for art she must pick up again and use in new ways. In fact, Cather makes it clear that without the integration of home Thea might never have become an artist. Moonstone, however, also has its materialists who obviously stand in opposition to the enduring, if sometimes conflicting, values of earth and art. The only villain of the piece is the wife of Thea's best friend and supporter, Doctor Archie. She is a mean, pinched woman, shriveled with stinginess.

Once Thea has left Moonstone and gone to Chicago to study music, the killing pace and the battle against mediocrity wear her to the breaking point. In an effort at self-renewal, she accepts an invitation to recuperate on a ranch near the Canyon de Chelly in Arizona. There, she spends many hours lying in the sun on the red rock, following the paths of ancient potters, examining the broken pieces of their pottery that still lie in the streambeds. It is there that Thea has the revelation that gives birth to her artist self. These ancient potters made art pieces of their pottery by decorating them. The clay jars would not hold water any better for the artistic energy expended upon them, but their makers expended that energy nevertheless. This revelation comes to Thea out of the landscape itself, and it gives her the knowledge she needs in order to continue her studies: Artistic desire is universal and ageless, and she is a part of it.

Something of an earth mother like Alexandra Bergson, yet more malleable and human, Ántonia Shimerda of *My Ántonia* is for many readers Cather's most appealing character. She becomes a total embodiment of the strength and generosity associated with those who are at one with the land and the forces of nature. Unlike Alexandra, her capacity for life finds expression not only in the trees and plants she tends but also in her many children, who seem to have sprung almost miraculously from the earth. It is in Jim Burden, who tells the story, and to some extent, in Ántonia's husband, Anton Cuzak, that the conflict between East and West occurs. Jim, like

Cather, comes to Nebraska from Virginia as a youngster, and though he has to seek his professional life in eastern cities, he never gets Nebraska out of his soul. Even as a student at the University of Nebraska in Lincoln, he gazes out of his window and imagines there the landscape and figures of his childhood. Ántonia represents for Jim, even after twenty years of city life, all the positive values of the earth for which no amount of civilization can compensate. At the end of the book, he determines to revitalize his past association with the land and yet still tramp a few lighted streets with Cuzak, a city man at heart.

The conflict between the harshness of life on the prairie and the cultural advantages of civilization is also presented in Ántonia's father, who had been a gifted musician in Europe but who now, poverty-stricken and overworked, no longer plays the violin. Ántonia's deep appreciation for Cuzak's quality and for his gentle city ways, as well as her pride in Jim's "city" accomplishments, bridges the gap between prairie and civilization.

The materialists are also evident in *My Ántonia*. In fact, one of Cather's most memorable villains is the lecherous and greedy Wick Cutter, Black Hawk's nefarious moneylender. His last act is to devise a scheme whereby he can kill himself and his equally greedy wife and at the same time guarantee that her relatives will not get a cent of his money.

Even though *Death Comes for the Archbishop* was not Cather's final novel, it was in a very real sense a culmination of her efforts at reconciling the central urges toward land and toward art, or civilization, that are the hallmark of her life and her work. Selfishness and greed are a threat in this book too, but their influence is muted by Cather's concentration on Father Jean Latour as the shaping force of her narrative. He is Cather's ideal human being, by the end of the book a perfect blend of the virtues of the untamed landscape and the finest aspects of civilization.

As a young priest, Latour is sent from a highly cultivated environment in his beloved France to revitalize Catholicism in the rugged New Mexico Territory of the New World. Learned in the arts, genteel in manner, and dedicated to his calling, this man of fine-textured intelli-gence is forced to work out his fate in a desolate, godforsaken land among, for the most part, simple people who have never known or have largely forgotten the sacraments of the civilized Church. His dearest friend, Father Joseph Vaillant, works with him—a wiry, lively man, Latour's complement in every way. Latour must bring a few greedy, unruly local priests into line, but his greatest struggle is internal as he works to convert himself, a product of European civilization, into the person needed to serve the Church in this vast desert land. In the end, his remarkable nature is imprinted indelibly on the barren landscape, and the landscape is imprinted indelibly on his nature. Instead of returning to France in his official retirement, he elects to remain in the New World. His total reconciliation with the land is symbolized in the fulfillment of his dream to build a European-style cathedral out of the golden rock of New Mexico. In that building, the art of civilization merges gracefully with the very soil of the Western landscape, just as Jean Latour's spirit had done.

Cather's work stands as something of an emotional autobiography, tracing the course of her deepest feelings about what is most valuable in human experience. For Cather, what endured best, and what helped one endure, were the values contained in the land, and in humanity's civilizing impulses, particularly the impulse to art. What is best in humanity responds to these things, and these things have the capacity to ennoble in return. Sometimes they seem mutually exclusive, the open landscape and civilization, and some characters never reconcile the apparent polarity. Cather says, however, that ultimately one can have both East and West. For her, the reconciliation seems to have occurred mainly in her art, where she was able to love and write about the land if not live on it. A conflict such as this can be resolved, for it involves a tension between two things of potential value. Thus, in her life and her art it was not this conflict that caused Cather to despair; rather, it was the willingness of humanity in general to allow the greedy and unscrupulous to destroy both the land and civilization. At the same time, it was the bright promise of youth, in whom desire for the land and for art could be reborn with each new generation, that caused her to rejoice.

Other major works

SHORT FICTION: *The Troll Garden*, 1905; *Youth and the Bright Medusa*, 1920; *Obscure Destinies*, 1932; *The Old Beauty and Others*, 1948; *Willa Cather's Collected Short Fiction: 1892-1912*, 1965; *Uncle Valentine and Other Stories: Willa Cather's Collected Short Fiction, 1915-1929*, 1973.

POETRY: *April Twilights*, 1903.

NONFICTION: *Not Under Forty*, 1936; *Willa Cather on Writing*, 1949; *Willa Cather in Europe*, 1956; *The Kingdom of Art: Willa Cather's First Principles and Critical Statements, 1893-1896*, 1966; *The World and the Parish: Willa Cather's Articles and Reviews, 1893-1902*, 1970 (2 volumes).

MISCELLANEOUS: *Writings from Willa Cather's Campus Years*, 1950.

Bibliography

Bloom, Edward A., and Lillian D. Bloom. *Willa Cather's Gift of Sympathy*. Carbondale: Southern Illinois University Press, 1962.

Bloom, Harold, ed. *Modern Critical Views: Willa Cather*. New York: Chelsea House, 1985.

Carlin, Deborah. *Cather, Canon and the Politics of Reading*. Amherst: University of Massachusetts Press, 1993.

Fryer, Judith. *Felicitous Space: The Imaginative Structures of Edith Wharton and Willa Cather*. Chapel Hill: University of North Carolina Press, 1986.

Gerber, Philip. *Willa Cather*. Boston: Twayne, 1975.

Middleton, Jo Ann. *Willa Cather's Modernism: A Study of Style and Technique*. Rutherford, N.J.: Fairleigh Dickinson University Press, 1990.

Murphy, John. *Critical Essays on Willa Cather*. Boston: G. K. Hall, 1984.

Stouck, David. *Willa Cather's Imagination*. Lincoln: University of Nebraska Press, 1975.

KATE CHOPIN

Born: St. Louis, Missouri; February 8, 1851   **Died:** St. Louis, Missouri; August 22, 1904

Principal long fiction

At Fault, 1890; *The Awakening*, 1899.

Other literary forms

In addition to her novels, Kate Chopin wrote nearly fifty poems, approximately one hundred stories and vignettes, and a small amount of literary criticism. Chopin's most important work, apart from her novels, lies in the short-story form. It was for her short stories that she was chiefly known in her time. Many of her mature stories are included in the two volumes published during her lifetime—*Bayou Folk* (1894) and *A Night in Acadie* (1897). All the stories and sketches have been made available in *The Complete Works of Kate Chopin* (1969). Had she never written *The Awakening*, these stories alone, the best of which are inimitable and gemlike, would ensure Chopin a place among the notable writers of the 1890's.

Achievements

Chopin's reputation today rests on three books—her two short-story collections, *Bayou Folk* and *A Night in Acadie*, and her mature novel, *The Awakening*. *Bayou Folk* collects most of her fiction of the early 1890's set in Nachitoches (pronounced Nack-i-tosh) Parish. Not all the stories in *Bayou Folk* are perfectly achieved, but three of the stories in this volume—"Beyond the Bayou," "Désirée's Baby," and "Madame Célestin's Divorce"—are among her most famous and most frequently anthologized. *A Night in Acadie* collects Chopin's stories from the middle and late 1890's, differing from *Bayou Folk* somewhat in the greater emphasis it gives to the erotic drives of its characters.

Chopin's authority in this aspect of experience, and her concern with the interaction of the deeply inward upon the outward life, set her work apart from other local-color writing of the time. In her early novel *At Fault*, she had not as yet begun to probe deeply into the psychology of her characters. David Hosmer and Thérèse Lafirme are drawn too much at the surface level to sustain the kind of writing that does best. After she had developed her art in her stories, however, she was able to bring her psychological concerns to perfection in *The Awakening*, her greatest work. Chopin's achievement was somewhat narrowly bounded, but in *Bayou Folk*, *A Night in Acadie*, and *The Awakening*, Chopin gave to American letters works of enduring interest—the interest not so much of local color as of a strikingly sensuous psychological realism.

Biography

Kate Chopin was born Katherine O'Flaherty on February 8, 1851, in St. Louis, Missouri, into a socially prominent family with roots in the French past of both St. Louis and New Orleans. Her father, Thomas O'Flaherty, an immigrant to America from Ireland, married into a well-known Creole family, but his wife died in childbirth only a year later. In 1844, he married Eliza Faris, the fifteen-year-old daughter of a Huguenot man who had migrated from Virginia and a woman who descended from the Charlevilles, among the earliest French settlers in America. Kate was one of three children and the only one to live to mature years. In 1855, tragedy struck when Thomas O'Flaherty, a director of the Pacific Railroad, was killed in a train wreck. In 1860, Kate entered the St. Louis Academy of the Sacred Heart, a Catholic institution where French history, language, and culture were stressed—as they were, also, in her own household. Such an early absorption in French culture would eventually influence Chopin's own writing, an adaptation in some ways of French forms to American themes.

In 1870, Chopin was introduced to St. Louis society.

The following year, she made a trip to New Orleans and met Oscar Chopin, whom she married in 1871. The couple moved to New Orleans, where Chopin's husband was a cotton factor (a businessman who financed the raising of cotton and transacted its sale). Oscar Chopin prospered at first, but in 1878 and 1879, the period of the great "Yellow Jack" epidemic and of disastrously poor harvests, he suffered reverses. The Chopin family then went to live in rural Louisiana, where, at Cloutierville, Oscar Chopin managed some small plantations he owned. The Chopin marriage was an unusually happy one, and in time Kate became the mother of six children. This period in Kate's life ended, however, in 1883 with the sudden death, from swamp fever, of her husband. A widow at thirty, Chopin remained at Cloutierville for a year, overseeing her husband's property, and then moved to St. Louis, where she remained for the rest of her life. She began to write in 1888, while still rearing her children, and in the following year she made her first appearance in print. Her marriage proved to be much more than an "episode" in her life, for it is from this period in New Orleans and Nachitoches Parish that she drew her best literary material and her strongest inspiration.

Chopin's first novel, *At Fault*, was published by a St. Louis company at her own expense. She then wrote a second novel, *Young Dr. Gosse*, which in 1891 she sent out to a number of publishers—all of whom refused it—and which she later destroyed. She then concentrated on the shorter forms of fiction, writing stories, sketches, and vignettes. By 1894, her stories began to find a reception in eastern magazines, notably in *Vogue*, *The Atlantic Monthly*, and *Century*. In the same year, her first short-story collection, *Bayou Folk*, was published by Houghton Mifflin to favorable reviews. Even so, because short-story collections were not commercially profitable, she had difficulty placing her second collection, *A Night in Acadie*, which was brought out by a relatively little-known publisher in Chicago in 1897. Although having achieved some reputation as an author of what were generally perceived to be local-color stories set in northern Louisiana, Chopin was still far from having established herself as a writer whose work was commercially profitable. Under the advice of editors that a longer work would have a broader appeal, she turned again to the novel form, publishing *The Awakening* in 1899. *The Awakening*, however, received uniformly unfavorable reviews, and in some cities was banned from library shelves. In St. Louis, Chopin was cut by friends and refused membership in a local fine arts club. Chopin had never expected such a storm of condemnation and was deeply hurt by the experience. She wrote little thereafter and never published another book. In 1904, after attending the St. Louis World's Fair, she was stricken with a cerebral hemorrhage and died two days later.

With her death, Chopin's reputation went into almost total eclipse. In literary histories written early in the century, her work was mentioned only in passing, with brief mention of her local-color stories but none at all of *The Awakening*. Even in the first biography of Chopin, Daniel S. Rankin's *Kate Chopin and her Creole Stories* (1932), *The Awakening* was passed over quickly as a "morbid" book. The modern discovery of Chopin did not begin until the early 1950's. By the mid-1960's, *The Awakening* was reprinted for the first time in half a century, and critics praised it warmly. With the publication of Per Seyersted's *Kate Chopin: A Critical Biography* (1969) and his edition of her writing, *The Complete Works of Kate Chopin* (1969), Chopin's work at long last became fully available. She has been of particular interest to feminist scholars, but interest in her has not been limited to a single group. It is now generally conceded that Chopin was one of the significant writers of the 1890's, and *The Awakening* is commonly viewed as a small masterpiece.

Analysis

Comparable in kind to Gustave Flaubert's *Madame Bovary* (1857), *The Awakening* is Kate Chopin's most elaborate orchestration of the theme of bondage and illusion. Dramatic in form, intensely focused, it makes use of imagery and symbolism to an extent never before evident in Chopin's work. The boldness of her possession of theme in *The Awakening* is wholly remarkable. Her earliest effort in the novel, *At Fault*, asked if the individual was responsible to others or to the self, a question that is raised again in *The Awakening*. *At Fault*, however, deals with its characters conventionally, on the surface only, while in *The Awakening* Chopin captures the deep, inner life of Edna Pontellier and projects it powerfully upon a world of convention.

In *The Awakening*, Chopin achieved her largest exploration of feminine consciousness. Edna Pontellier, its heroine, is always at the center of the novel, and nothing occurs that does not in some way bear upon her thoughts or developing sense of her situation. As a character who rejects her socially prescribed role as a wife and mother, Edna has a certain affinity with the "New Woman," much discussed in the 1890's, but her special modeling and the type of her experience suggests a French influence. Before beginning the novel, Chopin translated eight of Guy de Maupassant's stories. Two of these tales, "Solitude" and "Suicide," share with *The Awakening* the theme of illusion in erotic desire and the inescapability of the solitary self. Another, "Reveil," anticipates Chopin's novel in some incidents of its plot. At the same time, *The Awakening* seems to have been influenced by *Madame Bovary*. Certain parallels can be noticed in the experience of the two heroines—their repudiation of their husbands, estrangement, and eventual suicides. More important, Flaubert's craftsmanship informs the whole manner of Chopin's novel—its directness, lucidity, and economy of means, as well as its steady use of incident and detail as leitmotif. The novel also draws upon a large *fin de siècle* background concerned with a hunger for the exotic and the voluptuous, a yearning for the absolute. From these diverse influences, Chopin has shaped a work that is strikingly, even startlingly, her own.

The opening third section of *The Awakening*, the chapter set at Grand Isle, is particularly impressive. Here one meets Edna Pontellier, the young wife of a well-to-do Creole *negociant* and mother of two small boys. Mrs. Pontellier, an "American" woman originally from Kentucky, is still not quite accustomed to the sensuous openness of this Creole summer colony. She walks on the beach under a white parasol with handsome young Robert Lebrun, who befriends married Creole women in a way that is harmless, since his attentions are regarded as a social pleasantry, nothing more. In the background are two young lovers, and not far behind them, keeping pace, a mysterious woman dressed in black who counts her beads. Edna Pontellier and Robert Lebrun have just returned from a midday swim in the ocean, an act undertaken on impulse and perhaps not entirely prudent, in view of the extreme heat of that hour and the scorching glare of the sun. When Edna rejoins her husband, he finds her "burnt beyond recognition." Léonce Pontellier is a responsible husband who gives his wife no cause for complaint, but his mind runs frequently on business and he is dull. He is inclined to regard his wife as "property," but by this summer on Grand Isle she has begun to come to self-awareness, suppressed by her role as a "mother-

woman." Emboldened by her unconventional midday swim, she goes out swimming alone that night, and with reckless exhilaration longs to go "further out than any woman had ever swum before." She quickly tires, however, and is fortunate to have the strength to return to the safety of the shore. When she returns to their house, she does not go inside to join her husband but drowses alone in a porch hammock, lost in a long moonlit reverie that has the voluptuous effulgence of the sea.

As the novel proceeds, it becomes clear that Edna has begun to fall in love with Lebrun, who decides suddenly to go to Mexico, following which the Pontelliers themselves return to their well-appointed home in New Orleans. There Edna begins to behave erratically, defying her husband and leading as much as possible an independent existence. After moving to a small house nearby by herself, she has an affair with a young roué, Alcée Arobin; Lebrun returns from Mexico about the same time, and, although in love with her, does not dare to overstep convention with a married woman and the mother of children. Trapped once again within her socially prescribed role, Edna returns to the seashore and goes swimming alone, surrendering her life to the sea.

In its own time, *The Awakening* was criticized both for its subject matter and for its point of view. Reviewers repeatedly remarked that the erotic content of the novel was disturbing and distasteful, and that Chopin had not only failed to censure Edna's "morbid" awakening but also had treated it sympathetically. What the reviewers failed to take into account was the subtlety and ambiguity of the novel's vision. For if Chopin enters deeply into Edna's consciousness, she also stands outside it with a severe objectivity. A close examination of *The Awakening* reveals that the heroine has been involved in illusion from the beginning. Edna sometimes meditates, for example, on the self-realization that has been blunted by her role as wife and mother; but in her rejection of her responsibilities, she constantly tends toward vagueness rather than clarity.

The imagery of the sea expresses Edna's longing to reach a state in which she feels her own identity and where she feels passionately alive. The "voice" of the sea, beckoning Edna, is constantly in the background of the work. "The voice of the sea," Chopin writes, "speaks to the soul. The touch of the sea is sensuous, enfolding the body in its soft, close embrace." In this "enfolding," however, Edna discovers her own solitude, and loses herself in "mazes of inward contemplation." In *Moby*

Dick (1851), Herman Melville contrasts the land and the sea, the one convention-bound, the other "open" and boldly, defiantly speculative, but Edna is no thinker; she is a dreamer who, in standing apart from conditioned circumstance, can only embrace the rhapsodic death lullaby of the sea. At the end of her life, she returns to her childhood, when, in protest against the aridness of her Presbyterian father's Sunday devotions, she had wandered aimlessly in a field of tall meadow grass that made her think of the sea. She had married her Catholic husband despite her father's objection, or rather, one thinks, *because* of his objection. Later, discovering the limitations that her life with her husband imposes upon her, she rebels once again, grasping at the illusion of an idealized Robert Lebrun. Edna's habit of idealization goes far back in her past. As a girl, she had fallen in love with a Confederate officer whom she had glimpsed, a noble figure belonging to a doomed cause, and also with a picture of a "tragedian." The last lines of the novel, as Edna's consciousness ends, are: "The spurs of the cavalry officer clanged as he walked across the porch. There were the hum of bees, and the musky odor of pinks filled the air." Her consciousness at the end thus reverts back to its beginning, forming a circle from which she cannot escape. The final irony of *The Awakening*, however, is that even though Edna is drawn as an illusionist, her protest is not quite meaningless. Never before in a novel published in America was the issue of a woman's suppressed erotic nature and need for self-definition, apart from the single received role of wife and mother, raised so forcefully. *The Awakening* is a work in which the feminist protest of the present had already been memorably imagined.

Chopin was not prolific; all but a few of her best stories are contained in *Bayou Folk* and *A Night in Acadie*, and she produced only one mature novel, but these volumes have the mark of genuine quality. Lyric and objective at once, deeply humane and yet constantly attentive to illusion in her characters' perception of reality, these volumes reveal Chopin as a psychological realist of magical empathy, a writer having the greatness of delicacy.

Other major works

SHORT FICTION: *Bayou Folk*, 1894; *A Night in Acadie*, 1897.
MISCELLANEOUS: *The Complete Works of Kate Chopin*, 1969 (Per Seyersted, editor, 2 volumes).

Bibliography

Bloom, Harold, ed. *Modern Critical Views: Kate Chopin*. New York: Chelsea House, 1987.

Bonner, Thomas, Jr. *The Kate Chopin Companion*. New York: Greenwood Press, 1988.

Boren, Lynda S., and Sara deSaussure Davis, eds. *Kate Chopin Reconsidered: Beyond the Bayou*. Baton Rouge: Louisiana State University Press, 1993.

Ewell, Barbara. *Kate Chopin*. New York: Frederick Ungar, 1986.

Koloski, Bernard, ed. *Approaches to Teaching Chopin's "The Awakening."* New York: Modern Language Association of America, 1988.

Martin, Wendy, ed. *New Essays on "The Awakening."* New York: Cambridge University Press, 1988.

Seyersted, Per. *Kate Chopin: A Critical Biography*. Baton Rouge: Louisiana State University Press, 1969.

Skaggs, Peggy. *Kate Chopin*. Boston: Twayne, 1985.

Toth, Emily. *Kate Chopin*. New York: William Morrow, 1990.

AGATHA CHRISTIE

Born: Torquay, Devon, England; September 15, 1890   **Died:** Wallingford, England; January 12, 1976

Principal long fiction

The Mysterious Affair at Styles: A Detective Story, 1920; *The Secret Adversary*, 1922; *The Murder on the Links*, 1923; *The Man in the Brown Suit*, 1924; *The Secret of Chimneys*, 1925; *The Murder of Roger Ackroyd*, 1926; *The Big Four*, 1927; *The Mystery of the Blue Train*, 1928; *The Seven Dials Mystery*, 1929; *The Murder at the Vicarage*, 1930; *Giants' Bread*, 1930 (as Mary Westmacott); *The Sittaford Mystery*, 1931 (published in the United States as *The Murder at Hazelmoor*); *The Floating Admiral*, 1932 (with others); *Peril at End House*, 1932; *Lord Edgware Dies*, 1933 (published in the United States as *Thirteen at Dinner*); *Murder on the Orient Express*, 1934 (published in the United States as *Murder on the Calais Coach*); *Murder in Three Acts*, 1934; *Why Didn't They Ask Evans?*, 1934 (published in the United States as *Boomerang Clue*, 1935; *Unfinished Portrait*, 1934 (as Mary Westmacott); *Death in the Clouds*, 1935 (published in the United States as *Death in the Air*); *The A.B.C. Murders: A New Poirot Mystery*, 1936; *Cards on the Table*, 1936; *Murder in Mesopotamia*, 1936; *Death on the Nile*, 1937; *Dumb Witness*, 1937 (published in the United States as *Poirot Loses a Client*); *Appointment with Death: A Poirot Mystery*, 1938; *Hercule Poirot's Christmas*, 1939 (published in the United States as *Murder for Christmas: A Poirot Story*); *Murder Is Easy*, 1939 (published in the United States as *Easy to Kill*); *Ten Little Niggers*, 1939 (published in the United States as *And Then There Were None*, 1940); *One, Two, Buckle My Shoe*, 1940 (published in the United States as *The Patriotic Murders*, 1941); *Sad Cypress*, 1940; *Evil Under the Sun*, 1941; *N or M? The New Mystery*, 1941; *The Body in the Library*, 1942; *Five Little Pigs*, 1942 (published in the United States as *Murder in Retrospect*); *The Moving Finger*, 1942; *Death Comes in the End*, 1944; *Towards Zero*, 1944; *Absent in the Spring*, 1944 (as Mary Westmacott); *Sparkling Cyanide*, 1945 (published in the United States as *Remembered Death*); *The Hollow: A Hercule Poirot Mystery*, 1946; *Murder Medley*, 1948; *Taken at the Flood*, 1948 (published in the United States as *There Is a Tide . . .*); *The Rose and the Yew Tree*, 1948 (as Mary Westmacott); *Crooked House*, 1949; *A Murder Is Announced*, 1950; *Blood Will Tell*, 1951; *They Came to Baghdad*, 1951; *They Do It with Mirrors*, 1952 (published in the United States as *Murder with Mirrors*); *Mrs. McGinty's Dead*, 1952; *A Daughter's a Daughter*, 1952 (as Mary Westmacott); *After the Funeral*, 1953 (published in the United States as *Funerals Are Fatal*); *A Pocket Full of Rye*, 1953; *Destination Unknown*, 1954 (published in the United States as *So Many Steps to Death*, 1955); *Hickory, Dickory, Dock*, 1955 (published in the United States as *Hickory, Dickory, Death*); *Dead Man's Folly*, 1956; *The Burden*, 1956 (as Mary Westmacott); *4:50 from Paddington*, 1957 (published in the United States as *What Mrs. McGillicuddy Saw!*); *Ordeal by Innocence*, 1958; *Cat Among the Pigeons*, 1959; *The Pale Horse*, 1961; *The Mirror Crack'd from Side to Side*, 1962 (published in the United States as *The Mirror Crack'd*, 1963); *The Clocks*, 1963; *A Caribbean Mystery*, 1964; *At Bertram's Hotel*, 1965; *Third Girl*, 1966; *Endless Night*, 1967; *By the Pricking of My Thumb*, 1968; *Hallowe'en Party*, 1969; *Passenger to Frankfurt*, 1970; *Nemesis*, 1971; *Elephants Can Remember*, 1972; *Postern of Fate*, 1973; *Curtain: Hercule Poirot's Last Case*, 1975; *Sleeping Murder*, 1976 (posthumous).

Other literary forms

Agatha Christie published approximately thirty collections of short stories, fifteen plays, a nonfiction book (*Come Tell Me How You Live*, 1946), and many omnibus editions of her novels. Under the pen name "Mary Westmacott," Christie published six romantic novels. At least ten of her detective works were made into motion pictures, and *An Autobiography* (1977) was published be- cause, as Christie told *Publishers Weekly* (1966), "If anybody writes about my life in the future, I'd rather they got the facts right." Sources disagree on the total number of Christie's publications because of the unusual quantity of titles, the reissue of so many novels under different titles, and especially the tendency to publish the same book in England and America under differing titles.

Achievements

Among her many achievements, Christie bears one unusual distinction: She is the only writer whose main character's death precipitated a front-page obituary in *The New York Times*. Christie was a Fellow in the Royal Society of Literature; received the New York Drama Critics' Circle Award for Best Foreign Play of 1955 (for *Witness for the Prosecution*); was knighted Dame Commander, Order of the British Empire, in 1971; received the Film Daily Poll Ten Best Pictures Award in 1958 (for *Witness for the Prosecution*); and was made a Doctor of Literature at the University of Exeter.

Biography

Born at Torquay, Devon, England, on September 15, 1890, the impact of this location on Mary Clarissa Agatha Miller was enormous. Near the end of *Agatha Christie: An Autobiography*, Christie indicates that all other memories and homes pale beside Ashfield, her parents' home in Torquay.

Christie was educated at home chiefly by her parents and her nurse. She taught herself to read before she was five and from then on was allowed to read any available book at Ashfield. She was always allowed to use her imagination freely. Her sensible and beloved nurse went along with her early construction of plots and tales enlisting the nurse as well as dolls and animals to be the characters. Her mother invented ongoing bedtime tales of a dramatic and mysterious nature. Her elder sister, Madge, liked to write, and she repeatedly told Agatha one particular story: It was the "Elder Sister" tale. As a child, Agatha would ask her sister, feeling a mixture of terror and delight, when the elder sister was coming; Madge would indicate that it would be soon. Then a few days later, there would be a knock on Agatha's door and her sister would enter and begin talking in an eerie voice as if she were an elder, disturbed sister who was normally locked up somewhere but at large for the day.

In 1914, Agatha Miller married Colonel Archibald Christie in a hasty wartime ceremony. They had one daughter, Rosamund, whom Agatha adored but considered an "efficient" child. Agatha started writing on a dare from her sister but only began writing novels seriously when her husband was away in World War I and she was employed as a chemist's assistant in a dispensary. Finding herself with extra time, she wrote *The Mysterious Affair at Styles*. Since she was familiar with both poisons and death because of her hospital and dispensary work, she was able to distinguish herself by the accuracy of her descriptions. Several other books followed, which were increasingly successful, until *The Murder of Roger Ackroyd* became a best-seller in 1926. The death of her mother and a divorce from Archie Christie took place about the same time as her success. These sent her into a tailspin which ended in her famous eleven-day disappearance. She reappeared at a health spa unharmed but, to her embarrassment, the object of a great deal of attention; and the public was outraged at the large expense of the search.

In 1930, she married Sir Max Mallowan, an archaeologist. Her domestic life after the marriage was peaceful; in addition, she was able to travel with Mallowan to his archaeological dig sites in the Middle East. This gave her new settings and material for her books and enabled her to indulge in one of her greatest pleasures: travel.

In 1930, *The Murder at the Vicarage* was published; it introduced her own favorite sleuth, Miss Jane Marple, an old woman who observed the village scene. By this time, Christie was an established author, and in the 1940's, her books began to be made into plays and motion pictures. In 1952, *The Mousetrap* was launched in London theater and eventually became one of the longest running plays in that city's history. The film version of *Witness for the Prosecution* received awards and acclaim in the early 1950's. *Murder in the Calais Coach* became *Murder on the Orient Express*, a popular American film.

In 1971, she was knighted Dame Agatha Christie by Queen Elizabeth II and had what she considered one of her most thrilling experiences, tea with the queen. In 1975, she allowed the book *Curtain: Hercule Poirot's Last Case* to be published and the death of her chief sleuth, Hercule Poirot, to occur. By the time of her own death in 1976, more than four hundred million copies of her novels and short stories had been sold, and her works had been translated into 103 languages.

Analysis

Agatha Christie's trademarks in detective fiction brought to maturity the classical tradition of the genre, which was in its adolescence when she began to write. The tradition had some stable characteristics, but she added many more and perfected existing ones. The classical detective hero, for example, according to Ellsworth Grant, is of "superior intellect," is "fiercely independent," and has "amusing idiosyncrasies." Christie's Hercule Poirot was crafted by these ground rules and reflects them in *The Mysterious Affair at Styles* but quickly begins to deplore this Sherlock Holmes type of detecting. Poirot would rather think from his armchair than rush about, magnifying glass in hand, searching for clues. He may, by his words, satirize classical detection, but he is also satirizing himself, as Christie well knew.

Christie's own contributions to the genre can be classified mainly as the following: a peaceful, usually upper-class setting into which violence intrudes; satire of her own heroes, craft, and genre; a grand finale in which all characters involved gather for the dramatic revelation of truth; the careful access to all clues; increased emphasis on the "who" and the "why" with less interest in the "how"; heavy use of dialogue and lightning-quick description, which create a fast-paced, easy read; a consistent moral framework for the action; and the willingness to allow absolutely any character to be guilty, a precedent-setting break with the tradition. Her weakness, contemporary critics claim, is in her barely two-dimensional characters and in their lack of psychological depth.

Although *The Mysterious Affair at Styles* is marred by overwriting and explanations that Christie sheds in later books, it shows signs of those qualities that would make her great. The book is narrated in the first person by Hastings, who comes to visit his old friend John Cavendish and finds him dealing with a difficult family situation. His mother married a man who everyone agrees is a fortune hunter. Shortly afterward, she dies of poison in full view of several family members, calling her husband's name. Hastings runs into Hercule Poirot at the post office; an old acquaintance temporarily residing at Styles, he is a former police inspector from Belgium. (Christie's idea in this first novel seems to be that Hastings will play Watson to Poirot's Holmes, although she quickly tires of this arrangement and in a later book ships Hastings off to Argentina.)

Every obvious clue points to the husband as the murderer. Indeed, he *is* the murderer and has made arrange-ments with an accomplice so that he will be brought to a speedy trial. At the trial, it would then be revealed that the husband had an absolute alibi for the time when the poison must have been administered; hence, he and his accomplice try to encourage everyone to think him guilty. Poirot delays the trial and figures out that the real poison was in the woman's own medicine, which contained a substance that would only become fatal if released from other elements. It then would settle to the bottom of the bottle and the last dose would be lethal. Bromide is an ingredient that separates the elements. Bromide was added at the murderer's leisure, and he had only to wait until the day when she would take the last dose, making sure that both he and his accomplice are seen by many people far distant from the household at the time she is declared to have been poisoned. The plot is brilliant, and Christie received congratulations from a chemists' association for her correct use of the poisons in the book.

By the publication of *The Murder of Roger Ackroyd*, her sixth book, Christie had hit her stride. Although Poirot's explanations are still somewhat lengthy, the book is considered one of her best. It is chiefly noted for the precedent it set in detective fiction. The first-person narrator, Dr. Sheppard, turns out to be the murderer. The skill with which this is revealed and concealed is perhaps Christie at her most subtle. The reader is made to like Dr. Sheppard, to feel he or she is being taken into his confidence as he attempts to write the history of Roger Ackroyd's murder as it unwinds. Poirot cultivates Dr. Sheppard's acquaintanceship, and the reader believes, because he hears it from Dr. Sheppard, that Poirot trusts him. In the end, Dr. Sheppard is guilty. Christie allows herself to gloat at her own fiendish cleverness through the very words that Sheppard uses to gloat over his crime when he refers back to a part of his narrative (the story itself is supposedly being written to help Poirot solve the crime) where a discerning reader or sleuth ought to have found him out.

The Body in the Library, executed with Christie's usual skill, is distinctive for two elements: the extended discussions of Miss Marple's sleuthing style and the humorous dialogue surrounding the discovery of the body of an unknown young woman in the library of a good family. Marple, as well as the other characters, comments on her methods. Marple feels her success is in her skeptical nature, calling her mind "a sink." Another character, Sir Henry, describes her as "an old lady with a sweet, placid, spinsterish face and a mind that has plumbed the depths of human iniquity and taken it as all in the day's work."

Through a delightfully comic conversation between Mr. and Mrs. Bantry, the possibility of a dead body in the library is introduced, and, once it is discovered, the story continues in standard sleuth style; the opening dialogue, however, is almost too funny for the subject matter. Ralph Tyler in *Saturday Review* (1975) calls this mixture of evil and the ordinary a distancing of death "by bringing it about in an upper-middle-class milieu of consummate orderliness." In that milieu, the Bantrys' dialogue is not too funny; it is quite believable, especially since they do not yet know the body is downstairs.

In *Sleeping Murder*, written several years before its 1977 publication date, Christie achieves more depth in her portrayal of characters than before: Gwenda, her dead stepmother, Dr. Kennedy, and some of the minor characters such as Mr. Erskine are excellent examples. The motivation in the book is, at least, psychological as opposed to murder for money or personal gain, which are the usual motives in Christie's novels. There seems, in short, to be much more probing into the origin and motivation of her characters' actions. The novel ends with the romantic young couple and the wise old Miss Marple conversing on the front porch of a hotel in Torquay, Christie's beloved birthplace. Christie came full circle, celebrating her romantic and impulsive youth and her pleasant old age in one final reunion at home in Torquay, England.

Other major works

SHORT FICTION: *Poirot Investigates*, 1924; *Partners in Crime*, 1929; *The Mysterious Mr. Quin*, 1930; *The Thirteen Problems*, 1932 (published in the United States as *The Tuesday Club Murders*, 1933); *The Hound of Death and Other Stories*, 1933; *The Listerdale Mystery and Other Stories*, 1934; *Parker Pyne Investigates*, 1934 (published in the United States as *Mr. Parker Pyne, Detective)*; *Murder in the Mews and Other Stories*, 1937 (published in the United States as *Dead Man's Mirror and Other Stories)*; *The Regatta Mystery and Other Stories*, 1939; *The Labours of Hercules: Short Stories*, 1947 (published in the United States as *Labors of Hercules: New Adventures in Crime by Hercule Poirot)*; *The Witness for the Prosecution and Other Stories*, 1948; *Three Blind Mice and Other Stories*, 1950; *Under Dog and Other Stories*, 1951; *The Adventures of the Christmas Pudding, and Selection of Entrées*, 1960; *Double Sin and Other Stories*, 1961; *13 for Luck: A Selection of Mystery Stories for Young Readers*, 1961; *Star over Bethlehem and Other Stories*, 1965 (as A.C. Mallowan); *Surprize! Surprize! A Collection of Mystery Stories with Unexpected Endings*, 1965; *13 Clues for Miss Marple: A Collection of Mystery Stories*, 1965; *The Golden Ball and Other Stories*, 1971; *Hercule Poirot's Early Cases*, 1974.

PLAYS: *Black Coffee*, 1930; *Ten Little Niggers*, 1943 (published in the United States as *Ten Little Indians*, 1946); *Appointment with Death*, 1945; *Murder on the Nile*, 1946; *The Hollow*, 1951; *The Mousetrap*, 1952; *Witness for the Prosecution*, 1953; *The Spider's Web*, 1954; *Towards Zero*, 1956 (with Gerald Verner); *The Unexpected Guest*, 1958; *Verdict*, 1958; *Go Back for Murder*, 1960; *Afternoon at the Seaside*, 1962; *The Patient*, 1962; *The Rats*, 1962; *Akhnaton*, 1973.

POETRY: *The Road of Dreams*, 1925; *Poems*, 1973.

NONFICTION: *Come Tell Me How You Live*, 1946; *An Autobiography*, 1977.

Bibliography

Bargainnier, Earl F. *The Gentle Art of Murder: The Detective Fiction of Agatha Christie*. Bowling Green, Ohio: Bowling Green University Popular Press, 1980.

Hart, Anne. *The Life and Times of Miss Marple*. New York: Dodd, Mead, 1985.

Riley, Dick, and Pam McAllister, eds. *The Bedside, Bathtub, and Armchair Companion to Agatha Christie*. New York: Frederick Ungar, 1979.

Robyns, Gwen. *The Mystery of Agatha Christie*. Garden City, N.Y.: Doubleday, 1978.

Wagoner, Mary S. *Agatha Christie*. Boston: Twayne, 1986.

CHRISTINE DE PISAN

Born: Venice, Italy; c. 1365

Died: Probably at the Convent of Poissy, near Versailles, France; c. 1430

Principal poetry

Le Livre du chemin de long estude, wr. 1402-1403, pb. 1881; *Le Livre de la mutacion de fortune*, wr. 1400-1403, pb. 1959; *Cent Ballades*, wr. c. 1410, pb. 1886-1896; "Le Dittié de Jeanne d'Arc," wr. 1429, pb. 1838; *Œuvres poétiques de Christine de Pisan*, 1886-1896.

Other literary forms

Christine de Pisan's oeuvre was not limited to poetry but included an impressive number of prose works as well. Composed primarily between 1400 and 1418, these works cover a broad thematic range and bear witness to a powerful and erudite ability; they include letters, short narratives, memoirs, manuals, autobiography, treatises, allegorical psalms, and meditations. Many represent an expansion and development of ideas expressed initially in her poetry; her early poetic commitment to scholarship, political ethics, religious devotion, and women's rights was amplified in the prose works of her maturity.

Achievements

Christine de Pisan is rightly recognized as France's first woman of letters, professional writer, and feminist. Although scholars of the past acknowledged and respected her ability, modern scholarship has elevated Christine (as she is known by scholars) to a deserved place in world literature. If this recognition has been somewhat tardy, the delay has been the result of the general inaccessibility of her work, spread among dispersed manuscripts. In recent years, however, a number of modernized versions from the original Middle French, translations, editions, and critical studies have dramatically heightened interest in her work. Especially remarkable are her learned vocabulary, her knowledgeable use of mythological allusions, and her feminism.

Christine excelled thematically and structurally in both traditional and innovative forms. As an accomplished lyrical poet, she received acclaim from her contemporaries for her conventional courtly poetry. In this category, for example, she demonstrated mastery of the ballad, rondeau, lay, pastoral, and lover's lament. These poems were designed to please the aristocracy at court through an idealized concept of love. Her skill in writing traditional poetry earned the admiration and support of many important members of the nobility, such as the Dukes of Orléans, Burgundy, and Berry as well as King Charles V. Although she was composing in the conventional style, Christine often interjected her own personality by describing events in her life, by referring to a noble benefactor, or by expressing her opinions on the important issues of her day. In this regard, the works possess a documentary value.

Although Christine's poetry exhibits a high degree of technical mastery, she was never content with virtuosity for its own sake. Central themes of the necessity for justice and responsibility in government, concern for all women, and religious devotion imbue her writings. As a whole, Christine's works bear witness both to a vast knowledge of history and to a profound moral commitment to the age in which she lived.

Biography

Although Christine de Pisan ranks as France's first woman of letters, she was not of French but of Italian birth. Born about 1365 in Venice, she spent only her first years in Italy, leaving her birthplace when her father received the position of astrologer at the court of Charles V of France. Tommaso di Benvenuto da Pizzano, known as Thomas de Pisan after his arrival in France, brought his family to Paris around 1368, and it was there that Christine had an experience that was to shape the course of her lifework. With her father's encouragement, she received the kind of education usually reserved for boys in the Middle Ages. A precocious child, Christine was eager to learn, and this unique educational opportunity proved to be the single most important factor in her life, for it provided the young artist with the scholarly tools and knowledge upon which she was to draw during her entire career. On these early foundations in classical languages, literature, mythology, history, and biblical studies, Christine would build a rich and varied literary edifice. In addition, her educational background influenced her perspective by prompting her to view her subjects in a historical, comprehensive, and ethical light.

Because of her creative talent and her ability to please the court with her poetry, Christine became a favorite and never lacked noble patronage. Yet at age fifteen, in 1380, she married not a nobleman but a court notary from Picardy, Étienne de Castel. According to *Lavision-Christine* (wr. 1405, pb. 1969), an autobiographical work, it was a happy marriage, and the couple had three children. Two extremely unhappy events sharply influenced Christine's life and career before she was twenty-five years old. The first of these was the death of Charles V in 1380 and the subsequent government during the minority of Charles VI. During the regency period of the Dukes of Bourbon and Burgundy, Christine's father lost his court position. This demotion meant a loss of prestige as well as severe financial losses from which the scholar and former court astrologer never recovered. A few years later, in 1385, Thomas de Pisan died. Then, in 1389 or 1390, a second, even more devastating, event occurred when Christine's husband died in an epidemic. Thus, her ten-year marriage came to an abrupt end, leaving her with the heavy responsibility of rearing three children alone.

Instead of lamenting the loss of those who had supported and encouraged her literary talents. Christine turned to her art as a source of income as well as a refuge from grief. She was successful in her literary pursuits and regained noble patronage, moving gradually yet not exclusively into prose and producing a wide range of works. Although it is difficult to reconstruct her biography for these years, it is thought that she entered the Dominican convent at Poissy around 1418, the time of the Burgundian massacres. Scholars base this hypothesis on the description of a visit to her daughter at Poissy in "Le Dit de Poissy" (the proverb of Poissy) in the second volume of *Œuvres Poétiques de Christine de Pisan* (poetic works of Christine de Pisan). She did not break the silence of her retreat until 1429, when she composed the poem "Le Dittié de Jeanne d'Arc" (Joan of Arc). Thus, Christine concluded her literary career appropriately, honoring a woman who, like herself, had risen above adversity to pursue her goals. The exact date of her death is not known.

Analysis

The most striking characteristics of Christine de Pisan's work are her breadth of knowledge and her active engagement of the social and political issues of her day. While these attributes would be considered typical rather than extraordinary in a modern writer, they are indeed intriguing in a woman living at the beginning of the fifteenth century. Clearly, credit for the wealth of knowledge seen in her works must be given to the exceptional education that she received. Nevertheless, an analysis of the artist must include recognition of the artistic sensitivity and the reverence for life which she brought to her career. Because of the broadness of her vision, she transcended the traditional courtly style of poetry in which she was trained and began to include significant personal, political, and moral issues in her poems. Her works weave innovation into traditional background by passing from idealized medieval expression to realistic humanist concerns that are closer in spirit to the Renaissance.

Christine's first published works in verse reveal her conformity to the literary standards of the era. The aesthetic canon governing late medieval poetry did not accept expressions of individual joy or sorrow but instead required these emotions to be placed in a universal framework. Christine's early works demonstrate not only her respect for the existing literary system but also her mastery of it. In her ballads, lays, and rondeaux, there is a harmonious relationship between form and meaning. An example of the traditional mold can be seen in *Cent Ballades* (one hundred ballads). In ballad 59, following the social code of the era, the poet advises young lovers to be noble, peaceful, and gracious. Written in decasyllabic lines, the ballad follows the prescribed form in stanzaic composition, regular rhyme, and refrain. The tone is appropriately elevated by the use of virtuous, abstract vocabulary, and verbs in the imperative and subjunctive moods. This ballad is typical of Christine's courtly love poems in lines of two to four syllables in equally short stanzas. These poems, which in their grace and elegance meet and even surpass the criteria of the times.

At the beginning of her career, Christine was dependent upon the approval of her patrons, and it was important to please them by adhering to acceptable forms and also to amuse them with clever versatility and occasional flattery. She accomplished this by writing a group of rondeaux, very brief poems in lines of two to four syllables in equally short stanzas. These poems on the chagrin of love are typical of the clever, though sometimes exaggerated, metric exercises with which late medieval poets experimented. Christine also excelled at occasional verse; several of her poems in this category go beyond flattery by conveying a secondary message which in the course of the poem emerges as the main theme. For example, in a series of poems honoring Charles d'Albret, a patriotic high constable, Christine salutes his royal lineage, then hastens to one of her favorite and most important themes, the defense of the honor of women, particularly those in need. Although Christine continues to observe the fixed form of the ballad, she transmits her intense interest in her subject through a passionate tone, a concrete vocabulary, and a rhythmic pattern that dramatically emphasizes key words. The contemporary theme is anchored to ancient history as the poet compares the champion of her sex to virtuous Roman Brutus.

Many of Christine's poems are centrally concerned with women's rights. It would appear that the genesis of this theme in her work was twofold, First, as a woman who herself had to work for a living, Christine could identify with women who had suffered misfortune, most of whom did not have her advantages. Many times in her works, she pleads for widows and orphan girls. While Christine's feminism thus had its roots in her own experience, it was also given force by her rejection of widely accepted literary stereotypes of women. She abhorred, for example, the image of her sex in *Le Roman de la rose*

(thirteenth century; *The Romance of the Rose*), where women are portrayed as greedy, inconstant, and egocentric.

Christine's final literary work provides an appropriate conclusion to a survey of her poetic career. In terms of both theme and structure, "Le Dittié de Jeanne d'Arc" represents a culminating point because in it, the poet restates and unites both forcefully and creatively the concerns that inspired her whole literary career. Of the inspirations, the most prominent is religious devotion. The poem, which extols Joan of Arc's mission to save France, is a pious work, praising God's grace and power. Joan is uniquely qualified to champion France because she is God's handmaiden: "Blessed is He who created you!/ Maiden sent from God," exclaims the poet in the twenty-second stanza. Two secondary themes, patriotism and political concern, are welded to the religious motif; they also give the poem documentary value.

The poem reflects the attitude of a nation already weary from what was to be known as the Hundred Years' War (1337-1453) yet exhilarated by the victory of Orléans and the coronation of Charles VII at Reims in 1403. Christine's sense of reality does not allow her to be swept away by optimism. Instead, realizing that there are further civil dangers to be faced, she encourages mutual cooperation between citizens and their king.

The final theme of the poem, yet certainly not the least in importance, is explicitly feminist: The heroine, supported and uplifted by the author's belief that women are able to do all things, confers unity and balance to this hymn of praise. In her enthusiastic expression of admiration for Joan as a woman, Christine employs a range of technical devices that convincingly reinforce her message. Written in sixty-one stanzas of eight octosyllabic lines each, the poem adheres to a traditional stanzaic structure, yet within the stanzas, all formality disappears; marked by exclamations, direct address, rhetorical questions, concrete and picturesque vocabulary, and conversational movement, the style is highly innovative. In this final work, Christine left an eloquent testimony to her accomplishments as a woman and as a poet.

Other major works

NONFICTION: *L'Epistre d'Othéa le déesse à Hector*, wr. 1400, pb. 1970 (*The Epistle of Othea to Hector: Or, The Boke of Knyghthode*, c. 1470); *Espistres du débat sur le Roman de la rose*, wr. 1402, pb. 1976; *Le Livre des fais et bonnes meurs du sage roi Charles V*, wr. 1404, pb. 1936-1940; *Le Livre de la cité des dames*, wr. 1404-1405, pb. 1982 (*The Book of the City of Ladies*, 1521); *Lavision-Christine*, wr. 1405, pb. 1969; *Le Livre des trois vertus*, wr. 1405, pb. 1912; *Les Sept Psaumes allégorisés*, wr. 1409-1410, pb. 1965; *Le Livre des fais d'armes et de chevalerie*, wr. 1410, pb. 1488 (*The Book of Fayttes of Arms and of Chivalry*, 1489); *Le Livre de la paix*, wr. 1412-1413, pb. 1977; *L'Epistre de la prison de la vie humaine*, wr. 1416-1418, pb. 1924.

Bibliography

Bornstein, Diane, ed. *Ideals for Women in the Works of Christine de Pizan*. Detroit: Michigan Consortium for Medieval and Early Modern Studies, 1981.

Brabant, Margaret, ed. *Politics, Gender, and Genre: The Political Thought of Christine de Pizan*. Boulder, Colo.: Westview Press, 1992.

Hindman, Sandra L. *Christine de Pizan's "Epistre Othéa" : Painting and Politics at the Court of Charles VI*. Toronto: Pontifical Institute of Mediaeval Studies, 1986.

McLeod, Enid. *The Order of the Rose: The Life and Ideas of Christine de Pizan*. Totowa, N.J.: Rowman & Littlefield, 1976.

McLeod, Glenda, ed. *The Reception of Christine de Pizan from the Fifteenth Through the Nineteenth Centuries: Visitors to the City*. Lewiston, N.Y.: E. Mellen Press, 1991.

Richards, Earl Jeffrey, with Joan Williamson, Nadia Margolis, and Christine Reno. *Reinterpreting Christine de Pizan*. Athens: University of Georgia Press, 1992.

SANDRA CISNEROS

Born: Chicago, Illinois; 1954

Principal short fiction

The House on Mango Street, 1984; *Woman Hollering Creek and Other Stories*, 1991.

Other literary forms

Sandra Cisneros has published numerous uncollected poems and works of short prose as well as collections of poetry: *Bad Boys* (1980) and *My Wicked, Wicked Ways* (1987). Her writings also include literary criticism.

Achievements

Together with authors such as Ana Castillo, Denise Chávez, Alma Villanueva, and others, Cisneros is one of the literary voices that emerged in the 1980's that was responsible for securing Chicana fiction a place in mainstream American literature. Her collection of short stories *Woman Hollering Creek and Other Short Stories* was the first work by and about Chicanas—that is, Mexican American women—to receive a contract with a major publishing house (Random House). Cisneros was awarded the Before Columbus American Book Award for her first collection of short fiction, *The House on Mango Street*.

Biography

Sandra Cisneros was born in 1954 into a working-class family in Chicago, Illinois. Her mother is Mexican American, her father Mexican. She is the only daughter in a family of six brothers, a fact that she describes as being similar to having seven fathers. Because of close familial and cultural ties with Mexico, the Cisneros family moved back and forth between a series of cramped apartments in Chicago and the paternal grandmother's home in Mexico City. The concept of home or the lack of one would later weigh heavily in Cisneros' writing. The combination of an uprooted life-style with an ever-changing circle of friends, schools, and neighborhoods, and the isolation that resulted from her brothers' unwillingness to let a "mere" girl join in on their play, led Cisneros to turn inward to a life of books. That time spent alone allowed an observant, creative voice to take root in the author.

Cisneros considers her career as a professional writer to have begun in 1974—the year in which she enrolled in a writing class as a junior at Loyola University of Chicago, where she would later receive her bachelor of arts degree in English. It was her tenure at the University of Iowa's Writers' Workshop, however, that proved an invaluable aid in the formation of her own literary voice. During a discussion of Gaston Bachelard's *La Bétique de l'espace* (1957; *The Poetics of Space*, 1964), in which her classmates spoke of the house as a literary symbol complete with attics, stairways, and cellars of imagination and childhood, Cisneros realized that her experience was different from that of her college classmates. Her background was that of a multiethnic, working-class neighborhood complete with drunken bums, families sleeping on crowded floors, and rats. She ceased trying to make her style fit that of the perfect, white, and mostly male image that was foreign to her and, instead, undertook writing about that to which her classmates could not relate.

Cisneros' writing began to receive recognition in the 1980's. She is a two-time recipient of a National Endowment for the Arts Fellowship for Creative Writers for her poetry and fiction. In the winter of 1982-1983, she was a resident poet at the Michael Karolyi Artists Foundation in Venice, Italy. In 1985, Cisneros received a Dobie-Paisano Fellowship.

Cisneros has used her education to foster change within the Chicano community. She taught for three years in a Chicano barrio to high school dropouts. She has also worked as an administrative assistant at Loyola University, where she was involved in the recruitment of minority and disadvantaged students. In 1984, she was the literature director of the Guadalupe Cultural Arts Center of San Antonio, which she made her home.

Analysis

Sandra Cisneros has said that she writes about the memories that will not let her sleep at night—about the stories that are waiting to be told. Drawing on the memories of her childhood and her cultural identity—the rundown, crowded apartment, the double-edged sword of being American yet not being considered American, the sight of women in her community closed in behind apartment windows—Cisneros' fiction avoids any romantic clichés of life in the barrio. Despite the sobering themes upon which Cisneros touches—poverty, sexism, and racism—she tells her stories with a voice that is at the same time strong, playful, and deceptively simple. Cisneros' distinctive style is marked by the grace with which Spanish words and phrases are woven into her stories. Central to her stories is a preoccupation with the house, the community, and the condition of women. Her images are vivid and lyrical. She acknowledges that she was influenced in style by the mix of poetry and fiction in Jorge Luis Borges' *El hacedor* (1960; *Dreamtigers*, 1964). Indeed, while Cisneros herself classifies her fiction as stories that read like poems, critics have not reached an agreement, labeling her works *The House on Mango Street* and *Woman Hollering Creek and Other Stories* alternatively as novels, short-story collections, series of vignettes, and prose poems.

The series of sketches in *The House on Mango Street* offers a bittersweet view of life in a Chicago barrio. Readers follow the young adolescent narrator Esperanza—whose name (as explained in the story "My Name") means "hope" in Spanish and also implies too many letters, sadness, and waiting—as she makes the discoveries associated with maturing. She introduces the reader to her neighbors and her neighborhood, making them as familiar to the reader as they are to her. In the title story, Esperanza explains how her family came to live on Mango Street. The family had hoped that the house on Mango Street would be like the ones they had always dreamed of—with real stairs and several washrooms and a great big yard with trees and grass.

Esperanza sadly explains, however, that their house does not fulfill this wish at all. She is ashamed of her red brick house, as she has been of all of her family's previous dwellings. She succinctly describes the embarrassment that she felt when the family was living on Loomis and she had to show her apartment to a nun from her school. She pointed to the family's third-floor flat, located above a boarded-up laundromat, and suffered the blow of the nun's disbelieving response, "*there*?" From that moment, Esperanza knew that she had to have a house—one that she could show with pride to people as if it were a reflection of herself. She was sure the family would have such a house soon. Yet the house on Mango Street is not that house.

In "Bums in the Attic"—a sketch resembling one of Cisneros' favorite stories, Virginia Lee Burton's storybook *The Little House* (1978), in which the owners of a house on a country hill promise the house never to sell it—Esperanza again speaks of a house of her own. She speculates about the grand home on a hill that she will have someday. As much as she wants to leave Mango Street, she stresses that even in her country home she will not forget from where she came. Her house will not be a secured palace all her own; she will instead offer her attic to the homeless so that they too will have a home.

In "Those Who Don't," the young Esperanza discusses in a matter-of-fact tone the concept of being the other in society. She knows that people who happen into her neighborhood think that her community is dangerous, but she knows her neighbors by name and she knows their backgrounds. Among her Latino friends she feels safe. Yet Esperanza can understand the stranger's apprehension, for when she and her family venture out of the security of their neighborhood, their bodies get tense and their eyes look straight ahead.

Cisneros' concern for the place women hold in Latino society is evident in the powerful story "Alicia Who Sees Mice." Alicia, Esperanza's friend, must rise early every morning "with the tortilla star" and the mice in the kitchen to make her father's lunch-box tortillas. Alicia's mother had died, and, Esperanza remarks, Alicia has inherited her mother's "rolling pin and sleepiness." Alicia has dreams of escaping this life, however, with a university education. She studies hard all night with the mice that her father says do not exist. With its precise imagery, "Alicia Who Sees Mice" is at once a criticism of patriarchal oppression of women and a beacon for those women who would struggle to break away from that oppression.

The theme of education and writing as a means whereby women can escape from the barrio is also found in "Minerva Writes Poems." Minerva is only a bit older than Esperanza, "but already she has two kids and a husband who left . . . and keeps leaving." Minerva's husband reappears sporadically, but their reunion usually ends in violence and abuse. Minerva cries every day over her bad situation and writes poems at night. In an act of artistic and sisterly solidarity, she and Esperanza read their poems to each other, yet at this point, Esperanza feels helpless, unable to stop the beatings. In her reply, "There is nothing *I* can do," there is a sense that Esperanza is inciting Minerva to take action for herself as well as implying that society itself must change its attitudes.

Esperanza's passage into adulthood is not without setbacks. In "Red Clowns," she goes to the amusement park with her friend Sally. When Sally goes off with her boyfriend and tells Esperanza to wait for them by the red clowns, Esperanza is abducted and raped by a man who tells her, "I love you Spanish girl, I love you." She is angry and sad and confused over the loss of her innocence. She cannot understand why everyone told her that sex would be so wonderful when, in fact, she found nothing pleasant about the man's dirty fingernails and sour breath. She wants to forget that degrading experience; she does not want to speak its horror. She yells at her friend Sally for leaving her, but she also directs her anger at a society that is partner to such an awful lie.

Likewise, the stories of *Woman Hollering Creek and Other Stories* offer a glimpse into the lives of women who must confront daily the triple bind of not being considered Mexican, not being considered American, and not being male. Cisneros has said that while the pieces of *Woman Hollering Creek and Other Stories* function individually, there is a single, unifying thread of vision and experience that runs throughout the collection. While the names of narrators change with each work, each narrator retains a strong, determined, if not rebellious voice.

In "Eleven," eleven-year-old Rachel's birthday prompts her to consider what it means to grow older. The wisdom of her eleven years has taught her that it is the years "underneath" the birthday, like the rings inside a tree trunk, that makes one a certain age. When people want to cry, she reasons, it is the part of them that is three that makes them cry; when they are scared, it is attributable to the part in them that is five. For this reason, Rachel explains, she was not able to act eleven years old today in school when her teacher wrongly accused her of forgetting an ugly red sweater that had been in the coatroom for a month. All the years were welling up inside her, preventing Rachel from telling everyone that it is not her sweater. Instead, she is silent. She tries to be happy and remember that today she is eleven, and that

her mother will have a cake for her when she goes home. The part of Rachel that is three, however, comes out in front of the class instead. She wishes she were anything but eleven.

The narrator of the chilling "One Holy Night" is an adolescent girl who sells fruits and vegetables from her grandmother's pushcart. She meets a wanderer named Chaq who tells her that he is a descendant of a long line of Mayan kings. Intrigued by his story, the young woman begins to follow Chaq to his little room behind an automobile garage after she has sold each day's produce. Chaq spins mystic tales of the past and future greatness of his family's lineage as he entices the girl into her first sexual experience. She returns home to her grandmother and uncle a changed woman, barely able to contain her excitement. The young woman's secret, however, is soon discovered; she is pregnant. The family, in total disgrace, attempts to locate Chaq, who has since left town. Her uncle writes a letter in the hope of finding the man who could correct his niece's ruined life. A response arrives from Chaq's sister. She explains that her brother's name is actually Chato, which means "fat-face"; he is thirty-seven, not at all Mayan, and not at all royal. The girl's family sends her to Mexico to give birth and to avoid disgrace. It is later learned that Chato has been captured and charged with the deaths of eleven women. The girl appears unfazed by the news, however, and continues to plan her dreams of children. She becomes indifferent to love.

The collection's title story is one of its strongest. It is a story of Cleófilas, a woman reared in a small town in Mexico not far from the Texas border. Cleófilas dreams of the ubiquitous passion of the soap operas that she watches at her girlfriend's house. Her romantic fantasy is realized when she meets Juan Pedro, a Texan who wants to marry her right away, "without a long engagement since he can't take off too much time from work." Cleófilas is whisked away across the border to Seguin, Texas, a town like so many others, with nothing of interest to walk to, "built so that you have to depend on husbands."

Life on "the other side" is, at first, a blessing for Cleófilas. Texas is the land of Laundromats and dream homes. Running behind their new house is a creek that all call Woman Hollering. Cleófilas finds the name puzzling, since it is, like her, so ebullient and pretty. Her enthusiasm for her new life ends quickly, however, with a slap to her face by Juan Pedro. That slap will start a long line of abuse and cause Cleófilas to think flatly, "This is the man I have waited my whole life for." Although she had always promised herself that she would not allow any man to hit her, Cleófilas, isolated at home, not allowed to correspond with her family, hindered by not knowing English, and afraid of Juan Pedro's rage, stays with him. When she begins to suspect that Juan Pedro is unfaithful, she thinks about returning to her native town but fears disgrace and does not act. Cleófilas had always thought that her life would be like a soap opera, "only now the episodes got sadder and sadder. And there were no commercials in between for comic relief." She becomes pregnant with their second child but is almost too afraid to ask Juan Pedro to take her to the clinic for prenatal care. Once at the clinic, Cleófilas breaks down and tells her plight to a sympathetic doctor, who arranges a ride for her and her son to the Greyhound station in San Antonio. The morning of their escape, Cleófilas is tense and frightened. As they pass over Woman Hollering Creek in a pickup truck their spirited female driver lets out a Tarzan-like yell that startles her two passengers. On her way back to her father's home, Cleófilas catches a glimpse of what it is to be an autonomous woman.

Sandra Cisneros' refreshing style is enriched by Spanish-influenced images and phrases. In her fiction, she confronts issues of gender, race, nationality, religion, and economic status. Her characters may have come from a disadvantaged position in society, but Cisneros clearly empowers them and offers a means of confronting the status quo. She has an eye and ear for re-creating scenes particular to her Chicano heritage, yet her themes are universal and accessible to a wide variety of readers.

Other major works

POETRY: *Bad Boys,* 1980; *My Wicked, Wicked Ways,* 1987.

Bibliography

Cisneros, Sandra. "From a Writer's Notebook"; "Ghosts and Voices: Writing from Obsession"; "Do You Know Me? I Wrote *The House on Mango Street*." *The Americas Review* 15, no. 1 (1987): 69-73, 77-79.

_____. Interview by Jim Sagel. *Publishers Weekly* 238 (March 29, 1991): 74-75.

_____. "On the Solitary Fate of Being Mexican, Female, Wicked, and Thirty-three: An Interview with Writer Sandra Cisneros." Interview by Pilar E. Rodríguez Aranda. *The Americas Review* 18, no. 1 (1990): 64-80.

McCracken, Ellen. "Sandra Cisneros' *The House on Mango Street*: Community-Oriented Introspection and the Demystification of Patriarchal Violence." In *Breaking Boundaries: Latina Writing and Critical Readings*, edited by Asunción Horno-Delgado et al. Amherst: University of Massachusetts Press, 1989.

Olivares, Julian. "Sandra Cisneros' *The House on Mango Street*, and the Poetics of Space." *The Americas Review* 15, nos. 3/4 (1987): 160-170.

COLETTE
Sidonie-Gabrielle Colette

Born: Saint-Sauveur-en-Puisaye, France; January 28, 1873

Died: Paris, France; August 3, 1954

Principal long fiction

Claudine à l'école, 1900 (*Claudine at School*, 1956); *Claudine à Paris*, 1901 (*Claudine in Paris*, 1958); *Claudine en ménage*, 1902 (*The Indulgent Husband*, 1935; also as *Claudine Married*, 1960); *Claudine s'en va*, 1903 (*The Innocent Wife*, 1934; also as *Claudine and Annie*, 1962); *La Retraite sentimentale*, 1907 (*Retreat from Love*, 1974); *L'Ingénue Libertine*, 1909 (*The Gentle Libertine*, 1931; also as *The Innocent Libertine*, 1968); *La Vagabonde*, 1911 (*The Vagabond*, 1955); *L'Entrave*, 1913 (*Recaptured*, 1932; also as *The Shackle*, 1964); *Mitsou: Ou, Comment l'esprit vient aux filles*, 1919 (*Mitsou: Or, How Girls Grow Wise*, 1930; also as *Mitsou*, 1958); *Chéri*, 1920 (English translation, 1929); *Le Blé en herbe*, 1923 (*The Ripening Corn*, 1931; also as *The Ripening Seed*, 1955); *La Fin de Chéri*, 1926 (*The Last of Chéri*, 1932); *La Naissance du jour*, 1928 (*A Lesson in Love*, 1932; also as *Break of Day*, 1961); *La Seconde*, 1929 (*The Other One*, 1931); *La Chatte*, 1933 (*The Cat*, 1936); *Duo*, 1934 (*Duo*, 1935; also as *The Married Lover*, 1935); *Julie de Carneilhan*, 1941 (English translation, 1952); *Gigi*, 1944 (English translation, 1952); *7 by Colette*, 1955 (includes short fiction).

Other literary forms

Much of Colette's work defies ready classification. Aside from creating tales that are of such a length as to make it difficult to decide whether to term them short novels or long short stories (the term *nouvelle*, which Colette often used for her work, means both "novelette" and "novella"), Colette also frequently mixed fiction with fact in a confusing blend. *La Maison de Claudine* (1922; *My Mother's House*, 1953), for example, can pass for fiction; however, the book is essentially a series of sketches from Colette's life, primarily dealing with her mother, the famous Sido. Indeed, it has been observed that almost every page of this author's very personal writing contains something that can be traced to her life. Her works include, besides a number of short stories, a variety of reminiscences, adaptations of her tales for the stage and the cinema, and virtually unclassifiable publications on life as a music-hall performer, on cats, on writing, and on life in general. *Œuvres complètes de Colette*, the "complete" works of Colette (prepared under the eye of the author, who excised a number of titles that she considered unworthy of republication), published from 1948 to 1950, fill fifteen large volumes; these do not contain a sizable correspondence, most of which has been published separately.

Achievements

One indication of Colette's persisting appeal is the impressive number of republications of her chief works, including a sometimes bewildering array of retranslations. In her lifetime, she enjoyed an enormous popularity with everyday readers and eventually was recognized by the literary establishment as a genuine talent. She was elected to the Académie Goncourt (1945) and was the first woman to serve as its president (1949); she was given the Grand Cross of the Légion d'Honneur (1953); and she was the first woman in France to be accorded a state funeral. Perhaps a more significant index of Colette's literary importance is the record of her friendships with towering figures such as Marcel Proust and André Gide, both of whom admired her work. Since her death, numerous biographical and critical studies have attested Colette's impact on French letters and on world literature.

Biography

For a woman who was to become something of a symbol of feminism, Sidonie-Gabrielle Colette was born into the most unlikely surroundings. Saint-Sauveur-en-Puisaye was a small village in Burgundy, and little Sidonie grew up as a country girl—she retained a strong Burgundian accent until her death. Her mother, whose tremendous influence on Colette's life cannot be overestimated, was Adèle-Sidonie Landoy Robineau-Duclos, referred to as "Sido." She had two children by her first husband, Jules. After he died in 1865, she married Captain Jules-Joseph Colette and bore two more children: a ne'er-do-well son, Léopold, and Sidonie-Gabrielle, who made her mother famous.

Young Colette's family life was reasonably happy, although her father was somewhat shiftless. Through neglect and mismanagement, the Colette fortune was lost by 1890, forcing the family to move to a nearby village, to the home of Colette's half brother, Doctor Achille Robineau-Duclos. The move and the change in the family finances caused Colette to leave school at age sixteen, and her formal education ended at that point, although she continued to be an enthusiastic reader for the rest of her life, two of her favorite authors being Honoré de Balzac and Proust. Little is known of her life for the four years between the end of her schooling and her meeting with Henri Gauthier-Villars (known as Willy, one of his favorite pen names), who was to become her first husband. He was a gifted editor whose management of ghostwriters amounted to a career. After hearing his wife tell of her school days, he suggested that she write down some of the incidents, adding some spicy touches to make them more interesting. These sketches were to constitute her first published work, *Claudine at School*, which enjoyed a striking popular success.

Because of the success of *Claudine at School*, Willy forced Colette to turn out three sequels, one every year. The marriage, however, was not as successful as the series: Colette was simply too independent to live in Willy's shadow. They separated in 1906, and the divorce was finalized in 1910, by which time Colette was no longer the provincial girl who had to be introduced to Paris. As early as 1903, she had taken lessons in mime, and she appeared in several stage productions, the sensuality of which created something of a scandal but which enabled her to support herself. Also, she had met Henri de Jouvenel, the aristocratic editor of *Le Matin*, a leading newspaper, to which Colette contributed articles for many years.

Meanwhile, she continued writing, for herself rather than for Willy and under her permanent pen name, Colette; her novel *The Vagabond* was given serious consideration by the prize committee of the Académie Goncourt. The story of the rest of Colette's life is chiefly literary, the only striking personal note being her intimate friendships with several women (notably the Marquise de Belboeuf, nicknamed "Missy") and her amicable divorce in 1924 from Jouvenel, whom she had married in 1912. Aside from her writing, Colette's other activities were chiefly mime and, later, dramatic performances (occasionally in dramatized versions of her own works). As honors were offered to her and as her reputation grew, not only in France but also in England and the United States, Colette became something of a national treasure.

In 1924, Colette had met the much younger Maurice Goudeket. They were married in 1935 and had a very happy life together until her death in 1954. Perhaps the greatest irony of Colette's life story was the refusal of the Catholic church to allow her a religious funeral because of her two divorces. The funeral was one of the largest Paris had ever seen. It was noted that most of the mourners were women, evidently paying homage to the woman who had given them a voice.

Analysis

Almost all Colette's stories are told in the first person, a phenomenon that has encouraged autobiographical interpretations but that also gives her texts an impressive immediacy and warmth. Yet her detachment—refusal to theorize about life accompanied by a reluctance to judge other people and their modes of life—provided her with a sort of aesthetic distance from her subjects which helped to counter the elements of personal involvement that infuse her fiction. The most notable example of Colette's abandonment of the first person is the novel that many critics believe to be her masterpiece, *Chéri*, which, along with its sequel, *The Last of Chéri*, is possibly the closest thing to a truly "modern" novel in her entire canon. The modernity of *Chéri*, can be ascribed in part to the relatively detached tone of the narrative. All the emotion in this tragic story is felt only in relation to the characters; the author does not intrude at all.

Another aspect of *Chéri* that marks it as unusual among Colette's fictions is the fact that the central character is male, although several female characters play important roles in the novel. In most of Colette's works, the women are the outstanding figures; the male characters are often merely sketched in. Colette focuses on the problems and interests of women, particularly in their relationships with men but also in their position as human beings trying to come to terms with loneliness and failure. Again and again in her fiction, she dramatizes the failure of sexual relationships, usually placing the blame on the man but recognizing that the woman also bears responsibility in such matters. Although not a philosopher, Colette came to a number of reasonably profound and often unhappy conclusions about the battle of the sexes. One is that there is no guarantee of happiness in any liaison and that, indeed, happiness is not necessary for a meaningful life. She also concluded that a woman suffers fully only once, when her initial romance fades.

The Claudine series which comprises the first four novels of Colette, though inferior to her later masterpieces, displays several of the qualities that distinguish her work and reveals themes and topics that recur throughout her long career (Claudine, a character first conceived in 1900, has obvious affinities with Gigi, the heroine of the 1944 novella). Claudine is certainly a persona of Colette herself, and much of the first novel, *Claudine at School*, is taken directly from the author's experience, from the almost extravagant descriptions of the lush countryside to the delineation of real people as characters in the plot. (Colette, years later, learned that her portrait of the immoral headmistress, Mademoiselle Sergent, had seriously distressed the model for that character, and Colette regretted her callousness.) The opening novel in the series introduces Claudine as a lively, intelligent, fun-loving fifteen-year-old student whose life at school is enlivened by scandal, such as the "affair" between the headmistress and one of the younger instructors (a relationship that at first disturbs Claudine, since she has suffered from a powerful infatuation with the same young lady). An occasionally unnoticed quality of Colette's writing, her humorous irony, emerges in this first volume most agreeably. When Claudine discovers the "romance" between the headmistress and Mademoiselle Lanthenay (she secretly observes the two women in a passionate embrace), her first reaction is neither shock nor dismay; instead, she comments wryly to herself,

"Well done! No one could say this headmistress bullied her subordinates!" Apart from her escapes to the calming serenity of walks in the woods, Claudine's life is chiefly centered on events at her school. Her home life is quite dull; her father hardly notices her presence, and (perhaps because Colette was in reality very close to her mother) her mother is not on the scene. One feels, despite the frivolous adventures and trivial concerns of the girls, that Colette is sincere when she has Claudine remark, at the end of the novel, "Farewell to the classroom; farewell, Mademoiselle and her girl friend. . . . I am going to leave you to make my entry into the world . . . I shall be very much astonished if I enjoy myself there as much as I have at school."

In *Claudine in Paris*, Claudine and her father have moved to Paris, where she is unhappy at being isolated from the countryside that she loves. In this state of near-misery and surrounded by friends (one of whom was at school with her) who all seem to be engaged in some form of physical lovemaking (even her cat Fanchette is pregnant), including the homosexual Marcel, Claudine is an easy prey for Marcel's father, the forty-year-old roué Renaud. Instead of becoming his mistress, as she has decided, Claudine marries him (a plot turn revived effectively as the climax of *Gigi*). As might be expected, the marriage is not completely successful; in the next volume, *Claudine Married*, a triangle forms: Renaud, Claudine, and Rézi, the attractive woman with whom both of them have an intense love affair. The book ends with a rather contrived reunion of Claudine and her husband. It seems certain that the character of Renaud was at least partly based on Willy, though the happy ending is obviously not autobiographical.

In the fourth Claudine novel, *Claudine and Annie*, Renaud and Claudine are primarily observers of and commentators on the dissolution of the marriage of Annie and Alain, largely the result of Annie's awakening to life during her husband's prolonged absence on a trip to South America. Finally, after much sentimental advice from Claudine and a series of relationships of her own, Annie (who is the primary character in the story) decides to leave. Although this volume, like the others in the series, is marred by an occasional confusion of plot and uncertainty of theme, the Claudine series hints at the profound sensitivity, engaging irony, and perceptive vision of Colette's mature work.

This maturity is evident in *Chéri* and *The Last of Chéri*. The plot of the two volumes is direct and uncomplicated. Fred Peloux, nicknamed "Chéri," is spoiled by his immoral and malicious mother, Charlotte, whose indulgence is encouraged by his extreme good looks. Early in his life, his mother's old friend and fellow courtesan, Léa, becomes fond of the boy and later takes him as a lover, though she is nearly twice his age. When Chéri grows to manhood, his mother arranges a marriage for him to a lovely and acceptable young lady named Edmée. Like nearly every other girl that Chéri meets, Edmée is infatuated with the young man for his beauty (it was Colette's firm conviction that men can possess beauty just as women can), as well as for his talents in making love, developed with Léa's tutelage. The first volume closes with Chéri's resolve to abandon Léa, whom he believes to be no longer an important part of his life.

In the interval between *Chéri* and *The Last of Chéri*, five years have passed, the years of World War I; Colette captures the empty, futile mood of postwar France. Chéri is in gloomy harmony with this mood. He is idle, purposeless, and without substance. Nothing in his previous experience has prepared him for the challenge of creating some meaning for his life. In this vacuum, Chéri begins to think constantly of Léa and believes that he must attempt to revive their old romance, from a time when he felt really alive. In one of the most effective recognition scenes in literature, Chéri confronts Léa and for a time does not even recognize her: "A woman was seated at a desk, writing, her back turned to him. Chéri saw a great back, thick gray hair, cut short, like his mother's, a fat, bulging neck." It takes a few moments for Chéri to realize that this aging figure is his former lover. Léa has simply decided that, since she is nearing sixty, it is time for her to settle down to a comfortable old age. She has stopped dieting and dying her hair and performing the multifarious rituals required by her beauty regimen.

When Chéri finally realizes that his old life is gone and that he is unable to build a new one to replace it, he turns to the only escape possible: suicide. It is a clever touch of Colette's that he performs this ultimate act in a sordid room surrounded by old pictures of Léa as a youthful beauty. The compact development of the plot and the sure depiction of Chéri's decline give the climax a tragic stature; indeed, throughout the two novels, every scene clearly advances the plot and the characterization. Colette never exceeded the mastery displayed in these works. Seldom have such slender materials (the two volumes together occupy only a bit more than two hun-

dred pages) yielded such tragic power.

When Colette published the very short novel *Gigi* in 1944, she had not written a substantial piece of fiction for several years; it had been thought by some that she never would again. *Gigi* was therefore an especially happy surprise. In this, her last work of fiction, written when she was seventy, Colette produced a delightful tale with one of the few happy endings in all of her works. It is also one of her few novels to be narrated in the third person. Because the plot was based on an anecdote told to Colette many years earlier, her powers of invention were not taxed. Two wise decisions helped the novel to succeed: Colette set the story in 1899, and most of the text is in dialogue form. *Gigi* thus benefits both from a charming setting in an uncomplicated distant past and from a liveliness of presentation.

The tone of the narrative is ironic, but cheerfully so. Gigi, having just reached adolescence, is being reared by a grandmother and a great aunt, who are both retired courtesans, to follow in their "professional" footsteps. Fortunately, Gigi is too honest and skeptical to be much affected by this instruction; in the end, she outsmarts her teachers by marrying the bored and wealthy Gaston, whom they had only hoped to persuade to keep her as a mistress. The story abounds in jollity and good humor— it is no wonder that *Gigi* was very successfully adapted as a hit play and an Academy Award-winning film. There is a pleasing irony in that Colette's last story comes, at least in tone and atmosphere, full circle to the innocent ambience of her first novel, *Claudine at School*. Though Gigi's experience is told with far greater skill, she and Claudine seem sisters under the skin and even somewhat on the surface, especially in their eye for the ridiculous, their impatience with pompousness, and their sincere good intentions toward others.

The chief elements of Colette's fiction thus appear at the beginning and the end of her long career. She studied love—young love, ardent love, failed love, married love, illicit love, and also family love—as no other writer ever has studied it. Somerset Maugham once wrote that the truly great authors could see "through a stone wall," so great was their perception of life; he modestly claimed only that he could see very well what was right in front of him, hastening to add that such an accomplishment was not to be underrated. Colette looked at life in such minute detail and with such aesthetic integrity that one might say that now and again she penetrated the stone wall.

Other major works

SHORT FICTION: *Chambre d'hôtel*, 1940 (*Chance Acquaintances*, 1955); *Le Képi*, 1943; *7 by Colette*, 1955 (includes novels); *The Tender Shoot and Other Stories*, 1959.

NONFICTION: *Dialogues de bêtes*, 1904 (*Creatures Great and Small*, 1957); *L'Envers du music-hall*, 1913 (*Music-Hall Sidelights*, 1957); *La Maison de Claudine*, 1922 (*My Mother's House*, 1953); *Ces plaisirs*, 1932 (better known as *Le Pur et l'impur*, 1941; *The Pure and the Impure*, 1967); *Mes apprentissages*, 1936 (*My Apprenticeships*, 1957); *Journal à rebours*, 1941, and *De ma fenêtre*, 1942 (translated together as *Looking Backwards*, 1975); *L'Étoile vesper*, 1946 (*The Evening Star*, 1973); *Le Fanal bleu*, 1949 (*The Blue Lantern*, 1963); *Places*, 1970 (includes short sketches in English translation unavailable in a French collection); *Letters from Colette*, 1980.

MISCELLANEOUS: *Œuvres complètes de Colette*, 1948-1950 (15 volumes); *The Works*, 1951-1964 (17 volumes).

Bibliography

Cottrell, Robert D. *Colette*. New York: Frederick Ungar, 1974.

Crosland, Margaret. *Colette: A Provincial in Paris*. New York: British Book Centre, 1954.

_____. *Colette: The Difficulty of Loving*. London: Owen, 1973.

Goudeket, Maurice. *Close to Colette*. Translated by Enid McLeod. London: Martin Secker & Warburg, 1957.

Lottman, Herbert. *Colette: A Life*. Boston: Little, Brown, 1991.

Marks, Elaine. *Colette*. New Brunswick, N.J.: Rutgers University Press, 1960.

Peyre, Henri. *French Novelists of Today*. New York: Oxford University Press, 1967.

Phelps, Robert, ed. *Earthly Paradise: Colette's Autobiography Drawn from Her Lifetime Writings*. Translated by Helen Beauclark. London: Martin Secker & Warburg, 1966.

IVY COMPTON-BURNETT

Born: Pinner, England; June 5, 1884

Died: London, England; August 27, 1969

Principal long fiction

Dolores, 1911; *Pastors and Masters*, 1925; *Brothers and Sisters*, 1929; *Men and Wives*, 1931; *More Women Than Men*, 1933; *A House and Its Head*, 1935; *Daughters and Sons*, 1937; *A Family and a Fortune*, 1939; *Parents and Children*, 1941; *Elders and Betters*, 1944; *Manservant and Maidservant*, 1947 (published in the United States as *Bullivant and His Lambs*, 1948); *Two Worlds and Their Ways*, 1949; *Darkness and Day*, 1951; *The Present and the Past*, 1953; *Mother and Son*, 1955; *A Father and His Fate*, 1957; *A Heritage and Its History*, 1959; *The Mighty and Their Fall*, 1961; *A God and His Gifts*, 1963; *The Last and the First*, 1971.

Other literary forms

Ivy Compton-Burnett is known only for her novels.

Achievements

Compton-Burnett is a novelist's novelist, much appreciated by her peers. She has been compared by her partisans to figures as various as Jane Austen, Jean Racine, Henry James, Leo Tolstoy, George Eliot, Anton Chekhov, the Elizabethan tragedians, William Congreve, Oscar Wilde, George Meredith, Elizabeth Gaskell, Harold Pinter, and the cubists. Her appeal is to a growing circle of admirers, though her work has enjoyed neither popular adulation nor widespread critical attention. Her novels require slow and attentive reading and make heavy demands upon the reader, yet they do not offer the inviting depths of works such as James Joyce's *Ulysses* (1922) and William Faulkner's *The Sound and the Fury* (1929). Compton-Burnett's modernism is of a different kind: Her works present hard and brittle surfaces, and her style reaches its purest expression in pages of unbroken dialogue, highly stylized and crackling with suppressed emotion. Her uncompromising artistry won for her a small but permanent place in twentieth century world literature.

Biography

Ivy Compton-Burnett always thought she would write, even when she was quite young. She came from a well-to-do family: Her father, James Compton Burnett (no hyphen), was a doctor and direct descendant of the ecclesiastical writer Bishop Gilbert Burnett. Ivy adored her father and from him inherited a love of words and of nature. Her mother, Katharine Rees Compton-Burnett, was the second wife of her father: Katharine became stepmother to five children at marriage and mother of seven more, of whom Ivy was the oldest. Katharine seems to have been the prototype for several of the tyrants in Compton-Burnett's works: She was beautiful, autocratic, indifferent to her stepchildren and distant to her own. The real mother to the children was their nurse Minnie. Olive, the eldest of all the children, was bitterly jealous of her stepmother and of Ivy for her close relationship with their father.

Compton-Burnett's closest companions were her two younger brothers, Guy and Noel (Jim). The three were educated together, first by a governess, then by a tutor, and Compton-Burnett always remained proud that she had had a boy's education. She loved Latin and Greek. In 1902, she entered Royal Holloway College, London University; in 1904, she was awarded the Founder's Scholarship; and in 1906, she passed the Bachelor of Arts honors examination in the classics. Her love of the classic appears clearly in her works: Her plots, with their recurring motifs of incest and family murder, seem straight from Greek tragedy. Her characters often allude to Greek tragedy; her view of life as cruel and ironic is the tragic view of the Greek dramatists, skewed by modern experience and by her own temperament.

Compton-Burnett claims to have written very little before her first novel, *Dolores*, was published. She discounted *Dolores* entirely in later life, uncertain which parts were hers and which were the work of her overly enthusiastic brother Noel. Between the publication of *Dolores* and *Pastors and Masters*, her second novel, is a gap of fourteen years which was filled with family turbulence. After the death of both her parents, Ivy became head of the household and a bit of a tyrant herself. Her four younger sisters and Minnie moved out and set up their own household, which they refused to let Ivy visit. Compton-Burnett's only remaining brother, Noel—Guy had died earlier—was killed in World War I, and the author cared for his widow after she took an overdose of sleeping pills. Around the same time, Ivy's two youngest sisters committed suicide. She herself had a bout with Spanish influenza which drained her energy for some years.

In the early 1920's, Compton-Burnett settled in a flat in London with her friend, Margaret Jourdain, an author-ity on Regency furniture, with whom she lived for thirty years. Jourdain was the more famous and remained the dominant of the pair. The two women traveled abroad together every year, where Compton-Burnett pursued her passion of collecting wildflowers. Every odd-numbered year, with only a few exceptions, she produced a novel. World War II disturbed her greatly: She and Jourdain fled to the country to escape the bombing. When Jourdain died in 1951, Compton-Burnett felt betrayed by her "desertion."

In her later years, many honors were bestowed upon Compton-Burnett. She was made a Commander of the Order of the British Empire in 1951; was awarded the James Tait Black Memorial Prize in 1956; in 1960, received an honorary Doctor of Letters degree from the University of Leeds; and in 1967, was made a Dame Commander of the British Empire. She died in 1969 at the age of eighty-five.

Analysis

Ivy Compton-Burnett has no wide range of style or subject in her twenty novels. Like Jane Austen, she limits her characters to a few well-to-do families in the country. The action takes place in the late Victorian era, though there are few indications of any time period. Scenery is almost nonexistent, and no heavy Victorian furnishings clutter the scene.

Instead, Compton-Burnett concentrates entirely on her characters, not in describing them but in having them reveal (and sometimes betray) themselves in what they do and do not say. Her novels demand more of the ear than of the eye. They have been likened to plays in their spareness of description, narration, exposition, and their concentration on talk. Dialogue indeed is the reason that her novels draw readers and is her chief contribution to the art of the novel. Each chapter contains one event, which is discussed in detail by one family, and then perhaps another, or by the masters in the house and then the servants. Although Compton-Burnett as an omniscient author does not comment on or analyze her characters or their motives, her chorus of servants, children, neighbors, and schoolmistresses do so incessantly. In this way, she achieves many points of view instead of only one.

Compton-Burnett's novels have melodramatic and sometimes implausible plots with murders, incest, infidelity, and perversions of justice. At times, she drops enough clues for the reader to know what will happen; at other times, events occur arbitrarily. Shipwrecked characters often reappear; documents are stolen or concealed only to turn up later. Eavesdroppers populate her novels. Several people, for example, coincidentally walk into a room when they are being slandered. Although the events themselves are often too coincidental, the highly crafted conversations about them prove Compton-Burnett's talent as a writer. These witty and ironic conversations insist on the revelation of truth, on the precise use of language, making Compton-Burnett's novels memorable. Language insulates people against the primitive forces, the unmentionable deeds of which they are capable. Her witty dialogue tends to anesthetize the reader's response (and the characters' as well) to horrendous crimes of passion.

Compton-Burnett's novels explore all the tensions of family life—between strong and weak, between generations, between classes. Power is her chief subject, with love, money, and death as constant attendants. Her main foes are complacency, tyranny, and hypocrisy. Compton-Burnett deplores sloppy thinking and dishonesty, whether with oneself or with others. Her novels clearly indicate her view of human nature. She believes that wickedness is often not punished and that is why it is prevalent. When wickedness is likely to be punished, most people, she thinks, are intelligent enough to avoid it. She also sees very few people as darkly evil: Many people, when subjected to strong and sudden temptation without the risk of being found out, yield to such an urge. Even her bad characters have some good in them. Although the good points of the tyrants can be recognized, their cruelty can never be forgiven. Yet, ironically, their cruelty often produces good results. The victims build up bravery, loyalty, and affection as defenses against the wicked and cruel. Compton-Burnett's novels, above all, elicit concern for human suffering.

Though she does believe in economic and hereditary forces, Compton-Burnett also believes in free will. She is one of the rare novelists whose good-hearted characters are credible as well as likable. The good and innocent characters in her novels, particularly the children, are not corrupted and usually remain unharmed. They conquer by truth, affection, and, most important, by intelligence. Compton-Burnett shows the great resilience of the human spirit; her characters survive atrocities and then settle down to resume their everyday lives. In her novels, the greatest crimes are not crimes of violence, but crimes against the human spirit: one person beating down, wounding, or enslaving another's spirit. Yet her novels do not end with a feeling of despair. They end, rather, with a feeling of understanding. The good characters see the faults of the tyrants yet continue to love them and gallantly pick them up when they have fallen. The good characters realize that evil and good are inextricable.

Compton-Burnett's strengths and weaknesses as a novelist are both suggested by the fact that she has no masterpiece, no best or greatest novel. Her oeuvre has a remarkable consistency, the product of an unswerving artistic intelligence, yet also evidence of a certain narrowness and rigidity. By general consensus, her strongest works are those of her middle period, including *Brothers and Sisters, More Women Than Men, A Family and a Fortune*, and *Manservant and Maidservant*.

Manservant and Maidservant has been the most popular of all Compton-Burnett's novels; some critics have named it as their favorite, and Compton-Burnett even said it was one that she particularly liked. It is less spare than the other novels, with more exposition, more sense of place (a smoking fireplace begins and ends the novel, for example), and fully drawn characters. A story of reformation, it shows strong bonds of affection among Horace Lamb, his cousin Mortimer, and his counterpart in the servants' world, Bullivant, the butler.

Horace, a penny-pincher who makes his children do calisthenics to keep warm in winter, is one of Compton-Burnett's crotchety male tyrants. He often looks aside in apparent abstraction as "punishment to people for the nervous exasperation that they produced in him, and must expiate." His wife Charlotte and his cousin Mortimer plan to run away and take the children with them to save them from suffering. Horace finds a letter detailing their plans and becomes Compton-Burnett's first and only tyrant who attempts to reform. His reformation does not erase the past (his children, in particular, point this out); in fact, it makes the children suffer more because he inevitably has lapses. The ups and downs of being nourished, then starved, torture the children far more excruciatingly than would consistent oppression. Yet Horace draws forth deep love from Mortimer and devoted service from Bullivant. Mortimer explains the tyrant's appeal: "Is there something in Horace that twines itself about the heart? Perhaps it is being his own worst enemy." The wise characters may be victims of the tyrants, but they also understand and pity them.

Mortimer is an example of Compton-Burnett's unmarried, rather impotent characters who attach themselves to their richer relatives in the manor. Mortimer cares more about the children than their own father does. It is these dependent characters who have the strength to challenge the tyrant's ruthlessness, who speak with caustic honesty to expose the tyrant's pretentiousness. They act courageously, even though they must mortify themselves (thus Mortimer's name) and expose their own weakness in the cause of truth. The exploiter needs the exploited, and vice versa.

Manservant and Maidservant introduced an important new element in Compton-Burnett's novels: the servants. Like the children, they can mirror their masters or can serve as a chorus discussing the action. The characters of Compton-Burnett's servants are never better than in this novel: the timid maid; the motherly, nonconformist cook; George, the workhouse boy with grandiose pretensions; and Bullivant, the wonderfully comic butler. Bullivant holds both upstairs and downstairs together with his wry wit and firm hand. He knows everything that has transpired and anticipates what will come. He is also a character of great tenderness and protectiveness, though he hides it under a mask of strict propriety. His devotion to Horace is almost that of an elder brother, though he is always careful to keep his place.

Two important themes of *Manservant and Maidservant* are the conflict between instinct and social conventions and the pernicious effects of do-gooders' meddling. Compton-Burnett had no belief in God, but she was a great supporter of social conventions as necessary restraints on humanity's primitive instincts. The decent majority of people create social and moral rules; the unscrupulous minority violate them. Horace claims that civilized life consists of suppressing one's instincts, but his wife Charlotte corrects him by saying that all life consists of fulfilling them. Charlotte expresses the complexity of Compton-Burnett's vision: "There is so much truth on all the different sides of things."

Compton-Burnett's novels must be accepted on their own terms. She was not interested in realistic dialogue; she was concerned with speech as a means of revealing human character. Her tyrants tend to be careless in their speech, relying on clichés or using words inexactly, just as they are careless in the way they trample moral laws and people. Their victims, who seek truth, always correct the tyrants' misuse of language by questioning the real meaning of the words they use. Whatever her flaws as a novelist, Compton-Burnett was an artist of uncommon intelligence, originality, and control.

Bibliography

Baldana, Frank. *Ivy Compton-Burnett*. New York: Twayne, 1964.

Burkhart, Charles. *I. Compton-Burnett*. London: Victor Gollancz, 1965.

Nevius, Blake. *Ivy Compton-Burnett*. New York: Columbia University Press, 1970.

Sprigge, Elizabeth. *The Life of Ivy Compton-Burnett*. New York: George Braziller, 1973.

Spurling, Hilary. *Ivy: The Life of I. Compton-Burnett*. New York: Alfred A. Knopf, 1984.

SOR JUANA INÉS DE LA CRUZ
Juana de Asbaje y Ramírez de Santillana

Born: San Miguel Nepantla, Mexico; December 2, 1648

Died: Mexico City, Mexico; April 17, 1695

Principal poetry

The writings of Sor Juana Inés de la Cruz were first published in Spain toward the end of the seventeenth century. The initial volume of her works appeared in 1689, the second volume in 1690, and a third and final volume in 1700. No attempt was made to edit and unify her works until Alfonso Méndez Plancarte produced his definitive study and compilation, *Obras completas de Sor Juana Inés de la Cruz*, between 1951 and 1957. The four volumes of that collection include a number of selections omitted from the early editions as well as essays that reassess Sor Juana's place in literary history. Méndez Plancarte divides the works into four main sections, each given a separate volume: I, *Lírica Personal* (poetry); II, *Villancicos y letras sacras* (poetry); III, *Autos y Loas* (drama); IV, *Comedias, sainetes y prosa* (drama and prose).

Other literary forms

Sor Juana Inés de la Cruz's most readable prose work, the *Respuesta de la poetisa a la muy ilustre Sor Filotea de la Cruz* (1700; reply of the poetess to the illustrious Sister Filotea de la Cruz), is an appealing autobiographical defense of her precocious interest in learning, an emotional plea for acceptance as a woman and a scholar, and an obsessive declaration of faith. Sor Juana tries to convince her superiors that, despite her lifelong curiosity about the material world, theological concerns are still the most important to her. *El divino Narciso* (c. 1680; *The Divine Narcissus*, 1945), a religious one-act play, is a tasteful and imaginative treatment of divine love in which Narcissus, as a figure of Christ, falls in love with human nature as a reflection of himself. With this short play, the fantasy of desire which takes so many forms throughout Sor Juana's work finds its ultimate synthesis of *eros* and *agape*.

Achievements

Sor Juana Inés de la Cruz was a Mexican literary virtuoso who was called the "tenth muse" during her lifetime and who is generally considered the most important writer of colonial Spanish America. Although she wrote more than four hundred poems, twenty-three short plays, two full-length *comedias*, and various prose works, Sor Juana's reputation rests on a handful of poems (about two dozen in all), *The Divine Narcissus*, and *Respuesta de la poetisa a la muy ilustre Sor Filotea de la Cruz*. Although a reassessment of her works begun in the 1950's promises a more extensive list of her most important writings, it is likely that, with the exception of her extremely complex "Primero sueño" (first dream), the few pieces that earned for her the admiration of Marcelino Menéndez y Pelayo in the nineteenth century will continue to be the ones that will assure her a place of prominence in Spanish letters.

Biography

Juana de Asbaje y Ramírez de Santillana was born on December 2, 1648, in San Miguel Nepantla, some sixty kilometers southeast of Mexico City. She was the illegitimate child of a Spanish captain and a Creole mother. In the charming *Respuesta de la poetisa a la muy ilustre Sor Filotea de la Cruz*, she tells how she learned to read at the age of three and tagged along with one of her sisters to La Amiga, an elementary school, where she took her first formal lessons. She says that, at the age of eight, she begged her mother to let her cut her hair and dress like a boy so she could attend the university. That being denied her, she continued her self-education by reading the classics she found in her grandmother's house. Around 1659, she was allowed to go to Mexico City and live with the family of one of her aunts. Although not enrolled in the university, Juana privately continued her studies, which included twenty lessons in Latin. Twenty was apparently sufficient, for subsequently she was able to write Latin poetry as well as anyone in the viceroyalty.

By 1664, Sor Juana was a member of the viceregal court and was the darling of the vicereine. She so impressed the viceroy, the Marques de Mancera, with her knowledge, that he arranged for forty professors from the university to give her tests. Sor Juana passed them all, amazing the local elite. Her several years of court life must have been intense, emotional years. She was a beautiful woman and was doubtless wooed by gentlemen of some wealth and position. Nevertheless, by 1669, she had entered the convent and had taken religious vows, as much from aversion to marriage as from attraction to the celibate life. It was her desire to be free to learn, she states in the *Respuesta de la poetisa a la muy ilustre Sor Filotea de la Cruz*, that was the primary motivation for her vocation.

For the next twenty-three years, Sor Juana was the major literary figure in colonial Spanish America, composing everything from love sonnets to a treatise on music, almost all of her writing being done on request from high-ranking officials of the Church or the state. She wrote elaborate pieces for performance at liturgical functions, occasional verse for political events, and scenarios and scripts for afternoons of royal entertainment. Not long after the brilliant defense of her studies in *Respuesta de la poetisa a la muy ilustre Sor Filotea de la Cruz*, and at the height of her career, when her collected works were beginning to be published and acclaimed in Spain, pressures by her religious superiors induced her to give away her library of more than four thousand volumes and all of her scientific and musical instruments, and to abandon her writing altogether. Several years later, on April 17, 1695, she died in an epidemic that swept Mexico City.

Analysis

Sor Juana Inés de la Cruz was a deeply passionate and intelligent woman who dedicated her life to knowledge and spiritual perfection. On the one hand, she seems to have renounced love for intellectual freedom, and from her amatory and philosophical writings, it appears that her renunciation of the world, along with her commitment to learning, paradoxically caused an obsession with intimacy and a profound disillusionment with any reality except that of spiritual intimacy. On the other hand, judging from her other prose and verse, Sor Juana was also a writer engaged with her society, closely involved with its institutions and its native culture. An anthology of Sor Juana's most popular compositions may slight this more social side of her personality, but it is important to remember as one reviews her major poems of love and disillusionment that the poet wrote more concerning religion than about any real or imaginary love, and that she was as adept at elaborate versification about current events and visitors to the viceroyalty as she was at revealing her most private feelings. It is not difficult to dwell on the more romantic side of the "tenth muse," to use certain of her poems to enhance the image of a jilted, precocious, disenchanted teenage intellectual sequestering herself in a convent and spending her life in extremely elaborate sublimation. Her most famous pieces contribute to such an image, but as the reader is exposed to a wider spectrum of her talents, a more balanced picture emerges; a trajectory of maturation becomes visible in which Catholicism and the Baroque are means to the self-fulfillment and self-expression originally thwarted in her youth by her lack of social position and her fascination with scholarship.

If one reads Sor Juana's writings to observe a progression from human to divine love, it is appropriate to begin with the sonnet "Esta tarde, mi bien" (this afternoon, my love). The poem is one of the few in which she relates a moving encounter with another person, and it contrasts the impotency of words with the efficacy of tears in the communication of love. Here, there is none of the love-hate dialectic that colors most of her amatory poems; instead, one finds the description of a delicately feminine, sensitive, and formidably talented personality in a moment of unguarded abandon. It is only a slight exaggeration to say that after "Esta tarde, mi bien," one sees in Sor Juana's verse the psychological effects of an unhappy affair rather than the experience of love itself. Even the tender *lira* "Amado dueño mio" (my beloved master), while documenting in a poetic sense the dimensions of intimacy, is a conventional lament of the lover separated from the beloved. The lover, like a Renaissance shepherdess, tells her misfortunes to the wind, which carries her complaints, her passion, and her sadness to the distant partner. Alfonso Méndez Plancarte states that the poem contains some of Sor Juana's finest lines, and that it may surpass the eclogues of Garcilaso de la Vega. The comparison with Garcilaso is appropriate, and poetry in his likeness is fitting to express the absence of consummation rather than its presence; significantly, the *lira* keynotes a thematic transformation from completion to emptiness.

The sonnet "Detente, sombra de mi bien esquivo" (stay, shadow of my scornful love) can be considered an introduction to a series of poems which admit both the positive and the negative effects of passion, as well as the inconclusive status of unconsummated love. In "Detente, sombra de mi bien esquivo," the beloved himself eludes the poet, but his image cannot escape the prison of her fantasy. Important is the counterpoint of conceits and emotions about the love "por quien alegre muero" (for whom I would happily die), but also "por quien penosa vivo" (for whom I live in agony), which develops to an extreme in the sonnet "Al que Ingrato me deja, busco amante" (I seek the one who spurns me) and "Que no me quiera Fabio, al verse amado" (that Fabio does not love me as I love him), and the *redondilla* "Este amoroso tormento" (this torment of love). In the latter piece, as in the other poems of this group, the poet never finds fulfillment, "porque, entre alivio y dolar, hallo culpa en el amor y disculpa en el olvido" (because between relief and pain, I find blame in love and exoneration in forgetfulness).

Beyond frustration and the love-hate duality that the poet attributes to romantic feeling lie disillusionment and bitterness. The sonnets "Silvio, yo te aborezco" (I hate you, Silvio), "Amor empieza por desasosiego" (love begins uneasily), and "Con el dolor de la mortal herida" (with the pain of a mortal wound) are among Sor Juana's strongest denunciations of the men she once might have loved, as well as of herself for having given in to loving them: "no solo a tí, corrida, te aborrezco,/ pero a mí por el tiempo que te quise" (not only do I abhor you/but myself for the time that I loved you). Here the bittersweet of "Este amoroso tormento" turns to anger. The image of the lover purposely retained in "Detente, sombra de mi bien esquivo" is repeatedly banished, and it is a logical movement from such rejection to the *sátira filosófica,* "Hombres necios" (foolish men), one of Sor Juana's more popular denunciations of men as the source of all

women's problems. In these feminist *redondillas,* the poet exposes the ways in which men "acusan lo que causan" (blame us for the things they cause). Why, she asks, do men want women to be good if they tempt them to be bad? Who, she questions, is the greater sinner, "la que peca por la paga o el que paga por pecar" (she who sins for pay or he who pays for sin)?

Since Sor Juana's poems are not usually dated, there is no way of knowing whether the progression from the delicate, loving "Esta tarde, mi bien" to the sarcastic "Hombres necios" reflects the sequential effects of an increasingly unhappy situation. In any case, these poems of erotic experience do fit a pattern which begins with brief reciprocal affection and degenerates into ambivalence, then finally into contempt. There are, at the same time, a great number of poems written to women that do not fit this generalization. Sor Juana apparently had very meaningful relationships with the wives of two of the Mexican viceroys, and her many verses to Lysi show a far more consistent emotional response than that depicted in poems of male-female interaction. Certainly the Lysi poems, perhaps especially the ornate "Lámina sirva el cielo al retrato" (the sky is lamina of your portrait), are a moving contrast to her more widely read poems' heterosexual canon.

Sor Juana's philosophic poems complement her negative attitude toward worldly love. "Verde embeleso de la vida humana" (green charm of human life) rejects illusions and hope as deceptive: "solamente lo que toco veo" (I only see what I can touch). It represents the repression of vain dreams, the acceptance of life without romance or even platonic fantasy. "Diuturna enfermedad de la Esperanza" (lasting infirmity of hope) reiterates this concept, and "Este que ves, engaño colorido" (this painted lie you see), a sonnet on her portrait, is an intense affirmation of the Catholic view that the flesh is "polvo, es sombra, es nada" (dust, is a shadow, is nothing). Her "Rosa divina" (divine rose) is a variation on the universal theme of the brevity of beauty and life. Perhaps her most powerful renunciation is "Finjamos que soy feliz" (pretend that I am happy), in which she denies the validity of knowledge and maintains that because humanity can know nothing for certain, ignorance is preferable to imperfect knowing: "aprendamos a ignorar" (let us learn to not know). This poem is a moment of despair within the context of Sor Juana's self-confessed lifelong passion, the pursuit of knowledge. Her monumental "Primero sueño," the only work that she admitted to writing for her own pleasure and not to please someone else, is far more balanced in presenting her attitude toward learning.

The "Primero sueño," which is among the best philosophic poems in Spanish, is the height of Sor Juana's exploration of the Baroque. The poem begins with a description of nightfall, in which the entire physical world eventually succumbs to sleep. The human spirit, freed from the constraint of the body, soars upward to find a perspective from which it can comprehend the immensity of the universe. Once it glimpses the overpowering dimensions of creation, the soul retreats to the shadows. Finding a mental shore on the sea of knowledge, it decides to approach the challenge of learning by dividing things into categories and mastering each division separately. In spite of doubts that the mind can really know anything, echoes of the dark vision of "Finjamos que soy feliz," the soul continues its search for truth. Dawn arrives, however, and the dream ends inconclusively. Universal knowledge has eluded the soul, but the dreamer has not despaired.

Sor Juana's religious writings include several "sacred ballads," among which "Amante dulce del alma" (sweet love of my soul), "Mientras la Gracia me exita" (while Grace moves me), and "Traigo conmigo un cuidado" (I have a deep concern) are generally held in high regard. All three attempt to express the effects of divine love. "Amante dulce del alma" asks why Christ might have willed to visit the poet in Holy Communion: Has He decided to be present from love or from jealousy? She decides for the former, reflecting that God, knowing all things, can see into her heart and has no reason to be jealous. "Mientras la Gracia me exita" tries to clarify some of the feelings involved in the inner struggle between "la virtud y la costumbre" (virtue and habit). Like "Amante dulce del alma," this is a poem of scruples rather than a meditation of universal religious significance. "Traigo conmigo un cuidado" carries the analysis of spiritual love further and contrasts it with the poet's experience of human love. "La misma muerte que vivo, es la vida con que muero" (the same death that I live is the life in which I die), she writes at the end of the poem, attempting to sum up her contradictory mental state. Even though it is divine love that causes her to feel the way she does, there are parallels between the *contrarias penas* (contradictory anxieties) of "Este amoroso tormento" and those expressed in "Traigo conmigo un cuidado."

Sor Juana is easily anthologized, but such selectivity does not provide a proper perspective from which to view her talents or interests. The genius of the "tenth muse" offers almost unlimited fare for those who would dwell on the poems and techniques in themselves; similarly, literary historians will hardly want to limit their reading to Sor Juana's "best," but will find the richest commentary on colonial Mexico as well as the soul of the poet herself within the diversity of her complete works. There, instead of a facile trajectory from personal rejection to religion, one finds a maze of subtle rococo revelations.

Other major works

PLAY: *El divino Narciso*, pr. c. 1680, pb. 1690 (*The Divine Narcissus*, 1945).
NONFICTION: *Respuesta de la poetisa a la muy ilustre Sor Filotea de la Cruz*, 1700.
MISCELLANEOUS: *Obras completas de Sor Juana Inés de la Cruz*, 1951-1957 (Méndez Plancarte, editor, 4 volumes).

Bibliography

Abreu Gómez, Ermilo. *Sor Juana Inés de la Cruz: Bibliografía y biblioteca*. Mexico: Secretary of Foreign Relations, 1934.

Chávez, Ezequiel A. *Ensayo de psicologiá de Sor Juana Inés de la Cruz*. Barcelona: Araluce, 1931.

Paz, Octavio. *Sor Juana: Or, The Traps of Faith*. Cambridge, Mass.: Harvard University Press, 1988.

Pfandl, Ludwig. *Sor Juana Inés de la Cruz: La Decima Musa de Mexico*. Mexico: Instituto de Investigaciones Esteticas, Universidad Nacional Autonoma de Mexico, 1963.

Tavard, George H. *Juana Inés de la Cruz and the Theology of Beauty*. Notre Dame, Ind.: Notre Dame University Press, 1991.

Urbano, Victoria. *Sor Juana Inés de la Cruz*. Potomac, Md.: Scripto Humanistica, 1990.

SIMONE DE BEAUVOIR

Born: Paris, France; January 9, 1908

Died: Paris, France; April 14, 1986

Principal long fiction

L'Invitée, 1943 (She Came to Stay, 1949); Le Sang des autres, 1945 (The Blood of Others, 1948); Tous les hommes sont mortels, 1946 (All Men Are Mortal, 1955); Les Mandarins, 1954 (The Mandarins, 1956); Les Belles Images, 1966 (English translation, 1968).

Other literary forms

Simone de Beauvoir's novels as well as most of her other works have been published by Gallimard. Foremost among these is her four-volume autobiography, *Mémoires d'une jeune fille rangée* (1958; *Memoirs of a Dutiful Daughter*, 1959), *La Force de l'âge* (1960; *The Prime of Life*, 1962), *La Force des choses* (1963; *Force of Circumstance*, 1964), and *Tout compte fait* (1972; *All Said and Done*, 1974). Equally important is her monumental sociological study on women, *Le Deuxième Sexe* (1949; *The Second Sex*, 1953). Her most important philosophical essays include *Pyrrhus et Cinéas* (1944), *Pour une morale de l'ambiguïté* (1947; *The Ethics of Ambiguity*, 1948), *L'Existentialisme et la sagesse des nations* (1948), and *Privilèges* (1955; partial translation, "Must We Burn Sade?" 1953). She also wrote a chronicle of her travels in the United States, *L'Amérique au jour le jour* (1948; *America Day by Day*, 1953), a powerful account of her mother's illness and death, *Une Mort très douce* (1964; *A Very Easy Death*, 1966), and a tribute to Jean-Paul Sartre, *La Cérémonie des adieux* (1981; *Adieux: A Farewell to Sartre*, 1984).

Achievements

De Beauvoir was a presence felt in French intellectual life for almost forty years. She was one of the foremost examples of existentialist *engagement* and its most respected moral voice. Her novels, especially *She Came to Stay*, *The Blood of Others*, and *The Mandarins* (for which she won the Prix Goncourt in 1954), pose some of the central philosophical and ethical questions of modern times, exploring the problems of social morality, political commitment, and human responsibility. Along with her autobiography, her novels chronicle the time before and after World War II and the experiences that made her one of the most influential writers of the twentieth century.

De Beauvoir wrote numerous articles for *Les Temps modernes,* a periodical founded and directed by Sartre, and she was a member of its editorial board. In 1973, she became the editor of the journal's feminist column. *The Second Sex*, her carefully documented study of the situation of women, became one of the major theoretical texts of the women's movement. Her interest in women's rights and her concern for social justice were attested by her ongoing involvement in both. She demonstrated against France's restrictive abortion laws and signed the *Manifeste des 343*, a document listing women who admitted having had abortions. She served as president of Choisir (1971) and of the Ligue des Droits des Femmes (1974), an organization fighting sex discrimination. De Beauvoir was also one of the founders of the feminist journal *Questions féministes*. Her indictment of social injustice was evidenced by *The Coming of Age*, her defense of a free press (the Maoist underground newspaper *La Cause du Peuple*), and her political actions.

Biography

Simone de Beauvoir was born in Paris in January, 1908. Her father, Georges de Beauvoir, came from a wealthy family and was a lawyer by profession. A religious skeptic, he was openly contemptuous of the bourgeoisie and encouraged his daughter in intellectual pursuits. In contrast, her mother, Françoise, came from a provincial town, received her education in convents, and was a devout Catholic. Under her mother's supervision, the young de Beauvoir was educated at a conservative Catholic school for girls, the Cours Désir.

In *Memoirs of a Dutiful Daughter*—which covers the years from 1908 to 1929—de Beauvoir describes her early piety, her subsequent disenchantment with Catholicism, and the beginning of her rebellion against her middle-class background. Influenced by an early reading of Louisa May Alcott and George Eliot, she decided at age fifteen that she wanted to be a writer. After leaving the Cours Désir, she pursued the study of literature at the Institut Catholique in Paris. In 1926, she attended the Sorbonne and studied philosophy, Greek, and philology. Three years later, after a year at the prestigious École Normale Supérieure, she passed the examination for the *agrégation de philosophie*, the highest academic degree conferred in France.

In 1929, de Beauvoir met Sartre and began an association with him that lasted until his death in April, 1980. The years from 1929 to 1944 are chronicled in the second volume of her autobiography, *The Prime of Life*. Having completed her academic degrees, she was assigned a series of teaching positions, first in Marseilles and later in Rouen and Paris. Her first novel, *She Came to Stay*, appeared in 1943; it established her as a writer, and she stopped teaching. During the war years, she became interested in political action. By the end of World War II,

de Beauvoir and Sartre were labeled "existentialists," and their success and celebrity were assured. In 1947, de Beauvoir was invited on a lecture tour of the United States (described in *America Day by Day*) and began her four-year affair with Nelson Algren.

During the postwar years, de Beauvoir became increasingly preoccupied with the problems of the intellectual in society, and she continued to examine the relationship between freedom and social commitment. In *Force of Circumstance* (which spans the years 1944 to 1962), the third volume of her autobiography, political events such as the Korean War and the Algerian Crisis occupy progressively more space. She saw Sartre destroy his health to work on *Critique de la raíson dialectique* (1960; *The Critique of Dialectical Reason*, 1976) and became painfully aware of human mortality and solitude. Old age and death are themes that run through de Beauvoir's work done during this period, such as *A Very Easy Death, The Woman Destroyed, The Coming of Age*, and the last volume of her autobiography, *All Said and Done*. In spite of this, the general tone of *All Said and Done*—as well as of the frequent interviews she gave—is one of a woman content to have achieved her existentialist project. De Beauvoir died in 1986 at the age of seventy-eight.

Analysis

Simone de Beauvoir's novels are grounded in her training as a philosopher and in her sociological and feminist concerns. *She Came to Stay, The Blood of Others, All Men Are Mortal*, and *The Mandarins* all revolve around the questions of freedom and responsibility and try to define the proper relationship between the individual and society. Her characters search for authenticity as they attempt to shape the world around them. Their education is sentimental as well as intellectual and political. While most of her heroes accommodate themselves successfully to reality, the same may not be said of her heroines. In the later novels, *The Mandarins* and *Les Belles Images*, her female characters, who are successful by worldly standards, suffer a series of psychological crises. As they undertake what the feminist critic Carol Christ has called "spiritual quests," they often face suicide and madness. The existentialist enterprise of *engagement*, or commitment with a view of defining the self through action, seems more possible for the men in her novels than for the women. In *Simone de Beauvoir*

on Woman (1975), Jean Leighton has observed the absence of positive heroines in de Beauvoir's work: Woman seems condemned to passivity while man's fate is one of transcendence. Arguments from *The Second Sex* and from her philosophical essays echo in the novels. The tension between her philosophical ideas and their potential realization by the women characters is clearly visible in de Beauvoir's fiction.

De Beauvoir's first novel, *She Came to Stay*, is an imaginative transposition of her relationship with Olga Kosakiewicz. In 1933, de Beauvoir and Sartre had befriended Olga, one of de Beauvoir's students. They had attempted a *ménage à trois*; *She Came to Stay* is the story of its failure.

The heroine, Françoise Miquel, is a young writer who has lived with Pierre Labrousse, a talented actor and director, for eight years. They believe that their relationship is ideal since it allows them both considerable freedom. Françoise befriends Xavière, a young woman disenchanted with provincial life, and invites her to Paris, where she will help her find work. Once in Paris, Xavière makes demands on the couple and is openly contemptuous of their values. Pierre becomes obsessed with Xavière; Françoise, trying to rise above the jealousy and insecurity she feels, struggles to keep the trio together. Out of resentment, Françoise has an affair with Gerbert, Xavière's suitor. The novel ends as Xavière recognizes Françoise's duplicity; Xavière has now become the critical Other. Unable to live in her presence, Françoise turns on the gas and murders her.

She Came to Stay is a meditation on the Hegelian problem of the existence of the Other. The novel plays out the psychological effects of jealousy and questions the extent to which coexistence is possible. Critics such as Carol Ascher have noted the close ties between de Beauvoir's first novel and Sartre's *L'Être et le neant* (*Being and Nothingness*, 1956), published in the same year. Both texts deal with the central existentialist theme of letting others absorb one's freedom.

Despite Françoise's apparent independence, she needs Pierre to approve her actions and give them direction. Françoise's self-deception and the inauthenticity of her life anticipate de Beauvoir's analysis of *l'amoureuse*, the woman in love, in *The Second Sex*. Confronted with a rival, Françoise becomes aware that her self-assurance and detachment are illusory. Her growth as a character occurs as she sheds the unexamined rational premises she holds about herself and her relationship with Pierre. The gap between the intellect and the emotions continues to widen until it reaches a crisis in the murder of Xavière. Françoise is finally forced to confront her long-concealed hatred. In spite of the often-stylized dialogue, *She Came to Stay* is a lucid, finely executed study of love and jealousy and one of de Beauvoir's finest novels.

Although de Beauvoir was later to consider her second novel overly didactic, *The Blood of Others* is one of the best novels written on the French Resistance. The book opens with the thoughts of Jean Blomart as he keeps vigil over his mistress Hélène, who is dying from a wound received during a mission. The novel proceeds by flashback and alternates between the stories of Jean, a Resistance hero, and his companion Hélène. The son of a wealthy bourgeois family, Jean is plagued by feelings of guilt over his comfortable situation. He takes a job as a worker and tries to lead a life of uninvolvement. His attempted detachment is based on his belief that he can thus avoid contributing to the unhappiness of others. Passive at the outbreak of the war, he is finally drafted.

Upon his return to Paris, he realizes that his detachment is actually a form of irresponsibility. He organizes a resistance group and becomes its leader. As he watches the dying Hélène, he questions whether he has the right to control the lives of his comrades. Although he is doomed to act in ignorance of the consequences of his decisions, he decides that he nevertheless has an obligation to act. The novel ends with Hélène's death and his renewed commitment to the Resistance.

If *The Blood of Others* is the story of Jean's *engagement*, it is also the story of Hélène's political awakening. Like him, she is politically indifferent until a young Jewish friend is in danger of deportation. She then turns to Jean and becomes an active member of his group. Of all de Beauvoir's women, Hélène is one who, in her political commitment, manages to define herself through her actions rather than through her emotional attachments.

The Blood of Others recalls the discussion of individual freedom in *The Ethics of Ambiguity*. In both the novel and the philosophical essay, the problem of the Other is interfaced with the question of social responsibility. With its emphasis on the denial of freedom during the Occupation, the novel underscores the necessity of political action to ensure individual freedoms. The closed space of the love triangle in *She Came to Stay* is replaced by the larger obligations of the individual to a historical moment. *The Blood of Others* conveys the problematic quality of ethical decisions; as Robert Cottrell has noted in *Simone de Beauvoir* (1975), it evokes "the sense of being entrapped, of submitting to existence rather than fashioning it." Nevertheless, *The Blood of Others* is a more optimistic book than *She Came to Stay* in its portrayal of the individual working toward a larger social good.

The Mandarins, de Beauvoir's finest novel, covers the period from 1944 to the early 1950's and focuses on the relationship between political commitment and literature. The narrative voice shifts between Henri Perron, a novelist, journalist, and Resistance hero, and Anne Dubreuilh, a respected psychiatrist and the wife of Robert Dubreuilh, a prominent writer.

Robert, initiated into political activism during his years in the Resistance, believes that literature must now take second place to political concerns. He engages himself wholeheartedly in founding the S.R.L., an independent leftist political party. The problems that Robert confronts as a political figure point to the painful reality of making decisions that are not always satisfactory. He draws Henri into politics by convincing him that his newspaper, *L'Espoir*, should be the voice of the S.R.L. When they receive news of Soviet labor camps, they try to decide if they should publish it. Knowing that they will play into Gaullist hands and alienate the Communists to whom they are sympathetic, they reluctantly decide to print the story.

For Henri, questions of political commitment after the war are more problematic. He would like *L'Espoir* to remain apolitical and is nostalgic for the prewar years when literature and politics appeared to be mutually exclusive interests. Henri tries to act in good faith, but because of his sensitivity to others, he often opts for the less idealistically pure solution. He is reluctant to break with Paule, his mistress of ten years, and he protects acquaintances who were German collaborators because he fears that, like Paule, they could not survive without his help. Throughout the novel, he is torn between politics and a desire to return to literature. He gradually faces the impossibility of "pure" literature. At the end of the novel, having lost *L'Espoir*, he and Robert decide to found a new journal of the Left.

The questions that de Beauvoir examines through Robert and Henri have a striking immediacy that captures the problem of the intellectual in the modern world. Much of the action in *The Mandarins* is a fictionalized account of her experiences as a member of the intellectual Left during the postwar years. Critics have sought to identify Sartre with Robert, Albert Camus with Henri, and de Beauvoir herself with Anne. In *Simone de Beauvoir and the Limits of Commitment* (1981), Anne Whitmarsh notes that there is much of Sartre's experiences with the Rassemblement Démocratique Révolutionnaire in Robert's ties with the S.R.L. and that some of the early problems facing *Les Temps modernes* are reflected in the debates on the political role of *L'Espoir*.

The problems faced by the male characters are less pressing for Anne. Married to a man twenty years older, she seems out of touch with herself and her surroundings. Her work as a psychiatrist fails fully to occupy her, and her relationship with her unhappy daughter, Nadine, gives Anne little satisfaction. Encouraged by Robert, she accepts an invitation to lecture in the United States. In Chicago, she experiences an emotional awakening when she falls in love with Lewis Brogan, an up-and-coming writer. Her visits to Brogan are described in a highly lyric style full of images of country life and nature. The

physical and affective aspects of her life with Brogan form an effective counterpoint to the intellectual character of her relationship with her husband. The shifting loyalties she experiences for both men give Anne's narrative a schizophrenic quality.

Back in Paris, Anne tries to help Paule, who has suffered a nervous breakdown. Paule rarely leaves her apartment and is unable to function without Henri. Anne sends her to a psychiatrist, who "cures" her by having her forget the past. Like Françoise, Paule represents the temptation of living through others. In Paule's case, however, the dependence reaches an existential crisis from which she never fully recovers. Paule's illness is mirrored in Anne as the psychiatrist herself plunges into a long depression. When Brogan ends their relationship, she contemplates suicide. Thinking of the pain her death would cause Robert and Nadine, she decides to live. Despite this decision, Anne's alienation from her family and indeed from her own being is more acute than ever.

Anne's emotional awakening and Paule's mental breakdown leave them both as only marginal participants in life. Neither woman achieves the transcendence that characterizes the lives of her male counterpart. As Robert and Henri accommodate themselves to political realities, they become more integrated into society. The female quest for self-knowledge acts as a negative counterpoint to the male quest. The final scene is not unlike a collage in which the two parts of the composition are radically divided. The enthusiasm of Henri and Robert as they search for an appropriate title for their journal is juxtaposed to Anne's stillness; she sits off to the side, withdrawn, and hopes that her life may still contain some happiness.

All de Beauvoir's novels examine the relationship between the self and the Other that is at the heart of existentialist philosophy. In her early novels, such as *She Came to Stay, The Blood of Others*, and *All Men Are Mortal*, there is often an explicit existentialist premise underlying the action. In her later works, *The Mandarins* and *Les Belles Images*, the philosophical message, although still present, is clearly subordinated to the narrative. De Beauvoir's conclusions in *The Second Sex* appear to have led her to a closer examination of the lives of her women characters. Her later fiction adds another dimension to the quests for authenticity that mark her early production. For her heroes, the quest usually ends in some type of existentialist commitment; for her heroines, the quest seems to involve a withdrawal from harmful social myths. If at times the quests border on madness or isolation, they do so without losing their striking immediacy or their profound sense of reality. Like other great twentieth century quests, de Beauvoir's novels chart a journey into the heart of contemporary alienation.

Other major works

SHORT FICTION: *La Femme rompue*, 1967 (*The Woman Destroyed*, 1968); *Quand prime le spirituel*, 1979 (*When Things of the Spirit Come First: Five Early Tales*, 1982).

PLAY: *Les Bouches Inutiles*, 1945.

NONFICTION: *Pyrrhus et Cinéas*, 1944; *Pour une morale de l'ambiguïté*, 1947 (*The Ethics of Ambiguity*, 1948); *L'Amérique au jour le jour*, 1948 (*America Day by Day*, 1953); *L'Existentialisme et la sagesse des nations*, 1948; *Le Deuxième Sexe*, 1949 (*The Second Sex*, 1953); *Privilèges*, 1955 (partial translation, "Must We Burn Sade?," 1953); *La Longue Marche*, 1957 (*The Long March*, 1958); *Mémoires d'une jeune fille rangée*, 1958 (4 volumes; *Memoirs of a Dutiful Daughter*, 1959); *La Force de l'âge*, 1960 (*The Prime of Life*, 1962); *La Force des choses*, 1963 (*Force of Circumstance*, 1964); *Une Mort très douce*, 1964 (*A Very Easy Death*, 1966); *La Vieillesse*, 1970 (*The Coming of Age*, 1972); *Tout compte fait*, 1972 (*All Said and Done*, 1974); *La Cérémonie des adieux*, 1981 (*Adieux: A Farewell to Sartre*, 1984); *Lettres à Sartre*, 1990 (*Letters to Sartre*, 1992).

Bibliography

Ascher, Carol. *Simone de Beauvoir: A Life of Freedom*. Boston: Beacon Press, 1981.

Bieber, Konrad. *Simone de Beauvoir*. Boston: Twayne, 1979.

Cottrell, Robert D. *Simone de Beauvoir*. New York: Frederick Ungar, 1975.

Leighton, Jean. *Simone de Beauvoir on Woman*. Rutherford, N.J.: Fairleigh Dickinson University Press, 1975.

Whitmarsh, Anne. *Simone de Beauvoir and the Limits of Commitment*. Cambridge, England: Cambridge University Press, 1981.

ANITA DESAI

Born: Mussoorie, India; June 24, 1937

Principal long fiction

Cry, The Peacock, 1963; *Voices in the City*, 1965; *Bye-Bye, Blackbird*, 1971; *Where Shall We Go This Summer?*, 1975; *Fire on the Mountain*, 1977; *Clear Light of Day*, 1980; *In Custody*, 1984; *Baumgartner's Bombay*, 1988.

Other literary forms

Anita Desai is a well-known short-story writer as well as a novelist. Her first story was published in 1957, when she was twenty years old. Since then, she has contributed stories to magazines and periodicals such as *Envoy* (London), *Quest* (Bombay), *The Illustrated Weekly of India* (Bombay), and *Miscellany* (Calcutta). A collection of short stories, *Games at Twilight and Other Stories*, ap-peared in 1978. Desai has written three books for children, *The Peacock Garden* (1974), *Cat on a Houseboat* (1976), and *The Village by the Sea: An Indian Family Story* (1982). Finally, she has written a few articles, sketches, and reviews for some of the periodicals mentioned above.

Achievements

Desai is one of the more prominent contemporary Indian English novelists. With her first novel, *Cry, The Peacock* (1963), she added a new psychological dimension to Indian English fiction. Desai is probably the first Indian English novelist to be primarily concerned with the inner life of her characters—their fleeting moods, wisps of memory, subtle cerebrations. In her novels, Desai succeeds in capturing these evanescent moments of consciousness, preserving them from oblivion and investing them with the permanence of art. The result is that Desai not only creates something of value for herself out of the endless flux of her own psyche but also provides for her reader an opportunity to share this rich inner life through her characters.

Desai's stylistic accomplishment is noteworthy as well. Unlike many other Indian English novelists, she does not find it necessary to experiment with language. In her novels, no clash between English, her medium of expression, and the Indian subject matter is apparent. Indeed, her use of the language is natural and unselfconscious. Her writing is both supple and precise. Though each sentence is carefully crafted, the overall manner is easy, not precious or labored. Stylistically, Desai is thus in the mainstream of twentieth century English novelists.

With her novels, books for children, and collection of short stories, Desai is a writer of considerable achievement, perhaps the best contemporary Indian English woman novelist. Critical interest in her work has steadily grown since her first novel was published. Desai received the Royal Society of Literature Winifred Holtby Prize in 1978 and the Sahitya Akademi of India Award in 1979; she has been a member of the Sahitya Akademi English Board since 1972 and a fellow of the Royal Society of Literature since 1978.

Biography

Though born in Mussoorie, Anita Desai grew up in Delhi. Her father, D. N. Mazumdar, was Bengali, a businessman, and her mother, Toni, was German. Desai's mother met her father when the latter was a student in Germany. They were married and then moved to India in the late 1920's. As a child, Desai spoke German at home and Hindi to her friends and neighbors. She then learned English once she started school. She grew up during the war years of the late 1930's and the 1940's, sensing the anxiety in her mother about the situation in Germany. Fearing the devastation and change wrought by World War II, Desai's mother never returned to Germany, probably inspiring some of the facets of the character Hugo Baumgartner in *Baumgartner's Bombay*.

Desai was educated at Queen Mary's School, Delhi, and then at Miranda House at the University of Delhi. At

Miranda House she studied English literature, receiving her B.A. in 1957. Her studies helped to fuel her passion for writing, a compulsion which began at the age of seven. After working for a year in Max Muller Bhavan, Calcutta, she married Ashwin Desai, a business executive, in 1958. Since then, she has lived in Calcutta, Bombay, Chandigarh, Delhi, and Pune. She has four children, Rahul, Tani, Arjun, and Kiran.

Analysis

Anita Desai's novels reveal certain recurring patterns in plot, setting, and characterization. The plots of her novels fuse two opposing propensities—one toward the gothic mystery, and the other toward the philosophical novel. The gothic orientation, which Desai probably derived from Emily Brontë's *Wuthering Heights* (1847), is evident in varying degrees in all of her novels. *Fire on the Mountain*, the novel that comes closest to being purely a psychological thriller, ends with a half-insane, reptilelike child setting fire to the forest surrounding her house; in *Cry, The Peacock*, Maya, the neurotic heroine, kills her husband, thereby fulfilling the prophecy of an albino sorcerer; in *Voices in the City*, Monisha, an unsettled, manic-depressive housewife, pours kerosine over herself and burns herself to death. On the other hand, most of Desai's novels also contain a deep-rooted, philosophical concern about the meaning of life. From Maya to Bim, most of Desai's protagonists, dissatisfied with their routine existence, search for a more meaningful life.

Desai's novels also evolve a typical setting or "world" of their own. Most are set in the city, which comes to represent the undesirable, unimaginative reality; most also have a romantic counterpoint to the city in a hill-station or an island, which seems to represent a remote, romantic ideal but which is revealed to be an unreal or unsatisfying delusion. At the heart of the novels there is usually a big, old house with several verandas, green shutters, a garden, servants, and pets. The garden is extremely important in Desai's world because her characters show an unusual sensitivity to it. Trees, creepers, tendrils, flowers, fruits, seasons, pets—the concerns of the so-called "woman's world"—are more vividly perceived in Desai's novels than anywhere else in Indian English fiction. Also in Desai's world is a brooding, Faulknerian obsession with the past: The present is usually seen by the characters as a decadent remnant, a husk of a glamorous past. Finally, the characters are all upper class, belonging to once affluent, now decaying families.

Desai's work is respected worldwide. In Great Britain, she was Visiting Fellow at Girton College, Cambridge, in the late 1980's, during which time she wrote *Baumgartner's Bombay*, and both *Clear Light of Day* and *In Custody* were short-listed for the prestigious Booker Prize. She has taught writing at both Smith and Mount Holyoke colleges in the United States.

Desai's protagonists can be divided into essentially two types: One type possesses a neurotic, hypersensitive, artistic sensibility; the other is cynical, tough, and acerbic. Maya, Monisha, Sarah, Sita, and Tara belong to the first category, while Nirode, Amla, Dev, Nanda, and Bim belong to the second. In addition to these are two types of supporting characters: the old, ugly, sterile crone, who has been a failure; and the mysterious, insulated character, intriguing but ultimately inscrutable. The best example of the former is Ila Das of *Fire on the Mountain*; of the latter, Dharma of *Voices in the City*. The rest of the characters are the common crowd against whom the protagonist defines himself or herself: They have given up trying to make their lives meaningful and have accepted the full mediocrity of a futile existence.

Against such a backdrop, Desai's protagonists struggle to come to terms with their lives. They are usually in a state of conflict, either with themselves or with their environment. The results of this basic conflict are murder, insanity, suicide, compromise, death, or, in the rare instance of Desai's best novel, *Clear Light of Day*, balance, reconciliation, rich acceptance of reality, and a resolution of the conflict.

Clear Light of Day is one of her most accomplished novels. In it, the typical elements of her art merge to create a unique artistic triumph. The plot, for example, is a fine blend of the gothic and the philosophical, each strengthening the other. The mysterious well in the back, the drowned cow, Mira Masi's alcoholic disintegration, Tara's fear that her mother was murdered by her father, Baba's idiocy—all these contribute to the final resolution of the novel. One by one, these events are put into their place by the two heroines, Bim and Tara; the mystery, horror, or shame enveloping these events is slowly peeled away, and the past emerges in a new light of clarity and understanding by the end of the novel.

The setting, too, has the typical Desai elements—the ugly city, the large house with verandas, the garden, the servants' quarters, upper-class characters, and decadent families. These elements, however, are augmented by acute social observation and particularity of place and time. Not only the inner life of the characters but also their milieu is fully developed. Perhaps no other English novel so successfully immortalizes mid-twentieth century Delhi and its locales—Civil Lines, the old Delhi convent school, the Jamuna, Connaught Circus, Hindu College, Darya Ganj, Chandni Chowk, the Ridge, and the Lodi Gardens. *Clear Light of Day* is thus also valuable as a sociohistorical document, a feat rare in Desai's canon.

Desai's main concern, of course, remains with the characters and their conflicts. Bim is the tough, cynical heroine, the one who refuses to compromise. Tara is her softer, more sensitive, counterpart. Raja, the deserter, their brother, is Bim's double. Mira Masi and the sisters next door are the hags. Bakul, Tara's husband, is a shallower, stupider version of Guatama in *Cry, the Peacock*. Bim, Tara, and Raja share the same determination to live meaningfully, without compromise. At the beginning of the novel, when Tara returns to the old house, both sisters are equally distant from resolving their conflicts: While Tara is too weak, Bim is too harsh, too bitter. Both are uncertain about their past, about their relationships to each other and Raja, about the meaningfulness of their lives. Together, they slowly relive their entire past, which leads to the marvelous reconciliation in the last few pages of the novel. Bim, to her astonishment, realizes that Tara—despite her marriage to Bakul and several mundane years as the wife of a diplomat—whom she has always despised, is just like her, and that Tara, too, has managed to preserve her integrity. Tara and Bim reach a new understanding for the first time; through Tara, Bim at last relinquishes her grudge against Raja, reconciling herself to him again. After Tara's departure, Bim and Baba listen to Mulk and his Guru; Mulk is not after all merely a slothful drunkard as Bim has thought—he *can* sing, he is an artiste. Bim realizes that she does not have to degenerate into another Mira Masi; she fathoms the truth of T. S. Eliot's line from *Four Quartets* (1943): "Time the destroyer is also time the preserver." *Clear Light of Day* thus ends in balance, harmony, reconciliation, resolution, not in murder, suicide, death, insanity, or compromise, as do all Desai's previous novels, and as does *Baumgartner's Bombay*.

In *Baumgartner's Bombay*, the main character is neither Indian nor English—he is a German Jew. The story follows Hugo Baumgartner from childhood in pre-World War II Germany to his death in Bombay, India. The novel, however, starts with the ending (though the reader cannot realize it until the actual end of the book) and then jumps to the middle of the story. Baumgartner's past is relayed in a series of flashbacks from his time in India.

Baumgartner is forced to leave Germany when the Nazis' rise to power can no longer be ignored. Indeed, by the time Baumgartner leaves, his father has already committed suicide after being sent to a concentration camp, though he was later released. Interestingly, Desai has said about *Baumgartner's Bombay* that she "wasn't writing about the Nazis. I was writing about random evil." Baumgartner himself never expresses much feeling about the injustices done to him; about his six years in a British internment camp for German nationals, Baumgartner protests that "they were not such bad days."

Baumgartner's escape from Germany takes him to Venice, where he is to catch a boat for India. Venice remains in Baumgartner's mind as a kind of paradise, despite the troubles he has there and the fact that he is in the city for less than a week. These fabled and probably half-imagined qualities of Venice contrast sharply with the squalor and degradation of Bombay and of Baumgartner's life there. In fact, he spends most of his time going from restaurant to restaurant trying to find scraps for the multitude of cats with which he shares his dingy little flat.

Ironically, Baumgartner does die at the hands of a German, though not a Nazi: Rather, a German junkie whom Baumgartner has offered a place to stay kills him for his silver trophies. *Baumgartner's Bombay* marks a return for Desai to the twin themes of hopelessness and despair. Baumgartner, his aging friend Lotte, Julius Roth—all are stranded in India; none can return to Germany because the old Germany is gone forever, and they do not fit into the new Germany. Indeed, it is the new Germany that becomes the death of Baumgartner in the shape of the brutal junkie. Desai's picture of foreigners—or *firanghi*, as the Indians label these outcasts—is that they can never fit into Indian society no matter how hard they try. It is Desai's great talent, however, to be able to make these characters compelling despite their obvious fate, which is to be forgotten. They leave no mark or memory when they die, though Desai ensures that they do remain with the reader long past the end of the novel.

Other major works

SHORT FICTION: *Games at Twilight and Other Stories*, 1978.
CHILDREN'S LITERATURE: *The Peacock Garden*, 1974; *Cat on a Houseboat*, 1976; *The Village by the Sea: An Indian Family Story*, 1982.

Bibliography

Bande, Usha. *The Novels of Anita Desai: A Study in Character and Conflict.* New Delhi: Prestige Books, 1988.
Jain, Jasbir. *Stairs to the Attic: The Novels of Anita Desai.* Jaipur, India: Printwell, 1987.
Jena, Seema. *Voice and Vision of Anita Desai.* New Delhi: Ashish Publishing House, 1989.

EMILY DICKINSON

Born: Amherst, Massachusetts; December 10, 1830   **Died:** Amherst, Massachusetts; May 15, 1886

Principal poetry

The Poems of Emily Dickinson, 1955 (Thomas H. Johnson, editor, 3 volumes); *The Complete Poems of Emily Dickinson*, 1960 (Thomas H. Johnson, editor).

Other literary forms

In addition to her poetry, Emily Dickinson left behind voluminous correspondence. Because she was so rarely out of Amherst—and in her later life so rarely left her house—much of her contact with others took place through letters, many of which include poems. Like her poetry, the letters are witty, epigrammatic, and often enigmatic. They are available in *The Letters of Emily Dickinson* (1958, Thomas H. Johnson and Theodora Ward, editors, 3 volumes).

Achievements

By the mid-nineteenth century, American lyric poetry had matured, but it was still hampered by certain limiting assumptions about the nature of literary language; about the value of regular rhythm, meter, and rhyme; and about imagery as ornamental rather than organic. Into this situation came Emily Dickinson and Walt Whitman, poets who were alike only in their commitment to writing a personalized poetry unlike anything the nineteenth century had thus far read. Whitman, who rid himself of the limitations of regular meter entirely, identified with the common people and became a poet of the open road. Dickinson, however, was the poet of exclusion, of the shut door. She accepted the limitations of rhyme and meter and worked endless variations on one basic pattern, exploring the nuances that the framework would allow. No democrat, she constructed for herself a set of aristocratic images. No traveler, she stayed at home to examine small fragments of the world she knew. For Dickinson life was kinesthetic; she recorded the impressions of experience on her nerves and on her soul. Rather than being linear and progressive, it was circular. Whitman was a poet of explanation; Dickinson, having rejected expansion, exploited suggestion.

Although Dickinson was barely understood or appreciated in her own lifetime, she now seems a central figure—at once firmly in a tradition, and at the same time, a breaker of tradition, a revolutionary who freed American poetry for modern thought and technique.

Biography

Born in 1830 of a prominent Amherst family, Emily Dickinson rarely left the town, except for time spent in Boston and trips to Washington and Philadelphia. She attended the Amherst Academy and Mount Holyoke Female Seminary. Although she was witty and popular, she set herself apart from the other girls by her refusal to be converted to the conventional Christianity of the town. Her life was marked by a circle of close friends and of family: a stern and humorless father; a mother who suffered a long period of illness and whom Emily took care of; her sister Lavinia, who likewise never married and remained in the family home; and her brother Austin, who married Sue Gilbert Dickinson and whose forceful personality, like that of his wife, affected the family while Emily Dickinson lived, and whose affair with Mrs. Mabel Loomis Todd, the editor of Dickinson's poems, precipitated family squabbles that affected their publication.

Additionally, there was a series of men who formed a sort of emotional resource for her. The first of these was Samuel Bowles, the editor of the neighboring Springfield, Massachusetts, *Republican*, which published some of her poetry. Charles Wadsworth was the minister of a Philadelphia church; a preacher famous for his eloquence, he preached one Sunday when Dickinson was in Philadelphia, and afterward they corresponded for several years. In 1862, however, he and his family moved from Philadelphia to the West Coast. Dickinson immediately sent four of her poems to Thomas Wentworth Higginson, at *The Atlantic Monthly*, for his advice, and they began a long friendship; although Higginson was never convinced that Dickinson was a finished poet, he was a continuing mentor. Finally, late in life, Dickinson met Judge Otis Lord, and for a time it seemed as if they were to be married; this was her one explicitly romantic friendship, but marriage never took place. There were also less intense friendships with women, particularly Mabel Todd, who, despite her important role in Dickinson's life, never actually met her, and with the writer Helen Hunt Jackson, one of the few to accept Dickinson's poetry as it was written.

After 1862, Dickinson rarely left her house, except for a necessary visit to Boston where she was treated for eye trouble. She wore white dresses and with more and more frequency refused to see visitors, usually remaining upstairs, listening to the conversations and entering, if at all, by calling down the stairs or by sending in poems or other tokens of her participation. She became known as the "Myth of Amherst," and from this image is drawn the popular notion of the eccentric old maid that persists in the imagination of many of her readers today. Yet it is clear that Dickinson lived life on the emotional level with great intensity. Her poetry is dense with vividly rendered emotions and observations, and she transformed the paucity of her outward life into the richness of her inner life.

Analysis

During her lifetime, only seven of Emily Dickinson's poems were published, most of them edited to make them more conventional. After Dickinson's death, her sister Lavinia discovered about nine hundred poems, over half of the 1,775 poems that now compose the Dickinson canon. She took these to a family friend, Mrs. Todd, who, with Dickinson's friend Thomas Wentworth Higginson, published 115 of the poems in 1890. Together they published a second group of 166 in 1891, and Mrs. Todd alone edited a third series in 1896. Unfortunately, Mrs. Todd and Col. Higginson continued the practice of revision that had begun with the first seven published poems, smoothing the rhymes and meter, revising the diction, and generally regularizing the poetry.

In 1914, Dickinson's niece, Martha Dickinson Bianchi, published the first of several volumes of the poetry she was to edit. Although she was more scrupulous about preserving Dickinson's language and intent, several editorial problems persisted, and the body of Dickinson's poetry remained fragmented and often altered. In 1950, the Dickinson literary estate was given to Harvard University, and Thomas H. Johnson began his work of editing, arranging, and presenting the text. In 1955, he produced the variorum edition, 1,775 poems arranged in an attempt at chronological order, given such evidence as handwriting changes and incorporation of poems in letters, and including all variations of the poems. In 1960, he chose one form of each poem as the final version and published the resulting collection as *The Complete Poems of Emily Dickinson*. Johnson's text and numbering system are accepted as the standard. His job was thorough, diligent, and imaginative. This is not to say, however, that his decisions about dates or choices among variants must be taken as final. Many scholars have other opinions, and since Dickinson herself apparently did not make final choices, there is no reason to accept every decision Johnson made.

One of Dickinson's poems (#1129) begins, "Tell all the Truth but tell it slant," and the oblique and often enigmatic rendering of Truth is the theme of Dickinson's poetry. Its motifs often recur—love, death, poetry, beauty, nature, immortality, the self—but such abstractions do not indicate the broad and rich changes that Dickinson obliquely rings on the truths she tells.

Dickinson's truth is, in the broadest sense, a religious truth. Formally, her poetry plays endless variations on the Protestant hymn meters that she knew from her youthful experiences in church. Her reading in contemporary poetry was limited, and the form she knew best was the iambic of hymns: common meter (with its alternating tetrameter and trimeter lines), long meter (four lines of tetrameter), and short meter (four of trimeter) became the framework of her poetry. That static form, however, could not contain the energy of her work, and the rhythms and rhymes are varied, upset, and broken to accommodate the feeling of her lines. The predictable patterns of hymns were not for Dickinson, who delighted in off-rhyme, consonance, and, less frequently, eye-rhyme.

Dickinson is a religious poet more than formally, but

her thematic sense of religion lies not in her assurance, but in her continual questioning of God, in her attempt to define his nature and that of his world. Although she is always a poet of definition, straightforward definition was too direct for her: "The Riddle we can guess/ We speedily despise," she wrote. Her works often begin, "It was not" or "It was like," with the poem being an oblique attempt to define the "it." "I like to see it lap the Miles" (#585) is a typical Dickinson riddle poem. Like many, it begins with "it," a pronoun without an antecedent, so that the reader must join in the process of discovery and definition. The riddle is based on an extended metaphor; the answer to the riddle, a train, is compared to a horse; but in the poem both tenor (train) and vehicle (horse) are unstated. Meanwhile, what begins with an almost cloying tone, the train as an animal lapping and licking, moves through subtle gradations of attitude until the train stops at the end "docile and omnipotent." This juxtaposition of incongruous adjectives, like the coupling of unlikely adjective and noun, is another of Dickinson's favorite devices; just as the movement of the poem has been from the animal's (and train's) tame friendliness to its assertive power, so these adjectives crystallize the paradox.

Riddling becomes less straightfoward, but no less central, in such a representative Dickinson poem as "It was not Death, for I stood up" (#510), in which many of her themes and techniques appear. The first third of the poem, two stanzas of the six, suggest what the "it" is not: death, night, frost, or fire. Each is presented in a couplet, but even in those pairs of lines, Dickinson manages to disconcert her reader. It is not death, for the persona is standing upright, the difference between life and death reduced to one of posture. Nor is it night, for the bells are chiming noon—but Dickinson's image for that fact is also unnatural. The bells are mouths, their clappers tongues, which are "Put out"; personification here does not have the effect of making the bells more human, but of making them grotesque, breaking down as it does the barriers between such normally discrete worlds as the mechanical and the human, a distinction that Dickinson often dissolves. Moreover, the notion of the bells sticking out their tongues suggests their contemptuous attitude toward human beings. In stanza 2, it is not frost because hot winds are crawling on the persona's flesh. The hackneyed phrase is reversed, so it is not coolness, but heat that makes flesh crawl, and not the flesh itself that crawls, but the winds upon it; nor is it fire, for the persona's

marble feet "Could keep a Chancel, cool." Again, the persona is dehumanized, now grotesquely marble. While accomplishing this, Dickinson has also begun her inclusion of sensory data, pervasive in the first part of the poem, so that the confrontation is not only intellectual and emotional but physical as well.

The second third of the poem changes the proportions. Although the experience is not actually any of the four things she has mentioned above, it is like them all; but now death, the first, is given seven lines, night three, frost only two, and fire is squeezed out altogether. It is like death because she has, after all, seen figures arranged like her own; now her life is "shaven,/ And fitted to a frame." It is like night when everything that "ticked"—again mechanical imagery for a natural phenomenon—has stopped, and like frosts, which in early autumn morns "Repeal the Beating Ground." Her vocabulary startles once more: The ground beats with life, but the frost can void it; "repeal" suggests the law, but nature's laws are here completely nullified.

Finally, in the last stanza, the metaphor shifts completely, and the experience is compared to something new: drowning at sea. It is "stopless" but "cool"; the agony that so often marks Dickinson's poetry may be appropriate to the persona, but nothing around her, neither people nor nature, seems to note it. Most important, there is neither chance nor means of rescue; there is no report of land. Any of these conditions would justify despair, but for the poet, this climactic experience is so chaotic that even despair is not justified, for there is no word of land to despair of reaching.

Thus, one sees many of Dickinson's typical devices at work: the tightly patterned form, based on an undefined subject; the riddle-like puzzle of defining that subject; the shifting of mood from apparent observation to horror; the grotesque images couched in emotionally distant language. All this delineates that experience, that confrontation—with God, with nature, with the self, with one's own mind—which is the center of Dickinson's best poetry. Whether her work looks inward or outward, the subject matter is a confrontation leading to awareness, and part of the terror is that for Dickinson there is never any mediating middle ground; she confronts herself in relation to an abyss beyond. There is no society, no community to make that experience palatable in any but the most grotesque sense of the word, the awful tasting of uncontrollable fear.

Whenever Dickinson looks at nature, the moment

becomes a confrontation. Although she is superficially within the Puritan tradition of observing nature and reading its message, Dickinson differs not only in the chilling message that she reads but also because nature refuses to remain passive. It is not simply an open book to be read—for books remain themselves—but active and aggressive; personification suggests its assertive malevolence. In #348 ("I dreaded that first Robin, so"), the initial part of the poem describes the poet's fear: Spring is horrible; it shouts, mangles, and pierces. What Dickinson finally manages is merely a peace with spring; she makes herself "Queen of Calvary," and in deference to that, nature salutes her and leaves her alone.

The same accommodation with nature occurs in #986, "A narrow Fellow in the Grass," where the subject, a snake that she encounters, is first made to seem familiar and harmless. Then the poet suggests that she has made her peace with "Several of Nature's People," and she feels for them "a transport/ Of cordiality," although one expects a more ecstatic noun than cordiality after a sense of transport. Dickinson concludes with a potent description of her true feelings about the snake, "Zero at the Bone," a phrase which well reflects her emotion during most confrontations, internal or external.

Death is not merely metaphorical for Dickinson: It is the greatest subject of her work. Perhaps her finest lyrics are on this topic, which she surveyed with a style at once laconic and acute, a tone of quiet terror conveyed through understatement and indirection. Her power arises from the tension between her formal and tonal control and the emotional intensity of what she writes. She approaches death from two perspectives, adopts two stances: the persona as the grieving onlooker, attempting to continue with life and her own faith tested by the experience of watching another die; and the persona as the dying person.

By consensus the greatest of all Dickinson's poems, "Because I could not stop for Death" (#712) explores death from the second perspective, as do such poems as "I Heard a fly buzz—when I died" (#465) and "I died for Beauty" (#449). "Because I could not stop for Death" unites love and death, for death comes to the persona in the form of a gentleman caller. Her reaction is neither haste to meet him, nor displeasure at his arrival. She has time to put away her "labor and . . . leisure"; he is civil. The only hint in the first two stanzas of what is really occurring is the presence of Immortality, and yet that presence, although not unnoticed, is as yet unfelt by the persona. The third stanza brings the customary metaphor of life as a journey and the convention of one's life passing before one's eyes: from youth, through maturity, to sunset. Here, however, two of the images work against the surface calm: The children out for recess do not play, but strive; the grain is said to be gazing. "Grazing" might be the expected word, although even that would be somewhat out of place, but "gazing" both creates unfulfilled aural expectations and gives the sense of the persona as only one actor in a drama that many are watching.

Again, as is common in Dickinson, the poem is hinged by a coordinate conjunction in the exact middle. This time the conjunction is "Or," as the speaker realizes not that she is passing the sun, but that "He passed us." The metaphoric journey through life continues; it is now night, but the emotions have changed from the calm of control to fright. The speaker's "Zero at the Bone" is literal, for her clothing, frilly and light, while appropriate for a wedding, is not so for the funeral that is occurring. The final stop—for, like the first two stanzas, the last two are motionless—is before the grave, "a House that seemed/ A Swelling of the Ground." The swelling ground also suggests pregnancy, but this earth bears death, not life. The last stanza comments that even though the persona has been dead for centuries, all that time seems shorter than the one moment of realization of where her journey must ultimately end. Death, Dickinson's essential metaphor and subject, is seen in terms of a moment of confrontation. Absence thus becomes the major presence, confusion the major ordering principle.

Dickinson's poetry is at times sentimental, the extended metaphors occasionally too cute, the riddling tone sometimes too coy. Like any poet, that is, she has limitations; and because her poetry is so consistent throughout her life, those limitations may be more obvious than in a poet who changes more noticeably. They do not, however, diminish her stature. If she found her place in American literature only decades after her death, it is a place she will not forfeit. Her importance is, of course, partly historical: With Whitman she changed the shape and direction of American poetry, creating and fulfilling poetic potentials that make her a poet beyond her century. Her importance, however, is much greater than that. The intensity with which she converted emotional loss and intellectual questioning into art, the wit and energy of her work, mark the body of her poetry as among the finest that American poets have produced.

Other major work

NONFICTION: *The Letters of Emily Dickinson*, 1958 (Thomas H. Johnson and Theodora Ward, editors, 3 volumes).

Bibliography

Cameron, Sharon. *Choosing Not Choosing: Dickenson's Fascicles.* Chicago: University of Chicago Press, 1992.
Dickinson, Donna. *Emily Dickinson.* Oxford, England: Berg, 1985.
Farr, Judith. *The Passion of Emily Dickinson.* Cambridge, Mass.: Harvard University Press, 1992.
Ferlazzo, Paul, ed. *Critical Essays on Emily Dickinson.* Boston: G. K. Hall, 1984.
Howe, Susan. *My Emily Dickinson.* Berkeley, Calif.: North Atlantic Books, 1989.
Juhasz, Suzanne, ed. *Feminist Critics Read Emily Dickinson.* Bloomington: Indiana University Press, 1983.
MacNeil, Helen. *Emily Dickinson.* New York: Pantheon Books, 1986.
Robinson, John. *Emily Dickinson: Looking to Canaan.* Winchester, Mass.: Faber & Faber, 1986.
Sewall, Richard B. *The Life of Emily Dickinson.* 2 vols. New York: Farrar, Straus & Giroux, 1974.

JOAN DIDION

Born: Sacramento, California; December 5, 1934

Principal long fiction

Run River, 1963; *Play It As It Lays*, 1970; *A Book of Common Prayer*, 1977; *Democracy*, 1984.

Other literary forms

Joan Didion is respected as a novelist, but she has been even more highly acclaimed as an essayist. Her career as a writer was launched by a piece of nonfiction; in 1956, during her senior year at the University of California at Berkeley, her article on the San Francisco architect William Wilson Wurster won *Vogue's* Prix de Paris contest for young writers, and she was awarded a job with that magazine. Although she resigned her position at *Vogue* in 1963 to devote more time to her fiction, she continued as a film critic for the magazine and began publishing regularly in the *Saturday Evening Post*. She has also written articles for periodicals such as *The American Scholar*, *The New York Times Magazine*, *National Review*, *Esquire*, *New West*, and *The New York Review of Books*. Didion has also collaborated with her husband, John Gregory Dunne, on several screenplays.

Didion achieved national recognition with her first collection of essays, *Slouching Towards Bethlehem* (1968); her second collection, *The White Album* (1979), was a best-seller. Her books *Salvador* (1983) and *Miami* (1987) are more overtly political and have aroused considerable controversy.

Achievements

Didion's achievements are somewhat paradoxical. Despite her claims that she speaks only for herself, she has become a spokesperson for the anxiety-ridden generation of the late 1960's and early 1970's; as surely as F. Scott Fitzgerald became a chronicler of the jazz age, she has become the chronicler of a generation living, in her terms, "close to the edge." Didion has developed a reputation for cool, detached observation and for her syncopated but elegant style. James Dicky has called her "the finest woman prose stylist writing in English today," and even some who dismiss her as intellectually shallow respect her craftsmanship.

Didion has her detractors, as all writers have. Some, pointing to her detachment, have criticized her for not taking stronger moral and political stands. Others maintain that her pessimism is too overriding and that her criticism of society is too shrill. Whether one shares Didion's pessimistic outlook, however, her integrity and her style deserve respect.

Biography

Joan Didion was born to Frank Reese and Eduene Jarret Didion on December 5, 1934, in Sacramento, California. Both the date and the place are significant. Though Didion had just turned seven when Pearl Harbor was attacked, she is not, strictly speaking, a child of the postwar generation. This fact might explain some of her detachment from the 1960's and some of the nostalgia she evidently feels even when she is pointing out the shortcomings of the more traditional and more orderly values of pre-World War II America.

Didion's place of birth is even more important. Didion is a child of the West—not the West of Los Angeles, but of the more pastoral Sacramento Valley. The land on which Didion lived had been in her family for five generations, and as a child, she was expected to absorb the myth that America was a new Eden. Didion explores—and largely explodes—the myth of the Sacramento Valley as Eden in her first novel, *Run River*.

Didion's intellectual break from a more traditional world may have begun in high school, when she discovered literature, and it must have been accelerated by her studies at the University of California at Berkeley. She did not, as she points out with some regret, make Phi Beta Kappa, but she did win first prize in *Vogue*'s Prix de Paris contest. Given as an award the choice of a trip to Paris or a job on the magazine, Didion chose the more practical option and moved to New York.

At *Vogue*, Didion learned to write for the general public, and she began writing for several other magazines as well. She also seriously began writing fiction, and *Run River* was published in 1963. Her time in New York was important for her development as a writer, but she soon became disenchanted. Then, disenchantment turned to depression. In January, 1964, she married John Gregory Dunne, also a writer, and the couple moved to Los Angeles.

In Los Angeles, Didion's writing continued to go well—she published *Slouching Towards Bethlehem* in 1968, and she and Dunne wrote the screenplay for *The Panic in Needle Park* (1971)—but for some time, she continued to suffer from the depression and sense of disorientation she describes in *The White Album*. Her marital problems were publicized in her own essays and in Dunne's. In the 1970's, however, both her marriage and her emotional state improved, and her literary success continued to grow: *Play It As It Lays*, *The White Album*, and *A Book of Common Prayer* were all bestsellers. Financial success also came, not so much from the books as from Didion and Dunne's collaboration on screenplays. Besides *The Panic in Needle Park* and the film adaptation of Dunne's novel *True Confessions* (1977), the couple worked on the script for *A Star Is Born* (1976). Didion and Dunne moved to the affluent Brentwood section of Los Angeles.

Analysis

Almost all Joan Didion's works are concerned with similar themes, and there is an interesting complementary relationship between her essays and her novels. Her essays generally seem intended to force the reader to strip away illusions about contemporary life and accept realities, even if they are bleak. The novels are generally explorations of characters crippled by illusions. To some extent, in each novel, the heroine is disabused of her illusions. The fragile hope that each novel holds out, however, is not offered in terms of this disillusionment, but in terms of new illusions and almost meaningless gestures. Each novel ends with the heroine learning to care for others—for a husband, for children, for friends—and yet this caring is generally based on illusion and seems doomed to failure. Didion's final implication, then, seems to be that people need to strip away all illusions, except those which help them to care for others. Such illusions—even though they are doomed to lead to failure—are sacred.

Although Didion's first novel, *Run River*, is not autobiographical, it does explore the myth she absorbed in her childhood, the myth of America as the new Eden, the new Promised Land.

The ease with which *Run River* can be explained as an explosion of traditional American myths, however, probably suggests why the novel is generally considered Didion's most modest achievement: So many people have exploded traditional American myths since 1963 that it does not seem necessary to reread *Run River* to see it done again. In *Play It As It Lays*, Didion does something few writers have done as well as she; she turns the tables and explodes the myths and illusions surrounding the contemporary sensibility.

Perhaps no setting could be more appropriate for an illusion-hunter than Los Angeles. In *Play It As It Lays*, Didion places her heroine Maria (pronounced "Mar-eye-ah," like the west wind in the musical *Paint Your Wagon*) squarely in the fast lane of life in Southern California. The novel opens with Maria in a psychiatric ward. She has been placed there, presumably, for her failure to attempt to stop a friend from committing suicide in her presence. As the novel unfolds backward into the past, however, the reader comes to realize that if Maria has become unhinged, it is probably a result of the cumulative effect of her abortion, her divorce, and the miscellaneous acts of casual sex, drugs, and other perversities one might expect in a novel about Hollywood.

Maria was not reared with the traditional American values. Instead of the Puritan work ethic ("God helps those who help themselves"), she was taught the gambler's code: "My father advised me that life itself was a crap game." That view was infused with a faith in good luck: "I was raised to believe that what came in on the next roll would always be better than what went on the last." For a long time, Maria was content to wait for the rolls, to go with the flow, and to "play it as it lays." Unfortunately, Maria's luck runs out. The bad roll is an unwanted pregnancy. She thinks, but is not sure, that Carter, her husband, is not the father. He demands that she have an abortion and threatens to take away Kate, their brain-damaged daughter, if she refuses. Maria acquiesces, and her mental deterioration begins.

If Maria could completely accept the mores of her set, she would have no problem; for them, neither abortion nor divorce is anything over which to lose one's composure. Maria, however, does cling to one traditional dream; she wants a family. She fantasizes about living a simple life with Kate and some man—in almost identical fantasies, the man is either Ivan or Les, two of her steadier lovers. Abortion—the termination of another possible child—is almost more than Maria can contemplate, yet she undergoes it. Maria's reaction to the abortion is not philosophical, moral, or religious; it is emotional, physical, and psychological: She cries, hemorrhages, and reaches a point where she cannot easily use plumbing because she imagines pipes clogged with chopped-up pieces of flesh.

Didion does not attempt to make an abstract moral issue out of abortion. Maria's reaction is almost primitive, in the sense of being immediate and unreflecting. In Didion's view, however, abortion is a denial of the most basic social responsibility, that of mother to child. In *Play It As It Lays*, characters fail to fulfill their primal social responsibilities. Carter, Les (even Les's wife), Maria's friends, Helene and BZ, and a number of others all say that they are "seriously worried" about Maria as she slips more and more into self-destructive behavior; yet none of them take care of her.

Most of these characters profess not to be concerned with the sexual conduct of their spouses. When Helene, BZ's wife, drifts into an affair with Carter, BZ asks Maria if she cares. For a time, Maria tries to insist that she does care, but as the novel draws to a conclusion, BZ forces her more and more to a nihilistic position: "'Tell me what matters,' BZ said. 'Nothing,' Maria said." At the end of the novel, BZ kills himself with a bottle of vodka and a grain-and-a-half of Seconal. When Helene and Carter force their way into the room, BZ is dead and Maria is asleep next to him, holding his hand.

On the last page of the novel, Maria, from the psychiatric ward, affirms BZ's nihilism, if not his suicide: "I know what 'nothing' means, and keep on playing. Why, BZ would say. Why not, I say." That, however, is not all there is to it. Maria has already made it clear that she is playing for Kate. She wants to take Kate away from the hospital to a home by the sea where they can live a simple life. Given Kate's condition—to say nothing of Maria's—this future does not sound very likely. Despite her acceptance of nihilism, Maria holds on to one last romantic notion. Perhaps she realizes how illusory her hope is, but the illusion and the hope are necessary. They keep her in the game and away from the Seconal.

While *Play It As It Lays* demonstrates the failure of the nihilistic life-style, Maria survives. In Didion's third novel, *A Book of Common Prayer*, however, the reader is told on the first page that the protagonist, Charlotte Douglas, does not survive. The narrator comments that "she died, hopeful." Whether Charlotte's hope, like Maria's, is illusory is a central question of the novel.

It is the question that the narrator, Grace Strasser-Mendana (née Tabor), is trying to answer throughout the novel. Grace, originally from the United States, "married into one of the three or four solvent families in Boca Grande," the small Central American republic in which Charlotte Douglas is finally killed (or murdered—as Grace says, neither word seems to work). The death of Grace's husband has left her "in putative control of fifty-nine-point-eight percent of the arable land and about the same percentage of the decision-making process in La República." From this position of power, Grace observes the political scheming of her family. She also watches Charlotte walk barefooted into the scene and become caught up in it. Grace leaves the country before Charlotte dies, and the novel is her attempt to understand Charlotte.

Grace comments that Charlotte "dreamed her life," and much of what Grace says makes Charlotte seem a woman even more given to illusion than was Maria. Like Maria, Charlotte loses some of the optimism; her luck runs out. The more traditional life-style fails her. Her first husband, Warren Bogart (perhaps the name is meant to be halfway between those of actors Warren Beatty and Humphrey Bogart) had been "raised to believe not in 'hard work' or 'self reliance' but in the infinite power of the personal appeal." He is also sadistic, sexually perverse, and alcoholic. Charlotte is not perfect, either; one Easter, while their child Marin is still a baby, she gets drunk and sleeps with a man she does not even like (she later conveniently forgets the episode). Warren hits her, and she finally walks away from the marriage.

Her second marriage is not unlike Maria's life in the fast lane, except that the game is radical politics. Her husband is a radical chic lawyer who flies from one center of revolution to another. Leonard does seem genuinely to care for Charlotte, but there are complications. Marin, Charlotte's child by Warren, turns revolutionary; she and her friends hijack a jetliner, burn it in the desert, and join the underground.

Charlotte's main illusion, like Maria's, is centered around her daughter. She later tells Grace that she and

Marin were "inseparable" (a term she also uses to describe her relationship with Warren), and she spins out fantastic accounts of their visit to the Tivoli Gardens. As might be expected, the revolutionary Marin claims to have little use for her bourgeois mother.

After a disastrous reunion with Warren and after the birth and almost immediate death of her child by Leonard, Charlotte drifts to Boca Grande, where she meets Grace. At first, Charlotte gives Grace every reason to think that she is dreaming her life. For quite a while, she goes to the airport every day, on the offhand chance that Marin will pass through Central America. She drifts aimlessly into sexual relations with Victor, Grace's brother-in-law, and then with Gerardo, Grace's son. She seems not to notice the growing signs of revolution and refuses the attempts of Gerardo, Leonard, and Grace to persuade her to leave. Finally, the revolution begins, and she is arrested and killed. Her body is dumped on the lawn of the American embassy.

All this does seem to add up to a life of dreams and illusions, yet throughout the novel, Charlotte proves herself to be capable of very practical behavior.

If Charlotte is not as out of touch as she seems, it seems strange for her to stay in Boca Grande and risk her life. Leonard warns her, "You don't get any real points for staying here, Charlotte." Didion does not glorify Charlotte's decision to stay; it is not a self-defining existential act. She simply returns to her work at a birth control clinic (an ironic job for a woman whose passport lists her occupation as "*madré*"). Her work is not particularly meaningful, since Charlotte routinely advises women to use the diaphragm while the clinic stocks only IUD's. In any event, no clients come on Charlotte's last day of work, the last day of her life. In deciding to stay, Charlotte maintains something of her integrity, what Didion would call "character," but Didion allows the reader no illusions about the act; it is the integrity of a cardplayer playing out a losing hand.

Charlotte's integrity can be appreciated only in comparison to the values of the other characters, particularly those of Grace. Even though Grace has been trying to understand Charlotte throughout the novel, she is as much a victim of delusion as Charlotte is. For some time, Grace has realized the difficulty in understanding things, in trying to get the story straight. When Leonard reveals to her that her husband Edgar had been involved with the guerrillas himself, Grace is finally forced to realize that her life, as much as Charlotte's, has been one of delusion.

Grace's statement, "We all remember what we need to remember," is one of the lessons of the novel. All people prefer to believe their own versions of the stories in which they are trapped; all people accept delusions. Grace finally realizes that, "I am more like Charlotte Douglas than I thought I was." Perhaps Charlotte's death was something of a meaningless gesture, but beside her coffin, Grace can only make a small meaningless gesture of love; she places a T-shirt painted like an American flag on the casket. By way of comment, she borrows a phrase from Charlotte and Leonard: "There were no real points in that either." Neither Grace nor Charlotte— perhaps none of Didion's characters in any of her novels—scores any real points in the end.

Other major works

SHORT FICTION: *Telling Stories*, 1978.

SCREENPLAYS: *The Panic in Needle Park*, 1971 (with John Gregory Dunne); *Play It As It Lays*, 1972 (with Dunne); *A Star Is Born*, 1976 (with Dunne and Frank Pierson); *True Confessions*, 1981 (with Dunne).

NONFICTION: *Slouching Towards Bethlehem*, 1968; *The White Album*, 1979; *Salvador*, 1983; *Miami*, 1987; *After Henry*, 1992.

Bibliography

Friedman, Ellen G., ed. *Joan Didion: Essays and Conversations*. Princeton, N.J.: Ontario Review Press, 1984.

Henderson, Katherine Usher. *Joan Didion*. New York: Ungar, 1981.

Kazin, Alfred. "Joan Didion: Portrait of a Professional." *Harper's* 243 (December, 1971): 112-114.

Olendorf, Donna. "Joan Didion: A Checklist, 1955-1980." *Bulletin of Bibliography* 32 (January-March, 1981): 32-44.

Winchell, Mark Royden. *Joan Didion*. Rev. ed. Boston: Twayne, 1989.

ISAK DINESEN
Baroness Karen Blixen-Finecke

Born: Rungstedlund, Denmark; April 17, 1885

Died: Rungstedlund, Denmark; September 7, 1962

Principal short fiction

Seven Gothic Tales, 1934; *Vinter-Eventyr*, 1942 (*Winter's Tales*, 1942); *Sidste Fortællinger*, 1957 (*Last Tales*, 1957); *Skæbne-Anekdoter*, 1958 (*Anecdotes of Destiny*, 1958); *Ehrengard*, 1963; *Efterladte Fortællinger*, 1975 (*Carnival: Entertainments and Posthumous Tales*, 1977).

Other literary forms

In addition to her numerous tales and stories, Isak Dinesen wrote many letters and essays. She is particularly well known, however, for her narrative *Den afrikanske Farm* (1937; *Out of Africa*, 1937), which tells of her years in Kenya (a sequel was published in 1960). After her death, two volumes of letters, written while in Africa, were published, as were her essays.

Achievements

Dinesen has a special position in modern literature in that she is a major author in two languages. Although a native of Denmark, she wrote in both English and Danish, creating her tales as original works in both tongues. Popular with the critics as well as the general public, she was appointed an honorary member of the American Academy of Arts and Letters in 1957 and was repeatedly mentioned as a candidate for the Nobel Prize in Literature. Her initial success came in the English-speaking world. With time, however, she became successful also at home, where her magnetic personality and storytelling gifts gradually captivated the public. Aided by the medium of radio, she became a veritable cultural institution in Denmark. Since her death, her critical reputation has steadily grown both at home and abroad, and she has come to be considered a modern master of short fiction.

Biography

Isak Dinesen's life may be divided into three parts: her childhood and youth, her time in Africa, and her years as a recognized writer. Her parents came from very different social backgrounds. From her father, Wilhelm Dinesen, a landed proprietor, she inherited a love of adventure, nature, and storytelling. Her mother, on the other hand, came from a bourgeois family of merchants and attempted to foster a sense of duty, obligation, and guilt in her three daughters. Karen Christenze (Isak is a pseudonym that she assumed at the beginning of her writing career) was her father's favorite daughter and thereby was able to avoid some of her mother's puritanical manacles. At the age of ten, however, her father's suicide turned her youth into a period of mostly joyless desperation. Early she began writing stories and short plays, for which she had been prepared by an unsystematic private education. She also studied art and traveled abroad with her mother, sisters, and aunt.

The second period in Dinesen's life began in 1914, when she married her first cousin, the Baron Bror Blixen-Finecke, and with him settled down to manage a coffee plantation outside Nairobi, in British East Africa. Her husband infected her with syphilis and proved himself a poor manager of the plantation; the couple was separated in 1921 and divorced four years later. Living in what was then known as Kenya as the manager of a different, and larger, coffee farm, Dinesen cultivated a friendship with Denys Finch Hatton, whom she had met in 1918. A confirmed bachelor, Finch Hatton had no desire to marry Dinesen, which grieved her. Dinesen's African life came to an end in 1931, when the coffee farm had to be sold and Denys died in the crash of his private plane.

Dinesen returned to Denmark in a state of abject poverty. Supported by her family and inspired by the success of a few stories, which years earlier had been published under the pen name Oceola, she set out to create a new life for herself as a writer. Other stories, written during her African sojourn, existed in draft form, and some of these gradually became perfected and included in *Seven Gothic Tales*, the English-language edition of which became both a critical and popular success. Her autobiographical narrative *Out of Africa* established her as a major presence on the literary scene both in Denmark and in the English-language world, and the books that followed were also enthusiastically received.

An indication of Dinesen's popularity in the United States is the fact that five of her titles were chosen as Book-of-the-Month Club selections. Living at her birthplace, Rungstedlund, north of Copenhagen, Denmark, she gathered her admirers around her and tended her literary reputation.

During most of her adult life, Dinesen was plagued by illness, which was exacerbated by much strenuous travel abroad and the entertainment of numerous guests at home. After a particularly taxing summer, she died at her home on September 7, 1962.

Analysis

Isak Dinesen reacted against the psychological and social realism of contemporary Danish literature and looked back to the Romantic storytellers for inspiration. Like them, she preferred the longer, drawn-out tale to the short story proper, and authorial narration, often with overtly present narrators, is a hallmark of her narratives. Her chosen form therefore often struck her contemporaries as old-fashioned. This was also the case with her thematic concerns, for her stories take place mostly in the century between 1770 and 1870 and express the ethos of a bygone age. She speaks in favor of such aristocratic values as duty, honor, and justice, but she also rejects the Christian dualistic worldview and questions the role of religion and the place of women in contemporary bourgeois society. Above all, however, the role of art in human life constitutes a central theme of her authorship. Through art, a unified vision is possible, and such a monistic perception of reality is, for Dinesen, a primary source of meaning in general and of comfort in difficult times.

"Aben" ("The Monkey"), a long story from *Seven Gothic Tales*, is a good example of Dinesen's "gothic" or fantastic narratives that also exhibits many of her thematic concerns. Its setting is a noble milieu in northern Germany in the 1830's; its theme is the nature of love. Boris, a young lieutenant in the Prussian Royal Guards, has become involved in a homosexual scandal in the capital and is seeking the aid of his maiden aunt, Cathinka, the Prioress of Cloister Seven, a convent for spinsters of noble blood. In order to escape dishonor and almost certain death, Boris has resolved to marry, thus hoping to lay to rest the rumors of his homosexual involvement with other members of his regiment. His aunt, who is well acquainted with the various noble

families of the land, is being asked to select a suitable mate for him. The fantastic element of the story is found in the relationship between the Prioress and her little gray monkey, to which she has a mysterious bond and with which she, from time to time and in accordance with traditional Scandinavian folk belief in shape-shifting, exchanges her identity. The monkey is connected with the idea of love through the love goddess of an ancient Baltic people, the Wends. The goddess looks like a beautiful woman from the front and like a monkey from the back. Through this image, Dinesen argues against the Judeo-Christian distinction between the heteroerotic, which is acceptable to society, and the homoerotic, which is not. Speaking in favor of a monistic outlook on human sexuality, Dinesen, through the similarity between the Wendish love-goddess and the Janus face, problematizes the distinction between normal and abnormal sexuality. The text actually foregrounds the question of how it can be determined which side is the front and which is the back of the goddess, and the implied answer is that no such determination can be made on objective grounds.

There is, nevertheless, a recognition on Dinesen's part that people have to live up to the expectations of their society if they are to get along in life. Boris has certain duties to his family, and despite his sexual difference from the norm, he is obligated to repress his desires and to force himself to marry. The Prioress, who at this time and in a mysterious way is possessed by aspects of her monkey's personality, chooses as his bride the only daughter of a neighbor, a tall and strong young woman named Athena, whom Boris has known since childhood. Her father welcomes Boris as a suitor and says that he would delight in seeing the young man's features in the faces of his grandchildren. Athena rejects him, however, and states unequivocally that she will never marry; she will not, in other words, yield to her duty to her family. There is a strong implication in the text that Athena is as troubled by her gender role as Boris is by his.

Athena's rejection infuriates the Prioress, who arranges a supper of seduction during which Athena gets drunk. As the girl goes to her room, The Prioress gives Boris an aphrodisiac to help him complete his conquest, and he struggles with Athena, who knocks out two of his teeth. Boris interprets this as a symbolic castration and feels that he has been freed from his obligation to have a normal conjugal relationship with her, should they get married. She has won his battle with traditional sexuality for him, and he therefore triumphantly kisses her with his bloody mouth. The significance of this perverted and ironic image of defloration is not lost on Athena, who, in horror and disgust, loses her consciousness. Boris does not touch her further.

The next morning, Athena is told by the Prioress that she is now most likely pregnant and that her only hope of avoiding dishonor is to marry Boris. Together, they then watch as the Prioress, who all along has been in the grip of the personality of the monkey, reasserts her own true self through an intense struggle with the little animal. This astonishing event affects Athena deeply, and she resigns herself to marrying Boris, with the proviso, however, that she is to have dominion in their relationship. Athena and Boris' union is thus marked by the back side of the love goddess in several ways. Erotically, they are misfits in that they both look on heterosexuality with revulsion. Psychologically and emotionally, their union is a result of a power struggle, touched by the fantastic, rather than a consequence of the usual process of falling in love. Morally, their marriage represents a surrender to the expectations of their families, but it is unlikely that they will do their real duty and have children. Socially, their marriage will also be out of the ordinary, as, in opposition to the patriarchal norm of their time and place, the wife will rule the roost with the consent of her husband. Dinesen thus problematizes one of the fundamental oppositions of human life, namely that between male and female, and offers a critique of both sex roles and Christian dualism.

While the stories in *Seven Gothic Tales* touch on the fantastic and frequently present challenges to the reader, those of *Winter's Tales* are more traditional, and therefore also more accessible, narratives. Written during the German occupation of Denmark, they are tales for difficult times, in which the possibility of reconciliation and restoration is held dear.

Dinesen's often-gentle critique of Christianity becomes relentlessly satirical in "Heloise" ("The Heroine"), in which she casts a woman stripper in the role of the Christian savior. A young Englishman named Frederick Lamond, together with a company of French travelers, is caught in a German border town at the time of the Franco-Prussian war. A student of religious philosophy, Frederick is at the time writing a treatise on the doctrine of the Atonement. When the German army marches into town, he and the other stranded travelers are accused of espionage. A famous messianic prophecy from the Book of Isaiah, which is quoted in Frederick's manuscript, is read as a code by the Germans and forms the main proof of their accusation.

One of the travelers is a woman named Heloise, whose rare beauty greatly impresses one of the German officers. Realizing that the accusation of espionage may not have much merit, he offers the travelers a bargain: if Heloise will appear before him in the nude, they will be permitted to continue to France; otherwise, they will be shot. Heloise turns to the company and leaves the decision in their hands, and they all vote to refuse the German's demand. The officer, who respects the courage of both Heloise and her companions, then decides to let them go after all, and he apologizes to Heloise, whom he terms a heroine, by sending her a big bouquet of roses.

Six years later, Frederick is in Paris in order to attend some lectures in his field. Entertained by a friend, he is taken to a music hall, where the most beautiful woman in Paris is appearing nude in a show. It turns out that the woman is Heloise, whom Frederick still remembers well. They meet and reminisce after the show, and Heloise explains what in her opinion was at stake in the dramatic incident six years earlier. It was not only the lives of the travelers, she says, which hung in the balance, but their ability to live with their consciences. It would have cost her very little to comply with the German's demand; for her, it would have been a professional matter, not one of conscience. The other travelers, however, would have never gotten over it if Heloise were to have bought their freedom at the cost of exposing her body. Frederick now understands that her heroism did not consist in standing up to the German officer's demands but in looking after the welfare of her companions' souls. Heloise, who through the imagery in the story has been carefully presented as a kind of Christ-figure, now appears, to both Frederick and the reader, as a full-blown savior. Heloise's parting comment to Frederick is that she wishes that he might have seen her perform six years earlier, when her beauty was at its fullest. Heloise has the temperament of an artist in that art, in her case the beauty of her body, gives meaning to her life.

Portraying a stripper as someone who saves people from guilt constitutes a truly ironic comment on traditional Christian religion. Casting a woman in such a position undercuts the traditional conception of women's roles as well. "The Heroine," through its overt questioning of central religious and social norms, therefore becomes one of Dinesen's most radical stories.

Dinesen placed high demands on herself. She felt a strong sense of duty and loyalty to the artist within her, and her exquisitely crafted tales are not numerous. She relentlessly pursued her unitary vision, subtly criticizing those aspects of life that went against the grain of her thought, such as the dualism of received religion and traditional sex roles.

Other major works

NOVEL: *Gengældelsens Veje*, 1944 (*The Angelic Avengers*, 1946; as Pierre Andrézel).

NONFICTION: *Den afrikanske Farm*, 1937 (*Out of Africa*, 1937); *Skygger paa Græsset*, 1960 (*Shadows on the Grass*, 1960); *Essays*, 1965; *Breve fra Afrika 1914-1931*, 1978 (*Letters from Africa 1914-1931*, 1981); *Daguerreotypes, and Other Essays*, 1979; *Samlede essays*, 1985.

Bibliography

Bjornvig, Thorkild. *The Pact: My Friendship with Isak Dinesen*. Translated from the Danish by Ingvar Shousboe and William Jay Smith. Baton Rouge: Louisiana State University Press, 1983.

Johannesson, Eric O. *The World of Isak Dinesen*. Seattle: University of Washington Press, 1961.

Juhl, Marianne, and Bo Hakon Jørgensen. *Diana's Revenge: Two Lines in Isak Dinesen's Authorship*. Translated from the Danish by Anne Born. Odense, Denmark: Odense University Press, 1985.

Langbaum, Robert Woodrow. *The Gayety of Vision: A Study of Isak Dinesen's Art*. New York: Random House, 1964.

Migel, Parmenia. *Titania: The Biography of Isak Dinesen*. New York: Random House, 1967.

Stambaugh, Sara. *The Witch and the Goddess in the Stories of Isak Dinesen: A Feminist Reading*. Ann Arbor: UMI Research Press, 1988.

Thurman, Judith. *Isak Dinesen: The Life of a Storyteller*. New York: St. Martin's Press, 1982.

RITA DOVE

Born: Akron, Ohio; August 28, 1952

Principal poetry

The Yellow House on the Corner, 1980; *Museum*, 1983; *Thomas and Beulah*, 1986; *Grace Notes*, 1989; *Selected Poems*, 1993.

Other literary forms

Although Rita Dove is known primarily as a poet, she has also published *Fifth Sunday* (1985), a collection of short stories, and *Through the Ivory Gate* (1992), a novel.

Achievements

Dove's literary honors include grants and fellowships from the National Endowment for the Arts, the Academy of American Poets, the Guggenheim Foundation, and the General Electric Foundation. She spent 1988-1989 as a Senior Mellon Fellow at the National Humanities Center in North Carolina. In 1987 her collection *Thomas and Beulah* made her the first black woman since Gwendolyn Brooks to win the Pulitzer Prize. In 1993, Dove was named Poet Laureate of the United States.

Biography

Born in 1952 in Akron, Ohio, Rita Dove is the daughter of Ray and Elvira (Hord) Dove. She received a B.A. in 1973 from Miami University (Ohio) and then, on a Fulbright fellowship, attended the University of Tübingen to study modern European literature. She returned to the United States to earn an M.F.A. at the highly regarded University of Iowa Writers' Workshop in 1977. After holding a number of teaching posts and traveling widely in Europe and the Middle East, she became a professor of English at the University of Virginia.

Dove married Fred Viebahn, a writer, and they had a daughter, Aviva Chantal Tamu Dove-Viebahn.

Analysis

Rita Dove's poetry is characterized by discipline and technical proficiency, surprising breadth of reference, a willingness to approach emotionally charged subjects with aesthetic objectivity, and a refusal to define herself only in terms of blackness. She combines a novelist's eye for action and gesture with the lyric poet's exalted sense of language.

The startling scope of Dove's learning opens for her poetry a correspondingly vast range of topics and concerns, but the most persistent, and the one that most distinguishes her work from that of poets in the 1970's and 1980's, is history. She is constantly laboring to bring into focus the individual struggle in the ebb and flow of the historical tide. A second major concern is cultural collision, the responses of an outsider to a foreign culture, and she pursues this theme in a number of travel poems. Dove also plumbs the circumstances of her life as a way of confronting the puzzle of her own identity—as an African American, as a woman, as a daughter, as a parent—but she manages self-dramatization without self-aggrandizement.

Dove has been lauded for her technical acumen. While much contemporary poetry is best characterized by a certain casualness and laxity, she has created poetry in which no verse is "free." Each poem gives the impression of having been chiseled, honed, and polished. Her poems evolve into highly individual structures, rather than traditional forms, although it is possible to find an occasional sonnet neatly revised and partially hidden. More often she stresses rhythm and sound and uses interior rhyme, slant rhyme, and feminine rhyme to furnish her stanzas with a subtle organizing principle, what she calls the "sound cage" of a poem. Her idiom is predominantly colloquial, but she can adopt the stiffened, formal diction of the eighteenth and nineteenth centuries when evoking personas from those periods. In her mastery of the craft

Dove reveals an attitude toward poetry itself—a deeply felt love and respect—that also influences the approach a reader must take to it. Her work makes demands upon the reader because of that love.

Dove's first two volumes, *The Yellow House on the Corner* and *Museum*, both provide a balance between the personal or individual and the social or cultural. Each is divided into sections that allow the author to address concerns that she wishes for now to remain separate. Yet it has also been noted that the titles of these two books signal a shift in Dove's emphasis from the homely and familiar, "the yellow house," to the more sophisticated and arcane "museum." This generalization should not, however, obscure the fact that the poet's interests in these books overlap considerably. *Museum* is the more consciously organized, with its sections pointedly titled and each dealing with a central topic—history and myth, art and artifact, autobiography and the personal past, life in the modern world. *Thomas and Beulah* represents Dove's coming of age critically, a step into the position of a leading African American poet. It allows her to extend her continual dissertation on the single person striving in the midst of historical flux; at the same time she can pursue her abiding interest in her own family romance, the question of heritage. Still availing itself of a variety of themes, *Grace Notes* is by far the most intensely autobiographical of her works, becoming a study in limitation and poignant regret. How, she seems to ask here, does one grant to daily life, that ornament or variation that magically transforms it?

Poems in *The Yellow House on the Corner* often depict the collision of wish with reality, of heart's desire with the dictates of the world. This collision is made tolerable by the working of the imagination, and the result is, for Dove, "magic," or the existence of an unexplainable occurrence. It is imagination and the art it produces that allow the speaker in "This Life" to see that "the possibilities/ are golden dresses in a nutshell." "Possibilities" have the power to transform this life into something distinct and charmed. Even the woman driven mad with grief over the loss of her son (or husband?) in "The Bird Frau" becomes a testament to possibility in her desire to "let everything go wild!" She becomes a bird-woman as a way of reuniting with her lost airman, who died in the war over France. While her condition may be perceived as pathetic, Dove refuses to indulge sentimentality, instead seeing her madness as a form of undying hope.

The refusal to indulge sentimentality is a mark of Dove's critical intelligence. It allows her to interpose an objectifying distance between herself and the subject. She knows the absolute value of perspective, so that while she can exult in the freedom that imagination makes possible, she recognizes that such liberty has its costs and dangers too. Two poems in particular reveal this desire and her wariness: "Geometry" and "Sightseeing." In the former, Dove parallels the study of points, lines, and planes in space with the work of the poet: "I prove a theorem and the house expands:/ the windows jerk free to hover near the ceiling,/ the ceiling floats away with a sigh." Barriers and boundaries disappear in the imagination's manipulation of them, but that manipulation has its methodology or aesthetic: "I *prove* a theorem. . . ." In "Sightseeing," the speaker, a traveler in Europe after World War II, comes upon what would seem to be a poem waiting to happen. The inner courtyard of a village church has been left just as it was found by the villagers after an Allied bombing raid. It is filled with the shattered cherubim and seraphim that had previously decorated the inner terrace of the building: "What a consort of broken dolls!" Yet the speaker repudiates any temptation to view the sight as the villagers must—"A terrible sign . . ." Instead she coolly ponders the rubble with the detached air of a detective: "Let's look/ at the facts." She "reads" the scene and the observers' attention to it as a cautionary lesson. The "children of angels" become "childish monsters." Since she distinguishes herself from the devout villagers, she can also see herself and her companion in the least flattering light: "two drunks" coming all the way across the town "to look at a bunch of smashed statues."

This ability to debunk and subvert expectations is a matter of artistic survival for Dove and a function of her calm intelligence. As an African American poet she is aware of the tradition of letters into which she steps. Two other poems imply that this tradition can be problematic. In "Upon Meeting Don L. Lee, in a Dream" Dove encounters Lee (now known as Haki R. Madhubuti), a leading figure in the Black Arts movement, which attempted to generate a populist, specifically black aesthetic. The figure that emerges from Dove's poem, however, is unable to change except to self-destruct: "I can see caviar/ Imbedded like buckshot between his teeth." Her dream-portrait of Lee deflates not only his masculinity but his status as cultural icon as well. In "Nigger Song: An Odyssey" Dove seems to hark back further for a literary forbear and finds one in Gwendolyn Brooks, the first black woman to win the Pulitzer Prize. Although by 1967 Brooks had come to embrace the black nationalism that Don L. Lee embodied, Dove's poem echoes the Brooks of an earlier time, the composer of "We Real Cool." In her evocation of "the nigger night" Dove captures the same vibrant energy that Brooks both celebrates and laments with the realization that the energy of urban African American youth is allowed no purposeful outlet and will turn upon itself. She writes: "Nothing can catch us./ Laughter spills like gin from glasses."

Some of the most compelling poems in Dove's first book are in a group of vignettes and portraits from the era of American slavery. These poems not only reveal her historical awareness but also allow her to engage the issue of race from a distance. Dove wants her poetry to produce anger, perhaps, but not to be produced only by anger. One example of this aesthetic distance from emotion might be "The Abduction," a brief foray in the voice of Solomon Northrup. Northrup is a free black lured to Washington, D.C., by "new friends" with the promise of good work, and then kidnapped and sold into bondage. Dove dwells on the duplicity of these men and Northrup's susceptibility to them. Yet no pronouncements are made. The poem ends with the end of freedom, but that ending has been foreshadowed by the tightly controlled structure of the poem itself, with each stanza shortening as the scope of the victim's world constricts to this one-line conclusion: "I woke and found myself alone, in darkness and in chains." The indignation and disgust that such an episode could call forth are left entirely to the reader.

Dove's next volume, *Museum*, is itself, as the title suggests, a collection of historical and aesthetic artifacts. The shaping impulse of the book seems to be retrospective, a looking back to people and things that have been somehow suspended in time by legend, by historical circumstance, by all-too-human emotional wish. Dove intends to delve beneath the publicly known side of these stories—to excavate, in a sense, and uncover something forgotten but vital. The book is filled with both historical and mythical figures, all sharing the single trait of muted voice. Thus, "Nestor's Bathtub" begins: "As usual, legend got it all/ wrong." The private torment of a would-be martyr is made public in "Catherine of Alexandria." In "The Hill Has Something to Say," the poet speculates on the buried history of Europe, the cryptic messages that a culture sends across time. In one sense, the hill is a metaphor for this book, a repository of signs and images

that speak only to that special archaeologist, the reader.

In the section titled "In the Bulrush," Dove finds worthy subjects in unlikely places and draws them from hiding. "Banneker" is another example of her flair for evoking the antebellum world of slavery, where even a free man is wrongly regarded because of his race. In the scientist Benjamin Banneker she finds sensitivity, eloquence, and intelligence, all transformed by prejudice into mere eccentricity. Banneker was the first black man to devise an almanac and served on Thomas Jefferson's commission to lay out the city of Washington, D.C., but the same qualities that lifted him to prominence made him suspect in the eyes of white society. Dove redeems this crabbed conception of the man in an alliterative final passage that focuses attention on his vision:

> Lowering his eyes to fields
> sweet with the rot of spring, he
> could see
> a government's domed city
> rising from the morass and spreading
> in a spiral of lights . . .

A third section of the book is devoted entirely to poems about the poet's father, and they represent her efforts to understand him. It is a very personal grouping, made to seem all the more so by the preceding sections in which there is little or nothing directly personal at all.

In the final section, "Primer for the Nuclear Age," Dove includes what is one of her most impressive performances. Although she has not shown herself to be a poet of rage, she is certainly not inured to the social and political injustice she observes. Her work is a way of channeling and controlling such anger; as she says in "Primer for the Nuclear Age": "if you've/ got a heart at all, someday/ it will kill you." "Parsley," the final poem of *Museum*, summons up the rank insanity of Rafael Trujillo, dictator of the Dominican Republic, who, on October 2, 1957, ordered twenty thousand black Haitians killed because they could not pronounce the letter *r* in *perejil*, Spanish for parsley. The poem is divided into two sections: The first is a villanelle spoken by the Haitians, and the second describes General Trujillo on the day of his decision. The second section echoes many of the lines from the Haitians' speech, drawing murderer and victims together, suggesting a disturbing complicity among all parties in this episode of unfettered power. Even though Dove certainly wants to draw attention to this event, the real subject here is the lyric poet's realm—that point at which language intersects with history and actually determines its course.

Thomas and Beulah garnered the Pulitzer Prize, but it is more important for the stage it represents in Dove's poetic development. Her first two books reveal a lyric poet generally working within the bounds of her medium. The lyric poem denies time, process, change. It becomes a frozen moment, an emotion reenacted in the reading. In *Thomas and Beulah* she pushes at the limitations of the form by stringing together, "as beads on a necklace," a whole series of these lyric moments. As the poems begin to reflect upon one another, the effect is a dramatic unfolding in which the passing of time is represented, even though the sequence never establishes a conventional plot. To accomplish this end Dove creates a two-sided book: Thomas' side ("Mandolin," twenty-one poems) followed by Beulah's ("Canary in Bloom," twenty-one poems). The narrative moves from Thomas' riverboat life and the crucial death of his friend Lem to his arrival in Akron and marriage, through the birth of children, jobs, illness, and death. Beulah's part of the book then begins, moving through her parents' stormy relationship, her courtship with Thomas, marriage, pregnancy, work, and death. These two lives transpire against the historical backdrop of the Great Migration, the Depression, World War II, and the March on Washington; however, these events are practically the only common elements in the two sides of the story. Thomas and Beulah seem to live separate lives. Their communication with each other is implicit in the survival of the marriage itself. Throughout, Dove handles the story through exacting use of imagery and character.

Thomas emerges as a haunted man, dogged by the death of his friend Lem, which occurs in the opening poem, "The Event." Thomas drunkenly challenges Lem to swim from the deck of the riverboat to an island in the Mississippi. Lem drowns in the attempt to reach what is probably a mirage, and Thomas is left with "a stinking circle of rags/ the half-shell mandolin." In "Courtship" he begins to woo Beulah, but the poem implies that the basis of their relationship will be the misinterpreted gesture and that Thomas' guilt has left him with a void. He casually takes a yellow silk scarf from around his neck and wraps it around her shoulders; "a gnat flies/ in his eye and she thinks/ he's crying." Thomas' gift, rather than a spontaneous transfer of warmth, is a sign of his security in his relative affluence. The show of vulnerability and emotional warmth is accidental. The lyric poet in Dove allows her to compress this range of possibility in the isolated gesture or image. Beulah's life is conveyed as a more interior affair, a process of attaining the wisdom to understand her world rather than to resist it openly. In "The Great Palace of Versailles" Beulah's reading becomes her secret escape from the nastiness of the whites for whom she works in Charlotte's Dress Shoppe. As she lies dying in the final poem, "The Oriental Ballerina," her contemplation of the tiny figurine seems a similar invitation to fantasy, but her sensibilities have always been attuned to seeing the world as it is, as it has to be, and the poem ends in a brief flurry of realistic details and an air of acceptance; there is "no cross, just the paper kiss/ of a kleenex above the stink of camphor,/ the walls exploding with shabby tutus. . . ."

Grace Notes marks Dove's return to the purely lyric mode, but an autobiographical impulse dominates the work to an unprecedented degree. More than in any of her previous collections, the poet can be seen as actor in her own closet drama, whether as a young child learning a rather brutal lesson in the Southern black school of survival ("Crab-Boil") or as a mother groping for a way to reveal feminine mysteries to her own little girl ("After Reading *Mickey in the Night Kitchen* for the Third Time Before Bed"). The willingness to become more self-referential carries with it the danger of obscurity, the inside joke that stays inside. Dove, however, seems to open herself to a kind of scrutiny and challenge that offers no hiding place, and that assay extends to her own poetic practice. In "Dedication," a poem in the manner of Czesław Miłosz, Dove seems to question the veracity of her own technical expertise: "What are music or books if not ways/ to trap us in rumors? The freedom of fine cages!" In the wickedly ironic "Ars Poetica" she places herself on the literary chain of being with what might pass for self-deprecation. Her ambition is to make a small poem, like a ghost town, a minute speck on the "larger map of wills." "Then you can pencil me in as a hawk:/ a traveling x-marks-the-spot." Yet this hawk is not a songbird to be taken lightly. The very next poem in the book unleashes the bird of prey in Dove (a pun she surely intends); in the aptly titled "Arrow," she exposes the sexism and racism of an "eminent scholar" in all its condescending glory. This focus on the autobiographical element is not to imply that the range of subjects in *Grace Notes* is not still wide-ranging and surprising. Echoes of her earlier books sound clearly, so does the wit that makes them always engaging: "Here's a riddle for Our Age: when the sky's the limit,/ how can you tell you've gone too far?"

Dove's distinguishing feature is her ability to turn a cold gaze on the larger world with which she has to interact as a social being—and as an African American woman. That gaze is filtered through an aesthetic sensibility that regards poetry as a redemptive force, a transformational power. Her attention to the craft of poetry gives to her work a clarity, elegance, and naturalness.

Other major works

NOVEL: *Through the Ivory Gate*, 1992.
SHORT FICTION: *Fifth Sunday*, 1985.

Bibliography

Dove, Rita. "Coming Home." Interview by Steven Schneider. *The Iowa Review* 19 (Fall, 1989): 112-123.

_____. Interview by Judith Kitchen and others. *Black American Literature Forum* 20 (Fall, 1986): 227-240.

McDowell, Robert. "The Assembling Vision of Rita Dove." *Callaloo: A Black South Journal of Arts and Letters* 9 (Winter, 1986): 61-70.

Rampersad, Arnold. "The Poems of Rita Dove." *Callaloo: A Black South Journal of Arts and Letters* 9 (Winter, 1986): 52-60.

Shoptaw, John. Review of *Thomas and Beulah*. *Black American Literature Forum* 21 (Fall, 1987): 335-341.

MARGARET DRABBLE

Born: Sheffield, England; June 5, 1939

Principal long fiction

A Summer Bird-Cage, 1963; *The Garrick Year*, 1964; *The Millstone*, 1965 (published in the United States as *Thank You All Very Much*); *Jerusalem the Golden*, 1967; *The Waterfall*, 1969; *The Needle's Eye*, 1972; *The Realms of Gold*, 1975; *The Ice Age*, 1977; *The Middle Ground*, 1980; *The Radiant Way*, 1987; *A Natural Curiosity*, 1989.

Other literary forms

Margaret Drabble has combined literary scholarship with her career as a novelist. She has edited a collection of critical essays about Thomas Hardy, *The Genius of Thomas Hardy* (1975), and has edited three of Jane Austen's lesser-known works, *Lady Susan* (1974), *The Watsons* (1974), and *Sanditon* (1974). She has written biographies of William Wordsworth and Arnold Bennett and a literary travelogue of England, *A Writer's Britain: Landscape in Literature* (1979). Her edition of *The Ox-* *ford Companion to English Literature* was published in 1985 to great acclaim. Drabble has had a long-standing connection with drama and continues to write for the stage. Her works include *Bird of Paradise* (1969), a stage play; *A Touch of Love* (1969), a screenplay; and *Laura* (1964), a play for television. Drabble has also written a book for children, *For Queen and Country: Britain in the Victorian Age* (1978).

Achievements

Drabble's novels charm and delight, but perhaps more significantly, they reward their readers with a distinctively modern woman's narrative voice and their unusual blend of Victorian and modern structures and concerns.

Drabble seems to be able to evoke not only the female point of view but also the cadence of the female voice. Her ear for speech rhythms is exceptional, and each central female character has a distinct speech pattern and cadence. This is, of course, more intensely true in the first-person narratives of Drabble's earlier novels, but it is also true of her later novels in which the heroine's interior life is rendered by an omniscient narrator who mimes her speech in order to discuss her feelings and thoughts. Perhaps Drabble's artistry in portraying the sound of the female voice is among her most significant accomplishments.

Drabble has also begun to experiment with the return of the outspoken omniscient narrator. Drabble's rediscovery of an old literary technique seems timely rather than regressive. Her omniscient narrator gives the reader a sense of place, a sense of location and history, without forcing the characters to bear the burden of carrying all that perception in their minds. The narrator's involvement in place and history has important thematic implications for Drabble's fiction. She departs from the prevalent modern emphasis on the centrality of the individual sensibility to explore the consequences of choosing to submit to centrifugal forces, as opposed to struggling against them in an effort to be true to one's roots. This original blend of a deep concern for society's conventions and origins and an unusually sensitive evocation of the individual female sensibility gives Drabble's works their particular flavor.

Biography

Margaret Drabble was born into a family that at once reflects both the breakup of old patterns and the power of conventions, which may account for her receptiveness to both aspects of modern England. Her parents, John Frederick Drabble and Kathleen Marie (Bloor) Drabble, were the first of their families to attend a university. The results of her parents' upward mobility were both creative and destructive. Her father became a barrister and then a judge; her mother became an atheist and thus estranged herself from her fundamentalist parents. Drabble says that her mother was released from the harshness of her religious training when, as a young woman, she read George Bernard Shaw. As she turned the pages she had a revelation that there was no God. Drabble's mother had to struggle against clinically diagnosed depression and stabilized herself through drug therapy.

Drabble has a brother and two sisters, one of whom is Susan Duffy, a novelist whose pen name is A. S. Byatt. Drabble attended a Quaker boarding school in York, The Mount School, and then read English at the University of Cambridge, where she finished among the top of her class. In 1960, in the week that she finished at Cam-bridge, she married Clive Swift.

Swift was an aspiring actor who worked with the Royal Shakespeare Company. In the early years of their marriage, Drabble spent much of her time rearing three children, writing novels, and acting bit parts and under-studying for the Royal Shakespeare Company. Drabble separated from her husband in 1972; their divorce be-came final in 1975. In 1982, she married the biographer Michael Holroyd.

Analysis

Margaret Drabble's novels begin as elaborate embel-lishments on a simple series of events relative only to the first-person narrator, events that reflect a brief but for-mative time in the narrator's life. The early novels deal with the lives of rather ordinary middle-class girls and, but for their sensitivity and subtlety of insight, come dangerously close to being considered women's maga-zine fiction. The later novels are more complex, explor-ing the delicate webs of social interconnections and covering longer periods of time in which the conver-gences of many lives upon one another effect subtle and not-so-subtle changes. Both the early and later novels express concern with finding the legitimate sources of growth and development.

The Needle's Eyes, regarded by many readers as Drab-ble's finest novel, takes its title from Jesus' proverbial words to a rich young man: "It is easier for a camel to go through the eye of a needle, than for a rich man to enter into the kingdom of God" (Matthew 19:24). At the center of the novel are Simon Camish, a barrister from a poor background who would seem to have regretfully gained the world at the expense of his soul, and Rose Bryanston Vassiliou, a rich young woman who compulsively di-vests herself of the benefits of her inheritance but is not fully enjoying her flight into the lower classes.

Rose, a pale, timid girl, had created a tabloid sensation by marrying out of her class. Her choice was the disrepu-table, seedy, sexy Christopher Vassiliou, son of Greek immigrants whose pragmatic financial dealings are not solidly within the boundaries of the law. Rose sought to escape from the evils of wealth through Christopher, one of the downtrodden. Much to her consternation, how-ever, Christopher is not a "happy peasant." He detests poverty and associates it not with virtue but with humili-ation and deprivation, both of which he has endured.

Christopher's dream is to make something of himself.

This dream is only strengthened by the birth of their three children, for whom Christopher wants "only the best." He sees in Rose's war on wealth nothing but perverse self-destructiveness. His fury vents itself in physical abuse. Frail, pale Rose is equally adamant in the protec-tion of her children's future. To her mind, "the best" means freedom from possessions. Again Rose and Chris-topher become figures of tabloid fantasy, this time in a dramatic divorce case.

Rose is working out her divorce settlement when she meets Simon. Simon is introduced to the reader on the same night that he is introduced to Rose; the reader first sees him in a store, buying liquor. Simon feels estranged from the lower-class types who frequent and staff the store. Soon thereafter, this isolation is established as a sharp discontinuity in Simon's life, for he has risen from these ranks. He has been pushed upward by a mother embarrassed by the meanness of her lower-class life and determined that her son will have what she never had. Ironically, the essential gap in his mother's life is also left unfilled in Simon's—that is, the need for warmth and affection. Simon tried to marry into an inheritance of warmth and wealth by his alliance with what he thought was a good-natured girl of the comfortable upper-middle class, Julie Phillips. Their marriage, however, only re-vealed her fear and insecurity, her essential coldness. What Simon had mistaken for warmth was merely super-ficial brightness, a by-product of the Phillips' affluence.

Rose and Simon have attempted to gain what each personally lacked through marriage, as if one could graft onto oneself a human capacity with a wedding ring: Such marriages are doomed to failure. Also doomed has been Rose's attempt to meet human needs with "filthy lucre." She has given a huge portion of her inheritance to a schoolhouse in a lonely, little-known part of Africa. Within months, the school is demolished in the chaos of a civil war along with approximately one hundred children. Rose does not attempt to deny the futility of what she has done.

Simon and Rose strike up a professional acquaintance, casually, it seems, because Christopher has begun some devious maneuvers to get his children away from Rose. As he becomes increasingly involved in helping Rose, Simon realizes that he is in love with her. Rose reveals but a few of her feelings on this issue but does indicate the joy she takes in his company. While Rose and Simon are chasing around after Christopher, who appears to be in the process of abducting the children and taking them out of England, Simon finally tells Rose that, were they at liberty, he would marry her. He blurts out this sentiment as they are walking in a woodland setting. The moment of his revelation finds them in sudden confrontation with a dead stoat, hanging grotesquely in front of them, a dried-up little corpse. According to the narrator, this is "a warning" to Simon and Rose.

The satisfaction that Rose and Simon might find together is based on their shared concern for their obligations and duties. To turn to each other, a temptation for both of them, would be a betrayal of the very basis of their attraction to each other, as it would necessitate shirking their responsibilities. It is the grace in them that understands commitments beyond the self. Understanding this, Simon and Rose remain friends; Christopher and Rose are reunited. Rose has achieved a modus vivendi with Christopher, who goes to work for her father. There is no fully articulated happiness, but a kind of integrity exists at the heart of Rose's and Simon's arrangement.

In the novel's final tableau, Rose is looking at a vandalized lion outside a second-rate British edifice called the Alexandra Palace. The lion's plaster head is broken, revealing a hollow inside. It has been spray-painted red with the name of a local gang, but Rose decides that she likes it. Although beginning life as an anonymous, mass-produced piece of kitsch, the lion has been worn into something unique: "it had weathered into identity. And this she hoped for every human soul." Rose's final wish accepts the uniqueness of life, the beauty of its mere being. She rejects the vision of a life that is continually being held up to an intellectual ideal, by which standards the lion, like her life, is an awful mess.

Drabble has said in an interview that, had she written *The Needle's Eye* after her husband left her, she might

have altered Rose's destiny; perhaps she meant that Rose might have been sent off with Simon, after all. Perhaps these words reveal something of the personal Drabble, but they are a betrayal of the novel. The delicacy of Simon and Rose's poise in front of the dead stoat and the final image of the lion resist second thoughts.

In *The Ice Age*, Drabble considers the problem of survival within a dying tradition. England is enduring an ice age: Its social structure is collapsing. In a brilliantly dark vision, Drabble surveys the challenge this poses to personal resources.

As the novel begins, a reckless real estate speculator, Len Wincobank, is serving time in Scratby Open Prison for fraud. Len's technically innocent accomplice, Maureen Kirby, is wondering how to fit the pieces of her life back together again. A teenage girl, Jane Murray, daughter of an extremely beautiful former actress, Alison Murray, is on trial in the remote Communist country of Wallachia. Anthony Keating, a charming author of musical comedies turned real estate speculator, is recovering from a heart attack and the collapse of his financial empire.

All the characters are suffering through imprisonment in England. It is a time in which Max and Kitty Friedman are the victims of an IRA terrorist attack as they are having an anniversary dinner. England is plagued with degenerate youth, frightening in what it portends for the future. Jane Murray is an angry, shallow child, seemingly incapable of love or of true civility. Anthony Keating finds two young squatters on the empty floor of his former home. The girl is a heroin addict, pregnant and in labor. The boy is drunk and stoned, unable to summon assistance for the girl. Anthony's chance visit to his old house means that the girl gets to the hospital, but she dies and her baby is born suffering from prenatal heroin addiction.

Through the gloom of England's dark night, Drabble feels her way toward dawn, steadfastly refusing to deny the value of principle because history is suffering temporarily from chaos. She paints a damning picture of a contemporary of Anthony, Mike Morgan, a comedian who pointlessly and viciously ridicules his audience because he mistakes a bad patch for the end of coherence. She also, however, defends the human being as a flexible, creative source of energy not to be trapped within rigidities of principle.

Alison Murray emerges as the polar opposite to Mike Morgan. She too is a doomed soul, because as England flails about, she has chosen the sterility of a noble perfection over the struggles of possibility. Alison's choice has been to devote herself to her brain-damaged daughter Molly rather than to her normal daughter, Jane. Molly can never develop and grow, despite Alison's martyrdom, and Jane is wild and sullen as a result of her displacement. Drabble shows that Alison's choice is at least as bad as Mike's, leading directly to her own misery and indirectly to Jane's self-imposed troubles in Wallachia. Alison's choice also leads indirectly to Anthony Keating's downfall.

Anthony, Alison's lover, goes to Wallachia to escort Jane home when the authorities suddenly decide to return her to England. A civil war erupts, randomly freeing Jane and trapping Anthony. He is mistaken for a British spy and remanded to a Siberian-style forced labor camp.

Between the extremes of Mike Morgan and Alison Murray lies the possibility of working one's way back to continuity by keeping the spirit free. The major examples of such survival in the novel are Maureen Kirby and Anthony Keating. Maureen is a lower-class girl, sexy rather than beautiful, who falls somewhat short of conventional morality. Hardly a person who eschews extremes, Maureen has been the partner of Len Wincobank in his whirlwind financial spree. She has also temporarily retreated into her own selfish, protected world when Len is imprisoned, but she is resilient. In a striking narrative device, Drabble looks into the future at the end of the novel, coolly summarizing the fates of her characters. Maureen is projected as a woman of the 1980's who ultimately marries well and becomes a model to young women. Her coarse-grained vitality and common sense lack the charm of Alison's elegant self-immolation, but they radiate the warmth of survival.

Anthony Keating, in his frozen Wallachian prison, the ice age of England made palpable, turns also toward life in the only way that is available to him. He becomes enthralled with watching birds, symbols of his spirit which, despite everything, remains untrammeled.

At the close of the novel, the state of the nation is given a good prognosis. It will recover, asserts the narrator. Anthony has come to terms. Len will surely go on to further development and a financial comeback. Maureen's trajectory is in ascent, but, asserts the narrator, Alison Murray will never recover. The doom of Alison Murray strongly suggests that her kind of retreat from possibility is the worst prison of all, subject to no reprieve or amelioration. Here Drabble seems to have found the limits of what critics have called her conservatism. Cutting off from one's roots to rise in the world brings peril, denying one's context in order to acquire more brings suffering; these may reveal the flaws in the liberal dream. The ultimate horror, however, would seem to be turning away from growth, regardless of the reason.

Other major works

PLAYS: *Laura*, 1964; *Bird of Paradise*, 1969; *A Touch of Love*, 1969; *Isadora*, 1969 (with Melvyn Bragg and Clive Exton).

NONFICTION: *Wordsworth, Literature in Perspective*, 1966; *Arnold Bennett*, 1974; *A Writer's Britain: Landscape in Literature*, 1979.

CHILDREN'S LITERATURE: *For Queen and Country: Britain in the Victorian Age*, 1978.

EDITED TEXTS: *Lady Susan*, 1974; *The Watsons*, 1974; *Sanditon*, 1974; *The Genius of Thomas Hardy*, 1975; *The Oxford Companion to English Literature*, 1985.

Bibliography

Creighton, Joanne V. *Margaret Drabble*. New York: Methuen, 1985.

Moran, Mary Hurley. *Margaret Drabble: Existing Within Structures*. Carbondale: Southern Illinois University Press, 1983.

Myer, Valerie Grosvenor. *Margaret Drabble: Puritanism and Permissiveness*. London: Vision Press, 1974.

Rose, Ellen Cronan. *The Novels of Margaret Drabble: Equivocal Figures*. Totowa, N.J.: Barnes & Noble Books, 1980.

Sadler, Lynn Veach. *Margaret Drabble*. Boston: Twayne, 1986.

Schmidt, Dorey, ed. *Margaret Drabble: Golden Realms*. Edinburg, Tex.: Pan American University School of Humanities, 1982.

MARGUERITE DURAS

Born: Giadinh, Indochina; April 4, 1914

Principal long fiction

Les Impudents, 1943; *La Vie tranquille*, 1944; *Un Barrage contre le Pacifique*, 1950 (*The Sea Wall*, 1952; also as *A Sea of Troubles*, 1953); *Le Marin de Gibraltar*, 1952 (*The Sailor from Gibraltar*, 1966); *Les Petits Chevaux de Tarquinia*, 1953 (*The Little Horses of Tarquinia*, 1960); *Le Square*, 1955 (*The Square*, 1959); *Moderato Cantabile*, 1958 (English translation, 1960); *Dix heures et demie du soir en été*, 1960 (*Ten-Thirty on a Summer Night*, 1962); *L'Après-midi de Monsieur Andesmas*, 1962 (*The Afternoon of Monsieur Andesmas*, 1964); *Le Ravissement de Lol V. Stein*, 1964 (*The Ravishing of Lol Stein*, 1966); *Le Vice-consul*, 1966 (*The Vice-Consul*, 1968); *L'Amante anglaise*, 1967 (English translation, 1968); *Détruire, dit-elle*, 1969 (*Destroy, She Said*, 1970); *Abahn Sabana David*, 1970; *L'Amour*, 1971; *India Song: Texte-théâtre-film*, 1973 (English translation, 1976); *L'Amant*, 1984 (*The Lover*, 1985); *Les Yeux bleus, cheveux noirs*, 1987 (*Blue Eyes, Black Hair*, 1987); *Emily L.*, 1987 (English translation, 1989); *La Pluie d'été*, 1990 (*Summer Rain*, 1992); *Yann Andréa Steiner*, 1992 (*Yann Andrea Steiner: A Memoir*, 1993).

Other literary forms

In addition to her novels, Marguerite Duras has published short-story collections and short texts, including *Des journées entières dans les arbres* (1954; *Days in the Trees*, 1967), *L'Homme assis dans le couloir* (1980), and *L'Homme atlantique* (1982). A number of her plays have been published in the collections *Théâtre I* (1965) and *Théâtre II* (1968), and they continue to be performed on the French stage. After 1969, Duras turned to filmmaking as her principal activity, perhaps encouraged by the success of her scenario for Alain Resnais' *Hiroshima mon amour* (1959; *Hiroshima mon amour: Text by Marguerite Duras for the Film by Alain Resnais*, 1961). In 1969, she wrote and directed her first film, *Détruire, dit-elle*, avowedly inspired by the May, 1968, cultural and political revolution in France. Duras has evolved a new "hybrid" genre with works such as *India Song: Texte-théâtre-film*; the film version was awarded a special prize for the best experimental film at the Cannes Film Festival in 1975.

Achievements

Marguerite Duras' extensive work in the cinema has generated interest in her novels, which are being read and appreciated by a wide audience. Despite her affinities with the New Novelists, who gained prominence in the 1950's and 1960's, Duras steadfastly refrains from aligning herself with any one school of literature. She has a deep concern for human values, and some of her fiction of the early 1970's is definitely marked by the events in France of May, 1968, which proclaimed an end to excessive governmental control and sought a more egalitarian society. For the most part, however, Duras' novels address political issues indirectly. Her talents as a writer lie in character portrayal, particularly in her studies of female protagonists caught in the imaginative re-creation of a passionate love. In her later works, Duras eschews straightforward analysis of characters' emotions for an allusive style that evokes fantasies and imaginations through a lyric, often fragmented, prose. As a result of numerous interviews in periodicals and on television and through her prodigious output in fiction, drama, and film, Duras has become a highly visible, often controversial, figure on the French literary scene. The publication of *The Lover* in 1984 was met with widespread acclaim; the novel won the prestigious Goncourt Prize and the Ritz Paris Hemingway Award and expanded the audience for Duras' work.

Biography

Marguerite Duras was born Marguerite Donnadieu on April 4, 1914, in Giadinh, Indochina (now Vietnam), where her parents came to teach from northern France. Her father died when she was young, and her mother undertook the rearing of two sons and a daughter by farming a government land grant. Duras' attachment to her older brother and her ambivalent feelings toward her feisty and domineering mother are sketched in many of the novels, most particularly in *The Sea Wall*. The exotic landscape of Indochina, where Duras attended the *lycée* and took her *baccalauréat* in Vietnamese and French, colors her fiction. She excels at evoking a steamy, although oftentimes suffocating, atmosphere in settings that are rich in sensual vegetation.

In 1931, Duras went to Paris to continue her education, earning a *licence* in law and political science in 1935. A secretary for the Colonial Ministry from 1935 to 1941, she married Robert Antelme, an active member of the Communist Party and author of *L'Espèce humaine* (1947). Her own membership in the Party and her participation in the Resistance movement during World War II bespoke a strong sense of political commitment, which she later rejected. It was during the war that she began to work at Gallimard and to write fiction. Although her first manuscript, "La Famille Taneran," was never published, she was encouraged by Raymond Queneau to continue writing. Divorced from Antelme, Duras met Dionys Mascolo, a fellow Communist and author of a book about the Party; they had a son, Jean. In 1950, Duras was one of a number of intellectuals excommunicated from the French Communist Party. As a result of this experience and, later, the revolution of May, 1968, she has advocated a rejection of all ideology and a negation of bourgeois values and social conventions.

During the 1960's, Duras was a journalist and conducted interviews on French television. In 1963, she achieved notoriety for her exposé of the Ben Barka affair during the Algerian revolt. She has also written articles for *Vogue* magazine and, more recently, has published short texts for feminist publications such as *Sorcières*. Her country home in Neauphle-le-Château, outside Paris, served as the setting for some of her films.

Analysis

All Marguerite Duras' novels revolve around the central theme of love, a necessary and impossible passion that is most often addressed in a climate of violence and left unsatisfied. Duras' early works set forth most of the themes that are elaborated in her subsequent novels. *Les Impudents*, *La Vie tranquille*, and *The Sea Wall* are concerned with young heroines in search of a lover or husband to fill the emptiness of their existence. Passive, lethargic women, they seek incarnation in the other, and their inner void is indistinguishable from the ennui and stagnation of their environment. They must wrench themselves from the domination of a brother or a mother, and, at the novel's conclusion, their success is ambiguous.

In the novels from Duras' middle period, her protagonists are preoccupied with an unhappy love affair from the past, which they attempt to reenact in the present. Similarly, in the screenplay *Hiroshima mon amour*, the French actress confuses her adolescent affair during World War II with a present, illicit affair in a city that is a constant reminder of a tragic past. In *Ten-Thirty on a Summer Night*, a married couple turns to infidelity in order to mediate their past desires for each other. The wife's encounter with a criminal in a city besieged by violent storms is Duras' indirect affirmation of the destructive aspect of their love. Anne, in *Moderato Cantabile*, reenacts with Chauvin a crime of passion which they have both witnessed at the beginning of the novel. The re-creation of love provokes desires and fantasies associated with crime, disorder, death, and destruction. In these novels, Duras' style begins to conform to her subject matter. The verbosity of description and the careful delineation of narrative events that marked the earlier works are discarded for a more poetic, allusive style in which characters' motives and incidents of plot are evoked in a gesture or setting and emphasized through repetition. The atmosphere of violence associated with destructive passion begins to affect textual structure and style.

For the most part, Duras' later fiction embodies fragments both of *The Ravishing of Lol Stein* and of her earlier works. Thus, text mirrors content (characters' memory or re-creation of past events), and it becomes clear that protagonists' desires are equated with memory and writing, equally fictitious. Sentences and paragraphs are reduced to lyric fragments of the story, decor is stylized, characters' identities are blurred, chronological time yields to phenomenological duration, and narrative control is abandoned in favor of poetic evocation. Many of Duras' later novels are decanted versions of the same story, one that springs from Duras' childhood and adolescent experiences in French Indochina. In a sense, the story of love and desire is progressively internalized and made to reverberate in its repetitions.

Because of its critical success, *The Sea Wall* marks a turning point in Duras' career as a novelist. Published in 1950, the novel was translated into English in 1952 and was adapted for the screen by René Clément in 1967. Often compared with the fiction of Ernest Hemingway, *The Sea Wall* is a fictionalized account of Duras' experiences in colonial Indochina—the sentimental education of its eighteen-year-old protagonist, Suzanne, and, to a lesser degree, of her older brother Joseph. It is also the story of the siblings' mother, known as Ma. Like Duras' own mother, Ma is a widowed French teacher who had settled with her husband in the colonial city of Ram, near the Gulf of Siam. Forced to support the children after the death of her husband, she works nights as a piano player at the Éden Cinéma in order to buy a land grant from the French government. Her dreams of establishing a fortune by farming are shattered when she realizes that she, like the other settlers in the area, has been sold an uncultivable tract of land by the corrupt colonial government. The farmland is inundated by the Pacific during the summer rainy season. Ma's story is one of a herculean, almost ludicrous, attempt to hold back the forces of nature by constructing a dam at the ocean's edge. Her revolt against the Pacific and her angry protests against government corruption are evidence of her undaunted and overweening spirit. Suzanne and Joseph must liberate themselves from their mother's control if they are to pass from adolescence to adulthood.

Most of the novel centers upon Suzanne's relationship with the men who actively court her. The wealthy Monsieur Jo represents release from the hardships of life on the plains and from Joseph and Ma. Suzanne feels nothing for him, but she prostitutes herself in order to satisfy her family's materialistic longings. Passivity characterizes most of Duras' protagonists: Their desires remain lodged in the imagination. Suzanne's concept of love derives from long afternoons watching romantic films at the Éden Cinéma. A modern-day Emma Bovary, Suzanne's interpretation of the stormy, passionate affairs that she sees on the screen is that love is destructive and tinged with violence, a conclusion emblematic of her own repressed desire. Like so many of Duras' heroines, Suzanne fantasizes love, and, although she succeeds in working out some of her fantasies in other relationships, particularly with Jean Agosti, her emotional involvement is still characterized by passivity, and she retreats into a bitter stoicism. In the subplot concerning her brother, Joseph turns to women and drink to escape from the

quotidian boredom in this desolate outpost. At the novel's end, however, the only true release for the siblings comes with their mother's death.

The exotic Vietnamese landscape is a lush background for this novel of thwarted dreams and repressed sexuality. Duras' descriptions of the tropical forest and the forceful powers of the sea are rich in a feminine sensuality. The spiritual and physical misery of life on the plains, together with the sexual awakening of Suzanne and Joseph, bathe the novel in an atmosphere of morbidity and longing. The theme of desire is firmly implanted in Duras' corpus, to be picked up and elaborated in succeeding novels. The memories of a harsh yet sensuous childhood spent in Vietnam haunt the author and are reflected in practically everything that she has written. Her talent for dialogue—which sparks her plays and films—is evident in this novel, in which characters seem to talk past one another and in which the revelation of feeling resides in what is left unsaid rather than in what is explicitly stated.

The story of repressed desire that structures the plot of *The Sea Wall* also informs Duras' 1964 novel, *The Ravishing of Lol Stein*. Like the preceding works, this text excels in character portrayal and evocation of decor; its protagonist, a sensitive but passive young woman who thrives on reliving a thwarted passion, is but another version of Suzanne. In narrative form, however, *The Ravishing of Lol Stein* goes further in its subversion of traditional novelistic techniques. Conflicting elements of order and disorder, reason and madness, *eros* and *thanatos*, narrative control and narrative abdication serve to anchor the text in a series of contradictions. The very title, for example, suggests a dual interpretation of the heroine's predicament; the English title is an unfortunate mistranslation of the French. *Ravissement* is more accurately rendered as "ravishment," which can mean both ecstasy and ravage. *The Ravishing of Lol Stein* marks a reorientation in Duras' writing; successive works espouse a more open, less controlled form in a radical portrayal of the negation of self implicit in Duras' treatment of desire.

Set in a seaside village referred to as S. Thala, the decor is a stylized reflection of the lush, tropical landscape of Duras' youth in Vietnam. The site is emotionally charged in the novel and haunts the heroine of the story, Lola Valerie Stein, as a reminder of an unrequited love experienced when she was nineteen years old. At that time, she was engaged to be married to Michael Richardson, but, at a ball held at nearby T. Beach, she watched helplessly as her fiancé was seduced by an older, beautifully mysterious woman, Anne-Marie Stretter. In voyeuristic fashion, Lol observes their dance of desire from behind a row of plants. The scene of rejection that opens the novel has a tremendous impact on Lol. It crystallizes Lol's identity in a "lack"; the center of her personality (which, the narrator informs the reader, has always been distant and difficult to grasp) is paradoxically "grounded" in negation and unfulfilled desire. Although she later marries, has children, and leads a "respectable" life, an undercurrent of violent desire threatens to burst forth at any moment. Lol's passion is triggered by an amorous encounter that is a reliving of the primal scene of triangular desire and exclusion.

The triangular mediation of desire that serves as catalyst for the plot is underscored by the novel's tripartite division. Part 1 relates Lol's initial rejection and her temporary madness. Part 2 deals with her marriage and espousal of bourgeois values, reflected in an excessive orderliness of manner. In both parts, the style is clean and direct, and the narrative is in the straightforward mode of the third person. In part 3, the breakdown of Lol's compulsive behavior, induced by an affair, is reflected in the narrative style, which becomes rambling and confused. When Lol is seduced by Jacques Hold, the lover of her best friend, Tatiana, she is thrust once again into a triangular situation; part 3 repeats part 1. The revelation, by a sudden intrusion of first-person narration, that the narrator is Jacques Hold and that the reader's perspective on preceding events has been manipulated by an interested character-narrator, casts a different light on the story and accounts for the narrative confusion. Jacques's constant reminders in part 3 that he can only "believe" what happened and that he is "inventing" Lol's story erodes the reader's confidence and underlines the theme of memory as a fictive replay or rewriting of the past. Visually, the text betrays this erosion. Question marks, suppositions, hypothetical formulations, unfinished sentences, and blank spaces on the page convey an abdication of control and the very uncertainty of the text that is being read. Desire as lack is translated both formally and thematically.

Stylistic and narrational violence are complemented by subversive elements in time and place which enhance the portrayal of desire. Part 3, a replay or remembering of part 1 (which is itself a replay of preceding texts), continues the theme-and-variations pattern that characterizes the novels. The continual return to an elusive and illusional past succeeds in collapsing distinctions between past and present—a confusion supported by associations in the setting. Lol's seduction by Jacques Hold in part 3 takes place in a room reminiscent of the ballroom in part 1, to which Jacques and Lol make a pilgrimage. The site is consecrated as a sacred place of desire. Ambiguities resulting from confusion of past and present, ballroom and hotel room, occur also in character portrayal. The three female protagonists, Tatiana, Anne-Marie Stretter, and Lol, are variously described by the same characteristics of desire and death. They, like Duras' entire corpus, take on the attributes of allegory in a progressively stylized and thus universalized story of absolute passion.

Other major works

SHORT FICTION: *Des journées entières dans les arbres*, 1954 (*Days in the Trees*, 1967); *L'Homme assis dans le couloir*, 1980; *L'Homme atlantique*, 1982; *La Maladie de la mort*, 1982 (*The Malady of Death*, 1986); *La Douleur*, 1985 (*The War: A Memoir*, 1986).

PLAYS: *Les Viaducs de la Seine-et-Oise*, 1960 (*The Viaducts of Seine-et-Oise*, 1967); *Les Eaux et forêts*, 1965 (*The Rivers and Forests*, 1965); *Théâtre I*, 1965 (includes *The Rivers and Forests*, *Le Square* [*The Square*, 1975], and *La Musica* [English translation, 1975]); *Des journées entières dans les arbres*, 1966 (*Days in the Trees*, 1967); *Three Plays* (includes *The Square*, *Days in the Trees*, and *The Viaducts of Seine-et-Oise*); *Théâtre II*, 1968 (includes *Suzanna Andler* [English translation, 1975]; *Days in the Trees*; *Yes, peut-être*; *Le Shaga*; and *Un Homme est venu me voir*); *L'Amante anglaise*, 1968; *L'Eden Cinéma*, 1977; *Le Navire "Night,"* 1979; *La Musica, deuxième*, 1985; *Agatha; Savannah Bay*, 1992.

SCREENPLAYS: *Hiroshima mon amour*, 1959 (*Hiroshima mon amour: Text by Marguerite Duras for the Film by Alain Resnais*, 1961); *Une Aussi Longue Absence*, 1961 (with Gérard Jarlot; English translation, 1966); *Détruire, dit-elle*, 1969; *Nathalie Granger*, 1972; *La Femme du Gange*, 1973; *India Song: Texte-théâtre-film*, 1973; *Baxter, Véra Baxter*, 1976; *Des journées entières dans les arbres*, 1976; *Son nom de Venise dans Calcutta désert*, 1976;

Le Camion, 1977; *Le Navire "Night,"* 1978; *Cesarée*, 1979; *Les Mains négatives*, 1979; *Aurélia Steiner*, 1979; *Agatha: Ou, Les Lectures illisibles*, 1982; *L'Homme atlantique*, 1982.

NONFICTION: *Les Parleuses*, 1974 (*Woman to Woman*, 1987); *Les Lieux de Marguerite Duras*, 1977; *Outside, papiers d'un jour*, 1981 (English translation, 1986); *La Vie matérielle*, 1987; *Les Yeux verts*, 1987 (*Green Eyes*, 1990); *L'Amant de la China du nord*, 1991 (*The North China Lover*, 1992).

Bibliography

Cismaru, Alfred. *Marguerite Duras*. New York: Twayne, 1971.

Glassman, Deborah N. *Marguerite Duras: Fascinating Vision and Narrative Cure*. Rutherford, N.J.: Fairleigh Dickinson University Press, 1991.

Murphy, Carol J. *Alienation and Absence in the Novels of Marguerite Duras*. Lexington, Ky.: French Forum, 1982.

Seylaz, Jean-Luc. *Les Romans de Marguerite Duras: Essai sur une thématique de la durée*. Paris: Lettres Modernes, 1963.

MARIA EDGEWORTH

Born: Black Bourton, England; January 1, 1767

Died: Edgeworthstown, Ireland; May 22, 1849

Principal long fiction

Castle Rackrent, 1800; *Belinda*, 1801; *Leonora*, 1806; *Ennui*, 1809; *The Absentee*, 1812; *Vivian*, 1812; *Patronage*, 1814; *Harrington*, 1817; *Ormond*, 1817; *Helen*, 1834.

Other literary forms

Like a number of late eighteenth century and early nineteenth century authors, Maria Edgeworth did not intend to become a novelist, but began writing extended prose fiction as an outgrowth of other kinds of literary production. Her first works were children's tales, usually short and always with a clear and forcefully advanced didactic thesis. These tales were written largely at the behest of Edgeworth's father, Richard Lovell Edgeworth, a deeply committed moralist and a notable figure in the history of education in England and Ireland. Both father and daughter collaborated on many of the stories, as they did on most of what Maria Edgeworth wrote.

Apart from further essays on education, morals, Ireland, and culture, Edgeworth's primary emphasis was on fiction, usually of novel length. The only other form she attempted was the drama. The plays were composed essentially for the pleasure of the family, and the volume containing the best of them, *Comic Dramas in Three Acts* (1817), is now almost universally unread.

Achievements

During her long lifetime, Edgeworth helped to make possible the Victorian novel. She began to write at a time when female novelists were just beginning to be accepted—a few of them, such as Fanny Burney and Elizabeth Inchbald, managing to attain some popularity. The novel of manners was the prevailing genre produced by these "lady writers." The tight focus and excessively delicate feelings exhibited in this form limited its appeal and artistic possibilities. It lay to Jane Austen to instill clever, penetrating satire and a much greater sense of realism and to Maria Edgeworth to extend its bounds of character depiction, to include persons of the lower classes, and to broaden its range.

Edgeworth is bound to be compared with Austen, to the former's derogation; there can be no doubt that the latter is the greater novelist, from an artistic standpoint.

This judgment should not blind the reader to Edgeworth's accomplishment. Edgeworth's significance rests chiefly on two achievements: She widened the scope of the "female" novel, and, in her careful and detailed treatment of Ireland and its people, she made the regional novel possible. Sir Walter Scott, in the preface to *Waverly* (1814), gives Edgeworth full credit for inspiring him to essay regional fiction, a genre in which his work became a landmark. It has also been claimed that Stendhal and Ivan Turgenev were influenced by Edgeworth's sympathetic treatment of peasants. Some critics and literary historians have even given her the title of the first intelligent sociological novelist in English literature. More than any author up to her time, Edgeworth revealed human beings as related to, and partially formed by, their environment.

Biography

Maria Edgeworth was born in England, the child of Richard Edgeworth and his first wife, Anna Maria Elers Edgeworth, who died when Maria was five years old. By all accounts, Maria got along well with her three siblings, two sisters and a brother, and with her father's next three wives and her seventeen half brothers and half sisters, most of whom she helped to rear. The general harmony in the Edgeworth household may be seen as all the more remarkable when one considers that Richard Edgeworth's last wife, Frances Anne Beaufort Edgeworth, was a year or two younger than her stepdaughter.

Much of this impressive concord can be credited to

Richard Edgeworth, a man of enormous confidence and personal force. He took the typical eighteenth century view that, as the father in the household, he was the lord and master in a literal sense. Fortunately, he was a benevolent master. Although he believed firmly that he knew what was best for all of his wives and children, what he believed to be best was their relatively free development. Maria evidently accepted her father's guidance to the point of seeking and welcoming his advice. Richard Edgeworth informed his family of the reasons for nearly all of his decisions. The most important of these was his resolve to settle on his family estate in Ireland. He was convinced that Ireland could be one of the best and most productive areas in the British Empire.

To achieve the goal of proper estate management, a subject that was to engage the interest of Maria Edgeworth for the rest of her life, her father had to revolutionize the way in which he cared for his lands and tenants. The salient aspect of the change was a greater concern for genuine productivity and less for high rents. He was quite successful: The estate and the family survived riots, famines, and the very real threat of a French invasion of Ireland during the Napoleonic campaigns. From the time the Edgeworth family relocated to Edgeworthstown, in 1782, until her death, Maria Edgeworth lived in the family homestead. She managed to become acquainted, largely through her father's influence, with some of the leading thinkers and artists of the day, notably Sir Walter Scott, with whom she formed a warm personal friendship.

While visiting France in 1802, Edgeworth met the Chevalier Abraham Niclas Clewberg-Edelcrantz, a Swedish diplomat. For this somewhat shy, very small, not particularly attractive woman, the encounter was extraordinary. Edelcrantz was not handsome, and he was forty-six years old. On the positive side, he was very intelligent and quite well educated, a fact that appealed to Edgeworth. Although evidently astounded and pleased by Edelcrantz's proposal of marriage, she was wise enough to realize that his devotion to Sweden and hers to Ireland formed an absolute barrier to any happiness in such a union.

Apart from helping her father to manage the estate and looking after the family, Edgeworth devoted herself almost exclusively to writing. Some of her novels began as very short tales written for the entertainment of the younger members of the family circle. Richard Edgeworth, though, persuaded her to take her writing seriously. This she did for some fifty years, until shortly before her death in 1849, by which time she had become respected and famous.

Analysis

The novels of Maria Edgeworth are, to the modern reader, an odd combination of strengths and weaknesses. This phenomenon is not really very strange, given the times in which she lived and the progress of fiction-writing in the early nineteenth century. Edgeworth herself knew, for example, that her writings were didactic to an often annoying degree. Her father, who had much to do with her conviction that fiction should elevate the morals of its readers, even claims in one of his prefaces to her novels that a severe attempt had been made to subdue the moralistic features. By modern standards, the attempts never fully succeeded in any of Edgeworth's novels.

What is distressing in Edgeworth's "moral tales" are the improbable turns of plot such as those by which poor but honest people are suddenly discovered to be heirs to great properties or those believed to be orphans are revealed as the offspring of noble houses. This sort of device is especially dismaying in a story that is otherwise filled with convincing details about estate management (and mismanagement) in Ireland and fairly realistic studies of the lives of the common people.

The two types of novels that Edgeworth wrote—the Irish tales and, as the title of one collection indicates, the *Tales of Fashionable Life* (1809-1812)—manifest the poles of her thematic interest. She believed, as did her father, that Ireland could benefit and even prosper from a more responsible aristocracy, landowners who lived on their property and saw that it was fairly and efficiently managed. In her three best Irish tales, *Castle Rackrent, The Absentee*, and *Ormond*, Edgeworth underlines the virtues of fair play with tenants, caution in dealing with hired estate managers, and close attention to details of land and equipment.

In his introduction to the Oxford English Novels edition of *Castle Rackrent* (1964), George Watson claims for this unusual book the distinction of being "the first regional novel in English, and perhaps in all Europe."

Castle Rackrent is often praised for its lack of an obtrusive moral emphasis, but it would be a mistake to read the novel as having no message. The decline and fall of the Rackrent family is the story of irresponsibility and extravagance, and unfortunately common phenomenon in the history of Irish landowners.

The narrator, Thady Quirk, commonly called "honest Thady," tells the dismal but occasionally humorous tale of the several masters under whom he has served: Sir Patrick O'Shaughlin, who drinks himself to death early in the story; Sir Murtaugh Rackrent, who dies in a paroxysm of anger over a legalistic contretemps; Sir Kit Rackrent, who dies in a duel over the controversy stemming from his indecision regarding the choice of a new wife, when his first spouse seems on the point of death; and Sir Condy Rackrent, whose narrative is longer than the tale of the first three owners of Castle Rackrent. Another innovative aspect of the novel besides the use of such an authentic narrator is the consistent employment of dialect. The text is not difficult to read, but many of the expressions are not easily comprehensible to a reader unfamiliar with the Irish speech and mores of that era. Wisely, Edgeworth—with her father's help—appended a glossary which explains, occasionally in needless detail, many of Thady's locutions and references.

Perhaps the chief appeal of the work to the modern reader lies in the personality of Thady and in the folkways he embodies. The extraordinary loyalty of Thady to a family that seems not to deserve such fidelity is both exasperating and admirable. Thady is not, however, overcome with emotion when unfortunate circumstances arise. He speaks of a shocking event at the funeral with relative calm: "happy the man who could get but a sight of the hearse!—But who'd have thought it? Just as all was going on right, through his own town they were passing, when the body was seized for debt. . . ." Thady is moved enough to call the creditors "villains," but he swiftly moves on with his tale: "So, to be sure, the law must take its course—and little gain had the creditors for their pains." The old man spends more time on the legal implications of the seizure than on the event itself. This passage displays Edgeworth's understanding of the contentious element in the Irish personality and the formidable grasp of the law that even poorly educated people often had. Indeed, lawsuits and legal technicalities abound in Edgeworth's fiction.

Thady's almost eccentric equanimity and generous nature are further revealed when, after Sir Kit has gambled away virtually all the assets of the Rackrent estate, including the good will of his wealthy wife, the old retainer remarks, "the Castle Rackrent estate was all mortgaged, and bonds out against him, for he was never cured of his gaming tricks—but that was the only fault he had, God bless him!" Further, Thady seems untroubled by the confinement of Sir Kit's wife for seven years in her apartments, apparently lost in admiration of the fierce temper of his master, which not only caused the drastic action but also discouraged anyone from asking him about it.

Thady refers to Sir Condy Rackrent as "ever my great favorite, and indeed the most universally beloved man I had ever seen or heard of." Condy's chief attractions are a good nature and a propensity to spend excessively. Both of these qualities contribute to the further impoverishment of the estate, a condition that he does little to alleviate. Even his marriage to the daughter of a wealthy landowner on a nearby estate (who promptly disinherits his offspring as soon as he learns of the wedding, thus frustrating even this halfhearted attempt to repair the Rackrent fortunes) is a matter of chance: Condy, who actually loves Thady's pretty but fortuneless grandniece, Judy M'Quirk, flips a coin to determine whether he will propose to Judy or the moneyed Isabella.

Despite the disinheritance, Sir Condy is fond of Isabella; when financial disaster looms, he attempts to provide her with a generous allotment in his will. The closing of the novel exposes another theme that may be derived from the plot. The villain who buys up Sir Condy's debts and brings on his personal ruin is Thady's own son, the self-serving Jason. Edgeworth possibly had in mind to make some point about the difference between the single-minded loyalty and honesty of the older generation and the selfish heartlessness of the younger. Even the attractive Judy, when Thady suggests that she might become the next mistress of Castle Rackrent (Isabella has had an accident from which Thady believes she will die), tells him there is no point in marrying a poor man; she has evidently set her sights on Jason, much to Thady's dismay.

Typically, the novel ends with a lawsuit. Lady Condy, after her husband's death from drinking, sues for the title to the estate. Thady does not know how the suit will end, and he seems not to care: "For my part, I'm tired wishing for any thing in this world, after all I've seen in it." With this touching close to what is considered Edgeworth's best novel, the reader may well believe that the author has provided the opportunity for a greater understanding of those elements of Irish culture and history that impelled her to devote a lifetime of study to them.

During Edgeworth's lifetime, *The Absentee* was probably her most influential work. The central problem addressed in the novel is that of the absentee landlords, who left the management of their often vast Irish estates in the hands of inept and frequently unscrupulous agents. These agents robbed the landlords as well as the tenants, but the indifferent landowners took little interest in the lands so long as the rents were paid on time. As Edgeworth makes eminently clear by the contrast between the sensible and benevolent Mr. Burke, one of Lord Clonbrony's agents, and the other, Nicholas Garraghty, who is scheming and dishonest, not all agents were bad; the trouble was that the owners had no accurate way of knowing, since they were almost never on the scene.

The hero of this novel, Lord Colambre, is the son of Lord and Lady Clonbrony; it is around this unbelievably virtuous and somewhat stuffy young man that the several subjects subplots and themes are centered. The main plot line has to do with the Clonbronys, who live in London because Lady Clonbrony believes that high society is indispensable to her happiness. Lord Clonbrony would not mind returning to the family estate, and he realizes that remaining away may be ruinous, since he is already in considerable debt. Lord Colambre visits his father's lands in disguise, where he identifies the problem and recognizes the virtues and evils of the two agents. After vigorous efforts to repay his father's debts, he saves the situation and persuades his mother to return to Ireland. A related theme concerns the actions that Colambre will not take in order to pay the debts—chiefly, he will not marry for money, a time-honored method of acquiring funds in a short time. Edgeworth offers several illustrations of the folly of such a practice, though perhaps to the modern reader her emphasis on the legitimacy of the

birth of Grace Nugent, Colambre's cousin, as a criterion for his proposing to her may seem artificial and even essentially immoral. Interestingly, when Miss Nugent (who has been unaware of the "disgrace") learns of the reason for Colambre's erstwhile restraint, she fully agrees that it would have been improper for him to offer marriage when her birth seemed under a cloud. Through an unlikely and tiresome concatenation of circumstances and accidents, the problem is solved: It is proved that Grace's birth was legitimate, and the marriage is approved, even by Lady Clonbrony, who for most of the story has been trying to persuade her son to wed the wealthy Miss Broadhurst.

The Absentee is filled with flat characters created in the heroic model, most of whom befriend Colambre and impress him with a variety of sensible insights: the positive aspects of life in Ireland; the joys and satisfactions of the quiet country life; the emptiness and falseness of "society"; and the great importance of taking responsibility and performing one's duty well. *The Absentee* emphasizes two aspects of Edgeworth's philosophy of life. She fully accepted the eighteenth century conviction that the class structure of society was inevitable and proper, and she wholeheartedly believed in the primacy of duty as everyone's first responsibility. Thus, in *The Absentee* there is an interesting mingling of liberal attitudes toward the rights of the peasants and conservative views regarding the propriety of aristocratic privilege.

Edgeworth's novels are unfortunately little read today, except by students of the English novel. Aside from plainly revealing the significant lines of tradition and transition from the eighteenth century to the nineteenth century novel, her work is enjoyable in itself. Nowhere else can one find such a lively and fairly balanced picture of the life and values found in the Ireland and England of the late Georgian period.

Other major works

SHORT FICTION: *The Parent's Assistant: Or, Stories for Children*, 1796 (3 volumes), 1800 (6 volumes); *Early Lessons: Harry and Lucy, I and II; Rosamond, I-III; Frank, I-IV and Other Stories*, 1801-1802 (with Richard Lovell Edgeworth); *Moral Tales for Young People*, 1801; *The Mental Thermometer*, 1801; *Popular Tales*, 1804; *The Modern Griselda*, 1805; *Tales of Fashionable Life*, 1809-1812; *Continuation of Early Lessons*, 1814; *Rosamond: A Sequel to Early Lessons*, 1821; *Frank: A Sequel to Frank in Early Lessons*, 1822; *Harry and Lucy Concluded*, 1825; *Tales and Miscellaneous Pieces*, 1825; *Gary Owen, and Poor Bob, the Chimney-Sweeper*, 1832; *Tales and Novels*, 1832-1833, 1848, 1857 (18 volumes), 1893 (10 volumes), 1893 (12 volumes); *Orlandino*, 1848;

Classic Tales, 1883; *The Purple Jar and Other Stories*, 1931.

PLAYS: *Comic Dramas in Three Acts*, 1817; *Little Plays for Children*, 1827.

NONFICTION: *Letters for Literary Ladies*, 1795; *An Essay on the Noble Science of Self-Justification*, 1795; *Practical Education*, 1798 (also known as *Essays on Practical Education*, with Richard Lovell Edgeworth); *A Rational Primer*, 1799 (with Richard Lovell Edgeworth); *Essay on Irish Bulls*, 1802 (with Richard Lovell Edgeworth); *Essays on Professional Education*, 1809 (with Richard Lovell Edgeworth); *Readings on Poetry*, 1816 (with Richard Lovell Edgeworth); *Memoirs of Richard Lovell Edgeworth Esq.*, 1820 (Vol. II); *Thoughts on Bores*, 1826; *A Memoir of Maria Edgeworth*, 1867 (Francis Edgeworth, editor); *Archibald Constable and His Literary Correspondents*, 1873; *The Life and Letters of Maria Edgeworth*, 1894 (Augustus J. Hare, editor); *Chosen Letters*, 1931 (F. V. Barry, editor); *Romilly-Edgeworth Letters*, 1813-1818, 1936 (Samuel H. Romilly, editor); *Letters from England*, 1813-1844, 1971 (Christina Colvin, editor).

TRANSLATION: *Adelaide and Theodore*, 1783.

Bibliography

Butler, Marilyn. *Maria Edgeworth: A Literary Biography*. Oxford, England: Clarendon Press, 1972.

Harden, O. Elizabeth McWhorter. *Maria Edgeworth*. Boston: Twayne, 1984.

_____. *Maria Edgeworth's Art of Prose Fiction*. The Hague: Mouton, 1971.

Hurst, Michael. *Maria Edgeworth and the Public Scene: Intellect, Fine Feeling, and Landlordism in the Age of Reform*. Coral Gables, Fla.: University of Miami Press, 1969.

Newcomer, James. *Maria Edgeworth the Novelist*. Fort Worth: Texas Christian University Press, 1967.

GEORGE ELIOT
Mary Ann Evans

Born: Chilvers Coton, England; November 22, 1819   **Died:** London, England; December 22, 1880

Principal long fiction

Adam Bede, 1859; *The Mill on the Floss*, 1860; *Silas Marner*, 1861; *Romola*, 1862-1863; *Felix Holt, The Radical*, 1866; *Middlemarch*, 1871-1872; *Daniel Deronda*, 1876.

Other literary forms

George Eliot's three early stories, "The Sad Fortunes of the Reverend Barton," "Mr. Gilfil's Love Story," and "Janet's Repentance," originally published in *Blackwood's Magazine*, were collected as *Scenes of Clerical Life* in 1858. *The Impressions of Theophrastus Such*, a miscellany of sketches and essays, was published in 1879. Eliot's poetry does not achieve the high quality of her prose. Most notable examples are *The Spanish Gypsy* (1868), a verse drama, and *The Legend of Jubal and Other Poems* (1874). Eliot wrote more than seventy periodical essays and reviews; the most comprehensive collection is Thomas Pinney's *Essays of George Eliot* (1963). Eliot translated David Friedrich Strauss's *Das Leben Jesu* as *The Life of Jesus Critically Examined* (1846) and Ludwig Feuerbach's *Das Wesen des Christenthums* as *The Essence of Christianity* (1854).

Achievements

Eliot's pivotal position in the history of the novel is attested by some of the most distinguished English novelists. Reviewing *Middlemarch* in 1873, Henry James concluded, "It sets a limit, we think, to the development of the old-fashioned English novel"; and *Middlemarch* does, indeed, take what James calls the panoramic novel—"vast, swarming, deep-colored, crowded with episodes, with vivid images, with lurking master-strokes, with brilliant passages of expression," seeking to "reproduce the total sum of life in an English village"—to an unsurpassed level of achievement. Eliot was also an innovator. In the words of D. H. Lawrence, "It all started with George Eliot; it was she who put the action on the inside." thus giving impetus to the rise of the psychological novel, where the most significant actions derive from the motives of the characters rather than from external events. Eliot's work is, then, both the culmination of the panoramic Victorian novel as practiced by Charles Dickens and William Makepeace Thackeray and the beginning of the modern psychological novel as practiced by James, Lawrence, and many others.

Biography

The woman known to countless readers as George Eliot—a name she did not use until she was nearly forty—was born on November 22, 1819, and christened Mary Ann Evans, the third child of Robert Evans and his second wife, Christina Pearson. After her mother's death and her father's retirement, Eliot and her father moved to a new home outside Coventry. She soon established a close and lasting friendship with Charles and Cara Bray, Unitarians whose views of religion were more intellectual than those with which Eliot had been acquainted. At their suggestion, she began to translate *Das Leben Jesu*, a key work of the German theologian David Friedrich Strauss that questioned the divinity of Christ. Eliot's work on this translation completed the destruction of her religious orthodoxy.

Following the death of her father in 1849, Eliot moved to London, where she began to write for the *Westminster Review*. Although the *Westminster Review* was nominally edited by John Chapman—a man with whom Eliot may have been romantically involved—Eliot assumed most of the responsibilities of editorship and was, especially after Chapman bought the periodical in January, 1852, virtual editor.

One of the persons whom Eliot met at this time was

George Henry Lewes, who later became her common-law husband. Lewes was, with Thornton Leigh Hunt, coeditor of a weekly newspaper called *The Leader*. Lewes, Hunt, and Lewes's wife Agnes subscribed to the notion that passions could not be restricted by social conventions; thus, when Agnes delivered a son who had been fathered by Hunt, Lewes quietly registered the child as his own. By the time Agnes bore Hunt a second child, however, Lewes no longer considered her his wife. Victorian laws made divorce virtually impossible, and the fact that Lewes had accepted Hunt's child as his own precluded his citing adultery as possible grounds.

Under the circumstances, Eliot and Lewes decided to live together in a common-law marriage. On July 20, 1854, they traveled to Germany as husband and wife. Eliot wrote to her friends to explain her new status and to ask that from henceforth they address her as Marian Lewes. The irregularity of their relationship meant that only the most courageous Victorian women dared risk their own respectability by calling on her. Eliot's family also cut her off, condemning her relationship as adulterous.

Eliot published her first story in January, 1857. Because Eliot wished to protect her standing as an editor and reviewer and because she feared that her unconventional marriage would prejudice the reception of her fiction, she published under the pseudonym George Eliot. Encouraged by a favorable reception and protected by Lewes from adverse criticism, Eliot published her first full-length novel, *Adam Bede*, in 1859. Of her six other novels, only *Romola* was less than successful; the others won for Eliot both an enthusiastic popular audience and critical recognition as the major English novelist of her time.

Devastated by Lewes's death, Eliot married John Cross on May 6, 1880. In the eyes of her sternly conventional brother Isaac, this marriage conferred respectability; he wrote to his sister for the first time since 1854 to offer his "sincere congratulations." Their marriage, though happy, was brief: Eliot died in December 1880.

Analysis

Eliot conceived of fiction as a moral force, not because it is didactic in any narrow sense, but because it inculcates in the reader an attitude of sympathy for fellow human beings, which in turn leads to everyday acts of justice and compassion that lighten the burden of the human lot. As her career developed, Eliot's characters became complex moral paradigms that could serve her readers as both examples and warnings. The highest moral achievement of her characters is renunciation of their own claims to happiness in order to minister to the needs of others, sometimes less deserving, whose lives impinge on theirs. The act of renunciation involves acknowledgment of the claims of community and often provides a sense of continuity with the character's past or traditions. Conversely, the characters whom Eliot condemns most severely are those who evade their responsibilities by a process of self-delusion or self-indulgence, avoiding hard choices and hoping that chance will deliver them from the consequences of selfish actions.

Eliot's first full-length novel, *Adam Bede*, is built on two pairs of contrasting characters, one male and one female. Adam, a carpenter of consummate skill, is a model of rectitude and self-discipline whose only flaw is his intolerance of any weakness in others. Contrasting with Adam is Arthur Donnithorne, a well-intentioned young landowner whose moral weakness causes the principal catastrophe of the novel. There is a similar contrast between the two major female characters: Dinah Morris, a self-effacing Methodist preacher whose primary concern is doing what she can for others, and Hetty Sorrel, a young farm girl whose kittenish appeal conceals a hard core of egotism. The fact that both Adam and Arthur love Hetty intensifies the contrast between them. Adam, captivated by her charms, admires her as a paragon of femininity without ever perceiving her indifference to him. Arthur, without really intending to, takes advantage of Hetty's self-deluding dreams of being a wealthy landowner's wife to indulge in an affair with her. Frightened when she discovers that she is pregnant, Hetty runs away from home in a vain attempt to find Arthur, who has gone to rejoin his regiment. After her baby is born, she abandons it in a forest, where it dies of exposure. When she is arraigned for child murder, she appears hard and indifferent until Dinah moves her to repentance. Although Arthur succeeds in obtaining a pardon that saves Hetty from hanging, the young woman disappears from the story and, like the overwhelming majority of fallen women in Victorian fiction, dies. The somewhat improbable marriage of Adam and Dinah provides the happy ending that the contemporary audience expected.

The melodramatic aspects of *Adam Bede* tend to obscure Eliot's primary concerns in the novel. The relationship between Arthur and Hetty is not simply a trite story of a sexual encounter between a wealthy young man and a simple farm girl; the sexual aspect of their relationship is less important than their self-delusion, self-indulgence, and egotism. Arthur is attractive, likable, and well-intentioned, but he lacks both strength of purpose and self-knowledge. Intending to break off his relationship with Hetty, he finds himself contriving meetings with her. Hetty's flaw is even more damaging: Although she appears to be a creature of simple charm, her egotism makes her indifferent to almost everything except her own beauty and her self-deluding dreams. Similarly, Dinah's success in leading Hetty to repentance is a prototype of much more complex processes that occur in later novels. Dinah's willingness to take on responsibility for sympathetically ministering to the needs of people around her has to be learned by Adam, whose own stalwart rectitude causes him to scorn weakness in others.

Although it is a major achievement for a first novel, *Adam Bede* pales in comparison to Eliot's later fiction. Eliot's depiction of the self-deception and egotism of Arthur and Hetty looks ahead to the fuller development of this theme in later novels, but neither their characters nor their situation provides the opportunity for the depth of psychological insight Eliot shows later. Similarly, Arthur's last-minute rescue of Hetty from the very foot of the gallows is reminiscent of the clichés of nineteenth century melodrama and seems almost pointless in the light of Hetty's immediate disappearance from the story and her early death. The marriage of Adam and Dinah caters too obviously to the Victorian taste for this kind of conventional "happy ending" and seems inconsistent with the earlier description of Dinah. Adam himself is too idealized a character to be convincing.

Eliot's third and most perfectly constructed novel, *Silas Marner* embodies her complex moral vision with the precision of a diagram. Like *Adam Bede*, the novel is built on morally contrasting characters, but Silas Marner and Godfrey Cass reveal with much greater clarity than any of the characters in the earlier novel Eliot's concern with the moral patterns of renunciation and self-indulgence.

In a sort of prologue to the main action of the novel, Silas, a linen weaver who is a member of a pious religious sect in a large industrial city, is accused of stealing church funds by a close friend who actually stole the money. When a trial by lots sponsored by the sect declares Silas guilty, he loses faith in God and humanity and flees to a distant country village, where he isolates himself from the community and finds solace in constant weaving.

Through years of weaving, Silas accumulates a hoard of gold coins which becomes the only object of his affections. When his gold is stolen by Godfrey Cass's irresponsible brother Dunstan, Silas is utterly devastated until Godfrey's daughter by a secret marriage toddles into his house after her mother dies of exposure and an overdose of laudanum. The presence of this child, whom Silas rears as his own, restores the human contact that Silas had lost. Silas' spontaneous turns to the men assembled at the village tavern when his gold is stolen and to the New Year's assemblage at the Cass house when he finds the child suggest an instinctive searching for community. His heeding the parish clerk's admonition not to accuse the innocent after his gold is stolen and his choice of his younger sister's "Bible name" of Hepzibah (shortened to Eppie) for the child suggest the reestablishment of ties to his past.

Similarly, Godfrey embodies the consequences of a self-indulgent avoidance of one's responsibilities. Prevented by his secret marriage to the dissolute mother of Eppie from marrying Nancy Lammeter, he weakly trusts to chance somehow to relieve him of the consequences of his actions. Godfrey has none of the malice of his younger brother Dunstan; nevertheless, his anxiety is so great that his "one terror" when Silas comes to his house with Eppie is that his wife might *not* be dead. He sees that the child is his, but fails to acknowledge her, salving his conscience by giving Silas a half-guinea when he finds that Silas has determined to keep her.

The chance that has relieved Godfrey of the consequences of his secret marriage eventually brings retribution. His marriage to Nancy is childless, and when Dunstan's body is discovered with Silas' long-lost gold, Godfrey finally tells Nancy that Eppie is his child. Their plan of relieving their childlessness by adopting Eppie comes to nothing when Eppie tells them that she can only think of Silas as her father. With poetic justice that even Godfrey recognizes, the man who admits that he "wanted to pass for childless once" will now "pass for childless against my wish."

Middlemarch is unquestionably Eliot's finest achievement as a novelist. Whereas *Silas Marner* presented the moral patterns of renunciation and self-indulgence with unparalleled clarity, *Middlemarch* explores them with profound subtlety and psychological insight. The vast scope of *Middlemarch* gives Eliot room for a panoramic view of provincial life, and her focus on the upper-middle class and gentry gives her an opportunity to deal with characters whose experience is wider and whose motives are more sophisticated and complex than those of many of the characters in the early novels. Eliot explores the familiar moral territory of renunciation and self-indulgence by developing four more or less distinct plot lines: The most important of these concern Dorothea Brooke and Tertius Lydgate.

More than any previous novel, *Middlemarch* explores the moral achievements and failures of individuals against the background of an entire society, a society that does not provide many opportunities for people to put their best talents to use. These issues are perhaps most fully embodied in Dorothea Brooke, a young heiress with "a nature altogether ardent, theoretic and intellectually consequent" who is "struggling in the bands of a narrow teaching, hemmed in by a social life which seemed nothing but a labyrinth of petty courses, a walled-in maze of small paths that led no whither." Seeking a way to give her life consequence and purpose, she marries Edward Casaubon, a desiccated pseudoscholar, whom she naïvely thinks of as a John Locke or a John Milton, a "winged messenger" who can guide her along the "grandest path." She soon discovers that Casaubon is not a great man, but a rather pathetic egotist, morbidly sensitive to real or imagined criticism of his work, pettishly jealous of Dorothea's friendship with his nephew Will Ladislaw, and incapable of offering her any real affection. She also learns that his projected work, grandly entitled a "Key to All Mythologies," is nothing but a monumental collection of trivia, already rendered obsolete by superior German scholarship. Nevertheless, Dorothea prepares to promise her husband, who is suffering from a "fatty degeneration of the heart," that she will continue his work after his death, a sacrifice from which she is saved by his timely demise.

Like Dorothea, Tertius Lydgate finds his ambitions for significant achievement frustrated by social pressures, but unlike Dorothea he adds to his difficulties by a tendency toward heedless self-indulgence. His well-intentioned plans for medical reform are jeopardized by his lack of sensitivity to the feelings of both patients and other practitioners and by his regrettable involvement with Nicholas Bulstrode, an unpopular but powerful leader in community affairs. More important, he shackles himself by marriage to Rosamond Vincy, the beautiful and self-centered daughter of the mayor of Middlemarch. This marriage, which Lydgate slips into more or less intentionally, blights his hopes of success. He gets heavily into debt as both he and Rosamond carelessly incur expenses on the unconsidered assumption that they ought to live well. Rosamond, utterly unwilling to make any sacrifices, simply blames him for their problems.

These two plot lines come together when Dorothea, deeply moved by Lydgate's marital and financial problems and eager to clear him from blame in a scandal involving Bulstrode, offers to call on Rosamond. She finds Rosamond in what appears to be a compromising tête-à-tête with Will, whom she had come to love since Casaubon's death. Deeply distressed by what she assumes about Will's conduct, she nevertheless forces herself to "clutch [her] own pain" and think only of the "three lives whose contact with hers laid an obligation on her." Feeling "the largeness of the world and the manifold wakings of men to labour and endurance," she compels herself to make a second visit. She has some success in reconciling Rosamond to Lydgate and finds that Will's conduct was indeed blameless.

Although Dorothea's renunciation of herself has the unexpected result of opening the way for her marriage to Will, she never achieves her potential as a latter-day St. Theresa, "for the medium in which [her] ardent deeds took shape is forever gone." Her "full nature" spends itself "in channels which had no great name on earth" but which nevertheless bring benefits to others. Lydgate, who allowed himself to slip into marriage with the paralyzingly egotistical Rosamond, achieves financial success as a society doctor, but "always regarded himself as a failure; he had not done what he once meant to do."

The novel's subtitle, "Study of Provincial Life," calls attention to Eliot's recognition, more fully expressed in this novel than in any of the earlier ones, of the ways in which the circumstances of society limit her characters' options. Dorothea achieves the ideal of self-renunciation for which earlier characters have striven, but the conditions of her life prevent her from achieving her potential; Lydgate fails not only because of his ill-advised marriage but also because the community views his eagerness to advance medical practice with suspicion and prejudice. Conditions of society, as well as moral flaws, frustrate the ambitions of even the worthiest characters in Eliot's fiction.

Other major works

SHORT FICTION: *Scenes of Clerical Life*, 1858.
POETRY: *The Spanish Gypsy*, 1868; *The Legend of Jubal and Other Poems*, 1874.
NONFICTION: *The Impressions of Theophrastus Such*, 1879; *Essays of George Eliot*, 1963 (Thomas Pinney, editor).
TRANSLATIONS: *The Life of Jesus Critically Examined*, 1846; *The Essence of Christianity*, 1854.

Bibliography

Beer, Gillian. *George Eliot*. Brighton, England: Harvester Press, 1986.
Haight, Gordon. *George Eliot: A Biography*. New York: Oxford University Press, 1968.
Hardy, Barbara. *The Novels of George Eliot: A Study in Form*. London: Athone Press, 1959.
Newton, K. M. *George Eliot: Romantic Humanist*. Totowa, N.J.: Barnes & Noble Books, 1981.
Pinion, F. B. *A George Eliot Companion*. Basingstoke, England: Macmillan, 1981.

LOUISE ERDRICH

Born: Little Falls, Minnesota; July 6, 1954

Principal long fiction

Love Medicine, 1984, 1993; *The Beet Queen*, 1986; *Tracks*, 1988; *The Crown of Columbus*, 1991 (with Michael Dorris); *The Bingo Palace*, 1994.

Other literary forms

Jacklight (1984) and *Baptism of Desire* (1989) are books of poetry (and a few folktales) that present vivid North Dakota vignettes, as well as personal reflections of Louise Erdrich's relationships to her husband and children.

Achievements

A poet and poetic novelist, Erdrich has drawn on her Chippewa and German-immigrant heritage to create a wide-ranging chronicle of American Indian and white experience in twentieth century North Dakota. Since she began to publish her fiction and poetry in the early 1980's, her works have garnered high critical praise, and her three novels have been best-sellers as well. Love Medicine, Erdrich's first novel, won the National Book Critics Circle Award in 1984, and three of the stories gathered in that book were also honored: "The World's Greatest Fishermen" won the five-thousand-dollar first prize in the 1982 Nelson Algren fiction competition, "Scales" appeared in *Best American Short Stories, 1983* (1983), and "Saint Marie" was chosen for *Prize Stories 1985: The O. Henry Awards* (1985). Two of the stories included in the novel *Tracks* also appeared in honorary anthologies: "Fleur" in *Prize Stories 1987: The O. Henry Awards* (1987) and "Snares" in *Best American Short Stories, 1988* (1988).

Erdrich's works often focus on the struggle of Chippewas for personal, familial, and cultural survival. Yet her treatment of white and mixed-blood characters also reveals an empathic understanding of the ways in which North Dakota people of all races long for closer connection with other people and the land.

Biography

Louise Erdrich grew up in Wahpeton, a small town in southeastern North Dakota. Her father, Ralph Erdrich, is a German immigrant who taught in Wahpeton at the American Indian boarding school. Her mother, Rita Journeau Erdrich, is a three-quarters Chippewa who also worked at the school. Erdrich's mixed religious and cultural background provided a rich foundation for her later poetry and fiction.

Erdrich earned two degrees in creative writing, a B.A. from Dartmouth College in 1976 and an M.A. from The Johns Hopkins University in 1979. In 1981, she was married to Michael Dorris, a professor of anthropology and head of the Native American Studies Program at Dartmouth.

Erdrich and Dorris have devoted their lives to ambitious family, literary, and humanitarian goals. Like Erdrich, Dorris is three-eighths American Indian, and years before his marriage to Erdrich he had adopted three American Indian infants from midwestern reservations. Dorris and Erdrich produced three more children and moved into an eighteenth century farmhouse in Cornish, New Hampshire. Erdrich and her husband have said that they collaborate on virtually all the works that either one publishes—whether fiction, poetry, or nonfiction. Thus Erdrich acknowledges Dorris' important contribution to all of her fiction; similarly, she collaborated with him on his first novel, *A Yellow Raft in Blue Water* (1987), and on his study of fetal alcohol syndrome (FAS), *The Broken Cord* (1989). Erdrich and Dorris have donated money and campaigned for legislation to combat FAS, which afflicts the lives of many American Indian children born to alcoholic mothers.

Analysis

The essence of Louise Erdrich's writing emerges from her attachment to her North Dakota locale. The ways in which Erdrich has brought this region to literary life have been favorably compared by critics to the methods and style of William Faulker, who created the mythical Yoknapatawpha County out of his rich sense of rural Mississippi. Like Faulkner, Erdrich has created a gallery of diverse characters spanning several generations; she also uses multiple points of view and shifting time frames. Erdrich's stories generally begin with a realistic base of ordinary people, settings, and actions. As her tales develop, however, these people become involved in events and perceptions that strike the reader as quite extraordinary—as exaggerated or heightened in ways that may seem deluded or mystical, grotesque or magical, comic or tragic.

Erdrich's first novel, *Love Medicine*, spans the years 1934-1984 in presenting members of five Chippewa and mixed-blood families, all struggling in different ways to attain a sense of belonging through love, religion, home, and family. As originally published, the novel includes fourteen interwoven stories; though the title refers specifically to traditional American Indian magic in one story, in a broader sense "love medicine" refers to the different kinds of spiritual power that enable Erdrich's characters to transcend—however momentarily—the grim circumstances of their lives. Trapped on their shrinking reservation by racism and poverty, plagued by alcoholism, disintegrating families, and violence, some of Erdrich's characters nevertheless discover a form of "love medicine" that helps to sustain them.

The opening story, "The World's Greatest Fishermen," begins with an episode of "love medicine" corrupted and thwarted. Though June Kashpaw was once a woman of striking beauty and feisty spirit, by 1981 she has sunk to the level of picking up men in an oil boom-town. Unfortunately, June fails in her last attempts to attain two goals that other characters will also seek throughout the novel: love and home. Yet though she appears only briefly in this and one other story, June Kashpaw is a central character in the novel, for she embodies the potential power of spirit and love in ways that impress and haunt the other characters.

Part 2 of "The World's Greatest Fishermen" introduces many of the other major characters of *Love Medicine*, as June's relatives gather several months after her death. On the one hand, several characters seem sympa-

thetic because of their closeness to June and their kind treatment of one another. Albertine Johnson, who narrates the story and remembers her Aunt June lovingly, has gone through a wild phase of her own and is now a nursing student. Eli Kashpaw, Albertine's granduncle, who was largely responsible for rearing June, is a tough and sharp-minded old man who has maintained a traditional Chippewa existence as a hunter and fisherman. Lipsha Morrissey, who, though he seems not to know it, is June's illegitimate son, is a sensitive, self-educated young man who acts warmly toward Albertine. In contrast to these characters are others who are flawed or unsympathetic when seen through the eyes of Albertine, who would like to believe that her family is pulling together after June's death. These less sympathetic characters include Zelda and Aurelia (Albertine's gossipy mother and aunt), Nector Kashpaw (Albertine's senile grandfather), and Gordon Kashpaw (the husband whom June left, a hapless drunk). Worst of all is June's legitimate son King, a volatile bully. King's horrifying acts of violence—abusing his wife Lynette, battering his new car, and smashing the pies prepared for the family dinner—leave Albertine with a dismayed sense of a family in shambles.

Love Medicine then shifts back in time from 1981, and its thirteen remaining stories proceed in chronological order from 1934 to 1984. "Saint Marie" concerns a poor white girl, Marie Lazarre, who in 1934 enters Sacred Heart Convent and embarks on a violent love-hate relationship with Sister Leopolda. In "Wild Geese," also set in 1934, Nector Kashpaw is infatuated with Lulu Nanapush, but his affections swerve unexpectedly when he encounters Marie Lazarre on the road outside her convent. By 1948, the time of "The Beads," Marie has married Nector, had three children (Aurelia, Zelda, and Gordie), and agreed to rear her niece June. Nector, however, is drinking and philandering, and June, after almost committing suicide in a children's hanging game, leaves to be brought up by Eli in the woods. "Lulu's Boys," set in 1957, reveals that the amorous Lulu Lamartine (née Nanapush) had married Henry Lamartine but bore eight sons by different fathers. Meanwhile, in "The Plunge of the Brave," also set in 1957, Nector recalls the development of his five-year affair with Lulu's and tries to leave his wife Marie for her, but the result is that he accidentally burns Lulu's house to the ground.

The offspring of these Kashpaws and Lamartines also

have their problems in later *Love Medicine* stories. In "The Bridge," set in 1973, Albertine runs away from home and becomes the lover of Henry Lamartine, Jr., one of Lulu's sons, a troubled Vietnam veteran. "The Red Convertible," set in 1974, also involves Henry, Jr., as Lyman Lamartine tries unsuccessfully to bring his brother out of the dark personality changes that Vietnam has wrought in him. On a lighter note, "Scales," set in 1980, is a hilarious account of the romance between Dot Adare, an obese white clerk at a truck weighing station, and Gerry Nanapush, one of Lulu's sons who is a most unusual convict: enormously fat, amazingly expert at escaping from jail, but totally inept at avoiding capture. "A Crown of Thorns," which overlaps the time of "The World's Greatest Fishermen" in 1981, traces the harrowing and bizarre decline of Gordie Kashpaw into alcoholism after June's death.

Though in these earlier *Love Medicine* stories the positive powers of love and spirit are more often frustrated than fulfilled, in the last three stories several characters achieve breakthroughs that bring members of the different families together in moving and hopeful ways. In "Love Medicine," set in 1982, Lipsha Morrissey reaches out lovingly to his grandmother Marie and to the ghosts of Nector and June. In "The Good Tears," set in 1983, Lulu undergoes a serious eye operation and is cared for by Marie, who forgives her for being Nector's longtime extramarital lover. Finally, in "Crossing the Water," set in 1984, Lipsha helps his father, Gerry Nanapush, escape to Canada and comes to appreciate the rich heritage of love, spirit, and wiliness that he has inherited from his diverse patchwork of Chippewa relatives—especially from his grandmother Lulu, his aunt Marie, and his parents, June and Gerry.

In 1993, Erdrich published an expanded version of *Love Medicine*, with four new stories: "The Island," an undated piece narrated by Lulu Nanapush, coming between "Wild Geese" and "The Beads," and three other stories inserted near the end of the sequence: "Resurrection" (set in 1982), "The Tomahawk Factory" (1983), and "Lyman's Luck" (also 1983). In addition to these new stories, Erdrich expanded "The Beads," adding a second section. Taken together, these additions solidify the foundation for subsequent volumes in Erdrich's cycle of novels.

In *The Beet Queen*, her second novel, Erdrich shifts her main focus from the American Indian to the European-immigrant side of her background, and she creates in impressive detail the mythical town of Argus (modeled on Wahpeton, where she was reared, but located closer to the Chippewa reservation) in the years from 1932 to 1972.

The opening scene of *The Beet Queen*, "The Branch," dramatizes two contrasting approaches to life that many characters will enact throughout the novel. On a cold spring day in 1932, two orphans, Mary and Karl Adare, arrive by freight train in Argus. As they seek the way to the butcher shop owned by their Aunt Fritzie and Uncle Pete Kozka, Mary "trudge[s] solidly forward," while Karl stops to embrace a tree that already has its spring blossoms. When they are attacked by a dog, Mary runs ahead, continuing her search for the butcher shop, while Karl runs back to hop the train once again. As the archetypal plodder of the novel, Mary continues to "trudge solidly forward" throughout; she is careful, determined, and self-reliant in pursuit of her goals. On the other hand, Karl is the principal dreamer—impressionable, prone to escapist impulses, and dependent on others to catch him when he falls.

The Adare family history shows how Karl is following a pattern set by his mother, Adelaide, while Mary grows in reaction against this pattern. Like Karl, Adelaide is physically beautiful but self-indulgent and impulsive. Driven to desperation by her hard luck in the early years of the Depression, Adelaide startles a fairground crowd by abandoning her three children (Mary, Karl, and an unnamed newborn son) to fly away with the Great Omar, an airplane stunt pilot.

In Argus, Mary tangles with yet another beautiful, self-centered dreamer: her cousin Sita Kozka, who resents the attention that her parents, Pete and Fritzie, and her best friend, Celestine James, pay to Mary. Yet Mary prevails and carves a solid niche for herself among Pete, Fritzie, and Celestine, who, like Mary, believe in a strong work ethic and lack Sita's pretentious airs.

A number of episodes gratify the reader with triumphs for Mary and comeuppances for the less sympathetic characters of Karl, Adelaide, and Sita. Mary becomes famous for a miracle at her school (she falls and cracks the ice in the image of Jesus), gains Celestine as a close friend, and in time becomes manager of the Kozka butcher shop. By contrast, Karl becomes a drifter who finds only sordid momentary pleasure in his numerous affairs. Meanwhile, Adelaide marries Omar and settles in Florida, but she becomes moody and subject to violent rages. Similarly, Sita fails in her vainglorious attempts to become a model and to establish a fashionable French restaurant; she escapes her first marriage through divorce and becomes insane and suicidal during her second.

Yet even as Erdrich charts the strange and sometimes grotesque downfalls of her flighty characters, she develops her more sympathetic ones in ways which suggest that the opposite approach to life does not guarantee happiness either. Mary fails in her attempt to attract Russell Kashpaw (the Chippewa half brother of Celestine), and she develops into an exotically dressed eccentric who is obsessed with predicting the future and controlling others. Like Mary, Celestine James and Wallace Pfef are hardworking and successful in business, but their loneliness drives each of them to an ill-advised affair with Karl, and he causes each of them considerable grief. In addition, the union of Celestine and Karl results in the birth of Dot Adare (who grows up to be the ill-tempered lover of Gerry Nanapush in the *Love Medicine* story "Scales"); since Celestine, Mary, and Wallace all spoil the child, Dot turns out, in Wallace's words, to have "all of her family's worst qualities." As a teenager, Dot herself comes to grief when she is mortified to learn that Wallace has rigged the election for Queen of the Argus Beet Festival so that she, an unpopular and ludicrously unlikely candidate, will win.

Yet in addition to the defeats and disappointments that all the characters bear, Erdrich also dramatizes the joy that they derive from life. The compensations of family and friendship—ephemeral and vulnerable as these may be—prove to be significant for all the characters at various times in the story, particularly at the end. The irrepressible vitality of these people, troublesome as they often are to one another, keeps the reader involved and entertained throughout the novel.

Erdrich's third novel, *Tracks*, is her most concentrated, intense, and mystical. It covers a time span of only twelve years, and alternates between only two first-person narrators. This compression serves the story well, for the human stakes are high. At first, and periodically throughout the novel, the Chippewa characters fear for their very survival, as smallpox, tuberculosis, severe winters, starvation, and feuds with mixed-blood families bring them close to extinction. Later in the novel, government taxes and political chicanery threaten the Chippewas' ownership of their family homesteads. In response, Erdrich's Chippewa characters use all the powers at their command—including the traditional mystical powers of the old ways—to try to survive and maintain their control over the land.

Nanapush, one of the novel's two narrators, is an old Chippewa whom Erdrich names for the trickster rabbit in tribal mythology who repeatedly delivers the Chippewas from threatening monsters. In *Tracks*, Erdrich's Nanapush often does credit to his mythological model by wielding the trickster rabbit's powers of deliverance, wiliness, and humor. He saves Fleur Pillager, a seventeen-year-old girl who is the last of the Pillager clan, from starvation. Later he delivers young Eli Kashpaw from the sufferings of love by advising him how to win Fleur's heart. Also, Nanapush is instrumental in saving the extended family that forms around Fleur, Eli, and himself. This family grows to five when Fleur gives birth to a daughter, Lulu, and Eli's mother, Margaret Kashpaw, becomes Nanapush's bedmate. As these five come close to starvation, Nanapush sends Eli out to hunt an elk; in one of the most extraordinary passages of the novel, Nanapush summons a power vision of Eli hunting that the old man imagines is guiding Eli to the kill. Nanapush also demonstrates the humor associated with his mythological model in his wry tone as a narrator, his sharp wit in conversation, and the tricks that he plays on his family's mixed-blood antagonists: the Pukwans, Morrisseys, and Lazarres.

Foremost among these antagonists is the novel's other narrator, Pauline Pukwan. A "skinny big-nosed girl with staring eyes," Pauline circulates in Argus from the Kozkas' butcher shop to the Sacred Heart Convent, and on the reservation from the Nanapush-Pillager-Kashpaw group to the Morrissey and Lazarre clans. At first attracted to Fleur by the beauty and sexual power that she herself lacks, Pauline later takes an envious revenge by concocting a love potion that seems to drive Fleur's husband, Eli, and Sophie Morrissey to become lovers. Ironically, though one side of her believes in a Catholic denial of her body, Pauline later gives birth out of wedlock to a girl named Marie, and at the end of her narrative Pauline enters the convent to become Sister Leopolda— the cruel nun who later torments her own daughter, Marie Lazarre, in *Love Medicine*.

Though Erdrich clearly feels passionately about the sufferings visited on her Chippewa characters in *Tracks*, she treats this politically charged material with her usual disciplined restraint. Her dispassionate, deadpan use of first-person narrators (never broken by authorial commentary) matches the understated, stoic attitude that Nanapush adopts toward the numerous waves of hardship and betrayal that the Chippewas must endure.

If in some ways *Tracks* seems to conclude with a feeling of fragmentation and defeat, in other ways it strikes positive notes of solidarity and survival, especially when considered in relation to *Love Medicine* and *The Beet Queen*. Fleur disappears, leaving her husband and daughter, but Nanapush uses his wiliness to become tribal chairman and then to retrieve Lulu from a distant boarding school. At the end, the reader is reminded that Nanapush has addressed his entire narrative to Lulu: The old man hopes that his story will convince Lulu to embrace the memory of Fleur, "the one you will not call mother." Further, the reader familiar with *Love Medicine* will realize how this young girl, who becomes Lulu Lamartine, carries on the supernaturally powerful sexu- ality of her mother Fleur and the wily talent for survival of Nanapush, the old man who gave her his name and reared her.

If Louise Erdrich had been born two hundred years earlier, she might have become a traditional Chippewa storyteller, whose tales would have reminded her listeners of their unchanging relationship to the land and to the mythic and legendary characters who inhabited it. Now several generations removed from such a stable and undamaged culture, Erdrich nevertheless creates a richly neotribal view of people and place. Her novels testify to the profound interrelatedness of her characters—American Indian and white, contemporaries and ancestors—both with one another and with their North Dakota homeland.

Other major works

POETRY: *Jacklight*, 1984; *Baptism of Desire*, 1989.

Bibliography

Bly, Robert. "Another World Breaks Through." *The New York Times Book Review* 92 (August 21, 1986): 2.

Erdrich, Louise. "Where I Ought to Be: A Writer's Sense of Place." *The New York Times Book Review* 91 (July 28, 1985): 1, 23-24.

Strouse, Jean. "In the Heart of the Heartland." *The New York Times Book Review* 94 (October 2, 1988): 1, 41-42.

Wickenden, Dorothy. "Off the Reservation." *The New Republic* 195 (October 6, 1986): 46-48.

MRS. ELIZABETH GASKELL

Born: Chelsea, London, England; September 29, 1810   **Died:** Holybourne, England; November 12, 1865

Principal long fiction

Mary Barton, 1848; *Cranford*, 1851-1853; *Ruth*, 1853; *North and South*, 1854-1855; *Sylvia's Lovers*, 1863; *Cousin Phillis*, 1863-1864; *Wives and Daughters*, 1864-1866.

Other literary forms

Mrs. Elizabeth Gaskell published travel sketches, essays, and short stories. Her collections of stories which appeared in serial as well as hardcover form were *Lizzie Leigh and Other Tales* (1855); *Round the Sofa* (1859), containing also the separate tales inset in "My Lady Ludlow"; *Right at Last and Other Tales* (1860); *Lois the Witch and Other Tales* (1861); and *Cousin Phillis and Other Tales* (1865). Sketches of Manchester life appeared as *Life in Manchester* (1847) under the pseudonym "Cotton Mather Mills, Esq." A biography of Charlotte Brontë, still regarded as a standard source, appeared in 1857.

Achievements

Gaskell's reputation sank in the modernist reaction to Victorian literature in the post-World War I period. She was relegated to the status of a second- or third-rate novelist, considered markedly inferior to Charles Dickens, William Makepeace Thackeray, George Eliot, George Meredith, and Anthony Trollope and even placed below Charles Kingsley and Wilkie Collins. Since World War II, however, her reputation has risen, and the concerns of the feminist movement in the 1970's led to such a revaluation that the scholar Patricia M. Spacks refers to her as "seriously underrated." Other writers about the women's movement have praised Gaskell for detailing faithfully in her fiction the relation between women and marriage, the struggle for self-achievement, and the intermixture of women's careers and public history. The sense in her work of women of all classes as victims of economic and social restrictions has caused scholars to study her work and life more closely. She has been elevated to the ranks of the major Victorian novelists.

Biography

Mrs. Elizabeth Gaskell's life was divided between the industrial Midlands of the North and London and rural Hampshire in the South of England, as was that of her heroine, Margaret Hale, in *North and South*. Her mother's family, the Hollands, substantial landowners, were established near Knutsford, Cheshire, which became the "Cranford" of her best-known work. Elizabeth Cleghorn Stevenson was born on September 29, 1810, at Chelsea-on-Thames, just outside London. Because of her mother's death, Elizabeth was taken to Knutsford, where she spent the next thirteen years in the care of her aunt. Her brother, John, twelve years older, went into the merchant navy but disappeared on a voyage to the Far East in 1823, an event marked in Gaskell's fiction by various lost and recovered brothers.

Her father remarried, and at fourteen Elizabeth was sent to Avonbank School in Stratford, which was kept by the Byerley sisters, her stepmother's aunts. It was a progressive school by Victorian standards of feminine education, serving Unitarian and other liberal religious groups. She left school at seventeen to tend her paralyzed father, faithfully nursing him from 1827 until his death in 1829. The experience furnished the basis for Margaret Hale's nursing of her critically ill mother.

The experience of Margaret in the fashionable home of her London relations appears to parallel the months spent by Elizabeth with her uncle, Swinton Holland, a banker, and her cousin, Henry Holland, a London physician. Following the fashion for educated and leisured Victorian women, she visited various places during the next few years. At Manchester, she met William Gaskell, a minister, and their warm relationship eventuated in marriage at Knutsford in August, 1832. Gaskell became the mother of four daughters and a son, whose death at the age of ten months caused her great sorrow.

Gaskell's immediate impulse to write came from grief over her son's death. Her first attempt at a diary and encouragement from publisher friends resulted in sketches about *Life in Manchester*, but this was a prelude to her first success as a novelist, *Mary Barton*. This novel presented the sufferings of the workers during labor unrest, the resistance of the millowners, the failure of parliament to respond to labor grievances, and the need for reconciliation. The book was praised by Friedrich Engels and Karl Marx and condemned as unfair by her husband's wealthy parishioners, a denouncement that led Gaskell to present what she considered an account more favorable to the industrialists in *North and South*. The acclaim and damnation of *Mary Barton* made Gaskell rather visible among British intellectuals. Gaskell's friendship with Dickens, for example, created a writer-editor relationship that lasted more than a dozen years. Thus, Mrs. Gaskell joined the reforming group bent on altering the unsatisfactory living and working conditions among the laboring class in Britain.

Having become interested in the fate of the "fallen woman," she used, as the basis for her novel *Ruth*, the actual case of a sixteen-year-old girl who had been seduced, abandoned, and then imprisoned for theft in trying to keep herself alive. In the novel, a similar young girl is saved from a parallel disgrace by the intervention of a kindly minister and his sister and brought back to respectability and social usefulness by their tender concern. The presentation of Ruth's case, mild by modern standards, became almost instantly controversial.

While *Ruth* was exciting controversy, *Cranford*, the work which for a long time overshadowed Gaskell's reputation as a social critic, created a nostalgic and melancholic mood. Yet even in this novel, Gaskell expresses a concern for lives that are close to poverty, genteel survivors of once lively and secure families. In *North and South*, written two years after *Cranford*, Gaskell made a determined effort to present the mill-owner, Thornton, as a man with integrity, initiative, and humanitarian concern for his workers who weathers the financial crisis both with the support of his wife, Margaret Hale, and that of his workers. The leisurely description and extended characterization in *North and South*, together with difficulties of episodic compression for its weekly publication in his journal, strained her relationship with Dickens. Their editorial struggle induced Gaskell to look for publication elsewhere in more prestigious journals run on a monthly basis.

Gaskell employed rural settings in her next two novels, *Sylvia's Lovers* and *Cousin Phillis*. As *Cousin Phillis* was winding up its serial publication in August, 1864, She started what some critics consider her major work, *Wives and Daughters*, an exploration of the role of women in Victorian intellectual and social life. It was never completed. Gaskell's unceasing activity was taking its physical toll. Hoping to retire to Holybourne, Hampshire, which she had used a decade earlier as Margaret Hale's beloved home community, she had purchased a home there as a surprise for her husband. While spending a trial weekend at the house with family and guests, she suffered a sudden and fatal stroke on November 12, 1865.

Analysis

In Gaskell's fiction, there is a strong interest in natural scenery, in country customs, crafts, and tales; a sympathy for conservative small towns, yet equally a concern for working men and women; a desire for practical knowledge to enhance living; a focus upon the family as the stable social unit where affections are close but able, on occasion, to extend to others in need; and an insistence that violence is futile, the human condition precarious, faith necessary. In Gaskell's treatment of the laboring element, Jenni Calder sees her as avoiding the duality of other portrayers of working-class families—sympathetic yet condescending—and refers to Mrs. Gaskell as one of the few major Victorian writers showing marriage from

a woman's viewpoint and not simply as an escape, a bid for social status, or a profitable contract. Gaskell has been praised for her concrete presentation of social milieus and her gift for recording the relationship between work and home and between husbands and wives. Gaskell draws, tacitly, the analogy between the plight of women in their dependency and that of workers in relation to their employers. Gaskell's dilemma for feminists, however, lives in Victorian expectations of feminine domesticity and marriage as an end to intellectual creativity. Gaskell herself surmounted the problem, but her characters find it a difficult challenge.

In *North and South*, the protagonist Margaret Hale

must adjust to life in industrial Darkshire (Derbyshire) after living in rural Hampshire, and, through her perceptions, Margaret guides the reader to a major issue: the way in which a money-oriented competitive society challenges a more leisured, socially stratified one. The abrasive confrontations of Margaret and John Thornton, a mill-owner being tutored in classics by Margaret's father, define the mutual incomprehension of North and South in England. Thornton wants to have a "wise despotism" over his workers; Margaret contends for understanding based upon common destiny in the mills. The question of authority is raised in another dimension in the Hale family's personal travail over the enforced exile of Margaret's brother, Frederick, because of charges, unwarranted, of inciting the crew of his naval vessel to mutiny. Through friendship with Bessy Higgins, a mill girl dying of a disease fostered by textile manufacturing, Margaret, the central consciousness of the novel, is able to observe the sufferings of the working class during a strike caused by union efforts to prevent wage cuts which the mill-owners justify because of American competition. The owners themselves, while cooperating in opposition to workers, fight one another for economic survival, according to Thornton, who sees an analogy with survival of the fittest. Though Margaret can see the closeness of working men and women in their common suffering, a riot, instigated without union approval by Nicholas Boucher, a weak agitator, against Irish scab labor, seriously compromises the position of the union in terms of its own self-discipline. The issue is posed whether coercive tactics to enlist worker support of unions can be justified when a weak leader can jeopardize legitimate demands. Margaret terminates the riot, in fact, by heroically intervening between Thornton and the rioters. She quite literally mediates between the two sides.

The difficulty of reconciliation is made evident, however, when Bessy's father, Nicholas Higgins, a unionist, argues that Christian forbearance will not answer the industrialists, though he admits that workers and employers might compromise if they could understand one another. The blacklisting of Nicholas by other employers leads to Margaret's intervention, encouraging Thornton to rehire him, his own persistence equally helping to regain a job. Thornton realizes that employer responsibility must be broadened. The turmoil of the riot, in which Margaret must confront social disruption, has its counterpart in her own turmoil over the approaching

death of her mother and the secret reappearance of her brother to be with their mother. Unfortunately, Frederick's departure from town involves a scuffle with a drunken informer which later requires that Margaret lie to protect Frederick. This lie produces its painful outcome when Thornton, who has observed the scuffle, thinks that she is lying to protect a lover, thus causing further altercations. Margaret realizes, however, that her moral condemnation of manufacturers has been too harsh.

Margaret's opinions about the South as a preferable society also undergo change. She counsels Nicholas that his going to the South, when he is blacklisted, would lead to deadening toil, no real companionship, and intellectual decay because of the rural isolation. Visiting Helstone, her old home, Margaret encounters an old native superstition when a live cat is boiled to avert a curse. A meeting with her former lover, Lennox, confirms that Thornton is the more vital man. A fortunate inheritance from an old family friend, Mr. Bell, enables Margaret to save Thornton, who is faced with mounting debts because of competition. He, too, has faced a moral dilemma: whether it is right to borrow money to keep himself afloat knowing that the lenders are at a strong risk. Thornton wishes to start again, seeking an opportunity for social interchange with his workers beyond the cash nexus. Margaret, now an heiress, helps Thornton stay afloat and marries him. Higgins, providentially having witnessed the scuffle, knows who Frederick really is. Thus, North and South are united, and Thornton turns into a philanthropist.

In *Wives and Daughters*, Gaskell explores the question of the middle-class woman seeking to define herself and her goals in an atmosphere uncongenial to intellectual independence. Molly Gibson, whose mother has died, must cope in her teens with the remarriage of her father, who has sought a wife as much to guide Molly as out of real love. Her father's new wife, Hyacinthe Kirkpatrick, is the epitome of the parasitical woman, a former governess previously married out of necessity and then forced back into supporting herself and her daughter, Cynthia, upon her husband's death. She has become a companion to the newly aristocratic Cumnor family, but, wanting comfort, she can achieve it only by marrying Gibson. Molly receives her moral education, in part, by seeing through her stepmother's artificial pretenses. Cynthia, shuffled off while her mother has pursued Gibson, comes to reside in the household and establishes a close friendship with Molly despite her moral skepticism and social opportunism. Thus, the daughters are contrasted, not in black and white, but as possible responses to the dependency of women.

Cynthia's mother tries to marry her to Osborne Hamley, eldest son of an old family, not knowing that he is already married and that the child of the marriage has been kept secret for some time. The event has caused Hamley to fail in attaining his degree, and he returns home to mope, thus arousing the antagonism of his father, to whom he cannot acknowledge his liaison. Hamley finally dies, causing Mrs. Kirkpatrick to shift her sights for Cynthia to the second son, Roger. Molly meanwhile has naïvely pledged herself at sixteen to the odious Preston, a situation from which she is rescued by the more forthright Cynthia, who is in love with Roger but also the object of the affections of Walter Henderson,

Gaskell's ideal of the practical, creative scientist, a new social type. Cynthia, socially ambitious, realizes that the Hamley family enjoys ancient honor but is materially threatened, and she transfers her affections to a superficial, weak, but socially prominent young man. Molly is left to marry Roger, but the problem remains as to whether she can forge for herself a free life with her husband's support. The novel's probing analysis of the dilemma of femininity in a world guided by material values and restricted social consciousness, a world in which men too are caught by the inhibitions of social position and frozen into immobility, gives it peculiar power. It is an indication of what Gaskell could have accomplished if she had lived longer, and it shows her continuing effort to link broader social issues to very specific circumstances with careful attention to detail.

Other major works

SHORT FICTION: *Lizzie Leigh and Other Tales*, 1855; *Round the Sofa*, 1859; *Right at Last and Other Tales*, 1860; *Lois the Witch and Other Tales*, 1861; *The Cage at Cranford*, 1863; *Cousin Phillis and Other Tales*, 1865.
NONFICTION: *Life in Manchester*, 1847 (as Cotton Mather Mills, Esq.); *The Life of Charlotte Brontë*, 1857; *The Letters of Mrs. Gaskell*, 1966 (Arthur Pollard and J. A. V. Chapple, editors).

Bibliography

Craik, W. A. *Elizabeth Gaskell and the English Provincial Novel*. New York: Harper & Row, 1975.
Duthie, Enid. *The Themes of Elizabeth Gaskell*. Basingstoke, England: Macmillan, 1980.
Easson, Angus. *Elizabeth Gaskell*. London: Routledge & Kegan Paul, 1979.
Gerin, Winifred. *Elizabeth Gaskell*. New York: Oxford University Press, 1976.
Stoneman, Patsy. *Elizabeth Gaskell*. Brighton, England: Harvester Press, 1987.
Wright, Edgar. *Mrs. Gaskell: The Basis for Re-assessment*. New York: Oxford University Press, 1965.

NATALIA GINZBURG

Born: Palermo, Italy; July 14, 1916

Principal long fiction

La strada che va in città, 1942 (as Allesandra Tornimparte; *The Road to the City*, 1949); *È stato così*, 1947 (*The Dry Heart*, 1949); *Tutti i nostri ieri*, 1952 (*A Light for Fools*, 1956; also as *Dead Yesterdays*, 1956, and *All Our Yesterdays*, 1985); *Valentino*, 1957 (also includes *Sagittario* and *La madre*); *Le voci della sera*, 1961 (*Voices in the Evening*, 1963); *Lessico famigliare*, 1963 (*Family Sayings*, 1967); *Cinque romanzi brevi*, 1964; *Caro Michele*, 1973 (*No Way*, 1974; also as *Dear Michael*, 1975); *Famiglia*, 1977; *La casa e la città*, 1984 (*The City and the House*, 1987).

Other literary forms

Though Natalia Ginzburg is known primarily as a novelist and short-story writer, she is also a talented dramatist, essayist, and poet. She has published two collections of plays, *Ti ho sposato per allegria e altre commedie* (1967; I married you for the fun of it and other comedies) and *Paese di mare e altre commedie* (1973; sea town and other comedies), some of which have been performed in London and New York. Her three volumes of essays and articles, *Le piccole virtù* (1962; *The Little Virtues*, 1985), *Mai devi domandarmi* (1970; *Never Must You Ask Me*, 1973), and *Vita immaginaria* (1974; imaginary life), range over a wide variety of subjects, including literary and film criticism. Her scholarly biography of the family of Italy's greatest novelist of the nineteenth century, *La famiglia Manzoni* (1983; the Manzoni family), has won critical acclaim. Her poetry has been published in various newspapers and literary reviews.

Achievements

One of the best-known Italian female writers of the second half of the twentieth century, Ginzburg began her career by publishing short stories in *Solaria* and *Letteratura* in the mid-1930's. Her first short novel, *The Road to the City*, was published under the pseudonym "Alessandra Tornimparte" because of the anti-Jewish laws. Her narrative works of the 1940's and 1950's established her critical reputation and associated her with the brief but significant neorealist movement in Italian literature and film. In 1947, her second short novel, *The Dry Heart*, won the Tempo Prize. Her first long novel, *Dead Yesterdays*, was awarded the Veillon Prize in the year of its publication. In 1957, Ginzburg received the Viareggio Prize for the short novel *Valentino*. Ginzburg's second long novel, *Family Sayings*, which received the prestigious Strega Prize in 1964, is generally considered one of her strongest works, together with the novel that preceded it, *Voices in the Evening*. Ginzburg's uncomplicated narrative style, with which she recounts stories that hover between fiction and nonfiction, has made hers one of the most distinctive voices in postwar Italian letters. One of her several plays, *L'inserzione* (1967; *The Advertisement*, 1968), was honored with the Marzotto International Prize of 1968.

Biography

Although Natalia Levi was born in Palermo on July 14, 1916, she spent her childhood and adolescence in Turin, where her father was a professor of comparative anatomy. The daughter of a Catholic mother and a Jewish father (both nonpracticing), she acquired a sense of social isolation at an early age and was educated at home and in the schools of Turin. (She has told the story of her family in *Family Sayings*.) In 1938, she married Leone Ginzburg, a professor of Russian literature and an active anti-Fascist. From 1940 to 1943, the Ginzburgs, together with their three children, lived in compulsory political confinement in a remote district of the Abruzzi. After moving to Rome, Leone Ginzburg was arrested and imprisoned for the second time in November, 1943, and died in Rome at the Regina Coeli prison on February 5, 1944.

After the war, Natalia Ginzburg returned to Turin and worked there as a consultant for the Einaudi publishing firm. In 1950, she married Gabriele Baldini, a professor of English literature. When Baldini was named head of the Italian Institute of Culture in London, the family took up residence in that city, where they lived from 1959 to 1962, at which time they returned to the Italian capital. In 1968, her second husband died. Thereafter, she took up permanent residence in Rome, working as a consultant for Einaudi in addition to her writing and her occasional contributions to Italian newspapers and magazines.

Analysis

From her first short stories and novellas published in the 1930's and 1940's to her epistolary novels of the 1970's and 1980's, Natalia Ginzburg provides a female perspective on the Italian bourgeoisie during a period of widespread social change. Viewed in its entirety, her career shows a progression from the short story toward the more sustained form of the novel, with a developing interest in the theater. Her dominant themes, which can be related in part to her affinity to Cesare Pavese, revolve around the inevitability of human suffering and isolation, the impossibility of communication, the failure of love, the asymmetries in modern Italy between urban and rural existence, and the influence of the family on the individual. Her early novels, *The Road to the City* and *The Dry Heart*, both present first-person female narrators whose interior monologues focus on human emotions rather than external events. Relatively little happens in these early works, which are generally low-key in tone, straightforward in plot structure, and uncomplicated in lexicon and syntax. The elemental character of Ginzburg's prose makes her work accessible to students whose knowledge of Italian may still be rudimentary. In fact, her clear and direct approach to writing has won for her high praise as a stylist. Her later novels depend more on dialogue than on description, and her talent for reproducing realistic speech patterns expresses itself with equal felicity in her writings for the theater.

With *Family Sayings*, which is generally considered to be her best novel, Ginzburg introduced a more openly autobiographical element into her work. A chronicle of the author's family life during Fascism, the Resistance, and the immediate postwar period, *Family Sayings* testifies to the author's statement that memory provides the most important stimulus for her writing. Her interest in the family as a social unit is also manifest in her other works of the 1970's and 1980's and underlies such epistolary novels as *No Way* and *The City and the House*, as well as works as diverse as the novel *Famiglia* (family) and the scholarly biography *La famiglia Manzoni*.

The Road to the City recounts the experience of a sixteen-year-old-girl, Delia, whose boredom with her squalid peasant environment leads her into the trap for which she seems destined. Blinded by the glitter of city life (as personified in her older, more sophisticated sister), she allows herself to be seduced by a young law student named Giulio, for whom she feels only a superficial attraction. She becomes pregnant and marries Giulio while her cousin and true friend, Nino, dies from abuse of alcohol and frustration at being unable to establish a meaningful relationship with her. During the wedding ceremony, Delia realizes that she is marrying a man whom she does not love. Yet she fails to realize the underlying circumstances which have caused her to enter into a loveless marriage. This study in disillusionment contains the typical elements of Ginzburg's early work: Her narrator-protagonists are naïve and simple young women who find themselves attracted to the charms of city life but who are ultimately disappointed by the role that society offers them.

Relying on similarly uncomplicated stylistic devices, *The Dry Heart* recounts a murder story from the perspective of a first-person female narrator, a young schoolteacher from the country whose life in the city is full of disappointments. Like Delia, she enters into a loveless marriage. Unable to draw her husband away from his mistress, the unnamed narrator-protagonist kills him, seemingly against her own will. The murder is related in the novel's opening paragraphs, and the bulk of the novel is made up almost entirely of a monologue in which the protagonist seeks to justify and to understand her own actions. The detached, isolated "I" that appears throughout the narrative mirrors the naïveté, passivity, and resignation of the main character. Brief units of dialogue are embedded in blocks of the narrator's monologue, which is almost completely bereft of commas. This singular punctuation helps create the monotonous, despairing tone of a novel that treats the inability of human beings to establish mutually satisfactory relationships. The failure of a marriage leads to murder and to the protagonist's own drift toward suicide.

With *Dead Yesterdays*, Ginzburg's fiction took a significant step forward. Her first novel of a substantial length, this work seeks to add a historical dimension missing from her previous fiction. Composed while neorealism was enjoying its brief moment in the sun, *Dead Yesterdays* abandons the first-person narrative style of the early short novels in favor of the third person. The novel centers on the sufferings of two Italian families during the reign of Fascism, the war, and the Resistance; the book's plot structure is more developed than the author's previous work, and external events have a greater importance. Indeed, *Dead Yesterdays* seeks to tell the story of an entire generation. For the first time, Ginzburg's strange heroes become involved in the broader fabric of social reality. An unnamed industrial city in the North and a fictional village in the South constitute the settings. The main characters include Anna, the younger sister in the less wealthy of the two families; Concettina, her elder sister; and Cenzo Rena, an intellectual of the Left whose commitment to social problems furnishes Ginzburg's fiction with a successfully drawn portrait of an engagé figure. His decision to take the blame for the death of a German soldier is tantamount to suicide, but it saves the villagers from a brutal Nazi reprisal. His politically motivated self-sacrifice brings the novel to an end on a positive note.

The 1950's and the 1960's witnessed a fruitful development in Ginzburg's maturing narrative production. In 1951, she wrote *Valentino*, a novella published in 1957 together with *Sagittario* (Sagittarius) and *La madre* (the mother) in a single volume. These three novellas were awarded the Viareggio Prize of 1957 and further express Ginzburg's continuing preoccupation with the power of the family as a social unit. In the early 1960's, Ginzburg lived with her husband in London, where in the spring of 1961 she wrote *Voices in the Evening*. Set completely in Italy in an unnamed provincial town, *Voices in the Evening* chronicles the disintegration of an Italian middle-class family. Through a series of flashbacks (each one a portrait of a different member of the family), Ginzburg alternates dialogue with the narrator's monologue. Against a backdrop of Fascism and the war and its aftermath, once again the coming-of-age of a young woman, Elsa, provides the focal point for Ginzburg's

nostalgic narrative. Elsa's unhappy affair with Tommasino, a young man whose family background renders him incapable of giving love, is presented in the flat, unsentimental narrative style which has become Ginzburg's trademark.

Family Sayings was awarded the Strega Prize in 1964 and is regarded by many critics as the author's major work. Having grown up in the anti-Fascist atmosphere of Turin, Ginzburg manages to capture the feeling of an entire epoch in recounting the minimal details of her own family life. In *Family Sayings*, Ginzburg draws a portrait of the people who have mattered the most in her private world, many of whom, it should be noted, such as Leone Ginzburg, Filippo Turati, and Cesare Pavese, have also played a significant role in Italian culture and politics. Paradoxically, the openly autobiographical element of *Family Sayings*, the turning inward to mine her own private stock of memories, seems to have sharpened Ginzburg's abilities as an observer of social reality, abilities which she puts to good use in her three volumes of essays.

In the epistolary novel *No Way*, one finds the themes that Ginzburg elaborates throughout the previous four decades, but here they are brought into the context of the social unrest of Italy in the 1970's: The unhappy marriage of a middle-class Roman couple has disastrous effects on their offspring. The exchange of letters between the novel's various characters revolves around Michele, the young protagonist, who moves to London, where he marries an alcoholic divorcée, and who later dies in Bruges at the hands of a group of neo-Fascists. From a technical standpoint, the epistolary structure of the novel allows Ginzburg to experiment with multiple monologues and multiple points of view.

Famiglia and *Borghesia*, the titles of the two novellas that make up the volume *Famiglia*, indicate the twin themes that Ginzburg has pursued throughout her career. As in the novel that preceded this work, here she brings her focus on the Italian bourgeois family into the highly charged political atmosphere of Italy in the 1970's. With *The City and the House*, Ginzburg returns to the epistolary form used a decade earlier in *No Way*. Her cast of letter-writing characters includes the protagonist Giuseppe, a middle-aged Italian who, in emigrating to New Jersey, cuts himself off from his friends and his roots. The letter as a technical device also fits well with Ginzburg's attempt to fashion a sparse, unadorned style intended to reproduce the rhythms of actual speech. Her focus on the common objects and conflicting emotions of daily life has led critics to compare her work with that of Anton Chekhov. At the same time, as critic Allan Bullock has suggested (an intuition confirmed by the author herself), Ginzburg's use of dialogue beginning in the early 1960's owes a debt to a writer very different from Chekhov: the English novelist Ivy Compton-Burnett. Ginzburg's most accomplished novels, *Voices in the Evening* and *Family Sayings*, combine elements of autobiography, memory, and emotion within the broader context of historical events and social change. Ginzburg's gift for interweaving the private and the social, the personal and the historical in a simple, straightforward prose style may be her most significant contribution to Italian letters.

Other major works

PLAYS: *Ti ho sposato per allegria e altre commedie*, 1967; *L'inserzione*, 1967 (*The Advertisement*, 1968); *Paese di mare e altre commedie*, 1973.

NONFICTION: *Le piccole virtù*, 1962 (*The Little Virtues*, 1985); *Mai devi domandarmi*, 1970 (*Never Must You Ask Me*, 1973); *Vita immaginaria*, 1974; *La famiglia Manzoni*, 1983.

Bibliography

Bowe, Clotilde S. "The Narrative Strategy of Natalia Ginzburg." *Modern Language Review* 68 (1973): 788-795.

Bullock, Allan. "Natalia Ginzburg and Ivy Compton-Burnett: Creative Composition and Domestic Repression in *Le voci della sera*." *Rivista di letterature moderne e comparate* 30 (1977): 203-227.

Heiney, Donald. "Natalia Ginzburg: The Fabric of Voices." *The Iowa Review* 1 (Fall, 1970): 87-93.

Piclardi, Rosetta D. "Forms and Figures in the Novels of Natalia Ginzburg." *World Literature Today* 53 (1979): 585-589.

NIKKI GIOVANNI

Born: Knoxville, Tennessee; June 7, 1943

Principal poetry

Black Feeling, Black Talk, 1968; *Black Judgement*, 1968; *Black Feeling, Black Talk, Black Judgement*, 1970; *Re: Creation*, 1970; *Poem of Angela Yvonne Davis*, 1970; *Spin a Soft Black Song: Poems for Children*, 1971 (juvenile); *My House*, 1972; *Ego-Tripping and Other Poems for Young People*, 1973 (juvenile); *The Women and the Men*, 1975; *Cotton Candy on a Rainy Day*, 1978; *Vacation Time*, 1980 (juvenile); *Those Who Ride the Night Winds*, 1983 (juvenile).

Other literary forms

Besides her volumes of verse, Nikki Giovanni has made six poetry recordings. Some, such as *Truth Is on Its Way* (Right On Records, 1971), have gospel music accompaniment. Her recordings as well as her many public performances have helped to popularize the black oral poetry movement. Her two books of conversations with older, established black writers, *A Dialogue: James Baldwin and Nikki Giovanni* (1973) and *A Poetic Equation: Conversations Between Nikki Giovanni and Margaret Walker* (1974), offer the contrasting attitudes of two generations of African American writers on the aims of black literature in white America. *Gemini: An Extended Autobiographical Statement on My First Twenty-five Years of Being a Black Poet* (1971), which was nominated for a National Book Award in 1973, offers scenes from her life as a child and mother. She has edited *Night Comes Softly: Anthology of Black Female Voices* (1970), written syndicated columns, and contributed essays to many black publications. *Sacred Cows . . . and Other Edibles* (1988) collects a number of her essays.

Achievements

From the beginning of her career, Giovanni has combined private with public concerns, and her development has been toward the exploration of the inner life of one black female—herself—as a paradigm for black women's aspirations in contemporary America. An individualist who early admired Ayn Rand's concept of rational self-interest, Giovanni has a unique black identity. Her example of self-actualization embodied in her poetry has been not only influential but also inspirational, especially to African American youth.

Biography

Yolande Cornelia Giovanni was born on June 7, 1943, in Knoxville, Tennessee, but grew up in Wyoming and Lincoln Heights, Ohio, suburbs of Cincinnati. She described her childhood as "quite happy" in the poem "Nikki-Rosa," and her reminiscences in *Gemini* testify to her devotion to relatives, especially her sister Gary (who nicknamed her "Nikki") and her grandparents, John Brown Watson, one of the first graduates of Fisk University, and his wife Louvenia, whose strength of character she admired and emulated. Giovanni herself entered Fisk at sixteen and was graduated in 1967 with a B.A. magna cum laude in history. At Fisk, her independent spirit led to her being expelled after one semester, but when she reentered in 1964, she immediately became involved in politics, reestablishing the university's chapter of the Student Nonviolent Coordinating Committee (SNCC). She also became greatly interested in literature and participated in John Oliver Killens' writers' workshop. She briefly attended the School of Social Work at the University of Pennsylvania. It was African American politics and art, however, that held her interest. In 1967, a Ford Foundation grant enabled her to complete and publish her first book of poetry, *Black Feeling, Black Talk*, and its success led to a National Foundation of the Arts grant on which she attended Columbia University's School of Fine Arts in 1968. Instead of completing her proposed novel or work toward a graduate degree, she continued to work on a volume of poetry, *Black Judgement*, published through a grant by the Harlem Cultural Council on the Arts.

Her impact on African American literature was immediate and electric. Her celebration of blackness and her militancy placed her in the avant-garde. Hailed as the "Princess of Black Poetry," she began touring the United States, lecturing to college audiences, spreading her message of black cultural nationalism, "ego-tripping," and love. To raise black cultural awareness and to foster black art, she became an Assistant Professor of Black Studies at Queens College, Flushing, New York in 1968 and taught creative writing at Livingston College, Rutgers University, from 1968 to 1970. She organized the Black Arts Festival in Cincinnati in 1967, editing *Love Black*, a magazine of the people; participated in the 1970 National Educational Television program "Soul!"; and took part in the two-week black festival "Soul at the Center" at Lincoln Center in New York in 1972.

In 1969, her son Thomas Watson Giovanni was born: Her concern for him—indeed for all children—was the springboard for her volumes of children's poetry, which include *Spin a Soft Black Song, Ego-Tripping and Other Poems for Young Readers*, and *Vacation Time*. She also worked with the Reading is Fundamental Program in Harlem, the Jackie Robinson Foundation, and the President's Committee on the International Year of the Child (1979). She became an active member of black service organizations and an editorial consultant and columnist for *Encore American and Worldwide News Magazine*, a black news monthly with a Third World focus.

Analysis

Throughout Giovanni's poetry run two main themes, revolution and love—one destructive, the other creative. Even in her earliest verse, both strands are evident: Only the emphasis shifts from the former to the latter. The revolution that she calls for in *Black Judgement* is, on one level, literal. The revolution is also symbolic, striking out at the poisonous racial myths that have devalued blacks in America. In "Word Poem (Perhaps Worth Considering)" she writes: "as things be/come/ let's destroy/ then we can destroy/ what we be/come/ let's build/ what we become/ when we dream." The destruction here is of values and attitudes, seemingly in accord with the statement in *Gemini*: "Nobody's trying to make the system Black; we're trying to make a system that's human so that Black folks can live in it. This means we're trying to destroy the existing system." Giovanni's poems attack the American political establishment in a sweeping, generalized way; her analysis is simple—exterminate the white beast. Her real contempt is directed toward "Negroes" still in the service of white America: "The True Import of Present Dialogue, Black vs. Negro" is "Can you kill/ Can you kill a white man/ Can you kill the nigger/ in you." Aware that the future lies with the children, she urges in "Poem for Black Boys" new revolutionary games:

Ask your mother for a Rap Brown gun
Santa just may comply if you wish hard enough
Ask for CULLURD instead of Monopoly
DO NOT SIT IN DO NOT FOLLOW KING
GO DIRECTLY TO STREETS
This is a game you can win.

Her change from an incendiary radical to a nurturing poet is traced in the poem "Revolutionary Dreams": From dreaming "militant/ dreams of taking/ over america," she "awoke and dug/ that if i dreamed natural/ dreams of being a natural/ woman doing what a woman/ does when she's natural/ i would have a revolution." This changed perspective accords with the conclusion of "When I Die": "And if ever i touched a life i hope that life knows/ that i know that touching was and still is and will/ always be the true/ revolution." Love and sex form the subject matter of many of her poems. She will "scream and stamp and shout/ for more beautiful beautiful beautiful/ black men with outasight afros" in "Beautiful Black Men" and propose "counterrevolutionary" sex in "Seduction" and "That Day": "if you've got the dough/ then i've got the heat/ we can use my oven/ til it's warm and sweet." This bold and playful manner, however, is usually modulated by the complications of any long-term relationship between men and women. In "Woman" her acknowledgment of the difficulty of a black man maintaining his self-respect in America has led to her acceptance of his failings: "she decided to become/ a woman/ and though he still refused/ to be a man/ she decided it was all/ right."

This poem, like many others in *Cotton Candy on a Rainy Day*, bespeaks the tempering of her vision. The title poem tells of "the gray of my mornings/ Or the blues of every night" in a decade known for "loneliness." Life is likened to nebulous cotton candy: "The sweet soft essence/ of possibility/ Never quite maturing." Her attitude tired, her potential stillborn, she is unable to categorize life as easily as before, "To put a three-dimensional picture/ On a one-dimensional surface." One reason for her growth in vision seems to be her realization of the complexity of a woman's life. The black woman's negative self-image depicted in "Adulthood" was not solved by adopting the role of Revolutionary Black Poet. In "Woman Poem," "Untitled," "Once a Lady Told Me," "Each Sunday," and "The Winter Storm," the women with compromised lives are other women. In "A Poem Off Center," however, she includes herself in this condition: "maybe i shouldn't feel sorry/ for myself/ but the more i understand women/ the more i do." A comparison of "All I Gotta Do" ("is sit and wait") to "Choice," two poems alike in their subject matter and their syncopated beat, shows that a woman's only choice is to cry.

Two other themes in her poetry also ally Giovanni with the new black poets—Africa and black music. The romantic and exotic Africa of the Harlem Renaissance writers appears only in "Ego-Tripping," where Africa is personified as a beautiful woman. Her own African experience has produced poems that give a balanced recognition of the African's separate identity. In "They Clapped," African Americans are treated like any other tourists and African life is seen realistically.

they stopped running when they learned the packages
on the women's heads were heavy and that babies didn't
cry and disease is uncomfortable and that villages are
    fun
only because you knew the feel of good leather on good
    pavement.

Her conclusion—"despite the dead/ dream they saw a free future"—opens the way for a new hope in "Africa": "i dream of black men and women walking/ together side by side into a new world/ described by love and bounded by difference."

Black music forms the basis of many of her poems: Soul singer Aretha Franklin emerges as her personal idol, lines from popular songs are woven into "Revolutionary Music" and "Dreams," and several of her poems are based on traditional African American music. She has written a blues tune, "Master Charge Blues," in which a modern woman lets her credit card cure her troubles, and a song which could be set to music, "The Only Song I'm Singing."

The use of the ballad stanza in "On Hearing 'The Girl with the Flaxen Hair' " is effective in building a narrative about white and black art: The girl with flaxen hair gets

a song; the black woman does not because her man is tired after working. Her most successful adaptation of musical form comes in "The Great Pax Whitie," which recalls gospel music. Here Pax Whitie (a bitter parody of the Pax Romana) is described first in an inversion of the words beginning St. John's gospel: The word "was death to all life." Western history, its wars and brutality, is recounted with two alternating calls and responses: "ain't they got no shame?" and "ain't we got no pride?"Her historical account is heavily ironic:

So the great white prince
Was shot like a nigger in texas
And our Black shining prince was murdered
like that thug in his cathedral
While our nigger in memphis
was shot like their prince in dallas.

The irony here and in other political poems, such as "Oppression," will be directed in *Cotton Candy on a Rainy Day* toward herself in "Being and Nothingness" and "The New Yorkers."

As Giovanni's poems turned toward human relationships, there was a marked increase in her lyricism and especially in her use of imagery, both decorative and structural. Her lover's hands are compared to butterflies in "The Butterfly"; she feels like a falling leaf after a night of passion in "Autumn Poems." "Make Up" sustains the image of cosmetics to talk about the life of pretense that a woman must live. On the whole, her verse descends from William Carlos Williams and Langston Hughes, but her voice is her own. While she is neither a stylistic innovator nor a stunning image-maker, she has an ingratiating style, one that proceeds from the energy of her personality, and an increasingly sure command of phrasing.

In "The Wonder Woman (A New Dream—for Stevie Wonder)," Giovanni reviewed her life up to 1971: "i wanted to be/ a sweet inspiration in my dreams/ of my people but the times/ require that i give/ myself willingly and become/ a wonder woman." If her subsequent history has fallen short of this ideal, it is still her strong clear voice that one remembers after reading her poetry; her poems are ultimately the self-expression of an African American woman who has discovered that "Black love is Black wealth" and who has brought many people, both black and white, to poetry.

Other major works

NONFICTION: *Gemini: An Extended Autobiographical Statement on My First Twenty-five Years of Being a Black Poet*, 1971; *A Dialogue: James Baldwin and Nikki Giovanni*, 1973; *A Poetic Equation: Conversations Between Nikki Giovanni and Margaret Walker*, 1974; *Sacred Cows . . . and Other Edibles*, 1988.
ANTHOLOGY: *Night Comes Softly: Anthology of Black Female Voices*, 1970.

Bibliography

Baldwin, James, and Nikki Giovanni. *A Dialogue: James Baldwin and Nikki Giovanni*. Philadelphia: J. B. Lippincott, 1973.
Gould, Jean. "Nikki Giovanni." In *Modern American Women Poets*. New York: Dodd, Mead, 1984.
Mitchell, Mozella G. "Nikki Giovanni." In *Afro-American Poets Since 1955*, edited by Trudier Harris and Thadious M. Davis. Vol. 41 of *Dictionary of Literary Biography*. Detroit: Gale Research, 1985.

ELLEN GLASGOW

Born: Richmond, Virginia; April 22, 1873

Died: Richmond, Virginia; November 21, 1945

Principal long fiction

The Descendant, 1897; *Phases of an Inferior Planet*, 1898; *The Voice of the People*, 1900; *The Battle-Ground*, 1902; *The Deliverance*, 1904; *The Wheel of Life*, 1906; *The Ancient Law*, 1908; *The Romance of a Plain Man*, 1909; *The Miller of Old Church*, 1911; *Virginia*, 1913; *Life and Gabriella*, 1916; *The Builders*, 1919; *One Man in His Time*, 1922; *Barren Ground*, 1925; *The Romantic Comedians*, 1926; *They Stooped to Folly*, 1929; *The Sheltered Life*, 1932; *Vein of Iron*, 1935; *In This Our Life*, 1941.

Other literary forms

In addition to nineteen novels, Ellen Glasgow wrote a book of short stories, *The Shadowy Third and Other Stories* (1923); a book of poems, *The Freeman and Other Poems* (1902); a book on her views of fiction-writing (concerned primarily with her own works), *A Certain Measure* (1943); and an autobiography, *The Woman Within* (1954). She also wrote a number of articles on fiction for various periodicals and magazines. Her letters were published in 1958.

Achievements

Although Glasgow never believed that she had received the critical acclaim she deserved, she nevertheless played an important part in the development of Southern letters. She provided in her novels a new picture of the South, a region reluctantly ushered into the modern world. Against a sentimentalized view of the Old South, Glasgow advocated an acceptance of the inevitability of change.

Prior to 1925, Glasgow's critical reception was mixed—more positive than negative, but nothing that would mark her as a writer of the first rank. With *Barren Ground*, however, Glasgow's reputation began to grow with both critics and readers. That novel made the 1925 *Review of Review*'s list of twenty-five outstanding novels of the year. Glasgow's *The Sheltered Life* was a best-seller and greatly enhanced her reputation. *Vein of Iron* and *In This Our Life*, which received the Pulitzer Prize in 1942, helped to ensure her position as a writer of major significance.

Biography

Born in Richmond, Virginia, in 1873, Ellen Glasgow came from a combination of stern Scotch-Irish pioneers on her father's side and Tidewater, Virginia, aristocratic stock on her mother's side. Francis Glasgow was an ironworks executive, an occupation well suited to his Puritan temperament and character. Ellen Glasgow had little positive to say about her father. Her mother, on the other hand, was a cultivated, gracious, and humane woman. These divergent influences provided the crucible from which Glasgow's writings were to emerge.

The next to the youngest in a family of four sons and six daughters, Glasgow experienced a lonely childhood. Because of fragile health and a nervous temperament that precluded adjustment to formal schooling, her isolation was increased, and most of her education came from her father's extensive library. As a child, Glasgow admired the novels of Charles Dickens, Henry Fielding, and Jane Austen. From Dickens, she gained reinforcement for her already strong aversion to cruelty, and from the latter two, she learned that only honest writing can endure. Lesser novelists, she believed, lacked "the creative passion and the courage to offend, which is the essential note of great fiction."

Glasgow grew up in that period following the Civil War when, as she described it, the "prosperous and pleasure-loving" agrarians of the antebellum years were struggling for existence amid "the dark furies of Reconstruction." It was a conservative, even reactionary, time when, according to Glasgow, "being a rebel, even an intellectual one, was less exciting and more uncomfortable than it is nowadays." Rejecting the harsh Calvinism of her father and the bloodless social graces of Richmond society, she retreated even further into a life of the mind. Glasgow's growing sense of alienation and rebelliousness has been seen by critics as the wellspring of her literary vision.

By 1890, just one year after her hearing had begun to fade, Glasgow had produced some four hundred pages of a novel, *Sharp Realities* (unpublished). Putting that effort aside, she began writing *The Descendant* in 1891. Two years later, however, upon the death of her mother, with whom she had great affinity, she destroyed a good part of what she had written. Another two years passed before she returned to the novel and completed it. The following year, she made the first of numerous trips to Europe.

With the publication (anonymously) of *The Descendant* in 1897, Glasgow was launched on her prolific career. Writing became and remained her role in life, and she was ever mindful of the growth of her literary reputation, changing publishers when she thought it to her advantage and making sure that critics were fully aware of her books.

Presumably while on a trip to Europe in 1899, Glasgow fell in love with a married man, to whom she refers in her autobiography *The Woman Within* (1954) as Gerald B——. Another serious love affair was with Henry Watkins Anderson, a Richmond lawyer. He and Glasgow met in 1915 and were engaged in 1917. In July of the next year, Glasgow attempted suicide when she learned that Anderson, who was working with the Red Cross in the Balkan States, was attracted to Queen Marie of Romania. This turbulent love affair between Glasgow and Anderson was tacitly broken around 1920. In two novels, *The Builders* and *One Man in His Time*, Glasgow incorporated aspects of her relationship with Anderson.

As Glasgow began receiving the critical recognition for which she longed, her health began to fail. A heart condition worsened, and she died on November 21, 1945, in Richmond, Virginia.

Analysis

Turning away from a romanticized view of her own Virginia, Ellen Glasgow became a part of the revolt against the elegiac tradition of Southern letters. She strove for what she called "blood and irony"—blood because the South had grown thin and pale and was existing on borrowed ideas, copying rather than creating; and irony because it is the surest antidote to sentimental decay. She produced a series of novels that recorded the social history of Virginia through three generations, picturing sympathetically the social and industrial revolution that was transforming the romantic South. A central theme in this record is that of change—change brought about by the conflict between the declining agrarian regime and the rising industrial system. In pursuing the theme of change, however, Glasgow was careful not to go to the extreme in her presentation of deterioration.

In this respect, her works, unlike those of William Faulkner or Erskine Caldwell, lack shocking or sensational detail and maintain an almost Victorian sense of decorum.

Barren Ground marked Glasgow's emergence not only from a period of despondency regarding her social life but also as a novelist who had moved without question from apprentice to master. Certainly her finest work to that time, *Barren Ground* was to Glasgow the best of all her novels. One of her country novels, it deals with that class of people often referred to as "poor whites." Glasgow herself refutes this appellation, preferring instead to call them "good people," a label that distinguishes them from the aristocratic "good families." Lineal descendants of the English yeoman farmer, these people were the ones who pushed the frontier westward. In this novel, they stand as a "buffer class between the opulent gentry and the hired labourers."

Dorinda Oakley, the heroine, is the offspring of a union of opposites: Her father, Joshua, is a landless man whose industry and good nature do not compensate for his ineffectuality; and her mother, Eudora, the daughter of a Presbyterian minister, has a religious mania of her own. This background has kept Dorinda's heart "in arms against life." More important, however, she has also inherited a kinship with the earth that enables her to make something positive out of "barren ground."

Dorinda falls in love with Jason Greylock, a young doctor, seeing in him the promise of something more than the grinding poverty she has known. They plan to marry, but Jason cannot go against his father's wishes, and he marries Geneva Ellgood instead. Pregnant by Jason,

Dorinda flees to New York, where, after being struck by a taxi, she loses the baby. She works as a nurse for a Dr. Faraday until she learns that her father is dying. She returns home with enough money borrowed from Faraday to start a dairy farm. Back on the land, she becomes tough-minded and makes a success of the farm. Although she marries Nathan Pedlar, a storekeeper, she remains the head of the family. After his death in a train wreck, she is again alone, but happy, rearing Nathan's child by a previous marriage and managing the farm. Jason, in the meantime, has lost his wife by suicide and is forced to sell his farm to Dorinda. Because he is ill and an alcoholic, she unwillingly provides him with food and shelter. After a few months he dies, and once more she is alone. When a local farmer asks Dorinda to marry him, she responds, "I am thankful to have finished with all that."

A tragic figure of sorts, Dorinda sees herself trapped by fate, "a straw in the wind, a leaf on a stream." Even so, she is not content to be simply a passive victim of that fate. Unlike Jason, who through his inherited weakness, succumbs to the forces that beset him, Dorinda looks upon the land as a symbol of that fate against which she must struggle. Hardened by adversity and with a deep instinct for survival, she refuses to surrender.

Although Dorinda's life may be compared to barren ground because it has been emotionally unfulfilled, it nevertheless is a successful life in that she masters herself and, in turn, the land. Just as the broom sedge must be burned off the land, so must romantic emotions be purged from Dorinda's soul. In giving her life to the land, she, in a sense, gains it back—and is thus, ironically, both victim and victor.

Following *Barren Ground*, Glasgow turned to the novel of manners with a trilogy: *The Romantic Comedians*, *They Stooped to Folly*, and *The Sheltered Life*—the last novel regarded by some critics as Glasgow's finest. In *The Sheltered Life*, Glasgow employs two points of view—that of youth and that of age, in this case a young girl and an old man. Against the background of a "shallow and aimless society of happiness hunters," she presents characters as they are revealed through the mind and emotions of Jenny Blair and her grandfather, General David Archbald.

Glasgow intended General Archbald as the central character in the novel—a character who "represents the tragedy, wherever it appears, of the civilized man in a world that is not civilized." General Archbald sees before him a changing world, a world that is passing him by. Thus, he holds to the social traditions of the nineteenth century, which have provided little shelter for him. He was never a man for his time. A sensitive person who had wanted to be a poet, he was ridiculed in his earlier years. Poetry had been his one love in life; it was lost before it could be realized. He married his wife only because of an accidental, overnight sleigh ride that, in a tradition-bound society, demanded marriage to save appearances. A compassionate man, he gives up his desire to marry again after his wife dies in order not to disrupt the lives of his son's widow and her daughter Jenny. Jenny, too, unknowingly is caught in the patterned existence of the Archbald heritage. A willful girl, she has been sheltered from the real world by culture and tradition and can see things only in terms of her own desires. At eighteen, she falls in love with an older married man, George Birdsong. George's wife, Eva, eventually finds them in each other's arms. Jenny flees the scene, only to learn later that Eva has killed George.

Eva Birdsong is another perfect image of Southern womanhood, beautiful and protected all of her life. A celebrated belle prior to her marriage to George, she has striven to achieve a perfect marriage. Without children, she and George are thrown upon each other. Over the years, George has been a bit of a *roué* seeking pleasure where he could find it. In the end, Eva is left with the realization that what women "value most is something that doesn't exist."

When Jenny realizes what she has done, she flies to the General's understanding and sheltering arms, crying, "Oh Grandfather, I didn't mean anything. . . . I didn't mean anything in the world." Ironically enough, she is right. She did not mean anything.

The Sheltered Life is more a tragicomedy than simply a comedy of manners. It is also perhaps, Glasgow's best work, the novel toward which its predecessors were pointed. Symbol, style, characterization, and rhythm all combine to make *The Sheltered Life* a poignant and penetrating illustration of the futility of clinging to a tradition that has lost its essential meaning.

Glasgow's goal in all of her writing is perhaps stated best in *A Certain Measure*, when she says in reference to her last novel, *In This Our Life*, that she was trying to show "the tragedy of a social system which lives, grows, and prospers by material standards alone." One can sense in such a statement a conservative regard for tradition; even though Glasgow and many of her characters struggled against a shallow romanticism, a yearning for a genuine tradition was never far from her own artistic vision. The land seems to be the single sustaining factor in all Glasgow's novels—it was the land that gave rise to and nourished the so-called Southern tradition and that provides the "living pulse of endurance" to so many of her characters.

Other major works

SHORT FICTION: *The Shadowy Third and Other Stories*, 1923; *The Collected Stories of Ellen Glasgow*, 1963.
POETRY: *The Freeman and Other Poems*, 1902.
NONFICTION: *A Certain Measure*, 1943; *The Woman Within*, 1954; *Letters of Ellen Glasgow*, 1958.

Bibliography

Godbold, E. Stanly, Jr. *Ellen Glasgow and the Woman Within*. Baton Rouge: Louisiana State University Press, 1972.

Inge, M. Thomas, ed. *Ellen Glasgow: Centennial Essays*. Charlottesville: University Press of Virginia, 1976.

McDowell, Frederick P. W. *Ellen Glasgow and the Ironic Art of Fiction*. Madison: University of Wisconsin Press, 1960.

Raper, Julius Rowan. *From the Sunken Garden: The Fiction of Ellen Glasgow, 1916-1945*. Baton Rouge: Louisiana State University Press, 1980.

Scura, Dorothy M. *Ellen Glasgow: The Contemporary Reviews*. New York: Cambridge University Press, 1993.

Thiébaux, Marcelle. *Ellen Glasgow*. New York: Frederick Ungar, 1982.

SUSAN GLASPELL

Born: Davenport, Iowa; July 1, 1882

Died: Provincetown, Massachusetts; July 27, 1948

Principal drama

Suppressed Desires, pr. 1915, pb. 1917 (one act, with George Cram Cook); *Trifles*, pr. 1916, pb. 1917 (one act); *The People*, pr. 1917, pb. 1918 (one act); *Close the Book*, pr. 1917, pb. 1918 (one act; *The Outside*, pr. 1917, pb. 1920 (one act); *Woman's Honor*, pr. 1918, pb. 1920 (one act); *Tickless Time*, pr. 1918, pb. 1920 (one act, with Cook); *Bernice*, pr. 1919, pb. 1920; *Plays*, pb. 1920 (includes *Suppressed Desires, Trifles, Close the Book, The Outside, The People, Woman's Honor, Tickless Time*, and *Bernice*); *Inheritors*, pr., pb. 1921; *The Verge*, pr. 1921, pb. 1922; *The Chains of Dew*, pr. 1922; *The Comic Artist*, pb. 1927, pr. 1928 (with Norman Matson); *Alison's House*, pr., pb. 1930; *Plays by Susan Glaspell*, pb. 1987 (C. W. E. Bigsby, editor; includes *Trifles, The Outside, The Verge*, and *Inheritors*).

Other literary forms

Susan Glaspell began her long career, which lasted almost four decades, writing short stories that appeared in such popular magazines as *Harper's Monthly*, *Good Housekeeping*, *American Magazine*, and *Woman's Home Companion*. The short stories, in the tradition of local-color writing, generally romanticized the Midwest and its people. Thirteen of her forty-three stories have been collected in *Lifted Masks* (1912). While she enjoyed success as a short-fiction writer and a playwright, Glaspell regarded herself primarily as a novelist. Her nine novels include *The Visioning* (1911), *Ambrose Holt and Family* (1931), *Norma Ashe* (1942), and *Judd Rankin's Daughter* (1945). In addition, she is the author of a children's tale, *Cherished and Shared of Old* (1940), several essays, and a biography of her first husband, George Cram "Jig" Cook, entitled *The Road to the Temple* (1926).

Achievements

Glaspell received recognition in three of the genres that she utilized. Several of her short stories were selected for E. J. O'Brien's yearly anthology, *Best Short Stories*: "Jury of Her Peers" in 1918, "Government Goat" in 1920, and "His Smile" in 1922. Her novel *The Morning Is Near Us* (1940) was a Literary Guild selection, and another novel, *Brook Evans* (1928), was made into the film *The Right to Love* by Paramount Pictures. In addition, she won a Pulitzer Prize in 1931 for her play *Alison's House*. Her greatest achievement, however, was the work that she did with the Provincetown Players, a group that she helped found. The Provincetown Players, whose stated purpose was to produce new plays by American playwrights, was extremely influential and changed the direction of modern American drama, providing a forum where none had existed. From its inception to 1922, the group's theater produced ninety-three new American plays by forty-seven playwrights; all but two of these playwrights had their first plays produced by the theater. Glaspell, who wrote eleven of her fourteen plays for the group, was, after Eugene O'Neill, the group's most important playwright.

Biography

Born July 1, 1882, to Elmer S. and Alice Keating Glaspell, descendants of pioneer settlers, Susan Glaspell grew up in Davenport, Iowa, and attended public schools. She went to Drake University in nearby Des Moines, receiving her B.A. in 1899. While in college, she began writing stories and published her first one in the *Davenport Weekly Outlook* in 1896. After graduation, she spent two years working for *The Des Moines Daily News* and other newspapers as a reporter covering the court and legislative beats. She returned in 1901 to Davenport determined to become a writer. Her early stories, published in popular magazines, and her first novel, the best-selling *The Glory of the Conquered* (1909), were escapist, romantic, and conventional in form.

In 1907, Glaspell met Floyd Dell, future writer and

social critic; George Cram Cook, a socialist writer; and Cook's feminist wife, Mollie. Cook and Dell established the Monist Society, a discussion group formulated to expose provincialism and to introduce avant-garde ideas to Davenport. Glaspell fell in love with Cook, encountered the disapproval of her friends and family, and in 1909, in an attempt to end the affair, traveled to Europe, using the royalties earned from her first novel.

Upon returning to the United States, she spent time in Colorado, Davenport, Chicago, and Greenwich Village. She also finished her second novel, *The Visioning*, which shows Cook's influence in the seriousness of the issues it introduced—trade unions, evolution, and divorce, to name a few—and began a third, *Fidelity* (1915), which explores small-town life in the Midwest and examines the limits placed on women by traditional gender roles. In 1912, she published *Lifted Masks*, a collection of short stories based on her experiences as a reporter. She and Cook, who had divorced his second wife, were married on April 14, 1913, in Weehawken, New Jersey. As a result of being exposed to his ideas, she grew more radical and less conventional in her fiction. Her writing moved away from the sentimental and began to focus on more contemporary themes: the conflict between morality and individual freedom, the hypocrisy of small towns, and the evolution of the "new woman."

Glaspell spent the summer of 1914 writing and acting in plays with friends in Provincetown, and the following summer the Provincetown Players was formed. Thus began a period of playwriting that lasted about fifteen years, from 1915 to 1931. She and Cook, who had a strong interest in drama, collaborated on the first play, *Suppressed Desires*, a satire on Sigmund Freud's ideas. Unable to get the play produced by the Washington Square Players, the first little theater in New York City, and encouraged by friends, Glaspell and Cook formed the Provincetown Players in 1915 as an outlet for American plays. In 1916, the group moved to Greenwich Village and, with its emphasis on new ideas and techniques and its support of new American playwrights, strongly influenced American drama. Cook became

president and remained so until 1922, and Glaspell supported the endeavor primarily through writing plays but also through acting and directing, for the time being giving up her career as a novelist. She first wrote one-act plays; then in 1919, her first full-length play, *Bernice*, was produced, Glaspell performing the role of Abbie. As the Provincetown Players became more commercial, Glaspell and Cook grew disillusioned, and in 1922, they moved to Greece, fulfilling a lifetime desire of Cook, who wanted to live in the land where great drama began. There, in 1924 in the ancient town of Delphi, Cook died. During the years Glaspell spent with Cook, she wrote one novel, seven one-act plays, four full-length plays, and twenty short stories, the stories written to achieve some financial security. After her husband's death, she returned to Provincetown.

Later, traveling in Europe, Glaspell met Norman Matson, a writer, whom she married in 1925. In 1928, she returned to writing novels: *Brook Evans*, *Fugitive's Return* (1929), and *Ambrose Holt and Family*, the latter adapted from *The Chains of Dew*, the last play she wrote for the Provincetown Players. She also wrote *The Road to the Temple*, a biography of Cook in which she allowed, as much as possible, Cook's own words—garnered from letters, diaries, and other sources—to speak for him. She collaborated with Matson on a play, *The Comic Artist*, and wrote *Alison's House*, which received a Pulitzer Prize. In 1932, Glaspell was divorced from Matson. Her last play, "The Big Bozo," was not produced or published, and no copies are known to exist.

Glaspell did not see herself as a playwright and, without the Provincetown Players' demand for new plays and without Cook's encouragement, she ceased writing plays, although she retained an interest in the theater. In 1936, she went to Chicago to direct the Midwest Play Bureau of the Federal Theater Project, where she selected plays and organized productions. Returning to Provincetown in 1938, she wrote three more novels: *The Morning Is Near Us*, *Norma Ashe*, and *Judd Rankin's Daughter*. She died on July 27, 1948, in Provincetown, of viral pneumonia.

Analysis

Although Susan Glaspell considered herself a novelist, she is best known for her plays. Her playwriting period lasted fifteen years, seven of which were during the time of her association with the Provincetown Players. In only one season, that of 1919-1920, did Glaspell

not present at least one new play. While her work in short fiction and the novel is somewhat conventional, her work in the theater is not. She experimented, taking risks with her plays. She was an early advocate of expressionism, the use of nonrealistic devices to objectify inner experience. She experimented with language, sometimes incorporating poetry into the dialogue, and her plays are more often about ideas—feminism and socialism—than characters and plot. The general critical response of her contemporaries to her plays was praise for her realistic ones and a reaction of confusion to her more experimental ones.

Her plays have a range of themes, but most concern the individual and the individual's need to find self-fulfillment. Specifically, she focuses on women who attempt to go beyond societal roles, searching for independence and autonomy. Often, however, these women pay a price: in love or acceptance by family and friends, in money, or, in the case of Claire Archer in *The Verge*, in sanity. Sometimes the search is for the "otherness" of life, that which makes life worth living and takes one beyond the trivial and the commonplace. This search is often aided by a guide or mentor who, some critics argue, is patterned after Cook.

Glaspell's best-known and most anthologized play is the one-act *Trifles*, written for the Provincetown Players' second season, 1916-1917, to fill out a bill with Eugene O'Neill's play *Bound East for Cardiff* (pb. 1916) and later rewritten as the short story "A Jury of Her Peers" (1917). In *The Road to the Temple*, Glaspell describes the origin of the play, writing that she sat in the empty theater until the image of a Midwest farm kitchen with its occupants appeared before her. *Trifles*, based on an event that Glaspell covered as a reporter in Des Moines, takes place in the kitchen of Minnie Wright, a woman accused of murdering her husband. Minnie Wright, in jail, remains offstage for the entire play. *Trifles* marked Glaspell's first use of the device of the absent protagonist, which would be employed again in other plays, most notably in *Bernice* and *Alison's House*. The play, with its grounding in realism and regionalism, is not representative of her later, more experimental plays, but it is said to be the best structured of her plays, and it is certainly the most often performed.

Trifles opens as five people enter a farmhouse kitchen. The three men—the sheriff (Mr. Peters), the county attorney (Mr. Henderson), and a neighbor (Mr. Hale)—are there to uncover evidence to link Minnie to the murder of her husband, John Wright, who was choked to death with a rope while he slept. The two women—the sheriff's wife and the neighbor's wife—are there to gather a few items to take to Minnie. As the men examine the kitchen, the bedroom, and the barn, the women

remain in the kitchen. They notice the preserves Minnie had canned, the quilt she was sewing, things that the men belittle, but through their observations, the women solve the murder. The uneven stitching of the quilt indicates Minnie's anxiety, and when the women discover a canary with a broken neck, they know the motive, Minnie, who loved to sing as a young woman, was, in a sense, caged by John, cut off from her interests and isolated. She was figuratively strangled by John as the bird had literally been. After he killed what she loved, the only thing that gave her joy, she responded by choking him. Although the women have information that could convict Minnie, they remain silent. Mrs. Hale, the neighbor, had already failed Minnie by not visiting her when she knew that Minnie's life was bleak, and she will not fail her again. Mrs. Peters, the sheriff's wife, understands from her own experience—she had lost her firstborn—what loneliness is, and she, too, will support Minnie. In a sense, they are the jury of her peers, peers because only they can understand her loneliness and desperation. They try and acquit her. The play, thus, is about sisterhood and the need for women to sustain one another in a culture that is dominated by patriarchal attitudes, attitudes that trivialize women and the work—canning, quilting, baking—that they may do.

A more experimental play but one that also explores the limits placed on women is *The Verge*, a full-length play, produced in 1921 by the Provincetown Players. The play had a successful run at the New York MacDougal Street Theater, but when it moved uptown to the Garrick Theatre, the audiences became more conventional and less receptive to the experimental and expressionistic play.

Claire Archer, a Faust-like figure, wants to create new life-forms, plants that transcend the boundaries of reality, reaching for "otherness." Claire has spent years in her laboratory developing her plants, but when one of them, the Edge Vine, regresses, she unhesitantly destroys it because it "doesn't want to be—what hasn't been." Similarly, when Claire's daughter Elizabeth accepts conventional attitudes, Claire rejects her, as she does with her sister Adelaide, who urges her to "be the woman you were meant to be." Tom Edgeworthy, one of Glaspell's mentors or guide figures, also fails Claire when he cannot commit to a complete relationship that would include both the spiritual and the physical. He does not reach for the "otherness" but instead attempts to restrain Claire: "I'm here to hold you from where I know you cannot go.

You're trying what we can't do." She disagrees, "What else is there worth trying?" Because he refuses to accept the "otherness," she strangles him, destroying him as she did the Edge Vine. The play has strong feminist appeal in the character of Claire, who desires to go beyond the limits set by her culture. She does succeed with her plant, the Breath of Life, but the price she pays is her sanity.

Glaspell's last produced play, *Alison's House*, presented by the Civic Repertory Theater in 1930, received a Pulitzer Prize. As she had in earlier plays—for example, *The Comic Artist*—Glaspell developed the theme of the artist and his or her obligation to society. Alison Stanhope, whose story is loosely based on the life of Emily Dickinson, has died eighteen years earlier, but some of her poems, which obviously deal with a love affair, have recently surfaced. Her relatives are torn between destroying them because they would reflect negatively on the family—the love affair was with a married man—and publishing them because of the public's right to have access to them. The conflict is dramatized by the poet's brother, who wants the poems to remain unpublished, and his daughter Elsa Stanhope, who argues for publication. Elsa, who also had an affair with a married man, is forgiven by her father as they reach the decision that the publication of the poems should not be denied because of small-town morality and hypocrisy. In addition to these themes, the play exhibits other features common to Glaspell's plays: the absent main character and the setting of the small midwestern town.

While Glaspell did not see herself as a dramatist, the contribution she made in this area affected the future of modern American drama. Her willingness to experiment introduced American audiences to more than the traditional Broadway fare and encouraged other playwrights to follow her lead and to take risks.

Other major works

NOVELS: *The Glory of the Conquered: The Story of a Great Love*, 1909; *The Visioning*, 1911; *Fidelity*, 1915; *Brook Evans*, 1928; *Fugitive's Return*, 1929; *Ambrose Holt and Family*, 1931; *The Morning Is Near Us*, 1940; *Norma Ashe*, 1942; *Judd Rankin's Daughter*, 1945.
SHORT FICTION: *Lifted Masks*, 1912.
NONFICTION: *The Road to the Temple*, 1926.
CHILDREN'S LITERATURE: *Cherished and Shared of Old*, 1940.

Bibliography

Ben-Zvi, Linda. "Susan Glaspell's Contributions to Contemporary Women Playwrights." In *Feminine Focus: The New Women Playwrights*, edited by Enoch Brater. New York: Oxford University Press, 1989.
Bigsby, C. W. E. Introduction to *Plays by Susan Glaspell*. Cambridge, England: Cambridge University Press, 1987.
Dymkowski, Christine. "On the Edge: The Plays of Susan Glaspell." *Modern Drama* 1 (March, 1988): 91-105.
Ozieblo, Barbara. "Rebellion and Rejection: The Plays of Susan Glaspell." In *Modern American Drama: The Female Canon*, edited by June Schlueter. London: Associated University Presses, 1990.
Sarlós, Robert Károly. *Jig Cook and the Provincetown Players: Theatre in Ferment*. Amherst: University of Massachusetts Press, 1982.
Waterman, Arthur E. *Susan Glaspell*. New York: Twayne, 1966.

GAIL GODWIN

Born: Birmingham, Alabama; June 18, 1937

Principal long fiction

The Perfectionists, 1970; *Glass People*, 1972; *The Odd Woman*, 1974; *Violet Clay*, 1978; *A Mother and Two Daughters*, 1982; *The Finishing School*, 1985; *A Southern Family*, 1987; *Father Melancholy's Daughter*, 1991.

Other literary forms

In addition to her novels, Gail Godwin has published two collections of short fiction, *Dream Children* (1976) and *Mr. Bedford and the Muses* (1983). Godwin is also a frequent reviewer of contemporary fiction for *The New York Times Book Review* and other publications. In 1985, she served as editor for *The Best American Short Stories*.

Achievements

Godwin has done much to broaden the scope of the contemporary woman's novel. While the struggles of women who seek both an independent life and a productive connection to others are central to her work, she strives in her novels and short fiction to place those efforts within a larger context, especially within the framework of modern theories of art and psychology. In 1971-1972, Godwin was a fellow of the Center for Advanced Studies, University of Illinois at Urbana-Champaign. Her other awards include a grant from the National Endowment for the Arts in 1974 and a Guggenheim Fellowship in 1975. Her story "Amanuensis" was included in the *Prize Stories, 1980: O. Henry Awards* collection.

Biography

Reared by her mother and her widowed grandmother in Asheville, North Carolina, Gail Godwin was graduated in 1959 from the University of North Carolina at Chapel Hill with a B.A. in journalism. After working as a reporter for the *Miami Herald*, she lived in London and worked with the United States Travel Service at the American Embassy. After returning to the United States, she took an M.A. (1968) and a Ph.D. (1971) in English at the University of Iowa, where she later served on the faculty of the Writers' Workshop. She has been married twice, to *Miami Herald* photographer Douglas Kennedy and to British psychotherapist Ian Marshall. Her one-year marriage to Marshall is the basis for her first novel, *The Perfectionists*, as her early years with her mother and grandmother are for parts of *Glass People* and *The Odd Woman*. Her relationships with her father and her stepfather are also used in her fiction, especially in *Violet Clay* and *The Odd Woman* respectively.

Analysis

Gail Godwin's novels (and her short fiction as well) all deal with several easily identifiable themes. Most often cited is the theme of the modern woman, her dilemma in defining self and others in an era when the old frameworks and definitions have broken down, at least for the sort of women about whom Godwin writes. The conflict most often arises between the woman's work, usually an artistic pursuit of some kind, and her desire for security, love, and connection, most often through a relationship with a man. Thus, the theme of the woman struggling for identity divides into two separate thematic strands: her identity as artist and her identity as lover.

What makes Godwin an interesting and important figure in the world of contemporary fiction is the narrative technique by which she manages to develop and retell this essentially unchanging story. The noticeable and impressive growth in Godwin herself as an artist can be traced by examining the structural and technical variations in her telling of her stories. In the earlier novels, the distance between narrator and protagonist is less clearly defined. The overblown and romanticized version of the character sometimes seems to be an accurate representation of the narrator's perspective as well. Beginning with *The Odd Woman*, however, Godwin makes that distance itself a matter of chief concern. Her narrators seem acutely aware of the responsibility involved in entering into the lives and souls of "others." The characters seem to move from being primarily concerned with personal happiness and security to doing true and constructive work that recognizes the dignity in whatever lives the artist consumes for the sake of the work and that acknowledges the limitations and fallibilities of the artist herself. These later characters, by having real and constructive work to do, manage to be less obsessed with their personal lives as objects of art; they also manage to find satisfaction in the art and the work itself, whether their personal lives are or are not so satisfying at any given moment.

The perspective of Jane Clifford, the protagonist of *The Odd Woman*, marked a significant step forward for Godwin as a storyteller. First, her perspective is a much broader one than that of either of her predecessors, Dane Empson in *The Perfectionists* and Francesca Bolt in *Glass People*. Jane works as a teacher of literature, and her work as a graduate student writing her dissertation on George Eliot, in addition to her current work—grading the exams for her just-finished course in visionary literature and preparing to teach a course on women in literature—is an integral part of the narrative.

Furthermore, Jane Clifford has a family, a background, that is richly developed and explored across several generations. Unlike Francesca's fruitless journey back home, Jane's similar trip, to the funeral of her grandmother, produces extended encounters with her memories of the grandmother, her mother, stepfather, sister, and brothers. Kate, mother of Francesca, spends most of her daughter's visit behind the closed door of her bedroom. Jane is involved in talks, reminiscences, and arguments that test her perspective constantly.

Jane also has friends, male and female, to whom she talks, in whom she confides. There is the male colleague with whom she trades confidences about sex and bathroom regularity; there is her old college friend Gerda, the editor of a feminist newspaper in Chicago; and there is Sonia Marx, her colleague at the university where she teaches and the woman who serves as the role model for what Jane wants to be—someone with a career, husband, and family, managing it all with every sign of ease and brilliance. Again, although Jane's point of view is the

point of view of the novel, her constant encounters with these others broadens and modifies her view throughout.

Jane also has a married lover, Gabriel Weeks, an art historian. In him, Jane finds an alternative to the cynical and jaded perspective she finds pervasive in the academic world. She gradually comes to realize, however, that the Gabriel she has found is a creature of her own making. She has imagined him and orchestrated their relationship in such a way as to provide herself with a view of the world that must come from within, must be made from oneself, if it is to have true value.

Here, Godwin begins to develop the ironic awareness of self as artist that is crucial to the success of her subject matter. Jane Clifford is painfully aware of her life as an object of art, with herself as the artist. She sees the scenes of her life as just that, scenes, and she manipulates both her own part and the parts of others. The problem is that such a life will never reach the state of natural grace and spontaneity that is Jane's primary goal.

Thus, she is more like Dane and Francesca than she would like to be. She does not find a way to overcome her frustrations with her need to rewrite the role she has been given or has voluntarily taken on. Unlike those predecessors, however, she does not capitulate. She takes actions that give her a chance for progress. She ends her affair. She takes an extension on her temporary appointment at the university, meaning that she will have productive work for another year. She confronts the demons of her past as represented by the family, Greta, and the actor who has been for half a century the arch villain of the family history.

Through these actions and confrontations, she learns that all truths may be artificial and self-imposed, but she also comes to believe in some purer, more absolute version of her own life that will be possible for her, if she acts to pursue it. Thus, despite Jane's own limitations, because Godwin equips her with such an acute sense of irony about herself as well as others, Jane is the first step toward a successful Godwin protagonist.

Interestingly enough, the promise of a truly successful Godwin woman made with Jane is realized in Violet Clay, whose story is the first that Godwin told from a first-person point of view. Although it might seem that first-person narration would lead to even greater self-absorption, this does not happen. Using the same principles that make *The Odd Woman* such a step forward, Godwin generated a plot in *Violet Clay* with a death. Jane keeps her job and her lover through most of her story, however, while, in addition to losing her uncle—her only living relative—Violet loses what Jane has been able to keep.

She is forced by these events of plot to confront the essentials of her character, to test the view of herself that she has created. While she probes into her uncle's past to make sense of his suicide, Violet learns much about herself as well and about how the artist manufacturers both life and art, each feeding off the other. When she finally paints the painting that will set her on the road she has long aspired to travel, Violet uses some of the same material that her uncle failed to transform into the novel that he had struggled for decades to write.

Violet's success comes because she learns the limits of both life and art, partly through her uncle's example, his legacy to her, and partly through her own increasing ability to forget about "poor little me" and to enter into and learn from the struggles of those around her with compassion and respect. She learns that the artist must not and finally cannot both live and work successfully if she violates the integrity of the other, of the lives out of which her art and her own life are to be constructed.

In many ways Godwin's seventh novel, *A Southern Family*, is the aesthetic fruit of a challenge similar to the one her fictional alter ego raises at the end of *The Finishing School*. In *A Southern Family*, Godwin creates for herself a new role as author/narrator, using for the first time in her novels the narrative strategy of multiple limited perspectives. She also appears to be moving toward a new role for the "typical" Godwin woman within her fictional world. The Godwin woman in *A Southern Family* is Clare Campion, the author's first novel protagonist to share her profession. In fact, Clare is a writer whose career, as rendered in this fiction, closely parallels Godwin's own. The "new" role Godwin carves out for Clare is that of secondary, rather than primary, character; thus, her challenge is to accept this new (and inevitably "lesser") status without losing the power to make art (stories) from her experience.

The plot of *A Southern Family* is generated by the death of Clare Campion's half brother Theo Quick in an incident that the police rule a murder-suicide. The story is presented from the perspectives of Clare, her best friend Julia Richardson, Clare's mother and her stepfather, her surviving half brother, Theo's former wife, and Sister Patrick, a beloved nun who has taught Clare and her brothers. (That Godwin's half brother Tommy Cole died in circumstances similar to those described in the novel further suggests the strongly autobiographical nature of *A Southern Family*.)

Perhaps the most significant achievement of the novel is Godwin's broadening of her narrative spectrum to include male characters, characters from a variety of social classes, and characters with varying degrees of connection to the central action. There is no pretense of omniscience: The narrative in each section of the book is strictly limited to one or sometimes two perspectives.

A Southern Family opens up new narrative directions and a new approach to her "typical" protagonist for Godwin, but the novel also provides a clear culmination of other strands that are woven throughout the body of her fiction. The title makes clear that this is a family story, a Southern story—themes that have always been among the author's central concerns. The greater emphasis here on the family as a group, rather than on an individual's struggles, reinforces the narrative decision Godwin makes.

A Southern Family also continues Godwin's exploration of people, particularly women, who tend to see their lives as performances, themselves as actors in a drama partly of their own making, partly a by-product of their environment and conditioning. Theo's action causes everyone in his family to reexamine his or her role in the Quick family drama, causes each individual whose consciousness the novel explores to evaluate the role he or she plays in the events before and after the momentary act that calls the foundations of family life into question. In addition to generating the story this novel tells, this profound examination of self-as-actor that takes place in *A Southern Family*, read with full knowledge of the work that precedes it, is a reexamination of the author's body of work as well.

Godwin has grown in much the same direction as her characters and narrators. The movement has been in the life-affirming direction of compromise, recognition of others, acceptance of responsibility for the self, and productive creativity. The life that gets affirmed is the well-made life, the one shaped out of the complexities and ambiguities of human experience. Godwin's novels speak clearly of the enormous difficulty of being a sensitive and thoughtful woman in the modern world. They speak just as eloquently of what such women can make from those difficulties.

Other major works

SHORT FICTION: *Dream Children*, 1976; *Mr. Bedford and the Muses*, 1983.
PLAYS: *The Last Lover*, 1975; *Journals of a Songmaker*, 1976; *Apollonia*, 1979.
ANTHOLOGY: *The Best American Short Stories*, 1985.

Bibliography

Cheney, Anne. "Gail Godwin and Her Novels." In *Southern Women Writers: The New Generation*, edited by Tonette Bond Inge. Tuscaloosa: University of Alabama Press, 1990.

Frye, Joanna S. "Narrating the Self: The Autonomous Heroine in Gail Godwin's Violet Clay." *Contemporary Literature* 24 (Spring, 1983): 66-85.

Gaston, Karen C. " 'Beauty and the Beast' in Gail Godwin's *Glass People*." *Critique* 21 (1980): 94-102.

Lorsch, Susan E. "Gail Godwin's *The Odd Woman:* Literature and the Retreat from Life." *Critique* 20 (1978): 21-32.

Mickelson, Anne A. "Gail Godwin: Order and Accommodation." In *Reaching Out: Sensitivity and Order in Recent Fiction by Women*. Metuchen, N.J.: Scarecrow Press, 1979.

Rhodes, Carolyn. "Gail Godwin and the Ideal of Southern Womanhood." *Southern Quarterly* 21 (Summer, 1983): 55-66.

Smith, Marilyn J. "The Role of the South in the Novels of Gail Godwin." *Critique* 26 (1980): 103-110.

NADINE GORDIMER

Born: Springs, South Africa; November 20, 1923

Principal long fiction

The Lying Days, 1953; *A World of Strangers*, 1958; *Occasion for Loving*, 1963; *The Late Bourgeois World*, 1966; *A Guest of Honour*, 1970; *The Conservationist*, 1974; *Burger's Daughter*, 1979; *July's People*, 1981; *A Sport of Nature*, 1987; *My Son's Story*, 1990.

Other literary forms

Nadine Gordimer is one of the twentieth century's greatest writers of short stories. Her first collection of stories, *Face to Face: Short Stories* (1949), was published in Johannesburg by Silver Leaf Books. Her first story published in *The New Yorker*, where most of her stories first appeared, was "A Watcher of the Dead" (June 9, 1951). Gordimer's first collection of stories to be published in the United States was *The Soft Voice of the Serpent and Other Stories* (1952). This collection was followed by *Six Feet of the Country* (1956), *Friday's Footprint and Other Stories* (1960), *Not for Publication and Other Stories* (1965), *Livingstone's Companions: Stories* (1971), *A Soldier's Embrace* (1980), *Something Out There* (1984), and *Jump* (1991). *Selected Stories*, from her first five volumes, was published in 1975. Gordimer has also written or edited several volumes of nonfiction, most notably *The Essential Gesture: Writing, Politics, and Places* (1988).

Achievements

Gordimer won the W. H. Smith and Son Prize in 1971 for *Friday's Footprint and Other Stories*. In 1973, she won the James Tait Black Memorial Prize for *A Guest of Honour. The Conservationist* was cowinner of the Booker Prize. Gordimer also has received the French international literary prize, the *Grand Aigle d'Or*. In the United States, it is for her stories that Gordimer is best known. She has, however, received increased critical attention in the United States as an important novelist (*A Sport of Nature* became a Book-of-the Month Club dual selection). These honors culminated in the Nobel Prize in Literature for 1991.

Biography

Nadine Gordimer spent her childhood in a gold-mining town near Johannesburg, South Africa. Her father, Isidore Gordimer, was a watchmaker, a Jew who had emigrated from a Baltic town to Africa when he was thirteen; her mother was born in England. Gordimer did not care for the convent school to which she was sent as a day student, and she frequently played hooky. When she did attend, she would sometimes walk out. The pressures of uniformity produced revulsion and rebellion in the child.

Within Gordimer's environment, a white middle-class girl typically left school at about age fifteen and worked for a few years at a clerical job. Ideally, by her early twenties she would be found by the son of a family like her own and would then be ushered through her season of glory—the engagement party, the linen shower, the marriage, and the birth of the first child. There was no point in reading books; that would only impede the inevitable process by which the daughter was readied to fit the mold.

Gordimer, however, was an early reader and an early writer. By the age of nine, she was already writing; at fourteen, she won her first writing prize. She read the stories of Guy de Maupassant, Anton Chekhov, Somerset Maugham, D. H. Lawrence, and the Americans O. Henry, Katherine Anne Porter, and Eudora Welty. Reading these great artists of the short story refined her own story-writing, making her work more sophisticated. She found herself becoming increasingly interested in politics and the plight of black South Africans. Unlike other whites who rejected the white South African way of life, Gordimer did not launch into a writing career as a way to bring change.

Continuing to live at home, Gordimer commuted to

Johannesburg and the University of the Witwatersrand. While at the university, she met the Afrikaans poet Uys Krige, a man who had broken free of his Afrikaans heritage, lived in France and Spain, and served with the International Brigade in the Spanish Civil War. He had a profound effect upon Gordimer. She had bolted from school; she was in the process of bolting from family, class, and the superficial values and culture of white South Africa. Uys Krige gave her a final push. When she began sending stories to England and the United States, they were well received.

Despite her contempt for the social system and the economic exploitation that prevailed in South Africa

until the early 1990's, Gordimer continued to make Johannesburg her home. She gave birth to and reared her children there. She married a Johannesburg industrialist. She and her husband frequently traveled abroad, to Europe, to North America, to other African countries. She lectured at leading American universities such as Columbia, Harvard, and Michigan State, but she always returned to Johannesburg. She returned despite the censorship of and the prohibition against much of her writing, despite the fact that an arbitrary government could have prevented her from leaving again or restricted her freedom in other ways.

Analysis

Throughout most of Nadine Gordimer's life, to be personally liberated and to be South African was to be doomed to a continuing struggle between the desire for further freedom and development for oneself and the desire for the liberation of the oppressed masses. South Africa was a nation in which a white legislature promulgated laws that made it impossible for the overwhelming majority of nonwhite persons to advance themselves. For fifty years, apartheid, which in Afrikaans means "apartness," was the law of the land.

In her novels, Gordimer is engaged in an ongoing examination of the possible combinations of the private life and the public life. She has created a gallery of characters ranging from pure hedonists concerned only with their own pleasure to those who have committed their lives to bringing liberty, equality, and peace to South Africa. Her most interesting characters are those who are wracked and torn by the struggle, those who both want to be themselves and yet find it impossible to take personal goals seriously in a society built on the exploitation of the black masses.

Set in an invented nation in central Africa for which she has provided a detailed history and geography, *A Guest of Honour* does not deal with South Africa. Still, the kinds of events depicted in this novel could very well occur in South Africa at some future time. With independence gained and a native government functioning in the place of the former British colonial administration, there are expectations of dramatic changes: Civil rights will be respected, greater care will be taken in administering justice, natural resources will be used for the benefit of the people, and the standard of living of the masses will improve. President Mweta believes that

these legitimate expectations are being fulfilled in an orderly way and at a satisfactory rate. Edward Shinza, without whom independence might not yet have come, is dissatisfied. He believes that the country is no better off than it would have been under colonial rule. He is seeking a way to have an impact on the course of events. He may even be conspiring with the nation across the border. To Mweta, his former comrade Shinza is "a cobra in the house."

The novel's protagonist is Colonel James Bray, an Englishman who has been a district officer in the colonial administration. Bray is likable and loyal, a wholly sympathetic character. During the struggle for independence, he was of significant assistance to Mweta and Shinza. Now Mweta has invited Bray back to be an honored guest at Independence Day celebrations. Much to his chagrin, Bray discovers that while Mweta is covered with glory as the new nation's leader, Shinza, every bit Mweta's equal if not his better, has no role in governing the country and has not been invited to the celebrations; indeed, Shinza is living in obscurity in the bush. To Bray, this is an ominous sign.

President Mweta sends Colonel Bray on a mission to Gala, the district Bray formerly administered. He is to survey the district's educational needs. With Gala, Gordimer gives the first demonstration of her formidable knowledge of the life and people of rural Africa, of which she was to give further demonstrations in *July's People* and to a lesser extent in *The Conservationist*. With Gala, she has the opportunity to do a canvas of a whole province. She makes Bray pleased to be back in Gala and curious about what has happened in his absence. He knows the language, he likes the people, and he resonates sympathetically with the daily round of life. While in Gala, Bray will track down Shinza and get his viewpoint on the progress of the nation.

Shinza believes Mweta's principal concern is to consolidate his own power. He has no tolerance for dissent and is quite willing to use the police and torture to stifle it. Mweta allows foreign corporations to extract raw materials and export them rather than finding opportunities to make use of the country's natural wealth at home. Mweta will not allow any changes in the country that might give pause to these foreign interests. Shinza believes that Mweta's actions, taken together, make up a pattern of betrayal. While Shinza is trying to reassert himself by becoming a force within the trade-union movement, he also may be gathering a counterrevolutionary army, but his present intention is to attack Mweta through the unions and strikes.

Shinza comes onto center stage for the length of his impassioned speech on the ideals of the revolution at the congress of the People's Independent Party (P.I.P.), which has its factions but is still the only political party. Bray, who attends, cannot help but prefer the ideals of Shinza to the charisma and policies of accommodation of Mweta. In presenting the milieu of the party congress and in revealing the subtleties of motivations, alliances, and positions, Gordimer demonstrates a first-rate political intelligence. She has Shinza make use of his union support as the first phase in his scheme to dislodge Mweta; she has Mweta in turn capitalizing on the nationalistic fervor of the youth group within the P.I.P. to get them to attack strongholds of union supporters. Violence breaks out in Gala, and Bray is an accidental victim. *A Guest of Honour* shows a prescience and knowledge that carry it to the top rank of political novels.

Burger's Daughter is one of Gordimer's best novels. It is set between 1975 and 1977, as important changes are taking place in southern Africa but not yet in South Africa. The independence movements in Angola and Mozambique have succeeded. The Portuguese are in retreat, their colonial rule to be replaced by native governments. South Africa, however, remains firmly in the grip of the white minority. The white South African government will relinquish nothing.

Rosa Burger, the protagonist, is Gordimer's most fully achieved character. The hero of the novel, however, is Rosa's father, Lionel Burger. Just before he is to be sentenced to life imprisonment, Lionel Burger has the opportunity to address the court. He speaks for almost

two hours. He explains why he and the Communist Party, of which he is a leader, have been driven to engage in the acts of sabotage for which he has been on trial. For thirty years, to no avail, he and South African Communists had struggled without resort to violence to gain civil rights and the franchise for the country's black majority. The great mass movement that is the African Nationalist Congress has been outlawed. In desperation, selected symbolic targets have been sabotaged. If such symbolic actions fail to move the white ruling class, there will be no further careful consideration of tactics. The only way to a new society will be through massive, cataclysmic violence.

Rosa Burger is very different from her father. She is also different from her mother, who was familiar with prison and who from young womanhood was known as a "real revolutionary." Both her father and her mother regard the family as totally united in their dedication to the struggle. Rosa, named in tribute to Rosa Luxemburg, the German revolutionary Marxist, knows that the family is not united. While her parents are free and active, she has no choice but to be extensions of them. Her mother has died, however, and, after three years of his life term, her father dies. When they are gone, Rosa does not take up their work. She is twenty-seven and has been in her parents' revolutionary circle since childhood. She has carried out numerous secret missions. Recently, she has pretended to be the fiancée of a prisoner in order to bring him messages. With the death of her father, she cannot deny that she is tired of such a life. She does not want to have anything more to do with the endangered and the maimed, with conspiracies and fugitives, with courts and prisons. Much more pointedly, Burger's Daughter deals with questions first considered in A World of Strangers and Occasion for Loving: To what extent must individual lives be governed by the dictates of time and place and circumstances not of the individual's choosing? Can a person ignore the facts and conditions that circumscribe his or her life and still live fully, or must a meaningful life necessarily be one that is integrated with the "real flow of life"?

Rosa chooses to escape. At first she escapes within the city of Johannesburg, in the tiny cottage of a rootless young white man, a graduate student of Italian literature who survives by working as a clerk to a bookmaker. Rosa and Conrad start out as lovers; after a while they are more like siblings. Conrad, too, is struggling to be free, not of a revolutionary heritage but of his bourgeois heritage.

Even after she is no longer with him, Rosa continues to talk to Conrad, silently.

Rosa decides to leave South Africa, but she cannot get a passport because she is the daughter of Lionel Burger. Brandt Vermeulen is a cosmopolitan Boer, a new Afrikaner of a distinguished old Afrikaner family. He has studied politics at Leyden and Princeton and has spent time in Paris and New York. He is rooted, cultured, and committed to the status quo. His solution for South Africa is to create separate nations for whites and blacks. Rosa goes to see him because he has friends in the Ministry of the Interior, which issues passports. Playing on the fact that he and Lionel Burger emerged from very similar backgrounds, Rosa succeeds in persuading him to use his influence to get her a passport.

The second part of this three-part novel takes place in Europe. Rosa goes to the French Riviera and looks up the woman who had been Lionel Burger's wife before he met Rosa's mother. The woman, who used to be known as Katya and who now is known as Madame Bagnelli, is delighted that Burger's daughter has come to stay with her. Rosa is welcomed by Madame Bagnelli's circle, consisting of unmarried couples, émigrés, homosexuals, persons formerly prominent in Paris—rootless persons for the most part. On the Riviera, life is easy, difference is distinction. Survival is not an issue. Politics seems a waste of time, revolution a form of craziness.

There is great empathy between Rosa and Madame Bagnelli. As Katya, the latter, years before, found it a relief to give up the role of revolutionary that was required of her as Burger's wife. She had not always been able to put private concerns aside; she had been considered a bourgeoise or even a traitor and was subjected to Party discipline. She has no regrets at leaving that part of her life. Rosa is encouraged about her own course. She allows herself the luxury of a love affair.

After a summer of love, Rosa and Bernard Chabalier make plans to live together in Paris, where he is a teacher at a lycée. Rosa visits London while Bernard makes arrangements in Paris. She attends a party for South African exiles and is filled with joy at meeting her black "brother," Baasie, who as a child had been taken into the Burger home but whom Rosa has not seen for twenty years. Rosa is shocked by Baasie's attitude; he is hostile and sullen.

That night in London, Rosa's sleep is broken by a phone call from Baasie. He is angry. He wants her to know that he did not have the life Burger's daughter had. He had been pushed back to the mud huts and tin shanties. His father was a revolutionary who also died in prison, driven to hang himself. No one knows of Isaac Vulindlela, but everyone talks about Lionel Burger. He hates hearing about Burger, the great man who suffered for the blacks. He knows plenty of blacks who have done as much as Burger, but they go unknown. He does not want to be her black brother, he tells Rosa.

Rosa goes back to South Africa. She does not want the soft life Bernard will provide for her in Paris. Defection is not possible. Suffering cannot be evaded. Back in Johannesburg, Rosa takes up the occupation for which she trained, physiotherapy. She also works for the revolution. As the novel ends late in 1977, Rosa is in prison. The authorities have solid evidence of unlawful acts.

Gordimer has probed moral and political questions with honesty and unfailing courage, never being dogmatic or predetermining outcomes, allowing vividly imagined characters and communities lives of their own. Her work does more than shed light on the predicament of South Africa; it deals in depth with the problems of individual identity, commitment and obligation, and justice.

Other major works

SHORT FICTION: Face to Face: Short Stories, 1949; *The Soft Voice of the Serpent and Other Stories*, 1952; *Six Feet of the Country*, 1956; *Friday's Footprint and Other Stories*, 1960; *Not for Publication and Other Stories*, 1965; *Livingstone's Companions: Stories*, 1971; *Selected Stories*, 1975; *A Soldier's Embrace*, 1980; *Something Out There*, 1984; *Jump*, 1991; *Why Haven't You Written?: Selected Stories, 1950-1972*, 1993.

NONFICTION: *On the Mines*, 1973 (with David Goldblatt); *The Black Interpreters*, 1973; *Lifetimes Under Apartheid*, 1986 (with Goldblatt); *The Essential Gesture: Writing, Politics, and Places*, 1988.

EDITED TEXT: *South African Writing Today*, 1967 (with Lionel Abrahams).

Bibliography

Clingman, Stephen. *The Novels of Nadine Gordimer: History from the Inside*. London: Bloomsbury, 1993.

Cooke, John. *The Novels of Nadine Gordimer: Private Lives/Public Landscapes*. Baton Rouge: Louisiana State University Press, 1985.

Haugh, Robert F. *Nadine Gordimer*. New York: Twayne, 1974.

Heywood, Christopher. *Nadine Gordimer*. Windsor, England: Profile Books, 1983.

Wade, Michael. *Nadine Gordimer*. London: Evans Bros., 1978.

LORRAINE HANSBERRY

Born: Chicago, Illinois; May 19, 1930   **Died:** New York, New York; January 12, 1965

Principal drama

A Raisin in the Sun, pr., pb. 1959; *The Sign in Sidney Brustein's Window*, pr. 1964, pb. 1965; *To Be Young, Gifted, and Black*, pr. 1969, pb. 1971; *Les Blancs*, pr. 1970, pb. 1972 (edited by Robert Nemiroff); *The Drinking Gourd*, pb. 1972 (edited by Nemiroff); *What Use Are Flowers?*, pb. 1972 (edited by Nemiroff); *Les Blancs: The Collected Last Plays of Lorraine Hansberry*, pb. 1972 (includes *Les Blancs*, *The Drinking Gourd*, and *What Use Are Flowers?*).

Other literary forms

As a result of her involvement in the Civil Rights movement, Lorraine Hansberry wrote the narrative for *The Movement: Documentary of a Struggle for Equality* (1964), a book of photographs, for the Student Nonviolent Coordinating Committee (SNCC). Because she died at such a young age, Hansberry left much of her work unpublished, but her husband, Robert Nemiroff, the literary executor of her estate, edited and submitted some of it for publication and, in the case of *Les Blancs*, production. In addition, he arranged excerpts from Hansberry's various writings into a seven-and-a-half-hour radio program entitled *To Be Young, Gifted, and Black*, which was broadcast on radio station WBAI in 1967. This program was later adapted for the stage, opening at the Cherry Lane Theatre in New York on January 2, 1969, and becoming the longest running production of the 1968-1969 season. Many readers know Hansberry through the anthology of her writings edited by Nemiroff, *To Be Young, Gifted, and Black: Lorraine Hansberry in Her Own Words* (1969), a book which has enjoyed wide circulation.

Achievements

Hansberry's career was very brief, only two of her plays being produced in her lifetime, yet she recorded some very impressive theatrical achievements. She was only twenty-nine when *A Raisin in the Sun* appeared on Broadway, and its great success earned for her recognition that continues to this day. When *A Raisin in the Sun* was voted best play of the year by the New York Drama Critics Circle, she became the first black person as well as the youngest person to win the award. In 1973, a musical adapted from *A Raisin in the Sun*, entitled *Raisin* (with libretto by Nemiroff), won a Tony Award as best musical of the year (1974). She was respected and befriended by such figures as Paul Robeson and James Baldwin, and she helped in an active way to further the work of the Civil Rights movement.

Biography

Lorraine Vivian Hansberry was born on May 19, 1930, in Chicago. Despite her parents' affluence, they were forced by local covenants to live in the poor South Side. When Hansberry was eight years old, her father decided to test the legality of those covenants by buying a home in a white section of the city. Shortly after the family's move, a mob gathered outside their home, and a brick, thrown through a window, barely missed her before embedding itself in a wall.

In order to stay in the house, to which he was not given clear title, Carl Hansberry instituted a civil rights suit against such restrictive covenants. When he lost in Illinois courts, he and the National Association for the Advancement of Colored People (NAACP) carried an appeal to the United States Supreme Court, which reversed the ruling and declared the local covenants illegal. Thus, Lorraine had a consciousness of the need to struggle for civil rights from a very young age. Her father, despite his legal victory, grew increasingly pessimistic about the prospects for change and decided to retire in Mexico City. He had a stroke on a visit to Mexico and died in 1945.

Hansberry's uncle, William Leo Hansberry, was also an important influence on her. A scholar of African history who taught at Howard University, his pupils included Nnamdi Azikewe, the first president of Nigeria, and Kwame Nkrumah of Ghana. While Lorraine was growing up, she was frequently exposed to the perspectives of young African students who were invited to family dinners.

Lorraine, the youngest of four children, was encouraged to excel and was expected to succeed. After attending Englewood High School, she enrolled in the University of Wisconsin as a journalism student. She did not fare very well at the university, however, and felt restricted by the many requirements. After two years, she switched to the New School for Social Research in New York, where she was permitted greater leeway in choosing courses.

Once in New York, Hansberry began writing for several periodicals, including *Freedom*, Paul Robeson's monthly magazine. She quickly became a reporter and then an associate editor of the magazine. In New York, she met Robert Nemiroff, then a student at New York University, and they were married in June of 1953. By this time, Hansberry had decided to be a writer. When Nemiroff acquired a good position with music publisher Phil Rose, she quit working and began writing full-time.

Hansberry's first completed work was *A Raisin in the Sun*, which opened on Broadway at the Ethel Barrymore Theatre on March 11, 1959. The play was an enormous success, running for 530 performances and winning the New York Drama Critics Circle Award. Soon thereafter, Hansberry and Nemiroff moved from their apartment in Greenwich Village to a home in Croton, New York, in order for Hansberry to have more privacy for her work. At the same time, her success made her a public figure, and she used her newfound fame to champion the causes of civil rights and African independence.

It was not until 1964 that Hansberry produced another play, *The Sign in Sidney Brustein's Window*, and by that time she was seriously ill. The play opened at the Longacre Theatre on October 15, 1964, to generally good but unenthusiastic reviews, and Nemiroff had to struggle to keep it open. With an uncertain financial basis, production of the play continued from week to week. Meanwhile, Hansberry was in a hospital bed dying of cancer. She once lapsed into a coma and was not expected to recover, but for a brief time she did rally. Her strength gave out, however, and on January 12, 1965, she died. That night, the Longacre Theatre closed its doors in mourning, and *The Sign in Sidney Brustein's Window* closed after 101 performances.

Analysis

Lorraine Hansberry's realistic style and her stress on the possibilities for heroism within each of her characters have everything to do with the purpose that she saw in drama. As James Baldwin observed, Hansberry made no bones about asserting that art has a purpose, that it contains "the energy that could change things." In *A Raisin in the Sun*, Hansberry describes a poor black family living in Chicago's South Side, her own childhood home, and through her realistic portrayal of their financial, emotional, and racial struggles, as well as in her depiction of their ability to prevail, she offers her audience a model of hope and perseverance, and shows the commonality of human aspirations, regardless of color. In *The Sign in Sidney Brustein's Window*, she takes as her subject the disillusioned liberal Sidney Brustein, who has lost faith in the possibility of creating a better world. After all of Brustein's disillusionment, he realizes that despair is not an answer, that the only solution is hope despite all odds and logic, that change depends upon his commitment to it.

Hansberry's earliest play, *A Raisin in the Sun*, is also her finest and most successful work. The play focuses on the events that transpire during a few days in the life of the Younger family, a family headed by Lena Younger, the mother; the other family members are her daughter, Beneatha, her son, Walter Lee, and his wife, Ruth, and son, Travis. The play focuses on the problem of what the family should do with ten thousand dollars that Lena receives as an insurance payment after the death of her husband, Walter Lee, Sr.

The play's title is taken from Langston Hughes's poem "Harlem" and calls attention to the dreams of the various characters, and the effects of having those dreams deferred. The set itself, fully realistic, emphasizes this theme from the first moment of the play. The furniture, once chosen with care, has been well cared for, yet it is drab, undistinguished, worn out from long years of service. The late Walter Lee, Sr., was a man of dreams, but he could never catch up with them, and he died, exhausted and wasted, worn out like the furniture, at an early age. His family is threatened with the same fate, but his insurance money holds out hope for the fulfillment of dreams. Lena and Walter Lee, however, disagree about what to do with the money. Walter Lee hates his job as a chauffeur and plans to become his own man by opening a liquor store with some friends, but Lena instead makes a down payment on a house with one-third of the money and plans to use another third to finance Beneatha's medical studies. After the two argue, Lena realizes that she has not permitted her son to be a man and has stifled him, just as the rest of the world has. In order to make up for the past, she entrusts him with the remaining two-thirds of the money, directing him to take Beneatha's portion and put it into a savings account for her, using the final third as he sees fit. Walter Lee, however, invests all the money in a foolhardy scheme and discovers shortly thereafter that one of his partners has bilked him of the money.

The house that Lena has purchased is in a white neighborhood, and a Mr. Lindner has approached the Youngers, offering to buy back the house—at a profit to the Youngers—because the members of the community do not want blacks living there. Walter Lee at first scornfully refuses Lindner's offer, but once he has lost all the money he is desperate to recoup his losses and calls Lindner, willing to sell the house. The family is horrified at how low Walter has sunk, but when Beneatha rejects him, claiming there is "nothing left to love" in him, Lena reminds her that "There is always something to love. And if you ain't learned that, you ain't learned nothing." Lena asks Beneatha. "You give him up for me? You wrote his epitaph too—like the rest of the world? Well, who give you the privilege?" The epitaph is indeed premature, for when Lindner arrives and Walter is forced to speak in his son's presence, Walter gains heroic stature by rejecting the offer, telling Lindner in simple, direct terms that they will move into their house because his father "earned it." It is a moment during which Walter comes into manhood, and if it has taken him a long while to do so, the moment is all the richer in heroism.

The theme of heroism found in an unlikely place is perhaps best conveyed through the symbol of Lena's plant. Throughout the play, Lena has tended a small, sickly plant that clings tenaciously to life despite the lack of sunlight in the apartment. Its environment is harsh, unfavorable, yet it clings to life anyway—somewhat like

Walter, whose life should long ago have extinguished any trace of heroism in him. Hansberry gives her audience a message of hope.

Hansberry also reminds her audience of the common needs and aspirations of all humanity, and she does so without oversimplification. None of the characters in the play is a simple type, not even Lindner, who might easily have been presented as an incarnation of evil. Instead, Lindner is conveyed as a human being. When asked why she portrayed Lindner in this manner, Hansberry replied "I have treated Mr. Lindner as a human being merely because he is one; that does not make the meaning of his call less malignant, less sick." Here is where Hansberry calls her audience to action. She reminds the audience of what it is to be human and enjoins them to respect the dignity of all their fellows.

Hansberry's second play, *The Sign in Sidney Brustein's Window,* never matched the success of her first, but it, too, uses a realistic format and was drawn from her own life. Instead of South Side Chicago, it is set in Greenwich Village, Hansberry's home during the early years of her marriage with Robert Nemiroff, and the central character is one who must have resembled many of Hansberry's friends. He is Sidney Brustein, a lapsed liberal, an intellectual, a former insurgent who has lost faith in his ability to bring about constructive change. As the play opens, Sidney moves from one project, a nightclub that failed, to another, the publication of a local newspaper, which Sidney insists will be apolitical. His motto at the opening of the play is "Presume no commitment, disavow all engagement, mock all great expectations. And above all else, avoid the impulse to correct." Sidney's past efforts have failed, and his lost faith is much the same as Beneatha's in *A Raisin in the Sun.*

The surrounding environment goes a long way toward explaining Sidney's cynicism. His wife, Iris, has been in psychoanalysis for two years, and her troubled soul threatens their marriage. Iris' older sister, Mavis, is anti-Semitic, and her other sister, Gloria, is a high-class call girl who masquerades as a model. Organized crime controls politics in the neighborhood, and drug addiction is rampant; one of Sidney's employees at the defunct nightclub, Sal Peretti, died of addiction at the age of seventeen, despite Sidney's efforts to help him. Faced with these grim realities, Sidney longs to live in a high, wooded land, far from civilization, in a simpler, easier world.

The resultant atmosphere is one of disillusionment as characters lash out in anger while trying to protect themselves from pain. One of the targets of the intellectual barbs of the group is Mavis, an average, settled housewife who fusses over Iris and does not pretend to be an intellectual. When the wit gets too pointed, though, Mavis cuts through the verbiage with a telling remark: "I was taught to believe that creativity and great intelligence ought to make one expansive and understanding. That if ordinary people . . . could not expect understanding from artists . . . then where indeed might we look for it at all?" Only Sidney is moved by this remark; he is unable to maintain the pretense of cynicism, admitting, "I *care*. I care about it all. It takes too much energy *not* to care." Thus, Sidney lets himself be drawn into another cause, the election of Wally O'Hara to public office as an independent, someone who will oppose the drug culture and gangster rule of the neighborhood.

As Sidney throws himself into this new cause, he uses his newspaper to further the campaign, and even puts a sign, "Vote for Wally O'Hara," in his window. Idealism seems to have won out, and indeed Wally wins the election, but Sidney is put to a severe test as Iris seems about to leave him and it is discovered that Wally is on the payroll of the gangsters. Added to all of this is Gloria's suicide in Sidney's bathroom. Her death brings Sidney to a moment of crisis, and when Wally O'Hara comes into the room to offer condolences and to warn against any hasty actions, Sidney achieves a clarity of vision that reveals his heroism. Sidney says, *"This world*—this swirling, seething madness—which you ask us to accept, to maintain—has done this . . . maimed my friends . . . emptied these rooms and my very bed. And now it has taken my sister. *This* world. Therefore, to live, to breathe—I shall *have* to fight it." In this moment, Sidney learns true commitment and his responsibility to make the world what it ought to be. The play closes with Iris and Sidney holding each other on the couch, Iris crying in pain, with Sidney enjoining her: "Yes . . . weep now, darling, weep. Let us both weep. That is the first thing: to let ourselves feel again . . . then, tomorrow, we shall make something strong of this sorrow." As the curtain closes, the audience members can scarcely fail to apply these closing words to themselves. Only if they permit themselves to feel the pain, Hansberry claims, will it be possible to do anything to ease that pain in the future.

Other major works

NONFICTION: *The Movement: Documentary of a Struggle for Equality*, 1964 (includes photographs); *To Be Young, Gifted, and Black: Lorraine Hansberry in Her Own Words*, 1969 (Robert Nemiroff, editor).

Bibliography

Gomez, Jewelle L. "Lorraine Hansberry: Uncommon Warrior." In *Reading Black, Reading Feminist*, edited by Henry Louis Gates, Jr. New York: Meridian, 1990.

Lester, Julius. Foreword and afterword to *Lorraine Hansberry: The Collected Last Plays*, edited by Robert Nemiroff. New York: New American Library, 1983.

Miller, Jordon Y. "Lorraine Hansberry." In *Poetry and Drama*. Vol. 2 in *The Black American Writer*, edited by C. W. E. Bigsby. Baltimore: Penguin Books, 1971.

Nemiroff, Robert. "A Critical Background." In *Lorraine Hansberry: The Collected Last Plays*. New York: New American Library, 1983.

Russell, Sandi. *Render Me My Song: African-American Women Writers from Slavery to the Present*. New York: St. Martin's Press, 1990.

Wilkerson, Margaret B. Introduction to *Lorraine Hansberry: The Collected Last Plays*, edited by Robert Nemiroff. New York: New American Library, 1983.

H. D.
Hilda Doolittle

Born: Bethlehem, Pennsylvania; September 10, 1886   **Died:** Zurich, Switzerland; September 27, 1961

Principal poetry

Sea Garden, 1916; *Hymen*, 1921; *Heliodora and Other Poems*, 1924; *Collected Poems of H. D.*, 1925; *Red Roses for Bronze*, 1931; *The Walls Do Not Fall*, 1944; *Tribute to the Angels*, 1945; *The Flowering of the Rod*, 1946; *By Avon River*, 1949; *Selected Poems of H. D.*, 1957; *Helen in Egypt*, 1961; *Hermetic Definition*, 1972; *Collected Poems, 1912-1944*, 1983; *Selected Poems*, 1988.

Other literary forms

Although H. D. is known chiefly for her poetry, she did produce works in other genres, including novels, a verse drama, a screenplay, and a children's novel. The nonfiction trilogy *Tribute to Freud, Writing on the Wall, Advent* (1974), presents an account of her psychoanalysis with Sigmund Freud in the 1930's. *End to Torment* (1979) is a memoir of Ezra Pound.

Other posthumous publications have included *HER-mione* (1981), an autobiographical novel that was written in 1927, *The Gift* (1982), a memoir about her childhood that was written during the bombing of London in World War II, and *Asphodel* (1992), an experimental novel written in1921-1922 and revised several years later, tracing H. D.'s life from her departure for Europe in 1911 to the birth of her daughter in 1919.

Achievements

Doolittle, or H. D. as she signed her pseudonym, was at the center of the pre-World War I literary movement known as Imagism. It had a profound influence on twentieth century poetry, insisting on direct treatment through concrete imagery, freshness of language, economy of expression, and flexible versification. H. D. was a protégée of Ezra Pound, and the images in her poems best demonstrated Pound's definition of the image as "that which presents an intellectual and emotional complex in an instant of time. "Priapus" and "Hermes of the Ways," H. D.'s first Imagist poems, published in 1913, were hailed as innovative breakthroughs; with the publication of *Collected Poems of H. D.* in 1925, she came to be regarded as the finest of the Imagists. A number of these early poems, such as "Orchard," "Oread," "Heat," and "Sea Gods," have been repeatedly anthologized.

H. D.'s productive literary career spanned some fifty years. Her later poetry, somewhat neglected, included *Red Roses for Bronze;* the World War II trilogy *The Walls Do Not Fall, Tribute to the Angels*, and *The Flowering of the Rod;* her long "epic" poem, *Helen in Egypt;* and *Hermetic Definition*.

H. D. has received less critical attention than others of her generation. Although her early Imagist poetry was highly acclaimed, critical response to her later work has been mixed. Some critics have argued that this later work is marred by patches of triteness and sentimentality and a too-narrow focus; others have praised its spiritual richness and the undeniable beauty of many of its passages, and recent critics have called attention to its feminist aspects. Although she was awarded *Poetry*'s Levinson Prize in 1938, she was near the end of her life before there were signs of renewed interest in her work: She received the Harriet Monroe Memorial Prize in 1958; the Brandeis Award in 1959; and the presitigious poetry award of the American Academy of Arts and Letters in 1960—a prize given only once every five years. Several books appraising H. D. appeared in the 1960's, and since the mid-1970's numerous articles and the first full-length biography have been published. Her *Collected Poems, 1912-1944* was published in 1983.

Biography

Hilda Doolittle was born in Bethlehem, Pennsylvania, the first Moravian community in America, on September 10, 1886. Her mother, Helen Wolle Doolittle, was artistic and musical; her father, Charles Leander Doolittle, was professor of mathematics and astronomy at Lehigh, later director of the Flower Observatory at the University of Pennsylvania. Hilda had a rich childhood in a setting of mystical Moravianism that exerted a lasting influence on her poetry.

At the age of fifteen she met Ezra Pound, the first of several extraordinary figures who profoundly influenced her life. Pound, then a precocious graduate student at the University of Pennsylvania, encouraged her to become broadly read, and together they studied Latin, Greek, the classics, yogic texts, and a great diversity of authors. Pound, according to their fellow student William Carlos Williams, "was wonderfully in love with her," but their relationship was somewhat stormy. In 1908, he proposed that they elope to Europe, but her family ties and her suspicions of his other romantic liaisons deterred her. This estrangement was equivocal, however, and in 1911 Hilda joined Pound and his literary circle in London, never again to live in America. Her first Imagist poems were published in *Poetry* (January, 1913), under the signature that Pound suggested, "H. D., Imagist." Active in the Imagist movement, she published her first collection, *Sea Garden*, in 1916.

The intense experiences of the World War I years forever after dominated H. D.'s life and art. Although still attached to Pound, in 1913 she married fellow Imagist Richard Aldington. Their marriage, initially happy, was troubled by infidelity and the turmoil of war.

In 1914, H. D. met D. H. Lawrence. Their strong mutual attraction persisted through the war years, and their relationship was ever afterward present in H. D.'s life and work. In 1915, her first child was stillborn; in 1916, Aldington enlisted and at the same time began an extramarital affair. In 1917 H. D.'s favorite brother was killed in France, and in 1919 her father died. In 1919, gravely ill with pneumonia, she gave birth to her daughter, Perdita; H. D. never revealed who the father was, and she and Aldington separated. Distressed by these events to the point of collapse, she was aided by a young woman from a wealthy English family, Winifred Ellerman, known by her pen name Bryher. For a time, they lived together and traveled to Greece, America, and Egypt. In 1922, H. D. settled near Zurich, with Bryher nearby, to rear her daughter and write. Her literary reputation established by the 1925 publication of *Collected Poems of H. D.*, she lived an active though secluded life, dedicated to her art.

In 1933, dissatisfied with her imperfect understanding of the events of her life and how they related to her art, she entered analysis under Freud. This experience, together with her experiences in London during World War II, permitted her to crystallize her own "legend," to expand upon the multiple meanings in her writing. She wrote much during the last fifteen years of her life, including her most ambitious long poem, *Helen in Egypt*, and the autobiographical novel *Bid Me to Live* (1960). Following a brief visit to America to accept an award for her poetry, she was disabled by a stroke and died on September 27, 1961, at a clinic near Zurich, at the age of seventy-five.

Analysis

H. D. was a lyric poet with one overarching dramatic theme: a heroine's quest for love and spiritual peace. Her poetry about this one central drama, although written in concise and crystalline images, is an evocative and often enigmatic reworking of scenes, a retelling of tales, where new characters fuse with old, where meanings subtly shift with the perspective, and where understanding interchanges with mystery.

The early poem, "Oread"—one of the most often anthologized of H. D.'s poems—has been celebrated as the epitome of the Imagist poem. First published in February, 1914, this deft six-line poem not only illustrates the essence and freshness of the Imagist approach but also foreshadows and reflects many of the themes to which H. D. would turn and return in her art. The six lines of the poem rest upon a single image:

> Whirl up, sea—
> whirl your pointed pines,
> splash your great pines
> on our rocks,
> hurl your green over us,
> cover us with your pools of fir.

The image in this poem is a "presentation," not a representation; it is a tangible, immediate manifestation of a physical thing, not a description of a scene or an abstract feeling. On the immediate level, the poem is an image of a stormy sea whose wavecrests are like forest pines as they crash against the shore and recede, leaving rocky pools in their wake. The image evokes a complex picture suggesting color, the beating of waves on a coast, sounds crashing and hushed, and even fragrance.

"Oread" has, as the Imagists insisted free verse should have, a rhythmic and linguistic development that is musical rather than metrical, corresponding to the sense of the poem. The first three lines describe an active, thrashing sea advancing on a rocky coast, and the last three suggest a lessening forcefulness, still powerful but withdrawing. The rising and falling movement is created in part by emphatic, initial-stress spondees and trochees in the beginning lines of the poem, which then give way to the more yielding dactyls, anapest, and iambic of the last two lines. These prosodic modifications are paralleled by the vowel and consonantal sounds; rough plosives and fricatives dominate the first half; the last half employs liquid continuants to suggest waning flow and submarine calm. This shift in tone is also underscored by the appearance of back vowel sounds in the last three lines only, giving the lines a more sonorous and less frenzied sound.

Various devices give unity to the poem. It is set as one sentence, in lower case. The imperative mood of the verbs that begin all but the fourth line emphasizes the thrusting force of the waves. Internal rhymes subtly reinforce the central metaphor, fusing sea and forest. The aspirated *h* and the liquid *r* and *l* of "whirl" are repeated in "hurl"; the last word, "fir," is a partial assonantal echo of the first word, "whirl," and "green" similarly echoes "sea." Consonants are repeated with like effect. For example, the *h, l, p,* and *s* of "whirl up, sea" are forcibly compressed in "splash" and quietly recapitulated in "pools of fir." Line 4 ("on our rocks"), which introduces character and location, is distinguished from the preceding lines by its lack of a verb, its use of back vowel sounds, and its triseme (or anapest); yet it is yoked to line 3 by enjambment, again subtly sustaining the fusion metaphor.

"Oread" has an elusiveness that is typical of H. D.'s poetry: The identity of the speaker is obscure, the location of the seacoast is unspecified. Who is "us?" Why are the rocks "our rocks?" The answers lie hidden in the title, which contains much that is enigmatic and unspoken. An oread is a nymph of Greek myth—in particular, a mountain nymph. Like naiads, nereids, dryads, sylphs—the nymphs of rivers, the sea, woods, air—oreads were usually personified as beautiful young girls, amorous, musical, gentle, and shy virgins, although occasionally identified with the wilder aspects of nature and akin to satyrs. The oread is one of the multiple forms that H. D. used to develop the central feminine consciousness in her writings. The oread inhabits the lonelier reaches of nature, rocky places of retreat; as H. D. put it in her children's novel, *The Hedgehog* (1936), "The Oreads are the real mountain girls that live furtherest up the hill."

Mountain nymphs were especially identified in myth as companions of the goddess Artemis, the virgin huntress associated with the moon; Artemis guarded the chastity of her nymphs as jealously as her own. It is one of the finer aspects of H. D.'s poetry that she can evoke the presence of things that are not mentioned yet shimmer ghostlike somewhere just out of poetic range: The goddess Artemis is an offstage presence in this poem, as in others. Her figure, white, distant, cold, virginal, yet passionate, is another of the complex manifestations of consciousness that appear in odd guises throughout H. D.'s poetry. In *Helen in Egypt*, for example, the moon goddess is symbolized by the white island in the sea where Helen encounters her lover Achilles. Artemis is embodied in the form of another island in "The Shrine" (subtitled "She Watches over the Sea," and dedicated to Artemis when initially published); it is an island whose difficult approaches can wreck mariners but can also reward those who reach "the splendor of your ragged coast": "Honey is not more sweet/ than the salt stretch of your beach." There is a sexuality, even a bisexuality, about this Artemis apparent in such lines as these, or as in the opening lines of "Huntress": "Come, blunt your spear with us,/ our pace is hot."

The title "Oread" is an allusion to both the moon goddess Artemis, the virgin huntress, and her nymph companions, wild and free in the mountains. This allusion is but one of many in H. D.'s poems to the Greek world, which was, along with Egyptian, Roman, and other civilizations of antiquity, a frame of reference and an abiding source of inspiration for her. A reader with only a slight familiarity with H. D.'s writings will thus recognize in a title such as "Oread" resonances of the classical world. Virtually all of her poems and prose writings allude to it, either directly or by implication. Many of her early poems are explicitly set in the ancient world; others, such as "Sea Iris" and "Sea Lily," are located there only by reference to "temple steps" or "murex-fishermen," or, like "Oread" and "Lethe," have their settings implied solely by their titles.

In the classical world, H. D. found a metaphor for her own loneliness; as she once wrote to William Carlos Williams, "I am, as you perhaps realize, more in sympathy with the odd and the lonely—with those people that feel themselves apart from the whole . . . " It was a far country of the imagination where she could find retreat both from the pain of love and the strain of war and modern life. Ancient Greece or Egypt is envisioned as a stark and beautiful world, a world of cold purity in harmony with nature, where an austere peace could be found in the harsher aspects of the natural landscape. Cities are squalid (as in "The Tribute") or crowded, hideous, and menacing (as in "Cities"); H. D. finds the starker elements of sea, rocky coasts and mountains, trees and wild flowers, storms and wind, the moon and stars, rain, snow, and frost to be sympathetic as well as remote. "I go," she says in the epigraph to *The Flowering of the Rod*, "where I love and where I am loved: Into the snow." The wild seacoast of "Oread" is a manifestation of this nameless land. Linked to the classical world, it appears and reappears throughout H. D.'s work, a dense metaphor for the mental landscape of the particular consciousness present in her writings.

This piling up of associations to be evoked by allusion, as in "Oread," is a stylistic device that H. D. used in both poetry and prose. Her object was to create a many-layered work, dense with meaning, rich with metaphor, and evocative of mystery and legend. She labeled this style *Palimpsest* (also the title of her 1926 novel), a palimpsest being a parchment on which earlier writing has been erased but is still faintly discernible under new writing. H. D. thought of her writing as a superimposition of recurring, almost archetypal feelings and behaviors, like photographic negatives placed on top of one another, yielding a new yet old picture or pattern.

"Oread" illustrates this style. Against the background of rich allusion that is implied in the title, "Oread" is seen to have many layers of superimposed meaning. One step beyond the level of the surface imagery, the poem becomes an incantation, a prayer almost, spoken by the remote-dwelling oread on behalf of herself and her cloistered sisters. They seek, through communion with the elemental natural forces that sustain them in their retreat from the human world, to be cleansed and strengthened,

purified and rededicated to the harmonies of the natural world they have chosen for their refuge. There is also, in the call to the sea to "cover us with your pools," an implied wish to be suspended oblivious in the healing waters, to be reunited with the sea-matrix. This hint is echoed in many poems, such as the similar plea found in "Lethe" for release from the pain of loveless existence: "The roll of the full tide to cover you/ Without question,/ Without kiss." The subject of women hurt and deserted by men whom they loved recurs throughout H. D.'s poems about goddesses, demigoddesses, and other women of antiquity (of whom there are many in her verse—Demeter, Simaethea, Circe, Leda, Phaedra, Helen, Thetis, Cassandra, Calypso, Eurydice, and more). These poems present passionate women ill-treated by men.

At the same time that the poem invokes purification by a sort of baptismal rite, it is on yet another level wryly and compellingly sexual. In the first two lines of "Oread," the sea, traditionally a feminine metaphor, takes on masculine attributes as the image fuses sea and tree: "Whirl up, sea—/ whirl your pointed pines." The sea-crests, hardened by their fanciful merging with thrusting pines, are urged to "whirl up," to "splash" to "hurl" themselves against a rocky coast, to "cover us," as a male animal covers the female, perhaps to inseminate. The natural rhythm of the poem suggests arousal, climax, and commingled torpor. On an elementary level, "Oread" is about events in the natural world; on another level, the landscape pictured evokes the austere classical world to which consciousness may retreat; and, on still another level, the natural landscape becomes a metaphor for the landscape of the body.

H. D.'s poetic consciousness grew out of the events, situations, and characters of her life, and each of her poems is a symbolic re-creation of some part of her life, thus giving a further, hidden meaning to the poetry. For example, the knowledge that the nickname bestowed upon H. D. by the green-eyed Ezra Pound was "Dryad" adds another dimension to "Oread." A dryad is a wood nymph, and the nickname was perhaps a token of their early love among the apple trees of Pennsylvania, where H. D. was a virgin and Pound something of a satyr. Early poems such as "Oread" and "Priapus," with their bold sexual undercurrents, can thus also be read as amusing, half-mocking secret messages to the principal men in her life. Although not confessional poetry, H. D.'s work was intimately bound to her personal experiences, especially those of the period from 1911 to 1920.

H. D.'s poetry was original and manifested a new development in Western literature. Reversing the usual form of allegory, she drew images from the natural world and characters and situations from classical sources to transmute the story of her own life into poems expressing universal human experience. Exemplified by "Oread," her poems are like ideographic pictures or signs with many meanings coiled in single images—images that, in their distilled essence, contain the world seen by a gifted poet.

Other major works

NOVELS: *Palimpsest*, 1926; *Hedylus*, 1928; *Kora and Ka*, 1934 (includes *Mira-Mare*); *The Usual Star*, 1934 (includes *Two Americans*); *Nights*, 1935; *Bid Me to Live*, 1960; *HERmione*, 1981; *Asphodel*, 1992.

SHORT FICTION: *The Hedgehog*, 1936.

PLAY: *Hippolytus Temporizes*, 1927 (adaptation of classical text).

NONFICTION: *Tribute to Freud*, 1956; *Tribute to Freud, Writing on the Wall, Advent*, 1974; *End to Torment*, 1979; *The Gift*, 1982.

TRANSLATIONS: *Choruses from Iphigeneia in Aulis and the Hippolytus of Euripides*, 1919; *Euripides' Ion*, 1937.

Bibliography

Burnett, Gary Dean. *H. D. Between Image and Epic: The Mysteries of Her Poetics*. Ann Arbor, Mich.: UMI Research Press, 1990.

DuPlessis, Rachel Blau. *H. D., the Career of That Struggle*. Brighton, England: Harvester Press, 1986.

Friedman, Susan Stanford. *Psyche Reborn: The Emergence of H. D.* Bloomington: Indiana University Press, 1981.

Fritz, Angela DiPace. *Thought and Vision: A Critical Reading of H. D.'s Poetry*. Washington, D.C.: Catholic University of America Press, 1988.

Guest, Barbara. *Herself Defined: The Poet H. D. and Her World*. Garden City, N.Y.: Doubleday, 1984.

King, Michael, ed. *H. D.: Woman and Poet*. Orono, Maine: National Poetry Foundation, 1986.

Robinson, Janice S. *H. D.: The Life and Work of an American Poet*. Boston: Houghton Mifflin, 1982.

LILLIAN HELLMAN

Born: New Orleans, Louisiana; June 20, 1905

Died: Martha's Vineyard, Massachusetts; June 30, 1984

Principal drama

The Children's Hour, pr., pb. 1934; *Days to Come*, pr., pb. 1936; *The Little Foxes*, pr., pb. 1939; *Watch on the Rhine*, pr., pb. 1941; *The Searching Wind*, pr., pb. 1944; *Another Part of the Forest*, pr. 1946, pb. 1947; *Montserrat*, pr. 1949, pb. 1950 (adaptation of Emmanuel Robles' play); *The Autumn Garden*, pr., pb. 1951; *The Lark*, pr. 1955, pb. 1956 (adaptation of Jean Anouilh's play *L'Alouette*); *Candide*, pr. 1956, pb. 1957 (libretto; music by Leonard Bernstein, lyrics by Richard Wilbur, John Latouche, and Dorothy Parker; adaptation of Voltaire's 1759 novel); *Toys in the Attic*, pr., pb. 1960; *My Mother, My Father, and Me*, pr., pb. 1963 (adaptation of Burt Blechman's novel *How Much?*); *The Collected Plays*, pb. 1972.

Other literary forms

In addition to her original stage plays, Lillian Hellman published original screenplays, a collection of the letters of Anton Chekhov, her adaptations of two French plays (*Montserrat, L'Alouette*) and of an American novel (*How Much?*), an operetta adapted from Voltaire's *Candide*, many uncollected articles, and several volumes of memoirs, the first two of which have received as much acclaim as her best plays.

Achievements

Hellman was the most important American follower of Henrik Ibsen after Arthur Miller. She wrote strong, well-made plays involving significant social issues. She created memorable female characters, some strong and some weak; her most important female character, Regina Giddens of *The Little Foxes* and *Another Part of the Forest*, seems at least partially modeled on Ibsen's Hedda Gabler. Like his, some of Hellman's plays have a question ending, one in which the eventual outcome for the major characters is left ironically uncertain.

Hellman was, after Tennessee Williams, the most important dramatist writing primarily about the American South. Two of her plays, *Watch on the Rhine* and *Toys in the Attic*, won the New York Drama Critics Circle Award. Hellman received many other awards, including the Brandeis University Creative Arts Medal and the National Institute of Arts and Letters Gold Medal.

Biography

Lillian Florence Hellman was born in New Orleans of Jewish parents. Her father was also born in New Orleans, and her mother in Alabama, of a family long established there. Part of her mother's family moved to New York, and when Hellman was five years old, her parents moved there and commenced a routine of spending six months of each year in New York and six in New Orleans with her father's two unmarried sisters. As her memoirs make clear, Hellman's plays are strongly influenced by her Southern, urban background. Hellman attended New York University from 1922 to 1924 and briefly attended Columbia University in 1924, without completing a degree at either school. She worked for a time thereafter in New York and Hollywood in the areas of publishing,

book reviewing, and reading manuscripts of plays and film scenarios. In 1925, she married Arthur Kober; they were divorced in 1932. Two years later, her first play, *The Children's Hour*, was a tremendous hit, achieving a longer original run (691 performances) than any of her later plays. From that success until her last play in 1963, she was primarily a playwright and occasionally a scriptwriter, though she was never really happy in the theater.

Over the years, Hellman made various visits to Russia, to Civil War Spain, and elsewhere in Europe, including a very dangerous visit to Nazi Germany to take money to the underground at the request of a friend. For many years, she was the companion of the novelist Dashiell Hammett, though they lived together only sporadically.

Congressional investigations of Communism in the United States in the early 1950's caused serious trouble for both her and Hammett, though she denied having sufficiently consistent or deep political convictions to belong to any party. As a result of the investigations, Hellman and Hammett were both blacklisted in Hollywood; she also lost the home she owned and shared with Hammett in upstate New York, as well as various friends.

Hammett was imprisoned; soon after his release, he became ill, and Hellman took care of him until his death in 1961. In her later years, Hellman devoted herself to her four books of memoirs and taught at Harvard University, the Massachusetts Institute of Technology, and the University of California at Berkeley. She died of cardiac arrest on June 30, 1984, on Martha's Vineyard.

Analysis

The Children's Hour, Lillian Hellman's first play, was based on an actual lawsuit, the Great Drumsheugh Case. The play displays almost all the dramatic characteristics for which Hellman is noted: crisp, forceful, realistic dialogue; clear character construction and analysis; a clear-cut plot line in the tradition of the well-made play, with fast movement and adroitly handled suspense which kept (and can still keep) audiences enthralled. Some of Hellman's later plays display these characteristics with greater skill, but they are all there in her first. *The Children's Hour* and most of the others can also be called melodramatic, because of the suspense, because of the use of violence and of blackmail, and because of obvious authorial manipulation to achieve a neat conclusion. The plays are never, however, pure melodrama, since pure melodrama would not include valid, well-drawn characters or significant themes. *The Children's Hour*, like many of Hellman's plays, concerns the destructive power of evil, its ability to erode human relationships and destroy lives. In this play, evil is manifested by a child's malicious lie and its repercussions in the lives of two women.

The Children's Hour opens on a class in progress at a girls' boarding school in Massachusetts. The teacher, Lily Mortar, is the aunt of Martha Dobie, one of the two young women who own and operate the school. Presently, Mary Tilford enters, very late for class, carrying a bunch of flowers with which she appeases the teacher. Then the other owner, Karen Wright, enters. Karen has lost her bracelet and asks one of the girls, Helen, if she has found it, an important issue in the play. Karen asks Mary where she got the flowers. Mary repeats her claim that she picked them. Karen, apparently recognizing them, says Mary got them out of the garbage pail and has been lying. Mary says her heart hurts and pretends to fall into a faint.

Martha enters, and she and Karen discuss Mary as a troublemaker, send for Karen's fiancé (Joe Cardin, who

is a doctor and also Mary's cousin), and discuss getting rid of Mrs. Mortar. Martha is clearly upset at the imminent marriage. Although she likes Joe, she hates the possibility that Karen might leave the school. Joe arrives and goes off to examine Mary. Mrs. Mortar, deeply insulted at Martha's desire to get her away from the school, indirectly accuses her niece of homosexual feelings toward Karen. Mary's two roommates are caught eavesdropping. Mary comes in, and it is clear that Joe also considers her a troublemaker.

When the audience sees Mary for the first time alone with other girls, her character becomes only too clear. Her lies, her manipulation, her dictatorial attitude toward her schoolmates, and presently her outright blackmail of one of them represent more than mere naughtiness or adolescent confusion. Mary is psychotic, and dangerously so. She forces a girl named Rosalie to do some work for her by hinting of knowledge that Rosalie stole the bracelet that Karen asked about earlier. She forces her roommates to report the conversation that they overheard, and while Mary certainly does not completely understand its import, she nevertheless recognizes it as a weapon she can use.

Act 2 takes place in the living room of the home of Mary's grandmother, Mrs. Tilford. Mary arrives and is admitted by the maid, Agatha, who clearly does not trust her. Mrs. Tilford is an intelligent woman but, unlike Agatha, she can be taken in by her granddaughter, although not easily. Mrs. Tilford has supported Martha and Karen in their establishment of the school, has encouraged her friends to send their daughters there, and certainly trusts the schoolmistresses. Mary, therefore, begins to use the story she has heard secondhand. Mrs. Tilford is deeply disturbed and finds it difficult to believe that such a story could be invented. Scene 2 opens with Agatha telling Mary that Rosalie is coming to spend the night. The audience learns that Mrs. Tilford has told Mary's story to the parents of all the girls, all of whom have been called home. Rosalie is spending the night with Mary because her mother is in New York.

The scene develops very dramatically. Mary blackmails Rosalie into being prepared to support her lies if necessary. Joe arrives, and very soon he and his aunt are battling. Karen and Martha arrive, and the battle enlarges. Joe insists that Mary be questioned. Mary, genuinely nervous, tells her story, making it more and more circumstantial, until finally the circumstances catch her in a lie. She has said that she has seen things through Karen's keyhole, and Karen announces that her door has no keyhole. Mary is therefore forced to say that it was Martha's room, not Karen's; Martha announces that she shares her room with Mrs. Mortar. Backed into a corner, Mary says that it was not she but Rosalie who saw them, and that she saw them because Karen's door was halfway open. Rosalie is summoned and at first denies the story, but when Mary makes it plain that she will expose Rosalie as a thief, Rosalie agrees that the story is true and collapses in tears.

After so tense a moment, act 3 is almost anticlimactic. Karen and Martha are alone at the school. They have lost their case; the townspeople are against them. Martha hopes that Karen will escape through marrying Joe, but Karen seems doubtful. Mrs. Mortar, who would have been the key witness at the trial but who refused to testify, returns because she has run out of money, but Martha has no more to give her. She leaves the room, and Joe enters. He is planning for the marriage and for all three of them to leave together permanently, even though he would be giving up a promising career. Martha leaves, and in his words and attitude toward Karen it becomes clear that Joe is uncertain of the truth. Karen quietly denies any homosexual relationship, and he apparently accepts the denial. Karen asks him to think things over. He reluctantly agrees and leaves, insisting that he will come back, though Karen is sure that he will not. Martha returns and announces, in a scene of high emotion, that, though she had not previously been aware of it, she is in love with Karen. She leaves the room, and a muffled shot is heard. Karen opens the door and sees that Martha has killed herself. Mrs. Mortar rushes in, sees what has happened, and expresses her remorse. The doorbell rings, and it is Agatha; Mrs. Tilford is waiting outside in her car.

The final dialogue is between Karen and Mrs. Tilford, who has learned that Mary's story was a lie. The bracelet was found among Rosalie's things, and Rosalie confessed. Apparently, Mary has confessed, too. The judge at the trial will arrange a public apology and explanation, and Mrs. Tilford will pay the amount of the damages. Karen announces Martha's death and expresses her bitter feelings toward Mrs. Tilford, but she gradually recognizes Mrs. Tilford's sincerity. The old woman will be the greater sufferer: She has refused to commit Mary to an institution and will hence have to live permanently in her company. Karen agrees to accept Mrs. Tilford's money but disagrees with Mrs. Tilford's hope that she and Joe will marry. The two separate amicably, and Karen is left alone at the play's end.

The Little Foxes is, and almost surely will remain, Hellman's standard play. It represents significant advances in technique over *The Children's Hour* and is in various ways more typical of Hellman's overall production. First, it is set in the Deep South. Second, the characters are more sharply distinguished and more deeply realized, and the dialogue is more individualized. Third, Hellman displays compassion, humor, and irony. Fourth, *The Little Foxes* displays a sociopolitical theme: These are "the little foxes who spoil the vines" (a quotation from the Song of Solomon), whom Hellman sees as twentieth century capitalists in embryo.

The Little Foxes concentrates on a rapacious small-town Alabama family, the Hubbards, and on some of their victims. The year is 1900. As the play opens, Regina Giddens is giving a dinner party for a businessman from Chicago, William Marshall, with whom her brothers are negotiating to join them in opening one of the first cotton mills in the South. All the characters in the play are present except Regina's husband, Horace, the town banker, long confined to the hospital with a bad heart. The remaining characters are Regina's brothers, Ben and Oscar; Oscar's wife, Birdie; Oscar and Birdie's son, Leo; Horace and Regina's daughter, Alexandra; and the servants, Addie and Cal. Ben is a jovial hypocrite, and he and Regina are the dominant Hubbards. Oscar is relatively weak, obtuse, and blustery, while Leo is a lesser version of Oscar. Alexandra shares Birdie's cultural interests and seems not at all Hubbard-like. Regina herself is a handsome woman, a smooth and clever conniver, who takes in Marshall to a degree that Ben, for all of his hypocrisy, cannot.

When the deal for the cotton mill has been struck, the young couple drive Marshall to the station to return to Chicago. The Hubbards are triumphant, looking forward to being rich. One problem remains: The three siblings are supposed to contribute equal sums to the mill project, enough to make them together the majority shareholders, but while Ben and Oscar are ready to put up their share, Regina must get hers from Horace, who has ignored all letters on the subject. In a piece of typical Hubbard trickery, Regina declares that Horace is holding out because he wants a larger share, and Ben finally agrees that he should have a larger share and that the difference will come out of Oscar's. Oscar is furious, but he is mollified by Regina's assurance that she will consider a marriage between Leo and Alexandra. A plan is then made to send Alexandra, who is devoted to her father, to bring him home.

In *The Little Foxes*, the audience must wait, with anticipation, for what Horace's return in the second act will bring. Before Horace's arrival, Oscar and Leo conceive a plan to steal eighty thousand dollars' worth of bonds from Horace's safety deposit box, to finance their venture. (If they can do this, they will not need Regina as a partner.) Horace then arrives, stiff and ill, accompanied by Alexandra, who has his heart medicine. During the course of the act, it becomes clear that Horace and Regina are, and have been, at odds during most of their marriage, that Horace will not agree to finance the proposed project, and that he will not consent to a marriage between Alexandra and Leo. It is also clear that Regina will not be thwarted and that Horace is too physically frail to withstand her will.

In act 3, Horace, who has discovered the crime, informs Regina about the theft and tells her that he will pretend that the theft was a loan. Moreover, he will change his will, leaving Regina the bonds and all of his other property to Alexandra. Regina will thus lose the opportunity to invest in the business venture (since the partners will no longer need her money), and she will lose her inheritance from Horace. Furiously, she tell him that she married him only for money. He becomes distraught, reaches for his medicine, spills it, and asks her to get his new bottle. She simply stands there as he collapses and dies. Regina is now in a position to blackmail her brothers into assigning her a controlling interest in the mill, lest she prosecute them. Regina is triumphant; nevertheless, she now faces a life of loneliness because Alexandra has discovered her mother's treachery and will leave her.

The play ends with a question and is the better for it, since, if the ending represented a total and final triumph, it would emphasize the play's kinship to pure melodrama. Moreover, the Hubbard siblings are more complex than a recital of the plot might make them seem. Ben retains an incompetent servant because she has always been in the family. Ben and Oscar both seem genuinely moved by Horace's death. Ben and Regina are both capable of viewing their own, and others', behavior ironically, and there is humor in some of their dialogue. Regina is frightened at what she has done, or rather not done. These are highly individualized human beings, and the play is skillfully constructed, absorbing, and genuinely insightful.

Other major works

NONFICTION: *An Unfinished Woman: A Memoir*, 1969; *Pentimento*, 1973; *Scoundrel Time*, 1976; *Maybe*, 1980; *Eating Together: Recipes and Recollections*, 1984 (with Peter Feibleman); *Conversations with Lillian Hellman*, 1986.

SCREENPLAYS: *The Dark Angel*, 1935 (with Mordaunt Shairp); *These Three*, 1936; *Dead End*, 1937 (adaptation of Sidney Kingsley's play); *The Little Foxes*, 1941 (with Dorothy Parker, Arthur Kober, and Alan Campbell); *Watch on the Rhine*, 1943 (with Dashiell Hammett); *The North Star: A Motion Picture About Some Russian People*, 1943; *The Searching Wind*, 1946; *The Chase*, 1966.

EDITED TEXTS: *The Selected Letters of Anton Chekhov*, 1955; *The Big Knockover: Selected Stories and Short Novels of Dashiell Hammett*, 1966 (with introduction).

Bibliography

Adler, Jacob H. *Lillian Hellman*. Austin, Tex.: Steck-Vaughn, 1969.

Dick, Bernard F. *Hellman in Hollywood*. Rutherford, N.J.: Fairleigh Dickinson University Press, 1982.

Falk, Doris V. *Lillian Hellman*. New York: Frederick Ungar, 1978.

Feibleman, Peter. *Lily: Reminiscences of Lillian Hellman*. New York: William Morrow, 1988.

Lederer, Katherine. *Lillian Hellman*. Boston: Twayne, 1979.

Rollyson, Carl. *Lillian Hellman: Her Legend and Her Legacy*. New York: St. Martin's Press, 1988.

BETH HENLEY

Born: Jackson, Mississippi; May 8, 1952

Principal drama

Am I Blue, pr. 1973, pb. 1982; *Crimes of the Heart*, pr. 1979, pb. 1981; *The Miss Firecracker Contest*, pr. 1980, pb. 1982; *The Wake of Jamey Foster*, pr., pb. 1982; *The Debutante Ball*, pr. 1985, pb. 1991; *The Lucky Spot*, pr. 1986, pb. 1987; *Abundance*, pr. 1990, pb. 1992; *Beth Henley: Four Plays*, pb. 1992.

Other literary forms

In addition to her works for the stage, Beth Henley has written screenplays, including *Nobody's Fool* (1986); *True Stories* (1986), in collaboration with David Byrne and Stephen Tobolowsky; and the films *Crimes of the Heart* (1986) and *Miss Firecracker* (1989), adapted from her plays. She has also written the teleplays *Survival Guides* (1986) and *Trying Times* (1987), both with Budge Threlkeld.

Achievements

Henley is often compared to fiction writers Eudora Welty and Flannery O'Connor for her sympathetic portrayals of eccentric characters who lead deceptively simple lives in small Southern communities. Her work has also been identified with the literary traditions of the grotesque and the absurd. Henley's unique achievement, however, is the intermingling of absurdism and realism. Her plays realistically capture the Southern vernacular and take place in authentic Southern settings, yet they also exaggerate the recognizable and push the bizarre to extremes to reveal the underlying absurdity of the human condition. Loss and renewal, the vulnerability of loving, and the frail but indomitable human spirit are among her recurring themes; Henley delivers these serious concerns, however, through unpredictable characters, outra-geously witty dialogue, and offbeat humor. It is her insistence on the value of laughter in the face of adversity that places her within the tragicomic tradition of modern dramatic literature. Another of Henley's strengths is that she approaches her craft with a keen insight into what is stageworthy. This awareness, no doubt, is one of the reasons that her first full-length play, *Crimes of the Heart*, won the Pulitzer Prize in drama in 1981 with the distinction of being the first play to win the coveted award before appearing on Broadway. *Crimes of the Heart* also received the New York Drama Critics Circle Award in 1981, and, in the same year, Henley captured the prestigious George Oppenheimer/*Newsday* Playwriting Award.

Biography

The second of four daughters, Elizabeth Becker Henley was born May 8, 1952, in Jackson, Mississippi. Her parents, Charles Boyce and Elizabeth Josephine Becker, were reared in the neighboring communities of Hazlehurst and Brookhaven, locales that Henley adopted for two of her plays. Henley's father, an attorney, served in both houses of the Mississippi legislature. A shy child plagued with chronic attacks of asthma, Henley, often bedridden, entertained herself by reading play scripts that were in production at the New Stage Theatre in Jackson, where her mother, an amateur actress, regularly performed.

Selecting drama as her major, Henley enrolled at Southern Methodist University in Dallas, Texas, in 1970. While a sophomore, she wrote her first play as an assignment for a playwriting class. The play, a one-act comedy entitled *Am I Blue*, was produced at the university under a pseudonym in her senior year. After she was graduated in 1974 with a bachelor of fine arts degree, Henley taught creative dramatics and acted for the Dallas Minority Repertory Theatre. She earned a livelihood at odd jobs as a waitress, file clerk, and photographer of children at a department store. In 1975, she received a teaching scholarship from the University of Illinois, where she taught acting classes while pursuing graduate studies in drama. In the summer of 1976, she acted in the *Great American People Show*, a historical pageant presented at the New Salem State Park.

Hoping to break into films as an actress, Henley moved to Los Angeles in the fall of 1976. Failing to get auditions for parts, she turned to writing screenplays as a creative outlet, but without an agent to represent her, the studios would not read her scripts. Thinking that stage plays would have a better chance of getting performed, especially in small theaters, Henley began working on a comedy (set in Hazlehurst, Mississippi) about a crisis in the lives of three sisters. With production costs in mind, she deliberately limited the play to six characters and one indoor set. She finished *Crimes of the Heart* in 1978 and submitted it to several regional theaters without success, but Henley's friend and fellow playwright Frederick Bailey had faith in the play. Without Henley's knowledge, he entered *Crimes of the Heart* in the annual drama competition of the Actors Theatre of Louisville, Kentucky, where it was selected as a cowinner for 1977-1978. In February, 1979, the Actors Theatre produced the play as part of the company's annual Festival of New American Plays. The play was an immediate success. After productions in Maryland, Missouri, and California, *Crimes of the Heart* opened to full houses Off-Broadway on December 21, 1980. The public's high regard for the play was matched by critical acclaim. In April, 1981, at the age of twenty-eight, Henley was awarded the Pulitzer Prize in drama for *Crimes of the Heart*, the first woman so honored in twenty-three years. In the fall of 1981, after having been recognized by the New York Drama Critics Circle as the best American play of the season, *Crimes of the Heart* premiered on Broadway; it ran for 535 performances. Subsequent productions were staged in England, France, Israel, and Australia.

Within the next three years, two other comedies written before Henley won the Pulitzer Prize were produced in New York City. *The Wake of Jamey Foster* opened on Broadway on October 14, 1982, but closed after only twelve nights. Critics found the play, which was also set in Mississippi, too repetitious of *Crimes of the Heart*. Written before *The Wake of Jamey Foster*, *The Miss Firecracker Contest* was staged in New York in the spring of 1984. Again critics faulted the play for its similarity to her earlier works. Undaunted by these box-office failures, Henley kept writing for the stage. In the spring of 1985, the South Coast Repertory Theatre in Costa Mesa, California, produced her next play *The Debutante Ball*. In the following year, Henley's *The Lucky Spot* (set in a dance hall in Pigeon, Louisiana, in 1934) premiered in New York City. Reviews of the play varied, but one critic considered *The Lucky Spot* to be Henley's best play since *Crimes of the Heart*. In 1990, *Abundance*, Henley's drama about two mail-order brides whose lives become entangled in the American West of the late nineteenth century, opened in New York City to mixed reviews. Later in the same year, the New York Stage and Film Company staged a workshop production of Henley's *Signature* in Poughkeepsie, New York.

As a Pulitzer Prize winner, the playwright-actress also found herself in demand as a screenwriter. While continuing to write stage plays, Henley wrote the screenplay for the acclaimed film version of *Crimes of the Heart*; the script for another film, *Nobody's Fool*; and a screenplay based on her drama *The Miss Firecracker Contest*. Henley also collaborated with David Byrne and Stephen Tobolowsky on the screenplay for *True Stories* and with Budge Threlkeld on two television scripts, *Survival Guides* and *Trying Times*.

Henley's plays have reached audiences far beyond the regional theaters for which she first wrote, making her a significant contributor to American dramatic literature. Although the plays written after *Crimes of the Heart* have failed to bring her the critical praise she earned with that first full-length comedy, her dramatic output as a whole reveals a consistency in tone and theme.

Analysis

While the plays of Beth Henley are well constructed and provide ample conflict and suspense, the playwright's keen sense of place and character and her humorous yet compassionate view of the human predicament most typify her work. Her plays are set most often in her home state of Mississippi, where the innocent façade of friendly small-town life belies the horror and lunacy within. The dark side of humanity—the unpredictable, the irrational, the abnormal—attracts Henley, and her plays abound with stories of sickness, disease, and perversions. Ironically, however, Henley creates comedy out of the grotesque and fabricates endearing characters out of eccentricity.

Usually, Henley's plays depict the family in crisis joined by a close circle of friends and neighbors. From this basic situation, Henley makes her case for emotional survival. Guilt, despair, and loneliness are typical experiences of Henley's failed heroines, but each continues to search for some measure of happiness and often finds it, if only momentarily, in the community of others. Whereas Henley doggedly exposes human frailties, in the final analysis her view is a charitable one and her plays are optimistic, despite the fact that they offer no lasting resolutions to her characters' problems. The key to understanding Henley's optimism lies in the laughter that her plays evoke; laughter functions to undercut that which is horrifying in life—to render it less horrifying.

Henley's reputation as a major American playwright was established with two full-length plays, *Crimes of the Heart* and *The Miss Firecracker Contest*. These plays also best illustrate the qualities that shape her unusual talent: a uniquely comic but sad voice, a distinguishing preoccupation with the bizarre, and a gift for working out variations on the themes of loneliness, guilt, loss, and renewal. Set in Hazlehurst, Mississippi, five years after Hurricane Camille, *Crimes of the Heart* is about three sisters—Lenny, Meg, and Babe MaGrath. The immediate crisis is that the youngest sister, Babe, has shot her husband, Zackery Botrelle, who is the richest and most powerful man in the community. The plot is fairly easily resolved when Zackery recovers and his threat to confine Babe in a mental institution is thwarted. This, however, hardly accounts for the sisters' bizarre tale, which Henley unravels through exposition that is brilliantly interspersed with the main action. Babe's trouble is only one more disaster among many that the MaGrath women have experienced, beginning with their father's desertion and their mother's suicide (she hanged herself and the family's cat). The mother's death left the sisters under the supervision of their grandfather, and now the care of the sick old man has fallen to Lenny, the oldest sister, because Babe married young and Meg escaped to California to pursue a singing career. Growing up in the shadow of their mother's inexplicable suicide and the notoriety it brought, each of the sisters suffers silently and alone. Meg was especially affected. Fearing to show pity as a sign of weakness, she tested herself as a youngster by staring at a book full of pictures of people with horrible skin diseases. Remarkably, Henley wrings laughter out of the MaGraths' misfortunes: The sisters

suspect that Mama MaGrath killed herself because she was having a bad day; Lenny thinks that her prospects for marriage are bleak because she has a deformed ovary; and Babe shoots Zackery because she does not like his looks. To Henley's credit, the laughter is never at the expense of her characters, and there is a kind of bizarre logic to their eccentric behavior that makes the incredible credible. After Babe attempts suicide twice (because she, too, is having a bad day), she learns why her mother hanged the cat: She was afraid to die alone.

Of the same eccentric mold as the MaGrath women, twenty-four-year-old Carnelle Scott, the central character of *The Miss Firecracker Contest*, seeks to overcome her well-earned reputation as the town trollop by becoming Miss Firecracker at the annual Fourth of July celebration in her hometown of Brookhaven, Mississippi. Since Carnelle's determination to succeed is exceeded only by her lack of talent, the outcome is predictable. Carnelle loses (she comes in fifth in a field of five), but she manages to overcome her despondency over the loss and joins her friends to watch the fireworks display at the close of the play. Henley enlivens the simple plot with a number of very odd characters, all of whom, like Carnelle, seek redemption from their unhappy pasts. Delmount Williams, Carnelle's cousin, is a formal mental patient who wants to be a philosopher; his sister Elain finds it easier to desert her husband and sons than to abandon her clock collection; and Carnelle's seamstress, Popeye Jackson, who learned her trade by making dresses for frogs, hears voices through her eyes. Henley's propensity for the grotesque is even more marked in *The Miss Firecracker Contest* than in *Crimes of the Heart*. Carnelle recalls a childhood bout with ringworm, the treatment for which was to shave her head and cover it with a disgusting ointment; Delmount's last job was scraping up dead dogs from county roads; and all fondly remember Ronelle Williams, Delmount and Elain's mother, who died looking like a hairy ape after having her cancerous pituitary gland replaced by one from a monkey. Although in *The Miss Firecracker Contest* Henley tries too hard to be amusing at times, her characters are distinctly drawn and believable despite their whimsicality.

Henley's rise to prominence in the American theater is remarkable considering the regionalism that characterizes her work. The weaknesses of her plays, a penchant for telling tall tales that stretch credulity and a tendency to write gags that force laughter, are overcome by her gift for creating memorable characters. Whereas Henley's dramatic material is confined to small Southern towns and the misfits who inhabit them, her humorous but sympathetic treatment of human foibles has a universality and originality that make her one of the most imaginative dramatists writing for the American theater.

Other major works

SCREENPLAYS: *Nobody's Fool*, 1986; *Crimes of the Heart*, 1986 (adaptation of her play); *True Stories*, 1986 (with David Byrne and Stephen Tobolowsky); *Miss Firecracker*, 1989 (adaptation of her play).
TELEPLAYS: *Survival Guides*, 1986; *Trying Times*, 1987.

Bibliography

Haller, Scot. "Her First Play, Her First Pulitzer Prize." *Saturday Review* 8 (November, 1981): 40-44.

Harbin, Billy J. "Familial Bonds in the Plays of Beth Henley." *Southern Quarterly* 25 (Spring, 1987): 81-94.

Hargrove, Nancy D. "The Tragicomic Vision of Beth Henley's Drama." *Southern Quarterly* 22 (Summer, 1984): 54-70.

Jones, John Griffin, ed. "Beth Henley." In *Mississippi Writers Talking*. Vol. 1. Jackson: University Press of Mississippi, 1982.

McDonnell, Lisa J. "Diverse Similitude: Beth Henley and Marsha Norman." *Southern Quarterly* 25 (Spring, 1987): 95-104.

LINDA HOGAN

Born: Denver, Colorado; July 16, 1947

Principal poetry

Calling Myself Home, 1978; *Daughters, I Love You*, 1981; *Eclipse*, 1983; *Seeing Through the Sun*, 1985; *Savings*, 1988; *The Book of Medicines*, 1993.

Other literary forms

Linda Hogan has published critical and personal essays on American Indian literature and culture in popular and academic periodicals and anthologies. Her novel *Mean Spirit*, based on research initiated by Osage scholar Carol Hunter, appeared in 1990. She has also written a play, *A Piece of Moon*, which was produced in 1981, and with Carol Bruchac and Judith McDaniel she compiled the anthology *The Stories We Hold Secret: Tales of Women's Spiritual Development (1987)*.

Achievements

The publication of books and securing of teaching positions in universities represent in themselves major achievements for a woman who has said that as a young girl she did not plan to attend college because "I didn't know what college was." Through what she might call a combination of love and defiance, Linda Hogan has overcome many of the oppressive conditions and obstacles placed in the way of those she characterizes as the less privileged of society. Her writing challenges accepted standards of literary taste, being deliberately aimed at an audience that may be without formal education or training in complex literary forms. Her achievement and potential have been recognized: *Seeing Through the Sun* received an American Book Award from the Before Columbus Foundation, and Hogan has been awarded grants from the National Endowment for the Arts and the Minnesota State Arts Board.

Biography

Linda Hogan was born in Denver in 1947. Her ancestors include pioneer workers and farmers who had settled in Nebraska and Winchester Colbert, the nineteenth century head of the Chickasaw Nation. She grew up in Colorado, in Denver and later in Colorado Springs, and also spent much time in her childhood on her grandparents' farm in Oklahoma. The former experiences introduced Hogan to a multicultural, working-class environment, the latter to rural poverty and hardship as well as the beauty of nature and strong ties to the land. Leaving school at fifteen to begin work as a nurse's aide, Hogan worked at a series of low-paying jobs before and during her first years in college. She earned a bachelor's degree and, in 1978, received an M.A. in creative writing from the University of Colorado.

During the period of her self-education and formal education, Hogan began to write, seeking to formulate her own sense of pattern and significance in her existence. Her first book of poems was published in 1978; it was followed by the publication of several essays on American Indian and other writers. Since that time Hogan has been active both as writer and as teacher, teaching in colleges and universities in Colorado and Minnesota and publishing poetry, fiction, nonfiction, and drama.

Hogan has been politically active as well as articulate in her writing on issues relating to colonialism, human rights, and equitable treatment for working people. She participated with her family in an antinuclear encampment in the Black Hills of South Dakota during 1980; the experience was later commemorated in the poems collected in *Daughters, I Love You* (1981) and reprinted in *Eclipse*.

Analysis

Calling Myself Home, Linda Hogan's first collection of poems, showed the considerable promise of the young writer. The ambiguous title reflects the complexity of themes the author confronts: This phrase signifies a journey back to origins, but it can mean, as well, that home is to be found only within the self. Both these meanings reverberate in the poems in this collection, even as the struggle between the two senses permeates all Hogan's work and her relationship with her family and ancestors. "Landless Indians" is how Hogan describes the Chickasaw and other Oklahoma Indians, typified by her grandparents and relatives, who lost their allotment lands to bank failures, swindlers, and periods of depressed economy. Thus returning "home" means awareness of loss in the act of restoring ties to the land, and plumbing one's inner resources to create a psychological and spiritual "homeland" that maintains individual and collective identity.

The collection *Calling Myself Home* includes ten poems in the first section, "By the Dry Pond," dedicated to the author's sister; the second part has sixteen poems under the heading "Heritage." The first ten poems are reflective meditations that turn to an arid and materially impoverished landscape, yet the poems present memories full of wonder and reverent attention to details of landscape, as well as awareness of connectedness to a historic and prehistoric past. The frequent references to the ancient turtle inhabiting the now-dry pond, for example, offer both an image of patient endurance and survival and an allusion to the great tortoise that, in many American Indian mythologies, supports the world on its back. The title poem, "Calling Myself Home," weaves these themes together in its imaginative re-creation of "old women/ who lived on amber" and danced to the rattles they created of turtle shell and pebble. The speaker goes on to express an identity between herself, her people, and the ancient ones: "we are plodding creatures/ like the turtle." Such an affinity between people—especially women—and their land creates great strength. The generations of women forebears the author celebrates become part of the strength of the earth itself. Paradoxically, the speaker ends the poem on a note of farewell, stating that she has come to say good-bye, yet the substance of the poem indicates that the speaker, like the turtle, will carry her "home" with her always.

The second section of *Calling Myself Home* includes more poems meditating on Hogan's personal and family experience and also moves to larger themes of her heritage as a Chickasaw and as an American Indian woman. The section's title poem, "Heritage," alludes specifically to events she has elsewhere described as happening to her great-grandparents and other relatives: a plague of grasshoppers that destroyed her great-grandfather's farm in Nebraska, her uncle who carved delicate wood and bone objects and passed on traditional Chickasaw lore, her silent grandfather, and the counsel and practice of her grandmother. She alludes to secret wisdom, suppressed knowledge, and the sense, again, of "never having a home."

Other poems in *Calling Myself Home* celebrate metamorphosis and transformation, pervasive themes and modes of writing throughout Hogan's work. "The River Calls Them" offers close observation of the metamorphosis of tadpoles into frogs. In "Man in the Moon," the speaker identifies with the mutating phases of the moon, now emaciated and nearly invisible, now fat with a house that will "fill up with silver." In "Rain" metamorphosis becomes method as well as theme, as rainfall is portrayed as fish falling from the sky, while the actual fish revivified by the rain feed the exuberant children. In "Vapor Cave" the theme of metamorphosis extends to the speaker's reach beyond cultural past and identification with the earth itself. The vapor cave is a womblike hollow, both erotically steamy and innocently purifying; the speaker enters to be cleansed and restored and finds herself transmuting: "Legs and arms lose themselves/ lose their light boundaries of skin." The poem echoes the meditation in "Calling Myself Home" on women's bones transmuted into the calcified, tortoiselike skeleton of the earth itself.

Hogan's next major collection, *Eclipse*, comprises almost twice as many poems as *Calling Myself Home* and moves outward from the earlier book's grounding in personal memory and family history to embrace wider philosophical issues and topical concerns. *Eclipse* contains the poems published separately earlier in *Daughters, I Love You*, plus two sections of poems on animals ("Landscape of Animals" and "Small Animals at Night"), as well as poems grouped under the section titles "Who Will Speak?," "Land of Exile," and "Morning's Dance."

The first section groups poems affirming a sense of affinity and continuity with the natural world. Sometimes this affinity has the character of a spiritual, almost mystical union, as in these lines from "Landscape of Animals": "the birds/ fly through me/ a breath apart." Another poem, "Ruins," wonderfully evokes the atmosphere of vanished life within ruins of ancient peoples of the American Southwest: "the bare songs of a hundred flutes" are opened "out of stone/ to let themselves go/ with the wind." Another poem in this section, "Oil," reminds the reader of the fragility of the natural world: "The earth is wounded/ and will not heal." The last two sections of the book, "Small Animals at Night" and "Land of Exile," continue with poems on the theme of the continuity and interdependence the speaker perceives among herself, all human life, and the lives of animals.

In *Daughters, I Love You*, Hogan comes to grips with the nuclear menace and with historical and imminent guilt, fear, and danger. Most of the poems in this section allude to the atomic bombing of Japan, one focuses on an accident at an atomic reactor in Idaho, and at least one grew directly out of the experience of a peace encampment to protest the presence of nuclear missiles and bombs in the sacred Black Hills of South Dakota ("Black Hills Survival Gathering, 1980"). While they might loosely be categorized as poems of protest, the works in *Daughters, I Love You* are strongly unified in their underlying spiritual awareness, which Hogan sees as the most significant response she can make to the pure destructiveness represented by the dreams of power and poison with "a prayer that enters a house" to protect "the sleeping men and the gentle work/ of women."

The five poems grouped under the title "Who Will Speak?" explore the history of American Indian peoples in the United States. "A Place for the Eagle" evokes a sense of the ancient oral traditions, showing creation as the joint work of animal and spirit shapers. In "Stone Dwellers," the speaker gazes at a museum display of historic and prehistoric artifacts, reconstructing in her contemplation the vanished life of the people on the earth. Family history, including the astounding injustice and hardship of the removal of the five southern nations from their homelands in the South to the Oklahoma Indian Territory, is re-created in "Houses."

Seeing Through the Sun collects some fifty new poems grouped in four sections, entitled "Seeing Through the Sun," "Territory of Night," "Daughters Sleeping," and "Wall Songs." The third section echoes and continues themes opened in the earlier *Daughters, I Love You*, but focuses on a more personal vision of motherhood, moving at times into myth. "Tiva's Tapestry: La Llorona" is dedicated to a friend of the poet; the poem calls on the Mexican legend of La Llorona, the Weeping Woman, who is said to walk neighborhoods at dusk, weeping for her children whom she has killed, and seeking to kidnap replacements. The voice in the poem speaks of the sewing or embroidering of a picture that suggests the tragic mother ("She comes dragging/ the dark river/ a ghost on fire"), who moves into a figure of cosmic dimension: "on the awful tapestry of sky/ just one of the mothers/ among the downward circling stars."

The range of tone as well as subject matter expands in *Seeing Through the Sun*, "Death, Etc." offers a brittle, tightly rendered dialogue full of witty ambiguity: The speaker characterizes Death as a "Latin lover" who calls her "Señorita" and invites her to dance; she responds to his erotic advances by admonishing that "I am a taxpayer,/ I tell him,/ you can't do that to me." Other poems in the section titled "Territory of Night" move toward more outspoken erotic themes. A few of these, such as "Linden Tree," are tightly constructed, almost haikulike in their compression.

Savings, Hogan's next collection of poems, continues and expands themes initiated in the earlier works and provides a perspective on the development of the poet's work in the ten years since the publication of her first collection. The poems in *Savings* tend often to be more discursive than the tightly formulated associations of images in *Calling Myself Home*; many are longer, and there is some experimentation with form, as in the loose unrhymed couplets of "The New Apartment: Minneapolis."

Hogan's thematic preoccupations move from the sense of hardship endured and overcome in her personal, family, and tribal history to wider consideration of global issues of justice, care, and responsibility. The poems in *Savings* reach out from Chickasaw history and the Oklahoma landscape to embrace allusions to major contemporary injustices. Abuse of women, alcoholism, class hostility, the Holocaust, refugees from oppressive regimes, undocumented immigrants, poverty, and bigotry are all mentioned. The method in these poems differs somewhat from the focused topicality of the texts in *Daughters, I Love You*. In the earlier book, the poet's strategy is to weave related images around a central theme; for example, in "Black Hills Survival Gathering, 1980," the image and feeling of sunrise is collated with historical memory of Hiroshima, the presence of a Buddhist monk protesting nuclear war, and the appearance of a bomber flying overhead. The method in *Savings*, by contrast, is often both more discursive and more allusive. In "The Other Voices" the speaker attempts to come to terms with an overpowering evil by contrasting unspecified refugees fleeing a police state with the commonplace, unthreatening lives of domestic animals such as chickens and horses. In "Workday," a speaker meditates through a workday—going to work, sitting in a meeting, riding the bus—on torture and mutilation happening elsewhere in the world, past losses of children, and pervasive poverty and drudgery.

Hogan's development as a poet shows continuing commitment to certain ethical and emotional themes: problems of justice and injustice, the beauty and significance of the lives of ordinary people, strong bonds of family love, and a nurturing care for the natural world. The poet's method moves from very tightly structured, imagistic lyrics, focused in personal expression and feeling, outward to embrace issues wider in a geopolitical or ideological sense, though not in the moral or ethical dimension; her concerns become less immediately personal, at times, and more abstractly principled. The basic formula of the poems remains invariable: very brief to moderate length, first-person, free verse lyrics. The imagistic intensity of the earlier lyrics frequently gives way in later poems to more discursive expression, looser in construction and more focused in impact.

Other major works

NOVEL: *Mean Spirit*, 1990.
SHORT FICTION: *That Horse*, 1984.
PLAY: *A Piece of Moon*, 1981.
ANTHOLOGY: *The Stories We Hold Secret: Tales of Women's Spiritual Development*, 1987 (with Carol Bruchac and Judith McDaniel).

Bibliography

Allen, Paula Gunn. *The Sacred Hoop: Recovering the Feminine in American Indian Traditions*. Boston: Beacon Press, 1986.

Bruchac, Joseph. *Survival This Way: Interviews with American Indian Poets*. Tucson: University of Arizona Press, 1987.

Crawford, John, William Balassi, and Annie O. Eysturoy. *This Is About Vision: Interviews with Southwestern Writers*. Albuquerque: University of New Mexico Press, 1990.

Jaskoski, Helen. Review of *Calling Myself Home. SAIL: Studies in American Indian Literatures* 6, no. 1 (1986): 9-10.

SUSAN HOWE

Born: Boston, Massachusetts; June 10, 1937

Principal poetry

Hinge Picture, 1974; *The Western Borders*, 1976; *Secret History of the Dividing Line*, 1978; *Cabbage Gardens*, 1979; *The Liberties*, 1980; *Pythagorean Silence*, 1982; *Defenestration of Prague*, 1983; *Articulation of Sound Forms in Time*, 1987; *A Bibliography of the King's Book: Or, Eikon Basilike*, 1989; *The Europe of Trusts*, 1990; *Singularities*, 1990; *The Nonconformist's Memorial*, 1993.

Other literary forms

Susan Howe has also published unconventional literary criticism: *My Emily Dickinson* (1985), a book-length consideration of Dickinson's work, and *The Birth-mark: Unsettling the Wilderness in American Literary History* (1993). Those books are central to an understanding of Howe's oeuvre.

Achievements

In the years since she began to publish her poetry, Howe has established herself as a poet of profound engagement with the problematic of Being in the era she confronts. Her work also addresses the meaning of being American and being a woman in order to strip away obsolete ideas concerning both "America" and "Woman," the better to discover the realities of these conditions in the present.

Because her poetry is engendered both by a close attention to the minims of language and by a constant examination of the ground from which the language stems, Howe has come into association with the group known as the Language Realists, publishing in the magazines of that movement as well as in several anthologies predominantly or wholly of Language Realism: *The L=A=N=G=U=A=G=E Book* (1984), *21 + 1 American Poets Today* (a bilingual edition, 1986), *In the American Tree* (1986), and *Language Poetry* (1987).

Howe has twice received the American Book Award of the Before Columbus Foundation, in 1982 for *Pythagorean Silence* and again in 1985 for *My Emily Dickinson*. In 1980, she received a Pushcart Prize for "The Art of Literary Publishing," an interview she conducted with James Laughlin; in 1986, she was awarded a Writer's Fellowship by the New York State Arts Council; in 1989, she received a second Pushcart Prize. In 1985, she was writer-in-residence at New College in San Francisco.

Biography

Susan Howe was born in Boston, Massachusetts, on June 10, 1937. With the exception of a relatively brief period in Buffalo, New York, her childhood and adolescence were spent in Boston and Cambridge, where she attended the Beaver Country Day School, from which she was graduated in 1955. Also in 1955, she began a year's study at the Gate Theater, Dublin, Ireland, acting and designing sets. From 1957 to 1961, she attended the Museum School of Fine Arts in Boston. She next took up residence in New York City, working as a painter and exhibiting her paintings at a number of galleries, including the Kornblee. In 1961, she married Harvey Quayt-man, and their daughter Rebecca was born that same year. When her marriage ended in 1966, Howe began living with the sculptor David von Schlegell, and in 1967, their son Mark was born. The couple was married in 1976.

From 1975 to 1980, she produced the program *Poetry* for WBAI, New York City's Pacifica Radio station. In 1988-1989, she was Butler Fellow at the State University of New York, Buffalo, where she stayed on to teach; in 1990-1991, she was a visiting professor of writing at Temple University in Philadelphia.

Analysis

Susan Howe's poetry challenges habitual assumptions on many levels, but the level the reader is most likely to notice first is the syntactic; what Howe says of Dickinson can with equal force be applied to herself: "In prose and poetry she explored the implications of breaking the law just short of breaking off communication with a reader." Generally, Howe's poems make much use of the page, where the white space is allowed to interrupt the sequence of print, so that a variety of statements may be derived from relatively few phrases, and the overall thrust of the syntax is continually thwarted. Denied easy access to an overarching meaning, the reader must work with smaller units (phrase, line, couplet) and can only gradually constitute the meaning of the whole. This process parallels the approach to Being advocated both explicitly and implicitly in Howe's work. The presumptions of categorical value which modern Western culture persists in advocating are resisted at every turn, for Howe sees (and reveals) just how damaging such presumptions and categories can be.

Such a project inevitably must challenge received notions of the poetic. It is for this reason that traditional forms are absent from Howe's poetry. Such forms by their very ease of recognition would defeat her purpose. For Howe, the question then becomes, What portion of the inherited conceptions of beauty, truth, and the good ought to be retained (as inherent to the art of poetry), and what portion uprooted and discarded (as inimical to a faithful representation of the present)? Language, derived from Being, comes then to govern Being; the reader projects back onto the world expectations previously drawn therefrom. Yet the world is always in process, always changing, always endangering one's assumptions and rendering them obsolete. It is therefore to language itself, argues Howe, that the poet ought to draw attention; the reader must be kept aware of the ways in which language governs not only one's concepts but also one's perceptions.

"The lyric poet," Howe writes in *My Emily Dickinson*, "reads a past that is a huge imagination of one form," and while the labor of precursors in one sense is enormously beneficial, providing as it does countless elucidations of Being, in another sense it becomes a mighty burden, because of the irresistible nature of preexisting formulations, whether to the poet or to her audience, formulations that nevertheless demand to be resisted if one is to come to a personal definition of one's epoch. Howe, then,

in her determination to "make it new," aligns herself with such high modernists as Ezra Pound, Gertrude Stein, and William Carlos Williams. She must also keep her project distinct from theirs: Howe is among those who see the poet's calling as a demand to make forms consonant with her own day.

The analysis provided during the 1960's and 1970's of dominant patriarchal elements in Western society is one example of this altered ideology to which Howe would be responsible. *The Liberties* is a book of poetry whose sufficient cause is the largely masculine-engendered version of Esther Johnson, known as Jonathan Swift's Stella. Howe would liberate from this patriarchal version another picture of this historical personage. She begins by providing a prose sketch, "Fragments of a Liquidation," whose import can best be summarized by repeating the last two sentences of its first paragraph: "Jonathan Swift, who gave allegorical nicknames to the women he was romantically involved with, called her 'Stella.' By that name she was known to their close friends, and by that name she is known to history." The poems that follow spring from Howe's desire to liberate Esther from Stella and, by extension, Howe's own self from equally pernicious assumptions. In practice, it is not always possible to distinguish from each other these twin liberations, and so a composite woman, struggling to be freed from the roles provided for her by men and a male-dominated history, becomes the shadow heroine of Howe's pages.

If the method is to question in this manner, and to reconstitute a truer history, the technique that Howe develops and that is consonant with her method is to call meaning into question not only at the level of the sentence (these poems are so severely underpunctuated that the reader usually must decide the limits of the sentence) but also at the level of the phrase or even the word. One poem, for example, begins "and/ she/ had a man's dress mad/ e/ though her feet ble/ d/ skimming the surf/ ace," a series of ruptures which militates against any "skimming of the surface" on the reader's part.

In a subsequent section of *The Liberties*, Howe extends her attention to William Shakespeare's Cordelia, surely attractive to Howe for her refusal to accede to the patriarchal demand to accord with the picture of herself her father wished to perpetuate. This section, titled "White Foolscap," puns on "fool's cap" and thus reminds the reader that Cordelia is a dramatic character whose only "real" context is the play *King Lear*, complete with Fool. Yet the title also refers to the blank page that the writer addresses: metaphorically, the nothingness into which she throws herself, composing. In the next section, "God's Spies," a playlet, Stella and Cordelia meet, together with the ghost of Jonathan Swift; the women are dressed as boys in their early teens. The action is fragmented, the dialogue sparse, truncated, enigmatic. The longest speech is Stella's, a poem the historical Stella wrote, very much in the manner of Swift: When it is done, Stella shoots herself. To so sink herself in the style of another, Howe is saying, is tantamount to suicide.

The third and final section of *The Liberties*, "Formation of a Separatist, I," is prospective, as the previous sections were retrospective. Howe has composed these poems of isolated words—single words with white space between each, arranged in blocks—and celebrates their individual tones, rather than their syntactic possibilities. There are, however, other poems in this section that depend on phrases and sentences; in fact, the book ends with these lines: "Tear pages from a calendar/ scatter them into sunshine and snow." The nightmare of history disperses into a present which is subject to elements in their own nature.

Pythagorean Silence is also divided into three sections: The first, "Pearl Harbor," opens with a poem entitled "Buffalo, 12.7.41" and the announcement of the cataclysm that unleashed such terrible forces upon the second half of the century. A character in Howe's poem, who is called TALKATIVE, "says we are all in Hell": Howe suggests that a truer use of language can be found in biblical Rachel's inconsolable cry: "her cry/ silences/ whole/ vocabularies/ of *names*/ for *things*." The problem with the declaration that "we are all in Hell" arises from the clichéd nature of the phrase, which works against an experience of its meaning. Howe's "negative poetry" would undo prior namings where these have become impenetrably familiar. This is why she nudges her poems along through puns: In the pun, other meanings break through the intended singularity of usage, the law of logical syntax is transgressed by the play of several possibilities.

In section 2, the title section of *Pythagorean Silence*, the initial poem opens with a pun arising from the fracturing of a single word: "He plodded away through drifts of i/ ce." "Drifts of i" suggests the accumulation of personal, even egocentric, experience, with "drifts" implying the contingent nature of such accumulations, ac-

crued as "the wind listeth." The line's extension equates "i" with "ice"—a frozen lump of such subjectivity. Yet Pythagoras broke through the amassed subjectivity of his experience to accomplish, with his theorem, the objective; to the extent that he is the hero of this sequence and this book, Howe implicitly urges emulation of his persistence. The "silence" of her title refers to the silence maintained by initiates of the Pythagorean rites prior to their more active worship, a form of meditation. Yet if Pythagoras is the hero in her book, the reader must consider the possibility that he is also the villain, capable of leading the unsuspecting into frozen wastes of abstruse speculation. This afterthought does not annul the previous reading, but rather coexists with it. Howe's greatest clarity lies in her ability to imply and exemplify the insupportable partiality of any single answer.

Single answers, like universal concepts, are acts of enclosure, a delimiting of the possible; historically, they have been imposed by men upon women and children, by imperialists upon territories hitherto regarded as "unknown," terra incognita, full of hidden terrors—even as women and children for the dominant male. It has become part of the burden of Howe's poetry to confront readers with modes of capture and "unfreedom" of which they may have been unaware. Her method is to locate the influence of the past on the present in documents—narratives of escape and capture, for example—and in the persistence of past patterns into the conduct of the present. In this second endeavor, she may take herself as an instance, although her work never resembles autobiography in any of its conventional senses. When all is said and done, however, a poem itself is a form of enclosure, even as the choice of a place of one's own, an affirmation of belonging (as in Howe's case, being a New Englander). Such acceptance of limitation can be a source of strength, succor, and enabling. Even though Howe admits that all power is unstable, she does not deny its existence. There is a push-pull in her poetry, then, between the need for limits and a suspicion of them.

Inescapably, Howe is, by birth and gender, both American and a woman, subject to the assumptions of those categories, and at once in revolt against such predications and eager to discover their underlying realities. In *My Emily Dickinson*, she would rescue the Dickinson of her particular vision from the several inadequate characterizations which prevent, to Howe's view, a full experience of the poetry. To this end, Howe, in a work that is cousin to both William Carlos Williams' *In the Ameri-*

can Grain (1925) and Charles Olson's *Call Me Ishmael* (1947), rereads the contribution of figures vital to Dickinson's production: Elizabeth Barrett Browning and Robert Browning, James Fenimore Cooper, Emily Brontë, Charles Dickens, Jonathan Edwards, Ralph Waldo Emerson, Cotton Mather, Mary Rowlandson, William Shakespeare, Henry David Thoreau, and Thomas Wentworth Higginson. Howe finds that, approached from this rich assortment of angles, Dickinson's poetry yields a wealth of information not only about Being in general but also about being American and being a woman and about how a poetry grows consanguineously. Howe is severe with certain feminist critics who, while lauding Dickinson, laud a Dickinson who is essentially the creation of patriarchal vision, swallowing whole this distortion. Toward the end of *My Emily Dickinson*, Howe observes: "Victorian scientists, philosophers, historians, intellectuals, poets, like most contemporary feminist literary critics—eager to discuss the shattering of all hierarchies of Being—didn't want the form they discussed this in to be shattering." Howe's poetic practice is the negation of this widespread and persistent error.

Other major works

NONFICTION: *Religious Literature of the West*, 1971 (with John Raymond Whitney); *My Emily Dickinson*, 1985; *The Birth-Mark: Unsettling the Wilderness in American Literary History*, 1993.

Bibliography

Campbell, Bruce. "Ring of Bodies/Sphere of Sound." *The Difficulties* 3, no. 2 (1989).

Chamberlain, Lori. Review of *Defenestration of Prague*, by Susan Howe. *Sulfur* 9 (1984).

DuPlessis, Rachel Blau. " 'Whowe' On Susan Howe." In *The Pink Guitar*. New York: Routledge, Chapman & Hall, 1990.

O'Brien, Geoffrey. "The Way We Word." *The Village Voice Literary Supplement*, December, 1990.

Perloff, Marjorie. *Radical Artifice: Writing Poetry in the Age of Media*. Chicago: University of Chicago Press, 1992.

Quartermain, Peter. *Disjunctive Poetics: From Gertrude Stein and Louis Zukofsky to Susan Howe*. New York: Cambridge University Press, 1992.

Reinfeld, Linda. *Language Poetry: Writing as Rescue*. Baton Rouge: Louisiana State University Press, 1992.

ZORA NEALE HURSTON

Born: Eatonville, Florida; January 7, 1891   **Died:** Fort Pierce, Florida; January 28, 1960

Principal long fiction

Jonah's Gourd Vine, 1934; *Their Eyes Were Watching God*, 1937; *Moses, Man of the Mountain*, 1939; *Seraph on the Suwanee*, 1948.

Other literary forms

In addition to her four novels, Zora Neale Hurston produced two collections of folklore, *Mules and Men* (1935) and *Tell My Horse* (1938), and an autobiography, *Dust Tracks on a Road* (1942). Hurston also published plays, short stories, and essays in anthologies and in magazines as diverse as *Opportunity*, the *Journal of Negro History*, the *Saturday Evening Post*, the *Journal of American Folklore*, and the *American Legion Magazine*. Finally, she wrote several articles and reviews for such newspapers as the *New York Herald Tribune* and the *Pittsburgh Courier*. Hurston's major works have only recently been reissued. Some of her essays and stories have also been collected and reprinted. Although the anthologies *I Love Myself When I Am Laughing . . .* (1979) and *The Sanctified Church* (1981) have helped to bring her writing back into critical focus, some of her works are still not readily available, and her numerous unpublished manuscripts can only be seen at university archives and the Library of Congress.

Achievements

Hurston was the best and most prolific black woman writer of the 1930's. All of her novels were highly praised. Even so, Hurston never made more than one thousand dollars in royalties on even her most successful works, and when she died in 1960, she was penniless and forgotten. Hurston's career testifies to the difficulties of a black woman writing for a mainstream white audience whose appreciation was usually superficial and racist and for a black audience whose responses to her work were, of necessity, highly politicized.

Hurston achieved recognition at a time when, as Langston Hughes declared, "the Negro was in vogue." The Harlem Renaissance, the black literary and cultural movement of the 1920's, created an interracial audience for her stories and plays. Enthusiasm for her work extended through the 1930's, although that decade also marked the beginning of critical attacks. Hurston did not portray blacks as victims, stunted by a racist society. Such a view, she believed, implies that black life is only a defensive reaction to white racism. Black and left-wing critics, however, complained that her unwillingness to represent the oppression of blacks and her focus, instead, on an autonomous, unresentful black folk culture served to perpetuate minstrel stereotypes and thus fueled white racism. The radical, racial protest literature of Richard Wright, one of Hurston's strongest critics, became the model for black literature in the 1940's, and publishers on the lookout for protest works showed less and less interest in Hurston's manuscripts. Yet, when she did speak out against American racism and imperialism, her work was often censored. Her autobiography, published in 1942, as well as a number of her stories and articles were tailored by editors to please white audiences. Caught between the attacks of black critics and the censorship of the white publishing industry, Hurston floundered, struggling through the 1940's and 1950's to find other subjects. She largely dropped out of public view in the 1950's, though she continued to publish magazine and newspaper articles.

The African American and feminist political and cultural movements of the 1960's and 1970's have provided the impetus for Hurston's recent rediscovery. The publication of Robert Hemenway's excellent book, *Zora Neale Hurston: A Literary Biography* (1977) and the reissue of her novels, her autobiography, and her folklore collections seem at last to promise the sustained critical recognition Hurston deserves.

Biography

Zora Neale Hurston was born on January 7, 1891 (although she later listed the year of her birth as 1901). Her family lived in the all-black Florida town of Eatonville, in an eight-room house with a five-acre garden. Her father, the Reverend John Hurston, mayor of Eatonville for three terms and moderator of the South Florida Baptist Association, wanted to temper his daughter's high spirits, but her intelligent and forceful mother, Lucy Potts Hurston, encouraged her to "jump at de sun." When Hurston was about nine, her mother died. That event and her father's rapid remarriage to a woman his daughter did not like prematurely ended Hurston's childhood. In the next few years, she lived only intermittently at home, spending some time at a school in Jacksonville and some time with relatives. Her father withdrew all financial support during this period, forcing her to commence what was to be a lifelong struggle to make her own living.

When Hurston was fourteen, she took a job as a wardrobe girl to a repertory company touring the South. Hurston left the troupe in Baltimore eighteen months later and finished high school there at Morgan Academy. She went on to study part-time at Howard University in 1918, taking jobs as a manicurist, a waitress, and a maid in order to support herself. At Howard, her literary talents began to emerge. She was admitted to a campus literary club, formed by Alain Locke, a Howard professor and one of the forces behind the Harlem Renaissance. Locke brought Hurston to the attention of Charles S. Johnson, another key promoter of the Harlem Renaissance. Editor of *Opportunity: A Journal of Negro Life*, he published one of her stories and encouraged her to enter the literary contest sponsored by his magazine.

With several manuscripts but little money, Hurston moved to New York City in 1925, hoping to make a career of her writing. Her success in that year's *Opportunity* contest—she received prizes for a play and a story—won her the patronage of Fanny Hurst and a scholarship to complete her education at Barnard College. She studied anthropology there under Franz Boas, leading a seemingly schizophrenic life in the next two years as an eccentric, iconoclastic artist of the Harlem Renaissance on the one hand and a budding, scholarly social scientist on the other.

The common ground linking these seemingly disparate parts of Hurston's life was her interest in black folk culture. Beginning in 1927 and extending through the 1930's, she made several trips to collect black folklore in the South and in the Bahamas, Haiti, and Jamaica. Collecting trips were costly, however, as was the time to write up their results. Charlotte Osgood Mason, a wealthy, domineering white patron to a number of African American artists, supported some of that work, as did the Association for the Study of Negro Life and History and the Guggenheim Foundation. Hurston also worked intermittently during the 1930's as a drama teacher at Bethune Cookman College in Florida and at North Carolina College, as a drama coach for the WPA Federal Theatre Project in New York, and as an editor for the Federal Writer's Project in Florida.

Mules and Men and several scholarly and popular articles on folklore were the products of Hurston's collecting trips in the late 1920's and early 1930's. In 1938, she published *Tell My Horse*, the result of trips to Haiti and Jamaica to study hoodoo. As a creative writer, Hurston devised other outlets for her folk materials. Her plays, short stories, and three of her novels, *Jonah's Gourd Vine*, *Their Eyes Were Watching God*, and *Moses, Man of the Mountain*, make use of folklore. She also presented folk materials in theatrical revues, but even though the productions were enthusiastically received, she could never generate enough backing to finance commercially successful long-term showings.

Hurston's intense interest in black folklore prevented her from sustaining either of her two marriages. She could not reconcile the competing claims of love and work. She married Herbert Sheen, a medical student, in 1927 but separated from him a few months later. They were divorced in 1931. She married Albert Price III in 1939, and they too parted less than a year later. Other romantic relationships ended for the same reason.

In the 1940's, Hurston lost her enthusiasm for writing about black folk culture. She wrote her autobiography and in 1948 published her last novel *Seraph on the Suwanee*, a work which turns away from black folk culture entirely. The last decade of her life took a downward turn. Falsely accused of committing sodomy with a young boy, Hurston, depressed, dropped out of public view. Through the 1950's, she lived in Florida, struggling for economic survival. She barely managed to support herself by writing newspaper and magazine articles, many of which expressed her increasing political conservatism, and by working as a maid, a substitute teacher, and a librarian. In 1959, she suffered a stroke. She died on January 28, 1960.

Analysis

For much of her career, Zora Neale Hurston was dedicated to the presentation of black folk culture. She introduced readers to hoodoo, folktales, lying contests, spirituals, the blues, sermons, children's games, riddles, playing the dozens, and, in general, a highly metaphoric folk idiom. Although she represented black folk culture in several genres, Hurston was drawn to the novel form because it could convey folklore as communal behavior. Hurston knew that much of the unconscious artistry of folklore appears in the gestures and tones in which it is expressed and that it gains much of its meaning in performance. Even *Mules and Men* "novelizes" what could have been an anthology of disconnected folk materials. By inventing a narrator who witnesses, even participates in the performance of folk traditions, she combated the inevitable distortion of an oral culture by its textual documentation.

Hurston's motives for presenting black folklore were, in part, political. She wanted to refute contemporary claims that African Americans lacked a distinct culture of their own. Her novels depict the unconscious creativity of the African American proletariat, or folk. Yet Hurston also had a personal, psychological motive. She drew the folk materials for her novels from the rural, Southern black life she knew as a child and subsequently recorded in folklore collecting trips in the late 1920's and 1930's. She had fond memories of her childhood in the all-black town of Eatonville, where she did not experience poverty or racism. It was also there that she had a close relationship with and a strong advocate in her mother. In representing the rich culture of black rural Southerners, she was also evoking a happier personal past.

Although the witnessing narrator provided Hurston with the means to dramatize folklore, she also needed meaningful fictional contexts for its presentation. Her novels are a series of attempts to develop such contexts. Initially, she maintained the Southern rural setting for black folk traditions. In her first two novels, *Jonah's Gourd Vine* and *Their Eyes Were Watching God*, she re-created Eatonville and neighboring Florida towns. With her third novel, however, *Moses, Man of the Mountain*, Hurston turned in a new direction, leaving the Eatonville milieu behind. The novel retells the biblical story of Moses via the folk idiom and traditions of Southern rural blacks. Hurston leaves much of the plot of the biblical story intact—Moses does lead the He-

brews out of Egypt—but, for example, she shows Moses to be a great hoodoo doctor as well as a leader and lawgiver. In effect, Hurston simulated the creative processes of folk culture, transforming the story of Moses for modern African Americans just as slaves had adapted biblical stories in spirituals.

Seraph on the Suwanee, Hurston's last novel, marks another dramatic shift in her writing. With this novel, however, she did not create a new context for the representation of folk culture. Rather, she turned away from the effort to present black folklore. *Seraph on the Suwanee* is set in the rural South, but its central characters are white. Hurston apparently wanted to prove that she could write about whites as well as blacks, a desire that surfaced, no doubt, in response to the criticism and disinterest her work increasingly faced in the 1940's. Yet, even when writing of upwardly mobile Southern "crackers," Hurston could not entirely leave her previous mission behind. Her white characters, perhaps unintentionally, often use the black folk idiom.

Although Hurston's novels, with the exception of the last, create contexts or develop other strategies for the presentation of folklore, they are not simply showcases for folk traditions; black folk culture defines the novels' themes. The most interesting of these thematic renderings appear in Hurston's first two novels. Hurston knew that black folk culture was composed of brilliant adaptations of African culture to American life. She admired the ingenuity of these adaptations but worried about their preservation. Would a sterile, materialistic white world ultimately absorb blacks, destroying the folk culture they had developed? Her first two novels demonstrate the disturbing influence of white America on black folkways.

Jonah's Gourd Vine, Hurston's first novel, portrays the tragic experience of a black preacher caught between black cultural values and the values imposed by his white-influenced church. The novel charts the life of John Pearson, laborer, foreman, and carpenter, who discovers that he has an extraordinary talent for preaching. With his linguistic skills and his wife Lucy's wise counsel, he becomes pastor of the large church Zion Hope and ultimately moderator of a Florida Baptist convention. His sexual promiscuity, however, eventually destroys his marriage and his career. In its presentation of folklore and its complex representation of cultural conflict, *Jonah's Gourd Vine* is a brilliant first novel, although

Hurston does not always make her argument sufficiently clear. The novel lacks a consistent point of view. It was not until she wrote her next novel, *Their Eyes Were Watching God*, that Hurston learned to control point of view and presented a solution to the problem of white influences on black culture.

The life of Janie Crawford, the heroine of *Their Eyes Were Watching God*, is shaped by bourgeois values—white in origin. She finds love and self-identity only by rejecting that life and becoming a wholehearted participant in black folk culture. Her grandmother directs Janie's entrance into adulthood. Born into slavery, the older woman hopes to find protection and materialistic comforts for Janie in a marriage to the property-owning Logan Killicks. Janie, who has grown up in a different generation, does not share her grandmother's values. When she finds she cannot love her husband, she runs off with Jody Stark, who is on his way to Eatonville, where he hopes to become a "big voice," an appropriate phrase for life in a community which highly values verbal ability. Jody becomes that "big voice" as mayor of the town, owner of the general store, and head of the post office. Stark lives both a bourgeois and a folk life in Eatonville. He constructs a big house—the kind white people have—but he wanders out to the porch of the general store whenever he wants to enjoy the perpetual storytelling that takes place there. Even though Janie has demonstrated a talent for oratory, however, he will not let her join these sessions or participate in the mock funeral for a mule which has become a popular character in the townspeople's stories. For several years, Janie has no voice in the community or in her private life. Her life begins to seem unreal. One day, after Stark insults her in front of customers in the store, however, she speaks out and insults his manhood. The insult causes an irreconcilable break between them.

After Jody's death, Janie is courted by Tea Cake Woods, a laborer with little money. Though many of her neighbors disapprove of the match, Janie marries him. Marriage to Tea Cake lowers her social status but frees her from her submissive female role, from her shadow existence. Refusing to use her money, Tea Cake takes her down to the Everglades, where they become migrant workers. She picks beans with him in the fields, and he helps her prepare their dinners. With Tea Cake, she also enters into the folk culture of the Everglades, and that more than anything else enables her to shed her former submissive identity. Workers show up at their house every night to sing, dance, gamble, and, above all, to talk, like the folks in Eatonville on the front porch of the general store. Janie learns how to tell "big stories" from listening to the others, and she is encouraged to do so.

This happy phase of Janie's life ends tragically as she and Tea Cake attempt to escape a hurricane and the ensuing flood. Tea Cake saves Janie from drowning but, in the process, is bitten by a rabid dog. Sick and crazed, he tries to shoot Janie. She is forced to kill him in self-defense. Not everything she has gained during her relationship with Tea Cake, however, dies with him. The strong self-identity she has achieved while living in the Everglades enables her to withstand the unjust resentment of their black friends as well as her trial for murder in a white court. Most important, she is able to endure her own loss and returns to Eatonville, self-reliant and wise. Tea Cake, she knows, will live on in her thoughts and feelings—and in her words. She tells her story to her friend Pheoby—that storytelling event frames the novel—and allows Pheoby to bring it to the other members of the community. As the story enters the community's oral culture, it will influence it. Indeed, as the novel closes, Janie's story has already affected Pheoby. "Ah done growed ten feet higher from jus' listenin' tuh you," she tells Janie: "Ah ain't satisfied wid mahself no mo'."

In her novels, Hurston did not represent the oppression of blacks because she refused to view African American life as impoverished. If she would not focus on white racism, however, her novels do oppose white culture. In *Their Eyes Were Watching God*, Janie does not find happiness until she gives up a life governed by white values and enters into the verbal ceremonies of black folk culture. Loving celebrations of a separate black folklife were Hurston's effective political weapon; racial pride was one of her great gifts to American literature.

Other major works

SHORT FICTION: *Spunk: The Selected Short Stories of Zora Neale Hurston*, 1985.
NONFICTION: *Mules and Men*, 1935; *Tell My Horse*, 1938; *Dust Tracks on a Road*, 1942; *The Sanctified Church*, 1981.

MISCELLANEOUS: *I Love Myself When I Am Laughing . . . and Then Again When I Am Looking Mean and Impressive: A Zora Neale Hurston Reader*, 1979.

Bibliography

Gates, Henry Louis, Jr. *The Signifying Monkey: A Theory of Afro-American Literary Criticism.* New York: Oxford University Press, 1988.
Hemenway, Robert. *Zora Neale Hurston.* Urbana: University of Illinois Press, 1977.
Howard, Lillie P. *Zora Neale Hurston.* Boston: Twayne, 1980.
Johnson, Barbara. *A World of Difference.* Baltimore: The Johns Hopkins University Press, 1987.
Washington, Mary Helen. *Invented Lives: Narratives of Black Women, 1860-1960.* Garden City, N.Y.: Anchor Press, 1987.

SHIRLEY JACKSON

Born: San Francisco, California; December 14, 1919   **Died:** North Bennington, Vermont; August 8, 1965

Principal short fiction

The Lottery: Or, The Adventures of James Harris, 1949; *Come Along with Me*, 1968 (Stanley Edgar Hyman, editor).

Other literary forms

Shirley Jackson's dozen published books include novels, humorous fictionalized autobiographies, and children's books. Many of her stories, essays, and public speeches remain uncollected. Several works have been adapted to other media: "The Lottery" for television, *We Have Always Lived in the Castle* (1962) for stage, and *The Bird's Nest* (1954) and *The Haunting of Hill House* (1959) for the cinema.

Achievements

Jackson is probably best known for her short story "The Lottery," which was first published in the June 26, 1948, edition of *The New Yorker*. Like the majority of her works, both short stories and novels, "The Lottery" explores the darker side of the human psyche, in a manner often disturbing to the reader. In addition to using ordinary settings for extraordinary occurrences, Jackson often injects an element of the supernatural. This is seen, for example, in the story "The Visit" and in the novel *The Haunting of Hill House*. In addition, Jackson has published *Life Among the Savages* (1953), a highly humorous account of her home life. In 1961, Jackson received the Edgar Allan Poe Award for her story "Louisa, Please." She was awarded the Syracuse University Arents Pioneer Medal for Outstanding Achievement in 1965.

Biography

Shirley Jackson was born in California on December 14, 1919, and moved with her family to New York when she was sixteen. After an unsuccessful year at the University of Rochester, Jackson enrolled, at age twenty, in the University of Syracuse. This was to be the beginning of an independent life for the author, as she would finally be away from the dominating presence of her mother. At Syracuse, Jackson met Stanley Edgar Hyman, the man she would marry in 1940. Hyman achieved notoriety in his own right as a teacher, writer, and critic. The marriage between Jackson and Hyman was tumultuous in many ways but provided a stabilizing factor for Jackson. Her literary production increased markedly after the marriage and the birth of their four children. Jackson's own phobias, however, kept creeping into this successful, if odd, relationship. She was an agoraphobic and a depressive. Part of the latter affliction was contributed to by her asthma and arthritis, as well as Hyman's extramarital affair in the early 1960's. In addition, Jackson had never really been a social person—she was much too individualistic to fit into any of the polite social molds. In 1963, Jackson began to turn around psychologically. Her husband made a new commitment to the marriage and a psychiatrist began to help her work with the agoraphobia. Her writing continued to be an outlet for her. Although Jackson recovered emotionally, she never recovered physically. She was obese and a chain smoker. She died on August 8, 1965, at the age of forty-five.

Analysis

Shirley Jackson's stories seem to center on a single concern: Almost every story is about a protagonist's discovering or failing to discover or successfully ignoring an alternate way of perceiving a set of circumstances or the world. Jackson seems especially interested in how characters order their worlds and how they perceive themselves in the world. Often, a change in a character's perspective leads to anxiety, terror, neurosis, or even a loss of identity. While it is tempting to say that her main theme is the difference between appearance and reality, such a statement is misleading, for she seems to see reality as Herman Melville's Ishmael comes to see it, as a mirror of the perceiving soul. It is rarely clear that her characters discover or lose their grasp of reality; rather, they form ideas of reality that are more or less moral and more or less functional. For Jackson, reality is so complex and mysterious that one inevitably only orders part of it. A character may then discover parts that contradict a chosen order or that attract one away from the apparent order, but one can never affirm the absolute superiority of one ordering to another. In this respect, Jackson's fictional world resembles those of Stephen Crane and Ernest Hemingway. Perhaps the major differences between her fiction and theirs is that her protagonists are predominantly women; she explores some peculiarly feminine aspects of the problem of ideas of order.

Jackson's middle-class American women seem especially vulnerable to losing the security of a settled world view. Their culture provides them with idealistic dream visions of what their lives should be, and they have a peculiar leisure for contemplation and conversation imposed upon them by their dependent roles. Men in her stories seem so busy providing that they rarely look at and think about the order of things. Her career women are more like these men. In "Elizabeth" and "The Villager," the protagonists succeed, although precariously, in preserving ideas of themselves and their worlds despite the contradictory facts that seem increasingly to intrude. In these two stories, one sees a sort of emotional cannibalism in the protagonists as they attempt to preserve belief in an order that reality seems no longer disposed to sustain. Several stories show a woman's loss of an ordering dream. These divide into stories about women who experience the terror of loss of identity and those who may find a liberating and superior order in what would ordinarily be called infantile fantasy.

A closer look at three especially interesting stories reveals much about Jackson's themes and gives some indication of her technical proficiency. In "The Visit," Margaret comes to visit a school friend, Carla Rhodes, for the summer. The beautiful Rhodes estate includes a dream house with numerous fantastic rooms. The house seems not quite real; nearly every room is covered with tapestries depicting the house in different hours and seasons and there is a mysterious tower of which no one speaks. For Margaret, the house and the family are ideal, especially when Carla's brother, Paul, arrives with his friend, the Captain. This idyll lasts until the evening of Paul's departure, when Margaret discovers that Paul has been a hallucination or a ghost, for the Captain is Carla's brother and no one else has seen Paul. This revelation clarifies several mysteries that have developed, especially that of Margaret's strange visit to the tower. Paul has told Margaret that an old aunt often secludes herself in the tower. When Margaret pays her a visit, she undergoes a not frightening but certainly haunting experience with old Aunt Margaret. At the end of the story, the reader must conclude Aunt Margaret to be an apparition, that she is probably the Margaret who died for love and whose picture in mosaic appears on the floor of one room. Young Margaret has lost a phantom lover as old Margaret lost her Paul. Young Margaret realizes this at the same time that she is made aware of time's effect on the house: the age and weakness of the Rhodeses, the bitter darkness of their true son, and the physical decay of the buildings. Furthermore, she begins to doubt her own place and identity as she wonders if her visit to the house will ever end. The home of her dreaming now threatens to become an imprisoning nightmare.

In retrospect, the device by which Jackson encourages the reader to share Margaret's hallucination or haunting may seem contrived. This choice, however, seems effective because the more fully the reader shares Margaret's perceptions and the more subdued are the disturbing elements, the more fully will the reader share the shock of her awakening into nightmare. Also technically effective are the apparent connections with Poe's "The Fall of the House of Usher." Most important among these is the succession of mirror images: multiple pictures of the house, between the house and Mrs. Rhodes, among members of the family, between the two Margarets, and between the decline of the family and of the house. These connections seem deliberately chosen in part to emphasize the contrasts between Margaret and Poe's narrator. Because Margaret's response to the house is so positive, the shock of her discovery is greater by contrast. Furthermore, when she discovers this house to be like what one knows the House of Usher to be, one sees the analogy between her terror at imprisonment and that of Poe's narrator when he sees a universe unnaturally lit by a blood red moon, yet another image of the coffin lit from within. Margaret actually enters one of the dream worlds promised to American girls. Under its spell, she overlooks its flaws and forgets about time, but when the

Captain breaks the spell, pointing out signs of decay, Paul departs and Margaret becomes acutely aware of time as her nightmare begins.

Time is often the destroyer of feminine ideals in Jackson's stories because they seem to depend on a suspension of time. In "Pillar of Salt," another Margaret loses her secure world. A trip to New York City with her husband forces a new perspective on her that produces her anxiety and, finally, paranoia. It remains unclear, however, whether her paranoia is illness or a healthy reaction to an inimical environment.

The couple's first week in the city is idyllic, and the fast pace is a pleasant change from New Hampshire. At a party at the end of the first week, however, Margaret begins to feel isolated, unnoticed among strangers who behave in strange ways. She learns there is a fire in the building but is unable to persuade anyone else to leave. The fire turns out to be two buildings away, but she is the only one to heed the warning and flee the building. She comes to see this nightmarish experience as symbolic of her experience in New York and perhaps of her life as a whole. She begins to notice new details about the city: dirt, decay, speed, stifling crowds. She feels increasingly isolated and insignificant. Of this life she thinks, "She knew she was afraid to say it truly, afraid to face the knowledge that it was a voluntary neck-breaking speed, a deliberate whirling faster and faster to end in destruction." Even her friends' Long Island beach cottage shows the spreading blight: They find a severed human leg on the sand. Margaret comes to believe that her former order was illusory. Upon returning to the city, she begins to hallucinate, to see the destruction of the city in fast motion. Windows crumble. Her bed shakes. Driven from her apartment, she finds herself unable to return, paralyzed in a fast-moving, anonymous crowd on the wrong side of a mechanical and murderous river of traffic.

Margaret comes to see herself in a modern Sodom, paralyzed not because she has disobeyed God, but because she has seen in prophetic vision the truth about the city: It is impersonally intent upon destruction. The allusion of the title and her critique of city life verify her perception; however, those who do not share her vision remain capable of functioning. As in "The Visit," the internal view of Margaret encourages a close identification between reader and character that makes judgment difficult until the reader can step back; but stepping back from "Pillar of Salt" plunges the reader deeper into mystery. In both stories, the protagonist moves from dream to nightmare, but in "Pillar of Salt," the reader is much less certain that the move is to a better or more accurate view of reality.

Shirley Jackson's reputation rests primarily upon her most anthologized story, "The Lottery," Her lecture on this story (printed in *Come Along with Me*) suggests that her creation of a normal setting convinced many readers that the story was largely factual. In fact, the central problem of the story seems to be to reconcile the portrait of typical small-town life with the horrifying ritualistic killing these people carry out. Apparently incompatible ideas of order are thrust upon the reader for resolution, perhaps in order to complicate the reader's conceptions.

"The Lottery" develops by slowly raising the level of tension in the semipastoral setting until a series of carefully arranged revelations brings about a dramatic and shocking reversal. The villagers gather at mid-morning on a late June day for an annual event, the lottery, on which much excitement centers. Jackson supplies details that arouse reader curiosity: Nearly all towns have a similar lottery; it is as old as the town; it has an elaborate ritual form which has decayed over time; every adult male *must* participate; and some believe the orders of nature and of civilization depend on carrying it out correctly. The family of the man who draws the marked lot must draw again to determine the final winner. The tension built out of reader curiosity and the town's moods reverses toward the sinister when the "winner's" wife reveals that she does not want to win. Once this reversal is complete, the story moves rapidly to reveal the true nature of the lottery—to choose a victim for annual sacrifice by stoning. Jackson heightens the horror of this apparently unaccountable act with carefully chosen and placed details.

Several commentators have attempted to explain the story through reconstructing the meaning of the ritual and through carefully examining the symbols. Helen Nebeker sees the story as an allegory of "man trapped in a web spun from his own need to explain and control the incomprehensible universe around him, a need no longer answered by the web of old traditions." These attempts to move beyond the simple thriller seem justified by the details Jackson provides about the lottery. This ritual seems clearly to be a tradition of prehistoric origin, once believed essential for the welfare of the community. Even though its purpose has become obscure and its practice muddled, it continues to unify and sustain the community. Critics tend to underemphasize the apparent health and vitality of the community, perhaps feeling that this ritual essentially undercuts that impression. It is important to notice that one function of the lottery is to change the relationship between community and victim. The victim is chosen at random, killed without malice or significant protest, and lost without apparent grief. This story may be what Richard Eastman has called an open parable, a fable which applies at several levels or in several contexts. "The Lottery" creates an emotional effect of horror at the idea that perhaps in human civilization, the welfare of the many depends often on the suffering of the few: the victimized race, the exploited nation, the scapegoat, the poor, the stereotyped sex, the drafted soldier. In these cases, instead of a ritual, other aspects of the social order separate oppressor and victim, yet the genuine order and happiness of the majority seem to depend on the destruction of others. In this respect, "The Lottery" resembles many stories of oppression; its purpose may be to jar readers into thinking about ways in which their lives victimize others.

Jackson places the reader of "The Lottery," which lacks a protagonist, in a position similar to that of the protagonists of "The Visit" and "Pillar of Salt." The story moves from a relatively secure agrarian worldview to an event that fantastically complicates that view. Here, as in most of her stories, Jackson emphasizes the complexity of reality. Nature and human nature seem unaccountable mixtures of the creative and destructive. Her best people are in search of ways to live in this reality without fear and cruelty.

Other major works

NOVELS: *The Road Through the Wall*, 1948 (also published as *The Other Side of the Street*); *Hangsaman*, 1951; *The Bird's Nest*, 1954 (also published as *Lizzie*); *The Sundial*, 1958; *The Haunting of Hill House*, 1959; *We Have Always Lived in the Castle*, 1962.
PLAY: *The Bad Children*, 1959.
NONFICTION: *Life Among the Savages*, 1953; *The Witchcraft of Salem Village*, 1956; *Raising Demons*, 1957.
CHILDREN'S LITERATURE: *9 Magic Wishes*, 1963; *Famous Sally*, 1966.

Bibliography

Cleveland, Carol. "Shirley Jackson." In *And Then There Were Nine . . . More Women of Mystery*, edited by Jane S. Bakerman. Bowling Green, Ky.: Bowling Green State University Popular Press, 1985.
Friedman, Lenemaja. *Shirley Jackson*. Boston: G. K. Hall, 1975.
Kittredge, Mary. "The Other Side of Magic: A Few Remarks About Shirley Jackson." In *Discovering Modern Horror Fiction*, edited by Darrell Schweitzer. Mercer Island, Wash.: Starmont House, 1985.
Oppenheimer, Judy. *Private Demons: The Life of Shirley Jackson*. New York: G. P. Putnam's Sons, 1988.
Parks, John G. " 'The Possibility of Evil': A Key to Shirley Jackson's Fiction." *Studies in Short Fiction* 15, no. 3 (Summer, 1978): 320-323.

P. D. JAMES

Born: Oxford, England; August 3, 1920

Principal long fiction

Cover Her Face, 1962; *A Mind to Murder*, 1963; *Unnatural Causes*, 1967; *Shroud for a Nightingale*, 1971; *An Unsuitable Job for a Woman*, 1972; *The Black Tower*, 1975; *Death of an Expert Witness*, 1977; *Innocent Blood*, 1980; *The Skull Beneath the Skin*, 1982; *A Taste for Death*, 1986; *Devices and Desires*, 1989; *The Children of Men*, 1993.

Other literary forms

Though P. D. James is known principally as a novelist, she is also a short story writer and a playwright. The great bulk of James's work is in the form of the long narrative, but her short fiction has found a wide audience through its publication in *Ellery Queen's Mystery Magazine* and other popular periodicals. It is generally agreed that James requires the novel form to show her literary strengths to best advantage. Still, short stories such as "The Victim" reveal in microcosm the dominant theme of the long works. James's lone play, *A Private Treason*, was first produced in London on March 12, 1985.

Achievements

James's first novel, *Cover Her Face*, did not appear until 1962, at which time the author was in her early forties. Acceptance of her as a major crime novelist, however, grew very quickly. *A Mind to Murder* appeared in 1963, and with the publication of *Unnatural Causes* in 1967 came that year's prize from the Crime Writers Association. In the novels which have followed, James has shown an increasing mastery of the labyrinthine murder-and-detection plot. This mastery is the feature of her work that most appeals to one large group of her readers, while a second group of readers would single out the subtlety and psychological validity of her characterizations. Critics have often remarked that James, more than almost any other modern mystery writer, has succeeded in overcoming the limitations of the genre. In addition, she has created one of the more memorable descendants of Sherlock Holmes. Like Dorothy Sayers' Lord Peter Wimsey and Agatha Christie's Hercule Poirot, James's Adam Dalgliesh is a sleuth whose personality is more interesting than his skill in detection.

Biography

Phyllis Dorothy James was born in Oxford, England, on August 3, 1920. She was graduated from Cambridge High School for Girls in 1937. She was married to Ernest C. B. White, a medical practitioner, from August 8, 1941, until his death in 1964. James worked as a hospital administrator from 1949 to 1968 and as a civil servant in the Department of Home Affairs, London, from 1968 to 1972. From 1972 until her retirement in 1979, she was a senior civil servant in the crime department.

Analysis

P. D. James's work is solidly in the tradition of the realistic novel. Her novels are intricately plotted, as successful novels of detection must be. Through her use of extremely well delineated characters and a wealth of minute and accurate details, however, James never allows her plot to distort the other aspects of her novel. As a result of her employment, James had extensive contact with physicians, nurses, civil servants, police officials, and magistrates. She uses this experience to devise settings in the active world where men and women busily pursue their vocations. She eschews the country weekend murders of her predecessors, with their leisure-class suspects who have little more to do than chat with the amateur detective and look guilty.

A murder requires a motive, and it is her treatment of motivation that sets James's work apart from most mystery fiction. Her suspects are frequently the emotionally maimed who, nevertheless, manage to function with an apparent normality. Beneath their veneer, dark secrets fester, producing the phobias and compulsions they take such pains to disguise. James's novels seem to suggest that danger is never far away in the most mundane setting, especially the workplace. She avoids all gothic devices, choosing instead to create a growing sense of menace just below the surface of everyday life. James's murderers rarely kill for gain; they kill to avoid exposure of some sort.

The setting for *Shroud for a Nightingale* is a nursing hospital near London. The student nurses and most of the staff are in permanent residence there. In this closed society, attachments—sexual and otherwise—are formed, rivalries develop, and resentments grow. When a student nurse is murdered during a teaching demonstration, Inspector Adam Dalgliesh of Scotland Yard arrives to investigate. In the course of his investigation, Dalgliesh discovers that the murdered girl was a petty blackmailer, that a second student nurse (murdered soon after Dalgliesh's arrival) was pregnant but unmarried and had engaged in an affair with a middle-aged surgeon, that one member of the senior staff is committing adultery with a married man from the neighborhood and another is homosexually attracted to one of her charges. At the root of the murders, however, is the darkest secret of all, a terrible sin which a rather sympathetic character has been attempting both to hide and expiate for more than thirty years. The murder weapon is poison, which serves also as a metaphor for the fear and suspicion that rapidly spread through the insular world of the hospital.

Adam Dalgliesh carries a secret burden of his own. His wife and son died during childbirth. He is a sensitive and cerebral man, a poet of some reputation. These deaths have left him bereft of hope and intensely aware of the fragility of one man's control over his own life. Only the rules that humankind has painstakingly fashioned over the centuries can ward off degeneration and annihilation. As a policeman, Dalgliesh enforces society's rules, giving himself a purpose for living and some brief respite from his memories. Those who commit murder contribute to the world's disorder and hasten the ultimate collapse of civilization. Dalgliesh will catch them and see that they are punished.

In *An Unsuitable Job for a Woman*, published within a year of *Shroud for a Nightingale*, James introduces her second recurring protagonist. Cordelia Gray's "unsuitable job" is that of private detective. Gray unexpectedly falls heir to a detective agency and, as a result, discovers her vocation. Again, James avoids the formularized characterization. Gender is the most obvious but least interesting difference between Dalgliesh and Gray. Dalgliesh is brooding and introspective; although the narratives in which he appears are the very antithesis of the gothic novel, there are aspects of the gothic hero in his behavior. Gray, on the other hand, is optimistic, outgoing, and good-natured, despite her unfortunate background (she was brought up in a series of foster homes). She is a truth seeker and, like William Shakespeare's Cordelia, a truth teller. Dalgliesh and Gray are alike in their cleverness and competence. Their paths occasionally cross, and a friendly rivalry exists between them.

The publication of *Innocent Blood* marked a departure for James. While the novel tells a tale of murder and vengeance, it is not a detective story. Initially, the protagonist is Philippa Rose Palfrey—later, the novel develops a second center of consciousness. Philippa is eighteen, the adopted daughter of an eminent sociologist and a juvenile court magistrate. She is obsessed with her unremembered past. She is sustained by fantasies about her real parents, especially her mother, and the circumstances which forced them to give her up for adoption. Despite these romantic notions, Philippa is intelligent, resourceful, and tenacious, as well as somewhat abrasive. She takes advantage of the Children Act of 1975 to wrest her birth record from a reluctant bureaucracy.

The record shows that she was born Rose Ducton, to a clerk and a housewife in Essex. This revelation sends Philippa rushing to the dreary eastern suburb where she was born, beginning an odyssey that will eventually lead to her mother. She discovers that her fantasies cannot match the lurid realities of her past. Her father was a child molester who murdered a young girl in an upstairs room of his house. Her mother apparently participated in the murder and was caught trying to take the body away in her car. Her father has died in prison, and her mother is still confined. Though horrified, Philippa is now even more driven to find explanations of some sort and to rehabilitate the image of her mother. She visits Mary Ducton in prison, from which she is soon to be released, and eventually takes a small flat in London, where they will live together.

In chapter 8, James introduces the second protagonist,

at which time the novel becomes as much his as it is Philippa's. Norman Scase is fifty-seven and newly retired from his job as a government accounts clerk. Scase is the widowed father of the murdered girl. He retires when he learns of Mary Ducton's impending release, for all of his time will be required to stalk her so that, at the appropriate moment, he may kill her. The murder of young Julia Mavis Scase robbed her father of the same years it stole from Philippa. Philippa is desperately trying to reclaim these lost years by learning to know, forgive, and love her mother. Scase is driven to a far more desperate act.

In form, *Innocent Blood* resembles Tolstoy's *Anna Karenina* (1873-1877). Like Anna and Levin, the dual protagonists proceed through the novel along separate paths. Philippa has no knowledge of Scase's existence, and he knows her only as the constant companion of the victim he is tracking all over London. James makes the city itself a character in the novel, and as Philippa shares her London with her mother, it is fully realized in Dickensian detail. Philippa is the more appealing protagonist, but Scase is a fascinating character study: the least likely of premeditating murderers, a little man who is insignificant in everything except his *idée fixe*. James created a similar character in "The Victim," a short story appearing seven years earlier. There, a dim and diffident assistant librarian stalks and murders the man who took his beautiful young wife away from him. The novel form, however, affords James the opportunity to develop completely this unpromising material into a memorable character. As Scase lodges in cheap hotels, monitors the women's movements with binoculars, and stares up at their window through the night, the reader realizes that the little man has found a purpose which truly animates his life for the first time. He and Philippa will finally meet at the uncharacteristically melodramatic climax (the only blemish on an otherwise flawless novel).

Commander Adam Dalgliesh returns in *A Taste for Death* after an absence of nine years. He is heading a newly formed squad charged with investigating politically sensitive crimes. He is assisted by the aristocratic chief inspector John Massingham and a new recruit, Kate Miskin. Kate is bright, resourceful, and fiercely ambitious. Like Cordelia Gray, she has overcome an unpromising background: She is the illegitimate child of a mother who died shortly after her birth and a father she has never known. The title of the novel is evocative. A taste for death is evident in not only the psychopathic

killer but also Dalgliesh and his subordinates, the principal murder victim himself, and, surprisingly, a shabby High Church Anglican priest, reminiscent of one of Graham Green's failed clerics.

When Sir Paul Berowne, a Tory minister, is found murdered along with a tramp in the vestry of St. Matthew's Church in London, Dalgliesh is put in charge of the investigation. These murders seem linked to the deaths of two young women previously associated with the Berowne household. The long novel (more than 450 pages) contains the usual array of suspects, hampering the investigation with their evasions and outright lies, but in typical James fashion, each is portrayed in three dimensions. The case develops an additional psychological complication when Dalgliesh identifies with a murder victim for the first time in his career and a metaphysical complication when he discovers that Berowne recently underwent a profound religious experience in the church, one reportedly entailing stigmata.

Devices and Desires possesses the usual James virtues. The story is set at and around a nuclear power plant on the coast of Norfolk in East Anglia. The geographic details are convincing (even though the author states that she has invented topography to suit her purposes), and the nuclear power industry has obviously been well researched. Although the intricate plot places heavy demands of action upon the characters, the omniscient narrator analyzes even the most minor of them in such depth that they are believable. Finally, greater and more interesting than the mystery of "who did it" is the mystery of those ideas, attitudes, and experiences that have led a human being to murder. Ultimately, every James novel is a study of the devices and desires of the human heart.

In some ways, however, the novel is a departure. The setting is a brooding, windswept northern coast, the sort of gothic background that James largely eschewed in her earlier novels. *Devices and Desires* is also more of a potboiler than were any of its predecessors. As the story begins, a serial killer known as the Whistler is claiming his fourth victim (he will kill again during the course of the novel). A group of terrorists is plotting an action against the Larksoken Nuclear Power Station. The intrigue is so heavy and so many people are not what they seem that at one point the following tangled situation exists: Neil Pascoe, an antinuclear activist, has been duped by Amy Camm, whom he has taken into his trailer on the headland. Amy believes that she is acting as an agent for an animal rights group, but she has been duped by Caroline Amphlett, personal secretary to the Director of Larksoken. Caroline has, in turn, been duped by the terrorists for whom she has been spying—they plot her death when she becomes useless to them. Eventually, shadowy figures turn up from M15, Britain's intelligence agency. In this instance, so much exposition and explication is required of James's dialogue that it is not always as convincing as in the previous books.

Adam Dalgliesh shares this novel with Chief Inspector Terry Rickards. Rickards is a mirror image of Dalgliesh. He is less intelligent and imaginative, but he has the loving wife and infant child whom Dalgliesh has lost. While Dalgliesh is on the headland, settling his aunt's estate, he stumbles upon a murder (literally—he discovers the body). Hilary Robarts, the beautiful, willful, and widely disliked and feared acting administrative officer of the station, is strangled, and the Whistler's method is mimicked. As usual in a James novel, the suspects comprise a small and fairly intimate group. The author has totally mastered the detective story convention whereby at some point in the novel each of the suspects will seem the most plausible murderer.

The action of *Devices and Desires* affords James the opportunity to comment upon the use and potential misuse of nuclear power, the phenomenon of terrorism, the condition of race relations in London, even the state of Christianity in contemporary Britain. Still, what James always does best is to reveal, layer by layer, the mind which has committed itself to that most irrevocable of human actions—murder.

Other major works

PLAY: *A Private Treason*, 1985.
NONFICTION: *The Maul and the Pear Tree: The Ratcliffe Highway Murders, 1811*, 1971 (with T. A. Critchley).

Bibliography

Bakerman, Jane S. "Cordelia Gray: Apprentice and Archetype." *Clues: A Journal of Detection* 5 (Spring/Summer, 1984): 101-114.
Benstock, Bernard. "The Clinical World of P. D. James." In *Twentieth-Century Women Novelists*, edited by Thomas F. Staley. Vol. 16. Totowa, N.J.: Barnes & Noble, 1982.
Gidez, Richard B. *P. D. James*. Boston: Twayne, 1986.
Hubly, Erlene. "Adam Dalgliesh: Byronic Hero." *Clues: A Journal of Detection* 3 (Fall/Winter, 1982): 40-46.
Porter, Dennis. "Detection and Ethics: The Case of P. D. James." In *The Sleuth and the Scholar: Origins, Evolution, and Current Trends in Detective Fiction*, edited by Barbara A. Rader and Howard G. Zettler. Westport, Conn.: Greenwood Press, 1988.
Siebenheller, Norma. *P. D. James*. New York: Frederick Ungar, 1981.

SARAH ORNE JEWETT

Born: South Berwick, Maine; September 3, 1849

Died: South Berwick, Maine; June 24, 1909

Principal long fiction

Deephaven, 1877; *A Country Doctor*, 1884; *A Marsh Island*, 1885; *The Country of the Pointed Firs*, 1896; *The Tory Lover*, 1901.

Other literary forms

In addition to her novels, Sarah Orne Jewett wrote several collections of short stories and sketches, most of which were published initially in periodicals such as *The Atlantic*. The best known of these collections are *Old Friends and New* (1879), *Country By-Ways* (1881), *A White Heron and Other Stories* (1886), and *The King of Folly Island and Other People* (1888). Jewett also wrote a series of children's books, including *Play Days: A Book of Stories for Children* (1878), *The Story of the Normans* (1887), and *Betty Leicester: A Story for Girls* (1890). The posthumous *Verses: Printed for Her Friends* was published in 1916. Finally, Jewett was a voluminous writer of letters. Among the collections of her private correspondence are the *Letters of Sarah Orne Jewett* (1911), edited by Annie Fields and the *Sarah Orne Jewett Letters* (1956), edited by Richard Cary.

Achievements

Jewett is remembered today as perhaps the most successful of the dozens of so-called "local-color" or "regional" writers who flourished in the United States from approximately 1870 to 1900. She is especially noted for her remarkable depictions of the farmers and fishermen of Maine coastal villages at the end of the nineteenth century. Although Jewett was writing from firsthand observation (she was born and reared in Maine), she was not one of the common folk of whom she wrote. Wealthy, articulate, and well-read, Jewett was an avid traveler who moved within prominent literary circles. Her sophistica-tion imbued her best work with a polish and a degree of cosmopolitanism which renders it both readable and timeless; as a result, Jewett's reputation has been preserved long after the names of most other regional writers have been forgotten. Jewett is also regarded as something of a technical innovator. As modern critics of fiction attempt to establish specific criteria for novels and short stories, Jewett's best work—notably her classic *The Country of the Pointed Firs*—is seen as straddling both fictional categories. As such, her work is of great interest to contemporary literary theorists.

Biography

Sarah Orne Jewett was born in South Berwick, Maine, on September 3, 1849, the second of three daughters of a country doctor. The colonial mansion in which she was born and reared had been purchased and lavishly furnished by her paternal grandfather, Theodore Furber Jewett, a sea captain turned shipowner and merchant whose fortune enabled Sarah to live in comfort and to travel and write at leisure throughout her life. Her father and maternal grandfather were both practicing physicians who early imbued Sarah with a love of science and an interest in studying human behavior, as well as a passion for literature. Beginning in 1861, she attended the Berwick Academy, a private school; although for a while she considered pursuing a career in medicine, her formal education was in fact completed with her graduation from the Academy in 1865.

Under no pressure either to earn a living or to marry, Jewett went on trips to Boston, New York, and Ohio and began to write stories and sketches under various pseudonyms, including "Alice Eliot" and "Sarah O. Sweet." Her first published story, "Jenny Garrow's Lovers," was a melodrama that appeared in Boston's *The Flag of Our Union* in 1868, and the eighteen-year-old author was sufficiently encouraged by this to begin submitting children's stories and poems to such juvenile magazines as *St. Nicholas* and the *Riverside Magazine for Young Peo-*

ple, as well as adult stories and sketches to *The Atlantic*. Her tale "Mr. Bruce" was published in *The Atlantic* in December, 1869. The first of her Maine sketches, "The Shore House," appeared in that magazine in 1873, and a successful series of them rapidly followed. At the urging of *The Atlantic* editor William Dean Howells, she collected and revised them for publication in book form as *Deephaven*. By that time, Jewett was beginning to establish a circle of literary friends that eventually would include James Russell Lowell, John Greenleaf Whittier, Oliver Wendell Holmes, and Harriet Beecher Stowe.

Unquestionably the most significant of her literary relationships was that with James T. Fields of Ticknor and Fields, the Boston publishing house. When Fields died in 1881, his widow Annie established a close lifelong friendship with Jewett. The relationship inspired long visits to Annie's Boston residence at 148 Charles Street, as well as summer vacations at the Fields' cottage in Manchester-by-the-Sea. In addition, Jewett and Fields traveled extensively: In 1882, they visited England, Ireland, France, Italy, Switzerland, Belgium, and Norway, and met Alfred, Lord Tennyson, and Christina Rossetti. On other trips to Europe in 1892 and 1898, Jewett met Samuel Clemens, Rudyard Kipling, and Henry James, and in 1900 the pair traveled to Greece and Turkey.

Meanwhile, Jewett continued to write. *A Country Doctor* was published in 1884, and a visit to Florida with Fields in 1888 led to several stories with Southern settings. Jewett was strongest, however, in her fictional re-creation of Maine coastal life, as is evident from the popular and critical success of *The Country of the Pointed Firs*, published in 1896. She received an honorary Litt.D. degree from Bowdoin College in 1901, the same year she published her first (and only) historical novel, *The Tory Lover*. In 1902, an accident virtually ended her career: On her birthday, Jewett was thrown from a carriage when the horse stumbled, and she sustained serious head and spinal injuries. She never fully recovered either her physical health or her literary powers: Only two brief pieces were published during the remaining few years of her life, although she was able to write letters and to encourage the literary endeavors of the young Willa Cather. In March, 1909, she had a stroke while staying at Fields' Boston home; transported to South Berwick, Jewett died on June 24 in the house where she was born.

Analysis

The proper classification of Sarah Orne Jewett's first effort at long fiction, *Deephaven*, remains problematic even after a century. In some circles it is regarded as a novel, while many literary historians regard it as a collection of short stories, a contention immediately attributable to the book's genesis. It originated as a popular series of sketches that appeared in *The Atlantic* beginning in 1873. William Dean Howells encouraged Jewett to combine the sketches and flesh them out with a suitable dramatic framework and continuity, and the result—which was entitled *Deephaven* after the composite Maine seaport in which the sketches are set—was an immediate popular success. Even a reader unaware of the book's origins, however, still might be inclined to perceive it as a collection of stories, for the individual chapters—and, at times, even portions of chapters—tend to function as discrete fictional units rather than as elements subsumed within a satisfying whole. *Deephaven*'s confusing fictional status is caused in part by its young author's inexperience with revision, and as such it may be perceived as a flawed book; the fictional hybrid quality of *Deephaven*, however, ultimately became Jewett's stylistic trademark, and for many readers this blurring of the traditional distinctions between the novel and the short story is precisely the source of much of the charm and uniqueness of Jewett's work.

Regardless of whether one reacts to *Deephaven* as seriously flawed or charmingly eclectic, the fact remains that structurally speaking it is a sort of fictional quilt: The individual chapters retain much of their original discreteness, while the fictional framework that was constructed around them is patently an afterthought; in other words, the seams show. Jewett introduces two young ladies of Boston, Kate Lancaster and Helen Denis, who spend an extended summer vacation in Deephaven, Maine, at the home of Kate's late grandaunt, Katharine Brandon. The two women are wealthy, educated, and affectionate twenty-four-year-olds: All this background is revealed in a flurry of exposition within the first chapter or two, and in fact one learns nothing more of the women in the course of the next 250 pages. Their sole function in the story is to react to Deephaven and to record those reactions, and although Kate and Helen fulfill this function dutifully, their characterizations suffer accordingly. One has no sense of them as flesh-and-blood humans; indeed, they disappear from the text while some salty sea captain or rugged farmer, encouraged by an occasional "Please go only on!" from Kate, recounts a bit of folklore or personal history. This narrative frame, however annoying and contrived a technique it may be, suited Jewett's interests and purposes: Never skillful at portraying upper-class urbanites, she was strongest at presenting the colorful, dignified, and occasionally grim lives of common people clinging to a dying way of life in coastal Maine in the late nineteenth century. These farmers, villagers, and seafarers were a source of perennial interest to Jewett, and the rich variety of their life-styles, skills, and experiences were elements that she lovingly recorded, even as they were dying before her eyes. Ultimately, it is this impulse to record various aspects of a cross section of American life, rather than poor judgment or technical incompetence, which must be cited as the source of Jewett's distinctive fragmentary style.

That style was rapidly being crystallized in the creation of *Deephaven*. The book dissolves rapidly into a series of character studies, anecdotes, events, and descriptions of the landscape or homes. Individual characters are far more memorable than the volume in toto: The reader is inclined to recall Mrs. Kew, the lighthouse keeper; the widower Jim Patton, who repairs carpets; Danny the red-shirted fisherman, whose only friend is a stray cat; the "Kentucky Giantess," a local girl turned sideshow attraction; Captain Sands, a firm believer in thought-transference and the power of dreams; and Miss Sally Chauncey, the insane survivor of a once-prosperous family. Each character is painfully aware of the passing of the economic and cultural prominence of Deephaven and, concomitantly, the passing of each one's way of life; and accordingly, each (rather incredibly) recounts his or her life's high points, along with bits of folklore and anecdotes, to the two vacationing Boston ladies.

In addition to offering poignant and often penetrating studies of common folk, Jewett provides accounts of events that are symptomatic of the passing of Deephaven. These accounts include a circus full of tired performers and exhausted (or dead) animals, and a lecture on the "Elements of True Manhood" written for young men but addressed to a town whose young men have all died or departed to find new lives in urban factories or in the West. Finally, Jewett provides extended descriptions, often of home interiors. As a symbol

of the luxurious life of the past, she offers a chapter-long discussion of the house of the deceased Aunt Kate (an analysis so meticulous that it mentions the tiny spiders on the wallpaper), along with a companion study of the home of the mad Miss Sally, whose crumbling, furnitureless mansion is decorated with frames without paintings. Clearly this is not the sunny, sentimental world that is generally—and erroneously—attributed to local-color writing of the late nineteenth century. Although Jewett is often accused of avoiding the less positive aspects of life, this is certainly not the case with *Deephaven*: One finds a world of despair, poverty, unemployment, disease, alcoholism, insanity, and death. This is not gratuitous misery, but life as Jewett perceived it in coastal Maine.

Despite the book's rather unexpected acknowledgment of the unpleasant in life, however, it was warmly received not only because of the limitations Jewett set for herself (she was surely no literary naturalist when compared to Émile Zola, Stephen Crane, or Jack London) but also because of the two protagonists through whose eyes the reader experiences Deephaven. Early in the book, as they giggle and kiss their way through the alien environment of Deephaven, Kate and Helen generate a sentimentalized and frankly vacuous aura which is in keeping with the book's initial focus on the superficially picturesque aspects of the town; later in the story, as Jewett progressively focuses more on the grim side of life, the two girls begin to lapse frequently into improbable dialogues. For example, it is after a poor, unemployed widower dies of alcoholism that Kate reveals the lesson she's learned: "Helen, I find that I understand better and better how unsatisfactory, how purposeless and disastrous, any life must be which is not a Christian life. It is like being always in the dark, and wandering one knows not where, if one is not learning more and more what it is to have a friendship with God." Kate and Helen are ingenuous and often preachy; they offer a romanticized counterbalance to the realistic world of Deephaven. As such, the book was rendered palatable to a Victorian audience, but as a result, it appears disjointed, dated, and sentimental to modern readers. With the notable exception of *The Country of the Pointed Firs*, these unfortunate qualities tend to pervade all Jewett's attempts to write fiction of substantial length.

The Country of the Pointed Firs is unquestionably Jewett's masterpiece: An immediate popular and critical success, it is the only one of Jewett's five volumes of long fiction that is widely known today, and it is at the center of the perennial theoretical controversy as to how one should differentiate between a true novel and a collection of related short stories. As noted above, this situation exists with regard to *Deephaven*, but with an important difference: *Deephaven* was Jewett's first book, and so its hybrid quality is generally attributed at least in part to its author's inexperience. On the other hand, *The Country of the Pointed Firs* is clearly a more mature effort. Tight in structure, consistent in tone, complex in characterization, and profound in thought, it demonstrates how two decades of writing experience had honed Jewett's judgment and technical skill. Thus, the impression that *The Country of the Pointed Firs* somehow manages to straddle the two traditionally separate fictional classifications must be regarded as intentional. Yet *The Country of the Pointed Firs* is considerably more than a text for fictional theorists: It is a delightful book which shows Jewett at the height of her literary powers.

A comparison of *The Country of the Pointed Firs* with *Deephaven* gives some indication of the extent of those powers, for essentially *The Country of the Pointed Firs* is a masterful reworking of the earlier book. The premise is the same in both stories: A female urbanite visits a Maine coastal community for a summer and records her impressions. In *Deephaven*, the reader follows the experiences of two rather silly young women from Boston; in *The Country of the Pointed Firs*, there is only one visitor from an unspecified city, and even alone she is more than a match for Kate and Helen. A professional writer, she is by nature and training far more perceptive than the *Deephaven* girls. Well into middle age, she also has the maturity and experience to comprehend the residents of Dunnet Landing, who themselves are people who have led quite full, if not always pleasant, lives. The narrator of *The Country of the Pointed Firs* has credibility; One can believe that she enters into the world of Dunnet Landing and that people are willing to impart to her their most private and painful thoughts, whereas it is almost impossible to believe that any thinking person could be so intimate with giggly Kate and Helen. By the same token, although one knows little of the background and personal life of the narrator of *The Country of the Pointed Firs* (the reader is never told her name), one does know what goes on in her mind—her reactions, concerns, interests, misgivings—and as such she seems more like a real person than a fictional creation.

Closely aligned with this is the fact that the narrator of *The Country of the Pointed Firs* stays in focus throughout the story. Even though the book often breaks into little vignettes, character studies, or anecdotes, one never loses sight of the narrator, not only because she is the controlling consciousness who records the events at Dunnet Landing but also because one knows how she reacts to what she sees and hears. Those reactions are not always positive: She is initially annoyed by Captain Littlepage's account of the mythical Arctic place where souls reside; she is startled (and a bit disappointed) by the modernity of Elijah Tilley's cottage; and she feels the pang of young Johnny Bowden's glance of "contemptuous surprise" as she fails to recognize a local symbol pertaining to fishing.

The narrator's revelation of her inner life is perhaps most apparent in her dealings with Mrs. Almira Todd, the owner of the house where she stays for the summer. Whereas in *Deephaven* Kate and Helen stay in a relative's mansion and bring their Boston servants to run the household for them, the narrator of *The Country of the Pointed Firs* has a close link with the community in the form of her landlady: They live, eat, visit, and occasionally work together (Mrs. Todd grows and sells medicinal herbs), a situation which enables the narrator to acquire extensive firsthand knowledge of the people and lore of Dunnet Landing. Even so, she is aware that, as a nonnative, she can never truly be admitted into the community; she feels rather out of place at Mrs. Begg's funeral and at the Bowden family reunion, and her acute awareness of her being privy to many of the more intimate or concealed aspects of the community (such as Mrs. Todd's admission that she did not love her husband), while simultaneously being denied knowledge of many others, shows her to be a more complex, perceptive, and thoughtful character than either Kate or Helen could ever be. It also shows that Jewett was able to comprehend and convey the fundamental fact that life is far less cut-and-dried, far more rich and contradictory, than was indicated in her earlier fiction. This is perhaps most evident in her treatment of Dunnet Landing itself.

Jewett goes to great lengths to emphasize the local aspects of Dunnet Landing that make it unique in time and place. She carefully records local dialect by spelling phonetically; she presents characters whose values, interests, and activities mark them as a dying breed living in an isolated area; she reveals the ways in which the region's unusual environment and situation result in so-called "peculiar people," including the woman who designed her life around the fantasy that she was the twin of Queen Victoria. While emphasizing the uniqueness of this late nineteenth century coastal Maine village, however, Jewett also emphasizes its universality. It is significant in this regard that the reader is never told the year in which the events take place, and Jewett habitually draws analogies between the people of Dunnet Landing and those of biblical, classical, and medieval times.

Jewett's ability to strike a consistently happy balance between the universal and particular is quite remarkable, and equally remarkable is her talent for maintaining a tone which is profound without being obscure, touching without being sentimental. For once, Jewett also avoids preachiness: Captain Littlepage's discussion of the Arctic "waiting-place" inhabited by human souls does not lead into a lecture on Christian views of the afterlife nor a debate between matters of scientific fact and religious faith. Littlepage and his recital, like all the characters, anecdotes, and events of the novel, are allowed to speak for themselves, and the effect is a powerful one. Whether or not Willa Cather was justified in maintaining that *The Country of the Pointed Firs*, Nathaniel Hawthorne's *The Scarlet Letter* (1850), and Mark Twain's *The Adventures of Huckleberry Finn* (1884) were the only American books destined to have "a long, long life," it is true that *The Country of the Pointed Firs* does show Jewett in perfect control of her material and sure in her use of technique. Unquestionably, she had found the fictional milieu in which she functioned best.

Other major works

SHORT FICTION: *Old Friends and New*, 1879; *Country By-Ways*, 1881; *A White Heron and Other Stories*, 1886; *The King of Folly Island and Other People*, 1888.
POETRY: *Verses: Printed for Her Friends*, 1916.
NONFICTION: *Letters of Sarah Orne Jewett*, 1911 (Annie Fields, editor); *Sarah Orne Jewett Letters*, 1956 (Richard Cary, editor).
CHILDREN'S LITERATURE: *Play Days: A Book of Stories for Children*, 1878; *The Story of the Normans*, 1887; *Betty Leicester: A Story for Girls*, 1890.

Bibliography

Cary, Richard. *Sarah Orne Jewett*. Boston: Twayne, 1962.
Donovan, Josephine. *Sarah Orne Jewett*. New York: Frederick Ungar, 1980.
Magowan, Robin. *Narcissus and Orpheus: Pastoral in Sand, Fromentin, Jewett, Alain-Fournier, and Dinesen*. New York: Garland, 1988.
Nagel, Gwen L. *Critical Essays on Sarah Orne Jewett*. Boston: G. K. Hall, 1984.
Sherman, Sarah Way. *Sarah Orne Jewett: An American Persephone*. Hanover, N.H.: University Press of New England, 1989.

RUTH PRAWER JHABVALA

Born: Cologne, Germany; May 7, 1927

Principal long fiction

To Whom She Will, 1955 (published in the United States as *Amrita*, 1956); *The Nature of Passion*, 1956; *Esmond in India*, 1958; *The Householder*, 1960; *Get Ready for Battle*, 1962; *A Backward Place*, 1965; *A New Dominion*, 1972 (published in the United States as *Travelers*, 1973); *Heat and Dust*, 1975; *In Search of Love and Beauty*, 1983; *Three Continents*, 1987; *Poet and Dancer*, 1993.

Other literary forms

Though Ruth Prawer Jhabvala is known mainly as a novelist, she is also an accomplished writer of short stories, film scripts, and essays. Among her collections of short stories are *Like Birds, Like Fishes and Other Stories* (1963), *A Stronger Climate: Nine Stories* (1968), *An Experience of India* (1972), and *How I Became a Holy Mother and Other Stories* (1976); *Out of India* (1986) is a selection of stories from these volumes. Her best-known film scripts are *Shakespeare Wallah* (1965; with James Ivory), *Heat and Dust* (1983), *A Room with a View* (1986), and *Howards End* (1992), the latter two based on the novels by E. M. Forster. Jhabvala won an Academy Award for *Howards End*.

Achievements

Jhabvala has achieved remarkable distinction, both as a novelist and as a short-story writer, among writers on modern India. She has been compared with E. M. Forster, though the historical phases and settings of the India they portray are widely different. The award of the Booker Prize for *Heat and Dust* in 1975 made her internationally famous. Placing Jhabvala in a literary-cultural tradition is difficult: Her European parentage, British education, marriage to an Indian, and—after many years in her adopted country—change of residence from India to the United States perhaps reveal a lack of belonging, a recurring "refugee" consciousness. Consequently, she is not an Indian writing in English, or a European writing on India, but perhaps a writer of the world of letters deeply conscious of being caught up in a bizarre world. She is sensitive, intense, ironic—a detached observer and recorder of the human world. Her almost clinical accuracy and her sense of the graphic, the comic, and the ironic make her one of the finest writers on the contemporary scene.

Biography

Ruth Prawer was born in Cologne, Germany, on May 7, 1927, the daughter of Marcus and Eleonora Prawer; her family's heritage was German, Polish, and Jewish. She emigrated to England in 1939, became a British citizen in 1948, and obtained an M.A. in English from Queen Mary College, London, in 1951. That same year, she married C. H. S. Jhabvala, an Indian architect, and went to live in India. She resided there until 1975, when she moved to New York. She has three daughters, Renana, Ava, and Feroza, who live in India. Jhabvala's friendship and collaboration with filmmakers James Ivory and Ismail Merchant, that began in the 1960's, opened a new phase of her career; her work on film scripts enriched her technique as a writer of fiction and widened her vision.

Analysis

Ruth Prawer Jhabvala's distinctive qualities as a novelist grow from her sense of social comedy. She excels in portraying incongruities of human behavior, comic situations that are rich with familial, social, and cultural implications. Marital harmony or discord, the pursuit of wealth, family togetherness and feuds, the crisis of identity and homelessness—these are among the situations that she repeatedly explores in her fiction. She writes with sympathy, economy, and wit, with sharp irony and cool detachment.

Jhabvala's fiction has emerged out of her own experience of India. "The central fact of all my work," she once told an interviewer, "is that I am a European living permanently in India. I have lived here for most of my adult life....This makes me not quite an outsider either." Much later, however, in "Myself in India," she revealed a change in her attitude toward India: "However, I must admit I am no longer interested in India. What I am interested in now is myself in India . . . my survival in India."

This shift in attitude has clearly affected Jhabvala's fiction. There is a distinct Indianness in the texture and spirit of her first five novels, which are sunny, bright, social comedies offering an affirmative view of India. The later novels, darkened by dissonance and despair, reveal a change in the novelist's perspective.

Amrita inaugurates Jhabvala's first phase, in which reconciliation between two individuals (symbolic as well of a larger, social integration) is at the center of the action. Amrita, a young, romantic girl, has a love affair with Hari, her colleague in radio. Their affair is portrayed with a gentle comic touch: She tells Hari of her determination to marry him at all costs; he calls her a goddess and moans that he is unworthy of her. Jhabvala skillfully catches the color and rhythm of the Indian phraseology of love.

While this affair proceeds along expected lines, Pandit Ram Bahadur, Hari's grandfather, is planning to get his grandson married to Sushila, a pretty singer, in an arranged match. When Hari confesses to his brother-in-law that he loves Amrita, he is advised that first love is only a "game," and no one should take it seriously. Hari then is led to the bridal fire and married to Sushila. He forgets his earlier vows of love for Amrita, even the fact that he applied for a passport to go with her to England.

The forsaken maiden, Amrita, finds her hopes for a happy union revived when another man, Krishna Sengupta, writes her a letter full of love and tenderness. Enthralled after reading his six-page letter, she decks her hair with a beautiful flower, a sign of her happy reconciliation with life. Amrita shares in the sunshine of love that comes her way.

The original title of the novel, *To Whom She Will* (changed to *Amrita* for the American edition), alludes to

a story in a classic collection of Indian fables, the Panchatantra (between 100 B.C. and A.D. 500; *The Morall Philosophie of Doni*, 1570). In the story, which centers on a maiden in love, a Hindu sage observes that marriage should be arranged for a girl at a tender age; otherwise, "she gives herself to whom she will." This ancient injunction is dramatized in the predicaments of Hari, Amrita, Sushila, and Sengupta, the four main characters. The irony lies in the fact that Amrita does not marry "whom she will." Nevertheless, the regaining of happiness is the keynote of Jhabvala's first novel of family relations and individual predicaments.

The Householder is perhaps Jhabvala's most successful, least problematic, most organically conceived novel. A true social comedy, it is a direct, simple "impression of life." It centers on the maturation of its likable central character, Prem, a Hindi instructor in Mr. Khanna's private college. Prem is a shy, unassuming young man, in no way exceptional, yet his growth to selfhood, presented with insight and humor, makes for compelling fiction.

The title *The Householder* is derived from the Hindu concept of the four stages of a man's life; the second stage, that of a family man, is the one that the novel explores. Prem's relations with his wife, Indu, are most delicately portrayed. The scene of Prem loving Indu on the terrace in moonlight is both tender and touching. They both sense the space and the solitude and unite in deep intimacy. Prem realizes that Indu is pregnant and tenderly touches her growing belly—scenes which show Jhabvala at her best and most tender.

Prem's troubles are mainly economic—how to survive on a meager salary—and the comedy and the pathos which arise out of this distress constitute the real stuff of the novel. The indifference, the arrogance, and the insensitivity of the other characters are comically rendered, emphasizing Prem's seeming helplessness, as he struggles to survive and to assert his individuality. (A minor subplot is contributed by Western characters: Hans Loewe, a seeker after spiritual reality, and Kitty, his landlady, provide a contrast to Prem's struggle.) Nevertheless, Prem is finally able to overcome his inexperience and immaturity, attaining a tenderness, a human touch, and a balance which enable him to achieve selfhood and become a true "householder."

Get Ready for Battle, Jhabvala's fifth novel, resembles *The Nature of Passion*. Like that earlier novel, it pillories the selfish, acquisitive society of postindependence India. In particular, it shows how growing urbanization affects the poor, dispossessing them of their land. Like *The Nature of Passion*, *Get Ready for Battle* derives its title from the *Bhagavad Gita*, (c. fifth century B.C.), alluding to the scene in which Lord Krishna instructs Arjuna to "get ready for battle" without fear; similarly, Jhabvala's protagonist, Sarla Devi, urges the poor to get ready for battle to protect their rights. Get Ready for Battle is superior to The Nature of Passion, however, in its portrayal of interesting and believable characters. While the characters in the later novel still represent various social groups or points of view, they are not mere types.

The central character, Sarla Devi, deeply committed to the cause of the poor, is separated from her husband, Gulzari Lal. They represent two opposite valuations of life: She leads her life according to the tenets of the *Bhagavad Gita*, while he, acquisitive and heartless, is a worshiper of Mammon. The main action of the novel centers on her attempt to save the poor from being evicted from their squatters' colony and also to save her son from following his father's corrupt life-style. She fails in both these attempts, yet she is heroic in her failure.

Jhabvala brilliantly depicts the wasteland created by India's growing cities, which have swallowed farms and forests, at the same time destroying the value-structure of rural society. Yet *Get Ready for Battle* also includes adroitly designed domestic scenes. Kusum, Gulzari Lal's mistress, is shown with sympathy, while the relationship between two secondary characters, the married couple Vishnu and Mala, is portrayed with tenderness as well as candor. They show their disagreements (even speak of divorce), yet they are deeply in love. For them, "getting ready for battle" is a kind of game, a comic conflict, rather than a serious issue.

Jhabvala's next novel, *A Backward Place*, initiated the second phase of her career, marked by dark, despairing comedies focusing more attention on encounters between East and West and the resulting tensions and ironies. Jhabvala's most widely praised work, *Heat and Dust*, followed ten years later. The complex plot traces parallels between the experiences of two Englishwomen in India: the unnamed narrator and her grandfather Douglas' first wife, Olivia. In the 1930's, Olivia came to India as Douglas' wife. Bored by her prosaic, middle-class existence, Olivia is drawn to a Muslim nawab with whom she enjoys many escapades. Invited to a picnic close to a Muslim shrine, Olivia finds the nawab irresist-

ible. They lie by a spring in a green grove, and the nawab makes her pregnant. She then leaves Douglas, aborts her child, and finally moves to a house in the hills as the nawab's mistress.

After a gap of two generations, the narrator, who has come to India to trace Olivia's life story, passes through a similar cycle of experience. Fascinated by India, she gives herself to a lower-middle-class clerk, Inder Lal, at the same place near the shrine where Olivia lay with the nawab, and with the same result. The young narrator decides to rear the baby, though she gives up her lover; she also has a casual physical relationship with another Indian, Chid, who combines sexuality with a spiritual quest.

Heat and Dust is an extraordinary novel. Unlike many of Jhabvala's novels, it has a strong current of positive feeling beneath its surface negativism. Olivia, though she discards her baby, remains loyal to her heart's desire for the nawab, and the narrator, while not accepting her lover, wishes to rear her baby as a symbol of their love. This note of affirmation heightens the quality of human response in Heat and Dust, which is also notable for its fully realized characterizations.

In Search of Love and Beauty, set primarily in the United States but ranging widely elsewhere, centers on the experience of rootlessness which Jhabvala knows so well and which became so widespread in the twentieth century. The novel is a multigenerational saga, beginning with refugees from Nazi Germany and Austria and concluding in contemporary times. The rootlessness of that first generation to be dislocated from their culture is passed on to their children and their children's children, all of whom go "in search of love and beauty."

The first generation, represented by Louise and Regi, wishes to retain its German heritage, concretely symbolized by their paintings and furniture. The second generation, represented by Marietta, is partly Americanized. The restless Marietta travels to India, falls in love with Ahmad, an Indian musician, and befriends Sujata, a courtesan, sketched with deft accuracy. The image of India is lovable, vital, and glorious, and seems almost a counterpart to Germany's ideal image. The third-generation refugees, represented by Natasha and Leo, are more affluent and still more Americanized, yet they are trapped in drug abuse, depression, and meaninglessness.

In almost all of her novels, Jhabvala assumes the role of an omniscient narrator. She stands slightly aloof from her creations, an approach which has advantages as well as disadvantages. On the one hand, she does not convey the passionate inner life of her characters, many of whom are essentially stereotypes. Even her more fully developed characters are seen largely from the outside. On the other hand, she is a consummate observer. She has a fine eye for naturalistic detail, a gift for believable dialogue, but she is also an observer at a deeper level, registering the malaise that is characteristic of the modern world: the collapse of traditional values, the incongruous blending of diverse cultures—sometimes energizing, sometimes destructive, often bizarre. Thus, her fiction, while steeped in the particular reality of India, speaks to readers throughout the world.

Other major works

SHORT FICTION: *Like Birds, Like Fishes and Other Stories*, 1963; *A Stronger Climate: Nine Stories*, 1968; *An Experience of India*, 1972; *How I Became a Holy Mother and Other Stories*, 1976; *Out of India*, 1986.

SCREENPLAYS: *The Householder*, 1963; *Shakespeare Wallah*, 1965 (with James Ivory); *The Guru*, 1968; *Bombay Talkie*, 1970; *Autobiography of a Princess*, 1975 (with Ivory and John Swope); *Roseland*, 1977; *Hullabaloo over Georgie and Bonnie's Pictures*, 1978; *The Europeans*, 1979; *Quartet*, 1981; *Heat and Dust*, 1983 (based on her novel); *The Bostonians*, 1984 (with Ivory); *A Room with a View*, 1986; *Madame Sousatzka*, 1989 (with John Schlesinger); *Howards End*, 1992.

Bibliography

Gooneratne, Yasmine. *Silence, Exile, and Cunning: The Fiction of Ruth Prawer Jhabvala*. Hyderabad, India: Orient Longman, 1983.

Pritchett, V. S. "Ruth Prawer Jhabvala: Snares and Delusions." In *The Tale Bearers*. London: Chatto & Windus, 1980.

Shahane, V. A. *Ruth Prawer Jhabvala*. New Delhi: Arnold-Heinemann, 1976.

Sucher, Laurie. *The Fiction of Ruth Prawer Jhabvala*. New York: St. Martin's Press, 1989.

Updike, John. "Louise in the New World, Alice on the Magic Molehill." Review of *In Search of Love and Beauty*, by Ruth Prawer Jhabvala. *The New Yorker* 59 (August 1, 1983): 85-90.

ELIZABETH JOLLEY

Born: Birmingham, England; June 4, 1923

Principal long fiction

Palomino, 1980; *The Newspaper of Claremont Street*, 1981; *Mr. Scobie's Riddle*, 1983; *Miss Peabody's Inheritance*, 1983; *Milk and Honey*, 1984; *Foxybaby*, 1985; *The Well*, 1986; *The Sugar Mother*, 1988; *My Father's Moon*, 1989.

Other literary forms

Elizabeth Jolley's reputation was first established by her short stories, one of which, "Hedge of Rosemary," won an Australian prize as early as 1966. The first works she ever published were her short-story collections *Five Acre Virgin and Other Stories* (1976) and *The Travelling Entertainer and Other Stories* (1979); although her novel *Palomino* won a prize as an unpublished work in 1975, it did not appear in print until 1980. A third volume of short stories, *Woman in a Lampshade*, was published in 1983. Her radio plays have been produced on Australian radio and on the British Broadcasting Corporation (BBC) World Network.

Achievements

Jolley had been writing for twenty years before her first book, a volume of short stories, was published in 1976. In 1975, her novel *Palomino* was given the Con Weickhardt Award for an unfinished novel. *Palomino* was not published, however, until 1980, after a second volume of short stories had already appeared. Not until 1984 was Jolley widely reviewed in the United States.

Sometimes compared to Muriel Spark and Barbara Pym, Jolley is unique in her characterization and tone. Critics variously refer to her novels as fantasy combined with farce, comedy of manners, moral satire, or black comedy. Although most reviewers see a moral dimension beneath the slapstick surface of her work, noting her compassion, her wisdom, and her penetration of complex human relationships, some have insisted that she is merely a comic entertainer. Yet to most thoughtful readers, it is obvious that Jolley's humor often derives from characters who refuse to be defeated by their destinies, who boldly assert their individuality, and who dare to dream and to love, however foolish they may appear to the conformists.

Biography

Elizabeth Monica Jolley was born in Birmingham, England, on June 4, 1923. Her mother, a German aristocrat, the daughter of a general, had married a young Englishman who had been disowned by his father because of his pacifist convictions. Privately educated for some years, Jolley and her sister were then sent to a Quaker school. Later, Jolley was trained as a nurse at Queen Elizabeth Hospital, Birmingham, and served in that capacity during World War II. In 1959, she moved to Western Australia with her husband and three children. After her move, Jolley began increasingly to divide her time between writing, tending to her farm, and conducting writing workshops.

Analysis

In "Self Portrait: A Child Went Forth," a personal commentary in the one-volume collection *Stories* (1984), Elizabeth Jolley muses on the frequency with which the theme of exile appears in her works. Often her major characters are lonely, physically or emotionally alienated from their surroundings, living imaginatively in a friendlier, more interesting environment. Because of their loneliness, they reach out, often to grasping or selfish partners, who inevitably disappoint them. For Jolley's lonely spinster, widow, or divorcée, the beloved may be another woman. Sometimes, however, the yearning takes a different form, and the beloved is not a person but a place, like the homes of the old men in *Mr. Scobie's Riddle*.

If there is defeat in Jolley's fiction, there is also grace in the midst of despair. Despite betrayal, her characters reach for love, and occasionally an unlikely pair or group will find it. Another redeeming quality is the power of the imagination; it is no accident that almost every work contains a writer, who may, as in *Foxybaby*, appear to be imagining events into reality and characters into existence. Finally, Jolley believes in laughter. Her characters laugh at one another and sometimes at themselves; more detached, she and her readers laugh at the outrageous characters, while at the same time realizing that the characters are only slight exaggerations of those who view them.

The protagonist of Jolley's novel *Palomino* is an exile desperate for love. A physician who has been expelled from the profession and imprisoned, Laura lives on an isolated ranch, her only neighbors the shiftless, dirty tenants, who inspire her pity but provide no companionship for her. Into Laura's lonely life comes Andrea Jackson, a young woman whom the doctor noticed on her recent voyage from England but with whom she formed no relationship. Up until this point, Laura's life has been a series of unsuccessful and unconsummated love affairs with women. At one time, she adored a doctor, to whom she wrote religiously; when the doctor arrived on a visit, she brought a husband. At another period in her life, Laura loved Andrea's selfish, flirtatious mother, who eventually returned to her abusive husband. Perhaps, Laura hopes, Andrea will be different. She is delighted when Andrea agrees to run off with her, ecstatic when she can install her on the ranch, where the women live happily, talking, laughing, and making love. In her new joy, Laura does not realize that, like her other lost lovers, Andrea is obsessed with a man—her own brother, Christopher. It is Christopher's marriage and fatherhood that have driven her into Laura's arms, but Andrea continues to desire Chris, even at moments of high passion. When Andrea admits that she is pregnant with Chris's baby and tries to use Laura's love for her to obtain an abortion, Laura is forced to come to terms with the fact that the love between Andrea and her is imperfect, as it is in all relationships, and doomed to change or to dwindle. Obviously, loneliness is the human condition.

Although Jolley's characters must face hard truths

such as the inevitability of loneliness, often they move through suffering to new understanding. This is the pattern of *Palomino*. The novel derives its title from the horses on a nearby ranch, whose beauty Laura can appreciate even though she does not possess them. Joy is in perception, not possession; similarly, joy comes from loving, not from being loved. When Andrea and Laura agree that they must part, for fear that their brief love will dwindle into dislike or indifference, they know that they can continue to love each other, even though they will never again be together.

In the graphic dialogue of Laura's tenants can be seen the accuracy and the comic vigor which characterize Jolley's later works. *Mr. Scobie's Riddle*, for example, begins with a series of communications between the matron of the nursing home where the novel takes place and the poorly qualified night nurse, whose partial explanations and inadequate reports, along with her erratic spelling, infuriate her superior. At night, the nursing home comes alive with pillow fights, medicinal whiskey, and serious gambling, at which the matron's brother, a former colonel, always loses. In the daytime, the home is a prison: Old people are processed like objects, ill-fed, ill-tended by two rock-and-rolling girls, and supervised by the greedy matron, whose goal is to part her new guest, Mr. Scobie, from his property. Yet if the patients are prisoners, so are their supervisors. Having lost her husband to an old schoolmate, the matron cannot ignore the fact that the couple cavort regularly in the caravan on the grounds; in turn, the lonely matron saddles her schoolmate with as much work as possible. Meanwhile, the matron is driven constantly closer to bankruptcy by her brother's gambling and closer to a nervous breakdown by her inefficient and careless employees.

Some of the most poignant passages in *Mr. Scobie's Riddle* deal with the yearnings of two old men in Room One, who wish only to return to their homes. Unfortunately, one's has been sold and bulldozed; the other's has been rented by a voracious niece and nephew. As the patients are driven toward their deaths, no one offers rescue or even understanding. There are, however, some triumphs. The would-be writer, Miss Hailey, never surrenders her imagination or her hope; ironically, her schoolfellow, the matron, who has taken all of her money, must at last turn to Miss Hailey for understanding and companionship. In the battle for his own dignity, Mr. Scobie wins. Even though he is returned to the nursing home whenever he attempts to go home, and even though his uncaring niece and nephew finally acquire his beloved home, he wins, for he never surrenders to the matron. He dies before she can bully him into signing over his property.

The unique combination of farcical humor, lyrical description, pathos, and moral triumph which marks Jolley's later work is also exemplified in *Miss Peabody's Inheritance*. In this novel, a woman writer is one of the two major characters. In response to a fan letter from a middle-aged, mother-ridden London typist, the novelist regularly transmits to her the rough episodes from her new novel, a Rabelaisian story of lesbian schoolmistresses and the troublesome, innocent girl whom they escort through Europe. When at last the typist travels to Australia to meet her writer-heroine, she finds that the writer, a bed-bound invalid, has died. Yet her courage, her imagination, and her manuscript remain for Miss Peabody, an inheritance which will enable her to live as fully and as creatively as the novelist.

The characters in *Foxybaby* move through desperation to humor, love, imagination, and hope. The setting is a campus turned into a weight-loss clinic. Typically, the characters are trapped there, in this case by the rascally bus driver, who ensures a healthy wrecker and garage business by parking so that all approaching cars plow into him. The central character of *Foxybaby* is, once again, a woman writer, Alma Porch, who along with a sculptor and a potter has been hired to take the residents' minds off food by submerging them in culture. Miss Porch's mission is to rehearse an assorted group of residents in a film which she is creating as the book progresses. Brilliantly, Jolley alternates the wildly comic events at the campus with the poignant story that Miss Porch is writing, an account of a father's attempt to rescue his young, drug-ruined, infected daughter and her sickly baby from the doom which seems to await them. From his affectionate nickname for her when she was a little girl comes the name of the book.

The plot of *Foxybaby* illustrates the destructive power of love. Well-meaning though he is, the father cannot establish communication with his daughter. The reason is unclear, even to the writer who is creating the story, or, more accurately, is letting the characters she has imagined create their own story. Perhaps the father's love was crushing; perhaps in her own perverseness the daughter rejected it. At any rate, it is obvious that despite his persistence, he is making little headway in reaching the destructive stranger who is now his "Foxybaby" and

who herself has a baby for whom she feels nothing.

Meanwhile, like Jolley's other protagonists, Porch considers escaping from the place which is both her prison and her exile but is prevented from doing so by the very confusion of events. Loquacious Jonquil Castle moves in with her; a Maybelle Harrow, with her lover and his lover, invites her to an orgy; and the indomitable Mrs. Viggars brings forth her private stock of wine and initiates Porch into the joys of the school-like midnight feast. Offstage, the bus driver is always heard shouting to his wife or his mistress to drop her knickers. Love, in all its variety, blooms on the campus, while it is so helpless in the story being shaped in the same place.

Although the campus trap will be easier to escape, bus or no bus, than the nursing home in *Mr. Scobie's Riddle*, Jolley stresses the courage of the residents, a courage which will be necessary in the lives to which they will return, whether those lives involve battling boredom and loneliness, like Miss Porch's, or rejection, like that of Jonquil Castle, the doting mother and grandmother, or age and the loss of love, like the lascivious Maybelle Harrow's. Just as they will survive the clinic, though probably without losing any weight, they will survive their destinies. At the end of the novel, there is a triumph of love, when Mrs. Viggars, admitting her loneliness, chooses to take a young woman and her three children into her home, in order to establish a family once again. There is also a triumph of imagination, when Miss Porch actually sees the characters whom she has created. For her loneliness, they will be companions.

At the end of the novel, the bus stops and Miss Porch awakes, to find herself at the school. Jolley does not explain: Has Porch dreamed the events of the book? Will they now take place? Or is the awakening misplaced in time, and have they already taken place? Ultimately, it does not matter. What does matter is the power of the imagination, which, along with humor and love, makes life bearable.

Hester Harper, another unmarried protagonist, is somewhat like the doctor in *Palomino* in that she lives on an isolated ranch in Western Australia and yearns for love. In *The Well*, however, the beloved is an orphan girl, whom Hester takes home to be her companion. Refusing to admit her sexual desires, even to herself, Hester persuades herself that her feelings are merely friendly or perhaps maternal; yet she is so jealous of the orphan, Katherine, that she cannot bear to think of the friend who wishes to visit her or of the man who will ultimately take her away. The rival, when he appears, is mysterious, perhaps a thief, perhaps only an animal, whom Katherine hits on a late-night drive and whom Hester immediately buries in the well. Perhaps diabolical, perhaps distraught, Katherine insists that he is calling to her, demanding her love, threatening her and Hester. Although at last his voice is stilled, it is clear that Hester has lost control over Katherine, to whom the outside world of sexuality and adventure is calling with undeniable urgency. Unlike the doctor in *Palomino*, Hester cannot be contented with the memory of love. Imagination, however, once again mitigates the horror of life; at the end of the novel, Hester is making the mysterious nighttime adventure into a story to be told to children.

Because she deals with cruelty, indifference, greed, lust, and, above all, with loneliness, Jolley cannot be considered a superficial writer. The great distances of her Western Australia become a metaphor for the mysterious expanses of time; the small clumps of isolated individuals, trapped together on a ranch, on a weight-loss farm, or in a nursing home, represent society, as did Joseph Conrad's microcosmic ships on an indifferent ocean. Jolley makes it clear that love is infrequent and imperfect, that childhood is endangered by cruelty and that old age leads through indignity to death. Yet most of her works are enlivened by comic characters who defy destiny and death by their very insistence on living. Some of her characters transcend their isolation by learning to love, such as the doctor in *Palomino* or Mrs. Viggars in *Foxybaby*. Others, such as Miss Peabody and Miss Porch, triumph through their imaginations. There is also triumph in the isolated courage of a human being such as Mr. Scobie. If Jolley's characters are mixtures of the pathetic, the grotesque, and the noble, it is because they are human; if her stories keep the reader off balance between confusion, laughter, and tears, it is because they reflect life.

Other major works

SHORT FICTION: *Five Acre Virgin and Other Stories*, 1976; *The Travelling Entertainer and Other Stories*, 1979; *Woman in a Lampshade*, 1983; *Stories*, 1984.

RADIO PLAYS: *Night Report*, 1975; *The Performance*, 1976; *The Shepherd on the Roof*, 1977; *The Well-Bred Thief*, 1977; *Woman in a Lampshade*, 1979; *Two Men Running*, 1981.

Bibliography

Daniel, Helen. "A Literary Offering, Elizabeth Jolley." In *Liars: Australian New Novelists*. New York: Penguin Books, 1988.

Howells, Coral Ann. "In Search of Lost Mothers: Margaret Laurence's *The Diviners* and Elizabeth Jolley's *Miss Peabody's Inheritance*." *Ariel* 19, no. 1 (1988): 57-70.

Manning, Gerald F. "Sunsets and Sunrises: Nursing Home as Microcosm in *Memento Mori* and *Mr. Scobie's Riddle*." *Ariel* 18, no. 2 (1987): 27-43.

Westerly 31, no. 2 (1986).

Willbanks, Ray. "A Conversation with Elizabeth Jolley." *Antipodes: A North American Journal of Australian Literature* 3 (1989): 27-30.

ADRIENNE KENNEDY

Born: Pittsburgh, Pennsylvania; September 13, 1931

Principal drama

Funnyhouse of a Negro, pr. 1962, pb. 1969; *The Owl Answers*, pr. 1963, pb. 1969; *A Rat's Mass*, pr. 1966, pb. 1968; *The Lennon Play: In His Own Write*, pr. 1967, pb. 1969 (with John Lennon and Victor Spinetti); *A Lesson in Dead Language*, pr., pb. 1968; *Sun: A Poem for Malcolm X Inspired by His Murder*, pr. 1968, pb. 1971; *A Beast's Story*, pr., pb. 1969; *Boats*, pr. 1969; *Cities in Bezique: Two One Act Plays*, pb. 1969; *An Evening with Dead Essex*, pr. 1973; *A Movie Star Has to Star in Black and White*, pr. 1976, pb. 1984; *A Lancashire Lad*, pr. 1980; *Orestes and Electra*, pr. 1980; *Black Children's Day*, pr. 1980; *The Alexander Plays*, pb. 1992; *The Ohio State Murders*, pr., pb. 1992.

Other literary forms

In addition to her plays, Adrienne Kennedy has published a wide-ranging memoir, *People Who Led to My Plays* (1987). In 1988, she published *Adrienne Kennedy in One Act* and followed it two years later with *Deadly Triplets: A Theatre Mystery and Journal* (1990).

Achievements

Kennedy departs from the theatrical naturalism used by other African American playwrights in favor of a surrealistic and expressionistic form. Her plays capture the irrational quality of dreams while offering insight into the nature of the self and being. Most of her works are complex character studies in which a given figure may have several selves or roles. In this multidimensional presentation lies Kennedy's forte—the unraveling of the individual consciousness.

The playwright received an Obie Award in 1964 for *Funnyhouse of a Negro*, her best-known play; held a Guggenheim Fellowship in 1967; and received grants from the Rockefeller Foundation, the New England Theatre Conference, the National Endowment for the Arts, and the Creative Artists Public Service. She was a lecturer at Yale University from 1972 to 1974 and a Yale Fellow from 1974 to 1975. In addition to lecturing at Yale, Kennedy has taught playwriting at Princeton and Brown universities.

Biography

Adrienne Kennedy was born on September 13, 1931, in Pittsburgh, Pennsylvania, the daughter of Cornell Wallace Hawkins, a social worker, and the former Etta Haugabook, a teacher. She grew up in Cleveland, Ohio, and attended Ohio State University, where she received a bachelor's degree in education in 1953. A few years later, she moved to New York and enrolled in creative writing classes at Columbia University and the New School for Social Research. In 1962, she joined Edward Albee's Playwrights' Workshop in New York City's Circle in the Square. She wrote *Funnyhouse of a Negro* for the workshop. A decade later, she became a founder of the Women's Theater Council. In 1953, the playwright married Joseph C. Kennedy, whom she divorced in 1966. She has two sons.

Kennedy settled in New York, where she divided her time between writing and teaching. She continued to receive awards and recognition for her writing. The mayor of Cleveland proclaimed March 7, 1992, the opening date of her play *The Ohio State Murders*, to be Adrienne Kennedy Day.

Analysis

Adrienne Kennedy's plays are consistent in their exploration of the double consciousness of African Americans who are themselves inheritors of both African and European American culture and tradition. Symbolically represented by the split in the head of Patrice Lumumba, one of the selves in *Funnyhouse of a Negro*, this double identity frequently results in a schizophrenic division in which the character's selves or roles are at odds with one another. Typically it is the African identity with which the protagonist—who is often a sensitive, well-read young woman—is unable to come to grips. By using a surrealistic form to treat such a complex subject, Kennedy is able to suggest that truth can be arrived at only through the unraveling of distortion. Indeed, what Kennedy's protagonist knows of Africa and of blacks has come to her filtered through the consciousness of others who are eager to label Africans and their descendants "bestial" or "deranged." This seems to be what theater critic Clive Barnes means when he says that Kennedy "thinks black, but she remembers white." For this reason, animal imagery, as well as black and white color contrasts, dominates Kennedy's plays.

Kennedy's concerns with isolationism, identity conflict, and consciousness are presented primarily through character. She has called her plays "states of mind," in which she attempts to bring the subconscious to the level of consciousness. She achieves this essentially by decoding her dreams. Indeed, many of the plays were actually dreams that she later translated into theatrical form. This surrealistic or dreamlike quality of her work has been compared to August Strindberg's dream plays, in that both dramatists render reality through the presentation of distortion. Extracting what is real from what is a distortion as one would with a dream is the puzzle Kennedy establishes for her characters, as well as for her audience, to unravel in each of her major plays: *Funnyhouse of a Negro*, *The Owl Answers*, *A Rat's Mass*, and *A Movie Star Has to Star in Black and White*.

As in life, truth in Kennedy's plays is frequently a matter of subjectivity, and one character's version of it is often brought into question by another's. This is the case in *Funnyhouse of a Negro*, Kennedy's most critically acclaimed play. From the moment a somnambulist woman walks across the stage "as if in a dream" at the beginning of the play, the audience is aware that it is not viewing a realistic performance. Such figures onstage as the woman sleepwalker, women with "wild, straight black hair," a "hunchbacked yellow-skinned dwarf," and objects such as the monumental ebony bed which resembles a tomb, suggest a nightmarish setting. The action of the play takes place in four settings: Queen Victoria's chamber, the Duchess of Hapsburg's chamber, a Harlem hotel room, and the jungle. Nevertheless, it is not implausible to suggest that the real setting of *Funnyhouse of a Negro* takes place inside the head of Sarah, Kennedy's protagonist. As Sarah tells the theater audience in her opening speech, the four rooms onstage are "[her] rooms."

As with the four sets that are really one room, Sarah has four "selves" who help to reveal the complexity of her character. At first, Sarah appears to be a version of the kindhearted prostitute, or perhaps a reverse Electra who hates rather than loves her father. Kennedy builds upon these types to show Sarah's preoccupation with imagination and dreams, as well as her divided consciousness as a partaker of two cultures. Queen Victoria and the Duchess of Hapsburg are identified with Sarah's mother, or with her white European identity. The other two personalities, Jesus and Patrice Lumumba, the Congolese leader and martyr, on the other hand, are identified with Sarah's father, or with her black African heritage. Significantly, Sarah's four personalities tell the story of the parents' marriage and subsequent trip to Africa and the rape of her mother, which results in the conception of Sarah, each of which events can be called into question by the dreamlike atmosphere of the play and by the mother's insanity. One by one, the four alter egos add details to the story that allow the picture of Sarah's family to build through accretion. Even so, this story is undermined by the final conversation between the landlady and Sarah's boyfriend, Raymond. Doubling as "the Funnyman" to the landlady's "Funnylady," Raymond comes onstage after Sarah's suicide to tell the audience the truth about Sarah's father in the epilogue to the play. Although Sarah claimed to have killed her father, Raymond tells the audience that the father is not dead but rather "liv[ing] in the city in a room with European antiques, photographs of Roman ruins, walls of books and oriental carpets."

The same eschewal of linear progression in *Funnyhouse of a Negro* occurs in *The Owl Answers*, the first of two one-act plays appearing with *A Beast's Story* in the collection entitled *Cities in Bezique*. Clara Passmore, the protagonist in *The Owl Answers*, like Sarah in *Funny-*

house of a Negro, is a sensitive educated young woman torn between the two cultures of which she is a part. Riveted by her fascination for a culture which seems to want no part of her, Clara, a mulatto English teacher from Savannah, Georgia, learns from her mother that her father, "the richest white man in town," is of English ancestry. She comes to London to give him a fitting burial at Saint Paul's Cathedral, among the "lovely English." Once there, she has a breakdown and is imprisoned in the Tower of London by William Shakespeare, Geoffrey Chaucer, and William the Conqueror, who taunt her by denying her English heritage. Clara, who is both the daughter of the deceased William Mattheson and the Reverend Mr. Passmore (who, with his wife, adopted Clara when she was a child), is as firm in her claim to English ancestry as she is in her plans to bury her father in London. Like Sarah in *Funnyhouse of a Negro*, Clara's true prison exists in her mind. Ironically, Clara Passmore, whose name suggests racial passing, passes only from human into animal form. In a final, violent scene in which the third movement of Franz Joseph Haydn's Concerto for Horn in D accentuates the mental anguish of Clara and her mother, Clara's mother stabs herself on an altar of owl feathers. Clara, in the meantime, fends off an attack from a man whom she calls "God," who has assumed that the love she seeks from him is merely sexual. Sarah, who has grown increasingly more owl-like as the play has progressed, utters a final "Ow ... oww." In this play, as in *Funnyhouse of a Negro*, Kennedy leaves the audience with questions about the nature of spiritual faith in a world in which one calls upon God, yet in which the only answer heard comes from the owl.

Similar preoccupations with the clash of African and European culture in *Funnyhouse of a Negro* and *The Owl Answers* can be seen in *A Rat's Mass*, a one-act play set in the time of the marching of the Nazi armies. Brother and Sister Rat, who have a rat's head and a rat's belly, respectively, are both in love with Rosemary, a descendant of "the Pope, Julius Caesar, and the Virgin Mary." The two rat siblings struggle to atone for the dark, secret sin they committed when they "went on the slide together," which has forced them into hiding in the attic of their home. Alone together in their misery, Kay and Blake, the sister and brother, remember a time when they "lived in a Holy Chapel, with parents and Jesus, Joseph, and Mary, our wise men and our shepherd." Now they can only hear the gnawing of rats in the attic. In despera-

tion, they turn to Rosemary to help them atone for their sins. Rosemary refuses, stating that only through their deaths will there be a way of atonement. The way comes when Jesus, Joseph, Mary, two wise men, and the shepherd return as the Nazi army to open fire on the rats, leaving only Rosemary, like the evergreen shrub for which she is named, to remain standing.

The animal motif employed in *The Owl Answers* and *A Rat's Mass* is less apparent in *A Movie Star Has to Star in Black and White*. Clara Passmore of *The Owl Answers* returns for a "bit role" in which she reads from several of Kennedy's plays. The English literary tradition highly esteemed by the protagonist in *Funnyhouse of a Negro* and *The Owl Answers* is replaced by the American film tradition. Reinforcing the theme of illusion versus reality begun in *Funnyhouse of a Negro*, *A Movie Star Has to Star in Black and White* is actually a series of plays-within-a-play in which scenes from the films *Now Voyager* (1942), *A Place in the Sun* (1951), and *Viva Zapata!*, (1952) take place in a hospital lobby, Clara's old room, and Clara's brother's room, respectively. As the title of the play indicates—as well as a stage note directing that all the colors be shades of black and white—Kennedy continues her experimentation with black-and-white color contrasts onstage. As in other plays by Kennedy, linear progression is eschewed and the illusion of cinema merges with the reality of the life of Clara, a writer and daughter to the Mother and Father, the wife of Eddie, the mother of Eddie, Jr., and the alter ego to the film actresses.

Through lines spoken in the first scene by Bette Davis to Paul Henreid, the audience learns of Clara's parents' dream of success in the North, which ends in disappointment when they learn that racial oppression is not confined to the South. The scene takes place simultaneously in an ocean liner from *Now, Voyager* and a hospital lobby where Clara and her mother have come to ascertain the condition of Wally, Clara's brother, who lies in a coma.

Scene 2 moves to Wally's room, while Jean Peters and Marlon Brando enact lines from *Viva Zapata!* History repeats itself when it is revealed that Clara, like her mother before her, is having marital problems with her husband, Eddie. In the meantime, Brando's character changes the bed sheets onto which Peters' character has bled, reminding the audience of Clara's miscarriage while Eddie was away in the armed services.

In the following scene, Shelley Winters and Montgomery Clift appear onstage in a small rowboat from the film *A Place in the Sun*. In this scene, Clara reveals her frustration as a writer who is black and a woman. She says that her husband thinks that her life is "one of my black and white movies that I love so . . . with me playing a bit part." The play ends with the news that Wally will live, but with brain damage. In the interim, Winters' character drowns as Clift's character looks on, suggesting a connection between Clara's fantasy life in motion pictures and the real world, from which she struggles to escape.

Kennedy's other plays deal with themes similar to those in the works discussed. The animal motif, coupled with the theme of sexuality, is continued in *A Beast's Story* and *A Lesson in Dead Language*. In *A Beast's Story*, Beast Girl kills her child with quinine and whiskey and then kills her husband with an ax after he attempts to make love to her. Her parents, Beast Man and Beast Woman, preside over the dark course of events as shamans anxious for their daughter to rid the household of the "intruder" whose presence has caused a black sun to hover above them. Animal imagery is paired with the rite-of-passage motif in *A Lesson in Dead Language*. In this play, a schoolteacher who is a white dog "from the waist up" instructs seven young girls about menstruation. Similarly, the dreamlike quality of earlier plays continues in *Sun*, a play-poem written about the death of Malcolm X, and in *An Evening with Dead Essex*, based on the assassination of black sniper Mark James Essex.

With the 1980's, Kennedy branched out into the writing of children's plays on commission. Among these plays are *A Lancashire Lad, Orestes and Electra,* and *Black Children's Day.* Kennedy was a prolific writer in the late 1980's and early 1990's, with her esteemed "scrapbook of memories" *People Who Led to My Plays, Deadly Triplets: A Theatre Mystery and Journal,* and *The Alexander Plays,* the latter centering on the protagonist Suzanne Alexander and including such pieces as *The Ohio State Murders, She Talks to Beethoven, The Dramatic Circle,* and *The Film Club.*

Notable among her later works is her play *The Ohio State Murders,* the source of which was Kennedy's emotionally scarring experience as an undergraduate at Ohio State University. According to dramaturge Scott T. Cummings, "the play reflects [Kennedy's] abiding feeling that 'nothing has changed for American blacks,' that 'American blacks would have been better off leaving this country.'"

Kennedy dares to be innovative both in subject matter and in theatrical form. She writes difficult plays that raise questions rather than provide answers. From *Funnyhouse of a Negro* onward, Kennedy chose a subjective form that she has retained throughout her literary career. Her plays grow out of her own experiences as a sensitive and gifted African American who grew up in the American Midwest. There may be little plot in Kennedy's plays, but there is a wealth of symbolism concerning the inherent tensions of African American experience.

Other major works

NONFICTION: *People Who Led to My Plays,* 1987; *Adrienne Kennedy in One Act,* 1988.
MISCELLANEOUS: *Deadly Triplets: A Theatre Mystery and Journal,* 1990.

Bibliography

Benston, Kimberly W. "*Cities in Bezique*: Adrienne Kennedy's Expressionistic Vision." *College Language Association Journal* 20 (1976): 235-244.
Blau, Herbert. "The American Dream in American Gothic: The Plays of Sam Shepard and Adrienne Kennedy." *Modern Drama* 27 (1984): 520-539.
Bryant-Jackson, Paul, and Lois More Overbeck, eds. *Intersecting Boundaries.* Minneapolis: University of Minnesota Press, 1992.
Curb, Rosemary. "Fragmented Selves in Adrienne Kennedy's *Funnyhouse of a Negro* and *The Owl Answers.*" *Theater Journal* 32 (1980): 180-195.
Meigs, Susan. "No Place but the Funnyhouse: The Struggle for Identity in Three Adrienne Kennedy Plays." In *Modern Drama: The Female Canon,* edited by June Schlueter. Rutherford, N.J.: Fairleigh Dickinson University Press, 1990.
Sollors, Werner. "Owls and Rats in the American Funnyhouse: Adrienne Kennedy's Drama." *American Literature: A Journal of Literary History, Criticism, and Bibliography* 63 (1991): 507-532.

JAMAICA KINCAID
Elaine Potter Richardson

Born: St. Johns, Antigua, West Indies; May 25, 1949

Principal short fiction

At the Bottom of the River, 1983.

Other literary forms

In addition to her short stories, Jamaica Kincaid has written the novels *Annie John* (1985), *Lucy* (1990), and *The Autobiography of My Mother* (1994); a book-length essay concerning her native island Antigua entitled *A Small Place* (1988); and a children's book, *Annie, Gwen, Lilly, Pam, and Tulip* (1986), with illustrations by Eric Fischl.

Achievements

Kincaid is noted for her lyrical use of language. Her short stories and novels have a hypnotic, poetic quality that results from her utilization of rhythm and repetition. Her images, drawn from her West Indian childhood, recall Antigua, with its tropical climate, Caribbean food, local customs, and folklore laced with superstitions. Many of her stories move easily from realism to surrealistic fantasy, as would a Caribbean folktale. She is also praised for her exploration of the strong but ambiguous bond between mother and daughter and her portrayal of the transformation of a girl into a woman. Thus her work touches upon the loss of innocence that comes when one moves out of the Eden that is childhood. These are the features that are found not only in her short fiction but also in her novels, the chapters of which *The New Yorker* originally published as short stories, and in *Annie, Gwen, Lilly, Pam, and Tulip*, a children's book that was part of a project designed by the Whitney Museum of American Art, the original publisher, who sought to bring together contemporary authors and artists for a series of limited editions aimed primarily at collectors.

Kincaid's concern with racism, colonialism, classism, and sexism is rooted in her history: "I never give up thinking about the way I came into the world, how my ancestors came from Africa to the West Indies as slaves. I just could never forget it. Or forgive it." She does not hesitate to tackle these issues in her writing. In her nonfictional *A Small Place*, she directs the force of her language toward an examination of her native island of Antigua, presenting the beauty as well as the racism and corruption rooted in its colonial past. In her fiction, these same issues are not slighted; for example, *Annie John* and *Lucy* address various forms of oppression and exploitation.

Her short-story collection *At the Bottom of the River* received the Morton Dauwen Zabel Award from the American Academy and Institute of Arts and Letters in 1983. Her novel *Annie John* was one of three finalists for the international Ritz Paris Hemingway Award in 1985.

Biography

Born in 1949, Jamaica Kincaid, then Elaine Potter Richardson, lived with her homemaker mother and carpenter father on Antigua, a small West Indian island measuring nine-by-twelve miles. The family was impoverished: Their house had no running water or electricity. The young girl's chores included drawing water from a community faucet and registering with the public works so that the "night soil men" would dispose of the family's waste. Even so, her childhood was idyllic. She was surrounded by the extraordinary beauty of the island, was accepted by her community, and was loved and protected by her mother. When Kincaid was nine, however, her mother gave birth to the first of three more children—all boys. At that point, the closeness that Kincaid had enjoyed was at first disturbed and then destroyed. She credits the lies that she began to tell her mother as the catalyst for her fiction writing: "I wasn't really lying. I was protecting my privacy or protecting a feeling I had about something. But lying is the beginning of fiction. It was the beginning of my writing life." Also at this time, she began to comprehend the insidious impact of colonialism. (Antigua was a British colony until 1967, and only in 1981 did it receive full independence.) The Antiguans' docile acceptance of their inferior status enraged her. Thus the serenity she had known as a child was displaced by loneliness and anger.

In 1966, Kincaid, seeking to disassociate herself from her mother, left Antigua not to return for nineteen years and then only after she was a naturalized citizen of the United States and an established writer. Arriving in Scarsdale, New York, the seventeen-year-old Kincaid worked as a live-in baby-sitter. She did not open her mother's letters, and when, after a few months, she took an au pair position in New York City, she did not send her mother her new address. For the next three years, she cared for the four young girls of Michael Arlen, a writer for *The New Yorker* and a future colleague when she herself would become a staff writer for the magazine. Her childhood and early New York experiences are fictionalized in *At the Bottom of the River, Annie John*, and *Lucy*.

During her first few years in New York, she wanted to continue her education at a university but found her Antiguan schooling to be inferior; instead, she first studied for a high school diploma, took a few photography courses at a community college, and then attended Franconia College in New Hampshire on scholarship, leaving after a year because, although only in her twenties, she felt too old. After jobs as a secretary and receptionist, she wrote for a teen magazine. In 1973, she changed her name to Jamaica Kincaid, perhaps suggesting that she had achieved her own identity. Associating with New York writers and artists, she met George Trow (*Lucy* is dedicated to him), who wrote the column "Talk of the Town" for *The New Yorker*. She collaborated on a few columns, and eventually one of her pieces was accepted by editor William Shawn, who was known for encouraging fledgling writers. In 1978, the magazine published her first short story, "Girl." Soon after, she married Allen Shawn, the editor's son. In 1983, her first collection, *At the Bottom of the River*, was published to generally favorable reviews, as was her subsequent work, which has earned for her a devoted following. She continued to write short stories, usually published in *The New Yorker*, and give lectures and readings. She and Allen Shawn, a composer and professor at Bennington College, along with their two children—Annie, named after her mother, and Harold—settled in Bennington, Vermont.

Analysis

Jamaica Kincaid's short stories, strongly autobiographical, are often set in the West Indies or incorporate images from the islands and include many events from her youth and young adulthood. In general, her stories chronicle the coming-of-age of a young girl. Because the mother-daughter relationship is central to the process, Kincaid often examines the powerful bond between them, a bond that the child must eventually weaken, if not break, in order to create her own identity. Kincaid has been accurately called "the poet of girlhood and place."

The first of the ten stories in *At the Bottom of the River* is the often-praised and often-quoted "Girl." Barely two pages in length, the story outlines the future life of a young girl growing up on a small Caribbean island. The voice heard belongs to the girl's mother as she instructs her daughter in the duties that a woman is expected to fulfill in a culture with limited opportunities for girls.

Twice the girl interrupts to offer a feeble protest, but her mother persists.

The girl is told how to wash, iron, and mend clothes; how to cook fritters and pepper pot; how to grow okra; and how to set the table—in short, everything that will enable her to care for a future husband. She is told how to smile, how to love a man, and how to get rid of an unborn baby should it be necessary. Most important, however, her mother warns her about losing her reputation because then the girl (and this is unsaid) loses her value as a potential wife. Almost as a refrain, the mother cautions, "[O]n Sundays try to walk like a lady and not like the slut you are so bent on becoming" or "[T]his is how to behave in the presence of men who don't know you very well, and this way they won't recognize immediately the slut I have warned you against becoming." On the island, a girl's most important asset is her virginity.

The language is a prime example of Kincaid's ability

to work a hypnotic spell. The story consists of a series of variations of particular instructions: "[T]his is how to sew on a button; this is how to make a buttonhole for the button you have just sewed on; this is how to hem a dress when you see the hem coming down and so to prevent yourself from looking like the slut I know you are so bent on becoming." The rhythm and repetition create a lyric poetic quality that is present to some degree in all Kincaid's fiction. Her prose demands to be read out loud.

"Girl" suggests the child's future life on the island, but several stories in the collection re-create the atmosphere of her present existence. The story "In the Night" recounts her daily experiences. Thus, details such as crickets or flowers that would be important to her are recorded, often in the form of lists or catalogs: "The hibiscus flowers, the flamboyant flowers, the bachelor's buttons, the irises, the marigolds, the whiteheadbush flowers, lilies, the flowers on the daggerbush," continuing for a full paragraph. Here cataloging, a familiar feature of Kincaid's prose, represents a child's attempt to impose an order on her surroundings. The young narrator does not question her world but only reports what she observes. Thus witchcraft exists side by side with more mundane activities: "Someone is making a basket, someone is making a girl a dress or a boy a shirt . . . someone is sprinkling a colorless powder outside a closed door so that someone else's child will be stillborn." This melding of the commonplace with the supernatural occurs frequently in Kincaid's fiction. The narrator's troubles, such as wetting the bed, are those of a child and are easily resolved by her mother. Her plans for the future, marrying a woman who will tell her stories, also are typical of a child. This is an idyllic world before the fall from innocence, a world in which everything is ordered, listed, and cataloged. Nothing is threatening, since the all-powerful mother protects and shields.

In several other stories, including "Wingless" and "Holidays," the girl is again shown to be occupied by the usually pleasant sensations of living: walking barefoot, scratching her scalp, or stretching, but sometimes, as illustrated in "Holidays," experiencing pain: "spraining a finger while trying to catch a cricket ball; straining a finger while trying to catch a softball; stepping on dry brambles while walking on newly cut hayfields." The trauma, however, is clearly limited to physical sensations. When the child thinks of the future, the images are those of wishful thinking, similar to daydreams. This tranquil state of youth, however, is only temporary, as

the title "Wingless" implies. The narrator, wingless, is still in the "pupa stage."

In "The Letter from Home," the narrator's growing awareness makes it impossible for her to maintain the comforting simplicity of her child's world. Questions about life and death intrude: "Is the Heaven to be above? Is the Hell below?" These inquiries, however, are set aside in favor of the present physical reality—a cat scratching a chair or a car breaking down. Even love and conception are reduced to the simplest terms: "[T]here was a bed, it held sleep; there was movement, it was quick, there was a being." She is not ready to confront the idea of death, so when death beckons, she "turned and rowed away."

Just as the philosophical questions about life and death disrupt the bliss of childhood, so does the journey toward selfhood, which Kincaid symbolically represents as a journey over rough or impassable terrain or water. In "What I Have Been Doing Lately," the obstacle is water: "I walked for I don't know how long before I came to a big body of water. I wanted to get across it but I couldn't swim. I wanted to get across it but it would take me years to build a boat. . . . I didn't know how long to build a bridge." Because the journey is difficult, as any passage to adulthood would be, the narrator is hesitant, afraid of finding the world not beautiful, afraid of missing her parents, so she goes back to bed: She is not ready yet. Soon, however, she will not have that option of retreating and waiting.

The journey toward selfhood necessitates a separation from the mother, as is suggested in the story "My Mother." The protection that was vital during childhood becomes stifling in adolescence: "Placing her arms around me, she drew my head closer and closer to her bosom, until finally I suffocated." Furthermore, the girl's feelings are ambiguous. Realizing that she has hurt her mother, she cries, but then she utilizes those tears to create a pond, "thick and black and poisonous," to form a barrier over which they "watched each other carefully." The all-protecting mother of the earlier stories transforms herself into a mythic monster and thus threatens the emerging selfhood of the daughter. The daughter, however, also grows "invincible" like her mother, and she, too, metamorphoses into a similar beast. Strong as the daughter has become, however, she can never vanquish her mother: "I had grown big, but my mother was bigger, and that would always be so." Only after the daughter completes her own journey toward selfhood is her mother no longer a threat: "as we walked along, our steps became one, and as we talked, our voices became one voice, and we were in complete union in every way. What peace came over me then, for I could not see where she left off and I began, or where I left off and she began."

The concluding and title story is also the longest in the collection, at about twenty pages. "At the Bottom of the River" suggests answers to the questions raised in the other stories. Again, Kincaid employs the symbol of a journey through forbidding terrain to suggest traveling through life. What is the purpose of the journey, for what does one ultimately face but death? One man, overwhelmed, does nothing. Another discovers meaning in his family, his work, and the beauty of a sunrise, but still, he struggles and "feels the futility." How can one live with the paralyzing knowledge that "[d]ead lay everything that had lived and dead also lay everything that would live. All had had or would have its season. And what should it matter that its season lasted five billion years or five minutes?" One possible response is suggested in the life of "a small creature" that lives in the moment, aware only of the sensation of grass underfoot or of the sting of a honeybee.

The narrator, who at first knew only the love of her mother, suffers from its necessary withdrawal. Adrift, she embarks on a symbolic journey in which she submerges herself in a river-fed sea. Discovering a solution at the bottom of the river, she emerges with a commitment to the present. Death, because it is natural, cannot be destroyed, but the joys derived from the commonplace—books, chairs, fruit—can provide meaning, and she "grow[s] solid and complete."

Kincaid's stories are praised for their strong images, poetic language, and challenging themes, and they are criticized for their lack of plot and sometimes obscure symbolism. Yet any reader who, without reservations, enters Kincaid's fictive world will be well rewarded.

Other major works

NOVELS: *Annie John*, 1985; *Lucy*, 1990; *The Autobiography of My Mother*, 1994.
NONFICTION: *A Small Place*, 1988.
CHILDREN'S LITERATURE: *Annie, Gwen, Lilly, Pam, and Tulip*, 1986 (with illustrations by Eric Fischl).

Bibliography

Als, Hilton. "Don't Worry, Be Happy." Review of *Lucy*. *The Nation* 252 (February 18, 1991): 207-209.
Ellsberg, Peggy. "Rage Laced with Lyricism." Review of *A Small Place*. *Commonweal* 115 (November 4, 1988): 602-604.
Garis, Leslie. "Through West Indian Eyes." *The New York Times Magazine* 140 (October 7, 1990): 42.
Milton, Edith. "Making a Virtue of Diversity." Review of *At the Bottom of the River*. *The New York Times Book Review*, January 15, 1984, 22.
Onwordi, Iki. "Wising Up." *The Times Literary Supplement*, November 29, 1985, 1374.

MAXINE KUMIN

Born: Philadelphia, Pennsylvania; June 6, 1925

Principal poetry

Halfway, 1961; *The Privilege*, 1965; *The Nightmare Factory*, 1970; *Up Country*, 1972; *House, Bridge, Fountain, Gate*, 1975; *The Retrieval System*, 1978; *Our Ground Time Here Will Be Brief*, 1982; *Closing the Ring: Selected Poems*, 1984; *The Long Approach*, 1985; *Nurture*, 1989; *Looking for Luck: Poems*, 1992.

Other literary forms

Maxine Kumin's novels include *Through Dooms of Love* (1965), *The Passions of Uxport* (1968), *The Abduction* (1971), and *The Designated Heir* (1974). She has published a collection of short stories, *Why Can't We Live Together Like Civilized Human Beings?* (1982), and collections of essays, including *To Make a Prairie: Essays on Poets, Poetry, and Country Living* (1980) and *In Deep: Country Essays* (1987). Kumin has also published numerous volumes of children's literature, several coauthored with Anne Sexton.

Achievements

Most recognized for her rural poems, Maxine Kumin received a Pulitzer Prize in 1973 for her fourth volume of poetry, *Up Country*. She is applauded for her positive tone, her affirmation of life; for this life-affirming quality, her work is often contrasted to that of Anne Sexton and Sylvia Plath, in whose work critics find the negation of life. Among other awards, she has received a National Endowment for the Arts grant (1966), a National Council on the Humanities fellowship (1967), the Eunice Tietjens Memorial Prize from *Poetry* (1972), the American Academy and Institute of Arts and Letters Award for excellence in literature (1980), and an Academy of American Poets fellowship (1986). She has published regularly, throughout her career, in the most prestigious magazines in the country, including *Poetry*, *The New Yorker*, and *The Atlantic*.

Biography

Born of Jewish parents in the Germantown section of Philadelphia, Pennsylvania, in 1925 and educated as a child at a Catholic convent school, Maxine Kumin describes herself as an agnostic who believes passionately in poetry. Kumin's father, Peter Winokur, was a successful pawnbroker. As a teenager, Kumin trained to become an Olympic swimmer, but she abandoned this dream upon entrance to Radcliffe College, which lacked suitable training facilities. She received a bachelor's degree in 1946 and a master's in 1948, both from Radcliffe, but did not begin writing seriously until her late twenties, when, as a suburban housewife with small children, she turned to poetry for self-gratification. She met the poet Anne Sexton at a writing workshop at the Boston Center for Adult Education, and the two women developed a close personal and professional relationship, installing an extra telephone line in each of their homes so they could talk at length.

Kumin began her teaching career in 1958 at Tufts University in Massachusetts and has taught as visiting lecturer at Radcliffe, Columbia University, Amherst College, Princeton University, and Bucknell University, among others. She has been on the staff of the Bread Loaf Conference on numerous occasions, and she served as poetry consultant to the Library of Congress from 1981 to 1982. She prefers to spend much of her time at her horse farm in New Hampshire, where she lives with her husband, Victor Montwid Kumin, whom she married in 1946. They have three children: Jane Simon, Judith Montwid, and Daniel David.

Analysis

The poetry of Maxine Kumin is concerned with loss (particularly loss through death or separation) and surviving such loss. Equally at home with natural and domestic images, Kumin organizes most of her poems into groups of pastoral or tribal poems. These groupings allow her to explore relationships found in nature and also relationships within extended human families. These pastoral and tribal poems connect through Kumin's recurring emphasis on the seasonal patterns of nature and the regenerative cycles of familial generations.

Images of the body abound in Kumin's poetry: skin, bone, knees, ribs, and thighs. Swimming recurs as a metaphor with associated water imagery, especially in her first volume, *Halfway*. This first book also shows a concern for the instructor-student relationship and sometimes, as in the opening poem, "Junior Life Saving," explores this relationship within the context of water. The poem expresses concern with loss by drowning and the desire to prevent such loss. It begins with physical details, describing the young students, an "isosceles of knees," as they sit crosslegged and pick at their peeling sunburns. The lake assumes human powers; as the children enter the water to role-play the drowning victim and the rescuer, the lake seems to be smiling, "turned sudden to a foe." The speaker of the poem, who is aware of danger, gives instructions: "Class, I say, this is/ the front head release." Important is what the instructor, almost in a parental role, does not or cannot say: "Class, I say (and want/ to say, children, my dears,/ I too know how to be afraid)." Instead, the instructor remains firm and practical: " I tell you what I know:/ go down to save."

Both "High Dive: A Variant" and "The Lesson" suggest that mastery through practice can empower. The key word in "High Dive" (a sestina) is, in fact, "masterful": "Practice has made this come out right" so that "at peak" the male diver is "a schooled swan, arched and masterful." Although "The Lesson" (set in a natural body of water rather than a pool) approaches the theme more subtly, it announces itself flatly: "Eleven. Your hour of danger." The speaker-instructor continues to address the students, showing them how to do the sidestroke. Her directives are intertwined with observations of natural life in the water:

> it is the top leg goes forward
> forming the blade of the scissors,
> wherefore the cattails unseaming
> go rattletatat in the marshes,
> seeding the smallest of moments,
> all of us braver by inches.

The instructions seem themselves to cut through the poem and the water as if this concrete knowledge somehow lessens the danger of the lake. With the proper instruction, the swimmers learn to move through the water as if to do so were natural: "Up out and together we glide."

"Poems for My Son" and "The Journey: For Jane at Thirteen" are precursors of many poems in subsequent volumes on the separation of mothers and children. Relinquishment of the daughter in "The Journey: For Jane at Thirteen" is not only difficult but also perilous: "It is a dangerous time./ The water rocks away under the timber." Luckily, the daughter carries with her, in her purse, magical objects that will protect her, "pale lipstick, half a dozen lotions," and she bears history and mythology texts and wears pennies in her shoes. Ultimately, though, her own self-confidence is most powerful: "You lean down your confident head./ We exchange kisses; I call your name/ and wave you off as the bridge goes under."

The last poem in the volume, "For Anne at Passover," is the first of many poems dedicated to Kumin's friend Anne Sexton. The speaker of this poem, again an instructor, ironically addresses Socrates (rather than Sexton) when she states that "one student says you sinned the sin of pride./ Another consecrates your suicide." This poem alludes to ironies within the women's backgrounds—Sexton's Catholicism and Kumin's Judaism—yet it ends on a note of faith in love and the return of spring.

Kumin's poems celebrating love and spring (or summer) are among her most eloquent. Her rhythms soften. For example, in the conclusion of "We Are," from her fourth volume, *Up Country*, she uses enjambment rather than her usual end-stopped lines, allowing her sentences to flow over line and stanza breaks:

> Even knowing
> that none of us can catch up with himself
>
> we are making a run
> for it. Love, we are making a run.

Images of survival are lush and ripe; in "Five Small Deaths in May," for example, the speaker makes plans to bury a much-loved dog "under the milkweed bloom/ where in July the monarchs come/ as spotted as he, as rampant, as enduring." In "Watering Trough," water suggests richness and plenty. A footed Victorian bathtub has been set outside as a trough for farm animals, and the speaker invites "all longnecked browsers" to partake of its "green water for sipping/ that muzzles may enter thoughtful/ and rise dripping."

Kumin uses the image of water similarly in "Morning Swim," one of her most successful poems. Here water serves as nourishment:

> My bones drank water; water fell
> through all my doors. I was the well
> that fed the lake that met my sea
> in which I sang *Abide with Me*.

The speaker of the poem attains this state of immersion "in chilly solitude," and the act of swimming is not actually physical but a movement within the speaker's imagination: "Into my empty head there come/ a cotton beach, a dock wherefrom/ I set out, oily and nude."

The amenities of solitude appear again in Kumin's series of hermit poems. Like Kumin's love poems, several poems in this series are quite sensuous. The sequence opens with "The Hermit Wakes to Bird Sounds": "He startles awake. His eyes are full of white light./ In a minute the sun will ooze into the sky." Kumin's description of night in "The Hermit Has a Visitor" is similar but more richly fertile than her reference to "night fog thick as terry cloth" in "Morning Swim": "Night is a honey-comb./ Night is the fur on a blue plum." For Kumin, blue is a color of ripeness. In "The Hermit Picks Berries," she describes the ripening of blueberries by noting their transformation in color, from "wax white" to "the green of small bruises" to "the red of bad welts": "Now they are true blue."

In contrast to *Up Country, The Retrieval System* is structured thematically. In this book, Kumin confronts middle age and the loss of parents, children, and her friend Anne Sexton. In "Extrapolations from Henry Manley's Pie Plant" (one of a series of poems centered on Kumin's country neighbor), she reflects on the choices she has made: "I look at my middling self and recognize/ this life is but one of a number of possible lives." She considers some of these possible lives, then describes the one she as chosen: "Instead, mornings I commence with the sun,/ tend my animals, root in the garden/ and pass time with Henry." She does not regret this choice, because it has enabled her to live where the "goldfinches explode/ from the meadow."

In "Henry Manley, Living Alone, Keeps Time," the last and most successful poem of the series, Kumin considers the effects of aging: "Sundowning,/ the doctor calls it, the way/ he loses words when the light fades." Henry often cannot remember the names of those he loves, yet the poet recognizes that he "goes on loving them out of place." She is saddened by the separation of the body and the soul and notes his awareness of how loose his connection to life is becoming. At any moment his soul could slip out of his body, lightly and without warning, like the helium-filled balloon that floated from his grasp when he was a child.

Kumin explores more serious regrets in this volume, confronting losses very specific and real. She refers to them explicitly in "Address to the Angels." These losses include the suicide of Anne Sexton, her father's fatal heart attack, and her daughter's move to Europe. She thinks that if she could go back in time she could prevent these bad occurrences: "I am wanting part of my life back/ so I can do it over./ So I can do it better. In "How It Is," she thinks of the last day of Sexton's life, "how I would unwind it, paste/ it together in a different collage,/ back from the death car idling in the garage."

Several poems in this volume, which is dedicated to Kumin's daughters, concern the separation of parents and adult children, and particularly the separation of mothers and daughters. "Changing the Children" suggests the painfulness of adolescence and the distance it creates between parents and children. This distance is temporary, but by the time it closes, the relationship has changed: "Eventually we get them back./ Now they are grown up./ They are much like ourselves." In "Seeing the Bones," Kumin mourns her separation from her world-traveling daughter: "now you're off to Africa/ or Everest, daughter of the file drawer,/ citizen of no return." Again Kumin wishes to return to an earlier time: "Working backward I reconstruct/ you. Send me your baby teeth, some new/ nail parings." Yet in "The Envelope," Kumin, although fearful of her own death, looks forward—to the near-immortality that her daughters will give her: "we, borne onward by our daughters, ride/ in the Envelope of Almost-Infinity."

Assuming a voice more political than personal in her tenth volume, *Nurture*, Kumin frets about the condition of the environment and the actual physical survival of animals. In "Thoughts on Saving the Manatee," she questions the possibility of the manatee's survival, for "experts agree that no matter/ how tenderly tamed by philanthropy/ [their] survival is chancy." The poem ends with a possible solution and a call to action reminiscent of Jonathan Swift's "A Modest Proposal":

> Let's revert to the Catch of the Day
> and serve up the last few as steak marinara.
> Let's stop pretending we need them
> more than they need us.

In this volume, and especially in the animal poems, Kumin displays a recurring concern for mothers and children. In "Thoughts on Saving the Manatee," she notes that the manatee in her area are "mostly cows and their calves." Quite a different scenario is presented in "Catchment," in which the speaker watches a female leopard pounce on a newborn antelope. Here the speaker faces a dilemma and wonders which animal she should root for—the helpless baby antelope or "the big cat, in whose camouflaged lair/ three helpless youngsters wait/ so starved for meat."

In the title poem, "Nurture," Kumin states her motherly interest directly: "I suffer, the critic proclaims,/ from an overabundance of maternal genes." Touched by a televised report of the surrogate parenting of a baby kangaroo, she is willing to open her heart and home to such an orphan—or to a human orphan, however wild: "it is safe to assume,/ given my fireside inked with paw prints,/ there would have been room."

"Surprises," a "tribal poem," suggests a connection between Kumin and orphaned animals. Here, the poet, who is celebrating the success of her California peppers after fifteen years of failure, remembers how, when her mother's thriving roses finally caused the dilapidated trellis to collapse under their weight, "she mourned the dirtied blossoms more, I thought,// than if they'd been her children." While her mother "pulled on/ goatskin gloves to deal with her arrangements/ in chamberpots, pitchers, and a silver urn," Kumin was left to watch, "orphan at the bakeshop window."

Kumin moves forward to present time in "We Stood There Singing," which tells of a drive in Switzerland with her daughter and infant grandson. Kumin connects the grandson to the "wild child" in "Nurture" by using the verb "howled," again emphasizing the similarity between humans and animals. Kumin's grandson reappears in "A Game of Monopoly in Chavannes." Thinking of him, she contemplates the passing of her own generation. This grandson will someday replace her, will learn how to make his way through life, how to invest himself. Yet Kumin is not yet ready to leave. Mourning the deaths of her uncles in "Grappling in the Central Blue" makes her determined to hold onto life:

> Let us eat of the inland oyster.
> Let its fragrance intoxicate us
> into almost believing
> that staying on is possible
> again this year in
> benevolent blue October.

Some of Kumin's most beautiful poems, such as "Magellan Street, 1974," are about her daughter. Although she is again ruminating on the separation of mother and daughter, she is not sad, but hopeful. She stands in her daughter's kitchen, bright with potted herbs, and is able to envision how the younger woman's life "will open, will burst from/ the maze in its walled-in garden/ and streak toward the horizon."

Kumin's poetry is endlessly positive, celebrating the sensuousness of physical existence, the naturalness of movement and time. Had she published fewer volumes, choosing poems more selectively, her poetic achievement would have been more honed, her weaknesses less apparent. Yet solitary and social, personal and public, her poetry is a testament of affirmation within the context of painful losses.

Other major works

NOVELS: *Through Dooms of Love*, 1965; *The Passions of Uxport*, 1968; *The Abduction*, 1971; *The Designated Heir*, 1974.

SHORT FICTION: *Why Can't We Live Together Like Civilized Human Beings?*, 1982.

NONFICTION: *To Make a Prairie: Essays on Poets, Poetry, and Country Living*, 1980; *In Deep: Country Essays*, 1987.

CHILDREN'S LITERATURE: *Sebastian and the Dragon*, 1960; *Spring Things*, 1961; *Summer Story*, 1961; *Follow the Fall*, 1961; *A Winter Friend*, 1961; *Mittens in May*, 1962; *No One Writes a Letter to the Snail*, 1962; *Archibald the Traveling Poodle*, 1963; *Eggs of Things*, 1963 (with Anne Sexton); *More Eggs of Things*, 1964 (with Sexton);

Speedy Digs Downside Up, 1964; *The Beach Before Breakfast*, 1964; *Paul Bunyan*, 1966; *Faraway Farm*, 1967; *The Wonderful Babies of 1809 and Other Years*, 1968; *When Grandmother Was Young*, 1969; *When Mother Was Young*, 1970; *When Great Grandmother Was Young*, 1971; *Joey and the Birthday Present*, 1971 (with Sexton); *The Wizard's Tears*, 1975 (with Sexton); *What Color Is Caesar?*, 1978; *The Microscope*, 1984.

Bibliography

Gioia, Dana. Review of *Our Ground Time Here Will Be Brief*. *Hudson Review* 35 (Winter, 1982-1983): 652-653.

Harmon, William. Review of *Our Ground Time Here Will Be Brief*. *Poetry* 143 (April, 1983): 50-51.

Kumin, Maxine. *To Make a Prairie: Essays on Poets, Poetry, and Country Living*. Ann Arbor: University of Michigan Press, 1979.

Sexton, Anne, and Maxine Kumin. "A Nurturing Relationship: A Conversation with Anne Sexton and Maxine Kumin, April 15, 1974." Interview by Elaine Showalter and Carol Smith. *Women's Studies* 4 (1976): 115-136.

Shaw, Robert B. Review of *The Long Approach*. *Poetry* 148 (April, 1986): 36-38.

MADAME DE LA FAYETTE
Marie-Madeleine Pioche de la Vergne

Born: Paris, France; March (?), 1634

Died: Paris, France; May 25, 1693

Principal long fiction

Madame de La Fayette is the author of two novels: ZAYDE (also as *Zaïde*), in two volumes, published under the name of Segrais in 1670-1671, and *La Princesse de Clèves*, published anonymously in 1678 (*The Princess of Clèves*, 1679). She is also the author of two shorter works of fiction, often called historical novellas: *La Princesse de Montpensier*, published under the name of Segrais in 1662 (*The Princess of Montpensier*, 1666) and *La Comtesse de Tende*, published posthumously in 1724. Two other shorter works of fiction, published in 1909, have been attributed to her but are not generally recognized as authentic: *Histoire de Don Carlos D'Astorgas* and *Histoire espagnole*. The three works of fiction published during her lifetime appeared without her name apparently because of questions of decorum involved in women's literary activities. Although La Fayette explicitly denied having written *The Princess of Clèves*, the attribution is not seriously contested.

Other literary forms

Madame de La Fayette also wrote the following historical works: *Histoire de Madame Henriette d'Angleterre* (1720; *Fatal Gallantry*, 1722) and *Mémoires de la cour de France pour les années 1688 et 1689* (1731).

Achievements

Madame de La Fayette is frequently described as the first person to write a modern novel (as opposed to a romance) in French. La Fayette's plot construction in *The Princess of Clèves* clearly distinguishes between the main characters and those involved in the many subplots. The resultant concentration on the heroine allows readers to follow the development of her character and her motivations. Because the reader's attention is not dispersed over many plots, as in the romances, suspense and empathy are more intense. In fact, the public's identification with the novel's heroine reached such proportions that a torrent of letters and pamphlets appeared, taking passionately held positions on the heroine's conduct.

In purely literary terms, *The Princess of Clèves* constitutes a major change in the way fiction relates to history in French literature. Instead of placing her story in the distant past or in an exotic Oriental or African country, La Fayette blended real historical persons, well known to her readers, with purely imaginary characters. This proximity of the story to the life of the reader awakened an expectation of verisimilitude or realism that made the reader compare himself or herself with the characters. Reading thus became a critical activity of a new sort, for the reader could claim that a character behaved in an unlikely way or, on the contrary, could decide to identify with the character and try to model real-life action on the fictitious pattern. The so-called "quarrel of *The Princess of Clèves*" marks the historical beginning of the attempt to use the novel as a serious tool of social examination.

Biography

Born in Paris and baptized on March 18, 1634, Marie-Madeleine Pioche de la Vergne was well connected with the royal court. Her mother, Isabelle Pena, was the daughter of the physician of Louis XIII. La Fayette's father had an honorable career in the royal army until his death in 1649. Her mother's second husband, Renaud-René de Sévigné, was involved in the aristocratic rebellion known as the Fronde and was exiled from the court in 1652. Three years later, Marie-Madeleine married François, Comte de La Fayette. Madame de La Fayette spent less than four years at her husband's estate in the Auvergne. By 1659, they were back in Paris, where their second son was born. In 1661, the Count returned to the Auvergne, leaving Madame de La Fayette to live in the house built by her father and to participate in the life of the court. She was close to Madame de Sévigné and to Princess Henrietta of England, wife of Philippe d'Orléans, brother of the King. She frequented the salon of the literary Du Plessis-Guénégauds, held at the Hôtel de Nevers. In 1665, she began a long friendship with the Duc de La Rochefoucauld, a former leader of the Fronde and author of the well-known *Maximes* (1665-1678; *The Maxims*, 1670, 1706). After his death in 1680 and her husband's death in 1683, she renewed her friendship with the active literary figure Gilles Ménage. In the later 1670's, she was active in secret diplomatic negotiations with the Duchy of Savoy. After 1689, she turned toward religion under the direction of the Abbé de Rancé.

Analysis

Although it is frequently neglected by readers because of its exaggerated reputation as a difficult and complex novel, Madame de La Fayette's *Zayde* (often spelled *Zaïde*) is a highly polished, thoughtful work, containing many of the elements of La Fayette's undoubted masterpiece, *The Princess of Clèves*. Like the latter, *Zayde* contains a principal plot interrupted with less important plots appearing in inserted tales—that is, stories told by the characters. The inserted tales in *Zayde* are longer than those in *The Princess of Clèves* and differ also in that the characters in *Zayde* tell their own stories and not stories about other people. This constant changing of narrative voice and of character does make *Zayde* somewhat harder to follow than the later novel. Thematically, *Zayde* is closely linked to *The Princess of Clèves* by the characters' probing of the nature of reality in contrast to their presuppositions and fears about it. The heroes are their own worst enemies. They are paralyzed by assumptions about life and other people that simply do not match experience.

Consalve, a young courtier, leaves the court to seek utter solitude on the Spanish coast. There he meets another gentleman, Alphonse, who offers him a place to stay. The two exchange their stories of disenchantment. Consalve's story concerns his betrayal by his two best friends, the Prince Don Garcie and Ramir. The three of them had discussed whether love arises most strongly in a man for a woman he knows well or someone he does not know until the moment when he finds himself totally and irrationally attracted. Consalve claimed that he could not love a woman he did not know well. His two friends argued that acquaintance defeats love, and Ramir added that the desirability of the loved object increases if she already is attached to another. Yet Consalve's knowledge of his beloved was limited, because he did not know that she had the capacity to leave him for Ramir.

Alphonse, too, had developed a general concept of human conduct that subsequently failed him. He had decided that he would not marry a beautiful woman, because she would make him jealous of his rivals. In spite of this resolve, Alphonse had fallen in love and become jealous—to such an extent that he killed his best friend and drove his beloved into a convent. Alphonse's ideas about women were so rooted in his mind that he did not need a reason to be jealous. In many ways, Consalve's and Alphonse's stories are symmetrical. Consalve was betrayed by others in whom he placed excessive trust; Alphonse killed his best friend and ruined the life of his beloved because of an excessive lack of trust.

The vanity of trying to guide one's life by preconceived notions becomes evident in the course of the novel, which is largely devoted to Consalve's love for Zayde. She is a young woman whom Consalve finds washed up on the beach after a violent storm. Only Zayde and her woman companion have survived a shipwreck, and Consalve does not recognize their tongue. For months, he tries to converse with Zayde and fails. He intuits that Zayde finds in his face the likeness of someone else she has loved. Consalve is jealous when Zayde looks at him with tenderness, thinking that she sees him only as the image of her absent lover. The hero has proved that his initial assumptions about the relationship of love and knowledge are entirely wrong, and it takes many adventures and many more inserted tales before Consalve discovers what the relationship is. At the end of the novel, when he and Zayde meet after a long separation, they are able to speak to each other. She has learned Spanish, and he has discovered that her language is Greek and has learned it. He finds that she recognized in him the face from a portrait that had been identified for her as that of the Prince of Fez, to whom she had been promised in marriage. The portrait, however, is actually a lost portrait of Consalve. La Fayette concludes her novel with this trite mechanism for undoing complicated plots, but she uses the lost portrait for a specific reason that is quite original. One aspect of love, one that has afflicted both Consalve and Alphonse, is the attempt to impose on the outside world a conception of the way things are or ought to be. In a sense, both are seeking in love someone who will mirror themselves. Alphonse is punished by his inability to see that his beloved is not the mirror of his jealousy. Consalve's purgatory is the long quest to discover that it is his own image that stands in the way of his love for Zayde.

Although *The Princess of Clèves* is briefer than *Zayde* and has a less difficult plot, this acknowledged masterpiece addresses problems that are fully as complex as those in *Zayde*. In her second novel, La Fayette also treats the relationship between general assumptions and individual experience, but she does so by tracing the life of a woman, Mademoiselle de Chartres (the heroine has no first name), who comes to the court as an adolescent with her mother, who wants to arrange a good and prestigious marriage for her daughter. Since Mademoiselle de Chartres arrives at the court with neither opinions about nor acquaintance with its ways, she relies entirely on her mother to form her. In her educational endeavor, the mother uses two approaches: plain assertion and illustrative narration. The problem, however, is that the mother's assertions about the way a woman can be happy (the sole means of obtaining feminine happiness, she says, is to love one's husband and to be loved by him) and the story she tells about Madame de Valentinois (Diane De Poitiers), the mistress of King Henri II, do not coincide. The king's mistress is the most powerful woman at the court. She is faithful neither to her husband nor to her lovers, yet there is no indication of unhappiness on her part.

This contradiction is the starting point for one of the structural problems of the novel. Valincour, one of the earliest critics of *The Princess of Clèves*, felt that the internal narratives told by various characters to the heroine simply did not hold together. Surely, if the novelist wanted simply to create local color, she would not have needed to interrupt her narrative repeatedly to have characters fill in the gaps in the heroine's knowledge of court intrigue. The heroine could learn about these things without the reader of the novel having to listen verbatim to all the accounts given of the life of Mary Stuart or of Madame de Tournon, among others. It is more probable that the act of listening to such stories and trying to apply them to one's own life as models of conduct is a matter of interest in its own right. The heroine is trying to fit her general ideas about life—including such notions as men

never being faithful—to these stories in search of confirmation of her expectations. Even when she does not find her assumptions borne out, she clings to the instructions given to her by her mother.

The heroine's marriage to the Prince of Clèves does not give her happiness, but it does give her someone to talk to after her mother dies. The Princess has learned to seek guidance by using stories as examples of conduct and is accustomed to telling her own life, as a story, to her mother. When the Princess falls in love with the Duke of Nemours, the Princess' husband becomes the only person in whom she can confide. She believes that she must either yield to her passion or tell it to someone. The confession scene at Coulommiers, where she tells her husband that she is in love with someone else, is therefore a logical consequence of the mother's (and the novel's) insistence on telling stories.

The readers of the novel generally thought that no woman would ever make such a confession. Love and marriage were therefore strictly separate, despite the teachings of the Church and the somewhat utopian doctrine presented by the Princess' mother that women should love their husbands. Husband and wife frequently had little to do with each other, living separate lives, as did Madame de La Fayette and her husband. Under these circumstances, it would be either superfluous or imprudent for a wife to tell her husband about a love affair. To make matters worse, La Fayette multiplied the improbabilities of her novel. If the confession is in itself unlikely, how likely is it that Nemours, the object of the wife's adulterous passion, should be hidden in the trees, listening to everything she says? If his presence there is already stretching one's capacity to suspend disbelief, Nemours' secret return to the Clèves estate to spy on the Princess another time is certainly hard to credit. Finally, in the list of improbabilities detected by the early readers, the Princess' refusal to marry or to have an affair with Nemours after her husband's death (caused by a broken heart) raised numerous objections.

La Fayette seems to be playing with the reader's assumptions about what is normal. She can do so only by locating her novel in a time and space sufficiently close to the reader's own for the reader to apply the same standards to both book and world. If the Princess had been a figure in a romance, readers would probably have accepted anything she did. In *The Princess of Clèves*, however, there is a real tension between what critics and other readers found unbelievable and the historical accuracy of most of the setting.

The key to this puzzle may very well lie in the last sentence of *The Princess of Clèves*, in which, after having left the court for a remote country house, the widowed Princess dies and leaves the world "inimitable examples of virtue." The many inserted stories of this novel are used by the heroine as examples of conduct at the court. Despite the apparent educational value of these stories, they serve a strictly negative function, showing her what kind of conduct does not conform to her mother's precepts about feminine happiness. Furthermore, throughout the novel, the Princess is described as being unlike others. La Fayette squarely poses the problem of the usefulness of examples by confronting exemplary stories of the court with a heroine who is unique and who leaves behind examples that cannot be imitated.

The Princess of Clèves as been described as the first novel of psychological analysis. Although this description is in some ways a projection into the seventeenth century of late nineteenth century approaches, it does have the merit of emphasizing the heroine's role in seeking to understand her own desires and the conduct of those around her. Yet there are considerable areas of the mind and emotions of the principal characters that remain ambiguous. Even the heroine's decision to leave the court and not to marry Nemours remains a subject of great controversy. Some critics claim that she follows a religious impulse that leads her to flee from the man who led her to the brink of sin. Others see this ultimate refusal of love as a flight from unhappiness in view of her conviction that men are never faithful when they are satisfied both emotionally and sexually.

The persistence of mystery in the self is a link between *The Princess of Clèves* and *Zayde*. For all of their attempts to compress human conduct into clear definitions and rules, Consalve, Alphonse, and the Princess are never really certain what will happen or even precisely what passes through their own minds.

Other major works

NONFICTION: *Histoire de Madame Henriette d'Angleterre*, 1720 (*Fatal Gallantry*, 1722); *Mémoires de la cour de France pour les années 1688 et 1689*, 1731.

Bibliography

Durry, Marie Jeanne. *Madame de La Fayette*. Paris: Mercure de France, 1962.

Genette, Gérard. *Figures of Literary Discourse*. Translated by Alan Sheridan. New York: Columbia University Press, 1982.

Haig, Stirling. *Madame de La Fayette*. New York: Twayne, 1970.

Horowitz, Louise K. *Love and Language: A Study of the Classical French Moralist Writers*. Columbus: Ohio State University Press, 1977.

SELMA LAGERLÖF

Born: Värmland, Sweden; November 20, 1858

Died: Värmland, Sweden; March 16, 1940

Principal long fiction

Gösta Berlings saga, 1891 (*The Story of Gösta Berling*, 1898; also as *Gösta Berling's Saga*, 1918); *Antikrists mirakler*, 1897 (*The Miracles of Antichrist*, 1899); *Jerusalem I: I Dalarne*, 1901 (*Jerusalem*, 1915); *Jerusalem II: I det heliga landet*, 1902 (*The Holy City: Jerusalem II*, 1918); *Herr Arnes penningar*, 1904 (*The Treasure*, 1925); *Liljecronas hem*, 1911 (*Liliecrona's Home*, 1914); *Körkarlen*, 1912; *Kejsaren av Portugallien*, 1914 (*The Emperor of Portugallia*, 1916); *Bannlyst*, 1918 (*The Outcast*, 1922); *Löwensköldska ringen*, 1925-1928 (*The Ring of the Löwenskölds: A Trilogy*, 1928; includes *Löwenskölda ringen*, 1925 [*The General's Ring*, 1928]; *Charlotte Löwensköld*, 1925 [English translation, 1928]; *Anna Svärd*, 1928 [English translation, 1928]); *Höst*, 1933 (*Harvest*, 1935).

Other literary forms

Short stories, particularly tales drawn from oral traditions of her native Värmland, are Lagerlöf's most characteristic form. In *Osynliga länkar* (1894; *Invisible Links*, 1899), Lagerlöf relies on plots from Swedish folk legends. *Drottningar i Kungahälla* (1899; *From a Swedish Homestead*, 1901; also in *The Queens of Kungahälla and Other Sketches*, 1917) is based on the Norwegian royal sagas that record the careers and legends of medieval Scandinavian kings. Lagerlöf presented these well-known stories from the point of view of the women in them.

Lagerlöf is also the author of the classic Swedish children's literature, *Nils Holgerssons underbara resa genom Sverige* (1906-1907; *The Wonderful Adventures of Nils*, 1907; *The Further Adventures of Nils*, 1911), the story of a lazy and mischievous boy who is brought down to size by elves he has troubled. In Lagerlöf's *Kris-tuslegender* (1904; *Christ Legends*, 1908), the simple, compassionate stories of Christ's life are described as if they might be ordinary neighborhood occurrences.

In 1915, Lagerlöf wrote a volume of short stories entitled *Troll och människor* and completed a second volume of the same title in 1921. In 1920, she wrote a book-length biography of Zacharias Topelius, the Finnish poet who had been a major influence on the author's literary development.

Several of Lagerlöf's later works are autobiographical, among them her memoirs, which are collected in the three so-called Mårbacka volumes: *Mårbacka* (1922; English translation, 1924), *Ett barns memoarner* (1930; *Memories of My Childhood*, 1934), and *Dagbok, Mårbacka III* (1932; *The Diary of Selma Lagerlöf*, 1936). *Lilecrona's Home*, Lagerlöf's novel published in 1911, also has an autobiographical basis.

Achievements

Lagerlöf yearned to express what she believed were the heroic, elemental, and spiritual strains running through daily life. Therefore, she developed an epic fairy-tale atmosphere peopled with characters marked by tragedy, sorrow, and joy. With the appearance of her first book, Lagerlöf's distinctly unmodern aesthetic, perhaps more at home in the ninth century than the nineteenth, was warmly received by her countrymen, who communicated to her their gratitude that she expressed her subject matter in a mode entirely absent from contemporary literature.

In 1909, the Swedish Academy awarded to her the Nobel Prize in Literature, commending her noble ideal-ism, the richness of her imagination, and the generosity and beauty of forms that characterize her work. She was the first woman to win the prize. In characteristic fashion, her speech to the Nobel Commission took the form of a story: of a journey she made to Heaven to tell her father about winning the prize. Lagerlöf reviewed the several influences that had kindled her imagination, particularly honoring the "old country folk" who had taught her "to cast the glamour of poetry over grim rocks and grey waters."

Five years later, Selma Lagerlöf became the first woman to be elected to the Swedish Academy. Her works are widely translated.

Biography

Selma Ottiliana Lovisa Lagerlöf was born on November 20, 1858, at Mårbacka in Värmland, Sweden. Her parents, both members of aristocratic families, had moved to the estate of Mårbacka after Selma's father, Lieutenant Erik Gustav Lagerlöf, had failed to inherit the important post of Regimental Paymaster from his father. Lieutenant Lagerlöf 's annual birthday party, enlivened by pageants, theatricals, poetry recitations, dancing, and singing, became a social affair famous throughout the province.

Tales told from memory and read aloud at night—from local legend, from Hans Christian Andersen, and from Scandinavian sagas—were the essence of Selma Lagerlöf's early education; neither she nor her sister attended school. By early adolescence, Lagerlöf had determined that she would be a writer. During the next several years, she wrote novels, plays, and poems. In 1880, she attracted the notice of Eva Fryxell, a young author of the day, when she read an occasional poem at a friend's wedding. Despite Fryxell's sponsorship, Lagerlöf failed to place any of her work in literary journals. Fryxell encouraged the girl to broaden her education, a plan to which Lagerlöf eagerly subscribed. After a year's preparation at Sjöberg's Lyceum in Stockholm, Lagerlöf entered a teachers' college.

Lagerlöf taught school for ten years, during which time she wrote several stories which became part of *Gösta Berling's Saga*. In 1888, three years after her father's death, Mårbacka was sold. It was while she was at the homestead, watching her childhood home and family heirlooms sold, that she finally realized that her story of cavaliers living at a manor house should be told in a series of tales. With the five chapters she had completed by July of 1890, Lagerlöf won a competition sponsored by the women's paper *Idun*. She finished *Gösta Berling's Saga* by December of 1891, and it was published. While sales in Sweden were at first sluggish, the Danish version attracted the attention of the Danish critic and literary historian Georg Brandes, who immediately recognized it as a work of genius. His critical acclaim won widespread recognition for the book. By the time the second Swedish edition appeared, in 1895, recognition had come to Lagerlöf from all quarters.

After Lagerlöf was awarded the Nobel Prize in 1909, nearly all other literary honors offered in Sweden were awarded to her. The income associated with her success allowed her to repurchase the estate of Mårbacka, to which she moved with her mother. Until Lagerlöf's death in 1940, she oversaw the estate, entertained admirers and visitors from all over Europe and America, and sustained a large correspondence. She died at Mårbacka on March 16, 1940.

Analysis

Although Selma Lagerlöf wrote many distinguished novels, her countrymen have always considered the first to be her masterpiece. Whatever other merits later novels have—and they are more sophisticated in plot construction and theme—none compares to *Gösta Berling's Saga* for sheer concentration of vitality and idealism. The paeans of praise to Värmland's landscape and the detailed knowledge of Sweden's natural history, hallmarks of Lagerlöf's prose style, first appear here. As in later novels, the narrative voice in *Gösta Berling's Saga* is more prominent than those of the characters. The narrator is a storyteller; the raconteur never fades unobtrusively into the background. In Lagerlöf's novels, an air of reality surrounds the story but not the individual characters in it. One would never speculate about what a Lagerlöf character might be thinking when the character is not in the immediate scene.

The opening scene of *Gösta Berling's Saga* is characteristic of Lagerlöf's epic sweep, her comic tone, and, particularly, her eccentric character portraits. Gösta Berling, a young pastor, mounts the pulpit, pauses momentarily for inspiration, giving his congregation time to notice his exquisite features. His voice grows rich and strong as his images of God's glories ring through the chancel. At sermon's end, he has convinced the visiting bishop of his extraordinary merit; Gösta's triumph is particularly notable because on the previous Sunday he was not in church, nor was he there for many Sundays before that—each time he had been too drunk to preach. This day appears to be his redemption. One of Gösta's overzealous drinking companions, however—fearing that the bishop might still dismiss Gösta—takes the bishop on a carriage ride over ditches and half-plowed fields, counting on physical coercion to accomplish what the brilliant sermon may have fallen short of accomplishing. Hearing of his friend's misplaced loyalty, Gösta despairs of his future as a preacher and runs away. When next seen, he is stealing a sled loaded with grain from a child in another village.

In Lagerlöf's novels, human destiny is prey to violent turns of the sort Gösta's takes; the sheer speed with which a woman loses her beauty or a pastor becomes a derelict gives the work the flavor of fairy tale or allegory. This is particularly true in this first novel, in which Lagerlöf was finding a style suitable to her vision. Later novels possess a greater aura of realism but operate essentially upon the same premises. Although the first novel does have a plot of sorts, the power of the story is primarily its ability to render the life at the manor houses of a Sweden that was vanishing during Lagerlöf's childhood. The beautifully embellished descriptions of great balls and sleigh rides suggest a nostalgic longing for a life more elegant in manner and more mythic in perception than that of later eras.

The main body of *Gösta Berling's Saga* loosely centers on Gösta's reformation as he endures his humbled station as a pensioner. Gösta is rescued by the Mistress of Ekeby, the pipe-smoking, gracious, and powerful owner of seven mines and hostess to a group of pensioners. She makes Gösta one of her cavaliers. Gösta, "the strongest and weakest of men," is the center of provincial society, winning the affection of four of the district's loveliest women. The gentle influence of these good women and the subtler chastening of the Almighty lead Gösta from his impetuous youth to the verge of maturity.

The *Bildungsroman* begins on Christmas Eve, when the cavaliers make a pact with Sintram, a jealous blacksmith who comes to them disguised as the Devil. Sintram's predictions of doom are realized when the cavaliers take over the estate, bringing it to the brink of ruin through their wild dissipations and neglect of the industries. In turn, the district is blighted; unemployment, drunkenness, and general stagnation reign. In the novel's terms, God's Storm Year breaks over the countryside. Nearly every main character suffers a life-changing tragedy or loss, and these events represent a kind of spiritual cleansing. In the end, Sintram is arrested, and the Mistress of Ekeby returns home to die.

The thirty-six chapters of the book divide roughly into three sections. The first is dominated by Gösta's love affairs and the prosperous days the cavaliers enjoy before Ekeby slides toward destruction. The second section, centered on the sorrowful fate of the Countess Elizabeth, records the ongoing brilliant exploits of the cavaliers against scenes of impending doom. The cavaliers are in the background in the third section, which features great crowd scenes, emphasizing the desperate plight of the people during the year of devastation. This desolate course is altered at last by the noble Lennaert, who gives his life to defend a group of children and women. In the end, the chastened Mistress of Ekeby dies peacefully, and Gösta sets forth with his new wife to rebuild the district's fortunes.

In *Gösta Berling's Saga*, as in all Lagerlöf's novels, dramatic scenes of daily life give way to mythical, epic moments or insights. Neither mode prevails for long, and it is the tension between them that is the hallmark of Lagerlöf's style in this early novel. No event, however small, is conceived apart from the metaphysical claim that God's Storm Year has broken over the land. The morality implicit in such an idea emanates with epic force from natural causes—wind, storms, ice, and blizzard—and from the lake, invoked by the narrator as the district's guardian muse. Handsome Gösta is little more than a human embodiment of the same idea.

The second and third books of the trilogy *The Ring of the Löwenskölds* are among Lagerlöf's finer realistic novels. The whole of *Charlotte Löwensköld* and the first two-thirds of *Anna Svärd* form a compelling story of a young minister and the two women he courts. The final third of *Anna Svärd* reverts from realism to the fairy-tale tone that opens the trilogy. Despite their titles, the two novels are primarily the story of Karl Arthur Ekenstedt. Charlotte is his fiancée for five years and Anna Svärd is his wife; Thea Sundler is his confidante and later his illicit companion. Karl Arthur's mother, the Baroness, is the fourth woman whose life is interwoven with Karl Arthur's.

In many ways, Karl Arthur is a more realistic Gösta Berling. In the early novel, it is primarily a comic invention to have Gösta appear as a drunken preacher. Once he runs from his parish, Gösta's spiritual life is left behind, simply a passing stage of his youth. On the other hand, in Lagerlöf's more realistically conceived later work, Karl Arthur's concept of religion and his identity as a pietist are given a much larger part.

Karl Arthur Ekenstedt is a Löwensköld, a distant cousin to Charlotte. He is the youngest of three children, the apple of his mother's eye. Because she is the Baroness, the most popular woman in the district, outshining her daughters in all ways, her adoration of Karl Arthur becomes a district affair. Everyone knows that Arthur is off at the university taking Latin examinations or preparing for this or that degree. In fact, he is an ordinary boy, utterly spoiled by his mother's attentions. His extreme handsomeness, like Gösta's, attracts others to him, particularly women. While carrying out a mediocre study program at the university, Karl Arthur becomes acquainted with a young pietist who initiates him into the religion of austerity. Because Karl Arthur is unable to succeed in other ways, he determines to become a man of God. In subsequent years, his destructive jealousies, fired by a religious fanaticism, become the cover for his own weakness and also threaten to destroy others.

Despite his family's position and the possibility of acquiring a prestigious parish, Karl Arthur is content to remain at the deanery as curate. While there, he meets Charlotte, who is companion to the dean and his wife. Although Charlotte is amused by Karl Arthur's pietism, they become friends and Karl Arthur proposes. Five years pass, and Karl Arthur has made no attempt to start his career. Not knowing that Charlotte is engaged, a wealthy gentleman from the countryside asks for her hand. Charlotte, a spirited and loyal woman, refuses him. When Karl Arthur hears about the proposal, he remembers a single occasion when Charlotte suggested that he might try to find a post of his own. He uses what he terms Charlotte's "ambition" as an excuse for breaking with her, and she attempts to bring about a reconciliation. After Charlotte offers to accompany him to the poorest parish and to live in a humble hut, Karl Arthur is calmed, but a jealous thought sends him swiftly out the door, vowing that he will marry the first woman he sees.

Karl Arthur tells himself that he is submitting completely to God's Will, but once out on the road, he begins to regret his rash vow. The moment is one of Lagerlöf's most comic. The woman Karl Arthur meets is (to his great relief) a pretty Dalecarlian peasant girl, Anna Svärd, unschooled in the ways of the gentry but a skillful peddler woman, both bright and good-hearted—an acceptable alternative to Charlotte. Meanwhile, Karl Arthur's fierce jealousy of Charlotte and his overweening pride are both encouraged by Thea Sundler, wife of the church organist. Thea, who is herself in love with Karl Arthur, manages to convince him that Charlotte is unfaithful.

In the opening pages of *Anna Svärd*, Lagerlöf delineates life in the northern village where Anna lives, and the segment is as sympathetic and beautifully drawn as that describing Charlotte's life among the gentry. Lagerlöf lavishes scene after scene on Anna's wedding preparations, her acquisition of manners fitting to a minister's wife, and her innocent adoration of her handsome fiancé in the south. Great plans are made for the wedding, which Anna's uncle, a man of some means, will provide. Anna is believed to be favored above all peasant women; she will have "horse and cow, manservant and maidservant."

Karl Arthur has something quite different in mind. He arrives in the village one day, insisting that the marriage take place immediately, without ceremony. Karl Arthur is looking for a wife who is both manservant and maidservant. Anna, too stunned and too enamored of Karl Arthur to protest, sets off with him. Anna arrives at her new home to find that it is no more than a hut refurbished for the couple by Thea Sundler. To help keep Karl Arthur true to his pietist ways, Thea has prepared a comfortable couch for Karl Arthur in his study and a narrow cot for Anna in the kitchen. As she will do many times over the next several years, Anna outwits Thea and has her wedding bed. Years later, however, after Karl Arthur has callously ignored her feelings again and again, Anna finally leaves him. Karl Arthur himself, his preaching not going well, determines that God wants him to be out on the road preaching to the traveling folk, so he decides to take God's Word to the markets and fairs.

At this point, the novel loses its realistic foundation. Thea runs away to follow Karl Arthur, and the two become derelicts of the road; Anna, pregnant with Karl Arthur's child, finds a group of ten orphans, adopts them, and buys a farm with money from Karl Arthur's parents. Charlotte has long since married the country gentleman whose proposal she rejected when she was engaged to Karl Arthur.

Karl Arthur's pietism is equivalent to weakness of character. His absorption in himself, disguised as an ongoing search for God's way, is brilliantly portrayed and satirized. In the end, however, the narrator does not take her theme to a fittingly dismal conclusion. She attempts in the last chapters to thread Karl Arthur's tragedy and the deaths of other Löwensköld barons back to the curse of the ring described in the first book of the trilogy. The portrayal of a flawed man surrounded by good women is finally more memorable than the cursed ring motif; nevertheless, it is typical of the storyteller's mode not to wish any of her characters ill. In the final scene, Karl Arthur is planning to go to Africa to preach. Anna goes to church to hear him make his appeal and, recalling her youthful love, drops her wedding ring into the collection plate. The novel closes as Karl Arthur arrives at Anna's door, the storyteller asking, "How shall she answer him?"

In characteristic Lagerlöf style, then, the story resolves itself with a suggestion of enlightenment and joy. In this case, the ending and much of the narrative are also comic.

Lagerlöf's use of comedy bypasses her more serious themes rather than bringing them to a resolution. Even so, *Charlotte Löwensköld* and *Anna Svärd* are Lagerlöf's masterworks of character portrayal; they have been favorably compared to those of Jane Austen.

Other major works

SHORT FICTION: *Osynliga länkar*, 1894 (*Invisible Links*, 1899); *Drottningar i Kungahälla*, 1899 (*From a Swedish Homestead*, 1901; also in *The Queens of Kungahälla and Other Sketches*, 1917); *Kristuslegender*, 1904 (*Christ Legends*, 1908); *En saga om en saga och andra sagor*, 1909 (*The Girl from the Marshcroft*, 1910); *Troll och människor*, 1915, 1921 (2 volumes).

NONFICTION: *Zachris Topelius*, 1920; *Mårbacka*, 1922 (English translation, 1924); *Ett barns memoarner*, 1930 (*Memories of My Childhood*, 1934); *Dagbok, Mårbacka III*, 1932 (*The Diary of Selma Lagerlöf*, 1936).

CHILDREN'S LITERATURE: *Nils Holgerssons underbara resa genom Sverige*, 1906-1907 (2 volumes; *The Wonderful Adventures of Nils*, 1907, and *The Further Adventures of Nils*, 1911).

Bibliography

Berendsohn, Walter Arthur. *Selma Lagerlöf: Her Life and Work*. London: Nicholson & Watson, 1931.

Gustafson, Alrik. *Six Scandinavian Novelists: Lie, Jacobsen, Heidenstam, Selma Lagerlöf, Hamsun, Sigrid Undset*. Princeton, N.J.: Princeton University Press, 1940.

Larsen, Hanna Astrup. *Selma Lagerlöf*. Garden City, N.Y.: Doubleday, Doran, 1936.

Vrieze, Folkereina Steintje de. *Fact and Fiction in the Autobiographical Works of Selma Lagerlöf*. Assen, The Netherlands: Van Gorcum, 1958.

MARGARET LAURENCE

Born: Neepawa, Manitoba, Canada; July 18, 1926   **Died:** Lakefield, Ontario, Canada; January 5, 1987

Principal long fiction

This Side Jordan, 1960; *The Stone Angel*, 1964; *A Jest of God*, 1966; *The Fire-Dwellers*, 1969; *The Diviners*, 1974.

Other literary forms

Margaret Laurence published two short-story collections, *The Tomorrow-Tamer* (1963) and *A Bird in the House* (1970), and two children's books, *Jason's Quest* (1970) and *The Christmas Birthday Story* (1980). She also produced a translation of Somali folktales and poems, *A Tree for Poverty: Somali Poetry and Prose* (1954); a travelogue, *The Prophet's Camel Bell* (1963); and a study of Nigerian novelists and playwrights, *Long Drums and Cannons: Nigerian Dramatists and Novelists, 1952-1966* (1968). A collection of her essays, *Heart of a Stranger*, appeared in 1976. Because of her work on Nigerian fiction and drama, she is well known to students of African literature.

Achievements

From the beginning of her writing career, Laurence received much popular and critical recognition. *This Side Jordan* won the Beta Sigma Phi prize for a first novel by a Canadian; *The Stone Angel* received both critical and popular acclaim; *A Jest of God* was awarded the Governor General's Medal in 1966 and was adapted for motion pictures as *Rachel, Rachel*; *The Diviners*, despite less than universal critical acclaim, was at the top of the best-seller list for more than sixty consecutive weeks. Along with her popularity, Laurence enjoyed an international reputation as a consistently accomplished fiction-writer. Her special contribution to the novel was recognized by Jack McClelland of the Canadian publishing house of McClelland and Stewart when he first read *This Side Jordan*. The stories which were gathered in *The Tomorrow-Tamer* and *A Bird in the House* originally appeared separately in such Canadian, American, and British journals as *Prism, The Atlantic*, and *Queen's Quarterly*. Laurence also won respect as a lecturer and critic. United College, University of Winnipeg, made her an Honorary Fellow, the first woman and the youngest to be so honored. She received honorary degrees from McMaster, Dalhousie, Trent, University of Toronto, and Carleton University, and served as writer-in-residence at several Canadian universities. Her works have been translated into French, German, Italian, Spanish, Dutch, Norwegian, Danish, and Swedish.

Biography

Margaret Laurence was born Jean Margaret Wemyss on July 18, 1926, in Neepawa, Manitoba. When Laurence was four, her mother died, and her aunt, Margaret Simpson, left a respected teaching career in Calgary and went home to care for her niece. A year later, she and Robert Wemyss were married. They had one son, Robert, born only two years before his father died of pneumonia. In 1938, Margaret Simpson Wemyss took the two children and moved in with her father, the owner of a furniture store. Laurence lived in Grandfather Simpson's house until she left to attend United College, University of Winnipeg, in 1944.

John Simpson was a fierce and autocratic man of eighty-two when his widowed daughter and her two children moved in with him. Laurence resented his authority over her and her stepmother; this relationship fostered Laurence's empathy with women struggling toward freedom. All of her heroines struggle against oppressive forces, and Laurence's recurring theme of the lack of communication between men and women, as well as between women and women, is rooted in the domestic situation in Grandfather Simpson's house.

The encouragement and honest criticism given to Laurence by her stepmother were a great help to the girl, who started writing at an early age. At United College, she took honors in English, while her involvement with "The Winnipeg Old Left" during and after her college years reflected her dedication to social reform. After her graduation, she worked for a year as a reporter for the *Winnipeg Citizen*. Her experience covering the local labor news consolidated her social and political convictions.

In 1948, Laurence married Jack Laurence, a civil engineer from the University of Manitoba. They left Canada for England in 1949 and went to the British Protectorate of Somaliland in 1950, where he was in charge of a dam-building project. In 1952, they moved to the Gold Coast, now Ghana, where they lived until 1957. A daughter, Jocelyn, was born when they were on leave in England in 1952, and a son, David, was born in Ghana in 1955. Out of these African years came several early works, including *The Tomorrow-Tamer*, *This Side Jordan*, the translations of folktales, and the travel journal *The Prophet's Camel Bell*. During the years in Africa, Laurence read the Pentateuch for the first time, and these books of the Bible became a touchstone for her, especially pertinent to the African works and to a lesser extent to her Manawaka fiction. Here she developed the patience and discipline of a professional writer.

In 1962, Laurence and her children left Jack Laurence in Vancouver and moved to London. They remained in England until 1968, when Laurence returned to Canada to be writer-in-residence at Massey College, University of Toronto. She was affiliated with several other Canadian universities in the years that followed. In 1987, Laurence died in Lakefield, Ontario.

Analysis

The major emphasis of Margaret Laurence's fiction changed considerably between her early and later works. In a 1969 article in *Canadian Literature*, "Ten Years' Sentences," she notes that after she had grown out of her obsession with the nature of freedom, the theme of the African writings and *The Stone Angel*, her concern "had changed to that of survival, the attempt of the personality to survive with some dignity, toting the load of excess mental baggage that everyone carries. . . ." The more profound psychological realism of her later novels developed after a general awareness of the intractable problems of emerging African nations had matured both the Africans and their observers. The characters in the African works were products of a now-dated optimism which forced them into preconceived molds. The later novels reveal modified pessimism, but their vitality comes from Laurence's developing concern with psychological realism, which authenticates the characters and their voices.

In her first three novels, Laurence uses biblical allusions to provide a mythic framework for a psychological study of character and situation. All these allusions are from the Old Testament, which made a lasting impression on her when she read it for the first time in Africa. The names she chooses for the characters in the early fiction—Adamo, Jacob, Abraham, Nathaniel, Joshua, Hagar, Ishmael, and Rachel—provide ready-made dilemmas whose traditional solutions appear contrived and psychologically unrealistic. Biblical myth is replaced in *The Diviners* by the myths of Scottish immigrants and Canadian pioneers and Indians. The theme of the search for one's true origins also plays a prominent part throughout Laurence's fiction, but the issues become increasingly complex. Whereas a clear dichotomy between his Christian and African backgrounds divides Nathaniel Amegbe in *This Side Jordan*, Morag in *The Diviners*, a recognized novelist who was an orphan brought up by a garbage collector, is seriously perplexed by the bases of her identity.

The Stone Angel was published in 1964, two years after Laurence and her children moved to London. Laurence, in "A Place to Stand On" from *Heart of a Stranger*, states that the dominant theme of this novel is survival, "not just physical survival, but the preservation of some human dignity and in the end some human warmth and ability to reach out and touch others." The monument Hagar Shipley's father had built for her mother's tomb in the Manawaka cemetery is a stone angel, gouged out by stonemasons who were accustomed to filling the needs of "fledgling pharaohs in an uncouth land." Laurence's horror at the extravagance of the pharaohs' monuments at Luxor, recorded in "Good Morning to the Grandson of Rameses the Second" in *Heart of a Stranger*, is similar to her reaction to the material ambitions of the stern Scots-Irish prairie pioneers.

The story of Hagar Shipley is told in the first person

and covers the three weeks before her death, but in these weeks, long flashbacks depict scenes of Hagar's life in chronological order. Laurence gives sacramental overtones to the events of Hagar's last days: She confesses to a most unlikely priest in a deserted cannery over a jug of wine; in the hospital where she dies, she is able to overcome her pride and to enjoy and empathize with her fellow patients; after she accepts a previously despised minister sent by her son, she has an epiphany—"Pride was my wilderness, and the demon that led me there was fear"; and just before her death, she wrests from her daughter-in-law her last drink. Such sacramental overtones are not unusual in Laurence's works, but in her later works they become more subtle and complex than they are here.

Hagar Shipley is an old woman, an enormously fat, physically feeble old woman, grotesque and distorted in both body and spirit. She is mean-spirited as well as mean about her money and her possessions—almost a stereotype, an unlikely heroine, certainly not one who would seem to attract the sympathy of the reader. Hagar does, however, attract the reader; the genuineness of her portrayal makes her believable, and the reader empathizes with her plight, which she finally recognizes as self-made. The reader feels compassion for her in spite of and because of her pettiness. Her voice, even in her old age, is still strong, willful, and vital, and the development of her self-awareness and self-knowledge is gripping.

The Stone Angel is the first work in which Manawaka, Laurence's fictionalized hometown of Neepawa, Manitoba, serves as the childhood setting of the protagonist. She makes Manawaka a microcosmic world, the childhood home of all of her later protagonists, whose memories and friends carry over from one work to another. The mythic heritage of Hagar in *The Stone Angel*—the Scots-Irish pioneers and Metis Indians in Manitoba—is shared by Vanessa MacLeod in *A Bird in the House*, Rachel Cameron in *A Jest of God*, Stacey MacAindra in *The Fire-Dwellers*, and Morag Gunn in *The Diviners*, although Hagar is old enough to be the grandmother of the other four. Every one of these women leaves Manawaka in a search for identity and spiritual freedom, but none is able to escape her heredity and childhood environment entirely. The effects of environment and heredity were increasingly explored as Laurence became more and more concerned with the nature of identity. The Manawaka setting gave Laurence the opportunity to develop characters whose parents or grandparents en-gaged in a strenuous battle to open the frontier, founded what they hoped would be dynasties, and lived to see them fall because of the Depression. These stubborn and proud people begot children who had to find their own identities without the visible mansions their fathers had built to proclaim theirs. Pride in personal success became in the next generation pride in family and origin, and Hagar's inheritance from her father showed that the strength of the pioneer generation could destroy as well as build. The recognition of the double-edged nature of this strength enables Hagar, a stone angel in her former blindness, to feel at the end some human warmth for those around her.

Laurence worked on *The Diviners* from 1969 to 1973, at the old house she bought on the Otonabee River near Peterborough, Ontario. Unlike the earlier Laurence protagonists, apparently ordinary women who turn out to be extraordinary in their own way, Morag Gunn is an extraordinarily gifted writer who has quite ordinary and common concerns. The title, *The Diviners*, refers explicitly to gifted individuals, artists such as Morag who contribute to a greater understanding of life, as well as to her friend, Royland, a true water diviner. Indeed, Morag discovers that many of her acquaintances are, in some way, themselves diviners. At the end of the book, when Royland tells Morag he has lost the gift of divining, Morag muses, "At least Royland knew he had been a true diviner. . . . The necessity of doing the thing—that mattered."

The Diviners is the longest and the most tightly structured of Laurence's novels; it has three long parts framed by a prologue and epilogue. The plot is commonplace: Morag spends a summer worrying about her eighteen-year-old daughter Pique, who has gone west to find herself. In this action, Morag is only an observer, as all mothers must be in this situation. Her own story is enclosed within the action in the present, with chronological flashbacks such as those in *The Stone Angel*. The novel is presented in the first person, but with two new techniques: "Snapshots," meditations on the few snapshots Morag has from her youth; and "Memorybank Movies," Morag's memories from her past. The snapshots cover the lives of her parents before Morag was born through her early childhood and their deaths. Aware that she embroidered stories about the snapshots as a child, Morag looks at a snapshot, remembers her make-believe story, and then muses, "I don't recall when I invented that one." This comment, early in the novel, establishes the mythologizing of one's past as an important motif.

Morag's future as a writer is foreshadowed by her retelling of Christie Logan's tales when just a girl, adapting them to her own needs. In the prologue, Morag the novelist worries about diction, the choice of the proper words: "How could that colour be caught in words? A sort of rosy peach colour, but that sounded corny and was also inaccurate." Morag uses her hometown for setting and characters, just as Laurence herself does; the theme of where one belongs is as important to Morag as a writer as it is to Laurence.

The title of Morag's second novel, *Prospero's Child*, foreshadows the motif of the end-frame. Royland loses his gift of witching for water and hopes to pass it on to A-Okay Smith. Morag realizes that she will pass on to Pique her gift, just as Christie Logan's manic prophecies influenced her creativity. Among all Laurence's heroines, Morag Gunn is the closest in experience and interests to Laurence herself. Each successive protagonist, from Hagar and Rachel and Vanessa to Stacey, came closer and closer to Laurence's own identity. She said that she realized how difficult it would be to portray a protagonist so much like herself, but *The Diviners* is a risky novel, an ambitious book which only an established writer could afford to produce.

Presenting her characters as beings caught between the determinism of history and their free will, as individuals who are torn between body and spirit, fact and illusion, Laurence portrays life as a series of internal crises. Through the development of her protagonists, Laurence celebrates even the crises as she celebrates her protagonists' progress. The search for self involves both the liberation from and the embracing of the past. Survival with dignity and the ability to love, she remarks in *Heart of a Stranger*, are themes inevitable for a writer of her stern Scots-Irish background. Since these themes are of immense contemporary importance, her works explore problems that have universal appeal, a fact that goes far to explain her tremendous popularity.

Other major works

SHORT FICTION: *The Tomorrow-Tamer*, 1963; *A Bird in the House*, 1970.
NONFICTION: *The Prophet's Camel Bell*, 1963 (published in the United States as *New Wind in a Dry Land*, 1964); *Long Drums and Cannons: Nigerian Dramatists and Novelists, 1952-1966*, 1968; *Heart of a Stranger*, 1976.
CHILDREN'S LITERATURE: *Jason's Quest*, 1970; *The Christmas Birthday Story*, 1980.
ANTHOLOGY: *A Tree for Poverty: Somali Poetry and Prose*, 1954.

Bibliography

Kertzer, J. M. "Margaret Laurence and Her Works." In *Canadian Writers and Their Works: Fiction Series*, edited by Robert Lecker, Jack David, and Ellen Quigley. Toronto: ECW Press, 1987.
Sorfleet, John R., ed. "The Work of Margaret Laurence." *Journal of Canadian Fiction* 27 (1980).
Thomas, Clara. *Margaret Laurence*. Canadian Writers 3. Toronto: McClelland and Stewart, 1969.
Verduyn, Christl, ed. *Margaret Laurence: An Appreciation*. Peterborough, Ontario: Broadview Press, 1988.
Woodcock, George, ed. *A Place to Stand On: Essays By and About Margaret Laurence*. Western Canadian Literary Documents Series 4. Edmonton: NeWest Press, 1983.

URSULA K. LE GUIN

Born: Berkeley, California; October 21, 1929

Principal long fiction

Rocannon's World, 1966; *Planet of Exile*, 1966; *City of Illusions*, 1967; *A Wizard of Earthsea*, 1968; *The Left Hand of Darkness*, 1969; *The Tombs of Atuan*, 1971; *The Lathe of Heaven*, 1971; *The Farthest Shore*, 1972; *The Dispossessed: An Ambiguous Utopia*, 1974; *Very Far Away from Anywhere Else*, 1976; *Malafrena*, 1979; *Leese Webster*, 1979; *The Beginning Place*, 1980; *The Eye of the Heron*, 1982; *Always Coming Home*, 1985; *Catwings*, 1988; *Catwings Return*, 1989; *Tehanu: The Last Book of Earthsea*, 1990.

Other literary forms

Included in Ursula K. Le Guin's list of novels have been books specifically written for children and young adults: *A Wizard of Earthsea*, *The Tombs of Atuan*, and *The Farthest Shore* (the first three books of what is known as the Earthsea series); *Very Far Away from Anywhere Else*; *Leese Webster*; and *The Beginning Place*. Her other published works include a novella, *The Word for World Is Forest* (1972); several volumes of short stories, *The Wind's Twelve Quarters* (1975), *Orsinian Tales* (1976), *The Compass Rose* (1982), and *Buffalo Gals and Other Animal Presences* (1987); and several volumes of poetry, *Wild Angels* (1975), *Hard Words and Other Poems* (1981), *In the Red Zone* (1983), and *Wild Oats and Fireweed: New Poems* (1988). Le Guin's comments on the nature and meaning of fantasy, her own creative process, and science fiction in general are collected in *From Elfland to Poughkeepsie* (1973), *The Language of the Night: Essays on Fantasy and Science Fiction* (1979; Susan Wood, editor), *Dancing at the Edge of the World: Thoughts on Words, Women, and Places* (1988), and *Napa: The Roots and Springs of the Valley* (1989). With Brian Attebery, she edited *The Norton Book of Science Fiction: North American Science Fiction, 1960-1990* (1993).

Achievements

The quality of Le Guin's work has been apparent from the beginning of her writing career. Brian Attebery, a fellow writer, has stated that even her first published novels are superior to most works of science fiction written at that time. Public recognition of Le Guin's work began with the Boston *Globe*/Horn Book Award for *A Wizard of Earthsea* in 1969. Since then, Le Guin has amassed numerous prestigious awards. They include Nebula and Hugo Awards for *The Left Hand of Darkness* (1969, 1970); the Newbery Silver Medal Award for *The Tombs of Atuan* (1972); a Hugo Award for *The Word for World Is Forest* (1973); a National Book Award for Children's Books for *The Farthest Shore* (1973); a Hugo Award for "The Ones Who Walk Away from Omelas" (1974); Nebula, Jupiter, and Hugo Awards for *The Dispossessed* (1974, 1975); a Jupiter Award for "The Diary of the Rose" (1976); a Gandalf Award for achievement in fantasy (1979); and, in 1986, the Kafka Award. In addition to receiving these honors, Le Guin has been a writer-in-residence at the Clarion West workshop at the University of Washington and a teaching participant in a science-fiction workshop at Portland State University. Her stature among science-fiction writers was recognized on an international scale when, in 1975, Le Guin was the Guest of Honor at the 33rd World Science Fiction Convention (Aussiecon) in Sydney, Australia. The following year, she was a Visiting Fellow in creative writing at the University of Reading, England.

Biography

Ursula Kroeber Le Guin was born into a close, intellectual family in Berkeley, California, on October 21, 1929. Her father, Alfred, was an anthropologist distinguished for his studies of the California Indians; her mother, Theodora Krackaw Kroeber, a respected writer with an advanced degree in psychology. During the academic year, they lived in a large, airy house in Berkeley. Their summers were spent in their Napa Valley home, Kishamish. To these forty acres flocked writers, scholars, graduate students, relatives, and Indians.

Living among so many people rich in knowledge and curiosity, and having access to an almost unlimited supply of books, Le Guin began writing and reading quite young. She did not discover science fiction, however, until she was twelve. When she found, while reading Lord Dunsany one day, that people were still creating myths, Le Guin felt liberated, for this discovery validated her own creative efforts.

In 1947, Le Guin entered Radcliffe College in Cambridge, Massachusetts. After she was graduated magna cum laude in 1951, she entered Columbia University, where she majored in French and Italian Renaissance literature. After completing her master's degree in 1952, she began work on a doctoral program. En route to France as a Fulbright fellow, she met Charles Le Guin, a historian from Georgia also on a Fulbright. They were married in Paris on December 22, 1953.

When they returned from France, the Le Guins lived in Georgia. Ursula taught French at Mercer University in Macon, and Charles completed his Ph.D. in French history at Emory University. Afterward, they moved to Idaho, where their first child, Elisabeth, was born in 1957. Caroline, their second daughter, arrived in 1959, the year Charles accepted a position at Portland State University and the family moved to a permanent home

in Oregon. A third child, Theodore, would be born in 1964. Ursula, who had never stopped writing but had yet to find a proper market for her efforts, became reacquainted with science fiction when a friend encouraged her to borrow from his library. Cordwainer Smith's story "Alpha Ralpha Boulevard" proved to be a catalyst, a type of fiction approaching Le Guin's own attempts. Le Guin began thinking, not only about writing but also about publishing her work in something other than obscure magazines.

Since she had begun to write, she had been trying to get her work published, but except for one story, "An die Musick," and a few poems, her work was returned, some of it characterized as "remote." Her breakthrough came when *Fantastic* published "April in Paris" in September, 1962. The following year, *Fantastic* published her first genuine science-fiction story, "The Masters." After that time, Le Guin's literary output steadily increased, and her recognition as one of America's outstanding writers was assured.

During her writing career, Le Guin's work has expanded significantly outside the genre of science fiction. From "pro-choice" parables reprinted in *Ms.* magazine to advice to fellow authors, both from her book of essays *Dancing at the Edge of the World*, Le Guin has been prolifically diverse in her output.

Analysis

When Ursula K. Le Guin has Genly Ai state in *The Left Hand of Darkness* that "truth is a matter of the imagination," she is indirectly summarizing the essential focus of her fiction: explorations of the ambiguous nature of truth through imaginative means. Few other contemporary authors have described this process with the force and clarity of Le Guin. Her subject is always humankind and, by extension, the human environment, since humankind cannot survive in a vacuum; her technique is descriptive, and her mode is metaphoric. The worlds Le Guin creates are authentic in a profoundly moral sense as her characters come to experience truth in falsehood, return in separation, unity in variety. Frequently using a journey motif, Le Guin sends her characters in search of shadows, rings, theories, or new worlds—all of which are metaphors for undiscovered elements of the self. Once made, these discoveries allow her characters to be integrated into themselves and their worlds.

Unity is what Le Guin's characters seek: not a simple sense of belonging but a complex sense of wholeness which recognizes paradoxes inherent in human existence. Much of her outlook is derived from the Taoist philosopher Lao-tzu, who maintained that scientific, ethical, and aesthetic laws, instead of being imposed by any authority, "exist in things and are to be discovered." Thus, Le Guin's characters must learn to recognize the true natures (or true names) of people or objects—none of which yields easily to the protagonist—before apprehending their essence and role in the world. Tao is the ultimate unity of the universe, encompassing all and nothing. Built upon paradox, Taoist philosophy proposes that apparently opposing forces actually complete each other. Discovering this in a world enamored of dualist thought, however, requires attaining an attitude of actionless activity, an emptying of the self and at the same time the fullest self-awareness. This compassionate attitude establishes a state of attraction, not compulsion; a state of being, not doing. Indeed, because the cycle of cause and effect is so strong, the Taoist sage never tries to do good at all, for a good action implies an evil action. Discovering the correlation of life/death, good/evil, light/dark, male/female, and self/other requires a relativist judgment. The Indian lore Le Guin absorbed as a child also contributed to her sense of unity. In her writing, she has drawn upon her rich knowledge of myths and the work of C. G. Jung as well as her own fertile imagination to create intricate metaphors for psychic realities. In her own words, "Outer Space, and the Inner Lands, are still, and will always be, my country."

Le Guin arrived at a dense, original expression of Taoist thought in *The Left Hand of Darkness*. In this novel, she brings together previously expressed themes in a striking metaphor. Time levels, separate in former books, coexist in this novel, as do polarized political systems, philosophies, and genders. Genly Ai, the man sent to bring the planet of Genthen into the Ekumen (formerly the League of All Worlds), must come to see the relativity of truth. To do so, he must cross barriers of thought, barriers he is at first incapable of recognizing. Even when he does, Ai is reluctant to cross, for he must abandon his masculine-scientific-dualist training to become a relativist. He must believe that "truth is a matter of the imagination."

Ai's difficulty in arriving at this conclusion is complicated by his alien existence on Genthen, where he is not merely an outsider; he is a sexual anomaly, a pervert as far as the natives are concerned. Being a heterosexual male in an androgynous culture adds immeasurably to Ai's sense of distrust, for he cannot bring himself to trust "a man who is a woman, a woman who is a man." The theme of androgyny enriches this novel, not only because it develops the complex results of an androgynous culture but also because it demonstrates how gender affects—indeed prejudices—thought and explores the cultural effects of this bias. Initially, Ai can see only one gender, one side at a time. This limited vision leaves him vulnerable to betrayal, both by himself and by others. Through his friendship with Estraven, Ai begins to respect, even require, those qualities he at first denigrates until he and Estraven become one, joined in mindspeech. Ai's varied experiences on Genthen teach him that apparently polarized qualities of light/dark, male/female, rational/irrational, patriot/traitor, life/death are necessary complements. The order of the universe requires both.

The Left Hand of Darkness consolidates Taoist ideas expressed in Le Guin's previous books, places them in a dramatically unique culture, and develops them with a finesse lacking in her earlier novels. Ai discovers a fuller recognition of self through merger with the other. He does so in a complete way because Le Guin complicates *The Left Hand of Darkness* with questions of opposing political systems, the nature and consequences of sexism, the issue of personal and political loyalty, and the interrelatedness of different periods of time. While retaining her basic quest structure, Le Guin has Genly Ai construct his "report" by using multiple sources: Estraven's diary, folktales, ancient myths, reports from previous investigatory teams. This adds texture and depth by dramatizing the multiplicity of truth and the unity of time. In a sense, this mixture of sources, added to the seasonlessness of Genthen, where it is always winter, and the relentless journey over the Gobrin Ice, constructs a center of time for the reader, an objective correlative to Ai's state of mind. Within a circular framework, a sense of wholeness is achieved. Ai will set the keystone in the arch, the image that opens *The Left Hand of Darkness*, by adding Genthen to the Ekumen. Later, he cements his personal bond to Estraven by visiting his home, ostensibly to return Estraven's diary but actually to assuage a sense of betrayal for not having Estraven publicly absolved of his "crime" of supporting the Ekumen instead of his king. At the novel's end, however, when Ai meets in Estraven's son the father's limitless curiosity, Ai's journey begins anew.

Robert Scholes has stated that one of the great strengths of *The Left Hand of Darkness* is that it "asks us to broaden our perspectives toward something truly ecumenical, beyond racism and sexism, and even speciesism." Clearly Le Guin has opened up new territory for science-fiction writers to explore. In *The Dispossessed*, her next novel in what is called her Hainish cycle, she presses even further, bringing to full realization her heroic figure of the Taoist sage in the protagonist Shevek. Stoic, persistent, curious, and humane, he shares qualities with Estraven and Genly Ai. Shevek's character and journey, however, differ from his predecessors' in several important respects. Shevek's sense of alienation is tempered by his mature love for his partner Takver. No matter how alone he is on his journey, Shevek can and does turn to their mutually supportive relationship for solace. Shevek's sense of individual integrity is also more conscious than that of previous characters. Already aware of himself and his value, he is able to expand beyond both. Most important, Shevek has a clearly defined sense of purpose—a need to unbuild walls through communication—and a certainty of return. Early in the novel, Le Guin assures her readers that "he would most likely not have embarked on that years-long enterprise had he not had profound assurance that return was possible . . . that the very nature of the voyage . . . implied return." Buttressed by this conviction, Shevek goes forth, his empty hands signifying his spiritual values, and effects a revolution in both senses of the word: a completed cycle and a dynamic change. When he discovers his theory of temporal simultaneity, Shevek gives it away, for he knows that its value is not in its scarcity, but in its general use.

The Dispossessed is not simply a vehicle for Taoist philosophy; it is just as significantly a political novel. Le Guin subtitles the novel *An Ambiguous Utopia*, indicating her focus, and she directs her readers' attention by alternating chapters on Anarres, Shevek's home planet, and Urras, where he resides throughout much of the novel. Scenes from Anarres are recalled through flashback as Shevek, surrounded by an alien political and social system repugnant to much in his nature, reflects upon himself in relation to his culture. Anarres, founded by libertarian followers of Odo, a radical Urasti thinker, is at once dedicated to individual freedom and the good of the whole. There is no formal government, only a system of individually initiated syndicates, a Division of Labor to keep track of job needs, and the Production Distribution Committee to oversee production loosely. On Anarres nothing is owned; everything is shared. Since everyone is equal, there is no discrimination, no exploitation; but there are stringent societal responsibilities which all Annaresti share. Because Anarres is virtually a desert, with plant life so scarce that no animals are indigenous, careful conservation, voluntary labor, and a sense of duty to the whole are required of everyone.

By contrast, Urras is wealthy, lush with water, teeming with life. Its capitalistic system, however, encourages exploitation because profit is the motivating force. As a result, Urras has an entrenched class system, with women and workers considered inferior to the intellectual and governing classes, and a power structure intent on maintaining control. While much of this authority is exerted by custom, some is imposed by force. Shevek, unaccustomed to any type of exploitation, violence, discrimination, or conspicuous waste, needs to experience fully the benefits and detriments of Urras before he can make necessary connections. Once he recognizes that the seeds of his freedom germinated in the rich soil of Urras, he can declare his brotherhood with the Urrasti and offer them what he can: a way to the only future he knows, that of Anarres. Speaking from deep within himself, Shevek tells Urrasti rebels "You must come to it alone, and naked, as the child comes into his future, without any past, without any property, wholly dependent on other people for his life. . . . You cannot make the Revolution. You can only be the Revolution."

The essence of Le Guin's novels is that she compels her characters to undergo a reductive process in order to discover their identity. In the end, her characters stand for no one, no concrete meaning; they simply are. Along the way, Le Guin demands that they learn the paradoxes inherent in life, the ambiguous nature of creation, and the interrelatedness of all that seems to be opposed. By offering her readers characters motivated by intellectual curiosity, humanism, and self-determination; a nonviolent, nonexploitative philosophy capable of encompassing the unknown; and complex cultures in relation to one another, Le Guin is far more than a science-fiction writer. She is a novelist whose contribution to American literature will be valued for generations to come.

Other major works

SHORT FICTION: *The Word for World Is Forest*, 1972; *The Wind's Twelve Quarters*, 1975; *Orsinian Tales*, 1976; *The Compass Rose*, 1982; *Buffalo Gals and Other Animal Presences*, 1987.

POETRY: *Wild Angels*, 1975; *Hard Words and Other Poems*, 1981; *In the Red Zone*, 1983; *Wild Oats and Fireweed: New Poems*, 1988.

NONFICTION: *From Elfland to Poughkeepsie*, 1973; *The Language of the Night: Essays on Fantasy and Science Fiction*, 1979 (Susan Wood, editor); *Dancing at the Edge of the World: Thoughts on Words, Women, and Places*, 1988; *Napa: The Roots and Springs of the Valley*, 1989.

CHILDREN'S LITERATURE: *The Visionary*, 1984; *Solomon Leviathan's 931st Trip Around the World*, 1988; *Fire and Stone*, 1989; *Fish Soup*, 1992 (illustrated by Patrick Wynne).

EDITED TEXT: *The Norton Book of Science Fiction: North American Science Fiction, 1960-1990*, 1993 (with Brian Attebery).

Bibliography

Bittner, James W. *Approaches to the Fiction of Ursula K. Le Guin.* Ann Arbor, Mich.: UMI Research Press, 1984.

Bloom, Harold, ed. *Ursula K. Le Guin.* New York: Chelsea House, 1986.

Bucknall, Barbara J. *Ursula K. Le Guin.* New York: Frederick Ungar, 1981.

Selinger, Bernard. *Le Guin and Identity in Contemporary Fiction.* Ann Arbor, Mich.: UMI Research Press, 1988.

Spivack, Charlotte. *Ursula K. Le Guin.* Boston: Twayne, 1984.

DORIS LESSING

Born: Kermanshah, Persia; October 22, 1919

Principal long fiction

The Grass Is Singing, 1950; *Martha Quest*, 1952; *A Proper Marriage*, 1954; *Retreat to Innocence*, 1956; *A Ripple from the Storm*, 1958; *The Golden Notebook*, 1962; *Landlocked*, 1965; *The Four-Gated City*, 1969; *Briefing for a Descent into Hell*, 1971; *The Summer Before the Dark*, 1973; *The Memoirs of a Survivor*, 1974; *Shikasta*, 1979; *The Marriages Between Zones Three, Four, and Five*, 1980; *The Sirian Experiments*, 1981; *The Making of the Representative for Planet 8*, 1982; *Documents Relating to the Sentimental Agents in the Volyen Empire*, 1983; *The Diary of a Good Neighbour*, 1983 (as Jane Somers); *If the Old Could . . .*, 1984 (as Jane Somers); *The Diaries of Jane Somers*, 1984 (includes *The Diary of a Good Neighbour* and *If the Old Could . . .*); *The Good Terrorist*, 1985; *The Fifth Child*, 1988.

Other literary forms

In addition to her many works of long fiction, Doris Lessing has published numerous volumes of short stories, some of which are set in the Africa of her childhood. She has also written memoirs, documentaries, essays, plays, reviews, and a book of poems.

Achievements

Lessing has been one of the most widely read and influential British novelists of the second half of the twentieth century. Her works have been translated into many languages and have inspired critical attention around the globe. Generally serious and didactic, Lessing's fiction repeatedly urges the human race to develop a wider consciousness that would allow for greater harmony and less violence. Although known particularly as a master of realism, Lessing is often experimental or deliberately fantastic, as shown in her science-fiction novels. Her interests are far-ranging, from Marxism and global politics to the mystical teachings of Sufism to the small personal voice of the individual. Her awards include the Somerset Maugham Award, the German Shakespeare Prize, the Austrian Prize for European Literature, and the French Prix Médicis for Foreigners.

Biography

Doris May Lessing was born in Kermanshah, Persia (later Iran), in 1919, the first child of Alfred Cook Tayler and Emily Maude McVeagh Tayler, who had emigrated from England to Persia shortly after World War I. A brother, Harry, was born two years later, and in 1925 the family moved to a farm in Southern Rhodesia (later Zimbabwe). Her parents were never financially successful. Her father was a dreamer who became a cynic; her mother was domineering but ineffective. Despite Lessing's love of the African landscape and the isolated veld, she was eager to leave her family behind. She attended a Catholic convent school in Salisbury (now Harare) but left when she was fourteen, saying that she had eye problems, though she continued her voracious reading.

In 1938, Lessing moved to Salisbury to work in various jobs, mostly clerical, and began writing fiction. She was married to Frank Charles Wisdom, a minor civil servant, in 1939, and had a son, John, and a daughter, Jean. Divorced in 1943, she was remarried two years later to a German-Jewish refugee, Gottfried Lessing. They had a son, Peter, in 1947. She divorced Gottfried Lessing in 1949 and that same year moved to England, settling in London; in 1950, she published her first novel. Since then she has continued to live in London and to make her living as a professional writer, writing reviews, media scripts, and nonfiction in addition to her novels, short stories, drama, and poetry.

Lessing's interest in politics began with a Marxist group in Rhodesia, and in England she was briefly a member of the Communist Party, leaving it officially in

1956. In the late 1950's, she participated in mass demonstrations for nuclear disarmament and was a speaker at the first Aldermaston March in 1958. During the early 1960's, she worked in the theater, helping to establish Centre 42, a populist art program, and writing her own plays. In the late 1960's, Lessing's thinking began to be heavily influenced by the mystical teachings of Indries Shah and Sufism, which emphasizes conscious evolution of the mind in harmony with self and others. Although for many years Lessing resisted the role of public persona, since the mid-1980's she has made numerous public appearances in many countries.

Analysis

Doris Lessing is a powerful writer committed to the lofty goal of changing human consciousness itself. The narrative voice that weaves throughout her prolific fiction is that of an intense thinker who observes, explores, and describes the contemporary world but whose ultimate sense of human life is that the individual, and indeed the human race, is meant to go beyond mere recognition of perceived reality and to struggle with visions of the possible. Her novels repeatedly suggest that changes in the way humans view themselves, their world, and their relationships with others are imperative if life on this planet is to survive.

Lessing's scope is wide. Her creative imagination is able to provide a close analysis of a character—with all that individual's fears, longings, and contradictions—and to relate that individual not only to his or her circle of acquaintances but to patterns of global economics and politics as well, and then to sweep beyond even this planet to the cosmos and a perspective that encompasses the metaphysical questions of existence. Her fictional explorations are multiple, multidimensional, and overlapping, suggesting that no one viewpoint is adequate or complete. This range is also reflected in her varied narrative forms, which include realism, naturalism, science fiction, utopian and dystopian fiction, fantasy, fable, transcultural postmodernism, and experimental combinations of these. This heterogeneity of themes, techniques, and perspectives illustrates Lessing's overriding premise that truth and substance cannot easily be compartmentalized or assigned fixed labels: Existence is always process, always in flux.

Lessing's position as an exile is a prominent aspect of her work, both in content and in theme. Born in the Middle East of English parents, she spent her adolescence in Southern Rhodesia, first with her family on an isolated and impoverished farm whose workers were all native black Africans, and then on her own in Salisbury. In the city, she became involved with a group interested in international politics whose most specific focus was increased rights for black Rhodesians. Her experiences there in the 1940's, including two marriages and three children, became material for nearly all of her novels for the first twenty years of her writing career.

Martha Quest, A Proper Marriage, A Ripple from the Storm, Landlocked, and *The Four-Gated City* trace in detail the growth and development of Martha Quest, an autobiographical character who is intensely interested in knowing herself and making sense of the world. Together these novels make up the Children of Violence series. The first four are set in Africa, while *The Four-Gated City*, which nearly equals in length the preceding four, is set in London and traces Martha Quest from her arrival there around 1949 to the late 1990's. The novels set in Africa are categorized as social realism, while *The Four-Gated City* moves beyond that to discuss what are often considered paranormal capacities, and the work concludes after some unspecified disaster has destroyed much of life on Earth. The futurist world Lessing depicts here is neither entirely utopian nor dystopian, and despite forces beyond the control of the individual, Martha Quest and some of the other inhabitants of the postcatastrophic world epitomize the continuing need for individual responsibility and commitment to a more harmonious world.

Martha Quest, as her surname suggests, is a quintessential Lessing heroine, always examining the human condition and searching for a higher consciousness to change herself and her world. The characterization is detailed and frank, including descriptions of Martha's sexual relationships and, in *A Proper Marriage*, a lengthy and explicit description of childbirth. Yet Martha's perceptions and innermost thoughts also provide a historical overview of an entire era and a challenge to the status quo. Central to all Martha's struggles is her determination to grow and to envision a freer and more responsible world.

Lessing interrupted the writing of the Children of Violence series to work on *The Golden Notebook*, published in 1962 and generally acknowledged as her most impressive and influential novel. "The two women were alone in the London flat," begins the long novel, and from this simple statement Lessing creates a fascinating portrait of the modern world. The protagonist is Anna Wulf, a writer who says that she is suffering from writer's block after a successful first novel about racial problems in Africa. Anna's friend Molly is a divorced mother trying to make a life for herself. Through them Lessing perceptively examines the problems of the intelligent and disillusioned modern woman. Anna tries to create order out of chaos by keeping a diary, which she divides into four notebooks: a black notebook recounting her experiences as a young woman in Africa; a red notebook for her Communist and political activities; a yellow notebook, which includes her fictional attempts to understand herself, including the creation of an autobiographical character named Ella who is also writing a novel; and a blue notebook to record the factual details of her daily life and her relationships with men. Sections of these notebooks are repeated sequentially four times and are finally superseded by another notebook, the golden one of the novel's title, in which Anna attempts to integrate these compartmentalized and often-conflicting aspects of her life. In the golden notebook section, influenced by the mental breakdown of one of her lovers, Saul Green, Anna goes through layers of madness in herself and questions the idea of reality itself.

The shape of this pivotal metafictional novel is further complicated by sections called "Free Women," which open and close the book as well as separating the repeated sections of the black, red, yellow, and blue notebooks. The five "Free Women" sections together form a conventional novel about sixty thousand words long. Although it deals with the same characters and events recounted in the various notebook sections, it does so in a reductive and more structured way. It is as though the "Free Women" novel were what Anna is able to produce to end her writer's block, but a novel that shows that fiction is unable to capture the intricacies and complexities of actual existence. Since the sections of this conventional novel frame and appear throughout the larger work, the contrasts and variations with the notebook sections make The Golden Notebook as a whole a complex structural and stylistic achievement.

While The Golden Notebook elaborates Lessing's attitudes toward racism, sexism, and the interconnections between the personal and the political, it also shows the development of Lessing's thinking to include the benefits of the irrational and the necessity of exploring areas

beyond the layers of social pretense and conventionality. These areas are further addressed in The Four-Gated City and in three subsequent novels, Briefing for a Descent into Hell, The Summer Before the Dark, and The Memoirs of a Survivor. Each of these novels breaks from traditional versions of realism and insists upon a wider definition of the possible.

Lessing shows the conjunction between the individual and the larger society, including the importance of responsibility and direction, in The Memoirs of a Survivor. In this dystopian rendering of the "near future," the unnamed first-person narrator records her observations of a world in a state of cultural and social decline following an unexplained catastrophe. A stranger consigns into the narrator's care a girl of about twelve, Emily, who has with her Hugo, an ugly cat/dog creature. Much of the novel describes Emily's accelerated development through puberty and her association with Gerald, a young gang leader who, with Emily's help, tries to rebuild some semblance of order or at least some system of survival in a degenerated and nonfunctional society. From the window of her flat the narrator watches groups abandon the city, never to be heard of again, and she witnesses the collapse of civilization, demonstrated particularly in the very young children who fend for themselves and who have only fleeting connections to others for immediate gain. In these children, not only respect for others but also language itself has broken down, and they attack their victims or one another with barbaric yaps.

In the midst of all this collapse, the narrator has become aware of another layer of reality in and through the walls of her flat. When she enters this space, she is confronted with a variety of scenes from the past, not necessarily her own past, and usually she sees something that she must do. On one journey through the walls, she glimpses a figure of a woman, perhaps a goddess or some aspect of herself, who fills her with a sense of hope. Surrounded by despair in the present world, the narrator constructs an alternative visionary world, and at the end of the novel, when even the air is unbreathable, the collapsed world is left behind as the narrator steps through the wall through both a willed and a magical transformation. She takes with her Emily and Gerald and their group of youngsters as well as Hugo, transformed from an ugly beast into something shining with hope and promise.

In 1979, Lessing published Shikasta, which she announced was the first in a series called Canopus in Argos:

Archives, and in the next four years she published the other four books in the series. A number of loyal readers were disappointed with what Lessing called her "space fiction," with its undeveloped, stylized characters and strangely unexciting interplanetary rivalries. Yet the series attracted a new audience of science-fiction readers, and taken as a whole the series continues Lessing's themes: the individual versus the collective, political systems and their interference with racial and sexual equality, the interconnectedness of all life, and the need for a more enlightened consciousness.

None of the narrators and voices in the Canopus in Argos series is entirely reliable, and many questions are left unanswered. Perhaps this confusion is itself Lessing's goal: to make her readers question and reconsider ideas and actions. As Johor, an emissary to Shikasta (Earth), comments on the very first page of the series: "Things change. That is all we may be sure of. . . . This is a catastrophic universe, always; and subject to sudden reversals, upheavals, changes, cataclysms, with joy never anything but the song of substance under pressure forced into new forms and shapes."

The same year the final volume of Canopus in Argos was published, another novel appeared entitled *The Diary of a Good Neighbour*, purportedly by a new British writer, Jane Somers. It was not until the following year, and after the publication of another Jane Somers novel, *If the Old Could. . .* , that Lessing publicly revealed her authorship with the publication of the two novels together as *The Diaries of Jane Somers*. In her introduction to the book, Lessing discusses some of her reasons for having used a pseudonym. One was to create a new persona as the narrator: How would a real Jane Somers write? Another was to show the difficulties unestablished writers have in getting published, and indeed the first manuscript was rejected by several publishers before it was printed by Michael Joseph in London, the same firm that had accepted the unknown Doris Lessing's *The Grass Is Singing* nearly four decades earlier. Lessing also

says that she wanted the novels to be judged on their own merit, apart from the Lessing canon. When the Jane Somers novels first appeared, they sold in only modest numbers and received favorable but very limited attention from reviewers. Lessing notes that the modern publishing business markets high-volume, high-profile authors with the planned expectation that the novels will have a short shelf life—big sellers for a few weeks but soon replaced and out of print. Such policies do not favor new and experimental novelists.

The Diaries of Jane Somers focuses on old age, especially the relationship that develops between the middle-aged Jane Somers, head of a high-fashion magazine, and Maudie Fowler, a poor but proud woman in her nineties. Set in a realistic London, the novels, particularly *The Diary of a Good Neighbour*, give an insightful analysis of contemporary health care services and again show the impact of social attitudes and governmental policies on the individual. The social realism of the novel, with its discussions of aging and dying, is given contrast by the summaries of novels Jane writes about Maudie's life. Maudie tells stories of her long, hard life, and Jane transforms them into successful romanticized fictions, which Maudie then enjoys hearing. Jane, whose friends call her Janna, is repeatedly mistaken for a "Good Neighbour," a social worker, as though there could be no other explanation for her friendship with Maudie. The layers of illusion and reality, fictions and lives, add to the emotional power of the novel and make it an important addition to Lessing's later works.

Lessing's novels, far-ranging in scope and treatment, resist any easy labels. Still, her major themes, though presented in a variety of ways, have been remarkably consistent. The individual has responsibilities, Lessing always shows, not only to achieve self-knowledge and inner harmony but to contribute to the greater harmony of society as well. Human consciousness must expand and people's attitudes and actions must change if human life is to survive.

Other major works

SHORT FICTION: *This Was the Old Chief's Country*, 1951; *Five: Short Novels*, 1953; *The Habit of Loving*, 1957; *A Man and Two Women*, 1963; *African Stories*, 1964; *The Temptation of Jack Orkney and Other Stories*, 1972 (also known as *The Story of a Non-Marrying Man and Other Stories*); *This Was the Old Chief's Country: Volume 1 of Doris Lessing's Collected African Stories*, 1973; *The Sun Between Their Feet: Volume 2 of Doris Lessing's Collected African Stories*, 1973; *Sunrise on the Veld*, 1975; *A Mild Attack of Locusts*, 1977; *To Room Nineteen/Her Collected Stories*, 1978; *The Temptation of Jack Orkney/Her Collected Stories*, 1978; *Stories*, 1978; *The Real Thing: Stories and Sketches*, 1992.

PLAYS: *Each His Own Wilderness*, 1958; *Play with a Tiger*, 1962.
POETRY: *Fourteen Poems*, 1959.
NONFICTION: *Going Home*, 1957; *In Pursuit of the English: A Documentary*, 1960; *Particularly Cats*, 1967; *A Small Personal Voice*, 1974; *Prisons We Choose to Live Inside*, 1987; *The Wind Blows Away Our Words*, 1987; *African Laughter: Four Visits to Zimbabwe*, 1992.

Bibliography

Draine, Betsy. *Substance Under Pressure: Artistic Coherence and Evolving Form in the Novels of Doris Lessing.* Madison: University of Wisconsin Press, 1983.

Fishburn, Katherine. *The Unexpected Universe of Doris Lessing: A Study in Narrative Technique.* Westport, Conn.: Greenwood Press, 1985.

Rose, Ellen Cronan. *The Tree Outside the Window: Doris Lessing's Children of Violence.* Hanover, N.H.: University Press of New England, 1976.

Rubenstein, Roberta. *The Novelistic Vision of Doris Lessing: Breaking the Forms of Consciousness.* Urbana: University of Illinois Press, 1979.

Schlueter, Paul. *The Novels of Doris Lessing.* Carbondale: Southern Illinois University Press, 1973.

Seligman, Dee. *Doris Lessing: An Annotated Bibliography of Criticism.* Westport, Conn.: Greenwood Press, 1981.

Sprague, Claire, and Virginia Tiger, eds. *Critical Essays on Doris Lessing.* Boston: G. K. Hall, 1986.

DENISE LEVERTOV

Born: Ilford, Essex, England; October 24, 1923

Principal poetry

The Double Image, 1946; *Here and Now*, 1957; *Overland to the Islands*, 1958; *Five Poems*, 1958; *With Eyes at the Back of Our Heads*, 1959; *The Jacob's Ladder*, 1961; *O Taste and See: New Poems*, 1964; *City Psalm*, 1964; *Psalm Concerning the Castle*, 1966; *The Sorrow Dance*, 1967; *A Tree Telling of Orpheus*, 1968; *A Marigold from North Vietnam*, 1968; *Three Poems*, 1968; *The Cold Spring and Other Poems*, 1969; *Embroideries*, 1969; *Relearning the Alphabet*, 1970; *Summer Poems 1969*, 1970; *A New Year's Garland for My Students: MIT 1969-1970*, 1970; *To Stay Alive*, 1971; *Footprints*, 1972; *The Freeing of the Dust*, 1975; *Chekhov on the West Heath*, 1977; *Modulations for Solo Voice*, 1977; *Life in the Forest*, 1978; *Collected Earlier Poems, 1940-1960*, 1979; *Pig Dreams: Scenes from the Life of Sylvia*, 1981; *Wanderer's Daysong*, 1981; *Candles in Babylon*, 1982; *Poems, 1960-1967*, 1983; *Oblique Prayers: New Poems with Fourteen Translations from Jean Joubert*, 1984; *The Menaced World*, 1984; *Selected Poems*, 1986; *Breathing the Water*, 1987; *Poems, 1968-1972*, 1987; *A Door in the Hive*, 1989; *Evening Train*, 1992.

Other literary forms

The Poet in the World (1973) gathers prose articles, reviews, criticism, statements to the press, and tributes to fellow poets. *Light Up the Cave* (1981), Denise Levertov's second volume of prose pieces, includes three short stories; articles on the nature of poetry and politics; speeches and political commentary; and memoirs and notes on other writers.

Levertov has also written a novella *In the Night: A Story* (1968), and the libretto for an oratorio, *El Salvador: Requiem and Invocation* (1983). She has produced translations of other poets' works, including *In Praise of Krishna: Songs from the Bengali* (1967, with Edward C. Dimock, Jr.); *Selected Poems*, by Eugene Guillevic (1969); and *Black Iris*, by Jean Joubert (1988).

Achievements

Levertov's first book of poems, *The Double Image*, was published in England in 1946. It brought her to the attention of British and American critics and poets such as Kenneth Rexroth and Robert Creeley. Eleven years later, her first American book was published, followed by many volumes of poems and several translations of other poets' work. She has taught at many institutions, including Vassar College, Drew University, City College of New York, University of California at Berkeley,

Massachusetts Institute of Technology, Brandeis University, Tufts University, and Stanford University. As the poetry editor of *The Nation* in the 1960's, she influenced the critical reception of new poets. She was elected to the American Academy of Arts and Letters. Her many awards include a Guggenheim Foundation Fellowship in 1962, the Lenore Marshall Poetry Prize in 1975 for *The Freeing of the Dust*, and the Elmer Holmes Bobst Award in 1983.

Biography

Born near London, England, in 1923, Denise Levertov was reared in a multicultural environment: Welsh and Russian, Jewish and Christian. Beatrice Spooner-Jones, her mother, was a daughter of a physician and great-granddaughter of a tailor, teacher, and preacher, Angell Jones, made famous by Daniel Owen, "the Welsh Dickens," in the novel *Hunangofiant Rhys Lewis* (1885).

Spooner-Jones loved to travel, and in Constantinople, where she was a teacher in a Scottish mission, she met a young Russian Jew, Paul Peter Levertov, who had converted to Christianity. They were married in London, where he was ordained to the Anglican priesthood. His great passion in life was reconciliation between Christians and Jews. A daughter, Olga, was born to the couple, and seven years later, a second daughter, Denise.

Denise never attended a public or private school; her mother, her only teacher, read many classic works of fiction to her. She visited museums and libraries in London and studied ballet for many years. When World War II came, she worked in a number of London public hospitals caring for children, the aged, and the poor. She had been writing poems since childhood and published her first volume of poems in England shortly after the war.

Levertov met and married an American writer, Mitchell Goodman, who was studying abroad. They lived in Europe until 1948, returning to Europe from New York for a period in 1950-1951. Her son Nikolai was born in 1949. In 1956, she became an American citizen. For the next thirty years, she published more than a dozen volumes of poetry with the same publisher, New Directions. Levertov wrote and spoke passionately against the Vietnam War, and she vigorously supported protests against American involvement in civil wars in El Salvador, Honduras, and Nicaragua. She lived in Mexico for a number of years. Levertov then maintained a residence in Massachusetts but taught at Stanford during the academic year.

Analysis

Denise Levertov seems to have been uniquely placed in her family and time to inherit two great streams of lyric power—her mother's Welsh gift for song and speech and the profound religious thought of her father's Jewish-Christian search for truth. With such a combination of parental influences, the themes that prevail in Levertov's poetry—the nature and form of poetry, and the moral obligations of the poet to society—are hardly surprising. She has said that the Hasidic or mystical beliefs in her father's Jewish heritage gave her an ease and familiarity with spiritual mysteries. For the purpose of analysis, one can study these three areas of her concern—poetry, morality, and mystery—but in her poems they often appear not separately but together, coloring the mosaic of her words. She combines the skills of a craftsman and an artist, the vision of moral integrity and spiritual insight.

Levertov learned from modernistic poets such as Charles Olson and William Carlos Williams, who used concrete, everyday words and familiar settings and events to convey profound truths. She drew also from Welsh hymn-singing lines. Lines and line breaks are essential to the sound quality of her poetry. Some of her inspiration comes from dreams, images, and dream sounds.

The second preoccupation in Levertov's poetry, morality, was influenced by the Holocaust, as millions of innocent women, children, and men were gassed in death camps in Europe. The shock of this discovery in 1945 as World War II came to a close must have been intense for the young poet-nurse whose father was both Jewish and Christian. In later decades, Levertov felt an imperative to protest the horror and injustice of war. The effort to end the Vietnam War brought women together before the women's movement had gathered full force. Levertov's actions and her words expressed the outrage of many citizens. She explored the relevance of poetry to politics and questioned the moral responsibility of the poet in a time of peril.

Early in her career, Levertov expressed her vision of unity in the physical and spiritual worlds. "Taste and See," the title poem of her seventh volume, has a biblical sound. Insisting that one cannot know a divinity apart from what is given to the senses, she probes the meaning of physical experience—a life affirmation—and considers its relationship to religious values. Decades before the general public awakened to the need to respect the physical world, Levertov spoke of the mystery in the objects people taste, touch, and see: the moon, food, a glass of water. In her later poetry, the value of mystical and religious experience became her theme.

Levertov has expressed a modest view of the poet: a person who can articulate feeling through the medium of language. She refuses the exalted aura of a supersensitive person whose feelings are beyond the reach of ordinary human beings. It is the process of writing, not the result, that fascinates her. She sees poems as structures of meaning and sound that convey feelings accurately. The poet must revise and polish until the poem is complete. Technical skill with diction, form, rhythm, syntax, and sound—above all, sound—raise a poem from mediocrity to perfection. Her poems are more readily understood when one is familiar with these principles.

Levertov experimented in her early writings with various rhyme schemes, tones, and forms. A 1946 poem, "Folding a Shirt," uses Dante's interlacing *terza rima* rhyme pattern for six stanzas: *aba bcb cdc ded efe fgf*. "Midnight Quatrains" rhymes the second and fourth end words of each stanza. There are dramatic poems in dialogue form and ballads. Typically, however, Levertov's poems have no end rhyme or regular meter. Her rhythm is subtle, moving with the line break. Uneven lines are the rule, not the exception. The placement of words and indentations create rhythmic ebb and flow, abrupt interruptions, slow pauses, and dramatic suspense.

That the poet should be also a political person came as an early and natural revelation to Levertov. Her first published poem, "Listening to Distant Guns" (1940), tells of hearing " a low pulsation in the East" that "betrays no whisper of the battle scream." She actually heard the guns of World War II from the south coast of England, to where she, along with many young people, had been evacuated from the city of London. She describes the dismal feelings of the English people in "Christmas 1944," when no celebration could hide the blackout curtains on the windows, the knowledge of "fear knocking on the door" of so many Europeans. During her impressionable teens and early twenties, she was surrounded with war. Although two decades would pass before her active involvement in the American antiwar movement, she had already expressed her grief at the mass destruction war brings.

By 1966, Levertov was writing poems about the war in Vietnam. The most influential and famous of these is probably "Life at War." Speaking for her contemporaries, she tells of war's pervasive influence in her century—"We have breathed the grits of it in, all our lives"—and then begins a long lament over the damage war has done to people's imaginations. The modern imagination, she argues, is "filmed over with the gray filth of it," because humankind, "whose language imagines *mercy* and *lovingkindness*," can schedule the burning of children's bodies. "Burned human flesh/ is smelling in Vietnam as I write." As a former nurse, Levertov can bring her sensual awareness into her passionate denunciation of modern war. The poem closes with a statement that humankind needs the "deep intelligence" that living at peace can give. Other antiwar poems were composed in the form of dialogues such as questions and answers about Vietnamese people or a narrator questioning a bomber pilot. One poem honors her friend and fellow poet Muriel Rukeyser, who went to Vietnam with her in 1972.

Family life, and in particular marriage, has inspired many of Levertov's most memorable poems. In keeping with her insistence on the beauty of sensual experience, she celebrates the joy of marriage. The short poem "Bedtime" puts the contentment of fulfilled love in natural terms: "We are a meadow where the bees hum,/ mind and body are almost one." "Hymn to Eros" praises the "drowsy god" who quietly circles in "a snowfall hush." Two beautiful poems to her son, Nikolai, are spaced years apart—one before his birth, "Who He Was," and one, "The Son," as he becomes a man. The first tells of his conception, gestation, and birth, and the second of skills he has gained.

The death of love and the contemporary difficulties in male-female relationships also provide subjects for notable poems. The much-quoted "About Marriage" begins with a cry for freedom, "Don't lock me in wedlock, I want/ marriage, an/ encounter," and concludes, "I would be/ met/ and meet you/ so,/ in a green/ airy space, not/ locked in." As the women's movement and the antiwar movement seemed to merge, the desire for peace and independence became the message of many women writers and poets. "The Ache of Marriage" compares marriage to Jonah's life in the belly of a whale; the poet and her spouse are looking for joy, "some joy/ not to be known outside it." Marriage is not discarded as an ideal, but its confinement brings problems to women who feel an urge to work in a wider field. In "Hypocrite Women" Levertov tells women that they should not be ashamed of their "unwomanly" traits but should admit boldly the truth of their lives.

The mystical and religious tones of Levertov's poetry can be traced from their beginnings to their full flowering in the poems of the 1980's collected in two volumes, *Breathing the Water* and *A Door in the Hive*. The daughter of a clergyman who was steeped in mystical Jewish Hasidism, Levertov showed her familiarity with religious texts in early poems. "Notes of a Scale" gives four moments of wonder; its reference note directs the reader to Martin Buber's *Tales of the Hasidim: The Early Masters* (1975). The poem "Sparks" includes passages from the Old Testament book of Ecclesiastes. In this work, Levertov moves easily from the ancient Hebrew text to the circumstances of a modern life. Not only Jewish mysticism but also Christian tradition inspired her poetry. Later poems take as their themes the annunciation to Mary, Jesus' parable of the mustard seed, and the path of Calvary. Levertov's religious poetry is deeply imbued as well with thoughts on the lives and works of religious saints and writers. Saint Thomas Didymus, Julian of Norwich, William Blake, William Everson, and

W. H. Auden are evoked in various poems.

Levertov has written of two childhood dreams: One consisted of a violent transformation from a rustic scene of happiness to a scene of burning and devastation. The other recurring dream was of a large country house made of a warm pink stone; its name was Mazinger Hall. These two dreams, like the later ones she used in poems, carry emotional content of joy and sorrow, gain and loss, security and terror. Gradually, her dream material has been transformed into poems that evoke similar feelings in her readers. In Levertov's early dream-based poems, the process of transferring a dream to a poem involved describing the dream content. The poet has explained that later, after analytical work on her dreams, she abandoned that objectivity and gave her images stronger and clearer emotional force to present the dream content more directly to the reader. A third stage in this process came with the realization that the dream needs a literary form that cannot be imposed but must be listened for. Several times she found that a dream worked only as a prose tale. The stories "Say the Word" and "A Dream" began as poems that she transformed to a rhythmic prose. The experience of using dream material for a work of art teaches the poet that the poem must be not only visually clear but also morally or emotionally significant for the reader. An expression that is too private does not make an effective poem.

Another kind of dream may result from an auditory message received in a dream state, or as a combined visual and auditory dream. Levertov has experienced each type and has made poems of them. In "The Flight," she retells a vision of the poet and mystic William Blake, who spoke the words, "The will is given us that we may know the delights of surrender." She waited several years before composing a poem about that experience, to avoid a too-literal transcription. Again, an auditory message was received in a dream about the Russian poet Boris Pasternak. The visual scene disappeared from memory, but the words remained. In both instances, as Levertov explains, the quality of the resulting poem came from the poet's willingness to recognize and absorb a hidden quality that lay beyond the superficial appearances. Some dream images may indicate the questions or problems present at that moment in the poet's life. In that case, the truth of the life and the truth of the dream provide an interplay that makes a powerful poem.

The religious message that hums (a favorite Levertov verb) throughout her poetry is the oneness of all life: all human beings, animals, trees, and the great elements of earth, air, fire, and water. The vision of air and water blended comes in poems about bees, honey, and ocean currents that hold "my seafern arms." The cleansing properties of honey in the hive, she writes in "Second Didactic Poem," neutralize even the poison of disease organisms. That hive with its transforming power may be the same as human activity—"honey of the human." Transformation may also move in the opposite direction, from a joyful morning self-confidence to a rapid pace that diminishes the person ("Remembering"). These apparent divisions between good and evil in a person's emotional life can be harmonized from a point of view that is wide enough to encompass the other side, or opposite, in what is experienced.

Three qualities characterize Levertov's poetic work: music, morality, and mysticism. Her best poems are true lyrics—songs, in their flowing rhythms and enchanting sound patterns of vowel and consonant combinations. Moreover, she teaches lessons about respect for natural life and for unprotected, helpless human beings, especially children and the elderly. There is the wonder she shares in the magic of common things—the "gleam of water in the bedside glass" ("Midnight Gladness") and the moonlight crossing her room ("The Well"). Levertov says, "There is no magic, only facts"; her magic is found in accurate and loving observation of everyday shapes, colors, and sounds.

Yet beyond her mastery of the poem's form and even beyond the thought content, Levertov's poetry can be appreciated for the qualities of the poet herself. During the 1960's, before the women's movement had strengthened the fragile position of women poets, when a cult of death followed the suicides of Anne Sexton and Sylvia Plath, Denise Levertov lamented their loss, not only because they were fine poets but also because their deaths would confirm a popular conception of the poet as abnormally sensitive, often on the edge of madness. For her, alcoholism and nervous breakdowns were not signs of poetic talent. Creativity, she wrote, belongs to responsible, mature adults who take citizenship seriously. In the late 1960's and 1970's, she put this antiromantic view to the service of the peace and women's liberation movements—marching, protesting, speaking against social injustices. She called attention to the political poets imprisoned in many countries. In the 1980's, she produced poetry of great beauty on the human and material sources of her spiritual inspiration. She has shown that a poet in the United States can support herself economically. Generously and with humor, she shares with students the fruits of her years of practicing her craft. In all these ways, she has modeled a high standard for both poetry and the poet.

Other major works

NOVEL: *In the Night: A Story*, 1968.

NONFICTION: *The Poet in the World*, 1973; *New and Selected Essays*, 1992.

TRANSLATIONS: *In Praise of Krishna: Songs from the Bengali*, 1967 (with Edward C. Dimock, Jr.); *Selected Poems*, 1969 (by Eugene Guillevic); *Black Iris*, 1988 (by Jean Joubert).

EDITED TEXT: *Penguin Modern Poets 9*, 1967 (with Kenneth Rexroth and William Carlos Williams).

MISCELLANEOUS: *Light Up the Cave*, 1981; *El Salvador: Requiem and Invocation*, 1983.

Bibliography

Felstiner, John. "Poetry and Political Experience: Denise Levertov." In *Coming to Light: American Women Poets in the Twentieth Century*, edited by Diane Wood Middlebrook and Marilyn Yalom. Ann Arbor: University of Michigan Press, 1985.

Lacey, Paul A. "Denise Levertov: A Poetry of Exploration." In *American Women Poets*, edited by Harold Bloom. New York: Chelsea, 1986.

Marten, Harry. *Understanding Denise Levertov*. Columbia: South Carolina University Press, 1988.

Pope, Deborah. "Homespun and Crazy Feathers: The Split Self in the Poems of Denise Levertov." In *A Separate Vision*. Baton Rouge: Louisiana State University Press, 1984.

Wagner-Martin, Linda. *Denise Levertov*. New York: Twayne, 1967.

CLARICE LISPECTOR

Born: Chechelnik, Soviet Union; December 10, 1925   **Died:** Rio de Janeiro, Brazil; December 9, 1977

Principal long fiction

Perto do coração selvagem, 1944; *O lustre*, 1946; *A cidade sitiada*, 1949; *A maçã no escuro*, 1961 (*The Apple in the Dark*, 1967); *A paixão segundo G. H.*, 1964; *Uma aprendizagem: Ou, O livro dos prazeres*, 1969 (*An Apprenticeship: Or, The Book of Delights*, 1986); *Água viva*, 1973; *A hora da estrela*, 1977 (*The Hour of the Star*, 1986); *Um sopro de vida: Pulsações*, 1978.

Other literary forms

Clarice Lispector was a prominent short-story writer as well as a novelist; among her collections of stories are *Alguns contos* (1952; some stories) and *Laços de família* (1960; *Family Ties*, 1972). *A legião estrangeira* (1964; *The Foreign Legion*, 1986) is a collection of stories and brief miscellaneous prose pieces.

Achievements

Lispector is regarded as one of the most influential and important Brazilian fiction writers. A member of the revisionist school of writers that emerged in the period following World War II, she was a force in the move, in Brazilian fiction, from the regionalism and sociological orientation of the 1930's to an intense interest in subjective experience.

She first achieved general acclaim with *Family Ties*, a collection of inward-looking short stories. *The Apple in the Dark* marked Lispector's major artistic breakthrough. Lengthy and complex, symbolic and mythic, its intense, lyrical style recalls the works of Djuna Barnes, Virginia Woolf, and Katherine Mansfield.

Lispector was the recipient of many literary prizes. In 1943, the publication of *Perto do coração selvagem* (close to the savage heart) won for her the Graça Aranha Prize. She received the Cármen Dolores Barbosa Prize for *The Apple in the Dark* in 1961, a prize from the Campanha Nacional da Criança for a children's story, "O mistério do coelho pensante" (the mystery of the thinking rabbit) in 1967, the Golfinho de Ouro Prize for *An Apprenticeship* in 1969, and was awarded first prize in the tenth Concurso Literário Nacional for her overall contribution to Brazilian literature in 1976, one year before her death.

Biography

Clarice Lispector was born in Chechelnik, Ukraine, in 1925, of Jewish parents. The family moved to Brazil when the child was two months old. Lispector attended school first in Recife, then in Rio de Janeiro. In 1943, she was graduated from the Faculty of Law in Rio. She married a diplomat and lived in Italy, Switzerland, Great Britain, and the United States for many years. After her divorce, she settled permanently in Rio de Janeiro in 1959. She died from cancer in 1977.

Analysis

Most, but not all, of Clarice Lispector's protagonists are female, and the author is keenly aware of women's problems and of the female side of the psyche. Her major works deal with internal guests. An occurrence in the protagonists' lives causes them to move out of their daily routines and enter into new types of relationship with themselves and with the physical world. They live each moment intensely, as if every breath of existence is a major experience, tightly connected to the pulsating rhythm of life itself. The protagonist's quest has no specific goal except to move forward. Lispector's major protagonists are all making their way through the maze of life, lost at times, but always eventually able to resume their journey toward enlightenment.

The Apple in the Dark is considered to be Lispector's most important novel. Martim, the protagonist, is fleeing a crime. At the beginning of the novel, he is in bed in a womblike hotel room. The balcony outside his room overlooks a garden bathed in darkness. Still half asleep, Martim walks out onto the balcony, observes that a car which has been parked in front of the hotel has disappeared, and suspects that a German who lives in the hotel has gone to turn him in to the police. Totally awake now, Martim jumps from the balcony into the garden and begins a long, slow walk into the dark.

The Apple in the Dark is a dreamlike narrative of Martim's quest for a side of the self with which he has lost contact while living as a married man in a conventional social setting. Unsure of where he is going, his only goal is to move in a straight line so as to avoid a circular return to the walls of the hotel. Martim's quest ends on an ambiguous note, since at the end of the novel he appears to have given up and is ready to be captured and returned to the world he left behind.

Nevertheless, Martim's journey has provided him with experiences and insights that he did not possess at the beginning of the book. "We don't know where we came from and we don't know where we're going; but we just experience things, we experience! And that's what we have, Ermelinda." Surrounded by stones and plants, Martim experiences exquisite moments of connection with the mystery of the natural world, as all of his senses open and his mind abdicates its power and accepts being merely a part of life "with the nakedness of his lack of understanding." He makes the surprising discovery that "the more stupid he was the more face to face with things he was." In his new state of consciousness, Martim replaces understanding with awareness. He senses the air he breathes with the delicate tension of a plant and attempts to adopt the patient rhythm of grazing cows.

The Apple in the Dark is a novel about love, both for the world itself and for other human beings. A significant part of the book describes Martim's stay at a farm and his encounter with two women, Ermelinda and Vitória. Ermelinda seeks, in her love for Martim, protection against her obsessive fear of death, only to discover that physical love, on the contrary, brings her closer to an experience of dying than does any other emotion. This newly won insight finally enables Ermelinda to accept her own mortality. Martim's encounter with Vitória is different, a communion of souls rather than bodies. In a moving description, Lispector shows how Martim's resistance to intimate contact with another person is gradually broken down, as Vitória for the first time in her life gives expression to her innermost thoughts and emotions. While communication does not last, the experience proves crucial to Martim, who is finally able to look upon himself with love and respect: "The man was loving himself for the first time, which meant that he was ready to love others. . . ." Martim no longer needs to flee, and he willingly consents to cut short his quest and return to society.

The title of the novel is important. *The Apple in the Dark* can be read as a commentary on the biblical myth on the tree of knowledge. The understanding of the world that Martim achieves is intuitive rather than rational. He never actually eats the apple, he merely reaches out for it in the dark, hoping that he will be able to hold onto the fruit: "And I have that clumsy way of reaching for an apple in the dark—and trying not to drop it."

An Apprenticeship is Lispector's most optimistic novel. The novel has two protagonists, a woman and a man, engaged in an extensive dialogue. Lori, a physically attractive young teacher, lives an empty, nonreflective life until she falls in love with Ulysses, a professor of philosophy. Although Lori has had several affairs, Ulysses refuses to consummate their love until she has completed her "apprenticeship" and learned the secret meaning of life. Only then, he believes, is a permanent union of two people possible. Lori, feeling frustrated and rejected, reluctantly starts her slow, painful route toward self-discovery under his guidance.

Until the meeting with Ulysses, Lori had eliminated pain from her life, but she had also cut off any potential for meaningful contact either with herself, with other people, or with life itself: "Without pain, she had been left without anything, lost in her own world and that of others without any means of contact." Love, reduced to sex, failed to connect her to anything outside herself. Ulysses realizes this and decides that Lori must reestablish contact with her own body and soul before she will be able to love him or anybody else: "I could have possessed you already with my body and my soul, but I will wait even though it takes years, for you, too, to have a body and a soul to love with," he tells her.

During her apprenticeship, Lori experiences an increased sense of awareness of the world around her, and of the silence of death which perpetually lurks behind the bustling noises of life. Lori discovers that pain and pleasure, life and death, are inextricably linked. By attempting to escape from pain she has excluded pleasure from her life as well. Consequently, her new receptivity to pain will restore her ability to experience pleasure. It is only after having accepted the pain of death that she can start to feel a genuine joy of living.

The pleasure results from her growing ability to strip away façades and protective mechanisms and dare finally to be herself. Lori soon experiences flashes of communication and insights accompanied by a keen sense of genuinely existing. During this period of profound introspection, Lori needs to distance herself from society and from Ulysses as well, in order to be more fully with herself. Her ultimate goal, however, is connection, not isolation. First, she must be reattached to the earth itself. Then, she hopes to reestablish the link between herself and other people.

In an episode typical of Lispector's fiction, Lori is walking slowly and wearily down the street. She notices a girl waiting for the bus, and her heart begins to throb—she has decided to try to make contact with another person. After the brief encounter, Lori realizes that what she is looking for is more profound. She returns home and calls Ulysses. She bites into an apple and discovers that the eating of the fruit leads her to a state of grace rather than exile: "Unlike Eve, when she bit into the apple she entered paradise. . . . It was the beginning . . . of a state of grace." The state of grace is the state of someone who does not have to guess any longer, according to the narrator, someone who simply knows. The world around her acquires a kind of halo that radiates almost perfectly from things and people, a kind of energy consisting of very fine particles of light. Lori, at the same time, realizes that she does not want to experience grace often, she does not want to become addicted to it, because it would distance her from the struggle, from the perplexity and joy of an ordinary human destiny: "It was important not to forget that the state of grace was merely a small opening to the world which was like paradise—it was neither an entrance into it nor did it give one the right to eat from the fruits of its orchards."

Lori, then, does not stay in paradise but emerges from her experience of grace as a better human being. Ulysses, in the following chapter, tells her that she is now ready for love. Before leaving her apartment to join him, Lori stands by her window, watching the rain. She feels neither pain nor pleasure, only a keen sense of connection and release: "She and the rain were busy with their violent outpouring." She intuitively knows that she will be able to transfer her newly won intimacy with the world to her relationship with Ulysses, leaves her apartment without putting on her customary makeup, and takes a taxi to his place. Somehow, living and loving have finally become simple, as Lori has discovered that it is possible for her to give herself without losing herself. After a period of passionate lovemaking, she sees in a vision the fruit of the world, "And it was in midair that she placed her mouth on the fruit and managed to bite into it, yet leaving it intact gleaming in space." Ulysses is no longer a teacher to Lori. The two of them are equal, united through mutual love.

An Apprenticeship, with its vision of a mature, passionate, conscious relationship between a man and a woman, is an exception within Lispector's total work, a pleasant detour along the road. In *Água viva* (sparkling water), written four years later, the author returns once again to a solitary, questioning protagonist. The novel is an intense, fluid monologue addressed to an absent "you," a person with whom the narrator was once intimately involved. In the novel's first paragraph, the narrator bursts out in a cry of joy upon realizing that she is once again free. It is a joy mixed with the sadness of separation and the fear of an unknown future. Nevertheless, she wants to capture the present moment, to connect with the spirit of life, and to sing out the joy she experiences from being in the world: "And I sing hallelujah in the air like the bird does."

Água viva is a glorification of the self alone in the world, detached from material possessions and from other people. The prevailing emotion in the book is one of begin intensely alive, bought at the price of separation from the person she loves. Her new lover is nature, a feminine principle both soothing and ferocious. This love affair with life itself is for the narrator a way of approaching God. Such a radical break is necessary for Lispector's narrator in order to escape from a society which flattens out emotional lives and turns people into automatons, unable ever to grasp the present moment. Separation, thus, becomes a gift of life that she, through her writing, wants to bestow upon her former lover as well. Separation is seen as a birth trauma, painful but necessary for the lover to experience the exquisite joy of liberty: "I give you liberty. First I break the waterbag. Then I cut the umbilical cord. And you are alive in your own right." On the book's final page, she addresses the lover for the last time: "Look at me and love me. No: you look at yourself and love you. And that is what is just."

Água viva is a long meditation on love, separation, life, death, and God, seemingly inspired by Oriental mysticism: "Profound prayer is a meditation on nothingness," according to the narrator. Faced with the pain of separation, analogous to the pain of dying, the narrator chooses to respond with joy: ". . . because it is too cruel, so I respond by the purity of indomitable joy. I refuse to be sad. Let us be joyous." The style of *Água viva* is fluid and poetic, each sentence giving birth to the next with no preconceived structure, as Lispector attempts to capture the rhythm of her own respiration.

In her final novel, *Um sopro de vida* (a breath of life), Lispector returns for the last time to an intensely personal inquiry into the problems of life, death, and writing. Completed shortly before the author's own death, the novel is the ultimate statement of an artist whose own road has come to an end, for whom reality has caught up with her life's vision, and for whom each breath now literally encapsulates the essence of life itself. The novel was published posthumously.

Other major works

SHORT FICTION: *Alguns contos*, 1952; *Laços de família*, 1960 (*Family Ties*, 1972); *A legião estrangeira*, 1964 (*The Foreign Legion*, 1986); *Felicidade clandestina: Contos*, 1971; *A imitaçã da rosa*, 1973; *Onde estivestes de noite*, 1974; *A via crucis do corpo*, 1974; *A bela e fera*, 1979.

NONFICTION: *Para não esquecer*, 1978.

CHILDREN'S LITERATURE: *O mistério do coelho pensante*, 1967; *A mulher que matou os peixes*, 1968.

MISCELLANEOUS: *Selecto de Clarice Lispector*, 1975.

Bibliography

Borelli, Olga. *Clarice Lispector, esboço para um possível retrato*. Rio de Janeiro: Editora Nova Fronteira, 1981.

Campedelli, Samira Youssef, and Benjamin Abdalla, Jr. *Clarice Lispector*. São Paulo, Brazil: Abril Educãco, 1981.

Cixous, Hélène. *Reading With Clarice Lispector*. Edited and translated by Verena Andermatt Conley. Minneapolis: University of Minnesota Press, 1990.

Fitz, Earl E. *Clarice Lispector*. Boston: Twayne, 1985.

Lindstrom, Naomi. *Women's Voice in Latin American Literature*. Washington, D.C.: Three Continents Press, 1989.

Sá, Olga de. *A escritura de Clarice Lispector*. Petrópolis, Brazil: Editora Vozes, 1979.

AUDRE LORDE

Born: New York, New York; February 18, 1934

Died: St. Croix, U.S. Virgin Islands, November 17, 1992

Principal poetry

The First Cities, 1968; *Cables to Rage*, 1970; *From a Land Where Other People Live*, 1973; *New York Head Shop and Museum*, 1974; *Between Our Selves*, 1976; *Coal*, 1976; *The Black Unicorn*, 1978; *Chosen Poems, Old and New*, 1982; *Our Dead Behind Us*, 1986; *Undersong: Chosen Poems, Old and New*, 1992; *The Marvelous Arithmetics of Distance: Poems, 1987-1992*, 1993.

Other literary forms

The Cancer Journals (1980) is a personal account of Audre Lorde's struggles with breast cancer. *Zami: A New Spelling of My Name* (1982), which Lorde called a "biomythography," is a retrospective narrative of her emerging sexuality. *Sister Outsider* (1984) and *A Burst of Light* (1988) are collections of essays and speeches on poetry, feminism, lesbianism, and racism.

Achievements

Lorde received a National Endowment for the Arts grant and was a poet-in-residence at Tougaloo College in Jackson, Mississippi, in 1968. She received other recognitions, including the Creative Artists Public Service grant (1972 and 1976) and the Broadside Poets Award (1975). She called herself a "black lesbian feminist warrior poet." At the heart of her work as a poet, essayist, teacher, and lecturer lies an intense and relentless exploration of personal identity. Beyond the stunning portrayals of her deepest insights and emotions, her work is filled with powerful evocations of universal survival. The substance of her poetry and essays always reaches beyond the individual self into deep concerns for all humanity. Progressively, her work revealed an increasing awareness of her West Indian heritage in relation to her place in American society and its values.

Biography

Audre Lorde's parents emigrated from Grenada to New York City in 1924. Lorde, the youngest of three girls, was born in 1934. She recounted many of her childhood memories in *Zami*, identifying particular incidents that had an influence or effect on her developing sexuality and her later work as a poet. She attended the University of Mexico (1954-1955) and received a B.A. from Hunter College (1959) and an M.L.S. from Columbia University (1961). In 1962, she was married to Edwin Rollins, with whom she had two children before they were divorced in 1970.

Prior to 1968, when she gained public recognition for her poetry, Lorde supported herself through a variety of jobs, including low-paying factory work. She also served as a librarian in several institutions. After her first publication, *The First Cities*, Lorde worked primarily within American colleges and free presses. She was an instructor at City College of New York (1968-1970), an instructor and then lecturer at Lehman College (1969-1971), and a professor of English at John Jay College of Criminal Justice (1971-1981). In 1981, she became a professor of English at Hunter College and poetry editor of the magazine *Chrysalis*. She was a contributing editor of the journal *Black Scholar* and a founding member of SISA (Sisterhood in Support of Sisters in South Africa) and Kitchen Table: Women of Color Press. She also served on the board of the National Coalition of Black Lesbians and Gays. Lorde died on November 17, 1992, at the age of fifty-eight.

Analysis

All Audre Lorde's poems, essays, and speeches are deeply personal renditions of a compassionate writer, thinker, and human being. Indeed, she drew much of her material from individual and multifaceted experience; she rendered it in writing that seeks to reveal the complexity of being a black feminist lesbian poet. She expressed the feelings of being marginalized in an American society that is predominantly white, male, heterosexual, and middle-class. Her writings reflect the changing constitution and perspective of American life, but she never relented to an easy optimism, nor did she make uninformed dismissals of society's ills. Her personal experiences made her compassionate toward those who suffer under oppressive regimes all over the world. By drawing from the history and mythology of the West Indies, she was able to refer to the racism and sexism that exist in other cultures.

In her early collections of poetry, *The First Cities* and *Cables to Rage*, Lorde expresses a keen political disillusionment, noting the failure of American ideals of equality and justice for all. When Lorde uses the pronoun "we" in her poetry, she speaks for all who have been dispossessed. In "Anniversary," for example, she writes, "Our tears/ water an alien grass," expressing the separation between those who belong and those who do not. In poems such as "Sowing," the poet reveals the land's betrayal of its inhabitants by describing images of destruction juxtaposed to personal rage: "I have been to this place before/ where blood seething commanded/ my fingers fresh from the earth."

She also demonstrates a concern for the children of this earth in "Bloodbirth": Casting about to understand what it is in her that is raging to be born, she wonders how an opening will come "to show the true face of me/ lying exposed and together/ my children your children their children/ bent on our conjugating business." The image of the warrior, the one who must be prepared to go about the business of existing in an unjust world, signifies the need to take care of those not yet aware of unfulfilled promises.

If the rage in her early poems appears "unladylike," Lorde is setting out to explode sexual typecasting. Certainly, there is nothing dainty about her sharp images and powerful assessments of social conditions. As she confronts harsh realities, the portrayals must necessarily be clamorous. Yet the poet's rage does not lead to a blind rampage. In "Conversation in Crisis," the poet hopes to speak to her friend "for a clear meeting/ of self upon self/ in sight of our hearth/ but without fire." The poet must speak honestly and not out of false assumptions and pretenses so that real communication can occur. The reader and listener must heed the words as well as the tone in order to receive the meaning of the words. Communication, then, is a kind of contractual relationship between people.

In the collections *From a Land Where Other People Live* and *Between Our Selves*, Lorde uses a compassionate tone to tell people about the devastation of white racism upon African Americans. She mixes historical fact with political reality, emphasizing the disjunction that sometimes occurs between the two. In "Equinox," Lorde observes her daughter's birth by remembering a series of events that also occurred that year: She had "marched into Washington/ to a death knell of dreaming/ which 250,000 others mistook for a hope," for few at that time understood the victimization of children that was occurring not only in the American South but also in the Vietnam War. After she heard that Malcolm X had been shot, she reread all of his writings: "the dark mangled children/ came streaming out of the atlas/ Hanoi Angola Guinea-Bissau. . ./ merged into Bedford-Stuyvesant and Hazelhurst Mississippi."

From the multiplicity of world horrors, the poet returns to her hometown of New York, exhausted but profoundly moved by the confrontation of history and the facts of her own existence. In "The Day They Eulogized Mahalia," another event is present in the background as the great singer Mahalia Jackson is memorialized: Six black children died in a fire at a day care center on the South Side; "firemen found their bodies/ like huddled lumps of charcoal/ with silent mouths and eyes wide open." Even as she mourns the dead in her poems, the poet is aware of both the power and the powerlessness of words to effect real changes. In the poem, "Power," Lorde writes,

> The difference between poetry and rhetoric
> is being ready to kill
> yourself
> instead of your children.

Once the event has occurred, one can write about it or one can try to prevent a similar event from occurring; in either case it is not possible to undo the first event.

Therefore, as a society, people must learn from their errors and their failures to care for other people. Lorde even warns herself that she must discern and employ this crucial difference between poetry and rhetoric; if she does not, "my power too will run corrupt as poisonous mold/ or lie limp and useless as an unconnected wire."

For Lorde, the process of learning all over again how to transform thought into action begins with the awareness of her personal reality. In the collections, *Coal, The Black Unicorn,* and *Our Dead Behind Us*, the poet addresses more specifically the individual human beings in her life, creating vignettes of her relationships with other people. In particular, she returns again and again to images of her mother, Linda Belmar Lorde, whose relatively light-colored skin is mentioned in many of the poems. In "Outside," she links her mother's lightness to the brutal faces of racism: "Nobody lynched my momma/ but what she'd never been/ had bleached her face of everything." When Lorde questions, "Who shall I curse that I grew up/ believing in my mother's face," she is echoing the anger that also appears in the poem "Sequelae." There she states explicitly the rage that evolved from the mother's lies, white lies: "I battle the shapes of you/ wearing old ghosts of me/ hating you for being/ black and not woman/ hating you for being white." (*Zami* elaborates many of the specific events to which Lorde refers in her poems about her mother.)

The return to childhood allows the poet to come to new terms with her mother. In several of her poems, she also returns to even deeper roots constituting her identity. In "Dahomey," she refers to the African goddess Seboulisa, "the Mother of us all" or the creator of the world. In embracing the mother goddess, the poet is able "to sharpen the knives of my tongue." Because the subjects of her poetry are painful ones, Lorde empowers her own speech by always calling attention to the dangers of remaining silent. In "A Song for Many Movements," she states simply and precisely the project of her poetry: "Our labor has become/ more important/ than our silence."

The various forms of her writing provide many pieces to the whole picture that made up Lorde's life and work. She is unsentimental in naming the people who were a part of her life and in evaluating the events that made up her experiences. Her parents and her sisters are addressed with some frequency in her poems. A girlhood friend, Genevieve, appears in *Zami*, and Lorde eulogizes her death in a poem entitled "Memorial II." Many women are treated in several different poems, sometimes in cycles—for example, Martha and Eudora. In these ways, Lorde documented the people and the course of her life as she charted the changes and the progress that occurred; at each turn, she sought to understand more deeply the situation and to learn which detours to take next.

When she was in her forties, Lorde was diagnosed as having breast cancer. *The Cancer Journals* and the essay "A Burst of Light: Living with Cancer" are important pieces of personal writing that record her uncertainties, fears, and doubts about her mortality. Writing mostly in the form of a diary, Lorde allows the reader to enter into her most private thoughts and emotions, with the hope that others may be encouraged to fight cancer. Out of her determination to survive, Lorde converted her struggles with cancer into energy for battling in behalf of other humanitarian concerns.

She set out rigorously to combat racism, sexism, heterosexism, and homophobia in her work. At times she dealt with the issues separately, but more frequently she spoke of the whole gamut, since she perceived that each stems from human blindness about the differences among people. What is remarkable about Lorde's insights is the balance that she sought in presenting her view. Overtly political in intent and social in content, the essays and speeches ask all individuals to understand more deeply the ways in which human lives are organized. She then beckons people to take charge of their lives, to confront the tasks at hand, and to take responsibility for making changes.

Much of Lorde's mature work evolved from her identity as a black feminist lesbian poet. These terms are essential conjunctions that express her vision. In the essay "The Master's Tools Will Never Dismantle the Master's House," Lorde makes no apologies or defenses for her choices. She writes, "For women, the need and desire to nurture each other is not pathological but redemptive, and it is within that knowledge that our real power is rediscovered." For Lorde, the power to exist and be alive came from her love—in all senses of the word— for women.

In her most often cited essay, "The Uses of the Erotic: The Erotic as Power," Lorde dislodges some of the negative assumptions that have sprung up around the terms "erotic" and "power," and offers new perspectives on how an individual must use her power and ability to love. For Lorde, the erotic was "a resource within each of us that lies in a deeply female and spiritual plane, firmly rooted in the power of our unexpressed or unrecognized feeling." Through a redefinition of the terms, Lorde shows how societal oppression numbs a woman's ability to feel and act deeply. Often the two—emotion and action—are in conflict with the values of a "racist, patriarchal, and anti-erotic society." Before individual human beings can come together as one society, each person must be in touch with his or her own feelings and be willing to express and share with others. These are the necessary first steps to effecting real political change.

Lorde contended that the need to share is a fundamental one that all people feel. Unfortunately, the attitudes of American society often preclude true expression of individualism: If people do not fit into the norms or expectations of the dominant system of values, they are deemed "not normal" or deviant. Lorde argued against the hypocrisy of American values: Where is freedom if any forms of expression considered "unfit" are ex-

cluded? How might one such as herself, who is on the margins of all that is "normal," empower herself to take effective action?

These are the kinds of difficult questions Lorde raised from the beginning of her work as a writer and poet. She made efforts to answer them anew in much of what she produced. She emphasized the necessity of listening to others and teaching what she herself learned in the course of her work. Always receptive to the notion of difference that exists among all people, Lorde set out to consider the meaning of her own experiences first, before she attempted to convey to others what those experiences might mean in the larger context of existence. On the one hand, her work is intensely personal; it may even be considered self-absorbed at times. Yet on the other, she managed to transform her deeply private pains and joys into universal and timeless concerns.

Other major works

NONFICTION: *The Cancer Journals*, 1980; *Zami: A New Spelling of My Name*, 1982; *Sister Outsider*, 1984; *A Burst of Light*, 1988.

Bibliography

Avi-Ram, Amitai F. "*Apo Koinou* in Lorde and the Moderns: Defining the Differences." *Callaloo* 9 (Winter, 1986): 193-208.

Brooks, Jerome. "In the Name of the Father: The Poetry of Audre Lorde." In *Black Women Writers, 1950-1980: A Critical Evaluation*, edited by Mari Evans. Garden City, N.Y.: Anchor Press/Doubleday, 1983.

Hull, Gloria T. "Living on the Line: Audre Lorde and *Our Dead Behind Us*." In *Changing Our Own Words: Essays on Criticism, Theory, and Writing by Black Women*, edited by Cheryl A. Wall. New Brunswick, N.J.: Rutgers University Press, 1989.

Martin, Joan. "The Unicorn Is Black: Audre Lorde in Retrospect." In *Black Women Writers, 1950-1980: A Critical Evaluation*, edited by Mari Evans. Garden City, N.Y.: Anchor Press/Doubleday, 1983.

ALISON LURIE

Born: Chicago, Illinois; September 3, 1926

Principal long fiction

Love and Friendship, 1962; *The Nowhere City*, 1965; *Imaginary Friends*, 1967; *Real People*, 1969; *The War Between the Tates*, 1974; *Only Children*, 1979; *Foreign Affairs*, 1984; *The Truth About Lorin Jones*, 1988.

Other literary forms

Besides writing fiction, Alison Lurie has distinguished herself in two other areas, children's literature and the semiotics of dress, and her novels reflect both concerns as well. Real children's rhymes, Lurie has observed, are surprisingly subversive, not like the "safe" literature written for children by adults. She developed this insight in a nonfiction work, *Don't Tell the Grown-ups: Subversive Children's Literature* (1990). Lurie's fascination with the semiotics of clothing discussed in *The Language of Clothes* (1981), is reflected frequently in her novels, where she pursues the relationship between clothing and personal identity.

Achievements

Lurie's fiction has received much praise from critics, and her work has been very popular with the broader reading public. Her first novel, *Love and Friendship*, appeared in 1962 and was followed by several prestigious grants and fellowships: Yaddo Foundation fellowships in 1963, 1964, and 1966; a Guggenheim grant in 1965-1966; a Rockefeller Foundation grant in 1967-1968; a New York State Cultural Council Foundation Grant in 1972-1973. *The War Between the Tates* in 1974 brought Lurie a popular audience and more critical acclaim. An American Academy of Arts and Letters award followed in 1978, and for *Foreign Affairs* she was awarded a Pulitzer Prize in 1985. All Lurie's fiction displays a remarkable control of language, a style which surprises and amuses. She has often been compared to Jane Austen, both for her wit and for her sharp-edged, satiric depiction of human follies.

Biography

Alison Lurie was born September 3, 1926, in Chicago, Illinois, but grew up in White Plains, New York. An avid reader as a child, she began at about the age of thirteen or fourteen to read such authors as Charles Dickens, George Bernard Shaw, and Jane Austen. In 1947, she was graduated from Radcliffe, where she had met many people who later became important literary figures—Barbara Epstein, for example, later an editor of *The New York Review of Books*, and Jonathon Peale Bishop, a teacher, critic, and essayist whom she married in 1948. Lurie became professor of children's literature at Cornell University in Ithaca, New York, in 1969.

Analysis

Alison Lurie's novels are known for their comedy and satire, and her acute observation is most often trained on the complications of love, marriage, and friendship as they affect the lives of the upper classes, the educated, the academic. Many of her novels take place at the fictional Convers College in New England or at Corinth University in upstate New York (based on Cornell University, where Lurie has taught for many years) or concern characters who teach at or have been associated with Corinth. These novels are not, however, all academic satire; the academics often travel to other places or become involved in issues beyond the campus.

At the heart of Lurie's first two novels are couples trying to work out their relationship. Her first novel, *Love and Friendship* (a title taken from Jane Austen), draws out the main lines of the issue. What is love and what is friendship? Are they different in what is best and most enduring? In this novel, the main character, Emmy

Turner, "loves" her lover more than she does her husband. In the end, however, she chooses her husband over her lover because he needs her and to him she can be a friend. Indeed, what first led her to enter into a love affair was frustration with her husband's failure to make a friend of her, to discuss with her his work and his concerns. Ultimately, Lurie suggests, friendship is more satisfying and lasting than love; indeed, love at its best is friendship at its best.

Love and friendship in marriage are explored most intensively in Lurie's next and most celebrated novel, *The War Between the Tates*. Erica and Brian Tate, a young academic couple, are in their own eyes and the eyes of their friends the perfect couple, but as middle age looms, Brian becomes increasingly frustrated at not being famous, while the children become rebellious teenagers. True love and friendship appear to be lacking. Finally, Brian has an affair with a student whom he makes pregnant, Erica befriends the student, and both Brian and Erica, but especially Erica, wander through a bewildering maze of events that leave their earlier sense of themselves and their marriage damaged. As the novel ends, they drift back together, confused, "out of love," but basically seeking a peace they can find only with each other.

The love and friendship theme appears again in *Foreign Affairs*, which juxtaposes two main characters, one married and one not. Vinnie Miner, a middle-aged professor, finds love surprisingly where she had least expected it, in a friendship with a man totally unlike her, a retired sanitary engineer. The other main character, a handsome young man in Vinnie's academic department, begins the novel estranged from his wife, is temporarily dazzled and infatuated by a far more glamorous Englishwoman, but returns to his wife at the end, finding her superior in trust, honesty, and common decency.

Lurie's novels concern themselves with relationships between people, and these relationships are at the center of all her works. Yet the lives of Lurie's characters are affected by more than personal forces alone. Context, temporal and physical alike, is also central to these novels, and the direction of the lives of Lurie's characters is profoundly affected by the times and the places in which they live. The most persistent context, moreover, is academic, since many of these characters, like Lurie herself, are university professors or members of their families. In this case again, *Love and Friendship* sets a pattern which other novels will follow. Emmy Turner's husband, Holman Turner, is a young instructor at Convers, a small, exclusive liberal arts college in New England. Emmy wants to share her husband's academic interests but he shuts her out, treasuring her as an ideal wife and mother but bored by her attempts to enter into his intellectual concerns. Ironically, Emmy should be more at home at Convers (her wealthy father is a trustee, and two brothers are alumni), while Holman has come from a very different background, yet it is he, not Emmy, who seems the "Convers type." Emmy's love affair flaunts the Convers traditions, while Holman seems the perfect instructor. In the end, however, he falls afoul of those same Convers traditions, and it is Emmy who must stay to save him.

The War Between the Tates again makes the academy not only strong backdrop but also actor in the events. Brian Tate is a highly successful sociology professor at Corinth University in upstate New York, and his wife, Erica, is a faculty wife. Their two closest friends who divorce in the novel, are Leonard Zimmern, an English professor, and Danielle Zimmern, Erica's closest female friend, a part-time faculty member in the French department. The convulsions of America academe in the late 1960's interfere directly in Brian's and Erica's lives. Brian, though very successful academically, has always dreamed of fame as an advisor to governments and presidents, and his middle-aged frustration makes him susceptible to trying to recover his lost youth by mixing socially with his graduate students, increasingly adapting his clothing and other styles to theirs, finally indulging in his affair with Wendy. Erica attempts to preserve her traditional moral values in the face of all this upheaval and tries not only to adapt herself to these values but also to give direction to Brian and Wendy, even to the point of insisting that Brian divorce her and marry Wendy. She becomes peripherally involved, through her friend Danielle, in the Hens, a local feminist group, and finding the local Hare Krishna guru of the students to be an old school friend, under his guidance has her own adventure with LSD. Brian and Erica, then, experience their marital troubles amid the student rebellions of the 1960's. Though the novel does not probe as deeply as *Imaginary Friends* into the political and intellectual doubts and troubles of academe, these influences are present, shaping their reaction.

In *Foreign Affairs*, the two main characters are again college professors, both from the English department at Corinth University: the middle-aged, internationally famous expert in children's literature, Vinnie Miner, and the young specialist in the eighteenth century, Fred Turner, both on leave to do scholarly work in London. The novel for the most part tells their stories separately, their paths crossing significantly only twice. While their common background does make their lives cross in significant ways, and while both their lives are shaped by their academic backgrounds, the primary focus of the novel is on other aspects of their lives.

The university campus, then, demonstrates the importance of time and place in Lurie's novels. This is also true in a larger sense, since American culture itself, with its regional and sociological tensions, plays just as important a role as the characters do. If *Love and Friendship*, the first novel, works off a Jane Austen theme, it also echoes a peculiarly American, Fitzgeraldian theme in which the different regions and classes of America become important players in the conflicts of the novel. Emmy is New Jersey rich, her lover Will Thomas Southern shabby genteel, and her husband Holman Chicago shabby but respectable poor. As the marital couple work out their conflicts with traditions of Convers College playing an important role, these different regional and class conflicts do much to shape their actions and reactions.

Foreign Affairs enlarges on the Jamesian theme found in *Imaginary Friends* not only by explicitly introducing Henry James's work by name but also by exploring one of his most insistent themes: what happens when Americans encounter European society. In James's novels of this type, the balance is struck in favor finally of the basic, honest decency of Americans against the more sophisticated but possibly corrupt world of the Europeans, and Lurie's novel arrives at the same resolution. This exploration is complicated by the fact that, of the two Americans, Vinnie Miner knows the ways and customs of the English so well that she really feels more culturally at home there than in the United States. Fred Turner, on the other hand, despite his great physical charms and his knowledge of eighteenth century literature, is basically a raw recruit to European culture. Both, however, have "foreign affairs": Vinnie with an almost illiterate Oklahoman whom she meets on the plane on the way over, so embarrassingly crude that she dreads presenting him to her friends; and Fred with an English aristocrat and actress so elegant and sophisticated that his American life appears crude by comparison. Despite this structural converse—in which Vinnie loves an American far less

presentable than her European friends and Fred loves an Englishwoman far more sophisticated than his American wife and friends—both find, despite all their differences, their American loves superior after all, and their European friends, for all their sophistication, less satisfying morally as friends and lovers than their American friends. Thus, the pattern of James's international novels, in which superior American decency confronts and ultimately wins out over superior European elegance and sophistication, is repeated here in Lurie's fiction.

If Lurie's readers often spot resonances from other fiction, they also have the pleasure of recognizing characters they have met in other Lurie novels, for she frequently works with recurring characters. Emmy Turner's four-year-old boy Freddy from *Love and Friendship* is one of the grown-up main characters in *Foreign Affairs*, while Fred's wife Roo in that same novel appeared as a child in the earlier *The War Between the Tates*. Sometimes Lurie will in a later novel go back to an earlier period in a character's life: Miranda, the grown-up, married mother of three children in *Love and Friendship*, is seen as a child in the later novel *Only Children*. Of all the characters that recur, the most persistent one is Leonard Zimmern, first seen in *Real People* as a middle-aged, distinguished critic of American literature living in New York and later in *The War Between the Tates* as a friend of Brian and Erica. He is also the father of Roo, a child here but an adult in *Foreign Affairs*. In *Only Children*, the Depression-era story, Zimmern is a teenager, and in *Foreign Affairs* he is the father of a grown-up Roo, the famous critic whose harsh article on Vinnie Miner's work in children's literature haunts Vinnie as she goes to England. Roger Zimmern of *Imaginary Friends* is mentioned briefly in *The War Between the Tates* as Leonard Zimmern's cousin. This remarkable amount of recurrence suggests Lurie's strong interest in understanding how her characters came to be who they are, despite her novels' time frames. Her novels cover only short periods of time—one, *Only Children*, takes place in a single weekend. In order to continue her characters' development, then, Lurie often spreads out their lives over several novels, the recurrence of her characters in different novels doing much to tie their lives together.

As in the other novels, all the themes discussed so far are treated as well in *Imaginary Friends*. Their treatment in that novel, however, represents perhaps Lurie's broadest and deepest effort, for the academic backdrop she uses so often elsewhere is broadened here to embrace the most fundamental of human questions—questions of knowledge, of identity, of sanity, and finally of madness. The main character in this novel, sociologist Roger Zimmern—a young, brand-new Ph.D. at a large, upstate New York university—goes to Sophis, a nearby small town, as the research assistant of Thomas McCann. McCann is a famous senior professor in his department whom Roger admires despite rumors he has heard about him from other young faculty members and despite the realization that McCann's form of empirical sociology (the case-study method) is passé. To investigate McCann's hypothesis that small groups can build so powerful a belief system that it can withstand, rationalize, and incorporate doubting attacks from within and without, Roger infiltrates, under the cover of a public opinion seeker, a group of religious fundamentalists called the Truth-seekers, whose young leader, Verena, leads and directs through automatic writing from superior beings on a planet named Varna. McCann is introduced as a businessman friend, also interested in their theories. Roger's secure identity is overset by his mentor's unscientific attempt to control the experiment in the direction of this hypothesis rather than merely observe and record, by the degree to which he sees this tendency in his mentor, driven by academic rivalry and jealousy. Also tormented by his sexual attraction for Verena, he reaches a point where he no longer knows what he believes in, no longer knows who he is, no long knows whether there is in his discipline any objective basis for scientific inquiry. He believes that he is going mad but decides that it is, rather, his mentor who is insane and becomes unwillingly the primary witness whose testimony results in McCann's being committed to an asylum. The novel ends with Roger maintaining tenuous but commonsensical hold on his own sanity. Here, Lurie has touched upon questions central not only to academic life but to the lives of everyone else as well: How can one truly observe and know? How real is one's own sense of self?

Taken as a whole, Lurie's novels reveal a remarkable uniformity. Her own background in academe provides the most common setting for her novels, and frequently this setting is broadened to reflect the central questions with which Lurie is concerned. Her work is best considered not as a series of separate novels but as a continuity in which her characters' lives continue, not ceasing with the end of a particular novel but continuing as do all lives: growing and changing through time.

Other major works

NONFICTION: *The Language of Clothes*, 1981; *Don't Tell the Grown-ups: Subversive Children's Literature*, 1990.

CHILDREN'S LITERATURE: *The Heavenly Zoo: Legends and Tales of the Stars*, 1979; *Clever Gretchen and Other Forgotten Folktales*, 1980; *Fabulous Beasts*, 1981.

Bibliography

Evory, Ann, ed. *Contemporary Authors*. Rev. series, Vol. 17. Detroit: Gale Research, 1981.

Hall, Sharon D., ed. *Contemporary Literary Criticism*. Vol. 39. Detroit: Gale Research, 1986.

Helterman, Jeffrey, and Richard Layman, eds. *Dictionary of Literary Biography*. Vol. 2. Detroit: Gale Research, 1978.

Hite, Molly. *The Other Side of the Story: Structures and Strategies of Contemporary Feminist Literature*. Ithaca, N.Y.: Cornell University Press, 1989.

Riley, Carolyn, ed. *Contemporary Literary Criticism*. Vol. 4. Detroit: Gale Research, 1975.

MARY McCARTHY

Born: Seattle, Washington; June 21, 1912   **Died:** New York, New York; October 25, 1989

Principal long fiction

The Oasis, 1949; *The Groves of Academe*, 1952; *A Charmed Life*, 1955; *The Group*, 1963; *Birds of America*, 1971; *Cannibals and Missionaries*, 1979.

Other literary forms

First known as a book reviewer, drama critic, and essayist, Mary McCarthy also wrote short stories, collected in *The Company She Keeps* (1942) and *Cast a Cold Eye* (1950). Her drama criticism is collected in *Sights and Spectacles: 1937-1956* (1956) and in *Mary McCarthy's Theatre Chronicles, 1937-1962* (1963). *Venice Observed* (1956) and *The Stones of Florence* (1959) are books of travel and art history. *The Writing on the Wall* (1970) and *Ideas and the Novel* (1980) are literary essays and lectures. *On the Contrary: Articles of Belief* (1961) contains autobiographical essays and literary criticism. *Memories of a Catholic Girlhood* (1957) and *How I Grew* (1987) are memoirs of her childhood and youth.

Another autobiographical work, *Intellectual Memoirs* (1992), left unfinished at her death, was published posthumously. Her books *Vietnam* (1967) and *Hanoi* (1968) oppose United States involvement in the Vietnam War, an interest which she continued in *Medina* (1972) and in *The Seventeenth Degree (1974). The Mask of State (1974) presents impressions of the Watergate hearings*.

Achievements

From the appearance of her first book reviews, when she was just out of college, to the time of her death, McCarthy was one of the leading figures on the American literary scene. In her novels as much as in her essays and reviews, she was above all a critic, a sharp observer of contemporary society. Her work is indispensable for students of twentieth century American culture.

Biography

Born into an affluent family of mixed Irish and Jewish heritage on June 21, 1912, in Seattle, Washington, Mary Therese McCarthy had a segmented childhood. After six years of what she called a "fairy-tale" existence of happiness, both parents died of influenza in 1918 during a move to Minneapolis. Mary and her three younger brothers, placed with their grandaunt and uncle, then entered a bleak phase of intense, strict Catholicism, which Mary described in *Memories of a Catholic Girlhood*. In 1923, Mary's grandparents moved her to a convent school in Seattle for the seventh and eighth grades; she spent her ninth grade year in a public school and then her remaining high school years at the Annie Wright Seminary in Tacoma, from which she was graduated in 1929 at the top of her class. In the same year of her graduation as a Phi Beta Kappa from Vassar College in 1933, she married Harold Johnsrud; the marriage lasted three years. She reviewed novels and biographies for *The New Re-public* and *The Nation*, worked for the left-wing publishers Covici Friede, and, in 1937, involved herself in Trotskyite politics. In 1937, she became drama editor for the *Partisan Review*.

The next year, Mary McCarthy married Edmund Wilson and gave birth to a son, Reuel Wilson; also, at Wilson's urging, she wrote her first fiction, a short story. Thereafter, the stories she wrote for *Southern Review, Partisan Review,* and *Harper's Bazaar* were collected in 1942 in the book *The Company She Keeps*. She separated from Wilson in 1945, the same year that she was teaching literature at Bard College; and in 1946, she married Bowden Broadwater. In 1948, she taught one semester at Sarah Lawrence College and, in 1949, was a Guggenheim Fellow, an award which was repeated in 1959. Also in 1949, she received the *Horizon* literary prize from the publishers of her novel *The Oasis*. In 1961, she was divorced from Broadwater; that same year, she married

James Raymond West, a State Department official assigned to Paris—and went to live with him in France.

Two events dominated the 1960's for McCarthy. The first was the enormous popular success of her novel *The Group*, which became a best-seller. The second was the Vietnam War; she was an outspoken critic of United States policy in Vietnam. In the 1970's, she published two novels with social and political themes: *Birds of America* in 1971 and *Cannibals and Missionaries* in 1979.

In 1980, an offhand remark on *The Dick Cavett Show* embroiled McCarthy in a prolonged legal battle that became a *cause célèbre* in the literary community. Discussing Lillian Hellman's memoirs, McCarthy said that "every word she writes is a lie, including 'and' and 'the.'" Hellman sued. The resulting legal maneuvering was costly for McCarthy (in contrast, the wealthy Hellman did not count the cost) and ended only in 1984 when, after Hellman's death, the suit was dropped before going to trial. The controversy brought several of Hellman's autobiographical works under close scrutiny, and the consensus was that McCarthy's judgment, although stated in hyperbolic terms, was vindicated.

In 1987, McCarthy published *How I Grew*, the first installment in what was projected to be a multivolume intellectual autobiography. In general, critics found it inferior to *Memories of a Catholic Girlhood*, which had covered some of the same territory from a different perspective. McCarthy died in New York on October 25, 1989.

Analysis

Mary McCarthy's novels often feature herself, with an assumed name, as protagonist; she also exploited her husbands and other people close to her for fictional purposes. Her characters generally have a superior education and/or intellect so that citations and quotations from learned sources—mainly classical or artistic—spring into their conversations. This heightened discourse promotes compact paragraphs of dialogue, in which several persons speak to the same topic, in contrast with the usual fictional technique of a separate paragraph for each speaker. Yet, in the close conceptual unity of McCarthy's novels, lengthy paragraphs of extensive character analyses frequently fill several pages without interruption. As a result, the technique of several speakers in one paragraph seems to support the general schema. It supports, also, the paradigm of the group.

Structurally, the three novels preceding *The Group* develop around separate chapters, each presenting the viewpoints and the consciousness of the different characters; their point of unity is the common awareness of the social group. A protagonist, often a reflection of the author, generally emerges from among these peripheral persons, but the effect of each chapter remains that of the portrait or sketch.

Several factors of McCarthy's work can be inferred from this structure. As an orphan and a Catholic among Protestants, she no doubt had an early sensitivity to the significance of the group and the outsider. Furthermore, the intensely autobiographical nature of her work blurs the lines of genre, so that her essays read like short stories and her short stories like essays. Genre distinction, then, becomes a problem in any analysis of her work. For example, McCarthy did not term *The Oasis* a "novel" but called it a *conte philosophique*. Also, several chapters of her novels were published individually as short stories before being incorporated in the novels. The effect of this technique raises the question of whether she pushed the boundaries of the traditional novel outward or merely retreated to its earliest phases of development. She lamented the loss of a "sense of character" in modern novels, saying it began to fade with D.H. Lawrence. She admired Leo Tolstoy, Gustave Flaubert, George Eliot, Charles Dickens, and "all the Elizabethans."

The dominant quality of McCarthy's work is satire, and much of it is achieved by exaggeration and generalization. The dominant organization is the pairing of a separate character with each chapter, infused with an occasional chorus of viewpoints. McCarthy compared the technique to ventriloquism: The author throws her voice into various characters who speak for her. The long paragraphs of explication or character analysis tend to minimize plot; the concentration is on the psychological effects of what are frequently trivial incidents.

The themes of McCarthy's novels generally concern the social failures of a group—of Utopian communities in *The Oasis*, of progressive education in *The Groves of Academe*, or of cultural progress in *The Group*. The interest in group attitudes can be best observed in the political content of McCarthy's novels, many of which feature a person who had some affiliation with the Communist Party and defected or failed to become a member. Her work also shows a persistent aversion to the efforts of Senator Joseph McCarthy to eradicate Communists in the United States.

The Groves of Academe is set in a small Pennsylvania college called Jocelyn and resembling Bard College. Directing its satire at progressive education, this novel pits the progressive against the classical, satirizes the small college in general, and exposes the evils of McCarthyism, focused in Senator McCarthy's House Un-American Activities Committee. The group here is the English department faculty, from which Professor Henry Mulcahy finds himself dismissed. He rallies the faculty to his support, although he is a poor academician and deserves dismissal, and gains it through an appeal for sympathy for his wife and children. McCarthyism brought him to the position—the president hired him because he had been unjustly accused of being a Communist sympathizer—and, finally, it accounts for his retention. Mulcahy loses his chief faculty supporter when she discovers that Mulcahy lied about his wife's illness, but he gains another weapon through a visiting poet who recognizes him from Communist party meetings. At the climax of the novel, the McCarthy scare is shown at its most evil: Protecting the college, the well-meaning president conducts an interview into Mulcahy's past, which results in getting himself charged with libel. The unstable Mulcahy triumphs and secures his position at Jocelyn—certain to continue bullying students and colleagues alike—and the president resigns.

With a theme of the failure of modern progress, *The Group* was published in November, 1963. At that time, Betty Friedan's *The Feminine Mystique* (1962) and other feminist writings had focused on the problems of women, and the public was responsive to works focused on the problems of the emancipated woman. Although the novel is set in the seven years from 1933 to 1940, the progressiveness of the eight *cum* nine young Vassar women seemed to be the progress that was engulfing women of the 1960's. Like gleanings from an alumnae bulletin, the random appearances, different voices, and loose ends are not expected to be resolved. The undistinguished occupations of the group, confirm the alumnae magazine reports of most women graduates, but somehow more is expected of Vassar women. Not only the money but also increased competition for admission meant that, by 1963, most women could not get into Vassar. For the general public, there is some comfort in the failure of the culturally advantaged.

The novel begins with the wedding of Kay Strong in 1933 and ends with her death seven years later at the age of twenty-nine. Of the eight members of the group who had lived in the same dormitory, plus one outsider, Kay seemed to be most forward-looking and progressive. Like McCarthy, she comes from the West and, immediately upon graduation, she marries her lover of some time, a mostly unemployed playwright named Harald Petersen who resembles Harold Johnsrud. Part of McCarthy's personality is dispersed among the other characters, especially Libby MacAusland, a woman of formidable intellect who writes book reviews and becomes a literary agent.

The elegant, beautiful, and wealthy Elinor Eastlake disappears into Europe and reemerges a lesbian prior to Kay's death. Polly Andrews becomes attached to a married man who is obviously well adjusted except that he pays twenty-five dollars a week for psychiatric counseling. Working in a hospital, Polly becomes engaged to another man, a psychiatrist who has defected from the profession and thus augments the satiric attack on psychiatry. Helena Davison, in Cleveland, remains the stable rich girl, highly intelligent and analytic. Priss Hartshorn marries a pediatrician, and attempting to breast-feed her son and train him by modern theories, provides the satire on this aspect of progressivism. Pokey Prothero plans to become a veterinarian.

Kay, during a fight with Harald, gets a black eye and finds herself committed to a mental hospital. Despite Harald's admission that she does not belong there, she decides to stay for a rest and then disappears from the story until she reemerges after a divorce and a year in the West. Back East, ready to start a career again, she falls to her death while spotting planes from her window and becomes the first casualty of the war.

Representing a culmination of the group philosophy and the disjointed voices of the earlier novels, *The Group* with its timely feminist content earned for McCarthy much money and many appearances on talk shows and in magazines. Some Vassar alumnae were recognizable in it, and the film version omitted naming the college. This novel established McCarthy as a popular writer.

While *The Groves of Academe* is still highly esteemed as an example of the academic novel, and *The Group* is read by students of popular fiction and women's issues, McCarthy's novels considered by themselves do not make up a lasting body of work. Rather, they derive their lasting significance from their place in the life and work of an exemplary woman of letters.

Other major works

SHORT FICTION: *The Company She Keeps*, 1942; *Cast a Cold Eye*, 1950; *The Hounds of Summer and Other Stories*, 1981.

NONFICTION: *Sights and Spectacles: 1937-1956*, 1956; *Venice Observed*, 1956; *Memories of a Catholic Girlhood*, 1957; *The Stones of Florence*, 1959; *On the Contrary: Articles of Belief*, 1961; *Mary McCarthy's Theatre Chronicles, 1937-1962*, 1963; *Vietnam*, 1967; *Hanoi*, 1968; *The Writing on the Wall and Other Literary Essays*, 1970; *Medina*, 1972; *The Seventeenth Degree*, 1974; *The Mask of State*, 1974; *Ideas and the Novel*, 1980; *Occasional Prose*, 1985; *How I Grew*, 1987; *Intellectual Memoirs: New York, 1936-1938*, 1992.

Bibliography

Auchincloss, Louis. *Pioneers and Caretakers: A Study of Nine American Novelists*. Minneapolis: University of Minnesota Press, 1961.

Brightman, Carol. *Writing Dangerously: Mary McCarthy and Her World*. New York: Clarkson N. Potter, 1992.

Gelderman, Carol W. *Mary McCarthy: A Life*. New York: St. Martin's Press, 1988.

Grumbach, Doris. *The Company She Kept*. New York: Coward, McCann, 1967.

Munroe, Gretchen Himmele. "Mary McCarthy." In *American Novelists Since World War II*, edited by Jeffrey Helterman and Richard Layman. Vol. 2 in *Dictionary of Literary Biography*. Detroit: Gale Research, 1978.

Stock, Irvin. *Mary McCarthy*. Minneapolis: University of Minnesota Press, 1968.

CARSON McCULLERS

Born: Columbus, Georgia; February 19, 1917   **Died:** Nyack, New York; September 29, 1967

Principal long fiction

The Heart Is a Lonely Hunter, 1940; *Reflections in a Golden Eye*, 1941; *The Member of the Wedding*, 1946; *The Ballad of the Sad Café*, 1951; *Clock Without Hands*, 1961.

Other literary forms

Carson McCullers published a number of short stories, some of which are included in the volume containing *The Ballad of the Sad Café*, and some in a collection of short works, *The Mortgaged Heart* (1971), edited by her sister, M. G. Smith. The latter also contains some magazine articles and notes of her writing. McCullers adapted *The Member of the Wedding* for the stage in 1950 (a film version appeared in 1952). She wrote two plays, including *The Square Root of Wonderful* (1957). McCullers' poetry is published in *The Mortgaged Heart* and in a children's book, *Sweet as a Pickle and Clean as a Pig* (1964).

Achievements

Like William Faulkner, McCullers has literary kinship with those older, midnight-haunted writers—Edgar Allan Poe, Nathanial Hawthorne, and Herman Melville among them—who projected in fable and with symbol the story of America's unquiet mind. Against her Southern background she created a world of symbolic violence and tragic reality, indirectly lighted by the cool Flaubertian purity of her style. Of the writers of her generation, none was more consistent or thorough in achieving a sustained body of work.

Several of McCullers' works received critical acclaim. "A Tree, a Rock, a Cloud," a short story sometimes compared in theme to Samuel Taylor Coleridge's "The Rime of the Ancient Mariner," was chosen for the O. Henry Memorial Prize in 1942. The dramatic version of *The Member of the Wedding* was extremely successful, running on Broadway continuously for nearly fifteen months, and it was named for both the Donaldson Award and the New York Drama Critics Circle Award in 1950. In addition, McCullers was a Guggenheimer fellow in 1942 and 1946, and she received an award from the American Academy of Arts and Letters in 1943.

Biography

Carson McCullers was born Lula Carson Smith on February 19, 1917, in Columbus, Georgia. Marguerite Smith, McCullers' mother, was very early convinced that her daughter was an artistic genius and sacrificed herself and, to some extent, McCullers' father, brother, and sister, to the welfare of her gifted child. McCullers grew up, therefore, with a peculiar kind of shyness and emotional dependence on her mother, combined with supreme self-confidence about her ability. McCullers announced early in life that she was going to be a concert pianist. Smith placed her daughter under the tutelage of Mary Tucker, a concert musician, who agreed that McCullers was talented. McCullers came to love Mrs. Tucker and her family with an all-consuming passion, a pattern she was to follow with a number of other close friends during her life. McCullers suffered from despair when the Tuckers moved away from her hometown.

Writing was also an early enthusiasm of McCullers. As a child, she created shows to be acted by herself and her siblings in the sitting room. The shows stopped when she discovered Eugene O'Neill. Soon after, she became enthralled by the great Russian writers, Fyodor Dostoevski, Anton Chekhov, and Leo Tolstoy—a fascination she never outgrew.

Her family had enough money to send the seventeen-year-old McCullers to New York City to attend the famous Julliard School of Music, but she lost the tuition money in the subway and found herself almost penniless. One way or another, McCullers managed to support herself through the school term. By the time she came home in the summer, she had begun to write in earnest, and the dream of being a concert pianist was entirely displaced by the vision of becoming a great writer.

Back home, McCullers met a handsome young soldier Reeves McCullers; in 1937, they were married. Though idyllically happy at the first, their marriage became increasingly troubled. While McCullers' first novel, published when she was twenty-two, brought her immediate recognition in the literary world of New York, her husband met with continual frustration in his own ambitions. Moreover, both she and her husband were sexually ambivalent. The repressed homosexuality and odd love triangles that are so characteristic of McCullers' fiction had some correlation to real-life situations. McCullers had a disconcerting tendency to fall in love with either men or women, and to suffer inordinately when such attentions were repulsed.

In 1940, McCullers and her husband separated, and McCullers moved into a two-room apartment in a large Victorian house in Brooklyn Heights, owned by George Davis, editor of *Harper's Bazaar*. The old house became the temporary home for a stimulating group of artists, including novelist Richard Wright, and musicians and composers Aaron Copland, Leonard Bernstein, and David Diamond. Diamond was to become emotionally involved with both McCullers and Reeves. Also temporarily in residence were Salvador Dalí and his wife Gala,

as well as other prominent surrealist painters.

While McCullers and Reeves tried again to live together in New York, and for a time took comfort in a new intimacy with Diamond, she eventually divorced him. When he went back into the service and became a much-decorated war hero, however, McCullers was so admiring of his new role that they were remarried. Yet Reeves could not maintain the independence and pride he had so heartily won as a soldier. He turned increasingly to drink and eventually expressed the desire to commit suicide. When, in Europe, he seemed determined that they should both hang themselves, McCullers fled from him in terror and returned home alone. Shortly thereafter, Reeves was found dead in a Paris hotel.

After McCullers finished *The Member of the Wedding*, which proved immensely popular, her friendship with dramatist Tennessee Williams encouraged her to write a stage adaptation of the work, which starred Ethel Waters as the black maid and Julie Harris as the lonely adolescent. *The Member of the Wedding* was eventually adapted into a motion picture with the original cast.

McCullers' last years were a nightmare of pain. She had two strokes; underwent several operations on her paralyzed left arm, leg, and hand; had a cancerous breast removed; broke her hip and elbow in a fall; and finally died after another massive stroke. She was fifty years old.

Analysis

Carson McCullers' fiction has a childlike directness, a disconcerting exposure of unconscious impulses in conjunction with realistic detail. She is like the candid child who announces that the emperor in his new clothes is really naked. She sees the truth, or at least a partial truth of the human psyche, then inflates or distorts that truth into a somewhat grotesque fable which is sometimes comic, but always sad. Such a tragicomic effect derives, apparently from an unusual openness to the subconscious direction, combined with conscious cultivation of a style that best exploits such material, weaving into it just enough objectively observed reality to achieve plausibility.

The thematic content of McCullers' works is consistent: All her stories deal with a metaphysical isolation of individuals and their desperate need to transcend this isolation through love. Love is the key to a magnificent transformation of leaden existence into gold, but the exalted state is doomed because love is so seldom recip-

rocated. Though this feeling (and it is more feeling than thought) may stem from McCullers' early fears and dependence on her mother, it strikes a universal chord. That McCullers projects this terrible sense of unrequited love into all kinds of human relationships except that between mother and daughter may be suggestive in itself.

McCullers successfully universalizes that state of metaphysical isolation as a perennial human condition, not merely a neurotic regression to childhood. Her first novel, *The Heart Is a Lonely Hunter*, has as its child character Mick Kelly; she clings to John Singer, the deaf-mute who, she fancies, understands and sympathizes with her problems. McCullers' own definition of the character in "Author's Outline of 'The Mute'" (found in *The Mortgaged Heart*) reveals an almost transparent self-dramatization: "Her story is that of the violent struggle of a gifted child to get what she needs from an unyielding environment." Only metaphorically is Mick's struggle "violent," but even when McCullers presents physical violence in fiction it often seems to function as the objective correlative to mental anguish.

McCullers casts Jake Blount, the ineffectual social agitator, as a would-be Marxist revolutionary, but he may seem more like an overgrown frustrated child. Her outline says, "His deepest motive is to do all that he can to change the predatory, unnatural social conditions existing today. . . . He is fettered by abstractions and conflicting ideas. . . . His attitude vacillates between hate and the most unselfish love."

Dr. Benedict Copeland is the more believable character, representing the peculiar plight of an educated African American in the South, who has internalized white society's condemnation of black cultural traits. His daughter's black dialect and careless posture embarrass him, and he frowns on what he considers the irresponsible fecundity and emotionality of the black youth. What McCullers calls his "passionate asceticism" has driven away even his own family.

Biff Brannon, the proprietor of the local restaurant, is the dispassionate observer, sympathetic, in a distant way, with all human oddities. Like Mick, he seems almost a part of McCullers, but a grown-up version. Brannon is also sexually impotent, with homosexual leanings. He is cold and withdrawn with his wife and has a repressed attraction for Mick in her tomboyish prepuberty—an impulse that fades as soon as she shows sexual development.

All these characters pivot around the deaf-mute, John Singer, who is the central symbol of humanity's metaphysical condition. They take his silence as wisdom and pout out their hearts to his patient, but unreceptive ears. He does lipread, so he knows what they are saying, but he has no way to communicate with them in reply. Moreover, the experiences they confide to him seem so alien to his own that he does not really understand. Mick talks about music, which he has never heard; Jake Blount rants about the downtrodden working classes; Dr. Copeland speaks of his frustrations as a racial leader without any followers; and Biff Brannon simply looks on with no project of his own.

Yet, John Singer shares their universal need to love and communicate with a kindred soul. The object of his adoration is another mute, a sloppy, retarded Greek man named Antonopoulos, who loves nothing but the childish pleasure of a full stomach. When Antonopoulos dies in an institution, Singer commits suicide. The whole pyramid of illusion collapses.

This bleak tale suggest that the beloved is created in the lover's mind out of the extremity of his or her need, and projected upon whomever is available. Singer drew the love of these desperate souls because of his polite tolerance of their advances coupled with an essential blankness. They looked into his eyes and saw their own dreams reflected there, just as Singer himself read a secret sympathy and understanding in the blank round face of Antonopoulos, who was actually incapable of such sentiments.

The haunting quality of this story may derive partly from the impression of getting an inside look at a multiple personality. The young McCullers displays a curious ability to divide her ambivalent psyche to create new, somewhat lopsided beings. McCullers had never seen a deaf-mute, for example, and when Reeves wanted to take her to a convention of deaf-mutes, she declined, saying she already knew John Singer. Marxist political agitators may have been just as foreign to her actual experience, but she could create one from the jumble of liberal sentiment she acquired through educated friends and through reading. If the issues were not clear in her own mind, it did not really matter, because Jake was a confused and drunken loser. McCullers has been praised by African American writers for her sensitive portrayal of blacks, yet the peculiar warmth of the relationship between Dr. Copeland's daughter Portia, her husband, and her brother suggests the triangular love affairs McCullers sometimes acted out in her own life and dramatized several times in other fiction.

The Ballad of the Sad Café offers a successful treatment of archetypal myth, with its psychodramatic overtones tempered by humor. Like the true folk ballad, it is a melancholy tale of love. The setting is an isolated Southern village—little more than a trading post with a few dreary, unpainted buildings. The most prominent citizen is known as Miss Emelia, a strong, mannish, cross-eyed woman with a sharp business sense. She runs the general store and operates a still that produces the best corn liquor for miles around. There is nothing to do for entertainment in town except drink her brew, follow the odd career of this sexless female, and listen to the melancholy singing of the chain gang, which suggests a universal entrapment in the dreary reality of one's life.

The story concerns a temporary hiatus from boredom when Miss Emelia and the observing townspeople become a real community. Love provides the means for a temporary transcendence of Miss Emelia's metaphysical isolation, and through her, sheds a reflected radiance on all. Like John Singer, Miss Emelia chooses an odd person to love, a homeless dwarf who straggles into town, claiming to be her cousin and hoping for a handout. Although Miss Emelia had thrown out the only man who had ever loved her because he expected sexual favors when they were married, she unaccountably falls in love with this pathetic wanderer. She takes "Cousin Lymon" in and, because he likes company, begins a restaurant, which becomes the social center of the entire community. All goes well until the despised husband, Marvin Macy, is released from the penitentiary and returns to his hometown, bent on revenge for the monstrous humiliation Miss Emelia had visited upon him.

Another unusual threesome develops when Cousin Lymon becomes infatuated with Marvin Macy. The competition between Macy and Miss Emelia for the attention of Cousin Lymon comes to a tragicomic climax in a fistfight between the rivals. Miss Emelia, who has been working out with a punching bag, is actually winning when the treacherous Cousin Lymon leaps on her back, and the two men give her a terrible drubbing. Macy and Cousin Lymon flee after they vandalize Miss Emelia's store and her still in the woods. Miss Emelia is left in a more desolate isolation than she has ever known and becomes a solitary recluse thereafter. The coda at the end recalls again the mournful song of the chain gang.

There is no more somber image of spiritual isolation than the glimpse of the reclusive Miss Emelia at the window of her boarded-up café. "It is a face like the terrible, dim faces known in dreams—sexless and white, with two gray crossed eyes which are turned inward so sharply that they seem to be exchanging with each other one long and secret gaze of grief." This story, written in a style that precludes sentimentality, is surely McCullers' most successful treatment of unrequited love and betrayal. The fight scene is a satire of all traditionally masculine brawls for the love of a woman, witnessed by the entire community as a battle larger than life, for a prize both morally and physically smaller than life. Miss Emelia is certainly the absolute opposite to all conventions about the beautiful but fragile Southern lady, who is entirely useless.

The Member of the Wedding is possibly the most popular of McCullers' novels, partly because it was converted into a successful Broadway play—in defiance of one critic's judgment that the novel is entirely static, totally lacking in drama. In fact, the story has a quality

somewhat akin to closet drama. The endless conversation occurs in one spot, the kitchen of a lower-middle-class home in the South. There are occasional forays into the outer world, but always the principals return to the kitchen, where real experience and visionary ideals blend in an endless consideration of human possibilities.

The protagonist, a motherless adolescent girl named Frankie Addams, is the central quester for human happiness, foredoomed to disappointment. She is similar to Mick in *The Heart Is a Lonely Hunter*. It is not accident that both their names reflect the genderless state of prepuberty; moreover, neither has been indoctrinated into the attitudes and conventional expectations of little girls. In the isolation and boredom of Frankie's life, the only exciting event is the upcoming marriage of her older brother. Frankie conceives of the dream that will sustain her in the empty weeks of the long, hot summer: She will become a member of the wedding and join her brother and his bride on their honeymoon and new idyllic life of love and communion.

This impossible dream is the central issue of those long conversations in the kitchen where the girl is flanked by a younger cousin, John Henry, who represents the childhood from which Frankie is emerging, and the African American maid Berenice, who tries to reason with Frankie without stripping her of all solace. Ignorant as she is of the dynamics of sexual love, what Frankie aspires to is not a love so self-seeking as *eros*, nor quite so all-encompassing as *agape*. She envisions an ideal love which establishes a permanent and free-flowing communication among the members of a small, select group. This imagined communion seems to express an unvoiced dream of many, sometimes situated in a visionary future, or an equally visionary past. Berenice, for all her gentle earthiness, shows that her vision of a golden age is in the past, when she was married to her first husband. She admits that after that man died, her other two marriages were vain attempts to recapture the rapport she had known with her first husband.

A curious irony of the story is that Frankie, with her persistent goal of escaping her isolated personal identity in what she calls the "we of me," actually comes closest to that ideal in the course of these endless conversations with the child and the motherly black woman. This real communion also passes away, as surely as the imagined communion with the wedded pair never materializes. John Henry dies before the end of the story, symbolic perhaps of the passing of Frankie's childhood. Reality and banality seem to have conquered in a world unsuited to the dreams of sensitive human beings.

Although Carson McCullers will probably endure as a writer with a very special talent for describing the in-between world before a child becomes an adult, the no-man's land of repressed homosexuality, and the irrational demands of love in the absence of any suitable recipient of love, the range of her fiction is quite limited. Somehow, the "child genius" never quite achieved maturity. Nevertheless, all people are immature or maimed in some secret way; in that sense, every reader must admit kinship to McCullers' warped and melancholy characters.

Other major works

SHORT FICTION: *The Mortgaged Heart*, 1971 (M. G. Smith, editor).
PLAYS: *The Member of the Wedding*, 1950; *The Square Root of Wonderful*, 1957.
CHILDREN'S LITERATURE: *Sweet as a Pickle and Clean as a Pig*, 1964.

Bibliography

Carr, Virginia Spencer. *The Lonely Hunter: A Biography of Carson McCullers*. Garden City, N.Y.: Anchor Press, 1975.
Evans, Oliver. *The Ballad of Carson McCullers: A Biography*. New York: Coward, McCann, 1966.
_____. "The Theme of Spiritual Isolation in Carson McCullers." In *South: Modern Southern Literature in Its Cultural Setting*, edited by Louis D. Rubin, Jr., and Robert D. Jacobs. Westport, Conn.: Greenwood Press, 1961.
Graver, Lawrence. *Carson McCullers*. Minneapolis: University of Minnesota Press, 1969.
McDowell, Margaret B. *Carson McCullers*. Boston: Twayne, 1980.

KATHERINE MANSFIELD

Born: Wellington, New Zealand; October 14, 1888   **Died:** Fontainebleau, France; January 9, 1923

Principal short fiction

In a German Pension, 1911; *Bliss and Other Stories*, 1920; *The Garden Party and Other Stories*, 1922; *The Doves' Nest and Other Stories*, 1923; *Something Childish and Other Stories*, 1924 (also known as *The Little Girl and Other Stories*, 1924).

Other literary forms

Although Katherine Mansfield is best known as a writer of short stories, she also wrote poems and book reviews, which were collected and edited posthumously by her second husband, John Middleton Murry. She once began a novel, and several fragments of plays have survived. She left a considerable amount of personal documents; their bulk greatly exceeds that of her published work. Murry edited the *Journal of Katherine Mansfield* (1927; revised 1954), *The Letters of Katherine Mansfield* (1928), *The Scrapbook of Katherine Mansfield* (1939), and *Katherine Mansfield's Letters to John Middleton Murry, 1913-1922* (1951). A comprehensive scholarly edition, *The Collected Letters of Katherine Mansfield*, is published by Oxford University Press: *Volume I: 1903-1917* (1984), *Volume III: 1918-1919* (1987), *Volume III: 1919-1920* (1993).

Achievements

Although extravagant claims have been made for her, many critics insist that Mansfield's achievements were modest. She completed no novel, and, although she wrote about a hundred stories, her fame rests on no more than a dozen. Yet, in any age, her stories would be remarkable for their precise and evocative descriptions, their convincing dialogue, their economy and wit, and their dazzling insights into the shifting emotions of their characters.

In her own age, she was a pioneer. She and James Joyce are often credited with creating the modern short story. Though this claim may be an exaggeration, her stories did without the old-fashioned overbearing author-narrators, the elaborate settings of scenes, and the obvious explanations of motives and themes of earlier fiction. Instead, she provided images and metaphors, dialogues and monologues with little in between. Her stories have influenced such writers as Elizabeth Bowen, Katherine Anne Porter, and Christopher Isherwood.

Biography

The author was born Katherine Mansfield Beauchamp in Wellington, New Zealand, on October 14, 1888. (In her lifetime, she used many names. Her family called her "Kass." She took "Katherine Mansfield " as her name in 1910.) Her father, Harold Beauchamp, was an importer who rose to become chairman of the Bank of New Zealand and to be knighted in 1923. In 1903, the Beauchamps sailed for London, where Kass was enrolled at Queen's College, an institution for young women where she read advanced authors such as Oscar Wilde and published stories in the college magazine. Her parents brought her back to Wellington in 1906, where she published her first stories in a newspaper. She left new Zealand for London in 1908, never to return.

Her next decade was one of personal complexities and artistic growth. She was sexually attracted to both women and men. At Queen's college she met Ida Baker, her friend and companion for much of her life. Back in London, she fell in love with a violinist whom she had known in New Zealand. After she learned that she was pregnant by him, she abruptly married George C. Bowden on March 2, 1909, and as abruptly left him. At her mother's insistence, she traveled to Germany , where she had a miscarriage. The Bowdens were not divorced until April, 1918.

In Germany she met the Polish translator Floryan

Sobieniowski, who, in the opinion of biographer Claire Tomalin, infected Mansfield with gonorrhea. Most of her medical problems may have come from this infection: the removal of a Fallopian tube, rheumatic symptoms, pleurisy, and eventually tuberculosis. Back in London, Mansfield met the future editor and critic John Middleton Murry; they were married on May 3, 1918.

Mansfield and Murry knew many famous writers and artists, particularly those who frequented Lady Ottoline Morrell's famous salon at Garsington: Lytton Strachey, Dora Carrington, David Garnett, Aldous Huxley, Dorothy Brett, J. M. Keynes, T. S. Eliot. She and Virginia Woolf had an off-and-on friendship and professional association; she seriously flirted with Bertrand Russell. The Murrys' most notable friendship was with D. H. and Frieda Lawrence; "Gudrun" in D. H. Lawrence's *Women in Love* (1920) is said to be based on Mansfield. Both Woolf and Lawrence were influenced by Mansfield; both made nasty remarks about her in her last years.

During 1910 and 1911, she published a number of bitter stories with German settings, collected in *In a German Pension*. For the next seven years, Mansfield experimented with many styles and published stories in journals such as New Age, Rhythm, and Blue Review before she discovered a mature voice. Her first great story, "Prelude," was published as a booklet in July, 1918, by Virginia and Leonard Woolf's Hogarth Press.

Her health had not been good for several years; her gonorrhea remained undiagnosed until 1918. From the time she learned that she had tuberculosis in December, 1917, she spent most of each year out of England. Accompanied by Murry or Ida Baker, she traveled to France, Switzerland, and Italy, trying to fight off her disease. In 1922, her search lead her to Georges Ivanovitch Gurdjieff's Institute of the Harmonious Development of Man near Paris, where she seems to have been moderately happy until she died.

During her last five years, she wrote most of the stories for which she is best known. They were often published in journals such as *Athenaeum, Arts and Letters, London Mercury,* and *Sphere.* Many were then collected in *Bliss and Other Stories* and *The Garden Party and Other Stories.*

Analysis

Katherine Mansfield set herself the tasks of communicating the exhilarating delicacy and peacefulness of the world's beauty and of crying out against "corruption." A reader will soon make his or her own list of themes: the yearnings, complexities, and misunderstandings of love; loneliness, particularly of independent women; the superficiality of much of modern life; the erosions of time and forgetfulness; the beauty and indifferent power of the natural world, especially plant life and the sea. Her exact meanings are not so easily pinned down, for her tone is complex: She mixes witty satire and shattering emotional reversals. Moreover, she uses dialogue and indirect speech extensively, and she does not often seem to speak directly in her own voice; the reader is not sure exactly who is speaking. Mansfield does not conceal a hidden "message" in her stories. If a story appears to point in many directions, not all of which are logically consistent, that is the way she believes the whole truth is most honestly communicated.

Mansfield's stories often evoke the complexities of the conversational give-and-take between women and men and the unexpected courses that passion can take. Mansfield often portrays complex and ambiguous sexual and psychological relationships and, as usual, constructs her story to lead her reader in roundabout ways into unexpected territory. Though she often takes readers briefly into male minds, the story "Je ne parle pas français" has one of her rare male narrators. Raoul Duqette, a grubby Parisian writer, pimp, and gigolo, tells of an Englishman, Dick Harmon, and the woman nicknamed "Mouse," whom he brings to Paris. Not all critics agree on whom the story concerns. Although the reader learns much about the English couple's tortured relationship (Dick leaves Mouse because he cannot betray his mother, and Mouse knows she cannot return to England), many readers think that the story centers on the Frenchman. Incapable of deep emotion, Raoul spies on those with fuller lives than his own; he despises women, is sexually attracted to Dick, and is able to recognize only dimly the suffering that he has witnessed. At the end, he revels in Mouse's sorrow and imagines selling a girl like her to an old lecher.

The triangle in "Bliss" is different, and again, Mansfield mixes her tones. Bertha seems childishly happy in her marriage, her home, her child, and her arty friends. She gives a marvelous party in which sophisticated guests make inane, decadent conversation. Meanwhile, Bertha finds herself physically attracted to one of her guests, the cool Miss Fulton, and thinks that she detects Miss Fulton giving her a signal. Together in the garden, they contemplate a lovely, flowering pear tree, and Bertha senses that they understand each other intuitively. Again Mansfield surprises the reader. Bertha transfers her feelings for Miss Fulton to her husband; for the first time, she really desires him. When she overhears him making an assignation with Miss Fulton, however, her life is shattered. In "Bliss," as elsewhere, Mansfield's brilliant and precise descriptions of the nonhuman world are always evocative. Although sometimes nature simply reveals an unsympathetic force, allied to human passions but beyond human control, some natural features demand to be interpreted as symbols, such as the phallic pear tree in this story. Phallic it is, but it may be feminine as well, for Bertha identifies with it.

Mansfield also explores the problems of lonely women, often by showing the reader their inmost trains of thought. Perhaps Mansfield's best-known version of the lonely woman is the central character of "Miss Brill." The reader follows Miss Brill's thoughts as she arrives at the public gardens. The first faint chill of fall and the noise of the band signals that a new season has begun. Miss Brill's sympathetic interest extends to the various sorts of people in the park; the reader senses an older, precise woman who yearns that happiness and gentleness will come for herself and others. Even some unpleasantries fail to shake Miss Brill's enjoyment, as she rejoices that everyone there is performing in some wonderful, happy play. Her illusions, however, are shattered by two insensitive young lovers who simply wish that the fussy old woman would move. Again the reader is taken into a lonely woman's mind as she undergoes a psychic shock.

In "The Daughters of the Late Colonel," the shock is muffled, and the reader does not enter the two sisters' minds so deeply so soon. The story at first appears to center on the familiar Mansfield theme of male domination: The sisters seem to react alike to the death of their domineering father. They are still under his spell. Mansfield shows her dry wit as their hesitant and ineffectual efforts to assert themselves with the nurse and their maid are pathetic and hilarious at the same time. Even sisters, however, may be alone. Not only have they lost their father and are without prospects of marriage, but also they differ so much in temperament that they will never understand each other—the older sister is prosaic, the younger one dreamy. It is only at the end of the story that

each sister shows small signs of vitality. The prosaic sister hears a cry from within, muses on lost chances, and feels a hint of hope. When Mansfield takes readers into the thoughts of the younger sister, they discover that all along she has been living in a secret and extravagant imaginary world of repressed desire: her real life. For a moment, each sister thinks that some action could be taken, but the moment passes without communication. Their lives will never bear fruit.

Mansfield's modernist method seldom gives the reader straightforward statements of her themes; the reader needs to interpret them carefully. Her most deliberately ambiguous and hotly debated story is "The Fly." A businessman ("the boss") is reminded of his beloved son's death in World War I and how he has grieved. Now, however, the boss is troubled because he can no longer feel or cry. At this point, he rescues a fly caught in his inkwell; the fly carefully cleans itself. Then the Mansfield surprise: The boss drops another gob of ink on the fly, admires its courage as it cleans itself again, but then drops more ink. The fly is dead. The boss feels wretched and bullies an employee. The story may remind some readers of a line from William Shakespeare's *King Lear* (1605-1606): "As flies to wanton boys are we to the gods;/ They kill us for their sport."

Murry said that "The Fly" represents Mansfield's revulsion from the cruelty of war; other critics discover her antipathy to her own father. Whatever its biographical source, the reader must try to decide his or her reaction to the boss. Where are the readers' sympathies? At first they are with the aged employee who jogs the boss's memory and perhaps with the boss himself. When readers hear of the son's death, they do sympathize with the father. What do they make of his torturing—yet admiring—the fly? Do readers despise him as a sadistic bully? Do they sympathize with him? Is the fly simply another victim of society's brutality, the boss's brutality? Are readers to see Mansfield as the fly, unfairly stricken with tuberculosis? Does the boss refuse to admit his own mortality until he sees himself as a victim, like the fly? At the very end, is he repressing such thoughts again? Critics are divided about this story, but what is clear is that its ambiguities raise a host of issues for consideration.

Another story that poses problems is "The Man Without a Temperament." The reader has trouble establishing where the story is taking place and who its characters are. Gradually it can be determined that the story takes place at a continental hotel and that the central characters are The Man (Robert Salesby) and his invalid wife (Jinnie—Mrs. Salesby). The Mansfield woman here is not only lonely but also sick—sick with something that resembles the author's own tuberculosis. The readers' difficulties are slightly compounded when Mansfield manipulates time; readers soon decide that the dislocations in the story are Robert's memories of happier days in England. This story's greatest problem, however, is what the reader is to think of Robert. At first glance, he seems without temperament; all his care is for his wife, her comfort, her health, and her whims. Soon, the tension that he is under becomes obvious. He is tortured by his memories. When his wife encourages him to take a walk by himself, he quickly agrees and almost forgets to return. The exquisite tact and humor that his wife loves so much rings hollow: Readers know that he suspects that she will not live much longer. Is he an icy, resentful, and disgusting hypocrite? Some readers may think so. Is he admirably patient and forbearing? Murry, who acknowledged that Robert was a portrait of himself, thought it was drawn with admiration.

Soon after her return to London, Mansfield wrote some stories based on her experiences among the common people of New Zealand. The critic Rhoda B. Nathan thinks that the New Zealand stories, taken as a group, can be considered as a *Bildungsroman*, or story of an artist's growth. The family drama of Mansfield's childhood provided material for many of these stories. Her two longest works of fiction, "Prelude" and "At the Bay," are strikingly different from conventional short stories. Both take a slight narrative line and string on it a number of short episodes and intense renderings of the inner lives of members—mainly female—of an extended family. In both, readers are set down among these people without preparation; they must work out their relations for themselves. In both, readers must take time to discover the rich vision that Mansfield is giving them.

In "Prelude" the reader enters the consciousness of several members of the family as they adjust to a new house in the country. (The Beauchamps moved from Wellington to Karori in 1893). The reader is led from the minds of the child Kezia (the character who resembles the author as a girl), her hearty father (Stanley), her pregnant mother (Linda), and her unfulfilled aunt (Beryl). Their relations are strained, and they reveal their hopes, loves, and anxieties. Gradually, Mansfield's emphasis becomes clear. She gives most weight to Linda

and Beryl, whose inner worlds invite a range of analysis. Analysis begins with the aloe tree. Mansfield had earlier prepared readers for this huge, ugly, ominous growth, which flowers only once every hundred years. Readers sense that the tree is somehow symbolic. Linda is fascinated by it. When she sees the tree by moonlight, its cruel thorns seem to embody the hate that she often feels, or do they embody the masculine force that she hates? Either way, the aloe tree brings out for the reader the secret that Linda keeps from everyone else: Alongside her other emotions (dislike for her children, love and concern for her husband) is pure hatred. She wonders what Stanley would think of that. Beryl too has her secret self. The story ends with her taking an inventory of her attractive qualities and wondering if she can ever get beyond her poses, her false life, to the warm authentic life that she thinks is still within her. Mansfield's apparently haphazard plot has in fact been drawing the reader to two striking female visions.

"At the Bay" tells about the same household perhaps a year later. Some characters, such as Kezia, appear to have changed. Mansfield's methods, however, are much the same, though the sea that frames this story does not insist on its symbolic force so obviously as did the aloe tree. Stanley forges off to work. The women he leaves are happy that he is gone, especially Linda, his strangely passive wife, who still loves him but dislikes their children, including a new baby boy. The children and their cousins play games. Kezia almost faces death when she pleads with her grandmother not to leave them. Linda's weak brother does face his failure. Beryl has a new friend, a vivid witchlike woman with an attractive younger husband. Though Linda briefly finds love with Stanley, this story, like "Prelude," ends with two dissimilar kinds of unfulfilled love. Linda loves her baby only for a moment. Beryl yearns for sexual contact but is terrified and revolted when she finds the real thing. Perhaps at the end, the sea (as a possible symbol of female fecundity, time, and destruction) sympathizes with human desires, perhaps not. Mansfield's way of presenting her incidents and structuring her story creates intense sympathy for her characters, yet simultaneously lets readers see them, without obviously judging them, from a distance.

Two shorter New Zealand stories probably show Mansfield at her finest, and they show most clearly how her narrative surprises and moments of brilliant revelation of character and motive can be concentrated in a single phrase, in what might be called a domestic epiphany: a small moment of great importance not easily summarized. In "The Doll's House," Kezia and her sisters are given a vulgar plaything. The house is despised by Aunt Beryl but loved by the girls (Kezia is particularly enthralled by a tiny lamp in the diminutive dining room) and much admired by their schoolmates. The story seems to be about adult cruelty and juvenile snobbery. All along, however, there appear to be two social outcasts, Lil Kelvey and her silent little sister, Else, both daughters of a washerwoman and (perhaps) a criminal. When Kezia impulsively invites them to look at the house, Aunt Beryl orders them away. Lil says nothing, but her silent, wretched little sister had got one glimpse of the beautiful doll's house and remembers, not her humiliation, but that she saw the house's tiny lamp. A small human spirit asserts itself.

"The Garden Party" is based on what happened at a real party that the Beauchamps gave in Wellington in 1907. Part of its meaning concerns the relations between two social classes. The central character is Laura, clearly a Mansfield-like character, an adolescent Kezia. Laura is thrilled by the promise of festivity, but in the middle of the expensive preparations—canna lilies, dainty sandwiches, a small band to play under the marquee—she learns of the death of a poor man who lived close by in a wretched house. Readers see the clash of generations when Laura demands that the party be canceled, but her worldly mother says no. The party is a grand success. As usual in Mansfield, important matter slip the mind; Laura enjoys herself immensely, especially because her large new hat is widely admired. After the guests have left, her mother sends Laura with a basket of party food to the house of the dead man. Her journey at dusk is phantasmagoric. Her sympathies, forgotten at the party, return. She is shocked by the somber house of death and by the grieving wife, and overwhelmed by the stillness, even the beauty, of the corpse. Laura feels that she must say something: "Forgive my hat." What she says is certainly inadequate, but it seems to signal a moment of understanding and growth—or does it? Laura has found a moment of beauty in death. Is that evasive or profound? She accepts the sympathy of her brother at the very end. He understands—or does he?

Other major works

POETRY: *Poems*, 1923 (edited by J. M. Murry).
NONFICTION: *Novels and Novelists*, 1930 (edited by J. M. Murry).

Bibliography

Alpers, Antony. *The Life of Katherine Mansfield*. Rev. ed. New York: Viking Press, 1980.
Berkman, Sylvia. *Katherine Mansfield: A Critical Study*. New Haven, Conn.: Yale University Press, 1951.
Hankin, C. A. *Katherine Mansfield and Her Confessional Stories*. New York: St. Martin's Press, 1983.
Mansfield, Katherine. *The Complete Stories of Katherine Mansfield*, edited by Antony Alpers. Auckland: Golden press/Whitcombe & Tombs, 1974.
Meyers, Jeffrey. *Katherine Mansfield: A Biography*. New York: New Directions, 1980.
Nathan, Rhoda B. *Katherine Mansfield*. New York: Continuum, 1988.
Tomalin, Claire. *Katherine Mansfield: A Secret Life*. New York: Alfred A. Knopf, 1987.

MARIE DE FRANCE

Born: Normandy, France; c. 1150

Died: England (?); c. 1190

Principal short fiction

Lais, c. 1167 (*The Lays of Marie de France*, 1911).

Other literary forms

In addition to the *Lais*, Marie de France is also known for the *Isopet* (c. 1170; *Medieval Fables*, 1983), a translation of a Latin text by Aesop. Besides being a demonstration of Marie's poetic skill, the lively and witty *Medieval Fables* is historically important as the earliest existing collection of this material in the vernacular of Western Europe. She is also known for *Espurgatoire Seint Patriz* (c. 1190; the purgatory of St. Patrick), a translation of a Latin text attributed to a twelfth century Cistercian monk, to which she added a prologue and an epilogue.

Achievements

Although her identity remains unclear, France's first woman poet, known as Marie de France, emerges from the twelfth century as an important literary figure. As a writer of vernacular literature, she ranks, along with Chrétien de Troyes, among the best-known medieval writers of the period. Her ability as a writer has been noted by critics, who cite her mastery of irony and understatement, her creation of suspense and description, and her use of material from folktales. A product of her times, her work is a reflection of medieval attitudes and society.

Her best-known and most representative work, the *Lais*, is characterized by a view of the problems of a love that finds itself in confrontation with social conventions. In form, they are works in rhymed octosyllabic couplets. The *lais* have been much imitated, and there are several others attributed to Marie beyond the twelve that scholars are reasonably sure are her work.

Biography

Only two facts are certain about Marie: her name and her provenance. She names herself in each of her works, and in the *Medieval Fables* she says that she is "de France." Although there are several Maries mentioned in this period, notably Marie de Champagne, daughter of Eleanor of Aquitaine and patron of Chrétien de Troyes, the most appealing identification of Marie de France is with Marie, abbess of Shaftesbury, the natural daughter of Geoffrey of Anjou and half sister of Henry II of England. The precise date of Marie's birth is unknown, but a *floruit* of 1155-1215 seems reasonably firm. From the allusions in her works, she was obviously well educated (she mentions Priscian and Ovid), and she was aware of the conventions of "courtly" romance of her time, although her connections with and influence of and by her contemporaries are unclear.

Analysis

Marie is best known for the twelve *lais* that represent her earliest work and also present her narrative art in its fullest variety. The *Medieval Fables* and the *Espurgatoire Seint Patriz* are clearly derivative (more or less faithful translations of earlier works) and allow very little opportunity for the development of character, ironic situations, or the exploitation of supernatural elements that are hallmarks of Marie's work. It has been suggested that, in the *Lais*, Marie is the creator of a narrative form. Although this is a debatable point and one that is difficult to support, it is reasonable to say that the form Marie gave to the *lai* became normative in the centuries that followed.

Marie states that she is writing down *lais* that she has heard from Breton *conteurs* (storytellers) or from other sources. The titles of some of her *Lais*, "Yonec,"

"Eliduc," or "Laüstic," for example, are of Celtic provenance, but it is impossible to determine precisely how much and in what ways Marie depended on her "Celtic sources." Even the etymology of the word *lai*—possibly the Celtic *laid*, Latin *leudas* (*laus* or *laudis*?), meaning a tale to be sung—is in dispute and can give little substance to theories of the origin of this genre. If there were Breton minstrels who composed and performed, possibly with musical accompaniment, the short adventures known as "Breton lays," there is very little evidence of connection between such performers and the courts of Norman England.

The general prologue to the *Lais* provides Marie's definition of the genre and her own statement of purpose in writing the *Lais*. A *lai* is composed to commemorate an adventure, generally an affair of love, that had first become current as a *conte*, a tale which was then formulated in verse so that it could better be remembered. Marie desired to demonstrate her literary skills; she also saw in her writing a labor that would keep her from idleness and sorrow: "Who wishes to defend herself from wickedness should study and learn and undertake serious work."

Both the general prologue as well as the prologue to "Guigemar," her first *lai*, show an artist at once confident in her skill and defensively aware that her learning makes of her an anomaly in her culture, the object of jealousy and scorn. In a strongly worded passage, she compares her detractors to "evil, cowardly, felonious dogs/ who bite people treacherously," but she will not allow such opposition to stop her from writing. Isolated by her talents and quite possibly also isolated in her personal circumstances since "de France" indicates that she is not writing in her native land, it is not surprising that many of her characters find themselves in some form of alienation created by their own natures, by their societies, or by the love relationship that is the core of their adventure. This is not to suggest that the *lais* are autobiographical; rather, the theme of isolation or alienation is one of the most effectively expressed elements in the *Lais* of Marie.

Most notable in this regard is "Lanval." The protagonist, Lanval, a young knight of Arthur's court, finds himself neglected and unrewarded by the king he serves and envied by his fellows because of his prowess. His own pride prevents him from seeking help in his impoverished state and, near despair, he leaves the court to seek the consolations of solitude. He is approached by the handmaidens of a princess of the fairy realm. The princess welcomes him as a lover and promises to free him from want and loneliness as long as he keeps their relationship a secret. When he returns to court, he finds himself both the possessor of miraculous wealth and also the lover of the lady. He keeps his lady's identity a secret until he is taunted by Arthur's queen, whose efforts at seduction he has repulsed, claiming that the least of his lady's maidens is more beautiful than the queen. His words earn him the king's displeasure, and it is only at the last moment that he is rescued from the penalties of *lèse-majesté* by the arrival of his lady, who makes good his boast.

The theme of isolation is the most consistently developed element of "Lanval." Although Marie alludes specifically to the plight of one who finds himself a stranger in a foreign land, her implicit references to alienation are more effective. Lanval is wretched in his neglected state, but part of his plight is the result of his own prideful refusal to seek aid. His eminence in knightly skill—which should alleviate his difficulties—ironically worsens them since he earns only the envy of his fellows. Even in the consolations of love he finds himself shut out from the knightly community since he must keep secret his lady's existence. This same necessity for secrecy opens the way for the vicious taunts of the queen (spurned, she accuses Lanval of unnatural vice) that lead to Lanval's breaking of his oath to his lady. Marie's presentation of isolation in "Lanval" has a lyric force and intensity, yet Lanval is agent as well as victim; his own sexual pride is the cause of the betrayal that redoubles his isolation. The poignancy of his situation is balanced by the aesthetic distance that Marie provides in indicating that much of Lanval's distress can be attributed to his own nature. At the same time, she emphasizes the exclusivity of the love relationship, the effect of which is heightened by the use of the supernatural, since, in gaining the fulfillment of love, Lanval must leave behind the society that both nurtured and scorned him. Lanval's lady comes from the fairy realm, and it is to her land that Lanval is taken in the end. In this and in many others of the *lais* of Marie, the denouement is ambiguous at best.

If Marie's lovers are isolated in and by their loves, they are also, initially, deprived of love. In "Guigemar," "Laüstic," "Yonec," "Les Deus Amanz" ("The Two Lovers"), and "Milon," the protagonists either spurn love initially ("Guigemar") or are the victims of jealous mates (as are the wives in "Guigemar," "Laüstic," "Yonec," and "Milon") or of too-possessive parents (the daughter in "The Two Lovers"). The jealous husband in "Laüstic" is Marie's most distinct portrayal of this character type. He is aware that his wife is in love with their neighbor and that, although the two never meet, they exchange gifts and glances from the windows of their towers. The wife dissembles, claiming only her joy in the song of a nightingale (*L'eostic*) as the reason for her frequent risings at night. Her husband then sets his whole entourage to trap the nightingale. He confronts his wife with the bird, and when she demands it, he kills it and flings the corpse at her so that her shift is bloodied. The lady entombs the bird in a gem-ornamented casket and sends it, as a sign that their affair must end, to her lover, who treasures the casket as a relic.

In "Laüstic," Marie maintains dramatic contrast and tension between the highly idealized passion of the lovers and the debasing jealousy of the husband; between the two codes—social and amatory; and between the fragility of the affair and the violence unleashed on it and its symbol, the nightingale, by the opposing passion of jealousy. The husband has "right" on his side, as Marie attests in the words she chooses to conclude her description of the lover: "He loved his neighbor's wife." Nevertheless, the husband's rage is so exaggerated, and his vengeance aimed at a bird is so incongruous, that there is little to relieve his negative portrait. Marie does not wholly exonerate the lovers, especially the lady, who dooms the affair by her lack of prudence and her transparent guile. However sincere the lovers' passion might seem to be, it is no more concrete than the song of the nightingale. Even if, as some critics maintain, the lovers are only playing at love, the husband is sincere, and if the song of the bird corresponds to the love affair, the bird's corpse and, yet more graphically, the blood on the lady's garment correspond to the violence with which reality can destroy an ideal. Marie focuses the interplay of passions by means of the nightingale, a multiplex image whose song exemplifies unrestrained passion, destroyed nevertheless by the passions of which it becomes the focus.

The nightingale is one of several concrete focusing images that Marie uses in the *Lais*. Others are the lovers' knots in "Guigemar" which can only be untied when the lovers are reunited; the ring and coverlet in "Le Frêne" ("The Asa Tree"), signs of the heroine's noble birth; the sea in "Eliduc" with its complex referents of passion and isolation; and the double image of the interwoven honeysuckle and hazel in "Chèvrefeuille" ("The Honey-

suckle"). In the latter tale, which recounts an episode from the legend of Tristan and Iseult, Tristan, banished from court, uses a carved hazel twig wreathed with honeysuckle to convey this message: "Fair friend, thus it is with us/ not you without me, nor I without you." This image functions both within the *lai* and between the *lai* and the reader, who receives the message in the same moment as does Iseult. The elegant simplicity of the verse, which English cannot convey, reinforces the image of interdependence of the hazel and the honeysuckle.

Not all the *lais* deal with faithfulness in love. Two, "Equitan" and "Bisclayret," are tales of disloyalty and punishment. "Equitan" is as close to a *fabliau* as one can find among Marie's *Lais*: A pleasure-loving king commits adultery with his seneschal's wife. The two conspire to murder the husband, but they are destroyed in the trap they set for him. "Bisclayret" is the tale of a werewolf who, betrayed by his wife, is forced to remain in wolf-form while his wife lives with her lover. He is befriended by his king, and when the guilty couple come to court, he avenges himself, and his wife is forced to allow him to return to his human form. In both instances, the penalties for disloyalty in love are harsh and swiftly dealt out. At the same time, vengeance is insufficient since the survivor in both cases had been truly in love. There is thus a double condemnation of disloyalty—the simple wish fulfillment of justice meted out and the more complex implicit condemnation presented in the fate of the regretful survivor.

"Eliduc," the longest of Marie's *lais*, is one of the most problematic. Based on the folk motif of the "man with two wives," this *lai* presents a seemingly unresolvable dilemma and a barely probable solution. The happily married Eliduc, unfairly exiled, falls in love with the daughter of the king whose service he has entered. When he is allowed to return home, he is welcomed by his king and his wife Guildeluec whom he still loves. Yet Eliduc still yearns for Guilliadun, the princess. He returns to the land of his exile, ostensibly to aid Guilliadun's father, and she elopes with him. Their ship is caught in a storm, and the sailors blame Guilliadun's presence for their ill-fortune. When she learns that Eliduc is married, she falls unconscious and all believe her to be dead. Eliduc has her placed in a hidden chapel and visits her bier daily. Guildeluec learns of the visits, comes to the chapel, and finds Guilliadun. The princess is magically revived by an herb Guildeluec discovers by chance, and Guildeluec enters a convent to allow the lovers to marry. In their later years, Eliduc and Guilliadun also enter the religious life, and all spend their last years in holiness and charity.

The denouement of "Eliduc" is purest romantic wish fulfillment, although Guildeluec's abdication is not without overtones of much grimmer possibilities. Marie never suggests that the passionate affair is tarnished by any implicit contrast with the wife's sacrifice; Eliduc's new love is taken for granted. He can be considered an analogue to those other characters in Marie's *Lais* who are deprived of love. Although he is content in marriage, the new affair is the love of free consent, the romantic passion somewhat inaccurately called "courtly love." Guilliadun is exonerated by her innocence of Eliduc's obligations and, furthermore, she is quite similar to the lover of Lanval. Her role is analogous to that of a fairy princess: She lives in a realm apart, her lover is drawn or compelled to come to her, and her power is absolute. The element of conflict between "ideal" love and social reality is also present, but here a near-miraculous decision resolves the dilemma. The denouement moves the story from the secular context entirely, since it is only in the realm of *caritas*, Christian charity, that the complex loves of the "Eliduc" can exist.

No one *lai* of Marie can be selected as supremely characteristic of her work. All show the cool, ironic detachment that tempers the allegiances and responses of the readers as they observe her characters in their respective dilemmas of love. "Eliduc," however, may be seen as a compendium of motifs, technique, and thematic emphasis. From the all-powerful princess, the isolation and deprivation of the protagonist, the celebration of free passion tempered by the ironic observation of its consequences, to the validation of faithfulness in loving even when the *context* of that love must be transposed to a higher realm, "Eliduc" shows Marie at her best.

Perhaps the best evaluation of the *Medieval Fables* of Marie, her translation of a Latin text of Aesop, is that which, in one scholar's words, describes her work as a depiction not of "humanity" but of "feudalism." The moral application of a typically Aesopian tale, the lamb confronted by the wolf who chooses any imagined grudge as an excuse to devour his victim, is appropriate to twelfth century society. Marie's contribution to this genre was to bestow contemporary referents on these ancient tales and render them skillfully in the octosyllabic couplets popular with the readers and the listeners of her milieu.

Marie's *Espurgatoire Seint Patriz* is also a translation, this time of a Latin text attributed to Henry of Saltrey, a twelfth century Cistercian monk. Marie followed her Latin text very closely, adding a prologue and an epilogue of her own and a very small number of lines not in the original for purposes of clarification. The work narrates the adventures of an Irish knight, Owein, who serves as interpreter for an English monk who is establishing a monastery in Ireland. He visits the entrance to Purgatory established by the second St. Patrick, is allowed to enter, witnesses the various torments inflicted on sinners, and is himself menaced by demons. Later he is shown the Terrestrial Paradise. He survives the ordeal and lives for twelve years more as a lay Brother at the monastery established by the Englishmen. Although Marie states that she is translating the story for the purpose of spiritual edification, The *Espurgatoire Seint Patriz* has attractive literary qualities as well. It is vividly descriptive of Owein's experiences, and scholars have noted its resemblance to a tale of knightly adventure. The established sequence of Marie's works (the *Lais*, the *Medieval Fables*, and *Espurgatoire Seint Patriz*) might suggest a turning away on her part from purely secular works, but thematic and stylistic similarities, such as the journey, elements of the supernatural, the concern with moral obligations, and the verse form, show a basic consistency in her works. Although it pleased her to instruct, Marie did not allow didacticism to overshadow her impulse to produce a well-wrought narrative.

Other major works

TRANSLATIONS: *Isopet*, c. 1170 (*Medieval Fables*, 1983); *Espurgatoire Seint Patriz*, c. 1190.

Bibliography

Burgess, Glyn S. *The "Lais" of Marie de France: Text and Context*. Athens: University of Georgia Press, 1987.

Donovan, Mortimer J. *The Breton Lay: A Guide to Varieties*. Notre Dame, Ind.: University of Notre Dame Press, 1969.

Ferguson, Mary H. "Folklore in the *Lais* of Marie de France." *Romantic Review* 58 (1966): 3-24.

Mickel, Emanuel J. *Marie de France*. New York: Twayne, 1974.

_____. "Marie de France's Use of Irony as a Stylistic and Narrative Device." *Studies in Philology* 71 (1974): 265-290.

_____. "A Reconsideration of the *Lais* of Marie de France." *Speculum* 46 (1971): 39-65.

PAULE MARSHALL

Born: Brooklyn, New York; April 9, 1929

Principal short fiction

Soul Clap Hands and Sing, 1961; *Reena and Other Stories*, 1983.

Other literary forms

Paule Marshall is best known for her 1959 novel *Brown Girl, Brownstones*, which tells the story of Barbadian immigrants striving to surmount poverty and racism in their new home, as seen through the eyes of the young heroine, Selina Boyce, daughter of a hardworking, ambitious mother and an easygoing, romantic father.

Ten years after her first novel, *The Chosen Place, the Timeless People* (1969) was published, followed by *Praisesong for the Widow* (1983) and *Daughters* (1991). Marshall has also written a number of essays on African American women writers and her own experience as an artist.

Achievements

Marshall's first novel, *Brown Girl, Brownstones*, ushered in a whole new approach to the African American female protagonist; only Gwendolyn Brooks' *Maud Martha* (1953) and the earlier *Their Eyes Were Watching God* (1937) by Zora Neale Hurston had focused on an African American woman's search for identity within a black community and her own conscious, interior life. Marshall also has explored the experience of Americans of West Indian origin. Her writing is lyrical, capturing the grace and idiom of her protagonists. She was awarded a Guggenheim Fellowship in 1960, the Rosenthal Award from the National Institute of Arts and Letters in 1962, for *Soul Clap Hands and Sing*, a Ford Foundation grant for 1964-1965, a National Endowment for the Arts grant for 1967-1968, and the Before Columbus Foundation American Book Award in 1984 for *Praisesong for the Widow*.

Biography

Paule Marshall was born in Brooklyn in 1929, the daughter of Samuel and Ada Burke, émigrés from Barbados who arrived in the United States shortly after World War I. She thus grew up in a culture with its roots in the Caribbean, which she visited for the first time when she was nine years old, an experience that had a strong influence on her future writing. She wrote poetry as a child and listened to the talk of women, both of which prepared her for her career as a powerful and poetic writer. In the opening of *Reena and Other Stories*, she describes the influence of her mother, women relatives, and other female friends on her experience in an essay called "From the Poets in the Kitchen":

> They taught me my first lesson in the narrative art. They trained my ear. They set a standard of excellence. This is why the best of my work must be attributed to them; it stands as testimony to the rich legacy of language and culture they so freely passed on to me in the workshop of the kitchen.

Marshall attended Brooklyn College, receiving a B.A. cum laude in 1953; she was also a member of Phi Beta Kappa. She wrote her first novel, *Brown Girl, Brownstones*, while a graduate student at Hunter College. She married Kenneth E. Marshall in 1950; they had a child, Evan, but the marriage failed and a divorce was granted in 1963. In the meantime, Marshall worked as a librarian for the New York Public Libraries and as a staff writer for *Our World* magazine in New York; she also published her first collection of short stories for Atheneum, *Soul Clap Hands and Sing*.

With the help of grants from the Ford Foundation and the National Endowment for the Arts, she completed her second novel, *The Chosen Place, the Timeless People*, which, like her earlier work, was critically well received but commercially only marginally successful.

On July 30, 1970, Marshall married Nourry Menard, and that fall she took the position of lecturer on creative writing at Yale University. She has also been a lecturer on black literature at several colleges and universities, including the University of Oxford, Columbia University, Michigan State University, Lake Forest College, and Cornell University. In 1983, Marshall's third novel, *Praisesong for the Widow*, was published by Putnam; this work won the Before Columbus Foundation American Book Award in 1984. The Feminist Press published *Reena and Other Stories*, which includes the novella *Merle*, excerpted from *The Chosen Place, the Timeless People*, and the short stories "Brooklyn" and "Barbados," which originally appeared in *Soul Clap Hands and Sing*. Other stories in *Reena and Other Stories* appeared in various periodicals. This collection was reprinted in 1985 by Virago Press under the title *Merle: A Novella and Other Stories*. In 1991, Marshall published the novel *Daughters*, which was also greeted with great critical acclaim. Her influence on, and significance to, both African American literature and feminist scholars is gradually being recognized in the academy, but only time will tell if she will ever receive the popular attention that she so richly deserves.

Analysis

Paule Marshall's work has been concerned from the beginning with a number of major themes: the experience of growing up African American in the United States; the clash of cultures between Westerners and African Americans, West Indians and inhabitants of the American mainland; and the relationships between men and women.

Marshall's first collection of shorter works is *Soul Clap Hands and Sing*, which contains four longer short stories, almost novellas. They are given the title of the setting: "Barbados," "Brooklyn," "British Guiana," and "Brazil." In each, the main character is an older man, and the stories explore how that man has failed to live his life fully, for whatever reasons. This failure is indicated by the title of the collection, which is taken from the William Butler Yeats poem "Sailing to Byzantium," which included the lines "An aged man is but a paltry thing/ A tattered coat upon a stick, unless/ Soul clap its hands and sing." In each case, it is the failure of the man to allow his soul to "clasp hands" that has led to the emptiness or aridity of his life. Thus, he is forced to realize his failure to live truly through the intervention of a woman who, in some way, exposes his inadequacies.

For example, in "Barbados," Mr. Watford, who has returned to his native island after having worked single-mindedly throughout his adult life in the United States just so he can return for this purpose, lives like a white colonizer. He has built a house, bought plantation land, and planted coconut trees, which he tends faithfully, despite years of accumulated fatigue. He has never completely finished his house, however, and he lives in total isolation, proud of the fact that he needs no one and no one needs him. It takes a young native woman, foisted on him as a servant, to reveal the paucity of his life, the emptiness of his days. He recognizes that he has not been able to bear the responsibility for the meaninglessness of his life, but when he goes to confront the young woman with the hope of some renewal, he is capable only of attacking her verbally, to which she responds, "you ain't people, Mr. Watford, you ain't people." It is this that destroys him: that he has not been able to be a part of the people who bore him, and has not found sustenance living the same way as those who oppressed him.

In "Brooklyn," an aging Jewish professor, who has been banned from teaching by the Red-baiters of the McCarthy era, attempts to coerce a young black woman who is taking his class to spend some time at his summer home. She refuses but in the end returns to his class for the final and takes him up on his invitation, only to express her outrage but also the freedom that she now feels. She has also felt like an outcast from her own people, while unable to trust the whites. Now she has the courage to live not as her parents have taught her but as she chooses. Professor Max Berman, on the other hand, is forced to recognize that it is his failure to believe in or stand up for anything that has resulted in his loneliness and failure. Interestingly, in the first story the female protagonist is not given a name, while in the second she is named only in dialogue as Miss Williams.

"British Guiana" explores the present of Gerald Motley, a man who is indeed a motley collection of races; he could have been taken for white, because of the British army officer who was one of his ancestors, or black, for the slave woman that officer had used sexually, or East Indian, from a Hindu who also had a part in his creation. He has achieved a certain amount of success as the head of a radio station, but he knows that he has failed to live his life fully. Although as a young man he had shown a great ability and had rejected his middle-class background to organize a strike, he had been bought off by a job in radio, which forces him to copy the whites who have colonized his country. When he attempts to penetrate the jungle, to prove himself to himself, he is prevented by another motley person, Sybil, an African-Chinese woman with whom he is involved. He is forever conscious of his betrayal of himself and also of Sybil's part in this, which results in a life of cynicism and taking the easy way. At the end of the story, when Sybil, whom he might have married, returns to visit, his last act is to bargain with her for a protégé who despises him but deserves a chance. In the conclusion, he realizes that he is going to die a failure by his own doing.

The final story in the book, "Brazil," reminds the reader of Carson McCullers' *The Ballad of the Sad Café*. It is the story of what appears to be a strange love affair between a white woman of epic proportions and a black dwarf. In this story, the dwarf is a performer who goes by the name of O Grande Caliban and has teamed up with a blonde of Germanic appearance to perform a comic and athletic act. He, however, had decided that it is time to retire, but his mistress does not wish to do so. One of the interesting things about the story is the breaking of the traditional white reader's expectations; it is the undersized black man who is trying to end a relationship with the Aryan-looking female. He has become so famous as Caliban, however, that no one knows him as he had been. He has been living a lie so long that he cannot convince people of the truth anymore, and so he ends by destroying everything.

Reena and Other Stories is a collection of previously printed works gathered together for the first time in 1983 by the Feminist Press. It begins with Marshall's autobiographical essay, "From the Poets in the Kitchen," which had originally been published in *The New York Times Book Review*'s series called "The Making of a Writer." This essay celebrates the women in Marshall's life who helped form her thought and shape her voice. The collection includes two of the stories discussed above, "Brooklyn" and "Barbados," previously published in *Soul Clap Hands and Sing*. Also included is a novella, *Merle*, which has been excerpted from her 1969 novel *The Chosen Place, the Timeless People* but was extensively reshaped and rewritten. Marshall wrote autobiographical headnotes to each story, which help to place them in the context of her experience and development as a writer.

For example, the first story in the collection, "The Valley Between," was as Marshall explained, "my very first published story, written when I could barely crawl, never mind stand up and walk as a writer." In it, the characters are white, a deliberate decision as Marshall herself was at the time married to Kenneth E. Marshall, a marriage she describes as "an early, unwise first marriage," and she wished to disguise the autobiographical elements in it. It is the story of a marriage falling apart because the wife (and mother of a small child) continues to grow, while the husband wishes her to remain the same, to be nothing more than a wife and mother. Published in August, 1954, it is a story well before its time in its depiction of the stifling expectations placed upon a woman of talent and energy.

The title story, "Reena," is unusual in that it was commissioned by *Harper's Magazine* for a special supplement on "The American Female," published in October of 1962. Intended by the editors to be an article on the African American woman, the story instead became a thinly disguised fiction concerning the women whom Marshall knew best: "those from an urban, working-class and lower middle-class, West Indian-American background who, like [Marshall herself], had attended the free New York City colleges during the late forties and fifties."

A first-person narrator named Paulie recounts her meeting again after twenty years with a friend from her childhood, Reena, formally named Doreen but—being a child who shapes her own life as best she can in a world that discriminates against women, African Americans, and particularly African Americans from the West Indies—had transformed herself into Reena, "with two ees!"

The meeting place is at the funeral of Aunt Vi, Reena's aunt, a woman who represents the strong, nurturing, enduring women "from the poets in the kitchen," and who will reappear in Marshall's fiction. Having been out of touch for so long, Reena and Paulie have much to discuss, and much of the story is Reena's recounting of what has been happening in her life: the struggle for meaningful work; her relationship with her family, particularly her mother; relationships with white men (usually unsuccessful) and with black men, who have to learn how to relate to and accept a strong, educated, ambitious black woman; childbearing; radical politics; and loneliness. In almost essayistic form, this story provides an intimate glimpse into the struggle, suffering, and successes of these African American women.

"To Da-duh, in Memoriam" is based on a visit that Marshall made to her maternal grandmother in Barbados when she was nine. Da-duh is another of the ancestor figures who populate Marshall's fiction, like Aunt Vi in the previous story and Merle in the story of that same name; as Marshall says, "Da-duh turns up everywhere."

An example of this appears in the final selection in the collection, the novella *Merle*, excerpted from *The Chosen Place, the Timeless People*. Merle is "Part saint, part revolutionary, part obeah woman," a woman who, wherever she goes, exhorts people to resist oppression, while on a personal level she is "still trying to come to terms with her life and history as a black woman, still seeking to reconcile all the conflicting elements to form a viable self."

Merle is the woman whom Paule Marshall creates in various guises, calling into being a new character for twentieth century American literature. In her compelling portrayal of women in her works, she brings to life a vision of the direction the world should be going by showing readers the people whom they should emulate.

Other major works

NOVELS: *Brown Girl, Brownstones*, 1959; *The Chosen Place, the Timeless People*, 1969; *Praisesong for the Widow*, 1983; *Daughters*, 1991.

Bibliography

Brown, Lloyd W. "The Rhythms of Power in Paule Marshall's Fiction." *Novel: A Forum on Fiction* 7, no. 2 (Winter, 1974): 159-167.
Christian, Barbara. "Sculpture and Space: The Interdependency of Character and Culture in the Novels of Paule Marshall." In *Black Women Novelists: The Development of a Tradition, 1892-1976*. Westport, Conn.: Greenwood Press, 1980.
Collier, Eugenia. "The Closing of the Circle: Movement from Division to Wholeness in Paule Marshall's Fiction." In *Black Women Writers, 1950-1980*, edited by Mari Evans. Garden City, N.Y.: Anchor Press/Doubleday, 1984.
Kapai, Leela. "Dominant Themes and Technique in Paule Marshall's Fiction." *College Language Association Journal* 16 (September, 1972): 49-59.
McClusky, John, Jr. "And Called Every Generation Blessed: Theme, Setting, and Ritual in the Works of Paule Marshall." In *Black Women Writers, 1950-1980*, edited by Mari Evans. Garden City, N.Y.: Anchor Press/Doubleday, 1984.
Washington, Mary Helen. Afterword to *Brown Girl, Brownstones*. New York: Feminist Press, 1981.

EDNA ST. VINCENT MILLAY

Born: Rockland Maine; February 22, 1892   **Died:** Austerlizt, New York; October 19, 1950

Principal poetry

Renascence and Other Poems, 1917; *A Few Figs from Thistles*, 1920; *Second April*, 1921; *The Harp-Weaver and Other Poems*, 1923; *The Buck in the Snow and Other Poems*, 1928; *Edna St. Vincent Millay's Poems Selected for Young People*, 1929; *Fatal Interview*, 1931; *Wine from These Grapes*, 1934; *Conversation at Midnight*, 1937; *Huntsman, What Quarry?*, 1939; *Make Bright the Arrows*, 1940; *There are No Islands Any More*, 1940; *Invocation to the Muses*, 1941; *Collected Sonnets*, 1941; *The Murder of Lidice*, 1942; *Collected Lyrics*, 1943; *Poem and Prayer for an Invading Army*, 1944; *Mine the Harvest*, 1954; *Collected Poems*, 1956.

Other literary forms

Edna St. Vincent Millay was known during her early career for her verse plays, the most successful being the first, *Aria da Capo*, produced in 1919 and published in 1921, followed by *The Lamp and the Bell* and *Two Slatterns and a King*, also published in 1921, and *The Princess Marries the Page* (written during her student years at Vassar), published in 1932. Her reputation as a writer of verse for the stage was such that she was invited to write the libretto for a Deems Taylor opera commissioned by the Metropolitan Opera Company of New York. The result of her collaboration with Taylor was a successful presentation of *The King's Henchman* (1927), a variation of the Tristan story. Millay tried to rework the material of the opera libretto into a drama but finally condemned the result as hopelessly contaminated: She

was never able to rid it of the influence of the libretto.

In addition to working with dramatic forms, Millay, in the beginning years of her career, wrote topical commentaries for the New York weekly *Vanity Fair*, under the pseudonym "Nancy Boyd"; they were collected in a 1924 volume as *Distressing Dialogues*, the title used by the magazine as the pieces appeared. Although these early essays helped to support the young poet, Millay was never willing to have them published under her name. She was, however, proud of her collaboration on *Flowers of Evil* (1936), a translation of Charles Baudelaire's *Les Fleurs du mal* (1857), although scholars find more of Millay in the translations than the original may warrant. Millay's letters have been collected and published, and a recording she made of selected poems is still available.

Achievements

Millay's meteoric rise as a popular poet seems to have been, in part, a product of her times and the independent style of life that she represented. This fact may account for the later critical dismissal of her work. Millay's poetry is, in many ways, conventional in its formal aspects, often showing strict attention to rhyme and traditional metrical patterns. In her strong allegiance to the lyric, to traditional verse forms, and to conventional diction, she guaranteed that she would not take her place in the mainstream of influential twentieth century poets, although she was very much aware of contemporary currents.

Ironically, much of Millay's early popularity came from her image as a rebel and nonconformist—a representative of emancipated Greenwich Village culture, a

perfect example of the liberated woman of the 1920's. This reputation was primarily promoted by the publication of *A Few Figs from Thistles*, a collection of flippant and audacious poems which seemed a manifesto for the new woman and her independent, nontraditional attitude toward modern life. The image in "First Fig" of the short-lived candle burning at both ends and giving its lovely light forged an identity for Millay that her serious poems could never alter and seems in retrospect an ironic paradigm for her poetic career.

In spite of Millay's waning popularity in the last decades of her life and the harsh judgment of some critics, Millay's poetic accomplishment is considerable. She is very much an American poet in her eclecticism. Millay was a champion of the individual and of freedom from tyranny of any kind, a poet willing to insist on the validity and strength of real emotion and thought in women and on their individuality in relationships. In her frank introspection and exploration of psychological states, she opened the way for the modern confessional poets who followed her.

Biography

Edna St. Vincent Millay was born in Maine and spent the first twenty years of her life there, most of them in Camden, where her mother moved with her three young girls after a divorce in 1900. Millay and her sisters were encouraged to develop their musical and poetic talents and to read widely in the classics and in English and American literature. Millay's mother supported the family by working as a nurse, and from her example, Millay learned early the independence and self-reliance which were to influence her poetry.

With the aid of a patron, Millay was able to attend Vassar College the year after the publication of "Renascence," the beginning of her public career as a poet. After graduation from Vassar, Millay moved to New York and, living in poverty, began her association with Greenwich Village and the Provincetown Players. It was during this period that her famous friendships and love affairs with Floyd Dell, Arthur Fricke, and Edmund Wilson, among others, began, and during which the Provincetown Players produced *Aria da Capo*. She won fame and national popularity with the publication of *A Few Figs from Thistles in 1920. After several years in Europe, marked by the beginning of bad health that was to plague her for the rest of her life, Millay returned to the United States and in 1923 became the first woman to win a Pulitzer Prize for poetry. In the same year, she married a Dutch importer, Eugen Jan Boissevain, who gave up his business to provide a stable environment for her—on a farm at Austerlitz, New York, and in an island home off the coast of Maine.*

Taking an active part in the general outcry of Ameri-

can intellectuals and artists against the death sentencing of Nicola Sacco and Bartolomeo Vanzetti, Millay called on the governor of Massachusetts and wrote public statements and several poems, including "Justice Denied in Massachusetts." She was arrested along with others keeping vigil at the time of the execution. In this, as in everything she did, Millay acted with total conviction and unflinching courage—qualities which give strength to her poems, although these same unabashed qualities set her apart in an age that increasingly demanded ironic distance as a prerequisite for serious verse.

Millay received several honorary doctorates and was elected to both the National Institute of Arts and Letters and the American Academy of Arts and Letters. By the end of the 1930's, however, after publication of *Conversation at Midnight*, her reputation had suffered a serious decline, a decline accelerated by the work that she published too hurriedly in the service of wartime propaganda: *Make Bright the Arrows* and *The Murder of Lidice* represent the lowest ebb in her reputation as a serious poet. In the summer of 1944, she suffered a severe nervous breakdown accompanied by serious "writer's block" that lasted for more than two years. Just as she was beginning to take up her work again in 1949, her husband died suddenly. The shock resulted in hospitalization again. She returned later that year alone to her farm in Steepletop, New York, where she died of heart failure a little more than a year after her husband's death. A volume of new poems, *Mine the Harvest*, was published in 1954 and her *Collected Poems* in 1956.

Analysis

The theme of individual liberty and the frank acknowledgment of emotion are ever present in Edna St. Vincent Millay's poems. She speaks as clearly for a democracy of persons, in whatever relationship, as Walt Whitman does and with no hint of snobbery or elitism. She values the simple and common in nature; the reader never finds her straining after exotic effects. Millay is a realist in her expectations, and she refuses conventional romantic attitudes—a refusal which often results in the ironic tone of some of her love poems.

The one form in which Millay excelled is the sonnet, both Shakespearean and Petrarchan. She has been described as a transitional poet, and this is nowhere better borne out than in her control of a conventional and circumscribed form in which she was equally comfortable with traditional or modern subject matter and attitudes.

"Euclid Alone Has Looked on Beauty Bare," published in *The Harp-Weaver and Other Poems*, is an accomplished classical Petrarchan sonnet written early in Millay's career. It takes as its subject the holy, dazzling beauty of pure form or idea available only to the Greek mathematician, Euclid, who perceived a pure beauty which has not been matched by the prattling of subsequent generations seeking imitations of beauty clothed in human form. The octave ends with a command to let the geese gabble and hiss (an allusion both to the use of geese as watchdogs in ancient times and to those who mistakenly cry out that they have sighted Beauty). The sestet presents a vivid description of the blinding and terrible light that Euclid bore when he "looked on Beauty bare," suggesting that lesser men are fortunate that they have not seen Beauty whole, as it would be too much for them to bear. Lesser men are lucky if they have even once heard Beauty's sandal on a distant rock; those seekers after Beauty who are not Euclids are doubly fortunate to have heard only a distant echo of Beauty's step, for they could not have borne the blinding intensity of Euclid's vision.

Fatal Interview, the chronicling of a love affair from inception through intense passion to sad conclusion, represents Millay's longest sustained sonnet sequence. The book's title comes from John Donne's sixteenth elegy in a series about a tragic affair, beginning, "By one first strange and fatal interview." Although the sonnets do not evince the full range of intense emotion that one might expect, Millay manages to treat her subject with the objectivity, control, and irony that mark her love poems as the products of the modern woman, freed from the stereotype of woman as the passive, overwhelmed love object. The passions of love and sexual ecstasy find their way into these poems, but always present too is an awareness of the fleeting nature of even the most passionate relationships and a refusal to accept a bondage that involves the loss of individual integrity. She knows that love can be "stung to death by gnats."

"Well, I have lost you; and I lost you fairly" is the initial line of sonnet forty-seven, and there is a pride expressed in losing well on the speaker's own terms. Nights of weeping she will not deny, but day finds her dry-eyed and fully operative in the world that goes on after love is lost. A more slyly played relationship or one of lesser intensity might have preserved the relationship through another summer, but at too high a cost for lovers who have experienced so much intensity and honesty. The price in "words I value highly" is one that Millay as

poet and woman will not, cannot, pay. "Well, I have lost you" is simple and straightforward, a sign of control over pain and grief. Sonnet thirty and others preceding it have made it clear that Millay's realism, her defense against the grief of loss, is a reaction inherent in her philosophical stance in the world; this fact, however, does not lessen the real poignancy of the sonnet. These are the statements of a highly intelligent and sensitive woman who suffers because of the awareness that never leaves her. In "Love is not all: it is not meat nor drink" (sonnet thirty) the speaker is conscious that men have died for lack of love even though it is not technically one of the physical necessities of life such as food, drink, and shelter. The sonnet accepts love as a dear necessity for life, but there is in the concluding lines the nagging realization that if it were necessary, she might sell this love for peace, or these passionate memories for food. Although at this moment she is inclined to think she would not, the acknowledgment of the possibility clearly marks the distance between Millay's poem and Elizabeth Barrett Browning's "How do I love thee?" In a more flippant early lyric entitled "Thursday," the gulf between Millay and the more conventional Browning is absolute and unbridgeable.

Among Millay's poems for her mother, "The Ballad of the Harp-Weaver" and "In the Grave No Flower" are two which display careful simplicity and controlled depth of feeling. "The Ballad of the Harp-Weaver" was criticized by Edmund Wilson for being slight, superficial, and sentimental. He characterized it as a poem for a woman's magazine. The poem is more effective than Wilson suggested and wholly appropriate to its subject: the rich gifts of the spirit given to a child by a mother who, in her poverty, cannot provide the material food and clothing that her child needs. The ballad form controls the simple narrative of the parable, and if the reader accepts the perfect union of form and subject that Millay achieves, the poem is more than a modest success.

"In the Grave No Flower" names with loving specificity common weeds that, by their rank fecundity and stubborn resistance to the plow, inherit the earth, in contrast to the barren grave where there is and can be no flower. This lyric demonstrates Millay's control of intense grief, heightened by her ability to express it with devastating simplicity. The reader has only to compare "In the Grave No Flower" to the early "Elegy Before Death," written on the death of a close friend, to see the distance that Millay had come in her growth as a poet.

Millay's best poems may be love sonnets or lyrics of passion or elegy (even "The Buck in the Snow" is an elegy of sorts), but as a poet she is willing to risk the most ordinary of subjects. A poem called simply "Menses," although not one of her best, is an interesting example of the risk-taking that marked Millay both in her personal and in her poetic life. This poem celebrates the settled relationship, the accommodations made between two people out of the love and understanding that come with adjustments to the most unglamorous cycles of life. The occasion of the poem is a surface duel between a man and a woman who is undergoing the emotional upheaval associated with her monthly menstrual cycle. The poem is, for the most part, an interior dramatic monologue spoken by the man ("to himself, being aware how it is with her"), who turns aside an incipient quarrel, having "learned/ More things than one in our few years together." Millay's risk-taking in this poem is found with her decision to give to the man the voice in this special situation, and with the woman, driven by physical forces, half-awaiting the relief his understanding will bring her. A simple rendering of the symbiotic daily relationship of two people, this poem is deeply meaningful and, in its own way, as spectacular and surprising as a moment of passion might be in one of Millay's love sonnets.

Millay's poetic subjects range more widely than her reputation suggests, for the complexity of her poetry has been obscured by the personal image created during the early years of her career. She is not only the poet whose candle consumes itself and the night but also an accomplished poet of a wide range of complex emotions, themes, and forms.

Other major works

PLAYS: *Aria da Capo*, 1919; *The Lamp and the Bell*, 1921; *Two Slatterns and a King*, 1921; *The King's Henchman*, 1927 (opera libretto); *The Princess Marries the Page*, 1932.
NONFICTION: *Distressing Dialogues*, 1924 (as Nancy Boyd).
TRANSLATION: *Flowers of Evil*, 1936 (with George Dillon).

Bibliography

Brittin, Norman A. *Edna St. Vincent Millay*. 1967. Rev. ed. Boston: Twayne, 1982.
Cheney, Anne. *Millay in Greenwich Village*. Tuscaloosa: University of Alabama Press, 1975.
Drake, William. *The First Wave: Women Poets in America, 1915-1945*. New York: Collier Books, 1987.
Gould, Jean. *The Poet and Her Book*. New York: Dodd, Mead, 1969.
Sheean, Vincent. *The Indigo Bunting: A Memoir of Edna St. Vincent Millay*. New York: Harper, 1951.
Stanbrough, Vane. "Edna St. Vincent Millay and the Language of Vulnerability." In *Shakespeare's Sisters: Feminist Essays on Women Poets*, edited by Sandra Gilbert and Susan Gubar. Bloomington: Indiana University Press, 1978.

GABRIELA MISTRAL
Lucila Godoy Alcayaga

Born: Vicuña, Chile; April 7, 1889   **Died:** Hempstead, New York; January 10, 1957

Principal poetry

Desolación, 1922; *Ternura*, 1924, 1945 (enlarged); *Tala*, 1938; *Antología*, 1941; *Lagar*, 1954; *Selected Poems of Gabriela Mistral*, 1957; *Poesías completas*, 1958; *Poema de Chile*, 1967.

Other literary forms

Although the poems published in Gabriela Mistral's three main collections are the principal source for her recognition, she was active until her death as a contributor of prose to newspapers and journals throughout Latin America. She also wrote for newspapers whenever she was abroad, and her translated articles appeared frequently in the local press. Much of what she wrote supported principles espoused in her poetry. Though less introspective, the prose, like the poetry, relates closely to the author's life and derives from episodes that left a profound mark upon her.

Achievements

Latin America's most honored woman poet, Mistral was awarded the Nobel Prize in Literature in 1945. The first Latin American writer to be so honored, she was selected as the most characteristic voice of a rich literature which had until then been denied that coveted award. The intrinsic merits of her work, described as lyricism inspired by vigorous emotion, were representative of the idealism of the Hispanic American world.

Mistral's popularity was keen throughout her adult life, during which she received the National Award for Chilean Literature and honorary doctorates from the University of Florence, the University of Chile, the University of California, and Columbia University.

Mistral pressed her genius into the service of brotherhood among nations, responsibility in professional activity, regard for future generations, appreciation for native American culture, effective education, love for the weak and oppressed, and a yearning for social justice. All these endeavors are rooted in the principal sentiment of Mistral's poetry—her unsatisfied desire for motherhood. This emotion is in Mistral both a feminine instinct and a religious yearning for fulfillment. She elevates her great anguish to the heights of art; this is her originality.

Biography

Gabriela Mistral was born Lucila Godoy Alcayaga, the child of Chilean parents of Spanish heritage, probably mixed with Indian ancestry. When she was three years old, her father left home and never returned. The task of rearing Mistral was shared by her mother and her half sister, Emelina. Both women were teachers and provided the child with primary instruction and a thirst for additional knowledge. During her last year of primary instruction, falsely accused of wasting classroom materials and further victimized when classmates threw stones at her, she was sent home and was taught by Emelina. This first encounter with injustice and human cruelty left a profound impression on the future poet.

The family moved to La Serena on Chile's coast in 1901. Three years later, the fourteen-year-old Mistral's prose began to appear in local periodicals. These writings seemed somewhat revolutionary in a provincial town, and probably accounted for the poet's admission to, and then expulsion from, the normal school. Undeterred, the family continued tutoring her while she finished her studies. In 1905, she began to work as a teacher's assistant. For the next five years, she taught in the primary grades, while nurturing her early work as a writer. This initial poetry possessed a melancholy flavor in tune with poets with whom she was familiar. Certified as an educator in 1910, she began a career as a high school teacher that took her throughout her native country. All during her life she would characterize herself as a simple rural teacher. Near the end of her career as an educator, Chile named her "Teacher of the Nation." A good portion of her literary work, which has an educational motive, is directed toward young people. Behind the writer is the teacher who desires to encourage moral and spiritual awareness and aesthetic sensitivity.

With the publication of her first book in 1922, the poet's literary name, "Gabriela Mistral," definitively replaced her birth-name. The name "Gabriela" was chosen for the archangel Gabriel, one who brings good tidings, and "Mistral" was chosen for the dry wind that blows in the Mediterranean area of Provence. Also in 1922, Mistral left Chile for Mexico, to participate in a national program of educational reform. Intending at first to stay for six months, she remained in Mexico for two years. This sabbatical began a lifetime of travel. In 1932, Mistral became a member of the consular corps of the Chilean government, fulfilling various diplomatic assignments in Spain, Portugal, France, Brazil, and the United States. At the same time, she continued a life of writing and intellectual pursuits. She taught Latin American literature at the University of Puerto Rico and at several institutions in the United States. In 1953, she became the Chilean delegate to the United Nations, where she served until poor health forced her to retire. She died in 1957.

Analysis

Through a poetry that is at times deliberately crude and prosaic, Gabriela Mistral distinguished herself as an artist of tenderness and compassion. Her themes are nourished by her personal sorrow, which she ably elevates to the realm of the universal. Maternity, children, love, God, the fight against instinct, the soul of things, are voiced in anguish and in reverence by a poet whose vigor belies her sensivity and whose high concept of morality is always present but never militant.

Mistral's three major collections of poems, *Desolación, Tala,* and *Lagar*, were published at sixteen-year intervals. They contain a selection of poems from among the many that the poet produced in newspapers during the intervening years.

Desolación was compiled through the initiative of Federico de Onís, Professor of Spanish at Columbia University and founder of the Hispanic Institute. Onís had selected the poet's work as the theme for a lecture which he gave at the institute in 1921. The participants, primarily Spanish teachers from the United States, were deeply impressed by the depth and beauty of this vigorous new voice in Hispanic-American poetry, and when they discovered that the poet had not yet published a book, Onís insisted on publishing the collection under the auspices of the Hispanic Institute.

The unity of the book is the body of moving, impassioned poems which were inspired by two painful experiences in the life of the youthful poet. While a teacher in La Cantera, Mistral became romantically involved with an employee of the railroad company, but, because of bitter differences, they ended their relationship. When the young man later committed suicide for reasons unrelated to his association with the poet, Mistral was deeply affected. Several years later, she met a young poet from Santiago with whom she fell passionately in love. When he rejected her in favor of someone from Santiago's wealthy elite, Mistral was crushed. Shortly thereafter, she requested a transfer to Punta Arenas in Chile's inhospitable southland.

Inasmuch as the poems inspired by these devastating episodes do not appear in chronological order, one reads them as if the poet were relating the history of a single painful love. With great lyrical strength, she expresses the awakening of love, the joy and self-consciousness, the boldness, timidity, hope, humiliation, and jealousy. The poems that deal with suicide of the beloved reveal the poet's anguish and her petition to God concerning his salvation. The agony is tempered at intervals by tenderness, her disillusionment nurtured by hope, her pain anointed with pleasure, and the hunger for death soothed by a reverence for life.

The language of these poems is natural, simple, and direct. It is the realism of one who has lived close to the earth, who eschews delicate subtleties in favor of frankness. The lyrical roots of *Desolación* are not a product of imagination: They are a lived tragedy. When Mistral begins to regard her lost youth, foreseeing the seal of fate in her sterility, condemned to perpetual loneliness, she raises a prolonged, sharp moan. Overcome, the poet mourns her desolation, her martyrdom in not being able to be the mother of a child from the man she loved. This maternal yearning is the tender cry of one who loves, who lives in agony over the loss of that which is closest to the ultimate joy of her soul.

Mistral's poetry employs a great variety of verse forms. She freely used sonnets, tercets, quatrains, the five-line stanza, sextains, ballads, and other forms, with little regard for conventional patterns. She favored the Alexandrine, the hendecasyllabic line, and the nine-syllable line, which gradually became her preferred form; the latter seems to blend well with the slow pace of much of her poetry. The poems in *Desolación* do not follow classical models. Mistral toys with new rhymes, in which her consonants are imperfect or are interspersed with assonances. The artist has been accused of an inability to deal properly with metric forms. It is true that she lacked a musical sense. Her images, too, are frequently grotesque, too close to death and violence. Together with poems of rough, unpolished form in *Desolación*, however, there are others which are flawless in construction. Mistral reworked many of her poems repeatedly, the result generally being a refinement, although at times it was a disappointment. Her major objective was the power of the word rather than the meter of the lines.

Mistral concludes *Desolación* with the request that God forgive her for this bitter book, imploring those who consider life as sweetness to pardon her also. She promises in the future to leave her pain behind and to sing words of hope and love for others. *Tala* fulfilled this promise sixteen years later. She compiled these poems as a concrete gesture to relieve the suffering of the children of Spain who had been uprooted from their homes during the Spanish Civil War. Mistral was disappointed and ashamed that Latin America had not appeared to share her grief for the plight of these homeless children, and the proceeds from the sale of this volume alleviated the difficulties in the children's camps.

The title of the book refers to the felling of trees and applies both to the poems themselves and the purpose for which the author compiled them. The limbs are cut from the living trunk and offered as a gift, a part of oneself, a creation. From within the poet who has made her offering, there remains the assumption of the growth of a new forest. *Tala* has its pain (with allusions to the death of the poet's mother), but this volume is more serene than its predecessor. *Tala* speaks of the beauties of America, as the poet humanizes, spiritualizes, and orders the creatures of the continent around the human presence. Mis-

tral gathers all things together, animate and inanimate, nourishes them like children, and sings of them in love, wonder, thanksgiving, and happiness. Far from America, she has felt the nostalgia of the foreigner for home, and she desires to stimulate the youth of her native soil to complete the tasks that are ahead.

Mistral sees Hispanic America as one great people. She employs the sun and the Andes Mountains as elements that bind the nations geographically, and she calls for a similar spiritual kinship. She believed that governments should be born of the needs of nations; they should emphasize education, love, respect for manual labor, and identification with the lower classes. She invokes the pre-Columbian past with nostalgia, feeling remorse for the loss of the Indian's inheritance and his acceptance of destiny.

The maternal longing of the poet is the mainspring of Mistral's many lullabies and verses for children that appear in this and other volumes. The other constant, implicitly present in all the poems of *Tala*, is God. She approaches God along paths of suffering, self-discipline, and a deep understanding of the needs of her fellow people. Her ability to humanize all things grows from her desire to find God everywhere. Thus these objects and the wonder derived from them infuse the religious into the poet's creation. Her metaphors and images derive from the contemplation of nature and its relationship with the divine. More objective than the poetry of *Desolación*, this work retains its personal, lyrical quality.

Lagar (wine press) was published less than three years before Mistral's death. Together with the lack of world peace, the years brought new personal tragedies in the suicide of two of Mistral's closest friends and the devastating suicide of her nephew, Juan Miguel Godoy, whom she had reared like a son. Her health declined, and she became preoccupied with thoughts of death. Restless, Mistral moved frequently during this period. *Lagar* tells of the imprint of these experiences on her soul. The wine press of life and death, ever draining her heart, has left her weak and exhausted. In theme, *Lagar* refers back to *Desolación*, though Mistral no longer regards death with the anger of her frustrated youth. She bids it come in silence in its own due time. She is more confident of herself, eliminating the prose glosses which accompanied earlier collections. Her simple, prosaic verses are austere and purified. They beckon to the world beyond the grave in a poetic atmosphere which is as spiritual as it is concrete. Fantasy, hallucination, and dreams all contribute to an ethereal environment governed by imagination and memory.

Like Mistral's other published collections, *Lagar* lacks topical harmony. Mistral delights the reader with playful songs, revels in her creativity, and feels at one with God; yet the pain and weariness of the ever-draining wine press constitute the dominant mood. Other verses demonstrate the poet's concern with the effects of war. Mistral protests against injustice and identifies with those who suffer through no fault of their own. Religion, not according to a prescribed dogma but rather in a sense of spiritual communication between the living and the dead, along with the ever-present identification with nature, continue as important themes. In *Lagar*, the fusion of these two motifs is more complete than in the poet's earlier work. Nature is viewed in a spiritual sense. There appears a need to be in contact with the earth and the simplicity of its teaching in order to maintain spiritual harmony with the divine. This thought comforts the poet, who searches for a spiritual state of knowledge and intelligence.

By preceding her nouns with the first-person possessive, Mistral assumes a personal stance not found in her work before, as if she were participating more completely in the process of creation. Indeed, she begins to overuse the adjective, not so much to describe physical attributes as to personify the inanimate and to engender a mood. The mood thus created generally drains or destroys. Past participles used as adjectives (burned, crushed, pierced) fortify this effort, thus strengthening the theme of the title and suggesting the travail of life on earth as parallel to the crushing of grapes in the wine press.

Although much of her poetry has become dated, Mistral will continue to be recognized as a vital force in Latin American literature.

Bibliography

Arce de Vázquez, Margot. *Gabriela Mistral: The Poet and Her Work.* Translated by Helene Masslo Anderson. New York: New York University Press, 1964.

Castleman, William J. *Beauty and the Mission of the Teacher: The Life of Gabriela Mistral of Chile.* Smithtown, N.Y.: Exposition Press, 1982.

Gazarian-Gautier, Marie-Lise. *Gabriela Mistral: La maestra de Elqui.* Buenos Aires: Editorial Crespillo, 1973.

Rodriguez Pagan, Juan Antonio. *Gabriela Mistar, voz de la América hispánica.* Rio Piedras, San Juan, P.R.: Editorial San Juan, 1973.

MARIANNE MOORE

Born: Kirkwood, Missouri; November 15, 1887   **Died:** New York, New York; February 5, 1972

Principal poetry

Poems, 1921; *Observations*, 1924; *Selected Poems*, 1935; *The Pangolin and Other Verse*, 1936; *What Are Years*, 1941; *Nevertheless*, 1944; *Collected Poems*, 1951; *Like a Bulwark*, 1956; *O to Be a Dragon*, 1959; *Tell Me, Tell Me*, 1966; *The Complete Poems of Marianne Moore*, 1967, 1981.

Other literary forms

Marianne Moore left a voluminous correspondence with literary figures in America and England. She wrote occasional reviews and lectured on campuses and at poetry centers. A sampling of her prose as well as of her verse was published as *A Marianne Moore Reader* (1961). A selection of essays, *Predilections*, appeared in 1955.

Because Moore frequently revised extensively, a genuinely complete edition must be variorum; the best available selection is *The Complete Poems of Marianne Moore*. Most of Moore's manuscripts and correspondence, as well as a collection of her furnishings and personal items, are housed in the museum of the Philip H. and A. S. W. Rosenbach Foundation, Philadelphia. *The Complete Prose of Marianne Moore* (1986) includes all Moore's published prose work, from her early stories to her mature essays and reviews; as editor of *The Dial* from 1921 to 1929, and later, as her poetic reputation grew, she had the opportunity to write on a broad range of twentieth century poets and fiction writers.

Achievements

Praised by T. S. Eliot as "one of those few who have done the language some service," Moore quickly made a reputation among other poets. She won the Dial Award in 1924, and in 1925 was the object of discussion in five consecutive issues of *The Dial*. Her work, however, long remained little known to the public. The "beauty" that she sought was the product of an individualistic decorum, a discipline of self and art that yielded the quality she admired in the poem "The Monkey Puzzle" (*Selected Poems*, 1935) as "porcupine-quilled, complicated starkness." The quilled and stark imagery is slow to attract admirers other than the *cognoscenti*, but by the 1950's her work was receiving wide recognition.

She had, indeed, a year of wonder in 1952, receiving the National Book Award, the Bollingen Prize, and the Pulitzer Prize. Since that time, some of her poems have appeared in every reasonably comprehensive anthology of modern verse. Either the 1935 or the 1967 version of "Poetry" is almost always included. Other choices vary: "The Pangolin," "What Are Years?," "Virginia Britannia," and "A Grave" are among those poems most frequently anthologized.

Biography

Marianne Moore seems to have had an inborn disdain for the self-indulgent. After a girlhood in Missouri and Pennsylvania and an education at Bryn Mawr College, she taught commercial subjects at the United States Indian School in Carlisle, Pennsylvania, for three and a half years while perfecting her art as a poet. Her verse began to appear in *The Egoist* (London), *Poetry*, and other journals of the new poetry. By 1918, she had settled in Manhattan and become a member of the literary circle that included William Carlos Williams, Wallace Stevens, and Alfred Kreymborg. Her first volume, *Poems* (1921), was brought out in London. The period of the Dial Award was followed by her appointment in 1925 as an editor—soon to be editor in chief—of *The Dial*. She guided the journal through its heyday as the premier American periodical of literature and the arts. The work excited her, demonstrated her firm taste, and made her acquainted with most of the prominent writers of the time. After *The Dial* was discontinued in 1928, Moore never again worked at a salaried job. Although she earned occasional small checks for verse and reviews, her career as a writer was subsidized by the former backers of *The Dial*. In the same year that the publication ended, Moore and her mother—a close adviser until her death in 1947—moved to Brooklyn, where the poet's brother John, a Navy chaplain, was stationed.

Useful though it was, the period with *The Dial*, was an interruption. Moore had published *Observations* (1924) before going to work on the journal; her next book, *Selected Poems*, did not appear until 1935. This volume reprinted several pieces from earlier books and also some more recent work from magazines. The slim *The Pangolin and Other Verse* appeared in 1936. Moore lived quietly for the next two decades, publishing additional thin volumes. In the 1950's, the growing acceptance of modernism and the approval indicated by her numerous awards helped bring public attention; she became, indeed, something of a celebrity. Doubtless interest was furthered by her darting and witty conversation with interviewers, as well as her shrewd adoption of a three-cornered hat as a badge of eccentricity. It became routine to see a photo story in *Life* magazine on Moore's trip to the zoo, to read of her as unofficial hostess for the mayor of New York, and to find *The New Yorker* printing the hilarious exchange of letters that resulted from the request in 1955 that she think up names for a new model from Ford. (The final choice—not one of her suggestions—was "Edsel.") When in 1965 she left her Brooklyn apartment for one in Manhattan, the move was recorded on the front page of *The New York Times*.

Yet Moore could never be accused of self-importance. She enjoyed attention, but was wary—"I am often taken advantage of," she said—and continued to work at essays, reviews, and poetry. In some of her late verse she is sententious or playful. In other pieces she continues to focus on an object, a "thing" that provides her with observable fact that she can carpenter into an aesthetic stairway, a means of rising to discovery. Readers will frequently find in the work of her early and middle decades, and sometimes even in her late poems, the delight, the quilled beauty that is her legacy.

Analysis

In Moore's best work the imagined and the perceived are interdependent; she merges the two to create her usefully idiosyncratic reality. Often she finds in her universe suggestions of ethical principle. When she integrates statement of principle with sufficient circumstance, she makes the presentation seem not merely a lesson but also a fundamental component of the aesthetic structure of her world.

That "we"—speakers of English, one supposes—have not successfully integrated the world of imagination with that of the senses is part of the closing observation in her best-known poem, the 1935 version of "Poetry." This piece unfortunately has been the victim of ill-advised revision. Its argument was clear in the 1921 printing; after publishing a much-altered version in her 1924 book, Moore in 1935 returned to the 1921 version. The 1935 printing, however, introduced an ambiguity that illustrates how much may depend on so supposedly trivial a device as a punctuation mark.

The 1935 version, the one that became well known, opens with a first line that seems to dismiss poetry as "all this fiddle." This is best taken as a bit of rueful humor about Moore's own dedication, since she clearly was in no way contemptuous of her art. The poetry she likes is that which contains the "genuine," a quality that she shows by example and then by assertion to be equivalent to "useful." In what is perhaps a caution against the dangers of her own frequent practice of working from pictures or written descriptions rather than from firsthand experience, she remarks that the too "derivative" may become "unintelligible," and adds that people do not admire "what they cannot understand." In the 1921 version, a period followed "understand," making it clear that the next several examples that the poem gives are included in the "phenomena" mentioned in line 18. After "understand" in the 1935 version, however, Moore puts a colon, seeming to indicate that the content of the following lines is to be taken as examples of objects that, because they are unintelligible, are not admired. This material, however, consists of several notations of the sort of exact reality that Moore likes to use—a "tireless" wolf, a "twitching critic"—and lines 16 to 18 accept the usefulness of such detail by declaring that, together with other matter, all such "phenomena" are important. The reader not deterred by the apparent contradiction will next find a warning that mere specification of "phenomena" does not make art, followed by the observation that real poetry is not yet with "us," that it will arise only when poets become "literalists of the imagination" who produce "imaginary gardens with real toads in them." This much-discussed phrase is a careful statement of her own intention: to disclose the universe ("imaginary gardens") suggested by the objects perceived by the senses (such as "real toads"). The ending remark is that "in the meantime" the reader will have to be satisfied with one or the other of the two components of true art: raw material in "all its rawness" and "the genuine." The real poet, it appears, will be the one who merges these elements.

"Poetry" is uncharacteristically broad in its interests. Moore's usual stance in her early work is that of one on guard against threat, controlling and armoring the self. She sees humankind as living in danger, as though over an abyss, an emptiness largely composed of people's ignorance of purpose of significances, together with a suggestion that the universe, insofar as it may heed humankind at all, is indifferent or hostile. One must be rock-hard, alert, wary. In "The Fish" (*Poems*) she portrays the dark colorations, the lack of hiding places, the "iron edge" of the forces that impel life forms into seemingly chaotic motion. Yet these life forms represent the intelligence, the consciousness of an enduring cliff of reality and of spirit that withstands all "abuse" and "accident." The view is ultimately optimistic; but the optimism is sparse, the opponent determined, grim, almost victorious. The sense of threat, of a necessary caution in attempts to profit from or even to understand the oceanic indifference that surrounds humanity, is emphasized in "A Grave" (*Observations*). Here the "sea," the abyss of perhaps, the universe, society, or self-indulgence, offers the incautious nothing but a grave. It subdues the rapacious with its own superior rapacity; it lies under all activity of humanity and bird and shell, and though humans may at times create a harmony that seems to deny its power, in the end it extinguishes all that is "dropped," that thoughtlessly stumbles into it.

One protection is decorum, a discipline that keeps focus on the essential, that avoids all gluttony and greed. Moore frequently celebrates objects, creatures, and places that exemplify this spare rectitude. In "The Jerboa" (*Selected Poems*), stanzas headed "Too Much" condemn the wealth of Egyptian courtiers who accumulated luxuries while poverty and drought afflicted the common people; stanzas headed "Abundance" celebrate the true wealth of the jerboa, the self-sufficient rodent that, unlike the pharaoh's overindulged mongoose,

knows a natural "rest" in its desert home. In such early poems, Moore finds in the relatively uncomplicated lives of animals, usually exotic ones that have no traditional symbolism in the English-speaking world, and occasionally in examples from the worlds of flora and of human craftsmanship, the delight that arises from the primary values she recommends. These are the values that make for survival in a world of hard requirements: honesty in function and behavior, modest simplicity in bearing, and courage.

The combination of discipline and excitement, of decorum and ardor, is supported by Moore's style. Instead of using the accentual-syllabic measure that determines the length of lines in most poetry in English—a repetitive arrangement of stressed syllables which gives verse a sound quite different from prose—Moore counts syllables. This gives her the freedom to use the syntax normal to prose. Her syntax is at times exotic, but this results from her fondness for ellipses and abrupt juxtapositions that require of the reader some of the dexterity of her own perception. The syllabic measure enables her to use feminine rhyme, which puts the stress on syllables other than those that rhyme. She commonly parallels line lengths from stanza to stanza. In "The Jerboa," for example, the first and second lines of each stanza have five syllables, the third lines each have six, the fourth lines have eleven, and similar parallelism is maintained throughout. She also indents to put together those lines which rhyme. Internal correspondences of sound are frequent. Despite this workmanship, however, the effects are almost entirely visual: read aloud, a Moore poem sounds like thoughtful prose. Yet the suggestion of verse is there; and it is strengthened by Moore's obvious delight in accumulating specific, colorful detail.

The theme of most of Moore's early work is summed up in "An Octopus" (*Selected Poems*) as "relentless accuracy." Although in the poetry that she published in mid-career she continues to emphasize need for discipline and heroic behavior, she begins to relent a bit, to add to her exposition an emphasis on love and spiritual grace. She always gives particulars, grounding cautionary generalization firmly in sensory reality. She no longer limits her typical poem to one "thing," one animal or object, however, and she more often considers directly the human behavior that is the underlying subject. The broadening of range shows in the great poem "The Pangolin" (*The Selected Poems and Other Verse*), an admiration of the interrelationships of grace as that quality is seen in the observed features of the animal, the architecture and stone ornamentation of a cathedral, and the behavior of humans when "kindly" toward one another. In such "splendour" Moore finds a suggestion of the spiritual. The poem is a marvelous interweaving of delighted observations of the animal, appreciative examination of the cathedral, recognition of humanity's "vileness" but also of its "excellence," and intimation, by question and by assertion of renewal, of the existence of a grace beyond the mundane.

The poem "What Are Years?" is Moore's most direct presentation of her values. Perhaps too direct for some tastes, it appeals to others by its accessibility. After noting that people cannot understand the nature of their guilt or innocence, but that all are "naked" to the dangers of existence, the speaker moves on to define courage as "resolute doubt," the strength of spirit to remain strong even when defeated. The chief exponent of such strength is the one who "accedes to mortality," who accepts the fact of death and yet struggles to live, keeps returning to the struggle even though imprisoned in a world of mortality. An ambiguous "So" begins the last stanza: One who feels strongly, who is intensely aware of mortality, "behaves," keeps the ego disciplined. The pattern is that of the caged bird who, though captive, continues to sing. Despite his lack of "satisfaction," presumably of desire for flight and freedom, he knows "joy," the spiritual strength to go on living and to triumph over circumstance. This joyous discipline, it appears, "is" mortality, is knowledge of death, yet also "is" eternity, awareness of something beyond the mortal.

Moore's last three volumes continue to explore her familiar themes: resistance to threat and intrusion, admiration for the disciplined and delightful. She adds, however, much of what used to be called "occasional" verse, prompted by some event of the moment. The poems of *Like a Bulwark* show these late tendencies. The title poem admires one "firmed" by the assault of fate, leaned and strengthened by his sturdy resistance. Delight in a certain complexity in existence appears in "Then the Ermine": In a quotation that Moore may have devised, she describes the ermine's color as "ebony violet." In "The Sycamore," this pleasure in the parti-colored expands to glorification of "anything in motley." Too often overlooked is "Apparition of Splendor," wherein works of art, the forests of the earth, and traditional fairy tales all contribute to celebrate the courage of the porcupine, which defends itself without aggression. Observation of

particulars in skating, tennis, dancing, music, canoeing, pomology, and painting lead in "Style" to an exclamation of joy as the speaker rapturously contemplates artistry wherever it occurs.

In some poems of *Tell Me, Tell Me*, Moore's last book made up primarily of new poems, ardor is as warm as ever. "Arthur Mitchell," a brief admiration of a dancer, shapes its stanzas to imitate the twirl of the performer. The closing imagery of "Sun" (a poem first published in 1916) implies comparison of the power of the sun—standing, one deduces, for courage of spirit—to a work of spiritual art, a gorgeously wrought hourglass. The poem is almost a prayer: The speaker appeals to "Sun" to eradicate the "hostility" found in "this meeting-place of surging enmity," this world, or, even, one's own soul.

The reprinting of "Sun" implies a continuity of thought and feeling. Moore seems, however, to have been conscious of a lessening of her powers. "The Mind, Intractable Thing" is, despite its seemingly playful title, a saddening poem when compared with the sprightly dance of feeling in the earlier "The Mind Is an Enchanting Thing." In the late poem, the speaker still exclaims over her subject, but the details are autumnal, the delight colored by near despair as she complains that the "mind" does not help her, that she does not know how to "deal with" terror and wordcraft. One need not take the poem too literally for, as the several good poems in the volume show, Moore retained great abilities to the end of her life.

Most poet-critics have continued to be admiring of Moore's work. Randall Jarrell declared that Moore has discovered "a new sort of subject" and "a new sort of connection and structure for it," and John Ashbery speculated that she would eventually be ranked as the best American modernist poet. Yet Moore has had detractors. In her early years such traditionalists as Louis Untermeyer and Margaret Anderson denigrated her work because it does not have the marked rhythm and heightened language that their Romantic taste demanded. Somewhat later, such middle-of-the-road critics as Oscar Cargill and Babette Deutsch gave her writing only carefully qualified praise. Feminists have struggled to accommodate Moore in their systems. Emily Stipes Watts declares that her reputation is "evaporating" because she follows what are in Watt's view masculine standards. Helen Vendler and Bonnie Costello admire her greatly and are rather possessive about her as a fellow member of what they see as their beleaguered gender; but they are bothered by male critics' applause, suspicious that such praise is only another tactic for putting a woman on a pedestal. The quilled beauty of Moore's work may put off the timid, but it will nevertheless prevail, because by its rigor, grace, and artistry, it achieves aesthetic triumph.

Other major works

PLAY: *The Absentee*, 1962.
NONFICTION: *Predilections*, 1955.
TRANSLATION: *Selected Fables of La Fontaine*, 1955.
MISCELLANEOUS: *A Marianne Moore Reader*, 1961; *The Complete Prose of Marianne Moore*, 1986.

Bibliography

Costello, Bonnie. *Marianne Moore: Imaginary Possessions*. Cambridge, Mass.: Harvard University Press, 1981.

Diehl, Joanne Feit. *Elizabeth Bishop and Marianne Moore: The Psychodynamics of Creativity*. Princton, N.J.: Princeton University Press, 1993.

Hadas, Pamela White. *Marianne Moore: Poet of Affection*. Syracuse, N.Y.: Syracuse University Press, 1977.

Molesworth, Charles. *Marianne Moore: A Literary Life*. New York: Atheneum, 1990.

Stapleton, Laurence. *Marianne Moore: The Poet's Advance*. Princeton, N.J.: Princeton University Press, 1978.

Tomlinson, Charles. *Marianne Moore: A Collection of Critical Essays*. Englewood Cliffs, N.J.: Prentice-Hall, 1969.

TONI MORRISON

Born: Lorain, Ohio; February 18, 1931

Principal long fiction

The Bluest Eye, 1970; *Sula*, 1973; *Song of Solomon*, 1977; *Tar Baby*, 1981; *Beloved*, 1987; *Jazz*, 1992.

Other literary forms

Toni Morrison is primarily a novelist. She has published a short story, "Big Box," in *Ms.* magazine (1980), and many essays. In *Playing in the Dark: Whiteness and the Literary Imagination* (1992), Morrison argues that the presence of African Americans has had a formative influence on American literature. Morrison edited *Racing Justice, En-gendering Power: Essays on Anita Hill, Clarence Thomas, and the Construction of Social Reality* (1992) and contributed an introductory essay.

Achievements

Morrison is generally regarded as one of the most significant African American novelists to have emerged in the 1970's. Her novel *Sula* was nominated for the National Book Award in 1975. In 1977, *Song of Solomon* won the National Book Critics Circle Award. The former was a Book-of-the-Month Club alternate and the latter, a main selection. In 1988, *Beloved* was awarded the Pulitzer Prize. In 1993, Morrison was honored with the Nobel Prize in Literature for her lifetime body of work.

Morrison's fiction, especially *Song of Solomon*, has been compared to Ralph Ellison's *Invisible Man* (1952) for its mixture of the literal and the fantastic, the real and the surreal. Morrison has been praised for her use of language and for the sense of voice that emerges not only in her dialogue but also in the movement of her narratives. Morrison's novels are also remarkable for their sense of place, for the detailed, coherent physical worlds she creates. Finally, her fiction is noteworthy for its depiction of the deep psychic realities of women's experience.

Biography

Toni Morrison, daughter of George and Ramah (Willis) Wofford, was born Chloe Anthony Wofford on February 18, 1931, in Lorain, Ohio. Her father, a laborer, simultaneously held three jobs to take care of his family. Morrison was graduated from high school with honors and entered Howard University in Washington, D.C., where she received a B.A. degree in 1953. In 1955, Morrison earned a master's degree at Cornell University. She subsequently taught undergraduate English at Texas Southern University, and in 1957, she joined the faculty of Howard University, her alma mater. While there, she married Harold Morrison, an architect originally from Jamaica. Morrison became the mother of two sons, Ford and Slade, before being divorced. While in Washington, Morrison joined a writer's group and began the story that became her first novel, *The Bluest Eye*. In 1965, Morrison became an editor for Random House, first in Syracuse and later in Manhattan, where she became a senior editor. Beginning in 1967, she also taught as a visiting lecturer at Yale University and lectured at many other universities as well.

Analysis

In all of her fiction, Morrison explores the conflict between society and the individual. She shows how the individual who defies social pressures can forge a self by drawing on the resources of the natural world, on a sense of continuity within the family and within the history of a people, and on dreams and other unaccountable sources of psychic power.

Sula explores the oppressive nature of white society, evident in the very name of the "Bottom," a hillside community that had its origin in the duplicitous white treatment of an emancipated black slave who was promised fertile "bottom land" along with his freedom. In a bitterly ironic twist, the whites take over the hillside again when they want suburban houses that will catch the breeze. In taking back the Bottom, they destroy a place, a community with its own identity. In turn, the black community, corrupted by white society, rejects Sula for her experimenting with her life, for trying to live free like a man instead of accepting the restrictions of the traditional female role.

Sula provokes the reader to question socially accepted concepts of good and evil. As Sula is dying, she asks her girlhood friend Nel, "How do you know that you were the good one?" Although considered morally loose and a witch by the townspeople, the unconventional Sula cannot believe herself to be an inferior individual. Contrasting the traditional role of mother and church woman that Nel has embraced, Sula's individuality is refreshing and intriguing. Despite her death, Sula maintains an independence that ultimately stands in proud opposition to the established network of relationships that exist within conventional society.

The novel shows that the Bottom society encompasses both good and evil. The people are accustomed to suffering and enduring evil. In varying degrees, they accept Eva's murder of her drug-addict son, Plum, and Hannah's seduction of their husbands, one after another. The community, nevertheless, cannot encompass Sula, a woman who thinks for herself without conforming to their sensibilities. They have to turn her into a witch, so that they can mobilize themselves against her "evil" and cherish their goodness. Without the witch, their goodness grows faint again. Sula is made a scapegoat.

Growing up in the Bottom, Sula creates an identity for herself, first from the reality of physical experience. When she sees her mother Hannah burning up in front of her eyes, she feels curiosity. Her curiosity is as honest as Hannah's admission that she loves her daughter Sula the way any mother would, but that she does not like her. Hearing her mother reject her individuality, Sula concludes that there is no one to count on except herself.

In forging a self, Sula also draws on sexual experience as a means of joy, as a means of feeling sadness, and as a means of feeling her own power. Sula does not substitute a romantic dream for the reality of that physical experience. She does finally desire a widening of that sexual experience into a continuing relationship with Ajax, but the role of nurturing and possession is fatal to her. Ajax leaves, and Sula sickens and dies.

A closeness to the elemental processes of nature gives a depth to the lives of the Bottom-dwellers, although nature does not act with benevolence or even with consistency. Plum and Hannah, two of Eva's children, die by fire, one sacrificed by Eva and one ignited by capricious accident. Chicken Little and several of those who follow Shadrack on National Suicide Day drown because acts of play go wrong and inexplicably lead to their destruction. Sula's supposed identity as a witch is connected to the plague of robins that coincides with her return to the Bottom. The people of the Bottom live within nature and try to make some sense of it, even though their constructions are strained and self-serving.

On one level, Sula refuses any connection to history and family continuity. Her grandmother Eva says that Sula should get a man and make babies, but Sula says that she would rather make herself. On the other hand, Sula is a descendant of the independent women Eva and Hannah, both of whom did what they had to do. It is at least rumored that Eva let her leg be cut off by a train so that she could get insurance money to take care of her three children when BoyBoy, her husband, abandoned her. When her husband died, Hannah needed "manlove," and she got it from her neighbors' husbands, despite community disapproval. In their mold, Sula is independent enough to threaten Eva with fire and to assert her own right to live, even if her grandmother does not like Sula's way of living.

To flourish, Morrison suggests, conventional society needs an opposite pole. A richness comes from the opposition and the balance—from the difference—and an acceptance of that difference would make scapegoats unnecessary. The world of the Bottom is poorer with Sula dead and out of it.

In *Song of Solomon*, Morrison again traces the making of a self. The novel is a departure for Morrison in that the protagonist is not female, but a young man, Milkman Dead. Milkman grows up in a comfortable, insulated, middle-class family, the grandson of a doctor on his mother's side and the son of a businessman, whose father owned his own farm. Son of a doting mother, Milkman is nursed a long time (the reason for his nickname) and is sent to school in velvet knickers. Guitar Baines, a Southside black, becomes Milkman's friend and an ally against the other children's teasing.

As the novel progresses, though, and as Milkman discovers the reality of his family and friends as separate people with their own griefs and torments, Milkman comes to feel that everyone wants him dead. Ironically, Milkman's last name actually is "Dead," the result of a drunken clerk's error when Milkman's grandfather was registering with the Freedmen's Bureau.

Milkman learns that his mere existence is extraordinary, since even before his birth his father tried to kill him. Milkman survived that threat through the intercession of his mother and, especially, of his aunt, Pilate, a woman with no navel. After having been conjured by Pilate into making love to his wife again, years after he had turned against her, Macon Dead wanted the resulting baby aborted. Ruth, the baby's mother, out of fear of her husband, took measures to bring about an abortion, but Pilate intervened again and helped Ruth to find the courage to save the child and bear him.

In the present action of the novel, Hagar, Milkman's cousin, his first love and his first lover, pursues him month after month with whatever weapon she can find to kill him. Hagar wants Milkman's living life, not his dead life, but Milkman has rejected her, out of boredom and fear that he will be maneuvered into marrying her. At this point, he does not want to be tied down: He wants freedom and escape.

Hagar feels unlovely and unloved, rejected because Milkman does not like her black, curly hair. Pilate says that Milkman cannot *not* love her hair without *not* loving himself because it is the same hair that grows from his own body. Hagar is a victim of an absolutely univocal standard of beauty, and she is a character who needs a supporting society, a chorus of aunts and cousins and sisters to surround her with advice and protection. Instead, she has only Pilate and Reba, grandmother and mother, two women so strong and independent that they do not understand her weakness. Unhinged by Milkman's rejection of her, Hagar chases Milkman with various weapons, is repeatedly disarmed, and finally dies in total discouragement.

Trying to find out about his family's past, Milkman travels to Virginia, to Shalimar, a black town. The men in the general store challenge him to fight, and one attacks him with a knife. Milkman does not understand why these people want his life, but they think he has insulted and denied their masculinity with his powerful northern money and his brusque treatment of them, by not asking their names and not offering his own.

The most serious threat to Milkman's life, however, turns out to be Guitar, Milkman's friend and spiritual brother. When Guitar tries to kill Milkman, he is betraying the reality of their friendship for the idea of revenge against whites and compensation for the personal deprivation he has suffered. Guitar, thinking that Milkman has a cache of gold that he is not sharing with him, decides to kill him. Guitar rationalizes his decision by saying that the money is for the cause, for the work of the Seven Days, a group of seven black men sworn to avenge the deaths of innocent blacks at the hands of the whites.

Milkman's being alive at all, then, is a triumph, a victory that he slowly comes to appreciate after coming out of his comfortable shell of self-involvement. Unwillingly, Milkman comes to know the suffering and griefs of his mother and father and even his sisters Magdelene and Corinthians. The decisive experience in his self-making, however, is the quest for Pilate's gold on which his father sets him. In the first stage, the men are convinced that Pilate's gold hangs in a green sack from the ceiling of her house, and Guitar and Milkman attempt to steal it. The two friends succeed in taking the sack because the women in the house are simply puzzled, wondering why the men want a sack which is really full of old bones. In leaving the house, though, the two men are arrested, and Pilate must rescue them and the bones by doing an "Aunt Jemima" act for the white policemen. Milkman's father, Macon, is convinced that the gold still exists somewhere, and Milkman sets out to find it by going back to Pennsylvania, where Macon and Pilate grew up, and later to Virginia, where the previous generation lived.

Milkman's making of a self includes many of the archetypal adventures of the heros of legend and myth. Like other heros of legend, Milkman limps, with one leg shorter than the other, a mark of his specialness. Like Oedipus' parents, his parents try to kill him early in his life. There is a wise old lady who gives him help and advice. He goes on a quest for a treasure, and he hopes for gold and the hand of a beautiful princess. He solves a puzzle or riddle to achieve his quest and confirm his identity. He has a transcendent experience and reaches heights of prowess. When his people turn against him, he gives his life for them.

Like Sula, too, Milkman creates a self from the reality of physical experience, the processes of nature, a connection to history and family continuity, and springs of human possibility through myth, dreams, legends, and other sources of psychic power. Milkman reaches an understanding of physical experience and the processes of nature in a struggle against the physical environment. As a rich city boy, Milkman was insulated from nature, but in his trip south to try to get the gold, he overcomes a series of physical obstacles to reach the cave where Macon and Pilate in their youth encountered a white man and the gold. Milkman gets there only after falling into the river and climbing up twenty feet of rock, splitting his shoes and the clothes that mark him as a city man. During the trip, Milkman loses his possessions—trunk, clothes, and whiskey—and he makes it on his own, in a place where his father's name and father's money do not protect him. Milkman succeeds in finding Circe, who years ago sheltered Pilate and Macon when their father was killed, and he reaches the cave where there is no longer any gold.

Milkman also encounters nature as an obstacle to be overcome when, after the knife-fight in Shalimar, he is invited to go on a coon hunt into the woods with the older men of Shalimar. Again, Milkman undergoes a test, having to move through the woods in the dark, having to show the courage and physical endurance necessary to be one of the hunters. Milkman also experiences the music of the hunt, the communication between the men and the dogs, the language before language, of a time when men were so close to their physical reality that they were in harmony with all creatures.

Milkman also creates himself in searching for his origins. In searching for his fathers, he discovers himself; like Telemachus and Stephen Dedalus, Milkman must find the reality of his fathers to know his own potential. Milkman's original pursuit of the gold seems to be an impulse he gets from his father, the man of business, and even from his father's father, who was a lover of property. The quest, however, changes as Milkman pursues it, finding the thread of his family's history. Stopping in Pennsylvania, Milkman hears the stories of the men who knew his father and grandfather and who rejoice in their successes. The story of the Dead family dramatizes the dream and the failure of that dream for blacks in America. When the older Macon Dead was killed by white men for his flourishing farm, the possibilities of his neighbors were narrowed and their lives scarred. Seeing his father and grandfather through their former neighbor's eyes helps Milkman to understand better the pride that Macon had when he said that his father had let Macon work side by side with him and trusted him to share in his achievements.

In Shalimar, Milkman also learns about his great-

grandfather by piecing together the memories of people there and by deciphering the children's game and song, a song about Solomon and Rynah that seems to be interspersed with nonsense words. Milkman matches this song to a song that he had heard Pilate sing about Sugarman. He solves the riddle of the song, and he even figures out what the ghost of Pilate's father meant when he said, "Sing," and when he told Pilate to go get the bones. Finally, he discovers that his grandmother was an American Indian, Singing Bird, and that his great-grandfather, Solomon, was one of the legendary flying Africans, the father of twenty-one sons, a slave who one day flew back to Africa. His grandfather Jake had fallen through the branches of a tree when Solomon dropped him, trying to take his last baby son back with him. Learning about that magic enables Milkman himself to fly when he surrenders to the air and lets himself be upheld.

Milkman creates a self so that he can share it and even sacrifice it for a friend. With Pilate, Milkman buries the bones of Jake, his grandfather, on Solomon's Leap. Guitar, who has continued to stalk Milkman, shoots and kills Pilate, but Milkman, saying to Guitar, "Do you want my life? Take it if it is any good to you," leaps into the air and flies. Guitar is free to kill his friend, but Milkman soars.

The ending of the novel shows the transcendence of the spirit, as the hero achieves his destiny. The satisfaction of the ending, which also soars into legend, comes from the triumph of the human spirit, the triumph that even death cannot destroy. *Song of Solomon* is a beautiful, serious, comic novel that moves beyond the social to the mythic.

In her fifth novel, *Beloved*, Morrison confronts directly for the first time the institution of slavery. Morrison's intention is immediately apparent in the novel's dedication to the "Sixty Million and more" victims of slavery—a figure that is provocative not only in its sheer magnitude but also in its relation to the oft-cited "six million," that is, the number of Jews who perished in the Holocaust.

Spanning the period from 1855 to 1874, *Beloved* is at one level a powerful account of the slave experience, an intimate re-creation of suffering and struggle. Nevertheless, as readers of her previous novels might expect, to get at the deeper truth of her subject Morrison has created a lyrical, mythic narrative. At the heart of *Beloved* is a single terrible act: Sethe, a young slave, kills one of her children, a daughter not yet two years old. Much of the novel is devoted to making that act of murder comprehensible, not as an instance of insane cruelty but as an image of the legacy of slavery. That Morrison is thinking of that still-enduring legacy, a malign presence even in the late twentieth century, becomes clear when Sethe's murdered daughter, Beloved, appears as a young woman eighteen years after her death. A ghost story with echoes of Greek tragedy, an anguished, angry testament, *Beloved* is a significant addition to Morrison's body of work.

Other major works

NONFICTION: *Playing in the Darkness: Whiteness and the Literary Imagination*, 1992.

EDITED TEXT: *Race-ing Justice, En-gendering Power: Essays on Anita Hill, Clarence Thomas, and the Construction of Social Reality* (1992).

Bibliography

Bloom, Harold, ed. *Toni Morrison: Modern Critical Views*. New York: Chelsea House, 1990.

Heinze, Denise. *The Dilemma of "Double-Consciousness": Toni Morrison's Novels*. Athens: University of Georgia Press, 1993.

Holloway, Karen F. C., and Stephanie A. Demetrakopoulos. *New Dimensions of Spirituality: The Novels of Toni Morrison*. New York: Greenwood Press, 1987.

McKay, Nellie Y., ed. *Critical Essays on Toni Morrison*. Boston: G. K. Hall, 1988.

Middleton, David L. *Toni Morrison: An Annotated Bibliography*. New York: Garland, 1987.

Otten, Terry. *The Crime of Innocence in the Fiction of Toni Morrison*. Columbia: University of Missouri Press, 1989.

Samuels, Wilfred D., and Clenora Hudson-Weems. *Toni Morrison*. Boston: Twayne, 1990.

ALICE MUNRO

Born: Wingham, Canada; July 10, 1931

Principal short fiction

Dance of the Happy Shades, 1968; *Something I've Been Meaning to Tell You: Thirteen Stories*, 1974; *The Moons of Jupiter*, 1982; *The Progress of Love*, 1986; *Friend of My Youth: Stories*, 1990.

Other literary forms

Alice Munro is principally a writer of short stories, but she has published the novels *Lives of Girls and Women* (1971) and *The Beggar Maid* (1979), which was originally published in Canada under the title *Who Do You Think You Are?* (1978). Whether *The Beggar Maid* is a new kind of novel or an intricately related collection of short stories has been the subject of some debate, but since the ten stories follow the life of one woman over a period of thirty years, from childhood to maturity, many view it as a novel.

Achievements

Munro has gained recognition as a consummate writer, principally of short psychological fiction. She has received the Governor General's Award (Canada's highest literary award) for *Dance of the Happy Shades* and *The Beggar Maid*. Her novel *Lives of Girls and Women* won the Canadian Booksellers Association International Book Year Award in 1972. She has been nominated for the Booker Prize. Munro has been compared with Ernest Hemingway for the realism, economy, and lucidity of her style; with John Updike for her insights into the intricacies of social and sexual relationships; with Flannery O'Connor and Eudora Welty for her ability to create characters of eccentric individualism; and with Marcel Proust for the completeness and verisimilitude with which she evokes the past.

Munro is an intuitive writer who is less likely to be concerned with problems of form than with clarity and veracity. Some critics have faulted her for a tendency toward disorganization or diffusion—too many shifts in time and place within a single story, for example. On her strengths as a writer, however, critics generally agree: She has an unfailing particularity and naturalness of style, an ability to write vividly about ordinary life and its boredom without boring her readers, an ability to write about the past without being sentimental or romantic, and a profound grasp of human emotion and psychology. Chief among her virtues is her great honesty: her refusal to oversimplify or falsify human beings, emotions, or experience. Finally, her themes—memory, love, transience, death—are significant. To explore such themes within the limitations of the short-story form with subtlety and depth is Munro's achievement.

Biography

Alice Munro was born in the town of Wingham, Ontario, Canada, on July 10, 1931. She spent two years at the University of Western Ontario. She was married in 1951 and moved to Vancouver, British Columbia; she later lived in Victoria, British Columbia. She has three daughters by this marriage. In 1972, she returned to Southwestern Ontario; she settled in Clinton with her second husband.

Analysis

One of Munro's recurring themes is "the pain of human contact . . . the fascinating pain; the humiliating necessity." The phrase occurs in "The Stone in the Field" and refers to the narrator's maiden aunts, who cringe from all human contact, but the emotional pain that human contact inevitably brings is a subject in all of her stories. It is evident in the title story of her first collection, "Dance of the Happy Shades," in which an elderly, impoverished piano teacher, Miss Marsalles, has a "party" (her word for recital) for a dwindling number of her students and their mothers, an entertainment she can ill afford. The elaborate but nearly inedible refreshments, the ludicrous gifts, and the tedium of the recital pieces emphasize the incongruity between Miss Marsalles' serene pleasure in the festivities and the grim suffering of her unwilling but outwardly polite guests. Their anxieties are intensified by the mid-party arrival of Miss Marsalles' newest pupils, a group of mentally retarded people from a nearby institution. The other pupils and their mothers struggle to maintain well-bred composure, but inwardly they are repelled, particularly when one of the retarded girls gives the only accomplished performance of a sprightly piece called "The Dance of the Happy Shades." The snobbish mothers believe that the idea of a retarded girl learning to play the piano is not in good taste; it is "useless, out-of-place," in fact very much like Miss Marsalles herself. Clearly, this dismal affair will be Miss Marsalles' last "party," yet the narrator is unable at the end to pity her, to say "Poor Miss Marsalles." "It is the Dance of the Happy Shades that prevents us, it is the one communiqué from the other country where she lives." The unfortunate Miss Marsalles is happy; she has escaped the pain she would feel if she could know how others regard her, or care. She is living in another country, out of touch with reality; she has escaped into "the freedom of a great unemotional happiness."

Few of Munro's characters are so fortunate. In "The Peace of Utrecht," for example, the inescapable emotional pain of human contact is the central problem. Helen, the narrator, makes a trip with her two children to Jubilee, the small town where she grew up, ostensibly to visit her sister Maddy, now living alone in their childhood home. The recent death of their mother is on their minds, but they cannot speak of it. Maddy, who stayed at home to look after their "Gothic Mother," has forbidden all such talk: "No exorcising here," she says. Yet exorcism is what Helen desperately needs as she struggles with the torment that she feels about her sister's "sacrifice," her mother's life, and her own previous self which this return home so vividly and strangely evokes. Mother was a town "character," a misfit or oddity, even before the onset of her debilitating and disfiguring illness (she seems to have died of Parkinson's disease). For Helen, she was a constant source of anxiety and shame, a threat to Helen's own precarious adolescent identity. Recalling the love and pity denied this ill but incorrigible woman, Helen experiences raging guilt, shame, and anger that she and her sister were forced into "parodies of

love." Finally, Helen and her sister withdrew even the pretense of love, withdrew all emotion: "We took away from her our anger and impatience and disgust, took all emotion away from our dealings with her, as you might take away meat from a prisoner to weaken him, till he died." Still, the stubborn old woman survived and might have lived longer except that Maddy, left alone with her mother and wanting her own life, put her in the hospital. After she tried to run away, restraint became necessary; she did not survive long after that.

Critics have agreed that Munro's strongest works are those which draw on her own small-town origins in Western Ontario, stories of Jubilee, Tuppertown, Hanratty, Dalgleish. Munro has confessed in an interview that "The Peace of Utrecht" is her most autobiographical story and thus was difficult to write. Perhaps its emotional power derives in part from its closeness to her own experience, but it exhibits those qualities for which her writing has been praised: the effortless clarity of style, the psychological penetration of character, the evocation of time and place, the unfailing eye and ear which convey an impression of absolute authenticity—these are the hallmarks of Munro's finest fiction, and they are evident even in her earliest stories. For example, in "The Peace of Utrecht," Helen's visit to two memorable residents of Jubilee, her mother's sisters, Aunt Annie and Auntie Lou, demonstrates a deftness of characterization and a sureness of touch which are remarkable but typical of this writer at her best. Helen finds them

spending the afternoon making rugs out of dyed rags. They are very old now. They sit in a hot little porch that is shaded by bamboo blinds; the rags and the half-finished rugs make an encouraging, domestic sort of disorder around them. They do not go out any more, but they get up early in the morning, wash and powder themselves and put on their shapeless print dresses trimmed with rickrack and white braid.

Later, after tea, Aunt Annie tries to press on Helen a box of her mother's clothing (painstakingly cleaned and mended), seemingly oblivious to Helen's alarm and pain at the sight of these all-too-tangible reminders of her mother. To Aunt Annie, things are to be used up; clothes are to be worn. Yet she is not insensitive, nor is she a fool. Revealing to Helen (who did not know) the shameful facts about her mother's hospitalization against her will, her pitiful, frantic attempt to escape one snowy January night, the board that was subsequently nailed across the bed to immobilize her, and Maddy's indifference to it all, Aunt Annie begins "crying distractedly as old people do, with miserable scanty tears." Despite the tears, however, Aunt Annie is (as Helen is not), emotionally tough, "an old hand at grief and self control." Just how tough she is is conveyed by Aunt Annie's final, quietly understated words: "'We thought it was hard,' she said finally. 'Lou and I thought it was hard.'"

Helen and Maddy, with less emotional resilience, try to come to terms with their own complex anguish through evasion, rationalization, and finally, admonishment—"don't be guilty"—but Munro is too honest to imply that they can be successful. In the final lines of the story, Helen urges her sister to forget the past, to take hold of her own life at last. Maddy's affirmation, "Yes I will," soon slips into an agonized question: "But why can't I, Helen? *Why can't I?*" In the "dim world of continuing disaster, of home," there is not Peace of Utrecht, not for Munro's characters, perhaps not for Munro.

The preoccupation in Munro's fiction with family, usually as a "continuing disaster," is striking. Assorted eccentric aunts, uncles, and cousins appear and reappear; a somewhat miscreant brother appears in "Forgiveness in Families" and "Boys and Girls." Sometimes the family portraits are warmly sympathetic, as in the case of the grandmother in "Winter Wind" or especially the gentle father who calmly prepared for his death in "The Moons of Jupiter." Even the neurotic mother and father in "The Progress of Love" are treated sympathetically. There, the mother's fanatical hatred of her own father leads her to burn the desperately needed money she inherits from him at his death. Clearly, for Munro, family origins matter, sometimes as the source of humor and delightful revelation but more dependably as the source of endless mystery and pain. In Munro's fiction, the view of the emotional entanglements called "family" is unflinchingly honest, unsentimental, but always humane, at times even humorous.

Another important dimension of Munro's short stories is sexual relationship, particularly in the "feelings that women have about men," as she stated in an interview. In "Bardon Bus," the narrator, a woman writer spending time in Australia, meets an anthropologist (known as "X") and begins a deliberately limited affair, asking only that it last out their short time in Australia. After, when both have returned to Canada, she is miserable, tortured by memory and need: "I can't continue to move my body

along the streets unless I exist in his mind and in his eyes." Finally, she realizes her obsession is a threat to her sanity and that she has a choice of whether to be crazy or not. She decides she does not have the stamina or the will for "prolonged craziness," and further that "there is a limit to the amount of misery and disarray you will put up with, for love, just as there is a limit to the amount of mess you can stand around a house. You can't know the limit beforehand, but you will know when you've reached it. I believe this." She begins to let go of the relationship and finds "a queer kind of pleasure" in doing this, not a "self-wounding or malicious pleasure," but "pleasure in taking into account, all over again, everything that is contradictory and persistent and unaccommodating about life. . . . I think there's something in us wanting to be reassured about all that, right alongside—and at war with—whatever there is that wants permanent vistas and a lot of fine talk." This seeming resolution, however, this salvation by knowing and understanding all, is subtly undercut by the conclusion of the story. The narrator's much younger friend, Kay, happens to mention her involvement with a fascinating new "friend," who turns out to be "X," the anthropologist. The story ends there but the pain (presumably) does not.

Munro's clear-eyed, self-aware narrators are never easy on themselves. They are constantly requiring themselves to face reality, to be aware of and responsible for the consequences of their own choices. In "Labor Day Dinner," the narrator, forty-three-year-old Roberta, has for the past year been living on a run-down farm with George, a younger man and former art teacher. His ambitious plan is to restore the farm and create a studio in which to do his sculpture. Roberta's daughters Angela, seventeen, and Eva, twelve, are spending the summer with her. The atmosphere is emotionally charged, prickly and tense. George does not approve of the way Roberta indulges her daughters, allowing them to practice ballet instead of doing any work. George does not approve of Roberta, who seems to be indulging herself with tears and moody idleness. On the other hand, Roberta (weeping silently behind her sunglasses) does not approve of George's cooling ardor, his ungallant awareness of her age as evidenced by his request that she not wear a halter top to his cousin's Labor Day dinner because she has flabby armpits.

Despite such melodramatic subject matter, Munro is able to prevent her charcters from deteriorating into stereotypes or her theme into cliché.

Roberta's daughters are close observers of as well as participants in this somewhat lugubrious drama. Angela, watching the change in her mother from self-reliant woman too near wreck and viewing George as a despot who hopes to enslave them all, records in her journal, "If this is love I want no part of it." On the other hand, sensitive Eva, watching her older sister develop the unpleasant traits of a typical adolescent, wants no part of that—"I don't want it to happen to me."

They all nearly get what they want, a way out of the emotional trauma in which they find themselves. On the way home from the Labor Day dinner, the pickup truck in which they are riding (the girls asleep in the back) comes within inches of being hit broadside by a car that came out of nowhere traveling between eighty and ninety miles an hour, no lights, its driver drunk. George did not touch the brake, nor did Roberta scream; they continue in stunned silence, pull into their yard and sit, unable to move. "What they feel is not terror or thanksgiving—not yet. What they feel is strangeness. They feel as strange, as flattened out and borne aloft, as unconnected with previous and future events as the ghost car was." The story ends with Eva, waking and calling to them, "Are you guys dead?" "Aren't we home?"

The ending shocks everything in the story into a new perspective, making what went before seem irrelevant, especially Roberta's and George's halfhearted playing at love. For Munro, it seems that the thought of the nearness, the omnipresence, and the inevitability of death is the only thing which can put lives and relationships into true perspective, but this (as Munro states at the conclusion of "The Spanish Lady") is a message which cannot be delivered, however true it may be.

Munro has stated in an interview that her need and desire to write "has something to do with the fight against death, the feeling that we lose everything every day, and writing is a way of convincing yourself perhaps that you're doing something about this." Despite her characteristic concern for honesty and her determination to tell only the truth, it seems in this passage that she may be wrong about one thing: It seems clear that Alice Munro's writing is destined to last for a very long time.

Other major works

NOVELS: *Lives of Girls and Women*, 1971; *Who Do You Think You Are?*, 1978 (published in the United States as *The Beggar Maid: Stories of Flo and Rose*, 1979).

Bibliography

Blodgett, E. D. *Alice Munro*. Boston: Twayne, 1988.

Goldman, Marlene. "Penning in the Bodies: The Construction of Gendered Subjects in Alice Munro's 'Boys and Girls.'" *Studies in Canadian Literature* 15, no. 1 (1990): 62-75.

Martin, Walter. *Alice Munro: Paradox and Parallel*. Edmonton: University of Alberta Press, 1987.

Noonan, Gerald. "The Structure of Style in Alice Munro's Fiction." In *Probable Fictions: Alice Munro's Narrative Acts*, edited by Louis MacKendrick. Downsview, Ontario: ECW Press, 1983.

Rasporich, Beverly. *Dance of the Sexes: Art and Gender in the Fiction of Alice Munro*. Edmonton: University of Alberta Press, 1990.

Sheldrick Ross, Catherine. "'At Least Part Legend': The Fiction of Alice Munro." In *Probable Fictions: Alice Munro's Narrative Acts*, edited by Louis MacKendrick. Downsview, Ontario: ECW Press, 1983.

MURASAKI SHIKIBU

Born: Kyoto, Japan; c. 978   **Died:** Kyoto, Japan; c. 1030

Principal long fiction

Genji monogatari, c. 1004 (*The Tale of Genji*, 1925-1933, 1935, 1960, 1976).

Other literary forms

In addition to *The Tale of Genji*, Murasaki Shikibu is credited with two other works: her diary, *Murasaki Shikibu nikki* (eleventh century), and a collection of her poetry, *Murasaki Shikibu-shū* (eleventh century). Both of these works are translated and annotated in full in Richard Bowring's *Murasaki Shikibu: Her Diary and Poetic Memoirs* (1982); a partial translation of the diary may be found in Annie Shepley Omori and Kochi Doi's *Diaries of Court Ladies of Old Japan* (1920), excerpted in Donald Keene's *Anthology of Japanese Literature* (1955).

Achievements

Murasaki Shikibu's premier achievement is, without question, *The Tale of Genji*, which stands as perhaps the greatest monument of Japanese fiction. The work followed a tradition of several generations' standing of romances depicting life among the court nobility of Japan, most of which were written by women of rank, but in its length (more than one thousand pages in English translation), realism, psychological depth, and literary distinction, *The Tale of Genji* stands far above its predecessors and has subsequently been imitated but never equaled.

Prior to the advent of printing on a large scale in the seventeenth century, *The Tale of Genji* was circulated only in manuscript, but its influence was nevertheless immense. Its situations and the poetry exchanged by its characters quickly became a vital part of the literary canon, sources often exploited in later Japanese poetry, which was highly dependent upon allusion and reference. It became an important source for dramatists of the Nō theater in the fifteenth and subsequent centuries. By the seventeenth century, it had become the object of scholarly commentary and analysis and was seen by Motoori Norinaga (1730-1801), the foremost eighteenth century scholar of the native literature, as the *locus classicus* of ancient aesthetic, literary, and spiritual values.

Orthodox moralists of both the Confucian and the Buddhist schools condemned The *Tale of Genji* throughout the premodern period: What was fiction, after all, but a seductive tissue of lies? It was, moreover, a work steeped in carnality and moral inconsistency. Nevertheless, the work remained at the center of the Japanese literary tradition, and by the Tokugawa, or Edo, period (1603-1868), its influence was firmly embedded in popular culture as well. It was often retold and parodied, its characters were depicted in woodblock prints; it was the source of a popular card game, and the names of its characters were even taken as pseudonyms by courtesans in the urban brothel districts.

In more recent times, Murasaki and *The Tale of Genji* have continued to occupy a prominent place in Japanese letters. In the twentieth century, the poet Yosano Akiko and the novelists Jun'ichirō Tanizaki and Fumiko Enchi produced modern Japanese translations for a public no longer able to read the language of the original, and through translations into other languages, Murasaki's special vision of the world of the classical imperial court has shaped readers' perceptions of Japan around the world.

Biography

Lamentably, little is known of the life of Murasaki Shikibu. Scholars generally date her birth to sometime in the mid-970's, and guesses about the year of her death range between 1014 and about 1030. Even her real name is a mystery: "Murasaki" seems to have been taken from *The Tale of Genji* itself, where it is a name attached to one of the novel's most affecting female characters, and "Shikibu" (meaning "Bureau of Rights") is a court title that was borne by her father, Tametoki, a member of one of the lesser branches of the Fujiwara clan, which dominated court life and politics in Murasaki's day. (Court women were frequently referred to publicly in this way, by titles derived from those of male relatives; it is not unusual for a woman's real name not to have survived.)

On the evidence of her diary, Murasaki seems to have had a somewhat unusual upbringing from the perspective of the highest reaches of court society. She may have spent some time away from the imperial capital, Kyoto, in the company of her father, who served as a provincial governor in the late 990's; more important, she appears to have been unusually well educated in comparison with her peers, having acquired some knowledge of Chinese in addition to the facility in written Japanese that was expected of any aristocratic woman.

Murasaki appears to have married a nobleman and distant kinsman, Fujiwara no Nobutaka, in about 998. Nobutaka was nearly her father's age, and Murasaki was by that time well past the customary age for marriage, facts that suggest she had been married briefly before. In any case, in 999 she and Nobutaka had a daughter, who would become a poet in her own right under the names Echigo no Ben and Daini no Sammi, and who lived at least until 1078. Nobutaka, however, died in 1001, and it was as a widow that Murasaki became a lady-in-waiting to the Empress in 1005 or 1006.

It is probable that neither her rank nor her family connections would have been sufficient by themselves to account for Murasaki being called into service at the court of the Empress. It seems likely, therefore, that it was Murasaki's literary abilities that made her attractive as an attendant to the young Empress, who inhabited a rarefied and stylized subculture that had made poetry a principal mode of public and private expression. Most scholars agree that it may well have been the repute of *The Tale of Genji* itself, or some early portion of it, that originally gave Murasaki her entrée at court.

The Emperor Ichijō died in 1011, and his widow moved to different quarters, but Murasaki seems to have stayed with her at least until 1014, which is the earliest of several dates suggested by scholars for her death. There is rather clear evidence that Murasaki was no longer in the Empress' retinue in 1031, but there is only shaky evidence supporting any earlier date for her death.

Analysis

Murasaki Shikibu's novel *The Tale of Genji* both epitomizes and transcends the world of letters in which it found its origin. It is emphatically of its period, a work that has its roots in a highly stylized literary, primarily, poetic, subculture, yet it is also a work of sufficient universality and psychological depth to have a claim to be called the world's earliest novel. To read *The Tale of Genji* is not simply to acquit oneself of some imagined duty to cross-cultural understanding, but to step inside a fully realized fictional world. It should not be thought surprising that even to modern Japanese, that world is indisputably an alien one—the passage of nearly a millennium puts Murasaki and her fiction irretrievably in a place that even the remarkable continuity of Japanese literary culture cannot bring very close. It is a measure of Murasaki's art that *The Tale of Genji* can, nevertheless, still arouse the emotions of both non-Japanese and Japanese alike.

The Tale of Genji, as its title implies, is on its face the story of the princeling Genji, the son of an emperor by a concubine, who is so favored by nature with beauty and other, subtler gifts of character that he bids fair to replace in his father's favor the proximate heir to the imperial throne; to forestall disputes over the succession, the beautiful boy-child is given the nonimperial surname Genji and thus is removed from consideration as heir to the throne. He is a consummate musician on strings and flute, a specialist in the compounding of exotic fragrances, and a master of popular song—and of poetry, the primary and essential art of the courtier of the Heian era, the period in which Murasaki wrote.

Above all, Genji is a lover. He is both free and almost obliged to bestow his favors on the women with whom he comes in contact. His first love is his own father's concubine Fujitsubo, a woman who bears a strong resemblance to the kinswoman who was Genji's mother. Genji has a succession of affairs with women of varying degrees of quality, but his deepest and most enduring love is for Murasaki, who enters his life a waif in need of protection but whose first claim in Genji's affections derives from her resemblance to her cousin Fujitsubo, who takes her name from the "wisteria courtyard" that adjoins her quarters. As no reader of the original story would fail to note, *murasaki* is an herb whose roots yield a dye that mimics the hue of the wisteria in bloom.

Murasaki becomes the love of Genji's life but was not originally his principal consort. That honor went to the noblewoman known as Aoi, the daughter of a high minister of the Emperor. The marriage was arranged, as was proper, with a careful eye to the disposition of power in the court. A certain uneasy distance always prevails between Genji and Aoi. She is several years his senior when they marry, and Genji is then still young enough to find the difference in age disconcerting. As time goes by and Genji begins spending more and more of his nights away from her father's palace (highborn women of Heian lived under their fathers' roofs and received their husbands as guests), Aoi retreats from Genji into a mood of jealousy compounded with despairing yearning.

If the compelling power of beauty is one theme that is introduced early in the novel, another and more vivid one is jealousy. Aoi's jealousy is perhaps mitigated by her awareness of the circumstances of her marriage to Genji, but for another of Genji's early amours, The Rokujō lady, jealousy becomes literally a murderous passion. The first to suffer is Yūgao, the lady of the "evening faces" (a kind of flower), who is a mysterious woman of lesser rank who passively succumbs to Genji's courtship and allows him to spirit her off to a deserted mansion; a dreamlike interlude of lovemaking and deepening intimacy—the lovers engage in one of the subtlest poetic exchanges in the novel in trying to uncover each other's secrets—is shattered by Yūgao's sudden, inexplicable death. The second death is that of Aoi herself, less violent but no less devastating to Genji.

It becomes clear that both deaths resulted from possession by the avenging spirit of the Rokujō lady, whose jealous passion at her felt neglect by Genji is so strong that it has effected, quite without her knowledge, a separation of body and soul in life. In this respect, *The Tale of Genji* reveals itself to be something of a cautionary tale: Although love and sexual relations are a natural part of life, and men need not restrict themselves to a single partner, the bond between lovers must not be taken lightly.

Genji himself recognizes that he bears some responsibility in these deaths, but he is not shown to mend his ways, for in the world of the novel, they are not in any particular need of repair. The maturing Genji, chastened by Rokujō's excesses and sobered by his responsibilities to the young Murasaki, does not embrace monogamy, but he is careful to see that his attentions are spread among his dependent women in accordance with their respective expectations; none is simply ravished and then abandoned. Throughout his part of the novel, Genji remains a creature of his time and place, a man whose sex, social position, and physical and intellectual gifts allow him to make almost any woman his own, but he is almost invariably portrayed as a paragon of Heian virtue.

Modern Western readers sometimes find these virtues unredeeming. Genji is not a cad, but neither do his sensitivities keep him from imposing himself on women in ways that are no longer quite acceptable. Nevertheless, as Genji and Murasaki age, and as they mature in their ability to sympathize with their surroundings, the reader can begin to enter respectfully into their world of values. Among Genji's women, Murasaki in particular is a graceful model of adjustment to an awareness of the mutability and fragility of life; in her last appearances in the novel, she is on the verge of middle age, a gentle but somewhat troubled woman whose concern for the next life leads her to a nunnery to begin the necessary process of weakening and then severing the worldly bonds of Karma that will otherwise impede her movement toward rebirth on a higher plane. Genji himself remains something of an abstraction to the end, a bit too good to be true, perhaps. The reader can nevertheless share his grief at losing Murasaki, and his death, which comes unheralded some three-quarters of the way through the novel, leaves a void that is felt by the reader almost as strongly as by his survivors.

The world Genji leaves behind is a place of muted colors, dark, moody, and sometimes tormented. Its principal male characters are the young Niou and Kaoru, whose names translate as "glow" and "be fragrant," respectively—allusions, surely, to the "shining" Genji himself, so often described as possessing an ineffably sweet natural fragrance. The young nobles seem to split between them the vanished, larger-than-life Genji: Niou is impetuous, more than occasionally irresponsible, and inclined to force himself upon women; Kaoru is old beyond his years, sensitive to the transience of life to a painful degree, and so far from being impetuous as to be nearly paralyzed in his dealings with women. A trio of sisters, the protected, unworldly daughters of an aged and reclusive prince, are the primary female characters in this part of the novel, called the Uji chapters after the location of much of the action, in and around the old Prince's villa by the Uji River outside Kyoto.

The principal overt plot action in the Uji chapters

centers on the conflict between Niou and Kaoru, which in turn revolves around their relationships to the sisters. A subtler theme, however, is once again the matter of coping with the radical inconstancy of the things of this world—love, beauty, life itself. Here, the primary symbol of the natural world is the swirling waters of the Uji River, the sound of whose roaring current is a constant feature of life in the Prince's villa. It is into these waters, whose name poets have always associated with the adjective *ushi* (sorrowful), that the most sensitive of the Prince's daughters throws herself; the daughter's name, in the traditional reading of the novel, is Ukifune—"floating boat," but containing also *uki*, the attributive form of the same mournful word, *ushi*.

Appropriately enough, the Uji chapters end inconclusively. There is no wrapping up of the multiple stories of the scores of characters whose lives intersected with those of Genji and his dilute reincarnation in Niou and Kaoru, no resolution of the latter's inability to choose between life in the world and in the cloister. Some scholars argue that the tale is unfinished, that its ending has been lost or that Murasaki was for some reason unable to continue it; others find the indefiniteness of the ending, whether it is intentional or not, to be wholly satisfying.

The Uji chapters are of a gray and melancholy cast, and it is certainly possible to see the work as a whole as embodying a decidedly uncheerful and pessimistic statement of the futility of any but the contemplative life. It should not be imagined, however, that reading *The Tale of Genji* is a grim experience, for the novel is also a colorful artistic tapestry of life in a world that achieved a uniquely fine appreciation of the satisfactions of the life of the senses. *The Tale of Genji* deals with serious and sometimes unpleasant truths, but Murasaki Shikibu was an author who knew as well the importance of a well-told tale. Her novel is a literary achievement of the highest order; it is also a precious document that preserves a vanished way of life of astonishing refinement with a degree of detail and three-dimensionality.

Other major works

POETRY: *Murasaki Shikibu-shū,* eleventh century.
NONFICTION: Murasaki Shikibu nikki, eleventh century.
MISCELLANEOUS: *Murasaki Shikibu: Her Diary and Poetic Memoirs*, 1982 (includes poetry and nonfiction).

Bibliography

Bowring, Richard. *Murasaki Shikibu: Her Diary and Poetic Memoirs*. Princeton, N.J.: Princeton University Press, 1982.
Morris, Ivan I. *The World of the Shining Prince: Court Life in Ancient Japan*. New York: Alfred A. Knopf, 1964.
Pekarik, Andrew, ed. *Ukifune: Love in "The Tale of Genji."* New York: Columbia University Press, 1982.
Tokugawa, Yoshinobu. Introduction to *The Tale of Genji Scroll*, by Murasaki Shikibu. Translated by Ivan I. Morris. Tokyo: Kodansha International, 1971.

IRIS MURDOCH

Born: Dublin, Ireland; July 15, 1919

Principal long fiction

Under the Net, 1954; *The Flight from the Enchanter*, 1956; *The Sandcastle*, 1957; *The Bell*, 1958; *A Severed Head*, 1961; *An Unofficial Rose*, 1962; *The Unicorn*, 1963; *The Italian Girl*, 1964; *The Red and the Green*, 1965; *The Time of the Angels*, 1966; *The Nice and the Good*, 1968; *Bruno's Dream*, 1969; *A Fairly Honourable Defeat*, 1970; *An Accidental Man*, 1971; *The Black Prince*, 1973; *The Sacred and Profane Love Machine*, 1974; *A Word Child*, 1975; *Henry and Cato*, 1976; *The Sea, the Sea*, 1978; *Nuns and Soldiers*, 1980; *The Philosopher's Pupil*, 1983; *The Good Apprentice*, 1986; *The Book and the Brotherhood*, 1988; *The Message to the Planet*, 1989; *The Green Knight*, 1993.

Other literary forms

Iris Murdoch has produced a considerable amount of work in areas other than fiction, particularly in the areas of literary criticism, drama, and, most important, philosophy. Her first book, entitled *Sartre: Romantic Rationalist* (1953), was a critique of Jean-Paul Sartre's philosophy as it appears in his novels. She has written three plays for the theater and adapted several of her novels for the stage. *The Servants and the Snow* was first performed at the Greenwich Theatre in 1970, and *The Three Arrows* at the Arts Theatre, Cambridge, in 1972; the two plays were published together in 1973 as *The Three Arrows, and The Servants and the Snow: Two Plays*. Another play, *Art and Eros*, was performed at the National Theatre in 1980. Murdoch collaborated with J. B. Priestley to adapt her novel *A Severed Head* for the stage in 1963 (published in 1964), and with James Saunders to adapt *The Italian Girl* in 1967 (published in 1969). *The Black Prince* has also been adapted for the stage and was performed at the Aldwych Theatre in 1989. She has also produced several philosophical works, including *The Sovereignty of Good* (1970), which consists of three essays on moral philosophy: "The Idea of Perfection," "On 'God' and 'Good,'" and "The Sovereignty of Good over Other Concepts"; *The Fire and the Sun: Why Plato Banished the Artists* (1977), a study of Plato's objections to art and artists; and *Metaphysics as a Guide to Morals* (1992). In 1987 Murdoch added to her work on Plato in the form of two "platonic dialogues" entitled "Art and Eros: A Dialogue About Art" and "Above the Gods: A Dialogue About Religion" that she combined in a book entitled *Acastos: Two Platonic Dialogues*. She has also published several philosophical papers in the Proceedings of the Aristotelian Society and other important articles on philosophy and aesthetics, including "The Sublime and the Good" (*Chicago Review*) and "The Sublime and the Beautiful Revisited" (*Yale Review*). Her best-known essay, "Against Dryness: A Polemical Sketch," which appeared in the January, 1961, issue of *Encounter*, is a work of literary criticism which urges a return to the capacious realism of the great nineteenth century novelists.

Achievements

Murdoch, who is universally acknowledged as one of the most important novelists of postwar Britain, has combined a prolific output with a consistently high level of fictional achievement. From the beginning of her career as a novelist, she has been a critical and popular success in both Great Britain and the United States. In general, Murdoch is thought of as a "philosophical novelist"; and, despite her objections to this description, she has attempted a fusion of aesthetic and philosophical ideas in her fiction. Including her first novel, *Under the Net*, published in 1954, she has published twenty-four novels and has received a variety of literary awards and honors. In 1973, she was awarded the James Tait Black Memorial Prize for Fiction for *The Black Prince* and, in 1974, received the Whitbread Literary Award for Fiction for *The Sacred and Profane Love Machine*. *The Sea, the Sea* won the Booker Prize for Fiction in 1978. Murdoch became a member of the Irish Academy in 1970 and an honorary member of the American Academy of Arts and Letters in 1975, and she was awarded the honorary title of Commander of the British Empire in 1976. She was made a Dame of the Order of the British Empire in 1987, and in 1990 she received the Medal of Honor for Literature from the National Arts Club in New York.

Biography

Jean Iris Murdoch was born in Dublin, Ireland, on July 15, 1919, to Anglo-Irish parents, Wills John Hughes Murdoch and Irene Alice Richardson. The family later moved to London, where Murdoch attended the Froebel Education Institute; she finished her secondary education at the Badminton School, Bristol, in 1937. From 1938 to 1942, she attended Somerville College at Oxford University, studying classical literature, ancient history, and philosophy. After obtaining a first-class honors degree, she worked from 1942 to 1944 as the assistant principal in the British Treasury, and from 1944 to 1946 served as an administrative officer with the United Nations Relief and Rehabilitation Administration in England, Austria, and Belgium.

After the war, an interest in existentialism led Murdoch to turn her attention to philosophy. She was unable to accept a scholarship to study in the United States because she had become a member of the Communist Party while an undergraduate at Oxford, and instead attended Newnham College at the University of Cambridge from 1947 to 1948 after receiving the Sarah Smithson Studentship in philosophy. In 1948, she was made a fellow of St. Anne's College, Oxford, where she lectured in philosophy until 1963, when she was named an honorary Fellow of the college. In 1956, she married John O. Bayley, a novelist, poet, and literary critic and the author of *The Characters of Love* (1960) and several other well-known critical books; Bayley is Thomas Warton Professor of English Literature at Oxford. From 1963 to 1967, Murdoch lectured at the Royal College of Art in London, after which she stopped teaching in order to devote her time to writing novels, although she continues to do some work in philosophy. She lives with her husband in Oxford.

Analysis

A knowledge of Iris Murdoch's philosophical and critical essays is invaluable for the reader wishing to understand her fiction. Her moral philosophy, which entails a rejection of existentialism, behaviorism, and linguistic empiricism, informs her fiction throughout and provides a basis for an interpretation of both the content and the form of her work. Although she denies being a Freudian, Sigmund Freud's "realistic and detailed picture of the fallen man" is close to her own conception of human nature, and she agrees with what she calls Freud's "thoroughly pessimistic view" in which the psyche is described as an "egocentric system of quasi-mechanical energy" determined by its individual history; the natural attachments of this psyche are "sexual, ambiguous, and hard for the subject to control" The most important dimension of this description of the individual is a lack of rational free will. Murdoch's philosophical position is the basis for her choice of prose fiction as the most realistic literary genre. The novelist's advantage is a "blessed freedom from rationalism," and she sees the novel as the literary form that, because of its lack of formal restrictions, can best portray the "open world, a world of absurdity and loose ends and ignorance."

Murdoch's ambivalent attitudes about the role of art and artists are present in both her fiction and her philosophy. She has suggested to several interviewers that the basis of her novels is what she calls the conflict between "the saint and the artist," or the dichotomy between the "truthful, formless figure" and the "form-maker." The true or "good" artist must avoid the "ruthless subjection of characters" to his or her will and should use symbolism judiciously in a "natural, subordinate way" that attempts to be "perfectly realistic." In her fiction, Murdoch's artist-figures are often demonic individuals who manipulate people in real life without regard for their well-being or independence as persons. Her "saint" figures have a corresponding lack of form, or sense of self, and are frequently unable or unwilling to act in any way. Douglas Swann's comment in *An Unofficial Rose* that "nothing is more fatal to love than to want everything to have form" is also true of Murdoch's attitude toward art.

Jake Donaghue, the narrator-protagonist of *Under the Net*, informs the reader early in the novel that the story's central theme is his acquaintance with Hugo Belfounder. The relationship between the two men illustrates Murdoch's philosophical and aesthetic concerns, for the Hugo-Jake friendship represents the saint-artist dichotomy; this "philosophical novel" allows her to explore the problem of theoretical approaches to reality, the issue of contingency, the realization of the otherness of individuals, and the ambiguities of language and art.

The character of Hugo Belfounder is based in part on that of the enigmatic Elias Canetti, winner of the Nobel Prize in Literature in 1981; the Bulgarian-born Canetti, who moved to England in 1939, appears in various guises in several of Murdoch's early novels. Hugo, some of whose precepts suggest the influence of Ludwig Wittgenstein, is Murdoch's first "saint" figure, and he embodies many of the qualities of the "good" characters who appear later in her fiction. Hugo's saintliness is a result of his truthfulness and his lack of desire for form or structure in life and art. Opposed to him is Jake, who, fearing that he may actually tell the truth to Mrs. Tinckham about being evicted by Madge, delays telling his story until he can present it in a "more dramatic way . . . as yet it lacked form." Form, as Jake tacitly admits, is a kind of lying, an imposition of structure that distorts reality. Hugo, on the other hand, is attracted by the ephemerality and formlessness of the firework displays he has created, and he abandons them when they receive the attention of art critics who being to classify his work into styles. Hugo is also characterized by a selflessness that Jake finds astonishing: It does not occur to Hugo that he is responsible for the concepts discussed in Jake's book *The Silencer*, or that Anna Quentin's mime theater is based upon her interpretation of his beliefs.

The difference between the two men is also evident in their attitude toward theory. After his conversations with Hugo, Jake concedes that his own approach to life is "blurred by generalities," and he is entranced by Hugo's refusal to classify the world around him or to adopt any kind of theory about it. Annandine, Hugo's persona in *The Silencer*, says that "the movement away from theory and generality is the movement towards truth. All theorizing is flight. We must be ruled by the situation itself and this is unutterably particular." Theories, like form, distort what they attempt to explain and understand. Hugo's lack of a general theoretical framework for his ideas, the "net" of the novel's title, makes everything he encounters "astonishing, delightful, complicated, and mysterious."

Part of Jake's education and development as a potential artist is dependent upon relinquishing the need for theories and generalizations. In his first meeting with Anna, he notices that she is in "the grip of a theory," and one of the most important episodes in the novel is in Jake's realization that Jean-Pierre Breteuil, whose work he has previously translated into English, has finally written a good novel—a feat Jake had believed impossible. He understands that he has incorrectly "classed" Jean-Pierre and says that "It wrenched me, like the changing of a fundamental category." Similarly, when Jake becomes aware that Hugo is in love with Sadie Quentin rather than Anna, he says that "a pattern in my mind was suddenly scattered and the pieces of it went flying about me like birds." At the end of the novel, Jake has abandoned attempts to impose his own ideas onto his environment; rather, he decides to sit quietly and "let things take shape deeply within me," noting that he can "sense," beneath the level of his attention and without his conscious aid, "great forms moving in the darkness."

Jake's initial need to perceive form and to create theories is paralleled by his fear of contingency. One of Murdoch's major quarrels with Sartre is his inability to deal with the contingent, or, in her words, the "messiness" and "muddle" of human existence. Murdoch frequently forces her characters to come to terms with the physical world and the accidental and apparently chaotic nature of reality. Early in the novel, Jake announces that "I hate contingency. I want everything in my life to have a sufficient reason," and later, in a reference to Sartre's *La Nausée* (1938; *Nausea*, 1949), observes that Hugo's Bounty Belfounder film studio is situated in a part of London "where contingency reaches the point of nausea." The novel ends with Jake's laughingly admitting that he does not know why Mrs. Tinckham's kittens look as they do. "I don't know why it is," he says, "It's just one of the wonders of the world." In this scene, Jake focuses on the particular—the kittens—and is able to accept that their appearance cannot be explained by him, two actions which show that he has moved much closer to Hugo's position. Hugo had earlier advised Jake that "some situations can't be unravelled" and, as a result, should be "dropped."

This acceptance of contingency implies a realization that life cannot be completely controlled by human will. Jake also learns that other individuals exist independently of him and resist his efforts to explain and categorize their behavior. When he introduces his close friend Peter O'Finney to the reader, he claims that "Finn has very little inner life," and that, while Finn is an inhabitant of his universe, "I . . . cannot conceive that he has one containing me." Events in the novel force Jake to move out of his solipsistic consciousness, and at the conclusion he acknowledges that for the first time Anna exists "as a separate being and not as a part of myself," an experience he finds "extremely painful." She becomes "something which had to be learnt afresh," and he then asks if it is possible ever to know another human being. He answers himself in a statement that clearly belongs to his author: "Perhaps only after one has realized the impossibility of knowledge and renounced the desire for it and finally ceased to feel even the need of it." In the same way, Jake also grants Hugo a final mysteriousness and impenetrability, comparing him to a monolith whose purpose remains obscure.

Murdoch's suspicions about the nature of language are also evident in *Under the Net*. In a conversation between Hugo and Jake, Hugo maintains that, by definition, language lies: "The whole language is a machine for making falsehoods." Language is also vulnerable because of the human tendency to distort and to exaggerate experiences when attempting to articulate them; Hugo notes that when he speaks he does not state precisely what he thinks but rather what will impress Jake and force him to respond. Only actions, says Hugo, do not lie. This is not however, Murdoch's final word on language and literature, for Jake's development as a human being during the course of the novel culminates in his realization that he will be able to write creatively. The "shiver of possibility" that he feels at the novel's conclusion is his knowledge that his earlier writing has been merely a preparation for his emergence as a novelist.

Murdoch's first novel is clearly a *Künstlerroman* and her most overtly "philosophical" novel. In an interview in 1978 with Jack Biles, in *Studies in the Literary Imagination*, she said that she does not want to "promote" her philosophical views in her novels or to allow them to "intrude into the novel world." This attitude certainly seems more descriptive of the novels written after *Under the Net*. Although she paints an ironically amusing portrait of the novel's only professional philosopher, Dave Gellman, her major concerns in her first novel are clearly philosophical; *Under the Net* contains in more obvious form the philosophical issues that are transmuted into the fictional material of her subsequent work.

One of Murdoch's most critically acclaimed novels is 1986's *The Good Apprentice*, a novel that reflects her continuing desire to write fiction whose length and complexity embody her belief in a contingent, infinitely particularized universe in which goodness is easily discussed but achieved, if at all, with great difficulty and pain. The "good apprentice" can refer to either of two characters in the novel. Edward Baltram has recently been responsible for the death of his best friend and is attempting to deal with his resulting guilt and self-hatred; Stuart Cuno, his stepbrother, is, like many other Murdochian characters, seeking goodness and finding it a problematical goal.

Murdoch makes Stuart Cuno the mouthpiece of some of her most cherished ideas about the nature of goodness. Like Murdoch, Stuart acknowledges that goodness is often an unimaginable concept that involves inaction rather than action, and several times in the story he is referred to as a "negative presence." Stuart has rejected the entire concept of God and instead attempts to meditate blankly, to empty his mind out in order to perceive clearly, what Murdoch calls "an instinctive craving for nothingness which was also a desire to be able to love and enjoy and 'touch' everything, to *help* everything." Psychoanalyst Thomas McCaskerville, who stands in direct opposition to Stuart's nontheoretical approach to goodness, catechizes the younger man at length in an important conversation that reveals Thomas' dependence on the cozy theories of psychoanalysis that Murdoch mocked in her earlier novels. Thomas has a conceptual framework for almost any idea or event, and his discovery that his wife Midge has been having an affair with Stuart's father Harry Cuno only temporarily shocks him out of his comfortable mental and emotional world. His further realization that his supposedly psychotic patient Mr. Blinnet is actually quite sane and has been faking mental illness for years is another blow at Thomas' carefully constructed theoretical world.

It is the artist Jesse Baltram, Edward's father, who best represents one of the most enduring and interesting figures in Murdoch's fiction, the magician-artist power figure who mysteriously spellbinds those around him and functions as a catalyst for many important events. Edward goes to Seegard, Jesse's home, to be "healed" and "purified" of his friend's death. In the process, he meets May Baltram, Jesse's wife, his two half sisters, and, finally, his father, who has been reduced by an unspecified illness to childlike behavior and incoherence. Jesse's difficulty in making rational conversation is another alternative in the novel to Stuart's "blankness" and "whiteness" and Thomas' frenziedly articulate philosophizing: It signifies that the logical ordering principle of language ultimately cannot describe or explain a reality that is always "boiling over" with energy and creativity.

Jesse's description of the world and the relationship between good and evil, in which syntax and logic break down, is directly opposed to the other characters' slick facility with language. He tells Edward, "What I knew once—about good and evil and those—all *those* things—people don't really have them, meet them—in their lives at all, most people don't—only a few—want that—that fight, you know—think they want—good—have to have evil—not real, either—of course—all inside something else—it's a dance—you see—world needs power—always round and round—it's all power and—energy—which sometimes—rears up its beautiful head—like a dragon—that's the meaning of it all—I think—in the shadows now—can't remember—doesn't matter—what I need—is a long sleep—so as to dream it—all over again."

Jesse's connection with the supernatural and paranormal dimension of Edward's stay at Seegard reveals Murdoch experimenting with the limits of realistic fiction. She is willing to force the reader to accept the unexplained and acknowledge the thin line between the natural and supernatural, between distortion of perception and a glimpse into another world where the usual rational rules no longer apply. *The Good Apprentice* shows Murdoch at the height of her powers as a novelist, combining her "moral psychology" with her long-held aesthetic theories in a work that proves the undiminished fecundity of her imagination and intelligence.

Other major works

PLAYS: *A Severed Head*, 1963 (with J. B. Priestly); *The Italian Girl*, 1967 (with James Saunders); *The Servants and the Snow*, 1970; *The Three Arrows*, 1972; *Art and Eros*, 1980; *The Black Prince*, 1989.

NONFICTION: *Sartre: Romantic Rationalist*, 1953; *The Sovereignty of Good*, 1970; *The Fire and the Sun: Why Plato Banished the Artists*, 1977; *Acastos: Two Platonic Dialogues*, 1987; *Metaphysics as a Guide to Morals*, 1992.

Bibliography

Bloom, Harold, ed. *Iris Murdoch*. New York: Chelsea House, 1986.

Byatt, Antonia S. *Degrees of Freedom: The Novels of Iris Murdoch*. London: Barnes & Noble Books, 1965.

Dipple, Elizabeth. *Iris Murdoch: Work for the Spirit*. Chicago: University of Chicago Press, 1982.

Hague, Angela. *Iris Murdoch's Comic Vision*. New York: Associated University Presses, 1984.

Johnson, Deborah. *Iris Murdoch*. Bloomington: Indiana University Press, 1987.

Todd, Richard. *Iris Murdoch: The Shakespearian Interest*. New York: Barnes & Noble Books, 1979.

Wolfe, Peter. *The Disciplined Heart: Iris Murdoch and Her Novels*. Columbia: University of Missouri Press, 1966.

GLORIA NAYLOR

Born: New York, New York; January 25, 1950

Principal long fiction

The Women of Brewster Place: A Novel in Seven Stories, 1982; *Linden Hills*, 1985; *Mama Day*, 1988; *Bailey's Café*, 1992.

Other literary forms

In 1986, Gloria Naylor wrote a column, *Hers*, for *The New York Times* and published a work of nonfiction, *Centennial* (1986). She has also written a number of screenplays, short stories, and articles for various periodicals. She is known primarily, however, for her novels.

Achievements

Enjoying both critical and popular acclaim, Naylor's work has reached a wide audience. *The Women of Brewster Place* won the 1983 American Book Award for best first novel and was later made into a television miniseries. Naylor's other awards include a National Endowment for the Arts Fellowship in 1985 and a Guggenheim Fellowship in 1988.

Surveying the range of black life in America, from poor ghetto to affluent suburb to Southern offshore island, Naylor's work examines questions of black identity and, in particular, celebrates black women. In the face of enormous problems and frequent victimization, black women are shown coping through their sense of community and their special powers. Male readers might find less to cheer about in Naylor's work, as she writes from a feminist perspective, but her depictions of courage, community, and cultural identity have universal appeal.

Biography

The oldest child of black parents who had migrated from Mississippi, Gloria Naylor was born and reared in New York City. After graduation from high school, she spent seven years as a missionary for the Jehovah's Witnesses in New York, North Carolina, and Florida. She eventually found missionary life too strict, but her original zeal apparently carried over into her later feminism. Although her writings are not religious, a fundamentalist pattern of thinking pervades them. She tends to separate her characters into the sheep and the goats (mostly men), the saved and the damned, with one whole book, *Linden Hills*, being modeled after Dante's *Inferno* (c. 1320).

In high school, Naylor read widely in the nineteenth century British novelists, but later in a creative writing course at Brooklyn College she came across the book that influenced her most—*The Bluest Eye* (1970), by the African American novelist Toni Morrison. The example of Morrison inspired Naylor to write fiction and to focus on the lives of black women, who Naylor felt were underrepresented (if not ignored) in American literature. Naylor began work on *The Women of Brewster Place*, which was published the year after her graduation from Brooklyn College with a B.A. in English. By that time, Naylor was studying on a fellowship at Yale University, from which she received an M.A. in Afro-American studies in 1983.

Naylor's background and literary achievements won for her numerous invitations for lectureships or other appointments in academia. She has held visiting posts at George Washington University, the University of Pennsylvania, Princeton University, New York University, Boston University, Brandeis University, and Cornell University. She continued, however, to make her home in New York City.

Analysis

White people do not appear often and are certainly never featured in the work of Gloria Naylor. Yet their presence can be felt like a white background noise, or like the boulevard traffic on the other side of the wall from Brewster Place. White culture is simply another fact of life, like a nearby nuclear reactor or toxic waste dump, and the effects of racism and discrimination are omnipresent in Naylor's work. Against these stifling effects her characters live their lives and try to define their sense of black identity, from the ghetto women of Brewster Place to the social climbers of Linden Hills to the denizens of Willow Springs, a pristine Southern island relatively untouched by slavery and segregation.

Naylor writes about these settings and characters in a romantic mode that sometimes verges on the melodramatic or gothic. The influence of her earlier reading—such authors as Charlotte and Emily Brontë, Charles Dickens, William Faulkner, and Morrison—is apparent. The settings have heavy but obvious symbolic meanings, some derived from literary references: Brewster Place is a dead-end street, Linden Hills is a modern version of Dante's Hell, and Willow Springs recalls the magical isle of William Shakespeare's *The Tempest* (1611). The weather and numerous details also carry symbolic freight, almost as much as they do for such an emblematic writer as Nathaniel Hawthorne. In addition to literary influences, the symbolism seems to draw on Hollywood, particularly Hollywood's Gothic genre, horror films; for example, in *Linden Hills* the character Norman Anderson suffers from attacks of "the pinks"—imaginary blobs of pink slime—while the rich undertaker Luther Nedeed locks his wife and child away in the basement.

These two examples also show, in an exaggerated fashion, how Naylor's characters fit into the romantic mode. Her characters tend to go to extremes, to be emotional and obsessive, or to have a single trait or commit a single act that determines their whole life course. While being rather one-dimensional and melodramatic, they nevertheless linger in the memory. Such is the case with Luther Nedeed, who represents Satan in *Linden Hills*, and with the old conjure woman Miranda "Mama" Day, who represents Satan's usual opposition in the scheme of things.

In Naylor, this scheme of things illustrates how she has transferred her former missionary fervor, along with the framework of religious thought, over into her feminism. Luther Nedeed's behavior is only the most sensa-tional example of men's cruelty to women in Naylor's work; he has a large following. On the other hand, the mystical ability of Mama Day, the Prospero of women's liberation, to command the forces of nature and the spirit world is only the most sensational example of women's special powers in Naylor's thinking. Even the women of Brewster Place demonstrate these powers through their mutual love and support, enabling them to triumph over devastating personal tragedies and demeaning circumstances.

Naylor's men are another story: If not outright demons or headed that way, they seem to lack some vital force. Even the best men are fatally flawed—they are subject to "the pinks," are addicted to wine, or have a weak heart. Failing at key moments, they are useful only as sacrifices to the feminine mystique. A prime example is the engineer George Andrews of *Mama Day*, who, for all his masculine rationality and New York smarts, does not know how to handle, significantly, a brooding hen.

Naylor began fulfilling her commitment to make black women more prominent in American fiction with *The Women of Brewster Place*, subtitled *A Novel in Seven Stories*. The seven stories, featuring seven women, can be read separately, but they are connected by their setting of Brewster Place and by characters who carry over from one story to another (at least by brief mention). The women arrive on the dead-end street by different routes that exhibit the variety of lives of black women, but on Brewster Place they unite into a community.

The middle-aged bastion of Brewster Street is Mattie Michael, who over the course of her life was betrayed by each of the three men she loved—her seducer, her father, and her son. She mothers Lucielia Louise Turner (whose grandmother once sheltered Mattie) when Ciel's abusive boyfriend destroys her life. In addition, Mattie welcomes her close friend Etta Mae Johnson, who also once gave Mattie refuge. Etta Mae is a fading beauty who has used men all of her life but is now herself used by a sleazy preacher for a one-night stand. The other women featured are the young unwed Cora Lee, a baby factory; Kiswana Browne, an aspiring social reformer who hails from the affluent suburb of Linden Hills; and Lorraine and Theresa, two lesbians seeking privacy for their love.

Few men are in evidence on Brewster Place, and these few inspire little confidence. C. C. Baker and his youth gang lurk about the alleyway and, in the novel's brutal climax, rape Lorraine. The crazed Lorraine in turn kills the wino Ben, the old janitor who earlier had befriended her.

As these scenes suggest, Brewster Place is located in a ghetto plagued by social ills. The women must face these on a daily basis in addition to their personal tragedies and dislocations. Instead of being overcome by their sufferings, however, the women find within themselves a common fate and a basis for community. They gain strength and hope from their mutual caring and support. Besides their informal support system, they form a block association to address larger problems. The ability of women to unite in such a community inspires admiration for their courage and their special powers.

The community feelings of Brewster Place, from which the women gain a positive sense of identity, somehow make the ghetto's problems seem less awesome, paradoxically, than those of Linden Hills, an affluent suburb. If Brewster Place is a ghetto, Linden Hills is a hell. Naylor underlines this metaphor by deliberately modeling her novel *Linden Hills* after Dante's *Inferno*. Linden Hills is not a group of hills, but only a V-shaped area on a hillside intersected by eight streets. As one travels down the hill, the residents become richer but lower on the moral scale. Lester and Willie, two young unemployed poets who perform odd jobs for Christmas money (they are the modern counterparts of Vergil and Dante), take the reader on a guided tour.

The residents of Linden Hills have sold out for affluence: They suffer from a loss of black identity, or soul, as the result of adopting white attitudes, compromising their personal loyalties, and denying their kinship with other blacks. Lester's sister Roxanne deems black Africans in Zimbabwe unready for independence; one young executive, Maxwell Smyth, encourages another, Xavier Donnell, no longer to consider Roxanne as a prospective corporate bride; and Dr. Daniel Braithwaite has written the authorized twelve-volume history of Linden Hills without making a single moral judgment. Other sellouts are more personal: The young lawyer Winston Alcott leaves his homosexual lover to marry respectably, and Chester Parker is eager to bury his dead wife in order to remarry.

Significantly, Linden Hills is ruled over by men. The archfiend himself is Luther Nedeed, the local undertaker and real estate tycoon who occupies the lowest point in Linden Hills. Speaking against a low-income housing project planned for an adjacent poor black neighborhood, Nedeed urges outraged Linden Hills property owners to make common cause with the racist Wayne County Citizens Alliance. Most damning of all, however, is that Nedeed disowns his own wife and child and imprisons them in an old basement morgue; the child starves, but the wife climbs up to confront the archfiend on Christmas Eve.

It is clear that, while examining problems of middle-class black identity in *Linden Hills*, Naylor has not overlooked the plight of black women. In *Mama Day*, Naylor returns to a more celebratory mood on both subjects. The setting of *Mama Day* is unique African American culture presided over by a woman with even more unique powers.

The coastal island of Willow Springs, located off South Carolina and Georgia but belonging to no state, has been largely bypassed by the tides of American history, particularly racism. The island was originally owned by a white man, Bascombe Wade, who also owned slaves. Bascombe married Sapphira, one of his slaves, however, who bore their seven sons. In 1823 Bascombe freed his other slaves and deeded the island to them, his sons, and their respective descendants in perpetuity (the land cannot be sold, only inherited). Bascombe was more or less assimilated, and a black culture grew up on the island that was closely tied to the land, to the culture's beginnings, and to African roots. In other words, Willow Springs is definitely a mythical island—a tiny but free black state flourishing unnoticed under the nose of the Confederacy. Naylor underlines the island's mythic qualities by drawing parallels between it and the magical isle of *The Tempest*.

If Prospero presides over Shakespeare's island, then Prospero's daughter, Miranda "Mama" Day (actually a great-granddaughter of the Wades), presides over Willow Springs. Known and respected locally as an old conjure woman, Mama Day is a repository and embodiment of the culture's wisdom. In particular, she is versed in herbs and other natural phenomena, but she also speaks with the island's spirits. Mama Day uses her powers to heal and aid new life, but other island people who have similar powers are not so benevolent. One such person is Ruby, who stirs her knowledge with hoodoo to kill any woman who might take her man.

Unhappily, Mama Day's grandniece Cocoa, down from New York on a visit with her husband George, arouses Ruby's jealousy. By pretending to be friendly, Ruby is able to give Cocoa a deadly nightshade rinse, scalp massage, and hairdo. Just as a big hurricane hits the island, Cocoa begins to feel the effects of the poison. George, an engineer, native New Yorker, and football fan, works frantically to save Cocoa, but he is over-matched. With his urbanized, masculine rationality, he cannot conceive of what he is up against or know how to oppose it. Suffering from exhaustion and a weak heart, he is eventually killed in an encounter with a brooding hen.

Meanwhile, Mama Day has been working her powers. She confronts Ruby in a conjuring match, good magic versus bad magic, just as in Mali's oral epic tradition of the thirteenth century ruler Sundjata and in other tradi-tions of modern Africa. Ruby is destroyed by lightning strikes, and Cocoa is saved. It is too late for George the doubter, however, who learns about the mystical powers of women the hard way.

Mama Day provides Naylor's most advanced state-ments of her favorite themes, the assertion of black identity and the celebration of black women. There is much about her work that might ultimately prove self-limiting, mainly her doctrinaire feminism and her ten-dency to write in broad, sweeping gestures. Yet these same features give her work a mythic quality that is undeniably powerful. Naylor has obviously taken a few magical hints from Mama Day.

Other major work

NONFICTION: *Centennial*, 1986.

Bibliography

Bell, Bernard W. *The Afro-American Novel and Its Tradition*. Amherst: University of Massachusetts Press, 1987.

Braxton, Joanne M., and Andrée Nicola McLaughlin, eds. *Wild Women in the Whirlwind: Afro-American Culture and the Contemporary Literary Renaissance*. New Brunswick, N.J.: Rutgers University Press, 1990.

Carby, Hazel V. *Reconstructing Womanhood: The Emergence of the Afro-American Woman Novelist*. New York: Oxford University Press, 1987.

Gates, Henry Louis, Jr. "The Significant Others." *Contemporary Literature* 29 (Winter, 1988): 606-623.

Homans, Margaret. "The Women in the Cave: Recent Feminist Fictions and the Classical Underworld." *Contempo-rary Literature* 29 (Fall, 1988): 369-402.

Naylor, Gloria, and Toni Morrison. "A Conversation." *The Southern Review* 21 (Summer, 1985): 567-593.

ANAÏS NIN

Born: Paris, France; February 21, 1903   **Died:** Los Angeles, California; January 14, 1977

Principal long fiction

House of Incest, 1936; *Winter of Artifice*, 1939; *Winter of Artifice: Three Novelettes*, 1945 (contains *Winter of Artifice*, "Stella," and "The Voice"); *This Hunger*, 1945; *Cities of the Interior: A Continuous Novel*, 1959 (contains *Ladders to Fire*, 1946, *Children of the Albatross*, 1947, *The Four-Chambered Heart*, 1950, *A Spy in the House of Love*, 1954, *Solar Barque*, 1958); *Seduction of the Minotaur*, 1961; *Collages*, 1964.

Other literary forms

Anaïs Nin published numerous volumes of perceptive literary criticism. Highly acclaimed, her first book of nonfiction, *D. H. Lawrence: An Unprofessional Study*, appeared in 1932. In 1968, near the end of her career, she wrote *The Novel of the Future*, partly as an attempt to explain the literary philosophy that inspired her innovative fiction. Nin's published short stories, like her criticism, span her career. The most distinguished collection is *Under a Glass Bell and Other Stories* (1944). Her apprentice writing is available in another collection, *Waste of Timelessness and Other Early Stories* (1977), while two volumes of erotica were published after Nin's death: *Delta of Venus* (1977) and *Little Birds* (1979).

In addition to her works of fiction and criticism, Nin's extensive diary has been published. Edited from a vast manuscript, this autobiographical work has appeared in two series. The first series, entitled *The Diary of Anaïs Nin*, comprises seven volumes which appeared periodically beginning in 1966. The second series contains three volumes: *Linotte: The Early Diary of Anaïs Nin, 1914-1920* (1978); *The Early Diary of Anaïs Nin: Volume Two, 1920-1923* (1982); and *Journal of a Wife: The Early Diary of Anaïs Nin, 1923-1927* (1984). In addition, there is *Incest—from a Journal of Love: The Unexpurgated Diary of Anaïs Nin, 1932-1934* (1991).

Achievements

Nin's achievement in literature is of two distinct kinds: artistic and sociological. Strongly influenced by Arthur Rimbaud, Marcel Proust, and D. H. Lawrence, Nin conceived of and developed a uniquely personal approach to style and structure that places her within the modernist tradition as it evolved in the French literature of the early decades of the twentieth century. Nin persisted in articulating, refining, and extending an avowedly "feminine" ideal of the novel; this resulted in lyrical novels in which the imagistic manner of the poet is fused with the psychological penetration of the novelist.

The audience for Nin's novels is smaller than for either her diary or her collections of erotica. As the diary has increased Nin's audience, it has also brought her fiction to the attention of well-qualified critics and scholars, many of whom have been able to interpret it in ways that make it more accessible to a general readership trained on the conventions of realism. Considering the climate of growing respect for and interest in Nin's novels, it seems that her reputation as a literary artist is now securely established.

Biography

On February 21, 1903, Anaïs Nin was born in Paris, the oldest child of musicians Joaquin Nin and Rosa Culmell-Nin. Her parents' marriage was turbulent, and in 1913, Joaquin Nin deserted his family at Archachon, France. The following year, Rosa Culmell-Nin transported her daughter and two sons, Thorvald and Joaquin, to the United States. For some years, they lived in New York City and in Queens, actively participating in the lively Cuban community there, many of whose members were musicians. Nin has recorded this period of her life in *Linotte: The Early Diary of Anaïs Nin, 1914-1920*. What stands out most poignantly is her inconsolable grief at the loss of her father and her intense worship of her mother. At this time, Nin's aspiration to become an artist of one sort or another strongly manifested itself, and her account of her adolescence is a rich study of the formative years of an artist.

In 1918, Nin left school in order to manage the household for her mother, and in 1923, she married Hugh P. Guiler (known as an engraver and filmmaker under the name of Ian Hugo). As a young married woman, Nin lived in France. Marriage caused her to experience intense conflicts which she has described and analyzed in her diary. During those years, as in adolescence, Nin continued to write, and in 1932, she published her first book, *D. H. Lawrence: An Unprofessional Study*. This work brought about the explosive friendship with Henry and June Miller which she describes in the first published diary. Nin and Miller maintained a relationship until Nin's death.

In Paris during the 1930's, Nin embarked upon a lifelong devotion to psychotherapy. Her therapeutic relationship with the renowned Viennese psychoanalyst Otto Rank is recounted in the first volume of *The Diary of Anaïs Nin*. An independent, original, and forceful thinker whose special area of interest was the artist, Rank was of great assistance to Nin in the fulfillment of her artistic aspirations. His influence on her was so persuasive that for time she actually considered making a living as a lay psychoanalyst. For a few months in 1934, she lived in New York and assisted Rank with his practice. In 1935, however, she resumed her literary work and returned to France to rejoin her husband, but with the outbreak of World War II, she again returned to the United States. This move in 1939 was to become perma-

nent. It was not easy for Nin to give up her "romantic life" in Paris, as she called it, and her difficulty understanding Americans' disdain for the arts is a recurrent theme of her diary in the 1940's and 1950's.

Throughout her life, Nin maintained many friendships with writers and other artists. Nevertheless, she experienced continual frustration in the publishing world. On the whole, editors and critics were either hostile to her work or simply ignored it. The breakthrough of this period was the acceptance by publisher Alan Swallow of the five works that constitute *Cities of the Interior: A Continuous Novel*. For many years, Nin was an underground literary figure with a small but enthusiastic following.

In 1966, Nin's status changed suddenly; she had already published all of her fiction, the last book, *Collages*, appearing in 1964. When Harcourt Brace and World, with The Swallow Press, brought out the first volume of *The Diary of Anaïs Nin*, Nin quickly became a public figure. Because the content of the work expressed the feelings of many women who were experiencing deep evolutionary changes in their own lives, Nin involuntarily became a spokesperson for the women's movement.

During the remaining years of Nin's life, individual volumes of her diary continued to appear and received considerable public acclaim. Traveling throughout the United States, she gave hundreds of talks at colleges and universities and undertook trips to various countries, including Sweden and Bali. In 1970, she was awarded the French Prix Sévigné, and in 1974, she was elected to the National Institute of Arts and Letters.

Analysis

Anaïs Nin's approach to the novel was that of a poet with a heightened and highly developed sense of language. The image was her indispensable medium of expression; free association, which she learned to trust as a patient in psychotherapy, became the process through which she allowed literary structures to emerge. Always, Nin's subject was the self in its evolution, especially the self in relationships with others; her perspective was always psychological, though her books do not demonstrate any particular school of psychoanalytical thought.

Dispensing with conventional plots and with the framework of linear chronology, Nin portrayed her characters in a series of "shots" that derive their power from the carefully selected detail of their imagery. Her lan-

guage, never purely decorative, is metaphorical in a truly organic sense. Nin does not describe, she interprets, and in the act of interpretation, she re-creates her subjects. To know Nin's characters, the reader, too, must interpret their action, their gestures, look beneath the surfaces.

The five novels found in the final version of *Cities of the Interior* are *Ladders to Fire, Children of the Albatross, The Four-Chambered Heart, A Spy in the House of Love*, and *Seduction of the Minotaur* (which contains *Solar Barque*). They were first published individually during the 1940's and 1950's. An extraordinary work, it displays a brilliance of conception, a mastery of image and metaphor, and a refinement of structural technique. The title *Cities of the Interior: A Continuous Novel* suggests the timeless scope of this work. The "cities" are both ancient and modern. Nin set out to excavate the buried "cities" or the psychic worlds of her three main characters: Lillian, Djuna, and Sabina. The idea of "continuity," however, is more complex. A reader can begin with any one of the five volumes and move to the other four in any order, losing no essential connections. Nin's characters are totally immersed in the flow of internalized psychic time, in the patterns of their own growth. In *Cities of the Interior*, Nin has selected and expressed significant relationships and states of feeling in the ever-changing, continuous process of growth. Life, as distinct from existence, is possible only for those who can accept mutability, knowing that while change promises growth, it also demands inevitable loss.

Lillian's development spans *Cities of the Interior*, opening and closing the work when it is read in conventional sequence. The first part of *Ladders to Fire* describes "This Hunger," Lillian's ravenous need for love. Spontaneous, impetuous, unsure of her physical attractiveness, and compulsively generous, she gives up her career as a pianist so that she can support her lover's ambition to paint, but this sacrifice does not bring her the loyalty and security she desires. Jay repays Lillian's devotion by having affairs with other women.

The most threatening of Lillian's rivals is Sabina. The relationship between these two women is the most compelling in the novel and a superb example of Nin's brilliance at unmasking psychological motivations. When Lillian attempts to stop Sabina's pursuit of Jay by overwhelming the other woman with friendship, she discovers that she, too, is powerfully attracted to Sabina. For different reasons, both women are angry at Jay: Lillian because he has neglected her; Sabina because he would like to conquer her. The two women form an alliance against him. After dancing together in a working-class tavern, they go to Sabina's room to make love, but they discover that it is not sensuality they are seeking in each other so much as an exchange of feminine qualities. They both feel a "mysterious craving . . . to become each other."

During the dazzling party scene with which *Ladders to Fire* closes, Lillian commits "invisible hara-kiri" with an outburst of harmful self-criticism. It is clear to the reader that she has grown, that her anger at herself is partly an expression of this growth, and that she will soon end her unsatisfying relationship with Jay.

A delicate, playful book, with an undercurrent of sadness, *Children of the Albatross* traces a theme that is familiar in French literature but something of a novelty in the United States: the initiation of a young man by an older woman. Djuna, in her late twenties, becomes involved with Paul, seventeen. The other "children" of the novel's title are their friends, young gay men who meet with Paul and Djuna in her "house of innocence and faith." Here, they dance, paint, and play, celebrating their love of freedom from responsibility. The young men and Djuna are drawn together by their mutual fear of tyrannical, authoritarian fathers. For Djuna, this figure is represented by the cruel and lecherous watchman who terrified her when she was a child living in an orphanage. The positive creative act of evoking a counter-world to erect against the conventional and materialistic values of the "fathers" ignites sympathy among the rebellious "children."

From the start of *Children of the Albatross*, it is clear that Djuna's affair with Paul will be brief and will provide her with little emotional sustenance. Predictably, Paul's family disapproves of her, not only because she is "older" but also because she is a dancer. A crucial dream in which Djuna imagines herself as Adriadne predicts that after she has guided Paul safely through the passage from adolescence to early manhood, she will be abandoned. At the novel's end, Paul embarks upon an exciting journey to India, leaving Djuna behind. Feeling empty and dissatisfied, she searches the unexplored "cities" of her self. She begins to seek a fuller emotional life with a more mature partner.

In *The Four-Chambered Heart*, Nin explores the psychological complexity of a woman's involvement with a married man. Romantically ensconced in a houseboat on the Seine are Djuna and Rango, a tempestuous vagabond, so she imagines. Their relationship is initially enthralling but ultimately frustrating; both parties are weighed down by responsibilities to demanding hypochondriacs: he to his wife, Zora; Djuna to her father. Heavy rains force the lovers to move their houseboat up and down the river. Like their relationship, the boat does not "go anywhere"; it merely plies its way back and forth over the same area.

Djuna and Rango's passion attains its height in the novel's first thirty pages. After that, there is conflict and threatened violence. Zora makes a bizarre attempt to kill Djuna. Rango comes to the boat very late one night and falls into a heavy depressed sleep. Djuna, desperate to initiate a change of some sort, rips up floor boards in a wild attempt to sink the boat. It is swept down the river; everyone survives, though not in the same form. A fisherman rescues a doll from the water with a joke about its having tried to commit suicide. The doll is a comment on Djuna's passivity with regard to her own life and to the image of conventional femininity that she has been struggling to maintain, at the expense of her "true" self. It is time for her to move beyond the static situation she experiences with Rango, to give up the illusion of her generosity toward Zora, and to recognize and accept the negative qualities she has been "acting out" through Rango. Djuna must grow.

In *A Spy in the House of Love*, Sabina is portrayed as a glamorous woman seeking to express herself has "Don Juana." Married to a fatherly, indulgent man, she is free to fulfill her desire for adventure, which she experiences through relationships with men. Each of Sabina's partners embodies an aura, a sense of place, an ambience that lies waiting for her exploration and participation. There is the opera star Philip; he represents "Vienna before the war." There is Mambo, a black musician transplanted to Greenwich Village from a Caribbean island. There is John, a former aviator who has been grounded because of uncontrollable anxiety. Finally, there is Donald, a gay man who returns Sabina's maternal love with an irresistibly flattering letter-portrait of her idealized self. This balances the grossly sexual and cruel portrait given to her by her former lover, Jay, a painter.

A Spy in the House of Love is a musical novel both in style and structure. There is a prelude in which Sabina invites the detection of her "crime" (experiencing sex without feeling) by phoning a "lie detector." There is a coda in which Djuna, Sabina's consoling friend, plays a late Beethoven quartet to soothe and heal the dejected Don Juana. The body of the novel is a series of variations on the central theme: Sabina's attempt to live through her relationships with men who—so she deludes herself into believing—have far more exciting lives than she herself has. Each man is associated with a particular type of music, while Igor Stravinsky's "Firebird" is said to be Sabina's "unerring musical autobiography."

At once the most mature in theme and the most resplendent in imagery among Nin's novels, *Seduction of the Minotaur* takes up the story of Lillian. She has developed considerably since *Ladders to Fire*. Now a jazz performer instead of an interpreter of the classics, Lillian journeys to Mexico, imagining that she has finally freed herself from everything that imprisoned her in the past.

Traveling alone, Lillian meets a series of men, each of whom becomes a teacher or guide of sorts, revealing something of great significance in her own circuitous passage through the labyrinth of the self. The most engaging of these figures is Dr. Hernandez, a male version of Ariadne. He helps Lillian to see that she is not yet as free as she has imagined, wisely telling her that "we live by a series of repetitions until the experience is solved, understood, liquidated." The monster Lillian confronts is a "masked woman," the part of herself that she has previously been unwilling to recognize.

In Lillian's journey to Mexico and her confrontation with herself, Nin creates a living dream simultaneously in the past, present, and future. The meaning of freedom is not flight, as Sabina imagines, but commitment. If a woman can discover and love the many aspects of one man, she can be fulfilled with a single love. Lillian learns to see her husband Larry, from whom she has been separated, as a complex, multidimensional person. This discovery brings a new excitement, a forgiveness, the grace of understanding to her feelings about him. Because she untangles the knots in her own past, Lillian rediscovers the love of her husband. Thus, there is reconciliation instead of separation.

A more ambitious and a deeper book than its easy surface and gentle humor suggest, *Collages* is composed of nineteen short blocks of prose, showing once again Nin's preference for constructed rather than narrated fiction. *Collages* begins and ends with the same passage. Its circular structure encloses twenty-two characters portrayed in a wide variety of quickly sketched settings. The cement that binds these colorful elements into a composition is Renate, a woman artist who "makes her own patterns." She weaves in and out of the lives of the others, bringing inspiration not only to her paintings but also to her friends.

Collage art is shown to work magic transformations. In this book Nin once again stresses the many ways in which dream and fantasy enrich life. There is an intense relationship, for example, between a young woman and a raven. An elderly man feels closer to seals than to human beings; he finally develops the courage to renounce people in order to live with the animals he loves. A gardener pretends to be a millionaire in order to fulfill his dream of financing a literary magazine. A woman whose husband has rejected her for a younger woman replaces him with an exotic phantom lover. In *Collages*, imagination is sovereign.

The healing power of genuine relationships is shown

as complementary to that of creative fantasy. *Collages* closes with the reluctant emergence of a woman writer from a bitter, self-imposed isolation. Elderly Judith Sands allows herself to be "courted" by Renate and an Israeli admirer, Dr. Mann. Made more trusting by their friendship, Sands actually shows the visitors one of her manuscripts. Its opening words are the same words with which *Collages* begins. This repetition helps endow *Collages* with its circular form and also underscores Nin's

conviction that there is an unbroken connection from one person to another, one imaginative writer to another, and that life is redeemed through the alchemical transformation of art. *Collages* is an assured and accomplished example of Nin's skill at adapting techniques from the nonverbal arts to literature; it is also the most imaginative display of her convictions about the mutually nourishing exchange between art and life.

Other major works

SHORT FICTION: *Under a Glass Bell and Other Stories*, 1944; *Delta of Venus: Erotica*, 1977; *Waste of Timelessness and Other Early Stories*, 1977; *Little Birds: Erotica*, 1979.

NONFICTION: *D. H. Lawrence: An Unprofessional Study*, 1932; *Realism and Reality*, 1946; *On Writing*, 1947; *The Diary of Anaïs Nin : 1931-1934*, 1966; *The Diary of Anaïs Nin: 1934-1939*, 1967; *The Novel of the Future*, 1968; *The Diary of Anaïs Nin: 1939-1944*, 1969; *The Diary of Anaïs Nin: 1944-1947*, 1971; *Paris Revisited*, 1972; *The Diary of Anaïs Nin: 1947-1955*, 1974; *A Photographic Supplement to the Diary of Anaïs Nin*, 1974; *A Woman Speaks: The Lectures, Seminars, and Interviews of Anaïs Nin*, 1975; *The Diary of Anaïs Nin: 1955-1966*, 1976; *In Favor of the Sensitive Man and Other Essays*, 1976; *Linotte: The Early Diary of Anaïs Nin, 1914-1920*, 1978; *The Diary of Anaïs Nin: 1966-1974*, 1980; *The Early Diary of Anaïs Nin: Volume Two, 1920-1923*, 1982; *Journal of a Wife: The Early Diary of Anaïs Nin, 1923-1927*, 1984; *A Literate Passion: Letters of Anaïs Nin and Henry Miller, 1932-1951*, 1987; *Incest—from a Journal of Love: The Unexpurgated Diary of Anaïs Nin, 1932-1934*, 1991.

Bibliography

Evans, Oliver. *Anaïs Nin*. Carbondale: Southern Illinois University Press, 1968.

Fitch, Nöel Riley. *Anaïs: The Erotic Life of Anaïs Nin*. Boston: Little, Brown, 1993.

Franklin, Benjamin, and Duane Schneider. *Anaïs Nin: An Introduction*. Athens: Ohio University Press, 1979.

Hinz, Evelyn J. *The Mirror and the Garden: Realism and Reality in the Writings of Anaïs Nin*. 2d ed. New York: Harcourt Brace Jovanovich, 1973.

Spencer, Sharon. *Collage of Dreams: The Writings of Anaïs Nin*. Chicago: Swallow Press, 1981.

Zaller, Robert, ed. *A Casebook on Anaïs Nin*. New York: New American Library, 1974.

MARSHA NORMAN

Born: Louisville, Kentucky; September 21, 1947

Principal drama

Getting Out, pr. 1977, pb. 1978; *Third and Oak*, pr. 1978, pb. 1985 (includes *The Laundromat*, pb. 1980, 1985, and *The Pool Hall*, pb. 1985); *Circus Valentine*, pr. 1979; *The Hold-up*, pr. 1980, pb. 1987; *'night, Mother*, pr. 1982, pb. 1983; *Traveler in the Dark*, pr. 1984, pb. 1988; *Sarah and Abraham*, pr. 1987; *Four Plays*, pb. 1988; *The Secret Garden*, pr. 1991; *D. Boone*, pr. 1992.

Other literary forms

Though known primarily as a playwright, Marsha Norman began her career as a journalist, writing a number of highly regarded feature articles and reviews of books, plays, and films for the *Louisville Times* in the mid-1970's. During this same period, she created and edited that newspaper's celebrated children's weekend supplement, "The Jelly Bean Journal." She has continued to write reviews as well as articles on playwrights and on women's issues. Her first novel, *The Fortune Teller*, appeared in 1987.

Achievements

Norman's abilities as a playwright were first recognized in 1977 by Jon Jory, director of the Festival of New Plays, Actors Theatre of Louisville. Her first major play, *Getting Out*, was cowinner of the Actors Theatre's playwriting prize. Norman's other awards include the John Gassner New Playwright's Medallion (1979), the George Oppenheimer *Newsday* Playwriting Award (1979), and grants from the National Endowment for the Arts, the Rockefeller Foundation, and the American Academy and Institute of Letters. Her masterwork, *'night, Mother*, won the 1983 Pulitzer Prize in drama, the prestigious Hull-Warriner Award, the Susan Smith Blackburn Prize, and four Tony Award nominations. Norman also received a Tony Award and a Drama Desk Award for her Broadway musical *The Secret Garden*. She has been playwright-in-residence at the Actors Theatre of Louisville and the Mark Taper Forum in Los Angeles and has been elected to membership in the American Academy of Achievement.

Norman is known for her ability to write compellingly about the psychic pain of ordinary, often inarticulate, and generally forgotten people. Inevitably, she seizes upon the single moment of greatest crisis in the lives of these people, that which allows them to rise to their greatest nobility. Though she is from the South, she makes every effort to create characterizations and settings that rise above regionalism to stand as contemporary and universal.

Biography

Marsha Williams Norman was born on September 21, 1947, in Louisville, Kentucky. She was a solitary child, and she inevitably cites childhood loneliness as having led to writing as a profession. Her mother, a Fundamentalist Methodist, did not believe that the local children were "good enough," and so Norman spent her childhood reading, practicing piano, and playing with "Bettering," an imaginary friend, in her Audubon Park, Kentucky, home. A high school essay entitled "Why Do Good Men Suffer?" earned first prize in a local contest and was subsequently published in the *Kentucky English Bulletin*.

Norman's earliest works, whimsical reviews and essays published in the 1970's, appeared in local newspapers. Her most widely read pieces appeared in the *Louisville Times* starting in 1976 in "The Jelly Bean Journal," a weekend children's supplement which she created for that newspaper. It was only after Jory asked her to write a serious play that Norman recalled her counseling experiences with disturbed adolescents at Kentucky Central State Hospital (perhaps also the psychological imprisonment of her own childhood) and wrote *Getting Out*. This play was staged successfully by the Actors Theatre in 1977 and enjoyed Los Angeles and New York runs.

Norman's personal life changed greatly in the late 1970's, a period corresponding to her earliest theatrical success. Her first marriage, to Michael Norman, ended in divorce in 1974, and in November, 1978, she married Dann C. Byck, Jr., a Louisville businessman with an interest in the theater. After their marriage, Byck increasingly involved himself in theatrical production and support of Norman's work. The couple moved to New York despite Norman's apprehensions that Manhattan life would make her writing more difficult; in the event, Norman's most critically acclaimed works have all been written in New York. Norman continued to serve on the boards of the New York Foundation for the Arts and the Independent Committee for Arts Policy and to carry out her responsibilities as treasurer of the Council of the Dramatists Guild. Yet she remained closely associated with the Actors Theatre of Louisville, where her plays often open.

Analysis

Marsha Norman's plays often have small casts and deal with a single moment of overwhelming importance for the protagonist. The dramatic conflict centers on the recognition of this problem and its resolution. Though this does not seem very different from the pattern of classical drama, Norman's plays focus on some difficulty that relates to the inner life of the protagonist. In consequence, her dramas depend greatly on dialogue rather than stage action, physical movement, or change of scene. They are often the cathartic conversations of ordinary people, given in simple language and without learned allusions but nevertheless profound, because they mirror the unexpressed thoughts of many individuals. Normally inarticulate, often-nondescript protagonists find hidden strength and depth of feeling they had never before recognized in themselves, and they face their problems with determination. The solution is often a radical one. Though the outcome may be tragic, the central character is usually personally triumphant.

Getting Out, for example, deals with the difficulties of Arlene Holsclaw, a newly released parolee who served an eight-year prison term for robbery, kidnapping, and manslaughter. Eight years have greatly changed her, but she must still come to terms with her past as well as face an uncertain future. Her past is first represented by Arlie, her younger and uncontrolled self, that part of her capable of the earlier crimes. Played by a second actress, Arlie literally invades Arlene's shabby apartment on the first day of Arlene's new freedom. Arlie is foulmouthed, crude, and defiant in contrast to Arlene's attempt to be quiet, reserved, and self-confident. The alter ego declares that Arlene is not really free, that Arlene remains a prisoner to her younger self, and that this other part of her will surface again.

Though Arlene manages to quell Arlie, she is tormented by three other symbols of her past; a guard Arlene knew in prison who is concerned only with seducing her; her mother, who succeeds in revealing that she is domineering and selfish; and a former pimp who tries to enlist Arlene's help in supporting his addiction. The drama's tension mounts as Arlene, who could be destroyed at any moment, faces each of these temptations. She realizes that "getting out," winning personal freedom, must be accomplished by oneself and that psychological prisons are the most difficult to escape.

Norman always mentions in interviews the feelings of isolation and terror she had while writing the play, that *Getting Out* represented her own emotional release. The play was much acclaimed in its 1977 Actors Theatre production in Louisville; it was voted best new play produced by a regional theater by the American Theatre Critics Association, and it was published in extract in *The Best Plays of 1977-1978* (1980), the first non-New York production ever so honored. *Getting Out* was given an Off-Broadway production at Marymount-Manhattan Theatre, in the Phoenix Theatre's 1978-1979 season, as well as a revival in May, 1979, at the Theatre De Lys, which ran eight months with highly favorable notices.

Third and Oak comprises a pair of one-act plays that explore psychological terrain similar to that of *Getting Out*. In *The Laundromat*, a widow and a woman trapped in a loveless marriage meet by chance in a local Laundromat and fall into a discussion of the ironic similarity of their lives. Both desperately need love, though neither can find it. As she would often do subsequently, Norman imposes a strict time limit on conversation and action, as long as it takes to finish a week's washing, and the commonplace setting further highlights the banality of her characters' lives. *The Pool Hall*, the second half of *Third and Oak*, takes the form of a parallel conversation between the owner of the hall and the son of a famous pool shark. It similarly deals with personal frustrations and unrealized hopes. *Third and Oak* was the major success of the Actors Theatre's 1978 season, but, more important, it marks a further development of the kinds of characterizations and situations typical in Norman's plays and anticipates the playwright's great achievement *'night, Mother*.

The simple language and ordinary women presented in *'night, Mother* contrast with the magnitude of the question with which it deals; whether a woman presumably in control of her life can rationally and with dignity end it if she chooses. Jessie Cates is, accordingly, typical of many suicide victims. She has no compelling or overwhelming crisis in her life at the time she chooses to end it. It is simply that she recognizes her life's mediocrity and tedium. Significantly, she blames neither herself nor anyone else for the failure of her marriage or the delinquency of her son. Indeed, she calmly tells her mother, Thelma Cates, what she plans to do, not to be dissuaded but to allow Thelma to understand better why she wants to die and to satisfy her mother's last wants.

Thelma has turned off her television set on the night of her daughter's suicide, no doubt the first time she has changed her usual routine in many evenings. The irony is that it has taken the crisis of Jessie's imminent suicide to force her into frank conversation with her daughter. Apparently, Thelma's life is as unfulfilling as her daughter's, but it is clear Thelma will never take her own life. She seems content with her small house, her sweets, her insipid friendships, and the superficial contacts she has with her son and daughter-in-law. Clearly, Norman has isolated a genuine paradox of the modern world: Crisis or impending catastrophe seems required for simple conversation; communication is otherwise limited to trivialities or sacrificed to television.

Her mother learns more about Jessie in her final ninety-minute conversation with her daughter than she has in a lifetime. The modern world ironically sets a premium on time; Norman emphasizes this with onstage clocks set at real time, 8:15 P.M. at the beginning of the performance, and running to the time of Jessie's suicide just before 10:00 P.M. Jessie makes repeated references to the time, particularly when her conversation with her mother falls into trivialities or becomes repetitive. Jessie's last act is to bequeath her wristwatch to her son. She is determined to kill herself on this evening, while she is in relative control of her own life. She is, therefore, certain that it is a rational decision, not influenced by her epilepsy or depression concerning her failed marriage or delinquent son.

The play has only two characters: Jessie and Thelma.

Their conversation takes place in the small living room of Thelma's house, a room filled with Thelma's possessions: magazines, candy dishes, afghans, quilts, and other examples of Thelma's needlework. The house is cluttered but comfortable, and it is clearly Thelma's: Nothing is clearly identifiable as Jessie's. She does not even own the gun with which she kills herself.

Jessie is in her late thirties or early forties and seems pale and physically unsteady. She has come through a difficult period following her illness and divorce but now seems in complete control. She is systematic and disciplined in her behavior, and the lists she writes, the pencil behind her ear, and the arrangements she makes throughout the play for Thelma's comfort serve to confirm that her decision to take her life, announced to her mother at the play's outset, is both rational and carefully considered.

Thelma is in her late fifties or early sixties and has begun to feel her age. She allows Jessie to do even the simplest tasks for her. Indeed, without realizing it, she has become inordinately dependent on her daughter. The audience, accordingly, comes to realize that the real objections Thelma has to Jessie's suicide involve her concern for herself, not her daughter. By the play's end, it is clear that Jessie, despite her younger age, shows far greater maturity than her mother.

The conversation between Thelma and Jessie that forms this play is a confrontation of life and death. While nearly all the audience obviously would choose life, it is ironic that Thelma clearly loses the argument with her daughter. She is never able to give Jessie a solid reason for continuing a life so obviously unsatisfactory.

Yet it is a tribute to Norman's skill that she allows her audience to reach its own, although inevitable, conclusion about Jessie and Thelma. Aside from the plot's requirement that they live somewhere outside town. Thelma's house could be in any section of the country. Though nothing is said about their educational attainments, it is clear that neither woman is intellectually inclined. Jessie has the greater sensitivity and potential, but her inability to realize this potential is the very thing that causes her suicide.

Norman writes all of her plays about largely forgotten people, individuals whose lives seem small, perhaps even mean, but who, faced with some large and overwhelming problem, rise to their own variety of eloquence. It is for this reason that Norman keeps the dialogue simple in the extreme. There are few extended speeches and little that is philosophical. She does not intend her play as a polemic on the place of suicide in the modern world, and the audience correspondingly views Jessie and Thelma as full individualized characters. Though this violates a norm of classical tragedy, it intensifies the drama, because the audience, while not admitting the inevitability or irreversibility of Jessie's decision, remains intent on discovering just what provoked it.

Norman has always maintained that it was precisely because she had no models that she came so late to drama. Nevertheless, it is clear from her studies at New York's Center for Understanding Media that she is a serious student of the theater in addition to being one of its most important developing playwrights. Her style is taut and spare, like that of Samuel Beckett, though her setting and characters are realistic. She deals easily with psychological questions, as in *Getting Out*, in which a young woman moves easily between Arlene, her present

self, and Arlie, the girl who committed the murder which sent her to prison.

Both *The Hold-up*, about would-be cowboys at the beginning of the twentieth century in New Mexico, and *Traveler in the Dark*, about a brilliant surgeon unable to cope with the death of his closest coworker, retain this close psychological scrutiny of characters in pain, using dialogue that is witty and eloquent by turns. Throughout her work, Norman shows an interest in fundamental human relationships as fired in the crucible of both familial and generational conflict. All of her characters, in their own way, are struggling to survive, to find some inner strength to cope with the disabling emotions that their situation inevitably provokes. With similarities in both themes and technique, Norman's work fits easily into the traditional canon of American drama that includes such playwrights as Lillian Hellman, Tennessee Williams, and Arthur Miller, to whom she is often compared.

Other major works

NOVEL: *The Fortune Teller*, 1987.
TELEPLAYS: *It's the Willingness*, 1980; *In Trouble at Fifteen*, 1980; *The Laundromat*, 1985.

Bibliography

Hart, Lynda. "Doing Time: Hunger for Power in Marsha Norman's Plays." *Southern Quarterly* 25 (Spring, 1987): 67-79.
McDonnell, Lisa J. "Diverse Similitude: Beth Henley and Marsha Norman." *Southern Quarterly* 25 (Spring, 1987): 95-104.
Simon, John. "Theatre Chronicle: Kopit, Norman, and Shepard." *The Hudson Review* 32 (Spring, 1979): 78-88.
Spencer, Jenny S. "Marsha Norman's She-Tragedies." In *Making a Spectacle: Feminist Essays on Contemporary Women's Theatre*, edited by Lynda Hart. Ann Arbor: University of Michigan Press, 1989.
_____. "Norman's *'night Mother*: Psycho-Drama of Female Identity." *Modern Drama* 30 (September, 1987): 364-375.
Wolfe, Irmgard H. "Marsha Norman: A Classified Bibliography." *Studies in American Drama, 1945-Present* 3 (1988): 149-175.

JOYCE CAROL OATES

Born: Lockport, New York; June 16, 1938

Principal long fiction

With Shuddering Fall, 1964; *A Garden of Earthly Delights*, 1967; *Expensive People*, 1968; *them*, 1969; *Wonderland*, 1971; *Do with Me What You Will*, 1973; *The Assassins: A Book of Hours*, 1975; *Childwold*, 1976; *The Triumph of the Spider Monkey*, 1976; *Son of the Morning*, 1978; *Unholy Loves*, 1979; *Cybele*, 1979; *Bellefleur*, 1980; *Angel of Light*, 1981; *A Bloodsmoor Romance*, 1982; *Mysteries of Winterthurn*, 1984; *Solstice*, 1985; *Marya: A Life*, 1986; *Lives of the Twins*, 1987 (as Rosamond Smith); *You Must Remember This*, 1987; *American Appetites*, 1989; *Soul/Mate*, 1989 (as Rosamond Smith); *Because It Is Bitter, and Because It Is My Heart*, 1990; *I Lock My Door Upon Myself*, 1990; *The Rise of Life on Earth*, 1991; *Black Water*, 1992; *Foxfire: Confessions of a Girl Gang*, 1993.

Other literary forms

Oates's first play, *Miracle Play*, appeared in 1974, and others have since opened to appreciative audiences. In addition her short-story anthologies have been published with regularity. They include *By the North Gate* (1963), which predated her first novel; *Upon the Sweeping Flood* (1966); *The Wheel of Love* (1970); *Marriages and Infidelities* (1972); *The Goddess and Other Women* (1974); *The Hungry Ghosts* (1974); *Where Are You Going, Where Have You Been?* (1974); *The Poisoned Kiss* (1975); *The Seduction* (1975); *Crossing the Border* (1976); *Night-Side* (1977); *All the Good People I've Left Behind* (1978); *A Sentimental Education* (1980); *Last Days* (1984); *Raven's Wing* (1986); *The Assignation* (1988); and many others. Oates is the editor of several anthologies, including *Night Walks* (1982) and *First Person Singular* (1983). Her poems have also been anthologized, and in 1974 Oates and her husband founded *The Ontario Review*.

Achievements

As a writer who avidly embraces the contingencies of this world and a teacher who maintains her classroom along with an amazing proliferation of writing, Joyce Carol Oates has been awarded numerous and varied prizes. Among them are the 1967, 1969, and 1973 O. Henry Prize Awards, the Richard and Hinda Rosenthal Foundation Award from the American Academy of Arts and Letters (1968), the National Book Award for 1970, and the Lotos Club Award of Merit (1975).

Biography

Joyce Carol Oates was born on June 16, 1938, in Lockport, New York. She received a modest education in a one-room schoolhouse and, as a child, had very little exposure to literature. This, however, did not quell her desire to write, and she spent much of her time as a child writing stories and short books. Even with all the writing and composing experience from her childhood, she would not publish her first story until 1959. While studying at Syracuse University, she won the *Mademoiselle* college fiction award for her short story "In the Old World." This would be her first in a series of public recognitions for her writing.

After receiving her B.A. from Syracuse in 1960, where she was valedictorian, she went on to receive her M.A. from the University of Wisconsin. During her term at Syracuse, she met her future husband, Raymond J. Smith, and they married in 1961. The Smiths then moved to Beaumont, Texas, and Oates began to work on her Ph.D. at Rice University. She did not accomplish this task; she and her husband moved to Michigan in 1962. While in Michigan, she taught English at the University of Detroit. In 1967, she and her husband began teaching at the University of Windsor in Ontario. During their tenure at the university, Smith and Oates cofounded *The*

Windsor Review. After leaving the university in 1978, she went on to join the Princeton University Creative Writing Program. While a member of this program, she wrote not only fiction but also some brilliant essays on writers ranging from William Shakespeare to Norman Mailer.

Analysis

There have been few writers to match Joyce Carol Oates for sheer numbers—her novels, plays, short stories, and poems appear to multiply by themselves on library shelves. Yet even though the curse of quantity is normally mediocrity, Oates consistently supplies a product of the highest quality, dense with meaning and filled with beautiful words and full-blown characters.

Oates's poor, unimaginative characters typically ply their swords through a fogged-in existence inflicted upon them by a fatalistic creator. They cannot escape from the miasma they must breathe, and so they are poisoned by it, confused by muddled thoughts in an unkind world. The characters finally become enraged by their situation and so do bloody battle to extricate themselves from it.

In her first novel, *With Shuddering Fall*, Oates introduced a theme that would pervade almost all the rest of her fiction works: the awful responsibility of freedom. Her characters struggle to divest themselves of their little lives in order to achieve personal freedom, but they are unable to cope with the consequences of their release from their former lives. They learn that they have abandoned not only their pasts but also their identities. Then they must struggle either to reclaim their selves or to forge new ones.

With Shuddering Fall is one character's reconciliation with her life, and this treaty gains for her a new appreciation of her history and that of her family. Karen must endure a sort of familiar ritual under the hands of her father, Hert, and her lover, Shar. At first Karen rejects her father's values. He is a legendary figure who wields great power and enjoys a close relationship with Karen; however, this is destroyed by the arrival of the violent, virile Shar who deposes Hert. Shar is not a new ruler, however, but an anarchist who wishes only to topple kings, not replace them. He leaves, and Karen follows, not because she believes in him but because she seeks to escape Hert and "a life dominated by fathers." Once free from her father, Karen begins to feel uprooted, aimless and nameless. Without Hert, she has "nothing of herself but a face, a body, a set of emotions." There is nothing of depth to her being. She discovers that she needs her familial history to add meaning to her identity and so finally refuses the history-less Shar and his attempts at nihilism.

One of Karen's trials is Shar's proclivity for race-car driving in the lowland town of Cherry River. Cherry River is a town that seems to exist for the edification of the summer tourists and little else. It offers appreciation of self-gratification but not of history. The high point of the summer seems to be when Shar commits suicide on the race track. Oates seems to be saying that, in a community with no shared history, the only communal ties that exist are with shared acts of violence.

The spokesperson for the novel is Max, a self-centered businessman, who is the only one intelligent enough to share Oates's philosophy with the reader. He appears in many other novels as the maniacal oracle who tries to make Fate subservient to his will. He tries to cheat Karen of her birthright by confounding her with questions, but she eludes him and is, thus, saved. She returns to herself, her family.

It is not chance that Lewis Carroll's child adventure and Oates's novel *Wonderland* bear the same word in the title. Oates considers the work of this nineteenth century English mathematician to ask the pertinent questions of life: Can all of life be just a game, and am I the only one who is not cheating? Both protagonists in the novels—Alice and Jesse Harte—run and jump from square to square on a large, mostly unseen chessboard. Along the way they are both transmogrified into oddly sized versions of their original selves. Finally, in order to survive, Jesse and Alice regain their normal proportions and become resolved with their communities.

In the beginning of Oates's novel, the newly orphaned Jesse travels from his grandfather's farm to an orphanage and finally to the home of Dr. Pedersen, a brilliant but unbalanced surrogate father. He is the first of a triumvirate of adoptive fathers whom Jesse must survive. His biological father's initial attack has given Jesse the strength to deal with these surrogates. His father has slaughtered his wife and their unborn child and wounded Jesse before killing himself. Jesse escapes to his grandfather's farm, where he recuperates until he must start his strange odyssey. In the Pedersen family, Jesse learns of things small and fantastic. He studies cell life and becomes involved in Dr. Pedersen's cancer research. The more he learns, the more he is confused by his father's view of life, which is overshadowed by death. At last, Pedersen grows impatient with Jesse and dismisses him from the family, saying "You have no existence. You are nothing." Jesse must seek another, more receptive, lifestyle.

Jesse enters medical school, is graduated, marries, and tries to forge a new family, a home, for himself. He keeps returning, however, to the site of his father's tragic demise in his dreams. His own children gradually start to shrink away like the Cheshire cat. Michelle becomes Shelley and ultimately Shell, until Jesse can no longer grasp her—or the rest of his family—with any degree of certitude. Even Jesse's two father-figures, Drs. Cady and Perrault, become in turn distant and disdainful. Dr. Cady will not acknowledge anything but the ethereal, and Dr. Perrault will not admit that the mind is anything but actual. These two opposing views further succeed in alienating Jesse from a "real" life. To offset these unrealistic real people, Jesse creates an unreal friend, or series of friends, but she only promises disharmony and death, so he eventually rejects her, too.

In the end of the novel, the action picks up speed, racing toward the now of the narrative, 1971. Jesse finally returns to his father's psyche and discovers the final, perfect answer: "A clean, pure, empty being, a void." It is only through the total destruction of the universe that a peaceful existence (or nonexistence) can be enjoyed.

The setting of *Childwold* is again Eden Valley, scene of the action in *With Shuddering Fall* and *Wonderland*. The novel is peopled by a variety of characters and is narrated by several of them in turn, as each becomes the lover of the central figure's mother, Arlene Bartlett. Arlene's daughter, Laney Bartlett, is the unconscious catalyst for much of the violence in the novel.

The primary reaction occurs between Laney and Fitz John Kasch, a fiftyish hermit who lives among the debris of his large but deceased family. In Laney, Kasch sees not only his failed marriage but also his repressed desires. She becomes for him both icon and a Tantalus, love and passion. Unable to avail himself of her, Kasch woos and wins Arlene and becomes another in a lengthy retinue of lovers.

Arlene is a figure of the sex goddess, but, unlike so many untouchable figures, she is the small statue in the back of the church, worn down by the grasp of many hands. This, however, does not dismay her; indeed, it invigorates her. Where many single women would not welcome pregnancy, Arlene revels in it; her children reaffirm her existence in a world of many people. Kasch, on the other hand, is unable to enjoy the company of others. He secrets himself in a small part of what was once the family manse, now a museum. He blames his self-imposed isolation on his divorce, brought on by his former wife's infidelity. Retiring into his hermitage, however, only amplifies his feelings of detachment from life. Although he seeks to redefine himself in various ways (as a voyeur, among others), he remains at one, in harmony with only himself. When he finally becomes reconciled to the Bartletts' violent way of life, he remains unfulfilled. He can satiate himself neither with the daughter nor with the mother.

Instead of an object of violence, of rape or murder, Laney becomes an object of Kasch's creation. It is at this point that *Childwold* most neatly resembles Vladmir Nabakov's *Lolita*: the story of a middle-aged man's obsession with a nubile teenager. As did Humbert Humbert, Kasch casts a spell about Laney, using art as a medium, but she escapes, moving through the two-dimensional world of Kasch's photographs to the world of nature outside his museum/prison. She frees herself from the world he is doomed to inhabit.

It is a world that is of his own design. After Arlene has joined Kasch, her former lover, Earl Tuller, returns to threaten and bully her. In a rage, Kasch kills him and seals his fate as a prisoner. He has dreamed of being a murderer, but now that his fantasy has been accidentally granted, he is unable to bear the results. He has been defeated by his own desires mixed with the mindless tide of the universe. The novel ends with Arlene musing over the turn of events their lives have taken. Laney returns to Kasch's mansion, but he will not answer the door. Imagining that she sees him behind a curtained window, she calls out. She feels she is strong enough, has changed enough from the girl that she was, to save him, and so in a flash of anticipation she waits for "a sign, a sign," but it never comes. Oates demonstrates in *Childwold* the tragic consequences of the conflict between human ambitions and the machinations of the world.

In *Bellefleur*, Oates combines the Gothic grotesque and a sense of realism to create a novel that, incredibly, has believable unhuman creatures. If this type of book seems out of character for her, it may be she wishes to warn her audience that what seems extraordinary may, upon examination, be simply ordinary. In one episode, a huge rodent runs screaming into the house; the next morning, it is nothing but a cat. On the other hand, normality might suddenly become monstrous.

Bellefleur traces the history of the Bellefleur family through several generations and as many psychological aberrations. There are psychics in the family, the gnome who serves Leah Bellefleur, and several ghosts. Jedediah Bellefleur is the manifestation in this novel of the character who forces himself to exist against the will of nature. He is a recurring character in Oates's novels, and in *Bellefleur*, Jedediah is delightfully crazy. In the end, he is persuaded to continue the Bellefleur line despite his (and the reader's) misgivings.

The novel is difficult to read, because it jumps back and forth from past to present. Another difficulty stems from the fact that the main character of interest, the telepathic Germaine Bellefleur, ages only four years from her birth during the entire action of the novel, but her father ages two or three decades. The setting of the novel itself—the Adirondack mountain range—ages thousands of years. In addition, the mountains and the people shrink or grow spasmodically. The final chapters contain spiritual references that, at first, seem disjointed. After Gideon's transformation into the skeletal Angel of Death, however, an American Indian appears to the ancestral Jedediah and tells him to embrace the world that he has abandoned. This is Oates's final message to the reader, that only in a full and relished life is there union with God's body. Thus, as in her first novel, Oates's characters do battle with their own existences, their own beings. They struggle, escape, and wander only to return to their initial resting places within themselves and within the confines of their destinies.

The characters in *Mysteries of Winterthurn*, however, appear to have relinquished their resting places for ghostly—and ghastly—forays among the living. This Gothic mystery novel has been hailed as a feminist dissertation, a charge that has not been denied by Oates. Although the main character is male and the action in the novel is seen through his eyes, most of the victims are women and children, and it is to their plight that the narrator and the reader grow sympathetic. In *Mysteries of Winterthurn*, Oates discusses the existence of women in a male-dominated society, and a pitiable existence it is.

Even though Oates owes much of her presentation of

the situation of nineteenth century women and children to several other popular authors, her interpretation is uniquely her own. Her victims are disposable pawns in a society that is more than willing to sacrifice them for its own (male) devices. Oates inserts the supernatural into the novel to allow her women a modicum of revenge upon these perpetrators. If this seems to be impossible (the unreal attacking the real), Oates insists that once something is thought to be real, it becomes so whether it should be real or not. Thus, the view of women as passive, thoughtless beings is true for the males in her novel, even though it is a false concept. The women victims in the novel are freed by this misconception to react violently to those who misuse them because they (the women) cannot have acted in such a manner within the male scheme of things.

To drive this point home, Oates repeats it three times during the novel. The first story, "The Virgin in the Rose-Bower," deals with a sadistic husband and father, Erasmus Kilgarven, who has a hand in the brutal deaths of his two wives and commits incest for several years with his daughter, Georgina, causing her to become pregnant several times. Georgina kills her infants but claims that they have been destroyed by angels painted on the ceiling of her bedroom. The narrator, young Xavier Kilgarven, sees one painted angel bleed, and this leads to the discovery of several other infant corpses, silent witnesses to Erasmus Kilgarven's hideous habit. By claiming supernatural murder (and rape), Georgina is able to evade guilt and exact a small amount of revenge on her father.

In the persona of Iphigenia, her pen name, Georgina is also able to free her female family members by publishing poetry. The money she receives from this enterprise, until her father forbids it as unseemly, is later used to finance even more unfeminine exploits by a second sister, the young Perdita. Perdita needs no spectral avenger; she takes matters into her own hands, although she is never seen as a murderer by anyone but the reader. The only people who are capable of violent acts in *Mysteries of Winterthurn* are male; the females are those upon whom these acts are perpetrated. Thus, an invisible shield is created around Perdita, enabling her to murder several people in order to achieve her goal, union with young Xavier.

The third sister, Thérèse, is able to profit from her sisters' cloaked deeds, and, indeed, there are indications that she may be involved in Perdita's violent crimes in a peripheral manner. Yet this is only hinted at; outwardly, Thérèse appears to be a happy, modern woman. It is here that Oates's use of paradox—the woman who is both angel and demon, visible and invisible—culminates. All the women in the novel have been so seduced by the theory of their own guilt that they must violently oppose it in order to free themselves.

Other major works

SHORT FICTION: *By the North Gate*, 1963; *Upon the Sweeping Flood*, 1966; *The Wheel of Love*, 1970; *Marriages and Infidelities*, 1972; *The Goddess and Other Women*, 1974; *The Hungry Ghosts*, 1974; *Where Are You Going, Where Have You Been?*, 1974; *The Poisoned Kiss*, 1975; *The Seduction*, 1975; *Crossing the Border*, 1976; *Night-Side*, 1977; *All the Good People I've Left Behind*, 1978; *A Sentimental Education*, 1980; *Last Days*, 1984; *Raven's Wing*, 1986; *The Assignation*, 1988.

PLAYS: *Miracle Play*, 1974; *Three Plays*, 1980.

POETRY: *Women in Love*, 1968; *Anonymous Sins*, 1969; *Love and Its Derangements*, 1970; *Angel Fire*, 1973; *The Fabulous Beasts*, 1975; *Women Whose Lives Are Food, Men Whose Lives Are Money*, 1978; *Invisible Woman: New and Selected Poems, 1970-1982*, 1982.

NONFICTION: *The Edge of Impossibility: Tragic Forms in Literature*, 1972; *The Hostile Sun: The Poetry of D. H. Lawrence*, 1973; *New Heaven, New Earth: The Visionary Experience in Literature*, 1974; *Contraries: Essays*, 1981; *The Profane Art: Essays and Reviews*, 1983; *On Boxing*, 1987; *(Woman) Writer: Occasions and Opportunities*, 1988.

ANTHOLOGIES: *Scenes from American Life: Contemporary Short Fiction*, 1972; *The Best American Short Stories of 1979*, 1979 (with Shannon Ravenel); *Night Walks: A Bedside Companion*, 1982; *First Person Singular: Writers on Their Craft*, 1983.

Bibliography

Chell, Cara. "Un-tricking the Eye: Joyce Carol Oates and the Feminist Ghost Story." *Arizona Quarterly* 41 (Spring, 1985): 5-23.

Creighton, Joanne V. *Joyce Carol Oates*. Boston: Twayne, 1979.

_____. *Joyce Carol Oates: Novels of the Middle Years*. New York: Twayne, 1992.

Friedman, Ellen G. *Joyce Carol Oates*. New York: Frederick Ungar, 1980.

Grant, Mary Kathryn. *The Tragic Vision of Joyce Carol Oates*. Durham, N.C.: Duke University Press, 1978.

Waller, G. F. *Dreaming America*. Baton Rouge: Louisiana State University Press, 1970.

EDNA O'BRIEN

Born: Tuamgraney, Ireland; December 15, 1930

Principal long fiction

The Country Girls, 1960; *The Lonely Girl*, 1962 (reprinted in 1964 as *Girl with Green Eyes*); *Girls in Their Married Bliss*, 1964; *August Is a Wicked Month*, 1965; *Casualties of Peace*, 1966; *A Pagan Place*, 1970; *Zee & Co.*, 1971; *Night*, 1972; *I Hardly Knew You*, 1977; *The Country Girls Trilogy and Epilogue*, 1986; *The High Road*, 1988; *Time and Tide*, 1992.

Other literary forms

Edna O'Brien's short stories appear regularly in magazines such as *The New Yorker* and *The Atlantic*; some of them have been collected in *The Love Object* (1968), *A Scandalous Woman and Other Stories* (1974), and *Mrs. Reinhardt* (1978). O'Brien has also written plays, including *A Cheap Bunch of Nice Flowers* (1962) and *Virginia* (1980); screenplays, such as for *Girl with Green Eyes* (1964), *Time Lost and Time Remembered* (1966), *Three into Two Won't Go* (1969), and *X, Y, and Zee* (1971); television plays, including *Mrs. Reinhardt* (1981); and nonfiction, including the autobiographical *Mother Ireland* (1976), the travel book *Arabian Days* (1977), an anthology entitled *Some Irish Loving* (1979), and an essay on the Joyces, *James and Nora* (1981).

Achievements

Nearly always from a female narrator's point of view, O'Brien has brilliantly transmuted her personal experiences into art. Her recall and selection of the tiny details that make up the texture of life, particularly in her Irish scenes, are most dazzling. Impressive, too, is her evident love and savoring of words for their own sake and often in good dialogue. Perhaps because of the speed with which she works, the vivacity and brilliance of her prolific output is frequently marred by awkward grammar, punctuation, and syntax. Apparently, her editors have felt these stylistic lapses are all part of her Irish use of the language and have accordingly let them stand.

O'Brien was a feminist before the term became fashionable, but her works also affirm a wider humanistic sympathy for all people. Early, she took up the topics of women's attitudes toward their bodies, their sexuality, and their roles as mothers and daughters. In Ireland her books are banned because of their often negative comments on the Roman Catholic church, more common in her early work, and her frequent employment of graphic sexual terms and scenes. Outside Ireland, her reputation as a writer of fiction seems assured. Her acclaim will be even more certain when she can distance more effectively the bitterness she feels about her Irish upbringing, achieving the balance typical of the best of the many Irish writers in exile.

Biography

Edna O'Brien was born to Michael and Lena (Cleary) O'Brien in Tuamgraney, County Clare, Ireland, on December 15, 1930. She has one brother and two sisters. She first attended Scarriff National School in 1936, then boarded at the Convent of Mercy, Loughrea, County Galway, in 1941 before going off to the Pharmaceutical College in Dublin in 1946. In 1951, O'Brien married novelist Ernest Gebler (the marriage ended in 1964). Two sons were born, in 1952 and 1954. In 1959, the family moved to London and O'Brien's career as a published writer was quickly launched: In three weeks, far from County Clare, she wrote *The Country Girls*, tracing the development of fourteen-year-old Caithleen Brady. The trilogy was continued in *The Lonely Girl* and *Girls in Their Married Bliss*, and appended with *Epilogue* in 1986.

Since 1959, O'Brien has been based in London, frequently traveling abroad to Europe, the Middle East, and the Americas—for pleasure and profit, as a tourist and as a reader-lecturer.

Analysis

Edna O'Brien's concerns are most readily accessible in her very eccentric travel/autobiography *Mother Ireland*. Her Irishness is something of which O'Brien is proud: "It's a state of mind." She is not, however, blind to Ireland's faults, appreciating that there must be something "secretly catastrophic" about a country that so many people leave. After an iconoclastic opening chapter on Irish history, with its uncanonized patron saint and its paunchy Firbolgs, follow six chapters in which are sketched O'Brien's dominant themes: loneliness, the longing for adventure (often sexual), the repressive Irish Roman Catholic church, family ties (the martyred mother and the rollicking father), and the courageous hopelessness with which life at best must be lived.

It would be a melancholy picture if it were not for O'Brien's saving, ironic sense of humor and the skill with which she roots her observations in the sensual details of the actual world. Her readers share vividly in her world of wet batteries for radios, ink-powder, walls with fragments of bottles embedded in their tops, Fox's (Glacier) Mints, orange-boxes, and lice fine-combed from a child's head onto a newspaper. O'Brien's recurring themes, her experiments with form, and the feeling she succeeds in communicating that this Irish microcosm has its universal significance are all clearly present in *Mother Ireland*.

From its detailed, evocative opening page, redolent of genteel poverty, *The Country Girls*, O'Brien's first novel, serves notice of an unusual voice. The shy and sensitive Caithleen tells her first-person story and shares the action with her alter ego, the volatile and malicious Baba. It is a world divided into two warring camps, male and female, where Caithleen's aspirations toward romantic love are doomed to failure. Mr. Gentleman is the first in a long line of rotters (the drunken, brutal father; Eugene Gaillard; Herod; Dr. Flaggler), far outnumbering the few men with decent inclinations (Hickey, Auro); in such a world women stand little chance, single, married in the usual sense, or brides of Christ.

The repressive effects of poverty and a patriarchal society are hardly alleviated by the Church and its proscriptions. Her mother drowned, Caithleen spends her mid-teen years boarding in a strict convent-school from which Baba contrives their expulsion for writing a ribald note. In their late teens, joyously, they come up to Dublin, Baba to take a commercial course, Caithleen to work as a grocer's assistant until she can take the Civil Service

examinations. Loneliness, however, follows them: Baba contracts tuberculosis, and Caithleen's Mr. Gentleman lets her down. Yet, with the resilience of youth, her last line in this novel is, "I was almost certain that I wouldn't sleep that night."

The Lonely Girl continues the sage two years later, with Baba healthy again. It is, however, largely Caithleen's story; again she is the narrator. The repressive effects of her family, her village community, and her convent education are again in evidence. O'Brien has her heroine involved romantically with Eugene Gaillard, whose face reminds her of a saint, and who is about the same height as her father; he is a cultivated snob, and in an often cold fashion he begins the further education of his naïve, prudish, "student," both in bed and in the salon. (In *Edna O'Brien*, 1974, Grace Edkley points out that Caithleen's stiff tutor and O'Brien's former husband, Ernest Gebler, share the same initials.) At the novel's conclusion, Caithleen, wild and debased "because of some damned man," is learning, is changing; she is, as she says, finding her feet, "and when I'm able to talk I imagine that I won't be alone." Still seeking their connection, she and Baba sail on the *Hibernia*, from Dublin to Liverpool and London.

Girls in Their Married Bliss continues the story of the two in London, where, for the first time, Baba assumes the first-person narration, alternating with an omniscient voice distancing O'Brien and the reader from Caithleen's role. The women, now about twenty-five years old, have not left their Irish baggage behind in Dublin; there is a splendid, blustery Celtic quality to the scapegrace Baba's style. Kate (as Caithleen is called), too, has her share of one-liners, word associations, epigrams, and zany metaphors. "Self-interest," she observes on one occasion, "was a common crime." On another, at a party, she is amused by a girl wearing a strawberry punnet on her head to make herself taller.

In these early novels, O'Brien, like her leading characters, is learning and developing her skills. In *Girls in Their Married Bliss*, the topic is still the female search for love and connection: The novel is a precisely observed account of a marriage failing. People rub exquisitely on one another's nerves in the larger context of women's role in society; in the smaller context of bedroom politics, "Men are pure fools." Marriage, at least on the grounds on which the women enter it here, is evidently no end to the quest: Baba makes a calculated move for comfort; Kate sees that her interest in people is generated solely by her own needs. They have matured to the point where they no longer believe much in romantic plans. Kate's answer to the biological unfairness of God's scheme for women, as Baba sees it, is to have herself sterilized. She will not make the same mistake again: No other child of hers will be abducted by its father; no further child of hers will in its turn become a parent.

The complete trilogy was reissued in 1986 in one volume, with the brief *Epilogue* in the form of a monologue delivered by Baba. Here the ebullient Baba brings the reader up to date: The despairing Kate is dead; she drowned, perhaps deliberately.

In O'Brien's next novel, *August Is a Wicked Month*, an omniscient narrator describes the protagonist's abortive attempts at self-liberation, largely through sexual activity. Ellen is a Kate-like, superstitious, convent-bred, twenty-eight-year-old Irish magazine writer, formerly a nurse, living in London when the novel begins. She takes a trip to France when the husband from whom she is separated and their eight-year-old son, Mark, who lives with her, go on a camping holiday together. Her "pathetic struggles towards wickedness" involve rejecting the first sexual invitations she encounters. Eventually, however, when Ellen does become intimately involved with a high-living group, O'Brien subjects her to two catastrophic accidents: She receives a call from her husband, who tells her that her son has been killed by a car in a roadside accident, and she fears, wrongly as it turns out, that she has contracted a sexually transmitted disease. The guilt and the judgment are clear; perhaps they are too clear to make this novel an artistic success. Ellen finally finds an uneasy autumnal peace, unlike the women in O'Brien's next novel, who have a genuine joy ripped away from them.

In *Casualties of Peace*, Willa McCord, artist in glass, and her earthy domestic, Patsy Wiley, are the protagonists, exemplary victims of male violence. An omniscient narrator views the two unhappy women—Willa having escaped from a nightmarish marriage to the sadistic Herod, Patsy presently suffering her husband Tom's blows. Both have their dreams of happiness outside marriage shattered. There was a chance for peace for them, but accidents prevented them from knowing joy: Patsy blabs to Willa about leaving Tom rather than doing it immediately, as planned, and her lover, Ron, believes she has let him down; Willa, just when a loving connec-

tion with Auro seems possible, is murdered by Tom, who mistakes her for Pasty.

Patsy's love letters to Ron are reminiscent of the earthiest of James Joyce and Nora Barnacle's correspondence; Patsy indeed is a kind of Molly Bloom figure (more clearly developed in *Night*). Willa's letters to Auro, delivered posthumously, share the same stream-of-consciousness qualities: Words pile up into lists, associations trigger other more graphic associations, and "memory is the bugger." At times lyrical, at times humorous, O'Brien develops here the Celtic flair with words that is associated with Joyce or Dylan Thomas. Her theme is loneliness and its myriad causes; her characters search to alleviate their pain, to make connections, to overcome their feelings of guilt for being themselves.

A Pagan Place is a very odd novel; it is largely a sophisticated rewrite of *The Country Girls*, as O'Brien perhaps would have written that work had she had ten years more reading, writing, and living behind her at the time. Baba is dropped in favor of one unnamed, preadolescent girl whose sexual arousal when her father beats her accomplishes her move toward adolescence. Getting away from her Irish family and Irish community with their hereditary guilt will, it is suggested, take her yet a stage further. At the end of the novel, she leaves to the accompaniment of an eerie Hibernian howl.

Throughout the work an omniscient narrator, who sometimes uses dialect forms, sometimes very erudite words, and who is clearly unreliable in matters of fact (putting an English "general" on Nelson's pillar), places the reader at the center of the action by using the second-person narrative. No one but "you," then, is at the center of the action; the narrator and the writer are similarly distanced from the action. Perhaps in this novel O'Brien exorcised the worst of her Irishness; certainly, very violent feelings surface, all in the consciousness of a young girl. O'Brien, in contrast to her contemporaries among Irish writers of fiction, such as Brian Friel or Benedict Kiely, really seems to dislike her Celtic community. Here is a very bitter indictment of the Church, and perhaps its ultimate rejection in the priest's attempt to seduce "you." Here, too, is a savage, repressive, guilt-ridden world of so-called Christians, where unwed mothers receive no *caritas*, where legally wed mothers and fathers show no love either. It is a world where Holy Water is sprinkled on thoroughbred foals, where a black dog, chasing a frog that jumps out of the ashes at Della's wake, is seen as one and the same with the devil. All in all, it is, with few exceptions, a nightmarish community, especially for a child. For "you" as a child at the center of this world, deserted even by "your" mother at one period, a thing "you" thought would never happen, the only certainty is that "you" want to escape, whatever the burden of guilt "you" carry.

The theme of escape is continued in *Zee & Co.*, where O'Brien's heroines are back in London, and again, a pair. Zee moves increasingly aggressively and ruthlessly to hold her man, Robert, while dominating Stella, her rival. She succeeds in both endeavors. As the war of the sexes heats up, Zee refuses to be a victim: She is no patsy (or Patsy). O'Brien's long preoccupation with the defensive role of women in society appears to be shifting to the offensive in her later works as her heroines themselves become less fragmented. A person needs to be integrated psychically to withstand not only sexual partners and spouses but also all manifestations of phantoms, prejudice, repression, guilt, and loneliness. This new positive attitude is well illustrated in the rambunctious Mary Hooligan, whose nightlong monologue forms O'Brien's next work, *Night*.

In form and style, *Night* is O'Brien's most Joycean novel. In a harangue from her bed in England, Mary Hooligan—Irish, abused, divorced—delivers herself of an aggressive, courageous, independent, first-person autobiographical statement. Beginning with an Anglo-Saxon monosyllable in the opening paragraph, the non-conciliatory tone of her monologue is established. "I am a woman," Mary affirms, and proceeds to weave, in time and place, the story of her connection with her father and mother, her former husband—"the original Prince of Darkness"—and her son. It is an exuberant linguistic spree: from a "trepidation" of gelatin-like dessert to the welcome "tap o' the mornin'," metaphors and apt words are savored and invented. The pervasive humor is wry; the aggressive tone and confident technique perfectly match the content of a work whose burden is rebellion against loveless unions and ignorance.

Mary Hooligan is another in O'Brien's procession of outsiders, an Irish woman in England, merely house-sitting so even less important in the community. O'Brien, however, establishes Mary as a force on her own: Mary rejects her friend, Madge (Mary needs no Kate figure to complement her being). The theme under review remains the eternal search for love in its myriad manifestations; what is new here is the heroine's joyful attack as she continues her pilgrimage to "the higher shores of love."

Family, community, and marriage settings are again explored. Many of the details are familiar: the vicious father, the ignoramuses who could not tell cheese from soap, the cold-fish husband. Constant and familiar in O'Brien's work is the warm regard for children, particularly the mothers' regard for their sons. This aspect of love leads her to flirt with incest in her most violent work, *I Hardly Knew You*, where the narrator has an affair with and then murders her son's friend.

Nora, the protagonist of *I Hardly Knew You*, tells her story in yet another night monologue, from her prison cell, as she awaits trial for the murder of Hart, her young lover. Again, O'Brien's narrator is an Irish exile in England, divorced from an overly frugal husband, with a son, and literally in prison, isolated from all society. Loneliness is at the core of her existence, as it is, she remarks, at the core of Celtic songs. Her monologue shuffles time and space more formally than Mary Hooligan's in *Night* and reveals a world of increasing violence. Details and incidents from O'Brien's previous works, as far back even as *The Country Girls*, show up: the drunken father taking the cure; the abducted-child threat; the child scraping the toilet-seat paint; the kicking-match engaged in by the brutish relatives. The world has become an increasingly violent place, and the response of O'Brien's narrator matches it. Like Mary's, Nora's personality is integrated, but toward the Kate side. She engages in an explicitly lesbian encounter, but she needs no other woman to complement her. Indeed, she acts increasingly like the worst stereotype of the sadistic male predator, who uses and abuses other people, particularly women and especially wives. This is a chilling picture of a person driven to violence, to kill without regret. Here is a woman who has lost her balance and whose sweeping indictment of men must surely be viewed as just as reprehensible as male chauvinism. "I am proud . . . to have killed one of the breed to whom I owe nothing but cruelty, deceit, and the asp's emission," she avers, ignoring absolutely O'Brien's often stated support for "human decency" and kindness among people of whatever sex.

O'Brien is a writer from Ireland whose many years there profoundly affected her view of the world, and particularly of women's relationships and their place in society. Being Irish, she says in *Mother Ireland*, gives one a unique view of pleasure and punishment, life and death. O'Brien's work is lyrical and lively. Her memory for people and places, for the minutiae of daily living, is prodigious; her zest for language is Joycean. She is often on the attack, but at her best, which is often, she transcends her immediate cause to encourage, with a grain of humor, those who still dream of love achieved through kindness and decency—common virtues still no more common than they ever were.

Other major works

SHORT FICTION: *The Love Object*, 1968; *A Scandalous Woman and Other Stories*, 1974; *Mrs. Reinhardt*, 1978 (better known as *A Rose in the Heart*); *Returning*, 1982; *A Fanatic Heart*, 1984; *Lantern Slides*, 1990.
PLAYS: *A Cheap Bunch of Nice Flowers*, 1962; *A Pagan Place,* 1972; *Virginia,* 1980.
SCREENPLAYS: *Girl with Green Eyes*, 1964; *Time Lost and Time Remembered*, 1966 (with Desmond Davis); *Three into Two Won't Go*, 1969; *X, Y, and Zee*, 1971.
TELEPLAYS: *The Wedding Dress*, 1963; *Nothing's Ever Over*, 1968; *Mrs. Reinhardt*, 1981.
NONFICTION: *Mother Ireland*, 1976; *Arabian Days*, 1977; *Some Irish Loving*, 1979; *James and Nora*, 1981.
CHILDREN'S LITERATURE: *The Dazzle*, 1986.

Bibliography

Eckley, Grace. *Edna O'Brien*. Lewisburg, Pa.: Bucknell University Press, 1974.
Guppy, Shusha. "The Art of Fiction, LXXXII: Edna O'Brien." *Paris Review* 26 (Summer, 1984): 22-50.
Haule, James M. "Tough Luck: The Unfortunate Birth of Edna O'Brien." *Colby Library Quarterly* 23 (December, 1987): 216-224.
O'Brien, Peggy. "The Silly and the Serious: An Assessment of Edna O'Brien." *The Massachusetts Review* 18 (Autumn, 1987): 474-488.
Roth, Philip. "A Conversation with Edna O'Brien." *The New York Times Book Review*, November 18, 1984, 38-40.

FLANNERY O'CONNOR

Born: Savannah, Georgia; March 25, 1925   **Died:** Milledgeville, Georgia; August 3, 1964

Principal short fiction

A Good Man Is Hard to Find, 1955; *Everything That Rises Must Converge*, 1965; *The Complete Stories*, 1971.

Other literary forms

In addition to writing thirty-one short stories, Flannery O'Connor wrote two short novels, *Wise Blood* (1952) and *The Violent Bear It Away* (1960). A collection of her essays and occasional prose entitled *Mystery and Manners* (1969) was edited by Robert and Sally Fitzgerald, and a collection of letters entitled *The Habit of Being* (1979) was edited by Sally Fitzgerald. More correspondence is collected in *The Correspondence of Flannery O'Connor and Brainard Cheneys* (1986), edited by C. Ralph Stephens. O'Connor also wrote book reviews, largely for the Catholic press; these are collected in *The Presence of Grace* (1983), which was compiled by Leo J. Zuber and edited by Carter W. Martin.

Achievements

The fiction of O'Connor has been highly praised for its unrelenting irony, its symbolism, and its unique comedy. Today, O'Connor is considered one of the most important American writers of the short story, and she is frequently compared with William Faulkner as a writer of short fiction.

For an author with a relatively small literary output, O'Connor has received an enormous amount of attention. More than twenty-five books devoted to her have appeared beginning in the early 1960's, when significant critics worldwide began to recognize O'Connor's gifts as a fiction writer. Almost all critical works have emphasized the bizarre effects of reading O'Connor's fiction, which, at its best, powerfully blends the elements of southwestern humor, the Southern grotesque, Catholic and Christian theology and philosophy, atheistic and Christian existentialism, realism, and romance. Most critics have praised and interpreted O'Connor from a theological perspective and noted how unusual her fiction is, as it unites the banal, the inane, and the trivial with Christian, though fundamentally humorous, tales of proud Georgians fighting battles with imaginary or real agents of God sent out to shake some sense into the heads of the protagonists.

In her lifetime, O'Connor won recognition, but she would be surprised at the overwhelming response from literary critics that her fiction has received since her death. O'Connor won O. Henry Awards for her stories "The Life You Save May Be Your Own," "A Circle in the Fire," "Greenleaf," "Everything That Rises Must Converge," and "Revelation." *The Complete Stories*, published posthumously in 1971, won the National Book Award for Fiction. O'Connor received many other honors, including several grants and two honorary degrees.

Biography

Flannery O'Connor's relatively short life was, superficially, rather uneventful. O'Connor was born on March 25, 1925, in Savannah, Georgia, to Regina Cline and Edward Francis O'Connor, Jr. She was their only child. O'Connor's father worked in real estate and construction, and the family lived in Savannah until 1938, when the family moved to Atlanta. In that year, Edward O'Connor became a zone real estate appraiser for the Federal Housing Administration (FHA). Shortly thereafter, O'Connor and her mother moved to Milledgeville, Georgia, and her father became so ill that he had to resign from his job in Atlanta and move to Milledgeville. On February 1, 1941, Edward O'Connor died.

In her youth, O'Connor was diagnosed with the same disease that had killed her father when she was almost sixteen. Her short life would end tragically from complications related to disseminated lupus, a disease that attacks the body's vital organs. From the fall of 1938 until her death, O'Connor spent most of her life in Milledgeville, except for brief hiatuses. After graduating from the experimental Peabody High School in 1942, O'Connor entered Georgia State College for Women (now Georgia College) in Milledgeville, where she majored in sociology and English and was graduated with an A.B. degree in June, 1945. While in college, she was gifted both in drawing comic cartoons and in writing. In September, 1945, O'Connor enrolled at the State University of Iowa with a journalism scholarship, and in 1946, her first story, "The Geranium" (later revised several times until it became "Judgement Day," her last story), was published in *Accent*. In 1947, she received the master of fine arts degree and enrolled for postgraduate work in the prestigious Writers' Workshop. She was honored in 1948 by receiving a place at Yaddo, an artists' colony in Saratoga Springs, New York.

Planning never to return to the South, O'Connor lived briefly in New York City in 1949 but later moved to Ridgefield, Connecticut, to live with Robert and Sally Fitzgerald. Robert Fitzgerald is best known as a classics scholar and a translator of such works as the *Odyssey* and *The Theban Plays*. City life was too much for O'Connor, but she became quickly acclimated to life in slower-paced Ridgefield. In January, 1950, she underwent an operation while visiting her mother during Christmas. O'Connor remained in Milledgeville until she returned to Ridgefield in March.

In December, 1950, O'Connor became extremely ill en route to Milledgeville for Christmas. At first, it was believed that she was suffering from acute rheumatoid arthritis, but in February, after being taken to Emory University Hospital in Atlanta, O'Connor was diagnosed with disseminated lupus erythematosus. As a result of her illness, O'Connor would remain under the care of her mother for the rest of her life, and in March, 1951, she and her mother moved from the former governor's mansion in Milledgeville to Andalusia, the family's dairy farm. Though her illness restricted her life considerably, she was able to achieve greatness as a writer, with a literary output that had already become a permanent part of the canon of American literature from the post-World War II era.

Physicians were able to control the effects of lupus for years through the use of cortisone and other drugs, but in early 1964, O'Connor, suffering from anemia, was diagnosed with a fibroid tumor. The operation to rid her of the tumor reactivated the lupus, and O'Connor died of kidney failure in August, 1964. In her last months, most of which were spent in hospitals, O'Connor worked slowly but conscientiously on the fiction that was to appear in her second (and posthumous) collection of short stories, *Everything That Rises Must Converge*.

Analysis

Flannery O'Connor is uncharacteristic of her age. In writing about the pervasive disbelief in the Christian mysteries of contemporary times, O'Connor seems better suited to the Middle Ages in her rather old-fashioned and conventional Catholic and Christian conviction that the central issue in human existence is salvation through Christ. Perhaps the recognition that such conviction in the postmodern world is rapidly fading and may soon be lost makes O'Connor's concerns for the spiritual realm, what she called the "added dimension" in her essay entitled "The Church and the Fiction Writer," more attractive for a dubious audience.

Although O'Connor completed thirty-one short stories and two novels, she is best remembered for nearly a dozen works of short fiction. These major stories may be classified as typical O'Connor short stories for a number of reasons. Each story concerns a proud protagonist, usually a woman, who considers herself beyond reproach and is boastful about her own abilities, her Christian goodness, and her property and possessions. Each central character has hidden fears that are brought to surface through an outsider figure, who serves as a catalyst to initiate a change in the protagonist's perception. O'Connor's primary theme, from her earliest to her last stories is hubris—that is, overweening pride and arrogance—and the characters' arrogance very often takes on a spiritual dimension.

Closely connected with the theme of hubris is the enactment of God's grace (or Christian salvation). In an essay entitled "A Reasonable Use of the Unreasonable," O'Connor states that her stories are about "the action of grace in territory held largely by the devil" and points out that the most significant part of her stories is the "moment" or "action of grace," when the protagonist is confronted with her own humanity and offered, through an ironic agent of God (an outsider) and, usually through violence, one last chance at salvation. O'Connor's protagonists think so highly of themselves that they are unable to recognize their own fallenness because of Original Sin, so the characters typically are brought to an awareness of their humanity (and their sinfulness) through violent confrontations with outsider figures.

The first collection of O'Connor's fiction, *A Good Man Is Hard to Find*, consists mostly of previously published short stories and a short novella, *The Displaced Person*. The title story, which may be O'Connor's most famous, deals with a Georgia family on its way to Florida for vacation. As the story opens, the main character, the grandmother, tries to persuade her son, Bailey, to go to east Tennessee because she has just read about an escaped convict, The Misfit, who is heading to Florida. The next day, the family, including the nondescript mother, a baby, the other children, John Wesley and June Star, and Pitty Sing, the grandmother's cat, journeys to Florida. They stop at Red Sammy's Famous Barbeque, where the proprietor discusses his views of the changing times, saying "A good man is hard to find" to the grandmother, who has similar views.

The seemingly comic events of the day turn to disaster as the grandmother, upsetting the cat, causes the family to wreck the car, and The Misfit and two men arrive. The grandmother recognizes The Misfit, and as a result, brings about the death of the entire family. Before she dies, however, the grandmother, who has been portrayed as a self-centered, judgmental, self-righteous, and hypocritical Protestant, sees the humanity of The Misfit and calls him "one of my babies." This section of the story represents what O'Connor calls "the action or moment of grace" in her fiction. Thematically, the story concerns religious hypocrisy, faith and doubt, and social and spiritual arrogance. The Misfit, who strikes comparison with Hazel Motes of *Wise Blood*, is a "prophet gone wrong" (from "A Reasonable Use of the Unreasonable"), tormented by doubt over whether Christ was who he said he was.

The tale "The Artificial Nigger" is one of O'Connor's most important and complex. It has been subjected to many interpretations, including the suggestion by some critics that it contains no moment of grace on the part of Mr. Head and Nelson, the two main characters. The most Dantesque of all O'Connor stories, "The Artificial Nigger" concerns a journey to the city (hell), where Nelson is to be introduced to his first black person. As O'Connor ridicules the bigotry of the countrified Mr. Head and his grandson, she also moves toward the theological and philosophical. When Nelson gets lost in the black section

of Atlanta, he identifies with a big black woman and, comparable to Saint Peter's denial of Christ, Mr. Head denies that he knows him. Nevertheless, they are reunited when they see a statue of a black man, which represents the redemptive quality of suffering and as a result serves to bring about a moment of grace in the racist Mr. Head. The difficulty of this story, other than the possibility that some may see it as racist itself, is that O'Connor's narrative is so ironic that critics are unsure whether to read the story's epiphany as a serious religious conversion or to assume that Mr. Head is still as arrogant and bigoted as ever.

"Good Country People," which is frequently anthologized, concerns another major target of O'Connor's satirical fictions: the contemporary intellectual. O'Connor criticizes modern individuals who are educated and who believe that they are capable of achieving their own salvation through the pursuit of human knowledge. Hulga Hopewell, a Ph.D. in philosophy and an atheistic existentialist, resides with her mother, a banal woman who cannot comprehend the complexity of her daughter, because Hulga has a weak heart and has had an accident that caused her to lose one leg. Believing herself to be of superior intellect, Hulga agrees to go on a picnic with a young Bible salesman and country bumpkin named Manley Pointer, hoping that she can seduce him, her intellectual inferior. Ironically, he is a confidence man with a peculiar affection for the grotesque comparable to characters in the humor of the Old Southwest. As he is about to seduce Hulga, he speeds away with her wooden leg and informs her, "I been believing in nothing since I was born," shattering Hulga's illusion that she is sophisticated and intelligent and that her atheism makes her special. As the story ends, Hulga is prepared for a spiritual recognition that her belief system is as weak and hollow as the wooden leg on which she has based her entire existence. Pointer, whose capacity for evil has been underestimated by the logical positivist Mrs. Hopewell but not by her neighbor Mrs. Freeman, crosses "the speckled lake" in an ironic allusion to Christ's walking on water.

The final story in the collection, a novella entitled *The Displaced Person*, portrays the most positive of O'Connor's outsider figures, Mr. Guizac, a Pole. The story is divided into two sections. In the first part, to escape incarceration in the refugee camps after World War II, Mr. Guizac agrees to work for Mrs. McIntyre, a widow who runs a dairy farm. Unbeknown to him, Mr. Guizac arouses jealousy and fear in the regular tenant farmers, the Shortleys, and the black field hands. Because Mr. Shortley is lazy and lackadaisical, he particularly resents the productivity of Mr. Guizac. The story moves toward the spiritual dimension when Mrs. Shortley, who considers herself a model Christian, begins to see Mr. Guizac and his family as agents of the devil. After Mrs. Shortley learns that her husband is to be fired the next morning, the Shortleys drive away, and Mrs. Shortley dies of a stroke and sees her "true country," which is defined in one of O'Connor's essays as "what is eternal and absolute" ("The Fiction Writer and His Country"). At the time of her death, Mrs. Shortley, displaced like the poor victims of the Holocaust, which she has witnessed in newsreels, is redeemed through displacement and enters her spiritual home.

The story's second part concerns Mrs. McIntyre's growing fear of outsiders. Mr. Shortley reappears after his wife's death and learns that Mr. Guizac is arranging a marriage for, and taking money from, Sulk, a black field hand, so that Mr. Guizac's niece can earn passage to the United States. The Southern racial taboos are portrayed as fundamentally inhumane when confronted with the reality of human suffering, as seen in the niece, who is in a refugee camp. Father Flynn, the priest who has arranged for Mr. Guizac and his family to come to the United States to work for Mrs. McIntyre, tries to teach Mrs. McIntyre the importance of Christian charity and the fine points of Catholic theology. Unconcerned with these matters, which she considers unimportant, Mrs. McIntyre becomes neurotic about Mr. Guizac's inappropriateness and overlooks the spiritual for the material. Throughout the novella, O'Connor links the peacock, a symbol of Christ's transfiguration, with Mr. Guizac, and in the end, Mr. Shortley "accidentally" allows a tractor to run over Mr. Guizac while Mrs. McIntyre and the other field hands watch. As the human race is complicitous in the persecution and crucifixion of Christ, so are Mrs. McIntyre and the others in the death of Mr. Guizac, a Christ figure. At the story's end, Mrs. McIntyre, losing her dairy farm and all the material possessions in which she has put so much faith all of her life, becomes displaced, as do the others who have participated in the "crucifixion" of Mr. Guizac.

The second collection of O'Connor's short fiction, *Everything That Rises Must Converge*, shows the author's depth of vision as she moved away from stories rooted primarily in the tradition of Southwestern humor to heavily philosophical, though still quite humorous, tales of individuals in need of a spiritual experience. Most apparent is the influence of Pierre Teilhard de Chardin, the French paleontologist and Catholic theologian, on the title story as well as on the vision of the entire collection. Teilhard de Chardin argued that through the course of time, it was inevitable, even in the evolution of the species, that there was a process moving toward convergence with God.

This idea, though perhaps used ironically, appears as the basis for "Everything That Rises Must Converge," which is considered one of O'Connor's greatest works. O'Connor once said that this story was her only one dealing with the racial issue; even so, the tale still transcends social and political commentary. The main character, Julian, is another typical O'Connor protagonist. Arrogant and unjust to his more conventional Southern and racist mother, the adult college graduate Julian angrily hopes that his mother will be given a lesson in race relations by having to sit next to a black woman wearing a hat that is identical to her own. Outwardly friendly to the black woman's child, Julian's mother "converges" with the oppressed black race with characteristic O'Connor violence, after she offers a penny to the child. After the black woman hits Julian's mother with her purse, Julian becomes as helpless, lost, and innocent as the woman's child. He recognizes that his mother is dying and enters the world of "guilt and sorrow." Through this story, O'Connor reflects on the rising social status of blacks and connects this rise with a spiritual convergence between the two races.

"Greenleaf," also a major work, portrays still another woman, Mrs. May, attempting to run a dairy farm. Her two ungrateful bachelor sons refuse to take her self-imposed martyrdom seriously when she complains of the Greenleafs and their bull, which, at the beginning of the story, is hanging around outside her window. The Greenleafs are lower-class tenant farmers whose grown children are far more productive and successful than the bourgeois Mrs. May's. O'Connor moves to pagan mythology as she characterizes the bull as a god (compared to Zeus) and unites the Greenleaf bull symbolically with peculiarly Christian elements. The coming of grace in this story is characteristically violent. Mrs. May is gored by a bull, who, like the ancient Greek gods, is both pagan lover and deity (although a Christian deity).

O'Connor's last three stories, according to most critics, ended her career at the height of her powers. "Revelation," one of the greatest pieces of short fiction in American literature, is O'Connor's most complete statement concerning the plight of the oppressed. While her fiction often uses outsiders, she seldom directly comments on her sympathies with them, but through Ruby Turpin's confrontation with the fat girl "blue with acne," who is named Mary Grace, O'Connor is able to demonstrate that in God's Kingdom the last shall be first. Mary Grace calls Mrs. Turpin, who prides herself on being an outstanding Christian lady, a "wart hog from hell," a phrase that Mrs. Turpin cannot get out of her mind. Later, Mrs. Turpin goes to "hose down" her hogs, symbols of unclean spirits, and has a vision of the oppressed souls entering heaven ahead of herself and her husband (Claud). Critical disagreement has centered largely on whether Mrs. Turpin is redeemed after her vision or whether she remains the same arrogant, self-righteous, bigoted woman she has been all of her life.

"Parker's Back" is one of the most mysterious of O'Connor's stories. Obadiah Elihue Parker, a nonbeliever, marries Sarah Ruth, a fundamentalist bent on saving her husband's soul. After a mysterious accident in which he hits a tree, Parker gradually experiences religious conversion and, though tattooed all over the front of his body, is drawn to having a Byzantine tattoo of Christ placed on his back, thinking that his wife will be pleased. She is not, however, accusing him instead of idolatry. In reality, she is the heretic, for she is incapable of recognizing that Christ was both human and divine. Beating welts on her husband's back, Sarah Ruth fails to recognize the mystical connection between the suffering of her husband and that of the crucified Christ. By this point in her career, O'Connor was using unusual symbols to convey her sense of the mystery of God's redemptive power.

O'Connor's last completed story, "Judgement Day," is a revised version of her first published story, "The Geranium." The central character, a displaced Southerner living with his daughter in New York City, wishes to return home to die. Tanner, while an old and somewhat bigoted man, remembers fondly his relationship with a black man and hopes to befriend a black tenant in his daughter's apartment building. This story concerns Tanner's inability to recognize differences in Southern and Northern attitudes toward race, and, as with earlier O'Connor stories, "home" has more than a literal meaning (a spiritual destiny or heaven). Unlike almost all other O'Connor works, this story portrays racial relations as based on mutual respect. Also, Tanner, while attacked violently by the black tenant, is portrayed as a genuine believer and is sent to his eternal resting place (heaven), the destiny of a Christian. By the end of her life, O'Connor considered a return to a heavenly home much more significant than any other subject.

Other major works

NOVELS: *Wise Blood*, 1952; *The Violent Bear It Away*, 1960.
NONFICTION: *Mystery and Manners*, 1969; *The Habit of Being: Selected Letters of Flannery O'Connor*, 1979; *The Presence of Grace*, 1983; *The Correspondence of Flannery O'Connor and Brainard Cheneys*, 1986.
MISCELLANEOUS: *The Complete Works of Flannery O'Connor*, 1988; *Collected Works*, 1988.

Bibliography

Asals, Frederick. *Flannery O'Connor: The Imagination of Extremity*. Athens: University of Georgia Press, 1982.
Bacon, Jon Lance. *Flannery O'Connor and Cold War Culture*. New York: Cambridge University Press, 1993.
Feeley, Kathleen. *Flannery O'Connor: Voice of the Peacock*. New Brunswick, N.J.: Rutgers University Press, 1972.
Hendin, Josephine. *The World of Flannery O'Connor*. Bloomington: Indiana University Press, 1970.
Paulson, Suzanne Morrow. *Flannery O'Connor: A Study of the Short Fiction*. Boston: Twayne, 1988.
Walters, Dorothy. *Flannery O'Connor*. Boston: Twayne, 1973.
Westling, Louise Hutchings. *Sacred Groves and Ravaged Gardens: The Fiction of Eudora Welty, Carson McCullers, and Flannery O'Connor*. Athens: University of Georgia Press, 1985.

TILLIE OLSEN

Born: Omaha, Nebraska; January 14, 1913

Principal short fiction

Tell Me a Riddle, 1961.

Other literary forms

Besides her short stories and the novel *Yonnondio: From the Thirties* (1974), Tillie Olsen is also the author of "A Biographical Interpretation," a nonfiction essay published in Rebecca Harding Davis' *Life in the Iron Mills* (1972), which she edited, and *Silences* (1979), a collection of essays. She has edited two books: *Mother to Daughter, Daughter to Mother: A Daybook and Reader* (1984), a collection of excerpts, and *Mothers and Daughters: That Essential Quality* (1987), an exploration in photographs. In addition, she has written uncollected magazine articles on women and writing and many uncollected poems, several of which appeared in *Partisan Review*.

Achievements

Even though Olsen secured her literary reputation on the strength of one collection of short fiction, her voice as a humanist and feminist extends her influence beyond this small output. Olsen writes about working-class people who, because of class, race, or sex, have been denied the opportunity to develop their talents. Frequently she focuses on the obstacles women have experienced. She understands them well. Olsen was a victim of poverty during the 1930's, and then she worked and reared a family for more than twenty years until she could begin writing. Both her fiction and her nonfiction deal with the problem women face: that of developing individual talents while combating socially imposed views.

Olsen is also known as a leading feminist educator. Her courses have introduced students to forgotten writings, such as journals, to teach them about women's lives. The reading lists she developed have provided models for other women's studies' courses throughout the United States. Besides the O. Henry Award for the best American short story of 1961 for "Tell Me a Riddle," Olsen has also won the Award for the Distinguished Contribution to American Literature from the American Academy and the National Institute of Arts and Letters. Her short fiction appears in more than one hundred anthologies.

Biography

The daughter of Jewish immigrant parents, Tillie L. Olsen spent her youth in Nebraska and Wyoming. Her parents were active union members, so political commitment as well as economic pressures accompanied her early years. In 1933, she moved to California, where, in 1936, she married printer Jack Olsen. Because she reared four daughters and worked at full-time clerical jobs, she did not publish her first book until she was in her late forties. Then, with the help of a Stanford University Creative Writing Fellowship and a Ford grant in literature, she put together *Tell Me a Riddle*, the title story of which received the O. Henry Award for the best American short story of 1961. There followed a fellowship at the Radcliffe Institute for Independent Study, grants from the National Endowment for the Arts, and a Guggenheim Fellowship. A grant from the MacDowell Colony allowed her to complete *Yonnondio*, a novel she began in the 1930's. After its publication in 1974, Olsen continued writing essays and articles as well as editing collections of women's writings. In addition, she has taught at Amherst College, Stanford University, the Massachusetts Institute of Technology, and the University of Minnesota, among others.

Analysis

Tillie Olsen's *Tell Me a Riddle* contains four stories arranged chronologically in the order in which they were written: "I Stand Here Ironing," "Hey, Sailor, What Ship?," "O Yes," and "Tell Me a Riddle." All but the first story contain, as major or minor characters, members of the same family, whose parents emigrated from Russia. The characters in the first story could also belong to the same family, although there is no evidence to prove it and the names of the children are different; nevertheless in "I Stand Here Ironing" characters, situation, and tone are similar to those found in the other three stories. A difference between "I Stand Here Ironing" and the remaining stories in the volume is that the former story is told in the first person, being a kind of interior monologue (actually an imagined dialogue), whereas "Hey Sailor, What Ship?," "O Yes," and "Tell Me a Riddle" are told in varieties of the third person.

Exterior action in "I Stand Here Ironing" is practically nonexistent, consisting of a woman moving an iron across an ironing board. The interior action is much more complicated, being a montage of times, places, and movements involving a mother interacting (or not interacting) with her firstborn, a daughter, Emily. Questions arise as to whether the montage can define or even begin to define the daughter; whether the mother or anyone else can help the daughter or whether such help is needed; whether the daughter will continue to be tormented like the mother, who identifies herself with the iron moving inexorably back and forth across the board; or whether, as the mother hopes, the daughter will be more than the dress on the ironing board, "helpless before the iron." "She will leave her seal," the mother says, the only words spoken aloud in the story. Yet the words could express only the mother's fervent hope for the well-being of a daughter born to a mother of nineteen, impoverished, alone, distracted, in an age of depression, war, and fear.

"Hey Sailor, What Ship?" introduces Lennie and Helen and their children, Jeannie, Carol, and Allie. The story is not so much about them, however, as it is about "Whitey" (Michael Jackson, a sailor and friend of the family who seems more lost at sea than at home in any port or ship). Filtering through Whitey's consciousness, the story explores his frustrations and anger, pain and despair. At the same time, however, the living conditions of Lennie and Helen and their children and the relationships among the family and between various members of the family and Whitey are carefully delineated.

Whitey is a mariner, a perpetual wanderer whose only contact with family life is with Lennie, a boyhood friend. As the story opens, Whitey is drunk, a condition he finds himself in more and more, and with almost nothing left of his pay. His anguish, born of his desire to be with Lennie and the family and his reluctance to bear the pain of such a visit, is evident from the beginning, as is the shame and degradation he believes to be associated with his life-style. What had started out as a dream, a life of adventure on the sea with comrades who shared the good and the bad, has become a parade of gin mills and cathouses, clip joints, hockshops, skid rows, and lately, hospitals. Lennie's dreams, however, have also been frustrated. Lennie is a worn likeness of his former self; Helen is graying and tired from holding a job as well as caring for house and home. They live in poverty in cramped quarters. Still, as Helen explains to her oldest daughter Jeannie, this house is the only place where Whitey does not have to buy his way. The tragedy is that he believes that he does. He comes bearing presents, distributing dollars and at the same time too drunk to share in meaningful interaction with the family he loves, where he is brother, lover, and father to a family not his own.

"O Yes" picks up the family several years later when Carol, the second daughter, is twelve and about to experience the pain of parting with a close friend, Parry, a black girl. Carol and her mother, Helen, have accompanied Parry and her mother, Alva, to a black church to witness Parry's baptism. Carol is uncomfortable, however, both with the surroundings and with Parry, who is growing away from her. As the services rise to a crescendo of passion, Carol asks her mother to take her home and then faints. Later Alva tries to explain to Carol that the religion is like a hope in the blood and bones and that the music offers a release to despair, but Carol will not listen.

Later Jeannie tries to explain to her mother that Carol and Parry are undergoing an inevitable "sorting out" process, a sorting out demanded by the culture—their environment, their peers, their teachers—a sorting out that "they" demand. The separation is hard on both girls. Nevertheless, Parry seems better equipped to handle the crisis, while Carol continues to suffer and question. Helen knows that Carol, too, has been baptized, immersed in the seas of humankind, and she suffers with her daughter. The irony is that white people have no means of catharsis through their religion; they are unable to cry "O Yes."

The most haunting story in the collection *Tell Me a Riddle* is the title story. Longer than the other stories, this one focuses on Lennie's mother and father while at the same time bringing to a culmination themes Olsen explores in the other stories: the frustration of dreams unrealized; the despair of never having enough money; the anger and hostility of women who have had to cope with too much with too little and who have lost themselves in the process; the search for meaning and explanation; the continuing hope of the young in spite of the tensions around them; and the pain of mortality. If the story has a fault, it may be that it is too painful as it pulls the reader too close to raw feeling. "Tell me a riddle, granny," a grandchild demands. "I know no riddles, child," the grandmother answers; but she knows, and the reader knows, that the riddle is of existence itself. Why claw and scratch; why hold on? Aged and consumed by cancer, the grandmother's body will not let go.

Russian emigrants of Jewish extraction who have fled persecution to come to the American land of promise, the grandfather and grandmother have been married forty-seven years and have reared seven children, all of whom are married and have families of their own. Now the grandfather wants to sell the house and move to The Haven, a retirement community, where he will have freedom from responsibility, from fretting over money, and will be able to share in communal living, to fish or play cards or make jokes with convivial companions. The grandmother refuses, however, countering every argument her husband puts forth. She was the one who worked eighteen hours a day without sufficient money to keep the house together. Not once did he scrape a carrot or lift a dish towel or stay with the children. He is the one who needs companions; she lived a life of isolation. "You trained me well," she tells him. "I do not need others to enjoy." She is adamant: "Never again to be forced to move to the rhythms of others." The argument between them erupts continually, fanned by his desires and her anger and resentment.

The children do not understand. How can people married forty-seven years and now at a time of life when they should be happy get themselves into a power struggle that threatens to pull them apart? Unknowingly the children take their father's side, considering their mother to be unreasonable or sick. They advise him to get her to a doctor. The doctor finds nothing seriously wrong and advises a diet and a change in life-style—"start living like a human being." The grandmother continues to deteriorate; more and more she keeps to herself, stays in bed, and turns her face to the wall. One night she realizes that although the doctor said she was not sick, she feels sick, and she asks her husband to stay home with her. He refuses, once again bringing up the old argument, and as he leaves she sobs curses at him. When he returns he finds that she has left their bed and retired to a cot. They do not speak to each other for a week until one night he finds her outside in the rain singing a love song of fifty years ago. The husband and the children bring her to a son-in-law who is a physician, and during surgery he finds cancer. The children advise their father to travel with her and visit all the children; now begins an exodus of pain. She does not yet realize she is terminally ill, and the constant movement causes her utter despair. From house to house they carry her, and she refuses to participate, will not touch a baby grandchild, and retreats finally to sit in a closet when they believe she is napping. Once a granddaughter, herself upset, hauls her little body into the closet and finds her grandmother there—"Is this where you hide, too, Grammy?"

Finally the grandfather brings her to a new apartment close to a seaside resort, dismal in the off-season and filled with the impoverished aged. The grandmother, ill in bed for several days, is tended by her granddaughter, Jeannie, daughter of Lennie and Helen and now a visiting nurse. When she is better, the grandmother wants to go by the sea to sit in the sand. More and more now she loses control of her conscious self, sings snatches of songs, remembers pieces of quotations, tries in herself to find meaning while noticing that death, decay, and deterioration are all around her. Then she realizes that she, too, is dying and knows that she cannot tell her husband of her realization because a fiction is necessary to him; she wants to go home.

One day Jeannie brings her a cookie in the shape of a real little girl who has died and tells her of a Spanish custom of partying at funerals, singing songs, and picnicking by the graves. From this interaction Jeannie draws solace, from what she takes to be a promise from her grandmother that at death she will go back to when she first heard music, to a wedding dance, where the flutes "joyous and vibrant tremble in the air." For the others there is no comfort. "Too late to ask: and what did you learn with your living, Mother, and what do we need to know?"

Other major works

NOVEL: *Yonnondio: From the Thirties*, 1974.

NONFICTION: *Silences*, 1979.

EDITED TEXTS: *Life in the Iron Mills*, 1972; *Mother to Daughter, Daughter to Mother: A Daybook and Reader*, 1984; *Mothers and Daughters: That Essential Quality*, 1987.

Bibliography

Jacobs, Naomi. "Earth, Air, Fire, and Water in *Tell Me a Riddle*." *Studies in Short Fiction* 23 (Fall, 1986): 401-406.

Martin, Abigail. *Tillie Olsen*. Boise, Idaho: Boise State University, 1984.

Niehus, Edward L., and Teresa Jackson. "Polar Stars, Pyramids, and *Tell Me a Riddle*." *American Notes and Queries* 24 (January/February, 1986): 77-83.

Olsen, Tillie. "PW Interviews." Interview by Lisa See. *Publishers Weekly* 226 (November 23, 1984): 76.

Staub, Michael. "The Struggle for 'Selfness' Through Speech in Olsen's *Yonnondio*." *Studies in American Fiction* 16 (Autumn, 1988): 131-139.

CYNTHIA OZICK

Born: New York, New York; April 17, 1928

Principal short fiction

The Pagan Rabbi and Other Stories, 1971; *Bloodshed and Three Novellas*, 1976; *Levitation: Five Fictions*, 1982; *The Shawl*, 1989.

Other literary forms

Cynthia Ozick is the author of poems, articles, reviews, and essays as well as of short stories. She has also published several novels: *Trust* (1966), *The Cannibal Galaxy* (1983), and *The Messiah of Stockholm* (1987). Her poems have appeared in journals such as *Epoch,* *Commentary, The Literary Review*, and *Judaism*. Her other short works have been published frequently in journals such as those mentioned above and also in a wide variety of others.

Achievements

Often characterized as difficult and involved in syntax and ideas, Ozick's works have, nevertheless, received many awards. The short fiction especially has been judged prizeworthy, winning for her such prestigious awards and honors as the Best American Short Stories Award (five times), the National Book Award, the American Academy of Arts and Letters Award, the O. Henry Award, the PEN/Faulkner Award, and the Jewish Book Council Award. Immediately consequent to the publication of "Rosa," one of her prizewinning stories, Ozick was invited to deliver the Phi Beta Kappa oration at Harvard University, and she became the first person to receive the Michael Rea Award for career contribution to the short story.

As a Jewish American, Ozick has been bothered by the question of whether she can write imaginative works that call attention to themselves as art forms while remaining true to her faith. Literary artists involved in such activity, Ozick came to believe, are in great danger of becoming worshipers of themselves or, by extension, proponents of idolatry. Ozick seemed to believe that art existing entirely to delight and satisfy the senses can be argued to be inverted, narcissistic, and finally perverse. In the 1980's, however, Ozick began to realize that creative writers needed to use the highest powers of imagination to posit an incorporeal god, as exists in the Jewish faith, and to put forth a vision of moral truth rooted in the history, traditions, and literature of the Jewish people. Ozick's success in this endeavor is manifested not only in her identification as a Jewish American author but also in the number of awards she has received from representatives of the Jewish people. Perhaps most important, however, is her own satisfaction that in her writing she is and has continued to be serving the cause of moral truth according to Mosaic law.

Biography

Born of Russian immigrants who took up residence in the Bronx borough in New York, Cynthia Ozick and her parents and siblings worked in the family drugstore, which kept them in comfort and relative prosperity even through the years of the Great Depression. As a female child, Ozick was not marked for extensive education by her family and community. Nevertheless, she was enrolled at the age of five and a half in a Yiddish-Hebrew school so she could take religious instruction, and her family insisted that she be allowed to stay. The rabbi giving the instruction soon found that she had what he called a "golden head." Successful as she was in religious instruction, however, her public school experiences were difficult and humiliating. It was not until her entrance into Hunter College High School in Manhattan that she was once again made to feel part of an intellectual elite. Her years at New York University, where she earned a B.A. in 1949, were followed by attendance at Ohio State

University, where she received her M.A. in 1951.

In 1952, she married Bernard Hallote. One daughter, Rachel, was born in 1965. Early in her career, Ozick became interested in the Jewish textual tradition, and over the years she became an expert in it. In fiction and nonfiction, she has argued with passion concerning the vital role Judaism has played in Western culture, and she has become for many a spokesperson for the importance of art and artists in the Jewish tradition and for the role of women in Jewish culture.

Analysis

Cynthia Ozick's thesis for her M.A. degree was titled "Parable in the Later Novels of Henry James," an exercise that she later thought of as a first step in an act of devotion that resulted in her belief in the exclusivity of art. In effect, as a result of studying James, she became, she believed, a worshiper at the altar of art, a devotee of the doctrine of art for art's sake. This idea—one that many believe places art before life, form before content, beauty before truth, aesthetic enjoyment before moral behavior—became the belief system that led Ozick to conclude that to worship art is to worship idols—in effect, to break the Mosaic law. This kind of understanding led Ozick to study the Jewish textual tradition and the role of Judaism in Western culture.

A highly serious approach to art as embodying moral imperatives, however, is not necessarily one that eschews metafictional techniques, repetitions, reworkings, and story sequences. Happily, in her use of self-referential devices and other dazzling postmodern presentations of the fantastic, the irreverent, and the grotesque, Ozick's techniques are relevant to the traditions and teachings of Judaism, where magic, dreams, and fantastic occurrences are ways to embody and convey truth.

"The Pagan Rabbi" is a case in point. It is the story of Isaac Kornfeld, a pious and intelligent man who one day hangs himself from the limb of a tree. Isaac's story is told by a friend who has known Isaac since they were classmates in rabbinical seminary and who is a parallel character to Isaac. In the same way that the narrator and Isaac are counterparts, the fathers of both men are set up as opposites who agree on one thing only—that philosophy is an abomination that must lead to idolatry. Though the fathers are rivals, the sons accept the apparent differences in their own personalities and remain friends. In time, their different ambitions and talents separate them. The narrator leaves the seminary, marries a Gentile, and becomes a furrier; Isaac continues his brilliant career in the seminary and achieves the peak of his renown at the time of his death, when he has almost reached the age of thirty-six. The narrator, now a bookseller separated from his wife, learns that Isaac has hanged himself with his prayer shawl from a tree in a distant park. Immediately, the narrator takes a subway to the site of the suicide, since Isaac's behavior seems totally alien to his character and personality.

In the remainder of the story, Ozick attempts to explain the odd circumstances of Isaac's death and, by means of the parallelisms, inversions, and doublings, points to the ramifications of leaving the intellectual path for the mysteries and seductions of the unknown world of fantasy, magic, and dream. Apparently Isaac, shortly after his marriage, began to seek different kinds of pleasure that may have been associated with the marriage bed and beautiful Scheindel. In line with marriage customs, Scheindel covers her lustrous black hair after the wedding ceremony and subsequently bears Isaac seven daughters, one after another. As he fathers each daughter, Isaac invents bedtime stories for each, relating to such aberrations as speaking clouds, stones that cry, and pigs with souls. At the same time, Isaac shows an inordinate interest in picnics in strange and remote places.

As Isaac behaves in odder and odder ways for a rabbi, exhibiting unhealthy (because excessive) interest in the natural world, Scheindel becomes more and more puzzled and estranged, since she has no interest in old tales of sprites, nymphs, gods, or magic events. Scheindel's refusal to countenance anything magical is in counterpoint to her escape from the electrified fences in the concentration camp, which seemed a miracle of chance. Isaac's notebook offers little explanation for his behavior, though it is filled with romantic jottings, quotations from lyric poets, and a strange reference to his age, using the means of counting rings as for a tree. Below this unusual computation, Isaac has written a startling message: "Great Pan lives."

The narrator begins to understand more as Scheindel reads a letter written by Isaac and left tucked in his notebook. The letter makes clear that Isaac has eschewed deeply held Jewish beliefs to accept a kind of animism or pantheism, where all matter has life, and, moreover, soul, although all except humans can live separate from their souls and thus are able to know everything around them. Humans cannot live separate from their souls and thus are cursed with the inability to escape from their bodies except through death. Isaac concludes that there may be another route to freedom—exaltation and ecstasy by means of coupling with a freed soul. The idea, once conceived, needs a trial, and Isaac's efforts are subsequently rewarded by the appearance of a dryad, the soul of a tree. The dryad's lovemaking brings Isaac to marvels and blisses that no man, it is said, had experienced since Adam. Isaac errs, however, in trying to trap the dryad into his own mortal condition. In so doing, he loses his own soul. His soul free, Isaac's body is doomed to death. More important, however, the soul retains the visage of the rabbi, who has been and will be the one who walks indifferently through the beauties of the fields, declaring that the sound, smells, and tastes of the law are more beautiful than anything to be found in the natural world.

Scheindel's repugnance toward, and lack of charity for, her husband's folly surprises the narrator and turns him away from her. The narrator is able to appreciate the subtlety of the rabbi's thinking and the bravery of the pursuit, but Scheindel is one who guarded the Mosaic law with her own wasted body during the Holocaust, and Scheindel is the issue here, not intellectual subtlety—she who seemed doomed to death when she was seventeen years old, she who traded her youth and vitality for marriage to a Jewish rabbi. After his conversation with Scheindel, and as an ironic afterthought, the narrator goes home to clear his house of his three paltry houseplants. His gesture next to Isaac's forthright penetration into the forest, however, indicates something of the struggle of every Jew seduced by the pleasures of the beautiful but charged to interpret and guard the laws instead.

By the time of the publication of "The Shawl" in *The New Yorker* and "Rosa," also in *The New Yorker*, Ozick had come to articulate fairly clearly her recognition that imagination need not be a negative, leading to idolatry (the worship of false gods), but a positive, allowing Jews to imagine a god without image. These stories are of exceptional importance and significance in the Ozick canon. In them, Ozick deals directly with the horror of the Holocaust. Rosa is the focal character of both stories, each of which exists as a separate entity coherent in itself,

but also, when juxtaposed as in a diptych or modified story sequence, each takes added significance as the two parts interact with each other.

In "The Shawl," set in a concentration camp, Rosa is a young woman with a baby in her arms wrapped in a shawl that serves not only to shelter the child, called Magda, but also to hide it, to muffle its cries, and to succor it. With Rosa is her young niece, Stella, who is jealous of Magda and craves the shawl for her own comfort. Deprived of her shawl, the baby begins to cry and crawl around on the ground. Rosa's dilemma must be excruciatingly painful. She understands that her adolescent niece took the shawl, trying to cling to her own life, and she understands that if she chances getting the baby without the shawl to cover it up, she is likely to lose both her life and Magda's. She chooses to go after the shawl first, and the fatal moment arrives too soon. A German officer finds the child wandering about and hurls her against the electrified fence.

Complicating the issue is the question of who is Magda's father. Early in the story, it is suggested that the father is not a Jew, since Magda has blue eyes and blond hair and seems a pure Aryan, a situation that causes Stella to react even more bitterly. As in any nightmare, the dreaded occurs. Stella steals the shawl; the baby cries, wanders about, and is killed. Rosa survives the horrible ordeal as she has survived others, including repeated rapes by German soldiers. She knows that any action will result in her death, so she stuffs the shawl in her own mouth and drinks Magda's saliva to sustain herself.

For "Rosa," Ozick won four awards. On the basis of the story's publication, she was named one of three best short-story writers in the United States. Because the story does not proceed chronologically, a brief plot summary might be helpful. After Rosa and Stella are rescued from the camps, Rosa brings Stella to the United States, where Stella gets a job and Rosa opens an antique shop. The action takes place some thirty-five years after the occurrences described in "The Shawl." Rosa is still very angry with Stella for her role in Magda's death, and she is able to get little personal satisfaction from her activities in the antique shop. Apparently, her customers do not want to listen to the stories she has to tell, and one day, extremely angry and apparently insane, Rosa destroys her shop. To escape institutionalization, she agrees to move to what appears to be a poverty-stricken retirement hotel in Miami Beach. Life is difficult for her. The intense heat makes it hard for her to get out into the sunlight in order to shop. When she does eat, she scavenges or makes do with tiny portions, such as a cracker with grape jelly or a single sardine. The condition of her clothes seems to indicate that she has nothing to wear. One morning, however, Rosa makes her way to a supermarket, and there she meets Simon Persky. Persky is not a person in the ordinary mold. He notices Rosa on a personal level and insists that she respond to him. While Rosa's relationship with Simon Persky is developing, Ozick establishes two parallel plot lines having to do with Rosa's request of Stella that she send Magda's shawl and a request from a Dr. Tree asking Stella to help him conduct research on Rosa's reaction to her imprisonment and ill treatment.

These three plot lines weave about each other, providing the matrices for the action. Rosa is responsible for saving Stella's life in the concentration camp and bringing her to the United States, and Stella is indirectly responsible for Magda's death, perhaps the single most horrible thing that happened to Rosa in a life full of horrors—the internment, the death of family and friends, assaults and rape by brutal Nazis, near starvation, and finally Magda's execution by electric shock. Since Magda's death, Rosa has teetered on the brink of insanity, managing to hold herself together by working and by the creative act of writing letters to an imaginary Magda who, in Rosa's fantasy, has survived and become a professor of Greek philosophy at Columbia University. Stella too has survived in Rosa's imagination in another guise. She is a thief, a bloodsucker, evil personified, and the Angel of Death. To Magda, Rosa writes letters in perfect Polish, literary and learned. To Stella, Rosa writes in crude English, a language she never bothered to learn. To Stella, Rosa admits that Magda is dead; to Magda, Rosa explains that Stella is unable to accept and cannot be told the truth.

The shawl, which Stella agrees to send to Rosa and which finally arrives, acted in Poland during the worst years as an umbrella covering the three people—Rosa, prepubescent Stella, and baby Magda—and providing sustenance and security, even though illusionary. After Magda's death, the shawl becomes for Rosa an icon; "idol," "false god," Stella says, since Rosa worships it and prays to it.

Dr. Tree is another threat to Rosa; he is a kind of parasite, living to feed off the horrors attached to other people's lives. He wants to interview Rosa for a book that he is writing on survivors. His letter to Rosa calling her a survivor is replete with jargon, with clinical terms naming the horrible conditions with neutral language and hiding the grotesque reality under the name of his own Institute for Humanitarian Context. Rosa objects to being called a "survivor" because the word dehumanizes her and every other person on the planet. Persky, on the other hand, offers Rosa an actual friendship, a human relationship in concrete, not abstract, terms. Thus he emerges as winner of Rosa's attention, with Dr. Tree dismissed and memories of Magda put on hold for a while.

Discussions of Cynthia Ozick's fiction often include the descriptors "uncompromising," "demanding," "difficult," characteristics that can diminish a writer's popularity and, consequently, status. For Ozick, however, no such diminution has taken place. Indeed, her reputation has grown steadily and strongly, her writings gaining more attention and herself more rewards. The phenomenon is not, after all, that surprising. If her protestations are stronger than those of other Jewish American writers, her demands are based more clearly in moral imperatives of the Jewish tradition. Yet there is another tradition as truly her own, one that commentators sometimes forget: an American literary heritage, with Nathaniel Hawthorne, Herman Melville, Edgar Allan Poe, and William Faulkner, writers who also worked in a realm where the "power of blackness" wrestles with us all.

Other major works

NOVEL: *Trust*, 1966; *The Cannibal Galaxy*, 1983; *The Messiah of Stockholm*, 1987.
NONFICTION: *Art and Ardor*, 1983; *Metaphor and Memory*, 1989; *What Henry James Knew and Other Essays on Writers*, 1993.

Bibliography

Bloom, Harold, ed. *Cynthia Ozick: Modern Critical Views*. New York: Chelsea House, 1986.
Burstein, Janet Handler. "Cynthia Ozick and the Transgressions of Art." *American Literature: A Journal of Literary History, Criticism, and Bibliography* 59 (March, 1987): 85-101.

Fisch, Harold. "Introducing Cynthia Ozick." *Response* 22 (1974): 27-34.

Kauvar, Elaine M. *Cynthia Ozick's Fiction: Tradition and Invention.* Bloomington: Indiana University Press, 1993.

Lowin, Joseph. *Cynthia Ozick.* New York: Twayne, 1988.

Ozick, Cynthia. *Cynthia Ozick.* "An Interview with Cynthia Ozick," Interview by Elaine M. Kauvar. *Contemporary Literature* 26 (Winter, 1985): 375-401.

Pinsker, Sanford. *The Uncompromising Fiction of Cynthia Ozick.* Columbia: University of Missouri Press, 1987.

GRACE PALEY

Born: New York, New York; December 11, 1922

Principal short fiction

The Little Disturbances of Man: Stories of Men and Women in Love, 1959; *Enormous Changes at the Last Minute*, 1974; *Later That Same Day*, 1985.

Other literary forms

In addition to her short fiction, Grace Paley has published a collection of poetry, *Leaning Forward* (1985), and, along with the staff of the New America's Press, edited *A Dream Compels Us: Voices of Salvadoran Women* (1989). She has also contributed uncollected short stories to *The New Yorker* and essays on teaching to various journals.

Achievements

Despite her small literary output, Paley's innovative style and the political and social concerns she advocates in her work have enabled her to generate significant critical attention. Her stories treat traditional themes, focusing on the lives of women and the experiences of love, motherhood, and companionship that bind them together. She presents these themes, however, in inventive rather than traditional structures. Her stories are frequently fragmented and open-ended, without conventional plot and character development. Paley felt these structural innovations made her work more true to life. The stories gain their vitality by Paley's use of distinctive language—the voice, idiom, tone, and rhythms of the New York City locale. She writes best when rendering the razor-tongued Jewish American urban female, with an ironic wit, who does not hesitate to voice her opinions.

To speak out is a basic theme in Paley's stories, and it reflects her own life and political principles. The women in her stories are like her; they are political activists who speak on nuclear energy, the environment, and on all conditions that affect the world into which their children are born. This intermingling of politics and art brought Paley mixed reviews, but she has continued to stretch the limits of the short story, in both form and content. In 1970, she received an award for short fiction from the National Academy of Arts and Letters. She was elected to the American Academy and Institute of Arts and Letters in 1980 and, in 1988 and 1989, received the Edith Wharton Award. Paley is also the recipient of a Guggenheim Fellowship and a National Council of the Arts grant.

Biography

The daughter of Russian immigrant parents, Grace Paley was born and reared in New York City. Both her parents, Mary (Ridnyik) Goodside and Isaac Goodside, a doctor, were political exiles in their early years and passed on their political concern to their daughter. At home, they spoke Russian and Yiddish as well as English, exposing their daughter to both old and new cultures. She studied in city schools and after graduation attended Hunter College in 1938 and later New York University. Paley, however, was not interested in formal academic study and dropped out of college. She began to write poetry and, in the early 1940's, studied with W. H. Auden at the New School for Social Research. In 1942, she married Jess Paley, a motion picture cameraman. The couple had two children and separated three years later even though they were not legally divorced for twenty years. In the 1940's and 1950's, Paley worked as a typist while rearing her children and continuing to write. At this time, she began her lifelong political involvement by participating in New York City neighborhood action groups.

After many rejections, her first collection of eleven stories, *The Little Disturbances of Man*, was published in 1959. Even though the book was not widely reviewed, critics admired her work, and Paley's teaching career flourished. In the early 1960's, she taught at Columbia University and Syracuse University and also presented summer workshops. She also began writing a novel, a project that she did not complete. She increased her political activism, participating in nonviolent protests against prison conditions in New York City and the government's position on the war in Vietnam. A prominent member in the peace movement, she was a member of a 1969 mission that went to Hanoi to negotiate for the release of prisoners of war. In 1973, she was a delegate to the World Peace Conference in Moscow. In 1974, her second collection of stories appeared. It received sporadic condemnation from reviewers, partly because of her political views but also because the writing was termed uneven in quality.

Analysis

"Goodbye and Good Luck," the first story in Grace Paley's first collection, *The Little Disturbances of Man*, show her characteristic style and theme. The story begins, "I was popular in certain circles, says Aunt Rose. I wasn't no thinner then, only more stationary in the flesh." Aunt Rose knows what her sister—Lillie's "mama"—does not, that time rushes by relentlessly, that the old generation is quickly forgotten as the new generation supplants it, and that mama's life of stodgy domesticity (the "spotless kitchen") has meant little to her or anyone else as her life slips away. Mama, however, feels sorry for "poor Rosie" because Aunt Rose has not married and led a virtuous life. As a young girl, she could not stand her safe but boring job in a garment factory and took instead a job selling tickets at the Russian Art Theatre which put on Yiddish plays. The man who hired her said "Rosie Lieber, you surely got a build on you!" These attributes quickly gained the attention of the Yiddish matinee idol Volodya Vlashkin, "the Valentino of Second Avenue."

Although he was much older than her and had a wife and family elsewhere, he set her up in an apartment. Their affair went on—and off—over the years while he had many other lovers, but Rose was not lonely herself when he was gone. She never complained, but worshiped him when she had him and was philosophical about his infidelities: She convinced herself that an actor needs much practice if he is to be convincing on the stage. While she never asked anything from him, "the actresses . . . were only interested in tomorrow," sleeping

In the 1970's and 1980's, Paley continued her political activism as well as her writing and teaching. She joined with other activists in condemning the Soviet repression of human rights, was a leader in the 1978 demonstrations in Washington, D.C., against nuclear weapons, and in 1985, along with campaigning against American government policy in central America, visited Nicaragua and El Salvador. This trip resulted in *A Dream Compels Us: Voices of Salvadoran Women*, published in 1989. Her stories have appeared in *The Atlantic*, *Esquire*, *Accent*, and other magazines. She continues to teach in the New York City area, particularly at Sarah Lawrence College. Paley settled in Greenwich Village, in New York City, with her second husband, poet, playwright, and landscape architect Robert Nichols.

lovelessly with wealthy producers for advancement. They got their advancement; now they are old and forgotten. Vlashkin himself is old and retired, Aunt Rose fat and fifty, when his wife divorces him for all his past adulteries. He comes back to Rosie, the only woman who never asked anything of him, and they decide to get married. She has had her warm and love-filled life, and now she will have a bit of respectability, a husband—and, "as everybody knows, a woman should have at least one before the end of the story."

The theme is seen most clearly when Rose contrasts her life with her own mother's. Her mother had upbraided her when she moved in with Vlashkin, but her mother had "married who she didn't like. . . . He never washed. He had an unhappy smell . . . he got smaller, shriveled up little by little, till goodbye and good luck." Rosie, therefore, "decided to live for love." No amount of respectability, no husband, advancement, or wealth will save one from imminent change, decay, and death; so live for love, Aunt Rose would say, and have the last laugh.

The characters and tone may change in other stories, but the theme remains the same. In "The Pale Pink Roast" Anna sees her former husband and asks him to help her move into her new apartment. He is in "about the third flush of youth," a handsome, charming, but "transcient" man. In the midst of hanging her curtains, he stops and makes love to her. Then, admiring her fancy apartment and stylish clothes, he asks archly who is paying for it. "My husband is." Her former husband is furious with her.

The new husband, she tells him, is a "lovely" man, in the process of moving his business here. Why did you do it, then, her former husband wants to know: "Revenge? Meanness? Why?" "I did it for love," she says.

Over and over the female characters must choose between the safe and boring man and the charming but worthless lover. In "An Interest in Life," the girl has her secure but dull boyfriend, yet dreams of the husband who deserted her. In "Distance," Paley tells the same story over again, but this time from the point of view of another character in the story, a bitter old woman full of destructive meanness. She had been wild in youth but then had opted for the safe, loveless marriage, and it had so soured her life that she tried to force everyone into the same wrong pattern. Her own very ordinary son is the boring boyfriend the girl has while she dreams of her deserter husband. At heart, the bitter old woman understands the young girl, and this is her redeeming humanity.

In a slight variation of theme, "Wants" demonstrates why the love relationship between man and woman must be transitory. The desirable man wants everything out of life; the loving woman wants only her man. "You'll always want nothing," the narrator's former husband tells her bitterly, suggesting a sort of ultimate biological incompatibility between the sexes. The result assuredly is sadness and loneliness, but with islands of warmth to make it endurable.

In "Come On, Ye Sons of Art," Kitty is spending Sunday morning with her boyfriend ("Sunday was worth two weeks of waiting"). She is pregnant by him and already has a houseful of children by other fathers. She takes great pleasure in the fine morning she can give her boyfriend. The boyfriend, a traveling salesman, delights in his skill as a salesman. He only regrets he is not more dishonest, like his sister who, ignoring human relationships, has devoted herself to amassing an immense fortune by any means. Kitty's boyfriend wistfully wishes he too were corrupt, high, and mighty. They are listening to a beautiful piece of music by Purcell on the radio, which the announcer says was written for the queen's birthday; in reality, the music was not written for the queen, but rather for Purcell's own delight in his art, in the thing he did best, and no amount of wealth and power equals that pleasure.

Paley next began to strike out in new directions, away from the inner-city unwed mothers and the strongly vernacular idiom, to sparse, classical, universal stories. The theme, however, that there is no safe harbor against change and death, and that the only salvation is to live fully, realistically, and for the right things, did not change. "In the Garden" has, essentially, four characters who appear to be in some country in the West Indies. Lush gardens of bright flowers and birds surround them, suggesting a particularly bountiful nature. One character is a beautiful young woman whose children were kidnapped eight months ago and now are certainly dead, but she cannot face this fact, and her talk is constantly about "when they come home." Her husband is a rich landlord who did not give the kidnappers their ransom money; he shouts constantly in a loud voice that everything is well. There is a vacationing Communist renting one of the landlord's houses, who, out of curiosity, asks the neighbors about the case. He learns that the landlord had once been poor, but now is rich and has a beautiful wife; he could not believe that anything had the power to hurt his luck, and he was too greedy to give them the money. It is known that it was "his friends who did it." There is an elderly neighbor woman who is dying of a muscle-wasting disease. She had spent much time with the beautiful woman listening to her talk about when the children would return, but now she is fed up with her and cannot stand the husband's shouting. For a while, since she is too wasted to do much more, she follows with her eyes the movements of the Communist, but "sadly she had to admit that the eyes' movement, even if minutely savored, was not such an adventurous journey." Then "she had become interested in her own courage."

At first it may appear that nothing happens in the story, but it is all there. The garden is the world. The young woman with her beauty has won a rich husband; the landlord, through aggressiveness, has clawed his way to the top. Both these modes—beauty and aggressiveness—have succeeded only for a while, but inevitably whatever is gained in the world is lost because human beings are all mortal. The Communist—by being a Communist, "a tenderhearted but relentless person"—suggests someone who will try to find a political way to stave off chance and mortality, but in fact he merely leaves, having done nothing. The old woman, who realizes the fecklessness of trying to help and who has found mere observation of process insufficient, becomes more interested in the course of her own courage in facing up to inevitable change. She and her husband are the only ones who admit to change, and this seems the right position, the tragic sense of life that makes life supportable.

Other major works

POETRY: *Leaning Forward*, 1985; *New and Collected Poems*, 1992.
NONFICTION: *A Dream Compels Us: Voices of Salvadoran Women*, 1989.

Bibliography

Arcana, Judith. *Grace Paley's Life Stories: A Literary Biography*. Urbana: University of Illinois Press, 1993.

Baumbach, Jonathan. "Life Size." *Partisan Review* 42, no. 2 (1975): 303-306.

DeKoven, Marianne. "Mrs. Hegel-Shtein's Tears." *Partisan Review* 48, no. 2 (1981): 217-223.

Iannone, Carol. "A Dissent on Grace Paley." *Contemporary* 80 (August, 1985): 54-58.

Marchant, Peter, and Earl Ingersoll, eds. "A Conversation with Grace Paley." *The Massachusetts Review* 26 (Winter, 1985): 606-614.

Paley, Grace. "Grace Paley: Art Is on the Side of the Underdog." Interview by Harriet Shapiro. *Ms.* 11 (May, 1974): 43-45.

Taylor, Jacqueline. *Grace Paley: Illuminating the Dark Lives*. Austin: University of Texas Press, 1990.

DOROTHY PARKER

Born: West End, New Jersey; August 22, 1893   **Died:** New York, New York; June 7, 1967

Principal short fiction

Laments for the Living, 1930; *After Such Pleasures*, 1933; *Here Lies*, 1939; *The Portable Dorothy Parker*, 1944; *The Penguin Dorothy Parker*, 1977.

Other literary forms

Dorothy Parker's principal writings, identified by Alexander Woolcott as "a potent distillation of nectar and wormwood," are short stories and verse—not serious "poetry," she claimed. Her poetic volumes include *Enough Rope* (1926), *Sunset Gun* (1928), and *Death and Taxes* (1931)—mostly lamentations for loves lost, never found, or gone awry. She wrote witty drama reviews for *Vanity Fair* (1918-1920), *Ainslee's* (1920-1933), and *The New Yorker* (1931); and terse, tart book reviews for *The New Yorker* (1927-1933) and *Esquire* (1959-1962). "Tonstant Weader Fwowed Up," her provoked, personal reaction to A. A. Milne's *The House at Pooh Corner* (1928), typifies her "delicate claws of . . . superb viciousness" (Woolcott). Parker's major plays are *The Coast of Illyria* (about Charles and Mary Lamb's tortured lives) and *The Ladies of the Corridor* (1953; three case studies of death-in-life among elderly women).

Achievements

Parker's career flashed brilliantly in the 1920's and early 1930's and then faded equally quickly as the world she portrayed in her stories and poems disappeared into the hardships of the Depression. Her stories are sharp, witty portraits of an age when social and sexual conventions were changing rapidly. Her dramatic monologues, usually spoken by women without self-confidence, her sharp social satires, and her careful delineations of scenes and situations reveal the changing mores of the 1920's. They also, however, portray the attendants of rapid social change: anxiety, lack of communication, and differing expectations of men and women on what social and sexual roles should be. These problems continue into contemporary times, and Parker's incisive writing captures them well. Her writings are like herself—witty and sad.

Her stories, verse, and reviews appeared in, and helped to set the tone of, the newly founded *The New Yorker*, which began publication in 1925, and she remained an occasional contributor until 1955.

Biography

Educated at Miss Dana's School in Morristown, New Jersey, Dorothy Rothschild Parker wrote fashion blurbs and drama criticism for *Vanity Fair*, short stories for *The New Yorker* irregularly, Hollywood film scripts at intervals from 1934 to 1954, and *Esquire* book reviews from 1959 to 1962. Her marriage to Edwin Pond Parker lasted from 1917 to 1928, and was succeeded by two marriages to bisexual actor-writer Alan Campbell, from 1934 to 1947, and from 1950 to 1963, when Campbell died. Campbell, Lillian Hellman, and others nurtured Parker, but they could not control her drinking and her worsening writer's block that kept her from finishing many of her literary attempts during her last fifteen years.

Analysis

Dorothy Parker's best-known stories are "The Waltz," "A Telephone Call," and her masterpiece, "Big Blonde," winner of the O. Henry Memorial Prize for the best short story of 1929.

"The Waltz" and "A Telephone Call," both dramatic monologues, present typical Parker characters, insecure young women who derive their social and personal acceptance from the approval of men and who go to extremes, whether sincere or hypocritical, to maintain this approbation. The characters elicit from the readers a mixture of sympathy and ridicule. They evoke sympathy because each is agonizing in an uncomfortable situation which she believes herself powerless to control. The waltzer is stuck with a bad, boorish dancer—"two stumbles, slip, and a twenty-yard dash." The other woman is longing for a telephone call from a man she loves who does not reciprocate her concern: "Please, God, let him telephone me now, Dear God, let him call me now. I won't ask anything else of You. . . ."

These predicaments are largely self-imposed as well as trivial and so they are ludicrous, unwittingly burlesqued through the narrators' hyperbolic perspectives. Both women are trapped in situations they have permitted to occur but from which they lack the resourcefulness or assertiveness to extricate themselves. The waltzer not only accepts the invitation to dance but also hypocritically flatters her partner: "Oh, they're going to play another encore. Oh, goody. Oh, that's lovely. Tired? I should say I'm not tired. I'd like to go on like this forever." These cloying words mask the truth, which she utters only to herself and to the evesdropping audience: "I should say I'm not tired. I'm dead, that's all I am. Dead . . . and the music is never going to stop playing. . . ." Enslaved by an exaggerated code of politeness, therefore, she catches herself in the network of her own lies: "Oh, they've stopped, the mean things. They're not going to play any more. Oh, darn." Then she sets herself up for yet another round of hypocritical self-torture: "Do you really think so, if you gave them twenty dollars? . . . Do tell them to play this same thing. I'd simply adore to go on waltzing."

Like the waltzer, the narrator in "A Telephone Call" is her own worst enemy. Suffering from too much time on her hands—she is evidently not occupied with a job or responsibility for anyone but herself—she can afford the self-indulgence to spend hours focused exclusively on the dubious prospect of a phone call. She plays games with God; her catechism is a parody: "You see, God, if You would just let him telephone me, I wouldn't have to ask You . . . for anything more." She plays games with herself: "Maybe if I counted five hundred by fives, it might ring by that time. I'll count slowly. I won't cheat." She is totally preoccupied with herself and her futile efforts to fan the embers of a dying love; having violated the social code by phoning her former admirer at his office, by the monologue's end she is desperately preparing to violate it again by calling him at home. Nevertheless, she is ludicrous rather than pathetic because her

concern is so superficial (although her concentration on the anticipated phone call is also a barrier against the more serious reality of the estrangement); her calculations so trivial ("I'll count five hundred by fives, and if he hasn't called me then, I will know God isn't going to help me, ever again"); and the stakes for which she prays so low (attempting to manipulate God's will in such a minor matter). She, like the waltzer, envisions a simplistic fairy-tale solution dependent on the agency of another.

Thus the plots of these slight stories are as slender as the resources of the monologist narrators, for whom formulaic prayers or serial wisecracks ("I'd like to [dance] awfully, but I'm having labor pains . . . It's so nice to meet a man who isn't a scaredy-cat about catching my beri-beri") are inadequate to alter their situations. Such narratives, with their fixed perspectives, exploitation of a single, petty issue, and simple characters, have to be short. To be any longer would be to add redundance without complexity, to bore rather than to amuse with verbal pyrotechnics.

Although "Big Blonde" shares some of the features of the monologues, it is far more complex in narrative mode and in characterization. Rather than anatomizing a moment in time, as do the monologues, "Big Blonde" covers an indefinite span of years, perhaps a dozen. The story moves from comedy into pathos as its protagonist, Hazel Morse, moves from genuine gaiety to forced conviviality, undergirded by the hazy remorse that her name connotes.

Hazel, "a large, fair," unreflective, voluptuous blonde, has been, in her twenties, by day a "model in a wholesale dress establishment," and for "a couple of thousand evenings . . . a good sport among her [numerous] male acquaintances." Having "come to be more conscientious than spontaneous" about her enjoyment of men's jokes and drunken antics, she escapes into what she unthinkingly assumes will be a stereotype of marriage, isolation from the outer world à deux, but what instead becomes a travesty. She revels in honesty—the freedom to stop being incessantly cheerful and to indulge in the other side of the conventional feminine role that is her life's allotment, the freedom to weep sentimental tears over various manifestations, large and small, of "all the sadness there is in the world."

Her husband, Herbie, is "not amused" at her tears and impersonal sorrows: "crab, crab, crab, crab, that was all she ever did." To transform her from "a lousy sport" into her former jocular self he encourages her to drink, "Atta girl. . . . Let's see you get boiled, baby." Having neither the intellectual, imaginative, nor domestic resources to hold her marriage together any other way, Hazel acquiesces, even though she hates "the taste of liquor," and soon begins to drink steadily. Herbie, however, is as barren of human resources as is his wife, and alcohol only ignites their smoldering anger, despite Hazel's "thin and wordless idea that, maybe, this night, things would begin to be all right." They are not; Herbie fades out of Hazel's alcohol-blurred existence as Ed merges into it. He, too, insists "upon gaiety" and will not "listen to admissions of aches or weariness." Nor will Ed's successors, Charley, Sydney, Fred, Billy, and others, to whom Hazel responds with forced cordiality through her alcoholic haze in which the days and years lose "their individuality."

By now perpetually "tired and blue," she becomes frightened when her "old friend" whiskey fails her, and she decides, having no ties, no talents, and no purpose in living, to commit suicide by taking twenty sleeping pills—"Well, here's mud in your eye." In her customary vagueness she fails again, however, causing the impersonal attendants, a reluctant doctor and housemaid, more annoyance than concern. She concludes that she might as well live, but with a paradoxical prayer of diabolic self-destructiveness: "Oh, please, please, let her be able to get drunk, please keep her always drunk."

Although in both "Big Blonde" and the monologues Parker satirizes vapid, unassertive women with empty lives, her work carries with it satire's inevitable message of dissatisfaction with the status quo and an implicit plea for reform. For in subtle ways Parker makes a feminist plea even through her most passive, vacuous characters. Women ought to be open, assertive, independent; they should think for themselves and act on their own behalf, because men cannot be counted on to do it for them. They should be their own persons instead of allowing their happiness to depend on the waxing and waning affections and attentions of inconstant men.

To the extent that Dorothy Parker was a satirist, she was also a moralist. In satirizing aimless, frivolous, or social-climbing lives, she implied a purposeful ideal. In ridiculing self-deception, hypocrisy, obsequiousness, and flattery, she advocated honesty in behavior and communication. In her epigrams, the moralist's rapiers, she could hone a razor-edge with the best. In her portraits, cameos etched in acid, the touchstone of truth shines clear.

Other major works

PLAYS: *Nero*, 1922 (with Robert Benchley); *Close Harmony*, 1924 (with Elmer Rice); *The Coast of Illyria*, 1949 (with Ross Evans); *The Ladies of the Corridor*, 1953 (with Arnaud d'Usseau).

SCREENPLAYS: *Business Is Business*, 1925 (with George S. Kaufman); *Here Is My Heart*, 1934 (with Alan Campbell); *One Hour Late*, 1935 (with Campbell); *Mary Burns, Fugitive*, 1935; *Hands Across the Table*, 1935; *Paris in Spring*, 1935; *Big Broadcast of 1936*, 1935 (with Campbell); *Three Married Men*, 1936 (with Campbell); *Lady Be Careful*, 1936 (with Campbell and Harry Ruskin); *The Moon's Our Home*, 1936; *Suzy*, 1936 (with Campbell, Horace Jackson, and Lenore Coffee); *A Star Is Born*, 1937 (with Campbell and Robert Carson); *Woman Chases Man*, 1937 (with Joe Bigelow); *Sweethearts*, 1938 (with Campbell); *Crime Takes a Holiday*, 1938; *Trade Winds*, 1938 (with Campbell and Frank R. Adams); *Flight Into Nowhere*, 1938; *Five Little Peppers and How They Grew*, 1939; *Weekend for Three*, 1941 (with Campbell); *The Little Foxes*, 1941; *Saboteur*, 1942 (with Campbell, Peter Viertel, and Joan Harrison); *A Gentle Gangster*, 1943; *Mr. Skeffington*, 1944; *Smash-Up: The Story of a Woman*, 1947 (with Frank Cavett); *The Fan*, 1949 (with Walter Reisch and Ross Evans); *Queen for a Day*, 1951; *A Star Is Born*, 1954.

POETRY: *Enough Rope*, 1926; *Sunset Gun*, 1928; *Death and Taxes*, 1931; *Not So Deep as a Well*, 1936.

Bibliography

Freibert, Lucy M. "Dorothy Parker." In *Dictionary of Literary Biography: American Short Story Writers, 1910-1945*, edited by Bobby Ellen Kimbel. Vol. 86. Detroit: Gale Research, 1989.

Keats, John. *You Might as Well Live: The Life and Times of Dorothy Parker*. New York: Simon & Schuster, 1970.

Kinney, Arthur F. *Dorothy Parker*. Boston: Twayne, 1978.

Meade, Marion. *Dorothy Parker: What Fresh Hell Is This?* London: Heinemann, 1987.

JAYNE ANNE PHILLIPS

Born: Buckhannon, West Virginia; July 19, 1952

Principal short fiction

Black Tickets, 1979; *Fast Lanes*, 1984.

Other literary forms

Although Jayne Anne Phillips' oeuvre is dominated by her short fiction, which includes contributions to numerous anthologies, she has also written a highly acclaimed novel, *Machine Dreams* (1984). Indeed, *Machine Dreams* was such a critical and popular success that it was ultimately translated into fourteen languages.

Achievements

Phillips' work has been critically acclaimed throughout the world, and honors include the Pushcart Prize for her chapbook *Sweethearts* (1976), in 1977, as well as for several of her short stories in later years; the O. Henry Award for her short story "Snow," in 1980; and a National Book Critics Circle Award nomination, an American Library Association Notable Book citation, and a Best Books of 1984 citation for *Machine Dreams* from *The New York Times*, all in 1984.

Biography

Jayne Anne Phillips was born July 19, 1952, in Buckhannon, West Virginia. Her parents were Russell R. Phillips, a contractor, and Martha Jane Phillips (née Thornhill), a teacher. On May 26, 1985, Phillips married Mark Brian Stockman, a physician.

Phillips was graduated magna cum laude from West Virginia University in 1974 and received an M.F.A. from the University of Iowa in 1978. In 1982, she began working as adjunct associate professor of English at Boston University, and she also held the Fanny Howe Chair of Letters at Brandeis University, Waltham, Massachusetts, from 1986 to 1987. Despite her evidently academic career, however, Phillips has said that teaching does not really interest her and that she prefers to write.

Analysis

Jayne Anne Phillips' writing style in her short fiction varies in person and in tone. For example, in "How Mickey Made It" (first published in *Rolling Stone*, on February 5, 1981), the writing style suggests the rambling monologue that results from hearing only one side of a conversation. Phillips originally started her writing career as a poet, an influence that critics contend is apparent in her prose.

Many of Phillips' stories track the modern pursuit of happiness, which seems, for the most part, to be an unsuccessful quest: The main characters in stories such as "Fast Lanes" (first published in *Granta: More Dirt: The New American Fiction*, in the fall of 1986) and "Bess" (first published in *Esquire*, in August of 1984) are all trying to get away from their homes and families, either physically or mentally. The action often takes place around the time of the Vietnam War or soon thereafter. In "Blue Moon," the protagonist's younger brother, Billy, is told to improve his school grades, with his mother pleading, "Don't you know you'll get drafted? Vietnam is on the news every night now."

Many of Phillips' stories are drawn from observations made while traveling, during a period in the 1970's that one critic called "her rootless days on the road" wandering from West Virginia to California and back again. "Fast Lanes" concerns the travels of a pair of post-Vietnam era "dropouts," one a self-described "hippie carpenter" named Thurman and the other an unnamed, twenty-three-year-old cocaine addict who cannot face her addiction—or the consequences of her self-destructive behavior. During a conversation about their respective pasts, Thurman says about "the old days":

People weren't stupid; they just didn't worry. The war was over, no one was getting drafted. The girls had birth control pills . . . and everything was chummy.

Yet, he then negates this lotusland vision with a cynical "Ha."

Phillips' stories concentrate on the illusiveness of the sunny American Dream. Thurman's brother Barnes is killed in Vietnam, but his parents refuse to accept it; instead, his father believes that his eldest son's death was caused by drugs because he "wouldn't have died otherwise, he was an athlete." His mother, meanwhile, finds solace in alcohol, preferring to believe that Barnes is still alive, although she is upset that he never calls or writes.

Phillips does not accept "true love" as the panacea to these ills. In "Fast Lanes," the main character's addiction or self-destructive tendencies are too strong to allow her to accept healing in the form of love from Thurman. In "Blue Moon," the protagonist's mother is forever soured on football—she will not allow her son to play for the school team—when her first real love dies of a heart attack after a football game. Her marriage (to someone she clearly considers second best) disintegrates through the years, and she tries to break up her son's love affair with an "unsuitable" girl.

In "Bess," true love has become forbidden love, as it exists between a brother and a sister. It is not necessarily an incestuous love, for in this large family, each brother is described as having a favorite sister. Yet, as the main character, Bess, notes, "No love is innocent once it has recognized its own existence." For the title character in "Bess," the death of her brother Warwick ends her emotional life. She is left alone, with only memories of an event from years before to keep her company.

Many of Phillips' stories develop similar themes. In "Home," "The Heavenly Animal," "Souvenir," "Fast Lanes," and "Something That Happened," Phillips covers the problems of grown-up children and their aging parents. In "Home," a young woman comes home as an adult, forcing her mother to accept both her daughter's and her own sexuality. "The Heavenly Animal" addresses the failure that a father faces as he attempts to draw his adult daughter into his life as a senior citizen. "Souvenir" is the heartrending account of a mother dying of cancer who still can find the strength and courage to comfort her daughter. In "Fast Lanes," a son must accept the mental disintegration of his parents as age and emotional trauma take their toll. Conversely, "Something

That Happened" deals with a mother who must accept the strange behavior of her daughter, who morbidly forces her mother to celebrate her wedding anniversary even though her parents have been divorced for five years. In fact, the mother, Kay, notes, "the last sound of the marriage was Richard [her soon-to-be-former husband] being nervously sick in the kitchen sink."

Phillips' characters often seem on the verge of self-destruction or else eating themselves alive. The mother in "Something That Happened" has had to have half of her stomach removed because of ulcers—through stress and worry, she has chewed her way through her own stomach lining. In fact, she finally tells her children,

Look, I can't worry for you anymore. If you get into trouble, don't call me. If you want someone to take care of you, take care of each other.

Since then, she has gradually resumed what she calls her "duties," although she still draws the line at attending any of her children's weddings. "Something That Happened" looks at the family from the perspective of a woman trapped by society. The main character, Kay, notes that a woman's fertile years are called "the Child-Bearing Years, as though you stand there like a blossomed pear tree and the fruit plops off." Ironically, her first three daughters become feminist vegetarians, but her fourth, Angela, is a throwback to the days of women in marital bondage. Of her mother's former wedding anniversary, Angela says to Kay: "The trouble with you . . . is that you don't care enough about yourself to remember what's been important in your life," conveniently ignoring the destructiveness of this "something that happened." In addition, Kay has to contend with her daughter trying to feed her, as though if she eats "surely something good will happen."

The perspective of this story is multifaceted; it shows the hurt and anger of a daughter who feels betrayed by her parents' divorce while also presenting evidence that the marriage was literally eating up Kay. Kay's former husband, Richard, comes across as a selfish, sickening sort of personality. For example, after "the fourth pregnancy and first son," Richard is satisfied; he terms the fifth baby a "miscalculation" on Kay's part. This fifth pregnancy does not go as well as the others, however, and Richard feels guilty over not wanting the baby to begin with, so "he swore his love to [Angela]," giving her anything she wanted and a diamond ring on her sixteenth birthday. It is perhaps from this unhealthy aspect of the relationship that Kay is trying most to escape. She even bluntly tells Richard that Angela is his daughter, not his fiancée. The day that Richard "slipped the diamond on [Angela's] finger," Kay filed for divorce.

Dysfunctional though this family may be, it is not an obvious picture; characters are abused or degraded in very subtle ways. In fact, what Phillips writes about are the black undercurrents that slowly, inexorably drag her characters down, grinding the hope and joy out of their lives. One of the final images in "Something That Hap-pened" is Kay's recollection of "starting oranges for ten years, piercing thick skins with a fingernail so that the kids could peel them." After a while, she continues, she "didn't want to watch the skin give way to the white ragged coat beneath."

It is this "white ragged coat" that symbolizes the raw pain inside Phillips' characters, pain that is often never resolved or ameliorated. Yet, these people do not neces-sarily give up on life; rather, they live from day to day, surviving as best they can. Phillips' stories have a real-istically gritty finish.

Other major works

NOVEL: *Machine Dreams,* 1984.

Bibliography

Carter, Susanne. "Variations on Vietnam: Women's Innovative Interpretations of the Vietnam War Experience." *Extrapolation* 32 (Summer, 1991): 170-183.

Edelstein, David. "The Short Story of Jayne Anne Phillips: She Transforms Isolation and Dark Obsession into Exquisite Prose." *Esquire* 104 (December, 1985): 108-112.

Lassner, Phyllis. "Jayne Anne Phillips: Women's Narrative and the Re-creation of History." In *American Women Writing Fiction: Memory, Identity, Family, Space,* edited by Mickey Pearlman. Lexington: University Press of Kentucky, 1989.

Phillips, Jayne Anne. "Interview with Jayne Anne Phillips." Interview by Celia Gilbert. *Publishers Weekly* 225 (June 8, 1984): 65-67.

SYLVIA PLATH

Born: Boston, Massachusetts; October 27, 1932   **Died:** London, England; February 11, 1963

Principal poetry

The Colossus and Other Poems, 1960; *Three Women*, 1962; *Ariel*, 1965; *Uncollected Poems*, 1965; *Crossing the Water*, 1971; *Winter Trees*, 1971; *Fiesta Melons*, 1971; *Crystal Gazer*, 1971; *Lyonesse*, 1971; *Pursuit*, 1973; *The Collected Poems*, 1981; *Selected Poems*, 1985.

Other literary forms

Sylvia Plath was a prolific writer of poetry and prose. Her first publication was a short story, "Sunday at the Mintons'," which appeared in *Mademoiselle* in 1952. Throughout the remainder of her life, her stories and prose sketches appeared almost yearly in various journals and magazines. Ted Hughes edited a selection of these prose works, *Johnny Panic and the Bible of Dreams* (1977, 1979). Plath's extensive diaries and journals were also edited by Hughes; they were published as *The Journals of Sylvia Plath* in 1982. Her mother has edited a collection of letters written by Plath to her between 1950 and 1963, *Letters Home* (1975). Plath's work in other forms included a poetic drama, *Three Women*, that was aired on the BBC on August 19, 1962; an autobiographical novel, *The Bell Jar* (1963), published under the pseudonym "Victoria Lucas"; and a popular children's book, *The Bed Book* (1976).

Achievements

In spite of efforts to disentangle her poetry from her life and death, Plath's reputation and impact have fluctuated with public interest in her suicide. Almost immediately after her death, she was adopted by many members of the feminist movement as an emblem of the female in a male-dominated world; her death was lamented, condemned, criticized, and analyzed as a symbolic gesture as well as an inevitable consequence of her socialization. With the publication of *The Bell Jar* and the posthumous collections of poetry, however, her audience grew in diversity and appreciation. *The Collected Poems* (1981) was awarded the Pulitzer Prize in poetry in 1982. Sympathetic readers attempted to place her in a social and cultural context that would help to explain her artistic success and her decision to end her life.

Plath's poems transcend ideology. Vivid, immediate re-creations of mental collapse, they are remnants of a psyche torn by severely conflicting forces. Yet Plath's poems are not merely re-creations of nightmares; were they only that, they would hardly be distinguishable from reams of psychological case histories. Plath's great achievement was her ability to transform the experience into art without losing its nightmarish immediacy.

Biography

Few poets demand that we know as much about their lives as Sylvia Plath does. Her intensely personal poetry was often rooted in everyday experiences, the knowledge of which can often open obscure references or cryptic images to fuller meaning for the reader.

Plath's father, Otto, was reared in the German town of Grabow and emigrated to the United States at the age of fifteen. He taught applied biology at Boston University, where he met Aurelia Schober, whom he married in January, 1932. In 1934 his doctoral thesis was published by Macmillan as *Bumblebees and Their Ways*, and he became recognized as an authority on this subject. Beginning about 1935, Otto's health declined. When, in August, 1940, he stubbed his toe and suffered immediate complications, he was diagnosed as suffering from diabetes mellitus. The condition of his toe worsened, and his leg was amputated. He soon died from a pulmonary embolus.

Plath's mother had also been a teacher—of English and German. At Otto's request, she gave up her career and devoted her time to housekeeping. She took great interest in Otto's scientific research and writing as well as in her own reading and in the teaching of her children.

In September, 1950, Plath began her freshman year at Smith College in Massachusetts, the recipient of a scholarship. She continued her brilliant academic record, and at the end of her third year she was named guest managing editor of *Mademoiselle* and given a month's "working vacation" in New York. In August, 1953, after returning from New York, she suffered a nervous breakdown and attempted suicide. She was hospitalized and given shock treatments and psychotherapy. She returned to Smith for her senior year in February, 1954.

Plath won a full scholarship to study German at Harvard in the summer of 1954. She returned to Smith in September; in January, 1955, she submitted her English honors thesis, "The Magic Mirror: A Study of the Double in Two of Dostoevsky's Novels," and was graduated summa cum laude in June. She won a Fulbright Fellowship to study at Newnham College, the University of Cambridge, and sailed for England in September.

After one semester of study, she briefly toured London and then went to Paris to spend the Christmas break. Back in Cambridge, she met Ted Hughes at a party on February 25, 1956. They were married on June 16 in London. That summer she and Hughes toured France and Spain. She was awarded a second year on her Fulbright; Hughes began teaching at a secondary school. She completed her year of study, and, in 1957, she submitted her manuscript of poetry, "Two Lovers and a Beachcomber," for the English tripos and M.A. degree at Newnham College. In June, 1957, she and Hughes sailed for the United States, where she would be an instructor in freshman English at Smith College. She enjoyed her teaching and was regarded as an excellent instructor, but the strain of grading essays led her to abandon the academic world after one year. She and Hughes remained in Boston for the following year, both trying to earn a living by writing and part-time work. In the spring of 1959 Hughes was given a Guggenheim fellowship; meanwhile, Plath was attending Robert Lowell's seminars on poetry at Boston University.

In December of 1959 the couple returned to England, settling in London after a brief visit to Hughes's Yorkshire home. Plath was pregnant with her first child, and it was during these months in early spring that she learned of the acceptance by William Heinemann of her first book of poems, *The Colossus*, for publication in the fall. On April 1, Plath gave birth to her daughter, Frieda. Her book was published in October, to generally favorable reviews.

In February, 1961, Plath suffered a miscarriage, and in March she underwent an appendectomy. That summer, Plath and Hughes purchased a house in Croton, Devon, and went to France for a brief vacation. In August they moved into their house in Devon, and in November Plath was given a grant to enable her to work on *The Bell Jar*.

On January 17, 1962, Plath gave birth to her second child, Nicholas. Within a period of ten days in April she composed six poems, a sign of her growing desire to fit into the village life of Croton and of her returning poetic voice.

In June, Plath's mother arrived from America and remained until August. In July, Plath learned of Hughes's affair with Assia Gutman. On September 11, Plath and Hughes journeyed to Ireland; almost immediately Hughes left Plath and went to London to live with Gutman. Plath returned alone to Devon, where, with her children, she attempted to rebuild her life. She wrote extensively: twenty-three poems in October, ten in November. She decided, however, that she could not face another winter in Devon, so she found a flat in London and moved there with her children in the middle of December.

That winter proved to be one of the worst on record, and life in the flat became intolerable. The children were ill, the weather was cold, there was little heat, the pipes had frozen, and Plath was suffering extremes of depression over her separation from Hughes. On January 14, 1963, *The Bell Jar* was published to only lukewarm reviews. Her mood worsened, and on February 11, 1963, Plath committed suicide in the kitchen of her flat.

Analysis

In many ways, Sylvia Plath as a poet defies categorization. She has been variously described as a lyricist, a confessionalist, a symbolist, an imagist, and a mere diarist, but none of these terms can adequately convey the richness of approach and content of her work. Perhaps the proper way to identify Plath is not through a process of exclusive labeling but through inclusion and synthesis. All these terms aptly describe the various modes of discourse that work effectively in her poetry and her prose.

Plath's poetry is largely confessional, even when it is lyrical. Most of her confessional poetry, however, is not at all lyrical. Especially in her last years, she used this mode frequently, personally, and often viciously. She seldom bothered to create a persona through whom she could project feelings; rather, she simply expressed her feelings in open, exposed, even raw ways, leaving her self equally exposed. One such poem is "The Jailer," written after her separation from Hughes. The focus is the authorial "I," which occurs twelve times (together with the pronouns "my" and "me" that occur thirteen times) within the poem's forty-five lines. This thinly disguised persona imagines herself captive of her lover/husband (the jailer of the title), who has not only drugged her but also raped her; she has become, in her degradation, a "Lever of his wet dreams." She then imagines herself to be Prometheus; she has been dropped from great heights to be smashed and consumed by the "beaks of birds." She projects herself in the role of a black woman being burned by her captor with his cigarettes. Then she sees herself as a starved prisoner, her ribs showing after her meals of only "Lies and smiles." She sees herself as persecuted by him because of her rather frail religious belief (her "church of burnt matchsticks"). She is killed in several ways: "Hung, starved, burned, hooked." In her impotence to wish him the harm she feels he deserves, she retreats to slanders against his sexuality, making him impotent as well. She is paralyzed: unable to attain freedom through his death (by her wishes) and unable to escape her own imagination and her own psyche's fears.

Plath ends "The Jailer" by unconsciously revealing her worst fear: "What would the light/ Do without eyes to knife, what would he/ Do, do, do without me?" She seems reconciled to the pain and suffering that awareness brings, but, by repeating "do" three times, she shows that she cannot face her awareness that her lover has already assumed another active role, that he is performing on his new victim the same deeds he performed on her. Written only four months before her death, this poem shows Plath at both her strongest and her weakest. She is in command of the poetic form and language, but the emotions running through the words are in control of her. This same phenomenon occurs in many of Plath's other confessional poems, but especially in "Daddy," perhaps her most infamous poem. There she also seems able to

control the artistic expression within the demands of the poem, but she ultimately resorts to "screaming" at her father, who is transformed into a "Panzer-man," a "Fascist," and a "bastard."

Plath used many symbols throughout her poetry, some assuming the value of motifs. While her mode was not, in the strictest literary sense of the word, symbolic, she frequently resorted to symbols as primary conveyors of meaning, especially in some of her most personal and most obscure poems. The moon held a special fascination for her, and it recurs throughout her entire poetic output. Colors—especially white—take on greater significance with each appearance. In the same manner, trees become larger and more significant in her later poems. Fetuses and corpses, although less often used, are two prominent symbols in her poetry. Animals move in and out of symbolic meaning in both her poetry and prose. The sea is second only to the moon as one of her favorite symbols. Other recurring symbols include bees, spheres (skulls, balloons, wombs, heads), mirrors, flowers, and physical wounds. This is only a partial list, and the meaning of each of these symbols in any particular context is governed by many factors. The mere repetition, however, shows that Plath allowed them to assume special value in her own mind and imbued them with special meaning in her poems.

Perhaps Plath's greatest talent lay in her ability to transform everyday experiences—the kind that would be appropriate entries in a diary—into poems. Her poetry is a journal, recording not only full-fledged experiences but also acute perceptions and a wide range of moods. One such poem based on an everyday happening is "Medallion," in which the persona tells of discovering a dead snake. In fact, if the lines of the poem were simply punctuated as prose, the piece would have very much the appearance of a diary entry. This style in no way lessens the value of the piece as poetry. It is, indeed, one of Plath's most successful works because it is elegantly easy and colloquial, exemplifying one more mode of expression in which the poet excelled.

As Plath developed as a poet, she attempted to fuse these various modes, so that, by the end of her life, she was writing poems that combined any number of symbols and images into a quasilyrical confessional poem. What remains constant throughout her life and the various modes in which she wrote, however, is the rooting of the poem in her own experience. If Plath is to be faulted, this quality is perhaps her greatest weakness: She was not able to project her personae a great distance from herself. Plath was aware of this limitation—she once wrote, "I shall perish if I can write about no one but myself"—and attempted to turn it into an advantage. She tried to use her personal experiences and feelings to construct a vision. Her vision was in no way comprehensive, nor did it ever receive any systematic expression in prose, but it did govern many of her finest creations, especially in her later poetry.

Plath's recurring struggle was against uncontrolled subjectivity and self-dramatization. Two poems written in October, 1962, demonstrate the difficulties Plath faced when her poetic persona was simply herself, and her poetry less an act of communication than a private rite of exorcism. The first poem, "By Candlelight," presents a winter night's scene of a mother and her young son. The first stanza represents the exterior environment as threatening to break through the windows and overwhelm the two characters in cold and darkness. The next stanza focuses on the reality given the child by the light that fights the darkness (the candlelight of the title). The next stanza presents the awakening of the child and the poet's gazing on a brass figure supporting the candle. That figure is the focus of the final stanza, in which the little Atlas figure becomes the child's sole heirloom, his sole protection "when the sky falls." The poem is Plath's lamentation on her inadequacy, as a mother, as a human being, and as a poet, to ward off the world that threatens to break through the window. Her perception is made graphic and horrifying, as the surroundings take on an autonomy beyond human control. The tone of this poem is submissive, not even rebellious; the poet writes as therapy for her wounded self, as justification for resorting to words when all else fails.

"Nick and the Candlestick," written five days later, reveals changes in the poet's psyche that make the poem more assertive and alter its tone. Even the very beginning of the poem reflects this change of tone: "I am a miner." At least now the poet has assumed some sort of active role, she is doing something other than resorting to mere words to ward off mortality. She does, in fact, assume the role of a target, a lightning rod to attract the overwhelming forces toward her and away from the child. Even her small gestures—decorating their "cave" with rugs and roses and other Victoriana—have taken on great significance as acts to ward off the reality outside the window. The poet is able to end on a note of strengthened resignation, almost challenging the world to hurl its

worst at her, for her child has been transformed by her into her own messiah, "the baby in the barn." The process by which this quasi-religious transformation and salvation has occurred accounts for the major differences in tone in these two poems.

The tonal fluctuation and the inconsistent and varied personae in Plath's poems are rooted in her personality, which is capable of adopting numerous, almost infinite, masks. Plath played at many roles in her life: wronged daughter, brilliant student, coy lover, settled housewife, poet of promise, and mentally disturbed woman. Her life reflects her constant attempt to integrate these masks into what she could consider her identity—an irreproachable and independent psyche that needed no justification for its existence. Her life was spent in pursuit of this identity. She attempted to reassemble her shattered selves after her first suicide attempt, to exorcise selves that seemed to her too horrible, and to invent selves that she believed she should possess. Her poetry overwhelms its readers with its thematic consistency, drafted into this battle by Plath to help her survive another day, to continue the war against a world that seemed always on the verge of undoing the little progress she had made. Her personae were created from her and by her, but they were also created *for* her, with a very specific intent: survival of the self as an integrated whole.

In "Channel Crossing," an early poem, Plath uses the excitement of a storm at sea to suspend temporarily the identity of the persona, who reassumes her identity when the poem ends and she picks up her luggage. Identity is depicted as a fragile, dispensable entity. The nature of identity is also a theme in "The Lady and the Earthenware Head," in which the head is a tangible mask, a physically separate self that the persona seeks unsuccessfully to destroy. Here, instead of fragility, Plath emphasizes the oppressive durability of a prefabricated self. Identity's endurance, if it violates one's personal sense of self, is a terrible burden. That quality is displayed in "The Bee Meeting." Here the persona is a naked, vulnerable self that assumes identity only when the villagers surrounding her recognize her need for clothing, give her the clothing, and respond to the new self. The poem ends with the implication that her perceived identity will prove to be permanent, despite any efforts she might make to alter these perceptions. Identity becomes a matter of perception, as is clearly stated in "Black Rook in Rainy Weather." In this poem the persona concedes to the artist's perception the very power to establish the artist's identity. The dynamic of power between perceived and perceiver is finely balanced in this poem. In "A Birthday Present," the balance is tipped by the duplicity of veils and what they hide in identities that are established within personal relationships.

Toward the end of her life, Plath's concern with identity became defensively rebellious. In "Daddy," she openly declares her rebellion, severing the demands and ties of tradition that so strangled her earlier in her life and in her poetry. She adopts several methods to achieve her end of freedom: name-calling, new identities, scorn, humiliation, and transfer of aggression. Her freedom rings false, however; the ties are still there. "Lady Lazarus" reveals Plath's awareness of the lingering ties and stands as an encapsulation of her whole life's quest for identity—from passivity, to passive resistance, to active resistance, and finally to the violently imagined destruction of those people who first gave and then shattered her

self: men. This poem contains meaning within meaning and exposes much of Plath's feelings about where her identity arose. She saw herself as a product of a male society, molded by males to suit their particular whims or needs.

Plath finally conceded her failure to create a self that would satisfy her and the world about her. She reviewed a life that she had tried to end earlier. Even then she had been forced to regroup, forced to continue inhaling and exhaling. The truth of the real world that had threatened to overwhelm her collection of masks throughout her life had finally yielded to her on one point. She asked ten days before her death: "Once one has seen God, what is the remedy?" The perfection of death that had haunted her throughout her life seemed the only answer. Her final act was her ultimate affirmation of self in a world that would not let her or her words assume their holistic role.

Other major works

NOVEL: *The Bell Jar*, 1963.
NONFICTION: *Letters Home*, 1975; *The Journals of Sylvia Plath*, 1982.
CHILDREN'S LITERATURE: *The Bed Book*, 1976.
MISCELLANEOUS: *Johnny Panic and the Bible of Dreams*, 1977, 1979.

Bibliography

Alexander, Paul. *Rough Magic: A Biography of Sylvia Plath*. New York: Viking, 1991.
Axelrod, Steven Gould. *Sylvia Plath: The Wound and the Cure of Words*. Baltimore: The Johns Hopkins University Press, 1990.
Barnard, Caroline King. *Sylvia Plath*. Boston: Twayne, 1978.
Bundtzen, Lynda. *Plath's Incarnations: Woman and the Creative Process*. Ann Arbor: University of Michigan Press, 1983.
Newman, Charles, ed. *The Art of Sylvia Plath*. Bloomington: Indiana University Press, 1970.
Stevenson, Anne. *Bitter Fame: A Life of Sylvia Plath*. Boston: Houghton Mifflin, 1989.
Van Dyne, Susan R. *Revising Life: Sylvia Plath's Ariel Poems*. Chapel Hill: University of North Carolina Press, 1993.
Wagner-Martin, Linda. *Sylvia Plath: A Biography*. New York: St. Martin's Press, 1987.

KATHERINE ANNE PORTER

Born: Indian Creek, Texas; May 15, 1890

Died: Silver Spring, Maryland; September 18, 1980

Principal short fiction

Flowering Judas and Other Stories, 1930; *Hacienda*, 1934; *Noon Wine*, 1937; *Pale Horse, Pale Rider: Three Short Novels*, 1939; *The Leaning Tower and Other Stories*, 1944; *The Old Order*, 1944; *The Collected Stories of Katherine Anne Porter*, 1965.

Other literary forms

Katherine Anne Porter wrote, in addition to short stories, one novel, *Ship of Fools* (1962), parts of which were published separately from 1947 to 1959 in such magazines and journals as *The Sewanee Review, Harper's,* and *Mademoiselle*. She wrote essays of various kinds, some of which she published under the title of one of them, *The Days Before* (1952); these included critical analyses of Thomas Hardy's fiction and biographical studies of Ford Madox Ford and Gertrude Stein. Early in her career, she worked on a critical biography of Cotton Mather, which she never finished; she did, however, publish parts in 1934, 1940, 1942, and 1946. Her few poems and most of her nonfictional prose have been collected in *The Collected Essays and Occasional Writings* (1970) under the following headings: "Critical," "Personal and Particular," "Biographical," "Cotton Mather," "Mexican," "On Writing," and "Poems." In 1967, she composed *A Christmas Story*, a personal reminiscence of her niece, who had died in 1919. Her memoir of the Sacco and Vanzetti trial, *The Never-Ending Wrong*, was published in 1977 on the fiftieth anniversary of their deaths. She was a prodigious writer of personal letters; many have been published, first, by her friend Glenway Wescott, as *The Selected Letters of Katherine Anne Porter* (1970), and later by another friend, Isabel Bayley, as *Letters of Katherine Anne Porter* (1990).

Achievements

Porter is distinguished by her small literary production of exquisitely composed and highly praised short fiction. Although she lived to be ninety years old, she produced and published only some twenty-five short stories and one long novel. Nevertheless, her work was praised early and often from the start of her career; some of her stories, such as "Flowering Judas," "Pale Horse, Pale Rider," and "Old Mortality," have been hailed as masterpieces. Sponsored by Edmund Wilson, Allen Tate, Kenneth Burke, and Elizabeth Madox Roberts, Porter won a Guggenheim Fellowship in 1931 and went to Berlin and Paris to live while she wrote such stories as "The Cracked Looking-Glass" and "Noon Wine," for which she won a Book-of-the-Month Club award in 1937. After publication of the collection *Pale Horse, Pale Rider: Three Short Novels* in 1939, she received a gold medal for literature from the Society of Libraries of New York University, in 1940. Elected a member of the National Institute of Arts and Letters in 1943, Porter was also appointed as writer-in-residence at Stanford University in 1949, and, in the same year, she received an honorary degree, doctor of letters, from the University of North Carolina. Such awards and honors continued, with writer-in-residence appointments at the University of Michigan in 1954 and the University of Virginia in 1958 and honorary degrees at the University of Michigan, Smith College, and La Salle College. In 1959, she received a Ford Foundation grant, in 1962 the Emerson-Thoreau gold medal from the American Academy of Arts and Sciences, and in 1966-1967, the National Book Award for Fiction, the Pulitzer Prize in fiction, and the Gold Medal for fiction, National Institute of Arts and Letters.

Biography

There are conflicting reports of dates from Katherine Anne Porter's life, partly because Porter herself was not consistent about her biography. Nevertheless, the main events are fairly clear. Her mother, Mary Alice, died less than two years after Katherine Anne's birth. Subsequently, her grandmother, Catherine Anne Porter, was the most important adult woman in her life, and after the death of her grandmother in 1901, Katherine Anne was sent away by her father to an Ursuline convent in New Orleans, then in 1904 to the Thomas School for Girls in San Antonio. She ran away from her school in 1906 to marry John Henry Kroontz, the twenty-year-old son of a Texas rancher. She remained with him seven years (some reports say her marriage lasted only three years), and in 1911 she went to Chicago to earn her own way as a reporter for a weekly newspaper and as a bit player for a film company. From 1914 to 1916, she traveled through Texas, earning her way as a ballad singer. Then she returned to journalism, joining the staff of the Denver *Rocky Mountain News* in 1918. At about this time, Porter was gravely ill, and she thought she was going to die. Her illness was a turning point in the development of her character, and it was the basis for her story "Pale Horse, Pale Rider."

After she recovered her health, Porter lived briefly in New York and then Mexico, where she studied art while observing the Obregón revolution in 1920. Her experiences in Mexico provided material for Porter's earliest published stories, "María Concepción" and "The Martyr" in 1922 and 1923. She married and promptly divorced Ernest Stock, a young English art student in New York, in 1925. Soon after, she participated in protests against the trial of Nicola Sacco and Bartolomeo Van-

zetti, and then, in 1928, she began work on her biography of Mather, which was never completed.

After publication of her collection *Flowering Judas and Other Stories* in 1930, Porter was awarded a Guggenheim Fellowship to support her while living in Berlin and Paris, from 1931 to 1937. In 1933, she married Eugene Pressly, whom she divorced to marry Albert Erskine in 1938, when she returned to the United States to live with her new husband in Baton Rouge, Louisiana.

In 1941, Porter appeared on television with Mark Van Doren and Bertrand Russell; in 1944, she worked on films in Hollywood; and in 1947, she undertook a lecture tour of several Southern universities. The novel that she began as a story, "Promised Land," in 1936, was finally published in 1962 as *Ship of Fools* to mixed reviews. Apart from her work on this long fiction, Porter wrote little except for occasional essays and reviews, some of which she published as *The Days Before* in 1952. Porter spent most of her life after 1950 lecturing, traveling, buying and selling property, and slowly composing her novel along with her biography of Mather. In October, 1976, she read her essay "St. Augustine and the Bullfight" at the Poetry Center in New York City, and in 1977, she published a memoir of Sacco and Vanzetti, whose trials of injustice had haunted her for fifty years. When she died, in 1980, in Silver Spring, Maryland, she left behind a small canon of fiction and a great achievement of literary art.

Analysis

Katherine Anne Porter's short fiction is noted for its sophisticated use of symbolism, complex exploitation of point of view, challenging variations of ambiguously ironic tones, and profound analyses of psychological and social themes. Her career can be divided into three main (overlapping) periods of work, marked by publications of her three collections: the first period, from 1922 to 1935, saw the publication of *Flowering Judas and Other Stories*; the second, from 1930 to 1939, ended with the publication of *Pale Horse, Pale Rider: Three Short Novels*; and the third, from 1935 to 1942, shaped many of her characters who later appear in the collection *The Leaning Tower and Other Stories*. Her one novel and two stories "The Fig Tree" and "Holiday" were published long after the last collection of short stories, in 1962 and 1960, respectively. These constitute a coda to the body of her work in fiction.

From 1922 to 1935, Porter's fiction is concerned with the attempts of women to accommodate themselves to, or to break the bounds of, socially approved sexual roles. They usually fail to achieve the identities that they seek; instead, they ironically become victims of their own or others' ideas of what they ought to be. Violeta of "Virgin Violeta" fantasizes about her relationship with her cousin Carlos, trying to understand it according to the idealistic notions that she has learned from church and family; when Carlos responds to her sensual reality, she is shocked and disillusioned. The ironies of Violeta's situation are exploited more fully, and more artfully, in "María Concepción," "Magic," and "He."

In the first , María manages, through violence, to assert her identity through the social roles that she is expected to play in her primitive society; she kills her sensual rival, María Rosa, seizes the baby of her victim, and retrieves her wandering husband. Social norms are also triumphant over poor Ninette, the brutalized prostitute of "Magic," in which the narrator is implicated by her own ironic practice of distance from her story and her employer, Madame Blanchard. The mother of "He," however, cannot maintain her distance from the image that she has projected of her retarded son; she is willing to sacrifice him, as she had a suckling pig, to preserve the social image she values of herself toward others. In the end, however, Mrs. Whipple embraces, helplessly and hopelessly, the victim of her self-delusion: She holds her son in tragic recognition of her failures toward him, or she holds him out of ironic disregard for his essential need of her understanding. "He" does not resolve easily into reconciliation of tone and theme.

Images of symbolic importance organize the ironies of such stories as "Rope," "Flowering Judas," "Theft," and "The Cracked Looking-Glass." "Flowering Judas," one of Porter's most famous stories, develops the alienated character of Laura from her resistance to the revolutionary hero Braggioni, to her refusal of the boy who sang to her from her garden, to her complicity in the death of Eugenio in prison. At the center of the story, in her garden and in her dream, Laura is linked with a Judas tree in powerfully mysterious ways: as a betrayer, as a rebellious and independent spirit. Readers will be divided on the meaning of the tree, as they will be on the virtue of Laura's character.

In the middle period of her short fiction, Porter's characters confront powerful threats of illusion to shatter their tenuous holds on reality. Romantic ideals and family myths combine to shape the formative circumstances for Miranda in "Old Mortality." Divided into three parts, this story follows the growth of the young heroine from 1885, when she is eight, to 1912, when she is recently married against her father's wishes. Miranda and her older sister, Maria, are fascinated by tales of their legendary Aunt Amy, their father's sister whose honor he had risked his life to defend in a duel, and who died soon after she married their Uncle Gabriel. The first part of the story narrates the family's anecdotes about Aunt Amy and contrasts her with her cousin Eva, a plain woman who participated in the movement for women's rights. Part 2 of the story focuses on Miranda's disillusionment with Uncle Gabriel, whom she meets at a racetrack while she is immured in a church school in New Orleans; he is impoverished, fat, and alcoholic, remarried to a bitter woman who hates his family, and he is insensitive to the suffering of his winning racehorse.

Part 3 describes Miranda's encounter with cousin Eva on a train carrying them to the funeral of Uncle Gabriel. Here, Miranda's romantic image of Aunt Amy is challenged by Eva's skeptical memory, but Miranda refuses to yield her vision entirely to Eva's scornful one. Miranda hopes that her father will embrace her when she returns home, but he remains detached and disapproving of her elopement. She realizes that from now on she must live alone, separate, and alienated from her family. She vows to herself that she will know the truth about herself, even if she can never know the truth about her family's history. The story ends, however, on a note of critical skepticism about her vow, suggesting its hopefulness is based upon her ignorance.

Self-delusion and selfish pride assault Mr. Thompson in "Noon Wine" until he can no longer accept their terms of compromise with his life. A lazy man who lets his south Texas farm go to ruin, he is suddenly lifted to prosperity by the energetic, methodical work of a strangely quiet Swede, Mr. Helton. This man appears one day in 1896 to ask Mr. Thompson for work, and he remains there, keeping to himself and occasionally playing the tune of "Noon Wine" on his harmonica. The turn into failure and tragedy is more sudden than the turn to prosperity had been. Mr. Hatch, an obnoxious person, comes to Mr. Thompson looking for Helton, wanted for the killing of Helton's brother in North Dakota. Thompson angrily attacks and kills Hatch, and Helton flees. Helton, however, is captured, beaten, and thrown in jail, where he dies. Thompson is acquitted of murder at his trial.

Thompson, however, cannot accept his acquittal. He believes that his neighbors think that he is really guilty. His wife is uncertain about his guilt, and his two sons not only are troubled by his part in the deaths but also accuse him of mistreating their mother. Burdened by pains of conscience, Thompson spends his days after the trial visiting neighbors and retelling the story of Hatch's visit. Thompson believes he saw Hatch knife Helton, but no one else saw it, and Helton had no knife wound. The problem for Thompson is that he cannot reconcile what he saw and what was real. All of his life has been spent in a state of delusion, and this crisis of conscience threatens to destroy his capacity to accept life on his own visionary terms. The irony of the story is that Thompson must kill himself to vindicate his innocence, but when he does so, he paradoxically accepts the consequences of his delusions even as he asserts his right to shape reality to fit his view of it.

Love and death mix forces to press Miranda through a crisis of vision in "Pale Horse, Pale Rider." This highly experimental story mixes dreams with waking consciousness, present with past, and illness with health. Set during World War I, it analyzes the social consequences of a military milieu, and it uses that setting to suggest a symbolic projection of the pressures that build on the imagination and identity of the central character. Miranda is a writer of drama reviews for a newspaper. Although her small salary is barely enough to support herself, her patriotism is questioned when she balks at buying Liberty Bonds. This worry preoccupies her thoughts and slips into her dreaming experience. In fact, the opening of the story seems to be an experience of a sleeper who is slowly coming awake from a dream of childhood in which the adult's anxieties about money are mixed. Uncertainty about the mental state of Miranda grows as she mixes her memories of the past with the present, allowing past feelings to affect present judgments.

Miranda meets a young soldier, Adam, who will soon be sent to battle. They both know that his fate is sealed, since they are both aware of the survival statistics for soldiers who make assaults from trenches. Miranda becomes gravely ill just before Adam leaves for the war front, and he nurses her through the earliest days of her sickness. Her delirium merges her doctor with Adam, with the German enemy, and with figures of her dreams. By this process, Miranda works through her attractions to Adam, to all men, and survives to assert her independence as a professional artist. The climax of her dream is her refusal to follow the pale rider, who is Death. This feature of her dream is present at the beginning of the story, to anticipate that Miranda will have to resolve her inner battle even before the illness that constitutes her physical struggle with death. The men of her waking life enter her dreams as Death, and so when Adam actually dies in battle, Miranda is symbolically assisted in winning her battle for life. The story makes it seem that her dreaming is the reality of the men, that their lives are figments of her imagination. Her recovery of health is a triumph, therefore, of her creative energies as well as an assertion of her independent feminine identity.

In the final, sustained period of her work in short fiction, from 1935 to 1942, Porter subjects memories to the shaping power of creative imagination, as she searches out the episodes that connect to make the character of Miranda, from "The Source" to "The Grave," and as she traces the distorting effects of social pressures on children, wives, and artists in the remaining stories of the third collection. The crucial, shaping episodes of Miranda's childhood constitute the core elements of several stories in the collection called *The Leaning Tower and Other Stories*. Beginning with a sequence under the title "The Old Order," Miranda's growth is shaped by her changing perceptions of life around her. Helping her to interpret events are her grandmother, Sophia Jane, and her grandmother's former black slave and lifetime companion, Aunt Nannie; in addition, Great-Aunt Eliza plays an important role in Miranda's life in the story that was later added to the sequence, "The Fig Tree." Two of the stories of this collection, "The Circus" and "The Grave" are examples of remarkable compression and, particularly in "The Grave," complex artistry.

Miranda cries when she sees a clown perform high-wire acrobatics in "The Circus." Her fear is a child's protest against the clown's courtship with death. There is nothing pleasurable about it for Miranda. In fact, she seems to see through the act to recognize the threat of death itself, in the white, skull-like makeup of the clown's face. The adults enjoy the spectacle, perhaps insensitive to its essential message or, on the other hand, capable of appreciating the artist's defiance of death. In any event, young Miranda is such a problem that her father sends her home with one of the servants, Dicey. The point of poignancy is in Miranda's discovery of Dicey's warm regard for her despite the fact that Dicey had keenly wanted to stay at the circus. When Miranda screams in her sleep, Dicey lies beside her to comfort her, to protect her even from the dark forces of her nightmares. This sacrifice is not understood by the child Miranda, though it should be to the adult who recalls it. "The Grave" is more clear about the function of time in the process of understanding. Miranda and her brother Paul explore open graves of their family while hunting. They find and exchange a coffin screw and a ring, then skin a rabbit that Paul killed, only to find that the rabbit is pregnant with several young that are "born" dead. The experience of mixing birth with death, sexual awareness with marriage and death is suddenly illuminated for Miranda years later when she recalls her brother on that day while she stands over a candy stand in faraway Mexico.

The coda of her work in short fiction, "The Fig Tree" and "Holiday," are revisits to earlier stories, as Porter reexamines old themes and old subjects with new emphases. "The Fig Tree" relocates Miranda in the matriarchal setting of her childhood. Young Miranda buries a dead baby chicken beneath a fig tree and then thinks she hears it cheeping from beneath the earth. Frantic with anxiety, she is unable to rescue it because her grandmother forces her to leave with the family for the country. Later, Miranda's Great-Aunt Eliza, who constantly studies nature through telescopes and microscopes, explains to Miranda that she hears tree frogs when Miranda thinks she is hearing the weeping of the dead chicken. Her guilt is relieved by this, and since Miranda has emotionally mixed her burial of the chicken with burials of family members, resolution of guilt for one functions as resolution of guilt for the other.

The story of "Holiday" is much different in subject and setting, but its emotional profile is similar to "The Fig Tree." The narrator spends a long holiday with German immigrants in the backlands of Texas. The hardworking Müllers challenge, by their life-style, the values of the narrator, who only gradually comes to understand them and their ways. The most difficult experience to understand, however, is the family's attitude toward one of the daughters, Ottilie; at first, this girl seems to be only a crippled servant of the family. Gradually, however, the narrator understands that Ottilie is in fact a member of the family. She is mentally retarded and unable to communicate except in very primitive ways. Just when the narrator believes she can appreciate the seemingly heartless ways Ottilie is treated by her family, a great storm occurs and the mother dies. Most of the family follow their mother's corpse to be buried, but Ottilie is left behind. The narrator thinks Ottilie is desperate to join the funeral train with her family, and so she helps Ottilie on board a wagon and desperately drives to catch up with the family. Suddenly, however, the narrator realizes that Ottilie simply wants to be in the sunshine and has no awareness of the death of her mother. The narrator accepts the radical difference that separates her from Ottilie, from all other human beings, and resigns herself, in freedom, to the universal condition of alienation.

The critical mystery of Porter's work in short fiction is in the brevity of her canon. Readers who enjoy her writing must deplore the failure of the artist to produce more than she did, but they will nevertheless celebrate the achievements of her remarkable talent in the small number of stories that she published. Porter's finest ones please with their subtleties of technique, from point of view to patterned images of symbolism; inform with their syntheses of present feeling and past sensation; and raise imaginative energy with their ambiguous presentations of alternative ways of seeing.

Other major works

NOVEL: *Ship of Fools*, 1962.

NONFICTION: *My Chinese Marriage*, 1921; *Outline of Mexican Popular Arts and Crafts*, 1922; *What Price Marriage*, 1927; *The Days Before*, 1952; *A Defence of Circe*, 1954; *A Christmas Story*, 1967; *The Collected Essays and Occasional Writings*, 1970; *The Selected Letters of Katherine Anne Porter*, 1970; *The Never-Ending Wrong*, 1977; *Letters of Katherine Anne Porter*, 1990.

Bibliography

Bloom, Harold, ed. *Katherine Anne Porter: Modern Critical Views*. New York: Chelsea House, 1986.

DeMouy, Jane Krause. *Katherine Anne Porter's Women: The Eye of Her Fiction*. Austin: University of Texas Press, 1983.

Hardy, John Edward. *Katherine Anne Porter*. New York: Frederick Ungar, 1973.

Hartley, Lodwick, and George Core, eds. *Katherine Anne Porter: A Critical Symposium*. Athens: University of Georgia Press, 1969.

Hendrick, George. *Katherine Anne Porter*. New York: Twayne, 1965.

Liberman, M. M. *Katherine Anne Porter's Fiction*. Detroit: Wayne State University Press, 1971.

Nance, William L. *Katherine Anne Porter and the Art of Rejection*. Chapel Hill: University of North Carolina Press, 1964.

DAWN POWELL

Born: Mount Gilead, Ohio; November 28, 1897   **Died:** New York, New York; November 14, 1965

Principal long fiction

Whither, 1925; *She Walks in Beauty*, 1928; *The Bride's House*, 1929; *Dance Night*, 1930; *The Tenth Moon*, 1932; *Jig Saw: A Comedy*, 1934; *The Story of a Country Boy*, 1934; *Turn, Magic Wheel*, 1936; *The Happy Island*, 1938; *Angels on Toast*, 1940 (later as *A Man's Affair*, 1956); *A Time to Be Born*, 1942; *My Home Is Far Away*, 1944; *The Locusts Have No King*, 1948; *The Wicked Pavilion*, 1954; *The Golden Spur*, 1962.

Other literary forms

Though Dawn Powell is known primarily as a novelist, she had originally intended to write for the theater. Her play *Big Night* was produced by the Group Theatre in 1933, and *Jig Saw*, based on her novel *Jig Saw: A Comedy*, had a short run in 1934. Powell also wrote a musical comedy and scripts for radio, television, and film and published essays, reviews, and short stories in distinguished national magazines. A number of her short stories were collected in *Sunday, Monday, and Always* (1952).

Achievements

While such contemporaries as Ernest Hemingway and John Dos Passos considered Dawn Powell one of the finest writers of their time, she never attained their popularity. Shortly before her death in 1965, Powell was honored with an honorary doctorate and an award from the National Institute of Arts and Letters, but despite occasional attempts by her admirers, such as Edmund Wilson, to call attention to her achievements, she remained relatively obscure, and her sixteen novels, all out of print, were difficult to find. Fortunately, in the next two decades, there was a revolution in the American sensibility. One of the results of the feminist movement was that the critics and publishers had to admit sins of omission; they had minimized the talent of many fine women writers simply because they were women. Powell, who has been called an American equivalent to English satiric novelists such as Evelyn Waugh and Anthony Powell, is an obvious example. In 1987, author and critic Gore Vidal launched the campaign to obtain proper recognition for Powell. In a lengthy essay published in *The New York Review of Books*, he traced her life and her literary career and concluded by bemoaning the fact that the novels of the person he considered America's best comic novelist were all out of print. As a result of his article, several of her later books were reprinted, all with Vidal's essay as an introduction, and the reviews that followed suggest that Powell may at last receive the recognition denied her during her lifetime.

Biography

Dawn Powell was born in Mount Gilead, Ohio, on November 28, 1897, the daughter of Roy K. Powell, a traveling salesman, and Hattie B. Sherman Powell. After the death of her mother when Dawn was six, for six years she and her two sisters lived with various relatives on farms and in small towns. After her father's remarriage, the girls went to live with him and their stepmother on a farm. Dawn was already a dedicated writer; indeed, after her stepmother punished her by burning her stories, Dawn fled to the home of an aunt. After graduating from high school, Powell went to Lake Erie College, where she received her B.A. in 1918. That year she entered military service and moved to New York, where she remained, working in public relations and in advertising. In 1920, she married Joseph Roebuck Gousha, an executive with an advertising agency, by whom she had one son. Failing in her attempts to break into the theatrical world as a playwright, Powell began writing novels, publishing the first, *Whither*, in 1925. Over the next four decades, fifteen more were to appear, the early ones set in her native Ohio, most of the later ones in Greenwich Village. Without having been widely recognized, Powell died of cancer at St. Luke's Hospital in New York City on November 14,1965.

Analysis

The primary purpose of a Powell novel is to describe a society. To do so, she brings a number of characters together, perhaps in an Ohio boardinghouse, perhaps at a New York party or a bar. Then the characters seem to take over, as if they are determined to dramatize their own world. They act and interact, they talk, they boast, they scheme, they lie, and they confess to one another. To this extent, Powell's novels could be called realistic. They also, however, include an element of satire. It is primarily noticeable in the characters' inner deliberations, which Powell reveals to her readers in illuminating detail. The characters' confusion about facts, their muddled reasoning, and above all their clearly selfish motivations, reported with such painstaking care, leave the reader no doubt as to Powell's satiric intentions, which are further stressed in her occasional wry and witty comments.

Although Powell's first book, *Whither*, was set in New York City, all but one of the six novels published during the next six years were placed in the rural Midwest. These works introduce the themes that would dominate Powell's later work: the alienation of an individual from society, the frustration of the failing artist, the random nature of love, the limits of friendship, and above all the rule of money. Beginning with *Turn, Magic Wheel*, Powell wrote a series of seven novels to which Vidal refers as her "New York cycle." Most critics consider these novels to represent Powell's highest artistic achievement and, indeed, a unique contribution to American literature.

The third of these novels, *Angels on Toast*, illustrates Powell's approach. The world that she both summarizes and satirizes is defined in the first chapter of the book. The story begins with two businessmen, Jay Oliver and Lou Donovan, on the train from Chicago to New York. The self-absorption that marks most of Powell's characters is evident from the first. Their world is neither abstract nor cosmopolitan. At its simplest it is made up of their own bodies and their own clothes. Jay admires his own shoes, which he thinks reflect his polished personality, and his socks, which are so dazzling that he must mention how expensive they were. Lou contemplates and assesses his weight, his shoulders, then is delighted to tell Jay how much his shirt cost and to invite him to feel the material. For men so fascinated with the most trivial details about themselves, it is not surprising that both friendship and love are limited in depth. From the facile comment that Jay is his best friend, Lou soon has moved to the notion that Jay may know too much about him; indeed, it is Jay's company that is his best friend, not Jay himself, Lou muses. If Jay were replaced, the new man would become Lou's best friend. Lou's capacity for love is similarly limited by circumstances. For example, when he married above himself, he found it convenient to forget having been married before, and he is now worried because his former wife has turned up in Chicago. In a typical Powell passage, however, Lou congratulates himself because he has been faithful to his wife except for casual encounters in places where she would never go. Jay, on the other hand, is shockingly unfaithful, picking up his regular mistress on the train and taking her to New York with him. It is not adultery, but taking such chances, that Lou considers immoral.

In Powell's later novels, New York City itself might as well be listed as one of the characters. It is symbolic that the first chapter takes place on the way to New York, instead of on the way back to Chicago. In New York, the businessmen think, they can get away with anything. Ironically, the city proves to be much smaller than the out-of-town visitors think it is; paths do cross, and wives do find out what is occurring. The compelling attraction of New York City is also dramatized in the attitude of an eccentric old lady who lives in a seedy hotel. When her daughter suggests that they both move to Connecticut, the idea is greeted with horror. Obviously, even a dingy hotel in New York is better than a mansion anywhere else. Actually, the old lady's real home is the hotel bar; its inhabitants are the only people she needs or wishes to know.

The conflict between the creator and a crass, indifferent world is a major theme in Powell's last three novels. The cohesiveness of New York's literary and theatrical world is suggested by the title of the first of these books, *The Locusts Have No King*. The quotation, which comes from the biblical Proverbs, emphasizes the idea that although there is no single leader among locusts, that they seem to have a mysterious single direction. They move in hordes, and, it should be added, destructive hordes. It is such mindless human groups which can destroy the will and the hopes of an artist or, perhaps worse, turn an artist into a commercial success at the cost of creative integrity and personal relationships.

At the beginning of *The Locusts Have No King*, there seems to be no possibility that the protagonist, Frederick

Olliver, a writer of scholarly books, will ever become successful enough to find his soul endangered. In contrast, his mistress Lyle Gaynor, a successful playwright, is a celebrity who knows every other celebrity in the literary world. Lyle is completely devoted to Frederick. Indeed, she would marry him except for the fact that she feels a duty to remain with her ill-tempered husband because he is an invalid. In order to help Frederick, Lyle includes him in every party she gives and arranges for him to be invited to every party she attends. Nevertheless, Frederick always feels like an alien in Lyle's world. In response, he voices his scorn of the successful, including his generous mistress. The fact that one lover is inside the magic circle and that the other is outside it clearly imperils their relationship.

Powell's theme of alienation appears in three different typical situations. The first involves characters such as Frederick, who, though they are not new to New York, have simply not had enough success to be accepted. The second involves a young person who, like Jonathan Jaimison in *The Golden Spur* and like the young Dawn Powell herself in 1918, has recently arrived in New York City, usually from the Midwest, and must be initiated into its ways. Although the misunderstandings and mistakes of the innocent can be highly comic, they do not provide the occasions of satire that Powell sees in the third kind of alienation. Like all the great satirists, she delights in exposing the pretensions of characters who attempt to be accepted in a complex, cultivated society but who are too foolish to master its mannerisms or even its idiom.

An example of this kind of alienated character, who unlike the other types has no hope of being accepted as a result of eventual success or deliberate adaptation, is Dodo Brennan in *The Locusts Have No King*. Dodo has chosen to think of herself as a Southern belle, and she has come from Baltimore to conquer New York with cuteness. Unfortunately, her poses and her baby talk make her ludicrous. Although Frederick becomes involved with Dodo and introduces her into Lyle's circle, Dodo's vulgarity, her stupidity, and her inability to realize that her idiotic speeches have no resemblance to wit ensure her status as a permanent alien in the literary world.

In *The Locusts Have No King*, however, the theme of alienation is most important as it relates to the central love story. When by chance Frederick and Lyle reverse their places in society, when Lyle's fortunes decline and

Frederick becomes a commercial success, ironically the psychological barriers to their union disappear. Unlike most of Powell's lovers, whose short-term entanglements are motivated by chance, lust, and ambition, Frederick and Lyle prove to be capable of profound attachment, which only grows stronger in the face of change.

Even though sexual liaisons are important in Powell's novels, the real action takes place not in bedrooms but in the living rooms and bars where her characters gather. Although the title of her next novel, *The Wicked Pavilion*, is taken from a reference to the Brighton Pavilion in England, Powell's pavilion is simply a New York café, where many of the characters from her preceding books reappear, now older but hardly wiser. The book is carefully crafted, with two plots that are intertwined, both of which depend upon frequent appearances in the Café Julien. One of them involves an incomplete love story. Haunted by the memory of his passion for a young woman whom he met at the café during the war, Rick Prescott has returned to search for her and for the happiness he believes that he somehow lost. In developing this plot, Powell again emphasizes the transitory nature of most human relationships, especially love, which despite lovers' illusions depends heavily on chance and on the imagination.

The second plot exposes the phoniness of the artistic world. When a painter dies, two of his unsuccessful fellow artists discover that they can make a large amount of money by forging works supposedly painted by him; their scheme is complicated, however, when they find that he is not dead but has pretended to die and is now profiting by the greatly increased value of his old paintings, as well as of the new ones he is producing, which he can market as lost masterpieces. It is evident that Powell is in sympathy with the artists, who on at least one occasion have thus triumphed over the commerciality of art dealers and the arrogant stupidity of art critics.

In Powell's final novel, *The Golden Spur*, it is not the artist but the innocent who triumphs over the glittering and corrupt world that Powell knew, loved, and satirized. The Golden Spur is the name of a bar that has a special significance to a young man from the Midwest, Jonathan Jaimison. In her youth, his mother, then Constance Birch, had come to New York as a real innocent, had fallen in love with the city and with one of its residents, and then, pregnant, had returned to Ohio to marry an unsuspecting flour salesman named John Jaimison. Now another innocent, Connie's son, has come to New York City. In his response to the city, he is like his mother. Within eighteen hours, he is hopelessly in love with it. Unlike her, however, he is not destined to become a victim. As he seeks out the various men mentioned in the diaries, any of whom might possibly be his father, he finds that instead of being horrified at the prospect of scandal, they are all pleased. Even those who cannot remember Connie would like to talk themselves into the memory of an affair with her, which could have produced this appealing son. Yet the prospective son is less than enthusiastic about the various candidates, who, though they may be rich and famous, do not live up to the dream father who has appeared in his imagination.

Certainly, Powell is pointing out that reality rarely equals illusion. In this final book, however, there is a special significance in Jonathan's disenchantment. Like Powell herself, in her sixties at the time that *The Golden Spur* appeared, the people of the magic circle have aged, and the old New York is dead. At the end of *The Wicked Pavilion*, the Café Julien was torn down; at the end of *The Golden Spur*, an artist insists that the real money of the twenty-first century will be not in creation but in demolition. His ambition does not stop with seedy hotels and run-down cafés; he yearns to take the wrecking ball to the Metropolitan Museum. Thus Powell's final book does not mark merely the end of a young man's dream; it commemorates the end of the world she knew.

Other major works

SHORT FICTION: *Sunday, Monday, and Always*, 1952.
PLAYS: *Big Night*, 1933; *Jig Saw*, 1934.

Bibliography

Trilling, Diana. "Fiction in Review." *The Nation* 166 (May 29, 1948): 611-612.
Vidal, Gore. "Dawn Powell, the American Writer." *The New York Review of Books* 34 (November 5, 1987): 52-60.
Wilson, Edmund. "Greenwich Village in the 50's." *The New Yorker* 38 (November 17, 1962): 233-236.
_____. *The Thirties: From Notebooks and Diaries of the Period*, edited by Leon Edel. New York: Farrar, Straus & Giroux, 1980.

BARBARA PYM

Born: Oswestry, England; June 2, 1913

Died: Oxford, England; January 11, 1980

Principal long fiction

Some Tame Gazelle, 1950; *Excellent Women*, 1952; *Jane and Prudence*, 1953; *Less Than Angels*, 1955; *A Glass of Blessings*, 1958; *No Fond Return of Love*, 1961; *Quartet in Autumn*, 1977; *The Sweet Dove Died*, 1978; *A Few Green Leaves*, 1980; *An Unsuitable Attachment*, 1982; *Crampton Hodnet*, 1985; *An Academic Question*, 1986.

Other literary forms

In 1984, Hazel Holt and Hilary Pym published a one-volume edition of Barbara Pym's diaries and letters, entitled *A Very Private Eye: An Autobiography in Diaries and Letters*. In 1987, Holt edited a miscellany, *Civil to Strangers and Other Writings*, which contained mostly fiction but some nonfiction.

Achievements

Pym was a writer of distinctive qualities who, having suffered discouragement and neglect for fifteen years, was rediscovered toward the end of her life, to take her rightful place as a novelist of considerable originality and force.

Between 1949 and 1961, Pym wrote a novel every two years. As each manuscript was finished, she sent it off to Jonathan Cape. Her first six novels established her style, were well received by reviewers, and enjoyed a following among library borrowers. *Excellent Women*, her most popular novel, sold a little more than six thousand copies. Then, in 1963, Pym put her seventh novel, *An Unsuitable Attachment*, in the mail. A short time later, it was returned: Times, she was told, had changed. The "swinging sixties" had no place for her gently ironic comedies about unconventional middle-class people leading outwardly uneventful lives. Being a woman of determination and a certain modest confidence in herself, Pym went to work on an eighth novel, *The Sweet Dove Died*, and she sent it off to Cape; it too came back. She adopted a pseudonym—"Tom Crampton"—because "it had a swinging air to it," but twenty publishers turned down the novel. Despite signs of the continuing appeal of her work, Pym could not find a publisher, and by the mid-1970's, her name appeared to have been forgotten.

A renaissance in Pym's fortunes came with startling suddenness in 1977, when *The Times Literary Supplement* invited a number of well-known writers to name the most over- and underrated novelists of the century. Both Philip Larkin and Lord David Cecil—for years staunch admirers of hers—selected Pym as having been too long neglected, the only living writer to be so distinguished in the poll. Larkin praised her "unique eye and ear for the small poignancies and comedies of everyday life." Cecil called her early books "the finest example of high comedy to have appeared in England" in this century.

The publicity surrounding the article, not surprisingly, had positive effects on Pym's reputation. Macmillan published her new novel, *Quartet in Autumn*, near the end of 1977; later it was shortlisted for the Booker Prize. *The Sweet Dove Died* was published in 1978, followed by her last novel, the posthumously published *A Few Green Leaves* (1980). The manuscript of *An Unsuitable Attachment* was found among her papers after her death and published in 1982 with an introduction written by Philip Larkin. A book was prepared from her diaries and short stories.

Taken together, Pym's novels constitute that rare achievement: an independent fictional world, rooted in quotidian reality yet very much the creation of Barbara Pym. Central characters from one novel appear in passing or are briefly mentioned in another; delightful minor characters turn up in unexpected places. This pleasure of cross-references is characteristic of Pym's art, in which formal dexterity and a marvelous sense of humor harmonize with a modest but unembarrassed moral vision.

Biography

Barbara Mary Crampton Pym was born on June 2, 1913, in Oswestry, Shropshire, a small English town on the border of Wales. Like many of her characters, she led a quiet but enjoyable life among middle-class people with an Anglican background. Her father, Frederick Crampton Pym, was a solicitor and sang in the choir; her mother, Irena (Thomas), was of half Welsh descent and played the organ. Pym was given a good education (Huyton College, a boarding school near Liverpool; and St. Hilda's College, Oxford, from which she received a B.A., 1934, in English language and literature); saw some wartime service (Postal and Telegraph Censorship in Bristol, 1939, and the Women's Royal Naval Service in England and Italy, 1943-1946); and lived in various sections of London: Pimlico, Barnes, and Kilburn. She wrote down everything she saw in a series of little notebooks, and later "bottled it all up and reduced it, like making chutney."

In 1948, Pym began working at the International African Institute, first as a research assistant and later as an assistant editor of the journal *Africa*. She was given the job of preparing the research for publication, and regretted that more of the anthropologists did not turn their talents to the writing of fiction. In their work, she found many of the qualities that make a novelist: "accurate observation, detachment, even sympathy." Needed was a little more imagination, as well as "the leavening of irony and humour." Several of her novels draw on her years at the institute to study the behavior patterns and rituals of a group of anthropologists.

Although her first novel did not appear until 1950, Pym began writing when she was a schoolgirl and even completed a novel when she was sixteen. After leaving Oxford, she started to write seriously and finished two more novels, but she did not succeed in getting them published. By then, however, her literary tastes were well-set. Above all, she was addicted to novels. Anthony Trollope and Jane Austen were her favorite novelists, and she knew their works intimately. She read all the fiction she could, however, and listed among her favorites Ivy Compton-Burnett, Anthony Powell, and Iris Murdoch. She was less tolerant of contemporary novels and viewed popular and sentimental fiction with the critical eye of the satirist. Nowhere in her own fiction does the reader find sentimental excesses and sensational unrealities.

In 1971, Pym had a serious operation, and in 1974, she retired to live with her sister near Oxford. She died on January 11, 1980, at the age of sixty-six.

Analysis

Like most novelists, Barbara Pym was interested above all in human nature, and for most of her life she trained both eye and ear upon the exploration of that subject in its many fascinating dimensions. Her first published novel, *Some Tame Gazelle*, sets the tone and subject for what is to come as she casts her specialist's eye on British lower-class and lower-middle-class life and focuses on the quiet domestic lives of a few people. At the center are two unmarried women who have decided that they will be happier living alone together. An all-pervasive influence of the Anglican church, numerous references to anthropology and English literature, the weakness of men, realism, and a sometimes devastatingly comic tone are among the many distinctive features of not only this early novel but the later ones as well. Much the same judgment may be made for two posthumously published novels: *Crampton Hodnet*, which she had written in the 1930's but never intended to publish, and *An Academic Question*, for which she had written two drafts (one in first person, another in third person) but abandoned to write *Quartet in Autumn*. In 1986, Hazel Holt published an amalgamation of the two drafts. In spite of their thin plots and shallow characterization, both novels contain Pym's characteristically sharp observations and lively dialogue among the minor characters, as well as her concern with the elderly. Considered together, in all twelve of her novels Pym communicates her vision in an engaging, entertaining, and readable way. Her wit, her sense of style, her devotion to language and its revelation of character, and the richness of her invention all compel respect and critical attention.

"In all of her writing," Philip Larkin has written of Pym, "I find a continual perceptive attention to detail which is a joy, and a steady background of rueful yet courageous acceptance of things." In this statement, Larkin points to perhaps the single most important technique—and theme—in Pym's work. *Excellent Women, A Glass of Blessings,* and *Quartet in Autumn* develop their effects, as indeed do all Pym's novels, by exploiting the comedy of contemporary manners. Like her anthropologists, whom she quietly mocks for their esoteric detachment, Pym scrupulously notes and records the frustrations, unfulfilled desires, boredom, and loneliness of "ordinary people, people who have no claim to fame whatsoever." The usual pattern for the heroine is either retrenchment into her own world or, as a result of interaction with others, self-realization. By representing intensively the small world most individuals inhabit, it is Pym's method to suggest the world as a whole as well.

Usually Pym appoints a heroine to comment on the intimate details of social behavior. In *Excellent Women*, the assignment falls to Mildred Lathbury, who, as an observer of life, expects "very little—nothing, almost." Typical of Pym's "excellent women," Mildred is preoccupied with order, stability, and routine, but her special interest centers on the lives and crises of those around her—including her new neighbors, Rockingham and Helena Napier; the vicar, Julian Malory; and anthropologist Everard Bone. Faced with Mildred's honesty, diffidence, and unpretentiousness, the crises are resolved happily.

In Pym's fifth novel, *A Glass of Blessings*, the heroine is Wilmet Forsyth, a young and leisured woman bored with her excessively sober civil-servant husband. Her near-romances with a priest, her best friend's husband, and Piers Longridge (in whose friend Keith she discovers a rival) are only some of the pairings in this intricate drama of romantic errors. When the possibility of a love affair fails to materialize, Wilmet finds a different kind of consolation in religion.

Finally, Pym's anti-heroic view of life is particularly obvious in her most somber work, *Quartet in Autumn*, the first of her novels to be published after fifteen years of silence. Whereas her earlier work was a small protest against everyday life, *Quartet in Autumn* offered a formal protest against the conditions both of life itself and of certain sad civilities. The comedy is cold and the outlook is austere in this story of four people in late middle age who suffer from the same problem: loneliness. In its manipulation of the narrative among Edwin, Norman, Letty, and Marcia, the novel also represents Pym's greatest technical achievement.

Excellent Women, described by one critic as the most "felicitous" of all Pym's novels, explores the complications of being an unmarried woman (and a religious one, at that) in the England of the 1950's. The setting is a run-down part of London near Victoria Station, but the very high Anglican Church of St. Mary's also provides the background for some of the events described. In the quiet comfort of this world, where everything is within walking distance and a new face is an occasion for speculation, the pleasantness and security of everyday life dominate. Only small crises—such as an argument between Winifred and Alegra over how to decorate the church altar—form the counterpoint to comfort. As the narrator says, "life was like that for most of us—the small unpleasantnesses rather than the great tragedies; the little useless longings rather than the great renunciations and dramatic love affairs of history or fiction."

Mildred Lathbury, the narrator, is representative of one of Pym's favorite character-types: the "excellent woman." She lives very much as she did growing up in a country rectory, working part-time for the aid of impoverished gentlewomen and devoting herself to the work of the parish. As one who tends to get involved in other people's lives, she knows herself, she says, "capable of dealing with most of the stock situations or even the great moments of life—birth, marriage, death, the successful jumble sale, the garden fête spoilt by bad weather."

In all Pym's novels, says Larkin, "a small incident serves to set off a chain of modest happenings among interrelated groups of characters." In this instance, it is the entry into Mildred's life of Rockingham Napier. A flag lieutenant to an admiral, Rockingham has just returned from Italy, where he served his country by being charming to dull Wren officers. His wife Helena, an anthropologist, does not welcome his return. Scornful of his easy charm and lack of serious purpose, she has become infatuated with another anthropologist, Everard Bone, her coworker in Africa. As Helena pursues, however, Everard flees.

The reader depends upon Mildred for ironic commentary. Helena leaves her husband, who then departs for a cottage in the country. Excellent woman that she is, Mildred is invited by Rockingham to send him the Napier furniture, by Helena to get it back, by both to effect their reconciliation, and by Everard to read proof and make the index for his forthcoming book. Because the vicar, Julian Malory, needs to be protected from designing women and Everard needs her help with the book, it seems to Mildred that she may look forward to a "full life." Then she remembers Rockingham's smile and reads from Christina Rossetti: "Better by far you should forget and smile,/ Than that you should remember and be sad." "It was easy enough to read those lines and be glad at his smiling," she acknowledges, "but harder to tell myself there would never be any question of anything else." Still, Everard's affection is genuine, if undemonstrative—and not unmixed with a pragmatic desire to find a suitable typist, indexer, and all-around "helpmate"—and the reader is happy to learn, in a subsequent novel, that Mildred and Everard do indeed go on to wed.

Again set in the 1950's, town and country are contrasted in *A Glass of Blessings*, which Larkin regards as the "subtlest" of Pym's books. The novel opens in St. Luke's Church on the feast of its patron, the "beloved physician," as St. Paul called him. Celebrating the feast and her thirty-third birthday, Wilmet Forsyth, the narrator and heroine, is the well-to-do but aimless wife (subject to "useless little longings") of a typical Pym husband—hopelessly imperceptive, though well intentioned and reliable. Like Jane Austen's Emma, whom Pym has in mind throughout the novel, Wilmet is unused and spoiled. A beautiful woman, always exquisitely dressed, Wilmet is childless, idle, and snobbish. She is also utterly unknown to herself, unable to imagine another life, and afraid to risk herself, even on the London buses, certain that any disturbance will be disillusioning. Bored, without training for a career, despising routine, she plans "to take more part in the life of St. Luke's, to try to befriend Piers Longridge and perhaps even go to his classes."

Piers Longridge is sour, moody, and homosexual, the last of which Wilmet never quite seems to grasp until well into the novel. He has taken a seemingly useless degree and now teaches Portuguese in adult education classes. Believing that she might relieve his unhappiness, she forces herself on him, hoping for the grand passion of her life, another fact that she never really admits. Finally, in a scene of high comedy and bitter pain, exasperated by Wilmet's attentions and her naïveté, Piers confronts her with his secret lover, Keith, a male model, and accuses Wilmet of being incapable of affection. It is the first time anyone has told her anything near the truth, and in response, she says to Mary Beamish, "sometimes you discover that you aren't as nice as you thought you were—that you're in fact rather a horrid person, and that's humiliating somehow."

When she witnesses the courtship and marriage of Mary Beamish, an orphan and former Anglican nun, and Father Marius Lovejoy Ransome, Wilmet begins to perceive the possibilities of being useful in the parish and even of passion. After she finds out that Rodney has had an innocent flirtation with his secretary, Wilmet sees him differently, thinking, "I had always regarded Rodney as the kind of man who would never look at another woman. The fact that he could—and indeed had done so—ought to teach me something about myself, even if I was not quite sure what it was." The truth of it is that Wilmet has failed to recognize her society, including the parish of St. Luke's, for what it is—an erotic conclave of beauty and variety, both dangerous and enlivening. It is like George Herbert's "glass of blessings," full of the "world's riches"—"beautie . . . wisdome, honour, pleasure."

In her first six novels, Pym treats her characters with warm compassion and gentle irony. With *Quartet in Autumn*, however, her tone becomes harsher, more bitter, as she examines with bleak detachment the lonely rejection of the retired. Letty Crowe, another of Pym's excellent women, is sixty-five and faces retirement from the unspecified office job she has shared for many years with her colleagues, Marcia, Norman, and Edwin. For Letty, life in a rooming house is "a little sterile, perhaps even deprived." Retirement gives her a feeling of nothingness, as if she had never existed. During sleepless nights, her life unrolls before her: forty years wasted looking for love. Images of dead leaves drifting to the pavement in autumn and being swept away recur throughout the novel. Indeed, Letty tries not to dwell on the image of herself lying among the autumnal leaves "to prepare for death when life became too much to be endured."

Her former colleagues are of no help to Letty. Norman is a scrawny, sardonic bachelor. Edwin is a widower preoccupied with "the soothing rhythms of the church's year." Marcia is gravely ill and at least slightly mad—collecting tins of food she never opens and milk bottles which she hoards in a shed. The only pleasures Marcia knows are visits to the clinic for checkups and bus trips to look at the mansion of her adored surgeon. Incapable of thought, she is far more pathetic than Letty.

Unlike her colleagues, Letty does try to act bravely, reading books on sociology, participating in church activities, still caring for her hair and her dress. "She told herself, dutifully assuming the suggested attitude toward retirement, that life was still full of possibilities." At the close of the novel, she is, like Mildred and Wilmet, where she was at the beginning. Yet, at the slightest change in the routine of her eventless days, she courageously assures herself, "at least it made one realize that life still held infinite possibilities for change."

In *Excellent Women, A Glass of Blessings*, and *Quartet in Autumn*, Pym relies neither on violence nor on the bizarre. Nothing outwardly momentous happens, but the frustrations of a half dozen or more characters emerge clearly and poignantly. Beneath the calm surface of her novels, however, the events of the day do make an imprint—to a degree appropriate to the lives of ordinary middle-class people. Each novel is a miniature work of art, distinguished by an air of assurance, an easy but firm control of the material, and the economy of means to achieve it.

Other major works

NONFICTION: *A Very Private Eye: An Autobiography in Diaries and Letters*, 1984.
MISCELLANEOUS: *Civil to Strangers and Other Writings*, 1987.

Bibliography

Cotsell, Michael. *Barbara Pym*. New York: Macmillan, 1989.
Larkin, Philip. "The World of Barbara Pym." *The Times Literary Supplement*, March 11, 1977, 260.
Liddell, Robert. *A Mind at Ease: Barbara Pym and Her Novels*. London: Peter Owen, 1989.
Long, Robert Emmet. *Barbara Pym*. New York: Frederick Ungar, 1986.
Nardin, Jane. *Barbara Pym*. Boston: Twayne, 1985.

ANN RADCLIFFE

Born: London, England; July 9, 1764

Died: London, England; February 7, 1823

Principal long fiction

The Castles of Athlin and Dunbayne, 1789; *A Sicilian Romance*, 1790; *The Romance of the Forest*, 1791; *The Mysteries of Udolpho*, 1794; *The Italian: Or, The Confessional of the Black Penitents*, 1797; *Gaston de Blondeville*, 1826.

Other literary forms

In addition to her novels, Ann Radcliffe published *A Journey Made in the Summer of 1794 Through Holland and the Western Frontier of Germany* (1795). It recounts a continental journey made with her husband and includes copious observations of other tours to the English Lake District. The work became immediately popular, prompting a second edition that same year retitled *The Journeys of Mrs. Radcliffe*. Following a common practice of romance writers, Radcliffe interspersed the lengthy prose passages of her novels with her own verses or with those from famous poets. An anonymous compiler took the liberty of collecting and publishing her verses in an unauthorized edition entitled *The Poems of Ann Radcliffe* (1816). This slim volume was reissued in 1834 and 1845. Radcliffe's interest in versifying was further evident when her husband, in arranging for the posthumous publication of *Gaston de Blondeville*, included with it a long metrical romance, *St. Alban's Abbey* (1826). Radcliffe also wrote an essay, "On the Supernatural in Poetry," which was published in *The New Monthly Magazine* (1826).

Achievements

Radcliffe's fame as a novelist today in no way compares to the popularity she enjoyed in the 1790's. With the publication of her third novel, *The Romance of the Forest*, this relatively unknown woman established herself as the best-selling writer of the period, receiving rave reviews from the critics and increasing demand for her works from circulating libraries.

Radcliffe's five Gothic romances, published between 1789 and 1797, owed a portion of their motivation to Horace Walpole's *The Castle of Otranto* (1765) and two earlier Gothic writers, Sophia Lee and Clara Reeve. The Gothic tale reached its full development with Radcliffe's ability to manipulate the emotions of love and fear in such a manner as to provoke terror in both her characters and her readers. She offered her readers stereotyped plots, characters, and settings, and her disguises of foreign characters and lands were as thin as the supernatural illusions which often seemed anticlimactic in their emotional appeal. Yet these weaknesses did not deter Radcliffe's public, who remained fascinated by her distinctive brand of romanticism.

Radcliffe nurtured a cult of melancholy, primitivism, sentimentalism, exoticism, and medievalism in her novels, becoming the epitome of the Gothic genre to her contemporaries. *The Mysteries of Udolpho*, her best-known work, was satirized by Jane Austen in *Northanger Abbey* (1818) as representative of the entire mode. Her later importance was seen in a number of major Romantic writers who read her romances in their childhood. Percy Bysshe Shelley's *Zastrozzi* (1810), an extravagant romance, was a youthful answer to the genre. Lord Byron's *Manfred* (1817) appears as a Gothic villain committing spiritual murder in a landscape of "sublime solitudes." Matthew G. Lewis and Mary Wollstonecraft Shelley clearly benefited from Radcliffe's strengths as a novelist of suspense, mystery, and the picturesque. In America, Washington Irving's, Edgar Allan Poe's, and Nathaniel Hawthorne's tales of terror were suggested by Radcliffe's work.

As the most popular and perhaps most important novelist between the eighteenth century masters and Austen and Sir Walter Scott, Radcliffe continues to claim the attention of academicians. It is clear that there has been a remarkable revival of interest in the Gothic and in Radcliffe's work.

Biography

Ann Radcliffe, née Ward, was born on July 9, 1764, in Holborn, a borough of central London, the only child of William Ward and Ann Oates Ward. Her father was a successful haberdasher who provided the family with a comfortable life, allowing Radcliffe access to a well-stocked library and the time to read the works of every important English author, as well as numerous popular romances. This quiet, sheltered existence was enlivened by the visits of her wealthy and learned uncle, Thomas Bentley, who was the partner of Josiah Wedgwood, the potter. Bentley's London home was a center for the literati.

In 1772, Radcliffe joined her parents at Bath, where her father had opened a shop for the firm of Wedgwood and Bentley. She remained sequestered in this resort until her marriage to the young Oxford graduate, William Radcliffe, in 1788. William Radcliffe had first decided to become a law student at one of the Inns of Court but abandoned this for a career in journalism. The couple moved to London soon thereafter, where William subsequently became proprietor and editor of the *English Chronicle*. The marriage was happy but childless, and the couple's circle of friends were primarily literary, which added encouragement to William Radcliffe's argument that his wife should begin to write.

With her husband away on editorial business, Radcliffe spent the evenings writing without interruption. Her first book, *The Castles of Athlin and Dunbayne*, was unremarkable, but her next two novels established her reputation as a master of suspense and the supernatural. *A Sicilian Romance* and *The Romance of the Forest* attracted the public's voracious appetite for romances. Both works were translated into French and Italian and numerous editions were published, as well as a dramatization of *The Romance of the Forest*, performed in 1794. Radcliffe's success culminated in the appearance of *The Mysteries of Udolpho*; her decision to rely less on external action and more on psychological conflict produced ecstatic reviews. The excitement created by the book threatened the relative solitude of the Radcliffes, but the publisher's unusually high offer of five hundred pounds freed them to travel extensively on the Continent.

In the summer of 1794, the Radcliffes journeyed through Holland and along the Rhine to the Swiss frontier. On returning to England, they proceeded north to the Lake District. While traveling, Radcliffe took complete notes concerning the picturesque landscape and included detailed political and economic accounts of the Low Countries and the Rhineland. These latter observations were probably contributed by her husband, though both Radcliffes found the devastation of the Napoleonic Wars appalling. In 1795, there appeared *A Journey Made in the Summer of 1794 Through Holland and the Western Frontier of Germany*.

Radcliffe's interest in the human misery of these regions and the legends and superstitions of the great fortresses and Catholic churches of the Rhineland suggested her next work, *The Italian: Or, The Confessional of the Black Penitents*. As a romance of the Inquisition, it explored character motivation in great detail, while action became a method of dramatizing personalities and not a simple vehicle for movement from one adventure to another. *The Italian*, though not as popular as *The Mysteries of Udolpho*, was translated immediately into French and even badly dramatized at the Haymarket on August 15, 1797.

At the age of thirty-three, Radcliffe was at the height of her popularity; though she had never decided on writing as a potential source of income, her means by this time had become quite ample. With the deaths of her parents between 1798 and 1799, she found herself independently wealthy. Whether it was because of her secure financial condition or her displeasure with the cheap imitations of her novels, Radcliffe withdrew from the public domain and refrained from publishing any more works in her lifetime. Innumerable reports surfaced that she was suffering from a terminal illness, that the terrors of which she had written in her novels had driven her mad, or that she had mysteriously died. These reports were without substance; in fact, she wrote another novel, a metrical romance, and an extensive diary.

After her death, Radcliffe's husband found among her papers a novel, *Gaston de Blondeville*, which he arranged to have published. Written after Radcliffe's visit to the ruins of Kenilworth Castle in 1802, it came near to comparing with the historical romances of Scott but lost itself in a preoccupation with historical precision, leaving action and character to suffer from a lack of emphasis. The narrative poem, *St. Alban's Abbey*, appeared posthumously with this last novel; though Radcliffe had been offered an early opportunity for publication, she broke off negotiations with the publisher.

Content with retirement and relative obscurity, she wrote in her last years only diary entries concerning the places she and her husband had visited on their long journeys through the English countryside. From 1813 to 1816, she lived near Windsor and probably at this time began suffering from bouts of spasmodic asthma. From all reports, she enjoyed the company of friends, maintained a ready wit and a sly humor, but insisted on delicacy and decorum in all things. Shortly before her final illness, she returned to London; she died there on February 7, 1823, in her sixtieth year. The "Udolpho woman" or "the Shakespeare of Romance Writers," as one contemporary reviewer called her, has achieved a secure place in the history of English literature.

Analysis

The novels of Ann Radcliffe serve as a transition between the major English novelists of the eighteenth century and the first accomplished novelists of the nineteenth century. In the years between 1789 and 1797, her five novels established a style which profoundly affected English fiction for the next twenty-five years and had a considerable impact in translation as well. From the negligible first novel, *The Castles of Athlin and Dunbayne*, to the sophisticated romances, *The Mysteries of Udolpho* and *The Italian*, Radcliffe demonstrated an ability to enrich the motives, methods, and machineries of each succeeding work. Manipulating the conventions of the Gothic while introducing new thematic concerns and experiments with narrative techniques, Radcliffe became a master of her craft.

Improved control over the complex atmosphere of the Gothic romance proved an early factor in her success. Radcliffe went beyond the traditional Gothic devices of lurking ghosts and malevolent noblemen torturing innocent girls to an interest in natural description. This delight with nature's sublime scenery gave tone and color to her settings while emphasizing the heightened emotions and imagination that were produced in reaction to the landscape. A skillful use of numerous atmospherical factors such as sunsets, storms, winds, thunderclaps, and moonlight, intensified the romantic tendencies of her time. While she made landscape in fiction a convention, it was her combining of beauty in horror and the horrible in the beautiful that reflected the romantic shift away from order and reason toward emotion and imagination.

Radcliffe's novels rely not only on strategies of terror, but also on the psychology of feelings. Of particular psychological interest are Radcliffe's villains. Cruel, calculating, domineering, relentless, and selfish, they are more compelling than her virtuous characters. Since their passions are alien to ordinary people, she dramatically explores the mysteries of their sinister attitudes. Radcliffe's villains resemble those created by the Elizabethan dramatists, and their descendants can be found in the works of the great Romantics, Byron and Shelley.

With the publication of her third novel, *The Romance of the Forest*, Radcliffe moved from apprenticeship to mastery. Radcliffe's new emphasis on internal action makes her protagonist, Adeline, more credible than the stock romantic heroines whom she in many ways resembles. Adeline suffers from a nervous illness after mysteriously being thrust upon the LaMotte family, who themselves have only recently escaped, under curious circumstances, from Paris. Soon the group discovers a Gothic ruin, which contains the requisite underground room, rotten tapestries, blood stains, and a general aura of mystery.

Instead of the familiar chase scenes, a series of unified set-pieces portray the exploration of the ruin, the seduction of the heroine, and the execution of the hero. The entire plot depends upon the actions of a vicious but dominating sadist, the Marquis Phillipe de Montalt, and his conspiratorial agent, Pierre de LaMotte, against the unprotected Adeline. Because of the uncertainty of her birth, the sexual implications of this situation involve the risk of incest. Among contemporary readers, *The Romance of the Forest* became an immediate success, owing to its well-constructed narrative, the charm of its description of romantic landscape, and a consummate handling of the principle of suspense.

Radcliffe's next novel, *The Mysteries of Udolpho*, remains her best-known work. The sublimity of her landscapes and the control which she demonstrates in this novel mark an important change from her earlier novels; Radcliffe's handling of action and character also reached new levels of subtlety and success, moving the novel a step beyond the rather strict conventions of the sentimental mode to one of psychological inquiry.

The period of the novel is the end of the sixteenth century. The principal scenes are laid in the gloomy enclave of the Castle of Udolpho, in the Italian Apennines, but many glances are directed toward the south of France—Gascony, Provence, and Languedoc—and the brightness of Venice is contrasted with the dark horrors of the Apennines. Emily St. Aubert, the beautiful daughter of a Gascon family, is the heroine; she is intelligent and extraordinarily accomplished in the fine arts. Though revealing all the tender sensibilities of the characters associated with a hundred sentimental tales, Emily emerges as a credible figure who seems aware of the connections between the scenery around her and the characters who inhabit it. As a painter, she sees and thinks of life as a series of pictures. A further element of Emily's characterization that adds to her credibility is her internalizing of the suspense produced by the action in the narrative. Her heightened sensibility reacts to fear and terror in an all-inclusive way; this acuteness of sensibility makes her an easy prey for the villain, Signor Montoni. This sinister figure marries Emily's aunt for her money and then conveys Emily and her unhappy aunt to the "vast and dreary" confines of the castle.

There are certain shortcomings in Radcliffe's method: Landscape description strangles action; the visual aspects of the novel have been internalized; and the device of the chase over great stretches of land has been subordinated by mental recapitulation of past scenes—action becomes tableaux. This internal action is slow-moving, tortuously so in a novel of 300,000 words. Critics have also objected to Radcliffe's penchant for a rational explanation of every apparent supernatural phenomenon she has introduced; others, however, point out that Radcliffe's readers enjoyed terror only if they were never forced into surrendering themselves.

The Mysteries of Udolpho brought new energy to the picturesque, the sentimental, and the Gothic novel. Radcliffe alternated effectively between the picturesque vagueness of the landscape and the castle's hall of terrors. Her deft handling of sexual feeling, shown as antagonism between Montoni and Emily, is characteristic of her refusal to acknowledge sex overtly except as a frightening nameless power. The artificial terror, heightened sensibility, and the pervading air of mystery produced a powerful effect on her readers, yet many felt cheated by her failure to satisfy fully the intense imaginative visions awakened by the book. These readers would have to wait for *The Italian*, probably Radcliffe's finest work and the high-water mark of Gothic fiction.

The unity, control, and concentration of *The Italian* display a superb talent. Radcliffe's narrative technique is more sophisticated than at any previous time, particularly in the subtle revelation of the unreliability of feelings based on first impressions rather than on rational judgment. The dramatic pacing remains rigorous throughout and relatively free from digressions. The story's impulse depends upon the Marchesa di Vivaldi's refusal to allow her young son, Vincentio, to marry the heroine, Ellena di Rosalba, whose origins are in doubt. The Marchesa relies on the sinister machinations of her monk-confessor, Schedoni, who decides to murder Ellena. Radcliffe's antipathy to Roman Catholicism is evident in her account of the horrors of the Carmelite abbey and its order, including the labyrinthine vaults and gloomy corridors. A strange blend of fascination and disgust is evoked here and in the scenes of the trial in the halls of the Inquisition, the ruins of the Paluzzi, and in the prison of the Inquisition. Clearly, the Gothic aspects of *The Italian* function as representations of a disordered and morally evil past.

The vividness continues through to the climax of the story, when Schedoni, dagger in hand, prepares to murder Ellena but hesitates when he recognizes the portrait miniature she wears. Believing the girl is his lost daughter, he tries to make amends for his crimes. Though the solution involves more complex developments, the excitement of the confrontation between these two figures remains exceptional. Ellena has been a paragon of virtue, displaying piety, sensibility, benevolence, constancy, and a love of nature. To this catalog, Radcliffe adds intelligence, courage, and ingenuity. As an idealized character, Ellena represents the strengths necessary to prevail in the romantic conflict against external malign forces. Schedoni, the devil/priest, is a figure of strong and dangerous sexual desire, associated, as is often the case in Radcliffe's work, with incest. Radcliffe counters the passivity and weakness of Ellena's virtues with this masculine version of desire—the lust of unregulated ambition.

Radcliffe remains the undisputed mistress of the Gothic novel and a central figure in the Gothic revival that began in the late 1950's. The generous volume of Radcliffe criticism in recent decades has redefined her place in literary history, acknowledging the prodigious sweep of her influence. On first reading her works, one must remember to search behind the genteel exterior of the artistry to discover the special recesses of terror, subconscious conflict, and the psychology of feelings that played a major role in the evolution of dark romanticism.

Other major works

POETRY: *The Poems of Ann Radcliffe*, 1816; *St. Alban's Abbey*, 1826.

NONFICTION: *A Journey Made in the Summer of 1794 Through Holland and the Western Frontier of Germany*, 1795.

Bibliography

Durant, David S. *Ann Radcliffe's Novels: Experiments in Setting*. Rev. ed. New York: Arno Press, 1980.

McIntyre, Clara Frances. *Ann Radcliffe in Relation to Her Time*. New Haven, Conn.: Yale University Press, 1920. Reprint. New York: Archon Books, 1970.

Murray, E. B. *Ann Radcliffe*. New York: Twayne, 1972.

Sherman, Leona F. *Ann Radcliffe and the Gothic Romance: A Psychoanalytic Approach*. New York: Arno Press, 1980.

Smith, Nelson C. *The Art of the Gothic: Ann Radcliffe's Major Novels*. New York: Arno Press, 1980.

MARY RENAULT
Mary Challans

Born: London, England; September 4, 1905   **Died:** Cape Town, South Africa; December 13, 1983

Principal long fiction

Purposes of Love, 1939 (published in the United States as *Promise of Love*, 1940); *Kind Are Her Answers*, 1940; *The Friendly Young Ladies*, 1944 (published in the United States as *The Middle Mist*, 1945); *Return to Night*, 1947; *North Face*, 1948; *The Charioteer*, 1953; *The Last of the Wine*, 1956; *The King Must Die*, 1958; *The Bull from the Sea*, 1962; *The Mask of Apollo*, 1966; *Fire from Heaven*, 1969; *The Persian Boy*, 1972; *The Praise Singer*, 1978; *Funeral Games*, 1981; *The Alexander Trilogy*, 1984 (includes *Fire from Heaven, The Persian Boy*, and *Funeral Games*).

Other literary forms

All but two of Mary Renault's published works are novels. *The Lion in the Gateway: Heroic Battles of the Greeks and Persians at Marathon, Salamis, and Thermopylae* (1964) is a children's history of ancient Greek battles. *The Nature of Alexander* (1975) is a heavily documented biography placing the charismatic leader in the context of his time and customs.

Achievements

Critics praised Renault's first five novels, written and set around World War II, for their realism, psychological depth, and literary technique. In 1946, one year prior to its publication, *Return to Night* won the MGM Award, $150,000, then the world's largest literary prize. Although this novel was never made into a motion picture, the award brought Renault American acclaim, aug- mented later by the success of her Greek novels, but her work has never gained the academic attention it deserves. She received the National Association of Independent Schools Award in 1963 and the Silver Pen Award in 1971, and she was a Fellow of the Royal Society of Literature.

Biography

Mary Renault (the pen name of Mary Challans), a physician's daughter, was born on September 4, 1905, in London. At eight, she decided to become a writer, and she read English at St. Hugh's College, Oxford, from 1924 to 1927, where she preferred to study the Middle Ages, the setting of an attempted historical novel she destroyed after several rejections. She had once thought of teaching, but after graduation she entered nurses' training at Radcliffe Infirmary, Oxford, where she received her nursing degree in 1937. She dated her literary career from 1939, though she continued as a neurosurgical nurse at Radcliffe Infirmary throughout the war, writing in her off-duty hours. Her first novels were widely popular, but she claimed that "if her early novels were destroyed irrevocably, she would feel absolutely no loss" (Bernard F. Dick, *The Hellenism of Mary Renault*, 1972).

Renault's postwar travels in the eastern Mediterranean provided the impetus for a new literary phase marked by her emigration to South Africa in 1948. After this move, her exhaustive self-taught knowledge of ancient Greek history and philosophy made her a mesmerizing novelist able to re-create a lost world. In the estimation of Dick, Renault was "the only bona fide Hellenist in twentieth century fiction." Renault remained a resident of South Africa until her death on December 13, 1983.

Analysis

Mary Renault's novels celebrate and eulogize humanity's potential but transitory glory, a combination diffi- cult for a world that has relinquished its acquaintance with the classics. Renault's early work deals with the individual's freedom from contemporary power structures and stifling social conventions. Such topical concerns, however appealing to modern readers, are nevertheless peripheral to the core of Renault's art: the Platonism that she followed to the mythic depths of her later novels.

Renault's early novels have strong Platonic elements. In the first, *Promise of Love*, she shows Vivian, a nurse, and Mic, who loves her because she resembles her brother Jan, achieving self-knowledge not through sexual passion but by affection, the ultimate stage of Platonic love. *Kind Are Her Answers* foreshadows her interest in theater as mimetic form, Plato's first literary love, which she realized more fully in *The Mask of Apollo*. Her third novel, *The Middle Mist*, concludes with references to Plato's *Lysis*, his dialogue on friendship which claims that erotic satisfaction destroys *philia*, the more permanent nonphysical union promised by Platonic love, a theme to which Renault returned more successfully in *The Last of the Wine*. Renault attempted unconvincingly in *Return to Night* and *North Face* to state the *amor vincit omnia* tradition of "women's fiction" in mythological metaphors, and found that she had to develop a new fictional mode capable of expressing her archetypal themes with Platonic concepts.

Each of Renault's Greek novels focuses on a crucial nexus of physical and spiritual existence in Greek history. The age of legendary heroes such as Theseus of Athens, subject of *The King Must Die* and *The Bull from the Sea*, was followed by the Trojan War, 1200 B.C., the stuff of classical epic and tragedy and the harbinger of Greece's Dark Age, when only Athens stood against the Dorian invasion. By the sixth century B.C., the setting of *The Praise Singer*, Athens, under the benevolent tyrant Pisistratus, had become the model polis of the Greek peninsula, building a democracy that repelled imperial Persia and fostered the world's greatest tragedies in their Dionysian festivals. *The Last of the Wine* treats Athens' fall to Sparta in the Peloponnesian Wars, 404 B.C., torn by internal strife and bled by foreign expansion. The restored Athenian democracy of a half-century later is the milieu of *The Mask of Apollo*. Shortly after Plato's death, his pupil Aristotle taught a prince in Macedon who dreams of Homeric deeds in *Fire from Heaven*, accomplishes them in *The Persian Boy*, and leaves an empire to be shattered by lesser men in *Funeral Games*—Alexander the Great.

The Last of the Wine, like most of Renault's Greek fiction, is ostensibly a memoir, a form favored by classical authors. Its fictional narrator, a young and "beautiful" Athenian knight named Alexias, endures the agonizing aftermath of Athens' ill-fated Sicilian venture under Alkibiades, the magnetic but flawed former student of Sokrates. With Lysis, the historical figure on whom Plato modeled his dialogue on ideal friendship, Alexias begins the idealistic attachment they learned together from Sokrates, but physical passion, handled with sensitivity by Renault, overcomes them, and they ruefully must compromise their ideal. Sacrificing his honor for Lysis during the famine caused by the Spartan siege of Athens, Alexias models for sculptors, at least one lascivious, to feed his wounded friend, and in the battle to restore Athenian democracy, Lysis falls gloriously with Alexias' name upon his lips.

The novel's title, an allusion to the Greek custom in which the wine remaining in a cup is tossed to form the initial of a lover's name, metaphorically represents Athens' abandonment of the ideals of its Golden Age. Renault poignantly shows Lysis, a gentleman athlete in pursuit of *philotimo*, the hero's struggle for outward glory to emulate his ideal, beaten sadistically in the Isthmian Games by a monstrous professional wrestler, just as Athenian democracy is becoming warped by politicians such as the vicious Kritias and the cold-blooded Anytos, who will help condemn Sokrates. Alkibiades' personal disaster, abandoning Athens for its Spartan enemies, is an exemplary case of a leader who cannot resist abusing his charismatic gifts.

The Greek ideal of democracy learned at Sokrates' side and based on individual *arete*, inward pursuit of honor, still allows Lysis a moral victory often overlooked in this splendidly elegiac novel of the death of an era. "Men are not born equal in themselves," Lysis tells Alexias over wine one evening in Samos; "a man who thinks himself as good as everyone else will be at no pains to grow better." Lysis fights and dies for "a City where I can find my equals and respect my betters . . . and where no one can tell me to swallow a lie because it is expedient."

By the mid-fourth century B.C., late in Plato's life, sophisticated Athenians had accepted the gods as metaphysical forces within the human personality. In *The Mask of Apollo*, Renault poses the primal duality of Apollo and Dionysus in Greek culture, the calm, farseeing force of reason and art balanced against the irresistible force of ecstasy. An old mask of Apollo, reputedly from the workshop of the Parthenon's architect Phidias, accompanies Renault's narrator Nikeratos through his successful acting career, the fascinating backdrop to the political career of Dion of Syracuse, Plato's noble friend, who might have become the ideal philosopher-king Plato postulated in *The Republic*.

Though Dion is a model soldier and a principled statesman, circumstances force him to abandon his philosophical ideals to save Syracuse from devastation. Renault parallels his fall with Nikeratos' performance in Euripides' *The Bacchae* (405 B.C.), the enigmatic masterpiece named for the followers of Dionysus. As he meditates before Apollo's mask, Nikeratos hears his own voice: "With *The Bacchae* he [Euripides] digs down far below, to some deep rift in the soul where our griefs begin. Take that play anywhere, even to men unborn who worship other gods or none, and it will teach them to know themselves."

Plato's tragedy, acted out by Dion, was the "deep rift" that made men unable to follow him with united minds and hearts: "No one would fight for Dion, when he gave, as his own soul saw it, his very life for justice." By serving Apollo and Dionysus equally, however, Nikeratos the artist earns his gifts, one a Platonic dream of acting in a strange revenge drama, speaking lines beside an open grave to a clean skull in his hand. Through his love for his protégé Thettalos, whom he frees for achievements he knows will be greater than his own, Nikeratos plays Achilles in Aeschylus' *The Myrmidons* in a performance viewed by Alexander, a boy for whom men will fight and die, "whether he is right or wrong," a prince who "will wander through the world . . . never knowing . . . that while he was still a child the thing he seeks slipped from the world, worn out and spent."

Renault's Alexander grows from boy to king in *Fire from Heaven*, in which she abandons the memoir form for more objective narration, as though no single point of view could encompass Alexander's youthful ideals, fired by the blazing Homeric *philotimo* in Achilles' honor he learned at the epic-conscious Macedonian court. Modern archaeology supports Renault's conviction that Alexander deliberately patterned his actions, even his father Philip's funerary rites, upon the *Iliad* (c. 800 B.C.), which he read as though returning home, recognizing in his mutual love with Hephaistion the tragic bond of Achilles and Patroclus, the basis of the Western world's first, perhaps greatest, poem.

The novel in which Renault most precariously treats the question of homosexuality, *The Persian Boy*, is narrated by Bagoas, the handsome eunuch once King Darius' favorite and now the lover of Alexander. Renault's choice of Bagoas' point of view reflects her belief that Alexander was not corrupted by Persian luxury and imperial power, as many historians from classical times to the present have asserted, but that he sought to assimilate Eastern ways as a means of uniting his realm in spirit as well as military fact. Just as Alexander's "passionate capacity for affection" could allow him to accept affection wherever it was sincerely offered from the heart and yet remain wholly true to Bagoas' "victor now, forever," Hephaistion, who Renault feels is the most underrated man in history, Alexander felt "Macedon was my father's country. This is mine" — meaning the empire he had won for himself.

Renault believes that Alexander's eventual tragedy was that he was humanly unable to achieve equilibrium between his followers' personal devotion to him and their pragmatic selfish desires. Through Alexander's complex relationship with his dangerous mother Olympias, herself a devotee of Dionysus, Renault exemplifies the peril of neglecting the god of ecstasy basic to *The Bacchae*, in which Olympias herself had acted during Alexander's youth as a shocking challenge to Philip's authority. Toward the end of his own life, Dionysus' cruelty touches even Alexander. Renault shows his purported deterioration as less his own fault than his men's when he must hold them by force as well as by love, even violating Macedon's dearest law, killing before their Assembly had condemned a man to death. The powerful god leads Alexander to excess; Bagoas sees that "his hunger grew by feeding." The Roman historian Arrian, following the memoir of Alexander's only faithful general Ptolemy, commented, "If there had been no other competition, he would have competed against himself."

Bagoas better than any also sees that "great anguish lies in wait for those who long too greatly." Alexander loses Hephaistion and with him nearly abandons his own senses, emerging only after his friend's funeral, in which he watches Thettalos, without Nikeratos for the first time, perform *The Myrmidons* one last time; " 'perhaps,' Bagoas thought, 'the last of the madness had been seared out of him by so much burning,' "

At the close of *The Persian Boy*, Renault notes in her afterword, "When his [Alexander's] faults (those his own times did not account as virtues) have been considered . . . no other human being has attracted in his lifetime, from so many men, so fervent a devotion. Their reasons are worth examining." In her two novels of Alexander's life, Renault not only has examined the reasons but also has brilliantly probed to the heart of one of the greatest human mysteries: how one man can ask, as did Homer's Achilles, "now as things are, when the ministers of death stand by us/ In their thousands, which no man born to die can escape or even evade,/ Let us go." — and how other men, with all their hearts, can answer.

In Alexander's time, Renault has remarked, "the issue was not whether, but how one made [war]." At his death, brought about at least in part by his self-destructive grief for Hephaistion, Alexander's generals embarked on a cannibalistic power struggle—only Ptolemy, his half brother, emerging with any of the dignity Alexander had worn so easily in conquering his empire. Renault's *Funeral Games* is "the ancestral pattern of Macedonian tribal and familial struggles for his throne; except that Alexander had given them a world stage on which to do it." The most violent of Renault's Greek novels, *Funeral Games* contains a darkness that is alleviated only by flashes of Alexander reflected through the decency of the few who knew him best — Ptolemy, Bagoas, and Queen Sisygambis, who looked upon Alexander, not Darius, as her son.

In her eight novels of ancient Greece, Renault far surpasses conventional historical fiction. She achieves a mythic dimension in her balance of Apollonian and Dionysian psychological forces and philosophical precision in her treatment of Platonic doctrines. Her style is adapted to the Greek literature of each period she delineates, Attic elegance for *The Last of the Wine* and *The Mask of Apollo*, Hellenic involution counterpoised against Alexander's Homeric simplicity of speech. Renault links all eight novels with a chain of works of art, a finely crafted touch the classical Greeks would have applauded: the great tragedies, *The Myrmidons* and *The Bacchae*, Polykleitos' sculpture of Hermes modeled on Alexias, and the bronze of the liberator Harmodios in Pisistratos' day all serve as shaping factors in the portrait of her ultimate hero, Alexander. Mastering time, space, and modern ignorance of the classical world, Renault captures the "sadness at the back of life" Virginia Woolf so aptly cited as the essence of Greek literature, the inevitable grieving awareness of humankind at the impassable gulf between aspirations and achievement. In the face of the eternal questions of existence, Renault's novels offer a direction in which to turn when, in Woolf's words, "we are sick of the vagueness, of the confusion, of the Christianity and its consolations, of our own age."

Other major works

NONFICTION: *The Nature of Alexander*, 1975.

CHILDREN'S LITERATURE: *The Lion in the Gateway: Heroic Battles of the Greeks and Persians at Marathon, Salamis, and Thermopylae*, 1964.

Bibliography

Burns, Landon C., Jr. "Men Are Only Men: The Novels of Mary Renault." *Critique: Studies in Modern Fiction* 4 (Winter, 1963): 102-121.

Dick, Bernard F. *The Hellenism of Mary Renault*. Carbondale: Southern Illinois Press, 1972.

Sweetman, David. *Mary Renault: A Biography*. New York: Harcourt Brace, 1993.

Wolfe, Peter. *Mary Renault*. New York: Twayne, 1969.

JEAN RHYS
Ella Gwendolen Rees Williams

Born: Roseau, Dominica, West Indies; August 24, 1894

Died: Exeter, England; May 14, 1979

Principal long fiction

Postures, 1928 (published in the United States as *Quartet*, 1929); *After Leaving Mr. Mackenzie*, 1930; *Voyage in the Dark*, 1934; *Good Morning, Midnight*, 1939; *Wide Sargasso Sea*, 1966.

Other literary forms

Though Jean Rhys is now primarily remembered for her novels, her first published book was a collection of short stories, *The Left Bank and Other Stories* (1927). Rhys published two other collections of stories: *Tigers Are Better-Looking* (1968) and *Sleep It Off, Lady* (1976). In 1987, *The Collected Short Stories* brought together her work in this genre. At her death, she left an essentially completed first section of an autobiography with Diana Athill, who had edited *Wide Sargasso Sea* and *Sleep It Off, Lady*. Athill published this section and a less completed second section as *Smile, Please: An Unfinished Autobiography* in 1979. A collection of letters was published in 1984.

Achievements

When *Wide Sargasso Sea*, her last novel, was published, Jean Rhys was described in *The New York Times* as the greatest living novelist. Such praise is overstated, but Rhys's fiction, long overlooked by academic critics, is undergoing a revival spurred by feminist studies. Rhys played a noteworthy role in the French Left Bank literary scene in the 1920's, and between 1927 and 1939, she published four substantial novels and a number of jewellike short stories. Although she owes her current reputation in large measure to the rising interest in female writers and feminist themes, her work belongs more properly with the masters of literary impressionism: Joseph Conrad, Ford Madox Ford, Marcel Proust, and James Joyce. She began to publish her writing under the encouragement of her intimate friend Ford Madox Ford and continued to write in spite of falling out of favor with his circle. As prizes and honors came to her in her old age after the publication of *Wide Sargasso Sea*, it must have given her grim satisfaction to realize that she had attained entirely by her own efforts a position as a writer at least equal to that of her erstwhile friends.

Biography

Jean Rhys was born Ella Gwendolen Rees Williams in the West Indies on the island of Dominica in 1894, the daughter of a Welsh father and a part-Creole mother. English society classified her as "colored." Her child associates were often Creole, and she was surrounded by ideas peculiar to their culture, such as voodoo and witchcraft. At the same time, she attended a convent school and seriously considered the life of a nun. The colonial mentality was strong in Dominica, and the "proper" role for a well-bred young woman was sharply defined: passive, obedient, submissive.

In 1910, Rhys left Dominica and went to live in Cambridge, England, with her aunt, Clarice Rhys Williams. After a short term in a local school, she enrolled in the Royal Academy of Dramatic Art in London. Her father died soon after she arrived in England, and she found herself short of money. The transition from the West Indies to England must have been extremely painful for the sixteen-year-old girl: the climate harsh, the people cold, the social and economic situation threatening. Those who knew her as a young woman testified that she was strikingly beautiful. After a term at the Royal

Academy of Dramatic Art, she toured as a minor actress or chorus girl with provincial theater troupes and did modeling. Many of her stories and novels reflect scenes from her career on the stage, and most of them hinge on the theme of male exploitation of women through financial domination.

Near the end of World War I, Rhys married Jean Lenglet (alias Edouard de Neve), an adventurer who had served in the French Foreign Legion and who was probably employed by the French secret service during the war. The newlywed couple lived in Paris, constantly moving from one cheap hotel to another, although de Neve secured temporarily a position with the international mission administering Vienna. A son was born to them in 1919, but lived only three weeks. A daughter born in 1922 lived, but required special medical care. Rhys tried to earn a living in Paris by modeling and writing. Pearl Adam, the wife of a correspondent for *The Times* of Paris, took an interest in some of her sketches and introduced her to Ford Madox Ford, then editor of *The Transatlantic Review*. Through him, she entered into the expatriate community of the early 1920's, meeting James Joyce, Ernest Hemingway, and other prominent writers. Shortly after Rhys met Ford in the autumn of 1924, her husband was sent to prison for illegal dealing in antiques. Ford was living at the time with the artist Stella Bowen. Rhys, penniless, moved in with them and soon formed an intimate relationship with Ford. A casual episode in Ford's generally messy life was something much more serious for the young woman; Rhys treats this affair in her first novel, *Quartet*. De Neve never forgave her for her involvement with Ford. After her divorce from de Neve, Rhys became closely involved with a literary agent, Leslie Tilden Smith. They were eventually married and lived together until his death in 1945. Subsequently, she married his cousin, Max Hamer, who later served time in prison for mismanagement of his firm's funds. Throughout the 1940's and 1950's, Rhys suffered greatly from poverty, poor health, and family problems. Her books were all out of print.

She was not, however, entirely forgotten. The actress Selma Vaz Diaz adapted a dramatic monologue from *Good Morning, Midnight* for stage use in 1949. Eight years later, the BBC's third program presented Selma Vaz Diaz's monologue, which received excellent notices. The publication of *Wide Sargasso Sea* in 1966 and the rapid growth of feminist studies led to a Rhys revival, and the reprinting of all her works followed.

Analysis

Jean Rhys's first novel, *Quartet*, reflects closely her misadventures with Ford Madox Ford. The heroine, Marya Zelli, whose husband is in prison, moves in with the rich and respectable Hugh and Lois Heidler. Hugh becomes Marya's lover, while Lois punishes her with petty cruelties. The central figure is a woman alone, penniless, exploited, and an outsider. In her next novel, *After Leaving Mr. Mackenzie*, the central figure, Julia Martin, breaks off with her rich lover, Mr. Mackenzie, and finds herself financially desperate. *Voyage in the Dark* tells the story of Anna Morgan, who arrives from the West Indies as an innocent young girl in England, has her first affair as a chorus girl, and descends through a series of shorter and shorter affairs to working for a masseuse. In *Good Morning, Midnight*, the alcoholic Sasha Jensen, penniless in Paris, remembers episodes from her past which have brought her to this sorry pass. All four of these novels show a female character subject to financial, sexual, and social domination by men and "respectable" society. In all cases, the heroine is passive, but "sentimental." The reader is interested in her feelings, rather than in her ideas and accomplishments. She is alienated economically from any opportunity to do meaningful and justly rewarding work. She is an alien socially, either from a foreign and despised colonial culture or from a marginally respectable social background. She is literally an alien or foreigner in Paris and London, which are cities of dreadful night for her. What the characters fear most is the final crushing alienation from their true identities, the reduction to some model or type imagined by a foreign man. They all face the choice of becoming someone's gamine, *garçonne*, or femme fatale, or of starving to death, and they all struggle against this loss of personal identity. After a silence of more than twenty years, Rhys returned to these same concerns in her masterpiece, *Wide Sargasso Sea*. While the four early novels are to a large degree autobiographical, *Wide Sargasso Sea* has a more literary origin, although it, too, reflects details from the author's personal life.

Wide Sargasso Sea requires a familiarity with Charlotte Brontë's *Jane Eyre* (1847). In Charlotte Brontë's novel, Jane is prevented from marrying Rochester by the presence of his madwoman in the attic, an insane West

Indian wife who finally perishes in the fire which she sets, burning Rochester's house and blinding him, but clearing the way for Jane to wed him. The madwoman in *Jane Eyre* is depicted entirely from the exterior. It is natural that the mad West Indian wife, when seen only through the eyes of her English rival and of Rochester, appears completely hideous and depraved. Indeed, when Jane first sees the madwoman in Chapter XVI of the novel, she cannot tell whether it is a beast or a human being groveling on all fours. Like a hyena with bloated features, the madwoman attacks Rochester in this episode.

Wide Sargasso Sea is a sympathetic account of the life of Rochester's mad wife, ranging from her childhood in the West Indies, her Creole and Catholic background, and her courtship and married years with the deceitful Rochester, to her final descent into madness and captivity in England. Clearly, the predicament of the West Indian wife resembles that of Rhys herself in many ways. In order to present the alien wife's case, she has written a "countertext," an extension of Brontë's novel filling in the "missing" testimony, the issues over which Brontë glosses.

Wide Sargasso Sea consists of two parts. Part I is narrated by the girl growing up in Jamaica who is destined to become Rochester's wife. The Emancipation Act has just been passed (the year of that Imperial Edict was 1833) and the blacks on the island are passing through a period of so-called apprenticeship which should lead to their complete freedom in 1837. This is a period of racial tension and anxiety for the privileged colonial community. Fear of black violence runs high, and no one knows exactly what will happen to the landholders once the blacks are emancipated. The girlish narrator lives in the interface between the privileged white colonists and the blacks. Although a child of landowners, she is impoverished, clinging to European notions of respectability, and in constant fear. She lives on the crumbling estate of her widowed mother. Her closest associate is Christophine, a Martinique obeah woman, or voodoo witch. When her mother marries Mr. Mason, the family's lot improves temporarily, until the blacks revolt, burning their country home, Coulibri, and killing her half-witted brother. She then attends a repressive Catholic school in town, and her kindly colored "cousin" Sandi protects her from more hostile blacks.

Part II is narrated by the young Rochester on his honeymoon with his bride to her country home. Wher-

ever appropriate, Rhys follows the details of Brontë's story. Rochester reveals that his marriage was merely a financial arrangement. After an uneasy period of passion, Rochester's feelings for his bride begin to cool. He receives a letter of denunciation accusing her of misbehavior with Sandi and revealing that madness runs in the family. To counter Rochester's growing hostility, the young bride goes to her former companion, the obeah woman Christophine, for a love potion. The nature of the potion is that it can work for one night only. Nevertheless, she administers it to her husband. His love now dead, she is torn from her native land, transported to a cruel and loveless England, and maddeningly confined. Finally, she takes candle in hand to fire Rochester's house in suicidal destruction.

It is not unprecedented for a writer to develop a fiction from another writer's work. Yet Rhys's fiction permanently alters one's understanding of *Jane Eyre*. Approaching Brontë's work after Rhys's, one is compelled to ask such questions as, "Why is Jane so uncritical of Rochester?" and, "How is Jane herself like the madwoman in the attic?" Rhys's fiction reaches into the past and alters Brontë's novel.

Rhys's approach in *Wide Sargasso Sea* was influenced by Ford Madox Ford and, through Ford, Joseph Conrad. In the autumn of 1924, when Rhys first met Ford, he was writing *Joseph Conrad: A Memoir*. In it, Ford claimed that he and Conrad invented literary impressionism in English. Impressionist fiction characteristically employs limited and unreliable narration, follows a flow of associated ideas leaping freely in time and space, aims to render the impression of a scene vividly so as to make the reader see it as if it were before his or her eyes, and artfully selects and juxtaposes seemingly unrelated scenes and episodes so that the reader must construct the connections and relationships that make the story intelligible. These are the stylistic features of Rhys's fiction, as well as of Ford's *The Good Soldier* (1915), Conrad's *Heart of Darkness* (1899), Henry James's *The Turn of the Screw* (1898), and Joyce's *Ulysses* (1922).

An "affair"—the mainspring of the plot in an impressionist novel—is some shocking or puzzling event that has already occurred when the story begins. The reader knows what has happened but does not understand fully why and how it happened. The story proceeds in concentric rings of growing complication as the reader finds something once thought to be clear-cut becoming more and more intricate. Brontë's *Jane Eyre* provided Rhys with an impressionist "affair" in the scene in which the mad West Indian wife burns Rochester's house, blinding him and killing herself. Rhys takes up the affair of Rochester and reworks it into ever richer complications, making the initial judgments in *Jane Eyre* seem childishly oversimplified. "How can Jane simply register relief that the madwoman is burned out of her way? There must be more to the affair than that," the secondary fiction suggests.

One of the most important features of literary impressionism is the highly constructive activity that it demands of the reader. The tools for creating a verbal collage are limited, "unreliable" narration, psychological timeshifts, and juxtaposition. On the largest scale, *Wide Sargasso Sea* is juxtaposed with *Jane Eyre*, so that the two novels read together mean much more than when they are read independently. Within *Wide Sargasso Sea*, Part I (narrated by the West Indian bride) and Part II (narrated by Rochester) likewise mean more in juxtaposition than when considered separately. Throughout the text, the flow of consciousness of the storytellers cunningly shifts in time to juxtapose details that mean more together than they would in isolation.

The *Doppelgänger*, twin, or shadow-character runs throughout Rhys's fiction. All of her characters seem to be split personalities. There is a public role, that of the approved "good girl," which each is expected to play, and there is the repressed, rebellious "bad girl" lurking inside. If the bad girl can be hidden, the character is rewarded with money, love, and social position. Yet the bad girl will sometimes put in an appearance, when the character drinks too much or gets excited or angry. When the dark girl appears, punishment follows, swift and sure. This is the case with Marya Zelli in *Quartet*, Julia Martin in *After Leaving Mr. Mackenzie*, Anna Morgan in *Voyage in the Dark*, and Sasha Jensen in *Good Morning, Midnight*. It is also the case in Brontë's *Jane Eyre*. The education of Jane Eyre consists of repressing those dark, selfish impulses that Victorian society maintained "good little girls" should never feel. Jane succeeds in stamping out her "bad" self through a stiff British education, discipline, and self-control. She kills her repressed identity, conforms to society's expectations, and gets her reward—a crippled husband and a burned-out house. Rhys revives the dark twin, shut up in the attic, the naughty, wild, dark, selfish, bestial female. She suggests that the struggle between repressed politeness and unrepressed self-interest is an ongoing process in which total repression means the death of a woman's identity.

Other major works

SHORT FICTION: *The Left Bank and Other Stories*, 1927; *Tigers Are Better-Looking*, 1968; *Sleep It Off, Lady*, 1976; *The Collected Short Stories*, 1987.

NONFICTION: *Smile, Please: An Unfinished Autobiography*, 1979; *The Letters of Jean Rhys*, 1984 (also known as *Jean Rhys: Letters, 1931-1966*).

Bibliography

Angier, Carole. *Jean Rhys: Life and Work*. Boston: Little, Brown, 1991.

Benstock, Shari. *Women of the Left Bank: Paris, 1900-1940*. Austin: University of Texas Press, 1986.

Harrison, Nancy R. *Jean Rhys and the Novel as Women's Text*. Chapel Hill: University of North Carolina Press, 1988.

James, Selma. *The Ladies and the Mammies: Jane Austen and Jean Rhys*. Bristol, England: Falling Wall Press, 1983.

Staley, Thomas. *Jean Rhys: A Critical Study*. London: Macmillan, 1979.

ADRIENNE RICH

Born: Baltimore, Maryland; May 16, 1929

Principal poetry

A Change of World, 1951; *The Diamond Cutters and Other Poems*, 1955; *Snapshots of a Daughter-in-Law*, 1963; *Necessities of Life*, 1966; *Selected Poems*, 1967; *Leaflets*, 1969; *The Will to Change*, 1971; *Diving into the Wreck*, 1973; *Poems: Selected and New, 1950-1974*, 1975; *Twenty-one Love Poems*, 1975; *The Dream of a Common Language*, 1978; *A Wild Patience Has Taken Me This Far*, 1981; *Sources*, 1983; *The Fact of a Doorframe: Poems Selected and New, 1950-1984*, 1984; *Your Native Land, Your Life*, 1986; *Time's Power*, 1989; *An Atlas of the Difficult World: Poems, 1988-1991*, 1991; *Collected Early Poems, 1950-1970*, 1993.

Other literary forms

Of Woman Born: Motherhood as Experience and Institution (1976) is an analysis of the changing meanings of childbirth and motherhood in Anglo-American culture. Adrienne Rich draws upon personal experience as well as sources in mythology, sociology, economics, the history of medicine, and literature to develop her analysis. *On Lies, Secrets, and Silence: Selected Prose, 1966-1978* (1979) is a collection of essays on women writers (including Anne Bradstreet, Anne Sexton, Charlotte Brontë, and Emily Dickinson) and feminism. *Blood, Bread, and Poetry: Selected Prose, 1979-1985* (1986) and *What Is Found There: Notebooks on Poetry and Politics* (1993) offer further reflections on poetry, feminism, and politics.

Achievements

Rich's work has been at the vanguard of the women's movement in America. Her poems and essays explore her own experience and seek to develop a "common language" for women to communicate their values and perceptions. She has received numerous awards, including two Guggenheim fellowships, the National Institute of Arts and Letters award for poetry (1960), several prizes from *Poetry* magazine, the first annual Ruth Lilly Poetry Prize, the Shelley Memorial Award of the Poetry Society of America (1971), and the National Book Award for *Diving into the Wreck* in 1974. For several years she coedited (with Michelle Cliff) the lesbian feminist journal *Sinister Wisdom*.

Biography

Adrienne Cecile Rich was born in 1929, into a white, middle-class Southern family. Her father, Arnold Rice Rich, taught medicine at The Johns Hopkins University. Her mother, Helen Jones Rich, was trained as a composer and concert pianist but gave up her career to devote herself to her husband and two daughters. She carried out their early education at home, until the girls began to attend school in the fourth grade. Arnold Rich encouraged Adrienne to read and to write poetry. From his library, she read the work of such writers as Matthew Arnold, William Blake, Thomas Carlyle, John Keats, Dante Gabriel Rossetti, and Alfred, Lord Tennyson. Rich was graduated from Radcliffe College in 1951, the year her first volume of poetry was published. She traveled in Europe and England on a Guggenheim Fellowship in 1952-1953.

Rich married Alfred H. Conrad in 1953 and in the next few years gave birth to three sons. She lived with her family in Cambridge, Massachusetts, from 1953 to 1966, but spent 1961-1962 in The Netherlands on another Guggenheim Fellowship. In 1964, Rich began her involvement in the New Left, initiating a period of personal and political growth in which she reexamined her sexuality. In 1966, the family moved to New York, where Conrad taught at City College of New York. Rich also began to teach at City College, where she worked for the first time with disadvantaged students. After their separation, Conrad committed suicide in 1970. Rich contin-

436

ued teaching at City College and then Rutgers University until 1979, when she moved to western Massachusetts.

Rich eventually moved to California and continued her active career as poet, essayist, and speaker. Her

earliest work is a notable contribution to modern poetry. Her later work has broken new ground as she redefines and reimagines women's lives to create a female myth of self-discovery.

Analysis

Adrienne Rich's successive volumes of poetry chronicle a contemporary woman artist's odyssey. In her life and work she has been struggling to break out of patriarchal social and literary conventions, to redefine herself and create new traditions. W. H. Auden praised her first volume for its stylistic control, its skillful use of traditional themes such as isolation, and its assimilation of influences such as the work of Robert Frost and William Butler Yeats. (He wrote: "The poems . . . in this book are neatly and modestly dressed, speak quietly but do not mumble, respect their elders but are not cowed by them, and do not tell fibs." In *Snapshots of a Daughter-in-Law*, Rich began to move away from conventional poetic forms, to develop her own style, and to deal more directly with personal experience. Her attitudes toward literary tradition, history, and the home changed markedly. She questioned traditional attitudes toward home and family. As she found the patriarchal definitions of human relationships inadequate, her work became more personal and more urgent.

Snapshots of a Daughter-in-Law is written in a looser form than Rich's previous work. Language is simpler, texture less dense. The title poem is a series of vignettes of women's experiences. It fairly bristles with quotations drawn from Rich's wide-ranging reading. According to the poem, male authorities have always defined women in myths and literature. Thus, women lacked a literature of their own in which to define themselves. Rich wrote that she composed the poem "in fragments during children's naps, brief hours in a library, or at 3 A.M. after rising with a wakeful child." Because of these interruptions, she wrote the poem over a two-year period. In this poem, she wrote, "for the first time, directly about experiencing myself as a woman" rather than striving to be "universal." As the title indicates, these are static, fixed vignettes: the women are trapped, denied scope for action and choice.

Rich's first four books are built on linear oppositions. Balanced groups of stanzas articulate dichotomies between art and emotion, control and chaos, passivity and action, indoors and outdoors. Often characters must choose between alternatives. Tension between polarities

becomes a controlling force, focusing the poems' energies. In her next books of poetry, Rich would modify the dualistic structure of the earlier books. At the end of *Leaflets* (1969), she introduces the ghazal, a series of two-line units that conflate many ideas. These poems are collagelike, offering multiple perspectives.

Prompted by her increasing social concern and the leftist political critique evolving in the middle and later 1960's, Rich turned from personal malaise to political struggle, from private meditation to public discourse. Her jarring tone reflects her anger and impatience with language. Rhythms are broken, speech is fragmented. The poems suggest hurried diary entries. Images of violence, guerrilla warfare, and global human suffering suggest an embattled society. Yet, alongside the destruction, symbols of fertility and rebirth appear. The poems of this period describe Rich's heroines casting off traditional roles and preparing for journeys.

The evolution of *Leaflets* epitomizes Rich's movement from the personal to the political. The first poem, "Orion," is written in regular six-line stanzas and built on a typical pattern of balanced contrast. Indoors and outdoors, feminine and masculine, stagnation and adventure are the poles. The poem is a monologue in which the speaker blames herself for her failures as a woman. In contrast, the last poem in the book, "Ghazals," is a series of unrhymed couplets arranged in a seemingly random conflation of ideas and images. "Ghazals" is a multivoiced political critique of contemporary America. The heroes and heroines of the book are revolutionaries, protesters, challengers of an old order: Frantz Fanon, Walt Whitman, Galileo, LeRoi Jones (Amiri Baraka), Eldridge Cleaver, Dian Fossey. Turning her back on a political tradition that she now equates with death and destruction, Rich is saddened and estranged. Yet she not only wants to last until the new tradition begins but also will attempt to create that new tradition. Because the values and attitudes she wants to modify are so deeply entrenched in people's most fundamental assumptions, language itself must be reshaped to provide a vocabulary equal to her task of reconstruction.

Rich's poetry revises the heroic myth to reflect

women's experiences. *Diving into the Wreck* presents questing female heroes for the first time in her work. On their quests, they reconnect with lost parts of themselves, discover their own power, and build commonality with other women. Women's lives are the central focus as Rich's project becomes that of giving voice to women's experience, developing a "common language" that will bring the "dark country" of women's lives into the common light of day. Yet Rich also claims another task for women: They must struggle to redeem an endangered society. She argues that patriarchy's exaggerated aggressiveness, competition, and repression of feeling have led Western civilization to the brink of extinction. The task of reconstruction must be taken up by women. Working for change, the women in this book seek to turn civilization from its destructive paths by persuasion, creation of new myths, or redirection of anger.

Transformation is the cornerstone of *The Dream of a Common Language* and *A Wild Patience Has Taken Me This Far*. The poet wishes to effect fundamental changes in social arrangements, in concepts of selfhood, in governmental politics, in the meanings of sexuality, and in language. To that end, transformation supplants her earlier idea of revolution.

The title *The Dream of a Common Language* suggests vision, community, and above all a language in which visions and shared experience may be conceived and expressed. Dream is the voice of the nocturnal, unconscious self breaking into daytime existence. The terrain Rich explores here is the unknown country of the self, discovered in dream, myth, vision, ritual. Like dreams, the poems telescope time and space to make new connections among past, present, and future, between home and world. "Common" signifies that which is communal, habitual, shared, widely used, ordinary. Rich sets great value on the common, choosing it over the extraordinary.

In *The Dream of a Common Language*, the poet affirms that poetry stems from "the drive/ to connect. The dream of a common language." The book's central section, "Twenty-One Love Poems," orchestrates the controlling themes of women's love, power, language, world. Images of light and dark, dream and reality, speech and silence, home and wanderer structure the sequence. There are in fact twenty-two poems, for Rich has included an unnumbered "Floating Poem." Drawing from the sonnet tradition, Rich breaks formal conventions by varying the poems' lengths and departing from strict rhyme and meter. The sequence records a particular

lesbian relationship: its joyous beginnings, the difficulties encountered, and the termination of the affair. The poems ask questions about the meanings of self, language, and love between women, and about the possibilities of sustaining love in a hostile world. To be "at home" in the world requires coming to terms with the ugliness and brutality of the city, the pain and wounds, as well as the beauty of love and poetry. Deliberately, Rich situates the first sonnet of her sequence "in this city," with its "rainsoaked garbage."

Because she wishes to escape false romanticism, she seeks to connect the poems firmly to the world of daily life, to avoid sentimentality, and to speak honestly of her feelings. Because she wishes to transform the self-effacing behavior that has typically characterized women in love, she stresses self-awareness and deliberate choice. Caves and circles—images of roundness, completeness, wholeness—are dominant. Like the homes of Rich's earlier work, they are enclosures; however, the meaning of encirclement has been transformed, for in her new vision the poet no longer escapes from the world in her narrow room but reaches out to include the world, to bring it within her protected circle.

Poem XXI, the final poem of the sequence, is a complex network of dreamlike associations, of ritual and archetypal memory. In the sonnet, Rich moves from dark into light, from the prehistoric into the present, from inanimate nature ("the color of stone") into purposeful consciousness ("more than stone"). She becomes by choice "a figure in the light." The clarity of intelligence—"a cleft of light"—shapes her purpose. In drawing the circle she deliberately chooses her place.

Particularly in the last three poems of the book there is a sacramental quality, as Rich affirms her fusion with a world of women working together throughout time. Weaving, cooking, caring for children, they are crafting beautiful and utilitarian objects such as ceramic vessels, quilts, and clothing. Through these tasks, they create mementos of their lives and carry out the work of making a world.

"Transcendental Etude" is a long meditative poem of great richness and power. It traces the course of birth, death, and rebirth through a creativity that heals splits in the natural world and within the self. The poem begins in the pastoral imagery of an August evening and ranges over the realms of nature and of human life. Rich's vision here transforms the poet's craft. As a poet, she need not be, as she had once feared, an egocentric artist seeking undying fame at the expense of those she loves. Instead, through participation in the life of the physical universe, she articulates the patterns of her own being, of life itself. Thus, Rich's new metaphor of the poet is at once the most daring and the most simple: The poet is a common woman.

Achieving a selfhood that encompasses both creative work and human relationships, egotism and altruism, Rich and her women heal their psychic split in the symbolic return to home, to the full self represented by the circle. The voyage into history, the unconsciousness, the mind is completed in the return.

A Wild Patience Has Taken Me This Far is to a large extent a dialogue with nineteenth century women writers and thinkers: the Brontës, Susan B. Anthony, Elizabeth Barrett Browning. "Culture and Anarchy" takes its title from Matthew Arnold's essay on nineteenth century culture. Arnold longed for a literate, elite, verbal culture; Rich, on the other hand, celebrates a world of women's work, both verbal and nonverbal. Here, growing and cooking vegetables, responding to nature's seasonal rhythms, the simple tasks of women's lives, form a valuable cultural matrix out of which arise the heroic actions of individual women.

Rich's poem is a quilting together of the words of historical women (derived from the diaries and letters of Emily Dickinson, Anthony, Browning, and Jane Addams) and meditation on her own life and work. The women's voices here replace the quotations of male words in "Snapshots of a Daughter-in-Law." Again Rich telescopes time, bringing the earlier women into the circle of her life, joining them in their acts and visions.

In *Sources*, Rich returns to her past and engages in a dialogue with her dead father and husband. She is trying to come to terms with her own life and to put the lives of the others into perspective. *Your Native Land, Your Life* and *Time's Power* continue to develop the persona of the poet as representative woman facing the issues of her country and time. Language and poetry and their relation to history remain foci of concern: In "North American Time," she writes

> Poetry never stood a chance
> of standing outside history.
> ....
> We move   but our words stand
> become responsible
> for more than we intended

In the ruefully ironic "Blue Rock" she writes

> Once when I wrote poems they did not change
> left overnight on the page
> ....
> But now I know what happens while I sleep
> and when I wake the poem has changed:
> the facts have dilated it, or cancelled it

Rich's successive volumes of poetry reveal her development as poet and as woman. As she breaks out from restrictive traditions her voice is achieving power and authenticity. From a poet of isolation and withdrawal, of constraint and despair, she has become a seer of wide-ranging communal sympathy and great imaginative possibility. She is redefining in her life and poetry the meanings of language, poetry, love, power, and home. In her earlier life and work, she accepted patriarchal definitions. Consequently, she felt trapped in personal and poetic conventions: a marriage that curbed her creativity, an aesthetic that split form and feeling, a language that ignored her experience, a position of powerlessness.

At first she spoke in a derivative voice, the language of the "universal"; reluctant to speak as a woman, she echoed the tone of her male poetic ancestors. Because she hesitated to voice her own experience, her early poems are highly polished but avoid emotional depth. She grew to mistrust a language that seemed alien. The fragmented, provisional, stark poems of *Leaflets, The Will to Change*, and *Diving into the Wreck* record her groping toward a new language in which to voice her deepest concerns. In subsequent books, she wrote in a freer form, viewing poems as "speaking to their moment."

The transformations of Rich's home imagery parallel her growth of poetic force and political awareness. In early poems the home was entrapping, because patriarchal voices defined women's roles. As Rich's women became more self-defining, the old relationships were abandoned or modified to fit the real needs of the persons involved. Achieving selfhood, Rich's female heroes came to seize control of their homes, their lives. Through metaphorical journeys exploring the world, women's history, and their own psychic heights and depths, they struggle for knowledge and self-mastery. Healing their tormenting self-division, they grow more "at home" in the world. They recognize and cherish their links to a women's tradition of great power and beauty and to the natural world. In this process the idea of home has acquired new significance: From frail shelter or painful trap, it has grown to a gateway, the starting point for journeys of self-exploration, and the magic circle to which women return so that they may participate in the work of "making and remaking" the world.

Other major works

NONFICTION: *Of Woman Born: Motherhood as Experience and Institution*, 1976; *On Lies, Secrets, and Silence: Selected Prose, 1966-1978*, 1979; *Blood, Bread, and Poetry: Selected Prose, 1979-1985*, 1986; *What Is Found There: Notebooks on Poetry and Politics*, 1993.

Bibliography

Altieri, Charles. "Self-Reflection as Action: The Recent Work of Adrienne Rich." In *Self and Sensibility in Contemporary American Poetry*. Cambridge, England: Cambridge University Press, 1984.

Cooper, Jane Roberta, ed. *Reading Adrienne Rich: Review and Re-Visions, 1951-1981*. Ann Arbor: University of Michigan Press, 1984.

Gelpi, Barbara Charlesworth, and Albert Gelpi. *Adrienne Rich's Poetry*. New York: W. W. Norton, 1975.

Juhasz, Suzanne. *Naked and Fiery Forms: Modern American Poetry by Women—A New Tradition*. New York: Harper & Row, 1976.

Keyes, Claire. *The Aesthetics of Power: The Poetry of Adrienne Rich*. Athens: University of Georgia Press, 1986.

DOROTHY RICHARDSON

Born: Berkshire, England; May 17, 1873

Died: Beckenham, England; June 17, 1957

Principal long fiction

Pilgrimage 1938, 1967 (includes *Pointed Roofs*, 1915; *Backwater*, 1916; *Honeycomb*, 1917; *The Tunnel*, 1919; *Interim*, 1919; *Deadlock*, 1921; *Revolving Lights*, 1923; *The Trap*, 1925; *Oberland*, 1927; *Dawn's Left Hand*, 1931; *Clear Horizon*, 1935; *Dimple Hill*, 1938; *March Moonlight*, 1967).

Other literary forms

Dorothy Richardson wrote some essays and reviews for obscure periodicals edited by friends and also two books growing out of her interest in the Quakers. She contributed descriptive sketches on Sussex life to the *Saturday Review* between 1908 and 1914. During the years writing *Pilgrimage*, Richardson did an enormous amount of miscellaneous writing to earn money—columns and essays in the *Dental Record* (1912-1922), film criticism, translations, and articles on various subjects for periodicals including *Vanity Fair*, *Adelphi*, *Little Review*, and *Fortnightly Review*. She also wrote a few short stories, chiefly during the 1940's. None of this material has been collected.

Achievements

The term "stream of consciousness," adapted from psychology, was first applied to literature in a 1918 review of Richardson's *Pointed Roofs*, *Backwater*, and *Honeycomb*. In the twentieth century, novels moved from outward experience to inner reality. The experiments that marked the change were made almost simultaneously by three writers unaware of one another's work: the first two volumes of Marcel Proust's *Remembrance of Things Past* appeared in 1913; James Joyce's *Portrait of the Artist as a Young Man* began serial publication in 1914; the manuscript of *Pointed Roofs* was finished in 1913.

Richardson was the first novelist in England to restrict the point of view entirely to the protagonist's consciousness, to take for content the experience of life at the moment of perception, and to record the development of a single character's mind and emotions without imposing any plot or structural pattern. Her place in literature (as opposed to literary history) has been less certain; some critics feel that her work is interesting only because it dates the emergence of a new technique. The absence of story and explanation make heavy demands on the reader. Since the protagonist's own limited understanding controls every word of the narrative, readers must also do the work of evaluating the experience in order to create meaning.

Richardson deliberately rejected the description of events, which she thought was typical of male literature, in order to convey the subjective understanding that she believed was the reality of experience. Like her protagonist and like other women of her period, she broke with the conventions of the past, sought to create her own being through self-awareness, and struggled to invent a form that would communicate a woman's expanding conscious life.

Biography

Dorothy Miller Richardson, born on May 17, 1873, was the third of four daughters. Her father, Charles Richardson, worked in the prosperous grocery business that his father had established, but he wanted to be a gentleman. He abandoned Nonconformity for the Church of England and, in 1874, sold the family business to live on investments. During Dorothy's childhood, periods of upper-middle-class luxury (a large house, servants, gardens, membership in a tennis club) alternated with moves arising from temporarily reduced circumstances.

Charles Richardson had hoped for a son, and he took Dorothy with him to lectures in Oxford and meetings of scientific associations. She was sent at age eleven to a private day school for the daughters of gentlemen. It was late enough in the century for the curriculum to emphasize academic subjects; her studies included logic and psychology. In 1890, realizing that her family's financial condition had become seriously straitened, Dorothy looked to the example of Charlotte Brontë and *Villette* (1853) and applied for a post as pupil-teacher in a German school. Six months in Hanover were followed by two years teaching in a North London private school and a brief spell as governess for a wealthy suburban family.

By the end of 1893, Charles Richardson was declared bankrupt; in 1895, two of Dorothy's sisters married. Her mother, Mary Richardson, was troubled by an unusually severe bout of the depression that had gripped her for several years. Dorothy took her mother to stay in lodgings near the sea and found that she required almost constant companionship and supervision. On November 30, 1895, while her daughter was out for a short walk in the fresh air, Mary Richardson committed suicide.

At the age of twenty-two, responsible for her own support and severely shaken by the past two years' events, Richardson moved to an attic room in a London lodging house and took a job as secretary and assistant to three Harley Street dentists. For young women at that time, such a step was unusual, by taking it Richardson evaded the restraint, protection, and religious supervision that made teaching an acceptable profession for young women of good family. The nineteenth century was drawing to a close and London was alive with new ideas. Richardson explored the city, made friends with women who worked in business offices, and lived on eggs and toast so that she could afford concert tickets.

Soon after moving to London, she was invited for a Saturday in the country by an old school friend, Amy Catherine Robbins, who had married her science instructor at London University—a man named H. G. Wells. He had just published *The Time Machine* (1895). Richardson was fascinated by Wells and by the people and ideas she encountered at his house but angered by his way of telling her what to do. She was aware that she stood outside the class system and between the Victorian and modern worlds. She was drawn both to picnics with cousins at Cambridge and to Anarchist and Fabian meetings. She sampled various churches (including Unitarian and Quaker) but refrained from committing herself to any group or cause.

In 1902, Richardson began contributing occasional articles and reviews to *Crank* and other magazines edited by a vegetarian friend. She refused a proposal from a respectable physician and broke her engagement to a Russian Jew, Benjamin Grad. Her friendship with Wells passed at some point into physical intimacy, but she continued to struggle against being overwhelmed by his ideas and personality. In 1906, finding herself pregnant, she brought the affair to an end; she looked forward to rearing the child on her own and was distressed when she suffered a miscarriage.

Exhausted physically and mentally, Richardson left her dental job and went to Sussex to recover and think. In 1908, she began writing sketches for the *Saturday Review*. Then, as her fortieth year approached, she began deliberately searching for the form that would allow her to create what she called "a feminine equivalent of the current masculine realism."

Pointed Roofs was at first rejected by publishers; when it was published in 1915 it puzzled readers, distressed some reviewers, and failed to make money. Richardson persisted, however, on the course she had set, even while living an unsettled life in YWCA hostels and borrowed rooms and earning a minimal income by proofreading and by writing a monthly column for the *Dental Record*. In 1917, she married the artist Alan Odle, who was fifteen years younger than she and had been rejected for military service by a doctor who told him he had six months to live.

Richardson's books attracted some critical recognition in the years after World War I, but they never earned money; she was usually in debt to her publishers. She supported herself and Odle (who lived until 1948) and also coped with all the practical details of their life—housekeeping, paying taxes, writing checks, doing his business with publishers and exhibitors. The couple moved frequently, spending the off-season (when lodgings were less expensive) in Cornwall and going to rooms in London for the summer. During the early 1930's, Richardson took on the burden of five full-length translations from French and German. Returning to *Pilgrimage* and the state of mind in which it was begun became increasingly difficult for Richardson; the later volumes were weakened by extraliterary distractions and also by the psychological difficulty for the author in concluding the work that was based on her own life. The final segment, *March Moonlight*, was found unfinished among her papers after she died on June 17, 1957, at the age of eighty-four.

Analysis

Pilgrimage is a quest; the protagonist, Miriam Henderson, seeks her self and, rejecting the old guideposts, makes her own path through life. The book remains a problem for many readers, although since 1915 most of Dorothy Richardson's technical devices have become familiar: unannounced transitions from third-person narration to the first person for interior monologue, shifts between present and past as experience evokes memory, disconnected phrases and images and fragmentary impressions representing the continuous nonverbal operations of the mind. Looking back on the period when she was trying to find a way to embody Miriam Henderson's experience, Richardson described her breakthrough as the realization that no one was "*there* to *describe* her." Impressed by Henry James's control of viewpoint, she went one step further. The narrator and the protagonist merge; the narrator knows, perceives, and expresses only what comes to Miriam's consciousness. Furthermore, the narrator does not speak to any imagined reader and therefore does not provide helpful explanations. The scenes and people are presented as they impinge on Miriam's awareness—thus the most familiar circumstances are likely to be undescribed and the most important people identified only by name, without the phrases that would place them or reveal their relationship to Miriam. Many readers are discouraged by the attempt to follow the book and make meaning of it; some are tempted to use Richardson's biography as a pony to find out what "really" happened and others prefer to read isolated sections without regard to sequence, responding to the feeling and imagery as if it were poetry. Because there is no narrative guidance, meaning is continually modified by the reader's own consciousness and by the extent of identification.

The first three titles show Miriam Henderson in the last stages of her girlhood and form the prelude to her London life. *Pointed Roofs* covers her experience in Hanover; in *Backwater*, she is resident teacher in a North London school and still drawn to the possibility of romance with a young man from her suburban circle; in *Honeycomb*, she briefly holds a post as governess before her sisters' weddings and her mother's death complete the disintegration of her girlhood family. *The Tunnel* begins Miriam's years in London and introduces situations and characters that reappear in the next several volumes: the dental job, the room at Mrs. Bailey's lodging house, the new women Mag and Jan and the depen-

dent woman Eleanor Dear, a visit to her school friend Alma who has married the writer Hypo Wilson. In *Interim*, Miriam perceives the difficulty of communicating her current thoughts and experiences to her sister and other old friends. *Deadlock* treats her acquaintance—growing into an engagement—with Michael Shatov. In *Revolving Lights*, she has decided not to marry Shatov and becomes increasingly involved with Hypo Wilson. *The Trap* shows her sharing a cramped flat with a spinster social worker and growing despondent about the isolation which, she realizes, she imposes on herself to avoid emotional entanglements. *Oberland* is a lyrical interlude about a holiday in Switzerland. In *Dawn's Left Hand*, Miriam has an affair with Hypo Wilson and an intense friendship with a young woman (Amabel) who becomes a radical suffragist. *Clear Horizon* concludes much of the practical and emotional business that has occupied Miriam for several years; she disentangles herself from Wilson, Shatov, and Amabel and prepares to leave London. In *Dimple Hill*, she lives on a farm owned by a Quaker family, absorbs their calm, and works at writing. *March Moonlight* rather hastily takes Miriam up to the point of meeting the artist who would become her husband and to the beginning of her work on a novel.

This summary of events is the barest framework. Life, for Miriam Henderson, exists not in events but in the responses that create her sense of awareness. The books are made up of relatively independent sections, each treating a single segment of experience or reflection. Because of the depth with which single moments are recorded, the overall narrative line is fragmentary. Despite *Pilgrimage*'s length, it embodies isolated spots of time. Frequently, neither narration nor the memories evoked by subsequent experience indicate what events may have taken place in the gaps between. Furthermore, the book concentrates on those moments important to Miriam's interior experience, and it leaves out the times when she acts without self-awareness—which may include significant actions that take place when Miriam is so engrossed by events that she does not engage in thought or reflection.

Richardson disliked the phrase "stream of consciousness" because it implies constant movement and change. She preferred the image of a pool—new impressions are added, and sometimes create ripples that spread over the previously accumulated consciousness. Thus, Miriam's interior monologue becomes steadily more complex as she grows older. The earlier volumes have more sensory impression and direct emotion; later, as Miriam grows more self-aware, she has greater verbal skill and is more likely to analyze her responses. Because of her more sophisticated self-awareness, however, she also grows adept, in the later volumes, at suppressing impressions or fragments of self-knowledge that she does not want to admit to consciousness.

In many ways, Miriam is not likable—readers are sometimes put off by the need to share her mind for two thousand pages. In the early books, she is a self-preoccupied, narrow-minded adolescent, oppressively conscious of people's appearance and social class, annoyingly absorbed in wondering what they think about her, defensively judgmental. The wild swings in mood and the ebb and flow of her energies during the day appear to have little cause and to be unworthy of the attention she gives them. Most people, however, would appear unpleasantly selfish if their minds were open for inspection. Miriam creates her self by deliberate consciousness. The danger is that she tends to withdraw from experience in order to contemplate feeling.

Another continuing thread is created by Miriam's thoughts about men, about men and women together, and about the roles of women in society. Her basic animosity toward men gives shape to a series of statements on their personal, emotional, social, and intellectual peculiarities

that falls just short of a formal feminist analysis. Each possible romance, each rejected or forestalled proposal amounts to a choice of a way of life. The matter is, however, complicated by Miriam's sexual reticence. Even though she can talk about free love, she is not conscious—or perhaps will not permit herself to become conscious—of overt sexual urges or of physical attraction to men or to women. She struggles not to let her feeling for certain women lead her to be absorbed by their lives or roles. Struggling to know herself, Miriam is constantly faced with the problem of knowing other women.

Although Richardson struggled to bring the events in *March Moonlight* up to 1912, the year that she began writing *Pilgrimage*, her form and subject virtually required the book to remain unconcluded. The narrative techniques of *March Moonlight* grow more deliberate; when Miriam begins to write, she thinks and sees differently and is aware of selecting and arranging details. Thus, the book's ending is only a middle: Miriam's sense of self would inevitably change as she reexamined and re-created her experiences in order to write novels. Once traditional formulas are rejected and *being* itself becomes the subject, there can be no ending; there is no epiphany, no coming-of-age, no final truth but rather a continuous process of self-making through self-awareness.

Other major works

NONFICTION: *The Quakers Past and Present*, 1914; *Gleanings from the Works of George Fox*, 1914; *John Austen and the Inseparables*, 1930.

Bibliography

Fromm, Gloria G. *Dorothy Richardson: A Biography*. Champaign: University of Illinois Press, 1977.

Gregory, Horace. *Dorothy Richardson: An Adventure in Self-Discovery*. New York: Holt, Rinehart and Winston, 1967.

Labovitz, Esther Kleinbord. "Dorothy Richardson: *Pilgrimage*: Four Volumes." In *The Myth of the Heroine: The Female "Bildungsroman" in the Twentieth Century*. 2d ed. Vol. 4. American University Series 19. New York: Peter Lang, 1986.

Marcus, Jane, ed. "Political Aesthetics: Virginia Woolf and Dorothy Richardson." In *Virginia Woolf: A Feminist Slant*. Lincoln: University of Nebraska Press, 1983.

Rosenberg, John. *Dorothy Richardson, the Genius They Forgot: A Critical Biography*. New York: Alfred A. Knopf, 1973.

CHRISTINA ROSSETTI

Born: London, England; December 5, 1830

Died: London, England; December 29, 1894

Principal poetry

Verses, 1847; *Goblin Market and Other Poems*, 1862; *The Prince's Progress and Other Poems*, 1866; *Sing-Song*, 1872, 1893; *A Pageant and Other Poems*, 1881; *Verses*, 1893; *New Poems*, 1896.

Other literary forms

Commonplace and Other Short Stories (1870) suggests that Christina Rossetti may have once had the notion of becoming a novelist. Unlike other female poets of the period, she wrote much in prose, both secular and religious. The best of these prose pieces is "The Lost Titian," the plot of which revolves around two friends' competitive praise for another friend's painting. *Speaking Likenesses* (1874), a series of stories told to some girls by their aunt as they pass the time sewing, stands in the shadows of Lewis Carroll's and Jean Ingelow's works of the same period. *Annus Domini* (1874) is a devotional prose work, the first of several, which includes a prayer for each day of the year; these pieces were influenced by *The Book of Common Prayer*.

Achievements

Rossetti was praised in her time for the clarity and sweetness of her diction, for her realistic imagery, and for the purity of her faith. She was widely read in the nineteenth century, but not often imitated. The latter is true perhaps because she did not introduce innovative techniques or subject matter. She is not read widely today, either, and is usually treated as a minor poet of the Victorian period, being eclipsed by her brother Dante Gabriel Rossetti and his fellow Pre-Raphaelite writers. Perhaps the simplicity of Christina Rossetti's faith seems remote and unrealistic to many contemporary readers, but this fact should not diminish her artistic contributions.

Biography

Christina Georgina Rossetti was born on December 5, 1830, the youngest of four children. Her father, Gabriele, an Italian political refugee, was himself a poet and musician. Her mother, of half-Italian parentage, wrote a popular book on Dante, and her older brother, Dante Gabriel, became a noted poet and a leader of the Pre-Raphaelite Brotherhood.

Because of financial problems, the Rossettis moved from Portland Place to Mornington Crescent in 1851 in order for Mrs. Rossetti and Christina to open a small day school for children, thus providing a financial base for the family. By 1854, William Rossetti, Christina's brother, then a clerk in a revenue office, rented a house on Albany Street, where the family lived together. After Mr. Rossetti died in that year, Mrs. Rossetti and the children lived on there until 1867, and it was only because of William's marriage to Lucy Brown in 1874 that Mrs. Rossetti and Christina moved to Torrington Square.

Christina was not a world traveler, but her few experiences abroad did affect her poetry. She went abroad but twice, once in 1861 and again in 1865, and it was the Italian journey that is reflected in so much of her writing. She wrote some poetry in Italian, but her love for Italy can be seen in much of her English work. One excellent example is "Vanna's Twins," the story of an Italian family living in England.

Her first book, published in 1847 when she was seventeen, was a collection of poems privately printed by her grandfather Gaetena Polidori, himself a writer. The volume entitled *Verses* contained sixty-six pages of poems written by Rossetti between the ages of twelve and sixteen. By 1850, she had become a tangential member of the Pre-Raphaelite Brotherhood, of which her brother Dante was the center, and she published various poems in the Brotherhood's magazine *The Germ*. Although Christina loved her brother dearly and respected the other members of the group, she felt that they were too concerned with morally questionable subjects to engage herself directly in the work. It was, ironically, through the Pre-Raphaelites that she met a young man named James Collison, to whom she was greatly attracted and whom, had it not been for his Catholicism, she might well have married.

In 1862, after having gained much attention through the poems in *The Germ*, Rossetti published a volume entitled *Goblin Market and Other Poems*. The work was greeted with general acclaim, her only critics being metric purists such as John Ruskin. She brought out another volume in 1866, *The Prince's Progress and Other Poems*, which established her as England's greatest living woman poet, since Elizabeth Barrett Browning had died in 1861.

Although Christina was sickly in her youth, it was in 1871 that she became seriously ill with Graves' disease, which brought many periods of depression. During these years of severe illness, she experienced several unpleasant events: Her sister Maria died of cancer in 1876; in 1877 she and her mother began the nursing of Dante Gabriel through five years of psychotic depression; and in 1886 her mother died. In the midst of all this suffering, Rossetti continued to write. Her third volume of poetry, *A Pageant and Other Poems*, was published in 1881 and praised highly by Algernon Swinburne, the only remaining member of the old Pre-Raphaelite coterie. Between 1879 and 1892, she published five volumes of spiritual meditations.

In May, 1892, Christina submitted to an operation for cancer, another Rossetti to be the victim of that disease. The operation was not successful; the cancer reappeared in a few months. After considerable suffering, she died on December 29, 1894.

Analysis

Christina Rossetti, often thought of as a religious poet, actually became the major woman poet of mid-Victorian England. Her only true competitor, Elizabeth Barrett Browning, died a few months before Rossetti's *Goblin Market and Other Poems* appeared in 1862. "Goblin Market," the introductory poem of the volume, has remained her most famous work and illustrates her mastery of the lyric. Because much of her lyric poetry is oriented toward children, "Goblin Market" is often classified as a child's poem. Even though the characters in the poem are young girls and goblins with fairy-tale associations, the poem is actually an allegory of temptation and redemption meant for adult reading. Rossetti's common theme of the need for renunciation is prevalent, though in the disguise of whimsical child's play. The poem produces a grotesque comic effect, supported by irregular meter and cumulative cataloging. The tempting fruit of the goblins, described in Rossetti's typical sensual manner as "sweet to tongue and sound to eye," causes Laura to succumb, desiring more, only to discover that her pleasure is terminated.

Lizzie acts as the savior. Like Christ, she goes into the grove of the men selling their wares and offers to buy some, only to discover that they really want her, not her penny. Although she suffers much physical abuse, the evil people are "worn out by her resistance," and she returns home jubilant with her penny in hand, able to comfort Laura with the assurance that one can find happiness without the temptations of pleasure. Later, when both girls have married, they are able to relate to their daughters in didactic fashion how one can avoid the pitfalls of the evil world.

Rossetti's strong visual imagination aligns her with the Pre-Raphaelites' interest in painting. Although she did not paint, Christina had a painter's eye: The love of colors, particularly gold, rose, violet, blue, and green, and the delight in decorative detail inform all of her lyrics. Her eye often sees unexpected analogies. In "Goblin Market," for example, she compares Laura's arched neck to a swan and a lily, both natural phenomena, but also to a vessel being launched, a rather startling comparison somewhat in the vein of the seventeenth century metaphysical conceits. In fact, several critics have alluded to her love for seventeenth century poets, especially George Herbert and Henry Vaughan.

In addition to her lyrics, Rossetti wrote much narrative verse, characteristically on the theme of lost or frustrated love. Most of these love-narratives are romantic and otherworldly; when Rossetti does attempt realism, especially in describing marital love, her images are pale and flat. One of the longer narratives, "The Prince's Progress," developed out of a lyric of 1861; Rossetti expanded it at her brother's suggestion to provide a title poem for her next volume of poetry. Much like the tale of Edmund

Spenser's Red Cross Knight, this poem is the story of a princess waiting to be rescued by a prince.

The prince waits in his palace for a full month before leaving to meet his bride. When he finally hears the call, prompted by allegorical voices that represent fleeting time, he discovers that the journey will not be easy. It will be another *Pilgrim's Progress*. His first delay is the typical temptation of a beautiful maiden who keeps him as Dido detained Aeneas. Following his release, the prince finds himself in a nineteenth century wasteland with a blight lurking in the darkening air, "a land of neither life nor death." Here he discovers a cave with an old hermit who gives him the "Elixir of Life," but the elixir is insufficient. When he eventually leaves the cave, he is again diverted by self-indulgence, and when he finally arrives at his bride's door, he finds that she is dead, her body being prepared for burial. The poem is an interesting narrative in the vein of medieval romances, but it is obviously allegorical. The prince is admonished by the narrator, "You waited on the road too long, you trifled at the gate." The poem is permeated with ironies and allegorical symbolism proclaiming the vices of procrastination.

In "The Lowest Room," there is an evident implication that, bound by society's rules, women *must* be passive and *must* play given roles in life. Again, there are two sisters in the poem, but unlike those in other works, only the ideal sister is here rewarded with husband and child. The ideal one is described in feminine language; the other one, less attractive, dreams of Homer's soldiers. Masculine voluptuousness affects her. In projecting such a contrast, Rossetti implies that women in her society are told how to dress, how to act, and how to be successful. There is little room for individuality. The final acceptance of this less attractive female, the speaker of the poem, places her in the role of the typical passive woman waiting for her turn without being permitted to help in creating it.

Another narrative which takes a critical view of social conventions is "The Iniquity of the Fathers, upon the Children," in which a lady who has a child out of wedlock is tormented by the community. The only justice, the narrator concludes, is that all is "equal in the grave." On the other hand, Rossetti's narrative style can show a fairy-tale naïveté, as in "Maiden Song," a tale of three sisters, Meggan, May, and Margaret, all of whom desire husbands. The first two take the first man who comes along, afraid they will be like Margaret sitting at home

singing and spinning. Margaret's patience, however, is amply rewarded; she wins the king of the entire country for her husband.

Rossetti's strong religious faith supported her during continuing illnesses and she began to give most of her attention to writing devotional material. Her first poetry had shown her strong family affection and her religious feelings, particularly the sentiment of renunciation. The later poems (such as "A Novice," "A Martyr," and "I Have Fought a Good Fight") continue to focus on renunciation. The first is a flight from the world into the calm of the cloister; the latter two praise the eager laying down of life for the glory of God. Actually, religious ardour colors most of Rossetti's thoughts and results in much oversimplified verse echoing common platitudes about devotion. A poem such as "Whitsun Eve," however, illustrates poetic maturity, blending the love of God and the love of the beauty of creation. All that is pure in nature is pressed into the service of the one shining lamb.

An interesting aspect of Rossetti's style is her use of the Victorian motif of two voices, so prominently associated with Alfred, Lord Tennyson's poetry. The Victorian world attempted to synthesize the Romantic values of the early nineteenth century with the classical theories of order and restraint more prominently displayed in the eighteenth century. From this attempt came a strong clash of values and great personal frustration. Adding to this problem was the growth of the industrial world and the increase in scientific knowledge. Rossetti's dualism establishes the concept of a universe based on a conflict of opposites, as in "Life and Death," "Twice," "Today and Tomorrow," and "Two Parted."

"Two Parted" deals with one true lover and one betrayer. Ironically, the betrayer in this case is the woman. "Today and Tomorrow" creates a dichotomy of living life to the fullest on the one hand and wishing to die on the other. "Life and Death" begins with a negative statement about life's bitterness, juxtaposing the good things of life with the unpleasant. "Twice" uses the counterpoint of the narrator's offering her heart while the male suggests that her heart is not ripe. In the narrative poems this technique is carried out through the use of two opposing characters. Lizzie and Laura of "Goblin Market" illustrate the dualistic motif; in "Maiden Song" the conflict is between two plain sisters and the beautiful Margaret. This dualism is also apparent in Rossetti's religious poems, where there appears to be a confrontation between different views of salvation or different moral attitudes. A great number of traditional opposites are used here—time and eternity, earthly misery and heavenly bliss—demonstrating the torment of a trapped soul longing for escape. One such poem, "This near-at-hand," stresses the antithesis of heaven and earth.

The religious poems often describe a destructive end which results from the speaker's being torn between duty and desire. Sometimes the choice appears to have been made in error, and when it is, it seems to have arisen from weakness or beguilement. So choice itself becomes destructive: There is no solution; life is an absurdity. Even when the speaker is not caught in a personal dilemma, the poem repeats the impression that the world, as Matthew Arnold suggests in "Dover Beach," is a place of uncertainty, a virtual wasteland, a "darkling plain" where ignorant armies fight by night.

In the midst of all this dualism, the reader is left with the impression that Rossetti is earnestly searching for unity but cannot find it. In the secular love poems she goes so far as to suggest that perhaps as ghosts, removed from the flesh, lovers could achieve such a unity. In the religious poems, her solution is union with God through Christ in death. Much of her poetry reflects the struggle in her own life to find some solution to the paradox, irony, and bifurcation that life in general repeatedly offers. Rossetti's poetry reveals a dual personality—one side reflecting Pre-Raphaelite traits of fictional effects and sensual imagery, often set in a dream world; and the other reflecting the assurances of her orthodox faith.

Other major works

SHORT FICTION: *Commonplace and Other Short Stories*, 1870; *Speaking Likenesses*, 1874.
RELIGIOUS WRITINGS: *Annus Domini*, 1874; *Seek and Find*, 1879; *Called to Be Saints*, 1881; *Letter and Spirit*, 1882; *Time Flies*, 1885; *The Face of the Deep*, 1892; *Maude*, 1897.

Bibliography

Charles, Edna Kotin. *Christina Rossetti: Critical Perspectives, 1862-1982*. Selinsgrove, Pa.: Susquehanna University Press, 1985.

Harrison, Antony H. *Christina Rossetti in Context*. Chapel Hill: University of North Carolina Press, 1988.

Kent, David A., ed. *The Achievement of Christina Rossetti: England, Scotland, and the Union*. New York: Cornell University Press, 1988.

Mayberry, Katherine J. *Christina Rossetti and the Poetry of Discovery*. Baton Rouge: Louisiana State University Press, 1989.

Rosenblum, Dolores. *Christina Rossetti: The Poetry of Endurance*. Carbondale: Southern Illinois University Press, 1987.

MURIEL RUKEYSER

Born: New York, New York; December 15, 1913   **Died:** New York, New York; February 12, 1980

Principal poetry

Theory of Flight, 1935; *U.S. 1*, 1938; *A Turning Wind: Poems*, 1939; *Beast in View*, 1944; *The Green Wave*, 1948; *Elegies*, 1949; *Selected Poems*, 1951; *Body of Waking*, 1958; *Waterlily Fire: Poems 1935-1962*, 1962; *The Speed of Darkness*, 1968; *Twenty-nine Poems*, 1972; *Breaking Open*, 1973; *The Gates: Poems*, 1976; *The Collected Poems of Muriel Rukeyser*, 1978; *Out of Silence: Selected Poems*, 1992.

Other literary forms

In addition to her own poetry, Muriel Rukeyser published several volumes of translations (including work by the poets Octavio Paz and Gunnar Ekelöf), three biographies, two volumes of literary criticism, a number of book reviews, a novel, five juvenile books, and a play. She also worked on several documentary film scripts. The translations were exercises in writing during dry spells; the biographies, like her poetic sequence "Lives," combine her interests in the arts and sciences. The two volumes of literary criticism (along with her uncollected book reviews) are central for understanding her views concerning poetry and life.

Achievements

With the publication of *Theory of Flight* in the Yale Series of Younger Poets in 1935, Rukeyser began a long and productive career as a poet and author. Her work also earned for her the first Harriet Monroe Poetry Award (1941), a Guggenheim Fellowship (1943), the Copernicus Award and Shelley Memorial Award (1977), an honorary D.Litt. from Rutgers, and membership in the National Institute of Arts and Letters. She also won the Swedish Academy Translation Award (1967) and the Anglo-Swedish Literary Foundation Award (1978) for her translations.

While Rukeyser has been linked to W. H. Auden, Stephen Spender, and other political poets, her work more clearly evolves from that of Ralph Waldo Emerson, Herman Melville, and Walt Whitman. From Emerson and the Transcendental tradition, she developed her organic theory of poetry, from Melville, her poetry of outrage. From Whitman, however, she obtained perhaps her most distinguishing characteristics: her belief in possibility, her long, rhythmic lines, her need to embrace humanity, and her expression of the power and beauty of sexuality. Her feminist views link her also with Denise Levertov and Adrienne Rich, while her experimentation with the poetic line and the visual appearance of the poem on the page remind one at times of May Swenson.

Although Rukeyser's work has been relatively well regarded, she has received little critical attention. Yet the quality and quantity of her work and the integrity of her feminist and mythic vision suggest that she will come to be seen as a significant figure in modern American poetry.

Biography

Muriel Rukeyser was born on December 15, 1913, in New York City, the daughter of Lawrence B. Rukeyser, a cofounder of Colonial Sand and Stone, and Myra Lyons, a former bookkeeper. Her childhood was a quiet one, her protected, affluent life a source of her insistence on experience and communication in her poetry. In *The Life of Poetry* (1949), she tells of recognizing the sheltered nature of her life: "A teacher asks: 'How many of you know any other road in the city except the road between home and school?' I do not put up my hand. These are moments at which one begins to see."

Rukeyser's adult life was as eventful as her childhood was sheltered. In 1933, at age nineteen, she was arrested and caught typhoid fever while attending the Scottsboro trials in Alabama; three years later, she investigated at first hand the mining tragedy at Gauley Bridge, West

Virginia; and in 1936, she was sent by *Life and Letters Today* to cover the Anti-Fascist Olympics in Barcelona as the Spanish Civil War broke out around her. These crusades dramatize her intense conviction in the sanctity of human life and her desire to experience life actively, and they all served as inspiration for her poetry, fulfilling her declaration in "Poem out of Childhood" to "Breathe-in experience, breathe-out poetry."

Throughout the remainder of a life filled with traveling and speaking for causes in which she intensely believed, Rukeyser never stopped learning, teaching, and writing; she declared that she would never protest without making something in the process. The wide range of knowledge in her poetry and criticism and the large volume of poetry and prose she published testify to this fact. She attended the Ethical Culture School and Fieldston School, Vassar College, Columbia University, and the Roosevelt School of Aviation in New York City, and she learned film editing with Helen Van Dongen. Besides conducting poetry workshops at a number of different institutions, she taught at the California Labor School and Sarah Lawrence College and later served as a member of the board of directors of the Teachers-Writers Collaborative in New York.

Rukeyser made her home in New York City, except for the nine years she spent in California and the time she was traveling. She moved to California in 1945 and shortly afterward married painter Glynn Collins (although the marriage was soon annulled). Three years later, she had an illegitimate son and was disowned by her family, experiences which figure prominently in her poetry after this date. She moved back to New York in 1954 to teach at Sarah Lawrence College.

Rukeyser left Sarah Lawrence College in 1967. Although in failing health, she continued to write and protest. For the Committee for Solidarity, she flew to Hanoi in 1972 to demonstrate for peace, and later that year she was jailed in Washington, D.C., for protesting the Vietnam War on the steps of the Capitol. In 1974, as president of the American center for PEN, a society that supports the rights of writers throughout the world, she flew to Korea to plead for the life of imprisoned poet Kim Chi-Ha. Rukeyser died in New York City on February 12, 1980.

Analysis

Muriel Rukeyser was a poet of liberty, recording "the truths of outrage" she saw around her, and a poet of love, writing "the truths of possibility" in intimate human relationships. She wrote with equal fervor about social and humane issues such as miners dying of silicosis, the rights of minorities, the lives of women and imprisoned poets, and about universals such as the need for love and communication among people and the sheer physical and emotional joy of loving. Unlike many political poets, she tried to do more than simply espouse: to protect, but also to build, to create. For Rukeyser, poetry's purpose is to sustain and heal, and the poet's responsibility is to recognize life as it is and encourage all people to their greatest potential through poetry.

Refusing to accept the negation of T.S. Eliot's *The Waste Land* (1922), Rukeyser uses images of technology and energy extensively in her early volumes to find, in a positive way, a place for the self in modern technological society, thus identifying herself with Hart Crane and with the poets of the Dynamo school. "Theory of Flight" centers on the airplane and the gyroscope. The dam and the power plant become the predominant symbols in "The Book of the Dead," in *U.S. 1*, her next collection.

U.S. 1 also contains a series of shorter, more lyrical poems, entitled "Night-Music." While these poems are still strongly social in content, they are more personal and are based on what Rukeyser refers to as "unverifiable fact" (as opposed to the documentary evidence in "Theory of Flight" and "The Book of the Dead"). This change foreshadows the shifting emphasis throughout her career on the sources of power about which she writes—from machinery to poetry to the self. It is this change in conception that allowed Rukeyser to grow poetically, to use fewer of the abstractions for which many critics have faulted her, and to use instead more personal and concrete images on which to anchor her message.

This movement is evident in *A Turning Wind*. She begins to see the power and the accompanying fear of poetry, and her poetic voice becomes increasingly personal, increasingly founded in personal experience. Poetry becomes the means, the language, and the result of looking for connections or, in Jungian terms, a kind of collective unconscious. Rukeyser notices, however, that poetry is feared precisely because of its power: "They fear it. They turn away, hand up palm out/ fending off moment of proof, the straight look, poem." The fear of poetry is a fear of disclosure to oneself of what is inside, and this fear is "an indication that we are cut off from our own reality." Therefore, Rukeyser continually urges her readers to use poetry to look within themselves for a common ground on which they can stand as human beings.

The poetic sequence "Lives" (which extends through subsequent volumes as well) identifies another of Rukeyser's growing interests—"ways of getting past impossibilities by changing phase." Poetry thus becomes a meeting place of different ideas and disciplines. It is a place where the self meets the self, diving to confront unchallenged emotions in the search for truth, and a place where the self can face the world with newly discovered self-knowledge. Using the resources they discover both inside and outside themselves, people can grow to understand themselves and the world better. The subjects of the "Lives" exemplify values and traditions Rukeyser believes are important to the search.

Rukeyser's growth as a person and as a poet, then, was a growth of the self, realizing her capabilities and her potential and, in turn, the capabilities and potential of those around her. She becomes increasingly open in her later poems, discussing her failed marriage, her illegitimate son and subsequent disinheritance, her son's exile in Canada during the Vietnam War, and her feelings about age and death. Behind her search for self-knowledge and expansion of the self into the world is her belief in the necessity of communication. The silence she experienced at home as a child had a profound effect on her, and in many early poems, such as "Effort at Speech Between Two People," communication is ultimately impossible. This same silence appears to be at the root of many of the world's problems, and Rukeyser's open outrage and inner searching are attempts to right the problem, to achieve communication. By the time she wrote "Ajanta," silence had become a positive force, allowing her the opportunity to concentrate on her journey within.

One distinguishing mark of Rukeyser's poetry is the numerous poetic sequences (such as "Lives") which are connected by a common situation, theme, or character. "Waterlily Fire," for example, is a group of five poems about the burning of Claude Monet's *Waterlilies* at the Museum of Modern Art in New York City. "Elegies" is a collection of ten poems extending over three volumes. "Poem out of Childhood" is a cluster of fifteen poems, of which one is also a cluster of three, centered on Rukeyser's childhood—what she learns from it and how she uses it poetically. The sequence makes more apparent to readers the necessity of looking for connections among poems—recurring images, phrases, and sounds—than could separate poems.

In *The Speed of Darkness*, Rukeyser returns to her preoccupation with silence, expressing it both structurally in and as a subject. From her earliest poems, she used space within lines (often combined with a proliferation of colons) to act as a new type of punctuation—a metric rest—but in *The Speed of Darkness*, she places greater emphasis on the placement of the poem on the page to achieve this metric rest, for space on the page "can provide roughly for a relationship in emphasis through the eye's discernment of pattern."

Rukeyser's verse has often been characterized as half-poetry and half-prose because of the long, sweeping, encompassing, Whitmanesque free-verse lines especially noticeable in her early poems. In *The Speed of Darkness* and later poems, however, she moves toward shorter lines and works with smaller units of meaning in order to compensate for breathing. At times, her arrangement of these poems ("The War Comes into My Room," "Mountain: One from Bryant," and "Rune," for example) approaches Swenson's iconographs in their experimentation with the visual and physical movement of the line.

Perhaps another reason for the new, shorter lines is that they are more suited for the introspective journeys of Rukeyser's later work than are the long, flowing, altruistic lines she used earlier. They also help her to control more effectively her penchant for verbosity and maintain the development of her images. Yet the length and conclusion of the later lines are not without precedent. Many of the most powerful passages in the early poems were journalistic or cinematic passages, not yet matured but still effective in their performance. "The Book of the Dead" is especially noteworthy in this respect, for it contains the seeds of the concrete image and colloquial diction fully realized later.

Rukeyser's diction also gives ample reason for labeling her poetry half-prose. Yet as startling as it may be to encounter words such as "eugenically," "silicosis," and "cantillations" in her poems, these make the reader pay attention. She also employs words and even sounds as physical, musical, and thematic ties within and among poems in the same way other poets use rhyme and in the same way she uses image sequences.

With the variety of line length and placement evident in Rukeyser's work, it is not surprising that her canon is characterized by a rich variety of styles. Her experiments with language, line length, and rhythm easily lend themselves to experiments with different verse styles, including but extending beyond elegies, sonnets, odes, rounds, and rondels.

While she uses traditional as well as non-traditional verse patterns, she often treats even her most traditional subjects untraditionally. Because of her belief in the community of humankind, she has written many love poems, yet she approaches even the most personal subjects in an unexpected way. A notable example is "Letter, Unposted" from *Theory of Flight*, which is centered on the traditional theme of waiting for a lover. Yet it is distinguished from other such poems by the speaker's refusal to languish in love and to see nature languishing along with her. The letter remains unposted because the speaker cannot write all the traditional sentimental foolishness expected of her. Instead, as in even the bleakest situations about which Rukeyser writes, she sees the positive side: "But summer lives,/ and minds grow, and nerves are sensitized to power . . . and I receive them joyfully and live: but wait for you." The speaker rejoices in life rather than feeling sorry for herself.

Although a feminine consciousness is evident in every volume of Rukeyser's poetry, *The Speed of Darkness* also begins a new and more imperative feminist outlook. In the same way that she refused to be simply a Marxist poet, she is not simply a feminist poet. Rukeyser sees with a feminist point of view, but rather than rejecting the masculine, she retains valuable past information and revisualizes history and myth with female vitality. For example, in "Myth," one learns that Oedipus was not as smart as he thought he was; he did not answer the Sphinx's riddle correctly after all: " 'You didn't say anything about woman.'/ 'When you say Man,' said Oedipus, 'you include women/ too. Everyone knows that.' She said, 'That's what/ you think.' " "Ms. Lot" adds another perspective to the biblical story of Lot and his wife, and in "Painters" (from *The Gates*) she envisions a woman among the primitive cave painters.

Other poems written throughout her career on more contemporary issues reveal the strength of women while upholding their nurturing role. The mother in "Absalom" (from "The Book of the Dead") will "give a mouth to my son" who died of silicosis, and Kim Chi-Ha's mother in "The Gates" is portrayed as a pitchfork, one of Rukeyser's few uses of simile or metaphor. She also refuses to let women take the easy way out as some have been trained to do: "More of a Corpse Than a Woman" and "Gradus Ad Parnassum," for example, display the vapidity of the stereotypical passive rich woman.

Yet while women are strong in Rukeyser's verse, they are still human. Sex is one of the driving forces in her work, and she frequently expresses the joys of love and sex, especially in *Breaking Open*. Significant examples are the powerful eroticism of "Looking at Each Other," the honesty of "In Her Burning" and "Rondel," and the power of sexual renewal in "Welcome from War." Giving birth is also a powerful image in many of the poems.

"The Gates," a fifteen-poem sequence organized around Rukeyser's trip to Korea to plead for the release of imprisoned poet Kim Chi-Ha, synthesizes her recurring images and messages in a final, powerful poetic statement. Like "Night-Music," this sequence is at once social commentary and personal discovery, but it takes a much stronger stance in demanding freedom of speech and assessing Rukeyser's own development as a poet in the light of Kim Chi-Ha's life.

"Breathe-in experience, breathe-out poetry" begins "Poem out of Childhood," the first poem in Rukeyser's first collection. Muriel Rukeyser wrote a poetry developing organically from personal experience and self-discovery, a poetry bringing the anguishes, miseries, and misfortunes of human beings around the world to her readers' attention, a poetry demonstrating her exhilaration with life and love. Readers cannot hide from reality in her poetry, nor can they hide from themselves. There is always the journey, but possibility always lies at its end: "the green tree perishes and green trees grow." Rukeyser's challenge to the world she left behind is found near the end of "Then" (in "The Gates"): "When I am dead, even then,/ I will still love you, I will wait in these poems . . . I will still be making poems for you/ out of silence." The silence and passivity against which she fought throughout her life will not triumph if her readers are alive to her words and to the world around them.

Other major works

NOVEL: *The Orgy*, 1965.
PLAY: *The Color of the Day: A Celebration for the Vassar Centennial, June 10, 1961*, 1961.

NONFICTION: *Willard Gibbs*, 1942; *The Life of Poetry*, 1949; *One Life*, 1957; *Poetry and the Unverifiable Fact: The Clark Lectures*, 1968; *The Traces of Thomas Hariot*, 1971.

CHILDREN'S LITERATURE: *Come Back, Paul*, 1955; *I Go Out*, 1961; *Bubbles*, 1967; *Mayes*, 1970; *More Night*, 1981.

TRANSLATIONS: *Selected Poems of Octavio Paz*, 1963; *Sun Stone*, 1963 (of Paz's poems); *Selected Poems of Gunnar Ekelöf*, 1967; *Three Poems by Gunnar Ekelöf*, 1967; *Early Poems, 1935-1955*, 1973 (of Paz's poems); *Brecht's Uncle Eddie's Moustache*, 1974; *A Mölna Elegy*, 1984 (of Ekelöf's poem).

Bibliography

Bridgford, Kim Suzanne. "Discoverers of the Not-Known: Louise Bogan, Muriel Rukeyser, Sylvia Plath, May Swenson, and Adrienne Rich." *Dissertation Abstracts International* 50 (August, 1989): 558A.

Ciardi, John. *Mid-Century American Poets*. New York: Twayne, 1950.

Curtis, Jane Elizabeth. "Muriel Rukeyser: The Woman Writer Confronts Traditional Mythology and Psychology." *Dissertation Abstracts International* 42 (March, 1982): 3994A.

Kertesz, Louise. *The Poetic Vision of Muriel Rukeyser*. Baton Rouge: Louisiana State University Press, 1980.

NELLY SACHS

Born: Berlin, Germany; December 10, 1891   **Died:** Stockholm, Sweden; May 12, 1970

Principal poetry

In den Wohnungen des Todes, 1946; *Sternverdunkelung*, 1949; *Und niemand weiss weiter*, 1957; *Flucht und Verwandlung*, 1959; *Fahrt ins Staublose*, 1961; *Noch feiert Tod das Leben*, 1961; *Glühende Rätsel*, 1964 (2 parts of cycle), 1965 (3d part of cycle in *Späte Gedichte*), 1966 (4th part of cycle in the annual *Jahresring*); *Späte Gedichte*, 1965; *Die Suchende*, 1966; *O the Chimneys*, 1967; *The Seeker and Other Poems*, 1970; *Teile dich Nacht*, 1971.

Other literary forms

Nelly Sachs published the short play, or "scenic poem," *Eli: Ein Mysterienspiel vom Leiden Israels* (1951; *Eli: A Mystery Play of the Sufferings of Israel*, 1967). Her prose works are collected in *Legenden und Erzählungen* (1921).

Achievements

Acceptance of Sachs's poetry in West Germany was slow, partly because her main theme (Jewish suffering during World War II) stirred painful memories. In the late 1950's and 1960's, however, she was hailed as modern Germany's greatest woman poet and received numerous literary prizes. She was accepted for membership in several academies. In 1958, she received the poetry prize of the Swedish broadcasting system and in 1959, the Kulturpreis der Deutschen Industrie. The town of Meersburg in West Germany awarded her the Annette Droste Prize for women poets in 1960, and the city of Dortmund founded the Nelly Sachs Prize in 1961 and presented her with its first award. In the same year, friends and admirers published the first volume of a festschrift, followed by the second volume, *Nelly Sachs zu Ehren*, on the occasion of her seventy-fifth birthday in 1966. On October 17, 1965, she received the Peace Prize of the German Book Trade Association, and on December 10, 1966, she was awarded the Nobel Prize in Literature. Berlin, the city where she was born and in which she had lived for nearly half a century, made her an honorary citizen in 1967.

Biography

Leonie (Nelly) Sachs was born in Berlin on December 10, 1891, the only child of William Sachs, an inventor, technical engineer, and manufacturer, and his wife, Margarete (née Karger). The family lived in very comfortable financial circumstances, and Sachs was educated in accordance with the custom for daughters of the upper-middle class. Although both of her parents were of Jewish ancestry, Sachs's family had few ties with the Jewish community and did not practice their religion. Sachs attended public schools from 1897 to 1900, but for reasons of poor health was removed and received private instruction until 1903. She then attended a private secondary school for daughters of wealthy and titled families and finished her education in 1908 without any formal professional training. In the summer of that year, she fell in love with a man whose name she never revealed. That experience, which ended unhappily, escalated into a crisis, making Sachs consider suicide. The man was later killed in one of Germany's concentration camps.

For the next twenty-five years, even after the death of her father in 1930, Sachs led a sheltered and not particularly noteworthy existence. She produced some poetry, read extensively, and did watercolors, some of which have been preserved in the Nelly Sachs Archive in Stockholm. In 1906, Sachs received Selma Lagerlöf's novel *Gösta Berlings saga* (1891) as a birthday present. Her admiration for the writer resulted in a correspondence between the two, and Sachs sent Lagerlöf many of her own literary experiments. Through the intervention of Lagerlöf and the brother of the reigning Swedish king, Sachs and her mother received permission to emigrate to

Sweden in 1939. Shortly after Lagerlöf's death in 1940, Sachs received orders from German authorities to appear for deportation to a work camp. Leaving all of their possessions behind, Sachs and her mother fled Germany, arriving in Stockholm on May 16, 1940. They took up residence in a small apartment in the industrial harbor area, where Sachs remained until her death in 1970.

In 1960, Sachs returned to Germany for the first time since her exile in order to receive the Annette Droste Prize. Not wishing to spend a night in Germany, she stayed instead in Zurich, traveling the short distance to Meersburg only in order to accept the honor. Hearing the German language spoken again proved to be so traumatic, however, that she experienced a "memory trip to hell." In Zurich, she met Paul Celan, another exiled poet, who invited her to his home in Paris. The meeting resulted in a continuing correspondence, but Celan was in the midst of a personal crisis as well and the relationship may have contributed to Sachs's difficulties. After her return to Stockholm, Sachs suffered a mental breakdown and was hospitalized with severe delusions of persecution. Although she worked feverishly during the next decade, she continued to suffer periodic attacks in which she imagined herself persecuted and threatened with death. Her cycle *Noch feiert Tod das Leben* (death still celebrates life) was written while she recovered in the hospital. Celan attempted to aid her recovery through an intensive, supportive correspondence which was also, however, an attempt at self-healing, inasmuch as he suffered from a similar ailment. Their poetry, beginning with Sachs's *Noch feiert Tod das Leben* and Celan's *Die Niemandsrose* (1963), shows their continuing "dialogue in poems." In the spring of 1970, Sachs became mortally ill and thus was not informed when Celan was reported missing early in April of that year. He was later found— an apparent suicide by drowning. His funeral services took place in the Cimetière Parisien near Orly, France, on the same day in May on which Sachs died in a Stockholm hospital.

Analysis

It is difficult to speak of development in Nelly Sachs's poetic works, as she was well beyond fifty years old when she produced her first significant poems. It is true that she had published lyric poetry before the 1940's, but this early work has little in common with that of her mature years. Most of the poems from the 1920's and 1930's are thematically quite distinct from the later work, devoted to musicians such as Johann Sebastian Bach, Wolfgang Amadeus Mozart, Jean-Philippe Rameau, and Luigi Boccherini or dealing poetically with certain animals, such as deer, lambs, and nightingales. The Nelly Sachs archives in Dortmund and in Stockholm have copies of a substantial number of these early efforts.

In contrast, the work of Sachs's last twenty-five years concerns itself largely with existential problems, particularly with topics related to the Holocaust and rooted in personal experiences of flight, exile, and the death of friends. Her first collection of poems, *In den Wohnungen des Todes* (in the habitations of death), refers in its title to the Nazi death camps and is dedicated to those who perished there. It is a mistake, however, to perceive her work solely in the context of these historical events. Her topic is on a larger scale—the cycle of life itself—and Sachs develops various metaphors and her work. This difficulty is the result of her frequent use of ciphers to express the agony and the hope of this cycle.

While it is desirable to interpret Sachs's work separately from the context of specific historical events, it is almost impossible to analyze an individual poem without relying on information gained from a broader knowledge of her work. This difficulty is the result of her frequent use of ciphers, poetic images that can be "decoded" only by reference to other poems in which the same images occur. Such a cipher in Sachs's work is the stone. Its properties are chiefly those of inert matter: lack of emotion, or lifelessness. The cipher may depict human callousness, death, or desolation in different contexts, and it is related to similar poetic images such as sand and dust—decayed rock—which signify the mortal human condition.

The poem "Sinai" from the collection *Sternverdunkelung* (eclipse of the stars) contains entirely negative images of the stone. Sachs compares the ancient times of Moses, in which humanity was still in intimate contact with the divine and thus vibrantly alive, with the present state of lifelessness; there are only "petrified eyes of the lovers" with "their putrefied happiness." Recounting Moses' descent from Mount Sinai, Sachs asks: "Where is still a descendent/ from those who trembled?/ Oh, may he glow/ in the crowd of amnesiacs/ of the petrified!" The eyes of the lovers turned to stone signify the death both of sensibility and sensuousness, and the inability to re-create or reproduce. It is ultimately a death of humankind. The call is for one perhaps still alive among the multitude of those dead in mind and body.

In the poem "Chorus of the Stones," from *In den Wohnungen des Todes*, stones are venerable objects depicting the history of humankind. The stone is symbolic of all that has died, but it carries memories within it and thus is not entirely devoid of life. The last lines of the poem even offer the hope that the stone is only "sleeping," that it may come to life again: "Our conglomeration is transfused by breath./ It solidified in secret/ but may awaken at a kiss." Three ideas in "Chorus of the Stones" suggest that death is not the final answer to life: The lifeless entity (the stone) contains memories; it is imbued with breath, a necessary element of life; and it may be awakened by an act of love. Transformation, resurrection, and transfiguration are therefore within the realm of possibility.

Such a flight from lifelessness to a new beginning is nevertheless fraught with difficulties. In "Chassidische Schriften" ("Hasidic Scriptures," from *Sternverdunkelung*), Sachs writes: "And the heart of stones,/ filled with drifting sand,/ is the place where midnights are stored." "Drifting sand" is sand blown skyward by the wind; thus, while it is inert matter, it has lost this inertia momentarily on the wings of the wind. Midnight, on the other hand, represents the end of one day and the dawning of the next, a time of rebirth. Sachs contends that the stone, dead as it is, is imbued with the desire for rebirth and transubstantiation. Another possibility for the stone to attain a semblance of life is offered in "Golem Tod!" ("Golem Death!" from *Sternverdunkelung*). There, "The stone sleeps itself green with moss." The suggestion that the stone is merely sleeping, not dead, and that it is capable of producing living matter (moss) is also an affirmation of the possibility of renewal of life after death. The most dramatic depiction of the rebirth of the dead is to be found in the poem "Halleluja" ("Hallelujah"), from the volume *Flucht und Verwandlung* (flight and metamorphosis). The poem describes a mountain rising from the sea by volcanic action. The rock is portrayed as a beloved child, the crowning glory of its mother, the ocean, as it thrusts forth from the womb to the light of day. While still embedded in the sea, the rock showed signs of sustaining life. As in "Golem Death!" with its stone covered with moss, this rock has been nurturing life. For the sea algae, birth of the rock means death, which the "winged longing" of the rock will bring

about; although one form of life dies, another takes its place. These poems therefore encompass the cycle of life and death of living and inert matter on Earth.

In tracing the cipher of the stone, it is evident that the nihilism of the earlier cycles has given way to a guarded optimism in the later ones. A more traditional image of transfiguration is that of the butterfly. Its life cycle includes the apparent death of the homely caterpillar and its reemergence from the cocoon as a beautiful winged creature, and thus it is readily adaptable as a symbol of the soul's resurrection after physical death. Sachs uses the image of the butterfly within this tradition. The poem "In der Flucht" ("Fleeing," from the volume *Flucht und Verwandlung*) compares the flight of the Jews from their persecutors with the never-ending process of transformation, mutation, and metamorphosis. There is no rest and no end (no "Amen") for that which is considered mortal (sand, dust), for it experiences endless metamorphoses. The butterfly, itself a symbol of metamorphosis, will reenter the life-giving element at its death and complete the cycle of life.

In "Butterfly," from *Sternverdunkelung*, the butterfly is depicted as a mortal creature (one made of "dust") which nevertheless mirrors the beauty of a world beyond: "What lovely hereafter/ is painted in your dust." The butterfly is a messenger of hope for those who are dying, because it is aware through its own metamorphosis that death is only sleep. The butterfly is the symbol of farewell, just as it was the symbol of the last greeting before sleep.

More obscure than the image of the butterfly are Sachs's ciphers of music and dance. The dancer appears to be able to defy gravity in graceful and effortless leaps and spins. A new image of humanity is created in the dance—that of emancipation from earthly limitations and acceptance into the sphere of the incorporeal. On this premise, Sachs bases her depiction of the dancer as a re-creator, savior, and emancipator from material limitations. In the poem "Sie tanzt" ("She Dances," from *Noch feiert Tod das Leben*), the dancer rescues her lover from the dead. This act of rescue is not meant to save him from physical death, for he is no longer alive; metamorphosis is her aim. This she achieves, paradoxically, by her own death: "Aber plötzlich/ am Genick/ Schlaf beünt Sie hinüber" ("But suddenly/ at the neck/ sleep bends her over"). In German, the word "over" (*hinüber*) signifies "to the other side" and thus clearly suggests death; this connotation is underscored by the image of her bending at the neck (hanging) and by the word "sleep," which Sachs frequently uses as a synonym for physical, but not spiritual, death. In the act of dancing, the dancer has liberated both the dead lover and herself. The metamorphosis has released her from life and has rescued him from death. They are united in the spiritual realm.

In the poem "She Dances," the beginning and the end of life coincide at the point of metamorphosis, the dancer being the agent. The medium for transfiguration is music. The poem "O-A-O-A," in *Glühende Rätsel* (glowing enigmas), describes the rhythmic "sea of vowels" as the Alpha and Omega. Music is the means of metamorphosis: "Du aber die Tasten niederdrücktest/ in ihre Gräber aus Musik/ und Tanz die verlorene Sternschnuppe/ einen Flügel erfand für dein Leiden" ("But you pressed down the keys/ into their graves of music/ and dance the lost meteor/ invented a wing for your anguish"). The English word "keys" is ambiguous, but the German *Tasten* refers solely to the keys of a piano in this context. The graves, made of music, the transforming factor, are being played like the keys of a piano, while dance provides the wings for flight from the corporeal.

Finally, in the poem "In der blauen Ferne" ("In the Blue Distance," from *Und niemand weiss weiter*), the pregnant last lines combine the ciphers of stone, dust, dance, and music in the depiction of metamorphosis: "the stone transforms its dust/ dancing into music." The lifeless element needs no mediator here but performs the ritual of transubstantiation into music (release from corporeal existence) by "dancing" as "dust"—an action functionally identical to that of the drifting sand in the poem "Hasidic Scriptures."

It has frequently been assumed that Nelly Sachs is chiefly a chronicler of Jewish destiny during World War II, a recorder of death and despair. This narrow view does not do justice to her work. Sachs's poetry has many aspects of faith, hope, and love, and it need not be relegated to a specific historical event or ethnic orientation. Sachs writes about the concerns of every human being—birth, life, love, spiritual renewal, and the possibility of an existence beyond physical death. To diminish the scope of her appeal is to misunderstand her message and to misinterpret her work.

Other major works

SHORT FICTION: *Legenden und Erzählungen*, 1921.
PLAYS: *Eli: Ein Mysterienspiel vom Leiden Israels*, 1951 (*Eli: A Mystery Play of the Sufferings of Israel*, 1967); *Zeichen im Sand: Die szenischen Dichtungen*, 1962.
NONFICTION: *Briefe der Nelly Sachs*, 1984.

Bibliography

Bahr, Ehrhard. "Flight and Metamorphosis: Nelly Sachs as a Poet of Exile." In *Exile: The Writer's Experience*, edited by John M. Spalek and Robert F. Bell. Chapel Hill: North Carolina University Press, 1982.

Cervantes, Eleonore K. "A Woman's View of the Holocaust: The Poetry of Nelly Sachs." *Rendezvous: Journal of Arts and Letters* 22 (Spring, 1986): 47-50.

Foot, Robert. *The Phenomenon Of Speechlessness in the Poetry of Marie Luise Kaschnitz, Günter Eich, Nelly Sachs, and Paul Celan*. Bonn, Germany: H. Grundmann, 1982.

Holzer, Burghild Oberhammer. "Nelly Sachs and the Kabbala: A Dissertation on the Difficulty of Translating Her Poetry." *Dissertation Abstracts International* 44 (May, 1984): 3377A-3378A.

Thompson, Jane Hegge. "The Theme of Rebirth in Five Dramas of Nelly Sachs." *Dissertation Abstracts International* 42 (August, 1981): 721A.

GEORGE SAND
Amandine-Aurore-Lucile Dupin,
Baroness Dudevant

Born: Paris, France; July 1, 1804   **Died:** Nohant, France; June 8, 1876

Principal long fiction

Indiana, 1832 (English translation, 1881); *Valentine*, 1832 (English translation, 1902); *Lélia*, 1833, 1839 (English translation, 1978); *Mauprat*, 1837 (English translation, 1870); *Spiridion*, 1839 (English translation, 1842); *Le Compagnon du tour de France*, 1840 (*The Companion of the Tour of France*, 1976; also as *The Journeyman Joiner*, 1847); *Consuelo*, 1842-1843 (English translation, 1846); *La Comtesse de Rudolstadt*, 1843-1844 (*The Countess of Rudolstadt*, 1847); *Jeanne*, 1844; *Le Meunier d'Angibault*, 1845 (*The Miller of Angibault*, 1847); *Lucrezia Floriani*, 1846; *La Mare au diable*, 1846 (*The Devil's Pool*, 1929; also as *The Enchanted Lake*, 1850); *Le Péché de M. Antoine*, 1847 (*The Sin of Monsieur Antoine*, 1900); *La Petite Fadette*, 1848-1849 (*Fanchon the Cricket*, 1864; also as *Little Fadette*, 1850); *François le champi*, 1850 (*Francis the Waif*, 1889); *Les Maîtres sonneurs*, 1853 (*The Bagpipers*, 1890); *Elle et lui*, 1859 (*She and He*, 1902); *Le Marquis de Villemer*, 1861 (*The Marquis of Villemer*, 1871); *La Ville noire*, 1861; *Mademoiselle Merquem*, 1868 (English translation, 1868); *Historic and Romantic Novels*, 1900-1902 (20 volumes).

Other literary forms

George Sand, who was famous during her lifetime primarily as a novelist, earned a living for many years as a journalist. Some of her essays on art, literature, politics, and social questions are collected in two posthumous volumes, *Questions d'art et de littérature* (1878) and *Questions politiques et sociales* (1879). Her twenty-volume autobiography, *Histoire de ma vie* (1854-1855; *History of My Life*, 1901), is considered by some to be her masterpiece. Georges Lubin produced an excellent annotated edition of this work and other autobiographical writings for Gallimard in 1970. Other important nonfictional works include *Lettres d'un voyageur* (1837; *Letters of a Traveller*, 1847), *Lettres à Marcie* (1837), and *Un Hiver à Majorque* (1841). Sand's plays were published in five volumes in 1877. She wrote more than nineteen thousand letters and was called by André Maurois "the best French epistolary writer."

Achievements

To her contemporaries, George Sand was a great novelist and a "fallen woman." The controversy surrounding her life has continued into the twentieth century. Until recently, scholars have neglected her enormous production of literary works to concentrate on biographical quarrels. Sand was recognized as a major novelist by Honoré de Balzac, Ivan Turgenev, Victor Hugo, and Henry James. She was widely read in the United States and Great Britain, where she influenced writers such as the Brontë sisters and George Eliot. In Russia, where political treatises were banned, her novels passed on progressive ideas and inspired political thinkers such as Mikhail Bakunin as well as novelists such as Fyodor Dostoevski. Gustave Flaubert called Sand "My Dear Master," and Marcel Proust's most poignant childhood memories involved his mother reading Sand's rustic novels to him. This picture of Sand's pastoral or rustic novels persists in France today, where the average reader considers her a writer of sentimental stories for children. Because of this image, she has been attacked by political liberals who accuse her of supporting the status quo with her tales of happy peasants. Scholars, on the other hand, regard her rustic novels as the perfection of a literary genre. To the nineteenth century public, Sand's novels calling for the emancipation of women (and men) from arranged marriages, equality between the sexes, and education for women seemed outrageously feminist. Her novel *Lélia* shocked readers by its explicit analysis of female sexuality. Twentieth century feminists, however, point to the limits of Sand's feminism, especially to her opposition to the participation of women in political affairs (she believed that women should be educated before they were given the right to vote). Because of the volume of Sand's work and the speed at which she was forced to write to support her family, her artistic circle, and her charitable contributions, the quality of her fiction is uneven, yet literary critics admire her fluid style and her techniques of psychological analysis. All agree in considering *Mauprat, Consuelo*, and the rustic novels as powerful masterpieces.

Biography

George Sand was born Amandine-Aurore-Lucile Dupin in Paris on July 1, 1804, to parents who had been married scarcely a month. Her father, Maurice Dupin, was a descendant through bastard lines of the king of Poland, Augustus the Strong, and her mother, Sophie Delaborde, was a camp follower and the daughter of a Paris bird-seller. Thus, from the beginning, Sand was exposed to the class struggle. When she was four years old, her father was killed in a fall from a horse; three years later, her mother gave up custody of her to her aristocratic maternal grandmother, who brought her up as a lady at her country estate of Nohant in the Berry region. Sand nevertheless reached out to her mother in Paris and the working class she represented.

In 1817, Sand returned to Paris, where she entered the Couvent des Anglaises for her education. In 1820, she returned to the country while her grandmother attempted to arrange a suitable marriage for her; Sand preferred to read books and ride horses. After the death of her grandmother in 1821, Sand returned to Paris to live with her mother. This arrangement proved unsatisfactory because of her mother's violent temper, and the girl sought refuge at the country estate of her father's friends, the Roëttiers. Through the Roëttiers, she met Casimir François Dudevant, the illegitimate but recognized son of a baron; she married Dudevant in 1822.

At first, the couple seemed happy enough, but after the birth of their son Maurice in 1823, their incompatibility became evident. A second child, Solange, was born in 1828. After a fight with her husband, Sand arranged to spend half of each year in Paris, where Dudevant would send her an allowance from the revenues of her land. In 1831, she left for Paris to live with Jules Sandeau, a law student who aspired to become a writer. To supplement her meager pension, Sand obtained a job writing for *Le Figaro*, a newspaper run by Hyacinthe de Latouche, an acquaintance from Berry. In collaboration with Sandeau, Sand wrote several short stories and at least one novel, which was signed "J. Sand." When Sand wrote *Indiana* alone at Nohant and returned to Paris to publish it, de Latouche suggested that she keep the name "Sand" and choose another Christian name. She chose "Georges" (soon Anglicized to George) because it seemed to her to be typical of the Berry region. *Indiana*, the first novel signed "George Sand," was published in 1832. More than seventy others were to follow.

In 1833, Sand fell in love with the poet Alfred de Musset and left with him for Venice, the city that all the Romantic writers dreamed of visiting. There they both fell ill. Following several violent incidents resulting from Musset's overindulgence in wine and women, they agreed to separate. When Musset's illness recurred, Sand nursed him faithfully but fell in love with his Italian doctor, Pietro Pagello. Barely restored to health, Musset returned to Paris while Sand and Pagello stayed in Italy. Sand addressed much of her correspondence in *Letters of a Traveller* to Musset in Paris. In 1834, she returned to Paris with Pagello but neglected him, feeling herself drawn again to Musset. Musset wrote some of his most famous poems about this relationship and analyzed it in his *La Confession d'un enfant du siècle* (1836; *The Confession of a Child of the Century,* 1892). After Musset's death, in 1857, Sand re-evaluated their adventure in *She and He*.

After many painful scenes, Sand finally broke with Musset in 1835. Later that year, she met and fell in love with the Republican lawyer Michel de Bourges. When she returned to Nohant, she had a definitive fight with her husband and sued for a legal separation, since divorce did not exist in France at that time. De Bourges acted as her lawyer.

In 1838, Sand began a relationship with Frédéric Chopin, whom she met through a mutual friend, Franz Liszt. For nine years, Sand acted as Chopin's mother, mistress, and nurse, protecting him and enabling him to write some of his best music. The most famous event in their years together was the ill-fated trip they took with Sand's children to Majorca in the winter of 1838-1839, which she described in *Un Hiver à Majorque*. Most literary critics agree that Sand was satirizing her relationship with Chopin in her novel *Lucrezia Floriani*. Sand and Chopin separated in 1847, disagreeing over the marriage of her daughter Solange to the sculptor Jean-Baptiste Auguste Clésinger.

In 1848, Sand returned to Paris as soon as she received word that the monarchy had been overthrown. She wrote most of the official bulletins for the new Republican government, which included many of her old friends. When the Republicans were arrested in May, Sand took refuge at Nohant. Although she continued to intercede with the Emperor Napoleon III for her friends, Sand has been accused of turning her back on the Revolution to write bourgeois pastoral novels.

After 1848, Sand spent more time at Nohant than in Paris, but she returned to Paris often, frequently for the openings of her plays. From 1850 to 1865, Alexandre Manceau, an engraver and a friend of her son Maurice (who was an artist, a pupil of Eugène Delacroix), was Sand's private secretary and lover. In 1864, Manceau bought a small house near Paris, where they lived in order to leave Nohant to Maurice and his new wife, Lina, the daughter of the engraver Luigi Calamatta, an old friend of Sand. After Manceau's death from tuberculosis in 1865, Sand traveled, lived in Paris, visited Flaubert at Croisset, and went to the Ardennes region to document a novel, but she considered Nohant her home again. There, she received Flaubert and Turgenev as well as other friends. She died at Nohant of a painful intestinal blockage on June 8, 1876.

Analysis

Faced with the enormous number of George Sand's novels, literary critics quickly moved to divide them into categories. The traditional categories include feminist novels, socialistic novels, and rustic novels. While this oversimplification is inaccurate, it does help the reader to identify the major themes that recur in most of her novels.

Mauprat combines the beautiful exterior scenes of Sand's rustic novels with a historical adventure story of the type written by Sir Walter Scott or Alexandre Dumas, *père*. Political and philosophical reflections are carefully woven into the fabric of the work so as not to impede the swift movement of the plot toward its suspense-filled conclusion—for *Mauprat* also contains a detective story. These disparate elements are skillfully united to form a *Bildungsroman*. The central focus of the novel is the education of Bernard de Mauprat, that is, the transformation of a wild barbarian interested only in sensual gratification into a sensitive, loving, and cultured man. This transformation is the work of Bernard's cousin Edmée, who uses his love for her to force him to change.

From the outside, Edmée seems to be cold and proud; she dominates Bernard and treats him like her son. Yet Edmée is not frigid; she merely appears that way because she suppresses her own desire for Bernard and patiently waits for him to become her equal, emotionally and morally, before she agrees to marry him. Meanwhile, like Sand herself, Edmée carries a knife to commit suicide if necessary to protect her virtue.

Bernard, who was taken at age seven by his grandfather Tristan de Mauprat to a disintegrating castle, grew up in an atmosphere of violence and crime as his marauding uncles filled the countryside with terror, re-creating in the eighteenth century their family's feudal domination of the peasants. Bernard's slow progress from this life of darkness to the light of civilization begins when Edmée de Mauprat, the sole heir of the respectable younger branch of the family, loses her way in the forest and is captured by the evil uncles. She convinces Bernard, who only wants to make love to her, to rescue her and flee from the castle with her. In order to do this, she promises Bernard that she will belong to no other man before him.

This solemn promise shapes the future of both the young people. Bernard, who is seeking only instant physical gratification, slowly and painfully discovers that Edmée will withhold this from him for many years, while he, like the medieval knight, is forced to overcome obstacles to merit her love. Chivalrous motifs are reinforced by a young man named Arthur, who serves as Bernard's friend and guide in the American Revolution, explaining to him what he must do to earn the favors of the fair maiden. The medieval knight had to conquer dragons (exterior enemies) while Bernard must conquer his own savage nature. For Edmée, on the other hand, this promise to make love is tantamount to a promise of marriage.

As the love story gives unity to the plot, the theme of

the perfectibility of humankind forms the center of the philosophical framework of the novel. Edmée creates a utopia with the aid of Patience, an old hermit who gives up his solitary life-style to help Edmée build a life of dignity and honor for the peasants. Bernard and Edmée are happy to give up their wealth with the arrival of the French Revolution, which they see as a step toward a more equitable society. In *Mauprat*, Sand uses medieval trappings, the plot of an adventure story, and the psychological developments of a love story to interest her reader in the essential message that the human race can improve with education. This progressive theme signals Sand's own movement toward a more optimistic view of the world.

Consuelo and its sequel, *The Countess of Rudolstadt*, form another *Bildungsroman*. This time, however, the person who learns and grows by overcoming obstacles is a woman. *Consuelo*, considered by many to be Sand's masterpiece, is set in the eighteenth century. The title character is a talented singer, born in Spain of a Gypsy mother, who travels in Europe perfecting her voice and developing her career. She has the misfortune of being ugly until she is transformed by her music. Her ugliness may not be a disadvantage after all, however, because it saves her from easy success and venal protectors, enabling her to keep her independence and grow in her art.

The *Bildungsroman* operates on three levels as Consuelo follows an artistic itinerary which leads to becoming a composer, a political itinerary that makes her aware of the evils of despotism and dedicated to helping the poor and suffering, and a spiritual itinerary that culminates in her initiation into the secret society of the Invisibles, who work to correct social injustice. Consuelo's artistic voyage begins when the famous maestro Porpora agrees to give the poor girl free music lessons in Venice. After Porpora teaches her the fundamentals of her art, Consuelo becomes an opera star. At this point, Porpora feels he must warn her to beware of men—both would-be protectors such as Count Justiani and would-be lovers such as Anzoletto, her childhood friend. Porpora persuades Consuelo to devote her life to art and sends her off to the Castle of the Giants in Bohemia to give music lessons to the young Baroness Amélie.

In this castle, which has all the subterranean passageways and mysteries of the Gothic novel, Consuelo meets Albert de Rudolstadt, Amélie's cousin, who is subject to temporary mental disorders during which he imagines that he is the reincarnation of the Prince Podiebrand or the Hussite hero Jean Ziska. He plays violin music that has a magical influence on Consuelo. Albert and his deranged peasant friend Zdenko teach her the history of Bohemia and its suffering under political and religious oppression. They introduce her to folk music and begin her initiation into the occult. After saving Albert's life by carrying him through secret underground passages, tunnels, and wells, Consuelo becomes ill and is nursed back to health by Albert, who falls in love with her. She refuses to marry him and leaves the castle for Vienna to pursue her study of music.

On the trip to Vienna, Consuelo dresses up like a man to protect herself. This loss of female identity gives her a freedom that helps her develop as an artist. She accidentally meets young Joseph Haydn, who accompanies her on the long trip on foot. As a result of this journey, she learns about war, despotism, and the oppression of the peasants. In Vienna, she finds Porpora again and learns about tyranny from Maria Theresa.

As she is leaving Vienna for Berlin, Consuelo receives a message that Albert is dying. She rushes to the Rudolstadt castle and agrees to marry him *in extremis*. After his death, she renounces his wealth and title and continues on to Berlin, where she is imprisoned by Frederick the Great for conspiracy. In prison, she discovers the joys of musical composition and memorizes her creations, moving even closer to traditional folk music. She is freed from prison by the Invisibles, who take her to a palace where she studies their mysteries and decides to become a member of their secret society. She falls in love with her mysterious rescuer Liverani, only to discover that Albert is still alive and an Invisible. Forced to choose between love and duty, Consuelo follows her higher instincts and chooses Albert, who reveals that he is Liverani. After her initiation into the Invisibles, which takes place in another castle, with the symbolic name of Castle of the Grail, the marriage of Consuelo and Albert is renewed.

In the epilogue, the reader learns that the Invisibles have been forced underground, that Consuelo has lost her voice and Albert, his reason. She has become a composer writing music for Albert's poems. They wander with their children through the countryside, bringing hope to the poor and needy. Thus, Consuelo is as poor at the end of the novel as she was at the beginning, but she has become the "Good Goddess of Poverty." She has fulfilled her artistic destiny by becoming a creator—a complete Romantic artist. She has fulfilled her political and spiritual destiny by helping the needy. Finally, she has fulfilled her destiny as a woman by uniting physical and spiritual love in her relationship with Albert. She lives up to her name "Consuelo" by bringing "consolation" to those around her.

The religious and political philosophy of Albert and the Invisibles, which Consuelo adopts at the end of the novel, was inspired by Pierre Leroux, a Socialist thinker whom Sand admired. In *Consuelo*, the Invisibles base their doctrine on a belief in absolute equality between sexes and classes. They also proclaim the right of the people to participate as fully as the priests in religious sacraments. This desire to reform the Catholic church was a constant preoccupation of Sand, best expressed in *Spiridion*, which develops a religious philosophy of history. Parallel to her desire to reform the Church is her desire to reform society, which finds in *Consuelo* its most complete expression.

Other major works

SHORT FICTION: *Contes d'une grand'mère*, 1873, 1876 (*Tales of a Grandmother*, 1930).

PLAYS: *Théâtre complet de George Sand*, 1877 (5 volumes).

NONFICTION: *Lettres à Marcie*, 1837; *Lettres d'un voyageur*, 1837 (*Letters of a Traveller*, 1847); *Un Hiver à Majorque*, 1841; *Histoire de ma vie*, 1854-1855 (20 volumes; *History of My Life*, 1901); *Questions d'art et de littérature*, 1878; *Questions politiques et sociales*, 1879; *Letters*, 1896 (9 volumes); *Journal intime*, 1926 (*The Intimate Journal*, 1929); *Sketches and Hints*, 1926; *Correspondance*, 1964-1981 (15 volumes); *Œuvres autobiographiques*, 1970-1971 (2 volumes).

MISCELLANEOUS: *Works*, 1887 (38 volumes).

Bibliography

Barry, Joseph. *Infamous Woman: The Life of George Sand*. Garden City, N.Y.: Doubleday, 1976.

_____, ed. and trans. *In Her Own Words*. Garden City, N.Y.: Anchor Books, 1979.

Cate, Curtis. *George Sand: A Biography*. Boston: Houghton Mifflin, 1975.

Maurois, André. *Lélia: The Life of George Sand*. Translated by Gerard Hopkins. New York: Harper, 1953.

Moers, Ellen. *Literary Women*. Garden City, N.Y.: Doubleday, 1976.

SAPPHO

Born: Lesbos, Greece; c. 612 B.C. **Died:** Unknown

Principal poetry

Poetarum Lesbiorum Fragmenta, 1955; *Sappho: A New Translation*, 1958; *Lyra Graeca*, Volume 1, 1958; *Sappho: Poems and Fragments*, 1965; *The Poems of Sappho*, 1966.

Other literary forms

Sappho is known only for her poetry.

Achievements

One of the most admired poets of the ancient world, Sappho was widely popular not only during her lifetime but also for centuries after. Although she wrote nine books of poetry, very little of the corpus remains. Except for a very few phrases on vase paintings or papyri, Sappho's poetry has been preserved primarily in small bits that happened to be quoted by other writers. There are some 170 of these fragments extant, and although there may be among them one or two complete poems, most of the fragments consist of only a few lines or a few words. For Sappho's poem fragments, the numerical system of Edgar Lobel and Denys Page, *Poetarum Lesbiorum Fragmenta*, is used.

These fragments indicate that Sappho's poems were largely lyrical, intended to be sung and accompanied by music and perhaps dance. Although in form her poetry was thus traditional, in content it differed significantly from the larger body of Greek verse, which was written primarily by men. Whereas other Greek poets were mainly concerned with larger and more public issues and with such traditional masculine concerns as war and heroism, Sappho's poems are personal, concerned with the emotions and individual experiences of herself and her friends. In exploring and describing the world of passion, in particular, Sappho departed from conventional poetic themes. Perhaps that is one of the reasons that her poetry was so popular in the ancient world.

In addition to being well known for her subject matter, Sappho has come to be associated with a particular metrical form. Although she was probably not the inventor of Sapphic meter, it has been so named because of her frequent use of it. In Sapphic meter, the stanza consists of three lines, each of which contains five feet—two trochees, a dactyl, and two more trochees—with a concluding fourth line of one dactyl and one trochee. The first line of the "Ode to Aphrodite" in the original Greek illustrates this meter. This ode is thought to have been accompanied by music written in the Mixolydian mode, a musical mode with which Sappho is also associated. Plutarch, in fact, claims that this mode, which is said to arouse the passions more than any other, was invented by Sappho.

Sappho was praised and revered by a long line of ancients, including Solon, Plato, Aristotle, Horace, Catullus, Ovid, and Plutarch. Proving that imitation is the highest form of praise, some later poets actually incorporated her verse into their own compositions; Catullus' Poem 51, for example, is a slight reworking of a poem by Sappho. Plutarch, who, like Catullus, admired this particular ode, described it as being "mixed with fire," a metaphor which could accurately be applied to the entire body of Sappho's poetry which remains.

Biography

There are few details about Sappho's life which can be stated with certainty; the only evidence is what other writers said about her, and there is no way of knowing whether what they said is true. She is thought to have been of an aristocratic family of the island of Lesbos and to have had three brothers and a daughter named Cleis; dates of her birth and death, however, are not known. Athenaeus, writing around A.D. 200, claimed that Sappho was a contemporary of Alyattes, who reigned in Lydia from 610 to 560 B.C.; Eusebius, who was writing in the late third and early fourth centuries A.D., refers to Sappho in his chronicle for the year 604 B.C. Other writers indicate that Sappho lived at the time of another poet of Lesbos, Alcaeus, who seems to have been born around 620 B.C. It seems safe, therefore, to conclude that Sappho was born sometime during the last quarter of the seventh century and lived into the first half of the sixth century B.C.

Sometime between 604 and 592 B.C., Sappho seems to have been sent into exile in Sicily by Pittacus, who was then a democratic ruler of Mytilene on Lesbos; an inscription on the Parian marbles of the third century B.C. provides confirmation. Although it seems likely that such an exile would have been for political reasons, there are no clear references in any of the fragments of Sappho's poems to indicate that she was specifically concerned with political matters; in fact, based upon those fragments, her poetry appears to have been very much apolitical.

Whether Sappho was married is also uncertain; some say that she had a husband named Cercylas, but others believe this report to be a creation of the Greek comic poets. Sappho's poetry indicates that she was the leader of a group of young women who appear to have studied music, poetry, and dance and who seem to have worshipped Aphrodite and the Muses. As the daughter of an aristocratic family, Sappho would probably not have conducted a formal school, but was more likely the informal leader of a circle of girls and young women. Scholars know from other references in her poetry that there were several such groups on Lesbos, with leaders who were rivals of Sappho.

Many of Sappho's poems also concern her romantic relationships with various women of her group, a fact which has evoked various responses throughout history, ranging from vilification to denial. Her reputation seems to have been first darkened in the fourth century B.C., long after her death, when she was the subject of a number of comic and burlesque plays; it is believed that many of the unsavory stories that came to be associated with Sappho were generated during this period. A serious and most unfortunate effect of this created and perhaps inaccurate reputation was that much of Sappho's work was later deliberately destroyed, particularly by Christians whose moral sensibilities were offended by some of the stories that circulated in the second, fourth, and eleventh centuries A.D. Sappho's reputation was also reworked by later scholars who admired her poetry but who were discomfited by her love for women; among their efforts to dissociate Sappho from her sexuality was the widely circulated story that there were in fact two Sapphos, one the licentious and immoral woman to whom all the unsavory tales applied, and the other a faultless and asexual woman who wrote sublime poetry. Most scholars today believe that there was only one Sappho, but they also believe that most of the stories told about her were untrue.

Thus, because of the legendary tales that have come to be associated with Sappho, and because of the lack of reliable historical evidence, there is little knowledge about her life which is certain. It seems reasonable to assume that she lived on Lesbos, that she was a poet, and that she valued personal relationships, about which she wrote. Both during her lifetime and after, she was much admired; statues were erected in her honor, coins were minted bearing her likeness, and she is said to have been given a heroine's funeral. Beyond these small pieces of information, scholars must turn to the fragments of her poetry for knowledge and understanding.

Analysis

Since Sappho's poetry is largely personal, it concerns her immediate world: her dedication to Aphrodite, her love of nature and art, and her relationships with lovers, friends, and family. Her poetry reflects her enjoyment of beauty in the natural world and the close connection that existed between that world and the lives of herself and her friends. Their worship of Aphrodite, their festive songs and dances, are all celebrated with flowers from the fields and with branches from the trees. Her poetry also reflects her love of art, whether in the form of poetry, the music of the lyre, or the graceful movement of a maiden in a dance. Since these interests are, however, always presented through the perspective of a personal response, a chief defining characteristic of Sappho's poetry is that it is highly emotional.

Most of the extant fragments of Sappho's poetry were quoted by later writers to illustrate some point of dialect, rhetoric, grammar, or poetic style, and those writers usually quoted only that portion of Sappho's poem which was pertinent to their point. It is fortunate, then, that Dionysius of Halicarnassus, a Greek writer of treatises who lived in Rome around 30 B.C., quoted in its entirety

Sappho's "Ode to Aphrodite," to illustrate "the smooth mode of composition." This poem, the longest of several by Sappho honoring Aphrodite, appears to be the most substantial complete work of Sappho which remains.

The ode contains the usual components of a celebration prayer to Aphrodite: the Invocation, the Sanction, and the Entreaty. The Invocation to the goddess consists of a series of epithets, "Dapple-throned Aphrodite,/ eternal daughter of God,/ snare-knitter"; the Sanction asks the goddess' generosity and assistance and reminds her of past favors she has granted; and the Entreaty urgently appeals to the goddess for aid in the present situation. Sappho employs this traditional form in a fresh way, however, not only by her use of vivid metaphors and lyrical language but also by using the Sanction to reveal something of the goddess' character as well as something of Sappho's own psychology.

As Sappho employs it, the Sanction is a narrative passage within which both she and the goddess move back and forth in time. After describing a past occasion when the goddess came to Earth in a carriage pulled by sparrows, Sappho then recounts the goddess' questioning of her at that time. Using in her narrative the past tense and the indirect question, Sappho recalls the goddess' remarks: "You asked, What ailed me now that/ made me call you again?" Abruptly, then, Sappho places the goddess' gentle chiding within the present context; the poem shifts to direct discourse as the goddess questions Sappho directly: "Whom has/ Persuasion to bring round now/ to your love? Who, Sappho, is/ unfair to you?" This mix of the two temporal perspectives links and blends the present with the past, not only emphasizing Sappho's recurring states of anxiety over new love but also illuminating the special and friendly relationship between the poet and the goddess: Aphrodite has obviously assisted Sappho before in similar matters of the heart. Continuing to reveal Sappho's character, the goddess reminds her that they are beginning a now-familiar pattern: A bemused Aphrodite recalls, "If she [the desired lover] won't accept gifts, she/ will one day give them; and if/ she won't love you—she soon will/ love." Sappho, manipulating the tradition of the Sanction for new purposes of self-mockery and character revelation, thus discloses her love for the courting period, as well as the shift in attitudes which will inevitably occur between her and her new lover. After the goddess' assurance that the sought-after lover will very shortly be seeking Sappho, the reader is then returned to the poem's outer frame, the prayer, as Sappho begs the goddess to help at once, to "Come now! Relieve this intolerable pain!"

Within the form of a traditional prayer honoring Aphrodite, the poem thus presents a delightful variety of tone. It discloses the intensity of Sappho's passion for the desired lover and her wry recognition that this intensity will be limited by time and by her own nature. The poem similarly indicates not only the immensity of the goddess' power but also her gentle amusement at the joys and woes of her followers; although Sappho's present sufferings in love will soon be in the past, a pattern underscored by the poem's movement between present and past time, there is every reason to believe that the goddess will assist Sappho once again in achieving the lover who will end her present suffering. In revealing not only something of the character of Aphrodite but also something of the character of Sappho, the poem thus transcends the limitations of its genre.

Although there are a few other fragments of poems honoring Aphrodite, the largest number of Sappho's fragments which remain are concerned with love, a subject which occupied much of Sappho's attention. One love poem which may, like the "Ode to Aphrodite," be nearly complete, is the large fragment sometimes called the "Ode to Anactoria," although the poem may have been written for Atthis or even for some other woman whom Sappho loved. An unknown writer who has been labeled "Longinus," in a Greek work believed to date from the first or second century A.D., quoted this fragment to illustrate Sappho's mastery in depicting physical sensations. Extraordinary in its exquisitely precise delineation of the extremes of passion, the poem is also notable for the contrast between the control of its first section and the revealed intensity of its latter section, with the resulting alternations in tone as the speaker sits in the presence of two people, the woman she loves and the man who is evidently enjoying that woman's attentions.

Concisely and with control, the poem begins:

> He is a god in my eyes—
> the man who is allowed
> to sit beside you—he
> who listens intimately
> to the sweet murmur of
> your voice, the enticing
> laughter that makes my own
> heart beat fast.

This calm and steady beginning establishes an outer mood of control, an atmosphere of containment and casual social interplay; the poem turns, however, upon the word "laughter," and the rest of the fragment describes, rapidly and with great intensity, the physical symptoms of the poet's great passion. All of her senses are affected: Her "tongue is broken," and she sees nothing; she hears only her "own ears drumming" as she drips with sweat; and, as "trembling shakes" her body, she turns "paler than dry grass." In one of Sappho's most superb lines, she declares that "a thin flame runs under/ my skin." Then, ending this rapid and graphic description of the physical results of intense emotion, the poet remarks, in a powerfully reserved manner, that "At such times/ death isn't far from me."

Sappho's description in this poem of the effects of passion has not been surpassed, although a number of later poets, including Catallus, have imitated, translated, or adopted her ideas. None, however, has been able to convey such intensity of feeling with the economy and precision of Sappho. It seems safe to say that there are few who would dispute Longinus' claim that this poem illustrates "the perfection of the Sublime in poetry."

Several fragments of varying size treat the power of love, among them a particularly felicitous line quoted by Maximus of Tyre around A.D. 150: "As a whirlwind/ swoops on an oak/ Love shakes my heart." An overpowering natural phenomenon, love is presented here as an elemental force which completely overcomes the lover, both physically and emotionally. As the wind physically surrounds the oak, so does love overpower the lover physically as well as emotionally. Love, a force which cannot be denied, is thus depicted as a violent physical and emotional assault, to which one may well respond with mixed feelings.

Sappho explores the ambiguity of the lover's response to love's violent assault in another fragment, quoted by Hephaestion around A.D. 150: "Irresistible/ and bittersweet/ that loosener/ of limbs, Love/ reptile-like/ strikes me down." Again, love is depicted as an absolute power and as a violent force—in this instance as a reptile which, attacking a passive victim, creates in her a weakened state. That state is not, however, altogether unpleasant, as is indicated by the exquisite sensuality of the adjectival phrase describing love as "that loosener of limbs." Love's duality—its violence and its sweetness—and the lover's ambiguity of response—as the victim of assault and as reveler in love's sensuality—are further under-

scored by the oxymoronic adjective "bittersweet," an epithet for love which Sappho may have been the first to use.

In addition to analyzing the nature and effects of love, Sappho also writes of love's termination, of separation, loss, and grief. One such fragment, 94 L.-P., found in a seventh century manuscript in very poor condition, contains many lacunae and uncertain readings. Nevertheless, enough of the poem remains to prove that Sappho was defining the state of bereavement and the effectiveness of memory in alleviating that state. In the course of exploring these themes, however, the poem presents an enchanting account of the life led by Sappho and the members of her group as they worshipped Aphrodite, celebrated the beauty of nature, and gloried in one another.

Like the "Ode to Aphrodite," the poem uses a frame of present time to contain an account of past time; in this poem, however, the past time frames an even earlier period, so that there are three time periods represented. Beginning in her present situation, Sappho, alone, reveals her emotional state at the loss of her beloved: "Frankly I wish I were dead." Attempting then to console herself, Sappho recalls the occasion of their parting; at that time, in contrast to the present situation, Sappho controlled her grief in order to comfort her lover, who was overcome by weeping. On that occasion, Sappho urged her beloved to remember their former happiness and to comfort herself with the memory of their love. At this point in the past, the poem then removes to its third temporal setting, that idyllic period when the two were actually together. In a passage of great lyrical beauty, Sappho recalls the details of their life:

> think
> of our gifts to Aphrodite
> and all the loveliness that we shared
> all the violet tiaras
> braided rosebuds, dill and
> crocus twined around your young neck
> myrrh poured on your head
> and on soft mats girls with
> all that they most wished for beside them
> while no voices changed
> choruses without ours
> no woodlot bloomed in spring without song.

In re-creating, at the moment of their farewell, this earlier time of delight in love, nature, and each other, Sappho consoles her beloved by reminding her that the joys they shared are preserved in memories and that those memories can provide solace. At the same time, from her position in the outer frame of the poem—the present context—Sappho attempts to comfort herself by the same means. Yet, as Sappho tersely and flatly demonstrates by her opening statement, in no way can memory truly compensate for the beloved's absence.

Sappho's legacy is meager in size, consisting of one or two poems that may be complete, together with a number of shorter fragments that tantalize by their incompleteness even as they enchant with what they do provide. These few pieces clearly manifest the enormous poetic talent that Sappho possessed: a genius for capturing a mood, for portraying an experience, and for depicting an emotion. While her poetry is personal in dealing with her own responses to life, it is, paradoxically, also universal; the feelings she describes, even though they are her own, are shared by all human beings who ever love, lose, or grieve, or who experience jealousy, anger, or regret. One of the first poets to explore the range and depth of the human heart, Sappho well deserves Plato's epithet for her, "the tenth muse."

Bibliography

Bowra, C. M. *Greek Lyric Poetry from Alcman to Simonides*. 2d rev. ed. Oxford, England: Clarendon Press, 1961.

Page, Denys Lionel. *Sappho and Alcaeus: An Introduction to the Study of Ancient Lesbian Poetry*. Oxford, England: Clarendon Press, 1979.

Robinson, David M. *Sappho and Her Influence*. Boston: Marshall Jones, 1924.

Weigall, Arthur. *Sappho of Lesbos: Her Life and Times*. London: T. Butterworth, 1932.

Wharton, Henry Thornton. *Sappho: Memoir, Text, Selected Renderings, and a Literal Translation*. 2d ed. Chicago: A. C. McClurg, 1887.

NATHALIE SARRAUTE

Born: Ivanovo-Voznessensk, Russia; July 18, 1900

Principal long fiction

Portrait d'un inconnu, 1948 (*Portrait of a Man Unknown*, 1958); *Martereau*, 1953 (English translation, 1959); *Le Planétarium*, 1959 (*The Planetarium*, 1960); *Les Fruits d'or*, 1963 (*The Golden Fruits*, 1964); *Entre la vie et la mort*, 1968 (*Between Life and Death*, 1969); *Vous les entendez?*, 1972 (*Do You Hear Them?*, 1973); *"Disent les imbéciles,"* 1976 (*"Fools Say,"* 1977); *Tu ne t'aimes pas*, 1989 (*You Don't Love Yourself*, 1990).

Other literary forms

In 1932, Nathalie Sarraute began to write the short texts that make up *Tropismes* (1938, 1957; *Tropisms*, 1963). These short fictions cannot be called short stories because they have neither the plot nor the characters traditionally associated with the genre. Each text provides, rather, a glimpse into the inner psychological workings of anonymous beings designated only by pronouns. This book is the basis of Sarraute's later creations. While she was developing her novelistic techniques, Sarraute began to write critical essays on the evolution of the novel form. These essays were published in a collection entitled *L'Ère du soupçon* (1956; *The Age of Suspicion*, 1963). In 1963, Sarraute began writing plays as a form of "relaxation."

Achievements

The publication of Sarraute's *Tropisms* in 1938 went unnoticed by the general public, with only a single critical review. Yet the movement which Sarraute was unaware of starting became the "New Novel" movement of the late 1950's. When *Tropisms* was republished by Minuit in 1957, it was read in the light of the critical theories expressed in *The Age of Suspicion*, which was actually written after *Tropisms*. By this time, Sarraute had already published two novels, and her third, *The Planetarium*, received a friendly critical reception and became a best-seller. In 1964, *The Golden Fruits* won the Prix International de Littérature, and Sarraute became secure in her reputation as an established writer. Along with Alain Robbe-Grillet, with whom she sometimes disagreed, she was considered the leader and theorist of the New Novel movement. Although Sarraute likes to point out her differences with the New Novelists, there are many things on which they agree. They all see the traditional concepts of plot and character in a novel as outmoded and in need of renewal. It is certain that without the notoriety of this movement, the genius of Sarraute would have gone undiscovered for many more years.

Biography

Nathalie Sarraute was born Nathalie Tcherniak on July 18, 1900, in Ivanovo-Voznessensk, Russia. Her parents were Russian Jews who met in Geneva, where they had gone to acquire a university education because Nicholas II prevented Jews from attending universities in Russia. When she was two years old, her parents were divorced. French was her first language because she moved to Paris with her mother at age two and later attended nursery school there. Until the age of eight, when she settled in Paris with her father, who had remarried, she was shuttled back and forth between France, Switzerland, and Russia. At the age of seven she wrote a novel, which she timidly presented to a Russian writer, a friend of her mother. His only comment, "Learn to spell before you write novels," discouraged her for almost thirty years. By the age of twelve she was fluent in French, Russian, English, and German.

After studying at the Lycée Fénelon in Paris, Sarraute received the *baccalauréat* degree and then a *licence* in English from the Sorbonne in 1920. From 1920 to 1921, she studied toward a bachelor's degree in history at the University of Oxford. During the winter of 1921-1922, she studied sociology under Werner Sombart in Berlin. In 1922, she enrolled in the University of Paris Law School, where she met Raymond Sarraute in 1923. They were married in 1925 and were both admitted to the Paris bar. For twelve years, she worked as a lawyer, and during this time she gave birth to three daughters.

In 1932, Sarraute's literary career began, and her biography merges with the story of the long, painful process of getting her works recognized and published.

During World War II, Sarraute took refuge in the town of Parmain (Seine-et-Oise). There, under the name of Nicole Sauvage, she masqueraded as the governess of her own daughters in order to hide from the Germans.

Further biographical details about Sarraute are scarce: She maintains that this idea of a public persona has little relation to the consciousness of the writer who creates literary works.

Analysis

In her preface to *The Age of Suspicion*, Nathalie Sarraute attempts to explain the concept of "tropisms"—the subterranean movements she tries to capture in her fiction. She calls them "the secret source of our existence" and claims that they are "at the origin of our gestures, of our words and of the emotions that we believe we feel." Although few people recognize or pay attention to these rapid changes at the limit of consciousness, Sarraute insists that they occur in every human being. Because they are deeper than the "subconscious" mind and exist before thoughts are put into words, these emotional movements are extremely difficult to record. The method that Sarraute has adopted is to translate these tropisms into images—provoking in the reader an emotional reaction similar to the one she is seeking to portray. Because these movements are very rapid, she attempts to slow them down and take them apart so that the reader can follow the interaction of tropisms, usually between two or more people. Often, she devotes three or four pages to "events" that take place in a matter of seconds. Sarraute compares this technique to a slow-motion film.

In addition to showing the interaction of tropisms between different persons, Sarraute also studies the interplay of two levels of discourse. The first level, which she calls "conversation," realistically and sometimes ironically imitates the banal clichés that people exchange in everyday life or in the dialogues of a traditional novel. The second level, called "subconversation," contains the images that convey the tropisms and all the other unvoiced feelings and approximations of feelings that go on behind (Sarraute would say "below") ordinary conversation. Her later novels wander freely between these two levels, with few signposts for the reader. The extra work required from the reader, "collaboration" in making the novel, is one of the characteristics of the New Novel.

Because Sarraute has been fascinated by tropisms and seeks to portray them in her novels, she has discarded the traditional notions of plot and character, which, she believes, create an awkward distance between the reader and the tropisms she is trying to isolate. She numbers among her predecessors Fyodor Dostoevski, who also showed contradictory characters with illogical motivations; James Joyce, who pioneered in techniques of the interior monologue; and Franz Kafka, whose characters were caught in an irrational world where no human contact was possible. She is especially fascinated by Marcel Proust, who, according to Sarraute, was studying the same movements that interest her; however, he saw them only in the past, frozen by memory.

Sarraute captures her tropisms while they are still moving and makes the reader participate in this rapid movement. Otherwise, she sees her characters as dead, frozen, all of one piece, wax statues of the Musée Grévin—her most negative words of condemnation. In *Between Life and Death*, her writer-protagonist's alter ego explains that there are only two judgments possible for a work of art: It is alive, or it is dead.

After her first two novels, Sarraute abandoned first-person narration for a third-person technique permitting her to move rapidly from the inside of one character to another. These first two novels share a preoccupation with the notion of character. The third novel, *The Planetarium*, continues this exploration but also introduces a preoccupation with aesthetic values that becomes more important in *The Golden Fruits, Between Life and Death, Do You Hear Them?*, and the play *C'est beau* (1973; *It's Beautiful*, 1981). The notion of character has almost entirely disappeared from *The Golden Fruits*, where a novel of that name is the "protagonist." Sarraute's novel describes the tropisms surrounding the rise and fall of *The Golden Fruits* and incidentally provides an amusing satire of Parisian literary circles. *Between Life and Death* recounts the same process from the point of view of the artist. *Do You Hear Them?* and *It's Beautiful* center on intergenerational feuds over the definition of beauty in art. *"Fools Say"* returns to the paradox of the simultaneous necessity and impossibility of real human communication with words.

The Planetarium is both more complex and more traditional than Sarraute's first two novels. After the reader has mastered the technique of deciphering what critic Vivian Mercier calls Sarraute's "third person stream of consciousness," a traditional plot appears. This plot revolves around several questions concerning Alain Guimier, a young man supposedly working on a thesis in art history, who emerges as the central consciousness of the novel: Will Alain succeed in persuading his family to buy him an antique armchair rather than leather club chairs? Will Alain talk his Aunt Berthe out of her spacious apartment in a prestigious section of Paris? Will Alain be admitted into the circle of admirers of the famous writer Germaine Lemaire? In addition to this skeletal plot, *The Planetarium* has another vestige of the traditional novel—characters, who also have names if one is willing to search for them. Alain's wife is named Gisèle; his father, Pierre; and mother-in-law, Madeleine.

Despite these elements of the traditional novel, which tempt the reader to construct characters and adventure, the essence of the novel is elsewhere. In an interview with François Bondy published in *Der Monat*, Sarraute explained the symbolism of the title. A planetarium is a false sky, and the characters are like false stars rotating in elliptical orbits. This artificial reality—art objects, material success, social status—is the surface under which the real dramas, the tropisms, lie.

These dramas concern interpersonal relations in two worlds—the family and the social circle of the artist. Critics have variously suggested that Alain, Germaine Lemaire, or Aunt Berthe is the star at the center of this solar system, but the universe of *The Planetarium* seems to have no star, or at least no center of gravitational pull. The characters collide with one another at random. They are all seeking love, acceptance, possession (of other human beings), domination—in a word, human contact. Critics have said that Sarraute's novels contain no love or other warm human emotions, yet both Alain's father, with his desire for Spartan discipline, and his Aunt Berthe, with her need to lavish gifts on him, love Alain in their own way. Gisèle is torn between her love for her mother and her love for Alain. She seeks security and protection in his love. Even Alain has tender thoughts

about his aunt on occasion and takes refuge in the security of his wife's presence after his battles on the social front.

Beyond these psychological insights, Sarraute leads readers to question their own cherished values. The epigraph of the novel could be the reaction of Germaine Lemaire to a critical article which makes her see that her books are dead: "Alone on a burnt out star. Life is elsewhere." Lemaire quickly forgets this criticism, however, to bask in the praise of her admirers. Just as she refuses to search for authentic art, the other characters refuse to live authentic lives, taking refuge in shallow satisfactions.

Yet nothing is any more final in this novel than in everyday life. The reader is never sure that Alain is a spoiled brat, that Berthe is a possessive maniac. Their lives are filled with contradictory feelings and desires that resist all attempts to simplify them. In the last scene of the novel, Alain begins to have doubts about the good taste of his idol, Germaine Lemaire. Perhaps he is capable of finding the authentic existence she glimpsed briefly and brushed aside.

Sarraute's novel *"Fools Say"* weaves together several themes that interested Sarraute for many years, carrying them to their logical conclusion. In *Portrait of a Man Unknown, Martereau,* and *The Planetarium*, she was especially concerned by the masks people place on others. In *The Golden Fruits, Between Life and Death*, and *Do You Hear Them?*, a major theme was the relativity and subjectivity of aesthetic ideas. In *"Fools Say,"* Sarraute analyzes the processes by which people place masks, labels, or names on other people in order to denigrate their ideas. The ultimate insult to an idea, according to Sarraute, is to claim that it is said by a fool. By attacking the personality of the creator of the idea, one eliminates the necessity, or even the possibility, of a rational discussion of the merits of the idea itself.

The novel has no characters in the traditional sense—only voices that sometimes seem to coalesce to form a central consciousness. In certain sections, there are also relationships implied between people: grandmother-grandchild, master-admirers, two lovers, newlyweds, and so on. The central consciousness, which may belong to one person or to many, usually speaks in the first person and is almost always alone in protesting the use of "fools say" to silence opponents. He sees himself as infinite. He, like everyone, conceives of himself as a subject and cannot "see himself as others see him," as an object. For this reason, he does not recognize photographs of himself. The little boy who refuses to see his grandmother as "cute" is probably the same one who is shocked to be told he has Uncle Frank's undercut jaw. Then he overhears others saying that he is not really intelligent, he accepts their judgment at face value, until an adult points out to him that he must defend himself by calling the people imbeciles who say he is stupid. Later, he realizes that anyone who calls someone else an imbecile is one himself. (Sarraute cannot resist an ironic comment here: What does that make a person who writes a book on the subject?) When this boy, or another one, becomes more mature, he attempts to avoid this labeling by really examining a repugnant idea. This proves so distasteful that he is finally forced to use name-calling to escape from the situation.

The consciousness (or consciousnesses) who calls himself "I" fluctuates between a declaration that there are no limits between people ("There is no longer any I, any he, any separations, any fusion") and a recognition that individuals do exist ("Each in his place. Each is what he is"). This dilemma of identity makes the name-calling even more ludicrous. Finally, after starting a riot by declaring that he is "empty . . . a hole of air," he seems to be subdued by the "forces of order" and admits that ideas do come from people. He then becomes important; he is "someone." At the ironic ending of the novel, "he" is accused of conceiving and almost saying the words "That is what fools say."

In *"Fools Say,"* Sarraute points out how language can become a tool of repression and tyranny. By exploring the ambiguity of personal identity, she shows how futile it is to characterize a person by a word or a gesture. In this way, she protests against the use of language to attack individuals and to silence ideas.

Other major works

SHORT FICTION: *Tropismes*, 1938, 1957 (*Tropisms*, 1963); *L'Usage de la parole*, 1980 (*The Uses of Speech*, 1980).
PLAYS: *Le Silence*, 1964 (radio play; *Silence*, 1981); *Le Mensonge*, 1966 (radio play; *The Lie*, 1981); *C'est beau*, 1973 (*It's Beautiful*, 1981); *Théâtre*, 1978 (*Collected Plays*, 1981); *Pour un oui ou pour un non*, 1982.
NONFICTION: *L'Ère du soupçon*, 1956 (*The Age of Suspicion*, 1963); *Enfance*, 1983 (*Childhood*, 1984).

Bibliography

Besser, Gretchen Rous. *Nathalie Sarraute*. Boston: Twayne, 1979.
Kranake, Mimica, and Yvon Belaval. *Nathalie Sarraute*. Paris: Gallimard, 1965.
Temple, Ruth Z. *Nathalie Sarraute*. New York: Columbia University Press, 1968.
Tison-Braun, Micheline. *Nathalie Sarraute: Ou, La Recherche de l'authenticité*. Paris: Gallimard, 1971.

MAY SARTON

Born: Wondelgem, Belgium; May 3, 1912

Principal long fiction

The Single Hound, 1938; *The Bridge of Years*, 1946; *Shadow of a Man*, 1950; *A Shower of Summer Days*, 1952; *Faithful Are the Wounds*, 1955; *The Birth of a Grandfather*, 1957; *The Small Room*, 1961; *Joanna and Ulysses*, 1963; *Mrs. Stevens Hears the Mermaids Singing*, 1965; *The Poet and the Donkey*, 1969; *Kinds of Love*, 1970; *As We Are Now*, 1973; *Crucial Conversations*, 1975; *A Reckoning*, 1978; *Anger*, 1982; *The Magnificent Spinster*, 1985; *The Education of Harriet Hatfield*, 1989.

Other literary forms

A poet as well as a novelist, May Sarton has published a considerable number of volumes of verse. Her *Collected Poems, 1930-1993* appeared in 1993. She has also written a fable, *Miss Pickthorn and Mr. Hare* (1966); an animal fantasy story, *The Fur Person: The Story of a Cat* (1957); several volumes of autobiography, including *I Knew a Phoenix: Sketches for an Autobiography* (1959), *Plant Dreaming Deep* (1968), and *A World of Light: Portraits and Celebrations* (1976); and several journals of her life in Nelson, New Hampshire, and York, Maine.

Achievements

It was after World War II, with the novel *The Bridge of Years* and the poems collected in *The Lion and the Rose* (1948), that Sarton's reputation began to grow. Her novels have met with a mixed response from critics and reviewers, sometimes condemned for awkward or imprecise style, an odd charge against a practicing poet. Even Carolyn Heilbrun, Sarton's defender, admits that confusing shifts of viewpoint occur in her fiction. On the other hand, Sarton's honesty in presenting human problems, seeing them from varied perspectives, has generally been acknowledged. Sarton has also been accused of sentimentality and preciousness, and she has tried to shift her style to a more direct, less self-conscious one, perhaps answering critics of *Mrs. Stevens Hears the Mermaids Singing* who saw it as too arch, too knowing.

Sarton has complained of the lack of serious critical scrutiny of her work and has expressed disappointment as well at her failure to achieve a large popular success. She has been stereotyped as a woman's writer, presumably creating slick plot situations, overdramatic dialogue, and conventional characters in romantic duos or trios. Some of these charges are true; she herself, noting the difficulty of supporting herself by her work even as late as the 1970's although she is a prolific and well-established writer, has spoken of the difficulties of being a single woman writer not sustained by a family or a religious community. Nevertheless, she continues to affirm the possibility of self-renewal, commenting: "I believe that eventually my work will be seen as a whole, all the poems and all the novels, as the expression of a vision of life which, though unfashionable all the way, has validity." The recent surge of interest in her work, particularly among feminist scholars, would seem to confirm Sarton's hopes.

Biography

May Sarton was born Eléanore Marie Sarton in Wondelgem, Belgium, on May 3, 1912. Her mother, Mabel Elwes Sarton, an English designer who worked at Maison Dangette, Brussels, was a determined craftsperson and an uncompromising seeker of high standards. Her father, George Sarton, pampered by his Belgian upper-middle-class family after losing his mother early, was an active socialist who did mathematical studies at the University of Brussels before settling into his life's work as a major historian of science.

Sarton's earliest years were spent in Belgium, but with the coming of World War I, the family fled to England. In 1915, the Sartons went to America, staying briefly in New York before settling in Washington, D.C., where the Carnegie Institute gave support to Mr. Sarton's projected history of science. May's mother founded Belgart, specializing in handmade fashion apparel. May's father's somewhat informal appointment at Harvard University led the family to Cambridge, Massachusetts, in 1918. There, young May attended Shady Hill School, a Spartan institution run by an educational innovator, Mrs. Ernest Hocking, wife of a well-known philosopher, who combined the study of philosophy with poetry.

In 1919, the family briefly returned to settle their affairs in Belgium. For a short time, Sarton attended the Institut Belge de Culture Française, which she later attended for a year at age twelve. Literature was taught from great works, and memorization was required. Sarton spent that year with family friends while her parents were in Beirut so that her father could learn Arabic for his research. The literary atmosphere and general culture which she encountered there influenced Sarton greatly.

Sarton's parents settled into Channing Place, Cambridge, which was the center of Sarton's life until her parents' deaths. Sarton spent two years wanting to be an actress, doing summer stock in Gloucester before joining Eva LeGallienne's Civic Repertory Theater in 1929. She spent three years with the theater company; from 1931 to 1932, Sarton was in Paris working as director of the company's apprentices. While in Paris, she became friends with Aurélian-Marie Lugné-Poë, a founder of Théâtre de L'Œuvre, a theater which brought many new plays to France. Although he thought Sarton had more talent as a writer, he was willing to help her improve her acting skills. Their unsuccessful romantic relationship parallels that which occurs in *A Shower of Summer Days*, whose heroine goes to a country home in Ireland to overcome a love affair.

When LeGallienne ran out of money, Sarton, together with Eleanor Flexner and Kappo Phelan, kept the Apprentices Theater going, settling in Dublin, New Hampshire, and appearing elsewhere on tour. That venture failed after two years, a considerable shock for Sarton which turned her in the direction of writing fiction. In the following year, she wrote several short stories, none of which sold. In June, 1936, she went to Cornwall, England, first staying with Charles Singer, the historian of science, and then moving to London. She met Elizabeth Bowen, who was to become a friend over the next several decades and was the subject of passionate feelings; Juliette and Julian Huxley, at whose apartment over the London Zoo she spent a month; and Virginia Woolf.

From 1936 to 1940, Sarton visited Belgium each spring, and for decades she could not decide whether she was European or American. She began writing poetry at the age of twenty-six. Wanting funds and having no settled career, she returned to the United States in 1939 to read her poetry at various colleges.

During the years of World War II, she worked for the Office of War Information in the film department. In 1943, she set up poetry readings at the New York Public Library to provide cultural experience for wartime workers. She returned to England in 1944 to visit her friend Elizabeth Bowen, who also visited Sarton whenever she was in the United States. With *The Bridge of Years*, Sarton's novel-writing began again in earnest. Novels and other fiction and volumes of poetry have appeared at close intervals since. Her early poetry won for her the Gold Rose for Poetry and the Edward Bland Memorial Prize (1945).

Sarton supported herself by teaching, serving as Briggs-Copeland instructor in composition at Harvard from 1950 to 1952, poet-in-residence at Bryn Mawr from 1953 to 1954, and lecturing on poetry at Harvard, the University of Iowa, the University of Chicago, Colorado College for Women, and Wellesley and Beloit colleges. Other novels appearing in the early 1950's earned for Sarton a Guggenheim Fellowship from 1954 to 1955. Her reputation had grown with *A Shower of Summer Days*, though the critical reception, as with later novels, was mixed.

The Birth of a Grandfather came at a turning point in Sarton's life: Her mother had died in 1950 after a long illness and her father died quite suddenly in 1956. The family home in Cambridge was sold, and Sarton moved in October, 1958, to an old house equipped with a barn and thirty-six acres in Nelson, New Hampshire, a small village. *The Small Room*, a novel dealing with women training women as intellectual disciples in the atmosphere of a small women's college, was written there. It also introduced a lesbian love affair between Carryl Cope, a brilliant but flinty scholar, and Olive Hunt, a benefactor of the college. *Mrs. Stevens Hears the Mermaids Singing*, which was written at a time of gloom because of worries over her financial situation, was at first refused publication because it depicted a lesbian affair, and the publishers required excisions before the book was accepted.

Kinds of Love, As We Are Now, Crucial Conversations, and *A Reckoning* explore various marital or amatory dilemmas along with the problem of being feminine and an artist. During this period, Sarton settled briefly in Ogunquit, Maine, and then in York, Maine, in an old house on the coast, writing further volumes of poetry, autobiographical sketches, and journals.

Analysis

Based upon Sarton's student years in Belgium and memories of her own family, *The Bridge of Years* centers on a Belgian family, Paul and Melanie Duchesne, and their three daughters, during four segments of their lives. These periods, besides accounting for personal growth in the major characters, also demarcate the stages of political change after World War I: optimism in the immediate postwar period; the decline of public morale and search for political solutions to the Depression of the 1930's; the fear of renewed European conflict attendant upon the rise of Hitler; and the outbreak of that conflict as liberal, humanitarian values come under attack with World War II. The novel is, perhaps, Sarton's most complex work, partly because the prototypes of the main characters were close to Sarton's own experience and the themes were motivated by intellectual friendships established in Europe prior to World War II.

Melanie Duchesne, a designer of furniture, a stickler for fine craftsmanship, a courageous and optimistic woman whose country home is a model of stability, is based upon Sarton's mother and her long-time friend, Céline Limbosch. Paul, the temperamental philosopher who cannot express his thoughts, is partly based on Raymond Limbosch and partly on George Sarton, May's father, especially in his need for an ordered existence and exact routine. Paul's breakthrough into true philosophical statement under the pressure of the war is, as much as anything, Sarton's own search for authentic expression. Her father's leftist socialism and critical intelligence are reflected in Pierre Poiret, the university-student son of close friends of the Duchesnes. The immemorial Bo Bo, the stiff but protective Teutonic nursemaid, is a portrait of Sarton's childhood governess.

Of the daughters, Colette, the youngest, is the poet, a romanticist living in a fairy world, Sarton's view of herself as a child. Solange, who becomes a veterinarian, has the patient skill with animals that Sarton herself possesses. The eldest daughter, Françoise, with her long affection for Jacques Croll, a fatigued soldier from World War I, believes that art is everything, turning herself inward when Jacques, maneuvered by Melanie, marries a local girl. Françoise feels compromised when Jacques tips her a wink as he walks down the church aisle with his bride. Her resulting emotional breakdown, and the awareness that art cannot be everything when "life [is] lived near the point of conflict," reflect Sarton's own emotional turmoil in the 1930's as she sought to become an artist.

Paul Duchesne's skepticism about the perfectibility of the human spirit is tempered by his German friend, the intellectual Gerhard Schmidt, who sees the need for individual effort to resist tyranny. After escaping from his homeland during Hitler's purge of intellectuals, he goes to fight with the Loyalists in Spain while his son, Hans, hypnotized by the Nazis, becomes a storm trooper. This opposition of father and son is repeated in the case of Émile Poiret, a pious Catholic floral illustrator with a sense of cosmic presence in things, and his antireligious son, Pierre. The novel presents facets of the European response to the breakdown of democratic civilization in the 1920's and 1930's and, at a more personal level, reflects the idea that some persons must extend themselves in love if civilization is to continue.

Coming roughly at the middle of Sarton's career, *Mrs. Stevens Hears the Mermaids Singing* is the author's most intense study of the feminine artist. Her style received mixed reviews, one critic praising the music of the prose, another objecting to the fussiness and humorlessness of the writing. What one critic found to be a well-done presentation of the mystery of the creative impulse, a second found to be "an embarrassing probing of art" and "acute self-consciousness," and a third found the novel's characters "muse-chasers who believe themselves to be delicate vessels of talent." Carolyn Heilbrun, in noting that the novel deals with the poet Hilary Stevens' escape from the passivity of a feminine destiny, sees Sarton as aware that "the real artist is not the fantasy creature imagined by women trapped in domesticity." Art comes, as Hilary insists, at the expense of every human being, the self and the self's ties with other people.

The plot interweaves Hilary's initiation of Mar Hemmer, a potential poet recovering from an intense relationship with a man, with her reveries as she is being interviewed about her own poetic development. Mar, despite his lack of emotional proportion, helps her to see her own life in perspective. Married to an unstable war veteran in

England, Hilary began to write poetry after his sudden death. An intellectual friend, Willa MacPherson, encourages her to continue writing poetry and provides one night of passionate sexual exploration. Another friend, however, creates self-doubt, which Hilary identifies with the masculine force in herself. She knows that she can preserve her artistry only by caring about life, which does not necessarily mean sparing others from pain. As Hilary later points out to Mar, poetry and feeling are connected only if the poet understands that "true feeling justifies whatever it may cost." One cannot anesthetize the pain of life.

Philippa Munn, Hilary's proper girlhood governess with whom she is infatuated, plays the role which Sarton's own teachers did in her youth. Poetry diffuses sensuality, Hilary learns; it creates a moment of revelation, not simply of indulgence. As Hilary's wise physician tells her as she lies in the hospital recovering from a breakdown over her husband's death, she must write poems about objects and about a person to whom she can fasten herself deeply, but she should not confuse love for someone with poetry. Poetry can become "passionate decorum" in which love is presented as a mystique; what gives strength to poems is form.

Mrs. Stevens Hears the Mermaids Singing mixes the Platonic tradition of poet as maker whose creations surpass conscious understanding with an Aristotelian stress on the formal artifact that has its own laws of being and is autonomous. The notion of the poet as rapt by emotional experience lies also within the Platonic tradition of poetry as ecstasy. The events making up the life of Hilary Stevens have parallels with Sarton's own life, and the novel is a justification of that life. The presentation of the poet as a solitary individual misunderstood by the world reflects Sarton's Romanticism.

Other major works

PLAY: *Underground River*, 1947.

POETRY: *Encounter in April*, 1937; *Inner Landscape*, 1939; *The Lion and the Rose*, 1948; *The Land of Silence and Other Poems*, 1953; *In Time Like Air*, 1958; *Cloud, Stone, Sun, Vine: Poems, Selected and New*, 1961; *A Private Mythology*, 1966; *As Does New Hampshire and Other Poems*, 1967; *A Grain of Mustard Seed: New Poems*, 1971; *A Durable Fire: New Poems*, 1972; *Collected Poems, 1930-1973*, 1974; *Selected Poems of May Sarton*, 1978; *Halfway to Silence*, 1980; *Letters from Maine*, 1984; *The Silence Now*, 1989; *Collected Poems, 1930-1993*, 1993.

NONFICTION: *I Knew a Phoenix: Sketches for an Autobiography*, 1959; *Plant Dreaming Deep*, 1968; *Journal of a Solitude*, 1973; *A World of Light: Portraits and Celebrations*, 1976; *The House by the Sea*, 1977; *Writings on Writing*, 1980; *Recovering: A Journal*, 1980; *At Seventy: A Journal*, 1984; *After the Stroke: A Journal*, 1988; *Honey in the Hive: Judith Matlock, 1898-1982*, 1988; *Endgame: A Journal of the Seventy-ninth Year*, 1992; *Encore: A Journal of the Eightieth Year*, 1993.

CHILDREN'S LITERATURE: *Miss Pickthorn and Mr. Hare: A Fable*, 1966; *Punch's Secret*, 1974; *A Walk Through the Woods*, 1976.

MISCELLANEOUS: *The Fur Person: The Story of a Cat*, 1957.

Bibliography

Bloin, L. P. *May Sarton: A Bibliography*. Metuchen, N.J.: Scarecrow Press, 1978.

Evans, Elizabeth. *May Sarton*. Rev. ed. Boston: Twayne, 1989.

Grumbach, Doris. "The Long Solitude of May Sarton." *The New Republic* 170 (June 8, 1974): 31-32.

Martin, Lucy L. "May Sarton: Poetry (Life) Is a Discipline, Not a Self-Indulgence." *Maine Tribune*, June 20, 1975, pp. 22-23.

Sibley, Agnes. *May Sarton*. New York: Twayne, 1972.

DOROTHY L. SAYERS

Born: Oxford, England; June 13, 1893

Died: Witham, England; December 17, 1957

Principal long fiction

Whose Body?, 1923; *Clouds of Witness*, 1926; *Unnatural Death*, 1927 (also as *The Dawson Pedigree*); *Lord Peter Views the Body*, 1928; *The Unpleasantness at the Bellona Club*, 1928; *The Documents in the Case*, 1930 (with Robert Eustace); *Strong Poison*, 1930; *The Five Red Herrings*, 1931 (also known as *Suspicious Characters*); *The Floating Admiral*, 1931 (with others); *Have His Carcase*, 1932; *Ask a Policeman*, 1933 (with others); *Murder Must Advertise*, 1933; *The Nine Tailors*, 1934; *Gaudy Night*, 1935; *Six Against the Yard*, 1936 (with others; also as *Six Against Scotland Yard*); *Busman's Honeymoon*, 1937; *Double Death: A Murder Story*, 1939 (with others); *The Scoop, and Behind the Scenes*, 1983 (with others); *Crime on the Coast, and No Flowers by Request*, 1984 (with others).

Other literary forms

In addition to the twelve detective novels that brought her fame, Dorothy L. Sayers wrote short stories, poetry, essays, and plays, and distinguished herself as a translator and scholar of medieval French and Italian literature. She also edited a landmark anthology of detective fiction, *Great Short Stories of Detection, Mystery, and Horror* (1928-1934).

Outside of her fiction, the essence of Sayers' mind and art can be found in *The Mind of the Maker* (1941), a treatise on aesthetics; in her essays on Dante; and in two religious dramas, *The Zeal of Thy House* (1937) and *The Man Born to Be King* (1941-1942). The latter takes up what Sayers regarded as the most exciting of mysteries: the drama of Christ's life and death, the drama in which God is both victim and hero. Of her many essays, the 1946 collection *Unpopular Opinions* and the 1947 *Creed or Chaos?* provide a good sampling of the acumen, wit, and originality with which Sayers attacked a variety of subjects, including religion, feminism, and learning.

At her death, Sayers left unfinished her translation of Dante's *Cantica III: Paradise*, which was completed by her friend and colleague Barbara Reynolds and published posthumously in 1962 as the final volume in the Penguin Classics edition of Dante that Sayers had begun in 1944. An unpublished fragment of an additional novel, called *Thrones, Dominations* and apparently abandoned by Sayers in the 1940's, was also left unfinished.

Achievements

One of the chief pleasures for readers of Dorothy Sayers is the companionship of one of fiction's great creations, Lord Peter Wimsey, that extraordinarily English gentleman, cosmopolite, detective/scholar. Although the Wimsey novels were created primarily to make money, his characterization demonstrates that his creator was a serious, skillful writer. As the novels follow Wimsey elegantly through murder, mayhem, and madness, he grows from an enchanting caricature into a fully realized human being. The hallmarks of Sayers' art—erudition, wit, precision, and moral passion—provoke admiration in some readers and dislike in others.

Sayers' novels are filled with wordplay that irritates those who cannot decipher it and delights those who can. Her dialogue is embedded with literary allusions and double entendres in English, French, and Latin, and her plots are spun from biblical texts and English poetry. Reading a Sayers novel, then, is both a formidable challenge and an endless reward. Because of her exquisite language, her skill at delineating character, and her fundamentally serious mind, Sayers' detective fiction also largely transcends the limits of its time and genre. Certainly this is true of novels such as *Strong Poison, The Nine Tailors, Gaudy Night*, and *Busman's Honeymoon*, books which did much toward making the detective novel part of serious English fiction.

Biography

Dorothy Leigh Sayers was born on June 13, 1893, in the Choir House of Christ Church College, Oxford, where her father, the Reverend Henry Sayers, was headmaster. When Sayers was four, her father left Oxford to accept the living of Bluntisham-cum-Earith in Huntingdonshire, on the southern edge of the Fens, those bleak expanses of drained marshland in eastern England.

Sayers' fine education in Latin, English, French, history, and mathematics was conducted at the rectory until she was almost sixteen, when she was sent to study at the Godolphin School, Salisbury, where she seems to have been quite unhappy. Several of her happiest years followed this experience, however, when she won the Gilchrist Scholarship in Modern Languages and went up to Somerville College, Oxford, in 1912. At Somerville, Sayers enjoyed the congenial company of other extraordinary women and men and made some lasting friends, including Muriel St. Clare Byrne. Although women were not granted Oxford degrees during Sayers' time at Somerville, the university's statutes were changed in 1920, and Sayers was among the first group of women to receive Oxford degrees in that year (she had taken first honors in her examination in 1915).

Following her undergraduate days, Sayers worked as poetry editor for Blackwell's in Oxford from 1916 to 1918, then as a schoolmistress in France in 1919, and finally in London, where she worked as a free-lance editor and as an advertising copywriter for Benson's, England's largest advertising agency. Around 1920, the character of Lord Peter Wimsey was born, and Sayers' first novel, *Whose Body?*, introduced him to the world in 1923.

These early years in London were scarred by two bitterly disappointing love affairs, one of which left Sayers with a child, born in 1924. The novelist married Oswald Atherton Fleming, a Scottish journalist, in 1926, and shortly thereafter assumed financial responsibility for him as he became ill and ceased working several years after their marriage. Perhaps these pressures encouraged Sayers to keep turning out the increasingly successful Wimsey novels.

By the end of the 1930's, however, Sayers was in a position to "finish Lord Peter off" by marrying him to Harriet Vane, the detective novelist who first appeared in *Strong Poison* and who, like Wimsey, reflected part of Sayers' personality. After the Wimsey novels, Sayers was free to do the kind of writing she had always wanted to do: manifestly serious work such as religious dramas and a translation of Dante that would occupy most of her time from 1944 to 1957. Sayers also became something of a public figure, playing the role of social critic and Christian apologist. On December 17, 1957, Sayers died of an apparent stroke while alone in the house that she had shared with Fleming from 1928 until his death in 1950.

Analysis

If one should wish to know England as it was between the two world wars—how it was in its customs, among its different classes and in its different regions, how it regarded itself and the world, what weaknesses festered, what strengths endured—there is no better place than in the novels of Dorothy L. Sayers. When Harriet Vane marries Peter Wimsey in *Busman's Holiday*, she happily realizes that she has "married England," revealing that Sayers herself recognized the symbolic import of her hero. As a survivor of World War I, a war that decimated a generation of young Englishmen and left their society reeling, Wimsey represents England's fragile link with a glorious past and its tenuous hold on the difficult present. His bouts of "nerves" and persistent nightmares dramatize the lasting effects of this "War to End All Wars," while his noble attempts at making a meaningful life represent the difficult task of re-creating life from the rubble.

The most striking quality of *Whose Body?* as a first novel is the deftness with which it presents Sayers' hero and his world. In its opening pages, the reader gets to know Lord Peter Wimsey, the dashing man-about-town and collector of rare books (which, amazingly, he seems to read). Keen of mind and quick of tongue, Wimsey is also a wealthy man who knows how to spend both his time and his money. The product of an older England marked by civility, restraint, and order, Wimsey is accompanied in his first tale by two challengers to his wits and position: his valet, Bunter, and the middle-class Inspector Parker of Scotland Yard, who will make sure that Wimsey never nods during fourteen years of fictional sleuthing. Even his mother, the delightfully balmy Duchess of Denver, is introduced here, and the reader quickly guesses from their relationship that Sayers is interested in how men and women coexist in this world. The Dowager Duchess and her son are as different in appearance as they are similar in character, the narrator remarks, thus signaling that the superficial differences between men and women often conceal more important similarities. Wimsey and his entourage enter the world nearly complete, and their creator has a firm grasp of character, dialogue, and the mystery plot from the beginning of her career.

The theme of *Whose Body?* plants the seeds of one of Sayers' ever-flourishing ideas. Her first and perhaps most horrid villain, Sir Julian Freke, suffers from one of the great problems facing modern humanity: the disassociation from mind and heart that often renders "civilized" people incapable of moral behavior. The great surgeon Freke, who is aptly named because he is a freakish half-human, denies the importance of intangibles such as the conscience, which he considers akin to the vermiform appendix. With this perfectly criminal attitude, Freke coolly kills and dissects an old competitor, ironically from one of the oldest, least rational of motives, jealousy and revenge. Freke therefore demonstrates Sayers' point: that a human being, as a creature of both intellect and passion, must struggle to understand and balance both if moral action is to be possible. Freke, the dissector of life, destroys; the destruction he causes awaits the truly healing powers of a creative mind.

The somewhat surprising link between moral action and detective work is suggested by Wimsey, who observes that anyone can get away with murder by keeping people from "associatin' their ideas," adding that people usually do not connect the parts of their experience. The good detective, however, must study the fragments of human life and synthesize the relevant data. This synthesis, the product of imagination and feeling as well as reason, reveals not only "who did it," but how and why. Thus, according to Sayers' own definitions, her detective pursues moral action in his very sleuthing, not merely in its final effects of punishment for the criminal and retribution for society. Wimsey's detective method typifies this creative synthesis by incorporating different aspects of a rich experience: poetry, science, history, psychology, haberdashery, weather reports. When Wimsey finally realizes that Freke is the murderer, he remembers "not one thing, nor another thing, nor a logical succession of things, but everything—the whole thing, perfect and complete . . . as if he stood outside the world and saw it suspended in infinitely dimensional space." In this moment, Wimsey is not only a successful detective but also a creator, his mind flashing with godlike insight into human life. The story has moved, therefore, from destruction to creation because disparate aspects of life have been drawn together.

Freke's failure as a human being is exemplified in his failure as a physician, just as Wimsey's successful life is instanced in the skillful performance of his "job," his compulsive "hobby of sleuthing." More than a hobby, detection is actually Wimsey's "proper job." In a crucial discussion with Inspector Parker, Wimsey admits to feeling guilty about doing detective work for fun, but the perceptive Parker warns him that, as a basically responsible person for whom life is really more than a game, he will eventually have to come to terms with the seriousness of his actions. What is clear to the reader at this point is that Wimsey, an English aristocrat displaced by social change and scarred by World War I, is at least carving out a life that is socially useful while it is personally gratifying.

If Wimsey seems almost too perfect in the early novels, Sayers redeems him from that state by slowly revealing the finite, flawed, and very human man within the sparkling exterior. To make this revelation, she has to create a woman capable of challenging him, which she does in the character of Harriet Vane. By the time he appears in *The Nine Tailors*, Wimsey is less of a god and more of a human being. After all, the great lover has been humiliatingly unsuccessful in wooing Harriet Vane, whom he saved from the hangman four years earlier in *Strong Poison*. The greatest change in Wimsey's character and in Sayers' fiction, however, is evidenced in the novel's richer, more subtle structure, and in its newly complex view of crime and punishment, of good and evil.

Wimsey leaves this complex novel with greater insight into himself and the ambiguous nature of life; he is, therefore, finally ready to come to terms with the greatest mystery of his life, Harriet Vane, who is also about ready to accept his inquiry. In *Gaudy Night*, Wimsey reaches his fulfillment, a fulfillment that is expressed in terms of resolving the conflict between man and woman, between intellect and emotion, and between good and evil. In fact, Wimsey's fulfillment represents the culmination of Sayers' search for a resolution of these forces. The novel's subject is also one of Sayers' oldest: the moral imperative for every person to do good work that is well done, and the terrible consequences of not doing so. All these ideas come into play in this subtle novel, which is on one level the mystery of the "Shrewsbury Poison Pen" and on another, more important one, an unusual and profound love story. Reflecting the subtlety and delicacy with which Sayers spins her tale, there is not even a death in this book; the psychological violence caused by the Poison Pen is alarming, but here evil is banal, and all the more powerful for being so.

Gaudy Night takes place at Oxford, which held happy memories for Sayers as the place of her birth and formal education, and the entire novel is a paean to that golden-spired city. Harriet Vane goes to Oxford to attend the Shrewsbury Gaudy, an annual spring homecoming celebration, where she has the opportunity to judge her old classmates and teachers in terms of how well they, as women, have been able to live meaningful lives. Shrewsbury is obviously a fictional version of Somerville, Sayers' college, and just as clearly Vane, a famous detective novelist who is wrestling with the question of "woman's work" and with the problem of rendering reality in fiction, is to some extent Sayers, the self-conscious artist. Having been pursued by Wimsey for five frustrating years, Vane finally accepts him at the end of *Gaudy Night*. She accepts him because the experiences in this book teach her three interrelated things: that Wimsey, as an extraordinary man, will not prevent her from doing her "proper job," a consequence she feared from any relationship with a man; that men and women can live together and not destroy each other, but create a good life; and therefore, that there can be an alliance between the "intellect and the flesh." Vane's discoveries in this novel thus signal the solution of problems that had preoccupied Sayers throughout her career.

Vane learns all these things through Wimsey's unraveling of the mystery of the Poison Pen, who is a woman frightfully flawed because she has never been able to strike a balance between the intellect and the flesh, and therefore has never done her proper job. Annie Wilson, the Poison Pen who creates so much confusion and instills so much fear in the intellectual women of Shrewsbury, is the victim of sentimentality and a radically disassociated sensibility; she hates all learning because her dead husband was punished long ago for academic dishonesty. Ironically, Harriet Vane suffers from the same problem, but in its other manifestation; she begins the novel capable of trusting only the intellect, and fears any bonds of the flesh or heart. When she finally sees that neither the sentimentality of Annie nor the hyperintellectualism of Shrewsbury can solve the "problem of life," Harriet realizes that it is only through balancing intellect and passion that creative or truly human action is possible.

Wimsey, who solves the mystery because he is able to bring these forces into equilibrium and to acknowledge the potency of both, is rendered acceptable to Vane because of this ability. Her new willingness to admit her feelings reveals to her what Sayers' readers had known for a long time: She loves Wimsey. The man she loves has changed, too. He is no longer an unattainable paragon who sees good and evil as discrete and life as a game, but a middle-aged man who fears rejection and death, who is idiotically vain about his hands, and who, to Harriet's surprise, looks as vulnerable as anyone else when he falls asleep: the man behind the monocle. All of this does not argue that Wimsey is less extraordinary than he was; in fact, perhaps what is most extraordinary about him now is that he seems a real person—flawed, finite, vulnerable—who is yet capable of that rare thing, creative action. Indeed, his very life seems a work of art.

Other major works

SHORT FICTION: *Hangman's Holiday*, 1933; *In the Teeth of the Evidence and Other Stories*, 1939; *Lord Peter*, 1972 (James Sandoe, editor); *Striding Folly*, 1972.

PLAYS: *Busman's Honeymoon*, 1937 (with Muriel St. Clare Byrne); *The Zeal of Thy House*, 1937; *The Devil to Pay, Being the Famous Play of John Faustus*, 1939; *Love All*, 1940; *The Man Born to Be King: A Play-Cycle on the Life of Our Lord and Saviour Jesus Christ*, 1941-1942; *The Just Vengeance*, 1946; *The Emperor Constantine*, 1951 (revised as *Christ's Emperor*, 1952).

POETRY: *Op I*, 1916; *Catholic Tales and Christian Songs*, 1918; *Lord, I Thank Thee—*, 1943; *The Story of Adam and Christ*, 1955.

NONFICTION: *Papers Relating to the Family of Wimsey*, 1936; *An Account of Lord Mortimer Wimsey, the Hermit of the Wash*, 1937; *The Greatest Drama Ever Staged*, 1938; *Strong Meat*, 1939; *Begin Here: A War-Time Essay*, 1940; *Creed or Chaos?*, 1940; *The Mysterious English*, 1941; *The Mind of the Maker*, 1941; *Why Work?*, 1942; *The Other Six Deadly Sins*, 1943; *Unpopular Opinions*, 1946; *Making Sense of the Universe*, 1946; *Creed or Chaos? and Other Essays in Popular Theology*, 1947; *The Lost Tools of Learning*, 1948; *The Days of Christ's Coming*, 1953, revised 1960; *The Story of Easter*, 1955; *The Story of Noah's Ark*, 1955; *Introductory Papers on Dante*, 1954; *Further Papers on Dante*, 1957; *The Poetry of Search and the Poetry of Statement, and Other*

Posthumous Essays on Literature, Religion, and Language, 1963; *Christian Letters to a Post-Christian World*, 1969; *Are Women Human?*, 1971; *A Matter of Eternity*, 1973; *Wilkie Collins: A Critical and Biographical Study*, 1977 (edited by E. R. Gregory).

CHILDREN'S LITERATURE: *Even the Parrot: Exemplary Conversations for Enlightened Children*, 1944.

TRANSLATIONS: *Tristan in Brittany*, 1929 (by Thomas the Troubadour); *The Heart of Stone, Being the Four Canzoni of the "Pietra" Group*, 1946 (by Dante); *The Comedy of Dante Alighieri the Florentine*, 1949-1962 (Cantica III with Barbara Reynolds); *The Song of Roland*, 1957.

EDITED TEXTS: *Oxford Poetry 1917*, 1918 (with Wilfred R. Childe and Thomas W. Earp); *Oxford Poetry 1918*, 1918 (with Earp and E. F. A. Geach); *Oxford Poetry 1919*, 1919 (with Earp and Siegfried Sassoon); *Great Short Stories of Detection, Mystery, and Horror*, 1928-1934 (also as *The Omnibus of Crime*); *Tales of Detection*, 1936.

Bibliography

Brabazon, James. *Dorothy L. Sayers: A Biography*. New York: Charles Scribner's Sons, 1981.

Dale, Alzina Stone. *Maker and Craftsman: The Study of Dorothy L. Sayers*. Grand Rapids, Mich.: Wm. B. Eerdmans, 1978.

Gaillard, Dawson. *Dorothy L. Sayers*. New York: Frederick Ungar, 1981.

Hall, Trevor H. *Dorothy L. Sayers: Nine Literary Studies*. Hamden, Conn.: Archon Books, 1980.

Reynolds, Barbara. *Dorothy L. Sayers: Her Life and Soul*. New York: St. Martin's, 1993.

Scott-Giles, Charles Wilfrid. *The Wimsey Family: A Fragmentary History from Correspondence with Dorothy Sayers*. New York: Harper & Row, 1977.

Youngberg, Ruth Tanis. *Dorothy L. Sayers: A Reference Guide*. Boston: G. K. Hall, 1982.

ANNE SEXTON

Born: Newton, Massachusetts; November 9, 1928   **Died:** Weston, Massachusetts; October 4, 1974

Principal poetry

To Bedlam and Part Way Back, 1960; *All My Pretty Ones*, 1962; *Selected Poems*, 1964; *Live or Die*, 1966; *Poems*, 1968 (with Thomas Kinsella and Douglas Livingston); *Love Poems*, 1969; *Transformations*, 1971; *The Book of Folly*, 1972; *The Death Notebooks*, 1974; *The Awful Rowing Toward God*, 1975; *Words for Dr. Y: Uncollected Poems with Three Stories*, 1978; *The Complete Poems*, 1981.

Other literary forms

In addition to several articles on the craft and teaching of poetry, Anne Sexton authored the play *45 Mercy Street* (1969). It presents the struggle of a woman named Daisy to find meaning in a past and present dominated by religious and sexual conflicts objectified as demons and disembodied voices; critics find the thematic material important biographically and artistically in an analysis of Sexton's career. An important collection of her prose is *Anne Sexton: A Self-Portrait in Letters* (1977), and she also wrote several children's books in collaboration with Maxine Kumin.

Achievements

With little formal training in literature, Sexton emerged as a major modern voice, transforming verse begun as therapy into poetic art of the first order. Important for refining the confessional mode, experimenting with new lyrical forms, and presenting themes from the female consciousness, Sexton's work has the controversial impact of any pioneering artist. Despite periodic hospitalization for depression ultimately culminating in her suicide at age forty-six, Sexton contributed richly to her craft, receiving much critical recognition and traveling widely. Awarded fellowships to most of the major writing conferences, she worked closely with John Holmes, W. D. Snodgrass, Robert Lowell, Maxine Kumin, and others. She taught creative writing at Harvard, Radcliffe, and Boston universities, and she served as editorial consultant to the *New York Poetry Quarterly* and as a member of the board of directors of *Audience*

magazine. In 1963, her second collection of poetry, *All My Pretty Ones*, was nominated for a National Book Award; and in 1967, her fourth collection, *Live or Die*, received a Pulitzer Prize. Sexton also received a Guggenheim Fellowship in 1969 and many honorary degrees from major universities.

Although most critics believe the quality of her work deteriorated toward the end of her life, she had achieved by that time success with a new, highly personal voice in poetry and expanded the range of acceptable subjects to include the intimate concerns of women. In presenting the theme of female identity, Sexton began with a careful lyric formalism and then progressed throughout her career to experiment with open, dramatic forms, moving from the confessional to the surreal. She explored the limits of sanity and the nature of womanhood more fully than any poet of her generation.

Biography

The daughter of upper-middle-class parents, Anne Gray Harvey attended the public schools of Wellesley, Massachusetts, and spent two years at Rogers Preparatory School and one year at Garland Junior College before marrying Alfred Muller Sexton. After her marriage, she worked briefly as a model at the Hart Agency of Boston. Then, when she was twenty-five, her first daughter, Linda Gray Sexton, was born. The next year, Anne Sexton was hospitalized for emotional disturbance and several months later suffered the loss of her beloved great-aunt, Anna Ladd Dingley, nicknamed "Nana" in various poems and remembrances. The next year, Joyce Ladd Sexton was born, but within months her mother was again hospitalized for depression culminating in a suicide attempt on her twenty-eighth birthday.

Following her first suicide attempt, Sexton began writing poetry on the advice of her psychiatrist, Dr. Martin Orne, whose name appears in her first collection of poems. On the strength of her first work, she received a scholarship to the Antioch Writer's Conference where she worked with W. D. Snodgrass. Then she was accepted into Robert Lowell's graduate writing seminar at Boston University, soon developing friendships with Sylvia Plath, Maxine Kumin, and George Starbuck. The next year, both of Sexton's parents died in rapid succession. She continued her work, attending the Bread Loaf Writer's Conference and delivering the Morris Gray Poetry Lecture at Harvard, although she was hospitalized at intervals for pneumonia, an appendectomy, and an ovarectomy. In 1960, Sexton studied with Philip Rahv and Irving Howe at Brandeis University and developed a friendship with James Wright. She was appointed, with Kumin, to be the first scholars in poetry at the Radcliffe Institute for Independent Study. In 1962, she was again

hospitalized for depression, but by the end of the year, she recovered and toured Europe on the first traveling fellowship of the American Academy of Arts and Letters. She also received a Ford Foundation grant for residence with the Charles Playhouse in Boston.

In 1966, Sexton began a novel that was never completed. She again attempted suicide in July, 1966. In August, she took an African safari with her husband, but in November, she was hospitalized again when she broke her hip on her thirty-eighth birthday. In May of that year, she received the Pulitzer Prize for *Live or Die* and the Shelley Award from the Poetry Society of America. She taught poetry as a visiting professor in many schools and received many honorary degrees before again attempting suicide in 1970. In 1973, she divorced her husband during another period of hospitalization for depression. Although she continued to write and teach despite frequent intervals of hospitalization, in 1974, she committed suicide by carbon monoxide poisoning in the garage of her home.

Analysis

Anne Sexton's poetry presents a search for self and meaning beyond the limits of conventional expression and form. Although viewing her work autobiographically limits critical understanding of it, readers discover in her work a chronicle of experience that is intensely personal and genuine. Her poems are confessional in that they present statements about impulses formerly unknown or forbidden. Begun for self-revelation in therapy and initially sustained for the possible benefit of other troubled patients, Sexton's poems speak with penetrating honesty about the experience of mental illness, the temptation of suicide, and the dynamics of womanhood. Although less strident in tone than the work of Sylvia Plath, Sexton's work occasionally alienates readers who, like James Dickey, find her work too personal for literary evaluation. At its best, however, Sexton's poetry develops the confessional lyric into an effective modern form.

In her first collection, *To Bedlam and Part Way Back*, scenes from an asylum are set against those of life before and after the speaker's hospitalization. The perspective of these early poems is a daring interior one, underscored by the book's epigraph taken from a letter of Arthur Schopenhauer to Johann Wolfgang von Goethe, including the phrase "But most of us carry in our heart the Jocasta who begs Oedipus for God's sake not to inquire further." Sexton's poems pursue the inquiry into the

mental hospital and the mind of the patient as well. In the chantlike poem "Ringing the Bells," for example, Sexton projects the senseless rhythm of institutional life through the consciousness of a patient in the bell choir of a mental ward. The troubled women who "mind by instinct" assemble, smile, ring their bells when pointed to, and disperse, no better for their weekly music lessons. Another well-known portrayal of institutional life, "Lullaby," shows the figure of the night nurse arriving with the sleeping pills that, like splendid pearls, provide a momentary escape for the patients who receive them. Observing the moths which cling to window screen, the patient of "Lullaby" imagines that he will become like them after taking the sedative. "You, Doctor Martin" presents other figures in the mental hospital, including the large children who wait in lines to be counted at dinner before returning to the labor of making moccasins all day long. Although the portrayal of the mental hospital from an insider's perspective provides a fresh subject for experimental lyrics, Sexton's poems of the journey and return (suggested by the volume's title) are among her most complex and effective.

"The Double Image," for example, is a composite of experiences parallel to Sexton's own biography. In the poem, the speaker's hospitalization brings about a separation from her young daughter; the speaker's return to live in the home of her childhood coincides with the final illness of her own mother. Weaving together the present moment of her return home for a reunion with her daughter and events of the past, the speaker reflects on the guilt bounded by past and present sorrow. The three autumns explain her trouble better than any medical theories, and she finds that despair and guilt transform attempts at ordinary life into artifice. Portrait painting becomes a metaphor for control of time and emotions through the rest of the poem. Unable to adjust to the awkward period spent as a grown child in her parents' home, the speaker states repeatedly, "I had my portrait done instead." The same response belongs to her mother, who cannot forgive the speaker's attempt at suicide and so chooses to have the daughter painted as a measure of control. A double image forms when the mother learns of her own incurable illness and has her portrait done "instead." The portraits, facing each other in the parental home, serve as a mirror reflection with the figure of the speaker's child moving between them. As the speaker had been "an awkward guest" returning to her mother's home, so the young daughter arrives "an awkward guest" for the reunion with her recovering mother. The child provides both a measure of final identity and guilt.

Other poems in the first volume experiment with the voices of experience different from the poet's. "Unknown Girl in the Maternity Ward" attempts to voice the feelings of an unmarried girl who has just given birth. The emotions and imagery are generalized and undefined in presenting the setting of an urban hospital and the typical unmarried girl in trouble. According to Sexton, the poem marked a pivotal moment in her career, for after reading it, Robert Lowell advised her to develop the more personal voice that gives her finest poetry its power. A poem reflecting conflicting advice is "For John, Who Begs Me Not to Enquire Further." John Holmes, Sexton's teacher for a Boston University poetry workshop, recommended that she avoid the self-revelation becoming characteristic of her work. The directly personal voice won out, not only in this poem of apology to Holmes but also throughout her career. Another early poem, "Kind Sir: These Woods," indicates an awareness that readers in general may disapprove her probing of the psyche, "this inward look that society scorns." The speaker finds in her inward search, however, nothing worse than herself, "caught between the grapes and the thorns," and the search for herself continued to the end of her life.

An epigraph for Sexton's second collection, *All My Pretty Ones*, suggests a reason for the poet's insistence on inner exploration. According to a letter of Franz Kafka, "a book should serve as the ax for the frozen sea within us." Sexton similarly asserted in a later interview that "poems of the inner life can reach the inner lives of readers in a way that anti-war poems can never stop a war." The inner life revealed in *All My Pretty Ones* is primarily the experience of grief, the response to loss of the most precious others expressed in the lines from *Macbeth* (1606) that form the title. "The Truth the Dead Know" and the title poem deal with the death of Sexton's parents during the same year. The first poem eliminates personal references except for a dedication to the parents and simply contrasts the intensity of life and grief with the emptiness and stoniness of the dead. "All My Pretty Ones" addresses the lost father with memories of his belongings, his habits, and his hopes. Disposition of scrapbook photographs provides a way to accept and forgive the disappointments of the past, including the secret alcoholism his daughter can never forget.

The strongest poems of the second volume arise from Sexton's own experience. In "The Operation," the speaker's confrontation with death parallels the illness of her mother, and the speaker considers the uncertainty of life as much as the reality of death. Knowing that cancer, her mother's disease, the "historic thief" that plundered her mother's home is now invading her own domain, the speaker proceeds helplessly through the preparations for surgery, the experience of losing consciousness, and the recovery phase in doubt of her survival. Then, pronounced better, perhaps cured, by the doctors, she is sent home like a child, the stitches in her abdomen reminding her of the lacing on a football ready for the game. A similar sense of vulnerability appears in "The Fortress," wherein the speaker admits to her sleeping child that a mother has no ability to control life and that eventually it will overtake the child through the suffering of "bombs or glands" ending in death. Beyond the sense of relationships, especially those connected with motherhood, controlling many of Sexton's poems, there looms a sense of dark knowledge gained through poetry as a secret or forbidden art. In "The Black Art," for example, the speaker asserts that a woman who writes will not fit into society, for she "feels too much, these trances and portents." Home, family, social life are inadequate expressions for the one who wishes to know and control the mysterious forces of existence. The poem recalls an earlier statement of identity, "Her Kind," in which the speaker presents herself as a witch who is lonely, misunderstood, insane, and unashamed to die in the course of her journey. The comparison of Sexton's poetry with the black arts places her work on the level of myth, particularly in her pursuit of death itself.

Live or Die, Sexton's third collection, marks a high point in her career for handling intimate or despairing material with sure control and an element of self-irony. The epigraph for this book, taken from Saul Bellow's *Herzog* (1964), records the admonition to "Live or die, but don't poison everything." Certainly, the poems of this group reflect the impulse toward love and life as well as the impulse toward despair and death. The institutional setting appears in the volume but so does the home and family relationships of Sexton. "Flee on Your Donkey," one of her best-known poems, develops the tension between the worlds of private and institutional life. In the poem, a flood of scenes from the hospital culminates in a desire to escape back to the normal world that patients enter the hospital to avoid. Similarly, in "For the Year of the Insane," structured as a prayer to Mary, the speaker struggles to escape her mental as well as physical confinement. No longer at peace in the refuge of therapy, a mind that believes itself "locked in the wrong house" struggles in vain for expression and release. Poems of similar desperation, "The Addict" and "Wanting to Die," develop other means of escape. The speaker of the former poem yearns for the hallucinatory realm where drugs parcel out moments of deathlike experience. "Wanting to Die," one of Sexton's best-known poems, strives to explain for the uninitiated the hunger for death haunting the potential suicide. The obsession with methods of dying replaces the desire for experience of life. Love itself becomes "an infection" to those seeking the secret pleasure that final escape from the body will bring.

Love Poems, Sexton's fourth collection, examines the cycle of roles women play in life and love. Poems of separation and return, for example, include "Touch" and "Eighteen Days Without You," lyrics in which love between a woman and her lover controls survival and existence beyond their union. Throughout the volume, individual body parts achieve significance beyond their function in the physical realm. "Touch" begins, "For months my hand had been sealed off/ in a tin box." Following the arrival of her lover, life rushes into the fingers, spreading across the continent in its intensity. Other celebrations of physical contact include "The

Kiss," "The Breast," and "In Celebration of My Uterus." In this last poem, Sexton develops a great song which a whole catalog of women sing as they go about their daily work carrying the "sweet weight" of the womb. The negative side of experience returns in poems such as "The Break," which recounts the depression preceding a fall down the stairs which broke Sexton's hip and forced another lengthy hospitalization. Although the bones are sure to heal, the speaker's heart begins another building process to create a "death crèche," ready for the zeal of destruction when it returns.

The theme of self-destruction is hidden in *Transformations*, Sexton's collection of rewritten fairy tales narrated by a "middle-aged witch," the poet's name for her persona in the tales. For some critics, this collection provides a more objective scheme for Sexton's mythic quest; for others, the subject matter is quaint and unoriginal. Certainly the retold tales are entertaining and effective in the dark, modern twists Sexton creates. "Snow White," for example, tortures the wicked queen without mercy before returning to gaze triumphantly in her mirror "as women do." "Rumpelstiltskin" develops the figure of the dark one within, the *Doppelgänger* trying to escape every human being. Failing to gain the queen's child, he splits in two, "one part papa/ one part Doppelgänger," completing the division of the psyche. "Briar Rose (Sleeping Beauty)" becomes a tortured insomniac after being awakened by her prince and never knows the sleep of death.

Sexton's last collections, *The Book of Folly, The Death Notebooks*, and *The Awful Rowing Toward God*, contain many of her previous themes developed in experimental forms, including dramatic changes in style. Critics note a looser structure in the poems written late in Sexton's career; some believe it reflects a deterioration of her creative powers, while others find the experimentalism valuable for its innovation. One of the well-known late poems, "Hurry Up Please It's Time," reflects both the variety of thematic material, the variable stanza lengths, and the intrusion of dialogue, such as those between "Anne" and "The Interrogator." The poem reworks the approach of death and the obsessive derision of life on the part of the dying one. "Ms. Dog," one of Sexton's nicknames for herself and God spelled backward, figures in the poem as the troubled one facing guilt and rejection, the mystery and futility of death. In "Frenzy," another of the last poems, the speaker describes herself "typing out the God/ my typewriter believes in." Through the last years of Sexton's life, her writing sustained her even as her quest darkened. At the end of her life, she sought God when doctors, friends, and family were unable to help her; and her work reflected an outwardly religious search that had formerly been hidden. Although she never revealed that she found God within or without the lines of her poetry, she left behind a brilliant record of her heroic search.

Other major works

PLAY: *45 Mercy Street*, 1969.

NONFICTION: *Anne Sexton: A Self-Portrait in Letters*, 1977; *No Evil Star: Selected Essays, Interviews, and Prose*, 1985.

Bibliography

Hall, Caroline King Barnard. *Anne Sexton*. Boston: Twayne, 1989.

McClatchy, J. D. *Anne Sexton: The Artist and Her Critics*. Bloomington: Indiana University Press, 1978.

Markey, Janice. *A New Tradition? The Poetry of Sylvia Plath, Anne Sexton, and Adrienne Rich*. Frankfurt am Main, Germany: Peter Lang, 1985.

Middlebrook, Diane Wood. *Anne Sexton: A Biography*. Boston: Houghton Mifflin, 1991.

Schurr, William H. "Anne Sexton's Love Poems: The Genre and the Differences." *Modern Poetry Studies* 10, no. 1 (1980): 58-68.

Sexton, Linda Gray, and Lois Ames, eds. *Anne Sexton: A Self-Portrait in Letters*. Boston: Houghton Mifflin, 1977.

Wagner-Martin, Linda, ed. *Critical Essays on Anne Sexton*. Boston: G. K. Hall, 1989.

NTOZAKE SHANGE
Paulette Williams

Born: Trenton, New Jersey; October 18, 1948

Principal drama

for colored girls who have considered suicide/ when the rainbow is enuf, pr. 1976, pb. 1977; *A Photograph: Still Life with Shadows, A Photograph: A Study in Cruelty*, pr. 1977 (revised as *A Photograph: Lovers in Motion*, pr. 1979, pb. 1981); *Where the Mississippi Meets the Amazon*, pr. 1977; *From Okra to Greens: A Different Kinda Love Story*, pr. 1978, pb. 1985; *Spell No. 7*, pr. 1979, pb. 1981; *Boogie Woogie Landscapes*, pr. 1979, pb. 1981; *Mother Courage and Her Children*, pr. 1980 (adaptation of Bertolt Brecht's play); *Three Pieces*, pb. 1981; *Betsey Brown*, pr. 1991 (based on her novel); *The Love Space Demands: A Continuing Saga*, pb. 1991, pr. 1992.

Other literary forms

Ntozake Shange's three genres—plays, poems, and novels—so overlap that one might say she has invented a new genre, the "choreopoem." She has published several volumes of poetry, including *Nappy Edges* (1978, parts of which were included in her 1976 play *for colored girls who have considered suicide/ when the rainbow is enuf*), *Natural Disasters and Other Festive Occasions* (1979), *A Daughter's Geography* (1983), and *Ridin' the Moon in Texas: Word Paintings* (1987). Among her novels are *Sassafras, Cypress, and Indigo* (1982) and *Betsey Brown* (1985). She has gathered writings about her work into *See No Evil: Prefaces, Essays, and Accounts, 1976-1983* (1984), essential for study of her art.

Achievements

Shange's work embodies a rich confusion of genres and all the contradictions inherent in a world where violence and oppression polarize life and art. These polarizations in Shange's work both contribute to her artistry and complicate it. She has been criticized and praised for her unconventional language and structure, for her almost religious feminism, and for her stand on black/white and male/female issues. Her first play, *for colored girls who have considered suicide/ when the rainbow is enuf*, produced in 1976 by Joseph Papp's New York Shakespeare Festival, was honored in that year by the Outer Critics Circle, comprising those who write about the New York theater for out-of-town newspapers. Shange's 1980 adaptation of Bertolt Brecht's *Mother Courage and Her Children* won one of the *Village Voice*'s Obie awards.

Biography

Ntozake Shange (pronounced "En-to-zaki Shong-gay") was born Paulette Williams in Trenton, New Jersey, on October 18, 1948, daughter of a surgeon and a psychiatric social worker. She grew up surrounded by music, literature, art, and her parents' prominent friends, among them Dizzy Gillespie, Chuck Berry, and W. E. B. Du Bois, as well as Third World writers and musicians. Her ties with her family were strong; she also was close to her family's live-in black maids. She was graduated from Barnard College with honors in 1970, then received a graduate degree at the University of Southern Califor-nia in Los Angeles. While in California, she began studying dance, writing poetry, and participating in improvisational works (composed of poems, music, dance, and mime) at bars, cabarets, and schools. These gradually grew into *for colored girls who have considered suicide/ when the rainbow is enuf*, which she carried across the country to perform in workshops in New York, then at the Public Theatre, and eventually on Broadway. The contrasts between her privileged home and education and the realities of the lives of black women led her, in 1971, to change her name legally from what she called the "slave name" of Paulette Williams to Ntozake Shange, meaning "she who comes with her own things" and "she who walks like a lion" in Xhosa (Zulu). Her two failed marriages, her suicide attempts, and her contact with city violence resulted in an anger which found its outlet in her poems. During the late 1970's, she lived in New York City, but she later moved to Houston, Texas, with her daughter, Savannah. She has taught and lectured at many colleges and universities, including Mills College in Oakland, California; Rutgers—The State University in New Jersey; the University of California, Berkeley; and the University of Houston.

Her work with Emily Mann on the script version of

Betsey Brown brought her into prominence among feminists and experimental theaters. Working under the auspices of the New York Shakespeare Festival, the two women brought the play into its production form through a series of staged readings, workshops, and tryouts, and their collaboration techniques were the subject of forums among dramaturges in 1990.

Shange's poetic "reading/performance" piece, *The Love Space Demands*, in which she reads her own work (accompanied by guitarist Billie Patterson), was performed in New Jersey at the Crossroads Theatre and in San Francisco at the Hansberry Theatre in 1992.

Analysis

Ntozake Shange's plays have evoked a range of critical responses commensurate with their unconventional nature. Should her work be characterized as poetry or drama, prose or poetry, essay or autobiography? All these forms can be found in her plays, which are unified by a militant feminism in which some critics have seen a one-sided attack on black men. Others, however, point out the youthful spirit, flair with language, and lyricism that carry her plays to startling and radical conclusions. Her style and its contradictions (embracing black English and the erudite vocabulary of the educated) are at the heart of her drama. Influenced by their method of development—public poetry reading in bars, cafés, schools, Off-Off-Broadway theaters—the plays are generally somewhere between a poetry reading and a staged play.

First among the contrasts is her blending of genres: Her poems shade into drama, her dramas are essentially verse monologues, and her novels incorporate poetic passages. Second, her language varies radically—on a single page and even in a single phrase—from black dialect ("cuz," "wanna," "awready," "chirren") to the language of her middle-class upbringing and education ("i cant count the number of times i have viscerally wanted to attack deform n maim the language that i waz taught to hate myself in/"). In the published texts of her poetry, plays, and essays, in addition to simplified phonetic spellings, she employs the slash instead of the period and omits capitalization. Many recordings of her work are available, and these provide the reader with a much fuller sense of the dynamic quality of her language in performance.

Shange's first dramatic success, *for colored girls who have considered suicide/ when the rainbow is enuf*, she

called a "choreopoem"—the recital, individually and in chorus, of the lives and growth of seven different black women, named according to their dress colors: "lady in red," "lady in blue," "lady in orange," "lady in brown," "lady in yellow," "lady in purple," and "lady in green." The term "colored girls" in the title evokes a stereotype of black women yet also contains a germ of hope for the future (the "rainbow," both of color and of eventual salvation).

These seven stylized figures are representative voices of black women, and they express their fury at their oppression both as women and as blacks. The first segment shows high school graduation and the social and sexual rite of passage for "colored girls" in the working-class suburbs. Some of the women who have been cruelly disappointed in relationships with men discuss their spiritual quest. A black woman pretends to be Puerto Rican so that she can dance the merengue in Spanish Harlem. A woman breaks up with her lover by returning to him his plant to water. The scenes become more somber, portraying rape, abuse, city dangers, and abortion. Ties with a more heroic black past appear in "Toussaint," while the glamorized prostitute evicts her lover from her bed. The women begin to analyze their predicament and to assert their independence in segments entitled "somebody almost walked off wid alla my stuff" and "pyramid," in which three women console one another for the actions of the faithless lover whom they share. In the brutal culminating scene, a crazed Vietnam veteran, Beau Willie Brown, abuses his woman Crystal and kills their infant children, dropping them from a window.

Ultimately, the theme of the play is the thwarting of dreams and aspirations for a decent life by forces beyond one's control: war, poverty, and ignorance. There is, however, a saving grace. Toward the end of the play, the seven women fall into a tighter circle of mutual support, much like a religious "laying on of hands" ceremony, in which they say,

> i found god in myself
> (& i loved her / i loved her fiercely)

Their bitter pain, shown throughout the dramatic episodes, turns into a possibility of regeneration. Thus, the play is a drama of salvation for women who do not receive their full value in society.

Though it was a landmark in the emergence of new, black women playwrights, *for colored girls who have considered suicide/ when the rainbow is enuf* has been criticized for its lack of discussion of black traditions in religion, family, and ordinary work, and for its omissions of both black literary and political history and the influence of whites. Its style, considered as an attack on language, part of blacks' "enslavement," has also been criticized. Later plays, however, include these elements in a constantly enriching network of allusions.

Shange's second major work, *A Photograph: A Still Life with Shadows, A Photograph: A Study in Cruelty*, was produced in 1977; its title was changed in a later version to *A Photograph: Lovers in Motion* (which is the source of the text analyzed here). *A Photograph* is a set of meditations and sketches involving an ideal black woman named Michael and her lover Sean, a failed photographer. Sean, trying to objectify the world about him in his photographs, provides both the play's title and the technological representation of the play as a picture or mirror of the world. Rich allusions such as these, as in most of Shange's plays, are thickly sown throughout the characters' speeches and typically not explained. Sean and Michael's world is not that of *for colored girls who have considered suicide/ when the rainbow is enuf* (New York slums, ridden with violence) but that of San Francisco's arty world, peopled with dancers, lawyers, and intellectuals. The problems addressed are not those of Shange's previous play but those of middle-class, professional, and artistic blacks in a complicated urban society. In this play, Shange expands her black world's boundaries.

Sean tells Michael that she must share him, just as all sorts of women shared Alexandre Dumas in nineteenth century France. Michael dreams of an idealized lover who is not "all-American," while Sean boasts that "lil sean david who never got over on nothing but bitches/ is building a world in his image/" when one of his women, Nevada, an attorney, tears up his photographs. Michael expresses the world of her grandmother as "alla the blood & the fields & the satchels dragging in the dust. all the boogies & stairways late at night oozing the scent of love & cornbread/ the woods smelling of burnt flesh & hunger."

In addition, the idea of art as either survival (Sean's view) or love (Michael's) emerges. All the characters show insecurity and find no solution for their dilemmas, sexual or political. In manipulating one another, they realize how much they have been manipulated in the way they were reared and by the environment in which they live. They cannot love one another enough.

After examining the identity of isolated young black women in *for colored girls who have considered suicide/ when the rainbow is enuf* and of couples in *A Photograph*, Shange concentrates in her next play on one woman's visions, dreams, and memories. *Boogie Woogie Landscapes* was first produced as a one-woman poetry piece in 1978 and then cast as a play in 1979, with music and dance. Layla, a young black woman, entertains in her dreams a series of nightlife companions who exemplify her perceptions of herself and her memories. "Layla" means "night" in Arabic, and the whole play exists in Layla's subconscious, in her dreams. Layla's memories of Fidel Castro's Cuba, of primitive cruelties to African women, and of rock and roll and blues interweave with her feelings about growing up, family, brothers and sisters, parents, maids (some of which appear later in Shange's semiautobiographical novel *Betsey Brown*).

Shange's 1979 play *Spell No. 7*, as with her first play, is structured like a highly electric poetry reading, but this time the cast is mixed male and female. A huge blackface mask forms the backdrop for actors and actresses of an imitation old-time minstrel show (where actors did skits, recited, and joked) under the direction of a Mr. Interlocutor. The actors come offstage, relax at an actors' bar, and gradually remove their masks, revealing their true selves. One magician says that he gave up the trade when a colored child asked for a spell to make her white. The new spell the actors discover is a pride in their blackness. They arrive at this through telling classic "tall stories"; one of these concerns a child who thought blacks were immune to dread diseases such as polio since television pictures show polio victims as all white. She is disillusioned when she finds that blacks can hurt one another, so she buys South African gold to remind her of that pain. Another woman loves her baby while it is in the womb but kills it after it is born. Still another girl vows to brush her "nappy" hair constantly so that she can toss it like white girls. By these contrasts and by wry lists and surprising parallels, Shange shows the pain and difficulty, as well as the hopefulness, of being black. She concludes, "we gonna be colored & love it." As in her play *for colored girls who have considered suicide/ when the rainbow is enuf*, the power of love and self-realization becomes their salvation.

Shange has also done distinguished work as a director, of both her own work and that of others, notably Richard Wesley's *The Mighty Gents* in 1979. In 1980, Shange adapted Bertolt Brecht's *Mutter Courage und ihre Kinder* (1941; *Mother Courage and Her Children*, 1941), changing the scene from mid-seventeenth century Europe to post-Civil War America, making the protago-

nist an emancipated slave doing business with the army oppressing the Western Indians and changing the language to black English.

In 1991, Shange adapted her own novel *Betsey Brown* into a play. The semiautobiographical work tells the story of a thirteen-year-old African American girl growing up in a middle-class household in 1950's St. Louis. *The Love Space Demands*, a loosely connected series of poems and monologues that Shange performs with musical accompaniment, revolves around sexual relations in the age of acquired immunodeficiency syndrome (AIDS).

Though she has not always succeeded, Shange's bold and daring use of language, her respect for people formerly given little value, and her exploration of the roles of black men and women have opened a new dimension in theater. Her blendings of poetry, music, and dance bring theater back to its origins and simultaneously blaze a trail toward the drama of the future.

Other major works

NOVELS: *Sassafras: A Novella*, 1976; *Sassafras, Cypress, and Indigo*, 1982; *Betsey Brown*, 1985.
POETRY: *Nappy Edges*, 1978; *Natural Disasters and Other Festive Occasions*, 1979; *A Daughter's Geography*, 1983; *From Okra to Greens: Poems*, 1984; *Ridin' the Moon in Texas: Word Paintings*, 1987.
NONFICTION: *See No Evil: Prefaces, Essays, and Accounts, 1976-1983*, 1984.

Bibliography

Brown-Guillory, Elizabeth. *Their Place on the Stage: Black Women Playwrights in America*. New York: Greenwood Press, 1988.
Russell, Sandi. *Render Me My Song: African-American Women Writers from Slavery to the Present*. New York: St. Martin's Press, 1990.
Shange, Ntozake, and Emily Mann. "The Birth of an R&B Musical." Interview by Douglas J. Keating. *Inquirer* (Philadelphia), March 26, 1989, C12.
Sommers, Michael. "Rays of Hope in a Sky of Blues." Review of *The Love Space Demands*. *Star-Ledger* (Newark, N.J.), March 12, 1992, B10.
"*Spell No. 7* Takes Us on Magical Trip." Review of *Spell No. 7*. *Times* (Washington, D.C.), May 9, 1991, B1.

MARY WOLLSTONECRAFT SHELLEY

Born: London, England; August 30, 1797

Died: London, England; February 1, 1851

Principal long fiction

Frankenstein, 1818; *Valperga: Or, The Life of Castruccio, Prince of Lucca*, 1823; *The Last Man*, 1826; *The Fortunes of Perkin Warbeck*, 1830; *Lodore*, 1835; *Falkner*, 1837.

Other literary forms

Mary Wollstonecraft Shelley's short stories were firmly entrenched in the popular Gothic tradition, bearing such titles as "A Tale of Passion," "Ferdinand Eboli," "The Evil Eye," and "The Bride of Modern Italy." Her scholarly work included contributions to *The Lives of the Most Eminent Literary and Scientific Men* in *Lardner's Cabinet Cyclopaedia* (1830-1851). She wrote magazine articles of literary criticism and reviews of operas, an art form that filled her with delight. She wrote two travel books, *History of a Six Weeks' Tour Through a Part of France, Switzerland, Germany, and Holland* (1817) and *Rambles in Germany and Italy* (1844). Shelley edited two posthumous editions of her husband's poetry (1824 and 1839), and she wrote several poetic dramas: *Manfred* (now lost), *Proserpine*, and *Midas*. She wrote a handful of poems and two novellas: *Mathilda*, unfinished and unpublished, and *The Heir of Mondolfo*, published posthumously in 1877.

Achievements

Shelley's literary reputation rests solely on her first novel, *Frankenstein*. Her six other novels, which are of uneven quality, are very difficult indeed to find, even in the largest libraries. Nevertheless, Shelley lays claim to a dazzling array of accomplishments. First, she is credited with the creation of modern science fiction. All subsequent tales of the brilliant but doomed scientist, the sympathetic but horrible monster, both in high and mass culture, owe their lives to her. Second, the English tradition is indebted to her for a reconsideration of the Romantic movement by one of its central participants. In her brilliant *Frankenstein* fantasy, Shelley questions many of the basic tenets of the Romantic rebellion: the Romantic faith in humanity's blissful relationship to nature, the belief that evil resides only in the dead hand of social tradition, and the romantic delight in death as a lover and restorer. Finally, she has created one of the great literary fictions of the dialogue with the self. The troubled relationship between Dr. Frankenstein and his monster is one of the foundations of the literary tradition of "the double," doubtless an influence on the doubles in the works of such writers as Charles Dickens, Robert Louis Stevenson, Arthur Conan Doyle, and Joseph Conrad.

Biography

Mary Shelley, born Mary Wollstonecraft Godwin, lived the life of a great romantic heroine at the heart of the Romantic movement. She was the daughter of the brilliant feminist Mary Wollstonecraft and the equally distinguished scholar William Godwin. Born of two parents who vociferously opposed marriage, she was the occasion of their nuptials. Her mother died ten days after she was born, and her father had to marry for the second time in four years to provide a mother for his infant daughter. He chose a rather conventional widow, Mary Jane Clairmont, who had two children of her own, Jane and Charles. In her childhood, Shelley suffered the torments of being reared by a somewhat unsympathetic stepmother; later, she led the daughter of this extremely middle-class woman into a life of notoriety. The separation traumas in her early years indelibly marked Shelley's imagination: Almost all of her protagonists are either orphaned or abandoned by their parents.

Shelley's stormy early years led, in 1812 and until 1814, to her removal to sympathetic "foster parents," the Baxters of Dundee. There, on May 5, 1814, when she was seventeen years old, she met Percy Bysshe Shelley, who was then married to his first wife, Harriet. By March 6, 1815, Mary had eloped with Shelley, given birth to a daughter by him, and suffered the death of the baby. By December 29, 1816, the couple had been to Switzerland and back, had another child, William, and had been married, Harriet having committed suicide. Mary Shelley was then nineteen years old.

By the next year, Mary's stepsister, Jane Clairmont, who called herself Claire Clairmont, had a baby daughter by Lord Byron, while Mary was working on *Frankenstein*, and Mary herself had given birth to another child, Clara. While the Shelleys were touring Switzerland and Italy, they sent frantic communications to their friends, asking for financial help. There were also legal matters to be taken care of concerning publishing, Percy Shelley's estate, and the custody of his children from his previous marriage. Their letters and diaries are filled with urgent features for the safety of the Shelley children and the difficulties of what was in effect an exile necessitated by the Shelleys' unorthodox style of life. In 1818, Clara Shelley died, barely a year old, and in 1819, William Shelley died at the age of three. Five months later, a son, Percy Florence, was born, the only child of the Shelleys to grow to maturity.

In 1822, Mary Shelley's flamboyant life reached its point of desolation. Percy Shelley, while sailing with his close friend Edward Williams, in his boat, *Ariel*, drowned in the Gulf of Spezia. Mary's letters and diaries of the time clearly reveal her anguish, her exhaustion, and her despair. Many scholars have found indications that Percy Shelley was about to leave her for Jane Williams, the wife of the friend with whom he drowned. There is also some suspicion that Mary's stepsister had recently given birth to a baby by Percy Shelley, a rumor that Mary Shelley denied.

Mary's tragedy did not prompt warmth and help from her estranged father-in-law, Sir Timothy Shelley. He refused to support his grandson, Percy Florence, unless Mary gave the child to a guardian to be chosen by him. This she would not do, and she was rewarded for her persistence. Her son became heir to the Shelley estate when Harriet Shelley's son died in 1826. After the death, Mary's son became Lord Shelley. Just as important, however, was the warm relationship that he maintained with Mary until her death. Mary Shelley's life ended in the tranquil sunshine of family affection.

Analysis

Mary Shelley's six novels are written in the Gothic tradition. They deal with extreme emotions, exalted speech, the hideous plight of virgins, the awful abuses of charismatic villains, and picturesque ruins. The sins of the past weigh heavily on their plot structures, and often include previously unsuspected relationships.

Shelley does not find much use for the anti-Catholicism of much Gothic fiction. Her nuns and priests, while sometimes troublesome, are not evil, and tend to appear in the short stories rather than in the novels. She avoids references to the supernatural so common in the genre and tends instead toward a modern kind of psychological Gothic and futuristic fantasy. Like many Gothic writers, she dwells on morbid imagery, particularly in *Frankenstein* and *The Last Man*. Graphic descriptions of the plague in the latter novel revolted a reading public which had avidly digested the grotesqueries of Matthew Gregory Lewis' *The Monk* (1796).

With the exception of *Frankenstein*, Shelley's novels were written and published after the death of her husband; with the exception of *Frankenstein*, they appear to be attempting to work out the sense of desolation and abandonment that she felt after his death. In most of her novels, Shelley creates men and particularly women who resign themselves to the pain and anguish of deep loss through the eternal hope of love in its widest and most encompassing sense. Reconciliation became Shelley's preponderant literary theme.

Frankenstein is Shelley's greatest literary achievement in every way. In it, she not only calls into the world one of the most powerful literary images in the English tradition, the idealistic scientist Victor Frankenstein and his ironically abominable creation, but also, for the one and only time, she employs a narrative structure of daring complexity and originality.

The structure of *Frankenstein* is similar to a set of Chinese boxes, of narratives within narratives. The narrative frame is composed of the letters of an arctic explorer, Robert Walton, to his sister, Mrs. Saville, in England. Within the letters is the narrative of Victor Frankenstein, and within his narrative, at first, and then at the end within Walton's narrative, is the firsthand account of the monster himself. Walton communicates to England thirdhand and then secondhand accounts of the monster's thoroughly unbelievable existence. Here, it would seem, is the seminal point of Conrad's much later fiction, *Heart of Darkness* (1902): the communication to England of the denied undercurrents of reality and England's ambiguous reception of that intelligence. In *Frankenstein* as in *Heart of Darkness*, the suggestion is rather strong that England cannot or will not absorb this stunning new perception of reality. Just as Kurtz's fiancée almost a century later cannot imagine Kurtz's "horror," so Mrs. Saville's silence, the absence of her replies, suggests that Walton's stunning discovery has fallen on deaf ears.

The novel begins with Walton, isolated from his society at the North Pole, attempting to achieve glory. He prowls the frozen north "to accomplish some great purpose"; instead, he finds an almost dead Victor Frankenstein, who tells him a story which, in this setting, becomes a parable for Walton. Frankenstein, too, has isolated himself from society to fulfill his great expectations, and he has reaped the whirlwind.

Frankenstein tells Walton of his perfect early family life, one of complete kindness and solicitude. It is a scene across which never a shadow falls. Out of this perfection, Victor rises to find a way of conquering death and ridding himself and humankind of the ultimate shadow, the only shadow in his perfect middle-class life. Like a man possessed, Frankenstein forges ahead, fabricating a full, male, human body from the choicest corpse parts he can gather. He animates the creature and suddenly is overwhelmed by the wrongness of what he has done. In his success, he finds utter defeat. The reanimated corpse evokes only disgust in him. He abandons it in its vulnerable, newborn state and refuses to take any responsibility for it.

From that day, his life is dogged by tragedy. One by one, all of his loved ones are destroyed by the monster, who at last explains that he wanted only to love his creator but that his adoration turned to murderous hate in his creator's rejection of him. Ultimately, Frankenstein believes that he must destroy the monster, or, at the very least, die trying. He succeeds at both. After Frankenstein's death in the presence of Walton—the only man other than Frankenstein to witness the monster and live—the monster mourns the greatness that could have been and leaves Walton with the intention of hurling himself onto Frankenstein's funeral pyre.

The critical task regarding this fascinating work has been to identify what it is that Frankenstein has done that has merited the punishment which followed. Is the monster a kind of retribution for humanity's arrogant attempt to possess the secrets of life and death, as in the expulsion from Eden? Is it the wrath of the gods visited on humanity for stealing the celestial fire, as in the Prometheus legend, a favorite fiction of Percy Shelley? Or is this a rather modern vision of the self-destructiveness involved in the idealistic denial of the dark side of human reality? Is this a criticism of Romantic optimism, of the denial of the reality of evil except as the utterly disposable dead hand of tradition? The mystery endures because critics have suggested all these possibilities; critics have even suggested a biographical reading of the work. Some have suggested that Victor Frankenstein is Shelley's shrewd insight into her husband's self-deceived, uncritical belief in the power of his own intelligence and in his destined greatness.

Valperga, Shelley's second novel, has a fairy-tale aura of witches, princes, maidens in distress, castles, and prophecies. The author uses all these fantasy apparatuses, but actually deflates them as being part of the fantasy lives of the characters which they impose on a fully logical and pragmatic reality. The novel pits Castruccio, the Prince of Lucca, a worldly, Napoleonic conquerer, against the lost love of his youth, the beautiful and spiritual Euthanasia. Castruccio's one goal is power and military dominion, and since he is enormously capable and charismatic, not to mention lucky, he is successful. Nevertheless, that he gains the world at the price of his soul is clearly the central point of the novel.

To gain worldly sway, he must destroy Valperga, the ancestral home of his love, Euthanasia. He must also turn Italy into an armed camp which teems with death and in which the soft virtues of love and family cannot endure. His lust for power raises to predominance the most deceitful and treacherous human beings because it is they who function best in the context of raw, morally unjustified power.

In the midst of all this, Castruccio, unwilling to recognize his limits, endeavors to control all. He wants to continue his aggrandizing ways and have the love of Euthanasia. Indeed, he wants to marry her. She reveals her undying love for him, but will only yield to it if he yields his worldly goals, which he will not do. As his actions becomes more threatening to her concept of a moral universe, Euthanasia finds that she must join the conspirators against him. She and her cohorts are betrayed, and all are put to death, with the exception of Euthanasia. Instead, Castruccio exiles her to Sicily. En route, her ship sinks, and she perishes with all aboard.

Castruccio dies some years later, fighting one of his endless wars for power. The vision of the novel is that only pain and suffering can come from a world obsessed with power.

Surely the name Euthanasia is a remarkable choice for the novel's heroine. Its meaning in Shelley's time was "an easy death"; it did not refer to the policy of purposefully terminating suffering as it does today. Euthanasia's death is the best one in the story because she dies with a pure heart, never having soiled herself with hurtful actions for the purpose of self-gain. Possibly, the import of Shelley's choice is that all that one can hope for in the flawed, Hobbesian world of *Valperga* is the best death possible, as no good life can be imagined. It is probable that this bleak vision is at least obliquely connected with the comparatively recent trauma of Percy Shelley's death and Mary Shelley's grief and desolation.

The degenerating spirit of human history is the central vision of *The Last Man*. Set in the radically distant future of the twenty-first century, this novel begins with a flourishing civilization and ends with the entire population of the world, save one man, decimated by the plague. Lionel Verney, the last man of the title, has nothing to anticipate except an endless journey from one desolate city to another. All the treasures of humanity are his and his alone; all the great libraries and coffers open only to him. All that is denied to him—forever, it seems—is human companionship.

The novel begins before Lionel Verney's birth. It is a flashback narrated by Lionel himself, the only first-person narrator possible in this novel. Lionel describes his father as his father had been described to him, as a man of imagination and charm but lacking in judgment. He was a favorite of the king, but was forced out of the king's life by the king's new wife, a Marie Antoinette figure. The new queen, depicted as an arrogant snob, disapproves of Verney's father and effects his estrangement from the king by working on her husband's gullible nature.

Verney's father, in ostracized shame, seeks refuge in the country, where he marries a simple, innocent cottage girl and thus begets Lionel and his sister Perdita. Verney's father can never, however, reconcile himself to his loss of status and dies a broken man. His wife soon follows, and Lionel and Perdita live like wild creatures until chance brings the king's son, Adrian, into their path. Their friendship succeeds where the aborted friendship of their fathers failed.

What is remarkable to the modern reader is that Shelley, having set her story two hundred years in the future, does not project a technologically changed environment. She projects instead the same rural, agrarian, hand- and animal-driven society in which she lived. What does change, however, is the political system. The political system of *The Last Man* is a republican monarchy. Kings are elected, but not at regular intervals. The bulk of the novel concerns the power plays by which various factions intend to capture the throne by election rather than by war.

Adrian and Lionel are endlessly involved with a dashing, Byronic figure named Lord Raymond, who cannot decide whether he wants life in a cottage with Perdita, or life at the top. Ultimately, Raymond, like the protagonist of *Valperga*, wants to have both. He marries Perdita and gives up all pretensions to power, but then returns with her to rule the land. Power does not make him or his wife happy.

Despite the sublimation of the power process into an electoral system, the rage for power remains destructive, degenerating finally into war. The plague that appears and irrevocably destroys humankind is merely an extension of the plague of humanity's will to power. Not only Raymond and Perdita, but also their innocent children, Lionel's wife, Iris, and Adrian's sister, who stayed home to eschew worldly aspirations, are destroyed. No one is immune.

Lionel's survival carries with it a suggestion of his responsibility in the tragedy of humankind. His final exile in a sea of books and pictures suggests that those who commit themselves solely to knowledge and art have failed to deal with the central issues of life. In simply abdicating the marketplace to such as Lord Raymond, the cultivators of the mind have abandoned humanity. Through Lionel, they reap a bitter reward, but perhaps the implication is that it is a just reward for their failure to connect with their fellow human beings.

A number of critics consider *The Last Man* to be Shelley's best work after *Frankenstein*. Like *Frankenstein*, this novel rather grimly deals with the relationship between knowledge and evil. Its greatest drawback for modern audiences, however, is its unfortunate tendency to inflated dialogue. Every sentence uttered is a florid and theatrical speech. The bloated characterizations obscure the line of Shelley's inventive satire of humanity's lemming-like rush to the sea of power.

Yet in her last two novels, *Lodore* and *Falkner*,

Shelley's fictional involvement in the domestic sphere tones down her customary floridity and affords the reader fascinating insights into the thinking of the daughter of an early feminist, who was indeed an independent woman herself. It can only clarify history to know that such a woman as Shelley can write in her final novel that her heroine's studies included not only the "masculine" pursuits of abstract knowledge but also needlework and "the careful inculcation of habits and order . . . without which every woman must be unhappy—and, to a certain degree, unsexed."

Other major works

SHORT FICTION: *Mary Shelley: Collected Tales and Stories*, 1976.

PLAYS: *Proserpine*, 1922; *Midas,* 1922.

NONFICTION: *History of a Six Weeks' Tour Through a Part of France, Switzerland, Germany, and Holland,* 1817; *Lardner's Cabinet Cyclopaedia,* 1830-1851 (numbers 63, 71, 96); *Rambles in Germany and Italy,* 1844; *The Letters of Mary Shelley,* 1980 (Betty T. Bennett, editor, 2 volumes).

Bibliography

Baldick, Chris. *In "Frankenstein"'s Shadow: Myth, Monstrosity, and Nineteenth-Century Writing.* Oxford, England: Clarendon Press, 1987.

Forry, Steven Earl. *Hideous Progenies: Dramatizations of "Frankenstein" from Mary Shelley to the Present.* Philadelphia: University of Pennsylvania Press, 1990.

Mellor, Anne K. *Mary Shelley: Her Life, Her Fiction, Her Monsters.* London: Methuen, 1988.

Nitchie, Elizabeth. *Mary Shelley: Author of "Frankenstein."* New Brunswick, N.J.: Rutgers University Press, 1953.

Spark, Muriel. *Mary Shelley.* London: Constable, 1988.

Walling, William A. *Mary Shelley.* New York: Twayne, 1972.

LESLIE MARMON SILKO

Born: Albuquerque, New Mexico; March 5, 1948

Principal short fiction

Storyteller, 1981.

Other literary forms

Leslie Marmon Silko is known most widely for the novel *Ceremony* (1977). Her second novel, *Almanac of the Dead* (1991), also received significant attention. An early collection of poetry, *Laguna Woman* (1974), established her as an important young American Indian writer, and most of the lyric and narrative poems in that book are integrated with the autobiographical writings and short stories that make up *Storyteller*. Silko has also adapted, with Frank Chin, one of her short stories into a one-act play of the same title, *Lullaby*, which was first performed in 1976. Silko has also written film scripts; in one, she adapted a Laguna Pueblo myth, "Estoyehmuut and the Kunideeyah" (arrowboy and the destroyers), for television production in 1978.

Several of Silko's critical essays and interviews provide useful insights into her short fiction, as does her correspondence with the poet James Wright, which is collected in *The Delicacy and Strength of Lace* (1986).

Two particularly useful essays are "An Old-Time Indian Attack Conducted in Two Parts," published in *The Remembered Earth: An Anthology of Contemporary Native American Literature* (1981), and "Language and Literature from a Pueblo Indian Perspective," published in *English Literature: Opening Up The Canon* (1979). Silko's interviews often supply autobiographical and cultural contexts that enhance the understanding of her work; among the most insightful are "Leslie Silko: Storyteller," in *Persona* (1980), "Two Interviews with Leslie Marmon Silko," in *American Studies in Scandinavia* (1981), and the videotape *Running on the Edge of the Rainbow: Laguna Stories and Poems* (1979), which offers Silko reading from her work and is interspersed with her commentary on Laguna culture. A collection of Silko's work and related material is housed at the University of Arizona library in Tucson.

Achievements

Silko, along with Louise Erdrich, N. Scott Momaday, Simon Ortiz, and James Welch, is regarded by critics as among the best of the more than fifty American Indian writers with significant publications to have emerged between the mid-1960's and the mid-1980's. While she is well read in the canonical tradition of Anglo-American writing, having delighted particularly, at an early age, in Edgar Allan Poe, John Steinbeck, William Faulkner, Flannery O'Connor, and, later in college, William Shakespeare and John Milton, she brings to her own work the sensibility and many of the structures inherent in the Laguna oral tradition, creating, for example, a subtext of revisioned Laguna mythology to the more conventional aspects of her novel *Ceremony*. Although, in a manner similar to that of other American writers drawing upon an ethnic heritage, Silko chooses to place her work in the context of Laguna culture, her work appeals to diverse readers for its insights not only into the marginal status of many nonwhite Americans but also into the universal celebration of the reciprocity between land and culture.

Formal recognition of Silko's fiction came quite early in her career. Her story "Lullaby" was included in *The Best American Short Stories, 1975,* and "Yellow Woman" was included in *Two Hundred Years of Great American Short Stories* (1975), published to commemorate the American bicentennial. In 1974, she won the *Chicago Review* Poetry Award, and in 1977 she won the Pushcart Prize for Poetry. She has also been awarded major grants from the National Endowment for the Humanities and the National Endowment for the Arts for her work in film and in fiction. In 1981, Silko received a five-year fellowship from the MacArthur Foundation, permitting her the freedom to pursue whatever interests she wished to develop. In addition, Silko has held writing residencies in fiction at several universities and has been invited for lectures and readings at schools from New York to California.

Biography

Leslie Marmon Silko was born in Albuquerque, New Mexico, on March 5, 1948, the descendant of Laguna, Mexican, and Anglo peoples. Silko's mixed ancestry is documented in *Storyteller*, in which she recounts the stories of the white Protestant brothers Walter Gunn Marmon and Robert G. Marmon, her great-grandfather, who, with his older brother, settled in New Mexico at Laguna as a trader, having migrated west from Ohio in 1872. Her great-grandmother Marie, or A'mooh, married Robert Marmon, and her grandmother Lillie was a Model A automobile mechanic. Both were well educated and well informed about both Anglo and Laguna life-styles. Growing up in one of the Marmon family houses at Old Laguna, in western New Mexico, Silko inherited from these women and from her grandfather Hank Marmon's sister-in-law Susie Marmon a treasury of Laguna stories, both mythological and historical. Indeed, "Aunt Susie" is created in *Storyteller* as Silko's source for many of the traditional stories that shaped her childhood.

Silko's early years were spent in activities that neither completely included her in nor fully excluded her from the Laguna community. She participated in clan activities but not to the same extent as the full-bloods; she helped prepare for ceremonial dances, but she did not dance herself. Attending the local day school of the Bureau of Indian Affairs, she was prohibited from using the Keresan language which her great-grandmother had begun teaching her. She had her own horse at eight, and she helped herd cattle on the family ranch; at thirteen, she had her own rifle and joined in the annual deer hunts. From the fifth grade on, Silko commuted to schools in Albuquerque. After high school, she entered the University of New Mexico, also in Albuquerque, and, in 1969, she was graduated summa cum laude from the English department's honors program. After three semesters in the American Indian Law Program at the same university, Silko decided to pursue a career in writing and teaching. For the next two years, she taught English at Navajo Community College in Tsaile, Arizona. She spent the following two years in Ketchikan, Alaska, where she wrote *Ceremony*. She returned to teach in the University of New Mexico's English department for another two years before she moved, in 1980, to Tucson, where she became a professor of English at the University of Arizona for a few years.

Analysis

Leslie Marmon Silko's short fiction is "told" in the context of her personal experience as a Laguna Pueblo and serves as a written extension, continuation, and revitalization of Laguna oral tradition. Blurring the genre of the short story with historical anecdotes, family history, letters, cultural legacies, photographs, and lyric and narrative poems, *Storyteller* includes most of Silko's published short stories and poems. While the stories certainly stand on their own, and, indeed, many of them are included in various anthologies, Silko's matrix of thick description, conveying the mood of events as well as describing them, testifies to the essential role of storytelling in Pueblo identity, giving the people access to the mythic and historic past and relating a continuing wisdom—about the land, its animals, its plants, and the human condition—as an integral part of the natural process. About her collection, Silko has said, "I see *Storyteller* as a statement about storytelling and the relationship of the people, my family and my background to the storytelling—a personal statement done in the style of the storytelling tradition, i.e., using stories themselves to explain the dimensions of the process."

In unifying the past and the present to illuminate the kinship of land and people, Silko's story "Lullaby" evokes both beauty and loss. Set north of the Laguna Reservation, the story traces the life of an old Navajo couple, Chato and Ayah, from whose point of view the story is told by an omniscient narrator. While Ayah sits in the snow, presiding over her husband's death, she recalls various episodes in her own life just as if she were sharing in Chato's last memories. She is wrapped in an old Army blanket that was sent to her by her son Jimmie, who was killed while serving in the Army. She recalls, however, her own mother's beautifully woven rugs, themselves symbolic of stories, on the hand loom outside her childhood hogan. Again contrasting the past with the present, Ayah gazes at her black rubber overshoes and remembers the high buckskin leggings of her childhood as they hung, drying, from the ceiling beams of the family hogan.

What Ayah remembers seems better than what she has at present—and it was, but she does not escape into nostalgia for the old ways. Ayah remembers events and things as they were, for they have brought her to the present moment of her husband's death. She remembers Jimmie's birth and the day the Army officials came to tell Chato of his death. She remembers how doctors from the Bureau of Indian Affairs came to take her children Danny and Ella to Colorado for the treatment of tuberculosis, which had killed her other children. Despite their good intentions, the white doctors frightened Ayah and her children into the hills after she had unknowingly signed over her custody of the children to them. When the doctors returned with reservation policemen, Chato let them take the children, leaving Ayah powerless in her protest that she wanted first to try the medicine men. Chato had taught her to sign her name, but he had not taught her English. She remembers the months of refuge in her hatred of Chato for teaching her to sign her name (and thus to sign away her children) and how she fled to the same hill where she had earlier fled with her children. She remembers, too, Chato's pride during his years as a cattlehand and how, after he broke his leg in a fall from a horse, the white rancher fired him and evicted them from the gray boxcar shack that he had provided for the couple.

As Ayah recalls these losses, she also recalls the peacefulness of her own mother, as if she were rejoining her mother in contrast to the alienation of her own children from her after they had been away from home and learned to speak English, forgetting their native Navajo and regarding their mother as strangely backward in her ways. Now, with Chato reduced to alcoholism, senility, and incontinence, the old couple lives in the hogan of Ayah's childhood, and her routine is interrupted only by her treks to Azzie's bar to retrieve her husband. Ayah now sleeps with Chato, as she had not since the loss of Danny and Ella, because only her body will keep him warm. Fused with the heat of her body is the heat of her memory, as Ayah recalls how the elders warned against learning English: It would endanger them.

Ayah's recollection is presumably in Navajo (though Silko writes in English): The language is the story of her life and her relationship with the land on which she lived

it. Place dominates her values; an arroyo and a cowpath evoke precise memories, yet the evocation of her life culminates in her decision to allow Chato to freeze to death rather than see him suffer through the last days of his degradation. She wraps him in Jimmie's blanket and sings a lullaby to him which her grandmother and her mother had sung before her: "The earth is your mother,/ she holds you./ The sky is your father,/ he protects you./ Sleep. . . . / We are together always/ There never was a time/ when this/ was not so." Ayah's closing song in the story joins birth with death, land with life, and past with present. Through her story, Ayah creates an event that supersedes the oppression of the white rancher, the stares at the Mexican bar, the rejection of her acculturated children, and the apparent diminution of traditional ways: The story continues the timeless necessity of the people to join their land with the sacredness of their language.

In a later story set in Alaska, Silko focuses even more emphatically on the power of the story to create and to sustain the life of a people. By shifting from Laguna characters to Navajo characters and, finally, by using an Eskimo context, Silko stresses the universality of storytelling among peoples who codify the world through an oral tradition. Further, her contrast of orality with literacy is also a contrast in consciousness and values: In orality, meaning resides in the context of the linguistic event, be it in Keresan or Yupik, and that context implies an identification yet a diversity of nature and culture; in literacy, meaning resides in the coding of the script or print itself, be it the sign in English or in Chinese, and that coding implies a compartmentalization that permits abstract categories in both nature and culture. In short, orality encourages a holistic perspective while literacy seeks to preserve duality. The title story of the collection seeks to explore the ramifications of just such divergent ways of seeing the world (or hearing it), and, at the same time, the story models the process of the oral tradition: It is not a Yupik story so much as it is one that is written as if it were a Yupik story.

"Storyteller," like "Lullaby," begins *in medias res*, as do many stories in any oral tradition. It, too, is told from the point of view of a woman, but the Eskimo protagonist is a young girl, anonymous though universal as the storyteller. She is in jail for killing a "Gussuck" (a derogatory term for a white person) storekeeper. According to Anglo law and logic, however, the girl is innocent. Through juxtaposed flashbacks, Silko's omniscient narrator reconstructs the events that have led to her imprisonment. Moving away from the familiarity of a Pueblo context, Silko sets the story in Inuit country on the Kuskokwim River near Bethel, where she spent two months while she was in Alaska; she brings, then, her own attentiveness to the land to her fashioning of the story about attentiveness to storytelling. The imprisoned girl grew up with an old couple who lived in a shack outside the village, and she was nurtured by the stories of her grandmother. Although the girl had attended a "Gussuck school," she was sent home for refusing to assimilate, having been whipped for her resistance to speaking English. Sexually abused by the old man, the girl takes the place of her grandmother in the old man's bed after her death. Before the grandmother's death, however, the girl had learned about the death of her parents, who had been poisoned with bad liquor by a trader who was never taken to court for the crime. Her grandmother had not told her the complete story, leaving much of it ambiguous and unfinished. While the girl witnesses the destruction of village life by oil-drillers and listens to her "grandfather" ramble on and on with a story of a polar bear stalking a hunter, she recalls her grandmother's last words: "It will take a long time, but the story must be told. There must not be any lies." The girl believes that the "story" refers to the old man's bear story, but, in fact, it is the story which the girl herself will act out after the grandmother's death.

Bored by sex with the old man, the girl begins sleeping with oil-drillers, discovering that they are as bestial as the old man, who sleeps in a urine-soaked bed with dried fish while he adds to his story throughout the winter. When she is about to have sex with a red-haired oil-driller, he tapes a pornographic picture of a woman mounted by a dog to the wall above the bed, and then in turn mounts the girl. When she tells the old man about it, he expresses no surprise, claiming that the Gussucks have "behaved like desperate people" in their efforts to develop the frozen tundra. Using her sexuality to comprehend the strange ways of the Gussucks, the girl stalks her parents' killer as the old man's bear stalks the hunter. The Gussucks, seemingly incapable of grasping the old man's story, fail in their attention to the frozen landscape; they do not see or hear the place, the people, or the cold, blue bear of the story.

That failure to grasp the analogy of the bear story to the impending freeze of winter is what finally permits the girl to avenge the death of her parents. She lures the "storeman" from his store, which doubles as a bar, to the partially frozen river. Knowing how to breathe through her mitten in order to protect her lungs and wrapped in her grandmother's wolf-hide parka, the girl testifies mutely to the wisdom of her grandmother's stories. She knows where it is safe to tread on the ice and where it is not—she hears the river beneath her and can interpret the creaking of the ice. The storekeeper, taunted by her body, which is symbolic itself of her repository of knowledge for survival, chases her out onto the ice, trying to catch her by taking a single line to where she stands on the ice in the middle of the river. Without mittens and parka and oblivious to the warning sounds from below the ice, the storeman ignores the girl's tracks that mark a path of safety and crashes through the thin ice, drowning in the freezing river. He has had many possessions, but he lacked a story that would have saved him.

When the state police question her, the girl confesses: "He lied to them. He told them it was safe to drink. But I will not lie . . . I killed him, . . . but I don't lie." When her court-appointed attorney urges her to recant, saying, "It was an accident. He was running after you and he fell through the ice. That's all you have to say in court," the girl, disregarding the testimony of children who witnessed the man's death, insists: "I will not change the story, not even to escape this place and go home. I intended that he die. The story must be told as it is." Later, at home under a woman trooper's guard, the girl watches as the old man dies, still telling his story even as it evokes the death of the hunter; his spirit passes into the girl, who will now continue the story of the bear's conquest of the man.

Now the storyteller herself, the girl has become her story: The story has taken revenge on both the storeman and the old man, her first seducer, through her actions; namely, the telling of the stories. The story, then, does not end, but returns to itself, the bear turning to face the hunter on the ice just as the myth of natural revenge turns the story against the storeman and the seductive power of the story turns against the storyteller, the old man. Even, however, with a new storyteller, the girl, the story has no beginning and no end: It continues as long as the people and the land continue. Indeed, the story's survival is the survival of the people; ironically, the girl's story will provide the lawyer with a plea of insanity, ensuring the survival of the story and the storyteller despite the degradation involved in charging her with madness.

While Silko's stories are about the characterization of individuals, of a culture, of the land's significance to a people and their values, and of discrimination against a people, they are most fundamentally about the oral tradition that constitutes the people's means of achieving identity. Storytelling for Silko is not merely an entertaining activity reminiscent of past glories but an essential activity that informs and sustains the vitality of present cultures, shaping them toward survival and bestowing meaning for the future. The people, simply put, are their stories: If the stories are lost, the people are lost.

Other major works

NOVELS: *Ceremony,* 1977; *Almanac of the Dead,* 1991.
PLAY: *Lullaby,* 1976 (with Frank Chin).
POETRY: *Laguna Woman,* 1974.
NONFICTION: *The Delicacy and Strength of Lace: Letters Between Leslie Marmon Silko and James A. Wright,* 1986 (edited by Anne Wright).

Bibliography

Allen, Paula Gunn. "The Feminine Landscape of Leslie Marmon Silko's *Ceremony.*" In *Studies in American Indian Literature: Critical Essays and Course Design.* New York: Modern Language Association of America, 1983.
Brumble, H. David. *American Indian Autobiography.* Berkeley: University of California Press, 1988.
Larson, Charles R. *American Indian Fiction.* Albuquerque: University of New Mexico Press, 1978.
McAllister, Mick. "Homeward Bound: Wilderness and Frontier in American Indian Literature." In *The Frontier Experience and the American Dream: Essays on American Literature,* edited by David Mogen, Mark Busby, and Paul Bryant. College Station: Texas A&M Press, 1989.
Ronnow, Gretchen. "Tayo, Death, and Desire: A Lacanian Reading of *Ceremony.*" In *Narrative Chance: Postmodern Discourse in Native American Indian Literatures,* edited by Gerald Vizenor. Albuquerque: University of New Mexico Press, 1989.
Wiget, Andrew. *Native American Literature.* Boston: Twayne, 1985.

EDITH SITWELL

Born: Scarborough, England; September 7, 1887   **Died:** London, England; December 9, 1964

Principal poetry

The Mother and Other Poems, 1915; *Twentieth Century Harlequinade and Other Poems*, 1916 (with Osbert Sitwell); *Clown's Houses*, 1918; *The Wooden Pegasus*, 1920; *Façade*, 1922; *Bucolic Comedies*, 1923; *The Sleeping Beauty*, 1924; *Troy Park*, 1925; *Poor Young People*, 1925 (with Osbert Sitwell and Sacheverell Sitwell); *Elegy on Dead Fashion*, 1926; *Rustic Elegies*, 1927; *Popular Song*, 1928; *Five Poems*, 1928; *Gold Coast Customs*, 1929; *Collected Poems*, 1930; *In Spring*, 1931; *Epithalamium*, 1931; *Five Variations on a Theme*, 1933; *Selected Poems*, 1936; *Poems New and Old*, 1940; *Street Songs*, 1942; *Green Song and Other Poems*, 1944; *The Weeping Babe*, 1945; *The Song of the Cold*, 1945; *The Shadow of Cain*, 1947; *The Canticle of the Rose*, 1949; *Façade and Other Poems*, 1950; *Gardeners and Astronomers*, 1953; *Collected Poems*, 1954; *The Outcasts*, 1962; *Music and Ceremonies*, 1963; *Selected Poems*, 1965.

Other literary forms

In addition to her many collections of poetry, Edith Sitwell wrote several volumes of critical essays, biography, autobiography, social history, and fiction. Foremost among her critical studies are *Poetry and Criticism* (1925), *Aspects of Modern Poetry* (1934), and *A Poet's Notebook* (1943). Her critical biography *Alexander Pope* (1930) was meant to serve as a vindication of the man and poet. Having as much of an affinity for Queen Elizabeth as for Pope, she wrote of England's controversial monarch in *Fanfare for Elizabeth* (1946) and *The Queens and the Hive* (1962). *Bath* (1932) is a work of social history. *I Live Under a Black Sun* (1937) is a fictionalized biography of Jonathan Swift. She also edited several anthologies, of which *The Pleasures of Poetry* (1930-1932, 1934), *The American Genius* (1951), and *The Atlantic Book of British and American Poetry* (1958) are the best known. Her rather acerbic autobiography, which was published posthumously, is entitled *Taken Care Of* (1965).

Achievements

The best compliment ever paid Sitwell was Evelyn Waugh's statement that she took the dullness out of poetry. Never boring or tiresome, the worst her adverse critics could say about her was that she was eccentric and exhibitionistic, her poetry too experimental. A few of her literary enemies—and at one time they were almost as numerous as her friends—did go a step further, however, and labeled her early poetry pretentious, rambling, vacuous. Geoffrey Grigson, Julian Symons, and F. R. Leavis are only a few of the critics who thought her a dreadful poet; but William Butler Yeats, Cyril Connolly, Stephen Spender, Dylan Thomas, and T. S. Eliot believed she was one of the most creative artists of the twentieth century.

Sitwell's early poems produced a series of shocks. To some, her verse was artificial; others could see that she purposefully created an artificial world. Her teeming imagination fashioned a luscious, semimechanical microcosm, one having "furry light" from "a reynard-coloured sun," trees that "hissed like green geese" with leaves as "hoarse as a dog's bark," a domain populated by "poor flaxen foundlings . . . upon a darkened stair." The world she wrote about in her poetry was, as she put it, "like a bare egg laid by the feathered air."

Most admirers of her work rank the poems of her last years higher than the verbal legerdemain of her experimental period. In many of her early poems, Sitwell was more concerned with evoking beauty, with producing sonorous effects, than with communicating ideas; but in her later work she manifested a somberness and intensity, an almost grieving understanding of, and compassion for, the sufferings of humanity.

Biography

Edith Sitwell, daughter of Sir George and Lady Ida Sitwell and sister of the two writers Osbert and Sacheverell, was born in Scarborough, Yorkshire, in 1887. Though reared in an atmosphere of wealth and culture, her early years, as her brother Osbert wrote in his *Left Hand, Right Hand* (1944), were emotionally trying. An unwanted child, she suffered considerable physical and nervous anguish in being reared by a tyrannical father. At an early age she announced her intention of becoming a genius, and soon after she learned to write, she tried her hand at poetry. Early in the 1920's, Edith, Osbert, and Sacheverell emerged as a literary cult of three. Their circle was graced by such figures as Yeats, Virginia Woolf, Aldous Huxley, and Eliot. The most prolific of the three Sitwells, Edith produced volume after volume of poetry, and she took to reading her work to literary groups. *Wheels*, an iconoclastic annual publication which she founded and edited, outraged many.

Between 1914 and 1929, reacting strongly against the "banal bucolics" of the Georgian poets, she wrote nonrepresentational verse, which to some extent parallels the paintings of Pablo Picasso and the cubists. During her middle period, which extended from 1930 to 1940, she abandoned her dream world of sensuous mood and tonal patterns, her "pure poetry," to write poems that, like Eliot's *The Waste Land* (1922), denounced the barbarism, the hypocrisy, the misdirection of modern society. An eccentric but fascinating woman, Sitwell attracted the attention of many major celebrities and moved among them. Friendships, rivalries, and public spats made her life interesting, but the central theme of her life remained poetry. In 1933, she was awarded a medal by the Royal Society of Literature. Honorary degrees from Oxford, Leeds, Durham, and Sheffield universities followed, and she was made an associate of the American National Institute of Arts and Letters.

In 1941, she entered her final period and turned, like Eliot, to traditional values, spiritual matters, and orthodox Christianity. Thirteen years later, she was made a Dame Commander of the Order of the British Empire. The following year, Dame Edith Sitwell was received into the Roman Catholic church. Evelyn Waugh, who served as her godfather, cautioned her at the time that all too many Catholics were bores and prigs, crooks and cads, and that he himself was really pretty awful; but he added, mainly for Dame Edith's edification, how much worse he should be without the Faith. She took Waugh's words to heart, and shortly after her reception, when questioned what meant most to her, with the zeal of a convert she replied: "The love of God, the love of mankind, and the future of humanity." With such ideals uppermost in mind, she spent her final years in London, devoting herself even more zealously to literature. She continued to create and to encourage fledgling writers to do likewise, often writing warm introductions to their books. She died on December 9, 1964, after several months of illness.

Analysis

The pattern for much of Edith Sitwell's early verse can be found in her first published work, *The Mother and Other Poems*, wherein she deals with a prissy, dollhouse world full of such exotic objects as tambourines, mandolins, parakeets, nutmeg trees, and chinoiserie. Technically, the third poem in the collection, "Serenade," is one of the best. In its music of evening, the primacy of darkness is established in the opening lines: "The tremulous gold of stars within your hair/ Are yellow bees flown from the hive of night." In attributing the sun's color to the stars, she suggests a causal relationship between darkness and light, night and day. The yellow bees, born from the mothering hive of night to experience the darkness of the evening world, find the blossoms of the eyes of the beloved more fair "Than all the pale flowers folded from the light." Finally, "Serenade" pleads that the loved one open dreaming eyes "Ere those bright bees have flown and darkness dies."

Most of the poems in *Clown's Houses* and *The Wooden Pegasus* are similar to those in *The Mother and Other Poems*, but the poems making up *Bucolic Comedies* deal less with rhythm and exotica and more with what Sitwell labeled "sense transfusions." Though at first glance most of these poems may seem comedic nonsense, a careful reading indicates that even their oddest images have a purpose. In "Aubade," for example, Sitwell depicts the sad stupidity of a servant girl on a country farm coming down to light a morning fire: "Jane, Jane,/ Tall as a crane,/ The morning-light creaks down again." The dawn "creaks" about Jane because early light does not run smoothly. It is raining and Jane imagines each drop of moisture hardening into a "dull blunt wooden stalactite." Facing daily chores of weeding "eternities of kitchen garden," she senses flowers that cluck and mock her. (The flowers "cluck" for they are cockscombs.) The flames of the fire remind her of the carrots and turnips she has continually to clean and cook. Her spirits hang limp as "the milk's weak mind." Like so many of Sitwell's early poems, "Aubade" contains recollections of her own childhood. Thinking of the servant, Jane, brings to the poet's mind "The shivering movement of a certain cold dawn light upon the floor suggestive of high animal whining or whimpering, a half-frightened and subservient urge to something outside our consciousness."

Sitwell's early volumes caught the attention of only a limited number of readers, but on June 12, 1923, after reciting her *Façade* at London's Aeolian Hall, she achieved instant notoriety. Everything about her performance provoked controversy. She sat with her back to the audience, barely visible behind a transparent curtain adorned with a crudely painted moonface. Sitwell chanted her poems through an instrument called a "Sengerphone" (named after its inventor, George Senger). Out of the Sengerphone, which was made of compressed grasses meant to retain the purity of magnified tonal quality, came such baffling words as "The sound of the onycha/ When the phoca has the pica/ In the palace of the Queen Chinee!" After the performance, the audience became so threatening that the poet had to remain on stage behind the curtain. Disgruntled spectators had come to *Façade* expecting to hear some edifying verse, and what they heard sounded like gibberish. Had they listened more attentively they might have found subtle criticisms of modern life, innuendoes of decay, death, nothingness.

When Sitwell wrote *Façade* she believed a change in the direction, imagery, and rhythms of poetry had become necessary, owing "to the rhythmical flaccidity, the verbal deadness, the dull and expected patterns" of modern poetry. The poems in *Façade*, consequently, are in most cases virtuoso exercises in verbalizing, studies in rhythmical techniques. "Fox Trot," "Ass-Face," "Sir Beelzebub," "Waltz," and "Hornpipe" are excellent examples of her rhythmical techniques; these poems, in particular, consist of experiments concerning the effect that sound has on meaning.

One trisyllabic word, Sitwell discovered, had greater

rapidity than three monosyllabic words. Two rhymes placed immediately together at the end of each of two lines, furthermore, would be like "leaps in the air." In "Fox Trot," for example, she wrote: "'Sally, Mary, Mattie, what's the matter, why cry?'/ The huntsman and the reynard-coloured sun and I sigh." Other experiments were made to discover the influence of rhythm on the thickening and thinning, sharpening and softening, of consonants, as in certain lines of "Waltz": "The stars in their apiaries,/ Sylphs in their aviaries. . . . " These lines in turn are followed by others which end at times with a dissonance, at other times with a rhyme. To produce a waltz rhythm, she used disyllabic rhymes to begin as well as to end lines, "Daisy and Lily,/ Lazy and silly," followed by two long lines with assonance: "Walk by the shore of the wan grassy sea—/ Talking once more 'neath a swan-bosomed tree."

In "The Drum" the verse conveys a sense of menace, of deepening darkness, through the use of subtle dissonances. It opens: "In his tall senatorial,/ Black and manorial/ House where decoy-duck/ Dust doth clack—/ Clatter and quack/ To a shadow black." The words "black," "duck," "clatter," and "quack" with their hard consonants and dead vowels, Sitwell explained, are "dry as dust, and the deadness of dust is conveyed thus, and, as well, by the dulled dissonance of the 'a's,' of the 'u' in 'duck' followed by the crumbling assonance of 'dust.'" A duck's quacking, she obligingly added, was for her one of the driest of sounds: "It has a peculiar deadness."

Sitwell's verse was so radical that she often had to supply instructive analyses of individual poems. "Said King Pompey," she was kind enough to explain, is built upon "a scheme of R's . . . to produce a faint fluttering sound, like dust fluttering from the ground, or the beat of a dying heart." There are obvious *r* sounds in the opening lines of the poem, but to what extent, it is reasonable to ask, do the *r*'s suggest "dust fluttering from the ground"? Sitwell would respond by expatiating upon affective language and synaesthetic exchange. As soon as readers are willing to accept her theory of *r* sounds, they are then asked to consider other aural impressions. Certain words ending in *ck* "cast little imperceptible shadows." In "The Bat" she plays upon such words as "black," "quack," "duck," and "clack," in order, she says, to contrast shadows "so small yet so menacing, with . . . flat and shadeless words that end with 't' and with 'd.' Some of the *a*'s, she contends, have neither depth nor body, are flat and death-rotten, though at times the words in which they occur cast a small menacing shadow because of the *ck* ending, and frequently these shadows are followed almost immediately by flatter, deader, more shadeless words.

A few years after *Façade*, Sitwell turned from phonological hypothesizing to conceptualizations of time. Between 1924 and 1928, she devoted three long poems to finite time—*The Sleeping Beauty, Elegy on Dead Fashion*, and *Metamorphosis*. Each of these works has a richness that deserves critical attention; but, more important, she slowly overcame an agonized preoccupation with the destructiveness of time.

Of the three poems, *Metamorphosis* is the most important. Time initiates the metamorphosis of the poem's title, and in her verse Sitwell searches for a solution to the infernal behavior of contemporary humankind. Her hope at the end of the poem lies in the generative power of the sun, and she writes: "To rouse my carrion to life and move/ The polar night, the boulder that rolled this,/ My heart, my Sisyphus, in the abyss." The writing of *Metamorphosis*, however, left Sitwell in an even deeper spiritual abyss.

Sitwell followed *Metamorphosis* with one of the strongest poems of her early period, *Gold Coast Customs*. Admirers of her poetry thought it a sensation. William York Tindall labeled it "her *Waste Land*, footnotes and all." Yeats wrote that it was ennobled by the "intensity . . . endurance . . . wisdom" missing from much of contemporary poetry, the "something absent from . . . literature being back again. . . ." What Yeats especially liked about *Gold Coast Customs* was its concentration on the sterility of modern life.

Relying on G. F. W. Hegel's *The Philosophy of History* (1932) and anthropological findings as sources, Sitwell began *Gold Coast Customs* by drawing parallels between an African tribe of cannibals and a Lady Bamburger, a metaphorical goddess of materialism overly concerned with social rites. Convulsive rhythms suggest a *danse macabre*.

At the close of the poem, there is an intimation of the sacred, a quest for belief, some resolution of the futility of contemporary life. Sitwell's direction, broadly hinted at in the conclusion, was toward Christianity. Her lines allow the inference that she had become fully cognizant of the evil continuously erupting in human hearts. Convinced that there must be a greater design for life, that all moves toward a Day of Resurrection, she ends *Gold Coast Customs* with the words:

Yet the time will come
To the heart's dark slum
When the Rich man's gold and the rich man's wheat
Will grow in the street, that the starved may eat—
And the sea of the rich will give up its dead—
And the last blood and fire from my side will be shed.
For the fires of God go marching on.

"The Shadow of Cain," as its title indicates, is about modern fratricide. Its narrative concerns the second Fall, symbolized by the dropping of the first atomic bomb on Hiroshima. She wrote how, after "that epoch of the Cold," the victims of the immolation reached an open door. All that was left to them were primal realities:

The Fate said, "My feet ache."
The wanderers said, "Our hearts ache."
There was great lightening
In flashes coming to us over the floor:
The Whiteness of Bread
The Whiteness of the Dead
The Whiteness of the Claw—
All this coming to us in flashes through the open door.

These lines, Sitwell claims, came to her in a dream. The three flashes of lightning she explains as three primal realities of preservation, death, and struggle. Beyond the open door she saw spring returning; there was still the grandeur of the sun and Christ returning with the life-giving wheat of harvest. Then came the horror at Hiroshima. A gulf was torn across the world, stretching its jaws from one end of the earth to the other. Loud were the cries in the hollow from those who once were men, and yet "those ashes that were men/ Will rise again."

The horror of Hiroshima affected Sitwell deeply. Did God in some mysterious way declare Himself through such suffering? She began to incorporate into her work the re-creating energy of divine love. Her interest in prosodic experimentation was over. No longer would she tinker with sound effects, with the mechanics of rhyme. She encapsulated all of her principles of versification into one central dictum: "Poetry should always be running on pleasant feet, sometimes swift, sometimes slow." She wanted to vent the depths of her heart in sonorous, free-flowing lines that would touch the hearts of others. To express truths about human beings and the universe, to point them in the direction of salvation, became her purpose. In Sitwell's final period, her poems were hymns dedicated to the glory of life.

Other major works

NOVEL: *I Live Under a Black Sun*, 1937.

NONFICTION: *Poetry and Criticism*, 1925; *Alexander Pope*, 1930; *Bath*, 1932; *The English Eccentrics*, 1933; *Aspects of Modern Poetry*, 1934; *Victoria of England*, 1936; *Trio*, 1938 (with Osbert Sitwell and Sacheverell Sitwell); *A Poet's Notebook*, 1943; *Fanfare for Elizabeth*, 1946; *A Notebook on William Shakespeare*, 1948; *The Queens and the Hive*, 1962; *Taken Care Of*, 1965.

ANTHOLOGIES: *Wheels*, 1916-1921; *The Pleasures of Poetry*, 1930-1932, 1934; *Planet and Glow Worm*, 1944; *A Book of Winter*, 1950; *The American Genius,* 1951; *A Book of Flowers*, 1952; *The Atlantic Book of British and American Poetry*, 1958.

Bibliography

Brophy, James D. *Edith Sitwell: The Symbolist Order*. Carbondale: Southern Illinois University Press, 1968.

Cevasco, G. A. *The Sitwells: Edith, Osbert, and Sacheverell*. Boston: Twayne, 1987.

Elborn, Geoffrey. *Edith Sitwell: A Biography*. London: Sheldon Press, 1981.

Glendinning, Victoria. *Edith Sitwell: A Unicorn Among Lions*. London: Weidenfeld & Nicolson, 1981.

Pearson, John. *Façades: Edith, Osbert, and Sacheverell Sitwell*. London: Macmillan, 1978.

Salter, Elizabeth. *The Last Years of a Rebel: A Memoir of Edith Sitwell*. London: Bodley Head, 1967.

JANE SMILEY

Born: Los Angeles, California; September 26, 1949

Principal long fiction

Barn Blind, 1980; *At Paradise Gate*, 1981; *Duplicate Keys*, 1984; *The Greenlanders*, 1988; *A Thousand Acres*, 1991.

Other literary forms

Smiley's fiction-writing talents have assumed a wide variety of forms. Her novels include a mystery thriller (*Duplicate Keys*) and a medieval historical epic (*The Greenlanders*), as well as the contemporary Midwestern fictions for which she is best known. An accomplished short-story writer, she has produced a collection entitled *The Age of Grief* (1987), as well as additional short stories published in major periodicals. *The Age of Grief* and *Ordinary Love and Good Will* (1989) contain three of Smiley's novellas. Smiley's essays and opinion pieces have also appeared in prominent periodicals.

Achievements

Smiley's writing dramatizes the crises faced by "responsible" adults buffeted by the vagaries of human desire and its aftermath. Her preferred focus is the enormous emotional power wielded by each member of a family, an insight which enables her to expose the contradictions underlying the bourgeois idealization of the family. Among her recurrent themes are the paralyzing grip of the past; the capacities for selflessness, self-love, and betrayal within the same individual; and the terrible grief attendant upon all experiences of love.

Smiley's status as a medievalist informs her fiction, for her violently tragic universe recalls that of the Norse sagas. Whether her narratives deal with contemporary America or fourteenth century Greenland, prosperity, power, fame, and pleasure all prove ephemeral under the yoke of human mortality. Violence, sexual betrayal, greed, and envy continually disrupt the most strenuous efforts to create social harmony, and even love proves as likely to destroy as to create. Her most admirable characters are those who, despite their limitations and failures, stumble toward a personal vision of moral responsibility and communal obligation that both enables their survival and dignifies their self-awareness. Smiley compassionately expresses what one of her characters calls the "peculiar and fully branched inner life" of ordinary people who strive to cope with and comprehend the human condition.

Biography

Jane Graves Smiley was born in Los Angeles, California, in 1949 during her father's military posting to that area. Her midwestern parents, James La Verne Smiley and Frances Graves Nuelle, soon returned to that region, and although Jane herself never lived on a working farm, she claims deep "roots in rural country." After a childhood spent in St. Louis, Missouri, she attended Vassar College and in 1971 received a B.A. in English, writing her first novel as a senior thesis. Subsequent graduate studies at the University of Iowa led to a master of fine arts degree in 1976 and an M.A. and Ph.D. in medieval literature in 1978. She began teaching literature and creative writing at Iowa State University in Ames in 1981, becoming a full professor in 1989. Smiley served as a visiting professor at the University of Iowa in 1981 and 1987. Following a Fullbright Fellowship to Iceland in 1976-1977, she translated her study of Norse sagas into an epic novel of fourteenth century Scandinavian pioneers entitled *The Greenlanders*. Grants from the National Endowment for the Arts supported her work in 1978 and 1987.

Having begun her publishing career in 1980 with *Barn Blind*, Smiley published two more novels (*At Paradise Gate* and *Duplicate Keys*) by the time critical praise for her work exploded with the appearance of *The Age of Grief*, short fiction nominated for the National Book

Critics Circle Award. A similar excitement greeted publication of the novellas *Ordinary Love and Good Will*. With *A Thousand Acres*, Smiley won the National Book Critics Circle Award and the 1992 Pulitzer Prize; her subsequent fame led to the reissuance of all of her previous fiction.

A "vehement agnostic," Smiley suggests that her key themes—"sex and apocalypse"—derive from a childhood shadowed by the atomic bomb and an adolescence informed by "the Pill." Her personal history, like her fiction, reflects the complications of family life. A first marriage to John Whiston in 1970 ended in 1975. With second husband William Silag, whom she married in 1978, she bore two daughters, Phoebe and Lucy. A third marriage, to Stephen Mark Mortensen, began in 1987. Smiley regards her experiences as woman and mother as major influences on her imagination. Having envisioned herself as a "devoted modernist" infatuated with the nihilistic vision of early twentieth century literature, she found herself losing that alienated edge during her first pregnancy. Throughout her professional life, she has self-consciously challenged the Western prejudices embedded in the question, "Can mothers think and write?" Smiley unflinchingly probes areas of female subjectivity—including maternity—neglected until recently in creative literature.

Analysis

Jane Smiley's fiction involves the critical label "post-feminist" because of her attention to the competing goals of female experience, her resistance to polarized gender stereotypes, and her focus on the domestic sphere as a crucial arena of women's psychological struggles. As an avowed feminist, however, she critiques the hierarchical valuations through which power operates within society and its familial microcosm. Her novels depict the interior lives of women whose subjectivity has often been assumed nonexistent simply because it lies hidden or obscured by daily routines centered on the needs of others. In giving these women voice, Smiley dissects the platitudes about women's nature that cloud their ability to see themselves clearly and live authentically. Similarly, she exposes the social structures that encourage women toward economic and emotional dependency, challenging patriarchal hierarchies that devalue the female as "something to be used." Her characters are regularly buffeted by incompatible emotions, such as the intoxication and outrage accompanying motherhood. They also discover the falsity of sentimental formulas equating sexual desire and romantic love when they learn how easily the two may be split.

Finally, Smiley's writing typically shows women confronted with the demand that they take themselves seriously as moral beings responsible for their own self-definition as they maneuver through a treacherous universe. Often it is violence—actual, moral, or both—that wrenches a woman out of her assumed securities to undertake such reassessment. Smiley's fiction avoids the creation of idealized feminist saints and offers instead as wide an array of complex female psyches as exists in contemporary fiction.

Smiley's matriarchs present striking examples of women groping painfully toward a fuller understanding of their own female reality. Anna Robison, the septuagenarian Iowan protagonist of *At Paradise Gate*, initially offers the familiar and comfortable image of the *mater familias* whose steadfast self-sacrifice and loyalty have held her family together through decades of trouble, including business failure, geographical displacement, sibling rivalry, and the innumerable personal crises of her three daughters. Yet, as Anna stands watch over a dying husband with the rest of her female clan, she enters a life-spanning reverie about her own joys, griefs, and failings. Anna does not desert her post as the stalwart sensibility on whom the others rely, but her internalized narration allows the reader to see Anna as a woman hardly sanguine about the price that life has extracted from her, particularly a wrenching move east from her beloved Wyoming during the Depression. Her life of self-effacement leaves her a mystery to the very people who presume to know her best. In her tepid sympathy for her sick husband and her resentment of her demanding children, she broods on the insufficiency of all relationships to feed the deepest hungers of the solitary soul. Yet even as Anna wrestles with her bitterness at the years of compromise demanded by family life, she challenges her granddaughter Christine's panicky impulse to protect her own individuality by fleeing a repressive husband and aborting a pregnancy. In facing her existential loneliness Anna remains stoic and compassionate toward all those personalities to whom fate has bound her, finally achieving a state of grace as she sits alone with her now-dead husband, not only seeing but also accepting the full design of her life and generously offering her daughter the faith "that the family would go on" through the perseverance of its women. Others of Smiley's protagonist-mothers—Rachel Kinsella of *Ordinary Love*, for example—find themselves less noble than Anna, filled with greater grief over the consequences of their failings for the family members whom they had taught to idealize them.

While Anna recalls the Earth Mothers of Willa Cather's fiction, Kate Karlson, the matriarchal "antitype" of *Barn Blind*, wields her authority with a severity that, in seeming to hold her family together in shared purpose, actually fractures it, the "centripetal" energy of her will fueling the "centrifugal" counterforce of her children's resistance. Having established a marginally successful horse ranch and equestrian school in rural Iowa, Kate single-mindedly pursues her dream of training a truly champion horse and rider. To her delight, her oldest son Peter, seventeen years old and strikingly pliant, seems likely to fulfill her wishes mounted upon her favorite horse, the gifted but wayward MacDougal. It is in an effort to master the waywardness of the world that Kate spends her days, adopting the drill-like precision of classical riding technique as a self-conscious strategy for taming nature's—and humanity's—chaos.

Kate's temperament gravitates toward absolutes: When age and a leg injury end her own equestrian career, she converts to Catholicism and makes its observation an insistent feature of her family's life, embracing its theological clarity, ritual formality, and idealized self-discipline. Though she has borne four children, Kate seems fiercely virginal in her dedication to her work, rejecting the nurturing role and withdrawing from the intimacies of marriage. Yet her husband Axel remains steadfastly in love with her, titillated by a desire to pierce her aloofness. Kate's confident attempts to subdue nature's wild energies within her constrictive aesthetic unfold within an atmosphere of increasing threat, as Kate's hubris springs the tragic machinery that eventually engulfs the Karlson family.

Significantly, it is her own motherhood that undoes Kate's ambitions. Having taken for granted the parental right to subordinate her children to her own desires, she has failed to take seriously the power of their inner lives or their equally insistent hunger to possess her on their own terms. Oedipal tensions complicate her sons' adolescent drive toward independence and produce in them varying mixtures of attraction and repulsion: Peter shyly basks in her concentrated attention; Henry, age twelve, plots his escape from her suffocating authority; and John, age fifteen, chaotically vacillates between his rage at Kate's neglect of his limited talents and his desperate yearning for her approbation. Her lone daughter, Margaret, a college dropout at age eighteen, floats along in a dreamy stasis, trying to suspend time and deny the calls of a future apart from the family. Their respective struggles climax as John embarks on a wild ride that kills him—this in the midst of Peter's long-awaited championship performance, Henry's abortive runaway attempt, and Margaret's encounter with a seductive potential lover. After the boy's death, Kate refuses to confront the full weight of events and irrevocably alienates her devoted husband and daughter, freeing them from her power while ensuring the family's collapse.

Motherlessness and the patriarchal tyranny that grows unchecked in its absence lies at the heart of Smiley's award-winning novel *A Thousand Acres*, a fiction which audaciously sets William Shakespeare's *King Lear* in rural Iowa and shifts reader sympathy from father to children by telling the story through Ginny, the eldest daughter of Zebulon County's most successful farmer, Larry Cook. In flashback, Ginny tells the story of a family devastated by forces of love and hate that have fixed its members within unbearable and unbreakable bonds. Larry Cook is a man whose stunted interior life crashes in upon him as his family grapples with the emotional wreckage that he has wrought. The third generation heir to a homestead begun in 1890, Cook decides suddenly to retire and incorporate his land with his three daughters and their husbands as stockholders. In part a gesture prompted by his rivalry with neighbor Harold Clark, Larry's decision about the farm elicits mixed reactions from his extended family. While the elder two daughters, Ginny and Rose, support the plan, youngest daughter Caroline—the only one of the three to have left the farm, pursuing an independent career as an attorney in Des Moines—raises doubts that prompt Larry to disinherit her. When his subsequent loss of purpose and increasing eccentricity testify to the legitimacy of Caroline's concern, it is too late to reverse the furies that he has unleashed. Conflicts among the partners escalate, leading an increasingly erratic Larry to a showdown with Rose and Ginny in which he roars his loathing of them and storms off into a summer thunderstorm. His seeming abandonment by her sisters stirs Caroline to return to Larry's side, where she launches legal action to recover his property. In her smug self-righteousness and disregard for her sisters' perspective, however, she fails to win either the judge's approval or the reader's support.

Within Rose and Ginny's households, each marriage also deteriorates, in great part because of the intrusion of Jess Clark, Harold's prodigal son. Here Smiley reworks the Gloucester subplot of *King Lear* as Harold's two sons vie for his favor—and patrimony—while he in turn manipulates their loyalties. Here, as with the Cook sisters, the contrasts are vividly drawn: One son is dutiful if dull, while the other is a daring rebel who has lived on the West Coast since his Vietnam War era desertion from the Army. Returning home to reconcile with his father and explore the possibility of farming the family homestead organically, Jess also exploits the sexual hunger of Ginny and Rose, becoming each sister's lover. Jess thus exacerbates the disorder set in motion by Larry's egotism and provides another locus of male violation within the novel, though neither sister is freed from her own moral complicity in the situation that develops and each is profoundly tainted by it. Jess is not a complete villain: He speaks compellingly of the treachery of parents toward their children and recognizes the likely relationship between the region's aggressive farming practices and toxic environment that may have produced Ginny's repeated miscarriages and Rose's breast cancer.

Jess's sexual betrayal of the women mirrors the central revelation of the novel: Larry's incestuous relationships with both of his older daughters. Pressed by Ginny to explain her vindictiveness toward their increasingly pathetic father, Rose finally explains Larry's past transgressions; within a short time, the unbelieving Ginny is forced to confront her own suppressed memories of similar violation. Rose's anger poses one of the funda-

mental mysteries of the novel, for the fall from grace that has corrupted this Eden also blocks the victims' ability to forgive and fuels their lust for vengeance, conditions which ensure that the original crime will expand in waves of unrelieved horror. Forgiveness lies outside Rose's ken—grace evades her as it did her father, and before the book ends she has been widowed by her cuckolded husband's suicide and suffers a recurrence of her cancer. With her death, she leaves two motherless daughters for Ginny to rear. The homestead disappears, cannibalized by debt, and the family destiny is played out. Moral ignorance engulfs Caroline, who remains unaware of her father's sins and must suffer his humiliating inability to distinguish her from his other daughters. Larry himself retreats into insanity rather than accept the tragic moral lessons of his life.

Ginny ends the novel with the numbing discovery that her life had been built on fraudulent and self-deceptive assumptions. Divorced from a decent man, doubly bereft of the sisterhood by which she had defined herself, deprived even of the platitudes about human nature with which she had once contained her grievances, she lives an almost anonymous life as a waitress in St. Paul, Minnesota. At home, she finds herself in thrall to the teenage angst of the nieces who now live with her in a parody of the motherhood that she once craved. Trying to devise some means of coping with her awareness of her own debasement under the internal stresses of desire and rage, Ginny finds herself not exactly capable of forgiveness but willing to imagine herself into the psyche of her victimizer father. Smiley suggests that such a leap is the best grace allows in a fallen world.

Other major works

SHORT FICTION: *The Age of Grief*, 1987; *Ordinary Love and Good Will*, 1989.

Bibliography

Bakerman, Jane S. "Renovating the House of Fiction: Structural Diversity in Jane Smiley's *Duplicate Keys*." *Midamerica* 15 (1988): 111-120.

Bernays, Anne. "Toward More Perfect Unions." Review of *The Age of Grief. The New York Times Book Review*, September 6, 1987, 12.

Duffy, Martha. "The Case for Goneril and Regan." Review of *A Thousand Acres. Time*, November 11, 1991, 92.

Humphreys, Josephine. "Perfect Family Self-Destructs." Review of *Ordinary Love and Good Will. The New York Times Book Review*, November 5, 1989, 1, 45.

Klinkenborg, Verlyn. "News from the Norse." Review of *The Greenlanders. The New Republic* 198 (May 16, 1988): 36-39.

Leavitt, David. "Of Harm's Way and Farm Ways." *Mother Jones* 14 (December, 1989): 44-45.

STEVIE SMITH

Born: Hull, Yorkshire, England; September 20, 1902 **Died:** London, England; March 7, 1971

Principal poetry

A Good Time Was Had by All, 1937; *Tender Only to One*, 1938; *Mother, What Is Man?*, 1942; *Harold's Leap*, 1950; *Not Waving But Drowning*, 1957; *Selected Poems*, 1962; *The Frog Prince and Other Poems*, 1966; *The Best Beast*, 1969; *Scorpion and Other Poems*, 1972; *The Collected Poems of Stevie Smith*, 1981.

Other literary forms

Stevie Smith published three autobiographical novels, the best-received of which was her first, *Novel on Yellow Paper* (1936). A book of her drawings (with captions) called *Some Are More Human Than Others: Sketchbook* appeared in 1958. She also wrote short stories, essays, book reviews, and a one-act radio play.

Achievements

Smith's first novel received warm reviews in 1936, and she enjoyed a popularity that was sudden but relatively stable until the 1950's, when she fell out of fashion for a number of years. By the early 1960's, however, she was back in the public eye, and she remained popular giving readings in which she sometimes sang her poems in an odd, singsong voice, until her death in 1971. She won the Cholmondeley Award for Poetry in 1966 and was awarded the Gold Medal for Poetry by Queen Elizabeth II in 1969.

Biography

Born Florence Margaret Smith, Stevie Smith belonged to a family made up of women from the time she was four, when her father disappeared to make a career for himself as a sailor. That year, 1906, she moved with her mother, sister, and aunt to a house on Avondale Road in the London suburb of Palmers Green. Smith lived there for the rest of her life. By 1924 her mother had died and her sister had moved to Suffolk. From then on, she shared the house with her adored Aunt Margaret, whom Smith affectionately called "the Lion Aunt."

Smith was not university educated and was never married. The nickname "Stevie," acquired when she was eighteen, is a reference to Steve Donaghue, a famous jockey. After her graduation from secretarial training college, she got a job as a private secretary at a publishing firm in 1923. She kept this job for thirty years, until she finally devoted herself to writing full time. She died of an inoperable brain tumor in 1971.

Analysis

Stevie Smith populated the margins of her poems with idiosyncratic drawings of swimmers and potted plants, ghosts and dogs, howling children and flirting couples. She doodled this art herself, when, as she explained, she was "not thinking too much. If I suddenly get caught by the doodle, I put more effort into it and end up calling it a drawing. I've got a whole collection in boxes. Some are on tiny bits of paper and drawn on telephone and memo pads." Smith insisted that the drawings be published with her poems, even though they do not technically "illustrate" the words on the page. Instead, she chose drawings which seemed to her to illustrate "the spirit or the idea in the poem."

In some ways, reading Smith's poetry is like fishing in one of her boxes filled with drawings on loose sheets and tiny bits of paper. As one moves from one drawing to another, one poem to another, the habits of her imagination become familiar. One can identify concerns (death, spinsterhood, sexuality) that appeared early and persisted late, name maneuvers (analysis of myth, parody of family roles) that recur again and again. One learns to recognize the spatialization of her impatience with categories through images of claustrophobia ("Souvenir de Monsieur Poop"), to expect her assumption of the proximity between love and hate ("I HATE THIS GIRL"), to look for the ways in which grief feeds the heart ("So to fatness come"). She moves back and forth among forms—from rapid stanzas with fixed rhyme schemes ("Nourish Me on an Egg," "Do Take Muriel Out") to long poems constructed of rhyming couplets ("The Passing Cloud," "The Hostage"), to looser, more narrative lines ("Dear Karl," "The Abominable Lake"). Yet the procedure from one poem to another—or one collection to another—does not present itself as neat linear development.

It is possible, however, to sketch out a set of preoccupations that Smith found compelling enough to return to throughout her career. One of the most conspicuous of these concerns is her investigation of inherited stories: fairy tales, narratives from the Bible, legends, and myths. Smith takes as her premise that material culture and literary culture constitute overlapping territories and is at pains in many of her poems to demonstrate the ways in which Western culture has organized itself in response to certain famous stories. In a late poem called "How Cruel Is the Story of Eve," for example, she argues the disturbing repercussions that Genesis, with its snake and its apple and its falling woman, set in motion: "What responsibility it has/ In history/ For cruelty." She goes on to address the collective resistance of skeptical readers, who might call her estimation of the effects of Eve's story exaggerated: What is the meaning of this legend, she asks, "if not/ To give blame to women most/ And most punishment?"

If Smith's exploration of inherited stories uncovers some of the ways in which culture grids according to gender or species, her survey of the roles inherited and negotiated within families reduces the scale of the inquiry while maintaining precise attention to instances of ill fit between individuals and the roles in which they find themselves. Adults are irked at having to give up the colors and excesses of childhood ("To Carry the Child"); children with absent fathers are cynical from babyhood ("Infant"). Women with husbands and children weep over frying pans ("Wretched Woman") or lash out—"You beastly child, I wish you had miscarried,/ You beastly husband, I wish I had never married" ("Lightly Bound")—while women who refuse to compromise themselves by investing in less-than-adequate relationships doubt their own decisions and worry about isolation: "All, all is isolation/ And every lovely limb's a desolation" ("Every Lovely Limb's a Desolation"). Be-

cause Smith delights in circling round a situation, sizing it up from all angles, there also are poems that defend solitude—speakers who argue, for example, that the best personal prescription is to "shun compromise/ Forget him and forget her" ("To the Tune of the Coventry Carol"), despite the risks of isolation. The typical attitude of a wife toward her wifehood, a mother toward her motherhood, or a child toward her childhood is discomfort and cynicism. Figures in Smith's poems are perpetually chafed by the discrepancy between their needs and the roles into which they believe they have been, one way or another, stuck.

Smith pursues the possibility that "the love of a mother for her child/ Is not necessarily a beautiful thing" ("A Mother's Hearse"). "Mother, if mother-love enclosure be," one child protests, "It were enough, my dear, not quite to hate me." While another Brontë-like waif trails about tapping at windowpanes and crying that "you have weaned me too soon, you must nurse me again," the speaker corrects the misapprehension of the unhappy ghost. Would she indeed "be happier if she were within?" Smith guesses not: "She is happier far where the night winds fall,/ And there are no doors and no windows at all" ("The Wanderer"). Just as God and beasts are understood to restrict the possibility for human action by having prior claim on both divine instruction and animal instinct, claustrophobia of the will looms over the enterprise of motherhood. What Smith seems, in fact, to be suggesting is the unattractive possibility that domination is one of the primary (and primal) motivations of humankind. The desire to dominate warps even the best-intentioned of projects—warps even love.

If mothers threaten to smother their little darlings, the conspicuous absence of paternal will allows children to rule in worlds of lopsided power. The gigantic quantity of control one presumes that parents wield over their toddlers, for example, dwindles rather rapidly in "Papa Love Baby" when the child administers judgment:

I sat upright in my baby carriage
And wished mama hadn't made such a foolish marriage.
I tried to hide it, but it showed in my eyes unfortunately
And a fortnight later papa ran away to sea.

Such radical shrinkage of adult presumption would be comic except for the child's disturbing admission that its keen and unforgiving wit carries with it the burden of responsibility: "I could not grieve/ But I think I was somewhat to blame."

Even more disturbing than this image of a preschooler having to shoulder the blame for her own abandonment, the articulate baby of "Papa Love Baby" tells her brief tale in a way that hints darkly at incest:

What folly it is that daughters are always supposed to be
In love with papa. It wasn't the case with me
I couldn't take to him at all
But he took to me
What a sad fate to befall
A child of three.

The shrinking line lengths of this stanza, which ends with an admission of her tender age, remind us of the inevitable physical advantage that even a stupid papa enjoys over his little girl. The sexual suggestiveness of the poem stays, by all means, at the level of nebulous suggestion: The father "took to" the child who did not "take to him." Yet the reader can hardly help wondering why such a turn of events would constitute a "sad fate" and why, despite the fact that the poem concerns itself primarily with the child's disdain for her "unrespected" father, its title should highlight the fact that in spite of that childish contempt, "Papa Love Baby."

"Louise," the final poem in *A Good Time Was Had by All*, repeats the eerie childhood experience described in "Papa Love Baby": articulate intellectual power darkened by traces of sexual powerlessness. Louise sits on a suitcase in the "suburban sitting room" of Mr. and Mrs. Tease, having traveled all over Europe with her mother but having "never been long enough in any nation/ Completely to unpack." The only words she speaks in the poem are wistful ones—"Oh if only I could stay/ Just for two weeks in one place." Her thoughts are quickly followed by her mother's advice, "Cheer up girlie," because they will indeed be stopping here for at least two weeks, as it will take Louise's father that long to come up with the money they need to move on. As a result, "The poor child sits in a mazy fit:/ Such a quick answer to a prayer/ Shakes one a bit." That the near-instantaneous answer to her wish should send Louise down the emotional path of something as complicated as a "mazy fit" demonstrates part of what makes Smith's abnormally astute, hyperintuitive children such disturbing combinations of sophistication and vulnerability. While their wishes conform to a formula of Cinderella simplicity, their intuitive gifts expose the problems inherent in reductive answers. A homesick child gets to stay in one house for two weeks, but how reassuring is it when that house is presided over by hosts by the name of "Mr. and Mrs. Tease"? The predicament of Louise, caught between her apparent powers of shaping the adult world and her childish susceptibility to the adults who nevertheless continue to rule it, haunts the body of Smith's work right up to her death.

Sometimes children manage to elude adult authority—exhibiting, as a poem such as "'Duty Was His Lodestar'" gleefully demonstrates, particular skill in ducking out of verbal structures. As Smith herself has explained, the premise of this poem is a child's having "been told that duty is one's lodestar. But she is rebellious, this child, she will have none of it, so she says lobster instead of lodestar, and so makes a mock of it, and makes a monkey of the kind teacher." What the reader is presented with is "A song" (the poem's subtitle) in which speaker and lobster damage their relationship but then mend it and celebrate their reunification:

Duty was my Lobster, my Lobster was she,
And when I walked with my Lobster
I was happy.
But one day my Lobster and I fell out,
And we did nothing but
Rave and shout
Rejoice, rejoice, Hallelujah, drink the flowing champagne,
For my darling Lobster and I
Are friends again.

The seriousness of duty as presented by adult to child is replaced by the celebration of relationship. Duty, meant to fix the child's respectful attention and serve as a sober guide, gives way to friendship, charged with gospel-choir enthusiasm.

In "Our Bog Is Dood," Smith parodies the limits of the religious imagination in a humorous anecdote about the difficulties of achieving interpretive consensus. In this poem, the children chanting "Our Bog is dood" reveal to the speaker that they know their Bog is dood "because we wish it so/ That is enough." Here, Smith lays out for the reader's amusement the acts of sheer and reckless will by which both children and children of God collapse the distance between wish and belief, constructing verbal worlds that they inhabit with collective placidity until prodded to articulate the specifics of those worlds. "Then tell me, darling little ones," the speaker inquires, feigning innocence, "What's dood, suppose Bog is?" This flummoxes them, for though they give the irritating speaker an answer quick enough ("Just what we think it is"), they soon began arguing with one another, "for what was dood, and what their Bog/ They never could agree." The speaker proves to be exempt from this hostility not by virtue of having answers to the issues of Bog or dood but rather by a willingness to let the questions lie unanswered, to walk beside rather than into "the encroaching sea,/ The sea that soon should drown them all,/ That never yet drowned me."

An unblinking attitude toward death constitutes one of the most conspicuous stripes by which Smith's work may be recognized. Her stance toward it veers from the dismissive to the devoted but always takes careful account of its reliability as a solution. In "Death Bereaves Our Common Mother, Nature Grieves for My Dead Brother," an early poem from *A Good Time Was Had by All*, death is noted as a shift in verb tense: "He was, I am." The subject is a dead lamb, a drawing of which (lying on its back with its four legs straight up like a dead bug) decorates the poem. This ditty on death is casual to the point of flippancy, despite its professed compassion— "Can I see lamb dead as mutton/ And not care a solitary button?" Lest one suspect that she reserves this easy tone for animals, Smith describes the death of one Major Spruce in another poem in the same volume in nearly identical terms. "It is a Major Spruce/ And he's grown such a bore, such a bore . . . It was the Major Spruce./ He died. Didn't I tell you?" ("Progression").

In "The Doctor," from *Tender Only to One*, is the second stage of a doctor's prescription. When the solicitous physician observes that "You are not looking at all well, my dear,/ In fact you are looking most awfully queer," my dear replies that yes, indeed, the pain is "more than I can bear, so give me some bromide." She will go away to the seashore, where the tides, naturally, will take care of the situation, carrying the speaker "beyond recovery." "Come Death (I)," meanwhile, reprimands Christianity for teaching people to be brave in facing death, for courage is not even necessary. "Foolish illusion, what has Life to give?" the speaker inquires scornfully. "Why should man more fear Death than fear to live?" "From the Coptic" shapes the relationship between life and death into a narrative, as it describes three angels trying to coax clay into manhood. The first two angels promise the clay happiness, to little effect: "the red clay lay flat in the falling rain,/ Crying, I will stay clay and take no blame." Upon identifying himself as Death, however, the third angel produces immediate results: "I am Death, said the angel, and death is the end,/ I am Man, cries clay rising, and you are my friend."

Given the array of instances in which Smith warmly clasps the hand of death, that her most famous poem draws on the human dread of dying may say more about the kind of poems people wish to anthologize than it does about any alteration of her sensibility. "Not Waving but Drowning" is, however, the title poem of the 1957 collection, suggesting at the very least that she wished her readers to take a look at this fable of how gestures of despair and even catastrophe get mistaken for something else:

> Nobody heard him, the dead man,
> But still he lay moaning:
> I was much further out than you thought
> And not waving but drowning.

This poem, with its disturbing pun on panicky signal and casual acknowledgment, suggests that civilized systems of communication fail to accommodate emergencies. Schooled in polite noninterference and having no mechanism for detecting anything outside the bounds of that inarticulate propriety, one simply assumes that any waves at all are bound to be waves of greeting. This sorry state of communicative affairs is further complicated by the fact that the swimmer's ability to articulate difference is overwhelmed by the very medium through which he swims: How can he be expected to clarify for others the distinction between waves of greeting and waves of alarm when all of his waves are immersed in even more and perpetual waves of water? The enterprise seems doomed from the beginning.

Smith's refusal to desert these individual victims of isolation, her cocking of the ear to the persistent voice of a dead man, offers a fragile consolation. Her readers learn at least to recognize the coarseness of their own powers of interpretation. If one fails to make out the words of the drowned swimmer, one can at least be assured that it is not for the lack of his having gurgled out a message.

Other major works

NOVELS: *Novel on Yellow Paper*, 1936; *Over the Frontier*, 1938; *The Holiday*, 1949.

ANTHOLOGIES: *The Poet's Garden*, 1970; *The Batsford Book of Children's Verse*, 1970; *Me Again: Uncollected Writings of Stevie Smith*, 1981 (edited by Jack Barbera and William McBrien).

MISCELLANEOUS: *Some Are More Human Than Others: Sketchbook*, 1958.

Bibliography

Barbera, Jack, and William McBrien. *Stevie: A Biography of Stevie Smith*. London: Heinemann, 1985.

Bedient, Calvin. "Stevie Smith." In *Eight Contemporary Poets*. London: Oxford University Press, 1974.

Pumphrey, Martin. "Play, Fantasy, and Strange Laughter: Stevie Smith's Uncomfortable Poetry." *Critical Quarterly* 28 (Autumn, 1986): 85-96.

Sternlicht, Sanford. *Stevie Smith*. Boston: Twayne, 1990.

Storey, Mark. "Why Stevie Smith Matters." *Critical Quarterly* 21 (Summer, 1979): 41-55.

MURIEL SPARK

Born: Edinburgh, Scotland; February 1, 1918

Principal long fiction

The Comforters, 1957; *Robinson*, 1958; *Memento Mori*, 1959; *The Ballad of Peckham Rye*, 1960; *The Bachelors*, 1960; *The Prime of Miss Jean Brodie*, 1961; *The Girls of Slender Means*, 1963; *The Mandelbaum Gate*, 1965; *The Public Image*, 1968; *The Driver's Seat*, 1970; *Not to Disturb*, 1971; *The Hothouse by the East River*, 1973; *The Abbess of Crewe: A Modern Morality Tale*, 1974; *The Takeover*, 1976; *Territorial Rights*, 1979; *Loitering with Intent*, 1981; *The Only Problem*, 1984; *A Far Cry from Kensington*, 1988; *Symposium*, 1990.

Other literary forms

In addition to her novels, Muriel Spark has produced a sizable amount of work in the areas of poetry, the short story, drama, biography, and criticism. Her volumes of poetry include *The Fanfarlo and Other Verse* (1952) and *Collected Poems I* (1967). Her first collection of short stories, entitled *The Go-Away Bird and Other Stories*, appeared in 1958, followed by *Collected Stories I* (1967) and *The Stories of Muriel Spark* (1985). *Voices at Play*, a collection of short stories and radio plays, appeared in 1961, and a play, *Doctors of Philosophy*, was first performed in London in 1962 and published in 1963. *Curriculum Vitae: Autobiography* (1992) is the first installment of her autobiography.

Achievements

Critical opinion about Spark's status as a novelist is sharply divided. In general, she has been less highly valued by American critics; Frederick Karl, for example, has dismissed her work as being "light to the point of froth" and says that it has "virtually no content." English critics such as Frank Kermode, Malcolm Bradbury, and David Lodge, on the other hand, consider Spark a major contemporary novelist. Kermode compliments her on being "obsessed" with novelistic form, calls *The Mandelbaum Gate* a work of "profound virtuosity," and considers her to be a "difficult and important artist." Bradbury, who has regarded Spark as an "interesting, and a very amusing, novelist" from the beginning of her career, now thinks that she is also a "very high stylist" whose work in the novella shows a precision and economy of form and style. In a reassessment of *The Prime of Miss Jean Brodie*, Lodge comments on the complex structure of the novel and Spark's successful experimentation with authorial omniscience.

Throughout her career, Spark has been able to combine popular success with critical acclaim. In 1951, she received her first literary award, the *Observer* Story Prize for the Christmas story "The Seraph and the Zambesi." A radio drama based on *The Ballad of Peckham Rye* won the Italia Prize in 1962, and in the same year she was named Fellow of the Royal Society of Literature. In 1965, Spark received the prestigious James Tait Black Memorial Prize for Fiction for *The Mandelbaum Gate*.

Biography

Muriel Sarah Spark was born in Edinburgh, Scotland, on February 1, 1918, of a Jewish father, Bernard Camberg, and an English mother, Sarah Uezzell Camberg. She attended James Gillespie's School for Girls in Edinburgh, an experience that later formed the background for *The Prime of Miss Jean Brodie*. She lived in Edinburgh until 1937, when she married S. O. Spark and moved to Africa. She was divorced from Spark a year later and, in 1944, returned to England, after having lived in South Africa and Rhodesia. From 1944 to 1946, she worked in the Political Intelligence Department of the British Foreign Office. Her interest in poetry led to her serving as General Secretary of the Poetry Society in London from 1947 to 1949 and as editor of the *Poetry Review*; in 1949, she introduced a short-lived journal entitled *Forum Stories and Poems*. In the 1950's, she began a successful career as a critic and editor which included books on William Wordsworth, Mary Shelley, Emily Brontë, John Masefield, and John Henry Newman, publishing several of these works with her literary partner and friend Derek Stanford.

Brought up in the Presbyterian religion, she says that she had "no clear beliefs at all" until 1952, when she became "an Anglican intellectually speaking," although she did not formally join the Anglican Church until late in 1953. The Church of England was, however, a halfway house for Spark, who was an Anglo-Catholic for only nine months before her conversion to Roman Catholicism. Her conversion initially caused her much emotional suffering, and she says that her mind was, for a period of time, "far too crowded with ideas, all teeming in disorder." This feeling of mental chaos gave way later to what she has called "a complete reorganization" of her mind that enabled her to begin writing fiction. Several persons encouraged her to produce a novel, among them Graham Greene and Macmillan and Company, which was looking for new writers at the time; the result was *The Comforters*.

In 1961, Spark traveled to Jerusalem to research the background for *The Mandelbaum Gate*, and, in 1964, moved from her home in London to New York. She lived for less than a year in an apartment close to the United Nations Building, a location which later became the setting for *The Hothouse by the East River*. In 1967, she was awarded the Order of the British Empire and left England to settle in Italy. In 1982, after fifteen years in Rome, she moved to Tuscany.

Analysis

When Muriel Spark was writing her first novel, *The Comforters*, she thought that poetry was the only true literature, while the novel was an "inferior way of writing" whose "aesthetic validity" was very much in doubt. Although she has apparently revised her earlier low estimation of the novel, she says that she still thinks of herself as a poet rather than a novelist. Spark's distrust of the novel form also results from her suspicions about fiction's relationship to truth; she has said that she is interested in "absolute truth" and that fiction is a "kind of parable" from which a "kind of truth" emerges which should not be confused with fact. Spark perceives a parallel between God and the novelist, and the act of creating fiction is, in a sense, "dabbling in the devil's work."

As a result, Spark's novels are filled with would-be artists and artist-figures, people who attempt to create fictions in real life and consequently bring about discord and mischief. In *The Prime of Miss Jean Brodie*, Miss Brodie begins to view the people around her as characters in a story she is creating and attempts to bring about sexual pairings and heroic deeds in her self-made "plot," with disastrous results. Both Alex Warner in *Memento Mori* and Dougal Douglas in *The Ballad of Peckham Rye* are involved in "research" into the lives of the people around them; Douglas carries his curiosity about others a step further, fictionalizing an autobiography for an actress and later becoming the author of "a lot of cockeyed books." In two later novels, *The Public Image* and *Territorial Rights*, fictions are devised even more consciously—and are potentially more dangerous. Just as some characters are guilty of trying to manipulate reality by inserting carefully constructed "fictions" into the lives of real people, Sir Quentin Oliver in *Loitering with Intent* overtly plagiarizes a fictional model to accomplish his ends. After reading Fleur Talbot's novel *Warrender Chase*, he begins to orchestrate the lives of the members of the Autobiographical Association according to its plot, an action which causes Fleur to complain that "He's trying to live out my story."

Because Spark is so intent upon acknowledging her fiction as fiction, most of her novels are consciously artificial in both form and content. She has no desire to be a realistic novelist or to write the "long novel"; she said she grew bored writing her only lengthy novel, *The Mandelbaum Gate*, because of its length. Rather, she claims to speak in a "kind of shorthand" in which the narrative voice is curiously impersonal. Not surprisingly, in several novels, among them *Not to Disturb* and *The Driver's Seat*, she has experimented with her own version of the *nouveau roman*. In Spark's fiction, however, unlike that of many of the antinovelists, all details are ultimately significant.

In an interview, Spark has said that the eponymous protagonist of *The Prime of Miss Jean Brodie* represents "completely unrealised potentialities," a descriptive phrase which reflects the same ambiguity with which she is treated in the novel. The story of an Edinburgh schoolmistress and her effects on the lives of six of her pupils, *The Prime of Miss Jean Brodie* concentrates on the relationship between Jean Brodie and Sandy Stranger, the student who eventually "betrays" her. Like many other characters in Spark's fiction, Miss Brodie begins to confuse fact and fiction, and it is when Sandy perceives that her teacher has decided that Rose Stanley must begin an affair with art teacher Teddy Lloyd that Sandy realizes that Jean Brodie is no longer playing a game or advancing a theory: "Miss Brodie meant it." As David Lodge notes in his article on the novel in *The Novelist at the Crossroads* (1971), Sandy and Jenny intuitively understand when their fiction, a made-up correspondence between Miss Brodie and music teacher Gordon Lowther, should be buried and forgotten; unlike her students, Jean Brodie does not know when fantasies should be discarded.

In addition to seeing herself as an artist-figure who can manipulate the lives of her students and lovers, Jean Brodie is also guilty, in Sandy's eyes, of serious religious and political errors. Although she has not turned to religion at the time, a very young Sandy is frightened by her vision of all the "Brodie set" in a line headed by their teacher "in unified compliance to the destiny of Miss Brodie, as if God had willed them to birth for that purpose." Later, Sandy is horrified to discover that her former teacher "thinks she is Providence" and that she can see the beginning and the end of all "stories." Jean Brodie's lack of guilt over any of her actions results from her assurance that "God was on her side"; she elects herself to grace with an "exotic suicidal enchantment" which drives her to the excesses that eventually result in her forced retirement. Jean Brodie's view of herself as "above the common moral code," a phrase she applies to Rose, her chosen surrogate for an affair with Teddy Lloyd, is related to her political views as well. An early admirer of Benito Mussolini and Adolf Hitler whom Sandy later characterizes as a "born fascist," she sees herself as duty-bound to shape the personalities and the destinies of the young girls around her. "You are mine," she says to her "set," whom she has chosen to receive what she calls the "fruits of her prime," which will remain with the girls "always," a prophecy which is partially true.

The complexity of *The Prime of Miss Jean Brodie* lies in the fact that Jean Brodie is not simply a villainous character who oversteps her bounds as a teacher and begins to exert a potentially corruptive force on the young people entrusted to her. Although she flirts with Fascism (after the war she calls Hitler "rather naughty"),

she at the same time encourages a fierce individualism in her chosen students, who, as the headmistress of the Marcia Blaine School for Girls sadly learns, are totally lacking in "team spirit." She makes good her promise to "put old heads on young shoulders" and creates the "capacity for enthusiasm" for knowledge that remains with several of her students for life. The lecture to her girls on her theory of education—"It means a leading out. To me education is a leading out of what is already there in the pupil's soul. . . . Never let it be said that I put ideas into your heads"—is, like the portrait of Jean Brodie that Spark presents in the novel, open to several interpretations. Although in the later years of her prime, Miss Brodie *does* attempt to put "ideas" into the girls' heads, at the same time she bequeaths to her students a knowledge of and sensitivity to art, culture, and ideas that would have been impossible in a more conventional educational situation.

Just as *The Prime of Miss Jean Brodie* is about "unrealised potentialities," Miss Brodie also communicates to her students a knowledge of the unlimited potential inherent in all experience. In her late thirties, Jenny Gray has an experience that reawakens a memory of her "sense of the hidden possibility in all things" that she felt as an eleven-year-old student under the tutelage of Jean Brodie. More important, however, is the teacher's influence on Sandy Stranger. In his book on Spark, Derek Stanford says that "Truth, for Muriel Spark, implies rejection," and Sandy laments in the novel that she has had nothing, particularly in the religious realm, to react against or reject. Jean Brodie finally provides this catalyst, and Sandy's decision to "put a stop" to her results from a variety of reasons: her moral indignation over Miss Brodie's "plans" for Rose and Joyce Emily, sexual jealousy of Teddy Lloyd's continued infatuation with her teacher, and her awakening sense of Christian morals.

As an adult, however, Sandy acknowledges that Jean Brodie was her most important formative influence and in a sense responsible for the course her life has taken. Her conversion to Catholicism and taking of the veil are the result of her affair with Teddy Lloyd, an affair she instigates in order to subvert Jean Brodie's plans. Although Spark does not indicate the exact subject of the psychological treatise that has made Sandy famous, other than the fact that it concerns the nature of "moral perception," its title, "The Transfiguration of the Commonplace," reveals that it in some way deals with the mind's ability to alter everyday reality. Clearly, this topic owes a debt to Jean Brodie's communication to her students of the endless "possibilities" that surrounded them and is a reflection of Jean Brodie's constantly changing nature in the novel. The narrator observes that, unlike her colleagues, Miss Brodie is in a "state of fluctuating development"; like her students, her "nature was growing under their eyes, as the girls themselves were under formation." One element of Jean Brodie's "prime" is her nonstatic personality, and the problem is the direction in which the changes take place. As the narrator notes, "the principles governing the end of her prime would have astonished herself at the beginning of it."

In *The Prime of Miss Jean Brodie*, Spark is at the height of her powers as a novelist, and nowhere else in her fiction is she more in control of her subject. The "flash-forwards" which occur throughout the novel cause the reader to concentrate on the characters' motivations and interrelationships rather than on any intricacies of the plot, and Spark makes use of the principle of "economy" which she so values on almost every page, providing only the most telling details of the story while refraining, for the most part, from any authorial interpretation. In fact, the idea of economy is an important thematic element in the book. Sandy is first fascinated by the economy of Jean Brodie's fusing her tales of her dead lover, Hugh, with her current associations with Gordon Lowther and Teddy Lloyd, and later she is angered and intrigued by the economy of the art teacher's paintings, which make Jean Brodie's students resemble their teacher. When Sandy betrays Miss Brodie to the headmistress, she uses this principle after concluding that "where there was a choice of various courses the most economical was the best." Both in form and style, *The Prime of Miss Jean Brodie* shows Spark utilizing her own "intuitive artistic sense of economy."

Loitering with Intent is the fictional autobiography of its "author," Fleur Talbot, and a meditation by Spark on her own career as a novelist; it is, in addition, a meditation on the creative process and the relationship between fiction and autobiography. Fleur Talbot frequently comments on "how wonderful it is to be an artist and a woman in the twentieth century." At the conclusion, she admits that she has been "loitering with intent"; that is, she has used her observations about the people and events around her as fictional material, taking joy both in the comic and tragic occurrences in the lives of the individuals who become characters in her own "autobiography." *Loitering with Intent* calls into question the use "real" people

make of the fictions of others.

Fleur becomes the secretary of Sir Quentin Oliver, head of the spurious Autobiographical Association he has formed in order to bring people together to compose their memoirs. Like the character of Warrender Chase in the novel Fleur is in the process of completing, Sir Quentin begins to exert a devastating influence on the association's members, psychologically manipulating them not for blackmailing purposes but for the enjoyment of pure power. Instead of encouraging them to fictionalize their autobiographies, as Fleur attempts to do, Sir Quentin begins to fictionalize their lives with tragic results, Fleur says that

> I was sure . . . that Sir Quentin was pumping something artificial into their real lives instead of on paper. Presented fictionally, one could have done something authentic with that poor material. But the inducing them to express themselves in life resulted in falsity.

Fiction, when acknowledged as fiction, can help the individual to comprehend reality more clearly, as Fleur notes when she tells a friend that she will have to write several more chapters of *Warrender Chase* before she will be able to understand the events of the Autobiographical Association. In the same way, she says that one can better know one's friends if they are imaginatively pictured in various situations. Sir Quentin, however, inserts "fictions," frequently stories and events taken from Fleur's novel, into the lives of the association's members.

The relationship between Sir Quentin and Fleur symbolizes the battle between life and art that is waged in *Loitering with Intent*, for Fleur accuses him of "using, stealing" her myth, "appropriating the spirit" of her legend, and trying to "live out the story" she creates in *Warrender Chase*. Although she believes that it is wrong for Sir Quentin to take her "creation" from her, she in turn believes that he may well be a creation of hers, particularly when he begins to resemble her character Warrender Chase as the story progresses. She takes pride in saying that she could almost "have invented" Sir Quentin and that at times she feels as if she *has* invented him; in fact, this feeling so persists that she begins to wonder if it is Warrender Chase who is the "real man" on whom she has partly based the fictional character of Sir Quentin. From Fleur's point of view, this kind of inversion of life and art is necessary and productive for the artistic process and is not dangerous because it results in a bona fide fiction that acknowledges itself as fiction; Sir Quentin's appropriation of her "myth," however, is dangerous because he refuses to acknowledge the fictiveness of his creation. One irony of this situation is editor Revisson Doe's refusal to publish *Warrender Chase* because it too closely resembles the activities of the Autobiographical Association: Sir Quentin's literal and figurative theft of Fleur's novel almost results in its never becoming a work of art available to the public.

The relationship between life and art has another dimension in *Loitering with Intent*. In this novel, Spark is also concerned with the psychic potential of the artist, the ability of the creative imagination to foresee the future in the process of creating fictions. Just as Fleur remarks that writing a novel or imagining her friends in fictional situations helps her to understand them better, so does the artist often predict the future while constructing a work of art. At the end of the novel, Dottie admits that Fleur had "foreseen it all" in *Warrender Chase*, and the events of *Loitering with Intent* do bear an eerie resemblance to the plot of Fleur's first novel. In her book on Emily Brontë, Spark said that "Poetic experience is . . . such that it may be prophetic." In *Loitering with Intent*, Fleur uses reality as raw material for her novel, while Sir Quentin attempts to use art to tamper with the lives of real people; at another level, however, Fleur's poetic imagination perceives and creates future events.

Loitering with Intent also permits Spark to look back on her life as a novelist and defend many of her fictional techniques. Fleur's philosophy of art is, to a great degree, Spark's philosophy, and Fleur's descriptions and explanations of her craft could easily be addressed by Spark directly to her readers. Like Spark, Fleur is a believer in economy in art, observing "how little one needs . . . to convey the lot, and how a lot of words . . . can convey so little." Fleur does not believe in authorial statements about the motives of her characters, or in being "completely frank" with the reader; in fact, "complete frankness is not a quality that favours art." She defends herself against the charge of writing novels that are called "exaggerated" by critics and states that her fiction presents "aspects of realism." The novel, she believes, is not a documentary transcription of reality but should always seek to transform its subject. "I'm an artist, not a reporter," she informs her readers.

Fleur also answers the critics who in the past have accused Spark of treating her material in a flippantly detached manner. She says that she treats the story of Warrender Chase with a "light and heartless hand" which is her method when giving a "perfectly serious account of things" because to act differently would be hypocritical: "It seems to me a sort of hypocrisy for a writer to pretend to be undergoing tragic experiences when obviously one is sitting in relative comfort with a pen and paper or before a typewriter." At one point in the novel, Spark even challenges the "quality" of her readers, having her narrator remark that she hopes the readers of her novels are of "good quality" because "I wouldn't like to think of anyone cheap reading my books."

The most significant theme of *Loitering with Intent*, however, is joy: the joy the artist takes in the everyday reality that contributes to the imaginative act, and the euphoria the artist feels in the act of creation. Spark has indeed traveled a great distance from her early suspicions of the fiction-making process and of the novel as form.

Other major works

SHORT FICTION: *The Go-Away Bird and Other Stories*, 1958; *Voices at Play*, 1961 (with radio plays); *Collected Stories I*, 1967; *The Stories of Muriel Spark*, 1985.

PLAY: *Doctors of Philosophy*, 1963.

POETRY: *The Fanfarlo and Other Verse*, 1952; *Collected Poems I*, 1967.

NONFICTION: *Child of Light: A Reassessment of Mary Wollstonecraft Shelley*, 1951, 1987; *Emily Brontë: Her Life and Work*, 1953 (with Derek Stanford); *John Masefield*, 1953; *Curriculum Vitae: Autobiography*, 1992.

CHILDREN'S LITERATURE: *The Very Fine Clock*, 1958.

EDITED TEXTS: *Tribute to Wordsworth*, 1950 (with Derek Stanford); *Selected Poems of Emily Brontë*, 1952; *My Best Mary: The Selected Letters of Mary Shelley*, 1953 (with Stanford); *The Brontë Letters*, 1954; *Letters of John Henry Newman*, 1957 (with Stanford).

Bibliography

Bold, Alan, ed. *Muriel Spark: An Odd Capacity for Vision*. Totowa, N.J.: Barnes & Noble Books, 1984.

Kemp, Peter. *Muriel Spark*. New York: Barnes & Noble Books, 1975.

Page, Norman. *Muriel Spark*. New York: St. Martin's Press, 1990.

Randisi, Jennifer Lynn. *On Her Way Rejoicing: The Fiction of Muriel Spark*. Washington, D.C.: Catholic University of America Press, 1991.

Richmond, Velma Bourgeois. *Muriel Spark*. New York: Frederick Ungar, 1984.

Walker, Dorothea. *Muriel Spark*. Boston: Twayne, 1988.

Whittaker, Ruth. *The Faith and Fiction of Muriel Spark*. New York: St. Martin's Press, 1982.

JEAN STAFFORD

Born: Covina, California; July 1, 1915   **Died:** White Plains, New York; March 26, 1979

Principal short fiction

Children Are Bored on Sunday, 1953; *Bad Characters*, 1964; *The Collected Stories of Jean Stafford*, 1969.

Other literary forms

Jean Stafford's first three books were novels: *Boston Adventure* (1944), *The Mountain Lion* (1947), and *The Catherine Wheel* (1952). She also published juvenile fiction and a short, book-length interview with the mother of Lee Harvey Oswald, *A Mother in History* (1966).

Achievements

Although critics suggest that her insightful, carefully crafted fiction deserves more attention, Stafford is generally considered to be a minor writer. Best known for her more than forty short stories, which—like her novels—are largely autobiographical. Stafford investigates the complexities of human nature and explores the powerlessness of women in society as a major theme. Her treatment of women has generally been viewed as a metaphor for universal alienation in modern society.

Stafford's reputation as a fiction writer was established with the publication of *Boston Adventure* in 1944, the same year she was awarded a prize by *Mademoiselle*. Over the years, she received numerous other awards, including grants from the National Institute of Arts and Letters, the Guggenheim and Rockefeller foundations, and the National Press Club. She also received an O. Henry Memorial Award for her story "In the Zoo" in 1955 and the Pulitzer Prize for *The Collected Stories* in 1970.

Biography

Although born in California, where she spent part of her childhood, Jean Stafford grew up in Colorado, attended the University of Colorado (A.M., 1936), and did postgraduate work at the University of Heidelberg. Her father, at one time a reporter, had written a number of Western stories. After a year teaching at Stephens College in Missouri and then briefly at the Writer's Workshop in Iowa, Stafford decided to focus on her own writing and moved to Boston. There she married poet Robert Lowell in 1940; they were divorced in 1948. After a short marriage to Oliver Jensen in 1950, Stafford married again in 1959—to A. J. Liebling, critic and columnist for *The New Yorker*. After Liebling's death in 1963, Stafford withdrew from the New York literary world and made her home in Springs, Long Island. There she lived, becoming more and more reclusive, until her death in 1979.

Analysis

It is clear from a brief preface she wrote for *The Collected Stories* that Jean Stafford did not wish to be considered a regional writer. Her father and her mother's cousin had both written books about the West, but she had read neither before she began writing. Moreover, as soon as she could, she "hotfooted it across the Rocky Mountains and across the Atlantic Ocean" and came back to the West only for short periods. Her roots might therefore remain in Colorado but the rest of her abided "in the South or the Midwest or New England or New York." The short stories in this collection, which span twenty-five years of her productive life, she grouped under headings that both insisted on the national and international character of her art and echoed universally known writers with whom she clearly wished to associate herself: Henry James, Mark Twain, Thomas Mann.

It is true, as one discovers from the stories themselves, Stafford's fiction is not limited geographically but is set in such widely separated places as Colorado, Heidelberg, France, New York, and Boston; if, therefore, one thinks of these stories as the result of social observation they do indeed have the broad national and international scope their author claimed for them. Her stories, however—and this may have been as apparent to Stafford as it has been to some of her critics—are not so much the result of observation and intellectual response as they are expressions of Stafford's personal view of life, a reflection of her own feeling of having been betrayed by family and friends. Her protagonists are often girls or young women, pitted against persons who feel themselves superior but are revealed to be morally, emotionally, or even physically corrupt. Although Stafford's fiction was all but forgotten at the time of her death, it has been rediscovered by a new generation of readers, mainly through the work of feminist scholars. This is ironic because Stafford herself did not embrace feminist views and, in fact, spoke harshly about aspects of the feminist movement.

The thirty stories in Stafford's *The Collected Stories* are unified by one pervasive theme: illness (physical, mental, and emotional) and the accompanying snobbery of aberrant behavior. Fascinated, repelled, and at times outraged by the way illness can be used to purchase power over vulnerable individuals, Stafford describes the various forms of this currency, the number of places where it can be spent, and the way in which it can be used by those of any age or sex willing to employ it. The emotional and physical invalids in these stories clearly think themselves superior to ordinary folk, and the tensions built up in these stories are often the result of conflicts between a protagonist (who usually appears to speak for the author) and neurotic individuals who think themselves justified in exploiting others. Sometimes there is an actual physical sickness—disease, old age— but the illness or psychological aberration frequently becomes a metaphor for moral corruption.

In "Maggie Meriwether's Rich Experience," the protagonist is a naïve young American woman from Tennessee visiting in France, where she has been invited to spend the weekend at a fashionable country house. There she discovers a crowd of titled Europeans, rich, overdressed, and eccentric, who look down their collective nose at the simple girl from the American South. The reader, who sees through the eyes of the young American, sees how stupid and arrogant these aristocrats are and understands Maggie's relief at escaping to Paris. She

then telephones the older brother of her roommate at Sweet Briar and spends the evening delighting in the wholesome provincialism of her Southern American friends, regaling them with stories about her recent experience.

In "The Echo and the Nemesis," the combination of neurosis and snobbery becomes more convincingly sinister. The story is also set in Europe, in Heidelberg, but the two main characters are Americans. The protagonist, Sue, appears to be a rather unexceptional young woman from a family of ordinary means; the "invalid," Ramona, is an enormously fat girl from a very rich family (so she says), living permanently in Italy. Sue is at first impressed by Ramona's learning and by the stories she tells of her family's wealth, and the two girls become constant companions. At first the relationship, with frequent meetings in cafés, becomes routine, like another philosophy lecture or seminar in Schiller, but then Ramona begins a series of revelations about herself and her family that embarrass, mystify, and then entrance Sue. Ramona reveals that she had a twin sister who died at an early age, a beautiful girl of whom there are many drawings and paintings, and whose room had been turned into a shrine. Ramona next reveals that she has come to Heidelberg not to study but to lose weight, and she enlists Sue's aid. Captivated by Ramona's stories about her loose-living family, Sue readily accepts an invitation to visit Ramona's brothers at a ski resort in Switzerland.

Thereafter Ramona begins to change. She misses lunches, fails to show up for appointments, and wildly indulges herself in food. When Sue makes inquiries about the coming trip and questions her about her doctor, Ramona snaps at her and, once, even slaps her face. Ramona claims that Sue resembles her dead sister Martha and implies that the trip to Switzerland must therefore be called off, since Ramona's family would be too upset by the resemblance. Ramona's mysterious behavior is partially explained by Sue's discovery in Ramona's room of a photograph of a younger, thinner, and beautiful Ramona. In a final scene prior to Ramona's departure from Heidelberg, the revelation about her is made complete: Sue promises to remain her friend, and Ramona replies " 'Oh, no, no, there would be nothing in it for you. Thank you just the same. I am exceptionally ill.' She spoke with pride, as if she were really saying, 'I am exceptionally talented' or 'I am exceptionally attractive.'" When Sue responds, "I'm sorry," Ramona snaps back, "I'm not sorry. It is for yourself that you should be sorry. You have such a trivial little life, poor girl. It's not your fault. Most people do."

The neurotics in Stafford's stories are not always so aggressive and unappealing. In "The Bleeding Heart," an elderly dandy who is browbeaten by his invalid mother attempts to establish a "fatherly" relationship with a young Mexican girl who has come East and works as a secretary. The girl is at first impressed with the old gentleman's aristocratic bearing and imagines she would like him for a stepfather, but when she visits his mother with a plant, a gift from the school, she is appalled by the odors, the repellent condition of the mother, and the disgusting behavior of a parrot. When the old man attempts to force his attentions on her, she turns on him and tells him to leave her alone. "Rose," he tells her, "all I am asking is a little pity."

A briefer summary of several other stories will show the pervasiveness of this theme in Stafford's stories, both in the way that characters are conceived and relationships established and in the way that the main action is resolved. The point of the story "The Liberation" has to do with the way in which an old couple, pathetic in their loneliness, try to prevent their young niece from marrying. At her announcement of her forthcoming marriage in Boston to a teacher at Harvard (the story takes place in Colorado), the aunt (who "suffers" from chronic asthma) wrings her hands and her uncle glares at her. Both are outraged at the idea of her marrying and going off to live somewhere else. The story takes a curious turn as word comes that the girl's fiancé has died of a heart attack. The girl is at first stunned and about to resign herself to remaining in Colorado, but her uncle and aunt try to "appropriate" her grief and bind her even faster to themselves. In a panic, without luggage, the girl flees for Boston and her emotional freedom from the "niggling hypochondriacs she had left behind."

"The Healthiest Girl in Town" also takes place in Colorado, where a girl, whose mother is a practical nurse in a town inhabited mainly by tuberculous patients and their families, is forced to become friends with two sisters because her mother nurses the girls' grandmother.

At first the girl is impressed with the sisters (they also have illnesses) and their Eastern pretentiousness and ashamed of her own good health. After a quarrel with them, however, she proudly declares herself to be the healthiest girl in town.

Two other Easterners also proud of their abnormalities are a Boston spinster in "The Hope Chest" who delights in humiliating her maid and in tricking a boy who comes to her door selling Christmas wreaths into kissing her, and an elderly woman in "Life Is No Abyss" from a rich and socially prominent Boston family whom she punishes by going to the poorhouse and allowing them to come and observe her in her impoverishment. "A Country Love Story" also deals with an invalid, in this instance a writer who neglects his wife and then accuses her of being unfaithful to him and so drives her to the brink of insanity. Other such characters include a woman who devotes her life to looking beautiful and dies when her hands betray her age ("The End of a Career") and a woman who marries three times and each time selects the same brutal kind of husband ("Beatrice Trublood's Story").

"Bad Characters," which is perhaps Stafford's most amusing story, treats her usual theme comically. Here the neurotic invalid is cast as a vagabond girl with an appealing swagger, a female Huck Finn but without Huck's decency. She charms the daughter of a respectable family into shoplifting and, when the two are caught, pretends to be deaf and mute, allowing the respectable girl to bear the responsibility alone.

F. Scott Fitzgerald said that a writer has but one story to tell. Stafford tells hers in many different places, about people from rather different social levels, ages, education, and backgrounds: There is almost always an innocent charmed or somehow trapped by neurotic individuals from whom she finally escapes. Sometimes Stafford gives the stage to this neurotic individual and gradually peels away the mystery that always shrouds those who think themselves superior to others. The story holds up well in the retelling, for it is a universal and timeless theme.

Other major works

NOVELS: *Boston Adventure*, 1944; *The Mountain Lion*, 1947; *The Catherine Wheel*, 1952; *A Winter's Tale*, 1954.
NONFICTION: *A Mother in History*, 1966.
CHILDREN'S LITERATURE: *Arabian Nights: The Lion and the Carpenter and Other Tales from the Arabian Nights, Retold*, 1959; *Elephi: The Cat with the High I.Q.*, 1962.

Bibliography

Avila, Wanda. *Jean Stafford: A Comprehensive Bibliography*. New York: Garland, 1983.

Goodman, Charlotte. *Jean Stafford: The Savage Heart*. Austin: University of Texas Press, 1990.

Oates, Joyce Carol. "The Interior Castle: The Art of Jean Stafford's Short Fiction." *Shenandoah* 30 (Spring, 1979): 61-64.

Roberts, David. *Jean Stafford: A Biography*. Boston: Little, Brown, 1988.

Ryan, Maureen. *Innocence and Estrangement in the Fiction of Jean Stafford*. Baton Rouge: Louisiana State University Press, 1987.

Walsh, Mary Ellen Williams. *Jean Stafford*. Boston: Twayne, 1985.

CHRISTINA STEAD

Born: Rockdale, Australia; July 17, 1902

Died: Sydney, Australia; March 31, 1983

Principal long fiction

Seven Poor Men of Sydney, 1934; *The Beauties and Furies*, 1936; *House of All Nations*, 1938; *The Man Who Loved Children*, 1940, 1965; *For Love Alone*, 1944; *Letty Fox: Her Luck*, 1946; *A Little Tea, A Little Chat*, 1948; *The People with the Dogs*, 1952; *Dark Places of the Heart*, 1966; *The Little Hotel*, 1974; *Miss Herbert: The Suburban Wife*, 1976; *I'm Dying Laughing: The Humourist*, 1986.

Other literary forms

Christina Stead began her career with a volume of short stories, *The Salzburg Tales* (1934), and she has contributed short stories to both literary and popular magazines. A posthumous collection, *Ocean of Story: The Uncollected Short Stories of Christina Stead*, was published in 1985. Her volume *The Puzzleheaded Girl* (1967) is a collection of four novellas. Her other literary output includes reviews and translations of several novels from the French. She also edited two anthologies of short stories, one with her husband William Blake.

Achievements

Stead is considered to be in the first rank of Australian novelists; in 1974, she received Australia's Patrick White Award. One of Stead's novels, *The Man Who Loved Children*, received special critical acclaim. Stead resisted critics' attempts to represent her as a feminist writer, but she has received attention from feminist critics for her depiction of women constricted by their social roles.

Biography

Christina Ellen Stead's parents were David George Stead, a naturalist and fisheries economist, and Ellen Butters Stead, who died of a perforated appendix when Christina was two years old. David Stead then married Ada Gibbons, a society woman, and they had six children to whom Stead became big sister. Stead trained at the Sydney Teachers College, where she became a demonstrator in experimental psychology. As a public school teacher, she taught abnormal children and administered psychological tests in the schools. Stead suffered voice strain, however, and she later saw it as a symptom of her being unfit for the work. Stead studied typing and shorthand to embark on a business career. In 1928, she left Sydney, sailing on the *Oronsay* for England. In London and Paris, she worked as a grain clerk and a bank clerk, experiences that became background for her novel about finance, *House of All Nations*. By that time, Stead had met economist and writer William Blake (born William Blech), whom she married in 1952. Stead settled in the United States from 1937 to 1946, publishing several novels and working for a time as a screenwriter with Metro-Goldwyn-Mayer in Hollywood. At the end of World War II, Stead returned to Europe with Blake, living in various places on the Continent and returning to England when she feared that she was losing her feel for the English language. In 1968, Stead's husband died, and a few years later, in 1974, she returned to live with one of her brothers in Australia. She died in Sydney on March 31, 1983, at the age of eighty.

Analysis

Christina Stead was preeminently a novelist of character. She identified herself as a psychological writer, involved with the drama of the person. Her stories develop out of the dynamics of characters asserting their human energy and vigor and developing their wills. Stead established personality and communicated its energy and vitality through her creation of a distinctive language for each character. This individuating language

CHRISTINA STEAD

is explored in the characters' dialogues with one another (Sam Pollit talking his fantastic baby talk to his children), in their interior monologues (Teresa Hawkins walking miles to and from work, meditating on her need to find a life beyond the surface social conventions), and in letters (the letter to Letty Fox from her former lover, who wants his money back after she has had an abortion). The language establishes the sense of an individual person with obsessions and characteristic blindnesses. One gets to know the quality of the mind through the texture of the language.

Stead's masterpiece, critics agree, is the larger-than-life depiction of a family, *The Man Who Loved Children*. Out of print for twenty-five years, the book enjoyed a second life because of a partly laudatory review by the poet Randall Jarrell that was included as an introduction when the novel was reissued in 1965. *The Man Who Loved Children* immerses its readers in the life of the Pollit family, in its swarming, buzzing intimacy. The father, Sam Pollit, is a garrulous idealist who advocates eugenics for the unfit but who fantasizes for himself babies of every race and a harem of wives who would serve his domestic comfort. On the surface, Sam's passions are his humanitarian ideals and his love for his children, but his underlying passion is his own will. Sam is an egotistical child himself; he sees only what he wants to see. His characteristic talk is his overblown, high-sounding rhetoric expressing schemes to right the world and the fanciful, punning baby talk, whining and wheedling, that he uses with the children.

Henny, wife to Sam and stepmother to Louisa, is Sam's compulsive antagonist, worn down with child-bearing and the struggle to manage the overextended household. Henny's passion is to survive, to fight dirt and debt and the intermittent sexuality that involves her in continual childbearing. Henny's characteristic talk is insult and denunciation, castigating with graphic details and metaphors the revolting sights, sounds, smells, tastes, and touches that assault her. Stead emphasizes Henny's eyes in descriptions of the fierce eyeballs in her sockets and her mouth in descriptions of her incessantly drinking tea and mouthing insults.

Stead's way of explaining the unbridgeable gap between the minds and sensibilities of the marriage partners is to say that they have no words in common. Sam's abstraction can never communicate with Henny's particularity. They have no words that they understand mutually, and so for most of the book the two characters communicate with each other only through messages relayed by the children or by terse notes concerning household necessities. In spite of that essential gap, a sixth child is conceived and born to the couple during the novel, and the resources of the household are further strained, finally to the breaking point.

What brings the family to destruction is a complex of causes, many of which are fundamentally economic. The death of David Collyer, Henny's once-rich father, is a blow to the family's fortunes. The family loses its home, and Henny's creditors no longer expect that her father will pay her debts. Collyer's death also leaves Sam without a political base in his government job, and Sam's enemies move to oust him. The money crisis is intensified by Sam's refusal to fight for his job. Instead, he retires to their new ramshackle home to do repairs and to play with the children. Sam grandly waits to be exonerated, while Henny struggles to keep the family fed and clothed.

Another cause of the breakup of the family is the birth of Sam and Henny's newest baby. Part of the trouble is economic: The new child means more expenses when Henny had promised her money-conscious eldest son Ernie that there would be no more children. The birth also brings an anonymous letter charging falsely that the child is not Sam's because Sam has been away in Malaya for several months. The letter, filled with spite, probably has been sent by one of the Henny's disappointed creditors, but it exacerbates the mutual resentment of the couple and drives them closer and closer to serious violence against each other. (The pregnancy has not only invaded Henny's body and multiplied her worries but also cost her her lover, who deserts her when he hears of it. Henny is more than ever in Sam's power.)

A pivotal character in the fierce struggle between the parents is Louisa, oldest daughter of Sam and stepdaughter of Henny. Louisa's emergence from childhood upsets the hierarchy of the household. The man who "loved children" does not love them when they question his authority and threaten his position as "Sam the Bold," leader of the band of merry children. In retaliation, Sam calls Louisa names from "Loogoobrious" to "Bluebeak." In disputing Sam's ability to make it rain (his cosmic power), Louisa and Ernie—who is quick to jump in with what he has learned in school about evaporation—introduce norms from the world outside the family.

By the end of the novel, the family tears itself apart. Sam is unconsciously comparing himself to Christ and seeing Nature as his bride, while he says that women are "cussed" and need to be "run" and that he will send Henny away and keep the children. When Louisa asks for freedom to be sent to her dead mother's relatives, Sam says that he will never let her leave, that she must stay and help him with the children and his work. The quarreling between the parents increases until Louisa thinks that they will kill each other. The quarrels become physical battles, and Henny screams to the children to save her from their father. In despair, Ernie makes a dummy out of his clothes and hangs himself in effigy. Sam teases and humiliates the children, insisting that they stay up all night and help him boil down a marlin, an image that is reminiscent of Henny with its staring eye, deep in its socket, and its wound in its vitals.

Louisa sees the two parents as passionate and selfish, inexorably destroying each other and the children, completely absorbed in their "external married hate." To save the children, Louisa considers poisoning both parents. Sam provides both the rationale, that the unfit should make room for the fit, and the means, cyanide that he ghoulishly describes as the bringer of death. Louisa succeeds in getting the grains of cyanide into only one large cup of tea when Henny notices what she has done and drinks it, exonerating Louisa and saying "damn you all." Even with Henny dead and Louisa's confession of her plan and its outcome, Sam refuses to believe her and refuses to let her go. Louisa's only escape is to run away, thus seizing her freedom.

The power of the novel derives partly from the archetypal nature of the conflicts—between parents and children for independence; between man and woman, each for his own truth and identity; between parents for their children, their objects of greatest value. The power also results from the particularity of the characterization, the metaphors that Stead employs to communicate the nature of each family member, and the astounding sense of individual language mirroring opposed sensibilities.

The epigraph to another Stead novel, *Letty Fox: Her Luck*, says that one can get experience only through foolishness and blunders. The method that Letty follows in her adventures puts her in the tradition of picaresque heroes; the novel's subtitle, "her luck," makes more sense with reference to the notion of a submission to experience, to one's fate, than it does with reference to the common meaning of "luck" as "good fortune," Letty's "luck" is that she survives and learns something about the ways of the world.

Stead once said that in *For Love Alone*, the novel which preceded *Letty Fox*, she wrote about a young girl of no social background, who tries to learn about love, and that readers did not understand the story. Thus, in *Letty Fox*, she gave American readers a story which they could understand: the story of a modern American girl searching for love and trying to obtain status through marriage.

In both novels, the social structure tells young women that they have no valid identity except through the men they marry. In *For Love Alone*, Teresa Hawkins, like her friends, fears becoming an old maid. Even though Letty Fox has had a series of lovers and a series of responsible, interesting jobs, she does not feel validated without the security of marriage.

This firmly held conventional belief is belied by Letty's own family situation. Her beloved father Solander has a mistress, Persia, with whom he has lived faithfully for many years. The family women wonder how Persia can hold Solander without a paper and without a child. On the other hand, Mathilde, Letty's mother, has the marriage title but little else. She has three daughters—Letty, Jacky, and the much younger Andrea, conceived in a late reconciliation attempt—but Persia has Solander.

Like the picaresque hero, Letty learns the ways of the world on her own. She truly loves Luke Adams, who tantalizes her with pretended concern for her youth and innocence and fans her fascination with him. She lives for a summer with a married man and has an abortion for which she must repay him. Originally confused by Lucy Headlong's interest in her, Letty refuses a lesbian affair with her. Letty sees a range of choices in the lives of the women around her: from her sister Jacky, in love with an elderly scientist, to her younger sister Andrea, sharing the early maternal experience of her friend.

Letty wants the security of marriage, but the men she knows do not want to make serious commitments. In *For Love Alone*, Teresa remarks on the short season for the husband hunt, with no time for work or extended study. In the marriage market for the comparatively long season of seven years, Letty does not catch a husband, even when her vicious cousin Edwige does.

Except in the matter of marriage, Letty trusts her own responses and takes credit for her own integrity. When her lover Cornelius is about to leave her for his mistress in Europe and his wife, Letty faces him with the truth of relationships from a woman's point of view. She tells

Cornelius that she has got ambition and looks. She works for men, and she is their friend. She suffers without crying for help and takes responsibility for her life. Yet she sees men run after worthless, shiftless women and honor the formality of marriage when there is no substance to their relationships with them. All these facts might be just part of the injustice of the world, but Cornelius and many other men Letty knows also expect that she should be their lover and yet admit that there is no love involved by only a relationship of mutual convenience. Like the British poet William Blake, Letty sees prostitution as an invention of men who have tried to depersonalize the most intimate relationship between people. Letty affirms the reality of the sexual experience in its intimacy and its bonding.

With all her clear sight and all her independence, however, Letty does not feel safe and validated until she is married to her longtime friend Bill Van Week. Ironically, Letty marries Bill when he has been disinherited by his millionaire father, so the security Letty attains is not financial. In summing up her life to date, Letty does not claim total honesty, but—like a typical picaresque hero—she does claim grit. She says that with her marriage, her journey has begun. Here Stead limits the awareness of her character. At the end of the novel, Letty says that marriage gives her not social position but self-respect. In this retreat, Letty joins the social mainstream but denies her individual past experience. Self-respect is not an award; it is not issued like a diploma or a license. Letty, who may stand up very well to the practical problems of real life with Bill, is by no means liberated, and her awareness is finally limited.

Other major works

SHORT FICTION: *The Salzburg Tales*, 1934; *The Puzzleheaded Girl*, 1967; *Ocean of Story: The Uncollected Short Stories of Christina Stead*, 1985.

TRANSLATIONS: *Colour of Asia*, 1955; *The Candid Killer*, 1956; *In Balloon and Bathyscaphe*, 1956.

ANTHOLOGIES: *Modern Women in Love*, 1945 (with William Blake); *Great Stories of the South Sea Islands*, 1956.

Bibliography

Bader, Rudolf. "Christina Stead and the *Bildungsroman*." *World Literature Written in English* 23 (1984): 31-39.

Brydon, Diana. *Christina Stead*. London: Macmillan, 1987.

Jarrell, Randall. "An Unread Book." Introduction to *The Man Who Loved Children*, by Christina Stead. New York: Holt, Rinehart and Winston, 1965.

Lidoff, Joan. *Christina Stead*. New York: Frederick Ungar, 1982.

Ross, Robert L. "Christina Stead's Encounter with 'The True Reader': The Origin and Outgrowth of Randall Jarrell's Introduction to *The Man Who Loved Children*." In *Perspectives on Australia*, edited by Dave Oliphant. Austin: University of Texas Press, 1989.

Sheridan, Susan. *Christina Stead*. Bloomington: Indiana University Press, 1988.

Williams, Chris. *Christina Stead: A Life of Letters*. Melbourne: McPhee Gribble, 1989.

GERTRUDE STEIN

Born: Allegheny, Pennsylvania; February 3, 1874   **Died:** Neuilly-sur-Seine, France; July 27, 1946

Principal long fiction

Three Lives, 1909; *The Making of Americans*, 1925; *Lucy Church Amiably*, 1930; *A Long Gay Book*, 1932; *Ida, a Novel*, 1941; *Brewsie and Willie*, 1946; *Blood on the Dining-Room Floor*, 1948; *Things as They Are*, 1950 (later as *Quod Erat Demonstrandum*); *Mrs. Reynolds and Five Earlier Novelettes, 1931-1942*, 1952; *A Novel of Thank You*, 1958.

Other literary forms

Very few of Gertrude Stein's more than six hundred titles in more than forty books can be adequately classified into any traditional literary forms. Her philosophy of composition was so idiosyncratic, her prose style so seemingly nonrational, that her writing bears little resemblance to whatever genre it purports to represent. Depending on one's definition of the novel, Stein wrote anywhere between six and twelve novels, ranging in length from less than one hundred to 925 pages. The problem is that none of Stein's "novels" has a plot in any conventional sense, that few have conventionally developed and sustained characters, and that several seem almost exclusively autobiographical, more diaries and daybooks than anything else. If references to literary forms are made very loosely, Stein's work can be divided into novels, autobiographies, portraits, poems, lectures, operas, plays, and explanations. Other than her novels, her best-known works are *The Autobiography of Alice B. Toklas* (1933), *Tender Buttons* (1914), *Four Saints in Three Acts* (1934), *Lectures in America* (1935), *Everybody's Autobiography* (1937), and *Portraits and Prayers* (1934).

Achievements

Stein boasted that "the most serious thinking about the nature of literature in the twentieth century has been done by a woman," and her claim has great merit. During the course of her career, Stein finally managed to persuade almost everyone that there was indeed some point, if not profundity, in her aggressively enigmatic style. The ridicule and parody that frustrated so much of her early work had turned to grudging tolerance or outright lionizing by 1934, when Stein made her triumphant American lecture tour; for the last fifteen or so years of her life, she was published even if her editor had not the vaguest idea of what she was doing (as Bennett Cerf later admitted he had not). On the most concrete level, Stein's distinctive prose style is remarkably significant even when its philosophical dimensions are ignored. William Gass has observed, Stein "did more with sentences, and understood them better, than any writer ever has."

More important was Stein's influence on other leaders in the development of modernism. As a student of William James, a friend of Alfred North Whitehead and Pablo Picasso, Stein lived at the center of the philosophical and artistic revolutions of the twentieth century. She was the natural emblem for modernism, and in her person, career, and legend, many of its salient issues converged. It has also been argued that Stein was the first postmodernist, the first writer to claim openly that the instance of language is itself as important as the reality to which it refers. Among major writers, Ernest Hemingway was most obviously influenced by his association with her, but her genius was freely acknowledged by F. Scott Fitzgerald, Sherwood Anderson, and Thornton Wilder. William Saroyan explained her influence most directly when he asserted that no American writer could keep from coming under it.

Biography

Gertrude Stein was born on February 3, 1874, in Allegheny, Pennsylvania, but she was seven before her family settled into permanent residence in Oakland, California, the city she was later to describe as having "no there there." Her father was authoritarian, moody, aggressive, but vacillating. Her mother barely figured in her life at all: A pale, withdrawn, ineffectual woman, she left most of the rearing of her children to governesses. By the time Stein was seventeen, both parents had died and she had grown even closer to her immediate older brother, Leo. In 1893, she entered Harvard Annex (renamed Radcliffe College the following year), thus rejoining Leo, who was a student at Harvard. There, Stein studied with William James and Hugo Munsterberg and became involved in research in psychology. Together with the great influence exerted on her thinking by William James, this early work in psychology was to provide her with both a subject and a style that would continue in many forms throughout her career. She was awarded her A. B. by Harvard in 1898, almost a year after she had entered medical school at The Johns Hopkins University. Her interest in medicine rapidly waned, and she left Johns Hopkins in 1901, failing four courses in her final semester.

After leaving medical school, Stein spent two years moving back and forth between Europe and America. During that time, she was involved in an agonizing love affair with another young woman student at Johns Hopkins, May Bookstaver. The affair was painfully complicated, first by Stein's naïveté, then by the presence of a more sophisticated rival for May's love, Mabel Haynes. The resulting lover's triangle led Stein, in an effort to understand May, to begin formulating the theories of personality that dominated her early writing. The frustration and eventual despair of this lesbian relationship profoundly influenced Stein's view of the psychology of personality and of love.

After a brief stay in New York, she lived with Leo, first in Bloomsbury in London, and then, beginning in 1903, in Paris at 27 rue de Fleurus, the address she was to make so well known to the world. In Paris, Gertrude and Leo became more and more interested in painting, buying works by new artists such as Henri Matisse and Picasso. In 1907, Stein met another young American woman in Paris, Alice Toklas, and Alice began to displace Leo as the most important personal influence in Gertrude's life. Alice learned to type so she could transcribe Stein's handwritten manuscripts, beginning with portions of *The Making of Americans* in 1908. In 1909, Alice moved in with Gertrude and Leo at 27 rue de Fleurus, and by 1913, Alice had replaced Leo as Gertrude's companion and as the manager of her household. Stein later referred to her relationship with Alice as a "marriage," and few, if any, personal relationships have ever influenced a literary career so profoundly. Apart from providing Stein with the persona for her best-known work, *The Autobiography of Alice B. Toklas*, Alice typed, criticized, and valiantly worked to publish all Stein's work for the rest of her career and for the twenty years that Alice lived after Stein's death.

Gertrude and Alice spent the first months of World War I in England as houseguests of Alfred North Whitehead, returning to Paris briefly in 1914, then spending more than a year in Spain. They joined the war effort in 1917 when Stein drove a supply truck for the American Fund for French Wounded; she was later awarded the Medaille de la Reconnaissance Française for her work.

The Armory Show, which opened in New York in 1913, confronted Americans with the first cubist paintings and also led to the public's association of Stein's writing with this shockingly new art, particularly since Stein's first periodical publications had been "Matisse" and "Picasso" in *Camera Work*, the year before. Stein's mammoth, 925-page novel, *The Making of Americans*, was published in 1925, and in 1926, she lectured at the universities of Oxford and Cambridge, attempting to explain her idiosyncratic writing style. With the publication of the best-selling *The Autobiography of Alice B. Toklas* in 1933, Stein first captured the public's interest. She became front-page news the following year when her opera *Four Saints in Three Acts* was first performed and when she embarked on a nationwide lecture tour.

Stein and Toklas spent World War II in Bilignin and then in Culoz, France. While Stein and Toklas were both Jewish, they were never persecuted by occupying forces, owing in part to the influence of Bernard Fay, an early admirer of Stein's work who directed the Bibliothèque Nationale for the Vichy regime. When, after the war, Fay was sentenced to life imprisonment for his Vichy activities, Stein was one of his few defenders.

Stein died on July 27, 1946, following an operation for cancer. Alice Toklas' account of Stein's last words may be apocryphal: Stein asked her "What is the answer?" and, when Alice remained silent, added, "In that case, what is the question?"

Analysis

During the nearly fifty years of her writing career, Gertrude Stein's style developed in many related but perceptibly different stages, such as her "cubist" or her "cinema" phases. As a result, no single analysis can do more than describe the primary concerns and features of one of her stylistic periods. There are, however, three central concerns that underlie and at least partially account for all of the stages in the development of her style. These concerns are with the value of individual words, with repetition as the basic rhythm of existence, and with the related concept of "movement" in writing. Her articulations of these central concerns all run counter to her reader's expectations about the purpose and function of language and of literature.

One of Stein's goals was to return full meaning, value, and particularity to the words she used. "I took individual words and thought about them until I got their weight and volume complete and put them next to another word," she explained of seemingly nonsense phrases such as "toasted Susie is my ice cream," or "mouse and mountain and a quiver, a quaint statue and pain in an exterior and silence more silence louder shows salmon a mischief intender." This sort of paratactic juxtaposition of seemingly unrelated words rarely occurs in Stein's novels, but represents a problem for her reader in many other ways in her writing. She frequently chose to stress or focus on a part or aspect of the object of her description that the reader normally does not consider. The "things" Stein saw and wrote of were not the "things" with which readers are familiar: Where another observer might see a coin balanced on its edge, Stein might choose either of the descriptive extremes of seeing it literally as a thin rectangle, or figuratively as the essence of money. Characteristically, her most opaque parataxis refers to essences or processes rather than to objects or static concepts.

A related quirk in Stein's style results from her intellectual or emotional attachment to particular words and phrases at certain stages of her career. As she admitted in *The Making of Americans*,

> To be using a new word in my writing is to me a very difficult thing. . . . Using a word I have not yet been using in my writing is to me a very difficult and a peculiar feeling. Sometimes I am using a new one, sometimes I feel a new meaning in an old one, sometimes I like one I am very fond of that one that has many meanings many ways of being used to make different meanings to everyone.

Stein said she had learned from Paul Cézanne that everything in a painting was related to everything else and that each part of the painting was of equal importance—a blade of grass as important to the composition of the painting as a tree. She attempted to apply these two principles to the composition of her sentences, taking special delight in using normally "overlooked" words, arguing that articles, prepositions, and conjunctions—the transitive elements in grammar—are just as important and more interesting than substantives such as nouns and verbs.

By "movement," Stein referred not to the movement of a message to its conclusion or the movement of a plot or narrative, but to "the essence of its going" of her prose, a timeless continuous present in the never-ending motion of consciousness. Stein also credits Cézanne with discovering this concern, "a feeling of movement inside the painting not a painting of a thing moving but the thing painted having inside it the existence of moving." She seemed to understand Cézanne's achievement in terms of William James's model of consciousness as an ever-flowing stream of thought. Accordingly, she used her writing not to record a scene or object or idea (products of thought), but to try to capture the sense of the process of perceiving such things. Stein's subject is almost always really two things at once: whatever attracted her attention—caught her eye, entered her ear, or crossed her mind—and the mobile nature of reality, particularly as it is perceived by human consciousness. In fact, Stein was usually more concerned with the nature of her own perception and with that of her reader than she was with its objects. She wanted to escape the conventions of linguistic representation, arbitrary arrangements similar to the "rules" for perspective in painting, and to present "something moving as moving is not as moving should be." As confusing as her resulting efforts sometimes are, her concern with motion makes sense as an attempt to mimic or evoke the nature of consciousness as she understood it.

Three Lives is easily Stein's best-known and most respected piece of fiction. Technically three novellas, this work is unified by its three subjects, but its central concern with the nature of consciousness, and by its attempt to blend colloquial idioms with Stein's emerging style, here based largely on her understanding of Cézanne's principles of composition, particularly that "one thing was as important as another thing." "The

Good Anna," "Melanctha," and "The Gentle Lena" are the three sections of this work. Anna and Lena are poor German immigrants who patiently work as servants in Bridgepoint, Baltimore; Melanctha is a young black woman who discovers sexuality and love, then turns from a frustrating relationship with a sincere young black doctor to a dissipative affair with a gambler. Since all three women are essentially victimized by their surroundings and die at the end of their stories, this work is deterministic in the naturalist tradition, but *Three Lives* marks the transition from naturalism to modernism as Stein departs from nineteenth century literary conventions. She abandons conventional syntax to try to follow the movement of a consciousness rather than of events, and she develops a new narrative style only partially tied to linear chronology. The result is an interior narrative of consciousness in which Stein's prose style serves as the primary carrier of knowledge. Through the rhythms of her characters' speech and the rhythms of her narration, Stein gives her reader a sense of the basic rhythms of consciousness for these three women—what Stein would elsewhere refer to as their "bottom natures." Possibly Stein's most widely celebrated piece of writing, "Melanctha" has been praised by Richard Wright, among others, as one of the first realistic and sympathetic renderings of black life by a white American author, but Melanctha's race is actually incidental to Stein's central concerns with finding a style to express the rhythms of personality and the frustrating cycles of love.

While it was not published until 1925, Stein's *The Making of Americans* occupied her as early as 1903. This mammoth novel began as a description of the creation of Americans from a representative immigrant family: "The old people in a new world, the new people made out of the old, that is the story that I mean to tell, for that is what really is and what I really know." Stein's projected family chronicle soon lost its original focus, becoming first a history of every one, then a study of character types rather than of characters. Although the book ostensibly continues to follow events in the lives of two central families, the Herslands and the Dehnings, its real concern is almost always both larger and smaller, ranging from Stein's questions about her own life and identity to questions about various personality types. In a way, the book chronicles the "making" of Gertrude Stein, presenting a phenomenology of her mind as it works its way through personal problems toward a distinctive "cinema style."

Underlying a great part of the writing in this book is Stein's belief that human personality consists of variations on a few basic "bottom natures" or kinds of identity which can be perceived through a character's repeated actions. "There are then many things every one has in them that come out of them in the repeating everything living have always in them, repeating with a little changing just enough to make of each one an individual being, to make of each repeating an individual thing that gives to such a one a feeling of themselves inside them." There are two basic personality types, "dependent independent" and "independent dependent," polarities identified in part by the way the person fights: the first kind by resisting, the second by attacking. Concerns with character-typing dominate the book's first two sections. "The Dehnings and the Herslands" and "Martha Hersland," (the character most closely modeled on Stein's own life), while the third section, "Alfred and Julia Hersland," contains mostly digressions about contemporary matters in Stein's life. The fourth section, "David Hersland," becomes a meditation on the nature of aging and death ("He was dead when he was at the beginning of being in middle living,"), and the final section, "History of a Family's Progress," is—even for Stein—an incredibly abstract and repetitive series of reflections on the concerns that had given rise to the novel. This final section contains no names, referring only to "some," "any," "every," or "very many."

Stein later described her efforts in this book as an attempt "to do what the cinema was doing"; that is, to give a sense of motion and life through a series of highly repetitive statements, each statement only an incremental change from the preceding one, like frames in a strip of film. One of the main effects of this technique is to freeze all action into a "continuous present." Not only do Stein's sentences exist in overlapping clusters, depending more for their meaning on their relationships to one another than on individual semantic content, but also her verbs in *The Making of Americans* are almost exclusively present participles, suspending all action in the present progressive tense. "The business of Art," Stein later explained, "is to live in the actual present, that is the complete actual present, and to express that complete actual present." As a result, while *The Making of Americans* does ostensibly present a history of four generations of the Hersland family, there exists in it little or no sense of the passage of time. Instead, the book presents a sense of "existence suspended in time," a self-contained world existing quite independently of the "real world," a basic modernist goal that has also become one of the hallmarks of postmodernism.

A 416-page version, abridged by Stein, was published in 1934, but has not been accepted by Stein scholars as adequately representative of the longer work. For all its difficulty, *The Making of Americans* is one of modernism's seminal works and an invaluable key to Stein's literary career.

However idiosyncratic Stein's writing may seem, it must be remembered that a very strong case can be made for its substantial philosophical underpinnings. To her way of thinking, language could refuse few things to Stein, and the limitations of language were exactly what she refused to accept. She bent the language to the very

uses that process philosophers such as William James, Henri Bergson, and Alfred North Whitehead feared it could not be put. Her stubborn emphasis on the individual word—particularly on transitive elements—her insistent use of repetition, and her ever-present preoccupation with the essential motion of words were all part of Stein's monumental struggle with a language she believed was not accurately used to reflect the way people perceive reality or the motion of reality itself. In a narrow but profound sense, she is the most serious realist in literary history. Stein was not a philosopher—her magpie eclecticism, associational flights, and thundering *ex cathedra* pronouncements ill-suited her for systematic explanation—but in her writing a wealth of philosophy appears.

Other major works

PLAYS: *Geography and Plays*, 1922; *Operas and Plays*, 1932; *Four Saints in Three Acts*, 1934; *Lucretia Borgia*, 1939; *In Savoy: Or, Yes Is for a Very Young Man (A Play of the Resistance in France)*, 1946; *The Mother of Us All*, 1947; *Last Operas and Plays*, 1949; *In a Garden: An Opera in One Act*, 1951; *Selected Operas and Plays*, 1970.

POETRY: *Tender Buttons: Objects, Food, Rooms*, 1914; *Two (Hitherto Unpublished) Poems*, 1948; *Bee Time Vine and Other Pieces: 1913-1927*, 1953; *Stanzas in Meditation and Other Poems: 1929-1933*, 1956.

NONFICTION: *The Autobiography of Alice B. Toklas*, 1933; *Matisse, Picasso, and Gertrude Stein, with Two Shorter Stories*, 1933; *Portraits and Prayers*, 1934; *Lectures in America*, 1935; *Narration: Four Lectures*, 1935; *The Geographical History of America*, 1936; *Everybody's Autobiography*, 1937; *Picasso*, 1938; *What Are Masterpieces*, 1940; *Wars I Have Seen*, 1945; *Reflections on the Atomic Bomb*, 1973; *How Writing Is Written*, 1974.

CHILDREN'S LITERATURE: *The World Is Round*, 1939.

Bibliography

Doane, Janice L. *Silence and Narrative: The Early Novels of Gertrude Stein*. Westport, Conn.: Greenwood Press, 1986.

Hoffman, Michael J., ed. *Critical Essays on Gertrude Stein*. Boston: G. K. Hall, 1986.

_____. *Gertrude Stein*. Boston: Twayne, 1976.

Mellow, James R. *Charmed Circle: Gertrude Stein and Company*. New York: Praeger, 1974.

Neuman, Shirley, and Ira B. Nadel, eds. *Gertrude Stein and the Making of Literature*. Boston: Northeastern University Press, 1988.

Walker, Jayne L. *The Making of a Modernist: Gertrude Stein from "Three Lives" to "Tender Buttons."* Amherst: University of Massachusetts, 1984.

HARRIET BEECHER STOWE

Born: Litchfield, Connecticut; June 14, 1811   **Died:** Hartford, Connecticut; July 1, 1896

Principal long fiction

Uncle Tom's Cabin: Or, Life Among the Lowly, 1852; *Dred: A Tale of the Great Dismal Swamp*, 1856; *The Minister's Wooing*, 1859; *Agnes of Sorrento*, 1862; *The Pearl of Orr's Island*, 1862; *Oldtown Folks*, 1869; *Pink and White Tyranny*, 1871; *My Wife and I*, 1871; *We and Our Neighbors*, 1875; *Poganuc People*, 1878.

Other literary forms

In 1843, Harriet Beecher Stowe gathered a number of her sketches and stories into a volume called *The Mayflower: Or, Sketches of Scenes and Characters of the Descendants of the Pilgrims* (1843). For forty years thereafter, she published short fiction and miscellaneous essays in magazines. In *A Key to Uncle Tom's Cabin* (1853), she assembled a mass of sources and analogues for the characters and incidents of her most famous novel. Her 1869 *The Atlantic* article "The True Story of Lady Byron's Life," and a subsequent elaboration, *Lady Byron Vindicated* (1870), caused a sensation at the time. She also published a geography for children (1833, her earliest publication, issued under her sister Catharine's name), poems, travel books, collections of biographical sketches, and a number of other children's books.

Stowe's stories and sketches remain readable. Her best collection, *Sam Lawson's Oldtown Fireside Stories* (1872), differs from the novel *Oldtown Folks* mainly in degree of plotlessness. Selections from Stowe's frequently long and chatty letters can be found in the *Life of Harriet Beecher Stowe* (1889), written by her son Charles Edward Stowe, and in more recent biographies, but hundreds of her letters remain unpublished and scattered in various archives.

Achievements

Known primarily today for her antislavery novel *Uncle Tom's Cabin*, Stowe also interpreted the life of her native New England in a series of novels, stories, and sketches. Along with Ralph Waldo Emerson and Oliver Wendell Holmes, she contributed to the first issue of *The Atlantic* (November, 1857) and for many years thereafter contributed frequently to that Boston-based magazine. As an alert and intelligent member of a famous family of Protestant ministers, she understood the Puritan conscience and outlook as well as anyone in her time, and as a shrewd observer of the commonplace, she deftly registered Yankee habits of mind and speech. All of her novels feature authentic New England characters; after *Uncle Tom's Cabin* and *Dred*, she turned to settings that included all six New England states. Despite a contradictory idealizing tendency, she pioneered in realism.

One of the first American writers to apply a talent for dialect and local color to the purposes of serious narrative, she exerted a strong influence on Sarah Orne Jewett, Mary Wilkins Freeman, and other regionalists of the later nineteenth century. Without a doubt, however, her greatest achievement was the novel which, beginning as an intended short serial in a Washington anti-slavery weekly, the *National Era*, forced the American reading public to realize for the first time that slaves were not only a national problem but also people with hopes and aspirations as legitimate as their own. Critics as diverse as Henry Wadsworth Longfellow, Heinrich Heine, William Dean Howells, and Leo Tolstoy in the nineteenth century, and Edmund Wilson and Anthony Burgess in the twentieth, have used superlatives to praise *Uncle Tom's Cabin*.

Biography

When Harriet Elizabeth Beecher was born on June 14, 1811, the seventh child of Lyman and Roxana Beecher, her father's fame as a preacher had spread well beyond the Congregational Church of Litchfield, Connecticut. All seven Beecher sons who lived to maturity became ministers, one becoming more famous than his father.

Harriet, after attending Litchfield Academy, a well-regarded school, was sent to the Hartford Female Seminary, which was founded by her sister Catharine—in some respects the substitute mother whom Harriet needed after Roxana died in 1816 but did not discover in the second Mrs. Beecher. In 1827, the shy, melancholy girl became a teacher in her sister's school.

In 1832, Lyman Beecher accepted the presidency of Lane Seminary in Cincinnati, Ohio, and soon Catharine and Harriet had established another school there. Four years later, Harriet married a widower named Calvin Stowe, a Lane professor. In the years that followed, she bore seven children. She also became familiar with slavery, as practiced just across the Ohio River in Kentucky; with the abolitionist movement, which boasted several notable champions in Cincinnati, including the future Chief Justice of the United States Supreme Court, Salmon P. Chase; and with the Underground Railroad. As a way of supplementing her husband's small income, she also contributed to local and religious periodicals.

Not until the Stowes moved to Brunswick, Maine, in 1850, however, did she think of writing about slavery. Spurred by a vision she experienced at a church service, she began to construct *Uncle Tom's Cabin*. Even as a weekly serial in the *National Era*, it attracted much attention, and its publication in 1852 as a book made Stowe an instant celebrity. After that year, from her new base in Andover, Massachusetts, where her husband taught, she twice visited Europe, met Harriet Martineau, John Ruskin, the Brownings, and Lady Byron, among others, and the scope of her fame increased even further.

Stowe wrote another slavery novel, *Dred*, and then turned her literary attention to New England. The drowning of her son Henry, a Dartmouth student, in the summer of 1857, marred for her the successes of these years. In the fall of 1862, infuriated by the lack of British support for the North in the Civil War and skeptical that President Lincoln would fulfill his promise to issue a proclamation of emancipation, Stowe visited Lincoln, who is reported to have greeted her with the words, "So this is the little lady who made this big war." She left Washington satisfied that the president would keep his word.

Following Calvin Stowe's retirement from Andover, the family moved to Hartford, the winters usually being spent in northern Florida. Two of the most sensational scandals of the post-Civil War era involved Stowe, the first arising when she published an imprudent and detailed account of Lord Byron's sins as revealed to her some years earlier by the now deceased widow of the poet, the second being an adultery suit brought against her brother Henry in which Stowe characteristically defended him to the hilt. The Byron affair in particular turned many people against her, although her books continued to be commercial successes throughout the 1870's. The most severe personal abuse ever directed at a respectable nineteenth century woman bothered Stowe far less than another personal tragedy: the alcoholism and eventual disappearance of her son Fred in San Francisco in 1870.

In the last twenty-three years of her life, Stowe became the central attraction of the Hartford neighborhood known as Nook Farm, also the home of Charles Dudley Warner and Mark Twain, the latter moving there in part because of its Beecher connections. Her circle of friends included Annie Fields, wife of *The Atlantic* publisher; George Eliot, with whom she corresponded; and Oliver Wendell Holmes, always a staunch supporter. In her final years, her mind wandered at times, but she was still writing lucid letters two years before her death on July 1, 1896, at the age of eighty-five.

Analysis

The reader finds in Harriet Beecher Stowe's works a mingling of realistic and romantic elements. Her settings, particularly the New England ones, ring true. She understood her cultural roots, and she proved able to recollect childhood impressions almost photographically. She possessed a keen ear for dialect and a sharp eye for the idiosyncrasies of people she scarcely seemed to have noticed until they turned up in her writing. Stowe used the novel to probe urgent social issues such as slavery and women's rights. Although she liked nature and worked hard at describing it accurately, she disdained her native region's characteristic transcendental interpretations of it. She displayed the realist's aversion to mystery, mysticism, and the legendizing of history.

On the other hand, the romantic tendencies of Stowe's fiction stand out against its realistic background. Her heroines are invariably saintly, as are certain of her black males such as Uncle Tom and, in *Dred*, Uncle Tiff. Her recalcitrant heroes often undergo rather unconvincing conversions. Occasionally, she introduces a mythic, larger-than-life character such as Dred. In common with most of the generation of American realists who followed her, she never renounced the heroic but sought to demonstrate its presence among humble and common people. Her heroes differ from those of Twain, William Dean Howells, and Henry James, however, in drawing their strength from a firm Christian commitment: Stowe's piety has been something of an impediment to her modern readers.

One of Stowe's most persistent and indeed remarkable narrative traits also works against her realism on occasion. As she confides at the beginning of chapter 44 of *Dred*, "There's no study in human nature more interesting than the aspects of the same subject in the points of view of different characters." That she periodically allowed this interest to distract her from the task at hand is clear. Although she experimented with different points of view—omniscient, first-person, dramatic, and circulating (the last primarily through the use of the epistolary method)—she worked before the time when novelists such as Joseph Conrad, James Joyce, and William Faulkner developed techniques capable of sustaining this kind of interest. It should be pointed out that Stowe uses the expression "points of view" in the sense of "opinions," and she is more likely to present the conflict of opinions through conversations than through living, breathing embodiments of motivating ideas.

It is as a realist before her time that Stowe is most profitably considered. Even where her realism does not serve a socially critical purpose, as it does in *Uncle Tom's Cabin* and *My Wife and I*, she makes her readers aware of the texture, the complexity, of social life—particularly the conflicts, tensions, and joys of New England community life. Understanding how people grow from their geographic, social, religious, and intellectual roots, she is able to convey the reality of isolated Maine coastal villages and the jaunty postwar Manhattan of aspiring journalists. In her best work, she depicts evil not as the product of Mephistophelean schemers or motiveless brutes but of high-minded people incapacitated by a crucial weakness, such as the irresolute Augustine St. Clare of *Uncle Tom's Cabin*, the temporizing Judge Clayton of *Dred*, and the imperceptive Dr. Hopkins of *The Minister's Wooing*.

Uncle Tom's Cabin: Or, Life Among the Lowly, remains one of the most controversial of novels. Extravagantly admired and bitterly detested in the 1850's, it continues to arouse extreme reactions. An early barrage of challenges to its authenticity led Stowe to work furiously at the assembling of *A Key to Uncle Tom's Cabin*

the next year. In 262 closely printed, double-columned pages, she impressively documented horrors that verified "the truth of the work." This book unfortunately encouraged the development of an essentially nonliterary mass of criticism, with the result that the novel early gained the reputation of a brilliant piece of propaganda—even President Lincoln supposedly accepting the Civil War as its legacy—but unworthy of serious consideration on artistic grounds.

It did not help the novel's cause that the inevitable later reaction against this enormously popular story coincided with the effort, spearheaded by Henry James, to establish the novel as a form of art rather than as a mere popular entertainment. A writer who strove too single-mindedly for mere verifiability did not merit consideration as an artist. In the same year that *Uncle Tom's Cabin* began appearing serially, Nathaniel Hawthorne—James's chief example of the American artist—prefaced his *The House of the Seven Gables* (1851) with a firm declaration of its imaginary basis which contrasted sharply with his attempt to provide a "historical" one for *The Scarlet Letter* one year earlier. Hawthorne's star as a writer of fiction gradually rose; Stowe's sank. *Uncle Tom's Cabin* was relegated to the status of a work that made things happen—important historically but damned by that very fact to the region of the second-rate.

In *A Key to Uncle Tom's Cabin*, Stowe herself called the novel "a very inadequate representation of slavery," but her excuse is significant: "Slavery, in some of its workings, is too dreadful for the purposes of art." She was acknowledging a problem that would continue to bedevil realists for most of the rest of the century. The most prominent spokesman for realism, Howells, agreed with her, and until the 1890's, realists would generally exclude things considered "too dreadful."

Stowe sandwiched the story of Uncle Tom, the meek Christian capable of turning the other cheek even to the sadistic Simon Legree, between the resolute George and Eliza Harris' escape from slavery and the Harris family's fortuitous reunion at the end of the novel. If the plot is untidy and contrived, a number of the individual characters and episodes have remained among the most memorable in fiction. The famous scene in which Eliza crosses the Ohio River ice in early spring is "true" not because the feat had been accomplished (although Stowe knew it had) but because she makes the reader feel Eliza's desperation, the absolute necessity of the attempt, and the likelihood that a person who grew up in her hard school would develop the resources to succeed.

The meeting between Miss Ophelia and Topsy illustrates Stowe's talent for dramatizing the confrontation of stubborn viewpoints. Sold down the river by his first owner, Tom has rescued the angelic daughter of Augustine St. Clare and has been installed to the St. Clare household. Miss Ophelia, a Vermont cousin of St. Clare, has been brought south to take care of Eva, whose mother is languidly incompetent. St. Clare despises slavery but feels powerless to resist it; Ophelia's intransigent New England conscience will not permit her to acquiesce in it. After listening to a considerable amount of her antislavery rhetoric, St. Clare gives his cousin a little black girl rescued from alcoholic parents. Ophelia is revolted by Topsy, so utterly different from the golden, cherubic Eva. Topsy, shrewd and skeptical beyond her years, embodies the insidiousness of slavery itself. Ophelia must find room in her heart for the little "black spider" or lose face with her cousin. Her struggle with Topsy— and with her own physical aversion—is fierce and richly comical, and its successful outcome believable.

For the modern reader, the death scenes in the novel are more of a problem. Little Eva's protracted illness and beatific death exactly pleased the taste of Stowe's time. Today, her father's senseless and sudden death as a result of his attempt to mediate a tavern brawl seems more like real life—or would if Stowe had not permitted St. Clare to linger long enough to undergo a deathbed religious conversion. Modern reaction to Stowe's climactic scene is complicated by the hostility of writers such as James Baldwin to the character of Uncle Tom, who, in dying at the hands of Legree's henchmen, wins their souls in the process. Whether the conversion of Sambo and Quimbo convinces today's reader, Tom's character has been firmly established, and he dies in precisely the spirit the reader expects.

Far less satisfactory is the subsequent escape of two of Legree's slaves from his clutches. Stowe did nothing beforehand to induce belief in a brutal master who could melt into helpless impassivity at the sight of a lock of his dead mother's hair. Finding it expedient to make Legree superstitious, she established this side of his character belatedly and ineptly, and she failed to understand that

her conception of the power of motherhood was not universally shared.

In short, the reader's admiration is interrupted by idealistic and sentimental material that does not support Stowe's goal of depicting life as it was. Nor is this inconsistency surprising: No American had ever written such a novel, one realistic in impulse and directed at a current social problem of the greatest magnitude. She had no models and could not draw upon her own experiences.

Like Twain and Howells after her, Stowe did not banish Romanticism from her novels, but her commitment to realism is clear. Thirty years before Twain boasted of his accomplishments with dialect in *The Adventures of Huckleberry Finn* (1884), and nearly two decades before Bret Harte popularized the concept of local color, Stowe used dialects—not with perfect consistency but not for the conventional purpose of humor either. For the first time in major American fiction, dialect served the purpose of generating a credible environment for a serious narrative. In the process, Stowe changed the perceptions of hundreds of thousands of readers forever.

Stowe seldom brought her psychological insights to bear on the development of her main characters, with the result that the less important ones invariably seem more convincing. Whether because her most productive years antedated the time of the realistic novel and particularly the psychological novel, or because she felt too strongly the nineteenth century prohibition against a woman exploring the conflicts and repressions of her own life, Stowe left unwritten what might have constituted her richest vein of realism. She never wrote a novel expressing how it felt to be a vocationless Harriet Beecher approaching womanhood or the second Mrs. Calvin Stowe struggling with sickness, poverty, and the multitudinous demands of husband and children. The woman who wrote of domesticity in her time avoided calling attention to its tensions, exactions, and restrictions. Whatever else family life meant to Stowe, it helped prepare her to do what no American novelist had done before: write powerfully and feelingly about slavery.

Other major works

SHORT FICTION: *The Mayflower: Or, Sketches of Scenes and Characters of the Descendants of the Pilgrims*, 1843; *Sam Lawson's Oldtown Fireside Stories*, 1872.

POETRY: *Religious Poems*, 1867.

NONFICTION: *Sunny Memories of Foreign Lands*, 1854; *Lady Byron Vindicated*, 1870; *Palmetto Leaves*, 1873.
CHILDREN'S LITERATURE: *First Geography for Children*, 1833 (published under sister Catharine's name).
MISCELLANEOUS: *A Key to Uncle Tom's Cabin*, 1853.

Bibliography

Boydston, Jeanne, Mary Kelley, and Anne Margolis. *The Limits of Sisterhood: The Beecher Sisters on Women's Rights and Woman's Sphere*. Chapel Hill: University of North Carolina Press, 1988.

Hedrick, Joan D. *Harriet Beecher Stowe: A Life*. New York: Oxford University Press, 1993.

Stowe, Charles Edward. *Life of Harriet Beecher Stowe*. Boston: Houghton Mifflin, 1889.

Sundquist, Eric J., ed. *New Essays on "Uncle Tom's Cabin."* Cambridge, England: Cambridge University Press, 1986.

Tompkins, Jane. *Sensational Designs: The Cultural Work of American Fiction, 1790-1860*. New York: Oxford University Press, 1985.

Wagenknecht, Edward. *Harriet Beecher Stowe: The Known and the Unknown*. New York: Oxford University Press, 1965.

TATYANA TOLSTAYA

Born: Leningrad, Soviet Union; May 3, 1951

Principal short fiction

Na zolotom kryl'tse sideli, 1989 (*On the Golden Porch*, 1989); *Sleepwalker in a Fog*, 1992.

Other literary forms

Tatyana Tolstaya is known primarily for her short fiction.

Achievements

When her first collection of short stories was published in the United States in 1989 as *On the Golden Porch*, Tatyana Tolstaya was acclaimed by critics as an original and important new voice in Soviet literature. Her second book, also a group of stories, published in 1992 as *Sleepwalker in a Fog*, was generally conceded to be a worthy successor to her well-received first collection. Among those who paid enthusiastic tribute to Tolstaya were the American poet laureate Joseph Brodsky and Helena Goscilo, editor of *Balancing Acts: Contemporary Stories by Russian Women Writers* and *Heritage and Heresy: Recent Fiction by Russian Women*.

Biography

Tatyana Tolstaya was born in what was then the city of Leningrad in the Soviet Union (now St. Petersburg, Russia) on May 3, 1951, the daughter of Nikita Tolstoy, a professor of physics, and Natalia Lozinskaya. Her great-granduncle was the writer Leo Tolstoy, and her grandfather, also a writer, was Alexei Tolstoy. Tolstaya was graduated from Leningrad State University in 1974 with a degree in languages and literatures. She worked as a junior editor in the Oriental literature department of a publishing house in Moscow and later held the following positions in American universities: writer-in-residence at the University of Richmond, senior lecturer in Russian literature at the University of Texas at Austin, and writer-in-residence at Texas Tech University, Lubbock. In May, 1974, she married Andrei Lebedev, a professor of philology; with their two sons, they settled in Moscow. Her short stories were published in several Soviet journals as well as in *The New Yorker*.

Analysis

The title of Tatyana Tolstaya's story "Na zolotom kryl'tse sideli" ("On the Golden Porch") comes from an old Russian counting song that names several different unrelated persons—a czar, a king, a cobbler, and so forth. This is an appropriate allusion because the collection comprises stories about all sorts of people—a five-year-old girl and her nanny, a little boy in love with a beautiful neighbor, an old woman who still dreams of joining her first lover, a desperate young woman who traps a coarse and insensitive man into marriage, a shy fat man who dreams his life away—to mention only a few of the disparate and varied characters. The stories have some elements in common. Similar settings, themes, and style give the stories more unity and connection with one another than the nursery-rhyme title might suggest. A similar kind of variety, as well as unifying elements, characterizes the stories in *Sleepwalker in a Fog* as well.

The stories are all set in Moscow or Leningrad, with an only slightly less frequent setting being the dacha, or country summer home so often found in Russian literature. More particularly, the stories repeatedly contrast the cramped, drab, and dismal environments of late twentieth century Soviet citizens with the idyllic life in rural surroundings. There are exceptions to the idyllic quality of the dacha settings, but the connotation is always consistent with relaxation, plenitude, and natural beauty.

Tolstaya seems to have particular favorites among the kinds of characters she portrays; innocent though sometimes mischievous children; hardworking and loving elderly people, especially women; and a distinctive group of weak, deluded, and disillusioned persons of less determinate age but all suffering from vulnerability, deprivation of one sort or another, and a strong tendency to mix dreams and fantasy with harsh reality.

While there is not a completely cheerful story in the two collections, there is much that is joyful, merry, tender, and humorous. The stories are not tightly plotted. Incidents and events are used to reveal characters' interactions, situations, and conditions. Tolstaya seems to be more concerned with evoking moods and portraying unforgettable characters, whether a child dreaming of running away with a beautiful woman who betrays him, an old nanny who spends her life living for others, a weak and ineffectual librarian who longs for love, or a no-longer-young woman who traps a man into a loveless marriage. In fact, all the principal characters in her collections have stories that lift them out of the ordinary, into the realms of brilliant, rich imagination.

Tolstaya has been lauded as one of the most original and impressive writers of the late twentieth century in the Soviet Union. Her use of multivoiced narrators has been cited, as has her ability to combine sadness with humor, tenderness with cruelty. Her tendency to use objects in anthropomorphic ways has also been praised: Gardens wave handkerchiefs, cabbage soup talks to itself, dresses tuck up their knees inside dark trunks, and a lamp shade is young and skittish.

The metaphor of dream is one of Tolstaya's most distinctive devices. It appears in almost all of her stories; some of them consist almost entirely of dreams. The overall effect is evocative, evanescent, wry, and sometimes bizarre. Her stories have a natural, conversational style, whether in the narrator's voice, in the talk among characters, or even in a character's monologue. Tolstaya's themes reveal her special concerns: the dreadful contrasts between the disappointments and failures of everyday life and the joyful life of the imagination, between reality and fantasy, and between dream and nightmare.

Three stories of Tolstaya's first collection exemplify both the similarities and the contrasts in her writing. One is set in Leningrad, the other two in a dacha. All three stories are told from the point of view of a child, one of Tolstaya's favorite narrative forms. This method allows her to use a fluid, rambling conversational style, laden with images and strong feeling. In all three stories, the nature of childhood, which is not entirely innocent, is contrasted with cruel betrayals by adults, indeed, by life.

The differences, however, are what make each story distinctive and memorable in its own way.

The title story of the first collection alludes to a Russian counting rhyme in its title. Beginning with a brief poetic description of childhood as a garden, it shifts to the less idyllic aspects of childhood and uses several images of blood to convey the cruel and frightening side of that period. For example, a beautiful neighbor sells strawberries, her fingers red with berry blood. The narrator recalls how the same beautiful neighbor once smiled about her red hands after she had just killed a calf, and thus the contrast is established. The child narrator's fears are expressed in fantasies about her mother crawling over broken glass to steal a strawberry runner. Uncle Pasha, the scary neighbor's elderly, meek, henpecked husband, an accountant, runs every day to catch the commuter train to Leningrad. With his black cuff protectors, his scurrying to and from his job in a smoky basement, Uncle Pasha inevitably reminds one of Nikolai Gogol's Akaky Akakyevich. Uncle Pasha's house, however, is an Aladdin's cave of treasures, which are described in fantastic terms. With abrupt speed, the accountant grows old, and his treasure-filled room is now seen with the adult eyes of the narrator as filled with trash and rubbish, tacky, worn, cheap, fake. Uncle Pasha freezes to death on the porch. Juxtaposed against the picture of him face down in the snow are white snow daisies growing between his still fingers.

"Liubish'—ne liubish'" ("Loves Me, Loves Me Not"), the first story in the collection, is also told by a child, a five-year-old who resents having to be taken to the park by Maryvanna, an old servant, whom the child hates because of her ugliness, her poverty, her endless boring reminiscences. The old woman appears to be harmless, but the poems that she recites to the child are filled with frightening images that express night fears of monsters and other threatening creatures that never appear in the daytime. The child's occasional bouts of flu give rise to a different kind of fantasy, fever dreams of banging red drums, a round loaf of bread running along an airfield with a nasty smile, tiny planes like bugs with claws. A flea market provides another setting for fantastic people and objects. In contrast to Maryvanna, who personifies the self-absorption and silly, scary kind of adult, there is Nanny Grusha, who is too old and feeble to go out but who understands the child's anxieties and suffering and weeps compassionate tears with wordless love.

"Svidanie s ptitsei" ("Date with a Bird") is another story set in the country, told by a detached and omniscient narrator who observes the boyish play and infatuation with a beautiful, fantasizing woman named Tamila. Petya is completely captivated by her stories and her possessions—a ring in the form of a snake, a squashed silver toad, a black robe with a red dragon on the back. Petya vows to himself that he will marry Tamila and lock up Uncle Borya in a tower because he teases and torments the boy with ridicule and nagging. The contrast between the two male figures, the boy and the man, is sharply drawn. Between them is the seductive enchantress. Frightened by a nightmare, Petya wakes up and goes to the room where his grandfather has lain ill for a long time; he is dead. Petya runs to Tamila's dacha and there encounters the final betrayal and disillusionment.

Another group of stories illustrates the capacity to dream and apprehend fantasy on a somewhat more adult level. Among these stories, that of "Peters" serves as an outstanding example. Abandoned by his parents, Peters is brought up by his grandmother, is never allowed to play with other children, and imagines his scoundrel father living on a tropical island. He attends a library school and goes to work in a library after his grandmother dies. Fat and clumsy, Peters lives in fantasies about beautiful ladies and love. When Faina begins her employment in the library, Peters' dreamworld becomes connected to the real world, a trick that Tolstaya often plays on her characters. Then Peters happens to overhear Faina call him "a wimp . . . an endocrinological sissy," and he realizes that his youth is over. Nevertheless, when spring comes, he falls in love with Valentina, a young woman whom he happens to see buying postcards. He imagines that he might be able to astonish and impress her if he knew German; then, in a restaurant, he is picked up by a "flying flower" named Peri, who steals his money. Peters continues to live as in a dream, sleeping through several years of marriage to a stern, unfeeling woman who eventually abandons him. Now old, Peters feels stirring within him a renewed sense of life. He neither desires nor regrets but is simply grateful for life, though it is slipping past him indifferently, treacherously, mysteriously. Still, he sees it as "marvelous, marvelous, marvelous," and with these significant words, the book ends.

In the title story of *Sleepwalker in a Fog*, Tolstaya blends several of her characteristic devices and portraits. Denisov is one of her favorite types: middle aged, pensive, fearful of dying and being forgotten. His fiancée, Lora, is thoughtless, talkative, affectionate. With her in a cramped communal apartment lives her gentle widower father, a retired zoologist who is a bit strange but harmless. In her incessant, mindless chatter, Lora provides a considerable amount of humor in the story, while Papa, laboring over scientific articles for children, is the source of an anxious kind of pathos, wandering every night in his sleep.

Denisov, tormented by doubts and despair, lives in a constant round of visions, nightmares, and dreams. Thus he too, like the old somnambulist, walks through his troubled life in confusion, his waking life a dream. The story takes a bizarre turn as Denisov, attempting to do a favor for a young couple, looks up his comrade Bakhtiyarov, who is relaxing at the Woodland Fairy restaurant. There, events turn nightmarish, as Denisov envisions his friend Makov frozen to death on a mountaintop, while Bakhtiyarov teases and taunts Denisov, who slips into a state resembling the kind of rational illogic that one experiences in dreams. When he wakes up, he finds that everyone has gone. He calls Lora, who thinks that he has gone out of his mind when he tells her that he was locked in a fairy tale. She herself is in the middle of her own nightmare; having taken Papa to a healer in the country, she left him there, and he ran off in his sleep. The story ends in a poetic passage in which Denisov imagines the old man running through the night, through the forest, up and down hills, in the moonlight, smiling, fast asleep.

One of the longer works in Tolstaya's second collection, "Samaia liubimaia" ("Most Beloved"), is set, like many of her stories, in Leningrad and at the dacha. It is a vivid, poignant account of the narrator's recollections of Zhenechka, the woman who has worked for the family as nurse and governess for as long as the children can remember. She has always been there.

The narrator recalls especially the first summer morning at the dacha, when Zhenechka would walk through the house, distribute presents, clear the desk, and get organized for the daily lessons, much resented by the children. Zhenechka is implacable, having taught their mother, and before that, having been their grandmother's childhood friend. Zhenechka wears a hearing aid on her chest that chirrs like a nightingale. Walking with a limp, she wears an orthopedic shoe. She never takes off her amber necklace, because she believes that some sort of healthful electricity emanates from it. She is strict, loving, devoted. Once, Zhenechka gives one of the girls a box, on the cover of which she has written, "Don't wish to be the prettiest; wish to be the most beloved."

The motif of gift-giving is present throughout the story. Tolstaya uses this theme as a very effective way of characterizing Zhenechka. As the children grow up, she continues to bring presents when she comes to visit the family, which is all that she has left in the world. Aging, Zhenechka has become tiresome and boring, endlessly retelling her stories of bygone days. Interspersed with incidents from Zhenechka's last years are brief recollections of the first child she ever took care of, a little deaf boy, and of the only love in her life—"short, stunted, meager."

The story closes with a brief description of the deserted dacha, slowly deteriorating as the grasses take over the path, the mold blooms on the porch, and a spider spins the keyhole shut. The children have all grown up, Zhenechka has died. Although the narrator speaks of the old nurse's wish to be the most beloved as being naïve, the implication is clear that she really was just that. The greatest gift was herself, in her unthinking, simple, and total love.

"The Moon Came Out" is another story about an elderly figure, this time one named Natasha, born fifty years earlier. The story begins with childhood memories of a dacha near Leningrad, of games played to incantations such as "The moon came out behind the cloud." The parents died, but Grandmother hung on to life. Natasha's adolescence is described in Tolstayan fashion, with nightmarish images of filth and horror. There is a brief interlude when Konovalov is attracted to Natasha, but she feels unworthy and retreats into a world of dreams, which the author describes with images of flowers, wind, sleepy forests, bears, and friendly old women—images straight out of the Russian fairy tales on which Tolstaya draws so frequently and effectively.

Natasha becomes a teacher of geography and never mentions the world in her mind, Queen Maud Land.

Natasha lives in a communal flat, crowded, dismal, full of daily humiliations. She goes to Moscow once and falls in love with bearded, joyful Pyotr Petrovich, who has come into the city to shop for his family. As he leaves on the train, quite unaware of Natasha's short-lived devotion, she feels old age gripping her firmly by the shoulder.

Stories in which cruelty and death are themes include "Sarafim," about a misanthrope who kicks a small dog to death, and "Heavenly Flame," about a pointless practical joke played on a man awaiting death in a sanatorium. These themes are also fully expressed in "Limpopo," again a combination of burlesque and fantasy, reality and ridicule, revolving around the narrator's friends, Judy, from Africa, and Lyonechka, a poet who fights for truth. The dismal lives of Soviet citizens under the rule of the Communist Party are described with all the bite and snap of satire, with macabre humor and bitter irony. The political undertones are clearly present but under the guise of weird and grotesque incidents, such as an inexplicable massacre of innocent people by soldiers of "their own side." This story is Tolstaya's richest in terms of wild fancy, a large group of precisely and concisely delineated characters, a plot of complex and enigmatic events, and numerous and widely ranging literary allusions (to Dante, the Old Testament, Russian fairy tales, Don Juan, Alexander Pushkin, Dr. Doolittle, Søren Kierkegaard, and Homer, to mention only a few).

While critics have disagreed over which of her stories is her best, "Limpopo" exemplifies most of the distinctive features of her work. Critics do agree that Tolstaya is indebted to such writers as Gogol, Pushkin, Mikhail Bulgakov, and even Franz Kafka. She seems, however, to have drawn on these writers without losing her own wild imagination, deep and intense sympathy, and wry, sardonic humor. Tolstaya is a writer very much in the Russian tradition yet consistently retaining her own brilliant and original vision.

Bibliography

Goscilo, Helena, ed. *Balancing Acts: Contemporary Stories by Russian Women.* Bloomington: Indiana University Press, 1989.

_____, ed. *Heritage and Heresy: Recent Fiction by Russian Women.* Bloomington: Indiana University Press, 1988.

_____. "Tatyana Tolstaia's 'Dome of Many-Colored Glass': The World Refracted Through Multiple Perspectives," *Slavic Review* 47 (Summer, 1988): 280-290.

Zalygin, Sergei, comp. *The New Soviet Fiction: Sixteen Short Stories.* New York: Abbeville Press, 1989.

MARINA TSVETAYEVA

Born: Moscow, Russia; October 9, 1892

Died: Yelabuga, Soviet Union; August 31, 1941

Principal poetry

Vecherny albom, 1910; *Volshebny fonar*, 1912; *Iz dvukh knig*, 1913; *Razluka*, 1922; *Stikhi k Bloku*, 1922; *Versty I, 1922*; *Psikheya*, 1923; *Remeslo*, 1923; *Posle Rossii*, 1928; *Lebediny stan*, 1957 (*The Demesne of the Swans*, 1980); *Izbrannoe*, 1961; *Selected Poems of Marina Tsvetayeva*, 1971.

Other literary forms

Marina Tsvetayeva wrote a number of plays, including *Konets Kazanovy* (1922; the end of Casanova), *Metel* (1923; the snowstorm), *Fortuna* (1923; fortune), *Priklyuchenie* (1923; an adventure), *Tezey* (1927; Theseus), and *Fedra* (1928; Phaedra). Several of these were later expanded or combined and reissued under different titles. Tsvetayeva's prose is extensive. Parts of her diaries and her many memoirs have appeared in journals and newspapers, mostly abroad. Some of these prose pieces, together with literary portraits, critical essays, and letters, were collected in *Proza* (1953). A prose collection in English, *A Captive Spirit: Selected Prose*, appeared in 1980. Tsvetayeva also translated poetry, prose, and drama into French, and from French into Russian. A modest number of her plays and prose pieces were printed in Soviet journals.

Achievements

Recognition came to Tsvetayeva late in life, following decades of critical neglect, official Soviet ostracism, and émigré hostility. Her suicide during World War II, not known to the world for a long time, engendered critical fascination with the details of her life, eventually followed by publication, republication, and scholarly evaluation of her work. The creative variety and quality of Russian writing in the first quarter of the twentieth century created a situation in which many talented poets, among them Tsvetayeva, escaped public attention. Her adherence to the old orthography and to pre-Revolutionary values, cast into unconventional, awkward-seeming syntax, caused her work to appear disjointed. Only the subsequent careful study of her form and language has revealed the verbal and stylistic brilliance of a unique poetic voice. Political events forced Tsvetayeva to live in exile with artistically conservative Russians who did not understand her poetic experiments. She courageously developed her style, despite exclusion from émigré publishing houses and Soviet rejection of new forms, proudly suffering the ensuing material deprivation. Many of her themes are so closely linked to events in her life that it is difficult to comprehend them without biographical information; the publication of several critical and biographical studies has made her verse more accessible. Translations into English are beginning to appear, and literary scholars now acknowledge her as a major Russian poet.

Biography

Marina Tsvetayeva's birth on October 9, 1892, into an educated, artistic family augured well for her poetic future. Her mother, a talented amateur pianist, instilled in her an appreciation for the fine arts and insisted on rigorous musical training, while her father's respected position as a professor of art at Moscow University provided exposure to the creative community in Russia. Nicolas II himself, with his family, attended the opening of Professor Tsvetayeva's lifelong project, the Moscow Fine Arts Museum. This august event impressed Tsvetayeva and is reflected in both her poetry and prose, possibly contributing to the unswerving loyalty she displayed toward the imperial family, even when the expression of such sympathies proved dangerous. At age six, Tsvetayeva performed at a public piano recital and tried her hand at versification. Her mother's illness in 1902 necessitated a four-year stay abroad, during which Tsvetayeva developed her interest in literature at Swiss and German boarding schools. After the death of her mother in 1906, she reluctantly entered the Moscow *gimnaziya*, where she treated her courses rather casually. No longer attracted to music, she drifted in and out of schools, devoting all of her time to the writing of poetry. She barely managed to complete secondary education, lagging two years behind her graduating class. A collection of poems written in her teens, *Vecherny albom* (evening album), was privately published in 1910 in an edition of five hundred copies. Several critics generously noted artistic promise in the volume, and the poet-painter Max Voloshin introduced Tsvetayeva to Moscow's literary world.

Tsvetayeva's independent, sometimes provocative demeanor—she smoked, bobbed her hair, traveled alone abroad—coupled with a budding literary reputation, brought a measure of local fame. At Voloshin's Crimean house, which served as an artists' colony, she met and shortly thereafter, in 1912, married the eighteen-year-old Sergey Efron, member of a prominent Jewish publishing family. In the same year, she issued her second book of verse, *Volshebny fonar* (the magic lantern), dedicated to her new husband. Neither this collection nor her third, *Iz dvukh knig* (from two books), caused much of a critical stir, with public attention diverted by an abundance of other talented writers and the imminent war. When Tsvetayeva's daughter Ariadna was born in 1912, she immediately became a frequently mentioned star in her mother's verse. Tsvetayeva's writings during the next ten years, disseminated primarily through public readings and occasional journal printing, also failed to receive critical acclaim. These pieces saw publication only in 1922 under the title *Versty I* (milestones I).

The Bolshevik Revolution found the poet in Moscow, nursing her second daughter, Irina, while Efron fought with the White Army in the south. Tsvetayeva coped poorly with the hardships of civil war. Unwilling to waste time at nonliterary jobs, she lived on the edge of starvation, and Irina died of malnutrition in a government orphanage in 1920. These years, however, were poetically Tsvetayeva's most productive. Between 1917 and 1921, she completed work that was eventually assembled into "Versty II" (unpublished), *The Demesne of the Swans, Razluka* (separation), and *Remeslo* (craft), and she developed friendships with the foremost poets of the time, among them Aleksandr Blok, Vladimir Mayakovsky, Osip Mandelstam, and Boris Pasternak. By 1921, Efron had made his way to Prague, where Tsve-

tayeva joined him with their surviving daughter a year later. During the following years, much of her work was printed by émigré houses in Berlin, Paris, and Prague. In 1925, having expanded her range to epic poems and plays, and following the birth of her son Georgy, Tsvetayeva set up residence in Paris, where a large colony of anti-Communist Russians had gathered. While her contact with foreign writers remained limited, she corresponded regularly with Marcel Proust and Rainer Maria Rilke. The latter, deeply impressed by her talent, addressed a long elegy to her in 1926.

Tsvetayeva's poetic style developed in exile, heavily reflecting Futurist trends. Its experimental nature did not find favor with conservative émigré writers or the public, and her 1928 collection, *Posle Rossii* (after Russia), largely escaped notice. Reluctantly, Tsvetayeva turned to prose to support herself but never managed a comfortable existence. Her romantic involvements testify to a growing estrangement from Efron, who changed his political outlook in the 1930's and became a Soviet agent. This step had disastrous consequences for the poet. In 1937, her daughter, a confirmed Communist, returned to the Soviet Union. Later that year, Efron was implicated in several political murders, but he escaped to the Soviet Union before he could be brought to trial. Tsvetayeva, now ostracized by fellow exiles and in desperate financial straits, decided to follow her family back to Russia in 1939. Before her departure, she wisely left her manuscripts in several safe places. This collection later facilitated a Tsvetayeva revival by Western researchers.

The poet returned home to a chilly reception. Tsvetayeva's émigré status and well-known pre-Revolutionary sympathies precluded publication of her work. Only one poem appeared in print after her return, and no record of subsequent work exists or has been made public. Instead, a series of tragic events—the aftermath of Stalin's purges—drove her to record thoughts of suicide in her diary. Within months of her arrival, Ariadna was sent to a labor camp, where a Tsvetayeva's sister, Anastasia, also spent the last decade of Stalin's rule. Efron disappeared and was executed some time later. Fellow Russians, fearing political contamination, shunned Tsvetayeva. By 1941, wartime evacuation found her with her teenage son in the Tartar Autonomous Republic, east of Moscow. The village of Elabuga could offer the penniless poet only a job as kitchen maid. Proud and stubborn as always, she insisted on a more dignified occupation.

When an appeal to establishment writers quartered nearby failed, she hanged herself. The villagers, unaware of her artistic credentials, buried her without ceremony in an unmarked grave. Her son Georgy joined the army and is presumed to have been killed in action. When the "Thaw" began after Stalin's death, Ariadna returned from prison and, with the aid of no-longer-silent poets, devoted herself to promoting her mother's literary heritage. In 1956, a Soviet edition of selected poems appeared, followed by public readings and further publication, always in moderate proportion, carefully chosen to avoid anti-Soviet allusions. In 1980, the Moscow Excursion Bureau instituted a tour of places associated with Marina Tsvetayeva, during which the guide recited generous excerpts of her poetry. This revival, accompanied by an intense interest in her remarkable life, led to a Tsvetayeva cult in the Soviet Union and a lively black market in her work, finally giving her the recognition so long withheld.

Analysis

Marina Tsvetayeva's poetry is notable for its stylistic innovations, peculiarity of language, political sympathies, and autobiographical intensity. She did not immediately achieve mastery of style. Her early work shows that she was searching for a voice of her own, re-creating the language of Moscow's high society in a rather stilted, overly elegant fashion, punctuated by allusions to childhood and romantic longings that do not always mesh with her aristocratic tone. By the time she composed the poems collected in *Versty I*, the ornate phrasing had developed into a simpler language, but one reflecting old, already archaic Russian usage, thus evoking the poetic diction of earlier centuries. At the same time, Tsvetayeva destroyed this historic illusion by incorporating deliberately incongruous colloquialisms and by placing sacred Church Slavonic phrases in coarse contexts. This stylistic violence is redeemed by the expressive, sometimes whimsical quality of her language, which became the trademark of her later work. She selects significant words, often creating new ones by building on familiar roots, which can evoke extended images or form connections to the next phrase without any grammatical links. One of her favorite devices is the verbless stanza: She achieves the necessary cohesion by clever juxtaposition of sharply delineated nouns, producing a brittle, succinct, almost formulaic precision of line. Her lexical and phonetic experiments, especially her neologisms, evoke the work of Mayakovsky and other Futurists, but she manages to maintain a voice peculiarly her own, which is partially the result of her skill in combining archaisms with colloquialisms to produce an incongruous but striking blend of tradition and novelty.

In much of her later work, she also shifts the stress within the poetic line, carefully selecting her vocabulary to accommodate such prosodic deformation. Depending on the desired effect, Tsvetayeva drops unstressed syllables, adds dashes to represent syllables, or adds syllables to words, occasionally generating such awkward sequences that she feels it necessary to give intonation or pronunciation information in footnotes. Intensely interested in language expansion, she delighted in pushing poetic devices beyond existing limits. When employing enjambment, she broke the very word in half, creating odd, internal rhymes. These metric innovations, combined with her highly unusual diction, were responsible in part for the relative neglect which Tsvetayeva's work suffered for some time.

Theoretically, Tsvetayeva favored lost causes and failures. The most prominent example is *The Demesne of the Swans*, a cycle of mourning for the defeated White Army. The same compassion appears in the 1930 cycle on Mayakovsky, following his suicide, and in the poems condemning the German invasion of Czechoslovakia. Her loyalty to and love for the past led her again and again to reinterpret motifs from classical literature, with a particular emphasis on Russia's old epics and folklore.

A knowledge of Tsvetayeva's life does not merely enhance an understanding of her work; it is vital to it. Her poetry is a kind of diary in verse, a chronological account of her experiences, often inaccessible without further elucidation. When preparing her work for safekeeping before returning to Russia, she recognized the hurdles facing the reader and provided explanatory footnotes for many pieces. Even so, her verse demands time and attention before it yields its richness, and she is generally considered to be a difficult poet. The phonetic and semantic interplay which characterizes much of her work poses formidable challenges to the translator. Her inability or unwillingness to exist harmoniously with her surroundings—she continually stressed her otherness—led to a crippling isolation long before political exigencies forced her to extremes. While this withdrawal from the general community nourished her talents, it also lost her publishers, readers, friends, and family. In a December 30, 1925, letter to A. Tesková, she confessed that she had no love for life as such, caring only for its transformation into art. When that was no longer possible, she chose to end her existence.

Tsvetayeva's first book of verse, *Vecherny albom*, already shows the talent and originality of the later perfectionist, although it is still dominated by the immature, conventionally romantic confessions of a young girl. The poems are grouped around two thematic centers: hero worship and childhood feelings. She admires those who achieve a measure of exaltation and personal glory despite handicaps and mundane origin, among them Napoleon, Sarah Bernhardt, and Huck Finn. A special series is devoted to the doomed nobles featured in Edmond Rostand's works. When Tsvetayeva treats her early family life, she is equally idealistic, expressing impatience with the ways of the world: "I thirst for miracles/ Now, this minute, this very morning." The nursery verses also contain a fairy-tale dimension, filled with endearing diminutives, storytelling, the figure of her mother, and her own fear of leaving this shelter for adulthood. The metrical line and strophe are still traditional, although occasionally enlivened by flashes of lexical innovation. The second collection, *Volshebny fonar*, dedicated to her bridegroom, does not differ significantly in theme and style. The desire to linger in the safe haven of childhood remains strong. She implores Efron to honor these sentiments: "Help me to remain/ A little girl, though your wife," so that the marriage will proceed "From one fairytale into another." Family, friends, and husband are celebrated in sad and joyful verses. While a few snatches of brisk dialogue point to her later telegraphic style, rhyme and meter are strictly conventional. Forty-one poems from these first two volumes were collected in *Iz dvukh knig*, concluding Tsvetayeva's idealistic, romantic period.

Versty I (milestone I) represents the maturing of Tsvetayeva's poetry—hence the title. In this collection, she trims her lexical material to a minimum, focusing on sharply delineated images to produce an aphoristic style, and her rigid metrical design gives way to the more contemporary mixed meter, called *dolniki*, with which she had begun to experiment. The book serves as a poetic chronicle of the year 1916. Its unifying theme is the city of Moscow, to which she pays homage in every group of poems. She connects writers, friends, and family with various places in town, and she employs diverse poetic personae (tavern queens and beggars) and a range of colorful, lower-class expressions. Among those poets singled out are Anna Akhmatova, Blok, and Mandelstam. In cycles dedicated to the first two, Tsvetayeva cleverly rephrases the artists' own poetic idiom and adapts their metrical peculiarities to her own compositions, giving the reader the strange impression of two simultaneous poetic voices. A brief infatuation with Mandelstam resulted in an exchange of dedications. Finally, there are personal poems, walks around the city with Ariadna, and the poet's first separation from her daughter. In one striking composition, she envisions her own grand funeral procession winding through the streets of Moscow, quite unlike the pauper's burial for which she was destined. The voice of alienation, of being out of place, so dominant in her later verse, already prevails in a number of poems in this volume.

The Demesne of the Swans, Tsvetayeva's most controversial book, saw its first publication only in 1957, with a later edition in 1980 featuring English translations facing the original. The printings in the West evoked protest in the Soviet Union, where the work has never been published. Although Tsvetayeva's expressionistic technique and verbal brilliance are particularly evident in these cycles, the provocative theme of a noble, courageous White Army overrun by vile Bolshevik hordes dominates the book. Tsvetayeva's outrage at the destruction of venerated tradition by reincarnated Tartar hordes screams from almost every page. In chronicling the downfall of czarism, starting with Nicolas II's abdication and ending with the Communist victory in 1920, the poet reaches into Russia's epic past for motifs. She compares the White Army to the doomed troops of Prince Igor's campaign, whose defeat at the hands of looting Asiatics foreshadowed Russia's long suffering under the Tartar yoke. Conversely, the Red Army is depicted as an unseemly mob, stampeding all that is sacred and precious into the dust. Tsvetayeva's anguish concerning the unknown fate of Efron is evident but is overshadowed by the national tragedy, which she describes in dramatic effusion: "White Guard, your path is destined to be high/ . . . Godlike and white is your task/ And white is your body that must lie in the sands." Even the more personal poems in the volume are saturated with her hatred of the new regime. The intensity attending Tsvetayeva's treatment of the civil war is in marked contrast to the poet's customary nonpolitical, disinterested stance and affected her standing in the Soviet Union.

The remainder of Tsvetayeva's lyric output continues the driving rhythm, the aphoristically compressed line, and the discordant sound patterns introduced in *Versty I*. Rejection of the environment and notes of despair appear ever more frequently in her verse. Following the Russian Revolution, she also produced epic narratives, adding new dimensions to her style but still basing the narrative on private experience or reaching into Russian history to re-create its heroic legacy.

Tsvetayeva's verse is part of the general poetic flowering and experimentation of the early twentieth century. Her approaches reflect the innovations of Russian Futurists, but she manages to preserve a voice of her own. Despite isolation and hardship in exile, she continued to explore new means of poetic expression, maintaining an artistic link with developments in the Soviet Union. When her extensive output was finally collected and published, she began to emerge as a major Russian poet.

Other major works

PLAYS: *Konets Kazanovy*, 1922; *Fortuna*, 1923; *Metel*, 1923; *Priklyuchenie*, 1923; *Tezey*, 1927; *Fedra*, 1928; *Izbrannye proizvedeniya*, 1965.

NONFICTION: *Proza*, 1953; *A Captive Spirit: Selected Prose*, 1980; *Letters: Summer, 1926*, 1985 (with Boris Pasternak and Rainer Maria Rilke); *Art in the Light of Conscience: Eight Essays on Poetry*, 1992.

Bibliography

Glad, John, and Daniel Weissbrot, eds. *Russian Poetry: The Modern Period*. Iowa City: University of Iowa Press, 1978.

Grossman, Joan Delaney, ed. and trans. *The Diary of Valery Bryusov, with Reminiscences by V. F. Khodasevich and Marina Tsvetaeva*. Berkeley: University of California Press, 1980.

Karlinsky, Simon. *Marina Tsvetaeva: The Woman, Her World, and Her Poetry*. New York: Cambridge University Press, 1986.

Poggioli, Renato. The Poets of Russia, 1890-1930. Cambridge, Mass.: Harvard University Press, 1960.

Proffer, Ellendea, ed. *Tsvetaeva: A Pictorial Biography*. Ann Arbor, Mich.: Ardis, 1980.

Schweitzer, Viktoria. *Tsvetaeva*. London: Harvill, 1992.

ANNE TYLER

Born: Minneapolis, Minnesota; October 25, 1941

Principal long fiction

If Morning Ever Comes, 1964; *The Tin Can Tree*, 1965; *A Slipping-Down Life*, 1970; *The Clock Winder*, 1972; *Celestial Navigation*, 1974; *Searching for Caleb*, 1976; *Earthly Possessions*, 1977; *Morgan's Passing*, 1980; *Dinner at the Homesick Restaurant*, 1982; *The Accidental Tourist*, 1985; *Breathing Lessons*, 1988; *Saint Maybe*, 1991.

Other literary forms

In addition to her novels, Anne Tyler has published more than forty short stories, including several in *Harper's*, *Mademoiselle*, *The New Yorker*, *Seventeen*, and the *Southern Review*. Two stories appeared in the O. Henry Prize volumes for 1969 and 1972 and others in the first edition of the Pushcart Prize anthology (1976), *Best American Short Stories* (1977), *Stories of the Modern South* (1978, 1981), *The Editor's Choice: New American Stories* (1985), *New Women and New Fiction* (1986), *Louder Than Words* (1989), and several anthologies of American literature. Tyler has also written several autobiographical and personal essays, one for *The Washington Post* in 1976 and another for *The Writer on Her Work* (1980), edited by Janet Sternburg. Since 1975, her reviews of current fiction, criticism, and biography have appeared in major newspapers and magazines.

Achievements

Despite praise for the truth of her characterizations and her eye for details, Tyler did not receive much national recognition for her fiction until the publication of her sixth novel, *Searching for Caleb*. Prior to 1976, the largest segment of her audience was in the South, although her short stories appeared in prestigious national magazines throughout the 1960's and 1970's. Her strong supporters have included John Updike, who has favorably reviewed her novels for *The New Yorker*, and Reynolds Price, who was Tyler's professor at Duke University. Since 1976, Tyler has gained increasing recognition. In 1977, the American Academy and Institute of Arts and Letters cited her as a novelist of excellence and promise. *Earthly Possessions* and *Morgan's Passing* also received largely favorable national reviews. While a few critics, including Updike, expressed some disappointment in *Morgan's Passing*, the Writers Workshop of the University of Rochester awarded it the sixth annual Janet Heidinger Kafka Prize for fiction by an American woman.

With the publication of *Dinner at the Homesick Restaurant*, her first novel to make the best-seller list, Tyler at last acquired full national stature. As a result of this increasing recognition and praise, scholarly studies of Tyler's work, including her early novels, began to appear. Tyler's reputation as a major contemporary American novelist was fixed with the publication of *The Accidental Tourist*, which won the 1985/1986 National Book Critics Circle Award for fiction; the successful 1988 film version of the novel increased Tyler's popularity with the reading public. *Breathing Lessons* was nominated for the National Book Award and won the 1989 Pulitzer Prize for fiction.

Biography

Anne Tyler was born in Minneapolis, Minnesota, on October 25, 1941, to Phyllis Mahon, a social worker, and Lloyd Parry Tyler, an industrial chemist. She was the oldest of four children, the only girl. Both parents were Quakers dedicated to finding an ideal community, a quest that produced the theme of frustrated idealism in Tyler's fiction. Tyler spent most of her early years from infancy until age eleven in various rural Quaker communes scattered throughout the Midwest and South. When she was six, the family was settled in Celo, North Carolina—a large, isolated valley commune virtually independent of the outside world. Growing up in North

Carolina, she listened carefully to the stories of the tobacco handlers and tenant farmers, realizing that such stories could form the basis for literature. She was also to rely heavily on the North Carolina tobacco country as the setting for her early novels, especially *The Tin Can Tree* and *A Slipping-Down Life*. When Tyler was eleven, she and her family moved to Raleigh, where they finally settled into an "ordinary" middle-class existence. There, Tyler attended Broughton High School and received encouragement in her writing. She also discovered the work of Eudora Welty, which was to have great influence on Tyler's own fiction.

In September, 1958, Tyler entered Duke University as an Angier Duke Scholar majoring in Russian. She was encouraged by Price, who taught her freshman composition and later introduced her to his agent. At Duke, Tyler helped edit the *Archive* (the student literary magazine), published three early stories there, acted in several productions of the Wesley Players, and learned much about the craft of fiction from reading Leo Tolstoy and other major Russian novelists. She twice received the Anne Flexner Award for creative writing at Duke and was graduated Phi Beta Kappa, just three years after entering, in 1961. In September, 1961, Tyler began work on a master's degree in Russian at Columbia University. She completed the coursework for the degree but quit before writing her thesis. The following summer she spent in Maine, supporting herself by working on a schooner and proofreading for a local newspaper.

In 1962, Tyler returned to Duke University as the library's Russian bibliographer. That fall, she met her future husband, Taghi Modarressi, an Iranian child psychiatry student at the Duke Medical Center. The couple married in May, 1963, three months after the publication of Tyler's first short story in a national magazine. They moved to Montreal, Canada, that spring; during their four years there, Tyler wrote her first novel, taught herself Persian in anticipation of living in Iran, and worked as a librarian at the McGill University law library. In September, 1965, she gave birth to her first child, Tezh, a girl. The publication of *The Tin Can Tree* followed the next month.

In June, 1967, The Modarressis moved to Baltimore, Maryland. Tyler's short stories continued to appear frequently in national publications between 1965 and 1970. A second daughter, Mitra, was born in November, 1967. A dedicated mother and a productive, organized writer, Tyler managed her dual careers for years by writing in the mornings while her children were at school. Although her two daughters moved to other cities while attending college, Tyler and her husband continued to live in Baltimore.

Analysis

Reynolds Price once said that Anne Tyler is the closest thing the South has to an urban novelist, indicating her somewhat unusual position among late twentieth century American writers: a Southerner with a traditional interest in family, community, and the past; a modern woman fascinated with change and drawn to urban life; a writer with faith in humankind's ability to love and endure yet keenly aware of the difficulties of contemporary life, particularly the failure of communication within the family.

Tyler's view of human nature, her talent for realistically capturing generations of squabbling families, her keen ear for dialogue, and her interest in character and the isolation of the individual within the family derive from various sources. Her own "setting apart" experience in the North Carolina wilderness, her early childhood habit of telling herself bedtime stories for rest and amusement, and her long periods listening to tenant farmers' stories contributed substantially to her art. Shy, quiet, and keenly observant, she listened carefully to the stories the workers told. Later, she could call up the words of her own characters. "Having those voices in my ears all day," she has written, "helped me to summon up my own characters' voices." Additionally, with Price as her teacher and Eudora Welty as a model, Tyler saw early in her career the rich source of literary materials offered by commonplace experience. Critic Paul Binding also cites the influence of Tyler's study of the Russian masters, particularly Ivan Turgenev and Anton Chekhov, as a basis for her tolerant and warm portrayal of multiple generations of entangled and eccentric families. Finally, perhaps most prominent is Tyler's own witness to her parents' idealism, their quest for a perfect community throughout her youth, and later their apparently easy adjustment to an ordinary existence in a middle-sized Southern city. The heroes of Tyler's novels are complex people, enriched and deepened by experience and able to enjoy life because they view themselves and others with tolerance and wit.

Searching for Caleb marked a turning point in Tyler's

career. It was her first novel to receive national recognition, at a time when Tyler's own reviews began to appear in national publications. As Walter Sullivan commented in 1977 when reviewing *Searching for Caleb* for the *Sewanee Review*, Tyler "retained" in her work "a kind of innocence . . . a sense of wonder at all the crazy things in the world and an abiding affection for her own flaky characters." *Searching for Caleb* was also evidence that Tyler had retained her Southern literary roots and her delight in huge families and the range of human characters those families produce. The novel is something of a combined family history and detective story, tracing five generations of one large, dichotomous, and extremely long-lived clan, the Pecks of Baltimore, from the 1880's through 1973. Tyler shows her strong fascination with urban life, a result perhaps of her own early life in remote areas.

As the title suggests, *Searching for Caleb* involves a quest for the vanished Caleb, the great uncle of the novel's protagonists, Duncan and Justine Peck, and the half brother of their grandfather, Daniel Peck. Representing one side of the family, Caleb, Justine, and Duncan are outcasts of a sort: spirited, talented, imaginative, and free individuals unable or unwilling to live as family rules dictate. Caleb becomes a musician, Justine a fortune-teller. Duncan, her husband and first cousin, leads an unsettled life as a mechanic and jack-of-all-trades; Duncan dismays his family.

The other side of the family, the Pecks of Roland Park, headed by Daniel, are uniformly humorless and restricted. The women, though educated, are unthreatening; the men, all attorneys educated at the Johns Hopkins University, drive black Fords and dress in Brooks Brothers suits. They are, above all, clannish, living side by side in similar Roland Park houses. For them, family tradition and training—in effect, the past—are inescapable. Even Daniel's late-life quest for his half brother evolves from his ties to family and an unsettled conflict. It represents a delayed response to the question frequently asked in his childhood: "Daniel, have you seen Caleb?"

Searching for Caleb also illustrates the author's belief in the need for human adaptability, tolerance, and love. Justine epitomizes the philosophy. She weathers a dark and uncertain childhood with a depressive mother, frequent moves with her restless husband, the death of both parents and her grandfather, and the loss of her one daughter in marriage to a Milquetoast minister. Yet, she remains spirited and continues to love her family. She

insists on visiting Roland Park, a longing Duncan cannot understand, and she is committed to finding Caleb, not only out of a love of travel and adventure but also to share the experiences with her grandfather and to find her own roots. With its focus on community and family and its delineation of the unsettled conflicts of the past impacting on the present, *Searching for Caleb* indicates Tyler's own roots in the family of Southern literature.

Of all Tyler's novels, *Dinner at the Homesick Restaurant* most inspires comparison with the work of Flannery O'Connor. The title is reminiscent of O'Connor's wit and irony, and the mood of the novel, as one reviewer noted, is that of "O'Connor's Gothic South" with its "sullen, psychic menace." *Dinner at the Homesick Restaurant*, representing what Updike called a "darkening" of Tyler's art, focuses not on the husband who abandons his family to find a new life but on the family he left behind. It is a stunning psychological portrait of the Tulls, Pearl and her three children, and the anger, guilt, hurt, and anxiety they feel growing up in an uncertain world without a father. All carry their pain through life, illustrating more profoundly than any of Tyler's earlier books the past's haunting influence on the present.

Covering thirty-five years and three generations of Tulls, the novel opens with Pearl on her deathbed. This first chapter, reminiscent of Katherine Anne Porter's short story "The Jilting of Granny Weatherall," depicts Pearl as a stoical, frightened woman who has weathered a youth filled with dread of being an old maid, a quick marriage, and a lonely struggle to rear three "flawed" children: Cody, the oldest boy, a troublemaker from childhood "prone to unreasonable rages"; Jenny, the only girl, "flippant" and "opaque"; and Ezra, his mother's favorite, a gentle man who has not "lived up to his potential," but instead has become the ambitionless owner of the Homesick Restaurant. Not one of Pearl's children has turned out as she wished. Consequently, she, like other Tyler characters, feels "closed off" from her family, the very children to whom she has devoted her life. Later chapters reveal why, focusing on each of the children in turn and tracing the evolution of their lives as well as their fear of their mother's rages. All, like their mother, end up in some way "destroyed by love."

Tyler's compassionate portrayal of her characters and her characteristic humor do mitigate the darkness of this novel. Although Pearl, her forehead permanently creased from worry, verbally and physically abuses her children, Tyler lets the reader understand the reasons for Pearl's behavior and shows a far mellower Pearl in old age. Jenny, after struggling through medical school, two marriages, and a nervous breakdown, is nursed back to health by her mother. Cody spares no expense in caring for his family, even though he is unable to forgive Pearl for mistreating him as a child. The teenager Cody plays cruel but amusing tricks on his brother Ezra—partly out of resentment of Ezra's being the favorite, but also from Cody's own pain and sense of rejection. Taking slats from Ezra's bed, Cody strews the floor with pornographic magazines so Pearl will think Ezra the kind of disappointment she finds Cody to be. Later, after stealing Ezra's sweetheart, he recognizes not only his guilt but also his love for his brother. These tales fill out the dark psychological portrait Tyler draws, making *Dinner at the Homesick Restaurant* a confirmation of life's difficulty as well as of the value of love.

A mood of dark comedy pervades *The Accidental Tourist*. A murder occurs in this work, and a sense of the inexplicable, tragic nature of reality moves the plot and forms a backdrop for the novel. The book opens with Macon and Sarah Leary returning from a truncated beach vacation and the sudden announcement by Sarah that she wants a divorce. Macon, the central character, is a forty-four-year-old writer of guidebooks for business travelers who find themselves in foreign places but prefer the familiarity of home. The logo for the series, entitled Accidental Tourist, is a winged armchair, a motif suggesting Macon's attitude toward the disruptions of travel. In the opening pages of *The Accidental Tourist*, the reader learns of the death of Macon and Sarah's twelve-year-old son, Ethan, who was killed in a robbery at a burger stand. Besides their grief at the death of their son, Macon and Sarah must confront the permanent jarring of their world by the random nature of crime: The robber shot Ethan as an afterthought; Ethan and his friend had impulsively stolen away from a summer camp. With Sarah's leaving, Macon's life tailspins, yet he strives desperately to maintain control, to reduce life to its simplest terms. He sleeps in one sheet sewn together like a body bag and showers in his shirt to save on laundry. In a spirit of fun, Tyler gives Macon an alter ego, a Welsh corgi, Edward, who becomes increasingly surly as Macon's life disintegrates. Through Edward, Tyler introduces the unpredictable Muriel Pritchett, a dog trainer set on finding a father for her sickly son, Alexander.

Told from a limited third-person point of view, *The Accidental Tourist* displays Tyler's art at its best: her eye for idiosyncratic behavior and the accidental quality of reality, her focus on family as the center of life's triumphs and tragedies. The family here is not only Macon and Sarah but also Macon's siblings: his sister Rose, whose romance with Julian Edge, Macon's publisher, forms a dual plot to Macon's romance with Muriel, and his two brothers, Charles and Porter. For part of the novel, Tyler centers on the Leary siblings, all marred by their mother's carefree abandonment of them. Both Charles and Porter are divorced, and Rose now maintains her grandparents' home for her brothers. What is striking about the house is its orderliness—every item in the kitchen is shelved in alphabetical order—and its changelessness. When Macon breaks a leg in a freak accident, he returns to his siblings and resumes life just as if he had never been married, had a child, and lived away for years. The characteristics of families, Tyler suggests, are permanently etched. It is the occurrences of life that constantly shift.

In *The Accidental Tourist*, Tyler depicted the dissolution of a twenty-year marriage following the violent death of the Learys' son. In *Breathing Lessons*, she presents the opposite: the duration of Ira and Maggie Moran's marriage for twenty-eight years. Told primarily through flashbacks as the couple journeys to the funeral of a friend, the novel covers nearly thirty years in one September day and contrasts the Morans' courtship and marriage with the relationship of their son, Jesse, and his former wife, Fiona. From its beginning, *Breathing Lessons* concerns not only Ira and Maggie's bickering, love, and tolerance for each other but also Maggie's struggle to reconcile Jesse and Fiona.

Set in Pennsylvania and Baltimore, the novel has three principal divisions, each told from a restricted third-person point of view. The first and third sections focus on Maggie's consciousness, while the middle section, which constitutes something of an interlude, centers on Ira's thoughts. The first section wittily depicts the music and mores of the 1950's. The second part depicts a side trip in which Ira and Maggie temporarily become involved with an elderly black man who has separated from his wife of more than fifty years. This section also provides Ira's family history and his response to his wife and children. Tyler reveals here a masterful handling of exposition through internal thought sequences and flashbacks. The novel's third section, which introduces the characters of Fiona and Leroy, her daughter, returns to Maggie's thoughts and her memories of Jesse and

Fiona's relationship. A return to Baltimore with Fiona and Leroy completes the section, suggesting the cyclical nature of experience, a central theme in the novel.

From her earliest novels through *Breathing Lessons*, Tyler has skillfully balanced a lighthearted view of human nature with a depth of insight into the darker side of marriage. Maggie and Ira's marriage, while offering a sound balance of two contrasting personality types who can bicker and then reconcile, has its dark side also: a "helpless, angry, confined feeling" which Maggie experiences "from time to time." Ira, too, realizes that marriage involves "the same old arguments, . . . the same old resentments dragged up year after year." The joyful side of Tyler's fiction is her fondness for zany characters, her keen eye for the bizarre in human behavior, which she observes with amused detachment, and her finely tuned ear for human speech. *Breathing Lessons* offers many examples, beginning with the zesty, lower-class names of her characters: Serena, Fiona, Duluth. Maggie herself belongs to a long line of lively, unpredictable Tyler heroines—most expert caretakers. In fact, in both her acute observations of others and her repeated attempts "to alter people's lives," Maggie resembles her creator, the fiction writer who manipulates the lives of her characters to fill her plot.

Bibliography

Betts, Doris. "The Fiction of Anne Tyler." In *Women Writers of the Contemporary South*, edited by Peggy Prenshaw. Jackson: University Press of Mississippi, 1984.

Gullette, Margaret M. *Safe at Last in the Middle Years—The Invention of the Midlife Progress Novel: Saul Bellow, Margaret Drabble, Anne Tyler, and John Updike*. Berkeley: University of California Press, 1988.

Robertson, Mary F. "Anne Tyler: Medusa Points and Contact Points." In *Contemporary American Women Writers: Narrative Strategies*, edited by Catherine Rainwater and William J. Scheick. Lexington: University Press of Kentucky, 1985.

Stephens, C. Ralph, ed. *The Fiction of Anne Tyler*. Jackson: University Press of Mississippi, 1990.

Voelker, Joseph C. *Art and the Accidental in Anne Tyler*. Columbia: University of Missouri Press, 1989.

SIGRID UNDSET

Born: Kalundborg, Denmark; May 20, 1882   **Died:** Lillehammer, Norway; June 10, 1949

Principal long fiction

Fru Marta Oulie, 1907; *Fortaellingen om Viga-Ljot og Vigdis*, 1909 (*Gunnar's Daughter*, 1936); *Jenny*, 1911 (English translation, 1921); *Varen*, 1914; *Kristin Lavransdatter*, 1920-1922 (English translation, 1923-1927; includes *Kransen*, 1920 [*The Bridal Wreath*, 1923]; *Husfrue*, 1921 [*The Mistress of Husaby*, 1925]; *Korset*, 1922 [*The Cross*, 1927]); *Olav Audunssøn i Hestviken* and *Olav Audunssøn og hans børn*, 1925-1927 (*The Master of Hestviken*, 1928-1930, 1934; includes *The Axe*, 1928; *The Snake Pit*, 1929; *In the Wilderness*, 1929; *The Son Avenger*, 1930); *Gymnadenia*, 1929 (*The Wild Orchid*, 1931); *Den brændende busk*, 1930 (*The Burning Bush*, 1932); *Die Saga von Vilmund Vidutan und seiner Gefährten*, 1931; *Ida Elisabeth*, 1932 (*Ida Elizabeth*, 1933); *Den trofaste husfru*, 1933 (*The Faithful Wife*, 1937); *Madame Dorthea*, 1939 (English translation, 1940).

Other literary forms

Sigrid Undset's literary works include short stories, poetry, drama, essays, and autobiographies. In her youth, she favored shorter forms, following her first novel with a one-act play, *I graalysningen* (1908; in the gray light of dawn); a volume of lyrics, *Ungdom* (1910; youth); and four collections of short fiction, *Den lykkelige alder* (1909; the happy age), *Fattige skjæbner* (1912; humble existences), *Splinten av trold speilet* (1917; the splinter from the magic mirror), and *De kloge jomfruer* (1918; the wise virgins). She wrote in German and English as well as in her native Norse, and her numerous articles, essays, and speeches reflected the major social and spiritual concerns from which her fiction grew, such as her *Samtiden* article "Nogen kvindesaks-betragtninger" ("Reflections on the Suffragette Movement") in 1912 and the collection *Et kvindesynspunkt* (1919; a woman's point of view).

Undset's passionate interest in medieval Scandinavian history merged with her conversion to Roman Catholicism, to which she testified fervently in the essays collected in *Kimer i klokker* (1924: the bells are ringing), *Katolsk propaganda* (1927; Catholic propaganda), *Begegnungen und Trennungen: Essays über Christentum und Germanentum* (1931; meetings and partings: essays on Christianity and Germanism), and *Etapper I* and *II* (1929, 1933; *Stages on the Road*, 1934). In *De søkte de gamle stier* (1936; they sought the ancient paths) and *Norske helgener* (1937; *Saga of Saints*, 1934), she explored the lives of great European defenders of the faith.

As one of Nazi Germany's first and strongest opponents, Undset assailed totalitarian aims in "Fortschritt, Rasse, Religion" ("Progress, Race, Religion"), an essay that appeared in *Die Geföhrdung des Christentums durch Rassenwahn und Judenverfolgung* (1935), an anti-Nazi anthology published in Switzerland. Later, from the United States, she continued to attach Nazism and all other forms of modern paganism in the collections *Selvportretter og landskapsbilleder* (1938; *Men, Women, and Places*, 1939), *Tillbake til fremitiden* (1942; *Return to the Future*, 1942), and *Artikler og taler fra krigstiden* (1953; wartime articles and speeches). Her warm friendship with America and the American people is also reflected in her essays "Skjønne Amerika" ("Beautiful America"), "Amerikansk litteratur" ("American Literature"), and "Common Ground," all of which were written during World War II.

Toward the end of her life, Undset published several autobiographical fragments, of which the most detailed are *Elleve år* (1934; *The Longest Years*, 1935) and *Happy Times in Norway* (1942). Her last works, like her first, dwell upon her Christian Scandinavian heritage, and her last theoretical and historical essays, "Scandinavia and the New World" (in *The People's Century*, 1942), "Brotherhood," and "Scandinavian Literature," written in the early 1940's, all stress the peculiarly Scandinavian response to life she celebrated in her novels: "[The] preference for the realities of life . . . [the] interest in the innate disparities which condition our development."

Achievements

Undset's *Kristin Lavransdatter* and *The Master of Hestviken*, two multivolume novels treating the Norway of the thirteenth and fourteenth centuries, received the highest critical acclaim and were translated into every major European language. Undset received the Nobel Prize in Literature in 1928 for these novels, and on them her reputation beyond Norway largely rests. In *Kristin Lavransdatter*, European critics recognized a new dimension of historical fiction, with insights into love and marriage realistically portrayed in the context of an essentially moral universe. With *The Master of Hestviken*, Undset achieved a still greater triumph, a profound insight into the psychological ramifications of guilt which Sigurd Hoel has compared favorably with Fyodor Dostoevski's portrait of Raskolnikov in *Prestupleniye i nakazaniye* (1866; *Crime and Punishment*, 1886).

By 1945, Undset was exhausted from her own battles against Nazi Germany. She returned to Norway to find her home at Lillehammer sadly devastated by the wartime occupation, but on her sixty-fifth birthday, King Haakon awarded her Norway's highest honor, the Grand Cross of the Order of Saint Olav, "for eminent services to literature and to the nation."

Biography

Sigrid Undset was born at Kalundborg, Denmark, on May 20, 1882. Her father, Ingvald Undset, a famous Scandinavian archaeologist, had reacted against the provincial surroundings of his rural boyhood at Østerdal in Norway and the confining atmosphere of Norwegian Lutheranism. Undset's beautiful and intellectual mother, Anna Charlotte Gyth, had been reared by an indulgent Danish aunt and retained both a *grande dame* air and a rationalistic outlook after her marriage to Ingvald Undset, already not a well man. Not surprisingly, Sigrid Undset experienced only perfunctory religious training as a child.

In 1884, the Undsets moved to Christiania (now Oslo), where Undset's liberal parents allowed her to follow her own precocious interests. Her father's illness often shadowed the childhood memories she recorded in *The Longest Years*, which ends at his death when she was eleven, but her home was filled constantly with the atmosphere of the Middle Ages. She often read aloud to her father from medieval texts, perhaps only half understanding but wholly spellbound by the stern power and the splendor of Old Norse poetry.

At sixteen, Undset began to support herself and her family. Her ten years in an Oslo office made her familiar at first hand with the day-to-day struggles of ordinary women. She educated herself by reading voraciously, not only of Norway's past but also of the history of all Western Europe; in addition, she read widely in English literature. Her first literary attempt, a long medieval novel that later evolved into *The Master of Hestviken*, was rejected, and she turned to the problems of modern women, opening *Fru Marta Oulie* with the theme of marital conflict which she never abandoned in her fiction: "I have been unfaithful to my husband."

The first phase of Undset's literary activity extended through World War I as she unflinchingly portrayed women torn between their desire for independence and their yearning to be fulfilled in love and marriage. In 1912, she had married the divorced artist Anders C. Svarstad in Belgium. Despite his impetuosity, he was highly sensitive to color and artistic technique, a quality he shared with Undset. While rearing their three children and Svarstad's three from his former marriage, Undset wrote continuously, describing herself occasionally as "a bad housewife" and criticizing the egotistic materialism of the times that led to the evasion of responsibility. The moral position she had developed by 1918 depended on woman's traditional role. As she worked on her great medieval novels, Undset was increasingly drawn to the altar of the Roman Catholic church. Her marriage was disintegrating under insurmountable stresses, and in 1925, shortly before her formal conversion, it was annulled.

Between the two world wars, Undset firmly fixed her criticism of contemporary culture upon her religious ideals. Many commentators believe that the fiction she wrote during this time was impaired by her attempts to solve all human problems through the Catholic faith alone. Nazism for Undset was only one manifestation of the menace of modern society, and in her last novel, *Madame Dorthea*, she concentrated on the eighteenth century in the rationalistic spirit she had inherited from her mother. One of Undset's last works was the deceptively childlike memoir *Happy Times in Norway*, a celebration of traditional, home-centered Norwegian culture. Upon Undset's death in 1949, she was hailed as a Christian universalist, a relentless enemy of pseudoliberalism and irresponsible individualism.

Analysis

From her first work to her last, the central issue of Sigrid Undset's fiction is loyalty. In her epic medieval novels, Undset analyzed the development of the sense of loyalty to others, to self, and finally to God which motivates all lesser relationships in Christian morality. The pagan Scandinavia to which her father's work drew Undset worshiped gods who knew they themselves would die in flaming *Götterdämmerung*. Since the eventual defeat of good by evil was inevitable, only the manner in which the northern hero died could matter, and the old Nordic tales resound with the song of two-handed battle swords carving bitter destiny into the personal immortality of the saga. As she immersed herself in Scandinavian folklore and history in preparation for *Kristin Lavransdatter*, her reading of the thirteenth century *Njáls saga* became a turning point in Undset's life, she said, because she recognized there the intense psychological pressure exerted on the individual by the old pagan familial society. She came to believe, as she wrote in *Saga of Saints*, that the thirst for loyalty engendered by the ancient Germanic code, however noble its individual exemplifications, was fatally limited by the lack of "a door which leads to freedom for the soul of every human being, even though his deeds . . . have their inevitable consequences and defeat here on earth." In *De søkte de gamle stier*, a collection of sketches of "almost forgotten soldiers of Christ," Undset declared that the eventual victory of the good depends on "whether the wills of individual men and women are directed into an effort to do God's will—even if in life they have not been able to . . . without wavering, deviation and interruption."

Undset's *Kristin Lavransdatter* traces the life of a well-born woman of medieval Norway through youth in *The Bridal Wreath*, maturity in *The Mistress of Husaby*, and old age with *The Cross*. As in all of her fiction, Undset's characters are developed in an immensely detailed social and cultural milieu. By the time she wrote *Kristin Lavransdatter*, Norwegian scholars such as Magnus Olsen and Sigurðr Nordal had applied modern research methods to Scandinavian history, and Undset praised their respect for medieval documents as "examples of literary art," the basis for her re-creation of medieval Nordic life.

In *The Bridal Wreath*, Undset simultaneously depicted youthful love and mature marriage, both impeded by the tragic consequences of broken vows. Kristin's father, Lavrans Björgulfsson, all of his life had been devoted to doing the will of God, but the wife he took at his family's wish came to him secretly flawed by a previous affair. That hidden sin had to be faced and overcome before Lavrans and Ragnfrid could die at peace with God and each other. Kristin herself is betrothed to the good though dull Simon Darre, but she forces her father to break the vow and weds instead the dashing Erlend Nikulausson, a breach of faith which haunts them the remainder of their lives.

As *The Mistress of Husaby*, Erlend's manor, Kristin bears son after son in mounting frustration at Erlend's apparent lack of concern for their future. As she labors to rear their children and improve their estate, Erlend is drawn into a gallant yet abortive attempt to free Norway from the Swedish throne. Because Erlend fails and loses his inheritance, he must live on Kristin's land; his innate nobility however allows him to forget old injuries to an extent that Kristin, fatally, cannot.

In *The Cross*, Kristin's unwillingness to forgive will cause Erlend's needless death. They are separated, and he is living at his last holding, a little hut on the mountain at Haugen, when she visits him there briefly and conceives their last child. At its birth, the countryfolk accuse her of adultery, and in returning to defend her honor, Erlend is killed. Kristin's sons grow away from her, and she at last accepts the pilgrim's road to faith, dying of bubonic plague after she has nursed the poor and outcast as a lay sister in a convent not far from the road where she last saw the houses at Haugen, "high on the topmost mountain ridge."

In the story of Kristin Lavransdatter and Erlend Nikulausson, Undset championed the new, emerging Norway against the old. Kristin slowly and painfully wins her Christian faith, but Erlend perishes, unshriven, through the violence of his Scandinavian warrior's values. The old code of the sagas required the individual himself to execute the justice that he was due, but Undset's traditionally Christian orientation insisted upon the will of God before the will of humanity. Upon secretly plighting their troth, Erlend swears to Kristin, "May God forsake me if woman or maid ever rests in my arms, before I can possess you with law and honour." Kristin, however, replies, "May God forsake me if ever I take another man in my arms as long as I live." To Erlend, human law and honor are tragically uppermost; to Kristin, even though she does not fully understand until she bears her own cross, God's law is finally all.

Despite the great success of *Kristin Lavransdatter*, Undset considered the tetralogy *The Master of Hestviken* to be her masterpiece. Set in a slightly earlier historical period, *The Master of Hestviken* hinges on the conflict between ancient family honor and the new code in which Church and State, rather than the individual, must defend the law. While Kristin's redemption is earned by overcoming the pride that injures others, the long saga of Olav Audunssøn of Hestviken strikes inward to the tender spot of conscience, where a man stands loneliest before his God. Olav's revolt demonstrates the special Norse meaning of contrition as a power for rejuvenation. Henrik Ibsen hinted at such pagan redemption in *Rosmersholm* (1887), when Rebecca West recognizes that "What I have sinned—it is fit I must expiate, " as she goes "gladly" to her death with Rosmer. Undset carried Olav's redemption to its Christian extreme beyond physical death: "here on earth it would never be his to see the radiance of a standard under which he might fight."

The Axe, the first volume of the tetralogy, exposes the bloody family feuds that underlie Olav's exile from Norway and Ingunn, to whom he was betrothed as a child. Olav is nominally Christian, but when Ingunn's relatives deny their marriage, he kills one of them and must flee to Denmark. While waiting for Olav, Ingunn is trapped by a clever young rogue by whom she becomes pregnant; she confesses to Olav on his return. To preserve his own reputation, Olav secretly kills the youth who seduced Ingunn.

In *The Snake Pit*, Olav returns with Ingunn to Hestviken on the Oslo-fjord, where his life comes to resemble the old carving on the hall doorpost of Gunnar of the *Volsunga saga*, stricken by the one snake he could not charm. Olav's human loyalty to Ingunn and to Duke Haakon, whom he follows on an expedition to Norway, helps him restore his estate, but this is a pale shadow of his loyalty to God as Lord, which to Olaf only confirms the old morality. He still takes no account of the man he

secretly killed: "He had had to kill so many a better man in battle, and never taken it to heart." At Ingunn's death, Olav thinks of confession, but he draws back, not knowing whether something prevents him or whether "after all he dared not come forward."

Olav's middle years are spent *In the Wilderness*, as he now knows that he has chosen the path of Cain. Leaving Hestviken, he at last visits London and wins some respite from the snake gnawing at his breast: "It was not that he now thought less of his sin, but that he himself bulked far less in his own eyes." After he returns to defend Hestviken against marauding Swedes, the snake ceases to tear at his heart: "He saw now it was not his suffering that destroyed the happiness of his life . . . sufferings that are of some *avail*, they are like the spearpoints that raise the shield on which the young king's son sits when his subjects do him homage."

The final act of Olav Audunssøn's divine comedy is *The Son Avenger*, in which Olav reaches the end of his human resources and places himself, helpless, at the mercy of God. In solemn irony, Ingunn's illegitimate son Eirik helps Olav to contrition. Olav "must stand forth and could not declare one deed that he had performed from full and unbroken loyalty," but in a final ecstatic vision, "the very rays from the source of light" high on the hill above the fjord "broke out and poured down over him." Olav's loyal spirit had bowed at last before its true Lord.

Darker in spirit than *Kristin Lavransdatter* but no less evocative, *The Master of Hestviken* displays the essentially conservative theological position Undset adopted toward the psychological complex of guilt. Other views of Olav's tragic life are possible. As Sigurd Hoel noted in 1928, both the psychological theory of dangerously suppressing one's emotions and the biological explanation that certain minds are "disposed to melancholia, remorse, and all that is tragic" but Hoel concludes that Undset regarded Olav's "fixed ideas of sin and guilt" strictly from the religious viewpoint: "Olav's fate is the fate of one who disobeys the voice of God."

The twin purposes of Christianity and realism animated all Undset's work. Inspired by the intense attention to detail, the concentration upon personal loyalty, and the breadth of background of the Scandinavian family saga, she joined to these the considerable insight she achieved through her acceptance of Catholic tradition. She felt herself more at home in the Middle Ages than in modern civilization, and through her vividly realized characterizations of Kristin Lavransdatter and Olav

Audunssøn and the wealth of their environments no less than by her contemporary novels, she achieved a moral refuge for all who seek the personal relationship of faith, the only fellowship she thought worthwhile: the fellowship of individual souls in God.

Other major works

SHORT FICTION: *Den lykkelige alder*, 1909; *Fattige skjæbner*, 1912; *Splinten av trold speilet*, 1917; *De kloge jomfruer*, 1918; *Four Stories*, 1969.
PLAY: *I graalysningen*, 1908.
POETRY: *Ungdom*, 1910.
NONFICTION: *Et kvindesynspunkt*, 1919; *Kimer i klokker*, 1924; *Katolsk propaganda*, 1927; *Etapper I* and *II*, 1929, 1933 (*Stages on the Road*, 1934); *Begegnungen und Trennungen: Essays über Christentum und Germanentum*, 1931; *Elleve år*, 1934 (*The Longest Years*, 1935); *De søkte de gamle stier*, 1936; *Norske helgener*, 1937 (*Saga of Saints*, 1934); *Selvportretter og landskapsbilleder*, 1938 (*Men, Women, and Places*, 1939); *Happy Times in Norway*, 1942; *Tillbake til fremitiden*, 1942 (*Return to the Future*, 1942); *Artikler og taler fra krigstiden*, 1953.

Bibliography

Bayerschmidt, Carl F. *Sigrid Undset*. New York: Twayne, 1970.
Gustafson, Alrik. *Six Scandinavian Novelists: Lie, Jacobsen, Heidenstam, Selma Lagerlöf, Hamsun, Sigrid Undset*. New York: American-Scandinavian Foundation, 1940.
Solbakken, Elisabeth. *Redefining Integrity: The Portrayal of Women in the Contemporary Novels of Sigrid Undset*. New York: P. Lang, 1992.
Vinde, Victor. *Sigrid Undset: A Nordic Moralist*. Translated by Babette and Glenn Hughes. Seattle: University of Washington Book Store, 1930.
Winsnes, Andreas Hofgaard. *Sigrid Undset: A Study in Christian Realism*. Translated by P. G. Foote. New York: Sheed & Ward, 1953.

MONA VAN DUYN

Born: Waterloo, Iowa; May 9, 1921

Principal poetry

Valentines to the Wide World, 1959; *A Time of Bees*, 1964; *To See, to Take*, 1970; *Bedtime Stories*, 1972; *Merciful Disguises*, 1973; *Letters from a Father and Other Poems*, 1982; *Near Changes: Poems*, 1990; *If It Be Not I: Collected Poems, 1959-1982*, 1993; *Firefall: Poems*, 1993.

Other literary forms

Two short stories by Mona Van Duyn were published in *The Kenyon Review* in the 1940's. She has published reviews and criticism in *College English, American Prefaces*, and many literary magazines.

Achievements

One of the few poets today who succeed in incorporating a contemporary sensibility within tight and traditional forms. Van Duyn did not receive appropriate recognition until she won the Bollingen Prize in 1971 and her book *To See, To Take* received the National Book Award in the same year. She had, however, won several prizes previous to those—the Eunice Tietjens Award, the Harriet Monroe Award from *Poetry*, the Helen Bullis Award from *Poetry Northwest*, the Hart Crane Memorial Award from American Weave Press, and first prize in the Borestone Mountain Awards Volume of 1968. She was one of the first American poets to be awarded a grant from the National Endowment for the Arts. In 1972-1973 she held a Guggenheim Fellowship. The Loines Prize from the National Institute of Arts and Letters was given to her in 1976, and in 1980 she received a Fellowship of the Academy of American Poets. In recognition of her achievements, Van Duyn was named poet laureate of the United States, a one-year appointment which she held beginning in October, 1992.

Although she is not a prolific writer, she has always been known and admired by her peers. Her poems have been highly praised by poet-critics as diverse as Carolyn Kizer, Richard Howard, and James Dickey. The domestic world, as tightly enclosed as her chosen forms, is the most frequent source of her poetic content. Her achievement is that she makes the most of this material, shining so bright a light on subdued and quotidian events that their poignant and lasting aspects are revealed.

Biography

Born in Waterloo, Iowa, in 1921, Mona Van Duyn began her career by serving as class poet in the first grade in Eldora, Iowa, where her father ran a service station, a cigar store, and a soda fountain. She wrote poems throughout childhood and adolescence, then studied writing at Iowa State Teachers College and the State University of Iowa. She met her husband, Jarvis Thurston, later a professor of English at Washington University in St. Louis, while they were students. They were married on August 31, 1943.

In 1947, they founded and became coeditors of the magazine *Perspective, a Quarterly of Literature*, in whose pages were introduced such poets as W. S. Merwin and W. D. Snodgrass and other writers of stature. Van Duyn was instructor in English at the State University of Iowa in 1945, and at the University of Louisville from 1946 to 1950. In 1950 Van Duyn and her husband settled in St. Louis, where they formed the nucleus of a strong literary community including poets Donald Finkel, Constance Urdang, and Howard Nemerov and the novelists William Gass and Stanley Elkin. From 1950 to 1967, Van Duyn was a lecturer in English at Washington University and later taught at the Salzburg Seminar in American Studies, at Bread Loaf, and at various other writers' workshops throughout the United States.

Analysis

The life from which Mona Van Duyn writes is the life of the mind; there are few overtly dramatic events in her poetry. Her mind is excited by language—hence the frequent literary references in her poems—but it is also excited by everyday accidental happenings, intense emotions, whatever is irrational, recalcitrant, and unyielding to intellectual analysis or explanation. Her poems burst out of the tension between these polarities, the poem itself—often self-reflexive—being the only method she can find to maintain truth and sanity.

Compassion is an outstanding characteristic of Van Duyn's poetry, both as motive and expression, and yet it is manifested through a wrestling with intellectual questions and an urge to apply her knowledge. Van Duyn's long lines are particularly suitable for expressing discursive thought. Love and beauty are traditional themes of Romantic poets, but in Van Duyn they are united with an affinity for the forms and emphases of literary classicism reminiscent of the eighteenth century, with its bent toward philosophizing in poetry and its allegiance to strict and rhyming forms, especially the heroic couplet.

A classic philosophical problem therefore arises for Van Duyn in her early poems—the split between mind and body. In "From Yellow Lake: An Interval," she expresses discontent with her body as an impediment to overcoming the separateness she feels. The language of the poem has theological undertones: The beetles are "black as our disgrace," a reference to human sin and evil. Crows flying overhead become her dark thoughts, feeding upon "my mind, dear carrion." The poet sees each creature as an analogue of something human—the turtle is "flat as our fate" and the pike's "fierce faith" hooks him fatally on the fisherman's lure. Having a modern mind, the poet cannot find any theological answer to her questioning of the meaning of the creation that painfully yet beautifully surrounds her. The poem supplies the only resolution: Summer has warmed her but she must go back to "the wintry work of living"—that is, the life of the mind of an ordinary human being—and "conspire in the nailing, brutal and indoors, / that pounds to the poem's shape a summer's metaphors." The notion of Original Sin has here been given a new twist: The animal body is "innocent," a parable or metaphor, a natural "given," and the summer is the warmth of love, whereas the mind is that which creates separation, which construes evil and perversely invents the forms of pain. The mind, even if separated from the natural world, is still the only thing with which she can work. Only the poem—actually the process of making a work of art—can heal the split between mind and body, winter and summer, pain and love, by creating reality through metaphor.

"An Essay on Criticism" in *A Time of Bees*, is a tour de force in couplets that echoes Alexander Pope's eighteenth century poem of the same title and also explores the aesthetics of its day, leavening this subject matter with contemporary sensibility, idiom, and wit. In the frame of this poem, the poet, about to open and cook a package of dehydrated onion soup, is interrupted by the arrival of a friend, a young girl who has fallen in love and has discovered "how love is like a poem." In the dialogue that follows, many famous critical theories of poetry are cited and explored. The girl in love speaks first. She clutches the poet's arm "like the Mariner," an allusion to Samuel Taylor Coleridge's *The Rime of the Ancient Mariner* (1798) which the poet employs to join an intense, even obsessed, Romantic view of poetry in one embrace with the classic love of intellect and rationality. After the girl leaves, the poet continues to talk to herself as if gripping "a theoretical Wedding Guest"—Coleridge again—and to grapple inwardly and intellectually with various aspects of the interaction between life and art. She takes the side of the poem, "for I believe in art's process of working through otherness to recognition/ and in its power that comes from acceptance, and not imposition." At this point she finds tears falling into her onion soup, but onions did not cause them; the thought of love did. The poem has to be completed in a human reader's heart. In the complex punning of the last line—tears as "essay" (attempt)—life is asserted to be victorious over art, but poem-making is plainly what maintains their intricate and fruitful balance.

In Van Duyn's next volume, *To See, to Take*, she endeavored to step away from autobiographical reference and to elucidate her concerns by adopting the technique of the persona. In "Eros to Howard Nemerov," for example, she speaks through the traditional personification of love, the Greek god, who is addressing the representative modern American poet with a humorous eye turned on the posturings and vagaries of hippie love in the 1960's. Van Duyn's observant eye and sense of humor lead her directly to satire in "Billings and Cooings from 'The Berkeley Barb.'"

The theme of the passage of time emerges particularly

in this volume in two memorial poems, "The Creation" and "A Day in Late October." In "The Creation" Van Duyn mourns a friend's death; as art is a metaphor for life, she sees the friend's life as having been taken away as a pencil drawing is erased. "A Day in Late October," written after the death of Randall Jarrell, asserts the primacy of death, life's inseparable companion, over art—the art of poetry—by means of an extraordinary divagation for this poet: She breaks out of the poetic form altogether and falls back on prose, which is a kind of death of poetry, to express "what cannot be imagined: your death, my death." Death and the passing of time cannot fail to reinvoke a sense of the preciousness of love.

Two fine poems in this volume spring from autobiography, a mode in which she has both sharpened her technical skills and widened her attitude of appreciation. "Postcards from Cape Split" show her gift for straightforward description of the natural world. The facts of the place where she is vacationing in Maine carry their own intrinsic symbolic weight, so simply stating them is enough. The central motif of "Postcards from Cape Split" is abundance—unearned richness exemplified by hillsides covered with heliotrope, the sea surrounding the house whose interior mirrors the sea, a plethora of villages and shops, generous neighbors, flourishing vegetable gardens. The poet is dazzled and appreciative: "The world blooms and we all bend and bring/ from ground and sea and mind its handsome harvests." The mind remains a primary locus, but the emphasis here is on contentment and gratitude; the world's unasked for generosity is indispensable.

The second autobiographical poem, "Remedies, Maladies, Reasons" strikes quite a different note, although its power also stems from a straightforward statement of facts—the facts of Van Duyn's childhood. It is a record of her mother's acts and speeches that imposed on the child a view of herself as weak, ill, and in danger of dying. The record is brutal and nauseating; it continues in the mother's letters describing her own symptoms simply quoted in her own words, so overwhelming a body-hatred and self-hatred that it is miraculous that the poet survived it. The word "remedies" in the title has a heavily ironic ring, but by the time the poem ends, it has taken another turn of meaning: Implicitly, the act of making a poem from these horrors relieves them. It provides a remedy by evoking the sight of her mother as an attractive woman and as the mother the child wanted, who came in the night when called and defended the child against her felt enemy, sickness. The poem's last line—"Do you think I don't know how love hallucinates?"—constructs a complex balance, reasserting that love still exists but has maintained itself internally by a costly distortion of external fact. Without overtly referring to poetry as an aid, this poem is a remarkable testimony to the capacity of shaped language to restore a sane perspective and to enable one's mind to open to revision of memory, an act of love that is analogous to revision of the language of a poem.

The poem "The Stream," in *Letters from a Father and Other Poems*, is about the death of her mother. In an extended metaphor, Van Duyn sees love as a narrow stream running below ground, held down, unseen, but finally finding its way up until it is visible. This vision of the stream of love also suggests the stream of time flowing toward death, a flow echoed by the long flowing line whose form—the couplet with slant end-rhyme, Van Duyn's favorite—seems to constitute the same sort of facilitating obstacle that the rock and earth present to the underground stream of water. That water rises higher in a narrow tube is a physical fact; thus love rises under "the dense pressure of thwarted needs, the replay/ of old misreadings." Her mother's death has brought the stream of love to light, revealing to her "the welling water—to which I add these tears."

The tears and the poem, as in the earlier but different context of "An Essay on Criticism," join in felicitous confluence. The stringent form, when one gives in to it, is what produces genuine depth and maturation in life as well as in art. Van Duyn's development as a poet has been steady and straightforward, even relentlessly undeviating, without sudden switches of style or experimental or uncertain phases. She has never gone back on her commitment to work with tight forms, to deal with the world's pain, and to remain in love with the world despite its worst. Her poem "Since You Asked Me . . ." answers the question which must have been put to her a number of times: Why use rhyme and meter, since these are so old-fashioned and out of date? She says that she uses rhyme "to say I love you to language" and to combat the current linguistic sloppiness of "'y'know?' and 'Wow!'" She uses meter because it is "not just style but lifestyle."

Her manifesto is also a call to arms: She urges other poets to have "an almost religious/ regard for un-with-it truth." While love has always been her concern, as with the Romantic poets, she never neglects the classicist's need to take moral responsibility for the world, a responsibility that is not only compatible with art and creativity but also the whole motive for the artist's undertaking. The medium, rhyme, is "a challenge to chaos *hurled./ Why use it? Why, simply/* to save the world." That

commitment—to save the world—is the fullest anyone can make. Van Duyn's pledge to that goal has made her one of the most distinguished and accomplished contemporary poets.

Bibliography

Augustine, Jane. "Mona Van Duyn." In *Contemporary Poets*, edited by James Vinson and D. L. Kirkpatrick. 4th ed. New York: St. Martin's Press, 1985.

Grim, Jessica. Review of *Near Changes: Poems*, by Mona Van Duyn. *Library Journal* 115 (March 15, 1990): 94.

Jones, Debra G. "Mona Van Duyn." In *Contemporary Authors*, edited by Deborah A. Straub. Vol 7. New Revision series. Detroit: Gale Research, 1982.

Ludvigson, Susan. "Mona Van Duyn." In *American Poets Since World War 2*, edited by Donald J. Greiner. Vol. 5 in *Dictionary of Literary Biography*. Detroit: Gale Research, 1980.

Moss, Howard. *The Poet's Story*. New York: Macmillan, 1973.

ALICE WALKER

Born: Eatonton, Georgia; February 9, 1944

Principal long fiction

The Third Life of Grange Copeland, 1970; *Meridian*, 1976; *The Color Purple*, 1982; *The Temple of My Familiar*, 1989; *Possessing the Secret of Joy*, 1992.

Other literary forms

Alice Walker has published several volumes of short fiction, poetry, and essays in addition to her novels. Walker was an early editor at *Ms.* magazine, in which many of her essays first appeared. Her interest in the then little-known writer Zora Neale Hurston led to her pilgrimage to Florida to place a tombstone on Hurston's unmarked grave, to Walker's editing of *I Love Myself When I Am Laughing . . . And Then Again When I Am Looking Mean and Impressive: A Zora Neale Hurston Reader* (1979), and to her introduction to Robert Hemenway's *Zora Neale Hurston: A Literary Biography* (1977). With Pratibha Parmar, Walker wrote *Warrior Marks: Female Genital Mutilation and the Sexual Binding of Women* (1993), continuing the pioneering critique that she began with her novel *Possessing the Secret of Joy,* which brought the widespread practice of clitoridectomy to public attention for the first time. Parmar is a filmmaker, and the book is based on a documentary of the same title.

Achievements

Walker's literary reputation is based primarily on her fiction. *The Third Life of Grange Copeland* was widely and enthusiastically reviewed in journals as varied as *The New Yorker, The New Republic*, and *The New York Times Book Review*, although journals aimed primarily at a black readership were often silent or critical of the violence and graphic depiction of rural black life. With the publication of *Meridian*, Walker's second novel, her work as a poet, novelist, essayist, editor, teacher, scholar, and political activist came together. *Meridian* was universally praised in scholarly journals, literary magazines, popular magazines, and black-oriented journals. Some critics, mainly black male reviewers, objected again to the honest, straightforward portrayals of black life in the South and to Walker's growing feminism, which they saw in conflict with her commitment to her race. Walker's third novel, *The Color Purple*, was very widely acclaimed: Gloria Steinem wrote that this novel "could be the kind of popular and literary event that transforms an intense reputation into a national one," and Peter Prescott's review in *Newsweek* began by saying "I want to say at once that *The Color Purple* is an American novel of permanent importance." These accolades were substantiated when Walker received the 1983 Pulitzer Prize for fiction.

Biography

Alice Walker was born in Eatonton, Georgia, on February 9, 1944, the last of eight children of Willie Lee and Minnie Lou Grant Walker, sharecroppers in rural Georgia. Her relationship with her father, at first strong and valuable, became strained as she became involved in the Civil Rights and feminist movements. A moving depiction of her estrangement from her father occurs in her essay "My Father's Country Is the Poor," which appeared in *The New York Times* in 1977. For Walker, a loving and healthy mother-daughter relationship has endured over the years. An account of that relationship is central to her essays "In Search of Our Mothers' Gardens" and "Lulls—A Native Daughter Returns to the Black South."

One of the central events in Walker's childhood was a BB gun accident which left her, at age eight, blind in one eye. Scar tissue from that wound, both physical and psychological, seems to have left her with a compensating acuteness of vision, despite the conviction that she was permanently disfigured. Walker's partial blindness allowed her to attend Spelman College in Atlanta on a scholarship for the handicapped, following her graduation from Butler-Baker High School in 1961. She left Spelman after two years—which included summer trips to the Soviet Union and to Africa as part of a group called Experiment in International Living—for Sarah Lawrence College, where she was graduated in 1965.

Walker's political activity controlled her movements during the years immediately following her college graduation: She spent the summer of 1965 in the Soviet Union and also worked for civil rights in Liberty County, Georgia. The next year she was a case worker for New York City's Department of Social Services, and then a voter-registration worker in Mississippi. In 1967, she married Melvyn Leventhal, a civil rights lawyer, and moved to Jackson, Mississippi, where she continued her civil rights work, lived in the heart of the South as part of an interracial couple, and taught at Jackson State University, while continuing to write stories, poems, and essays. She taught at Tougaloo College in Mississippi for a year before returning to the East, where she was a lecturer in writing and literature at Wellesley College, an editor at *Ms.* magazine, and an instructor at the University of Massachusetts at Boston. By 1977, she had divorced her husband, accepted a position as an associate professor of English at Yale University, and written six books. Walker has continued to write, teach, edit, lecture, and read poetry across the nation from her base in rural Northern California.

Analysis

Alice Walker's work focuses directly or indirectly on the ways of survival adopted by black women, usually in the South, and is presented in a prose style characterized by a distinctive combination of lyricism and unflinching realism. Walker's women attempt not merely to survive, but to survive completely with some sense of stability, despite the constant thread of family violence, physical and mental abuse, and a lack of responsibility on the part of the men in their lives. Walker is simultaneously a feminist and a supporter of civil rights, not only for African Americans but also for minorities everywhere.

Walker's vision has been shaped in part by a work from the first flowering of black writing in America: Jean Toomer's *Cane* (1923). She said in 1974 about Toomer's book, "it has been reverberating in me to an astonishing degree. *I love it passionately*; could not possibly exist without it." Like *Cane*, the first part of which centers mainly on women in the South, Walker's novels are made up of nearly equal parts of poetry, portraiture, and drama, broken up into a series of sections and subsections. Other important literary influences on Walker include Zora Neale Hurston, from whom she inherited a love of black folklore; Flannery O'Connor, who wrote of Southern violence and grotesqueries from her home in Milledgeville, Georgia, less than ten miles from Walker's childhood home; and Albert Camus, whose existentialism speaks to the struggle for survival and dignity in which Walker's characters are engaged. Walker herself has defined her "preoccupations" as a novelist: "The survival, the survival *whole* of my people. But beyond that I am committed to exploring the oppressions, the insanities, the loyalties, and the triumphs of black women."

Meridian describes the struggles of a young black woman, Meridian Hill, who comes to an awareness of power and feminism during the Civil Rights movement, and whose whole life's meaning is centered in the cycles of guilt, violence, hope, and change characteristic of that dramatic time. *Meridian* explores the theme of self-sacrificial murder as a way out of desperate political oppression in the form of the constant question that drives Meridian Hill—"Will you kill for the Revolution?" Meridian's lifelong attempt to answer that question affirmatively (as her college friends so easily do) while remaining true to her sense of responsibility to the past, her sense of ethics, and her sense of guilt of having given to her mother the child of her teenage pregnancy, constitutes the section of the novel entitled "Meridian." The second third of the novel, "Truman Held," is named for the major male character in the narrative. At one time, Meridian loves Truman, but his callous treatment of her and of his desertion of her for Lynne Rabinowitz, a white civil rights volunteer from the North, causes their relationship to change. By the novel's end, Meridian has become teacher, confidante, and savior to both Truman and Lynne, whose eventual marriage is destroyed by the pressures of interracial tensions. The third major section of the novel, "Ending," looks back at the turmoil of the movement from the perspective of the 1970's. Long after others have given up intellectual arguments about the morality of killing for revolution, Meridian is still debating the question, still actively involved in voter registration, political activism, and civil rights organization, as though the movement had never lost momentum. Worrying that her actions, now seen as eccentric rather than revolutionary, will cause her "to be left, listening to the old music, beside the highway," Meridian achieves release and atonement through the realization that her role will be to "come forward and sing from memory songs they will need once more to hear. For it is the song of the people, transformed by the experiences of each generation, that holds them together."

In 1978, Walker described *Meridian* as "a book 'about' the civil rights movement, feminism, socialism, the shakiness of revolutionaries and the radicalization of saints. . . ." Her word "about" is exact, for all these topics revolve not chronologically but thematically around a central point—the protagonist, Meridian Hill. In some ways, Meridian *is* a saint; by the book's end she has sustained her belief in the Civil Rights movement without losing faith in feminism and socialism, despite family pressures, guilt, literally paralyzing self-doubts, the history of the movement, and the sexism of many of its leaders. In contrast, Truman Held represents those males who were reported to have said that "the only position for a woman in the movement is prone." Although Truman Held is Meridian's initial teacher in the movement, she eventually leaves him behind because of his inability to sustain his initial revolutionary fervor, and because of his misogyny. Truman argues that women are of less value than they should be because "Black women let themselves go . . . they are so fat." Later in the novel, Truman marries a white civil rights worker, whose rape by another black man produces disgust in him, as much at his wife as at his friend. When Truman seeks Meridian out in a series of small Southern hamlets where she continues to persuade black people to register to vote and to struggle for civil rights, he tells her that the movement is ended and that he grieves in a different way than she. Meridian answers, "I know how you grieve by running away. By pretending you were never there." Truman Held refuses to take responsibility for his own problems, preferring to run away to the North.

Meridian's sacrificial dedication to the movement becomes a model for atonement and release, words that once formed the working title of the book. Meridian leads three lives: as an uneducated child in rural Georgia who follows the traditional pattern of early pregnancy and aimless marriage; as a college student actively participating in political demonstrations; and as an eccentric agitator—a performer, she calls herself—unaware that the movement is ended. Meridian Hill is solid proof of the ability of any human to change dramatically by sheer will and desire.

Meridian is different from her friends, who, filled with angry rhetoric, ask her repeatedly if she is willing to kill for the revolution. This question haunts Meridian, because she does not know if she can or if she should kill, and because it reminds her of a similar request, posed in a similar way by her mother: "Say it now, Meridian, and be saved. All He asks is that we acknowledge Him as our Master. Say you believe in Him—don't go against your heart." In neither case, is Meridian able to answer yes without going against her heart. Unlike her college friends and Truman Held, who see the movement only in terms of future gains for themselves, Meridian is involved with militancy because of her past: "But what none of them seemed to understand was that she felt herself to be, not holding on to something from the past, but *held* by something in the past."

Meridian takes the form of a series of nonchronological sections, some consisting of only a paragraph, some four or five pages long, that circle around the events of Meridian's life. The writing is clear, powerful, violent, lyrical, and often symbolic. Spelman College, for example, is here called Saxon College. The large magnolia tree in the center of the campus, described with specific folkloric detail, is destroyed by angry students during a demonstration: "Though Meridian begged them to dismantle the president's house instead, in a fury of confusion and frustration they worked all night, and chopped and sawed down, level to the ground, that mighty, ancient, sheltering music tree." This tree (named The Sojourner, perhaps for Sojourner Truth) expands symbolically to suggest both the senseless destruction of black ghettos by blacks during the turmoil of the 1960's and Meridian Hill herself, who receives a photograph years later of The Sojourner, now "a gigantic tree stump" with "a tiny branch, no larger than a finger, growing out of one side." That picture, suggesting as it does the rebirth of hope despite despair, also evokes the last vision of Meridian expressed by the now-shamed Truman Held: "He would never see 'his' Meridian again. The new part had grown out of the old, though, and that was reassuring. This part of her, new, sure and ready, even eager, for the world, he knew he must meet again and recognize for its true value at some future time."

The Color Purple presents the author's familiar and yet fresh themes—survival and redemption—in epistolary form. Most of the novel's letters are written by Celie, an uneducated, unloved, black woman living in rural Georgia in the 1920's. Ashamed of having been raped by her stepfather, a man whom Celie thinks at the time is her father, she begins to send letters to God, in the way that children send letters to Santa Claus, because her rapist told her to tell nobody but God. Although her early letters tell of rape, degradation, and pain, of her stepfather's getting rid of the two children born of his cruelty, the tone is nevertheless captivating, ironic, and even humorous. Soon the despair turns into acceptance, then into understanding, anger, rebellion, and finally triumph and loving forgiveness as the fourteen-year-old Celie continues to write until she reaches an audience, some thirty years later. Like the author, who began writing at the age of eight, and who has turned her childhood experience in rural Georgia into three novels of violence, hatred, understanding, love, and profound hope for the future, Celie is a writer, a listener, a thinker, and a promoter of Walker's constant theme: "Love redeems, meanness kills."

Like Meridian Hill, Celie compares herself to a tree. After being repeatedly raped by her stepfather, Celie is sold into a virtual state of slavery to a man who beats her, a man she neither knows, loves, nor talks to, a man she can never call anything but Mr. ——, an ironic throwback to the eighteenth century English epistolary novel. Celie tries to endure by withholding all emotion: "I make myself wood. I say to myself, Celie, you a tree. That's how come I know trees fear man." Like The Sojourner, or like the kudzu vine of the deep South that thrives despite repeated attempts to beat it back, Celie continues to express her fears and hopes in a series of letters written in a form of black English that is anything but wooden. The contrast between the richly eccentric prose of Celie's letters and the educated yet often lifeless sentences of her sister Nettie's return letters supports Walker's statement that "writing *The Color Purple* was writing in my first language. . . ." The language of the letters is at first awkward, but never difficult to follow. As Celie grows in experience, in contact with the outside world, and in confidence, her writing gradually becomes more sophisticated and more like standard written English, but it never loses its originality of rhythm and phrase.

Based on Walker's great grandmother, a slave who was raped at twelve by her owner, Celie works her way from ignorance about her body and her living situation all the way through to an awakening of her self-worth, as well as to an understanding of the existence of God, the relations between men and women, and the power of forgiveness in uniting family and friends. Much of this transformation is brought about through the magic of a blues singer named Shug Avery, who guides Celie in understanding sexuality, men, and religion without causing her to lose her own fresh insights, naïve though they are.

The letters that make up the novel are something like the missives that the protagonist of Saul Bellow's novel *Herzog* (1964) writes but never sends, in that they are often addressed to God and written in an ironic but not self-conscious manner. Because of the combination of dark humor and despair, the letters also evoke memories of the desperate letters from the physically and spiritually maimed addressed to the hero of Nathanael West's *Miss Lonelyhearts* (1933). Although Celie is unlettered in a traditional sense, her ability to carry the complicated plot forward and to continue to write—first without an earthly audience, and then to her sister, whom she has not seen for more than twenty years—testify to the human potential for self-transformation.

Discussing Celie's attempts to confirm her existence by writing to someone she is not certain exists, Gloria Steinem says "Clearly, the author is telling us something about the origin of Gods: about when we need to invent them and when we don't." In a sense, Shug Avery becomes a god for Celie because of her ability to control the evil in the world and her power to change the sordid conditions of Celie's life. Early in the book, when Celie is worrying about survival, about rape, incest, beatings, and the murder of her children, her only source of hope is the name "Shug Avery," a name with a magical power to control her husband. Not even aware that Shug is a person. Celie writes "I ast our new mammy bout Shug Avery. What it is?" Finding a picture of Shug, Celie transfers her prayers to what is at that point only an image: "I see her there in furs. Her face rouge. Her hair like somethin tail. She grinning with her foot up on somebody motocar. Her eyes serious tho. Sad some. . . . An all night long I stare at it. An now when I dream, I dream of Shug Avery. She be dress to kill, whirling an laughing." Shug Avery becomes a god to Celie not only because she is pictured in the first photograph Celie has ever seen but also because she is dressed in a style that shows a sense of pride and freedom.

Once Celie's sister's letters begin to appear, mailed from Africa, where Nettie is a missionary, the ironic connection between the primitive animism of the Africans and Celie's equally primitive reaction to Shug's picture becomes clear. Although Nettie has crossed the ocean to minister to a tribe of primitive people, her own sister is living in inhuman conditions in Georgia: ignorance, disease, sexism, lack of control of the environment, and the ever-increasing march of white people. When Shug explains her own animistic religious beliefs—which include the notion that God is not a "he" or "she," but an "it" (just as Celie once thought Shug Avery was an "it")—Celie is converted to a pantheistic worship that makes her early identification with trees seem less naïve.

Celie's and Nettie's letters, ostensibly written to people long thought to be dead, speed across the ocean on errands of life, where they grow to sustain, not merely the sisters in the book, but all those lucky enough to read them. As the author says of *The Color Purple*, "It's my happiest book. . . . I had to do all the other writing to get to this point." Alice Walker's name could be substituted for Celie's in the author's statement about her novel: "Let's hope people can hear Celie's voice. There are so many people like Celie who make it, who come out of nothing. People who triumph."

Other major works

SHORT FICTION: *In Love and Trouble: Stories of Black Women*, 1973; *You Can't Keep a Good Woman Down*, 1981.
POETRY: *Once: Poems*, 1968; *Five Poems*, 1972; *Revolutionary Petunias and Other Poems*, 1973; *Goodnight, Willie Lee, I'll See You in the Morning: Poems*, 1979; *Horses Make a Landscape Look More Beautiful*, 1984.
NONFICTION: *In Search of Our Mothers' Gardens: Womanist Prose*, 1983; *Living by the Word: Selected Writings, 1973-1987*, 1988; *Warrior Marks: Female Genital Mutilation and the Sexual Binding of Women*, 1993 (with Pratibha Parmar).
EDITED TEXT: *I Love Myself When I Am Laughing . . . And Then Again When I Am Looking Mean and Impressive: A Zora Neale Hurston Reader*, 1979.
CHILDREN'S LITERATURE: *Langston Hughes: American Poet*, 1974; *To Hell with Dying*, 1988.

Bibliography

Bloom, Harold, ed. *Alice Walker: Modern Critical Views*. New York: Chelsea House, 1989.
Christian, Barbara. *Black Feminist Criticism*. New York: Pergamon Press, 1985.
Fairbanks, Carol, and Eugene A. Engeldinger. *Black American Fiction: A Bibliography*. Metuchen, N.J.: Scarecrow Press, 1978.
Pratt, Louis H., and Darrell D. Pratt. *Alice Malsenior Walker: An Annotated Bibliography, 1968-1986*. Westport, Conn.: Meckler, 1988.
Tate, Claudia. *Black Women Writers at Work*. New York: Continuum, 1983.

MARGARET WALKER

Born: Birmingham, Alabama; July 7, 1915

Principal poetry

For My People, 1942; *Prophets for a New Day*, 1970; *October Journey*, 1973; *This Is My Century: New and Collected Poems*, 1989.

Other literary forms

In addition to her poetry, Margaret Walker produced *Jubilee* (1966), which has the distinction of being the first realistic novel about slavery and the Civil War period to be written by an African American. So great was the interest in this best-selling work that in 1972 Walker brought out a book entitled *How I Wrote "Jubilee."* Walker later coauthored a transcription of unstructured conversations with Nikki Giovanni, a young black woman poet, published as *A Poetic Equation: Conversa-tions Between Margaret Walker and Nikki Giovanni* (1974). Her critical biography *Richard Wright, Daemonic Genius: A Portrait of the Man, a Critical Look at His Work* (1988) is considered a major contribution to scholarship in black literature. Walker has also published numerous articles in scholarly journals. An excellent source of some of her best essays is her collection *How I Wrote "Jubilee" and Other Essays on Life and Litera-ture* (1990).

Achievements

When Walker's *For My People* appeared in 1942, it marked the beginning of a new era. Unlike the writers of the Harlem Renaissance, who in the 1920's had taken refuge from the harsh realities of racism by romanticiz-ing the African past and postulating the existence of a pastoral present, and unlike the restrained black women who had preceded her, Walker revealed the ugly reality of racism and cried out for revolution. *For My People*, which won the Yale University Younger Poets Award, established her reputation as a new voice in African American literature.

Unfortunately, by the time she published her next volume of poetry, *Prophets for a New Day* (1970), much of which reflected the civil rights struggles of the 1960's, others had written works so much more radical that Walker now seemed temperate and even old-fashioned. Her reputation suffered, too, from the publication in 1966 of her novel *Jubilee*, based on the life of her great-grandmother, who had been born into slavery. Black nationalists were infuriated by the protagonist's display of Christian forbearance toward the whites who abused her, determinedly ignoring the fact that in the novel Walker also presented her militant great-grandfather, Randall Ware, as a sympathetic and admirable character.

The later volumes of Walker's poetry received only a lukewarm reception, not because they lacked merit but because they were out of style. Walker's militancy was too much tempered by Christianity and by humanism to be acceptable to radical blacks and liberal whites, who expected African American writers to voice only their hatred of whites and their demands for an apocalyptic end to an oppressive society.

Not until the late 1970's was this neglected writer rediscovered and reappraised. In *Jubilee*, critics finally saw a brilliant use of the folk tradition, and feminists in particular recognized in Vyry a prototype of the strong black woman who preserved and transmitted a sense of cultural identity despite her imprisonment, first as a slave and later as a victim of illiteracy, poverty, and systematic oppression. Walker's poetry was also reassessed. Not only in *For My People*, which had always been consid-ered a superior collection, but in her later work as well, scholars studied such subjects as Walker's biblical refer-ences and musical motifs; her use of ritual, myth, and folklore; and her original use of conventional poetic forms.

While some critics, such as Trudier Harris, categorize Margaret Walker as a transitional figure between the Harlem Renaissance of the 1920's and the Black Arts movement of the 1960's, the recent renewal of scholarly interest in her works suggests that Walker is at last being recognized as a writer of considerable merit. With their familiar references, their powerful images, their lucid style, and their thoughtful content, her poems should now be assured an important place in African American literature.

Biography

Margaret Walker was born in Birmingham, Alabama, on July 7, 1915. As she told John Griffin Jones, she was to grow up "in a home surrounded by books and music." Her father, Sigismund C. Walker, a classical scholar and a superb linguist, had originally come to the United States from Jamaica in order to become a Methodist minister. Her mother was Marion Dozier, a musician whose proudest possession was her piano. The two met in Marion's hometown of Pensacola, Florida, where Sigismund Walker was serving as a supply pastor. After Sigismund was graduated from Gammon Theological Seminary in Atlanta, he and Marion were married and moved to Birmingham, where he became the pastor of a church. There Margaret and there younger children were born, and there Margaret received all of her early schooling, with the exception of one year spent in Meridian, Mississippi.

When Margaret was ten, the family moved to New Orleans, Louisiana, where both Sigismund and Marion Walker were teachers. By the time she was twelve, Margaret was reading the poets of the Harlem Renaissance, such as Langston Hughes and Countée Cullen, and soon was jotting down her own poems in a little daybook which her father had given her. At sixteen, already attending New Orleans (later Dillard) University, the black college where her parents taught, Walker met Langston Hughes. She credits Hughes with persuading her parents to send her to the North in order to complete her education.

Transferring to Northwestern University as a junior, Walker soon met the second black writer to become her mentor and friend: W. E. B. Du Bois. It was Du Bois who was responsible for the first appearance of one of her poems in a major publication. Walker was also thinking about fiction; during her senior year, she began work on her great-grandmother's story, but, feeling uncertain about it, put it aside and turned her full attention to poetry.

After graduating from college in 1935, Walker joined a number of other unemployed writers at the WPA Writers' Project in Chicago. There she became a close friend of Richard Wright, the third black writer to influence her thinking. When her employment ended, Walker decided that it would be wisest to prepare herself for college teaching. During one arduous year at the University of Iowa Writers' Workshop, she worked feverishly on her M.A., completing it in 1940, when she was twenty-five. Her thesis was the collection of poems she called *For My People*.

From that point on, Walker began the difficult task of working at two full-time careers, teaching and writing. Her first position was at Livingstone College in Salisbury, North Carolina. After *For My People* won the Yale Series of Younger Poets Award in the summer of 1942, however, she received a better offer from West Virginia State College in Institute, West Virginia, where she spent the academic year of 1942-1943. In 1943, Walker married Firnist James Alexander. The following year, she was awarded a Rosenwald Fellowship to do concentrated research on *Jubilee*, and in 1948, at home with two small children, she was finally able to get her novel blocked out.

In September, 1949, Walker began to teach at Jackson State College in Jackson, Mississippi, which was to be her permanent home. Although she had occasional breaks, such as a semester at Yale in 1954 as a Ford Fellow, there was a period of some years when Walker published nothing: She was too busy with her family, her disabled husband, and her teaching responsibilities to do any writing. Further intensifying her frustration was the fact that, although as a poet she could advance in rank, she could not aspire to an adequate salary level without a doctorate. Clearly, she had to return to Iowa for a Ph.D. In September, 1962, Walker moved to Iowa City and began work, both on her doctorate and on her novel.

Walker remembers vividly the moment on that April day three years later when she typed the last word of her first draft of *Jubilee*. The novel was duly accepted as her doctoral dissertation, and a year later, it was published. Acclaimed as the first work by an African American writer that showed slavery from the black perspective, *Jubilee* won for Walker the Houghton Mifflin Literary Fellowship. The novel was also a popular success, going through thirty-six printings in its first two years. Translated and distributed worldwide, it sold more than a million copies. Ironically, during the very period when

Walker was completing her novel about the struggle for freedom a hundred years before, the battle of her people for civil rights against segregation was steadily intensifying. What she calls her "civil rights poems," many of which were written in 1963, while she was in Iowa City, later appeared in *Prophets for a New Day*.

The early 1970's were a particularly productive period for Walker. In addition to the two volumes of poetry, she published her account of the writing of *Jubilee* and, with the young poet Nikki Giovanni, coauthored a book of conversations about their craft. Nevertheless, Walker found the decade extremely stressful. She was concerned about her children, one of whom served in Vietnam, and she worried about new protests and new violence, such as that which resulted in the deaths of two Jackson State students. She was also involved in an unsuccessful suit against author Alex Haley, whom she accused of copy-right infringement, based on similarities she saw between *Jubilee* and his recently published novel *Roots* (1976). Before her retirement in 1979, however, she experienced what she calls the happiest period in her academic career, when at last she was able to create a full-fledged black studies program at Jackson State.

After her retirement, Walker continued to live on the street in Jackson that was renamed in her honor. Although her beloved husband passed away after thirty-seven years of marriage, Walker found support in her children and grandchildren. She also continued to write. In 1988, after winning a landmark suit which enabled her to "fair use" of unpublished materials, Walker brought out a brilliant biography of Richard Wright. The following year, the publication of *This Is My Century: New and Collected Poems* further enhanced her reputation.

Analysis

Walker points to her first published poem, which appears in *October Journey* as "I Want to Write," as a clear statement of her poetic aims. Quite simply, she speaks of the power of poetry to transform darkness into dawn and suffering into songs. In this context, even the militant poems of *For My People* can be seen as being written not to express hatred, but to exhort the oppressed to imitate the poet herself by using their anger to produce positive results.

The poems in *For My People* fall into three quite distinct categories. Some are visionary, such as the title work, "Dark Blood," "We Have Been Believers," "Southern Song," and "Sorrow Home." These poems are written in long verse paragraphs, reproducing the familiar cadences of sermons by black preachers, who since the time of slavery have led their people in the pursuit of freedom. Walker may even be presupposing that the expected "Amen"s and "That's right"s will fill the blank spaces between verses. The visionary poems, like the sermons on which they are modeled, are intended to arouse and inspire African Americans.

In her ballads, Walker uses the folk idiom to reinforce her call to action. Her admiring accounts of the exploits of "Bad-Man Stagolee," "Poppa Chicken," "Kissie Lee," "Teacher," and "Big John Henry" all suggest that there is nothing praiseworthy about consenting to be a victim. Stagolee, for example, is admired for killing a police officer and getting away from the lynch mob, and Kissie Lee would as soon cut out a man's heart as look at him. Even John Henry, who died trying to outwork a machine, is described as a person who drew his strength not from the acceptable Christian prayers, but from primitive rituals and even witchcraft.

In yet another way, the sonnets in *For My People* reflect the note of defiance that dominates this volume. By her deliberate use of inexact rhymes, Walker reminds her readers that the old forms must be newly cast. Moreover, often a specific misuse of the convention will emphasize the evil the poet is addressing. For example, in one of her best sonnets, "Childhood," Walker wrongly rhymes "miners" with "mines," suggesting that these workers have lost their individuality in their work, which is as "undermining" of their lives as their "grumbling" is of the words they say. In the sestet, Walker moves from the Birmingham of her childhood to the Delta, where "moonlight" can almost cause one to forget the signs of decay. This ambivalence toward her native South, so filled with natural beauty but so contaminated by the destructive combination of "sentiment and hatred," is one of Walker's major themes.

Another kind of ambivalence in Walker's work can be seen in her references to Christianity. Critics have cited another poem in *For My People*, "Since 1619," as evidence of Walker's rejection of the faith in which she was reared. Here, praise-songs and spirituals may well be equated with "dry bones." In "Childhood," however, there seems to be a call for a baptismal "flood" to wash away not the land, but the sins of its people.

By the time she was writing the poems in *Prophets for a New Day*, Walker had long since broken off with Richard Wright and totally rejected his anti-Christian materialism. In her new work, she identifies the heroes of the Civil Rights movement with the God-driven prophets of the Judeo-Christian tradition. Whatever white churches might do, Walker believes (as she indicates in "Sit-Ins") that the "Bold Young Galilean" would and will join the protesters at the lunch counter in Greensboro.

Many of the poems in *Prophets for a New Day* were composed in 1963, when newspapers were reporting new violence in the South almost daily. Not surprisingly, in these "civil rights poems" Walker uses many topical references. The epigraph in "Street Demonstration" quotes a young demonstrator; "Jackson, Mississippi," "Oxford Is a Legend," and "Birmingham" deal with three cities where violent confrontations occurred; and "For Malcolm X" addresses those who are mourning for a murdered martyr. Finally, in a number of poems, Walker labels the new leaders of her people with the names of the Old Testament prophets. She even makes references to biblical events that are relevant to her own troubled times. As a result, this collection is both rich in allusion and powerful in effect.

On the other hand, *October Journey*, a collection of poems written between 1934 and 1972, is generally unimpressive. Containing occasional and personal poems, many of them formal, as well as two ballads about black women of the past, and concluding with a formal, liturgical "Litany from the Dark People," this volume seems to lack a clear focus.

Nevertheless, the long title poem may well be Walker's most effective description of love and the anguish that Southerners have so often felt toward the South. In it, she skillfully alternates and intertwines references to the danger and the beauty of her native land. After vague warnings, derived from folklore, Walker moves to lyrical descriptions of a Southern spring. She soon reminds her readers, however, that this journey is actually taking place not in spring, but in the fall, when her South has diminished to a stopped clock and a "resentful," fearful world, "full of slimy things." "October Journey" is Walker at her best—passionate, lyrical, and lucid.

In an interview in 1973, Walker commented that she had been preoccupied for some five years with what she calls "Black humanism," which moves beyond any single race or religion to stress the value of every human being. This philosophy is evident in the two final segments of *This Is My Century*, which call for the spiritual renewal of all people.

While the poems in the section entitled "This Is My Century" are varied, each of them contributes toward Walker's vision of her past and of the society in which she is now living. There is much optimism in these poems. The title poem, for example, is a statement of pride in being black, being a member of the race that fought for a better world. Walker's delight in her gender is evident in such poems as "Black Paramour" and "My Truth and My Flame," as well as in the tender sonnet about her husband and her marriage, "Love Song for Alex, 1979." In "My Mississippi Spring," again the poet expresses her love of the South, which is seen in this poem, without ambivalence, as a place of Resurrection.

Yet if in this section Walker writes of reconciliation, acceptance, joy, and even triumph, she also utters some prophetic warnings, addressed not only to her own race but to all humankind as well. In "On Youth and Age," Walker describes a dark world in which "muggers" have moved into "multi-leveled offices." Elsewhere she points to the decline of the family, the dominance of drugs, the persistence of slums, and a pervasive spiritual emptiness.

Appropriately, the final section in this volume, "Farish Street," was patterned on T. S. Eliot's *The Waste Land* (1922). In this series of seven poems, Walker moves from the African past through recollections of slavery and martyrdom to a corrupt present, in which "we sell our souls daily." In her final poem, however, Walker deals with even this depressing reality. Because of her faith, she can view Farish Street as just "one slice of life," while she looks forward to "the glory of the morning of all life."

Throughout her distinguished career, Margaret Walker has been writing poems that speak to ordinary people. At first, her works were specifically addressed to African Americans, who were involved in a desperate struggle for freedom. Yet, because Walker's poems deal with universal experiences, with despair and poverty, with love, hope, and spiritual exaltation, they cannot be limited to any race, place, or time. Instead, they have meaning for all humanity.

Other major works

NOVEL: *Jubilee*, 1966.

NONFICTION: *How I Wrote "Jubilee,"* 1972; *A Poetic Equation: Conversations Between Margaret Walker and Nikki Giovanni*, 1974 (with Nikki Giovanni); *Richard Wright, Daemonic Genius: A Portrait of the Man, a Critical Look at His Work*, 1988; *How I Wrote "Jubilee" and Other Essays on Life and Literature*, 1990.

Bibliography

Davis, Arthur P. *From the Dark Tower: Afro-American Writers, 1900 to 1960*. Washington, D.C.: Howard University Press, 1974.

Evans, Mari, ed. *Black Women Writers, 1950-1980: A Critical Evaluation*. Garden City, N.Y.: Anchor Press/Doubleday, 1983.

Inge, Tonette Bond, ed. *Southern Women Writers: The New Generation*. Tuscaloosa: University of Alabama Press, 1990.

Miller, R. Baxter, ed. *Black American Poets Between Worlds, 1940-1960*. Knoxville: University of Tennessee Press, 1986.

Tate, Claudia C., ed. *Black Women Writers at Work*. New York: Continuum, 1983.

Walker, Margaret. "Poetry, History, and Humanism: An Interview with Margaret Walker." Interview by Charles Rowell. *Black World* 25 (1975): 4-17.

Young, James O. *Black Writers of the Thirties*. Baton Rouge: Louisiana State University Press, 1973.

WENDY WASSERSTEIN

Born: Brooklyn, New York; October 18, 1950

Principal drama

Any Woman Can't, pr. 1973; *Happy Birthday, Montpelier Pizz-zazz*, pr. 1974; *When Dinah Shore Ruled the Earth*, pr. 1975 (with Christopher Durang); *Uncommon Women and Others*, pr. 1975 (one act), pr. 1977 (two acts), pb. 1978; *Isn't It Romantic*, pr. 1981, pr. 1983 (revised version), pb. 1984; *Tender Offer*, pr. 1983 (one act); *The Man in a Case*, pr., pb. 1986 (one act; adapted from Anton Chekhov's short story of the same title); *Miami*, pr. 1986 (musical); *The Heidi Chronicles*, pr., pb. 1988; *The Heidi Chronicles and Other Plays*, pb. 1990; *The Sisters Rosensweig*, pr. 1992.

Other literary forms

Wendy Wasserstein, though best known for her plays, is the author of several teleplays, including *The Sorrows of Gin* (1979), an adaptation of John Cheever's short story. She has written several unproduced film scripts, among them an adaptation of her play *The Heidi Chronicles*. Her essays, which have appeared in numerous periodicals, including *Esquire* and *New York Woman*, have also been published in a collection entitled *Bachelor Girls* (1990).

Achievements

Wasserstein has been hailed as the foremost theatrical chronicler of the lives of women of her generation. Her plays, steeped in her unique brand of humor, are nevertheless moving, sometimes wrenching explorations—of women's struggle for identity and fulfillment in a world of rapidly shifting social, sexual, and political mores. Most often against the backdrop of the burgeoning feminist movement, her characters navigate through obstacle courses of expectations—those of their parents, their lovers, their siblings, their friends, and ultimately, themselves. They seek answers to fundamental questions: how to find meaning in life, and how to strike a balance between the need to connect and the need to be true to oneself. Wasserstein's works, which deftly pair wit and pathos, satire and sensitivity, have garnered numerous honors, including the Pulitzer Prize, the Tony Award, the New York Drama Critics Circle Award, the Outer Critics Circle Award, and the Susan Blackburn Prize.

Biography

Wendy Wasserstein was born on October 18, 1950, in Brooklyn, New York, as the fourth and youngest child of Morris W. Wasserstein, a successful textile manufacturer, and Lola (Schleifer) Wasserstein, a housewife and nonprofessional dancer, both Jewish émigrés from central Europe. When she was thirteen, Wasserstein's family moved to Manhattan, where she attended the Calhoun School, an all-girl academy at which she discovered that she could get excused from gym class by writing the annual mother-daughter fashion show. Some years later, at Mount Holyoke, an elite Massachusetts women's college, a friend persuaded Wasserstein, a history major, to take a playwriting course at nearby Smith College. Encouraged by her instructor, she devoted much of her junior year, which she spent at Amherst College, performing in campus musicals before returning to complete her B.A. degree at Mount Holyoke in 1971.

Upon graduating, Wasserstein moved back to New York City, where she studied playwriting with Israel Horovitz and Joseph Heller at City College (where she later earned an M.A.) and held a variety of odd jobs to pay her rent. In 1973, her play *Any Woman Can't* was produced Off-Broadway at Playwrights Horizons, prompting her to accept admission to the Yale School of Drama, turning down the Columbia Business School, which had simultaneously offered her admission.

It was at Yale University, where she earned an M.F.A. degree in 1976, that Wasserstein's first hit, *Uncommon Women and Others*, was conceived as a one-act play. Ultimately expanded, it was given a workshop production at the prestigious National Playwrights Conference at the O'Neill Theater Center in Connecticut, a well-known launching pad for many successful playwrights. Indeed, in 1977, the Phoenix Theater's production of *Uncommon Women and Others* opened Off-Broadway at the Marymount Manhattan Theater. Although some critics objected to the play's lack of traditional plot, most praised Wasserstein's gifts as a humorist and a social observer.

By 1980, Wasserstein, established as one of the United States' most promising young playwrights, was commissioned by the Phoenix Theater to write *Isn't It Romantic* for its 1980-1981 season. The play's mixed reviews prompted Wasserstein to rework it under the guidance of director Gerald Gutierrez and André Bishop, artistic director of Playwrights Horizons. There, with a stronger narrative line and more in-depth character development, it opened in 1983 to widespread praise.

In the meantime, Wasserstein had been at work on several new pieces—among them a one-act play, *Tender Offer*, which was produced at Ensemble Studio Theater, and, collaborating with Jack Feldman and Bruce Sussman, a musical, *Miami*, which was presented as a work-in-progress at Playwrights Horizons in 1986.

In 1988, one of Wasserstein's most ambitious works, *The Heidi Chronicles*, which had been previously performed in workshop at the Seattle Repertory Theater, had its New York premiere at Playwrights Horizons. It moved quickly to the larger Plymouth Theater on Broadway, where it opened to mostly positive critical response. The play earned Wasserstein the Pulitzer Prize, the Tony Award, and virtually every New York theater award.

Wasserstein's eagerly awaited *The Sisters Rosensweig* opened at the Mitzi E. Newhouse Theater at Lincoln Center in the fall of 1992. Receiving widespread critical acclaim, the piece augmented her already prominent presence on the American dramatic scene.

Analysis

Wendy Wasserstein's plays are, for the most part, extremely consistent in their emphasis on character, their lack of classical structure, and their use of humor to explore or accompany serious, often poignant themes. Throughout her career, Wasserstein's central concern has been the role of women—particularly white, upper-middle-class, educated women—in contemporary society. Though her plays are suffused with uproarious humor, her typical characters are individuals engaged in a struggle to carve out an identity and a place for themselves in a society that has left them feeling, at worst, stranded and desolate and, at best, disillusioned. This is not to say that Wasserstein's worldview is bleak. Rather, the note of slightly skewed optimism with which she characteristically ends her works, along with her prevailing wit, lends them an air of levity and exuberance that often transcends her sober themes.

These themes—loneliness, isolation, and a profound desire for meaning in life—are examined by Wasserstein chiefly through character. One of the playwright's great strengths is her ability to poke fun at her characters without subjecting them to ridicule or scorn. Her women and men, with all of their faults and foibles, are warmly and affectionately rendered. They engage their audience's empathy as they make their way through the intricate mazes of their lives, trying to con-

nect and to be of consequence in the world.

Wasserstein is best known for her four full-length, professional plays, *Uncommon Women and Others*, *Isn't It Romantic*, *The Heidi Chronicles*, and *The Sisters Rosensweig*. The first three plays have in common their episodic structure and non-plot-driven narrative. In each of the three, scenes unfold to reveal aspects of character. *Uncommon Women and Others*, for example, begins with five former college friends assessing their lives as they reunite six years after graduation. The body of the play is a flashback to their earlier life together at a small women's college under the often-conflicting influences of the school's traditional "feminine" rituals and etiquette and the iconoclasm of the blossoming women's movement. In each of the two time frames, events are largely contexts for discussions in which Wasserstein's women use one another as sounding boards, each one testing and weighing her hopes, fears, expectations, and achievements against those of her friends. Similarly, in *Isn't It Romantic*, two former college friends, Janie Blumberg, a free-lance writer, and Harriet Cornwall, a corporate M.B.A., move through their postcollege lives, weighing marriage and children against independence and the life choices of their mothers against their own. The play climaxes at the point where the two women diverge—Harriet, who has formerly decried marriage, accepting a suitor's proposal out of fear of being alone and Janie choosing to remain unattached and to seek happiness within herself.

The Heidi Chronicles, though more far-reaching in scope, is also a character-driven play. Here, Wasserstein narrows her focus to one woman, Heidi Holland, but through her reflects the changing social and political mores of more than two decades. From the mid-1960's to the late 1980's, Heidi, like Wasserstein's earlier characters, struggles to find her identity. Moving through settings ranging from women's consciousness-raising meetings and protests to power lunches in trendy restaurants and Yuppie baby showers, Wasserstein's Heidi functions as, in her words, a "highly-informed spectator" who never quite seems to be in step with the prescribed order of the day. In a pivotal scene, Heidi, now an art history professor, delivers a luncheon lecture entitled "Women, Where Are We Going." Her speech, which disintegrates into a seeming nervous breakdown, ends with Heidi confessing that she feels "stranded": "And I thought the whole point was that we wouldn't feel stranded," she concludes, "I thought the whole point was that we were in this together."

Isolation and loneliness and, contrastingly, friendship and family, are themes that run throughout these three earlier plays. Heidi's wish, expressed in that luncheon speech, is for the kind of solidarity that exists among the women in *Uncommon Women and Others*, who, while constantly comparing their lives, are not competitive in the sense of putting one another down. On the contrary, they are fervent in their praise and support of one another, a family unto themselves. Janie and Harriet, in *Isn't It Romantic*, share a relationship that is much the same until something comes between them; Harriet's decision to marry a man she hardly knows because he makes her feel "like [she has] a family." Heidi, on the other hand, at the point when she makes her speech, has no close women friends. Presumably, they are all off having babies and/or careers. Her decision, at the play's end, to adopt a Panamanian baby girl, thereby creating a family of her own, is much akin to Janie Blumberg's decision finally to unpack her crates in her empty apartment at *Isn't It Romantic*'s end and make a home for herself.

This desire on the part of Wasserstein's characters for a family and a place to belong has at its root the desire for self-affirmation. It is evident in the refrain that echoes throughout *Uncommon Women and Others*, "When we're twenty-five [thirty, forty, forty-five], we're going to be incredible," as well as in Janie Blumberg's invocation, "I am," borrowed from her mother, Tasha. Though failures by the standards of some, Janie, Heidi, and the others can be seen as heroic in their resilience and in the tenacity with which they cling to their ideals—however divergent from the reality at hand.

This aspect of Wasserstein's writing—that is, her tendency to create characters who resist change—can exasperate audiences, as her critics have noted. The women, in particular, who people her plays are often, like Janie with her unpacked crates of furniture, in a state of suspension, waiting for life to begin. In *Uncommon Women and Others*, there is a constant look toward the future for self-substantiation, as there is, to some extent, in Heidi's persistent state of unhappiness. Still, Heidi does ultimately make a choice—to adopt a baby, a step toward the process of growing up, another of Wasserstein's recurrent themes.

One of Wasserstein's greatest gifts is her ability to find and depict the ironies of life. This is evident in each of the three plays' bittersweet final images: the "uncommon women," their arms wrapped around one another, repeating their by now slightly sardonic refrain; Janie, tap-dancing alone in her empty apartment; and Heidi, singing to her new daughter "You Send Me," the song to which she had previously danced with her old flame, Scoop, at his wedding reception. These images are pure Wasserstein. In the face of the disappointment, even the disillusionment, of life, her characters manifest a triumph of the spirit and a strength from within that ultimately prevails.

Wasserstein's *The Sisters Rosensweig* is a departure from her earlier plays in a number of ways. Most overt among these differences are the play's international setting (the action takes place in Queen Anne's Gate, London) and its concern with global issues and events. Also of note is the playwright's uncharacteristic use of classical, nonepisodic structure, maintaining unity of time and place: in this case, several days' events in the sitting room of Sara Goode, the plays' main character and the eldest of the three sisters for whom the play is named.

Sara shares many of the characteristics of Wasserstein's earlier protagonists—that is, her gender (female), ethnic group (Jewish), social class (upper-middle to upper-class), and intelligence quotient (uncommonly high). She is, however, considerably older than her forerunners. *The Sisters Rosensweig* centers on the celebration of Sarah's fifty-fourth birthday. This is significant in that Sara, a hugely successful international banker who has been married and divorced several times, does not share the struggle for self-identity carried out by such Wasserstein heroines as Heidi Holland and Janie Blumberg. With a lucrative, challenging career (noteworthily, in a male-dominated field) and a daughter she loves, Sara has achieved, to some degree, the "meaning" in her life that those earlier characters found lacking and sought.

As the play progresses, however, it is revealed that Sara, despite her self-confidence and seeming self-sufficiency, shares with Heidi, Janie, and the others a deep need to connect—to find, create, or reclaim a family. As she fends off and at last gives in to a persistent suitor, Merv Kant, a false-fur dealer, and plays hostess to her two sisters—Pfeni Rosensweig, a socio-political journalist-turned-travel-writer, and "Dr." Gorgeous Teitelbaum, who hosts a radio call-in show—Sara manages, at last, to peel back the layers of defense and reserve that have seen her through two divorces and the rigors of her profession and to rediscover the joys of sisterhood and the revitalizing power of romantic love.

It is not Sara alone who serves Wasserstein in her exploration of her characteristic themes of loneliness, isolation, and the search for true happiness. Pfeni, forty years old, the play's most seemingly autobiographical character, a writer who has been temporarily diverted from her true calling, has been likewise diverted from pursuing "what any normal woman wants" by remaining in a relationship with Geoffrey, who is homosexual. Jilted, and distraught over the havoc that acquired immunodeficiency syndrome (AIDS) has played with the lives of his friends, Geoffrey has wooed and won Pfeni, only to leave her in the end to follow his true nature. Pfeni's ceaseless "wandering," as well as her self-confessed need to write about the hardships of others to fill the emptiness in her own life, is much akin to Heidi Holland's position as a "highly-informed spectator," waiting for her own life to begin.

The Sisters Rosensweig harks back to Wasserstein's Isn't It Romantic in its concerns with the profound role that both mothers and Judaism can play in shaping women's lives. Here, Sara rejects, and attempts to cast off, the influences of both. An atheist expatriate in London, she has reinvented her life, purging all memories of her Jewish New York upbringing and her deceased mother's expectations as firmly as she has embraced the habits and speech patterns of her adopted home. Sara's eventual acquiescence to Merv, a New York Jew, along with the rekindling of her emotional attachment to her sisters, represents, at the plays' end, an acceptance and embracing of the past that she has worked so hard to put behind her.

Like all Wasserstein's works, The Sisters Rosensweig presents characters whose spirits triumph over their daily heartaches and heartbreaks. While they long to escape the tangled webs of their lives ("If I could only get to Moscow!" Pfeni laments, in one of the play's several nods to Anton Chekhov's The Three Sisters), they manage to find within themselves and in one another sufficient strength not only to endure but also to prevail.

As in Uncommon Women and Others, Isn't It Romantic, and The Heidi Chronicles, there is a scene in The Sisters Rosensweig in which women join together to share a toast, affirming and celebrating their sisterhood and themselves. Be they blood sisters, sorority sisters, or sisters of the world, Wasserstein has made sisters her province. With The Sisters Rosensweig, she adds three more portraits to her ever-growing gallery of uncommon women—painted, as always, with insight, wit, and compassion.

Wasserstein is a unique and important voice in contemporary American theater. As a woman writing plays about women, she has been a groundbreaker, though never self-consciously so. Despite her often thin plot lines, she finds and captures the drama inherent in the day-to-day choices confronting the women of her generation. As a humorist, too, Wasserstein is unquestionably a virtuoso. Her ability to see the absurdity of even her own most deeply held convictions, and to hold them deeply nevertheless, is perhaps the most engaging and distinctive of her writing's many strengths.

Other major works

TELEPLAY: *The Sorrows of Gin*, 1979 (from a story by John Cheever).
NONFICTION: *Bachelor Girls*, 1990.

Bibliography

Bennetts, Leslie. "An Uncommon Dramatist Prepares Her New Work." *The New York Times*, May 24, 1981, p. C1-3.
Moritz, Charles, ed. "Wasserstein, Wendy." In *Current Biography Yearbook 1989*. New York: H. H. Wilson, 1989.

Nightingale, Benedict. "There Really Is a World Beyond 'Diaper Drama.'" *The New York Times*, January 1, 1984, p. C2-4.

Rose, Phyllis Jane. "Dear Heidi—An Open Letter to Dr. Holland." *American Theater* 6 (October, 1989): 26-31.

Shapiro, Walter. "Chronicler of Frayed Feminism." *Time* 133 (March 27, 1989): 90-92.

EUDORA WELTY

Born: Jackson, Mississippi; April 13, 1909

Principal short fiction

A Curtain of Green and Other Stories, 1941; *The Wide Net and Other Stories*, 1943; *The Golden Apples*, 1949; *The Bride of the Innisfallen and Other Stories*, 1955; *The Collected Stories of Eudora Welty*, 1980.

Other literary forms

In addition to her many short stories, Eudora Welty has published novels, essays, reviews, an autobiography, a fantasy story for children, and a volume of photographs of Mississippi during the Depression, *One Time, One Place: Mississippi in the Depression, a Snapshot Album* (1971), taken during her stint as photographer and writer for the Works Progress Administration.

Achievements

Welty possesses a distinctive voice in Southern, and indeed in American, fiction. Her vibrant, compelling evocation of the Mississippi landscape, which is her most common setting, has led to comparisons between her work and that of other eminent Southern writers such as William Faulkner, Carson McCullers, and Flannery O'Connor. Welty's graceful, lyrical fiction, however, lacks the pessimism that characterizes much of established Southern writing, and though her settings are distinctly Southern, her themes are universal and do not focus on uniquely Southern issues.

The honors and awards that Welty has amassed throughout her long career are so many as to defy complete listing in a short space. Among her major achievements are four O. Henry Awards for her short stories (first prizes in 1942, 1943, and 1968, and a second prize in 1941), two Guggenheim Fellowships (1942, 1949), honorary lectureships at Smith College (1952) and the University of Cambridge (1955), election to the National Institute of Arts and Letters (1952) and to the American Academy of Arts and Letters (1971), honorary LL.D. degrees from the University of Wisconsin (1954) and Smith College (1956), a term as Honorary Consultant to the Library of Congress (1958-1961), the William Dean Howells Medal of the American Academy of Arts and Letters for *The Ponder Heart* (1954), the Gold Medal for Fiction of the National Institute of Arts and Letters (1972), the Pulitzer Prize in fiction (awarded in 1973 for her 1972 novel *The Optimist's Daughter*), the National Medal of Literature and Medal of Freedom (1981), the National Medal of Arts (1986), and the naming of the Jackson Public Library in her honor (1986).

Biography

Eudora Welty was born on April 13, 1909, in Jackson, Mississippi. In the Welty household, reading was a favorite pastime, and Welty recalls in her autobiography, *One Writer's Beginnings* (1984), both being read to often as a young child and becoming a voracious reader herself. Her recollections of her early life are of a loving and protective family and of a close, gossip-prone community in which she developed her lifelong habit of watching, listening to, and observing closely everything around her. Her progressive and understanding parents encouraged her in her education, and in 1925, she enrolled at the Mississippi State College for Women. After two years there, she transferred to the University of Wisconsin and was graduated with a B.A. in English in 1929.

Welty subsequently studied advertising at the Columbia University Business School; her father had recommended to her that if she planned to be a writer, she would be well advised to have another skill to which she could turn in case of need. During the Depression, however, she had little success finding employment in the field of advertising. She returned to Mississippi and spent the next several years working variously as a writer for radio and as a society editor. In 1933, she began working for the Works Progress Administration, traveling throughout Mississippi, taking photographs, interviewing people, and writing newspaper articles. Her first short story, "Death of a Traveling Salesman," was published in 1936 by a "little" magazine called *Manuscript*. Her ability as a writer soon attracted the attention of Robert Penn Warren and Cleanth Brooks, editors of *The Southern Review*, and over the next years her writing appeared in that magazine as well as in *The New Yorker*, *The Atlantic Monthly*, and *The Sewanee Review*.

Her first collection of short stories, *A Curtain of Green and Other Stories*, appeared in 1941, with a preface by Katherine Anne Porter. Welty's reputation as an important Southern writer was established with this first volume, and, at the urging of her editor and friend John Woodburn, who encouraged her to write a longer work

of fiction, she followed it with her fabular novel *The Robber Bridegroom* in 1942. Thenceforth, she continued with a fairly steady output of fiction, and with each successive publication, her stature as a major American writer grew.

Welty has spent most of her life living in, observing, and writing about Jackson and the Mississippi Delta country. Her frequent visits to New York, and her travels in France, Italy, Ireland, and England (where she participated in a conference on American studies at the University of Cambridge in 1955) have provided her with material for those few stories that are set outside her native Mississippi. From time to time, she has lectured or taught but in general has preferred the quiet and privacy of her lifelong home of Jackson.

Analysis

Although some dominant themes and characteristics appear regularly in Eudora Welty's fiction, her work resists categorization. The majority of her stories are set in her beloved Mississippi Delta country, of which she paints a vivid and detailed picture, but she is equally comfortable evoking such diverse scenes as a Northern city or a transatlantic ocean liner. Thematically, she concerns herself both with the importance of family and community relations and, paradoxically, with the strange solitariness of human experience. Elements of myth and symbol often appear in her work, but she uses them in shadowy, inexplicit ways. Perhaps the only constant in Welty's fiction is her unerring keenness of observation, both of physical landscape and in characterization, and her ability to create convincing psychological portraits of an immensely varied cast of characters.

One relatively early story, "A Worn Path," recounts an ancient black woman's long and perilous journey on foot from her remote rural home to the nearest town. The frail old woman, called Phoenix, travels slowly and painfully through a sometimes hostile landscape, described in rich and abundant detail. She overcomes numerous obstacles with determination and good humor. Into the vivid, realistic description of the landscape and journey, Welty interweaves characteristically lyrical passages describing Phoenix's fatigue-induced hallucinations and confused imaginings. When Phoenix reaches the town, she goes to the doctor's office, and it is revealed that the purpose of her journey is to obtain medicine for her chronically ill grandson. A poignant scene at the

story's close confirms the reader's suspicion of Phoenix's extreme poverty and suggests the likelihood that her beloved grandson will not live long; old Phoenix's dignity and courage in the face of such hardship, however, raise the story from pathos to a tribute to her resilience and strength of will. Like her mythical namesake, Phoenix triumphs over the forces that seek to destroy her.

"Why I Live at the P.O." is a richly comic tale of family discord and personal alienation, told in the first person in idiomatic, naturalistic language that captures the sounds and patterns of a distinctive Southern speech. It is one of the earliest examples of Welty's often-used narrative technique, what she calls the "monologue that takes possession of the speaker." The story recounts how Sister, the intelligent and ironic narrator, comes to fall out with her family over incidents arising from her younger sister Stella-Rondo's sudden reappearance in their small Southern town, minus her husband and with a two-year-old "adopted" child in tow. Welty's flair for comedy of situation is revealed as a series of bizarrely farcical episodes unfolds. Through the irritable Stella-Rondo's manipulative misrepresentations of fact and Sister's own indifference to causing offense, Sister earns the ire of her opinionated and influential grandfather Papa-Daddy, her gullible, partisan mother, and her short-tempered Uncle Rondo. Sister responds by removing all of her possessions from communal use in the home and taking up residence in the local post office, where she is postmistress. Inability to communicate is a recurrent theme in Welty's short fiction; in this case, it is treated with a controlled hilarity that is chiefly comic but that nevertheless reveals the pain of a family's disunity. This story is one of the best examples of Welty's gift for comic characterization, her gentle mockery of human foibles, and her ear for Southern idiom and expression.

"The Wide Net" is a fabular tale of the mysteries of human relationships and the potency of the natural world. Young William Wallace returns home from a night on the town to find a note from his pregnant wife saying that she has gone to drown herself in the river. William Wallace assembles a motley collection of men and boys to help drag the river. The river's power as a symbol is apparent in the meaning that it holds for the many characters: To youngsters Grady and Brucie, it is the grave of their drowned father; to the rough, carefree Malones, it is a fertile source of life, teeming with catfish to eat, eels to "rassle," and alligators to hunt; and to the philosophical and somewhat bombastic Doc, it signifies that "the outside world is full of endurance." It is also, the river-draggers discover, the home of the primeval "king of the snakes."

Throughout the story, Welty deliberately obscures the nature of William Wallace's relationship with his wife, the history behind her threat, and even whether William Wallace truly believes his wife has jumped in the river. Characteristically, Welty relies on subtle hints and expert manipulation of tone rather than on open exposition to suggest to her readers the underpinnings of the events that she describes. This deliberate vagueness surrounding the facts of the young couple's quarrel lends the story the quality of a fable or folktale. The young lover must undergo the test of dragging the great river, confronting the king of snakes, and experiencing a kind of baptism, both in the river and in the cleansing thunderstorm that drenches the searchers, before he is worthy of regaining his wife's love. Like a fable, the story has an almost impossibly simple and happy ending. William Wallace returns from the river to find his welcoming wife waiting calmly at home. They have a brief, affectionate mock quarrel that does not specifically address the incident at all, and they retire hand in hand, leaving the reader to ponder the mystery of their bond.

"Livvie" has a lyrical, fabular quality similar to that of "The Wide Net." Livvie is a young black woman who lives with her elderly husband, Solomon, on a remote farm far up the old Natchez Trace. The strict old husband is fiercely protective of his young bride and does not

allow her to venture from the yard or to talk with—or even see—other people. The inexperienced Livvie, however, is content in Solomon's comfortable house, and she takes loving care of him when his great age finally renders him bedridden. One day, a white woman comes to her door, selling cosmetics. Livvie is enchanted with the colors and scents of the cosmetics but is firm in her insistence that she has no money to buy them. When the saleswomen leaves, Livvie goes into the bedroom to gaze on her ancient, sleeping husband. Desire for wider experience and a more fulfilling life has been awakened in her, and as her husband sleeps, she disobeys his strict command and wanders off down the Natchez Trace. There, she comes upon a handsome, opulently dressed young man named Cash, whom she leads back to Solomon's house. When Solomon awakes and sees them, he is reproachful but resigned to her need for a younger man, asking God to forgive him for taking such a young girl away from other young people. Cash steals from the room, and as Livvie gazes on the frail, wasted body of Solomon, he dies. In a trancelike shock, Livvie drops Solomon's sterile, ticking watch; after momentary hesitation, she goes outside to join Cash in the bright light of springtime.

"Livvie" is almost like a fairy tale in its use of simple, universal devices. The beautiful young bride, the miserly old man who imprisons her, the strange caller who brings temptation, and the handsome youth who rescues the heroine are all familiar, timeless characters. Welty broadens the references of her story to include elements of myth and religion. Young Cash, emerging from the deep forest dressed in a bright green coat and green-plumed hat, could be the Green Man of folklore, a symbol of springtime regeneration and fertility. In contrasting youth with age and old with new, Welty subtly employs biblical references. Old Solomon thinks rather than feels but falls short of his Old Testament namesake in wisdom. Youthful Cash, redolent of spring, tells Livvie that he is "ready for Easter," the reference ostensibly being to his new finery but suggesting new life rising to vanquish death. The vague, dreamy impressionism of "Livvie," which relies on image and action rather than dialogue to tell the story (except in the scenes featuring the saleswoman), adds to this folktale-like quality.

In "A Still Moment," Welty uses historical characters to tell a mystically imaginative tale. Lorenzo Dow, the New England preacher, James Murrell, the outlaw, and John James Audubon, the naturalist and painter, were real people whom Welty places in a fictional situation. Dow rides with an inspired determination to his evening's destination, a camp meeting where he looks forward to a wholesale saving of souls. With single-minded passion, he visualizes souls and demons crowding before him in the dusky landscape. Dow's spiritual intensity is both compared and contrasted to the outlook of the outlaw Murrell, who shadows Dow along the Natchez Trace. Murrell considers his outlawry in a profoundly philosophical light, seeing each murder as a kind of ceremonial drawing out and solving of the unique "mystery" of each victim's being. Audubon, like Dow and Murrell, has a strange and driving intensity that sets him apart from others. His passion is the natural world; by meticulously observing and recording it, he believes that he can move from his knowledge to an understanding of all things, including his own being.

The three men are brought together by chance in a clearing, each unaware of the others' identities. As they pause, a solitary white heron alights near them in the marsh. As the three men stare in wonder at the snowy creature, Welty identifies for the reader the strange similarity of these outwardly diverse men: "What each of them had wanted was simply *all*. To save all souls, to destroy all men, to see and record all life that filled this world." The simple and beautiful sight of the heron, however, causes these desires to ebb in each of them; they are transfixed and cleansed of desire. Welty uses the heron as a symbol of the purity and beauty of the natural world, which acts as a catalyst for her characters' self-discovery. Oddly, it is Audubon, the lover of nature, who breaks the spell. He reaches for his gun and shoots the bird, to add to his scientific collection. The magic of the moment is gone, and the lifeless body of the bird becomes a mere sum of its parts, a dull, insensate mass of feathers and flesh. Audubon, his prize collected, continues on his way, and the horrified Dow hurries away toward his camp meeting, comforted by the vivid memory of the bird's strange beauty. The dangerous Murrell experiences an epiphanic moment of self-realization; the incident has reminded him poignantly of the separateness and innocence of all human beings, a thought that reconfirms in him his desire to waylay and destroy. It is only through a brief but intense moment of shared feeling and experience that the men can recognize their essential loneliness. As in "The Wide Net" and "Livvie," the most important communication must be done without words.

"Moon Lake" is from the collection *The Golden Ap-ples*, the stories of which are nearly all set in or around the mythical community of Morgana, Mississippi, and feature a single, though extensive, cast of characters. Thematically, it shares with "A Still Moment" the sense of the paradoxical oneness and interconnectedness of the human condition. The story describes a sequence of events at a camp for girls at the lake of the story's title. The characteristically lushly detailed landscape is both beautiful and dangerous, a place where poisonous snakes may lurk in the blackberry brambles and where the lake is a site for adventure but also a brown-watered, bug-filled morass with thick mud and cypress roots that grasp at one's feet. The story highlights the simultaneous attraction and repulsion of human connection. Antipathies abound among the group assembled at the lake: The lake's Boy Scout lifeguard, Loch, feels contempt for the crowd of young girls; the Morgana girls look down on the orphan girls as ragged thieves; and rivalry and distrust crops up among individual girls. The sensitive Nina yearns for connection and freedom from connection at the same time; she envies the lonely independence of the orphans and wishes to be able to change from one persona to another at will, but at the same time she is drawn to Easter, the "leader" of the orphans, for her very qualities of separateness and disdain for friendship.

Nina and her friend Jinny Love follow Easter to a remote part of the lake in an unsuccessful attempt to cultivate her friendship, and when they return to where the others are swimming, Easter falls from the diving platform and nearly drowns. The near-drowning becomes a physical acting out of the story's theme, the fascinating and inescapable but frightening necessity of human connection. Without another's help, Easter would have died alone under the murky water, but Loch's lengthy efforts to resuscitate the apparently lifeless form of Easter disgust the other girls. The quasi-sexual rhythm of the resuscitation is made even more disturbing to the girls by its violence: Loch pummels Easter with his fists, and blood streams from her mud-smeared mouth as he flails away astride her. The distressing physical contact contrasts with the lack of any emotional connection during this scene. One orphan, a companion of Easter, speculates that if Easter dies she gets her winter coat, and gradually the other girls grow bored of the spectacle and resent the interruption of their afternoon swim. Jinny Love's mother, appearing unexpectedly at the camp, is more concerned with the lewdness that she imputes to Loch's rhythmic motions than with Easter's condition and she barks at him, "Loch Morrison, get off that table and shame on you." Nina is the most keenly aware of the symbolic significance of the incident and of the peril of connection; she reflects that "Easter had come among them and had held herself untouchable and intact. Of course, for one little touch could smirch her, make her fall so far, so deep."

"Where Is the Voice Coming From?" was originally published in *The New Yorker*, and it remained uncollected until the appearance of the complete *The Collected Stories of Eudora Welty* in 1980. In it, Welty uses a fictional voice to express her views on the civil rights struggle in the South. The story, written in 1963 in response to the murder of Medgar Evers in Welty's hometown of Jackson, is told as a monologue by a Southern white man whose ignorance and hate of African Americans is depicted as chillingly mundane. He tells how, enraged by black activism in the South, he determines to shoot a local civil rights leader. He drives to the man's home late on a hot summer night, waits calmly in hiding until the man appears, and then shoots him in cold blood. The callous self-righteousness of the killer and his unreasoning hate are frighteningly depicted when he mocks the body of his victim, saying "Roland? There was only one way left for me to be ahead of you and stay ahead of you, by Dad, and I just taken it. . . . We ain't never now, never going to be equals and you know why?

One of us is dead. What about that, Roland?" His justification for the murder is simple: "I done what I done for my own pure-D satisfaction." His only regret is that he cannot claim the credit for the killing.

Welty scatters subtle symbols throughout the story. The extremely hot weather, which torments the killer, reflects the social climate as the civil rights conflict reaches a kind of boiling point. To the killer, the street feels as hot under his feet as the barrel of a gun. Light and dark contrast in more than just the black and white skins of the characters: The stealthy killer arrives in a darkness that will cloak his crime, and he finds light shining forth from the home of his prey, whose mission is to enlighten. When the killer shoots his victim, he sees that "something darker than him, like the wings of a bird, spread on his back and pulled him down."

Unlike most of Welty's fiction, "Where Is the Voice Coming From?" clearly espouses a particular viewpoint, and the reader is left with no doubt about the writer's intention in telling the story. The story, however, embodies the qualities that typify Welty's fiction: the focus on the interconnections of human society; the full, sharp characterization achieved in a minimum of space; the detailed description of the physical landscape that powerfully evokes a sense of place; the ear for speech and idiom; and the subtle, floating symbolism that insinuates rather than announces its meaning.

Other major works

NOVELS: *The Robber Bridegroom*, 1942; *Delta Wedding*, 1946; *The Ponder Heart*, 1954; *Losing Battles*, 1970; *The Optimist's Daughter*, 1972.

NONFICTION: *Place in Fiction*, 1957; *Three Papers on Fiction*, 1962; *One Time, One Place: Mississippi in the Depression, a Snapshot Album*, 1971; *The Eye of the Story: Selected Essays and Reviews*, 1978; *One Writer's Beginnings*, 1984.

CHILDREN'S LITERATURE: *The Shoe Bird*, 1964.

Bibliography

Appel, Alfred, Jr. *A Season of Dreams: The Fiction of Eudora Welty*. Baton Rouge: Louisiana State University Press, 1965.

Evans, Elizabeth. *Eudora Welty*. New York: Frederick Ungar, 1981.

Prenshaw, Peggy Whitman, ed. *Conversations with Eudora Welty*. Jackson: University Press of Mississippi, 1984.

Vande Kieft, Ruth M. *Eudora Welty*. 1962. Rev. ed. Boston: Twayne, 1987.

Westling, Louise. *Sacred Groves and Ravaged Gardens: The Fiction of Eudora Welty, Carson McCullers, and Flannery O'Connor*. Athens: University of Georgia Press, 1985.

EDITH WHARTON

Born: New York, New York; January 24, 1862

Died: St. Brice sous Forêt, France; August 11, 1937

Principal long fiction

The Touchstone, 1900; *The Valley of Decision*, 1902; *Sanctuary*, 1903; *The House of Mirth*, 1905; *Madame de Treymes*, 1907; *The Fruit of the Tree*, 1907; *Ethan Frome*, 1911; *The Reef*, 1912; *The Custom of the Country*, 1913; *Summer*, 1917; *The Marne*, 1918; *The Age of Innocence*, 1920; *The Glimpses of the Moon*, 1922; *A Son at the Front*, 1923; *Old New York*, 1924; *The Mother's Recompense*, 1925; *Twilight Sleep*, 1927; *The Children*, 1928; *Hudson River Bracketed*, 1929; *The Gods Arrive*, 1932; *The Buccaneers*, 1938.

Other literary forms

In addition to her novels, of which several had appeared serially in *Scribner's Magazine*, *The Delineator*, and *The Pictorial Review*, Edith Wharton published eleven collections of short stories and three volumes of poetry as well as a variety of nonfiction works. She wrote an early and influential book on interior decorating, *The Decoration of Houses* (1897, in collaboration with architect Ogden Codman, Jr.), a short book on the art of narrative, *The Writing of Fiction* (1925) published originally in *Scribner's Magazine*, and a delightful if highly selective autobiography, *A Backward Glance* (1934), which includes among other things an amusing account of Henry James's circumlocutory manner of speech. Wharton, an indefatigable traveler, recorded accounts of her travels in *Italian Villas and Their Gardens* (1904), *Italian Backgrounds* (1905), *A Motor Flight Through France* (1908), and *In Morocco* (1920).

Achievements

Unlike Henry James, whose readership was small and intensely discriminating, Wharton managed to attract a large audience of general readers and at the same time command the interest of critics and fellow writers as well. Wharton's popularity remained high almost to the end of her career in the 1930's, but critical enthusiasm began to diminish after 1920, when the quality of her fiction declined. Even in the early years, 1905 to 1920, when Wharton's best fiction was being published, there were reservations expressed or implied by those who thought her a follower of and to some extent a lesser James, a charge easier to disprove than to eradicate. The truth is that, though Wharton learned from James, she had her own manner as well as her own subject; as she grew older, she continued to discover differences between her fiction and James's.

Wharton's major talent was for social observation. She filled her novels with precise accounts of the decoration of houses, of dress and of dinner parties, describing them often down to the cut of a waistcoat and the contents of the soup tureen. This is not to say that such details were signs of superficiality, but rather that Wharton's fiction depended heavily on the notation of manners and was the result of direct observation. Marriage was one of Wharton's principal subjects, and it provided her with a way of exploring and dramatizing her two main themes: the entrapment of an individual and the attempt by an outsider, often a vulgar lower-class individual, to break into an old, aristocratic society. In her best novels, there is both sympathy for the trapped individual and the invocation of an outside claim—marriage vows, moral code, traditional manners—with the balance of sympathy tipped to the individual.

Despite her later decline and the undeniable influence of James on some of her early work, Wharton produced a considerable body of original fiction, high in quality and superior to most of what was being published at the time. Her fiction also influenced other, younger American writers, notably Sinclair Lewis and F. Scott Fitzgerald. After a long decline in readership and a period of critical indifference, there now appears to be a renewal of interest in her writing, both by critics and scholars of the American novel and by feminist scholars interested in extraliterary issues.

Biography

Edith Wharton was born Edith Newbold Jones on January 24, 1862, in New York City. Her parents, George Frederic and Lucretia Rhinelander Jones, belonged to the pre–Civil War New York aristocracy, families whose wealth consisted largely of Manhattan real estate and who constituted in their common ancestry, landed wealth, and traditional manners a tightly knit, closed society.

Wharton was educated at home by governesses, and later, tutors, and it was expected that she would assume the role young women of her class were educated to play, that of wife, mother, and gracious hostess. From an early age, however, Wharton showed intellectual talents that, along with an acute shyness, kept her at the edge of conventional social life and later threatened to consign her at the age of twenty-three to a life of spinsterhood— the worst fate, so it was thought, that could befall a young woman of her class. After one engagement had been called off (because the young man's mother opposed it) and a promising relationship with a young lawyer, Walter Berry (who later became a close friend), had failed to develop romantically, Wharton married a man twelve years her senior, Edward ("Teddy") Robbins Wharton, a friend of her favorite brother.

Teddy Wharton was a socially prominent Bostonian without a profession or money of his own; Henry James and other friends in England were later incredulous that Wharton could marry a man so obviously her intellectual inferior and so incompatible in his interests; nevertheless, the marriage in the beginning must have been a liberation, both from the social pressure to marry and from her mother's domination. By marrying Teddy, she was at last free to come and go as she pleased, to establish her own residence, which she did on a grand scale at Lenox, Massachusetts, and to travel abroad as often as she liked. In time, however, the marriage to Teddy became irksome, partly from lack of deep affection for him, but also because of his increasing bout of depression and, later, his financial and sexual irresponsibilities. After revelations of his mismanagement of her estate and his adulterous affairs, she divorced Teddy in 1913. While researching his 1975 biography of Wharton, R. W. B. Lewis uncovered the fact that Wharton herself had a brief but intense affair in 1908 with American journalist Morton Fullerton; that relationship had a profound influence on her fiction.

Wharton had lived and traveled in Europe as a child with her parents and after her marriage had visited abroad as often as possible, alternating the seasons between her house at Lenox and an apartment in Paris, with shorter visits to England and rural France. In 1903, when she met James in England, there began an important friendship. The Whartons always traveled in luxury, and their style and Edith's energy quite overwhelmed James at the same time he delighted in them. Like James, and for somewhat the same reasons, Wharton became in time an expatriate, giving up the newer, rawer life of America for the rich, deeply rooted culture of Europe. She felt at home in the salons and drawing rooms of Paris and London, where art and literature and ideas were discussed freely, where women were treated by men as equals, and where life was more pleasing to the senses and to the contemplative mind. Wharton also believed that in Europe respect for the family, for manners, for learning, and for culture, even among the poorer classes, was very much alive.

Even before the final break with Teddy, Wharton had lengthened her frequent stays abroad and, finally, in 1911, allowed the house at Lenox to be sold. When World War I broke out, she remained in Paris and devoted her time, energy, and money to the relief of French and Belgian refugees; in 1916, she was officially recognized for her services to her adopted country by being made a Chevalier of the Legion of Honor. After the war, she bought a house just north of Paris and, later, another in the south of France. She made only one more trip home, in 1923, to receive an honorary degree at Yale. The remainder of her life was spent abroad.

According to those who knew her well, Wharton was a highly intelligent, well-read, brilliant conversationalist, somewhat remote at first, though the grand manner of which many complained was apparently a way of covering up her deep shyness. She read and spoke Italian and French fluently, and her salons in both Paris and Saint Clare were gathering places for literary, artistic, and social luminaries of the time, including such well-known figures as F. Scott Fitzgerald, Bernard Berenson, Jean Cocteau, Aldous Huxley, and Kenneth Clark. Despite the hectic pace of her social life and her frequent travels, Wharton continued to write regularly, turning out novels and short stories and articles, most of which sold well and brought a considerable amount of money. She suffered a slight stroke in 1935, which for a time curtailed her activities; two years later, she was fatally stricken. After a short illness, she died at her home in St. Brice sous Forêt on August 11, 1937.

Analysis

On a surface level, there is a surprising variety in the kinds of characters and the aspects of life with which Edith Wharton was familiar. In *The House of Mirth*, for example, one of her best novels, she was able to create characters such as the Trenors and the Van Osburghs, who belong to opposite ends of the upper level of old New York society, as well as Nettie Struther, the poor working-class girl who befriends Lily Bart when she has sunk from the glittering world of Fifth Avenue social life to a seedy, boardinghouse existence. In her two brilliant short novels, *Ethan Frome* and *Summer*, she managed to depict a life in rural Massachusetts that she could only have known by observation, rather than by direct experience. While Wharton is at times less than convincing, her ability to create realistic characters from a background quite different from her own is impressive, unrivaled in American fiction of the time.

Despite this surface breadth, this impressive range of social observation, Wharton's novels have a rather narrow thematic focus: It has been said that Edith Wharton's chief theme is entrapment. In many of the novels, a superior nature is caught in a wasteful and baffling submission to an inferior nature. It was a situation that Wharton herself must have experienced, not only with a mother who was obsessed with fashion and propriety but also in a society narrowly given up to the pursuit of pleasure. It was a situation in which she later found herself in her marriage to Teddy, who disliked and resented her interest in social and intellectual life.

In *The House of Mirth*, Lily Bart is impoverished by the bankruptcy and later the death of her father and is obliged to recoup her fortune by attempting to marry a rich man. Lily's situation was not Wharton's, but the social pressures on her must have been similar: to make a suitable marriage, with social position certainly, and, if possible, money as well. In the novel, Lily is given a choice that Wharton apparently did not have: an offer of marriage from Selden, an emancipated young lawyer of her own class (though Walter Berry, a lawyer, was thought at one time to have been Wharton's suitor). Wharton chose a passionless marriage with Teddy; Lily was not allowed that solution, as Selden deserts her at the crucial moment. Lily has in her possession a packet of letters which could be used to regain her social position, but the letters would involve the reputation of Selden. She also has an inheritance which could be used to establish herself in a profitable business, but she burns the letters and uses the money to repay a debt of honor. Lily dies of an overdose of sleeping medicine, but in choosing death rather than dishonor, she has escaped entrapment.

In *The Age of Innocence*, published fifteen years after *The House of Mirth*, the underlying conflict is the same, though the tone of the novel and the nature of the entrapment are somewhat different. Here, the trapped individual is a man, Newland Archer, a young lawyer who is engaged to marry May Wellend, a pretty and shallow young woman of respectable old New York society of the 1870's and 1890's. This is the world of Wharton's young womanhood, a society that is narrow and rigid and socially proper. Into this limited and self-contained world she brings Ellen Olenska, a cousin of May, who belongs to this world by birth but left it years before and has since married a Polish count. Ellen has now separated from her husband, who has been notoriously unfaithful, and has returned to the bosom of her family for support and comfort. Archer is engaged by the family to help her in her quest for a divorce settlement. The inevitable happens: Archer and Ellen fall in love. Archer is attracted by Ellen's European sophistication, her freedom of thought and manners, and her refusal to take seriously the small taboos of New York society. Archer considers breaking with May and marrying Ellen. The family, sensing his defection, contrive with other members of the society to separate the lovers and reunite Archer with May, his conventional fiancée. Social pressure forces Ellen to return to Europe, and Archer is again thinking of pursuing Ellen; then May announces that she is expecting a baby. Archer is finally and permanently trapped.

As though to drive home the extent to which Archer has been defeated, Wharton takes him to Paris years later. His son is grown, his wife dead, and Ellen Olenska is now a widow living alone. Archer makes an appointment to see Ellen but gets only as far as a park bench near her apartment. At the last minute, he decides to send his son to see her, while he remains seated on the bench, telling himself that it would be more real for him to remain there than to go himself to see Ellen. The trap has done its work.

While one can see resemblances between Ellen and Wharton—the expatriation, the charm, the liberated views, perhaps even the slight French accent with which Ellen speaks—Archer is also Wharton, or that side of her that could never entirely escape the past. *The Age of Innocence* was thought by some reviewers to be a glorification of the past, which it clearly is not. Wharton does evoke with some nostalgia the old New York of her youth, but she also sets forth with delicate but cutting irony that society's limitations and its destructive narrowness. Archer has led an exemplary life, one is led to believe, but the happiness he might have had was gently but firmly denied him. Whereas a more popular novelist might have allowed Archer to be reunited with Ellen at the end of the novel, Wharton insists that that would be unreal; for her, personal happiness in the real world is the exception rather than the rule.

Two of Wharton's best novels and also two of her shortest—some critics prefer to call them novellas—both deal with protagonists trapped by passionless marriages. The earliest of these, *Ethan Frome*, is about a Massachusetts farmer married to an older, neurasthenic wife, whose pretty young cousin Mattie has come to work for her. The inevitable again happens. Ethan falls in love with Mattie and dreams about running away with her. Ethan's jealous wife, however, arranges for Mattie to be sent away, and Ethan is obliged to escort her to the train station. It is winter, and the lovers stop for a brief time together. They embrace, realize the inevitability of separation, and decide to kill themselves by sledding down a steep hill into a great elm tree. During the ride down the steep hill, Ethan accidentally swerves the sled; a crash occurs, in which the lovers are seriously injured but survive. Mattie becomes a whining invalid, while Zeena, the neurotic wife, takes over the running of the household, and Ethan, who is severely disfigured, feels himself like a handcuffed convict, a prisoner for life.

As Lewis has pointed out, the situation in *Ethan Frome* is very much like the situation in Wharton's own life at the time. If one shifts the sexes, Frome is Wharton trapped in a loveless marriage with a neurasthenic Teddy and passionately in love with a younger man who shared her interests and feelings, Morton Fullerton. The violent ending may be seen as Wharton's passionate statement about her own desperate situation. The success of *Ethan Frome*, however, does not depend on making such autobiographical connections; the book is a brilliantly realized work of realistic fiction that owes its power not to

some abstractly conceived pessimistic philosophy of life, but to Wharton's successful transposition of her own emotional life into the language of fiction.

Summer was published six years after *Ethan Frome* and was called by Wharton and her friends the "hot Ethan." As in *Ethan Frome*, there is a triangle: Lawyer Royall, elderly guardian of Charity, a pretty young mountain girl, and a visiting architecture student, Lucius Harney. During the idyllic summer months, an intense and passionate affair takes place between Charity and Harney. Harney returns to Boston, and Charity is left to face her guardian, who is also in love with her, and the prospect of an illegal abortion. The novel concludes with a reconciliation between Charity and her guardian and a secure if passionless marriage with him. While it would be a mistake to overemphasize biographical parallels, they are unmistakable. The affair of Charity and Harney suggests Wharton's earlier affair with Fullerton, while the intrusive presence of the fatherly Lawyer Royall suggests Teddy's irksome claims on Wharton's loyalties. An interesting alteration of chronology is in making the marriage with the older man follow the affair rather than precede it, as it had in Wharton's own life. *Summer* was written four years after the Whartons were divorced, and by then, she may have had time to view her marriage to Teddy more dispassionately, as the practical solution it must originally have been. Like Lily's death, the surrender to marriage is a defeat as well as a moral triumph.

Wharton was a novelist of manners, not a chronicler of large social movements, and her real subject was the entrapment of superior individuals who keenly feel the pull of moral responsibility. Her talents for social observation, for noting subtleties of dress and decoration, for nuance of voice and phrase, and for language—precise and yet expressive—were essential instruments in the creation of her novels. Wharton has been unduly charged with pessimism; her characteristic tone is ironic, the product of a sensibility able to see and feel the claims on both sides of a human dilemma. If her voice faltered in her later years and she conceded too much to the popular taste for which she increasingly wrote, she nevertheless produced some of the finest American fiction published in the first two decades of the twentieth century.

Other major works

SHORT FICTION: *The Greater Inclination*, 1899; *Crucial Instances*, 1901; *The Descent of Man*, 1904; *The Hermit and the Wild Woman*, 1908; *Tales of Men and Ghosts*, 1910; *Xingu and Other Stories*, 1916; *Here and Beyond*,

1926; *Certain People*, 1930; *Human Nature*, 1933; *The World Over*, 1936; *Ghosts*, 1937; *The Collected Short Stories of Edith Wharton*, 1968.

POETRY: *Verses*, 1878; *Artemis to Actæon*, 1909; *Twelve Poems*, 1926.

NONFICTION: *The Decoration of Houses*, 1897 (with Ogden Codman, Jr.); *Italian Villas and Their Gardens*, 1904; *Italian Backgrounds*, 1905; *A Motor Flight Through France*, 1908; *Fighting France from Dunkerque to Belfort*, 1915; *French Ways and Their Meaning*, 1919; *In Morocco*, 1920; *The Writing of Fiction*, 1925; *A Backward Glance*, 1934; *The Letters of Edith Wharton*, 1988.

Bibliography

Fryer, Judith. *Felicitous Space: The Imaginative Structures of Edith Wharton and Willa Cather*. Chapel Hill: University of North Carolina Press, 1986.

Gimbel, Wendy. *Edith Wharton: Orphancy and Survival*. New York: Praeger, 1984.

Lewis, R. W. B. *Edith Wharton: A Biography*. 2 vols. New York: Harper & Row, 1975.

Lindberg, Gary H. *Edith Wharton and the Novel of Manners*. Charlottesville: University Press of Virginia, 1975.

Lyde, Marilyn Jones. *Edith Wharton: Convention and Morality in the Work of a Novelist*. Norman: University of Oklahoma Press, 1959.

Wolff, Cynthia Griffin. *A Feast of Words: The Triumph of Edith Wharton*. New York: Oxford University Press, 1977.

PHILLIS WHEATLEY

Born: Gambia, Africa; 1753(?)   **Died:** Boston, Massachusetts; December 5, 1784

Principal poetry

Poems on Various Subjects, Religious and Moral, 1773; *The Poems of Phillis Wheatley*, 1966 (Julian Mason, editor).

Other literary forms

Phillis Wheatley's cultivation of the letter as a literary form is attested by her inclusion of the titles of several letters in each of her proposals for future volumes subsequent to the publication of her *Poems on Various Subjects, Religious and Moral* (1773). Regrettably, none of these proposals provoked enough response to secure publication of any new volumes. Her letters display a graceful style and articulate some of Wheatley's strongest protestations in support of the cause of American independence and in condemnation of Christian hypocrisy regarding slavery.

Achievements

From the time of her first published piece to the present day, controversy has surrounded the life and work of America's first black poet, and only its second published woman poet, after Anne Bradstreet. Few poets of any age have been so scornfully maligned, so passionately defended, so fervently celebrated, and so patronizingly tolerated. Yet, during the years of her young adulthood, Wheatley was the toast of England and the Colonies. She was much sought after among the intellectual, literary set of London. Benjamin Franklin, to whom she would later inscribe her second book of poetry (never published), has even recorded that, while in London briefly, he called on Wheatley to see whether "there were any service I could do her."

In the opening pages of her 1773 volume appears a letter of authentication of Wheatley's authorship which is signed by still another of the signatories of the Declaration of Independence, John Hancock. During the early months of the American Revolution, Wheatley wrote a poem in praise of George Washington entitled "To His Excellency General Washington." As a result, she received an invitation to visit the general at his headquarters, and her poem was published by Tom Paine in *The Pennsylvania Magazine*. John Paul Jones, who also appreciated Wheatley's celebration of freedom, even asked one of his officers to secure him a copy of her *Poems*.

Nevertheless, she did not continue to enjoy such fame. A country ravaged by war has little time for poetry, and Wheatley faced the rejection of two more proposals for a volume of new poems. Her poetry has survived, however, and is now considered to be among the best of its period produced in America or in England. It is just beginning to be recognized that, contrary to the opinion of those who would dispose of Wheatley as a mere imitator, she produced sophisticated, original poems whose creative theories of the imagination and the sublime anticipate the Romantic movement.

Biography

The known details of Phillis Wheatley's life are few. According to her master, John Wheatley of Boston, she "was brought from Africa to America in the Year 1761, between Seven and Eight Years of Age." Her life with the Wheatleys, John and Susanna and their two children, the twins Mary and Nathaniel, was probably not too demanding for one whose disposition toward asthma greatly weakened her. The Wheatleys' son attended Harvard, so it is likely that Nathaniel served as the eager young girl's Latin tutor. At any rate, it is certain that Wheatley knew Latin well; her translation of the Niobe episode from Ovid's *Metamorphoses* (before A.D. 8), Book VI, displays a learned knowledge and appreciation of the Latin original. Wheatley's classical learning is evident throughout her poetry, which is thick with allusions to ancient historical and mythological figures.

The turning point of Wheatley's career, not only as an author but also as a human being, came when her *Poems on Various Subjects, Religious and Moral* was published in London in 1773. After she returned from England, having been recalled because of Susanna Wheatley's growing illness, she was manumitted sometime during September, 1773. It is probable that Wheatley was freed because of the severe censure that some English reviewers of her *Poems* had directed at the owners of a learned author who "still remained a slave." At this very point, however, the poet's fortunes began a slow decline. In 1778, at the height of the war and after the deaths of both John and Susanna Wheatley, she married John Peters, a black man of some learning who failed to rescue the poet from poverty.

Wheatley died alone and unattended in a hovel somewhere in the back streets of the Boston slums in 1784, truly an ignominious end for one who had enjoyed such favor. She was preceded in death by two of her children, as well as by the third to whom she had just given birth. She was at most only thirty-one years old.

Analysis

One of the major subjects of Phillis Wheatley's poetry is the American struggle for independence. Temporal freedom is not her only subject, however; she is also much concerned with the quest for spiritual freedom. Consequently, the elegy, in which she celebrates the Christian rewards of eternal life and absolute freedom after death, is her favorite poetic form. In addition, she delights in describing God's creation of nature's splendors and sometimes appears to enjoy the beauties of nature for their own sake and not simply as acts of God's providence. It is in her poem "On Imagination," however, that Wheatley waxes most eloquent; in this poem, perhaps her most important single work, she articulates a theory of the imagination which strikingly anticipates that of Samuel Taylor Coleridge. Indeed, Wheatley's affinities with Romanticism, which run throughout her poetry, may come to be seen as her surest claim to a place in literary history. Such an approach to this early American poet contradicts the widespread critical view that Wheatley was a highly derivative poet, inextricably mired in the neoclassical tradition. Her preference for the heroic couplet, one of the hallmarks of neoclassicism, has deceived many into immediately classifying her as neoclassical.

Her political poems document major incidents of the American struggle for independence. The poem "America" admonishes Britain to treat "americus," the British child, with more deference. According to the poem, the child, now a growing seat of "Liberty," is no mere adorer of an overwhelming "Majesty," but has acquired strength of his own: "Fearing his strength which she [Britain] undoubted knew/ She laid some taxes on her darling son." Recognizing her mistake, "great Britannia" promised to lift the burden, but the promise proved only "seeming Sympathy and Love." Now the Child "weeps afresh to feel this Iron chain." The urge to draw an analogy here between the poem's "Iron chain" and Wheatley's own predicament is irresistible; while America longs for its own independence, Wheatley no doubt yearns for hers.

The year 1770 marked the beginning of armed resistance against Britain. Wheatley chronicles such resistance in two poems, the second of which is now lost. The first, "On the Death of Mr. Snider Murder'd by Richardson," appeared initially along with "America." The poem tells how Ebenezer Richardson, an informer on American traders involved in circumventing British taxation, found his home surrounded on the evening of February 22, 1770, by an angry mob of colonial sympathizers. Much alarmed, Richardson emerged from his house armed with a musket and fired indiscriminately into the mob, killing the eleven- or twelve-year-old son of Snider, a poor German colonist. Wheatley calls young Christopher Snider, of whose death Richardson was later found guilty in a trial by jury, "the first martyr for the common good," rather than those men killed less than two weeks later in the Boston Massacre. The poem's fine closing couplet suggests that even those not in sympathy with the quest for freedom can grasp the nobility of that quest and are made indignant by its sacrifice: "With Secret rage fair freedom's foes beneath/ See in thy corse ev'n Majesty in Death."

Wheatley does not, however, ignore the Boston Massacre. In a proposal for a volume which was to have been published in Boston in 1772, she lists, among twenty-seven titles of poems (the 1773 volume had thirty-nine), "On the Affray in King Street, on the Evening of the 5th of March." This title, naming the time and place of the massacre, suggests that the poet probably celebrated the martyrdom of Crispus Attucks, the first African American to lose his life in the American struggle, along with two whites. Regrettably, the poem has not yet been recovered. Even so, the title alone confirms Wheatley's continued recording of America's struggle for freedom. This concern shifted in tone from obedient praise for the British regime to a supplicatory admonition and then to guarded defiance. Since she finally found a publisher not in Boston but in London, she prudently omitted "America" and the poems about Christopher Snider and the Boston Massacre from her 1773 volume.

She chose to include, however, a poem dedicated to the Earl of Dartmouth, who was appointed Secretary of State for the Colonies in August, 1772. In this poem, "To the Right Honourable William, Earl of Dartmouth, His Majesty's Principal Secretary of State for North America," she gives the Earl extravagant praise as one who will lay to rest "hatred faction." When the Earl proved to support oppressive British policies, the poet's expectations were not realized. Perhaps she was not totally convinced, however; the poem contains some unusually bold passages for a colonist who is also both a woman and a slave. For example, she remarks that, with Dartmouth's secretaryship, America need no longer "dread the iron chain,/ Which wanton *Tyranny* with lawless hand/ Had made, and with it meant t'enslave the land." Once again Wheatley uses the slave metaphor of the iron chain. Quite clearly she also accuses the Crown of "wanton *Tyranny*," which it had wielded illegally and with the basest of motives—to reduce the Colonies to the inhuman condition of slave states. Here rebellious defiance, no longer guarded, is unmistakable; the tone matches that of the Declaration of Independence. It is a mystery how these lines could have gone unnoticed in the London reviews, all of them positive, of her 1773 volume. Perhaps the reviewers were too bedazzled by the "improbability" that a black woman could produce such a volume to take the content of her poetry seriously.

In this poem, Wheatley also presents a rare autobiographical portrait describing the manner in which she was taken from her native Africa. The manuscript version of this passage is more spontaneous and direct than the more formally correct one printed in the 1773 volume, and thus is closer to the poet's true feelings. It was "Seeming cruel fate" which snatched her "from Afric's fancy'd happy seat." Fate here is only apparently cruel, since her capture has enabled her to become a Christian;

the young poet's piety resounds throughout her poetry and letters. Nevertheless, her days in her native land were happy ones, and her abduction at the hands of ruthless slavers doubtless left behind inconsolable parents. Such a bitter memory of the circumstances of her abduction fully qualifies her to "deplore the day/ When Britons weep beneath Tyrannic sway"; the later version reads: "And can I then but pray/ Others may never feel tyrannic sway?" Besides toning down the diction, this passage alters her statement to a question and replaces "Britons" with the neutral "others." In the fall of 1722, Wheatley could still think of herself as a British subject. Later, however, after rejoicing that the earl's administration had given way to restive disillusionment, perhaps the poet was less certain about her citizenship.

Three years after the publication of her 1773 volume, Wheatley unabashedly celebrated the opposition to the "tyrannic sway" of Britain in "To His Excellency General Washington," newly appointed commander-in-chief of the Continental Army; the war of ideas had become one of arms. In this piece, which is more a paean to freedom than a eulogy to Washington, she describes freedom as "divinely fair,/ Olive and laurel binds her golden hair"; yet "She flashes dreadful in refulgent arms." The poet accents this image of martial glory with an epic simile, comparing the American forces to the power of the fierce king of the winds:

> As when Eolus heaven's fair face deforms,
> Enwrapp'd in tempest and a night of storms;
> Astonish'd ocean feels the wild uproar,
> The refluent surges beat the sounding shore.

For the young poet, America is now "The land of freedom's heaven-defended race!" While the eyes of the world's nations are fixed "on the scales,/ For in their hopes Columbia's arm prevails," the poet records Britain's regret over her loss: "Ah! cruel blindness to Columbia's state!/ Lament thy thirst of boundless power too late." The temper of this couplet is in keeping with Wheatley's earlier attitudes toward oppression. The piece closes as the poet urges Washington to pursue his objective with the knowledge that virtue is on his side. If he allows the fair goddess Freedom to be his guide, Washington will surely emerge not only as the leader of a victorious army but also as the head of the newly established state.

In Wheatley's last political poem, "freedom's heaven-defended race" has won its battle. Written in 1784 within a year after the Treaty of Paris, "Liberty and Peace" is a demonstrative celebration of American independence. British tyranny, the agent of American oppression, has now been taught to fear "americus" her child, "And new-born *Rome* shall give *Britannia* Law." Wheatley concludes this piece with two pleasing couplets in praise of America, whose future is assured by heaven's approval:

Auspicious Heaven shall fill with favoring Gales,
Where e'er *Columbia* spreads her swelling Sails:
To every Realm shall *Peace* her Charms display,
And Heavenly *Freedom* spread her golden Ray.

Personified as Peace and Freedom, Columbia (America) will act as a world emissary, an emanating force like the rays of the sun. In this last couplet, Wheatley has captured, perhaps for the first time in poetry, America's ideal mission to the rest of the world.

Like many of the Romantics who followed her, Wheatley perceives nature both as a means to know ultimate freedom and as an inspiration to create, to make art. It is in her superlative poem, "On Imagination," however, that Wheatley most forcefully brings both aspirations, to know God and to create fine poetry, into clear focus. The piece opens with this four-line apostrophe:

Thy various works, imperial queen, we see,
How bright their forms! how deck'd with pomp by thee!
Thy wond'rous acts in beauteous order stand,
And all attest how potent is thine hand.

Clearly, Wheatley's imagination is a regal presence in full control of her poetic world, a world in which her "wond'rous acts" of creation stand in harmony, capturing a "beauteous order." These acts themselves testify to the queen's creative power. Following the four-line invocation to the muse, however, the poet distinguishes the imagination from its subordinate fancy:

Now, here, now there, the roving Fancy flies;
Till some lov'd object strikes her wand'ring eyes,
Whose silken fetters all the senses bind,
And soft captivity involves the mind.

Unlike the controlled, harmonious imagination, the subordinate fancy flies about here and there, searching for some appropriate and desired object worthy of setting

into motion the creative powers of her superior.

Following her description of fancy in "On Imagination," Wheatley details the role the imagination plays in her poetry. According to her, the power of the imagination enables her to soar "through air to find the bright abode,/ Th' empyreal palace of the thund'ring God." The central focus of her poetry remains contemplation of God. Wheatley exclaims that on the wings of the imagination she "can surpass the wind/ And leave the rolling universe behind." In the realm of the imagination, the poet can "with new worlds amaze th' unbounded soul."

Immediately following this arresting line, Wheatley illustrates in a ten-line stanza the power of the imagination to create new worlds. Even though winter and the "frozen deeps" prevail in the real world, the imagination can take one out of unpleasant reality and build a pleasant, mythic world of fragrant flowers and verdant groves where "Fair Flora" spreads "her fragrant reign," where Sylvanus crowns the forest with leaves, and where "Show'rs may descend, and dews their gems disclose,/ And nectar sparkle on the blooming rose." Such is the power of imagination to promote poetic creation and to release one from an unsatisfactory world. Unfortunately, winter and its severe "northern tempests damp the rising fire" cut short the indulgence of her poetic world, and lamentably force Wheatley to end her short-lived lyric: "Cease then, my song, cease the unequal lay." Her lyric must end because no poet can indefinitely sustain a mythic world.

Wheatley was, then, an innovator who used the imagination as a means to transcend an unacceptable present and even to construct "new worlds [to] amaze th' unbounded soul"; this practice, along with her celebration of death, her loyalty to the American struggle for political independence, and her consistent praise of nature, places her firmly in that flow of thought which culminated in nineteenth century Romanticism. Her diction may strike a modern audience as stiff and her reliance on the heroic couplet may appear outdated and worn, but the content of her poetry is innovative, refreshing, and even, for her times, revolutionary. She wrote during the pre-revolutionary and revolutionary war era in America, when little poetry of great merit was produced. Wheatley, laboring under the disadvantages of being not only a black slave but also a woman, nevertheless found the time to depict that political struggle for freedom and to trace her personal battle for release. If one looks beyond the limitations of her sincere if dogmatic piety and her frequent dependence on what William Wordsworth called poetic diction, one is sure to discover in her works a fine mind engaged in creating some of the best early American poetry.

Bibliography

Jones, Jacqueline. "Anglo-American Racism and Phillis Wheatley's 'Sable Veil,' 'Length'ned Chain,' and 'Knitted Heart.'" In *Women in the Age of the American Revolution*, edited by Ronald Hoffman and Peter J. Albert. Charlottesville: University Press of Virginia, 1989.

Richmond, Merle. *Phillis Wheatley*. American Women of Achievement series. New York: Chelsea House, 1988.

Robinson, William H., ed. *Critical Essays on Phillis Wheatley*. Boston: G. K. Hall, 1982.

_____. *Phillis Wheatley: A Bio-Bibliography*. Boston: G. K. Hall, 1981.

_____. *Phillis Wheatley and Her Writings*. New York: Garland, 1984.

CHRISTA WOLF

Born: Landsberg an der Warthe, Germany; March 18, 1929

Principal long fiction

Der geteilte Himmel, 1963 (*Divided Heaven: A Novel of Germany Today*, 1965); *Nachdenken über Christa T.*, 1968 (*The Quest for Christa T.*, 1970); *Kindheitsmuster*, 1976 (*A Model Childhood*, 1980; also as *Patterns of Childhood*, 1984); *Kein Ort: Nirgends*, 1979 (*No Place on Earth*, 1982); *Kassandra*, 1983 (*Cassandra: A Novel and Four Essays*, 1984); *Störfall: Nachrichten eines Tages*, 1987 (*Accident: A Day's News*, 1989).

Other literary forms

Christa Wolf's reputation rests primarily upon her novels. Her short stories were collected into one volume by Luchterhand in 1980, *Gesammelte Erzählungen*. A selection of stories and other prose pieces has appeared in translation as *What Remains and Other Stories* (1993). Her most important essays, reviews, speeches, and interviews are found in *Lesen und Schreiben* (1971; *The Reader and the Writer*, 1978) and *Die Dimension des Autors: Essays und Aufsatze, Reden und Gesprache, 1959-1985* (1987; selections translated as *The Fourth Dimension: Interviews with Christa Wolf*, 1988, and *The Author's Dimension: Selected Essays*, 1993). Her novel *Cassandra* was supplemented by an unusual companion volume, *Voraussetzungen einer Erzählung: "Kassandra"* (1983; *Cassandra: A Novel and Four Essays*, 1984), consisting of four essays which reveal the genesis of the novel and in so doing discuss a wide range of literary and social issues. She also collaborated on the screenplays of several East German films, and with her husband, Gerhard Wolf, wrote the script for *Till Eulenspiegel* (1972).

Achievements

Wolf's fame began with her first novel, *Divided Heaven*, a work which evoked lively discussion in both East Germany (the German Democratic Republic, or GDR) and West Germany (the Federal Republic of Germany, or FRG) and which quickly became known beyond the borders of the two German states. She received the National Prize III Class of East Germany's Academy of the Arts in 1964 for this novel. In 1972, she shared with Walter Kempowski the Wilhelm Raabe Prize of the city of Brunswick, West Germany, and in 1980 received the prestigious Georg Büchner Prize from the German Academy of Language and Poetry in Darmstadt, West Germany. In the spring of 1974, she was Max Kade Writer-in-Residence at Oberlin College, Ohio, and she returned to Ohio for a semester in the spring of 1983. In 1992 she came to Santa Monica, California, as a visiting scholar at the Getty Center for the History of Art and the Humanities.

Wolf has long been recognized as one of the most significant contemporary German writers by many of her literary peers as well as by critics, Germanists, and the reading public. Since the fall of the Berlin Wall in 1989 and the subsequent reevaluation of the East German experience, occasioned in part by the opening of the files of the Stasi, the East German secret police, Wolf has been the subject of intense criticism and controversy in the German press.

Biography

Christa Wolf was born March 18, 1929, in Landsberg an der Warthe, Germany (now Gorzów, Poland). Her youth was typical for many Germans of her generation: those old enough to have been influenced by the twelve years of Nazi rule, but too young at the end of the war to have participated actively in it. Wolf's autobiographical novel *Patterns of Childhood* deals largely with these twelve years and explores the connections that exist between the committed Socialist of the 1970's and the sixteen-year-old girl who confided to her diary that she would die if the Führer should. The flight of Wolf's family westward from her birthplace is documented in

Patterns of Childhood as well as in several of her other prose pieces. Allusions to her own years of studying German literature in Jena and Leipzig (1949-1953) may be recognized in *The Quest for Christa T.*

She joined the Socialist Unity Party (SED) in 1949, the year that the GDR was founded as a separate state with that party at its head. In 1951, she married Gerhard Wolf, a fellow Germanist and historian, and in the next years had two daughters. Her work as a reviewer and editor continued throughout these years. In 1959, she followed the suggestion of the SED leadership that writers go to work in the factories in order to gain working-class experience. She worked for a time in a train-car manufacturing plant in Halle.

In early 1963, her name was put on the candidate list for the Central Committee of the SED. At the December, 1965, plenary meeting of this body, she defended writers who acknowledge in their works that certain aspects of socialism were as yet unrealized in East German life. The defense of such literary works helped to bring her into disfavor with Party functionaries. She was later removed from the leadership of the Berlin branch of the Writers' Union for having cosigned an open letter protesting the expulsion of the poet Wolf Biermann from the GDR in 1976. Unlike some other prominent writers and intellectuals who signed the letter, Wolf remained in East Germany and enjoyed the freedom to write, lecture, and travel abroad.

Wolf's status changed radically with the downfall of Communism and the reunification of Germany. Having long enjoyed a reputation as a moral spokesperson in East Germany, she was widely criticized for her blindness to the real nature of the East German regime. Accusations of hypocrisy intensified when, in January, 1993, Wolf acknowledged that she met with Stasi representatives on several occasions between 1959 and 1962, though she said that the Stasi designation of her as an "informal collaborator" was misleading.

Analysis

In a 1974 interview with the East German critic Hans Kaufmann (reprinted in *Lesen und Schreiben: Neue Sammlung*), Christa Wolf used the term "subjective authenticity" to describe what she believes should be the methodology and the goal of contemporary prose writers: the intense involvement of the author's self in the work, along with an absolutely straightforward presentation of reality, as much as this is possible—given the unavoidable subjectivity of the author. Such an approach to writing prohibits the establishment of distance between the author and the work, the reading public, and society as a whole. In order to examine the problem of modern alienation and as part of the process of developing subjective authenticity, Wolf drew heavily on her own life as a literary source. She looked at East German society in order to understand alienation in herself and others. She wrote *Patterns of Childhood* in order to understand herself better as part of a whole generation of Germans who have been alienated from an important era of their lives and history. In *No Place on Earth*, she uses the figures of two writers, Heinrich von Kleist and Karoline von Günderode, both early victims of the alienation between art and life, both eventual suicides.

The selection of the almost forgotten poet Günderode as a subject fits another pattern in Wolf's work: her preoccupation with female figures. Women are the main characters in all of her novels and short stories. Where men play prominent roles, it is either as problematic, inwardly torn figures or as destructive forces. Wolf has claimed historical reasons for her depiction of women and men in seemingly stereotypical fashion. She asserts that women, because they have been excluded from power, also largely escaped the inner alienation from which modern men suffer. They are therefore a potential force for changing and even for saving contemporary human society. The problematic condition of the writer in the modern world is intensified when the writer is a woman.

When Wolf's second novel, *The Quest for Christa T.*, appeared in 1968, it was immediately sold out in East Germany. The Luchterhand edition the next year was eagerly awaited and greeted with positive reviews in the West. Within the GDR, however, only two reviews, largely critical, were published, and almost six years passed before a second edition was printed. *The Quest for Christa T.*, like its protagonist, came on the scene before its time. Only several years after its appearance did internal East German cultural politics acknowledge the need for constructive criticism within Socialist society. The potential for social criticism can be seen in one of the main themes of the novel: the question of how an individual can gain self-realization yet also be a productive member of a planned and carefully organized society. The background of GDR

Socialist society was essential to the novel, unclearly delineated as it seems at times, and unpolitical as the heroine seems to be. Christa T., the uncurable individual, believes in the rightness of the new world that socialism is to build yet finds it impossible to find a role for herself that will make her a useful member of the new society without necessitating her conforming to and stultifying within some given role. Left to assert her individualism outside a social context, she dies.

The extent to which Christa T.'s dilemma reflects Wolf's own experience is unclear; certainly, a close relationship exists among Wolf, Christa T., and the unnamed narrator, the latter's friend and a writer like Wolf. In "Selbstinterview" ("Self-Interview," in *The Reader and the Writer*), Wolf acknowledged the near-identity of the three. The biographical background of the novel is sufficiently complex to encourage what becomes an intermingling of personae: Both the narrator and Christa T. share elements of Wolf's biography, and Wolf has claimed that there was a real "Christa T." from whose life and posthumous papers she drew some of the facts and citations included in the work.

Aside from such factual cross-influences, the process of narration encourages identification of the narrator and the author with Christa T. This identification becomes one of the main themes of the novel. The narrator tries to be just to the person Christa T. was—indeed, to "rethink" her and thus let her go on living, for, she says, "we need her now." The English title does not transmit the wordplay which indicates this double function of the reflective, narrative process: both *nachdenken* (to reflect on) and *nach-denken* (to seek and re-create in thought). Christa T., ordinary and insignificant though she may seem, is the proper material for such a reciprocal, productive process. Unwilling and unable to compromise or commit herself and insistent on the necessity of conscience and fantasy for the continuation of the human race, she is an admonition to the narrator/author to maintain her own integrity and not to fall into complacency and self-satisfaction. Christa T.'s life is also a warning to her society. Her failure to find a useful place within it stems from the inconsistencies that result when a society calls for "new human beings" without making their development possible. The narrative process discloses the importance of Christa T. not only to the narrator/author but also to the reader and the society to which she so longed to contribute.

Closely connected to the theme of narration as a

creative and healing process is that of writing, for Christa T. is an aspiring writer, a role she shares with Wolf and the narrator. It is through writing that she seeks to close the "gaps" in life through which the cold, dark, destructive forces pour. For Christa T., as for the narrator and for Wolf herself, writing is a way of constructively processing the past, present, and future. Unlike Wolf herself, Christa T. lacks the strength to prevail against her time, which is still marked by many of the characteristics of the bourgeois and Nazi past. Yet the basic tone of the work is one of optimism, just as Christa T. also maintained her optimism and hope for a better future.

The tentative quality of Wolf's narrative style in *The Quest for Christa T.* is marked by "the difficulty of saying I," in the heroine's words. The difficulty stems in part from Christa T.'s own reluctance to commit herself to any role. This transmits itself to the narrator, who attempts to be absolutely accurate and at the same time nonautocratic in her statements in order to allow Christa T. to live again on her own terms. This effort causes her to draw closer to and understand her protagonist better and in turn invites a similar effort on the part of the reader to become an active participant in the text. In this novel, Wolf's subjective authenticity is at its best: the provocative evocation of an individual within an identifiable milieu; the weaving of a relationship among author, narrator, protagonist, and reader; and the general utopian impulse pointing the way to a reconciliation of individual fulfillment with common social goals.

The utopian import of *No Place on Earth* is indicated by its German title, *Kein Ort* (no place) and *Nirgends* (nowhere), being literal translations of the Greek term *utopia*. Here, Wolf uses in even more radical form than in her previous works the narrative technique associated with her subjective authenticity. She goes beyond her own past and social environment to examine the lives and times of two writers in the German Romantic era: Heinrich von Kleist and Karoline von Günderode. In her opening lines, she establishes the pertinence of these figures for herself. They are predecessors, for she has their "blood in her shoes." Wolf presents these writers as early victims of the alienation of the artist from society. The deep alienation from the self that ensued led to their youthful suicides. Their fate has broad implications, for it is a prophetic foreshadowing of that awaiting all those who cherish spiritual values in an increasingly materialistic world.

Wolf creates a fictional meeting between Kleist and

Günderode in Winkel along the Rhine in 1804. The couple's conversation and inner thoughts are interspersed with commentary by the narrator/author; at times it is difficult to be sure who is speaking. Wolf attempts to establish through narrative structure and style a close relationship between subject and object. She succeeds in this by projecting feelings and thoughts into these figures which are consistent with the excerpts from their diaries and letters that she also weaves into the text. As in *The Quest for Christa T.*, the artist is the one to sense the alienation between the spiritual and the material and is the most likely to be destroyed by it.

One is reminded of Christa T. when Günderode speaks of the necessity of hope, for, as she says, "when we stop hoping, that which we fear will certainly come." The belief that love can heal the self-alienation that modern materialistic life causes is also posited by Günderode, and this is an important theme in Wolf's fiction, especially in the short stories "Unter den Linden" and "Selbstversuch." In *No Place on Earth*, there is a utopian power and vision ascribed to literature, a power to remind human beings of the need to work continually toward their self-realization and a dynamic vision of humankind which, as Günderode says, is "contradictory to the spirit of every era." Kleist and Günderode may, like Christa T., have "died of their time," but our recognition of this, evoked by Wolf's re-creation of them, can become a first step in ending the historical process that began in their generation.

Although *No Place on Earth* is in some ways an artist's novel, its firm footing in a particular historical time and its concern with historical rather than literary forces put it in the tradition of themes and concerns familiar to Wolf's readers. Wolf has examined her historical and personal origins as a way of better understanding herself and modern society. It seems certain that the primary components of subjective authenticity, absolute integrity, and an intense involvement in the contemporary world will continue to characterize her works.

Other major works

SHORT FICTION: *Moskauer Novelle*, 1961; *Unter den Linden: Drei unwahrscheinliche Geschichten*, 1974; *Gesammelte Erzählungen*, 1980.

SCREENPLAY: *Till Eulenspiegel*, 1972 (with Gerhard Wolf).

NONFICTION: *Lesen und Schreiben*, 1971 (*The Reader and the Writer*, 1978); *Lesen und Schreiben: Neue Sammlung*, 1980; *Voraussetzungen einer Erzählung: "Kassandra,"* 1983 (*Cassandra: A Novel and Four Essays*, 1984); *Die Dimension des Autors: Essays und Aufsatze, Reden und Gesprache, 1959-1985*, 1987 (Selections translated as *The Fourth Dimension: Interviews with Christa Wolf*, 1988, and *The Author's Dimension: Selected Essays*, 1993).

MISCELLANEOUS: *What Remains and Other Stories*, 1993.

Bibliography

Baumer, Franz. *Christa Wolf*. Berlin: Colloquium Verlag, 1988.

Gitlin, Todd. "'I Did Not Imagine that I Lived in Truth.'" *The New York Times Book Review* 98 (April 4, 1993): 1, 27-29.

Kuhn, Anna K. *Christa Wolf's Utopian Vision: From Marxism to Feminism*. Cambridge, England: Cambridge University Press, 1988.

Love, Myra N. *Christa Wolf: Literature and the Conscience of History*. New York: P. Lang, 1991.

Stephan, Alexander. *Christa Wolf*. München, Germany: Beck, 1976.

VIRGINIA WOOLF

Born: London, England; January 25, 1882

Died: Rodmell, Sussex, England; March 28, 1941

Principal long fiction

The Voyage Out, 1915; *Night and Day*, 1919; *Jacob's Room*, 1922; *Mrs. Dalloway*, 1925; *To the Lighthouse*, 1927; *Orlando: A Biography*, 1928; *The Waves*, 1931; *Flush: A Biography*, 1933; *The Years*, 1937; *Between the Acts*, 1941.

Other literary forms

Virginia Woolf's output was both prodigious and varied; counting her posthumously published works, it fills more than forty volumes. Beyond her novels her fiction encompasses several short-story collections. As a writer of nonfiction, Woolf was similarly prolific, her book-length works including *Roger Fry: A Biography* (1940) and two influential feminist statements, *A Room of One's Own* (1929) and *Three Guineas* (1938). Throughout her life, Woolf also produced criticism and reviews; the best-known collections are *The Common Reader: First Series* (1925) and *The Common Reader: Second Series* (1932).

Achievements

From the appearance of her first novel in 1915, Virginia Woolf's work was received with respect—an important point, since she was extremely sensitive to criticism. Descendant of a distinguished literary family, member of the avant-garde Bloomsbury Group, herself an experienced critic and reviewer, she was taken seriously as an artist. Nevertheless, her early works were not financially successful; she was forty before she earned a living from her writing. From the start, the rather narrow territory of her novels precluded broad popularity; not until the brilliant fantasy *Orlando* was published did she enjoy a definite commercial success. Thereafter, she received both critical and popular acclaim; *The Years* was even a bona fide best-seller.

During the 1930's, Woolf became the subject of critical essays and two book-length studies. Yet at the same time, her novels began to be judged as irrelevant to a world beset by growing economic and political chaos. By the late 1960's, however, critical interest in her work accelerated dramatically for two reasons. First, Woolf's feminist essays *A Room of One's Own* and *Three Guineas* became rallying documents in the growing women's movement, and her novels were read primarily as validations of her feminist thinking. Second, with the appearance of her husband Leonard Woolf's five-volume autobiography from 1965 to 1969, her nephew Quentin Bell's definitive two-volume biography of her in 1972, and the full-scale editions of her own diaries and letters commencing in the mid-1970's, Woolf's life became one of the most thoroughly documented of any twentieth century author. Marked by intellectual and sexual unconventionality, mental illness, and suicide, it is for modern readers also one of the most fascinating. Such insatiable curiosity, while morbid, has led to serious, provocative revaluations of the political and especially the feminist elements in her work, as well as to redefinitions of her role as an artist.

Biography

Daughter of the eminent editor and critic Sir Leslie Stephen and Julia Jackson Duckworth, both of whom had been previously widowed, Virginia Woolf was born in 1882 into a solidly late Victorian intellectual and social milieu. Her father's first wife had been W. M. Thackeray's daughter; James Russell Lowell was her godfather; visitors to the Stephens' London household included Henry James, George Meredith, and Thomas Hardy. From childhood on, she had access to her father's superb library, benefiting from his guidance and commentary on her rigorous, precocious reading. Nevertheless, unlike her brothers, she did not receive a formal university education.

In 1895, when Woolf was thirteen, her mother, just

past fifty, suddenly died. The loss devastated Woolf, who experienced at that time the first of four major mental breakdowns in her life. On her father's death in 1904, Woolf sustained her second incapacitating breakdown. Yet she also gained, as her diary suggests, something crucial: freedom. Virginia, her sister Vanessa, and their brothers Thoby and Adrian set up a home in the seedy bohemian district of London known as Bloomsbury. There on Thursday evenings, a coterie of Thoby Stephen's University of Cambridge friends regularly gathered to talk in an atmosphere of free thought, avant-garde art, and sexual tolerance, forming the nucleus of what came to be called the Bloomsbury Group. The group eventually included such luminaries as biographer Lytton Strachey, novelist E. M. Forster, art critic Roger Fry, and economist John Maynard Keynes. In 1911, they were joined by Leonard Woolf, a colonial official just returned from seven years in Ceylon. Virginia married him the following year. Scarcely twelve months after the wedding, her third severe breakdown began, marked by a suicide attempt; her recovery took almost two years.

Leonard Woolf, himself a professional writer and literary editor, connected her mental illness directly to her genius: Her sanity was always most vulnerable im-mediately after a novel was finished. He learned to keep a daily record of his wife's health; throughout their life together, he would be alert for those signs of fatigue or erratic behavior that signaled approaching danger and the need for her customary rest cure.

Virginia Woolf displayed astonishing productivity after she recovered from her third illness. Although there were certainly periods of instability and near disaster, the following twenty-five years were immensely fruitful as she discarded traditional fiction to move toward realizing her unique vision.

After Woolf's seventh novel, *The Years*, was finished in 1936, however, she came closer to mental collapse than she had been at any time since 1913. Working at her Sussex home on her last book, *Between the Acts*, she could hear the Battle of Britain being fought over her head; her London house was severely damaged in the Blitz. The gradual symptoms of warning were absent this time. She began to hear voices and knew what was coming. On February 26, 1941, she finished *Between the Acts*. Four weeks later, she went out for one of her usual walks, placed a heavy stone in her pocket, and stepped into the River Ouse. Her body was recovered three weeks later.

Analysis

In an ordinary day, Virginia Woolf argued, "thousands of ideas" course through the human brain; "thousands of emotions" meet, collide, and disappear "in astonishing disorder." Thus, even personal identity becomes evanescent, continually reordering itself as "the atoms of experience . . . fall upon the mind." It follows, then, that human beings must have great difficulty communicating with one another, for of this welter of perceptions that define individual personality, only a tiny fraction can ever be externalized in word or gesture. Yet, people yearn to unite both with one another and with some larger pattern of order. Given the complex phenomenon of human subjectivity, Woolf asked, "Is it not the task of the novelist to convey this varying, this unknown and uncircumscribed spirit . . . with as little mixture of the alien and external as possible?" The conventional novel form is plainly inadequate for such a purpose.

Woolf first resolved the technical problems of her experimental fiction in *Mrs. Dalloway*. Though the freedom with which point of view shifts among characters and settings clearly posits an omniscient intelligence, the narrator's observations are subtly integrated with the thoughts of her characters, and the transitions between scenes flow organically. Woolf's subject is well suited to her method: *Mrs. Dalloway* is a novel of middle age, about what people have become as the result of choices made, opportunities seized or refused. The characters must come to terms with their pasts, sifting and valuing the memories that course through their minds.

The book covers one June day in the life of Clarissa Dalloway, fifty-two years old, an accomplished London political hostess and wife of a Member of Parliament. A recent serious illness from which she is still recovering has made her freshly appreciate the wonder of life as she prepares for the party she will give that evening. Peter Walsh, once desperately in love with her, arrives from India, where he has had an undistinguished career; he calls on her and is invited to the party, at which another friend from the past, Sally Seton, formerly a romantic and now the conventional wife of a Manchester industrialist, will also unexpectedly appear. Running parallel with Clarissa's day is that of Septimus Warren Smith, shell-shocked in the war; his suicide in the late afternoon delays the arrival of another of Clarissa's guests, the eminent nerve specialist Sir William Bradshaw. Learning of this stranger's death, Clarissa must confront the inevitability of her own.

Instead of using chapters or other formal sectioning, Woolf structures the book by counterpointing clock time, signaled by the obtrusive hourly tolling of Big Ben, against the subjective flow of time in her characters' minds as they recover the past and envision the future. Not only does she move backward and forward in time, however, she also creates an effect of simultaneity that is especially crucial in linking Septimus' story with Clarissa's. Thus, when Mrs. Dalloway, buying flowers that morning in a Bond Street shop, hears "a pistol shot" outside and emerges to see a large, official automobile that has backfired, Septimus is standing in the crowd blocked by the car and likewise reacting to this "violent explosion" ("The world has raised its whip; where will it descend?"). Later, when Septimus' frightened young Italian wife Rezia guides him to Regents Park to calm him before their appointment with Bradshaw, he has a terrifying hallucination of his dead friend Evans, killed just before the Armistice; Peter Walsh, passing their bench, wonders, "What awful fix had they got themselves in to look so desperate as that on a fine summer morning?" This atmosphere of intensely populated time and space, of many anonymous lives intersecting briefly, of the world resonating with unwritten novels, comic and tragic, accounts in part for the richly poignant texture of nearly all Woolf's mature work.

In her early thinking about *Mrs. Dalloway*, Virginia Woolf wanted to show a "world seen by the sane and the insane, side by side." Although the novel definitely focuses on Clarissa, Septimus functions as a kind of double, representing her own responses to life carried to an untenable extreme. Both find great terror in life and also great joy; both want to withdraw from life into blissful isolation, yet both want to reach out to merge with others. Though some critics condemn her partygiving as shallow, trivial, even corrupt, Clarissa considers her parties a form of creativity, "an offering," "her gift" of bringing people together.

In her most moving, complexly affirmative novel, *To the Lighthouse*, Woolf portrays another woman whose creativity lies in uniting people, Mrs. Ramsay. The plot is absurdly simple: An expedition to a lighthouse is postponed, then completed a decade later. Woolf's mastery, however, of the interior monologue in this novel makes such a fragile plot line quite sufficient; the real

"story" of *To the Lighthouse* is the reader's gradually increasing intimacy with its characters' richly depicted inner lives; the reader's understanding expands in concert with the characters' own growing insights.

Woolf again devises an experimental structure for her work, this time of three unequal parts. Approximately the first half of the novel, entitled "The Window," occurs during a single day at the seaside home occupied by an eminent philosopher, Mr. Ramsay, his wife, and a melange of children, guests, and servants, including Lily Briscoe, an amateur painter in her thirties, unmarried. Mrs. Ramsay is the dominant consciousness in this section. A short, exquisitely beautiful center section, "Time Passes," pictures the house succumbing to time during the family's ten-year absence and then being rescued from decay by two old women for the Ramsay's repossession. Periodically interrupting this natural flow of time are terse, bracketed, clock-time announcements like news bulletins, telling of the deaths of Mrs. Ramsay, the eldest son Andrew (in World War I), and the eldest daughter Prue (of childbirth complications). The final third, "The Lighthouse," also covers one day; the diminished family and several former guests having returned, the lighthouse expedition can now be completed. This section is centered almost entirely in Lily Briscoe's consciousness.

Woolf captures in the Ramsays' monologues the conflicting mixture of motives and needs that characterize human beings of either sex. For example, Mrs. Ramsay is infuriated that her husband blights their youngest son James's anticipation of the lighthouse visit by announcing that it will storm tomorrow, yet his unflinching pursuit of truth is also something she most admires in him. Mr. Ramsay finds his wife's irrational habit of exaggeration maddening, but as she sits alone in a reverie, he respects her integrity and will not interrupt, "though it hurt him that she should look so distant, and he could not reach her, he could do nothing to help her."

Amid these typical contradictions and mundane demands, however, "little daily miracles" may be achieved. One of Woolf's finest scenes, Mrs. Ramsay's dinner, provides a paradigm. As she mechanically seats her guests at the huge table, Mrs. Ramsay glimpses her husband at the other end, "all in a heap, frowning": "She could not understand how she had ever felt any emotion of affection for him." Gloomily, she perceives that everyone else is separate and out of sorts as well. For example, Charles Tansley, Mr. Ramsay's disciple, who feels the whole family despises him, fidgets angrily; Lily, annoyed that Tansley is always telling her "women can't paint," purposely tries to irritate him; and William Bankes would rather be home dining alone and fears that Mrs. Ramsay will read his mind. Mrs. Ramsay wearily recognizes that "the whole of the effort of merging and flowing and creating rested on her."

She instructs two of her children to light the candles and set them around a beautiful fruit centerpiece that her daughter Rose has arranged for the table. This is Mrs. Ramsay's first stroke of artistry; the candles and fruit compose the table and the faces around it into an island, a sheltering haven: "Here, inside the room, seemed to be order and dry land; there, outside, a reflection in which things wavered and vanished, waterily." All the guests feel this change and have a sudden sense of making "common cause against that fluidity out there." Then the maid brings in a great steaming dish of *boeuf en daube* that even the finicky widower Bankes considers "a triumph." As the guests relish the food and their camaraderie grows, Mrs. Ramsay, serving the last helpings from the depths of the pot, experiences a moment of perfect insight: "There it was, all around them. It partook . . . of eternity." She affirms to herself that "there is a coherence in things, a stability; something, she meant, that is immune from change, and shines out . . . in the face of the flowing, the fleeting." As is true of so much of Woolf's sparse dialogue, the ordinary words Mrs. Ramsay then speaks aloud can be read both literally and symbolically: "Yes, there is plenty for everybody." As the dinner ends and she exits the room triumphantly, she looks back on the scene and sees that "it had become, she knew . . . already the past."

The burden of the past and the coming to terms with it are the focus of Part III. Just as "a sort of disintegration" sets in as soon as Mrs. Ramsay sweeps out of the dining room, so her death has left a larger kind of wreckage. Without her unifying artistry, all is disorder, as it was at the beginning of the dinner. In a gesture of belated atonement for quarreling with his wife over the original lighthouse trip, the melodramatically despairing Mr. Ramsay insists on making the expedition now with his children James and Cam, although both hate his tyranny and neither wants to go. As they set out, Lily remains behind to paint. As she starts making rhythmic strokes across the canvas, she loses "consciousness of outer things" and begins to meditate on the past, from which she gradually retrieves a vision of Mrs. Ramsay that will permit her to reconstruct and complete the painting she left unfinished a decade ago, one in which Mrs. Ramsay would have been, and will become again, a triangular shadow on a step (symbolically echoing the invisible "wedge-shaped core of darkness" to which Mrs. Ramsay feels herself shrinking during her moments of reverie). Through the unexpectedly intense pain of recalling her, Lily also comprehends Mrs. Ramsay's significance, her ability "to make the moment something permanent," as art does, to strike "this eternal passing and flowing . . . into stability." Mrs. Ramsay is able to make "life stand still here."

Meanwhile, Mr. Ramsay and his children are also voyaging into the past; Cam, dreamily drifting her hand in the water, begins, as her mother did, to see her father as bravely pursuing truth like a tragic hero. James bitterly relives the childhood scene when his father thoughtlessly dashed his hopes for the lighthouse visit, but as they now near the lighthouse and Mr. Ramsay offers his son rare praise, James too is reconciled. When they land, Mr. Ramsay himself, standing in the bow, "very straight and tall," springs "lightly like a young man . . . on to the rock," renewed. Simultaneously, though the boat has long since disappeared from her sight and even the lighthouse itself seems blurred, Lily intuits that they have reached their goal and she completes her painting. All of them have reclaimed Mrs. Ramsay from death, and she has unified them; memory can defeat time. "Yes," Lily thinks, "I have had my vision." Clearly, Woolf had achieved hers too and transmuted the materials of a painful past into this radiant novel.

Although Woolf denied intending any specific symbolism for the lighthouse, it resonates with almost infinite possibilities, both within the book and in a larger way as an emblem of her work. Like the candles at the dinner party, it can be a symbol of safety and stability amid darkness and watery flux, its beams those rhythmically occurring moments of illumination that sustain Mrs. Ramsay and by extension everyone. Perhaps, however, it can also serve as a metaphor for human beings themselves as Woolf portrays them. The lighthouse signifies what can be objectively perceived of an individual—in Mrs. Ramsay's words, "our apparitions, the things you know us by"; but it also signals invisible, possibly tragic depths, for, as Mrs. Ramsay knew, "beneath it is all dark, it is all spreading, it is unfathomably deep."

Other major works

SHORT FICTION: *Monday or Tuesday*, 1921; *A Haunted House and Other Short Stories*, 1943; *Mrs. Dalloway's Party*, 1973 (Stella McNichol, editor); *The Complete Shorter Fiction of Virginia Woolf*, 1985.

NONFICTION: *The Common Reader: First Series*, 1925; *A Room of One's Own*, 1929; *The Common Reader: Second Series*, 1932; *Three Guineas*, 1938; *Roger Fry: A Biography*, 1940; *The Death of the Moth and Other Essays*, 1942; *The Moment and Other Essays*, 1947; *The Captain's Death Bed and Other Essays*, 1950; *A Writer's Diary*, 1953; *Granite and Rainbow*, 1958; *Contemporary Writers*, 1965; *Collected Essays, Volumes 1-2*, 1966; *Collected Essays, Volumes 3-4*, 1967; *The London Scene: Five Essays*, 1975; *The Flight of the Mind: The Letters of Virginia Woolf, Vol. I, 1888-1912*, 1975 (published in the United States as *The Letters of Virginia Woolf, Vol. I: 1888-1912*, 1975; Nigel Nicolson, editor); *The Question of Things Happening: The Letters of Virginia Woolf, Vol. II, 1912-1922*, 1976 (published in the United States as *The Letters of Virginia Woolf, Vol. II: 1912-1922*, 1976; Nigel Nicolson, editor); *Moments of Being*, 1976 (Jeanne Schulkind, editor); *Books and Portraits*, 1977; *The Diary of Virginia Woolf*, 1977-1984 (Anne Olivier Bell, editor, 5 volumes); *A Change of Perspective: The Letters of Virginia Woolf, Vol. III, 1923-1928*, 1977 (published in the United States as *The Letters of Virginia Woolf, Vol. III: 1923-1928*, 1978; Nigel Nicolson, editor); *A Reflection of the Other Person: The Letters of Virginia Woolf, Vol. IV, 1929-1931*, 1978 (published in the United States as *The Letters of Virginia Woolf, Vol. IV: 1929-1931*, 1979; Nigel Nicolson, editor); *The Sickle Side of the Moon: The Letters of Virginia Woolf, Vol. V, 1932-1935*, 1979 (published in the United States as *The Letters of Virginia Woolf, Vol V: 1932-1935*, 1979; Nigel Nicolson, editor); *Leave the Letters Till We're Dead: The Letters of Virginia Woolf, Vol. VI, 1936-1941*, 1980 (Nigel Nicolson, editor); *The Essays of Virginia Woolf*, 1987-1989 (3 volumes).

Bibliography

Abel, Elizabeth. *Virginia Woolf and the Fictions of Psychoanalysis*. Chicago: University of Chicago Press, 1989.

Baldwin, Dean R. *Virginia Woolf: A Study of the Short Fiction*. Boston: Twayne, 1989.

Beja, Morris. *Critical Essays on Virginia Woolf*. Boston: G. K. Hall, 1985.

Ginsberg, Elaine K., and L. M. Gottlieb, eds. *Virginia Woolf: Centennial Essays*. Troy, N.Y.: Whitston, 1983.

Gordon, Lyndall. *Virginia Woolf: A Writer's Life*. New York: W. W. Norton, 1985.

Guiguet, Jean. *Virginia Woolf and Her Works*. Translated by Jean Stewart. London: Hogarth Press, 1965.

Warner, Eric, ed. *Virginia Woolf: A Centenary Perspective*. New York: St. Martin's Press, 1984.

MARGUERITE YOURCENAR
Marguerite de Crayencour

Born: Brussels, Belgium; June 8, 1903   **Died:** Northeast Harbor, Maine; December 17, 1987

Principal long fiction

Alexis: Ou, Le Traité du vain combat, 1929 (*Alexis*, 1984); *La Nouvelle Eurydice*, 1931; *Denier du rêve*, 1934, revised 1959 (*A Coin in Nine Hands*, 1982); *Le Coup de grâce*, 1939 (*Coup de Grâce*, 1957); *Mémoires d'Hadrien*, 1951 (*Memoirs of Hadrian*, 1954; also as *Hadrian's Memoirs*, 1957); *L'Œuvre au noir*, 1968 (*The Abyss*, 1976); *Anna, Soror . . .*, 1981; *Comme l'eau qui coule*, 1982 (*Two Lives and a Dream*, 1987).

Other literary forms

Marguerite Yourcenar, though best known as a novelist, wrote in virtually every other literary form as well. *Feux* (1936; *Fires*, 1981) is a collection of prose poems about love centered on such characters and historical figures as Phaedra, Achilles, Antigone, Sappho, and Mary Magdalene, but shot through with images and allusions that reflect the modern world. The collection *Sous bénéfice d'inventaire* (1962; *The Dark Brain of Piranesi and Other Essays*, 1984) includes essays on such diverse subjects as the *Historia Augusta*, the engravings of Giambattista Piranesi, the château of Chenonceaux, Selma Lagerlöf, and Thomas Mann. *La Mort conduit l'attelage* (1934) and *Nouvelles orientales* (1938; *Oriental Tales*, 1985) are volumes of short stories. She also wrote many plays. *Les Yeux ouverts: Entretiens avec Matthieu Galey* (1980; *With Open Eyes: Conversations with Matthieu Galey*, 1984) is a series of interviews in which she talks about her life, her values, and her work.

Achievements

Yourcenar's greatest achievement is probably *Memoirs of Hadrian*, a novel in the form of a letter written by the emperor shortly before his death. Like nearly all of her mature works, it had a long gestation period—more than a quarter of a century. She destroyed some early versions of it and put it wholly aside between 1939 and 1948. *The Abyss* is another novel with a long history; the original impulse goes back to the early 1920's, and the final version is a development of material from the first story in the 1934 collection *La Mort conduit l'attelage*. A revised version of *A Coin in Nine Hands* appeared twenty-five years after the original. Such perfectionism is seldom rewarded with popular success, however respectful the critics may be. *Memoirs of Hadrian*, however, was not only very favorably reviewed but also widely read by a large and enthusiastic public. It won the Prix Femina-Vacaresco. Yourcenar was also awarded the Légion d'Honneur and the National Order of Merit. Other honors included membership in the Royal Academy of Belgium, the Prix Combat (1963), the Prix Femina for *The Abyss*, the Grand Prix National des Lettres (1974), and the Grand Prix de la Littérature de l'Académie Française (1977). In 1980, international attention was focused on her and her work when she was elected to the Académie Française, the first woman member in its history.

Biography

Marguerite Yourcenar was born Marguerite de Crayencour in Brussels in 1903. Her mother died a few days after Marguerite was born, and she was reared by her father, who supervised her education at home. They would read aloud to each other in French, English, Latin, and Greek. As a child, she lived sometimes at Mont Noir, the family home near Lille, and sometimes in Paris or the south of France. Her father took her to England in 1914, in flight from the Germans. A year later, they returned to Paris and then fled to the south of France.

In *With Open Eyes*, Yourcenar says that she felt herself and her father to be contemporaries from the time she was about thirteen. He paid for the publication of her first book, *Le Jardin des chimères*, as a Christmas gift and helped her to invent the anagrammatic pseudonym that she later made her legal name. He died when she was in her mid-twenties. His portrait is given at length in the second volume of her family chronicle, *Archives du nord*.

Yourcenar traveled extensively. She made her first visit to the United States during the winter and spring of 1937-1938. At the beginning of the war in 1939, she returned to the United States at the invitation of an American friend, Grace Frick, whom she had met in Paris two years earlier. Frick became Yourcenar's lifelong companion and her English translator. What was planned as a visit of six months became a permanent change of residence for Yourcenar. For a while she taught French and comparative literature part-time. She and Frick first visited Mount Desert Island in Maine in the early 1940's, and they eventually bought a house there. Frick died of breast cancer in 1979.

Yourcenar became an American citizen in 1947. Among her many interests was an active concern for the environment. She contributed to a variety of organizations for reducing overpopulation and pollution and for saving whales, seals, trees—whatever is threatened with extinction by avaricious exploiters.

Analysis

Most of Marguerite Yourcenar's novels have appeared in English, including *A Coin in Nine Hands, Coup de Grâce, Memoirs of Hadrian*, and *The Abyss*. *Memoirs of Hadrian* and *The Abyss* have large casts of secondary figures, but each is firmly centered on a single protagonist. *A Coin in Nine Hands*, in contrast, gives fairly full treatment to about a dozen characters, some of them only tenuously connected to one another. The looseness of structure that might have resulted is guarded by the concentration of the time scheme: Though the novel contains a certain amount of retrospective narrative (the past is always a concern for Yourcenar, the main action is confined to a period of about eighteen hours.

The English title refers to a unique structural feature of the novel, its tracing of the passage of a ten-lira piece from one character to another. The nine characters who handle the coin, and several others as well, are linked by a network of relationships, often casual or accidental, of which none of them sees the whole pattern.

The coin, though it is in itself of no great value to any of them and might seem a facile contrivance to a skeptical reader, in fact takes on considerable symbolic weight. In the afterword to the revised version of the novel, Yourcenar calls the coin "the symbol of contact between human beings each lost in his own passions and in his intrinsic solitude."

The coin is associated with the characters' dreams or illusions. The reader first sees the coin in the hand of Lina Chiari, a prostitute who received it from a man who has become a regular client since his wife deserted him. The narrator comments that although love cannot be bought, dreams can be, and adds, "The little money Paolo Farina gave Lina each week was used to create for him a welcome illusion; that is to say, perhaps the only thing in the world that does not deceive." Lina, after learning that she must have a mastectomy, uses the coin to buy a lipstick, makes up her face, and forces a smile that gradually becomes sincere: "Party to an illusion that saved her from horror, Lina Chiari was kept from despair by a thin layer of makeup." The storekeeper who sold her the lipstick buys votive candles to petition the madonna for relief from his domestic problems, and the candles "maintain the fiction of a hope." The candle vendor, learning of the sale of her childhood home in Sicily, to which she has long dreamed of returning, buys coals to light a fire to asphyxiate herself. Marcella, the seller of the coals, passes the coin to her estranged husband as payment for a gun she stole from him, with which she plans to shoot Benito Mussolini. Her husband is in good standing with the Fascists, and she hates herself for still feeling drawn to him in spite of his politics. The gesture of paying for the gun is intended to free her from any debt to him, to purchase an illusion of independence. He, in turn, uses the coin to buy flowers for a stranger to whom he has made love in a film theater, as if to mitigate the sordidness of the encounter. The flower vendor, uneasy at having been called a miser, proves to herself that the charge is untrue by passing the coin to a man that she takes for a beggar. He is in fact a famous painter, old and frightened by increasingly frequent attacks of angina. He throws the coin into the Trevi Fountain, like those tourists who hope to return, but thinking instead that he may soon see a quite different "Eternal City." Finally, under cover of darkness, a worker scoops up the coin with a handful of others and goes to a tavern to purchase a few hours of exaltation and oblivion in drink. Each character uses the coin to maintain a protective illusion or to soften the pain of a loss.

As the foregoing sketch indicates, death is a prominent theme in the novel. Lina thinks of her impending mastectomy as a death. The attempt on Mussolini's life is the novel's central event, and Marcella expects that even if she succeeds she will be killed. The settings often reinforce the novel's emphasis on death. The darkness in Marcella's little bedroom is repeatedly mentioned. As she moves toward the place where she hopes to kill and knows she will be killed, the street becomes a "river of shades . . . carrying along in its waves inert, drowned corpses who thought they were alive." The film theater that is the setting of the immediately succeeding chapter is a "cave full of specters," a version of the underworld of classical myth. The cinema offers illusory reflections of real life so distorted that they suggest life's opposite. Moreover, the fact that Marcella has been killed is withheld until the end of this scene. Thus, the whole chapter draws together the themes of illusion and death.

Memoirs of Hadrian is a first-person monologue in which a character confronts his past. This is a device Yourcenar used often because it eliminates the author's point of view and puts the reader in immediate contact with a character looking directly at his own life. The monologue is here cast in the form of a letter from the dying emperor to the young Marcus Aurelius.

Hadrian's attitude toward women is a positive one. As a young man, he had a string of mistresses whom he genuinely enjoyed, and his nonphysical relationship with Plotina, the wife of his predecessor Trajan, shows that his deeper friendships are not limited by considerations of gender. For Hadrian, however, the fully satisfying relationship is with one of his own sex—namely, the Bithynian youth Antinous. Antinous' suicide is a ritual offering which the youth believes will in some mystical way extend Hadrian's life. Hadrian is indirectly responsible for Antinous' death. Hadrian fails in wisdom, by a growing insensitivity to the youth's feelings, as he comes to take him increasingly for granted. Antinous' suicide is a complex act. It is both a gift and a reproach, and Hadrian sees that he has been master of Antinous' destiny but that he "must leave to the boy the credit for his own death."

The paradoxical link between love and hatred and the mysterious affinity between love and death make up only one of the novels' themes. Antinous, whom Hadrian calls "that fair stranger who each loved one is," is only one of several characters that evoke in the emperor an acute sense of the separateness of others. His friends Plotina and Attianus were present at the death of Trajan and may have been responsible for Hadrian's being named the successor. One of the few other witnesses, an enemy of Hadrian, died suddenly, shortly after Trajan did. Hadrian has never known for certain to what lengths his friends had to go in order to secure for him the imperial succession.

Hadrian is concerned at the start of the book with the shapelessness of his own life. By the end, however, one's strongest sense is not of shapelessness but of a clearly defined arc, or—to use a figure the author herself invokes in *With Open Eyes*—a pyramid. One follows Hadrian through the years of his education and his preparation for power, to the high point of public glory combined with personal happiness, thence to the loss of Antinous and a correspondingly important defeat in the public sphere— namely, the Jewish revolt under Simon Bar-Kochba. The phase of decline continued through the death of the brilliant and charming Lucius, whom he had adopted as his successor; the struggle for patience under the burden of failing health; and the difficult preparation for the attempt "to enter into death with open eyes." Without ever denying the considerable role of chance, the narrative succeeds in imposing a pattern on experience. Moreover, the emperor overcomes to some extent the isolation of the individual self, for he takes the reader with him virtually as far as he himself can go in the contemplation of his past and in the experience of his approaching death.

In preparing to write the novel, Yourcenar conducted long and painstaking historical research. Her bibliographic note attests the thoroughness and range of her reading of both primary and secondary sources, and professional historians have endorsed her scholarship. For her, the public and political aspects of Hadrian's life are at least as important as the private and philosophical: He was a man of action as well as of letters. With remarkable economy, the novel succeeds in conveying the extent of the Emperor's public achievements: his encouragement of trade, his interest in founding and rebuilding cities, his administrative reforms, his fostering of the culture of Greece, his reversal of the expansionist policies of Trajan in order to concentrate on a policy of stability within the existing frontiers of the already vast empire, his commitment to peace. In

Hadrian, supreme political power was united with an incisive and disciplined intellect as well as with a highly developed artistic sense. The convincing presentation of all of his facets evidences Yourcenar's extraordinary gifts, and *Memoirs of Hadrian* is a persuasive justification of the often-maligned genre of the historical novel.

Other major works

SHORT FICTION: *La Mort conduit l'attelage*, 1934; *Nouvelles orientales*, 1938 (*Oriental Tales*, 1985).

PLAYS: *Électre: Ou, La Chute des masques*, pb. 1954 (*Electra: Or, The Fall of the Masks*, 1984); *Rendre à César*, pb. 1961 (*Render unto Caesar*, 1984); *Le Mystère d'Alceste*, pb. 1963; *Qui n'a pas son Minotaure?*, pb. 1963 (*To Each His Minotaur*, 1984); *Théâtre*, pb. 1971 (partially translated as *Plays*, 1984).

POETRY: *Le Jardin des chimères*, 1921; *Les Dieux ne sont pas morts*, 1922; *Feux*, 1936 (*Fires*, 1981); *Les Charités d'Alcippe et autres poèmes*, 1956 (*The Alms of Alcippe*, 1982).

NONFICTION: *Pindare*, 1932; *Les Songes et les sorts*, 1938; *Sous bénéfice d'inventaire*, 1962 (*The Dark Brain of Piranesi and Other Essays*, 1984); *Souvenirs pieux*, 1973; *Archives du nord*, 1977; *Mishima: Ou, La Vision du vide*, 1980 (*Mishima: A Vision of the Void*, 1986); *Les Yeux ouverts: Entretiens avec Matthieu Galey*, 1980 (*With Open Eyes: Conversations with Matthieu Galey*, 1984); *Le Temps, ce grand sculpteur*, 1983 (*That Mighty Sculptor, Time*, 1988); *La Voix des choses*, 1987.

TRANSLATIONS: *Les Vagues*, 1937 (by Virginia Woolf); *Ce que savait Maisie*, 1947 (by Henry James); *Fleuve profond, sombre rivière*, 1964; *La Couronne et la lyre*, 1979; *Le Coin des "Amen,"* 1983 (by James Baldwin); *Blues et gospels*, 1984.

Bibliography

Horn, Pierre. *Marguerite Yourcenar*. Boston: Twayne, 1985.

Howard, Joan E. *From Violence to Vision: Sacrifice in the Works of Marguerite Yourcenar*. Carbondale: Southern Illinois University Press, 1992.

King, Katherine Callen. "Achilles on the Field of Sexual Politics: Marguerite Yourcenar's *Feux*." *Lit: Literature Interpretation Theory* 2, no. 3 (1991): 201-220.

Lydon, Mary. "Calling Yourself a Woman: Marguerite Yourcenar and Colette." *Differences: A Journal of Feminist Cultural Studies* 3, no. 3 (Fall, 1991): 26-44.

Savigneau, Josyane. *Marguerite Yourcenar: Inventing a Life*. Chicago: University of Chicago Press, 1993.

Shurr, Georgia H. *Marguerite Yourcenar: A Reader's Guide*. Lanham, Md.: University Press of America, 1987.

Tilby, Michael. "Marguerite Yourcenar." In *Beyond the Nouveau Roman: Essays on the Contemporary French Novel*. New York: Berg, 1990.

INDEX

"Na zolotom kryl'tse sideli." *See* "On the Golden Porch."

Nachdenken über Christa T. See *Quest for Christa T., The.*

"Narrow Fellow in the Grass, A" (Dickinson), 131.

Naylor, Gloria, 357-360; *Linden Hills,* 359; *Mama Day,* 359-360; *The Women of Brewster Place,* 358-359.

Needle's Eye, The (Drabble), 147-148.

"Nick and the Candlestick" (Plath), 407.

Night (O'Brien), 378.

'night, Mother (Norman), 368-369.

Nights at the Circus (Carter), 83-84.

Nin, Anaïs, 361-365; *Children of the Albatross,* 363; *Cities of the Interior,* 362-363; *Collages,* 364-365; *The Four-Chambered Heart,* 363; *Ladders to Fire,* 363; *Seduction of the Minotaur,* 364; *A Spy in the House of Love,* 364.

No Place on Earth (Wolf), 593-594.

No Way (Ginzburg), 176.

"Noon Wine" (Porter), 411.

Norman, Marsha, 366-369; *Getting Out,* 367; *'night, Mother,* 368-369.

North and South (Gaskell), 171-172.

"Not Waving but Drowning" (Smith), 512.

Nurture (Kumin), 260-261.

O Pioneers! (Cather), 87.

"O Yes" (Olsen), 386.

"O-A-O-A" (Sachs), 457.

Oates, Joyce Carol, 370-374; *Bellefleur,* 372-373; *Childwold,* 372; *Mysteries of Winterthurn,* 373-374; *With Shuddering Fall,* 371; *Wonderland,* 371-372.

O'Brien, Edna, 375-379; *August Is a Wicked Month,* 377; *Casualties of Peace,* 377; *The Country Girls,* 376; *Girls in Their Married Bliss,* 376-377; *I Hardly Knew You,* 378; *The Lonely Girl,* 376; *Night,* 378; *A Pagan Place,* 377; *Zee & Co.,* 378.

O'Connor, Flannery, 380-384; "The Artificial Nigger," 382; *The Displaced Person,* 382-383; "Everything That Rises Must Converge," 383; "Good Country People," 382; "A Good Man Is Hard to Find," 382; "Greenleaf," 383; "Judgement Day," 384; "Parker's Back," 384; "Revelation," 384.

"October Journey" (Walker), 569.

Odd Woman, The (Godwin), 191.

"Ode to Anactoria" (Sappho), 465-466.

"Ode to Aphrodite" (Sappho), 465.

Of Love and Shadows (Allende), 12.

Oh Pray My Wings Are Gonna Fit Me Well (Angelou), 18.

Olav Audunssøn i Hestviken and *Olav Audunssøn og hans børn.* See *Master of Hestviken, The.*

"Old Mortality" (Porter), 411.

Olsen, Tillie, 385-388; "Hey Sailor, What Ship?," 386; "I Stand Here Ironing," 386; "O Yes," 386; "Tell Me a Riddle," 387.

"On Imagination" (Wheatley), 589.

"On the Death of Mr. Snider Murder'd by Richardson" (Wheatley), 587.

"On the Golden Porch" (Tolstaya), 539.

"One Holy Night" (Cisneros), 104.

"Oread" (H. D.), 204-207.

"Our Bog Is Dood" (Smith), 511-512.

"Over 2000 Illustrations and a Complete Concordance" (Bishop), 36.

Owl Answers, The (Kennedy), 251-252.

Ozick, Cynthia, 389-393; "The Pagan Rabbi," 390-391; "Rosa," 391-392; "The Shawl," 391.

Pagan Place, A (O'Brien), 377.

"Pagan Rabbi, The" (Ozick), 390-391.

"Pale Horse, Pale Rider" (Porter), 412.

Paley, Grace, 394-397; "Come On, Ye Sons of Art," 396; "Goodbye and Good Luck," 395; "In the Garden," 396.

Palomino (Jolley), 247.

"Pangolin, The" (Moore), 336-337.

"Papa Love Baby" (Smith), 510-511.

Parker, Dorothy, 398-400; "Big Blonde," 399-400; "A Telephone Call," 399; "The Waltz," 398-399.

"Parker's Back" (O'Connor), 384.

Passion of New Eve, The (Carter), 83.

"Peace of Utrecht, The" (Munro), 345-346.

Persian Boy, The (Renault), 430.

"Peters" (Tolstaya), 540.

Phillips, Jayne Anne, 401-403; "Bess," 402; "Fast Lanes," 401-402; "Something That Happened," 402-403.

Photograph, A (Shange), 488.

Pilgrimage (Richardson), 443-444.

"Pillar of Salt" (Jackson), 231.

Pioche de la Vergne, Marie-Madeleine. *See* La Fayette, Madame de.

Plagued by the Nightingale (Boyle), 45.

Plan infinito, El. See Infinite Plan, The.

Planetarium, The (Sarraute), 470.

Plath, Sylvia, 404-408; "By Candlelight," 407; "The Jailer," 406; "Nick and the Candlestick," 407.

Play It As It Lays (Didion), 134-135.

Poem Without a Hero, A (Akhmatova), 4.

Poems, by Elizabeth Barrett Barrett (Browning), 70.

"Poetry" (Moore), 335-336.

Porter, Katherine Anne, 409-413; "The Circus," 412; "The Fig Tree," 413; "The Grave," 412; "Holiday," 413; "Noon Wine," 411; "Old Mortality," 411; "Pale Horse, Pale Rider," 412.

"Postcards from Cape Split" (Van Duyn), 559.

Pound, Ezra, 204, 206.

Powell, Dawn, 414-417; *Angels on Toast,* 415; *The Golden Spur,* 416-417; *The Locusts Have No King,* 415-416; *The Wicked Pavilion,* 416.

Prawer Jhabvala, Ruth. *See* Jhabvala, Ruth Prawer.

"Prelude" (Mansfield), 315.

Pride and Prejudice (Austen), 26-27.

Prime of Miss Jean Brodie, The (Spark), 515-517.

"Primero sueño" (Cruz), 117-118.

"Prince's Progress, The" (Rossetti), 446-447.

Princess of Clèves, The (La Fayette), 263, 265-266.

Princesse de Clèves, La. See *Princess of Clèves, The.*

Prophets for a New Day (Walker), 569.

Pym, Barbara, 418-422; *Excellent Women,* 420; *A Glass of Blessings,* 421; *Quartet in Autumn,* 421.

Pythagorean Silence (Howe), 222.

Quartet in Autumn (Pym), 421.

Quest for Christa T., The (Wolf), 592-593.

Radcliffe, Ann, 423-427; *The Italian,* 426; *The Mysteries of Udolpho,* 425-426; *The Romance of the Forest,* 425.

Raisin in the Sun, A (Hansberry), 200-201.

Rat's Mass, A (Kennedy), 252.

Ravishing of Lol Stein, The (Duras), 152-153.

Ravissement de Lol V. Stein, Le. See *Ravishing of Lol Stein, The.*

"Reena" (Marshall), 324.

Rees Williams, Ella Gwendolen. *See* Rhys, Jean.

"Remedies, Maladies, Reasons" (Van Duyn), 559.

Renault, Mary, 428-431; *The Last of the Wine,* 429; *The Mask of Apollo,* 429-430; *The Persian Boy,* 430.

Requiem (Akhmatova), 4.

"Revelation" (O'Connor), 384.

Rhys, Jean, 432-435; *Wide Sargasso Sea,* 433-435.